D0890045

CONCISE ENCYCLOPEDIA OF LANGUAGE AND RELIGION

CONCISE ENCYCLOPEDIA OF LANGUAGE AND RELIGION

Edited by

JOHN F. A. SAWYER
Lancaster University, UK

J. M. Y. SIMPSON
State University of Ceará, Brazil

Consulting Editor

R. E. ASHER
University of Edinburgh

2001

ELSEVIER

AMSTERDAM – NEW YORK – OXFORD – SHANNON – SINGAPORE – TOKYO

Elsevier Science Ltd, The Boulevard, Langford Lane,
Kidlington, Oxford OX5 1GB, UK

Copyright © 2001 Elsevier Science Ltd

All rights reserved. No part of this publication may be reproduced, stored in any retrieval system or transmitted in any form or by any means: electronic, electrostatic, magnetic tape, mechanical, photocopying, recording or otherwise, without permission in writing from the publishers.

Library of Congress Cataloging in Publication Data
Concise encyclopedia of language and religion / edited by John F.A. Sawyer, J.M.Y. Simpson ; consulting editor, R.E. Asher.
p. cm.
Includes bibliographical references and indexes.
ISBN 0-08-043167-4 (alk. paper)
1. Language and languages--Religious aspects--Encyclopedias. I. Sawyer, John F. A. II. Simpson, J. M. Y. III. Asher, R. E.

P41 .C65 2001
403--dc21

2001031550

British Library Cataloguing in Publication Data
A catalogue record for this book is available from the British Library.

ISBN 0-08-043167-4 (HC)

∞™ The paper used in this publication meets the minimum requirements of the American National Standard for Information Sciences—Permanence of Paper for Printed Library Materials, ANSI Z39.48–1984.

Typeset by MacMillan India, Bangalore, India.
Printed and bound in Great Britain by Polestar Wheatons, UK.

Dedicated to the memory of Ninian Smart (1927–2001),
world authority on the study of religion

कल्याण मित्र

kalyāṇa mitra

"beneficent friend"

Contents

Section II. Sacred Texts and Translations

Section III. Religious Languages and Scripts

Section IV. Special Language Uses

Section VI. Religion and the Study of Language

VII. Biographies

Section VIII. Glossary

Section IX. Transcriptional Conventions

Editor's Preface

The ten-volume *Encyclopedia of Language and Linguistics* (*ELL*) was but one of the many trail-blazing enterprises in the field of language-study conceived by Emeritus Professor Angus McIntosh of Edinburgh University. The publication of it in 1994 was the culmination of a period of preparation that had begun with discussions in 1987 and continued at a three-day-long meeting of some 30 experts in linguistics and related areas of study on the island of Jersey in April 1988; in the course of this meeting, the planning of the mammoth work was undertaken in detail. From the outset, the possibility had been kept in mind that there could be a series of 'spin-off' volumes deriving from it. These were intended to be collections of articles from *ELL*, each concerned with only one area within the vast field of language studies and appropriately updated to reflect the most recent research. This project was initiated with the appearance of *A Concise History of the Language Sciences* in 1995 and the present work is the latest in the series, produced under the sympathetic and authoritative guidance of Emeritus Professor R. E. Asher, Editor-in-Chief of *ELL*.

As was to be expected, the selection of articles from *ELL* devoted to the area of language and religion revealed the possibility of an even better publication that would be achieved by commissioning additional articles. Thus it is that articles on, for example, African traditional religions, feminism, Islamic calligraphy, missionaries, romanticism, syncretistic religions of the Caribbean, and many other important topics have now been included, as well as a number of new biographies of eminent scholars. Over 110 articles have been specially written for the present work. The editors are extremely grateful to the authors of these articles, and to the authors of those articles that had already appeared in *ELL* for revising and updating them.

Sadly, we have to record the deaths of several of the authors of *ELL* articles reprinted here, among them G. L. Bursill-Hall, F. W. Householder, R. H. Robins, and M. Weitzman. Other hands have undertaken the updating of their articles.

A feature of the present work is the Glossary; this is a selection of relevant entries from the splendid Glossary of linguistic and other terms in *ELL*, written by Marace Dareau, augmented by a few items from the pens of the present editors.

The present editors are indebted to the editorial and production staff of Elsevier Science, in particular to Dr Helen Collins, for immediate and good-natured attention to their many requests, expressed in e-mail communication between Brazil, Edinburgh, Lancaster, and Oxford. It is difficult to imagine a more helpful framework for working or a more enthusiastic team of collaborators. We would also like to say how much we have appreciated the willingness of many authors to go far beyond what would normally have been expected of them, and the scholarly advice freely given us by colleagues and friends, not all of them authors, especially in the Department of Religious Studies at Lancaster and the State University of Rio de Janeiro.

A noteworthy feature of *ELL* and the volumes derived from it has been renewing of old friendships and the forging of new ones as a result of the cooperation involved. The present editors may perhaps be forgiven for expressing their pleasure that a long-standing personal friendship, begun in the distinctly unacademic context of active service in the British Army in the 1950s, should have been complemented by professional collaboration in the publication of *ELL* and of the present work.

John F. A. Sawyer, *Lancaster, UK*
J. M. Y. Simpson, *Fortaleza-CE, Brazil*
May 2001

there are important philosophical discussions of religious language in Buddhism, Christianity, and Hinduism.

The next two sections focus on the influence of religion on the history of linguistics, a major element in our subject, due partly to the need for the accurate transmission of sacred texts and oral traditions from generation to generation, and partly to the impetus of missionary activity, especially Buddhist and Christian, in having them translated into the vernacular. Access to this vast subject is provided first by a series of general articles on 'Religion and the Study of Language' and then by a biographical section. Section VI includes articles on the contributions made by Plato, Aristotle, medieval Arab, Jewish, and Christian scholars, and the Arab, Persian, Chinese, Indian, Japanese, and Tamil linguistic tradition. There are also special studies of the Europeans' discovery of Sanskrit, Christian missionaries, the Summer Institute of Linguistics, and the role of computers in the modern study of language and religion. Finally, the biographical section contains over 100 short articles on religious leaders, missionaries, and theologians who have played a significant role in the history of language and linguistics, as well as linguists, orientalists, and philosophers who have played a significant role in the history of the study of religion.

SECTION I

Language in the Context of Particular Religions

Introduction

J. F. A. Sawyer

This section contains articles on all the major world religions: Bahā'ism, Buddhism, Christianity, Confucianism, Hinduism, Islam, Jainism, Judaism, Shintō, Sikhism, and Zoroastrianism, as well as a wide range of other religions or religious movements. Some of these, like the Hare Krishna Movement, Mormonism, Quakerism, Rastafarianism, Shamanism, and Theosophy, are quite well known, while others are less familiar such as Candomblé, Cao Dai, Kwanzaa, and Macumba. From the ancient world there are entries on the Etruscan Religion, Greek and Roman Religion, the religions of the Ancient Near East, Gnosticism, and Manichaeism. There are articles on various groupings, geographical like the indigenous religions of North and South America, the Caribbean, Africa, Australia and Melanesia, phenomenological like New Religious Movements and Ecstatic Religions, and both as in the case of New Religions in Japan. The entries on Buddhism, Christianity, and Islam are divided into geographical subsections (e.g. Chinese Buddhism, Tibetan Buddhism, Buddhism in the West), written by different authors.

These articles have two areas of interest: the role of language in the origins and development of each religion or religious movement, and the influence of religion on the history of language and linguistics. In some cases language and religion are inseparable, Sanskrit and Hinduism, for example, Hebrew and Judaism, Arabic and Islam. In the case of Islam the Qur'ān is traditionally believed to have been composed in an inimitable variety of Arabic in heaven and attempts to translate it into other languages have been strongly resisted by the religious establishment. The origins of Judaism and Christianity illustrate two quite different approaches to translation which are symptomatic of major theological differences between the two religions. While Judaism has always gone to great lengths to preserve Hebrew, 'the sacred language,' in worship and scholarly discourse, Christianity from the beginning gave no privileged position to Hebrew, although it was the original language of most of the books in their Bible, and instead have devoted vast amounts of energy and resources to translating it into every language. A similar contrast can be seen between Hinduism where Sanskrit has always played a central role, and Buddhism where Tibetan, Pali, Chinese, Japanese, and other translations have assumed the role of sacred texts.

The effect of this on the development of each distinctive religious tradition cannot be overestimated. It is hardly imaginable that the niceties of early Christian doctrine could have been defined with such precision in a language other than Greek, or that mediaeval Muslim theology would have taken the form it did take in a language other than Arabic. The sheer global power of a privileged language like Greek can be seen in its profound influence on the languages of all subsequent forms of Christianity, including Syriac, Coptic, Armenian, Latin, German, Russian, and English. The influence of Arabic on the vast Muslim world can be seen in the number of Arabic loan words in many of the languages of Africa and Asia, as well as the widespread use of the Arabic script for writing Ottoman Turkish, Persian, Pashtu, Urdu, Malay, and a variety of other languages. Early Christian scholars invented the Armenian, Georgian, Russian, and Gothic writing systems, to which many more must be added as a result of the tireless efforts of the last 300 years of missionary activity.

Many interesting linguistic phenomena are associated with particular religious movements: the Quakers' use of silence, for example, channeling in Spiritualism and some New Age movements, the unique combination of African languages with English, French, or Portuguese in the varieties used in the Caribbean and Brazilian syncretistic cults, and the status given to Jamaican creole by the Rastafarians and their method of giving positive meanings to words with negative associations in standard English (e.g. *dread* as a term of approbation). In some forms of ecstatic religion it has been suggested that the word *god* can function as a personal pronoun reflecting the experience of the speaker.

Most of these and other linguistic matters are dealt with in more detail in subsequent sections under separate headings, e.g. *Sacred Texts and Translations*; *Special Language Uses*; *Religion and the Study of Language*. But in many cases language is so closely related to religion that the articles in this first section, although intended to focus primarily on linguistic aspects of religion, go beyond that and are in effect useful introductions to each of the religions or religious movements described.

African Traditional Religions

I. A. Phiri

African Traditional Religion is the oldest and one of the major religions in Africa. It is African because it has its origins in the south of the Sahara desert. Since it was the first religion on this continent, it is also referred to as the primal religion of Africa. Historical studies have shown that before British, French, German, Portuguese and Belgium colonization in the nineteenth century there was no continent called Africa. Instead there were several communities with different languages, political, social, economic and religious systems. Therefore, the terms *Africa* and *African* are a construction of the European countries that colonized Africa. This historical truth has raised problems of identity. For example, can the European settlers in Africa be called Africans? Can Christianity and Islam, the two other major religions also be called African religions?

The world 'traditional' has been controversial among the scholars of this religion. It assumes that the religion is static, customary, and passed on from one generation to another without much thought and change. It may also imply something, which is old and out of touch with modern realities, and therefore needs to be discarded and replaced with something more modern and relevant to the present.

The reality is that African Traditional Religion is a dynamic religion in that over the centuries it has been adapting to the political, economic, geographical and social changes that have taken place among the people who have been and are still practicing it. For example, Matthew Schoffeleers' recent research has examined how African Traditional Religion speaks to issues of the AIDS pandemic and democratization process in Malawi (1999: 406–41). Traditional spirit mediums played a crucial role in the liberation war in what is now known as Zimbabwe (Ranger 1988: 867).

The term religion is also problematic in the title 'African Traditional Religion' for western scholars coined it. The practitioners of the faith do not call it 'African Religion.' It is simply referred to as 'our beliefs.' Thus the word religion is foreign to the indigenous African people. Before colonial rule in Africa, there was a holistic view of life in that there was no separation between culture and religion. To the indigenous African, religion is practiced in all areas of one's life. It is a way of life.

The fact that there are a variety of expressions of African Traditional Religion has led to discussions among the scholars as to whether one should talk about African Traditional Religion in plural or in singular. J.S. Mbiti, one of the outstanding scholars of this religion, argues for a plural description. He bases his arguments on the fact that the 1,000 ethnic groups of indigenous African people each have their own religious systems. Just as there are cultural differences between one African group of people and another, so there are differences in the expression of the religion. Even within one cultural group, the expression of the religion may vary slightly from clan to clan. One practices the beliefs of the people that one came from. Each ethnic group and family has its own founders who are revered. The family and community heroes are committed to memory and the information is passed on from one generation to the next generation orally.

On the other hand, another prominent scholar of African Traditional Religion, B. Idowu argues for a singular description of African Religion. He argues that despite the diversity found among the indigenous African people, one could still find sufficient shared societal traits as well as same cultural and religious beliefs that are worth maintaining. His study showed that the concept of the Creator God is found in all the African communities. Furthermore, he recorded similarities in the names given to God in different communities. One category of the names and concepts of God in Africa, present God as Creator or maker from the beginning. Examples are Mu'umba, among the Swahili, Lubumba among the Tonga of Zambia, and Karunga among the Herero of Namibia. What is common in all the words that they use is the root 'to mold.' God is viewed as the one who 'molded' creation. He therefore concludes that what brings Africa together is a strong belief in the existence of a living God. It is on this concept that he believes one should speak of African Traditional Religion in the singular. This is where one also notices more interaction between religion and language.

African Traditional Religion is oral. The first scholars of the religion were Christian missionaries who came to Africa with the intention to evangelise. They also came with the attitude that their culture and religion were superior. They could not fathom the African worldview. They therefore concluded that the African people had no religion. With the passing of time more and more Western scholars began to accept the existence of the African Traditional Religion. Nevertheless, misinterpretations of the beliefs and practices of African people have persisted to the present, due to what appears to be continuing lack of accurate knowledge of what African world view and religion are all about. The aim of such publications is not to promote dialogue but to give a Western interpretation of African Traditional Religion for the Western audience.

The scholarly works of Idowu and Mbiti, to mention a few African scholars, are attempts to give a systematic description and analysis of African Traditional Religion from an insider's perspective. The advantage of such writers was that they were able to find out what the religion is all about through a study of African proverbs, songs, art, prayers, riddles, names of people, places and objects. Others had first had experience of the religion, which previous Western scholars did not have. However, their writings came at a time when it was necessary to explain to the Western world as to what this religion is all about. In the process the early African writers fell in the trap of using Christian Western concepts and structure to describe African Traditional Religion. In so doing African Religion acquired, to a certain extent, a new understanding that was not there before.

Describing African Traditional Religion through Western concepts and language is bound to affect our understanding of the religion. For example, Western understanding of religion requires that there must be doctrines, founders, Scriptures, rituals, experience, and moral code. African Traditional Religion does not have one set of dogma, nor one founder or Scripture. Therefore, if the yardstick is Western religions, then African religion is forced to describe itself in terms of how it differs from the 'norm' rather than appreciating it for what it is, without apologies. Current approaches have been qualitative studies of African communities, which require knowledge of the people's language, observations over extended period of time, participation in events and the right attitude and language to describe the religion. The thematic approach has afforded scholars an opportunity to explore areas of commonality among the diverse indigenous African peoples. African traditional beliefs about the source of life are found in myths and names.

Each group of people has its own myths that help it explain where it came from and why things happen the way they do. The belief in the existence and religious powers of ancestors is also wide spread in Africa. In African worldview, death is not the end of life. After death, a person continues to live, and depending on his/her position in society, has an influence on the lives of the living relatives. Due to the interest that the ancestors have in the living relatives, John Mbiti has called them 'the living dead.' There is a controversy as to whether Africans worship their ancestors or not. Space does not allow us to go into that debate but the bibliography provided gives a balanced view. Another important concept is community. There is a religious basis for it in that most African communities maintain that from the beginning of creation, the people were created in community. Therefore, at every stage of growth, rituals are performed to incorporate a person into the community. In traditional African communities, every position of leadership is religious because the holder communicates with the ancestors and/or the Creator. In African Traditional religion(s), places, which are believed to be the dwelling places of ancestors, or places which are surrounded by mystery are said to be sacred. The totemic system, which is practised in some African communities, makes it possible to declare some animals and natural objects as sacred. At the heart of the belief in sacred places lies the African's regard of land as being sacred. Communication is through masks and symbols. Rock paintings, songs and the sounds of drums speak volumes about the people's beliefs.

See also: Christianity in Africa; Missionaries; Crowther S. A.; Candomblé; Caribbean Syncretistic Religions 1: Cuban Santeria and Haitian Voodoo; Caribbean Syncretistic Religions 2: Jamaican Cumina and Trinidadian Shango; Macumba.

Bibliography

Idowu E J 1973 *African Traditional Religion: A Definition*. SCM Press, London

Mbiti J S 1975 *An Introduction to African Traditional Religion*. Heinemann, London

Olupona J K 1991 *African Traditional Religions in Contemporary Society*. International Religious Foundation, New York

Phiri I A 1996 African Religion: The Misunderstood Religion. In: Steyn M E, Motshabi K B (eds.) *Cultural Synergy in South Africa: Weaving Strands of Africa and Europe*. Knowledge Resources, Randburg, pp. 55–64

Platvoet J, Cox J, Olupona J K 1996 *The Study of Religions in Africa: Past, Present and Prospects*. Roots and Branches, Cambridge

Ranger T O 1988 African Traditional Religion. In: Sutherland S, Beaver R P, Bergman J, Langley M S, Metz T W, Romarheim A, Walls A, Withycanbe R, Wootton R W F (eds.) *The World Religions*. Routledge, London

Schoffeleers M 1999 The AIDS Pandemic, the Prophet Billy Chisupe, and the Democratization Process in Malawi. *Journal of Religion in Africa* **XXIX**: 4

Ancient Near Eastern Religions

W. G. E. Watson

Knowledge of ancient near eastern languages has been seriously affected by the religious viewpoints of modern scholars. Most noticeable is the special attention they have given to religious texts, largely because of their possible connection with the Bible, and the corresponding neglect of administrative and other documents. Studies of vocabulary, for example, have tended to be based on the evidence of hymns, prayers and other religious texts.

It is of course a fact that a disproportionate amount of the surviving data from the ancient near east is of a religious nature, coming as it does mainly from cities with a strong temple establishment. Although the exact relationship between school and temple in the areas under discussion remains unknown, a significant part of the training of ancient scribes and scholars consisted of copying out and even composing religious documents. Certainly there were many secular compositions such as love songs and letters, but most of the literary texts were religious in character, and inevitably most of the literary languages of the ancient near east were influenced by religious factors. In general, the topic discussed here has not yet received the attention it merits. Although several indications are available in the works listed below, there is no book nor even a journal article specifically concerned with the influence of religion on the languages of the ancient near east. Moreover, due to the factor of chance involved in archaeological exploration and the random nature of epigraphic finds in the areas under consideration, our knowledge is very patchy. The rich material from Ebla and Emar is still being edited. Little is known of Hurrian, although the discovery of Hurrian–Hittite bilingual texts is promising. However, while more data would certainly be welcome, it is already apparent that in differing degrees the religions of the ancient near east left their mark on the languages of that region. This is most dramatically evident from the thousands of personal names which survive in the documents available to modern scholars.

For convenience, reference to each of the ancient near eastern religions discussed in this article will normally be by the name of a particular language (e.g., Assyrian, Babylonian, Hittite, Egyptian, Sumerian, etc.) because each religion was largely co-extensive with the language in which the documents were written, although occasionally geographical terms will be used instead (e.g., Anatolia, Mesopotamia, Syria, etc.).

1. Ordinary Vocabulary

Many personal names contain religious language even though it is more than probable that people using these names rarely if ever thought about what they meant. At birth, or when a baby was named, the parents often expressed their religious beliefs by their choice of name. 'Belshazzar,' for example, (from Babylonian *Bēl-šar-uṣur*) means 'May (the god) Bel protect the king'; and Egyptian 'Ramses' or 'Rameses' (from Egyptian *r'-ms-sw*) means 'child of (the sun-god) Ra.' Such names express many different theological beliefs, concerning, for instance, the relationship between the bearer and the gods. Even if in the common daily use of language these meanings probably went unnoticed, personal names in the ancient near east were usually quite easy to decipher and generally reflected the language used by the name-giver(s). In Hittite the king is generally referred to as UTU^{ši}, pronounced /*šamši*/ 'my Sun-god,' equivalent to 'his majesty' or 'your majesty.' The name is an Akkadian loanword, spelled in cuneiform with the Sumerian sign for 'sun' (UTU). The same usage was also current in Ugaritic, with the spelling *špš* for /šapšu/ or /šipšu/. In Anatolia, the queen had the very ancient Hattian title *tawanannas* 'mother of (the god) Tawa' (Tawa corresponds to later Zeus). In Mesopotamia too, royal epithets and titles, often very elaborate, included references to divine election or favor (e.g., *migir Enlil*, 'Enlil's favorite'—of Hammurapi, Merodach-baladan, etc. and *ša Aššur Marduk uttūšuma zikir šumišu ušēṣû ana rēšēte*, 'whom Ashur and Marduk have chosen and whose renown they extol to the utmost'—of Sargon II). The Egyptian pharaohs were addressed by traditional sequences of names which included the nomen 'son of (the sun-god) Re.'

Religious names were also given to certain places, parts of buildings and other constructions. In the city of Babylon there were, besides the famous Ishtar

Gate, seven others, all named after deities. Many of its walls, canals, streets and processional ways also had religious names. The very name *bāb-ili* 'Babylon' was understood to mean 'Gate of the God,' although it had another name, TIN.TIR (meaning unknown George 1992:238f.) which apparently was secular. The Egyptian king Akhenaten named his new capital 'Akhetaten' ('Horizon of the Sun-Disc'), after the Aten, the god he worshipped.

Many month names are religious in origin: for example, Babylonian *Du'ūzu* (a god) and *Tašrîtu* (a goddess) (from which Tammuz and Tishri in the Jewish calendar are derived); and Assyrian *bēlet ekalli* '(month of) the Lady of the Palace' and *Sîn* '(month of the mood-god) Sin.' At Ebla in Syria the new calendar introduced by king Ibbi Sipish (ca. 2500 BCE) replaced agricultural month-names by names which referred to religious festivals: e.g., *nidba kamiš* '(month of) the feast of (the god) Kemosh,' corresponding to August. Much the same was true of Emar. Most of the month names in Ugaritic are now known and some of them also apparently refer to festivals: e.g., *riš yn* '(the month of the feast of) First Wine' (September/October). Noteworthy is the Phoenician month name *zbḥ šmš*, '(Month of) sacrifice for the Sun(-god).' Similar names were used in the texts from Alalakh, also in Syria. In all these cultures the days of the week were simply referred to by number, although in Egypt each hour of the day and night had a name corresponding to a particular deity. In Babylonia the nineteenth day of the month was termed *ibbû* (a Sumerian loanword) '(the day of divine) wrath' and the twentieth was sacred to the Sun-god, Shamash.

2. Names

Some of the words for natural objects and phenomena, such as fire, rain, thunder, water, the subterranean waters, the sky, rivers, and mountains were probably religious in origin. Examples are Sumerian ^{d}GIŠ.BAR (also ^{d}BIL.GI)—(the ^{d} is an abbreviation of *dingir*, a determinative denoting a divinity)—both equivalent to Akkadian *girru*, 'fire' (used instead of common Semitic *išatu*); Akkadian and Babylonian *manzât*, 'rainbow'—the name of a goddess, written ^{d}TIR.AN.NA (literally, 'Bow of Heaven'); Hadad, 'thunder' (literally, the god Hadad) in Syria. In a letter from Mari (eighteenth century Syria) comes the descriptive expression *rigimšu udannin* '(the god) has intensified his growl,' that is to say, 'the storm has worsened.' In an Assyrian incantation each of the four cardinal points is addressed with reference to different gods (e.g., 'O South, beloved by (the god) Ea'), and in an inscription of the Assyrian king Esarhaddon (and in a wisdom text) the north wind is called *manīt bēl ilī ṭābu* 'that beneficial breath of the lord of the gods.' The names (and hierarchy) of the eight 'magnates' (lit. 'great men') making up the Assyrian cabinet exactly match the names of gods in the Assyrian Tree of Life, e.g. *ummânu* 'Scholar' corresponds to Ea, god of wisdom; *sartinnu* 'chief judge' corresponds to Shamash, god of justice (Parpola 1988).

As well as proper names, many items of everyday vocabulary contain elements, whose original religious meaning has long since been forgotten (cf. English *ladybird*, German *Marienkäfer*). Various Akkadian words for birds and animals, for example, contain the names of deities or demons: *kallāt šamši* 'the bride of Shamash' is a dragonfly; *iṣṣūr kilīli* 'the bird of (the female demon) Kilili' is an owl; and a species of reptile is known as *ḫumbabītu* after its similarity to Humbaba, a giant mythical monster. In Hittite the Sumerian loanword GIŠ ^{d}INANNA 'the (goddess) Ishtar instrument' is the name given to a musical instrument of some kind, frequently used in rituals.

3. Letter Writing and Greetings

It was quite common for letters to incorporate traditional expressions. For example, in Ugaritic the formula was *iluma taǵǵurūka tašallimūka* 'May the gods keep you safe and well!.' Other greetings were more elaborate and one salutation written in Akkadian (in an Akkadian letter from the archives of Ugarit) runs to several lines: 'May the gods of (the land of) Tipat and the gods of Ugarit and all the gods of our father's house keep you healthy, be favorable to you and give you many years (of life) in the presence of our father's house, forever!.' Sometimes the greeting was written in a language different from the rest of the letter. In some Hittite letters the opening lines (including the religious greeting formula) were written in a mixture of Sumerian and Assyrian. Within this tradition, however, there was some room for variation and expansion, which indicates that such greetings were not frozen expressions but part of everyday life. Some corroboration comes from the Epic of Gilgamesh which records the following farewell to a traveler: 'May Shamash open the obstructed path for you, keep the road in order for you to tread, the open country in order for your foot.'

Religion has left its mark on numerous other expressions. In Mesopotamia *ilam rašû* 'to acquire a (personal) god' means 'to have good luck,' and the phrase *qāt ili* 'the hand of the god' denotes an epidemic. In Babylonian medical texts language about venereal disease frequently contains the phrase *qāt ištar* 'the hand of Ishtar (goddess of love),' while other afflictions are named after a variety of demons, believed to be responsible. The expression *amāru šamaš* 'to see Shamash (god of justice)' can mean 'to be free, to be exposed.' More than likely there was wide variation in the extent to which the original theological content of such expressions was taken literally by individual speakers and writers. In Hittite the idiom ^{d}LIM-*iš kišat* 'he became a god' (used only of kings) means 'he died.' The Egyptian phrase *m3'-ḫrw* 'true of voice,' originally used only of Osiris, god of the underworld, was customarily added to the name of a deceased person and came to mean 'deceased' (or 'justified'). At Nuzi in Anatolia an accused person was given the option 'to lift the gods' (*našû ilāni*), that is, to challenge witnesses against him to perjure themselves at their peril. Several lists of offences against morals or manners in Mesopotamian wisdom and other literature end with the comment *nig.gig díngir.ra kam* 'these constitute an abomination to such-and-such a god.' However, unless committed on an unfavorable day, no actual religious taboo was involved: the expression simply implied profound disapproval. Occasionally the religious content of an idiom is present, perhaps, though in muted form. An Assyrian letter, for example, includes the statement: 'The following day we shall arrive safe and sound, the king's gods protecting' (DINGIR^{MEŠ} *ša* LUGAL *inaṣṣur*). The last phrase corresponds quite closely to English 'God willing.' The converse expression *ilum lā iddin* (or *ilum ay iddin*) 'May God not allow, God forbid!' is common in the Mari letters.

4. Special Languages

In Mesopotamia, as Sumerian was replaced by Akkadian, Sumerian was considered the prestige language especially in the liturgy even though it was no longer spoken. In Babylonian hymns and epics a special literary dialect was used, characterized by, for example, the preposition *el* for *eli* 'upon' and the pronominal suffix *-šun* for *-šunu* 'their.' Bilingual texts and some trilingual texts, including lists, vocabularies, interlinear translations and the like, were produced all over the ancient near east not only to facilitate international communication, but also to make some of the 'special languages,' used in rituals and elsewhere, such as Sumerian, Akkadian, Old Babylonian, Hieroglyphic Hittite (or Luwian) and Phoenician, intelligible.

By the Persian period (sixth century BCE) the cuneiform script had disappeared from ordinary, secular use but was maintained in the temples for religious, astronomical, and literary texts. Egyptian hieroglyphs were similarly reserved for sacred use and demotic for secular purposes, although a notable exception is the trilingual Rosetta Stone, in which both hieroglyphics and demotic are used along with a Greek translation. At Ugarit in Syria, Akkadian was used both for religious and literary texts, but also as the lingua franca for correspondence and diplomatic documents dealing with the outside world. Although few of the people living in Ugarit knew Hurrian, it is worth noting that a number of Hurrian documents, all of them religious in character, are actually written in the Ugaritic alphabetic script, rather than the normal syllabic cuneiform script used elsewhere (e.g., in Anatolia). Some documents were written purely for religious purposes and were not intended for human eyes: for example, foundation documents buried under buildings in Mesopotamia, Egyptian mortuary texts and generally certain magical texts such as amulets. Although essentially legal documents, many of the following texts were also couched in special religious varieties of language: boundary-stone inscriptions, inter-state treaties, marriage contracts, law codes. The law codes and treaties, for example, usually ended with a series of curses and blessings on those who either flouted or obeyed the stipulations contained in them.

The Babylonians in particular devoted a great deal of time and energy to determining the future from omens. To this end they produced highly technical lists of unusual phenomena of all kinds, and detailed descriptions of animal organs. For example, the umbilical fissure of the liver was called *bāb ekallim* 'the gate of the palace' as in the prophecy 'If the "gate of the palace" is absolutely straight the campaign will be peaceful.' Certain difficult and esoteric religious texts in Babylonian later engendered their own commentaries.

The most obvious example of a special language is the use of Sumerian for religious purposes and for documents produced by and for the establishment in Southern Mesopotamia long after it had ceased to be a spoken language (about 1800 BCE). It was also studied in the scribal schools of Syria, as texts discovered at Ebla prove, and in the first millennium certain classes of Sumerian text were provided with an interlinear translation into Akkadian, a clear indication that it was no longer understood. The use of Sumerian for religious purposes also served to maintain the study of Sumerian grammar. It is perhaps not entirely by chance that most of the epigraphic material in Phoenician and Punic comprises grave inscriptions and other texts of a religious character. Even the famous Phoenician (or possibly Punic) inscription from Pyrgi (present day Santa Severa, Italy) written on gold lamina is religious in content. The two accompanying versions of the text into Etruscan were written in Phoenician characters. A most significant exception, however, is the bilingual inscription in Phoenician and Hieroglyphic Hittite (Luwian), which is not a religious text but a royal inscription from Karatepe in Cilicia.

Due to the conservative nature of religion there is a tendency for language to remain unchanged over many centuries and therefore to become archaic in vocabulary and style. Eventually, a gap opens up between the living language used in letters, popular sayings, folktales and the like, and in the fixed patterns of religious texts. As a result, the language of religious texts becomes a dead language, surviving only in certain frozen expressions and in the cult.

See also: Names: Religious Beliefs; Myths About Language; Akkadian; Ancient Egyptian and Coptic; Egyptian Hieroglyphs; Phoenician/Punic; Rosetta Stone; Semitic Languages.

Bibliography

Arnaud D 1993 Jours et mois d'Ougarit. *Studi Micenei ed Egeo-Anatolici* **32**: 123–129

Cohen M E 1993 *The Cultic Calendars of the Ancient Near East*. CDL Press, Bethesda, MD

Cunchillos-Ilarri J L 1989 *Estudios de epistolografía ugarítica*. Fuentes de la ciencia bíblica 3; Institución San Jerónimo, Valencia, pp. 193–234

Gardiner A 1927 (etc) *Egyptian Grammar*. Oxford University Press, London

George A R 1992 *Babylonian Topographical Texts*. Orientalia Lovaniensia Analecta 40, Peeters, Leuven

Gibson J C L 1982 *Textbook of Syrian Semitic Inscriptions*, vol. III. *Phoenician Inscriptions*. Clarendon Press, Oxford

Groneberg B 1987 *Syntax, Morphologie und Stil der jungbabylonischen 'hymnischen' Literatur*. Steiner Verlag, Stuttgart

Gurney O R 1977 *Some Aspects of Hittite Religion*. Oxford University Press, Oxford

Hallo W W 1985 Biblical abominations and Sumerian taboos. *Jewish Quarterly Review* **76**: 21–40

Jacobsen T 1976 *The Treasures of Darkness: A History of Mesopotamian Religion*. Yale University Press, New Haven, CT

Lambert W G 1960 *Babylonian Wisdom Literature*. Clarendon Press, Oxford

McEwan G J P 1981 *Priest and Temple in Hellenistic Babylonia*. Franz Steiner, Wiesbaden

Olivier J P J 1971, 1972 Notes on the Ugaritic month names. *Journal of Northwest Semitic Languages* **1**: 39–45; **2**: 53–59

Parpola S 1995 The Assyrian Cabinet. In: Dietrich M, Loretz O (eds.) *Vom Alten Orient Zum Alten Testament*. Verlag Butzon and Bercker, Kevelaer/Neukirchener Verlag, Neukirchen-Vluyn

Seux M-J 1967 *Epithètes royales akkadiennes et sumeriennes*. Letouzey et Ané, Paris

Starr I 1983 *The Rituals of the Diviner*. Undena Publications, Malibu, CA

Australian Aboriginal Religions

C. H. Berndt and R. M. Berndt

Traditionally Australian Aborigines lived in partly separate but overlapping regional constellations cross-cut with similarities and differences in, for example, religion and language.

In the creative era mythic beings, some in human form, some male, some female, shaped the landscape. Their tracks and associated sites cover the whole continent. Knowledge of these is crucial in the process of 'reading the landscapes.' They located human populations, languages and dialects, and natural resources. They left general and specific instructions about a variety of sociocultural rules, including religious rituals, to ensure that people could maintain their divinely ordained life-style. The sacred time of spiritual continuity, sometimes called the Dreaming or Dreamtime, contrasts with everyday time: the cyclical rhythms of sun and moon, named seasons, and decay and renewal of physical organisms. As for the fate of the human spirit or soul, even where there is a belief in a Land of the Dead or in reincarnation or in mobile spirit manifestations, the emphasis is on a dead person's continuing association with his or her home country and language area. Almost everywhere there is a ban on uttering names of the recently dead, and in some regions alternatives must replace everyday words that resemble them.

Instead of written scripts, Aborigines traditionally relied on oral transmission, supplemented by material representations, rock and ground and body markings, dramatic actions, musical rhythms and songs, verbal and vocal styles, hand-sign vocabularies, speech taboos, and other constraints; and the unspoken understandings acquired in the course of socialization. Body scarring and other ritual operations can be conventionally identified within a varying regional range, but abstract designs in body and facial painting, emblems, ground and other surfaces, and Aboriginal art generally need verbal explanations and can have several layers of meaning. So does red ocher, which has ritual as well as decorative significance. Religious discourse, which up to a point embraces magic and sorcery, is not simply a matter of words and how these are deployed. It should involve a wider context: not only pauses, for instance, but rules about absence of words. In some regions circumcision novices have mandatory periods of silence (special vocabularies are another feature); or a girl at puberty is told to utter only a few words. Actors and dancers in major ritual events mostly do not speak but leave that to the singers (individual singers in much of the north, groups in the interior); or they join in various calls or wordless sounds or breathing effects in unison or harmony at stipulated junctures. Physical stance is important too.

A northeastern Arnhem Lander stands chanting invocations in a specific ritual setting and lifts his clapping sticks high, using them to emphasize his rapid calling of sacred place and other names. (In the same region a person with a grievance may harangue a camp of seated people for hours at a time, with a wealth of symbolic imagery.) Instruments such as clapping sticks, including boomerangs and other sound-making devices, come in various regional styles with various regional rules, but they are not merely accompaniments. They can constitute an acknowledged sign-vocabulary. In western Arnhem Land, for instance, a distinctive pattern of clapping sticks on a ritual occasion can alert women to the approach of men 'coming down' (the vernacular expression) from their men-only ritual ground. In an evening ceremony in the Victoria River area a change in the tempo and sound of the clapping boomerangs during a wordless pause by the male singers signals a change in the program to a men-only performance; at once all the women get up and move away into the darkness beyond the fires. The didjeridu is also a signaling instrument and even more versatile, capable of producing human-like and other vocal sounds. It has spread south from the northern coasts during the last 50 years to become (except for a few inland groups) a musical symbol of traditional Aboriginal identity.

Religious rules and authority are basic, but most conspicuous in sacred, especially secret-sacred, matters. In prose narratives and in songs and invocations and rites, modes of expression and layers of meaning vary according to age and ritual status, sex/gender, and territorial affiliations. Divisions of religious labor on a gender basis are more conspicuous in some areas, but least so among the Tiwe of Bathurst and Melville Islands and people of the lower River Murray and lakes in South Australia. Open-sacred affairs are for everyone in a community, but the elaborate patterning of participation and explanations involves rules of exclusion as well as inclusion: who is permitted to say or sing or hear or do what, when or where and at what distance. So, there is usually diversity even within one region. Versions of myths for children are simplified in language and imagery, as a traditional storehouse of information about their local environment and rules about 'good' and 'bad' behavior. Rituals include reenactment of mythic characters' activities, site-focused celebrations, and topics such as initiation, mortuary events, and fertility. In some areas women have secret or semi-sacred rites and songs, as men do, but the overall picture is one of multifaceted collaboration, in a kaleidoscopic cohesion of verbal, visual (art, emblems), musical, and dramatic ingredients. In a few cases the scope for individual expression and innovation extended to song composition, but usually the most sacred songs are seen as the least amenable to change.

Some words range from versions of ordinary spoken language to poetically dramatic forms and to compressed symbolic or cryptic statements, especially in the sphere of religion. At one extreme, Strehlow (1971: 207) refers to the language of Aranda 'ceremonial songs' as a 'highly artificial creation' that was 'never . . . a spoken language.' In some other areas untranslatable or 'nonsense' vocabularies are a minor feature of particular religious rites (as in northern Arnhem Land). More usually problems in translation are linked with the wide spread of song-sequences. Ritual gatherings between neighboring groups helped to communicate a large range of religious as well as everyday items, although specific translations of song words often get lost in long-distance transmission. Important 'traveling cults' such as the Kunapipi/Gunabibi were (like dreams) a blend of continuity and innovation; but the impact of European contact on Aboriginal religions has been almost wholly negative. Current efforts to sustain or restore a distinctively Aboriginal identity, including vernacular languages, face numerous difficulties. One is the problem of how to keep the details of local cultures within the new, overarching framework that incorporates urban people as well. Increasingly, for many of them now the distinctive feature of Aboriginality is its land-based religious quality, summed up as 'Aboriginal spirituality.'

See also: Ritual; Taboo, Religious.

Bibliography

Berndt R M 1951 *Kunapipi*. Hawthorne, Melbourne

Berndt R M 1974 *Australian Aboriginal Religion*. E. J. Brill, Leiden

Berndt R M, Berndt C H 1987 *The World of the First Australians*, 5th edn. Aboriginal Studies Press, Canberra

Durkheim E 1976 *The Elementary Forms of the Religious Life*. Allen & Unwin, London

Morphy H 1984 *Journey to the Crocodile's Nest*. Australian Institute of Aboriginal Studies, Canberra

Stanner W E H 1989 *On Aboriginal Religion*. Oceania Publications, University of Sydney, Sydney

Strehlow T G H 1971 *Songs of Central Australia*. Angus & Robertson, Sydney

Bahā'ism

S. Lambden and G. Lambden

The now globally diffused Bahā'ī religion originated in the Islamic Middle East. It evolved out of Bābism, a neo-Shī'ī religious movement founded by the Iranian martyr–prophet Sayyid 'Ali Muḥammad Shīrāzī ('the Bāb' = 'Gate') (1819–1850). His contemporary, Mīrza Ḥusayn 'Alī Nūrī, entitled Bahā'u'llāh ('the Glory of God') (1817–1892) spent 40 years or so living outside his native Iran in Ottoman Iraq, Turkey, and Palestine and founded the Bahā'ī Faith (Bahā'ism) in the middle of the nineteenth century. As independent and successive 'religions of the book,' Bābism and Bahā'ism have scriptures in the Persian and Arabic languages—both of which are regarded as 'languages of divine revelation.'

Between 1844 and 1850, the Bāb 'revealed' a very large number of Persian and Arabic books, treatises, and letters. He had something of a distaste for arid scholasticism and, in his revolutionary, ecstatic, 'stream of consciousness' (*shaṭḥ*), and sometimes esoteric–Kabbalistic type revelations, was moved to ignore or 'transcend' established rules of grammar and syntax. His linguistic innovations and idiosyncracies are championed or defended in a number of his works and letters, for example, his early and brief *Elucidation of Grammar and Syntax* (*Bayān fī naḥw wa ṣarf*), the *Equitable Tract* (*Ṣaḥīfa-yi 'adliyya*), and the Persian and Arabic *Expositions* (*Bayāns*). He exhibited a tendency, especially in certain late works, to neologize. Note, for example, his use of arcane locutions based upon words with identical numerical values according to the *abjad* system. A multitude of permutations or unused derivatives of Arabic roots are contained, among other places, in sections of his difficult *Book of Names* (*Kitāb al-asmā'*, e.g., *buhyān* and *mubti[a]hā* from the root *BHA'* 'to be beautiful,' splendid, glorious). Gnostic (*'irfānī*) terminology is in evidence in a good many of his works; a proportion of it rooted in the quasi-extremist (*ghuluww*) 'Sermon of the Gulf' (*Khuṭbah al-ṭutunjiyyah*) attributed to Imām 'Alī (died 661 CE, the cousin and son-in-law of the Prophet Muḥammad): including the etymologically opaque Arabic loanword *ṬTNJ* (spellings vary; Arabic (loosely) 'Gulf') and the Arabic *'Amā'* ((loosely) 'Cloud of Unknowing'), both of which, for doctrinal reasons, occur in the dual in the early *Commentary on the Suraih of Joseph* (*Tafsīr sūrat yūsuf*, mid-1844). The Shirāzī Sayyid, who claimed to be the expected Mahdi (or *Qā'im* ('Ariser'), the 'messiah figure' expected by Shī'ī Muslims), and one possessed of the station of subordinate divinity, has been much criticized for being ungrammatical both by Muslim divines and Western Orientalists.

In excess of 15,000 of Bahā'u'llāh's Arabic and Persian 'revelations' (or *alwāḥ*, 'tablets') are extant, dating from between 1852 and 1892. A considerable number of early poetical and related compositions draw on Sufi themes and exhibit such esoteric terminology as is typical of mystagogues of the school of Ibn 'Arabī (d. 1240). While a few of his Persian revelations are almost wholly devoid of Arabic (notably epistles to Zoroastrian converts), many mix and interweave the language of his homeland with that of the Qur'ān. On occasion Bahā'u'llāh ignored stylistic norms and revealed verses after the fashion of the Bāb. In his *Most Holy Book* (*al-Kitāb al-aqdas*, ca. 1873) he counsels governments to select an existing language and script (or invent new artificial ones) in order to facilitate global communication and encourage world unity. He referred to the Persian and Arabic languages as spiritual and linguistic 'milk' and 'honey.' Though Bahā'īs do not expect Arabic to be chosen as the anticipated international auxiliary language of the near or foreseeable future, the founder of their Faith viewed Arabic as a language of such supernal magnitude (Arabic *basṭ*) that it would be fit to become a global language in the distant future.

Bahā'u'llāh's eldest son 'Abdu'l-Bahā (head of the Bahā'ī community until his death in 1921), as the appointed interpreter of his father's teachings, wrote much in a highly polished yet inspirational Persian and Arabic, and occasionally in Turkish. He endeavored to promote the principle of an international auxiliary language encouraging Bahā'īs and others—as a temporary measure—to learn Esperanto.

As Guardian ('Head') of the Bahā'ī Faith (between 1921 and 1957), Shoghi Effendi, educated at Oxford for a while, translated 'several of the Founder's major works into elegant and 'Biblical' (King James Version) English and wrote thousands of expository letters in that language—as well as much in the 'languages of revelation.' In the early 1990s, the 5 or 6 million strong and rapidly expanding Bahā'ī community is headed by an elected body entitled the 'Universal House of Justice,' whose official communications are in either English or Persian. Further translation into Spanish or French is often made at the Bahā'ī World Centre in Haifa, Israel, and subsequently when required into other languages by Bahā'ī bodies internationally.

Regarded as the 'Word of God' Bahā'ī scripture, as indicated, consists primarily of the voluminous revelations of the Bāb and Bahā'u'llāh. Of central yet secondary importance is the authoritative exegesis of this scripture by Bahā'u'llāh's aforementioned eldest son and great-grandson. Translation of small portions of this scripture and the publication of a constantly expanding and multifaceted Bahā'ī literature—including expositions of Bahā'ī doctrine and its relationship to other religions and contemporary fields of learning—exists in well over 500 languages.

See also: Arabic; Ecstatic Religion; Persian; Qur'ān.

Bibliography

Note: Many relevant primary Bābī-Bahā'ī source materials only exist in Persian and Arabic manuscript sources. For Bābī scriptural sources see MacEoin (1992). A proportion of Western language materials are listed in Collins (1990)

Browne E G (ed.) 1891 *A Traveller's Narrative*, vol. II, Note R, p. 317f. Cambridge University Press, Cambridge

Collins W P 1990 *Bibliography of English Language Works on the Bábí and Bahá'í Faiths 1844–1985*. George Ronald, Oxford

MacEoin D 1992 *The Sources for Early Bābī Doctrine and History: A Survey*. E J Brill, Leiden

Momen M (ed.) 1987 *Selections from the Writings of E G Browne on the Bábí and Bahá'í Religions*. George Ronald, Oxford

British Israelites

W. L. Ingram

British-Israelism is a belief system which states the Caucasian people of Western Europe and the United States are the biological descendants of the ancient Israelites. Originating in England in the mid-nineteenth century, it was transported to the United States in 1887, where it found its most fertile ground. Joseph Allen published the first attempt to codify British-Israelite thought in 1901. In 1933, the British Israelites found their most successful voice in Herbert W. Armstrong, whose Radio Church of God, renamed The Worldwide Church of God in 1968, remained a bastion of British-Israelism. At its peak in the early 1970s, believers were estimated between 200,000 and 300,000 people. Following Armstrong's death in 1986, British Israelites have dwindled to less than an estimated 10,000 believers worldwide.

Biblical analysis supporting British-Israelism begins with the promises God gave to Abraham regarding his descendants. Via primogeniture, these promises were transferred to Abraham's grandson, Jacob/Israel and his 12 sons who are believed to be the ancestors of the individual Israelite tribes that bore their names. British-Israelism teaches that each of these tribes can be identified with a particular nation in Northern and Western Europe, and the United States. They believe all Jewish people are Israelites, but not all Israelites are Jewish. When Assyria conquered Israel in 722 BCE, only the tribe of Judah remained in historical documentation. Adherents of British-Israelism believe these 'lost' tribes of Israel were not assimilated, but migrated intact to western and northern Europe, where they became the ancestors of modern nations.

Particular importance is given to Jacob's blessing of his grandsons, Ephraim and Manasseh, the sons of Joseph: Ephraim father of a 'multitude of nations,' that is, ancestor of the British; and Manasseh father of 'a great nation,' that is, ancestor of the Americans. British-Israelism believes the true inheritors of the promises God gave to Abraham are the British and the Americans, because they are the 'true' Israelites.

British Israelites offer linguistic evidence to support their claims. They claim the Assyrians who conquered the Israelites called them 'Khumri,' and that Crimea, Cambridge, and Cambria are places named by Israelites. Northumberland is 'merely the land north of the Khumbris.' Reminding us that the ancient Hebrew alphabet contained no vowels, followers of British-Israelism point to the rivers Danube, Dnieper, Dniester, and the Don as evidence the tribe of Dan had passed close by. Place names such as Donegal, Dunsmor, and Denmark offer further evidence as does Jutland, that is 'land of the Jews,' in Denmark. British-Israelism also sees a connection between Irish *dunn* 'judge' and the tribe of Dan, since the descendants of Dan were a judgmental people (Genesis 49: 16).

The Angles are claimed to be descendants of the same people who worshipped the Golden Calf. (Hebrew *'egel* 'calf'): hence the British symbol 'John Bull.' The name Saxons originally 'Sac's sons' is derived from 'Isaac's sons.' 'British' is derived from the Hebrew words *berith* 'covenant' and *'ish* 'man' which proves that God's covenant has been properly passed down to King David's descendants, who, in the British monarchy, occupy his throne today.

British-Israelism lends itself well to a rhetoric of racist imperialism, through which Caucasian, English-speaking people maintain a divine right to dominate world events.

Bibliography

Allen J H 1997 *Judah's Sceptre & Joseph's Birthright*, 4th edn. Health Research, Pomeroy, WA

Armstrong G T 1981 *Europe & America In Prophecy*. Church of God, International, Tyler, TX

Armstrong H W 1980 *The United States & Great Britain In Prophecy*, 4th edn. Worldwide Church of God, Pasadena, CA

Ingram W L 1995 God & race: British Israelism and christian identity. In: Miller T (ed.) *America's Alternative Religions*. State University of New York Press, Albany, NY, pp. 119–26

Buddhism, Chinese

D. Lancashire

Buddhism in China is characterized by its interest in attitudes and teachings which reflect the cosmic invocations of the doctrine of metempsychosis and the experience of supreme enlightenment of the Buddha. These are commonly known as Mahāyāna, 'the Great Vehicle.' This does not mean that Chinese Buddhists are merely interested in philosophical speculation. Whether they explore the nature of being through concepts like 'voidness' (*śūnyata*), 'non-being' (*wu*), 'suchness' (*tathata*), and the like, or whether they stress the relations between Bodhisattvas and mankind, through the invocation, for example, of such figures as Avalokiteśvara (Guanyin), they seek to practice and present their faith in such a way as to cause themselves and others to attain Buddhahood.

1. The Introduction of Buddhism into China

A number of accounts exist of the manner of Buddhism's introduction into China, but a careful reading of Chinese historical texts suggests that Buddhism first became known in Chinese governmental circles about the middle of the first century CE. Pengcheng, an important center of commerce at the eastern end of the silk route, contained a community of foreign monks and Chinese laymen at the court of Liu Ying, king of the region, in the year 65 CE, and the evidence suggests that a community had also been established in Loyang, the Han dynasty capital, by the same date. Concerning Liu Ying, the records state that he kept the eight commandments laid down for lay Buddhists, and that he offered 'sacrifices.' He is said to have set up altars to both the Buddha and Lao-zi (the progenitor of Taoism) in his palace, which suggests that at the layman's level, at least, the Buddha was regarded as another 'divine' figure to be worshiped for whatever blessings he might be able to bestow.

Although the first Buddhists were, of necessity, foreigners, and although Chinese were forbidden during the Han dynasty (206 BCE–220 CE) to enter monastic life, the promulgation of the faith to the Chinese people was clearly felt to be important, and the translation of Buddhist texts was early seen to be a vital part of this task. The *Sutra of the 42 Sections* seems to have been the first major scripture to be translated, and by the year 189 over 50 works had been produced. Of this number, the Parthian, An Shigao, is said to have translated 31 books, and Zhi Loujiaqian 14. It should be noted, however, that the majority of these translations represented selections from larger Sanskrit works, and that with few exceptions, they consisted of little more than one or two chapters.

An Shigao's translations were mostly of meditation scriptures, which advocated techniques not unlike those found in Taoism—techniques which have been aptly described as 'Buddhist yoga.' Works translated by Zhi Loujiaqian were representative of the *prajñā* (wisdom, gnosis) system. Despite the poor quality of these translations, the impetus was provided for large translation projects in subsequent years.

2. Period of Consolidation and Growth

Towards the end of the second century CE, Confucianism underwent a major crisis, and both Mahāyāna Buddhism and Taoism were to be the beneficiaries. Events of the time opened the way to the second period of Buddhist history in China which covered the Wei and Jin dynasties (220–420). This was a period of consolidation and growth. It witnessed the entry of the first Chinese nationals into full monastic life following a monastic rule devised in China. An ever-increasing number of Buddhist scriptures were translated into Chinese, and Chinese translators appear in their own right in addition to those from abroad. Chinese commentators on scripture also emerged for the first time, which suggests a growing depth of understanding of the faith, and a greater self-confidence among the Chinese religious. Buddhist temples and monasteries sprang up in every part of the nation, and the number of religious showed a marked growth. In the two capitals of the Western Jin dynasty there were 180 centers with more than 3,700 monks and nuns, and in the Eastern Jin area there were said to be 1,768 centers and some 24,000 monks and nuns. Clearly, the growth of the Buddhist community to such proportions and the support it now received from ruling houses, meant that it had roots deep into Chinese soil.

Two translators of note during this period were Kang Senghui, who arrived in Jianye (the present Jiangningxian) in 247, and Kumārajīva (344–413) (see *Kumārajīva*). Born in China, but of Sogdian origin, Kang Senghui (d. 280) was the first Buddhist monk to have a thorough grasp of Confucian and Taoist thought, as well as of Buddhism. Although he would appear an 'idealist' in Buddhist terms, regarding 'mind' as the ground of all things, he promoted Confucian ethics, and in his exposition of 'mind' reflects Lao-zi's thinking on the Dao (see *Taoism*).

Records differ markedly regarding the number of works translated by Kumārajīva, but just over 30 comprising more than 300 chapters seem the most plausible figures. To produce such a number of works, Kumārajīva organized a Translations Bureau which employed between 500 and 800 persons selected from his more than 3,000 students.

Apart from Prajñā and Lotus-type ('One Buddha-Vehicle') scriptures, he also tackled a number of important works which had not previously been available in China in any form. These included the *mādhyamika* treatise *Zhonglun*, the *Shiermenlun*, and four of the *Bailun*. The importance of these excellent translations is that they clarified Buddhist thought and teachings, and provided foundation material for the growth of 'schools of thought.' The translations of the above three treatises, for example, were to give rise to the *Sanlun* (in Japanese *Sanron*) 'Three-Treatise' school.

Kumārajīva represents a watershed in the history of Buddhist scripture translation in China, and his translations are sometimes referred to as the 'new' as opposed to the 'old' translations.

3. Period of Maturity

The fourth century witnessed an outburst of creativeness through which the implications of the Taoist concepts of 'being' (*you*) and 'non-being' (*wu*) were related to Buddhist concepts of ultimate reality. Outstanding among the thinkers of this time were Zhi-dun (314–66) and Seng-zhao (384–414). The Sui and Tang dynasties (581–907) saw the full flowering of Buddhism in China and the establishment of all the major schools associated with Mahāyāna Buddhism, including the *Tiantai* 'Heavenly Terrace' (Japanese *Tendai*), *Huayan* 'Flowery Splendor' (Japanese *Kegon*), *Jingtu* 'Pure Land,' and *Chan* 'Meditation' (Japanese *Zen*).

Despite serious persecution in 845, Buddhist thought was a major factor in the emergence of Neo-Confucianism in the Song dynasty (960–1279). During the Mongol Yuan dynasty (1206–1368), an attempt was made by Phags-pa (1235–80), the lama of the powerful Sa-skya monastery, to introduce Tibetan Buddhism into China. Although appointed chaplain to the emperor, Kublai Khan, he found that Tantric literature did not appeal to the Chinese, and therefore confined himself to presenting summaries of basic Buddhist teachings to the Mongol princes.

Although the Mongol court was deeply influenced by the Tibetan form of Buddhism, Shamanism was the common religion of the Mongol people. Sensing the need for a more profound religious climate by which literacy and greater social sophistication could be encouraged, Altan Khan, in the mid-sixteenth century, invited a leading Tibetan monk to come to Mongolia where he was proclaimed Dalai Lama. Church and state were united through the system of reincarnation which resulted in the head of the Mongolian Tibetan Church being proclaimed Khan of all Mongolia. The Mongol synthesis was eventually disrupted by the Manchus (1644–1911), and this disruption was carried further by the Communist government of the twentieth century.

In China, Buddhism continues to have a profound influence on Chinese life where it is allowed freedom of expression.

See also: Buddhism in Southeast Asia; Buddhism, Tibetan; Buddhism, Japanese; Buddhist Canons: Translations; Confucianism; Apocrypha, Buddhist.

Bibliography

Chan Wing-tsit 1963 *A Source Book in Chinese Philosophy*. Princeton University Press, Princeton, NJ

Ch'en K K S 1964 *Buddhism in China: A Historical Survey*. Princeton University Press, Princeton, NJ

Conze E (ed.) 1954 *Buddhist Texts Through the Ages*. Penguin, Harmondsworth

Miller R J 1959 *Monasteries and Cultural Change in Inner Mongolia*. Harrassowitz, Wiesbaden

Welch H 1967 *The Practice of Chinese Buddhism 1900–1950*. Harvard University Press, Cambridge, MA

Zürcher E 1972 *The Buddhist Conquest of China*. Brill, Leiden

Buddhism, Indian

S. Collins

Buddhism in India probably began in the fifth century BCE; by the twelfth century CE it had virtually disappeared from the land of its birth, but was established throughout the rest of Asia. This article will deal with the languages used by Buddhists in India and with attitudes to language found in the philosophical thought and religious practice of the various Buddhist schools.

1. The Languages of Indian Buddhism

The Buddha was born as Siddhartha Gautama, from the Sākya clan in what is now southern Nepal. At the time of his birth that part of the subcontinent was gradually being 'Sanskritized'; that is, the Indo–Aryan (originally Indo–European) peoples, who had begun to conquer India from the Northwest perhaps 1,000 years earlier, were now spreading their language (Sanskrit, or Old Indo–Aryan) east and south, along with the religious culture of the Brahman priesthood. It is not known what language the Sākyan families had spoken previously; but it seems that when the Buddha began to teach in and around what is now Banaras in Northeast India, he used one or more forms of Middle Indo–Aryan, or Prakrit, although it is not known exactly which (see various authors in Bechert 1980).

Buddhist texts are extant in a number of forms of Middle Indo–Aryan and Sanskrit. The American scholar Franklin Edgerton called some of them 'Buddhist Hybrid Sanskrit'; not all scholars like the term, but no other has yet proved generally acceptable. Discoveries of manuscripts since the end of the nineteenth century have vastly increased the knowledge of Buddhist literature in Prakrit and Sanskrit, but the most extensive collection of extant writings is in what is now called Pali. The word originally meant 'a (canonical) text,' but it has come to be used in modern times for the language of those texts. It contains features of various North Indian dialects, and some forms which cannot have occurred through normal phonological development, but must be oral or scribal inventions or errors. On these grounds it has been claimed that Pali is an artificial literary language (von Hinüber 1982).

Later Pali texts regularly refer to their language (which they assume to be that of the Buddha) as 'Māgadhī': but philological analysis shows that this cannot be so. It is likely that the term was used in order to associate the language of early Buddhism with that of the Mauryan Empire, which was based in Magadha in Northern Central India, and particularly with the great Buddhist emperor Aśoka of the third century BCE (see Norman 1983; 2–7). Aśoka's edicts, preserved on pillars, rocks and religious monuments, and translated from Māgadhī into various dialects (some into Greek) represent the earliest decipherable writing in India. In fact Buddhist texts were at first preserved orally, and are said to have been written down for the first time in Sri Lanka in the first century BCE.

2. Buddhist Attitudes to Language

According to the usual interpretation of an enigmatic story in the Pali Canon, the Buddha refused to allow his words to be preserved in Sanskrit verse, on the model of the Brahmanical Vedas, and permitted different monks to learn his sermons in their own dialect (see the article by Brough in Bechert 1980). Philosophers of the later tradition, moreover, explicitly articulated a conventionalist view of language. Although by this time most Buddhist scholasticism had adopted Sanskrit, as the lingua franca of Indian intellectual tradition, they were consciously opposing the essentialist attitude to it found in Brahmanical thought, in which each Sanskrit word was held to be intrinsically connected with, or even part of, what it referred to. For Buddhists it was important for metaphysical and spiritual reasons that language should be, as they put it, merely a matter of 'conventional truth'; 'ultimate truth' was beyond words altogether. Some of them elaborated a complex theory of linguistic reference, called the *apoha* or 'exclusion' theory, in which words were held not to refer directly to their objects, but indirectly through the exclusion of what is other; any one referring term thus implies all others, all interrelated in a single, conventional network. Philosophy in India, in Buddhist, Hindu and other traditions, has always been grounded on an extensive and rich tradition of grammar and linguistics, one which Western scholarship has scarcely begun to explore.

Alongside these sophisticated conceptual developments can also be seen the emergence, or reemergence, of other attitudes to and uses of language. In the Pali commentarial texts, for example, Māgadhī is spoken of as 'the root language' of all beings, which children would speak naturally if they heard no other. In the same tradition various texts, normally taken from the Canon, are used in ceremonies of 'protection' (*paritta*), recited on a variety of ritual and practical occasions. Such uses may be called magical, in the sense that the language itself is credited with intrinsic and automatic practical efficacy. Similar attitudes are seen very widely in the northern, Mahāyāna tradition, particularly in the

Tantric schools. The actual words of sacred texts, whether recited orally or written in manuscripts, were themselves the objects of ritual and reverence, since they were thought to embody, in a more than merely semantic sense, the Buddha's saving Truth. Particular words or phrases, called *mantra* (see *Mantra*) or *dhāraṇī* (see *Dharani*), which are sometimes meaningful phrases and sometimes nonsense collections of syllables, were recited or written as part of an elaborate ritual and symbolic system, for propitiatory, apotropaic and other purposes, as well as for the more traditional soteriological goals of Buddhism. In the Pure Land schools repeated recitation of the name of the Buddha Amitābha was combined with visualization and meditation as means of salvation; in parts of China and Japan, it eventually came to be the sole means. (For a summary of these attitudes, and others, see Gomez 1987.)

See also: Pāli; Pali Canon; Buddhist Hybrid Sanskrit; Buddhism and Sanskrit Language.

Bibliography

Bechert H (ed.) 1980 *The Language of the Earliest Buddhist Tradition*. Vandenhoeck and Ruprecht, Göttingen

Gomez L O 1987 LANGUAGE: Buddhist views of language. In: Eliade M (ed.) *Encyclopaedia of Religion*, Vol. 8, pp. 446–51. Macmillan, New York

Hinüber O von 1982 Pali as an artificial language. *Indologia Taurinensia* **10**: 133–40

Norman K R 1983 *Pali Literature*. Harrossowitz, Wiesbaden

Buddhism, Japanese

I. Reader

Buddhism has had major linguistic influences in Japan, ranging from the development of classical Japanese literary forms and new syllabaries to the use of a wide vocabulary that has, in the course of time, become part of standard Japanese usage. It entered Japan along with many other facets of continental Asiatic culture from the sixth century onwards. Along with Buddhism the most significant cultural influence that entered Japan in this period was the Chinese writing system which the Japanese adopted. It was through the medium of Buddhist texts written in Chinese that the Japanese originally encountered and studied Buddhist thought. This Chinese orientation provided the predominant lens through which the Japanese viewed and learnt about Buddhism. Until the nineteenth century no systematic attempts were made to study such root languages of Buddhism as Sanskrit or Pali or to study early pre-Chinese Buddhist texts. There was, however, in the work of the eighteenth-century writer Tominaga Nakamoto, a recognition of the conditional nature of language, dependent on the time in which it was used, the form of expression used, and the intent of the user. Tominaga's studies of Buddhist texts and of the varying ways that Sanskrit terms had been translated, in different eras and by different authors, into Chinese, enabled him to come to an understanding of the relative nature of language and of religious forms, and to develop the foundations of a critical scholarship of religion and of Buddhist texts.

The entry of Buddhism into Japan led the Japanese to study Chinese culture in depth and, especially, to embark on an intensive study of the Chinese language and its writing system so as to facilitate study of the new religion. Consequently the entry of Buddhism was a powerful spur towards the Japanese adoption of the Chinese writing system. It also proved to be a major medium for its gradual transformation into a Japanese system, for in order to make the texts more readily comprehensible they were read in a Japanese syntactical style which applied Japanese pronunciations to the ideograms. Even in the present day, Japanese Buddhist priests intone, with Japanese pronunciations, texts written in Chinese. Because few understand Buddhist Chinese this has led to a situation in which most priests and worshippers do not understand the meanings of the texts they recite. Large numbers of contemporary Japanese translations and commentaries on Buddhist texts are, however, available to explain such texts.

Buddhism played a major part in the development and use of the phonetic syllabary *katakana* which forms an intrinsic part of the written language along with Chinese ideograms. *Katakana* developed as a mnemonic device for providing Japanese readings and pronunciations of Chinese Buddhist texts, and was widely used in the temples of Nara, the ancient capital, by the eighth century. Its use was subsequently diversified into the world of literature and eventually into general use. Although the earliest usages and development of the other phonetic syllabary, *hiragana*, occurred outside of Buddhist temples, it is clear that this syllabary was also widely used in the Buddhist world by the tenth century, and this further stimulated the emergence of an authentic written language combining ideograms and phonetic script.

Many Buddhistic words still in use in the modern era (e.g., the term *issai shujô*, 'all sentient beings') derive from the earliest wave of assimilation in the sixth century: although changes in the dominant form of Chinese in the seventh century affected the ways that the Japanese pronounced most Chinese ideograms, the Buddhist temples resisted this change and continued for the most part to preserve the earlier forms. For example, the ideogram meaning 'being, existence' is more commonly pronounced *sei*, but in Buddhist contexts generally retains the earlier pronunciation *jô*. To this extent, Buddhist Japanese as used in rituals has a rather archaic feeling compared to standard Japanese. Nonetheless many standard Buddhist terms based on these earlier forms of pronunciation, for example, *jigoku* (hell) and *gokuraku* (heaven), have become everyday terms still extant in contemporary Japanese and not limited to Buddhistic usage. Because of its close relationship with the Chinese language which formed the basis of the Japanese writing system and which added immeasurably to the Japanese vocabulary of the time, Buddhism has thus played an instrumental role in the evolution of the Japanese language and in augmenting its scope, both orally and in written forms.

See also: Buddhism, Chinese.

Bibliography

Matsunaga D, Matsunaga A 1978 *Foundation of Japanese Buddhism*, 2 vols. Buddhist Books International, Los Angeles

Miller R A 1967 *The Japanese Language*. Charles Tuttle, Tokyo

Nakamoto T 1990 *Emerging from Meditation* (transl. with an introduction by Pye M). Duckworth, London

Buddhism in Southeast Asia

G. Condominas

Born in India, Buddhism eventually disappeared from the subcontinent, but it spread to Sri Lanka, Southeast Asia, and Central and East Asia. While on the main part of the continent it was Mahayana Buddhism ('the Great Vehicle') which flourished, in Sri Lanka and Southeast Asia, it was for the most part Hināyāna Buddhism ('the Lesser Vehicle') or more precisely Theravāda ('of the Ancients'), in the Pali tradition, that encrusted itself onto the cultures and civilizations of these different countries. Vietnam which through Chinese influence belongs to Mahayana Buddhism, is the one exception (see *Buddhism, Chinese*).

At the level of language, the impact of Buddhism was considerable. In Burma, Laos, Thailand, and Cambodia (Malaysia is a Muslim country: see *Islam in Southeast Asia*), all the teaching is done in Pali. The writing systems of the national languages of these countries are all ultimately of Indian origin, in contrast to the ancient Vietnamese system, called *nōm*, which is based on Chinese characters. In these countries borrowings from Pali, and to a lesser degree from Sanskrit, are numerous, mainly in matters of religion. For example, *bun* (from Pali *puñña*) 'merit' in Lao and Thai is frequently used in the expression 'to acquire merit,' as in the daily offering of food to the monks and the giving of a feast at the pagoda. Such loanwords may acquire different meanings in neighboring languages: *sim* (from Pali and Sanskrit *símá*) keeps in Thai its original meaning of 'stone post,' marking the limits of the sanctuary, while in Lao it signifies the sanctuary itself, which in Thai is *bo:t*.

In Laos, many Buddhist texts are in Pali or *tham*, a mixture of Lao and Pali. In rural Laos, most of the monks who read or recite these texts do not understand them at all, a phenomenon one commonly encounters in the other Theravada Buddhist countries of Southeast Asia. The borrowing of Pali words is equally prominent in the domains of art, literature, and history: for example, Thai *rûup-pân* 'sculpture' is a combination of a Pali word and a Thai one. This corresponds to the modern introduction of French and English technological terms into the spoken language.

In the written language, not only in books but also in newspapers, there is a preference for Pali or Sanskrit words. The result is that people who understand borrowings from modern Indo–European languages such as French and English, do not recognize the synonyms borrowed from the ancient Indo–European languages Pali and Sanskrit, and this leads to the creation of two language levels, one for the literati and another for the general population. A Khmer peasant, for instance, easily understands and uses *laga* (from French *la gare*), but is perplexed by *thaniy ayahsmayien* (from Sanskrit *sthāna ayasmaya*, literally, 'locality iron-made,' i.e., 'the place (where is found) the iron-machine').

The introduction of Marxism in the east of Southeast Asia, combating all forms of religion, obviously had a crucial but nevertheless temporary effect on the situation. Among the Buddhist Dai Lü in Yunnan (China), for example, at the time of the liberalization in 1985, the first thing the people did was to rebuild the pagoda destroyed by the Red Guards and to call in Thai-speaking monks from Burma to reintroduce the teaching of Buddhist texts.

See also: Cao Daí; Pāli.

Bibliography

Bechert H 1966–1973 *Buddhismus: Staat und Gesellschaft in den Ländern des Theravāda–Buddhismus*, 3 vols. Otto Harrassowitz, Wiesbaden

Bechert H, Gombrich R (eds.) 1984 *The World of Buddhism*. Thames and Hudson, London

Bizot F 1976 *Le figuier à cinq branches: Recherches sur le bouddhisme khmer*. L'Ecole français Extrême Orient, Paris

Cadière L, Leopold P 1955–1958 *Croyances et pratiques religieuses des Viêtnamiens*, 3 vols. Ecole française Bulletin de la Société des Études Indochinoises, Saigon

Condominas G 1968 Notes sur le bouddhisme populaire en milieu rural lao. *Archives de Sociologie des Religions* **25**, **26**

Condominas G 1988 In search of a Vat: Lao external exile and Dai Lü internal exile. Third International Thai Colloquium. Canberra

Gabaude L 1988 Une herméneutique bouddhique contemporaine de Thailande. *Buddhadasa Bhikkhu*. Ecole française d'Extrême-Orient, Paris

Mus P 1935 *Barabudur. Esquisse d'une historie du Bouddhisme fondée sur la critique archéologique des textes*. Impr. d'Extrême-Orient, Hanoi

Tambiah S J 1976 *World Conqueror and World Renouncer: A Study of Buddhism and Polity in Thailand against a Historical Background*. Cambridge University Press, Cambridge

Zago M 1972 *Rites de cérémonies en milieu bouddhiste lao*. Documenta Missionalia 6. Universita Gregoriana, Roma

Buddhism, Tibetan

P. M. Williams

Tibetan Buddhism may be understood as both that form of Buddhism which normally looks to Tibet for its models of orthodoxy and excellence, and also the Buddhism which relies almost entirely upon the Tibetan language for its doctrinal and spiritual concerns. As well as Tibet proper, Tibetan Buddhism includes the Buddhism of Mongolia, and some of the southern Himalayan regions such as Ladakh, Bhutan, and Sikkim. The model for all religious usage in Tibetan Buddhism is Classical Written Tibetan, to all intents and purposes the language of the Tibetan translation of the Buddhist Canon. Thus the canonical language, a sophisticated technical language developed for the translation into Tibetan of Indian Buddhist concepts expressed in Sanskrit, has exercised a very strong normative role in Tibetan Buddhist practice and life. The great scholar mKhas grub rje /kai'drupdʒe/ (1385–1438) exhorts the learned to speak language free from fault 'like that which arises from the scriptures' (*gsung rab dag las 'byung ba bzhin*). He contrasts correct speech, known as the 'language of the (Buddhist) Teachings' (*chos skad*) or 'literary language' (*yig skad*), with the regional language (*yul skad*), which the learned scholar does not hesitate to call the language of fools. This normative and prestige value of Classical Written Tibetan pervades the world of Tibetan Buddhism.

Although the Canon was translated into Mongolian in the seventeenth century, still Mongolian religious practice continued to use Tibetan as the regular liturgical and doctrinal language, and young Mongolian monks of promise would be sent to Tibet to study. A number of important figures in the doctrinal history of Tibetan Buddhism were ethnically Mongols. Only in fairly recent years, as with the Dzongkha language in Bhutan, has there been any extensive and systematic effort to present Buddhist teachings in a regional language. Nevertheless there were conscious individual attempts in the past to express Buddhist ideas for the common people in a form influenced by regional languages. There remains a work written by the eighteenth-century scholar Gung-thang dKo mchog-bstan-pa'i sgron-me/guŋtaŋ kantʃoktɛnpai drənme/ in a colloquial nomad dialect of the Amdo region of northeast Tibet. Scriptural quotations, however, occur in their regular canonical form. The great saint and *yogin* Mi la ras pa (Milarepa 1040–1123) in his songs shows the adoption to Buddhist usage of a number of the structures and linguistic forms from an oral and secular folk literature.

It has been estimated that in some parts of the Tibetan world adult male lay literacy, understood as at least being able to recognize and pronounce the letters, may have reached 50 percent. The production of written literature, however, was mainly (although not completely) the preserve of monks. In spite of the dominance of Classical Written Tibetan, nevertheless in liturgical usage by no means the entire text would be in Tibetan. Parts of liturgical texts are in an Indian language, very often a form of Sanskrit which is rather corrupt by Classical standards. These are the *mantras*, sacred formulas imbued with particular power. In Vajrayāna (Tantric) Buddhist practice associated with particular forms of a Buddha or other spiritual figures, a *mantra* is repeated which may be thought to embody the qualities of that figure and connect the mind to the Buddha's spiritual being and realm. The recitation of these 'sacred words of power' is frequent in Tibetan Buddhism, and such expressions (for example, the famous *Oṃ maṇipadme hūṃ*) are carved, written, painted, wafted on the wind, and even written on water for the benefit of all sentient beings. Through the expression of *mantras* all Tibetan Buddhists, even the illiterate, take part in an articulation of religious identity and enthusiasm. As always in Buddhism its significance is thought to lie not in the act but in the mind from which it springs.

See also: Buddhism, Indian; Buddhist Canons: Translations; Tibetan; Mantra.

Bibliography

Ekvall R B 1964 *Religious Observances in Tibet*. University of Chicago Press, Chicago, IL.

Stein R A (transl.) Stapleton Driver J E 1972 *Tibetan Civilization*. Faber and Faber, London

van der Kuijp L W J 1986 Studies in the life and thought of Mkhas-Grub-Rje IV: Mkhas-Grub-Rje on regionalisms and dialects. *Berliner Indologische Studien* **2**: 23–49

Buddhism in the West

J. Cresswell

The early development and construction of Buddhism in the West is closely connected to scholarly interest in Asian texts and language. The term 'Buddhism' is itself a Western construct for which there is no Asian equivalent and misleadingly suggests that there exists such a unitary 'object.' The major Asian Buddhist languages are Sanskrit, Pali, Tibetan, Chinese, and Japanese.

As early as 1664 a Sanskrit grammar appeared in Germany and sections of Buddhist texts began to be translated from Pali and Sanskrit into European languages soon after. During the eighteenth and nineteenth centuries scholars including Alexander Csoma de Körös and Brian Hodgson uncovered and analysed texts from Tibet, Ladakh and Kathmandu, and many were sent back to Europe. The philologist, Eugène Burnouf made the first complete translation of a Buddhist sutra from Sanskrit in 1852—The *Saddharmapundarīkasūtra* or Lotus Sutra. The Pali Text Society, set up in the UK in 1881, has been pivotal in presenting Pali Buddhism to the West. Its voluminous translations of the Pali canon or Tipitaka (see *Pali Canon*) are to this day a major reference source for the study of Buddhism. However the early philological emphasis led to a textual presentation of 'original' Buddhism which viewed the Asian cultural manifestation as corrupt.

During the twentieth century, emphasis shifted from the scholarly to the religious. Groups from the majority of Asian Buddhist traditions began to emerge in the West, the earliest of which were often based on Pali and later, Japanese and Tibetan. The use of multiple languages for similar terms has led to a confusing array of interpretations and translations. Many prefer to leave terms untranslated, whilst others are seeking translations which more closely match Western culture, for example 'contingency' rather than 'co-dependent origination.' The use of Western religious terms such as 'faith,' 'prayer,' 'merit,' and 'worship' can lead to subtle though significant misinterpretations. Whilst there is no lingua franca in evidence there is a tendency, both in contemporary writing and between Buddhists, towards the use of Sanskrit.

Buddhist terms such as *karma, nirvana,* and *zen* now appear in popular usage and whilst broadly understood in their Buddhist usage they are also used in non-Buddhist contexts: a cosmetic called *Zen Blush*; a rock band called *Nirvana*; a pop song entitled *Karma chameleon*.

Many groups continue to chant mantras and texts in Buddhist languages for example *Om Mani Padme Hum* (Tibetan) and *Nam Myo Ho Renge Kyo* (Japanese). Often the Mantra is considered to hold inherent power and is therefore untranslatable. The Order of Buddhist Contemplatives chooses to chant in English and to use English terms for example 'contemplation' rather than 'Zen.' Within some

Buddhist groups language classes are made available to enable texts to be read in their native language though increasingly translated texts are relied upon.

See also: Mantra; Sutra; Meditation; Müller, F. M.; Buddhist Canons: Translations.

Bibliography

Batchelor S 1994 *The Awakening of the West, The Encounter of Buddhism and Western Culture 543 BCE–1992.* Aquarian, London

Fields R 1986 *How the Swans Came to the Lake: a Narrative History of Buddhism in America.* Shambala, Boston

Candomblé

C. H. Ribeiro dos Santos

Candomblé is one of the principal Black Brazilian manifestations of religion. The etymological origin of the word *Candomblé* is to be found in the Kimbundu (Loanda Mbundu) language: *ka* + *ndumbe* + *mbele* 'house of initiation.' Candomblé is practiced in almost all the territory of Brazil; the oldest houses of this sect, however, are in the states of Bahia, Rio de Janeiro, Maranhão, and Pernambuco. Its ceremonies are based on the worship of forces of nature (Orixás) and of ancestors. The sacerdotal structure is extremely hierarchical; a principal priest is called *babalorixá* (in Portuguese *pai-de-santo*) and a principal priestess *yalorixá* (*mãe-de-santo*).

Its origin dates back to the slave trade when Africans were taken to Brazil to serve as manpower in the plantations and in urban work. The principal three groups that came to make up Candomblé were the Nago, the Fon, and the Bantu. The Nago or Yoruba originated from different regions of present-day Nigeria; the Fon, also known in Brazil as Jeje, were natives of the ancient Kingdom of Dahomey (today the Republic of Benin), of Ghana and of Togo; and the Bantu came from the extensive territory of Southern African colonized by the Portuguese, such as Angola, the Congo, and Mozambique. These ethnic groups respectively brought the Yoruba, Ewe-Fon, and Kimbundu languages to Brazil.

The appearance of sects of African origin in the New World was an unforeseen result of the traffic in slaves and it forms one of the most important areas of the survival in Brazil of Black culture, including various African languages.

The investigation of the language of Candomblé shows that its traditional and conservative character—a fundamental facet of archaic cultures—encouraged the preservation of an immense richness of vocabulary, proverbs, and accents. The enduring African element, inherent in its forms of language and present in this manifestation of religion, has ensured a cultural continuity, in spite of the imposition of Portuguese as the official language of the country. Thus an amalgam, formed between the Portuguese language and the different African languages that arrived in Brazil, has given rise to the linguistic heterogeneity existing in the Candomblé communities, and equally to the elaboration of forms of communication and speech very typical of—and also peculiar to—this religious group.

Because of this, in the Candomblé communities it is possible to come across many different levels of expression in lexis and idiom that are attributable to their origin in varied linguistic situations. Such linguistic situations are of the following kinds. First, there is the common Portuguese spoken in Candomblé houses, with the use of regionalisms, colloquialisms, and expressions regarded as vulgar, used principally in non-religious contexts. Second, there is Portuguese with a strong idiomatic presence of terms in Yoruba, Ewe-Fon, and Kimbundu; this is used in conversations among novices, as an introduction to the language of ritual and of everyday life in the communities, either in non-religious activities or in the preparation of less complex rituals. Third, there is the Portuguese spoken by older initiates, in which Yoruba, Ewe-Fon, and Kimbundu terms predominate. The use of more African forms of speech appears as an additional affirmation of the power of the elders and as a form of excluding from conversations novices who are not yet prepared to have access to more profound knowledge of the rituals. Fourth, there is the exclusive use of Yoruba, Ewe-Fon, and Kimbundu, confined to the more complex moments of the ceremonies, in which the gods (Orixás, Voduns and Inquices) are invoked by means of hymns, prayers, and direct appeals.

In this cultural microcosm is found evidence of a vital linguistic force; it is separate from the power and ordinances of the state and in it the 'desire for blessing' is translated into the common speech of the Candomblé communities, such as *Motumbá* in the houses of Yoruba origin, or *Kolofé* in those of Fon or Jeje origin, and *Muculu* in those of Bantu origin. In these three words, of different origin yet of identical meaning, there is summed up the sense of reverence for the older initiates of the community and for the gods in whom they believe.

See also: African Traditional Religions; Caribbean Syncretistic Religions 1: Cuban Santeria and Haitian Voodoo; Caribbean Syncretistic Religions 2: Jamaican Cumina and Trinidadian Shango; Macumba.

Bibliography

Abraham R C 1981 *Dictionary of Modern Yorùbá*. Hodder and Stoughton, London

Fonseca Jr E 1993 *Dicionário Yorubá (Nagô)—Português*. Civilização Brasileira, Rio de Janeiro

Maia A da Silva 1964 *Dicionário Complementar Português-Kimbundo-Kicongo*. Editorial Missões, Cucujães

Maia A da Silva 1964 *Dicionário Rudimentar Português-Kimbundo*. Editorial Missões, Cucujães

Maia A da Silva 1964 *Epítome de Gramáticas Portuguesa e Quimbunda*. Editorial Missões, Cucujães

Muniz Sodré 1988 *O Terreiro e a Cidade: A Forma Social Negro-Brasileira*. Vozes, Petrópolis

Póvoas R do Carmo 1989 *A Linguagem do Candomblé*. José Olympio Editora, Rio de Janeiro

Ramos A 1979 *As Culturas Negras no Novo Mundo*. Companhia Editora Nacional, São Paulo

Verger P 1993 *Orixás—Deuses Iorubás na África e no Novo Mundo*. Corrupio, Salvador

Cargo Cults

K. O. L. Burridge

Cargo cults are socio-magico-religious activities which have been occurring in Oceania since at least the 1850s, the vast majority (say 97 percent) in Melanesia. Involving genuine socio-political and economic aspirations (a new earth) and also elements of spiritual and moral renewal (a new heaven), they are millennarian. The name cargo (=*kago* in Tok Pisin) derives from the overt aspirations and rites which—articulated and urged on others by a charismatic leader or 'prophet' after a revelatory experience—point to imminent access to quantities of processed foods and manufactured goods: the cargo imported from industrialized countries.

The recorded instances of cargo cults (more than 400) have much in common. Generally, following serious talk about activities elsewhere, which tends to arouse expectations, someone may have a dream or vision in which a traditional or Christian spirit entity reveals the means by which cargo will be obtained. Bizarre though these may seem at first (e.g., signaling for cargo with radios of palm thatch, grotesque baptismal rites, orgiastic dances, sexual promiscuity, destruction of crops, and traditional sacra), the word used to refer to the rites, both in Tok Pisin (*wok*) and in local vernaculars, means 'work': work in gardens which translates into food, exchanges, gaining status, and the power to attain, maintain, and be worthy of high status. Moreover, the symbolisms in the rites are clear: a fresh start to life in community; movement from an economy based on exchanges of food and valuables to one based on money; equal status and opportunity of access to cargo in relation to whites.

Cargo cults have generally been interpreted as reactions to the sociocultural changes attending colonialism, mission work, wage labour, two world wars, the several exchanges of one set of masters for another, and so on. Yet the incidence of the cults, in particular their high concentration in former New Guinea where Tok Pisin was most used and standardized by missionaries and administrators, shows that other factors may be at work. Also, accounting for the relatively few occurrences in Polynesia and Micronesia, where Tok Pisin is absent, and the Highlands of New Guinea, where the same general social conditions have obtained, presents problems. One answer is that in a cult context the Tok Pisin word *kago* carries a transcendent sense of final redemption from obligation which the English 'cargo' does not. And this seems to go with the fact that the cults are more frequent where infirm authorities and a shifting leadership give rise to ambiguities of obligation and identity, as in former New Guinea, and rarer where traditional political structures, identities and the loci of authority have persisted in reasonable certainty, as elsewhere in Oceania.

See also: Ecstatic Religion; Glossolalia; Melanesian Religions; New Religious Movements; Religious Symbols.

Bibliography

Burridge K O L 1960 *Mambu*. Methuen, London 1970 Harper Torchbooks, New York. Princeton University Press, NJ

Burridge K O L 1969 *New Heaven. New Earth*. Basil Blackwell, Oxford

Lawrence P 1964/1971 *Road Belong Cargo*, Manchester University Press, Manchester

Lindstrom L 1990 *Knowledge and Power in a South Pacific Society*. Smithsonian Institution Press, Washington
Steinbauer F 1971 *Melanesian Cargo Cults*. George Prior, London
Wilson B R 1973 *Magic and the Millennium*. Harper and Row, New York
Worsley P 1957/1968 *The Trumpet Shall Sound*. MacGibbon and Kee, London

Caribbean Syncretistic Religions 1: Cuban Santeria and Haitian Voodoo

C. H. Ribeiro dos Santos

Santeria is the generic term for the religious sects of African origin on the island of Cuba. Yorubas—a corruption of whose ancient name, Ulcumi, is preserved in Cuba as Lucumí—were the predominant group, in spite of the fairly important presence of Bantus (among others, speakers of (Ki)Kongo and Mbundu, as well as a group known in Cuba as Mayombe) and Dahomeans (speakers of Fon-Ewe) in the formation of Cuban culture. This culture is also the result of Spanish colonization, above all in the legacy of its language and of Roman Catholicism. The word *santeria* refers to the *santos* 'saints' and the sect's adherents combine devotions to the Orixás (divinities and forces of nature), known as *el santo*, and to Catholic martyrs in the same ritual. Oshún is associated with the Virgin of la Caridad del Cobre, Yemayá with the Virgin of Regla, Babáluayé with St Lazarus, and Changó with St Barbara.

Religious practices of several African ethnic groups are included under the name Santeria. Such rituals are popularly called *Regla* 'rule,' in the sense of 'sect' or 'religion.' The best known are the following. First, there is the *Regla de Ocha* or *Regla Lucumí*, the cultural and linguistic basis of which is Yoruba, consisting fundamentally in the worship of Orixás and of ancestors. Originally the term Santeria was applied to the *Regla de Ocha*. This religious ceremony is conducted by a priest known as *babalocha* or *santero*, and the novices are called *iyabó*. Second, there is the *Regla de Mayombe* or *Palo Monte*. It worships gods (*Nkisi*) and ancestors (*Fumbi*) and its main linguistic features are from Kongo. In the course of colonization, the *Regla de Mayombe* became closely associated with witchcraft. In this sect, the religious heads are called *mayomberos* or *Tata Nkisi*. Third, there is the *Regla Arárá-Dahomey*, originating among Fons from the ancient Kingdom of Dahomey (present-day Benin), devotees of divinities called *Voduns*. Their priests are called *bokono*.

In Cuba, the ceremonies for the dead and ancestors (*Egun*) and the oracular rituals invoking the mediation of the god of divination Orúmila are of great importance. Fate is revealed by a method of divination (*Ifá*), carried out by manipulating conch shells, oil palm seeds, and the like. These rituals are more characteristic of the Yorubas, the priest who consults the oracle being known as *babalawo*, a Yoruba expression meaning 'father of the secret.' Revelations are given by the interpretation of long poems (*Itá*), dealing with portents of fate, and of legends of the Orixás recited in Yoruba, such legends being called *pataki*. The *bokonos* of the *Regla Arárá-Dahomey* employ a roughly similar procedure, though the recitations are in the Fon-Ewe language.

It is noteworthy that the oral expressions of the followers of Santeria are made up of words in Spanish, Yoruba, Fon-Ewe, and different Bantu languages. However, the use of African languages is quite clear-cut in the caste of initiates. Thus, the higher the level of the celebrant in the hierarchy, the greater is his command of the African language of his sect.

In Haiti, a former French colony, the largest groups of Black slave labour who were taken to this island were of Fon origin (tribes from present-day Benin), Bantus (principally from the Congo and Guinea), and Yorubas. Among these ethnic groups Voodoo originated. Voodoo is a mystery religion, and at the same time, it is a word which for the Fons refers to a divinity. Its cultural diversity ensures that its religious observances form a multicolored mosaic of phenomena similar to a kaleidoscope: at each movement it presents a different appearance yet, by the same token, it is almost impossible to say what these appearances have in common.

Voodoo also represents a generic religious designation under which different rituals are encountered. First, there is the *Radá* sect, which worships and honours spirits and divinities of Dahomeyan origin, the latter being also syncretized with Catholic saints. Second, there is *Ginen*, originating in the beliefs of the Bantus of Guinea, in which good spirits or *loas* are honored. Third, there is *Kongo*, of Bantu origin. This is one of the least widespread rituals in Haiti, and one of its principal characteristics is the sacrifice of dogs. Fourth, there is *Petro*, whose divinities are all native to Haiti. This is a sect of national character, in which the so-called *loas créoles* are worshipped. The existing stereotypical macabre picture of Voodoo is due to *Petro*, since it is used to cause harm.

The singing, prayers and everyday conversation in Voodoo temples or *houmfort* are conducted in Creole, a mixture of French with African languages, such as Fon-Ewe, Yoruba, and Congo. In the Haitian countryside, the continued use of African languages in Voodoo is more deep-rooted and better preserved.

See also: African Traditional Religions; Candomblé; Caribbean Syncretistic Religions 2: Jamaican Cumina and Trinidadian Shango; Macumba.

Bibliography

Alfonso J H 1994 Santería: Uma Religião Cubana de Origem Africana. In: Moura C E M de (ed.) *As Senhoras do Pássaro da Noite*. Edusp, São Paulo

Alonso G A 1995 *Los Ararás en Cuba: Florentina, La Princesa Dahomeyana*. Editorial de Ciencias Sociales, La Habana

Benedicto J L L 1988 *Cuba*. Ediciones Anaya, Madrid

Cabrera L 1975 *El Monte: Notas sobre las Religiones, la Magia, las Superticiones y el Folklore de los Negros Criollos y del Pueblo de Cuba*. Ediciones Universal, Miami, FL

Chesi G 1980 *Voodoo*. Perlinger Verlag, Wörgl

Davis W 1986 *A Serpente e o Arco-Íris*. Jorge Zahar Editor, Rio de Janeiro

Helgueras A L, Salmoral M L 1988 *El Caribe*. Ediciones Anaya, Madrid

Laennec H 1987 *O Deus da Resistência Negra: O Vodu Haitiano*. Paulinas, São Paulo

Laennec H 1993 *Les Mystères du Vaudou*. Gallimard, Paris

Laennec H 1993 *El Bárbaro Imaginario*. Fondo de Cultura Económica, Mexico City

Métraux A 1989 *Le Vaudou Haïtien*. Gallimard, Paris

Price-mars J 1928 *Ainsi Parla L'Oncle: Essais D'Ethnografie*. Imprimerie de Compiegne, Port-au-Prince

Ramos A 1979 *As Culturas Negras no Novo Mundo*. Companhia Editora Nacional, São Paulo

Caribbean Syncretistic Religions 2: Jamaican Cumina and Trinidadian Shango

C. H. Ribeiro dos Santos

Jamaica, like the rest of Afro-America, was the birthplace of important religious and cultural phenomena among Blacks whose origins were on African soil but who were slaves for more than three centuries. The predominant ethnic group were the Kromanti of the Gold Coast (present-day Ghana), this name being used in the Americas to include speakers of Fante, Asante (Twi), Gã, and Agona; there were also Bantu cultural influences, principally from the Congo. The island was discovered in 1494 by the Spaniards, who governed it until 1655, when it was captured by an English expedition. Although English is the official language of the country, the majority of the population, especially in the rural central area, speak Creole or Black English, a mixture of African languages with the language of the colonizer. Anglicans and Baptists form the major religious groups and are the official religions recognized by the state; however, beliefs of African origin are extremely widespread. Because of this, on this particular island there is an interesting process of syncretization between Protestant and African religions; this is something different from the rest of Afro-America, almost all of which was colonized by Catholic nations.

Cumina is a religion closely bound up with beliefs about life after death and with the worship of ancestors. It is the product of cultural elements from ethnic groups from the Gold Coast (Fanti-Ashanti), mixed with a Bantu culture, probably from the Congo. In this religion, it is believed that man is endowed with two souls or spirits. One of these, after death, departs to a divine existence, never to return to the world of the living. The other soul, better known and called a *duppy*, is like a shadow. After death, it remains in the grave with the corpse and can walk about on earth and torment the living. The word *duppy* seems to be a corruption or Anglicization of the Jamaican word *jumbie*, itself originating from the Kimbundu *nzumbi*, meaning 'afflicted spirit' or 'spirit which wanders about to torment the living.' Among the Blacks of the island, it is common to meet proverbs which make reference to *duppies*, for example, *Duppy know who fe frighten in a dark night*, that is, 'A duppy knows whom it frightens on a dark night.'

It should be pointed out that in Jamaica we still find other Black religious movements, such as Obi or Obeah (associated with black magic, witchcraft, and other anti-social practices), Myalism, Rastafarianism (which has taken on political and ideological overtones, linked to the advancement of Black culture), Pocomania, and the Convince Cult. In all of these can be seen syncretism between elements of Protestant sects and of African cultures.

Trinidad was also colonized by the English. On this island we find Shango as the principal religious movement of African origin. In it the influence of Yoruba culture is predominant, originating from the peoples of present-day Benin and Nigeria. The word *shango* is the same as the name of the God of Thunder, of a mythical king, and at the same time of a historical person, who was a member of a long dynasty of rulers of the city of Oyo in Nigeria. One section of this cult is syncretized with Catholicism, there being links between the Orixás or Orichas (divinities and forces of nature) and Catholic saints. The other section became fused with Protestant sects, principally Baptists ('the shouters') and Adventists, and various Protestant hymns and customs were introduced into Shango. Practices from spiritualism, too, were introduced into these Afro–american sects.

The members of the religious community in general use a patois or dialect that mixes words from Yoruba and English. However, words in French are also used. It is interesting to note that in Shango the altars are called *stools*. Given the connotations of 'seat,' 'base' and 'support,' a *stool* can be either an altar or a stone dedicated to a divinity. The cult-house, properly speaking, is known by the French word *palais* 'palace.' The festivals in honor of the divinities are celebrated on the same days dedicated to the Catholic saints with which the Orixás are associated. Such ceremonies are accompanied by hymns, dances, and sacrifices of animals. In the course of the dancing trances are experienced in which African gods appear. The rituals are conducted by a director, who invokes the spirits to appear in his 'horses,' initiates who embody the Orixás.

The supreme divinity of the cult is Olorun. However, he does not have special rituals, a feature also observed in Africa, Brazil, and Cuba. It is Shango—the God of Thunder, symbolized by a double axe—who gives his name to this religion, since he is the most popular and important Orixá. Leba-Echu is also worshipped; he rules crossroads, roads, and the sexual act. Spirits of infants are also worshipped in the cult of Ibechi (the same Ibeji of the Yorubas), the twins associated with St Cosmo and St Damian, the protectors of children. Various other divinities are worshipped, there being a great similarity between them and the Yoruba gods worshipped in Cuba and Brazil. In Grenada there is also a cult of African origin called Shango, fairly similar to that of Trinidad with, however, rather less elaborate rituals.

See also: African Traditional Religions; Candomblé; Caribbean Syncretistic Religions 1: Cuban Santeria and Haitian Voodoo; Macumba; Rastafarianism.

Bibliography

Fichte H 1987 *Etnopoesia—Antropologia Poética das Religiões Afro–Americanas*. Editora Brasiliense, São Paulo

Franco M D G 1994 Antropología de lo Sagrado en el Caribe: Culto Obeah en Jamaica. In: *Boletin de Antropologia Americana* (No. 30), México, diciembre, 134–142

Maia A da Silva 1964 *Dicionário Complementar Português-Kimbundo-Kicongo*. Editorial Missões, Cucujães

Pollak-eltz A 1972 *Cultos Afroamericanos*. Universidade Católica Andrés Bello, Caracas

Pollak-eltz A *El Concepto de Múltiples Almas y algunos Ritos Fúnebres entre los Negros Afroamericanos*. Caracas: s/e, s/d

Ramos A 1979 *As Culturas Negras no Novo Mundo*. Companhia Editora Nacional, São Paulo

Cao Daí

C. Nguyen

Cao Daí is a popular religion that emerged towards the end of the period of French colonialism in South Vietnam. The movement never had any influence in North Vietnam. Cao Daí was 'founded' by a group of French-employed bureaucrats based on the claim of its original leader that in 1920 he had a series of revelations from the Supreme Being (Cao Daí) who referred to himself as 'Ngoc Hoang Thuong De' ('The Jade Emperor Lord on High') or 'Cao Daí Tien Ong Bo Tat Ma Ha Tat' ('The Supreme Immortal Bodhisattva Mahasattva'), a title suggesting the syncretism of Confucianism, Taoism and Buddhism.

Although presented as a self-styled reformed Buddhism, doctrinally, Cao Daí proposes a syncretistic ideology that represents the convergence and culmination of Eastern and Western religions. The Cao Daí pantheon includes, among others, Shakyamuni Buddha, Lao Tzu, Confucius, Jesus Christ, Socrates, Victor Hugo, Li Po, and Sun Yat-sen. At the center of Cao Daí teachings is the proclamation of the coming of the new era, a third era of general amnesty which would follow the first era of creation and the present era of decline. The Cao Daí teachings consist of a series of words spoken by Cao Daí Tien Ong to his disciples received through a spirit medium. It was imperative that the medium scribe write down faithfully to the minutest detail what was revealed to him. Absolutely no editing was allowed. The revealed words were in Vietnamese, Sino-Vietnamese and occasionally French. Stylistically, they were a mixture of prose and verse. The verses are written in 'Duong Luat' (Tang style) either of the 'that ngon tu tuyet' (four lines, seven syllables to a line) or 'that ngon bat cu' (eight lines, seven syllables to a line) style or the traditional Vietnamese 'luc bat' (a six-syllable line followed by an eight-syllable line) of various length. Most of them are in colloquial Vietnamese, some are in Sino-Vietnamese—Chinese characters with Vietnamese pronunciation written in the Roman alphabet. The prose part is a mixture of an awkward Sino-Vietnamese and an archaic colloquial southern Vietnamese with all its idiosyncrasies. Occasionally, there are mispellings typically of Southern Vietnamese. Since Cao Daí beliefs and practices draw on the main principles of Confucian ethics and popular Taoist/Buddhist tenets, a motley array of technical terms—in Sino–Vietnamese—from these religions are used throughout the canon. Western names are found in their French spellings. For instance, Moise (Moses), St. Jean-Baptiste (St. John the Baptist), Hebreux (Hebrew). Overall, the language of the Cao Daí scriptures is not readily intelligible and sounds hybrid and even comical to outsiders. However, it has become canonical language for the adherents of Cao Daí—the majority of them are Southern Vietnamese. Before the Fall of Saigon (1975) Cao Daí had about over 1 million followers. Nowadays, there are Cao Daí groups among the Vietnamese diaspora, particularly in California.

Bibliography

Do Van-Ly 1989 *Tim Hieu Dao Cao Dai*, Vol. I [*Understanding the Cao Dai Religion*]. Cao Dai Giao Viet Nam Hai Ngoai, Perris

Thanh Ngon Hiep Tuyen va Tan Luat Phap Chanh Truyen [*Selected Sacred Words and the New Orthodox Laws*]. Reprinted. Toa Thanh Tay Ninh, Tay Ninh, 1985

Vuong Kim 1965 *Tan The va Hoi Long Hoa* [*The End of the World and the Long Hoa Assembly*]. Tan Sanh, Saigon

Celtic Religion

H. Moisl

The language of pre-Christian Celtic religion was a version of the contemporary Celtic vernacular specialized to the point of obscurity. It was metrical in form, highly metaphorical, self-consciously recondite, and deliberately archaic. To understand why it was so, one has to consider the nature of the priesthood which cultivated it.

An identifiably Celtic culture emerged in central Europe round about the fifth century BCE, underwent a period of development and extensive geographical expansion in the centuries which followed, and then disappeared rapidly in the face of Julius Caesar's campaigns of conquest in the first century BCE and the subsequent romanization of Celtic regions. Most of the textual information about the continental Celts of this period comes from Greek and Roman historians of the first century BCE and the first century CE; vernacular continental Celtic material is limited to a relatively small number of short inscriptions. Thereafter, Celtic culture survived only in peripheral areas of Europe where Roman influence was weak or nonexistent, and which escaped the Germanic settlements which subsequently engulfed the western Empire: Ireland, Scotland, Wales, Cornwall, and Brittany.

Textual information about these areas begins to appear with the establishment of the Christian Church, which introduced literacy into the essentially preliterate Celtic culture and thereby made it possible for Celtic oral tradition to be recorded for the first time. Christianity was dedicated to the eradication of what it regarded as a heathen Celtic religion, and it succeeded rather quickly. But for various reasons the Church did record a substantial amount of information about the old paganism and its priesthood. The Irish material is the earliest and by far the most extensive: it begins ca. 650 CE with law tracts, royal dynastic history and mythological texts, and proliferates rapidly thereafter. The Welsh and Scottish records begin several centuries later and are relatively much sparser; for Cornwall and Brittany virtually nothing survives. For present purposes, therefore, 'Celtic' refers to the continental Celts up to about the first century CE, and to the Irish and Welsh from pre-Christian times into the early medieval centuries.

The priests of pre-Christian Celtic religion were the druids. Descriptions of them in Classical, Irish, and Welsh sources correspond in detail, and the account given here is composite. Like any preliterate society, the Celts needed some means of perpetuating the traditions which articulated and maintained their ethnic identity: history, law, mythology, and ritual. The cultivation of such tradition was entrusted to the druids, and in that task they were highly disciplined. Druidical schools existed in which students spent years—Caesar says 20, the Irish 12—memorizing the entire corpus of oral tradition. To aid memorization, the material was in verse form. Actual examples of such verse survive only in the Irish and, to a small extent, in the Welsh historical records. The basic metrical unit is the two-, sometimes three-stress line in which all stressed words alliterate; metrical lines are bound together by alliteration between the final stressed word of one line and the initial stressed word of the line following, which imparts mnemonic continuity. Because, moreover, this material was transmitted over successive generations in a fixed and memorized metrical format, its language tended to remain unchanged and thereby to become archaic relative to the current vernacular.

Like any priesthood, the druids' primary function was to mediate between the human and divine spheres. As part of their training, they learned mystical techniques which were intended to give them direct access to their gods, and by virtue of this access they claimed prophetic and magical powers. Divine invocations, prophetic pronouncements and magical spells were all couched in alliterative verse of the kind just described. In keeping with its numinous character, such verse tended to be syntactically convoluted and heavily metaphorical.

The druids occupied a socially prestigious and politically influential position by virtue of their learning and claimed mantic powers. The basis of Celtic political organization was tribal. Each tribe was ruled by a king, and each king had a druid in his court whose legally defined status was equal to his own. That status derived from the druid's broadly tripartite function. First, he administered the cult of sacral kingship, which derived royal authority from the sanction of the tribal deity. The druid was custodian of this mythology and associated ritual, and so was able to bestow and reiterate that authority on public occasions. By virtue of his prophetic powers, moreover, the druid advised the king in political matters, and used his claimed magical powers on the king's behalf, particularly to achieve victory in battle. Second, the druid maintained the history of the royal family, and was thus crucial in determining such things as historically based family prerogatives and rights of succession. Third, as custodian of law, the druid oversaw the administration of justice within the tribe, and advised the king in his role as ultimate arbiter. Because the druids occupied their privileged position by virtue of their learning, they were concerned to restrict that learning to themselves. They therefore deliberately accentuated the obscurantist characteristics already mentioned, and further increased its inaccessibility by liberal use of technical and exotic vocabulary.

The following verse fragment is characteristic. It comes from the Dindsenchas, a collection of Irish historical and mythological tradition which was almost certainly part of the curriculum in a druidical school. The Eo Rossa of the first line is a waterfall which, in pre-Christian mythology, was regarded as one of the places of contact between the world of men and the Otherworld:

Eo Rossa,	Eo Rossa,
roth ruirthech,	swift current,
recht flatha,	outpouring of water,
fuaimm tuinne,	noise of wave,
dech duilib,	excellent to men,
diriuch dronchrand,	straight firm tree,
dia dronbalc,	god vigorous and true,
dorus nime,	door to the Otherworld.

See also: Archaism; Incantations; Magic; Ogam; Shamanism.

Bibliography

Cunliffe B 1986 *The Celtic World*. Crown, New York
Ellis P B 1992 *Dictionary of Celtic Mythology*. Constable, London
Ellis P B 1994 *The Druids*. Constable, London
Ellis P B 1998 *The Ancient World of the Celts*. Constable, London
Green M 1986 *The Gods of the Celts*. Alan Sutton, Gloucester
Green M 1992 *Dictionary of Celtic Myth and Legend*. Thames and Hudson, London
Green M 1995 *The Celtic World*. Routledge, London
Green M 1997 *Exploring the World of the Druids*. Thames and Hudson, London
Ó Cróinín D 1995 *Early Medieval Ireland, 400–1200*. Longman, London

Christian Science

D. Treacy-Cole

Founded in the nineteenth century by a New England woman, Christian Science is described in and distinguished by its unique textbook *Science and Health with Key to the Scriptures*, first published in 1875. Audacious and radical, the language in *Science and Health* is described by its author, Mary Baker Eddy, as original, and decried by her detractors as incomprehensible.

Eddy struggled to find both terminology and a grammatical style to communicate her theology, often resorting to metaphorical language in the tradition of biblical writing. She employed a system of capitalization to distinguish seven synonymous terms (viz., Mind, Spirit, Soul, Principle, Life, Truth, Love) used 'to express the nature, essence and wholeness of Deity' (Eddy 2000: 465).

Critics accused Eddy of repetitiveness and circularity in her writing. However, a recent biographer points out that postmodernist and feminist critical theory do not necessarily consider non-linearity a failing (Gill 1998: 218). Objections to Eddy's style may be attributable to what has been called an oracular treatment of great theological themes, rather than the more common rationalistic and philosophical treatises of male theologians.

In an era that viewed the Christian God in patriarchal terms, Eddy emphasized God's motherhood. In her spiritual interpretation of the opening 'Our Father' of the Lord's Prayer, she offered 'Our Father–Mother God.' From the third edition of *Science and Health* published in 1881 through the fifteenth edition of 1885 Eddy went even further, using the feminine pronoun for God, although she subsequently reverted to the masculine form.

Science and Health also includes a glossary of 125 biblical terms. In some cases the original Hebrew or Greek word is mentioned, although the definitions correspond with Eddy's metaphysical interpretation of the subject.

See also: Feminism.

Bibliography

Eddy M B 2000 *Science and Health with Key to the Scriptures*. The Writings of Mary Baker Eddy, Boston

Gill G 1998 *Mary Baker Eddy*. Perseus Books, Reading, MA

Christianity in Africa

A. Hastings

The involvement of the Christian churches in issues of language has been central both to the modern linguistic history of sub-Saharan Africa and to the life of the churches themselves. Apart from Swahili in the east and Fulfulde and two or three others in the more islamicized west, none of the languages of Sub-Saharan Africa had been given a written form prior to the coming missionaries.

1. Early Missionary Translation Work

The earliest extant Bantu text is a lengthy catechism in Portuguese and Kongo produced by the Jesuit Mattheus Cardoso and printed in Lisbon in 1624. This, a subsequent Kongo dictionary by a Capuchin, Georges de Geel, and a grammar produced by another Capuchin, Giacinto Brugiotti da Vetralla in 1659, are immensely valuable for Bantu linguistic history. The last includes the Bantu noun-class and concord system. Unfortunately the Catholic missionaries of that era produced little work in any other language. It was the nineteenth-century Protestant missionaries with their far higher conviction of the necessity of Bible translation who produced a mass of linguistic work—the production of dictionaries, grammars, and biblical texts for scores of languages in every part of Africa. The pioneering work of Krapf in the east, van der Kemp, Moffat, Applevard, and Colenso in the south and Raban Schön, and Crowther in the west—to name but a few from the early and middle years of the nineteenth century—stands for a vastly larger undertaking which has as yet received no adequate historical survey. In almost every African language with a written literature missionaries have been responsible for the basic work and, indeed, for most subsequent published literature as well, except in a handful of the larger languages. The vast multiplicity of African languages and the policy of most colonial and postcolonial governments to use English, French, or Portuguese for educational purposes mean that (apart from some score of languages such as Yoruba, Swahili, Shona, and Ganda) there is still little, if anything, of any extent published in most languages except for church purposes.

2. Missionary Imposition of a Dialect as a Language

Missionaries could not, of course, have done this work without African collaborators who had themselves first learnt English. Inevitably the precise language canonized by missionaries, in the first dictionaries and New Testaments, was the dialect used by their assistants. As all languages inevitably varied geographically, so that it is indeed open to argument how far any specific language actually existed prior to its precise missionary-constructed form, the language of missionary literature represents in every case the particular local form in which the missionary's assistants were at home. Once printed it was, however, essential that it be used across a wider area in which people were much less at home with it. The missionary approach had mistakenly assumed a degree of linguistic uniformity which in fact it had rather to impose. This produced inevitable tensions and at times rebellions. Moreover, other missionaries working in the same general languages area but some distance away inevitably absorbed different dialectical forms. Missionaries certainly revised their translations as their language knowledge improved, but Africans had also to some extent to relearn their languages when they studied the Scriptures or other works in mission schools. Moreover, tensions between different forms of a language as fixed by a range of different missionary translations (so that, for instance, Protestant and Catholic Baganda could divide linguistically as well as theologically) continued for decades, at least until the 1930s or later when colonial governments insisted on standardized forms for state-assisted schools. Even then imposed uniformity such as 'Union Igbo' was not easily accepted.

The missionary preoccupation with the vernacular written word was quickly taken over by leading African Christians. The Reverend John Raban's initial work on Yoruba was continued by the Yoruba schoolteacher, and later bishop, Samuel Ajayi Crowther who made a major linguistic contribution in his recognition of the essential role of tone in Yoruba, Nupe, and other Nigerian languages. In southern Africa, the Presbyterian minister, Tiyo Soga, the translator of Bunyan's *Pilgrim's Progress* into Xhosa, died in 1871 while at work on the Acts of the Apostles. While some missionaries and African Christians, such as Schön and Crowther, were undoubtedly outstanding precisely as students of language, their primary preoccupation to translate as quickly as possible as much biblical and Christian literature as they could often, it must be said, weakened their achievement precisely as linguists.

3. The Name of God

For missionaries, the great question was a practical and pedagogical one: how far could they find suitable words already in existence for the special things they wished to teach about, how far had they instead to invent words in which to do so? In the latter case, how were they to arrive at the words they needed? It is striking that in the large majority of African languages, missionaries were content to use an existing vernacular name for the all-important name of God. In some places, at least at first, they felt unable to do this and imported foreign names like *Dio* or *Godi*. But these were exceptional and mostly short-lived. For the greater part, they became convinced that Africans had already sufficient belief in a single almighty spirit for it to be possible to adopt an African name for such a spirit to use for the biblical and Christian *Yahweh*, the Father of Jesus. Thus in East Africa, *Mungu*, *Mulungu*, or *Ruhanga*; in central Africa *Lesa* or *Nzambi*; in southern Africa *Molimo* all came—among many other names—to be used. In Zimbabwe, there were long hesitations among some over the use of *Mwari*—in this case because of its localized cult. It is noticeable that in many cases these names had already obtained a considerable degree of intertribal currency, in some cases overshadowing more local names. It seems clear that missionaries preferred words with the wider usage.

4. Other Key Christian Terms

This seems true for a wide range of religious terms. As missionaries advanced from one people to another, they inevitably carried words, especially key words, across intertribal boundaries. They did this particularly in eastern Africa in the early years with regard to Swahili. While Swahili is basically a Bantu language, it has incorporated a very large number of Arabic words, including especially religious words. Despite their Muslim origin, these seemed, with their theistic character and biblical links, ideal for missionary use. Hence words like *eddini*, *essala*, *injili*, *kanisa* ('religion,' 'prayer,' 'gospel,' 'church') were imported into many other inland Bantu languages from Swahili. They seemed to fill a gap, while avoiding the importation of purely European words to which many missionaries were driven in other circumstances, when no suitable vernacular word was discovered for some major Christian concept. However, a later generation of missionaries found this dependence upon Swahili regrettable, perhaps because of its apparent Muslim connotations, and in several languages such words were systematically eliminated if alternatives could be found.

'Gospel' and 'baptize' are typical cases. The root meaning of the one is 'good news,' of the other 'wash' or 'sprinkle,' but each has turned in Christian usage almost into a proper name. Many early missionaries (Catholics especially) were unwilling simply to find a vernacular phrase meaning 'good news' or 'wash' and render the words in this way. Hence vernacular Christian doctrinal texts could be peppered with strange-sounding terms, transliterations of Greek, Latin, or English. The tendency now is to eliminate these in favor of genuinely local words.

5. *Muzimu* and *Nganga*

In other cases, traditional words with a religious connotation were available but were avoided just because it seemed the wrong connotation. Words for 'spirit' are probably the clearest case. Missionaries were most anxious not to let the 'Holy Spirit' become identified with, or understood in terms of, the 'spirits' of traditional religion, especially spirits of the dead, which frequently possessed the living. Hence nearly everywhere the typical Bantu spirit word *muzimu* was rejected. Again, the almost universally used term throughout Bantu Africa for a priest, diviner, or medium *nganga*, was regarded as unusable for a Christian minister in the nineteenth century and since. The *nganga* became, instead, the stereotype of the pagan 'witchdoctor' against whose influence Christianity is battling. This is interesting because missionaries in the sixteenth and seventeenth centuries willingly described themselves as '*nganga*'. These are two cases in which the linguistic challenge of assimilation still remains to be met.

6. The Fluidity of Word Meanings

What seems clear is that language usage in nonliterate societies is far more fluid than might be imagined. It is less a matter of finding the right word than making it right by regular usage. Existing words had the flexibility of all language and missionaries could anyway not know how reliable were their informants. Words (and not only the name of God) moved easily across language groups in precolonial Africa. Missionary importations and adaptations were nothing new. Once a word was adopted, used in a certain way in scriptures, hymns, and sermons, it easily acquired the meaning now given it whether it had it before or not. Within a generation or so non-Christians too could be using it the missionary way. Thus, for instance, even where missionaries mistakenly adopted for 'God' a local name which had really belonged to a culture hero of quite limited importance (e.g., the Nyakyusa *Kyali*), the new missionary content for the word quickly became a normative one, recognized by all but the antiquarian.

7. The Lasting Language Impact of Missionary Translations

In the scores of African languages which have possessed a Bible, a hymn-book, a catechism for 50 to 100 years, but still very little more in the way of written literature, these books with their specific vocabulary and the meanings of the words which the content of the Bible and Christian tradition impose upon them may now be near the heart of living language usage. Rather little in that vocabulary was formally imported, but the conversion of traditional words to new meanings has effectively taken place. Nevertheless, the new meanings have not simply obliterated old meanings. African religion in most places is now an integrated mix of the traditional with the Christian (or the Islamic). That mix is one of concept, of ritual, and also, inevitably, of linguistic meaning. Moreover, the process described above has not proceeded everywhere at the same rate or gone so far. In some languages it began considerably later than in others. In many smaller languages little of scripture has even now been printed. Much has depended too on how skilled linguistically early missionaries were. In some places they did indeed master the language, translate intelligibly, preach eloquently, and in a way impose their meanings upon it. In others, missionaries were unable to do this. Their linguistic ability was simply inadequate. They preached through poorly trained interpreters and remained so marginal to the vernacular culture that what translations they produced had little impact upon its world of meaning. The very fact that schooling was in English or French might actually protect vernacular meanings from the impact of Western Christian verbal imperialism. Nevertheless, in most rural areas where Christian churches have been actively at work and (as in the case of most countries of Africa south of the Equator) now have a majority of the population considering itself Christian, biblical literature and a Christian interpretation of religious words may be almost has central to vernacular culture as was the King James version and its vocabulary specific to the culture of preindustrial Britain.

See also: African Traditional Religions; Missionaries; Bible Translations, Modern Period; Islam in Africa.

Bibliography

Bontinck F, Ndembe Nsasi D 1978 *Le Catéchisme Kikongo de 1624*. Réédition critique, Brussels

Coldham G 1966 *A Bibliography of Scriptures in African Languages*

Doke C M 1967 *The Southern Bantu Languages*. International African Institute, London

Fabian J 1986 *Language and Colonial Power: The Appropriation of Swahili in the Former Belgian Congo, 1880–1938*. Cambridge University Press, Cambridge

Hair P E H 1967 *The Early Study of Nigerian Languages.* Cambridge University Press, Cambridge
Hastings A 1989 The choice of words for Christian meanings in eastern Africa. In: *African Catholicism.* SCM Press, London
Rowling F, Wilson C 1923 *Bibliography of African Christian Literature*
Samarin W 1986 Protestant missions and the history of Lingala. *Journal of Religion in Africa* **16(2)**: 138–63

Christianity in East Asia

J. H. Grayson

1. China

The history of Christianity in China began with the establishment of the Nestorian Church during the T'ang Dynasty (618–907 CE) by missionaries and priests from Mesopotamia and the Near East who arrived in China in the year 635 and afterwards. In 638, the first of these missionaries, a Persian priest known in Chinese as Alopên (Abraham) is said to have written in Chinese an outline of the teaching of Christ entitled *Hsu-ting Mi-shih-so Ching* (The Gospel of Jesus the Messiah) which was a condensation of and exposition on St Matthew's Gospel. In 781, a great stela, inscribed in Chinese and Persian known latterly as the 'Nestorian Monument,' was erected in the T'ang capital, Ch'angan. Rediscovered by Roman Catholic missionaries in 1625, the stela is a primary document of the history and progress of the Nestorian Church (see *Chinese*: *Translation of Theological Terms*).

Following the collapse of the T'ang state, Nestorian Christianity survived mainly amongst the 'barbarian' peoples to the north of China. During the Mongol or Yüan Empire (1234–1368), which encouraged various religious traditions within their vast domains, the Nestorian Church again flourished within the bounds of the Chinese empire, although largely amongst non-Chinese peoples.

Also at that time, embassies from Europe to the Mongol court included priests or friars, and the first Roman Catholic missionary to arrive in China was the Italian Franciscan John of Montecorvino (sent after 1272, died before 1333), who translated the New Testament into Mongolian. An organized church was created with dioceses and an archdiocese located in the Mongol capital, Khanbalik, but this did not survive the collapse of the Mongol Empire in 1368 because the church was largely composed of non-Chinese members, has no native clergy, and was overly dependent on imperial patronage.

Permanent missionary work in China recommenced in 1573 with the arrival of the Jesuits, notably Matteo Ricci (1552–1610), who attempted to express Christian concepts through Chinese culture. The Jesuits were later joined by Franciscans and Dominicans who took a different view on 'The Term Question' concerning the appropriate word for the Supreme Being, and 'The Rites Controversy' over the propriety of Christian attendance at Confucian ancestral rituals. In 1773, the Jesuit order was suppressed by Papal command, a result of this interorder struggle, and the right to mission work in China given to the Paris Missionary Society.

Because the Roman Catholic Church traditionally emphasized the teaching of doctrine over scriptural study, translation of the Bible did not form a significant part of Catholic missionary endeavor before the early nineteenth century, although part of the New Testament was translated into Manchu in the seventeenth century. A number of apologetic works in Chinese were published. Most important of these was the *T'ien-hsüeh Shih-lu* ('The True Doctrine of the Holy Religion') by Matteo Ricci in 1595, revised in 1601 as the *T'ien-chu Shih-i* ('The True Doctrine of the Lord of Heaven'), which had an enormous influence in China, Korea, and Japan. The Lord's Prayer, Ave Maria, and the Apostles' Creed were also translated at an early stage, and then somewhat later the breviary, the missal, Aquinas's 'Summa Theologiae,' Thomas à Kempis's 'The Imitation of Christ,' and St Ignatius of Loyola's 'Spiritual Exercises' and several other liturgical and theological works.

Both Protestant and Roman Catholic missions expanded rapidly in China after the signing of the unequal treaties which concluded the 'Opium Wars' of 1839–44. Imperial edicts of toleration enabled the expansion of missions and the growth of the Protestant and Catholic churches. By the end of the nineteenth century there were over 530,000 Roman Catholics and 52,000 Protestants.

Because of the priority placed on Scripture, the first work undertaken by the earliest Protestant missionaries was the translation of the Bible into Chinese. The New Testament was first translated into a crude form of Chinese by Joshua Marshman (1768–1837) and others in Serampore, India in 1811, and the Old Testament by 1823. The finest early translation of the complete Bible was produced in Malacca by Robert Morrison (1782–1834) with the assistance of Robert Milne (1785–1822) in 1819. Morrison also prepared a valuable Chinese–English dictionary, and Chinese versions of the Church of Scotland Shorter Catechism and an abbreviated form of the Book of Common Prayer of the Church of England.

Bible translation continued to be one of the major efforts by Protestant missionaries throughout the nineteenth century. It was not only important to perfect the literary style and accuracy of the earlier translations, but it was also necessary to create translations which would be understandable to ordinary people rather than to the educated elite. A further problem was the translation of the Bible into the various 'dialects' (in reality different regional languages) of China. Like their Roman Catholic predecessors, early Protestant missionaries were also concerned about the selection of correct theological terms, especially the correct term for 'God' (see *Chinese*: *Translation of Theological Terms*).

Among the interesting techniques utilized by the missionaries was the transliteration of some of the southern coastal 'dialects' using Roman letters, rather than translation using Chinese characters. This was done both to facilitate literacy amongst the largely illiterate population and to represent words in those 'dialects' for which there were no Chinese characters.

The first attempt at a union Bible translation was made with the selection of a group of scholarly missionaries from various societies, The Delegates, who produced a common version of the New Testament in 1850. Unresolved questions of translation method prevented the Old Testament committee from producing a common translation. Two versions were produced, one more literary in form in 1853, and another in a more popular form in 1862. From the 1870s on, notable attempts were made to produce good translations in the Mandarin dialect of the north, and an easier form of the literary style called 'easy Wên-li.' By 1895, there were reported to be 10 missionary printing agencies to further literary mission work, and by the end of the missionary period in 1949, the Bible had been translated into 27 distinct Chinese 'dialects,' languages, or literary styles using Chinese characters, Roman letters, two different Chinese phonetic scripts, and a mixed script of Chinese characters and phonetic script.

Following the collapse of the Ch'ing Dynasty (1616–1912) and its society, many young Chinese turned to Christianity as a source of hope for the future of their country, and the number of Christians increased both numerically and in percentage representation within the population during the first half of the twentieth century. By 1949, there were over 3,500,000 Roman Catholics and 700,000 Protestants, forming roughly 1 percent of the Chinese population. This growth had been achieved under conditions of great economic hardship, foreign invasion, and civil war. In 1949, the Communist regime abolished all religious bodies formed by free association and created bodies subservient to the central, provincial, and local governments. The Three-Self Patriotic Movement and the Patriotic Catholic Movement had responsibility for Protestant and Catholic Christians respectively until the Cultural Revolution (1966–76) when churches and all other places of worship were closed.

Since 1979 the practice of religion has again been permitted and places of worship have been reopened. The main division in contemporary Chinese Christianity would appear to be between the officially sanctioned churches of the patriotic associations, and the semi-underground churches of the house church movement. By the mid-1990s, there may have been as many as six million Christians associated with the latter body and up to five times that many in the former grouping.

The translation of the Bible into Chinese still remains an important linguistic undertaking, the most notable recent example being the version based upon the *Good News for Modern Man* translation issued in 1975. As a result of the increased toleration of religion after the Cultural Revolution, the Three-Self Movement and its associated China Christian Council have acquired modern printing presses which have been used to produce hundreds of thousands of copies of the Bible in Chinese.

Modern translations into the languages of the minority peoples of China include New Testaments in the Kalmuk dialect of Mongolian (in the Mongolian script, 1815 and 1897), in Literary Mongolian (using the Manchu script, 1846 and 1952), in Manchu (1835), and in Tibetan (1903 and 1948). Parts of the New Testament were translated into the Khalka dialect of Mongolian (1872) and the Buriat dialect of Mongolian in the Cyrillic script (1909 and 1912).

2. Korea

Although knowledge of Christianity and Western customs was available to the Korean scholarly class from the early seventeenth century on, there appears to have been no missionary contact or Christian influence on Korea until the late eighteenth century. In the winter of 1777, a group of Korean scholars gathered to study Matteo Ricci's *T'ien-chu Shih-i*. In 1784 one of their number went to Peking with a royal embassy, and was baptized. Upon his return, he began to evangelize and baptize his friends so that by the time the first missionary, a Chinese priest, arrived in 1795, there were 4,000 believers. But with the death of the tolerant King Chŏngjo in 1800, an edict to suppress the 'pernicious superstition' was promulgated and until the 1880s, the history of the Roman Catholic Church in Korea was one of persecution and martyrdom. The first Western missionaries from the Paris Missionary Society entered Korea in 1836, but the Church had to remain underground for fear of persecution. By the end of the nineteenth century, the Catholic Church had become primarily a church of the lower and outcaste classes of society.

The establishment of diplomatic relations with Western nations in the 1880s brought the Hermit Kingdom into intercourse with the outside world and religious toleration was permitted. The Catholic Church began to come out from its ghetto, and Protestant missionaries established schools, a university, and hospitals which attracted large numbers of young progressive Koreans. At this time, mission schools created and helped to propagate new scientific and technical terms which were required for a Western-style academic curriculum.

The first Korean translation of the New Testament by John Ross (1842–1915), completed in 1887, not only was instrumental in the initiation of Protestant Christianity in Korea, but through its exclusive use of the indigenous Korean alphabet, disdained by the Confucian literati, had a profound effect on Korean literature and education. The alphabet, which Ross saw as the perfect tool for Christian evangelism, is today the symbol of Korean nationalism. Ross's choice of theological terms, especially his use of the native term for the 'High God,' *Hananim*, influenced every subsequent translation.

Later translations were usually printed in a mixed script of Chinese characters and Korean letters rather than solely in the Korean script as Ross had preferred. There are two contemporary translations of the Bible, the more colloquial *Common Translation* (1978) and the *New Standard Version* (1993) which is more traditional in style. Both of these translations use only the Korean alphabet and not Chinese characters. Other early missionary translation work includes the outstanding contribution of James Scarth Gale (1863–1938) who translated John Bunyan's 'Pilgrim's Progress' into Korean, and compiled a 'Korean–English Dictionary' which is the basis for all subsequent works of its type. As the singing of hymns is an important aspect of Protestant worship, it is not surprising to learn that by 1896 there were at least three different hymnals in use. However, ecumenical cooperation was early encouraged and since 1905, there has been only one hymnal in use throughout the Protestant denominations.

Under Japanese rule (1910–45), Korean nationalism and Protestant Christianity became closely linked. In the 1930s, Protestant Christian refusal to participate in the worship conducted at Shintō shrines in Korea, lead to the persecution and, in a few instances, the death of Christians. The Catholic Church, because of the Concordat signed between the Vatican and Japan, accepted participation in Shintō rites as a 'patriotic act.'

Liberation from Japanese rule led to the division of the Korean peninsula into American and Soviet zones of influence, the Republic of Korea in the south, and the Democratic People's Republic of Korea in the north. In the north, as in China, the government suppressed free religious associations and created bodies directly controlled by the government. In the south, religious bodies were permitted to form freely and Protestant and Roman Catholic Christianity have both seen spectacular increases in membership. Ten million people, approximately one quarter of the population, are Christians. By the mid-1990s, there were more than two million Catholics and eight million Protestants, largely Presbyterians and Methodists.

The situation in the north is hard to assess. Since 1987, delegations representing the Christian community there have traveled abroad, and two Protestant churches and a Catholic church have been built and opened for worship. Claims are made that there are 10,000 Catholic and 10,000 Protestant believers, but as northern Korea was the heartland of Korean Protestant Christianity before Communism, it is conceivable that, if there is an underground church, its size may be many times larger than that.

3. Japan

Christianity was brought to Japan in 1549 by St Francis Xavier (1506–56). Under the supervision of Xavier, the Gospel of St Matthew and the Catechism were translated and devotional literature was written. Christianity was suppressed ruthlessly throughout the Tokugawa shogunate (1603–1867) and these materials were destroyed. With the collapse of the shogunate, and the opening of Japan to the West, Christian mission work was again possible, and nineteenth-century Roman Catholic missionaries discovered underground Christian communities which had maintained their faith for over 200 years. Protestant missionaries also arrived in 1859 and by the end of the nineteenth century, it seemed possible that Japan might become a 'Christian country,' such was the reception given to the new religion by the educated elite. By 1880, the first complete translation of the New Testament appeared (revised 1917) and in 1888, the Japanese Old Testament was published, which remained the standard Protestant Bible for nearly 50 years. Colloquial Japanese translations of the New Testament appeared in 1953 and 1955, and the ecumenical *Common Bible* in 1978.

Japan did not become Christian in part as a result of the revival of Shintō and the connection which was made by the government between adherence to Shintō rituals and nationalism. Throughout the first half of the twentieth century, the Church was often treated with suspicion by the government, especially during the era of military governments in the late 1920s to the mid-1940s. It was during this era that the various Protestant denominations were 'Japanized' by amalgamating them into one government supported group, the Kyodan. The Catholic Church was likewise 'Japanized' by the removal of all foreigners in authority.

Although the impact of the Church on Japanese society has been relatively small, the Christian churches have produced some outstanding persons in the areas of the arts, letters, and philosophy, notably Uchimura Kanzō (1860–1930) and Kagawa Toyohiko (1886–1960).

Following the conclusion of World War II, contrary to expectations, the Christian percentage of the population remained at about 0.8 percent until the early 1980s, when there was a remarkable increase until it represented about 1 percent of the population in the early 1990s. A significant difference between the Korean and Japanese churches is that Japanese Christians have tended to be more intellectual and less evangelical than their Korean neighbors.

See also: Chinese: Translation of Theological Terms; Ricci, M.; Ross, J.; Korean; Missionaries.

Bibliography

Cary O 1976 *A History of Christianity in Japan: Roman Catholic, Greek Orthodox and Protestant Missions*. C. E. Tuttle, Rutland, VT

Clark D N 1986 *Christianity in Modern Korea*. University Press of America, Lanham, MD

Grayson J H 1989 *Korea: A Religious History*. Oxford University Press, Oxford

Jennes J 1959 *History of the Catholic Church in Japan from Its Beginnings to the Early Meiji Period, 1549–1873: A Short Hand-book*. Committee of the Apostolate, Tokyo

Lambert T 1991 *The Resurrection of the Chinese Church*. Hodder & Stoughton, London

Latourette K S 1929 *A History of Christian Missions in China*. SPCK, London

Latourette K S 1939–45 *A History of the Expansion of Christianity*, vol. 5. Eyre and Spottiswoode, London

Lee S K 1971 *The Cross and the Lotus*. The Christian Study Centre on Chinese Religion and Culture, Hong Kong

Paik L-G G 1971 *The History of Protestant Missions in Korea: 1832–1910*. Yonsei University Press, Seoul

Whelan C 1996 *The Beginning of Heaven and Earth: The Sacred Book of Japan's Hidden Christians*. Hawai'i University Press, Honolulu

Zetzsche J O 1999 *The Bible in China: The History of the Union Bible or the Culmination of Protestant Bible Translation in China*. Monumentica Sericam Institute, Sankt Augustin

Christianity in Europe

J. F. A. Sawyer

Despite its Near Eastern origins within the context of ancient Judaism, the dominant language of early Christianity was a European language. Many Jews were Greek-speakers, and the Hebrew scriptures had been translated into *koine* Greek (see *Bible Translations, Ancient Versions*) long before the time of Christ. To these were added the Gospels, Paul's Letters, and the rest of what later became Christian scripture, all originally written in Greek. Even the Coptic, Syriac, and later Arabic varieties of Christianity were strongly influenced by Greek. The shift from Jerusalem to Greece and Rome, represented already in the life and work of the Apostle Paul and described in the Book of Acts, was thus from a linguistic point of view less significant than might appear at first sight, and the rapid spread of Christianity through the Roman Empire, mostly among the lower classes of society, more understandable.

By the end of the fourth century, Christianity had become the official religion of the Roman Empire. The final split between the Western Church under the Papacy at Rome and the Eastern or Orthodox Church, with its center until 1453 at Byzantium/Constantinople, took place in the eleventh century. In the sixteenth century, European Christianity was further fragmented by the Protestant Reformation, and at about the same time began to spread in its various forms to North America, Latin America, Africa, and Asia.

Latin was the sole liturgical language of Western Christianity until the Reformation, and continued to hold this position in the Roman Catholic Church until the Second Vatican Council in 1962–65 which encouraged the use of the vernacular in the mass (see *Church Latin*). The Eastern Orthodox Church, in contrast, familiar with established Syrian and Armenian traditions, did not insist on linguistic uniformity, and it was with the blessing of Constantinople that Ulfilas (see *Wulfila*) (ca. 311–83 CE), originally from Cappadocia in Asia Minor, invented the Gothic alphabet and translated the Bible into Gothic for his mission to eastern Europe.

It was an Eastern emperor, too, who commissioned Cyril (826–69) to take the Gospel to the Slavs, for whom he invented the Glagolitic script, based on the Greek alphabet, and wrote his Slavonic translation of the Bible (see *Cyril and Methodius*; *Old Church Slavonic*; *Church Slavonic*). The influence of the Church on the Slavonic languages can still be seen in the use of the Cyrillic alphabet in Russia, Bulgaria, and Serbia, which are historically Orthodox, in contrast to the use of the Roman alphabet in Catholic regions like Poland, Czechoslovakia, and Croatia. By far the most influential among the other European Bible translations are Martin Luther's German Bible (see *Luther, Martin*) and the 'Authorized Version' of King James (1611).

1. Conservatism

Out of respect for tradition, the languages and language varieties used by the Church in Europe as elsewhere, especially in the liturgy, are mostly characterized by conservatism which separates them from everyday language. The retention of Latin by the Roman Catholic Church throughout the world until the latter part of the twentieth century is the most obvious example, and corresponds to the use of Arabic in Islam and Hebrew in Judaism. The first of the Vatican II documents, published in 1963, acknowledges that 'the use of the vernacular in the Mass... may frequently be of great advantage to the people' and authorizes translations from the Latin 'approved by the competent territorial ecclesiastical authorities.' Similar concerns have led to the publication of numerous new translations of the Bible, official and unofficial, in every European language.

Conservative opposition to these developments, due as a rule to a mixture of theological, aesthetic, and political factors, and rearguard actions of various kinds, have never been lacking. Reactions to vernacular translations range from the violence that led in the sixteenth century to the execution of the Bible translator, William Tyndale, in 1536 and the break-up of the Roman Catholic Church in Europe, to sardonic comments like that of Thomas Hobbes: 'After the Bible was translated into English, every man, nay, every boy and wench that could read English, thought they spoke with God Almighty and understood what he said.' The 'Tridentine Mass' movement led by the rebel Archbishop Lefebvre, and the 'High Church' Anglican 'Prayerbook Society,' dedicated to preserving the use of the 1661 Book of Common Prayer, are twentieth-century examples.

In most English-speaking varieties of Christianity, however, archaic forms like *thou*, *thee*, and *ye* have now been dropped, except, significantly, in the 'Lord's Prayer' and the 'Hail Mary' (see *Prayer*). Much traditional biblical and liturgical language which was borrowed, via Latin, from Ancient Hebrew and Greek, has also been abandoned. Thus, for example, modern vernacular translations no longer preserve English Hebraisms like *all flesh* 'all mortals,' *children of Israel* 'Israelites,' *beast of the field* 'wild animals,' *and with thy spirit* 'and also with you,' and *the bowels of Christ* 'Christ's compassion.' A few words of Greek (notably *Kyrie Eleison* 'Lord, have mercy') and Hebrew (e.g., *Hosanna* 'give victory'; *Hallelujah* 'Praise the Lord') still survive, as do a number of simple Latin hymns and chants popularized by the international and ecumenical Taizé community in France (see *Hymns*).

2. Sectarianism and Prejudice

Divisions within the Church are clearly reflected in language variation. In Britain, a Catholic priest lives in a *presbytery* and an Anglican in a *vicarage* or a *rectory*, while a Protestant minister lives in a *manse*, and for Presbyterians a *presbytery* is not a building at all, but one of the Church councils. Catholics *go to mass* on Sunday with their *missals*, Anglicans *go to church* with their *prayer books*. The distinctions and many others, such as that between Roman Catholic *Derry* and Protestant *Londonderry*, can be a matter of life and death in a situation like that in Northern Ireland in the late twentieth century. Until the Act of Union in 1800, Irish Gaelic was associated with Roman Catholicism, while English was the language of the powerful, landowning Protestant settlers, including the Scots in Ulster, and even today IRA graffiti are often in Irish. Sectarian conflict has spawned many terms, such as *papist* 'Roman Catholic' and *proddie* 'Protestant,' and some, like *Roman candle*, a type of firework burnt on Guy Fawkes night, have an obvious and gruesome origin in the history of persecution in England, even though this is no longer known to most people.

The history of the Church's attitude to Jews in Europe has been characterized by prejudice and hatred, frequently erupting into persecution, and, since the Holocaust, attempts have been made in the Protestant and Catholic Churches, though not so far in the Eastern Orthodox Church, to remove or reword some of the blatantly antisemitic language of the Good Friday liturgy, including the 1661 prayer for 'Jews, Turks, and infidels,' and to revise some passages in the Gospels where the Greek word for 'the Jews' can arguably be translated 'the Judaeans' or even, in some contexts, 'the people.' The term 'Old Testament,' however, is still used, often unthinkingly, in such expressions as 'Old Testament ethics' and 'the God of the Old Testament,' which tend to denigrate Judaism and perpetuate traditional antisemitic attitudes.

The language of the Church has also been affected by the changing role and status of women. In 1983, the Methodist Church in the UK published a hymnbook which 'takes equal account of the place of both women and men in the Church,' omitting or altering such compositions as 'Rise up, O men of

God.' In the ecumenical 'New Revised Standard Version' of the Bible (published in 1991) 'inclusiveness has been attained by simple rephrasing or by introducing plural forms.' Female images of God are now common in the language of worship and theological discourse, especially that of God as Mother, for which the authority of a number of scriptural passages can be cited (e.g., Deuteronomy 32: 18; Isaiah 42: 14), and a Trinity of 'Mother, Lover, and Friend' has been introduced as an alternative to the patriarchal 'Father, Son, and Holy Spirit' (McFague 1987). As expressions like 'my brothers and sisters,' 'men and women,' and 'humankind' become more frequent and more accepted in the liturgy, it will become harder to retain relics of the past, such as 'for us men and our salvation,' which is still current in modern translations of the Nicene Creed.

3. Influences on Secular Language

Christian beliefs and practices have left their mark on many aspects of secular vocabulary, even though their original Christian connection has long since been forgotten, from the commonest personal names like *John* and *Joanna* (cf. Gaelic *Iain*, German *Johann*, *Johannes*, or *Hans*, French *Jean* and *Jeanne*, Italian *Giovanni*, Spanish *Juan* and *Juanita*, Greek *Iōannēs*, Russian *Ivan*, Hungarian *Janos*: see *Names: Religious Beliefs*), to hundreds of items of vocabulary. These include not only specifically religious terms like French *Pâques* 'Easter' (from Greek *pascha*, Hebrew *pesaḥ*) and *bishop* (cf. French *évêque*, Greek *episkopos*), but also common everyday words like *ladybird* (cf. German *Marienkäfer*, Spanish *vaca de San Antón*, French *bête à bon Dieu*).

The days of the week in the European languages present an interesting variety, clearly related to the differing degrees of success among the indigenous cultures in withstanding the influence of Christianity. Thus in English and other Germanic languages they bear the names of the sun, the moon, and the five planets, called after the deities Tewis, Wotan, Thor, Freya, Saturn, and have no Christian associations at all (although in some very religious communities *the Lord's Day or the Sabbath* is preferred to *Sunday*). Greek, on the other hand, following Jewish and biblical tradition, uses the ordinal numerals 2–5 for 'Monday' to 'Thursday,' and the specifically religious terms *paraskeuē* 'preparation,' *sabbaton* 'sabbath,' and *kuriakē* 'the Lord's Day' for Friday, Saturday, and Sunday. Some Latin languages compromise with a combination of both systems, Christian and pre-Christian, by calling 'Sunday' the *Lord's day* (French *dimanche*, Italian *domenica*, Spanish *domingo*), and using the names of the moon and planets, called after the Roman deities Mars, Mercury, etc., for the rest of the week: French *lundi*, *mardi*, etc., Italian *lunedì*, *martedì*, etc. The Russian for Sunday, *Voskresenye*, literally '(the day of) the resurrection,' survived 70 years of official atheism.

In a number of countries, including England, Christian language and beliefs have a privileged status not afforded to other religions, in that they are protected by blasphemy laws (see *Blasphemy*).

Through the global activities of Christian missionaries from the sixteenth century on, who to begin with believed it to be their right and duty to impose their own beliefs and practices wherever they worked, it was European Christianity and with it some extraordinarily influential European Christian languages, especially English, Dutch, French, Spanish, and Portuguese, that established itself in many other parts of the world, including, ironically, Western Asia where it originated.

See also: Christian Views on Language; Feminism; Christianity in the Near East; Byzantine Greek; Vulgate.

Bibliography

Cross F L, Livingstone E A (eds.) 1997 *The Oxford Dictionary of the Christian Church*, 3rd edn. Oxford University Press, Oxford
Hastings A H, Mason A, Pyper H (eds.) *Oxford Companian to Christian Thought*. Oxford University Press, Oxford
Martin D (ed.) 1979 Crisis for Cranmer and King James. *PN Review* **13**: 1–64
McFague S 1987 *Models of God: Theology for an Ecological Nuclear Age*. Fortress Press, Philadelphia, PA
Ruether R R 1983 *Sexism and God-talk*. SCM, London
Sawyer J F A 1991 Combating prejudices about the Bible and Judaism. *Theology* **94**: 269–78

Christianity in Iran and Central Asia

N. Sims-Williams

By the end of the third century CE, the Syrian church had expanded southwards and eastwards from its earliest strongholds in northern Mesopotamia and Adiabene to become well established in many parts of western Iran. Here the Christians suffered from intermittent persecution, for reasons which were political as well as religious, since the ruling Sasanian dynasty, which adhered to the Zoroastrian religion, was often at war with the neighboring Christian state of Byzantium. However, the church in Iran received unintended reinforcement from the policy of Shapur I (ca. 240–270 CE), who deported large numbers of Greek speakers, including Christians, from Roman territory into Iran. These settlers retained their own ecclesiastical language and hierarchy as late as the fifth century, when some cities still had both a Greek-speaking and a Syriac-speaking bishop.

Early in the fifth century the church in Iran demonstrated its independence from Byzantium by refusing to accept the authority of the Patriarch of Antioch, a breach which became permanent when the doctrinal formula adopted by the Council of Chalcedon (451 CE) was rejected by the great majority of the Christians of Iran in favor of the so-called 'Nestorian' christology. Towards the end of the century, isolated both administratively and theologically from Western Christendom, the Nestorian church of Iran became more inward-looking. This is the period from which comes the first reliable evidence of the composition of Christian literature in Middle Persian, the Iranian dialect of the south-western province of Fars, and the state language of the Sasanian empire. One such work was a summary of Christian theology, which the Catholicus Acacius (d. 496) translated from Syriac into Middle Persian for submission to the Sasanian monarch Kawad I. Others included treatises on canon law, some of which are extant in Syriac translation, as well as hymns and other liturgical texts. The linguistic nationalism which may have given the first impetus to this literary activity is clearly seen in an episode in the Life of the East Syrian saint John of Dailam (d. 738), which describes a quarrel between Persian and Syriac-speaking monks over the language to be used in the liturgy. Later, Syriac regained its exclusive status as the language of Iranian Christendom, with the result that no Christian literature in Middle Persian survives. The only exception is a fragmentary psalter found in Chinese Turkestan (see below); other parts of the Bible are not known to have been translated into Persian before the thirteenth and fourteenth centuries.

The evangelization of Central Asia, which had begun by the fifth century, was principally due to the missionary zeal of the Nestorian church of Iran, though the Jacobites (the monophysite branch of the Syrian church) set up bishoprics as far east as Herat in Afghanistan, and the Melkites (the Syrian Christians who accepted the doctrine of the Council of Chalcedon) also had important centers in eastern Iran and Choresmia. In these distant outposts of the Syrian church, amongst speakers of languages such as Choresmian (Khwarizmian), Sogdian (the Iranian dialect of the Samarkand area, which had become a lingua franca of the trade route between Iran and China), Turkish, and Chinese, there is little evidence of knowledge of Greek, let alone Hebrew. Only the Melkites continued the use of Greek, beside Syriac, in their liturgy. For most Christians in Iran and Central Asia, the Syriac Peshitta version effectively took the place of the original texts of both Old and New Testaments. The prestige of Syriac, as the language of Scripture and of central parts of the liturgy, led to its continued use for religious and formal purposes, even amongst people whose grasp of Syriac grammar and orthography was shaky, such as the thirteenth and fourteenth century Christians, of mainly Turkic origin, whose gravestones have been found in great numbers in the region of Frunze (Kirghizia).

The position of Syriac in the Nestorian church was thus somewhat comparable to that of Latin in the West, a parallel noted by the Franciscan traveler William of Rubruck in the mid-thirteenth century, who wrote of the Central Asian Nestorians: 'They say their services and possess sacred books in Syriac, a language which they do not understand, so that they sing like those monks amongst us who are ignorant of grammar' (Pelliot 1973: 136–37). Unlike the Roman church, however, the Nestorian church had always allowed the vernacular a place in the liturgy, in particular for hymns, psalms, and Bible readings (Hage 1978). As the church expanded eastwards, a wide range of languages came to be employed in its worship, as has been demonstrated by the discovery, in the ruins of a Nestorian monastery at Bulayiq (in the Turfan oasis, Chinese Turkestan), of a library of fragmentary manuscripts in Sogdian, Syriac, Turkish, and other languages, including the Middle Persian psalter mentioned above. Most of these manuscripts are written in Syriac script, which was adapted to the phonology of non-Semitic languages such as Sogdian, New Persian, and Turkish by the addition of a few extra letters. Neither this modified Syriac script nor the Syriac vocabulary employed in these manuscripts (mainly technical terms such as 'bishop,' 'monastery,' 'canonical hour'; see Sims-Williams 1988) were ever adopted by non-Christian users of the languages concerned.

The use of Middle Persian for the vernacular parts of the liturgy was probably introduced into Central Asia during the initial stages of the Nestorian mission from Iran, but Middle Persian, which would not have been understood by the local population, was soon superseded by Sogdian. Later, but still before the end of the first millennium, Christianity became well established amongst the Turkic peoples of Central Asia, some of whom continued the by then traditional use of Sogdian—beside Turkish and Syriac—as a language of Christian literature and liturgy. Later still, certain Mongol rulers of Central Asia and Iran were attracted to Christianity and some Christian texts are said to have been composed in Mongolian. However, the Nestorian church in the

East did not long survive the ravages of the Mongol hordes of Timur in the late fourteenth century, after which the Christians were soon reduced to an insignificant minority in western Iran, Turkey, and Iraq, where the so-called 'Assyrian' church survives to the present day (see *Christianity in the Near East*).

See also: Byzantine Greek; Persian; Peshitta; Semitic Scripts; Syriac, Christian.

Bibliography

Hage W 1978 Einheimische Volkssprachen und syrische Kirchensprache in der nestorianischen Asienmission. In: Wiessner G (ed.) *Erkenntnisse und Meinungen* 2. Otto Harrassowitz, Wiesbaden

Pelliot P 1973, 1984 *Recherches sur les Chrétiens d' Asie Centrale et d'Extrême-Orient* [1], 2(1). Imprimerie Nationale, Paris

Sims-Williams N 1988 Syro–Sogdica. III: Syriac elements in Sogdian. In: *A Green Leaf. Papers in Honour of Professor Jes P Asmussen* (*Acta Iranica* **28**). E J Brill, Leiden

Sims-Williams N 1991a Christianity in Central Asia and Chinese Turkestan. In: Yarshater E (ed.) *Encyclopedia Iranica*. Mazda, Costa Mesa, CA

Sims-Williams N 1991b Christian literature in Middle Iranian languages. In: Yarshater E (ed.) *Encyclopedia Iranica*. Mazda, Costa Mesa, CA

Christianity in the Near East

J. N. Birdsall

The Christian communities of the Near East, together with their members forced by circumstances to emigrate, are the descendants of the earliest adherents of the faith, in and about the lands of its origin. Their fragmented aspect is the result of the divisions of the Church in the fifth and sixth centuries over the details of the doctrinal definition of the relationship of the divine and human natures in the person of Christ, especially as these had been decided in the Council of Chalcedon (451 CE). Divisions based on beliefs and formulae, both traditional and subtly defended, were intensified by the support given by successive rulers to one side or another, or by their attempts to enforce their own formulae of intended reconciliation. Sections of the population of the Eastern Roman Empire were alienated by the proscription of their beliefs, the exile of their leaders, and the legal sanctions invoked against them. Thus, when in the seventh century and afterwards, Islam grew and spread, the conquerors were welcomed as liberators.

There were regimes and periods where Christians were respected and protected sections of the population, playing an active part in the service of the state. Yet slowly but surely more repressive tendencies asserted themselves. Persecution and the more insidious pressures of legal, political, and social disabilities hemmed the Christian communities in. Proselytizing and conversion to Islam, massacre, and emigration led to numerical decline. Even protective measures, such as the Ottoman institution of the *millet* whereby each minority group had rights and representatives, led to the formalization and fossilization of the religious and social patterns inherited from earlier times.

The divisions were rendered more complex when after minimal contact for some centuries, Eastern Christians again met Western Christians in the period of the Crusades, and throughout the following centuries. The Roman Catholic Church sought to bring the churches of the Christian East into formal communion with itself and it sometimes appeared politic to the Eastern leaders to accept such overtures. But the people, whose experience was frequently of being despised, conquered, and exploited by Western liberators, would often fail to go along with their leaders, and thus new schisms and divisions were created within those already existing, leading to duplications of the old alignments: one group in communion with Rome, the other, as a rule the majority, still dissident. Only the submission of the Maronites to the claims of the Roman Church resulted in a simple transference from the Eastern to the Western camp.

The division of the Western Church at the Reformation in the sixteenth century intensified Roman Catholic missionary effort, especially through the Society of Jesus. Protestant interest in the Eastern churches was never absent but missionary activity producing separated churches began only in the late eighteenth century. Western nations, especially Britain and France, took an interest in the political fortunes of groups religiously affilitated to them, up to the mid-twentieth century.

If should be noted that when Eastern churches were reconciled with the Roman Catholic Church, accepting papal supremacy, their liturgical language remained unchanged. The objective of reconciliation was not the imposition of uniformity in this or other matters of practice, but doctrinal authenticity brought about by the acknowledgement of one ecclesiastical head. Thus Syriac, Arabic, Armenian, Coptic, Ethiopic, Greek, and Old Slavonic continued to be used in Catholic churches of the 'oriental rite,' as they are termed.

This brief survey begins with the Nestorians or Assyrians. These are the survivors of a church separated from orthodoxy by the decisions of the Council of Ephesus in 431. They prospered outside the Roman Empire in northern Mesopotamia and Iran, and during the Middle Ages their missionary zeal established Christianity in Central Asia, Mongolia, China, and South India. Most of these communities were destroyed by Timur-Lenk in the fourteenth century. Communities in Iraq, Iran, and Syria, still speaking a form of Syriac, however, have survived in spite of much persecution and massacre. In the territories of the former Soviet Union small communities are found in the Caucasus. Many have emigrated, especially to the USA. A great part of the indigenous Christians of South India are of this stock too. In communion with Rome, they are called 'Chaldaeans' in Iraq, Syria, the former Soviet republics, and elsewhere, or 'Syro–Malabars' in India. Their Bible and liturgy are in Syriac.

Jacobites or Syrian-Orthodox, together with Copts, Ethiopians, and Armenians, are descended from groups which opposed the formulations of the Council of Chalcedon in 461. 'Jacobite' is derived from their organizer in secession, Jacob Baradai (sixth century). They survive in Lebanon, Syria, Iraq, and Turkey, although in the latter they too have suffered persecution. Large-scale emigration has taken place to the USA and South America. Some South Indian Christians are in communion with them. A few villages in Turkey and Syria speak a form of Syriac, and another form is found in Lebanon, but most have Arabic as their mother tongue. Their Bible and liturgy, however, are in Syriac. In communion with Rome they are known as 'Catholic Syrians,' in India as 'Syro–Malankars.'

Maronites, found mainly in Lebanon and in emigrant groups from there, descend from a distinct theological stream. Having taken refuge in the Lebanon mountains in the ninth century, they accepted Roman supremacy in 1182 (those in Cyprus not until 1445). Their liturgy is mainly in Syriac, with parts in Arabic. Arabic is their mother tongue.

The Armenians have been a Christian nation since the end of the third century. They have known periods of independence but have often been subject to neighboring states, generally Muslim. In 1915–16 they were subjected to ferocious massacres at Turkish hands, in which almost all the Armenians in eastern Anatolia were exterminated. Two million now live in the republic of Armenia, and there is a worldwide diaspora. Modern Armenian flourishes in two dialects, eastern mainly in the territories of the former USSR and western elsewhere. Classical Armenian is the language of liturgy. The main Christian group opposed to Chalcedon is called 'Gregorian,' after the third-century evangelizer, Gregory the Illuminator, or 'Armenian Orthodox.' Those in communion with Rome are known as 'Armenian Catholics.'

The name 'Copt,' used to describe the indigenous Christians of Egypt, derives from the Greek *Aigyptios* 'Egyptian,' via the Arabic. The Coptic Church is descended from the Church in Egypt in late Roman and Early Byzantine times, which, through its large monastic component, vigorously rejected the decisions of Chalcedon. In spite of the very great pressures towards apostasy for social advantage, it maintains its existence with about four million adherents. It gained some advantages from Egyptian nationalism, but is now again at a disadvantage with the growth of Muslim fundamentalism. Its liturgical language is the Bohairic (Northern) dialect of Coptic, the latest form of the Old Egyptian language. Early Christian literature survives in several other dialects, none of which survives as a spoken tongue. Arabic was gaining ground in liturgical settings, but the renewed threat of Islam has given a certain strength to the retention of a distinctive ancient language. The Catholic Copts numbered over a million in a count made in 1973.

South of Egypt lay Nubia, where Christianity flourished from the fourth to the fourteenth centuries. Excavations there have brought many Christian documents to light, including scripture, liturgy, and hagiography, and fragmentary inscriptions. Translations were from Greek; and the Nubian language was written in the Greek alphabet, with five additional characters. The relationship of Old Nubian to the language families of the Sudan and the Horn of Africa has not been precisely defined as yet, although it is known to be related to modern dialects in the area (for Ethiopian Christianity, see *Ge'ez*).

Orthodox Chalcedonian Christianity is found in the Near East, first in Cyprus, and the Greek Orthodox presence in Turkey, Egypt, and Palestine, and second in the churches which were from early times supporters of Chalcedonian theology. In Syria, Egypt, and elsewhere they are known as 'Melkites,' that is to say, the 'Emperor's men,' seen from the viewpoint of their opponents who would not yield to government pressure. There are patriarchates of Antioch and Alexandria. These groups are Arabic speakers, and Arabic is also their liturgical language, following the Orthodox practice of using the vernacular for liturgy. The other main Orthodox Christian body is the Georgian Church, found mainly in the republic of Georgia, as there is no significant Georgian diaspora. Georgian Christianity goes back to the fourth century: like the Armenians they have known periods of independence and periods of foreign rule. They too are not without martyrs. In the late eighteenth and early nineteenth centuries they sought Russian suzerainty and were at length incorporated into the Russian empire. Their liturgical language remains Old Georgian.

Another form of Eastern Christianity in the Caucasus region was Christian Albania, situated in modern Azerbaijan. It was wiped out by Timur-Lenk, and few remains survive except for ruins and a few inscriptions. Its alphabet is recorded in Armenian manuscript lists. A modern survival of this Albanian (or Agvan) language is Udi, a North-east Caucasian language related to Lezgi and spoken in a few villages in Azerbaijan and Georgia. Some of the inscriptions have been deciphered, using the records of the alphabet and knowledge of modern Udi grammar.

Important documents of which the originals are lost or have only very recently come to light, have been preserved in the 'Near Eastern Christian languages.' These include Jewish and Christian pseudepigrapha, Gnostic and Manichean material, and lost patristic texts. These churches may also sometimes preserve ancient material otherwise unknown in their liturgical texts and practices. This raises the difficult question of the possibility of tracing an original language beneath the translations. It is not infrequently asserted, for example, that clear signs of an Armenian intermediary are to be found in early Georgian versions of the Bible, and of Syriac originals in both Armenian and Georgian texts. But such conclusions are seldom convincing. The insights of modern research on bilingualism have yet to be applied here. Improved knowledge of Syriac, Armenian, and Georgian palaeography also needs to be brought to bear on some earlier hypotheses which are in danger of assuming the status of fact.

Churches at the end of the twentieth century are caught up in many of the problems of the Near East and the Caucasus. They lack friends amongst the mighty, such as those they had in previous centuries. Nevertheless they continue to maintain a tenacious existence in their native lands, while, where there is a diaspora, their church migrates with them, as amongst Armenians worldwide and Syrian–Orthodox Gastarbeiter in Western Europe. There are often in such churches those who are eager to maintain the group's traditions of liturgical and even spoken language, and where there are means, academic study of the tradition is promoted, the Armenian case being the most striking example. These beleaguered churches and their cultural heritage may, against the odds, yet survive.

See also: Syriac, Christian; Ge'ez; Christianity in Iran and Central Asia; Arabic; Armenian; Ancient Egyptian and Coptic; Byzantine Greek; Georgian; Missionaries; Cyril and Methodius.

Bibliography

Arberry A J (ed.) 1969 *Religion in the Middle East.* Vol. 1. *Judaism and Christianity.* Cambridge University Press, London

Assfalg J, Krüger P (eds.) 1975 *Kleines Wörterbuch des Christlichen Orients.* Harrassowitz, Wiesbaden

Atiya S 1968 *A History of Eastern Christianity.* Methuen, London

Attwater D 1961–2 *The Christian Churches of the East*, 2 vols. Bruce, Milwaukee, WI

Blau J 1966–7 *A Grammar of Christian Arabic.* Secrétariat du Corpus SCO, Louvain

Brown L 1956, 1982 *The Indian Christians of St Thomas.* Cambridge University Press, Cambridge

Janin R 1955 *Les églises orientales et les rites orientaux*, 4th edn. Letouzey & Ané, Paris

Korolevskij C 1957 (trans. Attwater D) *Living Language in Catholic Worship: An Historical Inquiry.* Longmans, Green & Co., London

Schultze W 1982 *Die Sprache der Uden.* H. Fähnrich, Wiesbaden

Christianity in South Asia

C. Shackle

Christianity is the third most widespread religion in South Asia. Census returns for 1981 record some 19,000,000 Christians of different denominations in South Asia. Most of this figure is accounted for by the 16,000,000 Christians in India (2.6 percent of the total population), while there are also 1,350,000 in Pakistan (1.5 percent), and 1,100,000 in Sri Lanka (10 percent). In these three countries (numbers elsewhere being insignificant) Christians exist as small minorities, often thinly spread, among majority populations of Hindus, Muslims, and Buddhists respectively. The general sociolinguistic patterns of the local language area to which they belong have thus tended to be the prime determinants of language use among the various Christian communities.

Their linguistic profile has naturally also been formed by their origins in one or other of the missions to South Asia launched by various churches at different historical periods. Three principal phases of missionary activity may be distinguished, of which only the first predates the colonial period. This was the early spread of Nestorian Christianity from the

Middle East to Kerala in southwest India. Roman Catholicism was brought to the western and southern coasts of India and to coastal Sri Lanka by the Portuguese in the sixteenth century. The substantial spread of Christianity to other parts of South Asia took place only after 1800, when the efforts of mostly British and American missionaries founded numerous Protestant churches (as well as further spreading Roman Catholicism) with particular appeal both to the lowest castes and to linguistically isolated tribal communities.

1. Christianity in Kerala

The oldest community is that of the St Thomas or Syrian Malayalam-speaking Christians (Brown 1982) of Kerala, a region long associated with the Middle East through the Indian Ocean spice trade. A local Nestorian community, claiming to have been founded by the Apostle Thomas himself, was certainly in existence there by the sixth century, acknowledging the distant supremacy of the Jacobite patriarch of Antioch and having Syriac as the sacred language of its priests and monks, but fully integrated into the highly stratified society of precolonial Kerala. There still exists a distinctive spoken Christian dialect of Malayalam (Nair 1971), resembling the dialect of the Nairs, the warrior caste with whom Christians were traditionally ranked, though differentiated by such features as the loss of aspiration from the voiced aspirate series, the absence of a morphologically distinct honorific plural imperative, or the use of distinctive kinship terminology, e.g., *pempiḷa* 'wife' for standard *bhārya*.

Later Roman Catholic and Protestant missions, directed towards 'reconversion' of the Syrians or proselytization of lower castes, have created numerous rival churches in Kerala, where the 5,000,000 Christians constitute one-fifth of the population. Although Syriac survives as a liturgical language among the Jacobites and some other churches, it is being displaced even in this role by standard Malayalam, the cultural language of the Keralan Christians, with English being cultivated in the usual South Asian fashion by the more educated.

2. Roman Catholicism and Portuguese

A Roman Catholic presence in India was forcibly established by the Portuguese in the early sixteenth century. From their headquarters at Goa on the Konkan coast, vigorous proselytization was undertaken along the coasts of South India and Sri Lanka. A leading role was played by Jesuit missionaries, following the example of St Francis Xavier (1506–52) and his successful mission to the Parava fisher caste of coastal Tamil Nadu, where there were nearly 3,000,000 Tamil-speaking Christians in the early 1990s. The Tamil and Sinhala-speaking Christian communities of northwestern Sri Lanka are also largely the product of these Jesuit missions, whose emphasis upon working through local languages yielded the first Western descriptions of them.

While Latin long remained the liturgical language of all South Asian Roman Catholics (except in Kerala, where the Syriac liturgy was permitted), the first printed books in local languages were produced to propagate the faith, e.g., the Konkani *Doutrina Cristã* (1622), an elementary manual by the English Jesuit Thomas Stephens. Unusually for South Asia with its wealth of indigenous scripts, Christian Konkani literature (in a variety of dialects defined by both caste and locality) has traditionally been recorded in the Roman script, writing retroflexes as geminates and giving ⟨x⟩ its Portuguese value /ʃ/ e.g., the Goan place-name Saxtti (for *saṣṭi*). Portuguese influence on formal Christian Konkani extended beyond loans even to syntax, e.g., *te cottat xeva devachi* 'they perform the service of God,' with SVP for Indo–Aryan SPV (Miranda 1978). With the expulsion of the Portuguese from Goa in 1961, however, such Lusitanisms are becoming less characteristic as the Christians of Goa (300,000) draw closer to the Hindus in the common cause of maintaining Konkani as a language distinct from Marathi.

The former role of Portuguese as the premier language of Christianity in South Asia is still evidenced by the diffusion throughout New Indo–Aryan of such basic loanwords as Hindi *girjā* 'church' or *pādrī* 'priest' (<*igreja*, *padre*). Indo–Portuguese dialects formerly spoken by local Christians of mixed race (Dalgado 1900) are virtually extinct in the early 1990s, having been replaced as social markers by local 'Anglo–Indian' varieties of English.

3. Protestantism and English

While early Protestant missionaries were drawn from several north European countries, the main thrust of mission activity from 1800 was conducted by English-speaking missionaries who extended Christianity from the south to northern India. In keeping with the scriptural emphasis of Protestantism, much effort was devoted to Bible translations (Hooper 1963) and to practical descriptions of many hitherto unknown minor languages.

Work among the non-Indo–Aryan tribal populations proved particularly effective, as among the Santals and other Munda-speaking tribes of central India. On the north-east frontier, mass conversions of the Naga (600,000) and Mizo-speaking (400,000) tribes led to their Christian identity becoming a major factor in their successful campaigns for territorial recognition, the primacy of English as the medium of their conversion being reflected in its status as the state language of Nagaland.

Among the Indo–Aryan speakers of the northern plains, the appeal of Christianity was largely restricted to the lowest castes, converted in mass movements (1880–1947). Conformity to prevailing sociolinguistic patterns is illustrated, e.g., by the triglossia of church services in Pakistan, where an English liturgy caters for the small elite, with its Urdu counterpart for the mass of believers, who chiefly participate in the enthusiastic singing of the Psalms in metrical Panjabi translation to turn-of-the-century popular tunes.

The currency of English loans with a Christian connotation in non-Christian usage is restricted to such popular items as the public holiday *k(a)rismas* 'Christmas,' hardly including such coinages as *lāṭ pādrī* 'bishop' (<'lord'). The Anglo–Indian Christians of mixed race continue, however, to maintain their distinctively pronounced variety of English (Spencer 1966).

See also: Missionaries; Carey, W.; Nobili, R. de.

Bibliography

Brown L 1982 *The Indian Christians of St Thomas*, 2nd edn. Cambridge University Press, Cambridge

Dalgado S R 1900 *Dialecto indo-português de Ceylão*. Imprensa Nacional, Lisbon

Hooper J S M 1963 *Bible Translation in India, Pakistan and Ceylon*, 2nd edn. Oxford University Press, Bombay

Miranda R V 1978 Caste, religion and dialect differentiation in the Konkani area. *International Journal of the Sociology of Language* **16**: 77–91

Nair B G 1971 Caste dialects of Malayalam. *Proceedings of the First All India Conference of Dravidian Linguists*: 409–14

Spencer J 1966 The Anglo–Indians and their speech. *Lingua* **16**: 57–70

Christianity in Southeast Asia

E. U. Kratz

The role of Christianity in the cultural and linguistic development of Southeast Asia differs from that of other world religions, because a distinction has to be made between the influence of Christianity and that of the individual missionaries who with their various languages, brought Christianity to Southeast Asia. Also, despite obvious and undeniable links, the expansion and influence of Christianity must be seen separately from the expansion and impact of Western colonialism, and of Western thinking and technology. From the lexis of the diverse Southeast Asian languages which belong to several major language families (the Sino–Tibetan, the Mon–Khmer, the Tibeto–Burman, and the Austronesian group), it is obvious that 'Christian' languages such as Spanish, Portuguese, Dutch, French, and English have had a considerable impact on Southeast Asia as a whole, while Christianity itself has not.

With the exception of the Spanish-ruled Philippines, Christianity, which first took hold among those ethnic groups least affected by Indian religions and by Islam, has never made major inroads. This is not to say, however, that there are not substantial Christian minorities in some of the countries of Southeast Asia. Quite often, these minorities are of a political and social significance which is in stark contrast to their numerical strength. Yet, the religions which have had the greatest social and cultural impact are, successively, Hinduism and Buddhism, and then Islam. They had made their mark before Christianity even appeared in the region after the Portuguese victory over Malay Malacca (1511). Interestingly, one of the first names under which Europeans were known in Southeast Asia, the *Buran-gyi* of the Burmese (meaning 'Roman Catholic' in the late twentieth century), the *farang* of the Thai, the *baarang* of the Khmer, and the *feringgi* or *peringgi* of the Malays (through Arabic and Persian), harks back to the Franks of the Crusades whose reputation had preceded their actual arrival.

Unlike the present, when English is the most influential foreign language throughout the region, in the past the combined interests of colonial powers and missions determined (except in independent Thailand) which European language exerted most influence on the languages of the region. Thus Burmese and Malay as spoken in Malaysia, Singapore, and Brunei were influenced mostly by English; Khmer, Vietnamese, and Laotian by French; Malay in its Indonesian form by Dutch, prior to which there was the Portuguese contribution; and finally, Tagalog (and Pilipino) were beholden to Spanish.

Christian missionaries played an important part in the development of these Southeast Asian languages, and their lexicography, linguistic analysis, and description ever since they made first contact. The codification of a Latin script for Vietnamese (*Quoc ngu'*) and the Romanization of Malay both occurred in the seventeenth century; the first Vietnamese dictionary, by Alexandre de Rhodes, appeared in

1651 in Rome; a Burmese dictionary by Judson was published in 1826 in Calcutta by the Baptist Board of Publications; a Thai dictionary, by the Bishop of Mallos, Jean Baptiste Pallegoix, in 1854 in Bangkok by the Collegium Assumption is BMV. The normative influence of printing, which was first introduced by missionary presses, on the development of the modern national standard languages in the region, is undeniable.

Many of the first bilingual wordlists and dictionaries of all the national languages of Southeast Asia and of many of its regional languages were initiated and compiled by missionary societies. What is interesting, however, is the fact that only a few 'Christian' terms such as (Portuguese) *gereja* for church, and Indonesian *zending* (from the Dutch) and Thai *mitchan* for mission can be found in Southeast Asian languages. Even for borrowing Christian terminology, they turned sooner to their traditional donor languages, thus, to take the Indonesian example, producing (Arabic) *Al-Kitab* (The Book) for the Bible and (Sanskrit) *pendeta* for the (Protestant) clergyman.

By and large, loans from European languages lack a distinct religious association but they embrace all aspects of modern Western life, material culture, and political and scientific thinking.

See also: Missionaries.

Bibliography

Herbert P, Milner A 1989 *South-East Asia Languages and Literatures: A Select Guide*. Kiscadale Publications, Whiting Bay

Judson A 1826 *A Dictionary, Burmese and English*. Baptist Mission Press, Calcutta

Pallegoix J B 1854 *Dictionarium linguae Thai, sive Siamensis, interpretatione Latina, Gallica et Anglica*. Paris

Rhodes A de 1651 *Dictionarium Annamiticum* [*sic*] *Lusitanum, et Latinum*. Sacrae Congregationis de Propaganda Fide, Rome

Confucianism

L. Pfister

Confucius (or 'Master Kong'), born as Kong Qiu and styled Kong Zhongni (551–479 BCE), taught as a member of a new class of militarily capable and ritual-sensitive scholars known as '*ru*.' Although ultimately a political failure, his ideals of personal cultivation designed for aspiring political leaders at various levels of contemporary Chinese societies to prompt the establishment of a harmonious and humane society governed by a traditionally recognized supreme king won him a place among later generations as a cultural hero. The texts he considered to be sagely sources of political, religious, historical and moral teachings portrayed the fortunes and failures of various ancient kings and cultures in and around the 'Middle Kingdom'. Master Kong's fundamentalist turn toward these teachings and examples of these ancient sages, all who lived within a thousand year period starting from the early part of the second millennium BCE, oriented him to be culturally elitist and linguistically conservative. After the death of Master Kong, political and linguistic conditions continued to be disunified and diversified. Ru followers promoted his ideal return to a golden age of political unity, employing the complicated calligraphic scripts of the Zhou dynasty (c. 1100–700 BCE) as the appropriate linguistic medium for humane government and elite education. Competition from other teachings and finally military conquests by the ruler of the Qin state, a ruler not interested in Master Kong's political vision, oppressed Ru scholars and united the new empire under a totalitarian system which also enforced the use of a newly determined set of simplified Chinese characters. Though this brought about a political and cultural crisis for Ruist scholarship, within one hundred years after the first Qin emperor united China, Ru scholars adjusted and their venerated scriptures regained a place in prevailing imperial institutions. Since then they have continued to influence Chinese language relating to ethical, ritual, religious, educational, and political forms of life. Throughout its subsequent history of more than two millennia of fairly regular cultural and political dominance, Ru scholars following Master Kong were able to establish the language and texts of the northern Chinese plain as the standard for elite culture throughout China. Described in elevated terms as 'the Teacher of ten thousand ages,' Master Kong symbolized the power and interests of what at times was a vast bureaucracy of cultivated elites in political authority, many times including the ruling emperor among his devotees. The teachings associated with his name were called *rujiao*, the teachings of the Ru. Only in the seventeenth century AD were these teachings dubbed by foreign Roman Catholic missionaries as 'Confucianism,' due to the ritualized reverence they saw displayed by Ruists on special ceremonial days before images of Master Kong and his major disciples in imperially sanctioned temples. The first emperor united China (221 BCE), have influence Chinese language in its expressions relating to ethical, educational, and political forms of life.

1. The Influence of Master Kong's Language and Teachings

The teachings and manners of Master Kong, which were originally recorded on collated bamboo strips by second-generation disciples, are now referred to as the 'Analects' or 'Conversations'. Often couched in pithy aphorisms and sometimes in the context of a dialogue, Confucius' style was notably, but not exclusively, this-worldly. He frequently made appeals to antiquity to support his ideals, and used rhetorical chain arguments and arguments by analogy. These were emphasized and expanded by later *ru* (Wyatt 1990), especially after the *Analects* itself in the seventh century CE became a part of the canonical Ruist literature (Pfister 1993).

According to Master Kong's influential doctrine of 'rectification of names' (*Zhengming*), there is a correspondence between certain names and the social roles they describe which have a moral function: if I am to be called a ruler or a father, then I must act like one. This is found in the analects (12: 17; 13: 3) and is prominent in making the ruler act as a ruler should. Later Ru scholars developed this doctrine into a broader thesis about the relationship between names and the empirical or 'actual' world, seeking to align all human actions to a pre-established cosmic harmony which these words were meant to indicate. (see also *Names*: *Religious Beliefs*; Makeham 1994). So important were the scriptures and sayings associated with Master Kong that at seven times in imperial history – during the second, third, ninth, eleventh, twelfth, and eighteenth centuries – stone inscriptions of the then recognized Ruist scriptures were ordered by imperial authorities to be prepared. Once completed, they were displayed in imperially sanctioned sites in order to establish for that age the permanent and standard texts of this canonical literature (Tsien 1962). Consequently, "classical" Ruist language greatly influenced the foundations of all public life, education, and political discourse for most periods of Chinese dynastic history.

2. Dialectal Diversity and the Consolidation of Ruism ('Confucianism')

The early texts honoured by Master Kong as canonical scriptures reflected broad periods of time as well as different levels of society and political context. The *Book of History* (*Shangshu* or *Shujing*) dealt primarily with the ancient regal history of the State of Lu, where Kong Qiu much later was born. Yet the differences between this state's style of calligraphy, use of terms, and forms of rituals were manifest in the varieties of vocabulary found in both the *Book of Poetry* (*Shijing*), which contained in its standard form more than three hundred poems from more than a dozen states, and the compendium of social forms described and explained in the less ancient but still authoritative *Book of Rites* (*Liji*). These dialectial differences in vocabulary and written styles were recognized by various Chinese scholars of the pre-Christian era, and extensively described in the earliest dictionaries and commentaries on the Confucian canon. Very soon after Ruist scriptures and commentaries were adopted as a major element in political ideology and the standard for cultured education, important philological works were published which compiled multitudinous details about Chinese calligraphic and lexical differences in order to decipher the Ruist scriptures and other texts written in ancient scripts. In addition, dictionaries based on rhymes found in the *Book of Poetry* systematized this complicated vocabulary for future learners and scholars. So significant was this effort that one of these philological compendia, the *Erya* or *Approaching the Elegant and Refined*, was later considered to be part of the canonical literature as well.

In another of these important Ruist dictionaries, the *Shuowen* or *Explanations of Characters*, an early Ru scholar developed a system known as '*fanqie*' to identify ancient pronunciation. Since there was no phonetic alphabet available to Chinese literati, the *fanqie* method involved the use of two characters in sequence, representing the initial consonant and vowel-tone combination of the character studied. Although this method could not solve all pronunciation problems, it did standardize throughout later Chinese dynasties the Qi-Lu dialect in which Confucius and his followers spoke and wrote. On the basis of the knowledge gained by these philological works, rhyming dictionaries could be arranged according to more general rhymes and more specific homophone groups. Studies in these philological areas continued to develop across dynastic histories, so that more precise, comprehensive, and critical methods of philological understanding were developed for the texts and terms which had become archaic. At the same time, these studies provided a justified means for throwing doubt on the historical reliability of certain scriptures, issues which did arise at critical points in imperial Chinese history.

Traditional Chinese societies in different dynastic periods, but especially later in the fourteenth to the nineteenth centuries CE, was deeply impressed by the style, lexis, and ethical principles of the *Analects* and its associated ancient Ruist scriptures. Scholars memorized them word for word; poets and novelists subtly referred in their works to key phrases and concepts from them (such as 'benevolence,' 'faithfulness,' 'filiality,' and 'propriety'). In many dynasties these scriptures were the standards for civil examinations, and so framed the intellectual life and social aspirations of all educated Chinese male persons. Chinese literature on academic and noble life inevitably couched its relational terms in the forms of standard Ruist pairs of relationships (lord and minister, husband and wife, father and son, elder and younger brothers, friend to friend). The consolidation of several traditional records on proper ritual etiquette during the first century CE was motivated by Ruist virtues, and so imbued Ruist and imbued Confucian ways of thinking into the intimate details of daily decorum and less frequent ceremonial festivities. This was particularly the case with the important rites of passage such as marriage, coming of age ('capping' at 20 years old for males), funerals, and the imperial ceremonies and sacrifices maintained by a dynastic series of emperors.

A critical dilemma arose regarding the authenticity of the Ru scriptures during the later Han Dynasty (125–220). Although largely motivated by political desires to justify a secessionist dynastic takeover, the basis of the claims rested on new readings in certain ancient scriptures found in putatively more reliable ancient versions of these scriptures. This so-called 'Old and New Text controversy' focused significantly on matters of texts written in ancient or modern calligraphic styles. Ideologically it was also clear that the New Texts contained more radical political ideas and an image of Master Kong as the creator (and not merely the transmitter) of the tradition. Because proponents of the New Text school argued the 'ancient texts' were actually forgeries, they consequently presented a challenge to the reliability and authenticity of the Old Texts. Though their arguments did not ultimately succeed at this time, the claims motivated by these skeptical questions returned to haunt the last of the imperial epochs, the Qing dynasty, during its final years (1890–1911 CE).

3. A New Orthodoxy and Later Responses

The invention of paper in the later Han Dynasty made possible an extensive commentarial tradition on the *Five Classics* and other related texts. The emphasis was on philology, etymology, and exegesis. By the end of the second century CE, a small but burgeoning religious Daoism as well as an inchoate and not yet sinicized Buddhism from India did not pose a political, cultural or ideological challenge to Ruism. But with the breakdown of the later Han dynasty early in the third century CE, this situation changed dramatically. While Ruist language retained an uneasy dominance in the public sphere, Daoism's esoteric transmissions of visionary messages and elixirs for immortality were influential in shaping popular terms in medical spheres as well as in contemporary literature. The more foreign and technical Chinese vocabulary of Buddhism developed in the subsequent three centuries, ultimately adapting itself, as did Daoism, to the ethical vocabulary and values of the mainline Ruist traditions. Daoist and Buddhist terms gradually came to dominate the religious and aesthetic spheres of Chinese language, and for nearly seven centuries—from the third to the tenth centuries—almost succeeded in overcoming the Confucian claim to political dominance.

A response was slow in forming, but in the Song Dynasty (968–1279) it did finally reach a comprehensiveness, metaphysical subtlety, and sensitive reorientation which could counter the challenge. Daoist interests in immortality and magical arts were criticized by Ruist skeptics and replaced by an egalitarian ideal in which all could become sages like Master Kong. This prompted the liberalization and popularization of Ruist values which were quite successful in solidifying an orthodox Ruist form of life and its expressions in Chinese language. The subtleties of Buddhist logic and meditative arts were countered by the polar dialectic of the *Book of Changes* and Ru studies on its ancient commentaries, all of which portrayed a more integrated cosmology. Methods of self-cultivation, consciously responsive to and critical of Buddhist and Daoist alternatives, were developed and promoted from certain basic texts. A more sophisticated system of education and growth toward sagehood also entered into the mainstream of civil life during the last century of this period. Its methods and problems formed the linguistic categories and context for the subsequent development of other schools of Ru scholars. The literary gem of this period which was culled in part from the *Five Classics*, centering around Master Kong's teachings, was systematically organized and elaborated by Zhu Xi (Chu Hsi) (1130–1200) and called the *Four Books*.

This new orthodoxy stimulated numerous responses. Some Ru scholars argued for a more intuitive approach to self-cultivation, based on both textual and metaphysical grounds. One famous example was published in the dialogues of Wang Yangming (1472–1528), and was criticized as being too Buddhistic. This suggests how deeply embedded the forms of language has become: any hint toward an independent and aesthetic level of enlightened experience immediately smacked of something less than the Ruist cultural and political norms (Henderson 1998). Nevertheless, Wang's influence was not negligible in China and had a major impact on Japanese scholars of the Tokagawa era.

Zhu Xi himself prepared a highly systematic treatise from sayings and commentaries of his Song predecessors, *Reflections on Things at Hand* (*Jinsi lu*), which became a classic in its own right. It established a new vocabulary of investigations on the nature of reality, the process of self-cultivation, the ethical bonds of life, and the political duties of peaceful and intelligent subjects. Later Korean Ru scholars followed his teachings, developing further diagrams and systematizing further acceptable answers to both metaphysical and practical dilemmas in the tradition (DeBary and Haboush 1985; Kalton 1988). These Ru traditions are still actively developed and taught in twenty-first century CE Korean educational institutions.

Educational tools, made for young men to prepare them for civil service examinations in their mature years, were a unique cultural contribution. Starting with more commonly used characters and ending with the less well known ones, texts such as the *Elementary Learning* (*Xiaoxue*) and the *Three Character Classic* (*Sanzi jing*), set out the most basic principles and history of a humane Ruist life in patterns of three characters without repeating any earlier term. These prepared more advanced students for the four-character phrases, *chengyu,* or "perfected sayings", which concisely summarized a philosophical position or the message of a classical text. Even in the twenty-first century dictionaries of *chengyu*, many being influenced by Ruist values and originating from their scriptures and related texts, are regularly consulted, so that these *chengyu* continue to be studied, memorized, and employed in everyday life and writings by educated Chinese persons.

In addition, a special set of texts, one of the most influential being called the *Woman's Four Books* (*Nu sishu*), was published in the seventeenth century, elaborating restrictive standards of feminine virtue and women's duties to submit to male authorities. They followed writings and attitudes first promoted by a Han dynasty woman scholar and politician, Ban Zhao (c.48–c. 120 CE), but became broadly influential only at this later time (Lee 1994). The Manchurian rulers of the Qing dynasty greatly enhanced the dominance of all these elements of a general Ruist worldview especially along lines of Zhu Xi's interpretations, making it the orthodoxy for cultural and political institutions from the seventeenth to the early twentieth centuries.

4. Internationalization and Postrevolutionary Quandaries

Renditions of various Ruist scriptures and teachings in European languages began to appear during the seventeenth century and went through a great series of transmogrifications before arriving at some relatively authoritative texts. Concerns for evangelism and other cultural–political aims often distorted the earlier translations. Less self-conscious errors of misunderstanding also crept in eisegetically. The extensive research and translations of the so-called *Chinese Classics* and *Sacred Books of Confucianism* by James Legge (1815–97) helped to correct many of these abuses, setting international standards for subsequent translations, interpretations and criticism of Ruist canonical literature (Pfister 1993, 1994).

The failure of the Qing Dynasty (1644–1911) threatened the very existence of Ru teachings and institutions. Bureaucratic structures, including the educational system dependent on the Ruist scriptures, were dismantled, and their commitment to Ru interpretations became less relevant to the workings of state and daily life. Ideological antagonism intensified after 1919, when movements to promote vernacular learning atracked the use of pedantic exercises in the old style (*guwen*) most often identified with Ru scholarly translations. Straightforward attacks against Ruism, and, after the Communist revolution in 1949, against Master Kong himself, left deep wounds in the legitimation processes underpinning Ruist scholarship. Perhaps even more significant linguistically was the gradual process of simplifying the Chinese script during the first two decades of the existence of the People's Republic of China. This Maoist policy, much like the precedent set by the Qin emperor two millennia before him, not only reshaped the linguistic reference points for common Chinese persons in everyday language, but also strained the already weakened access to traditional Ruist terminology even among educated modern Chinese persons.

Nevertheless, vital but relatively much smaller communities of Ruist scholarship remained active and developed even more fully after 1949 in expatriate Chinese communities in Taiwan, Hong Kong, Singapore, Europe, and the USA. Significantly, a 'Confucian Manifesto' written in 1958 and signed by four major 'New Ru scholars' (*xin rujia*) in Hong Kong and Taiwan signalled an intention by some to develop a viable modern form of Ru teachings for a globalizing age. Consequently, vernacular renditions of the Ruist scriptures, both in contemporary Chinese as well as in other Asian and European languages, have been published and widely distributed. In the 1980s an attempt was made to provide an optional syllabus in 'Confucian' ethics as a national standard for teenage education in Singapore. Some contemporary Ru philosophers have left the exclusiveness of the Chinese setting and, especially among expatriate communities and non-Chinese Ru scholars, have sought by means of books, lectures, research centers, and international organizations to bring to light the global relevance and contemporary philosophical importance of 'Confucianism.'

See also: Buddhism, Chinese; Chinese; Confucianisn; Christianity in East Asia; Missionaries; Naming; Ritual; Taoism.

Bibliography

DeBary W T, Haboush J K (eds.) 1985 *The Rise of Neo-Confucianism in Korea*. Columbia University Press, New York

de Francis J 1984 *The Chinese Language: Fact and Fantasy*. University of Hawaii Press, Honolulu

Henderson J B 1998 *The Construction of Orthodoxy and Heresy: Neo-Confucian, Islamic, Jewish and Early Christian Patterns*. State University of New York Press, Albany

Kalton M C 1988 *To Become a Sage: The Ten Diagrams on Sage Learning by Yi T'oegye*. Columbia University Press, New York

Lee L X H 1994 *The Virtue of Yin: Studies on Chinese Women*. Wild Peony Pty Ltd, Broadway, NSW, Australia

Legge J 1893–1895 *The Chinese Classics*. (5 vols. in 8 tomes, 2nd partially revised edition). Clarendon Press, Oxford

Legge J 1879–1885 *The Sacred Books of China: Confucianism* in Mueller F. M. (ed.) *The Sacred Books of the East* (vols. 3, 16, 27–28). Clarendon Press, Oxford

Makeham J 1994 *Name and Actuality in Early Chinese Thought*. State University of New York, Albany

Pankenier D 1974 *On Script and Writing in Ancient China*. Association for Oriental Studies, Stockholm

Pfister L 1993 Reassessing Max Weber's Evaluation of the Confucian Classics. In: Davies J, Wollaston I (eds.) *The Sociology of Sacred Texts*. Sheffield Academic Press, Sheffield

Pfister L 1994 James Legge. In: Chan S W, Pollard D (eds.) *An Encyclopedia of Translations: Chinese-English, English-Chinese Translation*. Chinese University Press, Hong Kong.

Pulleyblank E G 1995 *Outline of Classical Chinese Grammar*. University of British Columbia Press, Vancouver

Tsien T H 1962 *Written on Bamboo and Silk: The Beginnings of Chinese Books and Inscriptions*. University of Chicago Press, Chicago

Tu C I (ed.) 2000 *Classics and Interpretations: The Hermeneutic Traditions in Chinese Culture*. Transaction Publishers, New Brunswick and London

Schwartz B I 1985 *The World of Thought in Ancient China*. Harvard University Press, Cambridge, MA

Wyatt D 1990 A language of continuity in Confucian thought. In: Cohen P, Goldman M (eds.) *Ideas Across Cultures*. Harvard University Press, Cambridge, MA

Yao X Z 2000 *An Introduction to Confucianism*. Cambridge University Press, Cambridge

Zhang D N 1997 *A Handbook of Categories and Concepts in Classical Chinese Philosophy*. Trns. and ed. by Edmond Ryden. Fujen Catholic University, Taipei

Ecstatic Religion

W. S. Bainbridge

'Ecstasy' is often defined as a state of overwhelming emotion, superficially erotic in nature, marked by irrationality and loss of self-control. Although shunned by staid, respectable churches, ecstasy can take the form of a mystic or prophetic trance, and it has played a formative role in the religious traditions of the world. In Eastern traditions, religious ecstasy is often achieved through meditating on or chanting a mantra (see *Mantra*), a word or phrase said to have unique spiritual powers. But perhaps more interesting for linguistics are the social–scientific interpretations of ecstasy that see it as a facilitator of communication and a source of meanings.

1. Ecstasy as Communication

Sociologist Rodney Stark noted that religious experiences can be defined as such only by the person having them, and that they constitute occasions felt to be an encounter with a supernatural consciousness. He identified four categories a religious experience, distinguishable in terms of the degree of communication between the person and the deity, arranged from the dimmest and most distant to the most frenzied and intimate: confirming, responsive, ecstatic, and revelational. In a confirming experience, the person feels the presence of God, and in the responsive experience the person senses that God is aware of him. In an ecstatic religious experience, a person feels intense involvement with God and a glorious physical thrill may diffuse the person's body. To this ecstasy, the revelational experience adds visions, voices, and a message from God that may even conflict with prevailing theology.

Questionnaire poll data reveal that most religious experiences are of the milder varieties, and several social factors tend to increase both their likelihood and intensity. Respectable denominations, in modern societies, tend to discourage emotionality, and religious ecstasies are thus more common among members of fundamentalist sects and innovative cults. The emotionality of sects probably expresses the frustrations felt by their members, who tend to be of low socioeconomic status. In contrast, many religious cults are vehicles of experimental exploration for well-educated persons. For historical reasons, religious traditions differ in the emphasis they place upon emotionality. In any denomination, those members most firmly embedded in the social life of the church, thus receiving the most unanimous spiritual messages from fellow believers, will be more apt to have powerful religious experiences.

2. Possession: Speaking with a New Voice

Premodern societies, which typically postulate numerous supernatural beings, tend to believe in spirit possession. Ioan Lewis called possession an 'oblique redressive strategy,' used by powerless people to increase their bargaining position. The victim of possession is someone oppressed by close relatives or powerful groups in society: for example, women in male-dominated societies and minority ethnic groups overpowered by an unsympathetic elite. Victims might like to escape the oppression, but they are economically and socially dependent upon the oppressors, and thus they cannot express their anger directly. The possessing spirit speaks for them, and the victim avoids responsibility for what it says. If the oppressor believes in the doctrine of possession, the victim may even be able to use the spirit to gain substantial concessions.

A good example is the Zar cult of Ethiopia, Somalia, and Sudan, in which women are seized by spirits known variously as *shaytan*, *afreet*, *abless*, *jinn*, or *zar*. A woman begins to complain of vague but disturbing symptoms, and a Zar healer is called in. In a lengthy and often emotional interview, the healer ostensibly determines whether possession is at fault, but really looks for signs that the victim is ready to use possession as a means of self-expression and negotiation with her husband. If so, she is invited to participate in a session of ecstatic religion that may last several days, in which other sufferers will shower spiritual gifts upon her, the spirit will make her dance to exhaustion, and she will learn new tactics for handling her husband and communicating her needs more effectively within the harsh limits of her oppression.

3. In the Name of God

New religions are often born in ecstatic revelational experiences. Weston La Barre has suggested that the word *god* is really a pronoun, whose referents, connotations, and denotations differ with every person and society using it. And it is a first person singular pronoun at that, being a projection into the void of a person's private fears and longings. Although the viewpoints from which religion may be analyzed are almost infinite, many social scientists believe that messiahs discover their messages in episodes of temporary insanity, usually separated from the rest of society, like Moses on the mountain top, yet channeling the longings of the multitude that later accepts their sacred visions.

Such episodes may be induced by injuries, consciousness-altering drugs, high fevers, unremitting emotional stress, sensory deprivation, and social isolation. Many religious traditions have special methods to induce ecstasy, often defined as techniques for communicating with spirits, but messiahs frequently appear on the fringes of society and may not have been trained in them. All large cultures seem to have a concept equivalent to our psychosis, and individuals who experience visions may seek a religious definition in order to avoid the stigmatizing label of insanity.

In many societies, the role of vision-inspired sorcerer may be highly respected, and at times of societal crisis the entire population may clamor for a savior. Claude Lévi-Strauss suggests that sorcerers participate in an economy of meaning: their clients seek the meaning of things which refuse to reveal their significance, while the unusual psychological state of the sorcerer provides him with a surfeit of emotional interpretations. In addition to numerous redefinitions of familiar concepts, the novel faith may be expressed through new words, including the proper names of spirits and terminology describing new ritual actions.

The danger that religious ecstasy may lead to heterodox revelations is a major reason why the respectable denominations discourage emotionality. This is a struggle between the written and the spoken word, the static church and the dynamic sect or cult, the bureaucratic organization and the charismatic movement. Scriptures written in ancient days are the support for contemporary religious hierarchies, while modern ecstatic revelations challenge the traditional power structures of religion. Established churches encourage their parishioners to pray to God, but strongly discourage them from hearing his voice and thus from experiencing the ecstasy of intimate communication with the divine.

See also: Glossolalia; New Religious Movements.

Bibliography

Glock C Y, Stark R 1965 *Religion and Society in Tension*. Rand McNally, Chicago, IL

La Barre W 1969 *They Shall Take Up Serpents: Psychology of the Southern Snake-Handling Cult*. Schocken, New York

La Barre W 1972 *The Ghost Dance: Origins of Religion*. Allen and Unwin, London

Lévi-Strauss C 1963 *Structural Anthropology*. Basic Books, New York

Lewis I M 1971 *Ecstatic Religion*. Pelican, Baltimore, MD

Sargant W W 1959 *Battle for the Mind: A Physiology of Conversion and Brain-washing*. Harper and Row, New York

Stark R, Bainbridge W S 1985 *The Future of Religion*. University of California Press, Berkeley, CA

Etruscan Religion

L. Aigner-Foresti

In the ancient world the Etruscans were regarded as a nation that devoted itself to the maintenance of religion with great diligence (Livy 5.1, 6). The doctrine of the 'immortal gods' is said to have been revealed to them by a superhuman being, Tages (Cicero, *De divinatione* 2.50). The Romans termed this etrusca disciplina (Cicero, *De haruspicum responso* 9, 18); it contained principles for the interpretation and the placating of celestial signs and divine intimations (Pliny the Elder, *Natural History* 2.199), together with ritual and social precepts. The original text has not been preserved. Translations into Latin date from Aulus Caecina and Nigidius Figulus (first century BCE). However, longer religious texts have come down to us from the Etruscans, so that the Etruscan language possesses a relatively rich vocabulary precisely in the area of religion. The cloth-bound Book of Zagreb (*liber linteus Zagrabiensis*), which contains a fairly lengthy ritual with recurring verses, belongs to the most significant religious literature of the whole ancient world. We have in addition: a calendrically arranged list of sacrifices on a clay tablet from Capua (*tabula capuana*); 38 names of gods which were carved into a bronze representation of a liver, found in Piacenza in Northern Italy, to indicate divine signs; and finally thousands of votive inscriptions. Remains of temples and tombs, sacred utensils and votive offerings are preserved equally plentifully.

Although those texts are written in the Etruscan alphabet, which is derived from the Greek, and hence they are not hard to read, nevertheless their interpretation is difficult insofar as our knowledge of Etruscan vocabulary is somewhat sketchy. Assistance can be sought from comparison of words, as well as from comparison of the structure of the Etruscan texts, with the structure of religious texts of the contemporary peoples of ancient Italy. In Etruria religious texts were probably sung (Dionysius of Halicarnassus, *Antiquities* 1.21); the recurrent formulae of the Book of Zagreb argue for a type of litany similar to the ritual of the Umbrians of Iguvium (*tabulae iguvinae*) and the metrical chanting of the Arval Brethern; the list of sacrifices from Capua, written in Schlangenschrift, suggests a special ritual, unknown to us. (Schlangenschrift, literally 'snake script,' is a form of boustrophedon in which not only is the direction of writing reversed in alternate lines, but the outlines of the letters are reversed and, for good measure, inverted.)

The Etruscan religion is many-layered. From about the eighth century BCE, due to Greek influence, high gods in human form become prominent. Tinia and Sethlans, Turan and Laran, Turms and Fufluns belong to the most ancient nucleus of Etruscan religion, which dates back into the second millenium BCE; they bear names that are linguistically different from the corresponding gods of the Greeks and Romans, as is respectively shown by Zeus–Iupiter, Hephaistos–Vulcanus, Aphrodite–Venus, Ares–Mars, Hermes–Mercurius, and Dionysos–Bacchus. Other gods, such as Aplu and Artumes are borrowed from Greek religion in the fifth century BCE, Aplu through Latin mediation, Artumes directly from the realm of Greek culture. However, the Greek Artemis corresponds to the Latin Diana. Others again, such as Uni, Menvra, and Nethuns, bear common italic names, which differ respectively from those of the Greek Hera, Athena, and Poseidon, and can be traced back to a Common Italic, pre-Greek pantheon.

According to Etruscan doctrine the gods express their will through signs (Cicero, *De divinatione* 1.1 ff) which are revealed in lightning and in the livers of animal sacrifices. The most important task of Etruscan priests was to determine from which god the sign came, for what reason he had sent it, what it could mean, and, if negative, how it could be placated. The examination of lightning and livers depended on the belief in the division of heaven, earth and the livers of animal sacrifices into sixteen regions; lightning was interpreted by the observer of lightning (Latin *fulgurator*, Etruscan *trutnvt*) and the signs on livers by the observer of livers (Latin *haruspex*, Etruscan *netsvis*). Concerning beliefs about the hereafter, the Etruscans provided for the preservation of the likeness and the name of the deceased. Not until Imperial times did the belief appear that through certain sacrifices human souls are transformed into gods (Servius, Commentary on Virgil's *Aeneid* 3.168); in this an influence from Christianity cannot be ruled out. The Emperor Constantine sought to diminish the activity of the divinators; however, Etruscan soothsayers are still mentioned by Zosimos (*History* 5.411, 1) and Procopius (*De bello Gothico* 8.21, 16).

Bibliography

Aigner Foresti L 1993 *Religioni dell' età classica.* Milan

Aigner-Foresti L 1998 *N(euer) P(auly) 4,* col. *189–195 s.v.* (Etruskische) Religion

Pallottino M 1950 La religione degli Etruschi. In: Turchi N (ed.) *Le Religioni del Mondo.* Rome, p. 313

Pfiffig A J 1975 *Religio Etrusca.* Graz

Rix H 1981 Rapporti onomastici fra il panteon etrusco e quello romano. In: *Incontro di Studio in Onore di Massimo Pallottino.* Rome, pp. 104–126

The Family (Children of God)

W. S. Bainbridge

This worldwide missionary communal movement was founded in California in the late 1960s by David Brandt Berg and his family. Members call it 'The Family,' but journalists dubbed it 'The Children of God.' Culturally, it was an amalgam of the Holiness Movement and the 'hippie' or New Age counterculture, stressing the intense spiritual experiences that were common to both. Unrelated to the Adventist tradition, which is the source of most millenarian movements in the United States, it did not attempt to decode precise prophecies from the Bible, but was guided by messages Father David received directly from Jesus and various lesser spirits.

Father David quoted divine guidance in hundreds of 'Mo [Moses] Letters' and other internal publications that held the movement together. When he passed away in 1994, at first his successors struggled to receive the gift of prophecy, but then a torrent of messages came not only to the new leadership but to the majority of members. In 1997, fully 95 percent of 1,025 members who responded to a sociological questionnaire said they had 'received prophecy, visions, or messages from the spirit world.' Some of these contacts were with departed friends and relatives, for example when a girl killed in a vehicle accident sent consoling words from the beyond. Many deceased celebrities wrote letters about their lives and afterlife experiences, including Marilyn Monroe, Elvis Presley, John Lennon, Albert Einstein, Richard Nixon, and Martin Luther King, Jr. The Family began publishing works of literature written posthumously, such as *The Return of the Seven Keys* by C. S. Lewis, *The Greatest of These* by William Shakespeare, *Nancine* by Guy de Maupassant, and *Amaris* by Scheherazade.

The Family believes that the spirit world is an eternal, invisible dimension which exists concurrently with the physical world. Heaven is a realm of action and delight, where people experience lives like those on Earth but much better. Thus, great writers continue to produce literature after their deaths, and the prayerful sensitivity of living helpers can channel their words to us. The fact that Shakespeare, de Maupassant and Scheherazade write in modern colloquial English is not strange, because God has given them the power to communicate effectively with their modern audience. In his preface to *The Perfect Ones*, an adventure novel about the Cathars, the spirit of Sir Walter Scott explains that his living helper convinced him to adopt a more contemporary style of writing. By the end of 1997, 381 'spirit stories' had been fully written down, and many were distributed within the group as an inspirational Heaven's Library. The booklet, *Hearing from Heaven*, and other internal publications instruct members on how to open their hearts in prayer to receive such messages themselves.

The primary language of The Family is English, although Spanish is widely used as well. Children are home schooled, using English-language lessons, but they frequently learn the rudiments of many other languages as they travel from country to country. There are roughly ten thousand missionaries, born in more than 90 nations.

See also: New Religions Movements; Spiritualism.

Bibliography

Bainbridge W S 1997 *The Sociology of Religious Movements*. Routledge, New York

Bainbridge W S 2001 *The Endtime Family*. SUNY Press, Albany, NY

Holding R 1999 *Hearing from Heaven*. Aurora, Thailand

Lewis J R, Melton J G (eds.) 1994 *Sex, Slander and Salvation*. Center for Academic Publication, Stanford, CA

Gnosticism

A. Crislip

Gnosticism is a modern term used in two different senses: (a) philosophically, a type of religious thought generally characterized by dualism and an emphasis on esoteric knowledge, and (b) historically, a specific religious movement of the ancient Mediterranean world, i.e., the Gnostics. This article will discuss the latter, historical, use of the term. The Gnostics are among the earliest Christian schools of thought. Their self-designation, the Gnostics (Gk *hoi gnōstikoi*) means 'those capable of knowledge.' They are attested as early as the second century CE. Another sect, the Valentinians, developed out of the Gnostic movement around 150 CE in Rome, around the theologian Valentinus.

Our sources for Gnosticism fall into two groups, those written by their opponents and those written by the Gnostics themselves. Literature written by the Gnostics is contained in sixteen ancient books written in Coptic, 13 of which were discovered together in 1945 in Egypt (see *Nag Hammadi Texts*).

Gnostic scripture presents a distinctive myth, often in the form of a revelation from or to biblical characters, such as Adam or Seth. Gnostic myth is a 'philosophical myth,' in the tradition of Plato's *Timaeus*. The myth begins with a single divine being, which emanates a series of 'aeons' or 'realms,' filling the spiritual universe. An intermediate being, Ialdabaoth, steals power from the spiritual realm and creates the material universe, a flawed copy of the spiritual realm. Gnostic scripture generally equates this 'craftsman' (Gk *dēmiourgos*) with the god of the Hebrew Bible. Wisdom, a spiritual aeon, attempts to regain the lost power from Ialdabaoth. The power, or light, is deposited in Adam, and is subsequently dispersed through one line of his offspring. The Gnostics view the return of the dispersed power to the spiritual realm as the goal of human history, effected as individuals come to gain knowledge (*gnōsis*) of their true divine nature.

While the term 'Gnostic' does not occur in Gnostic scripture, Gnostic writers use jargon or in-group language to refer to themselves, e.g., 'the seed of Seth' or 'the immovable race.' Gnostic scriptures also widely use 'magical' names in their myths, drawing on Hebrew and Greek roots. Gnostic literature, especially Valentinian literature, employs sophisticated allegory in its exegesis of Christian scripture.

Gnosticism was one of the most important early Christian sects and consistently challenged the supremacy of other Christian movements in the Roman Empire. The Gnostics are well attested throughout the Roman Empire into the third and fourth centuries CE, but after the imperial recognition of a single branch of Christianity in 381 CE, the Gnostic church dwindled, and is from then on attested only in the outskirts of the Roman and Persian empires, finally disappearing with the arrival of Islam (seventh century CE).

See also: Allegory; Magic; Manichaeism; Pseudepigrapha; Nag Hammadi Texts.

Bibliography

Layton B 1987 *The Gnostic Scriptures*. Doubleday, New York

Layton B 1996 Prolegomena to the study of ancient Gnosticism. In: White L M, Yarborough L O (eds.) *The Social World of the First Christians*. Fortress Press, Minneapolis, MN

Greek Religion

R. C. T. Parker

A form of ancient Greek religion is attested for almost two millennia, from the earliest writings in Greek on Linear B tablets c. 1400 BCE to the final triumph of Christianity c. 430 CE. The greatest god, Zeus, has unquestioned Indo–European origins (cf. Vedic *Dyaus*). Alongside gods, Greeks worshipped 'heroes,' normally envisaged as mortals who remained powerful after death (similar to saints, but less virtuous). Each Greek city or tribe honored overlapping but not identical groups of gods (usually many more than the 12 main figures) and heroes; therefore there was no single Greek religion. The names of gods were usually nontransparent, but those of Hephaestus and Ares were used in poetry for, fire and warfare, respectively; and certain abstract qualities such as love, Eros, social order, Themis, and righteous indignation, Nemesis, were also recognized as gods. Each sanctuary of a major god was normally dedicated them under a particular epithet; Athene, for instance, might be 'of the city' or 'of Horses' or 'Athene Victory' or 'Athena of Health' or 'Athene of Pallene' (a place), and so on through a long list. It was quite common to avoid using the name of frightening underworld powers. 'Theophoric' names, i.e. mortal names formed from those of gods (Artemisia, Dionysodoros ('gift of Dionysus') and so on) were widespread.

State was church in Greece. Decisions in religious matters were taken by the same individuals or bodies that took secular decisions; they then might decide to refer a problem to the gods themselves for resolution, by consultation of an oracle. Priests were attached to particular shrines; they did not constitute a unified group, and at most only had influence, not power. Numerous techniques of divination were in use, some institutionalized in fixed oracles linked with particular gods (trance mediumship, as at Delphi; drawing of lots; incubation in quest of prophetic dreams), some performed by self-employed seers (from the flight of birds; from sacrificial omens; from prophetic books) (see *Oracle*).

In Greek as opposed to Roman religion, the exact reproduction of formulae was seldom of importance (except in magic); there existed templates, for hymns, for instance, but not fixed forms. The request for blessings that accompanied every sacrifice was typically very simple.

There is no single Greek word for 'religion' or for 'cult.' 'Believing in the gods' cannot be translated without introducing an overtone of 'worshipping' the gods. 'Sacrifice' is divided between numerous overlapping sub-vocabularies. There are two words for 'sacred', one (*ἱερός*) merely identifying objects or persons associated with the gods, and one (*ἁγνός*) emphasizing the respect that such association demands; this latter word was believed in antiquity, perhaps correctly, to be etymologically connected with *ἐναγής*, accursed, polluted. When applied to things *ὅσιος* is the opposite of *ἱερός* and means 'not sacred'; when applied to persons it is something closer to 'pure' or 'upright.' The sense that underlies and unites the two usages is 'free from religious danger.'

See also: Etruscan Religion; Roman Religion.

Bibliography

Benveniste E 1973 *Indo–European Language and Society* [trans. E. Palmer]. Faber, London

Bremmer J 1994 Greek Religion. *Greece and Rome New Surveys in the Classics*, **24** reprinted with addenda 1999. Oxford University Press, Oxford

Bruit Zaidman L, Schmitt Pantel P 1992 *Religion in the Ancient Greek City* [trans. Cartledge P]. Cambridge University Press, Cambridge

Burkert W 1985 *Greek Religion* [trans. W. Raffan]. Blackwell, Oxford

Casabona J 1966 *Recherches sur le vocabulaire des sacrifices en grec*. Publications des Annales de la Faculté des lettres, Aix-en-Provence

Parker R 1983 *Miasma: Pollution and Purification in Early Greek Religion*. Oxford University Press, Oxford

Price S 1999 *Religions of the Ancient Greeks*. Cambridge University Press, Cambridge

Pulleyn S 1997 *Prayer in Greek Religion*. Oxford University Press, Oxford

Hare Krishna Movement

K. R. Valpey

The International Society for Krishna Consciousness (ISKCON), sometimes referred to as the 'Hare Krishna Movement,' is a worldwide mission-oriented branch of the Gauḍīya Vaiṣṇava or Caitanya Vaiṣṇava tradition of Hinduism. With theological roots in theistic Vedanta systematized by followers of Śrī Caitanya (1486–1533), ISKCON aims to transmit in as many languages as possible the teachings of its founder, A C. Bhaktivedanta Swami Prabhupāda. Although Swami Prabhupāda took the translating into English of Sanskrit texts of the Caitanya Vaiṣṇava *bhakti* tradition as his primary task, translation was not to obscure or replace Sanskrit, seen as the most sacred of languages (see *Hinduism*). Hence Prabhupada's books are notable for the presence of Sanskrit throughout, in both *devanāgarī* script and Roman transliteration, in word-for-word glosses of each text, and in proof-texts quoted within his extensive 'purports' based largely on commentaries of earlier preeminent Vaiṣṇavas.

This privileging of Sanskrit has carried over into daily temple worship, where morning and evening readings of the sacred texts (especially Bhāgavata Purāṇa and Bhagavad-gītā) include congregational repetition of the text or texts of the day to form the basis for subsequent homily.

From these books and from the daily readings, followers ('bhakta-s' or 'devotees'—stress on the middle syllable) encounter a substantial corpus of Sanskrit terminology. This vocabulary is then subject to translation into English, and eventually from English into other languages. Thus, for example, *parameśvara bhagavān śrī kṛṣṇa* is rendered by Prabhupāda as 'Krishna, the Supreme Personality of Godhead,' to become in German 'Krishna, die höchste Persönlichkeit Gottes.' Similarly, the Sankhya typology of *prakṛti* into *guṇa-s* becomes 'the modes of material nature,' which in German becomes 'die Erscheinungsweisen der materiellen Natur.'

Despite Sanskrit's privileged position as sacred language, Prabhupāda insisted that competence in the language was not a prerequisite for the spiritual perfection aspired for in the practice of *bhakti*. He even indicated that rituals performed in the worship of temple deities could be accomplished with translations of the liturgical Sanskrit mantras into vernacular languages. Despite this expression of adaptability by the Society's founder, an attempt by some of his followers to introduce an English version of a Sanskrit song in morning congregational worship in one American temple (in the early 1980s) led to strong worldwide ISKCON condemnation of the practice.

Much Sanskrit terminology used in ISKCON has to do with social identity and position. An ongoing discourse within ISKCON over '*varṇāśrama*' has devotees pondering about its proper application to themselves in the modern context. These designations, in turn, are held in tension with the overriding Vaiṣṇava conception that spirituality aims at becoming free from *all* designations except those indicating one's eternal servitorship to Krishna.

With a predominance of leadership coming from America, ISKCON's *lingua franca* is English (see *Hinduism*, section 7). Yet recent missionary advances in Russia could be the preliminary indications that its language, coupled with Russia's geographic proximity to India, could eventually become a more prominent if not dominant medium for the expanding 'Krishna consciousness' mission.

See also: New Religious Movements; Hinduism; Buddhism in the West.

Bibliography

Bhaktivedanta Swami Prabhupāda A C 1998 *The Complete Teachings of His Divine Grace A. C. Bhaktivedanta Swami Prabhupāda*. CD-ROM. Sandy Ridge, NC: The Bhaktivedanta Book Trust

Brooks C R 1989 *The Hare Krishnas in India*. Princeton University Press, Princeton, NJ

Goswami S D 1987 *Prabhupāda-Līlā*: *Around the World 1967–1969 & 1972–1975*. Gita-nagari Press, Potomac, MD

Internet Website: www.chakra.org

Hinduism

D. H. Killingley

The term 'Hinduism' covers a variety of religious traditions linked by Indian cultural history, and to some extent by the use of the Sanskrit language. Sacred texts, in Sanskrit and other languages, play a large part in Hindu religion, and distinctive ideas about language developed (see *Hindu Views on Language*; *Mantra*; *Pali*).

1. The Term 'Hinduism'

'Hinduism' was first used in English in the early nineteenth century; corresponding words in other languages, both European and Indian, were probably formed later. 'Hindu' was the Middle Iranian name of the river Indus and the land around and beyond it. It was also used as an ethnic term; the Persian-speaking Muslims who invaded North India from the eleventh century onwards applied it to those inhabitants of the region who were not Muslims. The word passed into South Asian languages, and has been current in English since the seventeenth century.

Since differences or religion in South Asia are closely correlated with ethnic differences in dress, diet, kinship systems and also language, the shift of meaning by which the ethnic term Hindu became a religious term is both natural and hard to trace. The nineteenth-century phrase 'Hindu Christian' indicates that at that time Hindu could still be primarily an ethnic term; and since one need not be religious to be a Hindu, it is still an ethnic or cultural term as well as a religious one. When traditional Hindus identify themselves by their religious affiliation, they use terms such as 'Vaiṣṇava' (worshiper of Viṣṇu, or of Kṛṣṇa), 'Śaiva' (worshiper of Śiva) or 'Śākta' (worshiper of the Goddess), or narrower terms. The boundaries between Hindu, Buddhist, Jain, Sikh, etc. have only during the latter half of the twentieth century been made firmer than tradition seems to warrant. Hinduism as a religious label was imposed from the outside, first by Muslims and later by Europeans. In the course of the nineteenth century, however, in response to attacks on Hinduism by Europeans and Westernized Indians, a unitary concept of Hinduism developed.

The self-understanding of Hinduism has been greatly facilitated by modern Indological scholarship, largely based on Sanskrit. The nineteenth-century search for the true Hinduism was conducted mainly by English-educated Hindus, and largely in English. It was largely concerned with literary sources, especially the more ancient ones, and tended to override the differences between regional traditions handed down in vernacular languages. From around 1890, the growing Indian nationalism became increasingly a religious nationalism, using Hindu symbols such as worship of the Goddess and protection of the cow.

2. Language and Religion in South Asia

In South Asia, choice of language correlates to some extent with religion. In a part of southern Maharashtra, for instance, Hindus speak Marathi, Muslims Urdu, and Jains Kannada (Shapiro and Schiffman

1981: 190). Differences of pronunciation have been found between Hindu and Muslim or Christian speakers of Hindi (Chandola 1962), and this situation is paralleled in a number of other languages of India. Even where the spoken language differs little, people of different religions may be literate in different writing systems, and regard themselves as speaking different languages: speakers of Panjabi use Devanāgarī, Gurmukhī or Urdu script, and consider themselves Hindi, Panjabi, or Urdu speakers, according as they are Hindus, Sikhs, or Muslims.

Hindu nationalism has been closely linked with the promotion of Hindi as the modern all-India language, and of Sanskrit as the language of scholarship and as a source of new words, not only for new concepts but to replace Persian and English words. Such words are associated by Hindu nationalists with Muslim and British rule respectively, though they are used freely by Hindus when not under the influence of Hindi purism. The most distinguished and thoroughgoing advocate of Sanskrit vocabulary was Dr Raghu Vira (1902–63), who recommended that the same Sanskrit words should be adopted not only in Hindi but in other Indian languages, both Indo–Aryan and Dravidian.

Such views aroused opposition, particularly in Tamil Nadu. A Tani Tamil (pure Tamil) movement was started in 1916 by Maraimalai Adikal (1876–1950), who himself had Tamilized his former Sanskrit name Svāmī Vedācalam. This movement was linked with opposition to the dominance of brahmins, who were disproportionately represented in education and the professions, to the political dominance of the Hindi-speaking region, and to the promotion of Hindi as an all-India language. Opposition to brahmins had religious implications, and sometimes took the form of atheism.

3. Sanskrit as a Sacred Language

The oldest known South Asian religious texts, collected in the corpus known as the Veda (Sanskrit *veda* 'knowledge'), are in Sanskrit. The Veda includes hymns in verse, composed perhaps as early as 1500 BCE, to which are added some prose texts recited in ritual (see *Mantra*), and a much larger body of prose texts, the Brāhmaṇas, which discuss various rituals and explain their purpose. Two further classes of texts, the Āraṇyakas and Upaniṣads, appear first as parts of Brāhmaṇas, but were later classed as separate literary genres. The Āraṇyakas continue the Brāhmaṇas, describing further rituals, some of which may not actually have been performed. The Upaniṣads, though containing some ritual matter, turn increasingly to theological and philosophical speculation, and in some passages explicitly reject ritual.

The main bulk of the Veda was composed gradually over a period of about 1,000 years; but it never formed a fixed canon, and Upaniṣads continued to be added during the second millennium CE. The language of the oldest hymns differs from Classical Sanskrit in some phonological, morphological, and lexical features which show that it is a related dialect rather than simply an earlier form of the same dialect. It is referred to by modern scholars as 'Vedic Sanskrit,' or sometimes simply as 'Vedic'; in the latter case the name 'Sanskrit' is restricted to the Classical language, the name 'Old Indian' being used to cover both.

As a language of ritual, Sanskrit holds a special place which is quite independent of its cultivation as a language of courtly literature and of secular learning. In the school of Vedic interpretation and ritual known as Pūrva-Mīmāṃsā ('earlier exegesis'), the Veda is regarded as eternal and without an author, and thus exempt from the errors to which all authors are liable. Since the mantras are used in dealing with the gods, they have a sacred character which was accentuated by the increasing differences between the current form of Sanskrit and the Vedic language. Already in the Brāhmaṇas, a distinction was being drawn between the language of the gods, as used in the mantras, and human language (see *Mantra*).

Throughout the Hindu tradition, including the Vedic period, the primary form of language is speech, not writing. Writing, apart from the pre-Vedic Harappan civilization, was not known until the third century BCE; the Veda was transmitted orally from teacher to pupil. Because the success of the ritual depended on the mantras being repeated exactly as they had been by earlier generations, great care was taken to memorize the text. The result was an astonishing feat of memory on the part of countless reciters, who transmitted the text unchanged for thousands of years with far greater accuracy than most manuscript traditions. Even when writing was known, recitation of the Veda from a written text was condemned (Allen 1953: 16). Because the Veda consisted essentially of spoken words that had previously been heard by the speaker from his teacher, it was known as *śruti* 'hearing,' as opposed to *smṛti* 'memory, tradition,' which referred to the less consistently transmitted, but still authoritative, non-Vedic texts. Post-Vedic tradition regards śruti as an eternal body of sound which was revealed by the *ṛṣis* ('sages, seers') who then passed it on to their pupils (see *Hindu Views on Language*).

4. Hindu Theories of Language

The importance of language in Vedic ritual gave it a prominent place in Vedic thought which it retained in later times (see *Hindu Views of Language*). Hindus have a long tradition of the study of actual language, applied primarily though not exclusively to Sanskrit, which may be accounted for by the importance of speech in Vedic ritual. The training of a Vedic priest included phonetics (*śikṣā*), grammar (*vyākaraṇa*), etymology (*nirukta*), and meter (*chandas*). This reflects a concern to ensure that the texts were properly pronounced and understood at a time when their language was becoming archaic.

Etymology was not concerned with the diachronic derivation of words, but sought synchronic relations between them, both in form and in meaning. In the Brāhmaṇas, it is used as a way of finding a hidden significance in a word, or of establishing a link between its referent and something else. Thus the head is called *śiras* because when the seven vital powers (*prāṇa*, literally 'breath') combined to form the original man, they placed their glory (*śrī*) in his head, and also because they relied (*śri*) on the head (*Śata-patha Brāhmaṇa* 6, 1, 1, 4). Where two etymologies are found for the same word, as in this example, there is no question of one being accepted and the other rejected; each of them reveals an aspect of the referent. Where such etymologies do not match those set up by modern linguists (though many of them do), they have been misleadingly referred to as folk etymologies. In fact they were devised and taken seriously by the learned of the Vedic period, and continued to be taken seriously later.

The use of etymology as a way of expounding the meaning of a word, without any reference to its diachronic origin continues in post-Vedic times. The second-century Sanskrit law book ascribed to Manu explains *māṃsa* 'meat' as *māṃsa* 'me he (will eat),' indicating the fate of the meat-eater after death (Manu 5, 55). The underlying assumption of natural affinity between words which reveals eternal truth persists in popular Hindu discourse, and is not confined to Sanskrit. Even in English, the word *God* has been explained as the acronym of 'generator, operator, destroyer,' a version of the ancient view of the threefold relation of Brahman with the world (cf. *Taittirīya Upaniṣad* 3, 1).

5. Sanskrit as an All-India Language

Because of the widespread use of Sanskrit in ancient and medieval India, not only in ritual and religious literature but in secular literature and for political and administration purposes, most Indian vernaculars, both Indo–Aryan and Dravidian, have many words in common. The frequent use of Sanskrit words is associated with Brahmins and the learning, and confers a certain kind of prestige implying attachment to the Brahmanical tradition. This prestige is not the only kind; other kinds of prestige may be conferred by the use of indigenous Tamil words in Tamil, for instance, or of English words in Bengali, or of Persian words in Urdu. The forms of Sanskrit words (even those words called *tatsama* 'the same as it,' i.e., of the same form as the Sanskrit etymon) usually differ according to the phonologies and sometimes the morphologies of different languages. Some of these differences appear in writing as well as in pronunciation, and sometimes there are differences of meaning; *kalyāṇa* means 'welfare' in Sanskrit and Hindi but 'wedding' in Tamil (*kaliyāṇam*).

Despite these differences many Hindus have a considerable passive knowledge and some active knowledge of Sanskrit vocabulary, which is independent of knowledge of Sanskrit itself. Sanskrit is also widely used in ritual in the form of mantras (see *Mantra*) and stotras (hymns of praise), so that the sound of it is familiar to many Hindus.

6. Devotional Movements and the Vernaculars

It was implied above (Sect. 5) that Sanskrit is not uniformly esteemed by Hindus. It is by no means invariably associated with Hinduism, and vernacular languages are also used for religious purposes.

Poetry expressing and inspiring religious devotion (bhakti) began to be composed in Tamil in the seventh century. It drew on the Tamil poetic tradition, which can be traced at least as far back as the first century, and is largely independent of Sanskrit literature. Devotional poetry fostered a form of religion which was independent of ritual, and often expressed contempt for brahmins and their practices.

Devotional poetry was composed in Kannada from the twelfth century, in Marathi from the thirteenth century, and in Hindi from the fifteenth century. Since these languages, unlike Tamil, had no previous literary tradition, it was bhakti that first led to their being developed for literary purposes.

7. English as a Hindu Language

In the nineteenth century, English became one of the languages of Hinduism. The identification of 'Hinduism' described in Sect. 1 was largely the work of English-educated Hindus writing in English, and using Western concepts, including the concept of Hinduism itself. At the same time, Western concepts were legitimated by the use of Sanskrit words. Bankim Chandra Chatterji (1838–94), writing in Bengali, pointed out that Bengali had no word for 'independence,' but he had no difficulty in forming one, by using the Sanskrit word *svādhīnatā*. Vivekananda legitimated the concept of evolution by identifying it with *vikāsa* 'opening (of a flower),' the term used by the eleventh-century theologian Rāmānuja to refer to the expansion of the self's awareness. The word *Hinduism* itself was adapted for use in Indian languages as *Hindutva*—a Persian word with a Sanskrit suffix—and was also identified with the traditional phrase *sanātana dharma* 'eternal law.'

The English language itself was used in Hindu discourse, being more extensively known throughout India than Sanskrit or Persian. This led to the development of what has been termed Neo-Hinduism, particularly among those English-educated Hindus who felt a need for a form of Hinduism that they could understand and respect. Neo-Hindu discourse developed its own English vocabulary, e.g., *spiritual*; *spiritualism* (in a different sense from the Western one); *realization*—all words with no exact Sanskrit equivalent. Sanskrit words such as *bhakti* 'devotion' and *dharma* 'law' are also used in this vocabulary.

Outside India, and in some families in India, generations have grown up with English as their most familiar language. In English-speaking countries, Hindus use Sanskrit in rituals, especially weddings and other life-cycle rituals; but since it is harder to understand these rituals outside their traditional social context, there is a need for explanation, and the brahmins who conduct them often add vernacular or English glosses. Devotional songs in vernacular languages are used in temples, but sometimes the words are written in roman script, on posters or typed sheets, for those who do not read Indian scripts. Hindus often substitute roughly homologous English terms for Indian ones, so that Diwālī is called 'Christmas,' muṇḍan (the ritual first cutting of a boy's hair) is called 'christening,' the oil lamps used in worship are called 'candles'—originally perhaps in an attempt to make themselves understood to non-Hindus, but increasingly among themselves.

Hindu, and also Buddhist, words, most of them Sanskrit, have entered the vocabulary of European languages. Many of them appeared in the technical vocabulary of Indology in the eighteenth and nineteenth centuries, and were popularized by Transcendentalism in the mid-nineteenth century and by Theosophy in the late nineteenth and early twentieth centuries, as well as by the British connection with India. In the 1960s, the International Society for Krishna Consciousness and other Hindu movements in the West gave them further currency. These three stages account for the currency in English of the words *ashram*, *avatar*, *Brahma*, *dharma*, *guru*, *karma*, *linga*, *mandala*, *mantra*, *prana*, *puja*, *sadhu*, *sannyasi*, *shanti*, *swami*, *swastika*, *tantra*, *upanishad*, *Veda*, *yantra*, *yoga*. The presence of substantial numbers of Hindus in the UK, together with interest in Hinduism fostered by religious education, has brought a fourth stage. Here, because of closer contact between English speakers and popular Hinduism, many of the words are Hindi or Gujarati, though some are also Sanskrit. Examples from Hindi are *ārti* 'ritual waving of lamps,' *dīwā* 'lamp,' *diwālī* 'an autumn festival' (Sanskrit *ārātrika*, *dīpa*, *dīpāvali*). Many more words are current as elements in Hindu personal names.

The currency of such words among nonspecialists, both Hindu and non-Hindu, brings problems of orthography and pronunciation. The name *Sītā* is sometimes written Siitaa or Seethaa (double letters being used to indicate vowel length, and *th* to represent an unaspirated interdental stop). On the other hand, some publications, notably those of the International Society of Krishna Consciousness, use the standard transcription for Sanskrit given in this Encyclopedia. Pronunciations such as [mæn'da:lə] for *maṇḍala* ['mʌɳɖʌlʌ] are common among English speakers.

See also: Sanskrit; Sanskrit: Discovery by Europeans; Ritual; Hare Krishna Movement.

Bibliography

Allen W S 1953 *Phonetics in Ancient India.* Oxford University Press, London

Chandola A 1962 Two social dialects of Hindi. *Orbis* **11**: 486–90

Gonda J (ed.) 1975 *A History of Indian Literature.* Harrassowitz, Wiesbaden

Killingley D H 1986 Om: The sacred syllable in the Veda. In: Lipner J J, Killingley D H (eds.) *A Net Cast Wide: Investigations into Indian Thought in Memory of David Friedman.* Grevatt and Grevatt, Newcastle upon Tyne

Shapiro M C, Schiffman H F 1981 *Language and Society in South Asia.* Motilal Banarsidass, Delhi

Islam in Africa

L. Sanneh

The records first linking Islam with Africa go back to the lifetime of the Prophet. In the fifth year of his preaching in Mecca, in 615 CE, groups of Muslim refugees, fleeing persecution in Mecca, began arriving in Abyssinia, and the fledgling religion gravitated towards an organized state, introducing an enduring structural theme in the subsequent expansion of the religion in Africa. By the end of the seventh century, Islam had been implanted in Egypt (642 CE) and North Africa (689 CE).

Political factors competed with trade to accompany further expansion, and the organized structures of the religion coalesced with appropriate indigenous institutions to facilitate its reception. Islamized groups were widespread in Sub-Saharan Africa from a very early time, particularly with the rise of states and kingdoms such as ancient Mali (1235–ca. 1450), Songhay (1460–1591), both in West Africa, and, beginning in the seventeenth century, with the populations of Futa Toro in Senegal, the Fulbe (Fulani) of Futa Jallon in Guinea, and the populations of Songhay in modern Mali and Kanem-Bornu in present-day Chad. On the east coast, Islam had spread among the populations of Eritrea and the Red Sea coast from a very early time, with other coastal populations (Arabic *sawāhil*, sg *sāhil*) also being subsequently affected. Beginning in the nineteenth century, with the onset of the *jihād* ('holy war') movement, Islam was enthroned or strengthened among the Hausa of north Nigeria, and the Fulbe of Masina and Futa Jallon. Later, with the coming of European colonial rule, it expanded among the Bambara of modern Mali, the Wolof of Senegal, and the Yoruba of western Nigeria, among others. In these expansions, especially those taking place under *jihād*, the military/political instrument was sometimes introduced to consolidate religious gains.

Nevertheless, in spite of the appeal of the sword, Islam is the religion of the word par excellence, the word enshrined in the Qur'ān and promoted in the canonical devotions. An influential class of religious specialists, devoted to Qur'ān study, including the Jakhanke Muslim clerics and others described as *karamokos*, *alfas*, *tchernos*, *tamsirs*, *marabouts*, *bookmen*, *morimen*, etc., was established among islamized and semi-islamized groups, strengthening and extending the cause. The word of the Qur'ān comes into contact with mother tongues by a process of displacement, at first gradually, at times by superscribing a lingua franca, sometimes by a major infusion of new terms, but always on its own terms. As pointed out by M. S. El-Garh, an Egyptian scholar then teaching at the University of Ibadan, Nigeria, 'whenever Arabic encountered another language, it was Arabic that... prevailed in the end' (El-Garh 1970: 19). Among educated and illiterate alike the Qur'ān is a potent oracle, a repository of infallible commandments, and an arbiter of dreams and visions, a subject of special significance in Muslim Africa.

A real obstacle confronts new Muslim Africans, namely, how to observe the obligations in the sacred but unfamiliar Arabic. At first there might be only blind imitation of sounds and syllables with little understanding of their meaning or source. Ordinary believers as well as new converts would defer to the experts for example and guidance. Some teachers taught that Muslims lacking knowledge of Arabic would, nevertheless, obtain at the resurrection the gift of perfect Arabic speech. Thus ignorance of Arabic, though an inadequacy, was not, however, considered a permanent injury to faith. Such an outlook also explains why mother tongues might survive under Islam without any enduring value. In the meantime, those who know Arabic have some of the prestige of the resurrection dispensation accruing to them, with many turning that knowledge and prestige to good account. As such they preside over courtly ceremonials, taking charge of functions natural to a literate elite. Many supplement these activities by operating Qur'ān schools, where for a fee instruction is offered to Muslim and non-Muslim alike.

European observers have always been struck by the educational and social role of the Muslim missionary, in particular his mobility and adaptability, and the relatively scant resources he needs to operate. Christian missionaries, for example, commented on the absence of any bureaucratic organization to support Islamic expansion in Africa, saying the simplicity of the Qur'ān school adds considerably to its utility and effectiveness.

Writing in the fourteenth century, the celebrated Arab geographer, Ibn Baṭṭūṭa, tells of draconian measures being adopted in these Qur'ān schools, such as shackling children, to ensure proper learning of the holy book.

Among the Fulbe four categories of study are recognized: *jangugol*, reading; *windugol*, writing; *firugol*, vernacular exegesis, and *fennu̱* (Arabic *funūn*), higher studies, *Firugol*, based on the vernacular, may lead to the more rigorous *kebbé*, vernacular scholastic theology which had the effect of mobilizing Fulbe pastoral and nomadic communities, and evoking Fulbe ethnic feeling. However, what energetic vernacular literary activity there was in the Fulfulde remained fixed in standard Islamic subjects, from theology, ritual, and devotion to linguistics, ethics, and law. Haafkens (1983) has collected some major Fulfulde religious texts that indicate the vernacular tradition is well established among Muslim Fulbe, where it imitates the superior Arabic.

The Qur'ān school is thus a rivet binding society to the word, its nontranslatable status allowing it to be transmitted without indigenous compromise, whatever extramural permutations might occur.

The educative power of the Qur'ān in time brings about reform. 'Abd al-Karīm al-Maghīlī (d. 1505), a North African scholar and the intellectual father of African reform Islam, charged scholars with not being 'Arabic-speaking,' thus making Arabic competence a condition of faithfulness. This placed the majority of Muslim Africans on the defensive, since only a tiny minority at any given time could thus acquit themselves, although in practice faithfulness is imputed vicariously, and the organized state, buttressed with Islam, becomes sufficient vindication of the truth.

Religious itinerancy, of which al-Maghīlī was such an outstanding example, contributed to the spread of Islam. The circulation of books and similar religious materials belongs to this tradition. The first published account of the Kanuri language (1854), for example, spoken by Muslims in the Lake Chad region, was prepared in Freetown by the linguist Sigismund Koelle who worked with freed slaves. It was subsequently checked and corrected in Cairo by another scholar working with students at Al-Azhar.

In numerous communities in Sub-Saharan Africa, too, Muslim religious practice has brought with it knowledge or veneration of Arabic as a prerequisite. Consequently, even outside the formal canon, Arabic has influenced religious and social culture, so that 'the literary language of the law books has enriched the languages of Muslims with hundreds of religious, political, commercial, and abstract words and expressions' (Spencer Trimingham 1959: 83).

Religious and cultural change in Muslim Africa implies linguistic change. Arabic terms and concepts flooded into the languages, claiming the high ground given to religion and metaphysics. Mandinka examples include *lakira* (Arabic *al-ākhirah*), 'afterlife,' *niyo*, *qaniya* (Arabic *nīyah*), 'soul, intention, volition,' *kaburo* (Arabic *qabr*, *maqbar*), 'tomb, grave,' and *baraka* (Arabic *barakah*), 'blessing, virtue.' Even in the Wolof language spoken in Senegal, West Africa, only relatively recently exposed to Islam, similar influences occur: for example, the word for 'language' *lagha* from Arabic *lūghah*, and words for knowledge (Wolof *ham ham*, Arabic *fahm*), confidentiality (Wolof *sutura*, Arabic *satara*, 'to cover, veil, shield or guard'), and the wooden tablet used in Qur'ān schools (Wolof *alluwa*, Arabic *al-lawḥ*).

Sometimes the old words and terms are retained but assigned almost exclusively to Islam. The Wolof *seringe* (Arabic *shaykh*), for example, is the holy man who now performs a number of Muslim religious functions: as Qur'ān expert (*tamsīr*), schoolmaster (*seringe daara*), provider of amulets, scribe, vendor of Muslim goods and general wares. His counterpart in Mandinka is the *karamokho*, in Hausa the *mallam* (Arabic *mu'allim*), and among the Fulbe the *alfa* (Arabic *alif*).

For indigenous populations, perhaps the most radical change comes with the adoption of the Islamic 'Allāh' as the name of the Supreme Being, and the accompanying loss of the indigenous name. Thus Muslim Hausa, Mandinka, Fulani, and Wolof, to take a random list, have now only variants of the Arabic 'Allāh' as the name for God, and even non-Muslim members of those ethnic groups have no other name for God available to them. Similarly, the Maguzawa, the non-Muslim Hausa of north Nigeria, employ Islamic terminology for their cosmology and ritual observances. Even the name *Maguzawa* (sg *Maguje*) is derived from the Arabic *majūs*, 'heathen, pagan,' a name given to unrepentant Hausa by Muslim jurists in order to incorporate them in the Islamic state as a tribute-paying people (*dhimmī*). Other non-*dhimmī* 'pagans' were called *arne*.

The novelist, Cheikh Hamidou Kane describes the word of the Qur'ān as 'not like other words. It was a word which demanded suffering, it was a word come from God, it was a miracle, it was as God Himself had uttered it... The word which comes from God must be spoken exactly as it has pleased Him to fashion it. Whoever defaces it deserves to die.' It ensures Arabic supremacy over mother tongues in Muslim Africa.

See also: Qur'ān.

Bibliography

El-Garh M S 1970 Arabic in Nigeria. Research Seminar, 24 November. Department of Arabic and Islamic Studies. University of Ibadan, Nigeria

Haafkens J 1983 *Les chants Musulmans en Peul*. E J Brill, Leiden

Levtzion N, Hopkins J F P (transls. & eds.) 1981 *Corpus of Early Arabic Sources for West African History*. Cambridge University Press, Cambridge

Sanneh L 1989 *The Jakhanke Muslim Clerics: A Religious and Historical Study of Islam in Senegambia*. University Press of America, Lanham, MD

Santerre R 1973 *Pédagogie musulmane d'Afrique noire*. Press de l'université de Montréal, Montreal

Spencer Trimingham J 1952 *Islam in Ethopia*. Clarendon Press, Oxford: repr. 1976. Frank Cass, London

Spencer Trimingham J 1959 *Islam in West Africa*. Clarendon Press, Oxford

Islam in Central Asia

S. Akiner

Some 60 million Muslims (1989) live in the territories of the former Soviet Union, a Muslim population second in size only to that of such countries as Indonesia, Pakistan, Bangladesh, and India. Almost all are Sunni (as are the majority of Muslims in general) of the Hanafi school. There are, however, some Shi'ites in Azerbaijan and several thousand Ismailis, followers of the Aga Khan, in the Pamir mountains of Tadjikistan, in the regions adjacent to Pakistan, Afghanistan, and China.

Taken as a whole, the Muslims amount to some 20 percent of the total population of the old Soviet territories. However, there is considerable ethnic diversity among them. Some 85 percent are Turkic; of these, the Uzbeks (16.7 million) are the most numerous, constituting the third largest nationality after the Russians and the Ukrainians. Those belonging to the Iranian family account for 8 percent; the Tadjiks (4.2 million) are by far the largest nationality in this group. The Caucasian family includes such peoples as the Avars, Laks, Lezgis, and Dargis; none very large in size, they speak languages that are almost wholly mutually incomprehensible.

Muslims are concentrated in three regions: in Central Asia (60 percent), Transcaucasia (20 percent), and the Volga region and Siberia (20 percent). Islam was brought to Central Asia and Transcaucasia by Arab invaders in the seventh century, scarcely 20 years after the death of the Prophet. It gradually gained ascendancy, to become in time the dominant force in those societies. The Tatars and Turkicized Mongols of the Golden Horde, who accepted Islam during the thirteenth and fourteenth centuries, carried the religion to the far side of the Urals, along the Volga and Siberia; it remained restricted to the tribes of the Golden Horde, however, and did not spread to the Slav population, who remained Christian.

The power of the Golden Horde began to wane during the fifteenth century, while that of Muscovy grew ever stronger. The capture of the Tatar strongholds of Kazan (1552) and Astrakhan (1556) by Ivan the Terrible brought Muslims under Russian control for the first time. For much of the next two centuries, the Tatars suffered severe repression and religious persecution. It was not until the reign of Catherine the Great (1762–96) that matters improved. During this period the community revived. A Muftiat was created in Orenburg in 1788 with responsibility for Muslim affairs. Tatars were granted a number of concessions in both religious and secular affairs; the latter included the restoration of the privileges of the Tatar nobility.

In the nineteenth century many more Muslims came under Russian rule. Azerbaijan and the Caucasus were incorporated into the empire in the first half of the century, Central Asia in the second. For the most part, however, the Russian colonial administration interfered little in the everyday life of the indigenous peoples. Muslim institutions continued to function as before. Christian missionary activity was minimal.

When the Bolsheviks took power after the 1917 Revolution, one of their first acts was to reassure the 'toiling Muslims of Russia and the East' that their beliefs and customs were henceforth 'inviolable.' Yet by the end of the 1920s a fierce antireligious campaign had been launched throughout the USSR. In the Muslim regions, mosques were closed, the Qur'ān and other religious works confiscated, Muslim courts and schools abolished, teachers and scholars killed or imprisoned. The Arabic script, used for centuries by all the Muslims of Central Asia, Transcaucasia, Siberia, and the Volga, the visible symbol of Islam and symbolic link with fellow believers throughout the world, was replaced first by the Latin (1930), then the Cyrillic (1940). These changes of script effectively ensured that all forms of pre-Revolutionary literature, secular and religious alike, became inaccessible to future generations because, quite simply, they became illegible.

During World War II, the Soviet government adopted a more conciliatory attitude towards religion. For the Muslims, four regional Spiritual Directorates were created, each headed by a Mufti, to administer such manifestations of Islam as were now allowed to reappear. The largest and most important Directorate was seated in Tashkent, the capital of Uzbekistan; its Mufti played the role of unofficial ambassador to Muslim communities abroad, acting as a mouthpiece for Soviet views on such matters as the Arab–Israeli conflict. Two *madrasa* (religious colleges) were reopened for the training of Muslim functionaries (in Tashkent and Bukhara) and public worship was permitted in a small number of mosques. Twenty to thirty carefully chosen representatives were allowed to go on the *hajj* (annual pilgrimage to Mecca); a tiny amount of religious literature was printed. Most of these measures were intended to impress Muslims abroad. They were too limited to have any real effect on the life of Soviet Muslims.

Truly fundamental changes did not come until the late 1980s, when the policy of *perestroika* ('restructuring') resulted in more mosques being opened in 1989 than had previously been allowed over several decades. Extensions to the two existing *madrasa* were sanctioned, and two new ones opened in Baku and Kazan. A new edition of the Qur'ān (50,000 copies) was printed in 1989 and translations into the local languages (Uzbek, Kazakh, etc.) were put in hand. A small but growing number of works on Islam are becoming available to the public at large. The Arabic script is being taught in schools (as an optional subject) and in evening classes; in some republics (e.g., Uzbekistan) there is a movement to have it reintroduced as the national script in place of the Cyrillic script. The *hajj* has been made more accessible; in 1990, more than 1,500 pilgrims went to Mecca. Far greater freedom of contact with Muslims abroad is now permitted, both to organizations and individuals. Substantial gifts of money, Qur'āns, and religious educational material are being received, with full official blessing, from countries such as Saudi Arabia, Libya, and Pakistan.

The languages of Soviet Muslims underwent considerable change between the 1920s and the 1990s. Language planning policies were introduced in the 1920s. Consequently, new literary languages were consciously developed on the basis of selected dialects for many large and small ethnic groups. Some Muslim groups had had no standard, unified written form of their language before this period; for others, such as the Uzbeks, the classical literary medium (Chagatai/Old Uzbek) was replaced by a form closer to the vernacular dialects. Large numbers of Russian loanwords (more accurately, Western European loanwords borrowed through Russian) were incorporated into these languages. In some cases, they introduced new concepts (e.g., in the fields of ideology, administration, Western-style science and technology); in others they replaced existing Arabic/Persian terms (e.g., in Uzbek, Arabic *dārilfunūn* was replaced by Russian *universitet* 'university'). Occasionally, old and new forms coexisted as synonyms (e.g., in Uzbek, Arabic *iqtisād* and Russian *ekonomika* 'economy' are used as exact equivalents). Towards the end of the 1980s a growing sense of resentment against the Russification of these languages became apparent. This heralded a move to reinstate the Arabic/Persian elements, parallel to the move to change the script from the Cyrillic back to the Arabic.

Following the disintegration of the Soviet Union the great problem that faces the leaders of Islam is how to respond to the changed situation; in the past, their principal concern was to preserve the basic functional framework of the religion: now they are able, and indeed encouraged, to take a more active role in society, to help in its moral regeneration. It is not an easy task. They have yet to come to terms with it.

See also: Arabic Script: Adaptation for Other Languages.

Bibliography

Akiner S 1986 *The Islamic Peoples of the Soviet Union*, 2nd edn. Kegan Paul, London. [Contains some information on scripts and vocabulary]

Sjoberg A F 1963 *Uzbek Structural Grammar*. Indiana University Press, Bloomington, IN

Waterson N 1980 *Uzbek–English Dictionary*. Oxford University Press, Oxford

Islam in East Asia

J. H. Grayson

Traversing Central Asia, Arab and non-Arab Muslims entered and settled in western China and in the imperial capital of the T'ang empire (618–907 CE), Ch'angan, within one generation of the death of the prophet Muhammad in 632. Coming via the sea, other Muslim traders settled in the port cities of southeast China. Until the eleventh century or later, there seems to have been no Islamic contact with Korea, and apparently none with Japan until contemporary times. For centuries, Manchuria has received small numbers of Muslims who are members of Central Asian ethnic groups. Thus, the history of Islam in East Asia is largely confined to China proper, and this history is principally the history of non-Chinese ethnic groups within the Chinese state.

During the T'ang Dynasty, Muslims—like other foreign peoples—were granted extraterritorial status and established their own Islamic quarters within the major ports and inland commercial centers. Any mosques built during that period would have been on a small scale and none have survived to the present day. Under the Yüan Dynasty (1234–1368), Muslim communities were flourishing in the major centers in the northwest of the empire, the modern province of Szechuan in the southwest, and in the coastal cities of the southeast; and the ruling Mongols used these Muslims to staff the bureaucracy of their empire, oversee medical services and hospitals, design buildings and cities, and perform astronomical observations to regulate the imperial calendar.

During the Ming Dynasty (1368–1662), there was a policy of forced cultural assimilation on the part of the government to which the Muslims conformed in outward matters such as dress. But they still lived in Islamic quarters, kept to Islamic social customs, and learned Arabic and Persian in order to read the Qur'ān and its commentaries. The succeeding Ch'ing Dynasty (1616–1912) treated Muslim groups well, and it was then that the first known Islamic works in China proper were published. The Qur'ān remained in Arabic, but important works from the period explaining Islam in Chinese included '*Chêng-chiao Chên-ch'uan*' (A Veritable Explanation of the True Religion) by Wang Tai-yu (1580–1650), and the '*T'ien-fang Hsing-li*' (The Philosophy of Arabia), '*T'ien-fang Tien-li*' (Islamic Law and Ritual), and '*Chih-sêng Shih-lu*' (The Veritable Record of the Prophet) by Liu Chih (1662–1736).

From the collapse of the Ch'ing Empire in 1912 to the establishment of the People's Republic of China in 1949, the Muslims in Sinkiang were recognized as one of the five nationalities of China. The

Communist government of China continued to pursue this policy by setting up Autonomous Regions in various parts of the country. As with all religious groups, the Muslims and their places of worship suffered greatly during the Cultural Revolution of 1966–76, but since 1976, mosques in many cities have been reopened and the publication of the Qur'ān in Arabic and Chinese has been permitted.

Islam was first brought to Korea by groups of Koreans who had settled in Manchuria at the end of the nineteenth century and returned after World War II. This Korean Muslim community was supported by the Turkish government during the Korean War, and later given considerable assistance in the construction of mosques and other facilities by Saudi Arabia and other Muslim nations in the 1970s. There are now about 20,000 ethnic Korean Muslims and there is a Korean translation of the Qur'ān.

See also: Qur'ān.

Bibliography

Broomhall M 1910 *Islam in China: A Neglected Problem*. Morgan and Scott, London

Grayson J H 1989 *Korea: A Religious History*. Oxford University Press, Oxford

Israeli R 1980 *Muslims in China: A Study in Cultural Confrontation*. Curzon Press, London

Israeli R, Gorman L 1994 *Islam in China: A Critical Bibliography*. Greenwood, London

Islam in the Near East

J. N. Mattock

While Islam numbers among its adherents speakers of very many languages, it is dominated linguistically by Classical Arabic (*al-lugha al-fuṣḥā* 'the pure language') to an extent that not even medieval Christianity can be said to have been dominated by Latin. The Qur'ān, as the actual word of God, must be read, or recited, in Arabic. It is widely disputed whether it is permissible to translate the Qur'ān and thus modify, if not pervert, the divine revelation. Many translations have, of course, been made, by Muslims as well as by non-Muslims, and an English translation was authorized in 1984 by the University of al-Azhar in Cairo, the most widely respected repository of Sunni orthodoxy, but the permissibility of translation remains a live issue. The prayers of the five canonical times must also be recited in Arabic. Only the Friday sermon is generally given in the vernacular in non-Arab communities.

1. Islam and Classical Arabic—A Symbiosis

It may reasonably be argued that it is the universal use of Arabic for religious purposes that largely sustains the very considerable cohesion of the Muslim brotherhood, bridging as it does the gulf between Sunni and Shi'i Islam, and even that between the Ahmadi movement and the rest. However imperfect a Muslim's command of Classical Arabic may be, it has become, as the medium in which the word of God was revealed, part of his heritage, which is to be revered and cherished.

It may also be argued that, to an even greater degree, it is Islam that has, reciprocally, sustained Classical Arabic. The idiom of the Qur'ān is not precisely that of the other surviving literature of its period—the pre-Islamic and early Islamic poetry—or of that of later periods. This is inherent in the doctrine of the inimitability (*i'jāz*) of the Qur'ān. It is, however, closer to the language that has survived, with remarkably little change, to become what is now known as 'Modern Standard/Formal Arabic,' than are, for example, most sixteenth-century forms of European languages to their modern counterparts. It is this language that the Arabs use for writing of all kinds, for formal oral communication—lectures, broadcasts, speeches, etc.—and, to some extent, for communication with speakers of 'dialects' that differ greatly from their own. It is the spoken native tongue of no one, and proficiency in its use varies greatly according to the degree of education of the user.

It is still uncertain what the relationship is between Classical Arabic and the various forms of speech (which are not generally represented in writing) that are familiarly referred to as the Arabic 'dialects,' collectively known in Arabic as *al-lugha al-'āmmiyya* 'the common language,' *al-lugha al-dārija* 'the current language,' or *al-lahajāt* 'the idioms, the dialects.' Traditionally, it has been claimed that these are simply offshoots of the Classical language that have become differentiated from it and from one another in the course of time. However, the theory has been advanced that a more complicated process of pidginization and creolization among the non-Arab subject peoples of the Islamic empire should be recognized as having taken place. Whatever the answer, the result has been that these 'dialects' are as different from one another as are the various languages of the Romance group.

They are, to all intents and purposes, separate languages and might well already have been recognized as such but for two factors, which are partly interconnected.

The first of these factors is Arab nationalism. This, although fostered by those who have had an interest in so doing, has never proved particularly powerful and is, indeed, somewhat specious; the greater majority of those who consider themselves Arabs have little enough direct link with the original Arab conquerors of the seventh century. The second is the importance that the Arabic language has for Islam. It is this that has, on the one hand, preserved it virtually in its pristine form and, on the other, given it a status that has caused its offspring to be regarded, even by those who speak them, as inferior. The 'dialects' are referred to in terms of greater or lesser 'purity' according to the degree to which they diverge from the Classical norm. That this is attributable to the influence of Islam is suggested by the case of Maltese; here one finds a descendant of Arabic that has developed in an entirely non-Muslim environment over more than six centuries, has adopted its own Romanized system of writing, and has been recognized as a language in its own right. Elsewhere, non-Muslim speakers of various 'dialects' have formed minorities within territories under Muslim domination.

Classical Arabic, then, is, in effect, a hieratic language for Muslims, although it is hardly recognized as such by those who consider themselves Arabic-speaking. The extent to which the vernaculars are permeated with Classical expressions, largely of a religious nature, perhaps tends to disguise the fact. Thus, the frequent citation of verses from the Qur'ān and the Hadith of the Prophet, exclamations such as *al-ḥamdu li-Lāh* 'praise be to God!,' *bismi l-Lāhi r-Raḥmāni r-Raḥīm* 'in the name of God, the Compassionate, the Merciful,' *a'ūdhu bi-l-Lāh* 'I take refuge in God (i.e., God forbid!),' and even the customary exchange of greetings, *as-salāmu 'alaykum* 'peace be upon you!'—*wa-'alaykumu s-salām* 'and upon you be peace!,' in all of which the inflections of the Classical language, absent from the vernaculars, are generally retained, strengthen the belief that other features of everyday speech represent a falling-short from a Classical perfection. On a secular level, the predilection of the educated for quoting medieval Classical poetry, in which the inflections are necessary for the meter, also reinforces this. Thus, although Classical Arabic is not a natural medium for them, 'Arabic-speaking' Muslims do not feel it to be so divorced from their own native speech as, for example, Russian-speakers regard Old Church Slavonic. For non-Arab Muslims, of course, Arabic is a hieratic language. Since, however, in many cases, their familiarity with it is exclusively in a religious context—whether simply as used in worship, or also as encountered in the study of secondary theological literature—they may not be in a position to differentiate between 'varieties' of 'Arabic.' In addition, they are disposed to follow the Arabs in regarding 'Arabic' as one language, proficiency in which is attained by different people to different degrees. Thus, although it is to them a hieratic language, it is not one that is equally remote from all believers; their Arab coreligionists have the enviable advantage of possessing it as their native medium of communication.

2. Other Islamic Languages

There is no documentation extant for the evolution of Pahlavi into Islamic Persian during the first three centuries after the Arab conquest; all Persians apparently wrote in Arabic, even though they presumably still spoke some form of their native tongue. When Persian emerged, it was heavily arabicized. A large proportion of its vocabulary was borrowed directly, and Arabic phrases were also adopted wholesale—not merely pious expressions and other religious idioms, but ordinary secular elements as well. It was, at first, still possible to use a less arabicized version, as can be seen in Firdawsi's epic the *S̲h̲āhnāmah*, in which, since it is concerned with preconquest history, Arabic phraseology would clearly be inappropriate. This, however, appears to have been regarded as delibrate archaizing, and, although the *S̲h̲āhnāmah* has always remained immensely popular, no subsequent writers followed Firdawsi's example. The degree to which the language of individual authors is consciously arabicized, however, differs greatly; in general, prose is more affected than verse, and the more orotund the style adopted, the more Arabic it appears.

Oddly enough, some items of Persian religious terminology survive, used interchangeably with their Arabic equivalents, and sometimes in preference to these, for example *namāz* 'prayer' (Arabic *ṣalāt*), *payghāmbar* 'messenger, prophet' (Arabic *rasūl, nabī*) and *K̲h̲udā* 'God' (Arabic *Allāh*). Arabic, however, was a dominant influence; sometimes even Persian syntax seems to be approximating to Arabic. Persian and Arabic words were readily compounded, as in *k̲h̲idmatgar* 'servant' (Arabic *k̲h̲idma* 'service' + *-gar*, a Persian suffix indicating 'one who does something'), and *dawlat-bar-andāz* 'revolutionary' (Arabic *dawla* 'state' + *bar-andāz*, a participial form from the Persian verb *bar-andāk̲h̲tan* 'to cast down'); Persian plural endings were attached to Arabic singular nouns, side by side with Arabic plurals, e.g., *ḥālathā* (Persian plural suffix *-hā*, for inanimate objects) and *ḥālāt* as plurals of *ḥāla* 'state/condition' and *g̲h̲ulāmān* (Persian plural suffix *-ān*, generally for animate beings) and *g̲h̲ilmān* as plurals of *g̲h̲ulām* 'boy/slave.' It appears possible that the Persian word *musulmān* 'Muslim' may have come into existence through a misreading of such a hybrid, *muslimān* 'Muslims' (*muslim* + pl suffix *-ān*), requiring the formation of a further plural *musulmānān*.

The languages that appeared somewhat later on the Islamic scene, such as Turkish and Urdu, borrowed largely from Persian, taking over in the process the Arabic borrowings already naturalized there. Persian itself, from about the fifteenth century, came to replace Arabic as the principal cultural, if not religious, language of Eastern Islam. It continued to enjoy this position until this century; of the poetry of Muhammad Iqbal, the celebrated Urdu poet, a sizeable proportion is in Persian.

Attempts have been made to 'purify' both Turkish and Persian by replacing the 'alien' elements with 'native' ones. Atatürk's efforts, in the 1920s, to do this for Turkish, had some success; modern Turkish contains a great deal less Arabic and Persian vocabulary than Ottoman Turkish, although much remains, some of it, no doubt, unrecognized as such. The last Shah, Muhammad Reza, became an enthusiastic propagandist for the 'Aryan' character of Persian civilization, and accordingly encouraged the resurrection of Persian terms to replace Arabic; thus 'agriculture' became *ka<u>sh</u>āvarzī* instead of *zirā'at* and 'student' *dāni<u>sh</u>jū* (literally, 'knowledge-seeker') instead of *ṭālib*. How much of this linguistic engineering will survive the Islamic revolution, with its inevitable emphasis on Arabic, remains to be seen. In fact, both the Turkish and the Iranian initiatives may be regarded as moves in campaigns of secularization. In Atatürk's case, the campaign has overt and acknowledged; in Muhammad Reza's case, it was covert, but nevertheless real, consequent upon the opposition that both his and his father's policies of modernization had encountered from the Iranian religious leaders.

3. The Arabic Script

The Arabic script, with various modifications, was almost universally adopted for other languages of the Muslim world (see *Arabic Script: Adaptation for Other Languages*); this remained the case until earlier this century, constituting a further bond between Muslims. The respect in which it was held amounted almost to reverence. The art of calligraphy was highly valued, and the Arabic script, often in highly ornate and fantastic forms, became one of the principal features of all the decorative arts. Poetry abounds in metaphors and similes taken from the shapes of the letters.

It has been retained for Persian, Urdu, and Pashto, all three of which are, of course, the languages of regions in which Islam is particularly strong. With some qualifications, it is reasonably well suited to these languages, although the absence of short vowels means that they cannot be read aloud by someone who does not know them. Turkish abandoned the Arabic script in 1928. It was not well suited to a language with a sophisticated vocalic system, but this reform was also a further step in Atatürk's attempt to diminish the influence of Islam in Turkey; it distanced the newly literate both from the Qur'ān and associated Arabic writing and from the corpus of Islamic Turkish and Persian literature. The modified Latin orthography of modern Turkish works well, but it does tend to disguise the Arabic and Persian borrowings in its reproduction of their Turkish pronunciation: the elements *ajzā'* 'components, drugs' (pl of Arab *juz'*) and *<u>kh</u>ānah* 'house, shop' (Persian) are barely recognizable in *eczane* 'chemist's shop'; *fevkalâde* 'extraordinary' appears somewhat far removed from its Arabic original *fawq al-'āda*. Kurdish, which is, somewhat distantly, related to Persian, has modified the Arabic script in such a way that short vowels can be represented; this expedient also disguises the shape of the Arabic, Persian, and Turkish elements, but it appears to have had no antireligious origin.

See also: Qur'an; Arabic; Arabic Script: Adaptation for Other Languages; Islamic Calligraphy.

Bibliography

Fārūqī I R, Fārūqī L L 1986 *The Cultural Atlas of Islam*. Macmillan, New York

Gibb H A R et al.(eds.) 1960 *The Encyclopedia of Islam*. E J Brill, Leiden [esp. articles 'Arabiyya, Islām, Lugha].

Holt P M, Lambton A K S, Lewis B (eds.) 1970 *The Cambridge History of Islam*. Cambridge University Press, Cambridge

Versteegh K 1984 *Pidginization and Creolization: The Case of Arabic*. Amsterdam Studies in the Theory and History of Linguistic Science, series IV, Vol. 33, Benjamins, Amsterdam

Islam in South Asia

C. Shackle

Islam was typically introduced through the original media of Arabic or Persian into the linguistically varied societies of South Asia, where the total Muslim population numbers some 250,000,000 in the early 1990s, whether concentrated in Islamic republics of Pakistan and Bangladesh or unevenly distributed across India. The long history of complex patterns of language use in South Asian Islam is reflected both in their regional variation and in the different degrees to which Perso–Arabic elements have become intrinsic to many South Asian languages.

1. Arabic and Persian in South Asia

The sacred primacy of Arabic has been almost universally accepted within South Asian Islam since its first beginnings around 700 CE. Muslim communities were established early in the Dravidian territory of coastal South India through direct maritime links with Arabia which have continued to ensure living local traditions of Arabic learning (Bayly 1990). Long social segregation has resulted in the emergence of distinctive varieties of Malayalam and Tamil among these Muslim communities which, like those of Sri Lanka and the Maldives, have remained historically isolated from the northern mainstream of South Asian Islam (Schimmel 1980).

From about 1000 CE, Islam spread throughout the vast New Indo–Aryan (NIA) area of the northern plains as a consequence of overland invasions from the lands of eastern Islam where Persian was the dominant language, with Arabic largely confined to the purely religious sphere. Down to the final decline of the Mughal empire in the mid-eighteenth century, the Indo–Muslim elite was continually reinforced by fresh immigration of Persian-speakers. The spread of Islam in South Asia was however chiefly due to mass conversions from among the local population, for whom Persian was a learned language. Indo–Persian accordingly developed as a distinctive variety marked both by conservative adherence to eastern Dari norms and by innovations due to Indo–Aryan influence in phonology, lexis, and syntax.

Throughout the medieval period, Persian remained the standard medium of Muslim education, government, and literature (Schimmel 1973) over almost the entire NIA territory, besides the northern Dravidian area of the Deccan. Its morphological simplicity and genetic similarity to NIA languages facilitated its long maintained status, in partial succession to Sanskrit, as a pan-Indian standard language with wide geographical distribution if narrow social currency. Its cultural prestige survived until the late twentieth century after the gradual British abrogation of its official status after 1800.

2. Islam and the New Indo–Aryan Languages

The cultural development and standardization of the NIA languages was long inhibited by the traditional concentration of lay Muslim education in South Asia upon formal instruction in Persian as a written language. This was accompanied, as it still is in the late twentieth century, by the ritual inculcation of a more or less mechanical recognition of Arabic sufficient for recitation of the Qur'ān, pro-founder knowledge being required only of religious specialists.

From the fourteenth century there is nevertheless evidence of some written Islamic cultivation of the local languages (Schimmel 1980), whether in the humble versified bilingual glossaries termed '*Khāliq bārī*,' or in the remarkable poetic romances and Sufi hymns which form some of the chief glories of many premodern NIA literatures, from Sindhi to Bengali. From the eighteenth century, there was a great expansion in the number of such vernacular Islamic genres, such as the *na't* and *maulūd* in praise of the Prophet, or the Shi'a *marsiya*, the elegy for the martyrs of Kerbela.

At no time, however, have such vernacular compositions seriously impinged upon the central place of Arabic in the orthodox ritual of the mosque in North or South India. The Qur'ān was first translated into Persian in 1737, followed in 1790 by the first of several Urdu versions, which in turn inspired later renderings into numerous South Asian languages, e.g., Tamil (1873), Gujarati (1879), Telugu (1938), Kannada (1949). Though quite widely used for private reference, such translations (Troll 1982: 135–67) have remained controversial alternatives to reliance on the sacred Arabic text. The one significant exception to this ritual primacy of Arabic is provided by the sacred literature of the Nizārī Ismā'īlī followers of the Āghā Khāns in western India, whose separate ritual is based on the singing of hymns (*ginān*) composed in a distinctive literary idiom, characterized by the grafting of Perso–Arabic loans on to a mixed Sindhi–Gujarati base (Shackle and Moir 2000).

From about 1750, Persian began quite rapidly to be replaced as the major cultural language of South Asian Islam by Urdu (Shackle 2000), the Persianized standard developed from the widely spoken lingua franca, loosely termed 'Hindustani,' based on the Kharī bolī dialect of the Delhi area. By the mid-nineteenth century, Urdu was fully developed as a literary language for all types of secular as well as religious writing, including both the traditional genres previously written in Persian and the new forms cultivated by Islamic reformers (Shackle and Majeed 1997). This was partly due to its promotion by the British as an administratively convenient local adjunct to English, whose wide diffusion has resulted in educated South Asian Muslims having more direct access to the modern international language than any of their coreligionists elsewhere.

The strong challenges to Urdu which emerged from the late nineteenth century have determined the different language patterns which characterize the Muslims of the modern countries of South Asia. In Bengal, the mass appeal of Urdu was inhibited by its close association with the local elite (Ahmed 1988). Exacerbated after 1947 by Pakistani attempts to impose Urdu, pro-Bengali sentiment was a principal motivation for the establishment of Bangladesh in 1971 as a Muslim state with Bengali as its national language.

In the Urdu-speaking heartlands of northern India, the successful promotion by Hindu activists of modern Hindi as a structurally identical rival standard, however sharply distinguished in both script and vocabulary, defined with increasing sharpness the status of Urdu as a language of Muslims (Shackle and Snell 1990). Even this status has been much weakened in post-1947 India by large scale Muslim emigration to Pakistan, and subsequent shifts in provincial policies encouraging the linguistic assimilation of local Muslim populations.

The role of Urdu as the premier language of South Asian Islam has been most strongly promoted in Pakistan (Rahman 1996), where its status as the national language commands powerful patriotic and religious loyalties, also characteristic of the Pakistani diaspora. Only recently has the growing strength of movements favoring the developing of provincial languages at the expense of Urdu, narrowly identified as the language of the *muhājir* refugees from India, begun to suggest that the diglossia which has so long characterized South Asian Islam may here too be beginning to break down. For the foreseeable future, however, Urdu will retain its present status as principal learned and formal medium of Islam in South Asia.

3. Script and Phonology

As the sharp visual contrast between Urdu and Hindi so clearly shows, choice of scripts is still a major shibboleth of religious allegiance in much of South Asia. This phenomenon is also illustrated by the use of Perso–Arabic script to write Punjabi in Pakistan versus the Sikh use of Gurmukhi in India, or the employment of the Arabic script for the Arabic–Malayalam religious literature of the Mappila Muslims of Kerala (see *Arabic Script: Adaptation for Other Languages*).

Only to some South Asian Muslims have the sacred associations of the Arabic script been outweighed by the intrinsic advantages of native scripts, whether in their quite precise notation of vowel quality and nasalization or in their clear indication of such typical consonantal contrasts as retroflex/dental and unaspirated/aspirated. The most notable illustration of this choice is provided by the universal Bengali Muslim preference for the Bengali over the Arabic script to write Bengali.

The Islamic character of Urdu, as of other languages of northern India and Pakistan with a majority of Muslim speakers, is however strongly reinforced by its use of the Perso–Arabic script, still characteristically reproduced by professional calligraphers in the *nasta'līq* style, with the minimum modifications needed to distinguish retroflexes from dentals, aspirated consonants from /h/, final nasalization from /n/, and final masc pl /-e/ from fem /-i/. Greater cultural significance is attached to the script's clear notation of the fricative series so uncharacteristic of most South Asian phonological systems, and the careful distinction of /x ɣ/ from /khg/ (also of /q/ from /k/) is a prized marker of educated Urdu speech. Although equally preserved in written spellings of Arabic loans, such distinctively Arabic phonemes as the pharyngeals /ʕ ħ/ are phonetically distinguished only in the highly Arabicized Urdu used in formal contexts by religious specialists.

Urdu orthography is followed by other languages with further modifications, maximally illustrated by the major restructuring of the script required to write the 15-term Kashmiri vowel-system. An independent modification of the *naskh* alphabet is employed for Sindhi with elaborate additional dotting to differentiate both aspirates and implosives, resulting in single graphs for, e.g., /b/, /bh/, and /ɓ/.

The intimate association between the Arabic script and Islam has generally inhibited the development of independent Muslim scripts. Here again, however, a notable exception is provided by the Ismā'īlī use of the hermetic Khojkī script, derived from Sindhi commercial shorthands (Asani 1987), now replaced by Gujarati script, or by roman transliterations.

4. Lexis

It is in lexis that Persian influence is most marked. Only in the most Persianized NIA languages does this influence extend to core grammatical markers, e.g., Urdu *khud* 'self' for Hindi *āp*, or phrasal structures like the postmodification exemplified by Urdu *daryā-e gangā* 'the river Ganges' for Hindi *gangā nadī*, whereas the early wide diffusion of large numbers of Perso–Arabic loans is well attested even from non-Muslim sources (Shackle 1978).

Within this wider pattern of borrowing, Islamic terminology as such forms a specialized category distinctive of Muslim usage, as seen in such phrases as the invocation *allāhu akbar*, the greeting *as-salāmu 'alaikum*, or the semi-Persian *khudā hāfiz* 'goodbye.' Specifically Islamic items are naturally represented by large numbers of Arabic loans, often with phonetic modifications unrepresented in the script, e.g., Arabic *wuḍū*>Urdu *vuzū* 'ritual ablution,' or semantic shifts of the type seen in Urdu *sunnat* 'circumcision.' Core items are often taken from Persian rather than Arabic, e.g. *khudā* 'God,' *namāz* 'prayer,' *roze* 'the fast.' Muslim names are both similarly distinctive and of similar Perso–Arabic origin, with phonetic deformations more prominent in the Dravidian than the NIA area.

The social segregation historically so characteristic of the religiously plural societies of South Asia has caused an equally natural differentiation of Muslim vocabulary in many other areas of social practice. Dietary codes govern the extension of Persian *gosht* 'meat,' with connotations different from NIA *mās*, or Muslim euphemisms for Indo-Aryan *sūar* 'pig,' e.g., Arab *khinzīr*, with alternative differentiations in other contexts, e.g., the Sanskritic associations of *jal* 'water' characterizing Hindu usage versus Muslim preference for common NIA *pānī*. Associated specialisms provide, e.g., *qasāī* (<Arabic *qaṣṣāb*) 'butcher,' or Persian *bāvarcī-khāna* 'kitchen,' versus Hindu *rasoī*. Muslim family practices result in further characteristic special vocabularies, e.g., *āpā* 'elder sister' and Arabic *khāla* 'mother's sister,' for common Hindu *dīdī* and *māsī*, not to speak of the very institution of *parda* itself.

Bibliography

Ahmed R 1988. *The Bengal Muslims 1871–1906: A Quest for Identity*, 2nd edn. Oxford University Press, Delhi

Asani A S A 1987 The Khojkī script: a legacy of Ismaili Islam in the Indo-Pakistan subcontinent. *JAOS* **107**: 439–49

Bayly S 1990 *Saints, Goddesses and Kings: Muslims and Christians in South Indian Society. 1700–1900*. Cambridge University Press, Cambridge

Rahman T 1999 *Language and Politics in Pakistan*. Oxford University Press, Karachi

Schimmel A 1973 *Islamic Literatures of India*. Otto Harrassowitz, Wiesbaden

Schimmel A 1980 *Islam in the Indian Subcontinent*. E J Brill, Leiden

Shackle C 1978 Approaches to the Persian loans in the *Ādi Granth*. *BSOAS* **41**: 73–96

Shackle C 2000 Urdū. *The Encyclopaedia of Islam* **9**: 873–81. E J Brill, Leiden

Shackle C, Snell R 1990 *Hindi and Urdu since 1800: A Common Reader*. School of Oriental and African Studies, London

Shackle C, Majeed J 1997 *Hali's Musaddas, the Flow and Ebb of Islam*. Oxford University Press, Delhi

Shackle C, Moir Z 2000 *Ismaili Hymns from South Asia*, 2nd edn. Curzon, Richmond

Troll C W (ed.) 1982 *Islam in India: Studies and Commentaries*, vol. 1: *The Akbar Mission and Miscellaneous Studies*. Vikas, New Delhi

Islam in Southeast Asia

E. U. Kratz

Islam came to Southeast Asia peacefully and over several centuries. While mainland Southeast Asia by and large remained faithful to Buddhism in its various forms and expressions, Islam had a particular impact on the peoples of insular Southeast Asia speaking Western Austronesian or Indonesian languages. Islam thus took hold of the Indonesian archipelago, parts of the southern Philippines and of the Malay Peninsula, a region often referred to as 'the Malay world.' Southeast Asian Muslims generally follow Sunnite traditions and adhere to the Shafi'i school of law. There are doubts whether traces of an earlier presence of Shi'ite elements in West Sumatra indicate a significant change of allegiance or are due to fairly recent contacts with Indian Shi'ites brought to the region under the British at the beginning of the nineteenth century.

Although Islam found a more ready acceptance among (coastal) ethnic groups which had previously had contact with Indian religions, it did not, however, replace these completely. But, just as there are pockets of Hinduism and Buddhism alive in the archipelago and in particular on Java and Bali, so too Islam is to be found beyond the Peninsula—on the mainland in Burma, and among the Cham of Cambodia and Vietnam who, significantly, speak an Indonesian language. The Cham, like so many Southeast Asian peoples, were converted to Islam through the Malays and are said to have received the faith from Brunei and Aceh. Yet, the importance of strong links with Kelantan in the north of the Peninsula, which appear to be of a more recent date, should not be underestimated. The origins of the small, indigenous Muslim community found in Burma must be sought entirely with Indian immigrants, and a once famous Muslim settlement in seventeenth-century Ayudhya was probably mainly populated by foreign merchants. In the year 2000, there are more than 20 million Muslims living in Malaysia and Brunei (where they form the great majority), Singapore, Southern Thailand (Patani), and the Southern Philippines, Vietnam and Cambodia. Indonesia, with approximately 180 million Muslims, is the country with the largest number of Muslim citizens in the world.

There is no comprehensive theory to explain the process of Islamization of the Malay world, which followed a different course in almost every ethnic (and thus linguistic) group in which it occurred in the region. One assumes, however, that traders of various nationalities played an important part and that, at least in its early years, Islam came via the southern ports of the Indian subcontinent, totally bypassing Moghul culture in the process. This is an important point, since Islam hardly influenced Southeast Asian sciences or culture in the broader sense, focusing almost exclusively on theology and law. As far as existing forms of art were concerned, it would appear that the acceptance of Islam led to the disappearance of many artistic and creative expressions which were not of an immediately religious nature. Others had to adapt radically in order to survive.

The Trengganu Stone inscription of the thirteenth century, which perhaps not surprisingly deals with legal matters, is the first example of Malay written in Arabic script and clear proof of the even earlier presence of the religion in the region, yet historical evidence would indicate that a more widely spread Islamization only began from the fifteenth century onwards. This was also the period when Sufi brotherhoods flourished internationally and when, after the Mongol conquest, Indian Ocean trade reached new peaks of intensity.

Once Islam had reached the archipelago and established a first foothold in the coastal trading cities of Sumatra, the Malay language became its main carrier, and it is not surprising that of the languages of Southeast Asia, it is Malay which has been influenced most by Islamic traditions. At some point, being a Malay even became synonymous with being a Muslim. Through Malay, the religion reached the northern coast of Java and most other islands. By the end of the nineteenth century, the process of Islamization of the Malay world can be said to have been completed, even though some Indonesian Muslims argue that after the conversion of the body, there still remains the task of converting the soul.

In the process of Islamization, Indian scripts and their derivatives were gradually replaced by a modified Arabic script which is closer to its Persian form. This is called *Jawi* in the Malay world where it is still used widely in preference to 'Roman' script, and *pegon* in Javanese (which otherwise adhered to its original, Indic script), where it is used exclusively for writing Islamic texts. Most significantly, *Jawi* provided for additional letters to convey the sounds of *ch*, *g*, *ng*, *ny*, *p* which are not found in standard Arabic.

Arabic also exerted its influence on syntax, morphology, and lexicography. While it is true to say that the influence on syntax and morphology is more clearly felt in the realm of theological literature, Qur'ānic exegesis, grammar, and jurisprudence, the influence of lexicography extended much further and led to the reception and total absorption of a wide range of words of Arabic and Persian origin, extending well beyond the purely religious sphere. The important concept of traditional (non-Islamic) law and custom, which is seen in opposition to Islamic law, is only known under its Arabic term '*adat*.'

It is interesting, however, that even under the influence of Islam the Indic heritage was not completely suppressed, as is evinced by the survival of a Tamil word such as *lebai* for the mosque official, and Sanskrit terms for key Islamic concepts such as the fast—*saum* in Arabic, but Sanskrit *puasa*, in most Indonesian languages—and the religious disciple, who is still called a *santri*. Equally interesting is the fact that the planners of modern Indonesian, besides drawing on European languages, turn to Sanskrit rather than Arabic when it comes to the coining of new words and expressions. It is worth remembering, however, in this connection that in the late twentieth century the influence on Indonesian of Javanese, which had always been more influenced by Sanskrit, became stronger than that of Malay. In view of the ethnic distribution of Indonesia's population, 60 percent of whom speak Javanese and only 5 percent Malay as their first language, this would appear natural, although non-Javanese Muslims find this Javanese influence hard to accept.

See also: Arabic; Arabic Script: Adaptation for Other Languages; Islamic Calligraphy; Qur'ān.

Bibliography

Bausani A 1975 Is classical Malay a 'Muslim language'? *Boletin de la Asociación Española de Orientalistas* **11**: 111–21

Jones R (ed.) 1978 Indonesian etymological project III: Arabic Loan-words in Indonesian. School of Oriental and African Studies, London

Kratz E U 1990 Islam in Indonesia. In: Clarke P B (ed.) *The World's Religions: Islam*. Routledge Reference, London

Ronkel P S van 1899 Over invloed der Arabische syntaxis op de Maleische. *Tijdschrift voor Indische Taal-, Land- en Volken-kunde* **41**: 498–528

Yegar M 1972 *The Muslims of Burma: A Study of a Minority Group*. Otto Harrassowitz, Wiesbaden

Jainism

P. Dundas

Jainism is a religious tradition which evolved in approximately the sixth century BCE in the Ganges basin of eastern India. Its doctrines are ascribed to a line of 24 teachers called 'ford-makers,' although only the last two of these, Pārśva (who lived perhaps in the eighth century BCE) and Mahāvīra, can be regarded as historical figures. The tenets of Jainism center around the attempt to show mankind how to win through to spiritual salvation by eliminating the material karma which has been attracted to the soul by its activity and which occludes the soul's natural qualities of energy, omniscience, etc. There are two main sects in Jainism: the Śvetāmbaras, whose male and female ascetics wear white robes; and the Digambaras, whose male ascetics are naked.

According to tradition, the Jain scriptures were preached by Mahāvīra and collected and organized by his immediate disciples. However, it is clear that the scriptural canon of the Śvetāmbaras, a portion of which has from an early period been accepted as lost, evolved gradually until its final version in the fifth century CE. The language in which it was composed is a Middle Indo-Aryan dialect called 'Ardhamāgadhī' (Half-Māgadhī), the name referring to the provenance of the language in the region of Magadha in eastern India. It seems clear that even the oldest texts of the canon do not represent the language in which Mahāvīra preached and that, rather, an original dialect has been reworked or refined. The Digambaras reject the authority of the Śvetāmbara scriptures, claiming that the canon has been lost, and have evolved their own scriptures in a dialect called, somewhat inaccurately, 'Jaina Sauraseni' owing to its slight resemblance to the Śaurasenī found in Sanskrit dramas.

Very few Jains today have any direct familiarity with the scriptural texts in the original languages. Indeed, while translations into modern Indian languages, especially Hindi, do exist, some sects place a ban on their being studied by lay people, restricting access to the ascetic community alone. However, a few Prakrit formulas are widely known and recited on specific ritual occasions, the most celebrated of which is the mantra known as the 'Five Homages,' a benediction uttered to the five most significant spiritual types in Jainism (namely the omniscient preachers, the liberated souls, the teachers, the preceptors, and the ordinary monks), and which is felt to be able to confer great benefits. Mantras are important in other contexts. For example, they are widely used in worship of the tutelary deities of Jainism, while the 'Five Homages' serves as an important focus for monastic meditation.

According to the Jains, language is atomic. An individual soul accrues language particles through the agency of bodily and vocal activity and transforms them into spoken language and then expels them. Philosophically, the Jains take a straightforward approach to language. Words stand to objects in the relation of signifier to signified, signification taking place because of the innate force of the word whose natural function is to reveal an object in the same manner as light. In its relativistic logic, Jainism has also shown an awareness that language has to be interpreted with full awareness of the context in which it occurs.

Over the last two millennia, Jains have written a vast amount of literature on many themes. From the linguistic standpoint should be noted the production of a Jain tradition of Sanskrit grammatical analysis, designed to rival and supplant the authority of the great Hindu grammarian, Pāṇini (see *Pāṇini*). The most significant Jain grammarian was Hemacandra (eleventh century CE), whose work is still in use in the late twentieth century. Also of particular importance is the role of Jainism in the origin and development of literature in vernacular languages in India. Perhaps the most striking example of this is the Kannada language of South India whose earliest, and in some respects greatest, poets were Jains writing on Jain mythological themes.

See also: Mantra; Hinduism.

Bibliography

Hinüber O von 1986 *Das Ältere Mittelindisch im Überblick*. Osterreichische Akademie der Wissenschaften, Vieena

Jain S 1989 *Jaina Philosophy of Language*. Ahomsa International, New Delhi

Jaini P S 1979 *The Jaina Path of Purification*. University of California Press, Berkeley, CA

Jehovah's Witnesses

W. S. Bainbridge

The movement alternately called Jehovah's Witnesses or The Watchtower Bible and Tract Society began when 18-year-old Charles Taze Russell was attracted by the singing of a group of Adventists in 1870. At the time, a large number of individuals and small groups in the United States were still carrying on the diffuse millenarian movement founded 30 years earlier by William Miller, and like Miller many of them attempted to decode from the Bible precise prophecies of the date of Christ's Second Coming. Russell became extremely active in religious publishing and wrote extensive decryptions of the Bible, initially calculating that the Second Coming would occur in 1874. A religious movement rapidly coalesced around Russell, who proved to be an able leader as well as writer. When he died in 1916, his successor Joseph Franklin Rutherford built a very strong central organization that easily survived his own death in 1942. Today the movement counts about 90,000 congregations with 6,000,000 members worldwide, but this is a conservative estimate, including only those adults who are actively involved in proselytizing.

More than a thousand volunteer translators help the Society publish in 354 languages. Other volunteers created a special multilanguage electronic photo-typesetting system to publish in 28 alphabets and character sets. Literature is published in Braille and in the form of 'video books' in American Sign Language and Japanese Sign Language. Documentary videos have been produced in 35 languages. More than 20 million copies of a typical issue of *The Watchtower* magazine are published in 126 languages. The Society has published more than one hundred million Bibles in 34 languages.

Central to the group's mission is *The New World Translation of the Holy Scriptures*, an English version of the Bible that supports a distinctive theology. For example, Jehovah's Witnesses reject the idea of a Trinity, asserting that Jehovah alone is God, and Jesus is a secondary and separate creation of God. Witnesses believe that Jesus currently rules God's Heavenly Kingdom and will soon extend his reign to the Earth. The other large branch of the Adventist tradition, the Seventh-day Adventist Church, has never made millenarian predictions, but Jehovah's Witnesses have done so several times, most notably 1914 and most recently 1975.

There is a significant degree of tension between Jehovah's Witnesses and the surrounding society, in part because Witnesses give their allegiance not to any nation but to Jehovah, refuse to salute national flags or serve in the military, and avoid blood transfusions. In the Second World War, many were imprisoned in the United States, Britain, and Canada for refusing to bear arms, and many others died in German concentration camps. The Witnesses have become a world leader in the fight for religious freedom, for example taking more legal cases to the US Supreme Court than any other group, winning most of them.

See also: Seventh Day Adventist Church.

Bibliography

Bainbridge W S 1997 *The Sociology of Religious Movements*. Routledge, New York

Beckford J A 1975 *The Trumpet of Prophecy*. John Wiley and Sons, New York

Curry M D 1992 *Jehovah's Witnesses*. Garland, New York

Rogerson A 1969 *Millions Now Living Will Never Die*. Constable, London

Judaism

M. Weitzman

Judaism could be defined as acceptance of the authority of the Hebrew Bible, and in particular the commandments of the Torah (i.e., Pentateuch), as interpreted by tradition. Both the Torah itself (Deuteronomy 29: 28) an its rabbinic interpreters stress practical observance of the commandments rather than a fixed set of beliefs. Nevertheless, certain beliefs are central in Judaism, and these include the utter unity and justice of God, the Torah as the unchangeable revelation of His will, and the future coming of a Messiah with whom war and suffering will cease. Judaism is not confined to a system of observances and beliefs. It is also the ancestral faith of the Jewish people, with a perceived common history reaching back to the Exodus from Egypt and beyond.

This article is concerned with Judaism since 70 CE, when the Jews were vanquished and their temple destroyed by the Romans. An early monument was the Mishnah, a digest of the discussions aiming to fill out the laws of the Torah with sufficient detail for practical implementation, compiled in the land of Israel before 200 CE. The regular public prayers replacing the temple sacrifices arose in the same area and period. Over the centuries up to ca. 400, this center also produced Midrash and Talmud, works which discussed and interpreted in detail the Bible and the Mishnah respectively. The main center, however, had become Babylonia (Iraq) and the Babylonian Talmud, a record of the discussion of the Mishnah between the third and fifth centuries, became the most authoritative source for Jewish law. The Arab conquests of the eighth century brought Babylonia into contact with centers to the west, which drew upon, and by 1000 had eclipsed, the scholarship of Babylonian Jewry.

Two streams emerged in European Jewry: the Sephardi ('Spanish'), in the Iberian peninsula; and the Ashkenazi ('German'), in France and Germany. The Ashkenazi schools produced what have become the most popular commentaries on the Bible and Babylonian Talmud. These commentaries move within the world of those sources, with very little recourse to external matter. The Sephardi Jews, however, brought to their commentaries an openness to Arabian science and literature. They also produced philosophy, Hebrew poetry, and mystical literature (the Zohar, which perhaps draws upon older esoteric traditions). Persecutions in Western Europe, culminating in the expulsion of the Jews from Spain in 1492, drove most Jews eastwards—the Ashkenazi branch to Poland, the Sephardi to Turkey. From the eighteenth century onward, however, there was a steady drift (much intensified by the Russian pogroms which began in 1881) to Western Europe and eventually to the USA. Another haven for Jews under persecution, since the expulsion from Spain, has been the land of Israel. Here, in 1564–65, Joseph Caro reduced the centuries of discussion on Jewish law to a definitive code, the Shulchan Aruch ('prepared table'). Nevertheless, Eastern Europe remained the center of Jewish life until the Nazi massacres, which left Israel and the USA as the principal Jewish centers.

In the belief that the Torah is the revelation of God's will, Jews have spared no effort on its interpretation. This was no easy task, because, on a literal reading of the Torah, the laws do not always cover the full range of possibilities, and moreover one law contradicts another. Yet Jews needed to work out, as a matter of practical urgency, what God required. Language has also been (in the form of prayer) the only vehicle for communication in the opposite direction, from man to God, since the cessation of sacrifice in 70 CE.

1. The Language of Prayer

Some prayers—notably Psalms—appear in scripture and have passed into the liturgy. Again, a central component of both the morning and evening services is the recitation of three biblical passages (Deuteronomy 6: 4–9, 11: 13–21; Numbers 15: 37–41) to affirm faith in the unity of God and in His commandments. These passages are collectively called '*Sh̲ĕma*'' ('hear') after the opening word. In public prayer, moreover, three days never pass without a reading from the Torah. Hence the service typically includes communication not only from man to God, but also from God to man. Indeed, according to the traditional interpretation of Exodus 33: 19, prayer is simply a form of revelation. God's words to Moses: 'I shall call upon the Lord's name before thee,' were taken to mean that God taught Moses—and demonstrated—how to pray (TB Rosh ha-Shanah 17b).

In its selection of material from scripture, Jewish prayer is particularly influenced by courtly speech. Nearly all the Psalms that have been adopted in Jewish liturgy are hymns. The many laments in the Psalter have been almost wholly rejected, as an unacceptable criticism of God's justice. One must bless God even for (apparent) evil (cf. already 2 Chronicles 20: 21). In the Bible, the proper form to entreat a king was not direct complaint but the simple cry: 'Save!' (*hōs̲h̲īa'*: 2 Samuel 14: 4; 2 Kings 6: 26). Already in the Psalter (notably at Psalm 118: 25) entreaty is sometimes expressed in this restrained form. In Jewish prayer this courtly entreaty has given rise to the *hosanna* liturgy of the Tabernacles festival, and also to strings of biblical verses which entreat God to 'save' (the beginnings of this form already appear in 1 Chronicles 16: 8–35). The verse in which many of these strings culminate is Psalm 20: 10: 'O Lord, save us; O King, answer us on the day that we call.'

An influence upon postbiblical compositions is the language of the law-court, which results in an insistent heaping-up of synonymous expressions—just as an advocate reiterates his arguments until he has hammered them home. In the Aramaic Kaddish and several Hebrew prayers, eight or more synonyms for praise of God are used in rapid succession. Sequences of synonyms are also common in entreaty and in public confession (compare already Daniel 9: 19; Psalm 106: 6). Indeed, the Hebrew word for 'prayer' *tĕp̲hillā* may by etymology mean a speech before the judge.

Postbiblical prayers continue to make constant biblical allusions, in the belief that scripture provides the model for prayer. Thus the opening words of the Amidah (literally 'standing'), which is a component in every service, are stitched together from Psalm 119: 12 ('blessed art thou O Lord'), Exodus 3: 6 ('our God and the God of our fathers...'), Deuteronomy 10: 17 ('the great mighty and revered God'), and Genesis 14: 19 ('highest God... possessor of all'). Medieval compositions continue to draw upon the Bible but delight in witty reapplication. For example, Tamar's challenge: 'Whose are this seal and these tassels?' (Genesis 38: 25) is placed in the mouth of Israel, who faithfully observes the seal of circumcision and the tassels of Numbers 15: 38, and now calls on God, from whom these come, to save her from persecution.

Another factor that tended to reshape biblical language is preference for communal prayer. Thus a prayer for the sick is based on Jeremiah 17: 14 but transposed to the Plural: 'Heal us, O Lord, and we shall be healed... .'

The rabbis of the second century insisted that prayer required the worshiper's understanding and attention (*kavanah*), even though recitation of scripture might not. In the late twentieth century, however, few worshipers are sufficiently versed in Hebrew to be able to follow the meaning at the pace at which the prayers are recited—particularly in the case of the intricate medieval poems so prominent in the festival services. Most worshipers, therefore, are reciting prayers which they do not fully understand. It is perhaps not appropriate to describe such recitation as prayer at all; it is rather a matter of ritual.

In order that people should understand the prayers that they address to God, the main public prayers could be said in any language (Mishnah Sotah 7: 1). In practice, however, Hebrew has been used almost exclusively, at least up to the nineteenth century. This ensured a large measure of uniformity in the prayers of Jews in every age and land. (It should however be noted that Sephardi and Ashkenazi Jewry differ in their exact wording of many prayers as well as their pronunciation of Hebrew.) At the end of the twentieth century, Orthodox Judaism permits no more than marginal use of modern vernaculars, e.g., in the prayer for the royal family or president. Reform Judaism uses both Hebrew and modern vernaculars, the mix varying between different congregations.

Other languages play only a limited role in prayer. Aramaic is represented chiefly by the doxology called 'Kaddish,' which entered the liturgy perhaps in the second century CE. Aramaic, when first introduced, was more familiar than Hebrew; at the present time, the opposite is true, and this lends the Kaddish a certain mystique. Among Jews hailing from Eastern Europe, Yiddish was never used for public prayer, but serves as a medium for private prayer of set form. A famous example is a supplication, recited by women at the termination of the Sabbath, that the coming week should bring health, life, and 'all good.' Yiddish is also the medium for spontaneous private prayer—often addressed to *Gottinyu*, diminutive of *Gott*.

2. Scholarship and Daily Life: Hebrew Language and Script

After the completion of the Mishnah, Hebrew remained the language of Midrash, liturgy (including the medieval poems called *piyyut*), and biblical exegesis. However, Jews came to conduct their detailed legal discussions in Aramaic, which is thus the language of much of both the Palestinian and the Babylonian Talmud. Even now, Aramaic remains the language of rabbinic responses to new questions of Jewish law. However, comprehensive codes of the law—notably by Moses Maimonides in 1170–80 and by Joseph Caro in 1564–65—were drawn up in Hebrew.

Aramaic is also the language of the Zohar, the main mystical text. The prevailing view is that the Zohar was composed in Spain shortly before 1300, and that Aramaic, the language of earlier rabbinic literature, was employed to give the appearance of antiquity.

For philosophy, however, the medieval Jews used Arabic, which had the requisite technical terms readily available. Their work was soon translated into Hebrew (for example, Maimonides' works were translated in his own lifetime in the twelfth century), and in these translations may be seen the efforts to create the necessary vocabulary from the resources of earlier Hebrew literature.

Over the centuries Jews have written a number of vernaculars in Hebrew script—hence Judeo–Arabic and Ladino (Judeo–Spanish) among Sephardi Jews, and Yiddish (Judeo–German) among Ashkenazi Jews. In particular, the Bible has been translated into these languages, with the use of Hebrew script. Children in fact learnt no script other than the Hebrew, until acculturation was advanced (which in the case of Eastern Europe was as late as the nineteenth century).

Ladino was preserved by Jews expelled from Spain, and prayers in Spanish were retained by those who remained in Spain and observed Judaism in secret (*marranos*). In both communities, Ladino became almost a second holy language. Yiddish, which at one time was the lingua franca of a majority of the entire Jewish people, could be said to enjoy a similar status.

Hebrew has never ceased to be a language of scholarship, but since the end of the nineteenth century it has also been revived as a spoken language in the land of Israel. The official pronunciation follows the Sephardi norm, which became established in the land of Israel after the influx of refugees from the Spanish expulsion. As a result, the Sephardi pronunciation now tends to dominate, even in Ashkenazi synagogues.

3. Beliefs About Language

Language is the distinguishing characteristic of humanity. Hence, while according to the original text of Genesis 2: 7 God created the first human being as a 'living creature,' the Targums (ancient Jewish Aramaic translations) instead refer to its 'spirit of speech.' Similarly, the Hebrew word coined (probably in the twelfth century) to mean 'rational' is *dĕḇhārī* or *daḇhrānī*, literally meaning 'capable of speech.'

Adam's first act (Genesis 2: 19) was to use language to name the animals and so classify the world. This imposition of order is comparable with the act of creation itself, which really meant imposing order on the preexisting 'emptiness and waste' (Genesis 1: 2).

Without language, it is impossible for humans to communicate. Modern linguists suppose that language diverged because people spread out over a wide area. The Bible (Genesis 11) reverses cause and effect; once languages were divided, people could no longer live together and were inevitably scattered over the world (see *Babel*).

In Jewish tradition, Hebrew was the original language, spoken at creation. The rabbis argued (Genesis Rabba 18: 6) that only in Hebrew is the word for 'woman' (*'ishshā*) a simple feminine of the word for 'man' (*'ish*), as demanded by Genesis 2: 23. The many other languages had arisen as a divine punishment at Babel, which would be reversed in the messianic age, when all mankind would revert to 'pure speech,' that is, Hebrew (Zephaniah 3: 9).

Hebrew is also the language of almost the entire Jewish Bible (see *Bible*). As medium of the sacred text, the language itself is holy. Its commonest name in rabbinic literature is 'the holy tongue' (*leshon ha-qodesh*). Tattered texts in Hebrew are buried, and this veneration is even extended to mundane documents in vernaculars written in the Hebrew script.

The modern term *'Ivrit'* for the Hebrew language significantly breaks with the rabbinic designation. It is in fact exceedingly rare before modern times, and is thus essentially a calque on German *Hebräisch*. Apparently it reflects an anxiety, going back to the Jewish Enlightenment in the eighteenth century, that the revival of Hebrew should not be dominated by religion.

Jewish biblical interpretation is typically concerned with close reading of individual verses or smaller units. For example, the rule that in a mixed marriage the child follows the mother's religion is derived from Deuteronomy 7: 4: '[lest] he remove your son from following me.' Where 'he' (the father) is not Israelite (since he might alienate the son from God), the son is still 'yours,' i.e., Israelite. The wider context tends to be ignored. Thus Job 8: 7 ('however small your beginning, your end will be great') is taken to mean that the righteous suffer in this world for their few sins, so that they may go hence straight to Paradise. It does not matter that the context shows no awareness of any other world than this, or that the speaker is Bildad, whose words are condemned as wrong at the end of Job. Such interpretations are often read into Scripture rather than derived from it.

In the Middle Ages, Jews again became concerned with the 'plain' meaning, which did not however displace the traditional meaning. For example, Exodus 13: 9 ('it shall be as a sign on your heart and a memorial between your eyes') means, traditionally, the binding of phylacteries (leather thongs affixed to boxes containing scriptural verses) upon the arm and forehead. The twelfth-century French rabbi Samuel ben Meir accepted this interpretation for the purposes of Jewish law, but observed that the plain meaning differed: God's command should always be in one's mind.

The last few centuries BCE found Jewry in the Holy Land outnumbered by the Diaspora, which in Mesopotamia spoke Aramaic, and in Egypt and westwards spoke Greek. Hence the need for versions in Greek (the Septuagint) (see *Septuagint*) and Aramaic (the Targums) (see *Targum*). Attitudes to such versions are ambivalent. Thus, on the one hand, Greek is praised as the only language into which the Bible could be adequately translated, and the translation was hailed as fulfilling Noah's blessing: 'let Japheth dwell in the tents of Shem' (Genesis Rabba 36: 12). On the other hand, the day that the Septuagint was made 'was as harsh for Israel as the day of the Golden Calf, since the Torah could not be adequately translated' (Soferim 1: 7). Attitudes to translations into Aramaic are likewise ambivalent. The rabbis were in a dilemma. They recognized that translations were needed, to make the text intelligible to the populace. At the same time, they were concerned for the unique status of the Hebrew original. In particular, they feared that a sectarian translator could purvey his own doctrines under the very guise of scripture, and in the case of the Septuagint they saw the translation hijacked by a rival faith.

4. Mystical Function of Language

The idea that words have independent power already occurs in the Bible. Thus Hebrew *dābhār* means both 'word' and 'thing'; a word is as real as a concrete thing. The word (as in the case of Isaac's blessing) generates occurrence. Isaac's blessing could not be revoked (Genesis 27: 37). Had Balaam been allowed to curse Israel, the Moabites might have smitten them (Numbers 22: 6). The language of the Torah had especial power, since it had preceded creation and been its blue-print (Genesis Rabba 1: 2). God had in fact created the universe by the utterance of *Hē*, one of the four letters of His holy name YHWH. That divine name was considered so holy that it was replaced in pronunciation by *'Adōnāy* ('Lord'). Already the Septuagint renders it by *kurios* 'lord.' All memory of the vowels has been effaced in Jewish tradition, but the reconstruction 'Yahweh' seems likely, being attested by Christian Fathers (ἰαβε, ἰαουε) and accounting for the shortened form *-yahu* (in names; see *Names: Religious Beliefs*).

Speculation on the mystical power of the alphabet, and particularly of the letters of the divine name, appears in the Sēpher Yēsīrā ('a book of creation'), perhaps dating from the fourth century CE. The 22 Hebrew letters are the raw material which God 'carved out and combined ... to form the life of all creation' (Sect. 19). Just as a magician uses amulets to protect a house, so God sealed the boundaries of the universe with the six possible permutations of two letters from His name YHWH. Thus the Hebrew language, which no heathen power could wrest from Israel, was the basis of creation, and its power lay at a level deeper than semantic meaning, in its inarticulate alphabetic letters. The Sēpher Yĕṣīrā became a favorite book among mystics, who found there the record of God's creative thoughts, which they could now think after him (see *Alphabet: Religious Beliefs*). The Hebrew language was also believed to enshrine numerical codes, according to a system called 'gematria' (cognate with 'geometry'; see *Gematria*).

Mystical ideas of the power of language have also had an impact on prayer. For example, the evening service begins on weekdays with the sequence Psalm 78: 38 ('He is merciful, forgives sin and destroys not . . .') and Psalm 20: 10, calling for God's salvation. That sequence is omitted, however, on Sabbath eve. The Zohar explains that the Sabbath establishes cosmic harmony, in which the divine wrath and judgement are banished; and that harmony would be destroyed by the mere utterance of Psalm 78: 38, with its references to sin and destruction.

5. Influence of Judaism

The Bible has brought into the languages of Christian Europe a number of expressions laden with religious meaning, either directly from Hebrew (e.g., 'Messiah') or in translation (e.g., 'almighty God'). It has also introduced some concepts for which it offers no explicit term; for example, the idea of the brotherhood of man goes back to the family tree of all humanity in Genesis 10.

Many words for biblical and Jewish institutions have naturally passed into the European languages, and some have developed new meanings (e.g., 'sabbatical' and 'jubilee'). The King James Version has introduced many common English expressions, e.g., 'escape with the skin of one's teeth' (from Job 19: 20), 'the race is not to the swift' (Ecclesiastes 9: 11). The influence of the idioms introduced by this version is not lessened by modern doubts regarding their accuracy as renderings of the Hebrew (e.g., 'scapegoat' from Leviticus 16: 8, 'see eye to eye' from Isaiah 52: 8).

The Jewish population has also enriched the European languages in less exalted registers. German underworld slang contains many expressions of Hebrew origin, such as the unlikely farewell *Hals- und Beinbruch*, which ostensibly means 'breakage of neck and leg' but is in fact a corruption of Hebrew *haṣlakha u-brakha* 'success and blessing.' In colloquial English, Yiddish *makkes* 'plagues' (from Biblical Hebrew *makkoth*) apparently became 'mockers' ('put the mockers on'). Yiddish expressions abound in American English (e.g., *goniff* 'thief,' *shlep* 'drag').

The medieval scholars, called 'Masoretes,' who meticulously recorded how the biblical text was to be written and pronounced, were the pioneers of statistical linguistics. To prevent error, they counted the number of verses, words, and letters. There are stylistic implications—though the Massoretes never drew them—in the results. The middle verse of the Torah (Leviticus 8: 8) occurs before the middle word (Leviticus 10: 16), which in turn occurs before the middle letter (Leviticus 11: 42). This demonstrates that verses have more words, and words have more letters, in the latter half of the Torah than in the former. In other areas too the influence of Hebrew scholarship is apparent. The term '*shwa*,' common among linguistic scholars for an unstressed central vowel, arose in Hebrew grammer. Judaism's abiding contribution to linguistics, however, is its tradition of close analysis of texts on both the phonetic and semantic levels.

See also: Hebrew Grammarians; Cairo Genizah; Hebrew, Biblical and Jewish; Talmud; Masoretic Tradition.

Bibliography

Barr J, Tené D 1971 Linguistic literature. *Encyclopedia Judaica*, vol. 16, columns 1352–1401. Macmillan, Jerusalem

Hayman P 1989 Was God a magician? Sefer Yĕṣīrā and Jewish magic. *Journal of Jewish Studies* **40**: 225–37

Lange N R M de 1986 *Judaism*. Oxford University Press, Oxford

Loewe R 1990 La linguistica ebraica. In: Lepschy G C (ed.) *Storia della linguistica*. Mulino, Bologna

Kwanzaa

W. S. Bainbridge

An African–American holiday celebrated from December 26 through January 1, Kwanzaa takes its name from the Swahili word *kwanza* 'first' and emulates traditional harvest or 'first fruits' festivals. The names of the seven principles of Kwanzaa are also adapted from Swahili: *umoja* (unity), *kujichagulia* (self-determination), *ujima* (collective work and responsibility), *ujamaa* (cooperative economics), *nia* (purpose), *kuumba* (creativity), and *imani* (faith). The chief aim of this holiday is to recreate a distinctive Black community, so each of these terms acquired a special meaning. *Nia* refers to the intention to restore African–Americans to the traditional greatness they possessed before they suffered enslavement. *Ujamaa*, which in Swahili means family, refers in Kwanzaa to the creation of a distinctive Black economy based in ethnic businesses, thus an economic family unit created artificially on the basis of racial identification rather than kin ties.

Kwanzaa was created in 1966 by Maulana Ron Karenga, then a graduate student and Black nationalist leader who later became the chairman of the Black Studies department of California State University at Long Beach. In the aftermath of the 1965 riots that had devastated the largely African–American Watts section of Los Angeles, Karenga sought a way to create Black solidarity nonviolently, bringing African–American Christians, Black Muslims, and nonreligious political radicals together. Therefore Kwanzaa was presented as a cultural but not a religious holiday. For example, *imani* refers to faith in the Black community, not in God. The classic sociological theory of religion of Emile Durkheim suggests Kwanzaa was religious nonetheless, because in this theory God is simply a community's sacralized image of itself.

Today, several million people celebrate Kwanzaa, and it has spread from the United States to other nations. Participants exchange gifts, prepare special foods, utter Swahili greetings, and share a rich symbolic life. Recently, Kwanzaa literature has begun to develop an ecumenical spirituality, extending the religious holiday of Christmas. Adopted by many in the Black middle class, commemorated by a US postage stamp, and respected by many schools, Kwanzaa seems to be evolving from a tool of separatist politics into a quasi-religious contribution to multicultural society.

See also: New Religious Movements.

Bibliography

Durkheim E 1915 *The Elementary Forms of the Religious Life*. Allen and Unwin, London

Harris J B 1995 *A Kwanzaa Keepsake*. Simon and Schuster, New York

Karenga M 1998 *Kwanzaa: A Celebration of Family, Community and Culture*. University of Sankore Press, Los Angeles

Wilde A D 1995 Mainstreaming Kwanzaa. *The Public Interest* issue **119**: 68–79

Macumba

C. H. Ribeiro dos Santos

Macumba is one of the various manifestations of religion of African origin. It is one of the products of the assimilation of traditional Bantu religion. The etymology of the name is controversial, although it is certain that its origin is in the Kimbundu (Loanda Mbundu) language. One suggestion is *ma* ('everything that is alarming') + *kumba* ('to sound'). This seems to refer to the sounds of the musical instruments used in their ceremonies, generally percussion instruments—types of drums struck with the hands (such drums were probably copied from the Yoruba cultural group). There is also the suggestion that it is a compound of the plural prefix *maku* + the root *mba* 'sorcery.' The term *macumba* also refers to an ancient musical instrument of African origin, consisting of a bamboo tube with cuts made across it, on which two sticks are scraped. Yet another proposal identifies the word *macumba* with the name given to female initiates of the Kabinda tribe, a group of Bantu origin taken to Brazil as slaves employed as African labor.

Macumba was the form of Afro–Brazilian religion predominant in Rio de Janeiro until the beginning of the twentieth century. However, its influence is also met within the states of Minas Gerais and São Paulo. Its religious ceremonies were generally performed in places known as *terreiros* ('shrines') or *centros* ('centres'); there invocations were made to spirits called *Pretos-Velhos* (literally 'Old Blacks,' the spirits of dead slaves), *Caboclos* (the spirits of Brazilian Indians) and *Beijadas* (literally 'the kissed ones,' the spirits of infants), among countless others. Such rituals were carried out by the *chefe de terreiro* 'head of the shrine,' who could be a *pai-de-santo* 'principal priest' or a *mãe-de-santo* 'principal priestess,' always assisted by an acolyte called a *cambone*. Macumba was a strongly syncretistic sect, to a great extent combining Catholic religious practices and the 'spiritism' of the French thinker Allan Kardec (1804–69), a type of spiritualism that incorporated a belief in reincarnation. This religious denomination practically disappeared after the end of the first decade of the twentieth century, at the same time as the rise of Umbanda—a word found in Kimbundu and Kicongo, the meaning of which has to do with witchcraft and magic spells—in the city of Rio de Janeiro. Umbanda is composed of various cultural and religious elements, such as African and indigenous beliefs, Catholicism, spiritualism and oriental rituals. It is a religion of the urban popular classes of the Brazilian southeast.

Both Macumba and Umbanda use Portuguese as the principal language of their chants, prayers and everyday conversation within the religious community. However, the names of divinities—the Orixás—were taken from Yoruba, although syncretized with Catholic saints; examples are Oxalá, Ogun, Oxum, and Iansã, associated respectively with Jesus Christ, St George, Our Lady of the Immaculate Conception, and St Barbara. The entities known as Caboclos illustrate the borrowing of names from indigenous Brazilian elements, such as Jurema, Jupira, Jandira, Iara, Ubirajara, Aimoré, Araribóia, Tupinambá, among others. These names derive from Tupi–Guarani languages.

Nowadays the word *macumba* has rather interesting connotations. It has generally become an affectionate and humorous form for the practitioners of Afro–Brazilian religions who call themselves *macumbeiras*. On the other hand, for persons outside the sect it is a pejorative term, synonymous with witchcraft, black magic, and evil-provoking rituals. It is noteworthy that one of the main popular attractions of Macumba and Umbanda is the above-mentioned use of the Portuguese language as the principal language of the sects. This aspect gives their religious ceremonies a fairly comprehensible character, involving very little that is obscure, as well as making participation in their rituals possible for people of different levels of education.

See also: Candomblé; Caribbean Syncretistic Religions 1: Cuban Santeria and Haitian Voodoo; Caribbean Syncretistic Religions 2: Jamaican Cumina and Trinidadian Shango; African Traditional Religions.

Bibliography

Cacciatore O G 1988 *Dicionário de Cultos Afro-Brasileiros*. Forense Universitária, Rio de Janeiro

Carneiro E 1991 *Religiões Negras/Negros Bantos*. Civilização Brasileira, Rio de Janeiro

Lopes N 1988 *Bantos, Malês e Identidade Negra*. Forense Universitária, Rio de Janeiro

Pinto A 1971 *Dicionário da Umbanda*. Editora Eco, Rio de Janeiro

Ramos A 1934 *O Negro Brasileiro*. Civilização Brasileira, Rio de Janeiro

Ramos A 1935 O *Folklore Negro do Brasil*. Civilização Brasileira, Rio de Janeiro

Manichaeism

S. N. C. Lieu

Founded by Mani (c. 216–276 CE) a gnostic teacher who was brought up in a Jewish or Christian community in South Babylonia, Manichaeism preaches an elaborate cosmogonic myth which seeks to explain the dualism of body (evil) and spirit (divine). The myth tells of an accidental invasion of the Kingdom of Light (which is entirely good) by the forces of the Realm of Darkness (which is dominated by concupiscence and strife). To repel the attack, a redeemer figure called the Primal Man was sent by the Father of Greatness to battle with them, equipped with armour composed of light. The Primal Man fell into a drugged sleep and another deity, the Living Spirit, was dispatched to rescue him. This marks the beginning of a complex process for the redemption of the Elements of Light held captive in the bodies of the Archons of Darkness. A series of heavens and earths were created and in their lower sections were imprisoned the Archons of Darkness. A new evocation, the hermaphroditic (Third) Messenger, then seduced the male and female Archons with his/her good looks and induced them to ejaculate and abort the Light Particles held captive in them. These fell to earth and bought forth plant and animal life, but through sexual desire and human conception, were perpetually enslaved in bodily flesh. They could only be redeemed through special knowledge (gnosis) provided by the sect, who thus played a direct role in the redemptive process. The sect was organized as a dyarchy of Elect members who had to adhere to a strict code of chastity, vegetarianism, and quietism, and Hearers who could follow a more normal way of life and whose main task was to administer the daily, especially the alimentary, needs of the Elect.

As Mani had intended his religion to be truly universal, Manichaean scriptures, mostly composed in Syriac and Middle Persian, were translated into Greek, Coptic, and Latin in the West and into Parthian, Bactrian, Sogdian, Turkish, Tocharian B, and Chinese. Though the translators were expected to be faithful to the original, they showed remarkable ability to adapt new religious concepts and terms as the religion diffused in new cultural zones. Its Christian roots were given strong emphasis in the West, shown especially by the newly discovered texts from Kellis in the Dakhleh Oasis. In the East, adaptation of Zoroastrian terms happened early. Thus in many Central Asian texts the Father of Greatness was called Zurvan and the Primal Man Ohrmezd. A more complex but important example of the missionary transformation of Manichaean theology can be seen in the adoption of the Zoroastrian deity Mihr or Mithra. In Middle Persian texts, Mihr was identified with the Living Spirit because of their common function as warrior gods. In Parthian texts, however, because of the local emphasis placed on Mihr as a sun-god, he was identified with the Third Messenger who dwelt in the sun. Once this identification was made, the function of the Third Messenger as a sun-god significantly increased. In China, Mani was worshipped as a Buddha of Light and also as an avatar of Lao-tzu (the traditional founder of Taoism) and Chinese Manichaean texts rarely contain references to accounts of incest and cannibalism, which abound in texts from Central Asia and the Near East. Despite the cultural and linguistic adaptations, the religion maintained a strong sense of self-identification through its veneration of Mani as a special envoy: as Apostle of Jesus Christ in the West and as the Envoy of Light in the East.

See also: Gnosticism; Zoroastrianism.

Bibliography

Asmussen J P 1975 *Manichaean Literature, Representative Texts Chiefly from Middle Persian and Parthian Writings, Persian Heritage Series, XXII.* New York

Klimkeit H-J 1994 *Gnosis on the Silk Road, Gnostic Parables, Hymns and Prayers from Central Asia.* San Francisco

Lieu S N C 1992 *Manichaeism in the Later Roman Empire and Medieval China.* Tübingen

Reeves J 1992 *Jewish Lore in Manichaean Cosmogony, Studies in the Book of the Giants Traditions.* Cincinnati

Melanesian Religions

G. W. Trompf

Melanesia includes the major island of New Guinea and its outliers, the Solomon Islands, Vanuatu, New Caledonia, and Fiji. It is known for its astounding array of traditional religions, famed as the world's 'last unknown' which has turned from cannibalism to Christianity over the last hundred years, and widely publicized as the region which spawned the unusual movements called 'cargo cults.'

1. Traditional Religions

Since there are as many as 1,500 discrete languages in Melanesia (from the Kai Islands and Vogelkop in the west to Fiji's Vanua Levu in the east), there is virtually the same number of indigenous cultures and religions. The region thus turns out to harbor between one quarter and a third of humanity's religions over 570,000 sq km of scattered islands. The religions belong to small-scale, stateless societies, individual tribes within language blocks typically acting as the executive, jural and custodial groups concerned to maintain long-inured traditions. There are various characteristics which are very common in these traditions—such as veneration of the ancestors, a warriorhood ethos whereby the deaths of kin must be avenged, and the enactment of ceremonial exchanges between tribes—but diversity of ritual life, legal—or regulative prescriptions, and of beliefs about the spirit order, is remarkable.

A greater degree of commonality exists between religions sharing the same language phyla, but much less so than might have been expected. Such phyla, after all, are in evidence over vast areas (e.g., Austronesian languages from western Irian Jaya to Vanuatu). There are some debates over the coextensibility of language and culture. One concerning the Sepik region, for instance, has arisen because some languages (e.g., Boiken) are shared by distinct enough cultures (e.g., Negrie and Yangoru), and because some cultures are remarkably similar (various middle Sepik) in spite of language differences.

Aspects of traditional religion of most interest to linguists include special terminology and occult languages in secret societies and among grades of initiates; symbolism and 'natural language' in ritual and in attitudes towards bodily functions; metaphor in the interplay between worldviews and collective activity; in-depth use of story and parabolic materials by religious custodians; and a relaying of messages between clans and groupings. Some linguistic problems for interpreting Melanesian cultures include the absence of lexical equivalents for such words as 'religion' (unless read as 'worship'); the temptation to use the term 'magic' instead of religion; and the false literalization of phrases denoting spirit beings (e.g., among the Papua New Guinea highland Wahgi, 'red spirit' means 'distant ancestors'). In larger culture areas, dialectal differences have led to semantic and orthographic difficulties.

2. Christianity (and Other Introduced Faiths)

Although almost every Melanesian culture still retains some practitioners of 'precontact' ways, the vast majority of the traditional religions have been seriously modified through the impacts of missionization, new religious movements, and general social change. The effects of Christianity on Melanesia have been immense, and by the 1990 census in Papua New Guinea, for example, 96.4 percent of the population declared itself connected to one Christian mission or another. (Adoption of Islam by Melanesians is known in Irian Jaya but is thus far minimal, and the following of Baha'ism in Papua New Guinea and New Caledonia still tiny.) On the other hand, Christianity has not arrived in the southwest Pacific as a unified whole, and while the larger missions and churches (those of the Catholics, Lutherans, Anglicans, Dutch Reformed, Methodists, and United Church) came to hold a traditional sway over given districts, many minor (frequently sectarian) Christian organizations later carved out evangelistic fields for themselves as well.

Most of the older 'mainline' missions were first established with some connection to patterns of colonial overlordship: the Lutherans in the Morobe Province at the time of the German colony in New Guinea, for example; the Marists on New Caledonia under French protection; and so forth. Approaches to grammar and orthography among missionaries and other researchers have consequently reflected different European and American schools. Highly impressive scholarly work on traditional languages has been achieved under mission auspices, nonetheless, and noted among earlier grammarians are Lutheran H. Zahn (on Jâbem, New Guinea), French Protestant M. Leenhardt (on Houailou, New Caledonia) and Anglican A. Capell (on comparative Pacific linguistics).

Since intertribal tensions could be kept alive by a disaffected group welcoming in another brand of missionary, many sectarian Christian groups have gained a foothold in Melanesia, the largest being Seventh Day Adventist. Representatives of up to 75 different denominations in the Eastern Highlands of Papua New Guinea may make that region the most missionized on earth, and it is there that the Summer Institute of Linguistics (see *Summer Institute of Linguistics*) and the Wycliffe Bible Translators have established their headquarters (at Ukarumpa). Translators in these organizations often belong to minor American sectarian churches; and some important work has been done under the sponsorship of such churches in mission (e.g., E. Ramsey's Wahgi dictionary for the Church of the Nazarene).

3. New Religious Movements

In reaction, often in open protest, against both colonialism and the missions, new religious movements have appeared in Melanesian history, and some of these endure to the present day. The best known of these have been dubbed 'cargo cults,' because their adherents have expected the return of their ancestors (and sometimes Jesus) with an abundance of European-style goods. These items, partly because they were not readily accessible to the Blacks, and partly because their origins were placed in the spirit world (rather than in factories, etc.), became symbolic of salvation, i.e., redemption from a loss of autonomy and the breakdown of old reciprocities. In most cases the expected arrival of the dead would produce a dramatic retributive reversal against the Whites' (and other expatriates') interests. Over and above cargo cults, a whole variety of protest and independent religious movements have been known, including insurrections, plainly millenarian cults, prophet movements, and independent churches. Because many of these reactions catch on across cultural boundaries, lingua francas are used as media of communications (see below).

4. Traditions, Religious Change, and the Language Factor

Rapprochement or three-way dialogue between traditional religions, universalizing Christianity, and regional cultic experimentations often centres on notions of deity and the role of the ancestors. Many Melanesian religions had 'high(er) gods,' and a rare few were monotheistic. Key missiological and linguistic issues revolve around the extent to which deities analogous to the Christian God remain conceptually localized (as mountain gods, for instance), or responsible only for a given district's fertility. If many of the old place-spirits, spirit-stones, and minor deities have disappeared from view upon mission impact, moreover, belief in the ancestors has usually remained strikingly resilient, the Catholic Church (with its Masses for the Dead) appearing to many to make more provision for ancestor 'veneration' as a component of a 'Melanesianized' Christianity. Because of linguistic diversity, there has been extensive use of lingua francas for the spreading of Christian, cargo-cultist and other more-than-local messages. With Austronesian languages prevailing on the coasts, it was natural that use would be made of these for evangelization purposes (Yabêm by the Lutherans in German New Guinea, for instance, or Motu by the London Missionary Society (later

United Church) in Papua, with Kâte from the Trans-New Guinea phylum being used by the Lutherans in Highland areas). Still wider in their implications for communication across cultures were the various (and not too dissimilar) pidgins in Papua New Guinea, the Solomons, and Vanuatu (formerly the New Hebrides), and Malay in Irian Jaya (formerly Dutch New Guinea or West Irian). In most cases missionaries played a key role in the grammatical study of the lingua francas, while the rhetorical usage of them was at its height on the lips of Melanesian religious leaders (including cargo-cultist prophets, who were often brilliant at exploiting the ambiguities of pidgins). Religious rhetoric and speech change in plantation, mining and urban contexts are of interest to linguists, including the use of pidgins and patois as first languages.

See also: Cargo Cults; Missionaries; New Religious Movements.

Bibliography

Capell A, Court C, Treefly D, Johnson R 1972 *Linguistic Papers*. Oceania Linguistic Monographs No. 15. Oceania Publications, Sydney

Dempwolff O 1937 *Vergleichende Lautlehre des Austronesischen Wortschatzes (Beihefte zur Zeitschrift für Eingeborenen-Sprachen 16)*. Reimer and De Gruyter, Berlin

Lawrence P, Meggitt M J (eds.) 1965 *Gods, Ghosts and Men in Melanesia*. Oxford University Press, Melbourne

Leenhardt M 1946 *Langues et dialectes de l'austro-Melanésie*. Institut d'Ethnologie, Paris

Leenhardt M 1971 *Do Kamo; la personne et le mythe dans le monde mélanesien*. Editions Gallimard, Paris

Loeliger C E L, Trompf G W (eds.) 1985 *New Religious Movements of Melanesia*. University of Papua New Guinea Press and Institute of Pacific Studies, Port Moresby and Suva

Meier J 1909 *Mythen and Erzählungen der Küsten-bewohner der Gazelle-Halbinsel (Neu-Pommern). Im Urtext aufgezeichnet und ins übertragen* (Bibliothèque/Bibliotek Anthropos, 1). Verlag der Aschendorffschen Buchhandlung, Münster

Ramsey E M *Middle Wahgi Dictionary*. Church of the Nazarene, Mount Hagen

Steinbauer F 1979 (transl. Wohwill M) *Melanesian Cargo Cults*. University of Queensland Press, St Lucia

Trompf G W 1991 *Melanesian Religion*. Cambridge University Press, Cambridge

Zahn H 1940 *Lehrbuch der Jabêmsprache* (*Beihefte zur Zeitschrift für Eingeborenen-Sprachen 21*). Reimer and De Gruyter, Berlin

Native American Religions, North

Å. Hultkrantz

Native American religions cannot be understood in detail without a knowledge of the relevant languages and their structure. At the same time it is difficult to decipher religion through language. Religions and religious concepts are draped in language forms that only vaguely, and often as symbols, mediate the message of the individual's religious conviction. American Native languages exhibit certain peculiarities that according to some writers may have influenced religion. Conversely, religio-magic conditions may have contributed to linguistic development.

Whorf's famous hypothesis of language impact on (Hopi) religion does not stand alone. It has long been suggested that the polysynthetic compounds characteristic of most Native American languages may preclude abstract thought (Boas 1911). This has a bearing on religious thought which is often blurred. It has also been noted that verbs rather than nouns tend to dominate these compounds, which may imply a factor of movement in conceptual constructions, thus restricting the growth of static concepts (Witherspoon 1977, Kinkade 1983). Besides being polysynthetic many languages are pathocentric, that is, they express an action with reference to the individual rather than the individual's action (Holmer 1949). This could possibly indicate the individual's passive adaptation to the supernatural world, for instance, in his or her vision quest. Vision quests, which are common over most of North America, involve fasting and meditation in isolation whereby the native hopes to have a vision of a spirit who then becomes his or her guardian spirit.

American Native vocabulary does not always correspond to Euro–American religious terminology. For instance, the very word 'religion' is usually missing, being covered by terms for rites, like the Zuni word *tewusu* 'a sacred custom, an urgent request.' It is obvious that many of the subtle abstractions of the Euro–American terminology are foreign to native Americans. On the other hand, native Americans believe that the content of religion is 'supernatural,' in Shoshoni *nanaṣuiga'nt* 'wonderful, extraordinary.' To the Lakota (Sioux) all divine beings are *wakan* 'supernatural,' and most of them are somehow parts of *Wakan Tanka*, 'the great mystery.' It is possible that the inclusive character of the godhead has a relation to the sometimes distributive meaning of nouns. Also the Algonquian (*Kitchi*) *Manitou* '(great) spirit' has similar connotations, but has at the same time a clearer personal import.

The tendency in American native languages to view concepts and ideas as concrete phenomena, devoid of abstractions, makes these languages good instruments for mythology. This mythology, it has been said, reveals a kind of visual experience, graphic scenes that can be extremely impressive. It is also interesting to watch how the personalities of mythical beings are expressed through sounds. The culture hero of the Nootka, for example, a strange trickster and introducer of culture, employs alliteration to achieve a humorous effect, while 'Deer' and 'Mink,' characters in the same mythology, turn all sibilants into laterals (Sapir 1949). There is another example of word play in Chinook mythology, where the culture hero discovers a man who catches fish by dancing, and tells him to do it with a net. The Chinook words for 'dancing' and 'catching with a net' sound identical.

When talking to each other and to supernatural powers, medicine men in some tribes use a sacred language, incomprehensible to the common people. Referring to the Lakota, Powers (1986) thinks that sacred language emerges from a continuous process by which secular words are transformed into sacred ones. If even a few words are unintelligible to ordinary people, then the whole language becomes incomprehensible. Among the Tillamook (Chinook), small children are believed to have their own special language in the world of the dead.

There is much debate as to whether some supposed religious concepts are in fact just metaphors. Gill (1987), for example, suggests that the idea of Mother Earth only existed as a metaphor among native Americans, and was interpreted by Europeans as an native Americans goddess. It was then accepted as such by the Indians at the beginning of the twentieth century. Such a development is difficult to prove, however, and most scholars prefer to regard Mother Earth as an ancient American deity.

Name taboos after the death of a person are common among native American Indians. Among the Mescalero Apache, for example, some personal names referring to, or sounding like, plants and animals may become taboo and have to be replaced by new names. It is possible to measure the rate of change in a tribe's basic vocabulary as affected by the operation of word taboos: e.g., among the Salish Twana, 15 percent of the vocabulary was replaced in this way (Elmendorf 1970).

Sign language is a system of gestures used for intercommunication over long distances or with foreign tribes on the Plains, and can express religious ideas. Thunder, for instance, is indicated by signs for bird and fire or bird and medicine, referring to the idea of a supernatural thunderbird (Clark 1885).

Bibliography

Boas F (ed.) 1911 Introduction. *Handbook of American Indian Languages*, Bulletin 40, part 1. Bureau of American Ethnology, Washington, DC

Clark W P 1885 *Indian Sign Language*. Hamersly, Philadelphia, PA

Elmendorf W W 1970 Word tabu and change rates: Tests of a hypothesis. In: Swanson E H Jr. (ed.) *Languages and Cultures of Western North America*. Idaho State University Press, Pocatello, ID

Gill S D 1987 *Mother Earth: An American Story*. University of Chicago Press, Chicago, IL

Holmer N 1949 Amerindian structure types. *Språkliga bidrag* **2(6)**

Kinkade M D 1983 Salish evidence against the universality of 'noun' and 'verb.' *Lingua* **60**: 25–39

Powers W K 1986 *Sacred Language: The Nature of Supernatural Discourse in Lakota*. University of Oklahoma Press, Norman, OK

Sapir E 1949 *Selected Writings of Edward Sapir in Language, Culture and Personality*, Mandelbaum D G (ed.). University of California Press, Berkeley, CA

Witherspoon G 1977 *Language and Art in the Navajo Universe*. University of Michigan Press, Ann Arbor, MI

Native American Religions, South

P. P. Arnold

Indigenous religions of South America are primarily noted for their wide diversity of cultural forms and expressions. Within its geographical limits religions ranging from hunting and gathering tribal groups of the Amazon Basin to urban centered civilizations of Mesoamerica and Peru have been generated and have prospered. Given this diversity, however, religions of these cultures can be defined as being manifold strategies of articulating a human orientation to the substantive conditions of existence. Various referents of religious action include the earth, water, animals, sky, and plants, to name only a few. These realities are engaged through a wide variety of creative means, including music, oral recitation, sacrifices, etc., but which are all characterized by the necessity of human action. Rituals are thus the primary means by which one can meaningfully investigate these religions. Human action, unlike more textually based world religions, focuses a community to a meaningful orientation with reference to the world in which they live.

1. Religious Activity

Myths of creation, usually tied to the actions of primordial beings, often dramatize specific attributes of the world while connecting to it the creativity of the actions of divine ancestors. For example, according to the Mataco of Paraguay and Argentina, after the Great Fire had destroyed the world a little bird, Icanchu, roamed in search of the First Place. Upon finding it he unearthed a charcoal stump on which he pounded. Without stopping he played, chanted, and danced. At dawn of the New Day a green shoot sprang from the coal drum and flowered into the Firstborn Tree. From this was created all forms of life of the present world. From the death of destruction new life was created primarily through the life affirming activity of the Mataco primordial ancestors. In addition, Icanchu's creative activity was expressed through music, song, and dance.

The activities of the ancestors are explicitly correlated to the daily life of humans in order that individuals within the community may directly participate in the creative activities of the cosmos. For example, among the Yąnamamö of Venezuela, penises of males are tied up so that droplets of rain, which carry the souls of the dead distilled in lakes of blood on the moon, can be sucked into the reproductive organ by the foreskin. Human orientation is an ongoing activity which perpetuates those features of the universe fashioned at the beginning of life while directly referring to them.

Likewise rituals are a primary means by which indigenous South Americans articulate their specific relationship with the cosmos. Many rituals mark the passing of human beings from one stage of existence to another. Called 'rites of passage,' these rituals celebrate occasions of birth, puberty, marriage, and death. For many, these occasions express an essentially optimistic vision of a life cycle in which, through the measured expenditure of creative energies, people are renewed and revitalized. Corresponding to rites of passage, however, are rites committed to the revitalization of the world. Among the Aymara of Bolivia, for example, their mountain home is seen as a living body. During important points in the year (i.e., days which mark the transition of seasons), rituals are performed to feed the mountain body at important earth shrines. In a ceremony called 'New Earth,' a field is ceremonially 'opened' for planting. Feeding the mountain body expresses a reciprocity between the Aymara and the earth which is substantive and material. Just as the human body must undergo rites which mark its existence, so the corresponding mountain body must be ritually addressed.

The religious activities of indigenous South Americans, variously expressed in myth and ritual, meaningfully orient their communities to their specific living conditions. In this way, their religions are primarily practical in character, application, and scope.

2. Indigenous Texts

While emphasis here has been on the oral attributes of South American religions, among some groups there existed distinct types of writing. For the Inca of the fifteenth and sixteenth centuries, a *quipu* was used to record information. This was an arrangement of knotted cords which would radiate out from a central knot. Knots along the cords directly corresponded to earth shrines in and around the imperial city of Cuzco. The *quipu*, closely linked with textiles, was a type of record which articulated an Incan strategy of marking their territory. In this sense, it was a device which directly correlated a text with their landscape.

Among the pre-Colombian Aztec and Maya there existed pictorial books on which were inscribed mythic accounts of ancestors and/or their calendrical count of days. These books, of which only 15 existed in the late twentieth century, needed to be 'activated,' however, by recitation or other ritual actions. The *huēhuetlahtōlli* (literally 'old words') among the Aztec were speeches, delivered by only the most esteemed people of their society, on the creation and their ancestors. While these were based on a written text, it was speech which brought them to life for a given community.

One of the most developed systems of writing in the Americas comes from the Maya civilization (200–1200 CE). Knowledge of their written traditions comes primarily from large stone monuments, called 'stelae,' which recount the successful conquests and successions of various rulers of a given region.

Indigenous texts of South America had religious significance only when activated by a human geography, human voice, and human action. In this way they are similar to the use of other ritual artifacts such as the drum, flute, and dance costume. They differ dramatically, however, from the textual tradition which was thrust upon them with the coming of Europeans. While the European tradition primarily organized meaning intertextually, the indigenous peoples of America would refer their religious expressions directly to the understanding of their place with reference to the phenomena of the world.

Bibliography

Bastien J W 1978 *Mountain of the Condor: Metaphor and Ritual in an Andean Ayllu.* Waveland Press, Prospect Heights, IL

Hanks W F 1990 *Referential Practice: Language and Lived Space Among the Maya*. University of Chicago Press, Chicago, IL
Lizot J 1985 *Tales of the Yanomami: Daily Life in the Venezuelan Forest*. Cambridge University Press, Cambridge
López Austin A 1988 *The Human Body and Ideology Concepts of the Ancient Nahuas*. University of Utah Press, Salt Lake City, UT
Schele L, Miller M E 1986 *The Blood of Kings: Dynasty and Ritual in Maya Art*. George Braziller, New York
Sullivan L E 1988 *Icanchu's Drum: An Orientation to Meaning in South American Religions*. Macmillan, New York
Todorov T 1984 *The Conquest of America: The Question of the Other*. Harper and Row, New York
Zuidema R T 1977 The Inca calendar. In: Aveni (ed.) *Native American Astronomy*. University of Texas Press, Austin, TX

New Religions, Japan

I. Reader

The most striking religious phenomenon in modern Japan has been the rise of a large number of religious movements that, while drawing on traditional elements within Japanese religion, express new forms of religiosity and teaching intended to meet with the needs of the modern age. Collectively known as the 'new religions' (*shin shûkyô*) several hundred such movements, usually founded and led by charismatic figures proclaiming newly discovered or revealed spiritual truths intended to save humanity from its present condition, have emerged since the mid-nineteenth century to attract the support of millions of Japanese followers.

While the new religions have taken many concepts and sacred texts from the established traditions of Buddhism and Shinto in Japan, they have also developed their own vocabularies and sacred texts, usually based in the writings or utterances of their charismatic founders, which express their understandings of the world and emphasize their particular spiritual claims. Generally these sacred teachings are in modern, everyday Japanese, and the new religions are characterized by their use of modern Japanese forms which makes their teachings readily accessible to ordinary Japanese, in contrast to the liturgies and sacred texts used in Buddhism and Shinto (which normally are in premodern Japanese or classical Chinese). Such sacred writings normally form the basis for subsequent exegetical developments and doctrinal clarification within the new religions after the deaths of their founders.

Among the most famous texts in the new religions are the *Ofudesaki* ('writings at the tip of an ink brush') of Nakayama Miki (1798–1887), founder of Tenrikyô ('the teaching of heavenly principles') and of Deguchi Nao (1837–1918) founder of Ômoto ('religion of the great origin'). Both these charismatic women were illiterate but according to their respective religions each received direct spiritual transmissions from the respective deities of their religions and wrote them down in a trance, using automatic writing. The *Ofudesaki* of both religions, which are written in simple style using only the *kana* (simple phonetic Japanese syllabary) script rather than the more complex *kanji* (Chinese ideograms) normally used in formal Japanese, form the basis of each religion's creed. Much of the subsequent doctrinal development and understanding of each movement consists of exegetical studies of these sacred writings, which, with their simple and direct language, are considered as revelatory messages from the divine realm.

The new religions also make use of basic Japanese terminology to transmit messages and meanings. A good example of this can be seen in the ways in which polite Japanese forms of greeting have been used in some new religions in innovative ways that implicitly express their respective truth claims and teachings. For example, visitors to Tenrikyô's sacred centre at Tenri are greeted with the words *okaerinasai* 'welcome back,' a greeting commonly used in Japan to greet someone returning home. According to Tenrikyô, the human race emerged onto this earth at Tenri (where Nakayama Miki lived and where God the Parent, the creator deity of Tenrikyô was first revealed to her). Hence anyone going to Tenri is returning to their roots and to the home of humanity. This same greeting has been adopted by other new religions (e.g., Agonshû), which see their sacred centres in a similar light.

In linguistic terms, then, the new religions contrast with the older established Japanese traditions of Shintō and Buddhism, in their use of language that is accessible to ordinary people. Behind their use of simple and everyday Japanese linguistic forms, however, are specific meanings and understandings of such forms that are specifically relevant to, and impart messages about, each individual new religion.

See also: New Religious Movements; Shintō; Buddhism; Japanese.

Bibliography

Hardacre H 1986 *Kurozumikyô and the New Religions of Japan*. Princeton University Press, Princeton, NJ

Kitagawa J 1966 *Religion in Japanese History*. Columbia University Press, New York

Ooms E G 1993 *Women and Millenarian protest in Meiji Japan: Deguchi Nao and Omotokyo*. Cornell East Asia Papers, Ithaca, NY

Reader I 1991 *Religion in Contemporary Japan*. Macmillan, Basingstoke, UK

Thomsen H 1963 *The New Religions of Japan*. Tuttle, Rutland, VT

New Religious Movements

W. S. Bainbridge

New religious movements are extremely fertile sources of new language, and they frequently put language to unusual tasks. The first linguistic challenge is the difficulty of classifying these groups. Following many scholars, the term 'cult' is used here to describe religious organizations with novel or exotic beliefs and practices, but other scholars apply the word to any system of devotional practice, whether deviant or not, and journalists reserve it for only the most dangerous and reprehensible small religions. Although claiming to be a science, Scientology fought in the courts to be labeled a church, while Transcendental Meditation simultaneously struggled to avoid legal definition as a religion. Many pseudoscientific psychotherapies, communes, life-style fads, and popular mythologies have so much in common with formally incorporated religious movements that it is difficult to distinguish them and, from the standpoint of linguistics, their common characteristic is the tendency to invent new words and concepts at a prodigious rate.

1. Cultic Neologisms

Practically every cult generates fresh terminology, partly just to name its innovations and partly to create an air of transcendence and exoticism. Among the most prolific is Scientology, which was inspired by the general semantics movement that explicitly based its cultism on linguistic theory. The prime goal for neophyte Scientologists is to 'go clear,' that is, to achieve a distinctive state of high mental functioning. The term comes from the belief that the human mind is a perfect computer that is suffering from false data, making it give wrong answers, so that pressing the computer's 'clear' button will erase these data. By extension, a person who has gone clear is 'a clear,' and someone working for this goal is 'a preclear.' This new religious movement has published several dictionaries, and the French word for 'preclear' is *préclair*.

Competition between religious movements is a potent stimulant of neologizing, especially when a new movement is born. The typical pattern is for a disaffected or ambitious member of one cult to leave and form his own. Apprenticeship to the leader of a successful group is the best way for a person to learn the skills required for this difficult business, and the founder of a new cult will want to imitate the success of the one he left. But he also needs to distinguish his approach, achieving what economists call 'product differentiation,' and one of the best strategies is to keep the beliefs, practices, and social roles of the earlier, successful cult, but give them all new names. Jack Horner served a long apprenticeship as lieutenant to L. Ron Hubbard of Dianetics and Scientology, and when he created his imitation, Dianology and Eductivism, he quickly published a dictionary filled with neologism and adaptations of Hubbard's terms.

Detailed research has not yet been done on the linguistic mechanisms by which this new terminology is generated, but clearly several principles are at work. New terms are often very similar in form to the old ones; Scientology's 'E-meter,' an electronic device used like a lie detector in counseling sessions, was renamed the 'P-scope' by The Process. If a sacred term was drawn from conventional language, a substitute for it may be found in a term with similar secular meaning; when The Foundation emerged from the wreckage of The Process, it renamed all membership ranks, and Prophets became Mentors. Slight alterations of orthography turn an ordinary word into an exotic one; several cults practice 'magick,' spelling the word this way to distinguish their 'real' magic from mere stage prestidigitation. In other cases, an exotic element is grafted onto an ordinary word; after living in Xtul on the Yucatán coast of Mexico, Processeans began using the letter *x* to indicate *sh* /ʃ/, and the slang term for a voluble line of extravagant talk, *spiel*, was spelled *xpiel*. Acronyms are also common; *mest* is Scientologese for the physical universe (matter, energy, space, time), having a filthy connotation rather like *messed*.

Imported cults, especially those brought to the West from Asia, bring their exotic words with them, often giving them new meanings. In the International Society for Krishna Consciousness (ISKCON), *sankirtana* originally meant public chanting, but it came to mean simply money gathering. Exotic terminology undoubtedly provides a quality of transcendence for otherwise commonplace things. It is far grander to proclaim, 'I am practicing Zen Buddhist *zazen*,' than to admit, 'I am just sitting and resting.'

Although ISKCON was founded by a native of India, some orientalizing cults were created by Westerners who claimed to have studied in remote parts of Asia, despite the doubts of their critics and of some scholars. Nothing could give their followers greater proof of the founders' veracity than the liberal use of Asian or Asian-sounding words. A fine example is the long glossary of Asian and exotic-sounding words in the book that Paul Twichell wrote for his ECKANKAR cult. There one learns that the ECK, the 'audible life current' that is God, can also be called *Ism-I-Asm*, *I Yuan*, *Nada*, and *Ousia*—terms derived, respectively, from Arabic, Chinese, Spanish, and Greek.

Exotic alphabets and picture scripts are also commonly used by new religious movements. Seattle's Love Family gave each inner member a name and an associated hieroglyph reflecting one of the virtues of Christ, nouns or adjectives like *logic*, *fresh*, and even *definition*. Members wore their personal glyphs as rings or embroidered into their robes, and the sacred writings included passages written in these symbols. Indeed, one could write a doctrinal sentence simply by getting the appropriately-named people to stand in a line.

Perhaps the most successful of the Rosicrucian groups, the Ancient and Mystical Order of the Rosae Crucis, in San José, California, capitalized on the mystique surrounding Ancient Egypt by claiming to be derived from it and covering its buildings and literature with hieroglyphics, Often the interpretations of these symbols diverged from the contemporary consensus of Egyptologists. The familiar *ankh* glyph meaning 'life,' the looped crux ansata, was believed to represent the human sexual organs, rather than a prosaic sandal strap as suggested by scholars. An imitative rival, The Order of the Ancient Mayans, substituted Mayan hieroglyphics. Both of these groups also employed secret code scripts, based on cutting pieces off different complex geometric designs and letting each piece represent a letter of the Roman alphabet.

2. Language Rituals and Mysticisms

In chants and rituals, language is believed to have supernatural power, and the new religious movements have not ignored this possibility. ISKCON, founded by A. C. Bhaktivedanta Swami, employs a variant of *bhakti yoga* which involves chanting 'Hare Krishna' almost endlessly. Combined with the high-carbohydrate diet of their *prasadam* meal, this chanting not only announces participants' devotion but also produces a transported sense of bliss.

Transcendental Meditation gave each of its Western recruits a personal Sanskrit mantra (see *Mantra*), supposedly selected to express a unique quality of the individual. However, the mantras were in fact assigned merely on the basis of the new meditator's age, and were taken from a list of just 16 words. The meditator was not supposed to know what the word meant, but to focus on the pure sound of it when meditating, and the power of the mantra would be lost if it were told to somebody else.

Several new religious movements discovered mystical significance in ordinary language. Max Freedom Long, founder of Huna Research Associates, believed that several Hawaiian words had double *huna* meanings, and he professed to discover some of the same words encrypted in the New Testament. Richard S. Shaver contended that each letter of the Roman alphabet actually expressed a word from the lost Lemurian language, and every English word was a cryptic sentence containing wisdom from a civilization that had died when its continent sank beneath the sea. For example, *big* meant 'I am pregnant,' because G stands for 'generate' and the three-letter word is really the three-word sentence 'be I generate,' or 'I am in the act of generation.'

Among the first experiences a new Scientologist will have is the HAS (Hubbard Apprentice Scientologist) of HTHP (how to handle people) course, which presents itself as a class on how to communicate better and consists of a series of highly structured verbal exercises between a pair of students. To pass the exam for TR-0 (training routine zero), the student must sit immobile for two hours, without responding at all to anything said to him. In TR-1 and TR-2, the 'Alice games,' students take turns reciting passages from *Alice in Wonderland* as if they were their own serious comments, for example: 'However, I know my name now, that's some comfort.' The student receiving such a comment has to *acknowledge* it, with one of the following: 'alright, okay, thank you, good, fine.' Everything is supposed to be spoken in a firm, flat tone, and no conversation or expressions of emotion are permitted. TR-3 and TR-4 are similar, except that Alice is replaced by two nonsense questions, asked over and over: 'Do fish swim? Do birds fly?'

The explicit purpose of these communication exercises is to give a person complete, conscious command over his speech, and to deny anybody else the capacity to fluster him. But the latent function seems to be to detach words from their meanings, so that participants could cheerfully profess faith in even the most bizarre notion. Outsiders often wonder how members of new religious movements could believe the strange creeds of these groups, and one answer is that, in a sense, they do not. Not only do particular words mean different things to members, but often the social meaning of language itself has been altered. Although self-proclaimed Satanists, Processeans did not actually believe in the Devil. For one thing, they held that Satan was the abstract principle of separation, having nothing to do with either Lucifer or the Devil, and for another, their symbol system was not a creed demanding belief but a set of evocative symbols designed to promote spiritual exploration.

Words have magical power (see *Magic*) in the minds of members of new religious movements. Frequently, cultic speech is a status contest, with the prize going to the person with the greatest command over the neologisms and exoticisms. Or, a verbal interchange can be an episode of pure social interaction, devoid of the information transfer often associated with conversations. The tremendous variety of novel ideas, practices, and social roles of new religious movements demands new terminology. But before it is anything else, the strange language of new religious movements is a social marker, possessed by members and withheld from outsiders, distinguishing participants from the rest of the world.

See also: Ecstatic Religion; Evangelism; Hare Krishna Movement; Buddhism in the West; Scientology.

Bibliography

Bainbridge W S 1978 *Satan's Power: A Deviant Psychotherapy Cult*. University of California Press, Berkeley, CA

Bainbridge W S 1985 Cultural genetics. In: Stark R (ed.) *Religious Movements*. Paragon, New York

Melton J G 1978 *The Encyclopedia of American Religions*, vol. 2. McGrath, Wilmington, NC

Stark R, Bainbridge W S 1985 *The Future of Religion*. University of California Press, Berkeley, CA

Wallis R 1976 *The Road to Total Freedom*. Columbia University Press, New York

Quakerism

M. P. Graves

Quakers, or the Society of Friends, began in mid-seventeenth-century England in the seedbed of radical Puritanism. They believed in the possibility and necessity of inward revelation, most often referred to as the 'Inward Light of Christ,' which drew persons into a right relationship to God, became a key to interpretation of the Bible, and provided a motivation and power to live a holy life (sanctification or 'perfection'). From the start the Quaker approach to the understanding and practice of Christianity involved implications on their style of life, and in particular upon their language use, the most significant tendencies of which still find widespread practice among contemporary Quakers.

1. Tensions Between Silence and Speech

Quakers have had a tendency to perceive all of life in spiritual terms, making no distinction between secular and sacred. Thus, the Quaker approach to worship, which exists amidst the tensions between silence and speech, influences the patterns of speech and silence in everyday affairs. Ideally, words used in worship, commerce, and relationships are to be weighed, and when spoken are to be intentionally truthful. The common early Quaker injunction, 'Let your words be few,' applied both to meetings for worship and Quaker lives during the rest of the week.

Quakers are commonly known for holding 'silent' meetings for worship, but in fact silence among early Friends and many contemporary Quakers is not seen as an end in itself, but as a means of quieting the inward person to hear the voice of Christ. Words 'heard' inwardly might be judged to be messages only for the individual or for the group gathered for worship. Words thus spoken 'out of the silence' take on significance *because* of the silence, because they have been 'weighed.' Particularly among the early Friends, words spoken in meetings—and there were few gatherings that were entirely silent—were regarded as words from God because the speakers believed they acted as God's oracles. Quaker preaching, until the last century, has been entirely impromptu, ostensibly motivated by the Inward Light of Christ speaking in the silence prompting the spoken word to be delivered to the gathering.

2. The Phenomenon of 'Plain Speech'

Early Quakers followed the Puritan movement toward plain speech, a radical move away from the Renaissance rhetoric of ingratiation with its inherent acceptance and promotion of an hierarchical social structure. Quakers agreed with the Puritan tendency toward plain language, a style focused more on content than adornment through figures of speech. But Quakers went much further and insisted on a range of language choice the set them apart from their contemporaries and expressed their own conception of truth-telling. The well-known early Quaker pronominal usage—the refusal to use 'you' in the singular and the substitution of 'thee' or 'thou'—was not only intended as a more truthful and grammatically accurate linguistic choice, but it also functioned as a symbol of Quaker insistence on not using any language form that imparted unmerited pride or promoted vainglory. Quakers also rejected use of titles, honorific greetings and salutations for the same reason. The language use was accompanied by nonverbal manifestations of the same principles, such as the wearing of plain apparel and the refusal to doff the hat in honor of person of rank.

Like the early Baptists, Quakers also rejected 'pagan' words for the days of the week and the months of the year, referring to them instead as 'First Day,' 'Second Day,' 'First Month,' 'Second Month,' etc.

Another manifestation of the Quaker plain style was the refusal to swear on oath before a magistrate, based on the biblical teaching: 'Swear not at all .... But let your communication be, Yea, yea; Nay, nay ....' Quakers thought that all speech should be truthful, and that oath-taking implied a double standard. Their refusal to swear before officials became the most common cause of Quaker imprisonment during the sect's first half century. The insistence on truthful speech carried over into business transactions where Quakers set a fair price on their goods and refused to bargain. Their 'Yea' and 'Nay' eventually helped break the back of an economic system based upon barter.

This peculiar verbal and nonverbal behavior set a newly 'convinced' Quaker apart from the rest of society, and persecution became very common during the early years of Quakerism. The subsequent ostracism would put the person's decision to the test. Throughout the eighteenth and nineteenth centuries, the peculiar pronominal use became less a witness to truth and more simply a sign of membership. Eventually it passed out of use. The use of nonpagan names for days and months continues among some contemporary Quakers. Emphasis on truth-telling and plain, unostentatious language use are still prized by the Friends.

3. Characteristics of Quaker Style

The earliest Quaker style has been described as 'incantatory' in nature, involving an 'incredible repetition, a combining and recombining of words and phrases drawn from scripture' (Cope 1956: 733). As the movement moved beyond its earlier stages, the style became 'catechetical,' and characterized by the use of language choices, such as rhetorical questions, which invited introspection and reflection (Bauman 1983: 147). From the beginning, Quakers have exhibited the tendency to view existence, knowledge, and spirituality in spatial terminology, the most commonly used terms to express this concept being 'inward' and 'outward' to denote everything from profound Christian experience and its counterfeit, to a dualism between the real world of the mind and the shadow world of the senses, a kind of 'spiritual Cartesianism' (Creasey 1962: 23).

In spite of the Quaker rejection of stylistic devices employed strictly for ornament, Quaker writers and speakers have expressed their theological beliefs in terms of metaphors rather than in terms of propositions or creedal statements. Some of the most commonly discovered metaphor groups or clusters in Quaker writings include the light/dark family, the Voice (part of a larger metaphor cluster that includes several terms for sound and silence), hunger and thirst metaphors, growth metaphors (including the early Quaker use of the term 'seed' to denote the new life and potential for growth through the Light), and the metaphor of the journey (Graves 1983: 364—65). Of this list, probably the light/dark, sound/silence, and journey clusters find the most use among contemporary Friends.

See also: Silence; Preaching.

Bibliography

Barbour H, Frost J W 1988 *The Quakers*. Greenwood Press, New York

Bauman R 1970 Aspects of seventeenth-century Quaker rhetoric. *Quarterly Journal of speech* **56**: 67–74

Bauman R 1983 *Let Your Words Be Few: Symbolism of Speaking and Silence among Seventeenth-century Quakers*. Cambridge University Press, Cambridge

Cope J I 1956 Seventeenth-century Quaker style. *PLMA* 71: 725–54

Creasey M A 1962 *'Inward' and 'outward': A Study in Early Quaker Language*. Friends' Historical Society, London

Graves M P 1983 Functions of key metaphors in early Quaker sermons, 1671–1700. *Quarterly Journal of Speech* **69**: 364–78

Graves M P 1994 Mapping the metaphors in George Fox's Sermons. In: Mullet M (ed.) *New Light on George Fox, 1624–1691: A collection of Essays*. William Sessions, York

Harvery T E 1928 *Quaker Language*. Friends' Historical Society, London

Rastafarianism

J. C. Beal

Rastafarianism is a messianic cult originating in Jamaica but now practiced elsewhere in the West Indies, the UK, the USA, Canada, Australia, and New Zealand, and also in Europe and the former colonies of France, Holland, and Spain. Its roots can be traced back to the teachings of Marcus Mosiah Garvey, who is said to have declared, on leaving Jamaica for the USA in 1916: 'Look to Africa for the crowning of a Black King: he shall be the Redeemer.' When, in 1930, the then Ras ('prince') Tafari was crowned Emperor of Ethiopia and given the titles Haile Selassie I, King of Kings and Lion of the Tribe of Judah, Garvey's followers in Jamaica recognized that his words had been prophetic and the Ras Tafari movement was born.

Rastafarian beliefs are centered on the divinity of Haile Selassie, who is seen to be the returned Christ. The divinity is addressed as *Jah*, as in the Bible (Psalm 68: 4) and much of Rastafarian doctrine involves the reinterpretation of the Bible to apply specifically to Black people, who are said to be the true Israelites, exiled as slaves in 'Babylon' (a term used by Rastafarians to refer to Jamaica, the Western world generally, or even the police). In the early days of the movement, repatriation of Africa was seen as the only means of redemption, but more recently greater emphasis has been placed on liberation in situ; a general consciousness of African roots, a sense of history, and positive self-image to counter the negative one imposed by Babylon since the days of slavery.

There is no special ceremony involved in becoming a Rastafarian: one simply has to recognize the presence of Ras Tafari within—to experience a revelation of self-knowledge. However, many of the symbolic practices of Rastafarians identify them as separate from mainstream (White or colonial) society. As well as restricting themselves to a practically vegetarian diet, composed only of naturally produced food (*I-tal*), they identify themselves with the Nazarites of the Bible in abstaining from strong drink and, in the case of men, by allowing their hair and beards to grow (see Numbers 6: 5). The resulting 'locks' or 'dreadlocks' are the most distinctive external trait of the Rastafarian. Since these 'locks' are curly, they also give positive value to a typically Afro-Caribbean physical trait which had been viewed negatively in colonial society.

Like these physical symbols of Rastafarian identity, the language used by Rastafarians is one that was formerly heavily stigmatized. The use of Jamaican Creole by Rastafarians has contributed to a greater acceptance of this variety, both in Jamaica and in the UK, where it is beginning to be used by young Afro-Caribbeans whose parents came from other islands.

Apart from conferring status on Jamaican Creole, Rastafarianism has contributed several distinctive words, some of which have been adopted by non-Rastafarians. Many of the words coined by Rastafarians have multiple meanings and some involve a play on homophones. The most important of these, because of its centrality to the cult and its subsequent use in many compounds is *I*, which involves a play on the homophones *I* and *eye*, incorporating concepts of identity and vision. In Rastafarian language, the pronoun *I* or *I-and-I* is used for both *I* and *we*, emphasizing the oneness of all Rastafarians if not all humanity. Cashmore (1979: 170) quotes a Rastaman as saying: 'I and I are one people... Ras Tafari is in all of I.' *I* is also substituted for the first syllable of several English words and names: *I-drin* for *brethren*; *I-vid* for *David*; and *I-tal* for *vital*. This last example, the word for food acceptable to Rastafarians, is 'fast becoming part of Jamaican speech' (Barrett 1977: 141), and words for common Jamaican foods are being remodeled on the Rastafarian pattern: thus *Callalu* is now called *Illalu*. Other English words are refashioned in order to substitute 'positive' morphemes for 'negative' ones. Thus *appreciate* and *create* become *apprecilove* and *crelove*, whilst *understand* becomes *overstand*.

On the other hand, Rastafarians tend to give positive meanings to words which are negative in standard English: *dread* is thus a term of great approbation amongst Rastafarians, for whom *Natty Dread*, immortalized in song by Bob Marley, has become a folk-hero. (The same semantic shift is found in the use of *bad* and *wicked* in US and British Black English respectively, and can possibly be attributed to the underlying influence of African languages which have this trait.)

In the UK and the USA as well as Jamaica, Rastafarian words are entering the general vocabulary as a result of the popularization of Rastafarian beliefs and practices, largely through the medium of Reggae music.

See also: Caribbean Syncretistic Religions 1; Caribbean Syncretistic Religions 2.

Bibliography

Barrett L E 1977 *The Rastafarians*. Sangsters Book Store, Kingston, Jamaica/Heinemann Educational, London

Bones J 1986 Language and Rastafari. In: Sutcliffe D, Wong A (eds.) *The Language of the Black Experience*. Blackwell, Oxford

Cashmore E 1979 *Rastaman: The Rastafarian Movement in England.* Allen & Unwin, London
Edwards V 1986 *Language in a Black Community.* Multilingual Matters, Clevedon
Garrison L 1979 *Black Youth, Rastafarianism and the Identity Crisis in Britain.* ACER Project, London
Murrell N, Spencer W D, McFarlane A A, Chisholm C (eds.) 1998 *Chanting Down Babylon: The Rastafari Reader.* Temple UP, Philadelphia
Pollard V 1986 Innovation in Jamaican Creole: the speech of Rastafan. In: Görlach M, Holm J A (eds.) *Focus on the Caribbean.* Benjamins, Amsterdam, pp. 157–66

Roman Religion

J. G. F. Powell

The religion of ancient Rome, a highly ritualistic polytheism, was traditionally supposed to have been codified by Numa Pompilius, the successor of Romulus as king of Rome. Religious law (*ius divinum*) regulated the relations of men with the gods, as civil law regulated their dealings with one another. Public sacrifices and festivals, celebrated by the magistrates, maintained the *pax deorum* or 'peace of the gods,' while the divine will was manifested through divination, prophecies, and omens. The state ritual was principally supervised by the College of Pontifices headed by the *Pontifex Maximus.* The science of divination (from the flight of birds, the entrails of sacrificed animals, meteorological phenomena, etc.) was greatly elaborated under Etruscan influence. The Romans saw the kinship between their religion and that of the Greeks, and syncretistic identifications of Roman and Greek gods were easily made. Sometimes these were supported by an etymological connection (Jupiter = Zeus) but more often a Roman divinity was assimilated to the Greek god or goddess whose sphere of influence was most nearly equivalent; thus Mars = Ares, Minerva = Athena, etc. Some had no equivalent in Greek religion or mythology, e.g., Janus (god of doorways and of beginnings—hence January). The Romans perhaps derived from the Greeks a tendency to deify abstractions; thus there were temples and public cults of Victory, Concord, Fortune, etc. A host of minor spirits (*numina*) were invoked in specific contexts. Elaborate rituals surrounded birth, marriage, and death, and private cults (*sacra*) were handed down in the family or attached to particular localities. Every individual Roman had a tutelary spirit (*genius* if a man, *Juno* if a woman) and every Roman family had its *Lares* (gods of the household) and its *Penates* (gods of the storecupboard); household worship was in the hands of the head of the family (*paterfamilias*). During the Principate, divine honors were paid to present and past emperors.

Roman ritual was an elaborate discipline with its own technical terminology. Accurate enunciation of ritual formulae (*carmina* or *verba concepta*) in prayers, vows, sacrifices, oaths, and other ceremonial acts was considered most important. If a sacrificing magistrate made a slip of the tongue, it was considered a bad omen; the whole sacrifice might have to be repeated (*instauratio*) and the fault expiated with a further sacrifice (*piaculum*). The language of ritual was often old-fashioned (as was the language of Roman law). Some extant items of religious Latin, such as the Saliar and Arval Hymns, are so archaic as to be largely unintelligible even with the help of philological research, and it is doubtful whether the Romans of the classical period understood them any better than modern scholars do. Latin prayers, such as those preserved by Cato the Elder in *De Agricultura* (139–41), show a standard pattern: first the god or gods concerned are invoked by name, then the petition is made, and finally the sacrifice (i.e., the payment for the granting of the request) is offered, with the formula *macte esto* (possibly meaning 'be thou increased'). Alliteration, isocolon, rhyme, and collocations of synonyms are all common in Latin ritual formulas, and these features combine with archaism in vocabulary and accidence to form a distinctive register of Latin, touches of which could be employed to good literary effect by authors such as Virgil and Livy.

Verbal prophecies were accepted as a potentially valid communication from the gods. The Roman state kept a collection of oracles (apparently written in Greek) known as the Sibylline Books, which were consulted on occasions of national emergency. Prophets (*vates*), diviners, and (later, under Graeco-Oriental influence) astrologers were taken seriously; an accidental utterance by an ordinary person could be regarded as an omen in certain circumstances. The verbal declaration of a god's will was called *fatum* (from *fari* 'to speak'), whence the use of this word to mean 'destiny' or 'fate.'

In general, Rome was receptive to foreign religious influences, although cults which threatened public order were from time to time officially suppressed. Cults of various origins were transported around the Empire by soldiers, tradesmen, and others; among these were the so-called mystery religions (Greek *mysteria* 'initiatory rites' from *myeo* 'initiate,' *myo* 'shut the eyes'), of Greek or Near Eastern origin, whose devotees progressed through various stages of initiation of a more or less secret nature. Temples of the Egyptian deities Isis and Serapis were established at Rome by the end of the Republic, while the religion of Mithras, 'the Unconquered Sun'—who probably bore an extremely tenuous relationship to the ancient Iranian god Mithra—was particularly congenial to the military classes. Owing to the secrecy of Isiac and Mithraic ritual, very little is known about its language; some Egyptian or Iranian formulas may have been preserved in it (as in contemporary magical documents), but it is likely that the main language was originally Greek, the lingua franca of the Eastern Mediterranean since the time of Alexander the Great, while Mithraists in the West probably used Latin.

Some central items of Christian Latin vocabulary derived directly from Roman paganism, though their meaning was altered (often consciously) by the influence of the Greek and Hebrew words which they were used to translate. Examples are *sacer*, *sanctus*, *sacramentum*, *sacrificium*; *pius*, *pietas*; *votum*, *devotio*; and of course *religio* itself. However, some other pagan terms, such as *pontifex*, were imported into ecclesiastical usage as a result of classicizing revival in the Renaissance.

See also: Etruscan Religion; Greek Religion.

Bibliography

Beard M, North J, Price S 1998 *Religions of Rome* (2 vols). Cambridge University Press, Cambridge
Liebeschuetz J H W G 1979 *Continuity and Change in Roman Religion*. Clarendon Press, Oxford
Ogilvie R M 1969 *The Romans and Their Gods in the Age of Augustus*. Chatto and Windus, London
Palmer L R 1954 *The Latin Language*. Faber, London
Scullard H H 1981 *Festivals and Ceremonies of the Roman Republic*. Thames and Hudson, London
Warde Fowler W 1922 *The Religious Experience of the Roman People*. Macmillan, London
Wardman A 1982 *Religion and Statecraft among the Romans*. Granada, London
Wissowa G 1912 *Religion und Kultus der Römer*. Beck, Munich

Scientology

W. S. Bainbridge

Scientology is not only one of the most innovative and influential new religious movements, but it is also an applied religious philosophy that seeks to help people in many practical spheres of life, notably language and communication. In 1950, explorer and author L. Ron Hubbard announced his discovery of Dianetics, a new communication-based technique designed to improve an individual's mental health. After five further years of spiritual research, Hubbard founded the Church of Scientology in Washington DC. Its fundamental religious practice is *auditing*, a form of spiritual counseling in which a trained *auditor* counsels a *preclear*, a Scientologist who is on the way toward a level of spiritual advancement called *clear*. This process of religious communication is assisted by the *E-Meter* electronic device, chiefly to help preclears address past experiences which have impaired their spiritual functioning.

Scientology has developed a number of communication courses, partly to train auditors for professional counseling, and partly to improve any Scientologist's accuracy of speech in everyday life. For example, in 1970 the introductory communications courses centered on training routines (TR-0 through TR-9), practised by students in pairs under the direction of a coach. TR-0 involved simply being aware of the presence of another person without speaking, retreating, or reacting to what the other might say or do. In TR-1, the student learned to speak sentences drawn from *Alice in Wonderland*, handling the words simply as words, without the need to flinch, stammer, or overwhelm the listener with superfluous emotions. TR-2 is the mirror image of TR-1, and the student responded to such sentences with words (*all right*, *okay*, *thank you*, *good*, or *fine*) that acknowledged the other person's speech and brought the cycle of communication to a full stop. Today, Scientology's communication training offers a rich collection of courses and publications.

L. Ron Hubbard was familiar with Alfred Korzkysbi's General Semantics theory that imprecise verbal communication causes many mental problems, and he concluded that clear thinking required rigorous use of words. Thus, Scientologists are taught to learn the precise meanings of terms, and the Church has published its own extensive dictionaries. For example, the *Dianetics and Scientology Technical Dictionary* defines *understanding* in terms of three elements often referred to by the acronym

ARC: affinity, reality, and communication. *Affinity* is defined as 'the feeling of love or liking for something or someone,' and *reality* as 'agreement as to what is.'

Because Scientology has many technical terms, and the church believes that precision is essential, translating the literature from English to other languages has been a challenge. Sometimes, the most equivalent word in the other language is used. For example, *ARC* is *ARK* in German (Affinität, Realität, Kommunikation), and *clear* is *clair* in French. In many other cases, technical terms are transferred from English. Thus, Scientologists speaking Italian use the English-derived term *beingness* (the assumption or choosing of a category of identity). By 1998, Scientology churches or missions had been established in 48 nations, and literature was being distributed in 138. In the middle of 2000, Scientology literature was available in 56 languages.

Bibliography

Church of Scientology International 1998 *Theology and Practice of a Contemporary Religion*. Bridge Publications, Los Angeles

Church of Scientology International 1998 *What is Scientology?* Bridge Publications, Los Angeles

Hubbard L R 1950 *Dianetics, the Modern Science of Mental Health*. Paperback Library, New York

Hubbard L R 1978 *Dianetics and Scientology Technical Dictionary*. Bridge Publications, Los Angeles

Hubbard L R 1992 *Grammar and Communication for Children*. Bridge Publications, Los Angeles

Seventh-day Adventist Church

W. S. Bainbridge

This global religious movement is the largest of the churches in the Adventist tradition, which emerged in the United States in the middle of the nineteenth century. The Seventh-day Adventist Church claims more than 10,000,000 members and a growth rate that doubles the membership every 15 years. It is active in 215 countries in the world, broadcasts radio programs in 40 languages, and publishes in 272 languages.

William Miller and Ellen White employed two diametrically opposite methods to receive the communications from God that created the Seventh-day Adventist Church. While serving in the Vermont militia in the 1812–16 war between the United States and Britain, Miller was horrified to see men killed by cannon and disease. In peacetime, seeking solace in the Bible, he concluded that it must contain all the clues needed for deciphering divine messages intended for his own historical era. He identified the Second Coming with the cleansing of the sanctuary which Daniel 8:14 says would take place after 2,300 days, and in Ezekiel 4:6 he found that each day represented a year. Comparing Biblical references with the works of secular historians, he counted forward 2,300 years from 457 BCE and predicted Christ would return about 1843.

A vast millenarian movement arose around Miller's calculations leading to the 'Great Disappointment' when a series of specific dates passed apparently without incident. Some Millerites, however, offered alternative interpretations, including the idea that Christ had indeed cleansed the sanctuary, but in Heaven rather than on Earth.

A few weeks later, a vision came to seventeen year old Ellen G. Harmon, one of the people who had listened to Miller. She saw a straight and narrow path up in the air, along which believers were ascending toward the New Jerusalem. Whereas Miller had employed logic to decode hidden messages in the Bible, Ellen entered trances that allowed her to see prophetic images. One of Ellen's visions, possibly influenced by contact with the Seventh Day Baptist Church, revealed that the Sabbath should be held not on Sunday but Saturday. In 1846, Ellen married James White, a Millerite preacher who believed that her visions were entirely real contacts with the supernatural, and the two of them built a small movement out of the wreckage of Millerism that was formally organized as a denomination in 1863.

Many religious movements are shaped by the personal experiences of their founders, and Ellen's own medical problems gave her movement a strong focus on healing and on proper nutrition. In Battle Creek, Michigan, they established the Western Health Reform Institute that became the hub of a network of medical facilities that spread across the world and today includes 162 hospitals and 361 clinics.

See also: Jehovah's Witnesses.

Bibliography

Bainbridge W S 1997 *The Sociology of Religious Movements*. Routledge, New York

Bliss S 1853 *Memoirs of William Miller*. Joshua V. Himes, Boston

Doan R A 1987 *The Miller Heresy, Millennialism, and American Culture*. Philadelphia University Press, PA

Numbers R L 1992 *Prophetess of Health: Ellen G. White and the Origins of Seventh-day Adventist Health Reform.* University of Tennessee Press, Knoxville, TN

White E G 1888 *The Great Controversy Between Christ and Satan.* Pacific Press Publishing Association, Mountain View, CA

Shamanism

C. E. Hardman

The term *shaman* comes from the Evenks, a people of eastern Siberia, whose Tungus-Manchu word *šaman* means 'one who knows.' It has also been translated as 'one who is excited, moved or raised' (Lewis 1971, p. 51), emphasizing the ecstatic trance state of some shamans. Although there is no agreed definition of the word, in present common usage the label of 'shaman' and the derivative 'shamanism' have become categories to describe a spiritual specialist, who is able to enter a trance state at will to communicate with spirits and gods on behalf of a community. It has also been appropriated by members of modern urban society to describe a new spirituality (Harner 1980). The most accepted definition is that of Mircea Eliade (1964, p. 5) 'the shaman specializes in a trance during which his soul is believed to leave his body and ascend to the sky or descend to the underworld.' However, this is limited, ruling out spirit possession as an element, and spirit possession does occur alongside soul journeying, especially in Siberia and in South East Asia. Eliade simply rejected possession as the later historical development. Two other features of shamanism are important; the 'mastery of spirits' (Shirokogoroff 1935), or the voluntary and controlled nature of the trance, and the assistance of helper spirits (Hultkranz 1973). Shamans have the ability to enter a trance voluntarily to make a soul journey or become possessed by a spirit, often with the help of one particular spirit. Hallucinogens, and some form of repetitive drumming or chanting may be used to facilitate entry into the trance state.

See also: Ecstatic Religion; Spiritualism; Native American Religions.

Bibliography

Eliade M 1951 [1964] *Shamanism, Archaic Techniques of Ecstasy*. Routledge London

Harner M 1980 *The Way of the Shaman.* Harper San Francisco, New York

Hultkranz Å 1973 A Definition of Shamanism. *Temenos*, Vol. 9

Lewis I 1971 *Ecstatic Religion.* Penguin, London

Shirokogoroff S 1935 *Psychomental Complex of the Tungus.* Kegan Paul, London

Shintō

I. Reader

Shintō is a Japanese religious tradition centered on the relationship between the Japanese people and the native deities, *kami*, and closely associated, both at national and local community levels, with issues of Japanese identity and with social and cultural belonging. With no fixed doctrines, its focus is primarily expressed in ritual actions that are concerned with the celebration and promulgation of life, and with issues of spiritual purity and ritual performances that uphold and maintain the relationship between the human world and the world of the *kami*. Although its influence on the Japanese language has never been as pronounced as that of the imported religion, Buddhism (see *Buddhism, Japanese*), it has nonetheless played a role in the development of philological studies in Japan as well as producing important texts and specialist vocabulary.

1. Shintō: Meaning and Derivation

The word '*Shintō*' itself comes from two Sino–Japanese ideograms in their *on* (Japanese approximations of the original Chinese) readings. The first, *shin* (Chinese *shen*), also has the Japanese reading *kami*, the word used to refer to Shintō deities or powers, and the second *tō* (Chinese *tao* or *dao*), whose *kun* or Japanese reading is *michi*, means 'way' or 'path.' Together they signify the *kami no michi*, or *Shintō*, the 'way of the *kami*', a word developed to identify the rather amorphous and undifferentiated native Japanese religious tradition centered on its native *kami* from the new religious entities and traditions, notably Buddhism, that were introduced to Japan from the Asian mainland from the sixth century CE onwards. Shintō as a named and identifiable entity thus evolved as a result of this cultural interaction with the outside. Although thereby identified as separate from the continental traditions and as specific to the Japanese experience, Shintō has generally existed in tandem with Buddhism in a mutually interpenetrating process. This interpenetration has not, however, prevented each from retaining its separate identity and form, including specialized linguistic forms.

2. Textual Traditions, Forms of Prayer and Linguistic Specialities

The introduction of Buddhism and the Chinese writing system provided the means by which a Shintō textual tradition and prayer forms specific to Shintō could be established and recorded. Because the myths and legends associated with Shintō were written at the instigation of the Imperial Court, they tended to legitimate the rule of the Imperial household as well as posit a special relationship of descent between the Japanese and their *kami*. The major text, the *Kojiki* or 'Record of Ancient Affairs,' and the *Nihon Shoki* or *Nihongi* ('Chronicles of Japan'), were written in the early eighth century in a Classical Japanese style strongly influenced by Chinese (indeed the *Nihongi* also contains sections from Chinese and Korean classical works) and describe the creation of Japan by the *kami*, the prominence of Amamterasu the Sun Goddess, and the descent of the Imperial lineage from her.

The adopted writing system provided the vehicle through which to record the *norito*, the sacred incantations and prayers used in Shintō rituals. According to the *Kojiki*, the first *norito* date from the mythical period of Japanese history described in the *Kojiki*, although in reality the earliest recorded extant examples only date to the early tenth century. *Norito* developed their own specialized style and linguistic structure, making use of the textual form of ideograms but adopting it into a style specific to Shintō ritual and terminology. In particular they used Chinese ideograms not simply in terms of meaning but also as phonetic devices: various grammatical nuances, such as verb endings and particles were denoted by ideograms inserted in the text in reduced size, to indicate that they were to be read for their sound rather than meaning. While the use of ideograms indicates the extent to which the indigenous religion was dependent on the linguistic forms provided by the adopted writing system to express itself, the specialized structure of *norito* equally reflects a dynamic within Shintō to create its own linguistic forms that could continue to differentiate it from Buddhism. Closely aligned to the concept of *norito* is that of *kotodama*—the notion that words used in sacred Shinto rituals, prayers, and invocations to the gods may contain within them a particular spiritual power or resonance that in itself can have magical and transformative effects.

Shintō has also developed its own ritual vocabulary that serves to distinguish it both from Buddhism and from everyday affairs. Much of this revolves around taboos, either of words associated with death (a taboo subject in Shintō) or of words associated with Buddhism. In ritual terms, also, specialized Shintō terms are used for everyday words so as to differentiate them from ordinary life and transpose them to the purified realms of the *kami*. Many foodstuffs, for example, which are important offerings in Shintō rites, have Shintō as well as ordinary names; rice wine, for example, is normally known as *sake* but in Shintō contexts is called *miki*.

3. Linguistic Studies and the Purity of Language

Its close associations with Japanese identity have often placed Shintō in the forefront of moves to assert the indigenous culture over and against any external influences. Shintō itself was largely an amorphous tradition until attempts were made by various scholars and nationalists from the eighteenth century onwards to codify it as part of a wider design to distinguish Japanese from Chinese and continental influences in Japanese culture, and to attempt to assert the superiority of the former over the latter. Prominent in this was Motoori Norinaga (1730–1801) whose studies of early Japanese texts and pre-Buddhist Japanese as part of his endeavors to assert the culturally unique content of Shintō were—despite their chauvinistic themes—a major starting point for modern philological understandings of the Japanese language. Motoori considered Japanese to be culturally and spiritually superior to Chinese, and, for early Japanese nationalists, such assertions served to attribute to the Japanese language sacred dimensions, and thereby create a unity between Shinto as a religion of national consciousness, and the Japanese language through which that consciousness was expressed.

In the following centuries until 1945, Shintō was a focal rallying point for successive governments in their attempts to assert the purity of Japanese cultural identity over and against the outside world, and this led to further codifications of Shintō and the formation of state Shintō (*kokka Shintō*). While the attempts made by the government, especially in the 1930s and 1940s, to 'purify' Japanese by excising foreign loanwords have no direct and overt connection to Shintō in religious terms, the close association between the Shintō of that period and the state, and Shintō's association with and legitimation of concepts of Japanese national identity, did mean that Shintō had some influence in this issue.

Since 1945 and the legal separation of religion and state, Shintō has reverted more clearly to its basic connections with local communities and with rites, festivals, and celebrations. Nonetheless, its continuing and underlying associations with issues of purity and identity mean that its potential as a rallying point and medium for the expression of nationalistic reactions to the increasing numbers of loan-words in Japanese, and hence its subliminal influence and image as a defender of the purity of the Japanese language, cannot entirely be dismissed. This is perhaps somewhat ironic considering that its linguistic influences were never as far-reaching as those of Buddhism and that its very emergence as a named entity was very much dependent on the tools provided by Japan's cultural borrowings from Chinese culture.

See also: Japanese Linguistic Thought; Buddhism, Japanese

Bibliography

Breen J, Teeuwen M (eds.) 2000 *Shinto in History: Ways of the Kami*. Curzon Press, Richmond, UK

Herbert J 1967 *Shinto*. Stein and Day, New York

Miller R A 1967 *The Japanese Language*. University of Chicago Press, Chicago, IL

Ono S 1962 *Shinto: The Kami Way*. C. E. Tuttle, Rutland, VT

Sonoda M (ed.) 1988 *Shintō: Nihon no minzoku shūkyō*. Kōbundō, Tokyo

Sikhism

C. Shackle

Sikhism has always had a close territorial connection with the Panjab, still the homeland of the great majority of Sikhs. The historic link between Sikhism and Panjabi, while undeniably close, is however more complex than their close modern identification might suggest.

1. The Scriptural Language of the Sikhs

One of the most vital religious currents in medieval North India was the reformist monotheism of the lower caste Sants, whose hymns were composed in the dialectically mixed idiom loosely termed 'Santbhāṣā'. Very much in general line with those of the Sants, though distinguished by their exceptionally coherent articulation, the teachings of Gurū Nānak (1469–1539), the founder of the Sikh faith who was born in Shekhupura district west of Lahore, were similarly couched in a mixed poetic language well suited to extend their geographical appeal. Since Gurū Nānak's magnificent hymns formed the model for his immediate successors whose compositions are collected in the *Ādi Granth*, the Sikh scripture assembled by Gurū Arjan (1563–1606), their language may properly be termed the sacred language of the Sikhs (SLS) (Shackle 1983), a distinctive variety of Santbhāṣā.

Drawing freely for its technical lexicon upon assimilated Perso–Arabic loans besides the usual Sanskritic *tatsama* vocabulary (Shackle 1995), the core dialectal elements of SLS are Nānak's own speech and the Kharī bolī lingua franca, in roughly equal measure. The parallel use of such 'Old Panjabi' and 'Old Hindi' elements is exemplified by many common alternations, e.g., PRES 1SG *karā̃/karaū̃*, 3PL *karanhi/karaṃhi*. The location of Nānak's own dialect in the borderland between central Panjabi and the western 'Lahndā' dialects with their typical sigmatic future is reflected in further alternations, e.g., FUT 3SG *karegā/karasī*. More peripheral dialectal components are drawn from the Siraiki of Multan to the west, and Braj bhāṣā to the east.

Apart from this dialectal mixture, the most striking feature of SLS from a modern perspective is its marked archaism (Shapiro 1987), notable in its retention of the morphologically important final short vowels since lost in modern Panjabi, e.g., SG DIR *guru*, SG OBL/Pl DIR *gura*, SG LOC/INSTR *guri*, versus modern *gur[ū]*. By making recourse to modern patterns of postpositional extension redundant, this permits a conciseness of expression more typical of older Apabhraṃśa norms than of later Indo–Aryan, where such characteristic constructions as the locative absolute (e.g., *satiguri miliai* 'through the True Guru's meeting') have long been unfamiliar.

2. The Gurmukhi Script and Postscriptural Literature

The *Ādi Granth* is written in the Gurmukhi script, whose standardization is attributed to the second Gurū, Angad (1504–52). This is superficially similar to Nagari, albeit with the confusing assignation of different values to identical graphs (e.g., Gurmukhi [s p m] = Nagari [m dh bh]) and the addition of a separate sign for [ṛ]. In such characteristics as the general avoidance of consonant clusters, Gurmukhi is however closer to original Brahmi norms than to learned South Asian scripts of the Nagari type. Gurmukhi may rather be regarded as occupying an intermediate position between the latter and the commercial shorthands known in the Panjab as *laṇḍe*, which it resembles in the alphabetic order of its 35 letters and their distinctive names. These features, plus the reduction of vowel-bearers to three and of the sibilants to a single graph, are seen in the first five letters of the alphabet: *ūṛā* [u], *aiṛā* [a], *īṛī* [i], *sassā* [s], *hāhā* [h].

Religions tend to be linked more closely to scripts than to languages (see *Alphabet*: *Religious Beliefs*), and postscriptural Sikh literature is recorded in the same sacred Gurmukhi, irrespective of its language. The seventeenth-century prose hagiographies (called *janamsākhī*, already show many more modern features, with increasing confusion in the notation of final short vowels indicating their gradual disappearance in contemporary speech.

Though not included in the *Ādi Granth*, particular liturgical importance attaches to the compositions of the tenth and last Gurū, Gobind Singh (1666–1708). Born in Patna and throughout his life involved in the militant struggle against the Muslim imperial power which was to dominate Sikh affairs throughout the eighteenth century, Gobind Singh mainly wrote not in SLS but in Braj bhāṣā, then the premier non-Muslim literary language of North India. Much of the later Sikh literature down to the time of the kingdom of Maharājā Ranjīt Singh (1799–1839) was similarly composed in Braj bhāṣā, though recorded in Gurmukhi.

3. Reformist Sikhism and the Rise of Modern Standard Panjabi

The British conquest of the Panjab in 1849 reduced the Sikhs to the unprivileged status of a minority to both Muslims and Hindus. From the 1870s the assimilationist claims of revivalist Hinduism were vigorously combated by the Sikh reformers of the Singh Sabhā movement. This religious controversy quickly assumed a linguistic dimension, as Panjabi Hindus identified with Hindi while the Sikhs identified with Panjabi (Brass 1974).

Owing much to the conscious efforts of such reformist writers as Vīr Singh (1872–1957), a modern standard Panjabi based on the central Mājhī dialect was evolved, drawing increasingly on Sanskrit rather than Perso–Arabic for its learned vocabulary (Shackle 1988). Although very different in character from SLS, the continued use of the Gurmukhi script (with the addition of appropriately standardized diacritics) has aided this modern Panjabi in becoming the unquestioned language of contemporary Sikhism.

Campaigns to secure its official recognition continued after Indian independence, until the demand for a Sikh-majority state, made politically acceptable by being defined as one with Panjabi as its official language, was eventually achieved in 1966. In the Sikh diaspora in Britain and North America, too, claims for its recognition overseas are frequently raised, in spite of the growing importance of English even within nonliturgical parts of the temple services themselves.

See also: Granth; Gurmukhi; Panjabi (Gurmukhi) Sacred Texts.

Bibliography

Brass P R 1974 *Language, Religion and Politics in North India*. Cambridge University Press, Cambridge

Shackle C 1983 *An Introduction to the Sacred Language of the Sikhs*. School of Oriental and African Studies, London

Shackle C 1988 Some observations on the evolution of modern standard Panjabi. In: O'Connell J T (ed.) *Sikh History and Religion in the Twentieth Century*. University of Toronto, Toronto

Shackle C 1995 *A Gurū Nānak Glossary*, 2nd edn. Heritage, New Delhi

Shapiro M C 1987 Observations on the core language of the Adigranth. *Berliner Indologische Studien* **3**: 181–93

Singh H 1995–8 (ed.) *The Encyclopaedia of Sikhism*. Panjabi University, Patiala

Spiritualism

J. Algeo

Spiritualism or *spiritism* is the belief that spirits of the dead communicate with the living, usually through an intermediary or medium. Spiritualistic practices have been found all over the world from ancient times to the present. The visit of Saul to the Witch of Endor (1 Samuel 28.7–19) is an early Hebrew account of communication with the dead. Similar practices are attested among Vietnamese, West Africans, Haitians, and American Indians, among others.

Modern spiritualism dates from March 31, 1848, when *rapping* sounds were heard in the house of the Fox family, which included two young girls, Margaret and Kate. The raps, which were interpreted as messages from a dead spirit, became the vehicle of both a religious revival and a pastime curiosity. As the practice of spiritualism spread, *rappings* were succeeded by a variety of other means of communication: *automatic writing and drawing*, *glossolalia* (shared with Pentecostal Christianity), *materializations* in *seances*, speech through a *medium*, *ouija boards*, and *table-tilting*. The Spiritualist movement, which was religiously and socially liberal, democratic, pro-feminist, and politically active, included such notable American figures as Susan B. Anthony, William Cullen Bryant, James Fenimore Cooper, William Lloyd Garrison, Horace Greeley, George Ripley, Elizabeth Cady Stanton, and Harriet Beecher Stowe.

Scandals in the early movement, of both fraud and immorality (free love), did not prevent Spiritualism from becoming institutionalized as the National Spiritualist Association and as various Spiritualist churches and communities, some of which still survive, such as that at Cassadaga, Florida. From its earliest days, Spiritualism assumed a number of forms. The French medium Allan Kardec, a proponent of reincarnation, was influential in Latin countries. The Theosophist H. P. Blavatsky unsuccessfully attempted a reform of Spiritualism by denying that its communications originated with the spirits of the dead.

Spiritualism has contributed to the vocabulary such terms, in addition to those above, as *cabinet* (a box or curtained space in which the medium concentrates the spiritual force needed for a materialization), *control* or *guide* (an intermediary between the communicating spirit and the medium), *ectoplasm*, types of mediums such as a *psychic medium* (who transmits messages received telepathically) or a *trance medium* (who enters into a trance to make contact with the dead), and *spirit world*.

See also: Channeling; Glossolalia; Shamanism; Theosophy.

Bibliography

Braude A 1989 *Radical Spirits: Spiritualism and Women's Rights in Nineteenth-Century America*. Beacon Press, Boston

Haynes R 1982 *The Society for Psychical Research, 1882–1982: A History*. Macdonald, London

Oppenheim J 1985 *The Other World: Spiritualism and Psychical Research in England, 1850–1914*. Cambridge University Press, Cambridge

Taoism

D. Lancashire

Taoism is an expression of the metaphysics and religious life indigenous to China, and has shared with Confucianism (see *Confucianism*) the moulding of Chinese culture over a period of 2,000 years. For many Chinese, Taoism has served as a counterweight to orthodox Confucianism with its emphasis on community life and social responsibility, government, and ethics. It has also been the source of China's imaginative life, providing inspiration for poetry and painting, and an escape from convention, a charter for freedom and joy.

The *Daodejing* ('Classic of the Way and its Power'), which is regarded as the foundation text for both philosophical Taoism (*Dao-jia*) and religious Taoism (*Dao-jiao*), is held to have been composed by the sixth-century BCE thinker, Lao-zi (Lao-tzu). His ideas were further developed in the fourth century BCE by the philosopher Zhuang-zi (Chuang-tzu).

In the second century CE, Taoism expressed itself in revolutionary movements of a messianic character in eastern China, culminating in the Yellow Turban Rebellion in 184. In 142 CE in west China a certain Zhang Daoling was given the title Celestial Master, and is regarded as the founder of organized religious Taoism. Taoism always had connections with court life. The founder of the Tang dynasty (618–907) declared himself a descendant of Lao-zi, and within Taoism was regarded by many as the fulfillment of messianic prophecy. Not surprisingly, the Tang dynasty was to see a rapid growth in religious Taoism throughout the land.

New Taoist sects were founded during the Song dynasty (960–1279), and the Ming dynasty

(1368–1644) witnessed the strengthening of syncretistic tendencies through, for example, the popularization of the Three Religions (*San Jiao*) movement in which Taoist, Buddhist, and Confucian elements were woven together.

Taoism spread to Korea in the third century CE and thrived between the eighth and fifteenth centuries, becoming fused with ancestor worship and local shamanism. It is estimated that in South Korea today there are some 820,000 followers of Taoism with approximately 3,000 priests.

Evidence of Taoist influence on Japanese Shintō ('Way of the Gods') is less clear, but that there has been some seems likely in view of certain similarities. Taoism is widespread throughout Southeast Asia, particularly where there are large Chinese communities.

The concept at the heart of the *Daodejing* is that of the Dao (Tao), the original meaning of which is 'road' or 'way.' It came to signify the 'Way of Nature' and the 'Way' of the sage kings of ancient times. In the *Daodejing*, however, it is regarded as the ground of all being, transcending time and space, the universe, and all things. All attributes are held within it, as are all of nature's ways and principles. It is beyond all names and descriptions: the nameless from which heaven and earth spring; the 'uncarved block'; the mystery which is 'darker than any mystery.'

Neither Lao-zi nor Zhuang-zi regarded it as an object of worship, but rather as a fundamental reality governing the rhythms of life and nature to which the mystic should seek to adapt himself. Thus to be in tune with the Dao and to give free play to its power or virtue De (*te*), is to be totally in tune with Nature. According to Lao-zi, 'The one who follows Dao is identified with Dao. The one who follows virtue (the power of the Way) is identified with virtue.' From the first century CE at the latest, however, Lao-zi is equated with the Dao and is also seen as the embodiment of it, so that he becomes a high god and an object of faith and worship for the faithful.

At the heart of the Taoist religion is the quest for immortality, which is attained through 'cultivation of the Dao,' by a variety of religious 'arts' or 'methods' practiced by devotees. These are primarily concerned with diet, but also with inner refinement, involving among other things, breathing exercises and meditation, talismans for healing and protection from demons, and sexual disciplines. A considerable body of scripture pertaining to these interests was to grow up.

For the ordinary worshiper who seeks only spiritual aid, prayers and sacrifices and can be addressed and offered to deities. Sins can be repented of, scriptures recited, techniques for receiving messages from the gods employed, and the gods persuaded to descend. Prayers, offerings, and the like are accompanied by texts similar in character to those used in ordinary life when addressing rulers and government officials.

As the indigenous expression of the Chinese religious spirit, Taoism appropriated to itself the religious vocabulary current from earliest times. The word *Shen*, so much used, is the generic term for gods and spirits. The term *Shangdi* ('sovereign on high') which figures in Confucian texts along with *Tian* ('heaven') as the supreme deity, is also employed by Taoists. By the end of the Song dynasty, the Taoist religion had assimilated and developed a hierarchy of *Shen* ('gods') and *Xian* ('immortals'), which clearly reflects patterns of government common to China.

Humanity occupies a position of centrality between heaven and earth, and is thought to possess a *shen* ('spiritual principle' or 'soul'). Our spiritual makeup is said to consist of *hun* ('the positive' or '*yang* soul,' also described as 'threefold' *san hun*) and *po* ('the negative' or '*yin* soul,' also described as 'sevenfold'). At death, the *hun* lives on, but the *po* is dissolved with the body. Humanity's role is to maintain a right relationship with Heaven, and to be so in sympathy with the spiritual realm as to be capable of perceiving it and bringing the spirit environment into service. The interrelationship between man and the realm of the spirit is such that there can be both the embodiment of spirit (*huashen*, 'transformation into bodily form'), and the divinization of humanity (*huashen*, 'transformation into a divine being').

Immortals (*xian*) who achieve this status through attainment of the Dao can be both 'heavenly' and 'earthly.' Heavenly Immortals have the potential to become deities, whereas the earthly are content to remain in the human realm. There are also Dispersed Immortals (*sanxian*) who may roam between both spheres.

The importance of meditative breathing or 'breathing exercises' (*qigong*) in the task of spiritual refinement cannot be overestimated. Hints of its practice are found in literature predating the Taoist religion, but it is in Taoism that it becomes central to the search for immortality.

See also: Chinese: Translation of Theological Terms; Buddhism, Chinese; Apocrypha, Buddhist.

Bibliography

Chan Wing-tsit 1963 *A Source Book in Chinese Philosophy*. Princeton University Press, Princeton, NJ

Lau D C 1963 *Tao Te Ching*. Penguin, Harmondsworth

Saso M 1978 *The Teachings of Master Chuang*. Yale University Press, New Haven, CT

Welch H 1965 *Taoism: 'The Parting of the Way,'* rev. edn. Beacon, Boston, BA

Welch H, Seidel H 1979 *Facets of Taoism*. Yale University Press, New Haven, CT

Theosophy

J. Algeo

Theosophy is a religious philosophy emphasizing personal experience of the transcendent. In a general sense it is present in such diverse traditions as Gnosticism, Vedanta, Sufism, Mahāyāna Buddhism, and Taoism. The term was used by Neoplatonists, the Protestant mystic Jakob Böhme, and early Swedenborgians. It is best known, however, through the Theosophical Society of H. P. Blavatsky and H. S. Olcott, founded in 1875. That organization was a major influence on the twentieth-century revival of Buddhism and Hinduism and on the introduction of Eastern concepts to the West. While identifying Theosophy as a contemporary statement of the 'perennial philosophy' or 'Wisdom Tradition,' the Theosophical Society has also been a primary source for ideas identified as 'New Thought' or 'New Age.'

The first popular use of the term *karma* in the *Oxford English Dictionary* is by the theosophist A. P. Sinnett. Other terms, with the concepts they represent, also owe their current use in large measure to theosophical literature: *akashic records* (the memory of nature), *astral* (as in *astral body* or *astral plane*, referring to a subtler form of matter than the dense physical but coexisting in the same space as the physical world), *aura* (a subtle energy field around people and things), *chakra* (an energy center in the subtle counterparts of the human body), *elemental* (an entity or energy capable of producing physical manifestations), *mahatma* (literally 'great soul,' one who has evolved beyond the ordinary human state), *mantra* (a formula of language whose repetition has a psychological or physical effect), *the Path* (a way of life involving study, meditation, and service as a regimen of spiritual development), *plane* (a dimension of space extending into other forms of matter than the physical), *pralaya* (a quiescent state between periods of activity), *prana* (vital energy), *ray* (any of seven emanations from the divine source of life, of which all beings are expressions), *reincarnation*, and *yoga* (with much of its terminology).

Theosophy developed an extensive but less well-known technical vocabulary, much of it borrowed from Sanskrit. Certain of its foundational works ('Stanzas of Dzyan' and *The Voice of the Silence*) are supposed to be translated from a mystery language called Senzar, which is in a sense the 'sacred language' of contemporary Theosophy but whose identity is moot. Blavatsky's comments about Senzar suggest it is comparable to Jungian archetypes rather than an ordinary spoken language.

Bibliography

Algeo J 1988 *Senzar: The Mystery of the Mystery Language*. Theosophical History Centre, London

Cranston S 1993 *HPB: The Extraordinary Life and Influence of Helena Blavatsky, Founder of the Modern Theosophical Movement*. Putnam's, New York

Ellwood R 1986 *Theosophy: A Modern Expression of the Wisdom of the Ages*. Theosophical Publishing House, Wheaton, IL

Zoroastrianism

A. V. Williams

Zoroastrianism is the ancient religious tradition, otherwise known as 'Mazdaism' or 'Zarathuštrianism,' founded by the Iranian prophet Zarathuštra. Precise dating of Zarathuštra is impossible, but it is widely thought that he must have flourished before 1000 BCE and probably around 1200 BCE in the area northeast of present day Iran. The religion has been transmitted in a faithful form down to the twentieth century thanks to the highly conservative priesthood who have maintained both a scriptural and liturgical tradition of high antiquity. There are presently about 140,000 Zoroastrians in the world, belonging to two language groups: the Persian-speaking Iranian Zoroastrians and the Gujarati- and English-speaking Parsis of India.

The scriptures preserved as supremely holy by Zoroastrians throughout history are the *Gāthās*, 17 metrical 'hymns' composed in an otherwise unattested Eastern Iranian language known as 'Gathic Avestan' (see *Avestan*). This is an archaic form of Younger Avestan in which the rest of the Avesta was transmitted orally for centuries and which was eventually committed to writing, probably in the fifth century CE. The *Gāthās* are a small part of the surviving canon in Avestan, but that too is only a fraction of the original Great Avesta of 21 divisions (Avestan *nask*) which has been lost since the Arab conquest of Iran in the seventh century CE.

The *Gāthās* are believed to be the inspired compositions of Zarathuštra himself. They are lyrical, poetic dialogues and meditations between the supreme divinity Ahura Mazdā, 'the Wise Lord,' and himself. They are difficult to translate, not least because they are highly condensed in expression and cryptic in metaphorical allusion. Linguistic and content interpretation is helped by comparison with the contemporary Indian *Rig Veda*. The *Gāthās* are arranged according only to their metrical schemes and it is thus impossible to be certain of the evolution of Zarathuštra's thought from a straightforward reading. The prophet's teachings, which inform all the Zoroastrian religion, are moral and ethical in character, with a strong spiritual urgency exhorting humankind to follow divinely created 'truth,' or 'righteousness' (Avestan *Aša*), rather than the demonically created 'lie' (Avestan *druj̆*). Ahura Mazdā created all good creatures, both spiritual beings (his 'blessed immortals,' Avestan *aməša spənta* and 'worshipful beings,' Avestan *yazata*) and physical creations (humankind, benevolent animals, plants, water, fire, and sky). An entity wholly other than Ahura Mazdā, known as Angra Mainyu 'the hostile spirit,' perpetrates evil in the universe, having invaded it and brought death to the world with his own evil creation of spiritual demons (Avestan *daēva*) and evil physical agents corrupted by him, evil men (Avestan *drəgvant*), the wolf species and noxious creatures (Avestan *xrafstra*). Through worship and through cultivation of the spiritual qualities exemplified in the 'blessed immortals,' men and women may cultivate their own righteousness and thereby help Ahura Mazdā to overcome the forces of Angra Mainyu in the physical world. The religion is strongly eschatological in character, from the *Gāthās* onwards, as it looks forward to the complete victory of goodness and wisdom over Angra Mainyu and all his evil brood at a time called 'the making wonderful' (Avestan *frašōkərəti*). This is a regeneration of the whole cosmos, whereafter evil will have been expelled forever, and it is preceded by a resurrection and last judgement of all souls. In the present time before the end, each soul is judged soon after it leaves the physical state, and according to its accumulation of merit it goes either to a heavenly or to a hellish state to await the final judgment and *Frašōkərəti*. The individual human soul is seen to be directly engaged in the cosmic struggle against evil and the ethos of the religion is one of valiant and active participation in a corporate endeavor for the sake of truth.

The *Gāthās* are enclosed in the manuscripts and in the liturgical rites (Avestan *Yasna*) by the *Yasna Haptanhaiti* ('Worship of the Seven Sections'), which is also in Gathic Avestan (see *Avestan*). The Younger Avesta comprises liturgical texts and prayers, the *Yašts*, hymns to the *yazatas*; *Vīdaēvadāta*, 'Law Against the Demons'; *Visperad*, 'Worship of All the Masters'; *Nyāyeš* and *Gāh*, regular prayers; *Xorda Avesta*, prayer book. All these texts, except the *Yašts*, have traditionally been interpreted in the light of the *Zand*, 'scriptural elucidation,' in a Middle Iranian language, Pahlavi (see *Pahlavi*). Some lost Avestan texts survive only in their Pahlavi *Zand*. There was originally a *Zand* in the Avestan language and in other Iranian languages, but these were replaced by the imposition of the Pahlavi *Zand* by the last Zoroastrian dynasty, the Sasanians (224–651 CE). The Pahlavi books are the principal sources for knowledge of Zoroastrian cosmology and eschatology, mythology, philosophy, ritual, and theology, composed between the sixth and tenth centuries CE on the basis of the much older, oral religious tradition and knowledge of the *Avesta*. The main record for Zoroastrian cosmology and religious mythology is the so-called '*Bundahišn*,' 'Creation.' For theology and philosophy, there is the voluminous *Dēnkard*, 'Acts of the Religion,' in seven extant books. Many other smaller texts in Pahlavi survive, most of which have now appeared in scholarly editions and translations.

After the tenth century Zoroastrians abandoned writing in Pahlavi in favor of New Persian in Arabic script. The Zoroastrians of Iran were subjected to forcible conversion and oppression by Islam until the present century. In the tenth century AD a group of the faithful migrated to western India where they settled and became known as 'Parsis' (i.e., 'Persians'), enjoying religious freedom and material success in trade and, in modern times, in commerce and industry. They adopted Gujarati as their language, and from the twelfth century translated the Avestan texts, and some of the Pahlavi texts, into Sanskrit and Old Gujarati. Other texts were transcribed, and hence interpreted, from the cryptic Pahlavi script into the clearer Avestan alphabet: in this form they are known as 'Pazand' texts (literally 'by interpretation'). There is also a group of texts known as the 'Persian *Rivāyats*' dating from the fifteenth to eighteenth centuries which were Irani Zoroastrian written answers to Parsi questions on matters of religious ritual, observance, and morality.

In modern times, the main population center of the Zoroastrian community has been in urban Bombay and, to a lesser extent, Tehran, although small rural communities do survive in India and Iran. The Parsi and Irani Zoroastrians (the latter since the declaration of the Islamic Republic of Iran) have formed diaspora communities abroad on all five continents. The religion continues to be a mainstay of identity for Zoroastrians, although change in the structure of the community, through education and economic improvement, has brought with it a polarization of 'orthodox' and 'reformist' tendencies into disharmonious sectarian divisions.

Bibliography

Boyce M 1968 Middle Persian literature. In: Spuler B (ed.) *Iranistik* I.4.2.1. E. J. Brill, Leiden

Boyce M 1975, 1982 *A History of Zoroastrianism. Vol. I: The Early Period. Vol. II: Under the Achaemenians.* E. J. Brill, Leiden

Duchesne-Guillemin J 1962 *La religion de l'Iran ancien.* Paris

Gershevitch I 1968 Old Iranian literature. In: Spuler B (ed.) *Handbuch der Orientalistik.* E. J. Brill, Leiden

Menasce J de 1983 Zoroastrian Pahlavi writings. In: Yarshater E (ed.) *Cambridge History of Iran*, vol. 3. Cambridge University Press, Cambridge

West E W 1904 Pahlavi literature. In: Geiger W, Kuhn E (eds.) *Grundriss der Iranischen Philologie*, vol. II. K. J. Trübner, Strasbourg

Zaehner R C 1956 *The Teachings of the Magi: A Compendium of Zoroastrian Beliefs.* George Allen and Unwin, London

SECTION II

Sacred Texts and Translations

Introduction

J. F. A. Sawyer

Sacred texts have a central role to play in most religious traditions and the language in which they are written and read is often a matter of crucial importance. In Islam the Qur'an represents the actual words of the deity, which were delivered directly, in Arabic, to Muhammad in the early seventh century CE, and must only be read in Arabic. Thus for the majority of ordinary Muslims throughout the world, who have no knowledge of Arabic, translation into the vernacular is officially discouraged and the Qur'an recited in the original language with amazing devotion and accuracy, but minimal understanding. Similar conservatism applies to the reading of Sanskrit texts· in modern Hindu temples, Avestan texts in Zoroastrian worship, and the Bible in Hebrew, even in the more liberal or progressive Jewish synagogues. In some cases it is the language of a widely used translation that assumes this role as in some varieties of Christianity where Greek, Latin, Slavonic, Syriac, Ge'ez, and other versions, not to mention King James Authorized Version, have been treated with the same awe as if they were the original. The same applies to some translations of the Buddhist canon which are in many cases preferred to the original Pali.

Elaborate scribal and grammatical techniques were worked out to ensure that the sacred text was accurately transmitted. Scribes engaged in copying a sacred text, the Jewish masoretes, for example, and Japanese Buddhist scribes, worked under the strictest rules governing writing materials and procedures. They also devised elaborate systems of 'pointing' to preserve correctly every minute detail of the text after Hebrew had ceased to be the first language of the Jews. Sacred scripts or 'hieroglyphics' were sometimes invented with a special religious function, and exquisite calligraphy evolved as in Islamic art and the great monastic manuscript traditions of mediaeval Europe. In the Hindu tradition, by contrast, the primary form of language is speech, not writing, and the Veda was transmitted orally. Here too linguistic precision was necessary for the success of the ritual, and astonishing feats of memory are documented which preserve the text over thousands of years as accurately as any manuscript tradition. Concern for the accurate oral transmission of Sanskrit texts also led to the development of a sophisticated theory of phonetics, pioneered by Pāṇini in the fourth century BCE.

The authorship and date of most of the world's sacred texts are often surrounded in legend. This applies to the Hebrew Bible, reputed to go back to Moses at Sinai, and the Qur'an believed to have been revealed to Muhammad in early seventh century CE Arabia. A similar miraculous aura surrounds the origin of the Septuagint, an official Greek translation of the Hebrew Bible, said to be the work of seventy two scholars who produced identical versions of the Hebrew text though working independently. The Book of Mormon is believed to have had an equally miraculous origin in nineteenth century America. Modern scholars of ancient texts have devised elaborate techniques of textual and literary criticism, often backed up with archaeological evidence, such as the Dead Sea Scrolls, the Nag Hammadi texts, and the Cairo Genizah, to establish as accurately as possible what the situation actually was. But in most communities, the authority of a sacred text is closely bound up with firmly held beliefs about its origin and special nature.

Canonization is a complex and lengthy process culminating in a decision taken by a religious leader or institution at a definite point in time, as to which texts are sacred and which are not. Such a decision may then be challenged at a later period, as for example, in the history of Christianity where many of the sixteenth century Reformers, led by Martin Luther, rejected as noncanonical certain Old Testament books which had been part of Christian scripture since the Church councils of the fourth and fifth centuries. Such rejected books are known collectively as the Apocrypha. There are apocryphal Buddhist texts as well. In the history of the Bible some books were accepted as canonical by the Coptic

Church of Egypt, the Ethiopian Church and other forms of Eastern Christianity, but never canonized elsewhere in Christian tradition: these are collectively known by the modern term Pseudepigrapha.

Translations frequently come to be treated almost as sacred texts in their own right. The legend of the miraculous origin of the Septuagint has already been mentioned, but the Latin Vulgate, the Syriac Peshitta, Luther's German Bible and King James' Authorized Version assumed a similar role in terms of authority and even infallibility. Augustine is said to have used the Vulgate as a means of divination; and there are tales of English speaking believers using the Authorized Version in the same way.

Apocrypha, Buddhist

L. Lancaster

Starting in the middle of the second century CE, Buddhist monks from Central Asia began to translate Sanskrit and Prakrit texts into Chinese. These texts were called *ching*, the term used to define the classics of Chinese philosophy and statecraft. In the following centuries, especially the fifth to the tenth, texts began to appear that claimed to be from India or copied the style of Buddhist sutras. However, from the vocabulary and the style of composition it can be established that these were written or compiled within China. The term apocrypha refers to these pseudographs.

The early cataloguers of the Buddhist texts were aware of these apocryphal materials and there was an attempt to purge the monastic libraries of this type of text. Therefore, many of the texts were not widely disseminated because they were not included in the copy centers that preserved and distributed the manuscripts of the translations of Indian originals. In other cases, the apocryphal texts came to be fully accepted as authentic translations of the teaching of the Buddha and are still held in high esteem. The *Ta cheng ch'i hsin lun* ('Awakening of Faith'), for example, which has been central to the development of East Asian Buddhism, is sometimes given the Sanskrit title *Mahāyānaśraddhotpadaśastra* and said to have been composed by the great Indian Buddhist master Aśvaghoṣa. Another example is the *Śuraṅgama Sutra* which is said to have been translated by Pāramiti in 705 CE. For those that were included in the accepted list of Buddhist *ching*, the printing of the canon by the Northern Sung dynasty insured continued access by the Buddhist community.

In the early part of the twentieth century, Cave 17 at Dunhuang in Western China was found to contain thousands of manuscripts, all dating before 1000 CE. Among these were a number of previously unknown apocryphal texts. Using these, scholars are able to give a better view of the nature of lay and even monastic practices not reported in the canonic literature. In the apocryphal texts, we see Buddhist thought from India brought into the Chinese sphere, and such items of doctrine as the Five Precepts of the Buddhist community in India associated with the Five Virtues of Confucian teachings and the Five Elements, that held such an important place in Chinese philosophical discourse. An example of this is the *T'i wei po li ching* 'The Sutra of Trapuśa and Bhallika' compiled in the Northern Wei about 460 by T'an ching. The use of this type of material has been of importance to scholars who study Chinese popular culture and religion.

See also: Buddhist Canons: Translations; Buddhism, Chinese.

Bibliography

Buswell R E 1990 *Chinese Buddhist Apocrypha*. University of Hawaii Press, Honolulu

Apocrypha, Christian

J. F. A. Sawyer

The Old Testament apocrypha contains those books accepted as scripture by the early Church, but not in the Hebrew Bible. They are also referred to as 'ecclesiastical' (as opposed to Jewish) and 'deutero-canonical.' The following are the apocryphal works contained in both Catholic and Orthodox Bibles: *Wisdom of Solomon, Ecclesiasticus* (*Wisdom of Jesus ben Sira* or *Sirach*), *Baruch, Tobit, Judith, 1 & 2 Maccabees, Additions to Esther and Additions to Daniel* (*Prayer of Azariah, Song of the Three Young Men, Susanna, Bel and the Dragon*). They are examples of Hellenistic Jewish literature, most of them originally written in Greek between 200 BCE and 70 CE, and preserved in early manuscripts of the Greek Bible (see *Septuagint*). Although never included in the Hebrew Bible, some remained part of Jewish tradition, particularly Sirach, Judith, Tobit, and Maccabees. A Hebrew text of Sirach is known from a fragment discovered at Massada (first century CE) and extensive manuscripts from the Genizah (see Cairo Genizah). Already Jerome had doubts about the apocryphal books, and did not include them in his Latin version (see Vulgate). But it was Luther and Calvin who finally separated them from the rest of scripture, and most Protestant Bibles now omit them altogether.

The 'Apocryphal New Testament' contains a collection of writings, mostly similar in form to the canonical Gospels and Acts, but of later and sectarian origin, e.g. Gospel according to the Hebrews, Gospel of Thomas, Acts of Pilate, Acts of Paul and Thecla, Acts of Thomas, the Apocalypse of Peter. As such texts were officially rejected from the canon of Greek and Latin scripture at an early stage, they survive for the most part in Coptic, Syriac, Armenian, and Arabic versions, the languages of oriental Christianity.

See also: Bible; Christianity in the Near East; Luther, M.; Nag Hammadi Texts; Peshitta; Septuagint.

Bibliography

Charles R H 1913 *The Apocrypha and Pseudepigrapha of the Old Testament in English*, vol. 1. Oxford University Press, Oxford

Henneke E, Schneemelcher W, Wilson R McL 1963–5 *New Testament Apocrypha*, 2 vols., Lutterworth

Kraft R A, Nickelsberg G W E (eds.) 1986 *Early Judaism and its Modern Interpreters*. Scholars Press, Atlanta, GA/ Fortress Press, Philadelphia, PA

Metzger B 1957 *An Introduction to the Apocrypha*. Oxford University Press, Oxford

Bible

J. C. L. Gibson

1. The Biblical Languages

The earliest part of the Bible, the 'Hebrew Bible,' comprising most of what Christians call the 'Old Testament,' was composed in a literary form of the Hebrew language spoken in ancient Israel before the Babylonian Exile of the sixth century BCE. This classical language was, because of its prestige, still being used for literary purposes as late as the time of Christ, as the Dead Sea Scrolls have shown. But after the Exile, it came increasingly under the influence of a still evolving spoken Hebrew which itself eventually attained literary status with the publication of the Mishnah around 200 CE. It was during the post-Exilic period that Aramaic, originally the language of Syria but by this time an official language of the Persian Empire, also began to be spoken in Palestine and as time went on to affect (and be affected by) Hebrew (see *Aramaic, Jewish*). A literary form of Imperial Aramaic gained entrance to the Hebrew Bible with the books of Ezra and Daniel. By the time of Christ, spoken Aramaic was especially strong in Galilee, but probably most of Palestine's population were at least competent in it as well as in spoken (i.e., proto-Mishnaic) Hebrew. This spoken Jewish Aramaic also attained literary status in the early Christian centuries, notably in the Targums (Aramaic translations of the Old Testament for Palestinian and other Eastern Jews who no longer knew Hebrew) and the Talmud. (The contemporary Aramaic used by Christians in the Levant and Mesopotamia is known as 'Syriac' (see *Syriac, Christian*).

The picture sketched above is a complicated one, and it becomes even more complicated when the long centuries of scribal transmission are taken into account. The manuscript sources on which modern printed Hebrew Bibles are based reflect the work of the so-called 'Masoretes,' the Jewish scribes and editors responsible in the final centuries of the first millennium CE for preserving, annotating and above all adding vocalization and accentual signs to the received consonantal text. This in effect means that students of Biblical Hebrew work with texts whose consonantal shape is ancient but whose vocalization records developments in phonology which were still taking place in the academies (if not by this late date in daily life) up to 1,000 years after the last words of the Hebrew Bible were written (see *Masoretic Tradition*).

But that is not all. The consonantal text itself shows evidence of having been heavily standardized before the Massoretes received it. In the case of the individual books, it can therefore be taken as representing only very partially the state of the language when each of them was first committed to writing. This means that to a very large extent, particularly for the period before the Exile, the evidence of Hebrew dialectal variation and of phonological and morphological change has been suppressed. Some reconstruction is possible with the aid of epigraphic finds in Hebrew, Aramaic, and other related northwest Semitic languages like Phoenician and Ugaritic (see *Ugaritic*). But welcome as such extrabiblical sources are, whether early like the Ugaritic tablets or late like the Dead Sea Scrolls (see *Dead Sea Scrolls*), there is still a long way to go before a fullscale Grammar of Biblical Hebrew from its beginnings in the time of David to the time of the Masoretes nearly two millennia later can be written.

With the Septuagint, a third-century BCE translation of the Hebrew Bible for the use of Jews living in Egypt and the wider Mediterranean diaspora, a non-Semitic language appears on the biblical scene. Hellenistic Greek had by this time become the lingua franca of the whole eastern Mediterranean, and in Egypt especially, but also all along the Levantine coast, it was beginning to contest the sphere of currency of Imperial Aramaic. The language of the Septuagint reflects the variety of Hellenistic (or as it is sometimes called 'koine' or 'common') Greek spoken in Alexandria but, being translation Greek, it is also suffused with Hebrew stylistic, and even sometimes grammatical, features (see *Septuagint*).

The Greek of St Paul, the Gospels and the other Christian writings which make up what is known as 'the New Testament' part of the Bible, is everywhere affected by Septuagint Greek but in itself reflects a rather later variety of Hellenistic Greek spoken in Palestine. How far this spoken Greek had spread among the general population of the country is uncertain, but the fact that some of Jesus' disciples had both Semitic and Greek names (e.g., Simon Peter) suggests that it was well known at least in Galilee and that therefore many people in Palestine were able with varying competencies and in varying situations to use three spoken languages (Hebrew, Aramaic, and Greek). In some books, the Greek is of a high literary quality, like the Hellenistic Greek written by contemporary Jewish authors like Philo and Josephus, but in others it is closer to the demotic Greek of the thousands of papyri known from Egypt; and particularly in the Gospels and the opening chapters of Acts it exhibits many features that are best explained from Aramaic interference. The survival of a few transliterated Aramaic words and phrases in these books certainly suggests that Jesus did his public preaching in Aramaic; and the presence of these and of the other features just mentioned has given rise to a long-running debate about whether parts of the Gospels and Acts, notably those containing the recorded sayings of Jesus, may not go back to sources or earlier drafts in Aramaic. Early Syriac and Coptic sources are an important additional source in this detective pursuit.

The linguistic data with which New Testament scholars have to deal are therefore also complex, though they cover a shorter time-scale than the Old Testament data.

2. Biblical Scholarship and Linguistics

The biblical languages were, along with Classical Greek and Latin, at the center of language study in the period of the Renaissance and for several centuries thereafter when language as a topic of academic investigation meant the language of prestigious literary texts. Biblical scholars also took enthusiastically to the rise in the nineteenth century of the discipline of comparative philology which gave them the tools with which to trace and evaluate the development and relationship of the northwest Semitic languages and the various forms of Hellenistic Greek. The same century saw, moreover, a massive influx of written archaeological finds bearing on the Bible, to the decipherment and editing of which the techniques of comparative philology seemed eminently suited. Finally, such philological and textual activities fitted neatly into the wider program of biblical scholarship in that period which was chiefly historical in its thrust as it attempted to get behind the traditional text of Scripture and uncover its literary and theological origins and growth. Ecclesiastical feathers may have been ruffled by its findings, but academically at the beginning of the twentieth century biblical philology was confident about its role and its methods.

It should come as no surprise therefore to find it reacting with suspicion to the revolutionary trends in language study set in motion by Saussure in the 1920s. All of a sudden living and spoken and nonliterary languages were being given priority, and synchronic interests were taking precedence over diachronic. Biblical scholars like other Classical linguists felt threatened and did not immediately see the relevance of the new ways to their kind of problems. But revolutions pass, and before long a partial consensus began to emerge between traditional and modern linguists. The real surprise is that at this stage biblical linguists should have chosen to retreat further into their inherited fortress. They have continued to produce accurate editions of newly discovered texts like the Ugaritic tablets or the Dead Sea Scrolls, already mentioned, or like the Coptic library from Nag Hammadi (see *Nag Hammadi Texts*). But in more central language pursuits there is a distinct impression of a once formidable machine faltering through neglect and running out of steam. Most of the major reference grammars and dictionaries in use are reprints or updatings of works issued at the end of nineteenth century or the beginning of twentieth; and with very few exceptions (e.g., Sawyer 1976) student textbooks are still thirled to latinate terminology and latinate models of analysis.

Fortunately, the picture is not all black. Since 1960, there have been a number of studies of biblical languages which have either been consciously based on the methods of this or that modern school or, perhaps more encouragingly, have shown their authors to be instinctively au fait, in a way that linguists trained today would recognize, with how things should be done. Of the first kind one might mention in phonology S. Morag's (1961) analysis of the Hebrew vocalization system; and in grammar F. I. Andersen's (1974) 'tagmemic' treatment of the Hebrew sentence, and G. Niccacci's (1990) 'text linguistics' study of the Hebrew verb. The second kind is represented by works such as R. Polzin's (1976) typological examination of late Biblical Hebrew prose and E. C. Maloney's (1981) investigation of Semitic influence on the Greek of St Mark's Gospel. These still look broadly traditional, but in their different ways show a modern understanding of what is involved in language contact and interference. The Hebrew Syntax study by Waltke and O'Connor (1990) makes considerable use of linguistics and has some pages explaining its terminology and possible application, as do D. A. Dawson's monograph for Hebraists and D. A. Black's for students of New Testament Greek. These should help future biblical specialists to get on terms, if very belatedly, with what is 'old hat' to students in other language disciplines. But at the moment, most of the books mentioned above are not well known or, where they are known, are not the first to be consulted.

The same judgment holds in the case of E. G. Nida's excellent work on translation theory on behalf of the Bible Societies, which is frequently mentioned with approval by modern linguists but is rarely listed in the bibliographies produced by biblical scholars (Nida 1964) (see *Nida, E.*). The work of James Barr is perhaps the exception that proves the rules; for it has had a very noticeable effect (see *Barr, J.*). Possibly it is because he has used linguistics to illumine areas of language study, in particular semantics, that impinge closely on theological concerns (see also Louw 1982). A study by Cotterell and Turner (1989), which is devoted largely to the bearing of linguistics on New Testament interpretation, follows and extends Barr's critique in the direction of discourse analysis. Finally, two important new dictionaries, a Hebrew one from Sheffield and a Greek one from the Bible Societies, deserve to be mentioned. Both are based on sound modern semantic and lexicographical principles and they ought, as they become more widely used among students, to have a major influence for good.

It looks as though at long last biblical scholarship is beginning to work with rather than against the grain of contemporary linguistic endeavor. It is not before time. But a warning too is needed. The recourse to linguistics by biblical scholars cannot be unconnected with a general moving away on their part from earlier historical and source-critical concerns towards studying 'the text as it is.' the emphasis of linguistics on the synchronic level accords well with this new interest—but so does a conservative attitude to Scripture! That is why it must be stressed that there are many diachronic problems in the biblical languages still awaiting solution.

See also: Hebrew, Biblical and Jewish; Bible Translations, Ancient Versions; Judaism; Christianity in the Near East; Apocrypha, Christian.

Bibliography

Andersen F I 1974 *The Sentence in Biblical Hebrew. JanL*, Series Practica 231, Mouton, The Hague

Barr J 1961 *The Semantics of Biblical Language*. Oxford University Press, London

Barr J 1968 *Comparative Philology and the Text of the Old Testament*. Clarendon Press, Oxford

Black D A 1988 *Linguistics for Students of New Testament Greek*. Baker Book House, Grand Rapids, MI

Clines D J A (ed.) 1989 *Dictionary of Classical Hebrew*, Sheffield Academic Press, Sheffield

Cotterell P, Turner M 1989 *Linguistics and Biblical Interpretation*. SPCK, London

Dawson D A 1994 *Text-Linguistics and Biblical Hebrew*. Sheffield Academic Press, Sheffield

Louw J P 1982 *Semantics of New Testament Greek*. Fortress Press, Philadelphia, PA

Maloney E C 1981 *Semitic Interference in Marcan Syntax*. Scholar's Press, Chico, CA

Morag S 1961 *The Vocalization Systems of Arabic, Hebrew and Aramaic. JanL*, **XIII**. Mouton, The Hague

Niccacci A 1990 *The Syntax of the Verb in Classical Hebrew Prose* (transl. Watson W G E). Sheffield Academic Press, Sheffield

Nida E 1964 *Towards a Science of Translating: With Special Reference to Principles and Procedures Involved in Bible Translating*. E. J. Brill, Leiden

Polzin R 1976 *Late Biblical Hebrew: Toward an Historical Typology of Biblical Hebrew Prose*. Harvard Semitic Monographs 12. Scholar's Press, Chico, CA

Sawyer J F A 1976 *A Modern Introduction to Biblical Hebrew*. Oriel, Stocksfield

Waltke B K, O'Connor M 1990 *An Introduction to Biblical Hebrew Syntax*. Eisenbrauns, Winona Lake, IN

Bible Translations, Ancient Versions

T. Muraoka

Ancient versions of the Bible are early translations of the Bible made from the original Hebrew/Aramaic and Greek. Some scholars include also translations indirectly made from primary versions. Because of the religious nature of the Bible, the general cultural significance of Judaism and Christianity, and the antiquity of these versions, they present a range of unique linguistic features.

1. Reasons for Translating the Bible

Written translation as distinct from oral interpreting has been, and still is, an important cultural and sociolinguistic phenomenon. This is particularly true of the Bible, largely due to its contents, its literary quality, and the place the religions based on it have occupied, and continue to occupy, in the private and communal lives of religious communities throughout history. In many speech communities a Bible in their own speech marks the first written expression of their language or dialect. A translation or a retranslation of the Bible may set a new benchmark in the written form of the language concerned, as happened in the case of Luther's German translation of the Bible (see *Luther, Martin*) or the King James Version of the English Bible (see *English Bible*). There are countless examples of Bible translation and translators contributing significantly to linguistics and philology: for example, William Carey (see *Carey, William*), an eighteenth-century English Baptist missionary to India, and the work associated with the Summer Institute of Linguistics (see *Summer Institute of Linguistics*). In certain cases the Bible is the oldest, or even the only, written record of a particular language as in the case of Old Church Slavonic and Gothic.

Bible translation has a very long history. The oldest of the ancient versions, the Greek translation of the Hebrew Bible, commonly known as 'Septuagint,' must, at least in part, date back to the third century BCE. Whilst written translation was practiced extensively in the ancient Near East, the production of the Septuagint must have been an unprecedented event in the literary history of the ancient world. Even the Pentateuch, believed to have been done in Greek first, is a sizeable piece of work.

One important and interesting question is why the Bible was translated into a particular language. In modern times, Bible translation is either part of missionary efforts or a response to the liturgical and educational needs of a particular religious community. Such an explanation would most likely apply to many ancient translations of the Bible, for example, the Old Latin version, and the Syriac Bible, the so-called 'Peshitta.' The same applies to many 'daughter' versions, that is, translations done not directly from the original Hebrew/Aramaic or Greek, but from one of the major ancient versions. In the case of the Septuagint there exists an ancient document of uncertain date (probably second century BCE), the so-called '*Letter of Aristeas*,' which purports to inform the reader precisely on this matter. According to this document, the translation was officially commissioned by the king, Ptolemy II Philadelphus (285–246 BCE) on a recommendation from the librarian of the famed library in Alexandria, who wished to fill the striking gap in its collection. This would seem to imply that the Greek Old Testament or the Pentateuch owes its origin to the intellectual curiosity of the pagan world. This information as well as other details in the document are dismissed by most scholars as historically unreliable. They conjecture, instead, that a more plausible reason for the production of the translation was the internal need of the Hellenized Jewish community in Alexandria and other parts of the Diaspora where the knowledge of Hebrew had sunk to a very low level.

A similar argument is often put forward to account for the genesis of a great variety of Aramaic renditions of the Hebrew Bible, the so-called 'Targum' (plural Targums or Targumim). A serious difficulty with this thesis has been presented by a fragment of the Targum of the book of Job from Qumran Cave 11, datable to the second century BCE at the latest, and another much smaller fragment from Cave 4 (first century CE). Whether the version was produced at Qumran or imported from outside, members of the religious community were certainly capable of a respectable Neo-Classical Hebrew attested by many of their compositions. Furthermore, the book of Job has never had a place in the official Jewish liturgy. It may be suggested that the book was read in Aramaic there to meet, at least in the case of this particular book, the intellectual need of the resident Jewish community.

A particular line of interpretation or range of possible interpretations embodied in a given version constituted a major reason for the activity of subsequent revision in the case of versions for which one can postulate a single original translation. Likewise, the possibility of publicizing a particular interpretation of the original text led to parallel or independent translations as in the case of a great variety of partial or fragmentary pre-Vulgate Latin translations of the Bible. Jerome's fresh retranslation of the Hebrew Bible into Latin, which would subsequently form part of the Vulgate, stemmed from his dissatisfaction with what he regarded as imperfections in the current Latin version which was based on a form of the Greek version: he strove after what he called '*hebraica veritas*,' 'Hebrew truth,' to attain which he sought Hebrew tuition by Jewish scholars. Incidentally, the Vulgate is one of those very few ancient Bible translations the circumstances of whose origin are well documented as they were endeavors undertaken by well-known individuals.

2. Translator-oriented and Reader-oriented Approaches

A whole corpus of commentaries by the Church fathers, most of whom were ignorant of Hebrew/Aramaic and some of whom will have had little Greek, were engaged in the exegesis of biblical books through the medium of these translations. This interest in the meaning of versions of the Bible on their own merits may be characterized as reader-oriented in contradistinction to a translator-oriented approach whose primary concerns are the relationships between the translation and its original text or texts. Such a concern is represented first and foremost by textual critics attempting first to establish the translation's *Vorlage* (i.e., the original text which lay before the translator) and then to use the critical text of the version thus established for the purpose of an enquiry into the history of the original text and its ultimate recovery. Practitioners of the reader-oriented approach, however, are more interested in how the translation was understood and interpreted, most of the time independently of the original text. Modern examples include an ongoing series *La Bible d'Alexandrie* (1986–) under the general leadership of M. Harl, and *The Aramaic Bible* (1987–) under the editorship of M. McNamara. An attempt to produce a modern Septuagint lexicon (T. Muraoka) is another expression of the same interest.

3. Basic Philological Work

Any serious work on a Classical text necessarily involves text-critical and philological work aimed at either establishing a critical (original) text of the version concerned, or tracing the evolution of various independent translations or revisions of an originally single translation. In spite of considerable advances made in the late twentieth century, this text-critical work is not yet complete for any of the major ancient versions of the Bible. A great deal of impetus is provided for this type of work by the occasional discovery of new written materials such as the Dead Sea Scrolls and related documents, the Cairo Genizah fragments, and the complete Palestinian Targum of the Pentateuch known as 'Codex Neofiti 1.'

This text-critical concern is by no means a modern phenomenon. As early as the second/third centuries CE the noted theologian and Bible scholar Origen of Caesarea appreciated the importance of the transmission history of the Greek Bible, and produced a gigantic six-column version of the entire Old Testament, the *Hexapla*, which set out the Hebrew text, its transliteration in Greek letters, and four different Greek versions. Three centuries later, Paul, Bishop of Tella in Mesopotamia, conscious of the importance of Origen's work, prepared a literal Syriac translation of a Greek column of the *Hexapla*, hence known as 'Syro–Hexapla.'

4. Versions as Sources of Linguistic Information

Apart from exegetical interests arising from the ancient versions, they are also a rich source of linguistic information. Thus the Septuagint is a document of major importance for those interested in Hellenistic (Koine) Greek. A substantial proportion of examples quoted by Theodor Nöldeke (see *Nöldeke, T.*) in his standard reference grammar of Classical Syriac come from the Syriac Bible. The Aramaic Bible, due to its importance in the Jewish liturgy, not only provides a considerable amount of lexical and grammatical data on Jewish Aramaic, but one important version of it (Targum Onkelos and Jonathan) has also preserved the all-important reading tradition with vowels. This applies to the Syriac Bible too.

Whilst interference of the source-language with the target-language, whether conscious and deliberate (a slavishly literal rendition) or subconscious (an idiomatic rendition), is always real, and means that not every linguistic feature of a given translation reflects the genuine usage of the target-language, this very interaction between the two languages provides valuable material for philological/linguistic inquiries. A considerable amount of work has already been done on translation techniques in these various versions. Furthermore, when one is dealing with a source-language which itself is still imperfectly known and understood, a translation from it into a better-known target-language can be useful. There are, for example, frequent references to the ancient versions in Biblical Hebrew lexicons because very many Hebrew words occur only very rarely in the Bible and other meager ancient Hebrew documents.

5. Place of the Versions in the Jewish and Christian Communities

Serious interest in the Bible in its original languages is, in the long history of the Christian Church, a relatively recent phenomenon, going back to the Renaissance with its motto of *ad fontes* 'back to the sources,' and the Reformation with its aversion to the Vulgate. In the Jewish community too, vernacular versions, notably the Aramaic Targum and Saadia's Arabic Bible (tenth century), have played a significant role (see *Saadya Gaon*). The impact of a Bible translation is well illustrated by the Septuagint. The prestigious position held by Greek and the Hellenistic culture in the Mediterranean world and the Levant in the Hellenistic and Roman periods was a major factor in its wide acceptance and long history in the Church. Augustine, Bishop of Hippo (fifth century CE), though a native speaker of Latin, declared the Septuagint divinely inspired (*The City of God* 18: 42–43). Its acceptance by the early Church as authoritative Scripture, however, led to its rejection by Jews. It is to be assumed that all New Testament writers were thoroughly familiar with the Septuagint, and thus their writings are abundantly imbued with Septuagintalisms, in grammar and phraseology and semantics. The Greek Bible then influenced subsequent Christian writings, and certain features of Byzantine and Modern Greek become intelligible only in the light of the Septuagint and the New Testament Greek. The Septuagint further served as the version from which several ancient daughter versions were produced: Old Latin (see above), Armenian, Ethiopic, Coptic, etc. Even if it was not directly translated, it was widely consulted by many translators, revisers of earlier translations, and exegetes: Origen (see above), an old Arabic version by Hunayn (ninth century), Gothic, Syro–Hexapla (see above), and Old Church Slavonic (ninth century).

See also: Old Church Slavonic; Syriac, Christian; Aramaic, Jewish; Gothic; Peshitta; Septuagint; Targum; Vulgate; Byzantine Greek; Church Latin.

Bibliography

Ackroyd P R, Evans C F 1970 *The Cambridge History of the Bible*, vol. 1. Cambridge University Press, Cambridge

Brock S P, Fritsch C T, Jellicoe S A 1973 *A Classified Bibliography of the Septuagint*. E J Brill Leiden

Dorival G, Harl M, Munnich O 1988 *La Bible grècque des Septante: Du judaïsme hellénistique au christianisme ancien*. Edition du Cerf, Paris

Jellicoe S 1968 *The Septuagint and Modern Study*. Oxford University Press, Oxford

McNamara M 1976 Targums. In: Crim K (ed.) *The Interpreter's Dictionary of the Bible: An Illustrated Encyclopedia*. Abingdon, Nashville, TN

Metzger B M 1962 Ancient versions. In: Buttrick G A (ed.) 1976 *The Interpreter's Dictionary of the Bible: An Illustrated Encyclopedia*. Abingdon, Nashville, TN

Metzger B M 1977 *The Early Versions of the New Testament: Their Origin, Transmission, and Limitations*. Clarendon Press, Oxford

Mulder M J (ed.) 1988 *Mikra: Text, Translation, Reading and Interpretation of the Hebrew Bible in Ancient Judaism and Early Christianity*. Van Gorcum, Assen/Fortress Press, Philadelphia, PA

Swete H B 1914 *An Introduction to the Old Testament in Greek*, 2nd edn. Cambridge University Press, Cambridge

Tov E, Kraft R A 1976 Septuagint. In: Crim K (ed.) *The Interpreter's Dictionary of the Bible: An Illustrated Encyclopedia*. Abingdon, Nashville, TN

Tov E 1981 *The Text-critical Use of the Septuagint in Biblical Research*. Simor, Jerusalem

Vööbus A 1976 Syriac versions. In: Crim K (ed.) *The Interpreter's Dictionary of the Bible: An Illustrated Encyclopedia*. Abingdon, Nashville, TN

Bible Translations, Modern Period

P. C. Stine

Historically, translations of the Bible have closely followed the spread of the Church. In the earliest centuries the Church took hold and grew because its languages were the two languages used throughout the Roman Empire: Greek, the original language of the New Testament and of the first translation of the Old Testament; and Latin, the first translation of the whole Bible. By the second century CE, Syriac had become the language of the Church in the eastern Mediterranean and in Asia and as the Church spread to other areas so the need grew for further translations. The appearance of the Gothic translation in the fourth century CE (see *Wulfila*) preceded the appearance of the Latin Vulgate by Jerome (see *Jerome*) in the fifth century, which became the standard Bible of Western Christianity for over 1,000 years (see *Vulgate* and *English Bible*). Nonetheless, other translations appeared in Georgian, Armenian (see *Mesrob*), Slavonic (see *Cyril and Methodius*), German, Dutch, Spanish, Norwegian, and Hungarian, and outside Europe in Chinese (seventh century), Arabic (eighth century), and Persian (fourteenth century).

Since the late eighteenth century, the number of languages into which the Bible has been translated has grown so rapidly that there are now every year between 20 and 30 languages in which a book of the Bible is published for the first time. With very rare exceptions, these languages are spoken in Africa, Asia, or the Pacific, or are indigenous to North or South America. To render the biblical texts in these languages, translators face great linguistic and cultural barriers, and they have been forced to develop techniques and methods significantly different from those used by translators of literary or technical works in Western European languages. This has been especially true because the focus of the Bible translation has been on the information content almost to the exclusion of the literary and aesthetic.

1. The Modern Missionary Movement

The growth of the modern missionary movement and the establishment of various Bible Societies in the early part of the nineteenth century brought an astronomical increase in the number of languages into which the Bible or some part of it was translated. Whereas in the first eighteen centuries of the Common Era an average of 1.9 new translations were added per century, 448 languages were added in the nineteenth century, and in the twentieth century there has been an average of 160 new languages per decade. Table 1 shows this growth through the centuries, and for the nineteenth and twentieth centuries, through the decades. Table 2 is a statistical summary of publication in languages according to geographical distribution through 1999.

2. The Development of Professionalism in Translation

Until the mid-twentieth century, most translations were prepared by missionaries with the assistance of native speakers as informants. There were exceptions, of course, one of the most notable being the translation of Samuel Ajayi Crowther into Yoruba (see *Crowther, S. A.*).

The promotion of professional expertise, the development of translation theory, and the systematic application of principles of translation based on such theory, began with Eugene A. Nida in 1943 when he joined the staff of the American Bible Society (see *Nida, E. A.*). He recruited a professional team of linguists and biblical scholars to serve as advisers to translators all over the world. Parallel with this was the development of the Summer Institute of Linguistics which has also promoted the professionalization of translation. The focus of the work of both groups is to render the meaning of the original texts in a way which modern readers can understand. Since this can best be done by translators working in their own languages, many older missionary translations prepared in the nineteenth century and the first half of the twentieth century are being replaced by new ones prepared by native speakers. Consequently, a major thrust of both the United Bible Societies (a cooperative association of more than 100 national Bible Societies including the American Bible Society) and the Summer Institute of Linguistics has been to train people to work as translators in their own languages.

3. Principles Followed

3.1 Goals of Translation and Basic Theory

Elsewhere in the *Encyclopedia* are discussed different theories which have guided the translation of both literary and technical materials (see *Translation: History*). Translation of written documents, mainly of literary works, has been practiced for at least 2,000 years, and discussions of theory which did occur usually centered around the dichotomy of word or form versus sense.

However, the development of the discipline of linguistics, wherein the study of language changed from primarily historical and prescriptive to theoretical and descriptive, led to a number of linguistically oriented theories of translation. For Bible translation, the most influential scholar was Eugene A. Nida, who seized on a number of the features of early transformational generative grammar as basic tools of analysis. These included the concepts of surface and deep structure, and componential analysis of lexical items.

In various writings, Nida and his colleagues developed a theory of translation which was called 'Dynamic Equivalence' (see in particular Nida 1947; Nida 1964; and Nida and Taber 1969). More recently, Nida has used the term 'Functional Equivalence' (see de Waard and Nida 1986). Such translations aim at producing the closest natural equivalent in the target or receptor language. Although closeness of form is desirable, the major emphasis is on closeness of meaning, which should be expressed as naturally as possible. A popular way of expressing this approach has been to say that translators want the understanding and response of the modern readers to be as close as possible to the understanding and response of the original readers of the various books of the Bible.

To achieve functional equivalence, Nida proposes a system of translation with three stages: the first is analysis, in which the surface structure of the source language text is analyzed in terms of the grammatical relationships and the meanings of the words and combinations of words; the second stage is transfer, in which the analyzed material is transferred from the source language to the receptor language; and the third stage is restructuring , in which this material is restructured in order to make the final text acceptable and natural sounding in the receptor language.

To analyze the source texts, translators are taught how to look behind the grammatical forms of utterances to the underlying semantic categories. For example, 'the will of God' is shown to be a matter of God willing something, that is, B (God) does A (wills); 'the Book of Moses' means 'the book Moses wrote,' that is, B (Moses) does X (wrote) A (the book); and 'baptism of repentance' means 'people have someone baptize them to show that

Table 1. First-time translation into new languages.

	Century	Languages added	Decade	Language added	Cumulative total
BCE	300	1			1
	200	0			1
	100	0			1
	0	1			2
CE		3			5
	100	1			6
	200	4			10
	300	2			12
	400	0			12
	500	2			14
	600	1			15
	700	2			17
	800	0			17
	900	2			19
	1000	3			22
	1100	4			26
	1200	6			32
	1300	3			35
	1400	14			49
	1500	11			60
	1600	13			73
	1700		1800	7	80
	1800		1810	27	107
			1820	42	149
			1830	26	175
			1840	29	204
			1850	52	256
			1860	71	327
			1870	38	365
			1880	60	425
			1890	96	521
			1900	100	621
	1900		1910	103	724
			1920	97	821
			1930	147	968
			1940	78	1046
			1950	144	1190
			1960	258	1448
			1970	286	1734
			1980	153	1887
			1989	41	1928
			1999	295	2233

(Smalley W A (1991) *Translation as Mission: The Role of Bible Translation in the Modern Missionary Movement*.
Mercer University Press, Macon, GA: Update *Bulletin 188/189*, 2000, United Bible Societies, Reading, UK).

Table 2. Summary of scripture publications in 1999 by geographical area.

	At least one book	New Testaments	Complete Bibles	Total
Africa	218	267	142	627
Asia	228	212	113	553
Australia/ New Zealand/Pacific Islands	172	194	30	396
Europe	106	29	62	197
North America	41	25	7	73
Caribbean Islands/Central America/Mexico/South America	135	233	16	384
Constructed languages	2	0	1	3
Total	902	960	371	2233

Bulletin 188/189, 2000, United Bible Societies, Reading, UK.

they have repented,' that is, X (someone not specified) does A (baptizes) Y (someone else not specified) as a sign that Y does B (repents). Thus although the three have similar genitive constructions, they do not represent similar semantic relations.

Words are analyzed on the basis of componential analysis, the distinctive features being ascertained by comparing related words. Thus a word such as *remorse* has features of [+ prior bad behavior] and [+subsequent sorrow], but [−change in behavior]; the features of *conversion* include [+ prior bad behavior] and [+ change in behavior], but [−sorrow]; but the word *repentance* has the components of [+prior bad behavior], [+ sorrow], and [+ change of behavior].

Similarly, metaphors and similes are analyzed as having three features: objects of comparison, which are compared to some image of the comparison, and a basis or ground of comparison. Not all of these features are necessarily explicit in either the source or receptor language texts. In the expression. 'All ye like sheep have gone astray,' the object of comparison is 'all ye,' the image of comparison is 'sheep,' and the basis for the comparison is 'gone astray.' But in 'faith as a grain of mustard seeds,' while 'faith' is the object of comparison and 'grain of mustard seed' is the image of the comparison, the basis for the comparison is not given. Translators, when they analyze the expression, may decide to give it their own basis of comparison, and indeed, some translations have 'faith as small as a grain of mustard seed.'

What is most striking at the second or transfer stage of translation is the emphasis on preserving the content of the message at the expense of the form of the message. Idioms, for example, often must be shifted to nonidioms or to new idioms. 'To gird up the loins of the mind' may need to become 'to get ready in one's thinking.' A nonidiom such as 'faith' is quite often conveyed with an idiomatic expression in the receptor language. In Tzeltal the expression is 'to hang on to God with the heart.' In fact, much figurative language becomes nonfigurative in the transfer stage, and very often there is a shift from either generic to specific or specific to generic. In translating 'Philip' was the brother of Herod,' a word as simple as 'brother' is a problem in languages which identify only older siblings and younger siblings. Translators are forced to specify whether Herod or Philip was the elder. *Denarius*, on the other hand, is often translated simply as a 'kind of money.' (Below are listed a number of other problems in transfer.)

The third stage is restructuring. The translators need to have some understanding of varieties of language and levels of language in both the source and receptor languages so that the final text is as close as possible to the original in the way it effects the readers. Finding the right style and genre is particularly difficult. For example, while poetry is a very prominent feature of the Old Testament, poetry in modern English is not commonly read and is not a major medium of communication. In fact, to convey very weighty theological ideas through poetry would be considered laughable by many, and certainly would not reach most readers. Very commonly, then, poetry is translated as prose, although it may be printed in poetic lines.

A problem in the Gbaya language of Cameroon illustrates another common restructuring problem in Africa (see Noss 1981). There are three types of oral discourse in Gbaya. One, called *nyere mo*, refers to history. It is everyday life and expression, what a person remembers, possibly even things as far back as his grandfather, but no further. A second, called *to*, is the tale. It is transmitted narrative, that is, myths and folktales. Stories about the great heroes of long ago are used for teaching about eternal truths and what is always relevant. The third type is *lizang*, the parable. With this form past experiences or tales from times of old are applied to current situations. Each of these types of discourse has its own linguistic forms, its own special use of verb forms and action words and types of descriptive phrases.

Parables in the Bible can use the *lizang* form, but the others pose more of a problem. For the Gbaya, what is true in a Western sense, that is events that actually occurred in time, only relates to *nyere mo*, and can only refer to recent events. Things that have lasting value are the teachings of *to*, the myths. Translators must decide whether to treat Genesis, for example, as *nyere mo*, as something that actually happened (and therefore something that would be perceived as irrelevant by the Gbaya), or as *to*, myth, and therefore 'true' and relevant for the Gbaya. Obviously different styles and forms of language affect the meaning of the text quite significantly.

This system of translation recommends a series of priorities. One states that contextual consistency takes priority over verbal consistency, so that a Greek word such as *sarx* 'flesh' may in various contexts be rendered as 'flesh,' 'body,' 'human nature,' 'ethnic group,' and 'men.' Another priority is that language as it is heard when read aloud takes priority over written language, so that features such as punctuation and capitalization are never used to disambiguate. Further, the needs to the audience take priority over the actual forms of the language, so that if the audience is one not initiated into religious jargon, then theological terminology is avoided as much as possible.

Most translations prepared under this method also aim at using 'popular language.' Popular language has been defined by William Wonderly as 'the contemporary language in a form that is shared by the entire population that speaks it (Wonderly 1968). It is used primarily for languages with 'little specialization along social, occupational, and literary lines.' Such situations occur in languages where most speakers share a common cultural heritage and where the language has not been used in higher education, with the result that there has not developed a wide difference in 'educated' and 'uneducated' styles. Most languages without written literary traditions would be included.

An important related concept has been to use 'common language.' Such translations also try to reach as wide a segment of the population as possible, but in these languages there are important differences in speech within the culture, for example, between social classes or between the more highly educated and those with less schooling in the language. Examples are English, Japanese, Hindi, Russian, and Spanish. There are also differences in the language of older people and that of youth, but they do share a common vocabulary and syntax. There are differences between dialect areas, but, again, there is common ground which these dialects share. Thus common language translations do not use the full resources of the language but limit themselves to language forms that are widely understood within the area.

Although Nida's theory was based on early transformational generative grammar, translators did not have to learn that theory to practice his principles of translation. Many translators were not linguists at all, and those who were often used a variety of other theoretical models for their own linguistic analyses. One of the most prominent of these models was that of tagmemics as developed by Kenneth Pike, Robert Longacre, and others from the Summer Institute of Linguistics (SIL) (see particularly Pike 1967, Longacre 1964; see *Pike, K.*). SIL began as an organization which sent out missionaries to work in Bible translation in languages where there was no Bible, and generally no system of writing. These translators needed basic tools to help them with the analysis of the languages which they were learning. Pike, one of the early members of the organization, developed tagmemics as a very practical heuristic and field-methods' analysis system. One of the major features of the system was that it acknowledged that language was a part of the behavior of a culture, and therefore should be studied in the context. It was not used as the basis for a translation theory, however, and members of SIL have generally followed Nida's model of translation both in translation practice and in scholarly writings (see for example Larson 1984, Beekman and Callow 1974).

One of the major weaknesses of Nida's early writings was that he did not account for ways that the discourse shaped a text, and consequently much of the investigation of discourse as a feature to handle in translation has been initiated by members of SIL. Some, such as Longacre 1983, essentially expanded Pike's basic theory of tagmemics to include discourse. On the other hand, Grimes (1975), among others, used different models.

The first problem that many translators face in non-European languages is the need to develop a writing system. Many early orthographies were based on rather poor phonological analyses, and consequently were difficult to read. For example, many missionaries working in Africa failed to recognize that the languages were tonal, and published their translations using orthographies that did not mark tone. For this very simple reason, even readers who were literate in the major language of education such as English or French, often were unable to read the materials prepared in their own languages. Other features such as marking phonemic differences between aspirated and unaspirated stops could have the same effect, and if there were a number of such failures the published materials were unusable. One of Pike's greatest strengths has been in the area of phonological analysis, and in teaching methods of phonemic analysis which help ensure that translators can prepare orthographies that are both usable and teachable (see Pike 1947).

Of course, in addition to developing a writing system, it was necessary to encourage literacy. If there were no readers, no one would use the translation when it was prepared. Consequently a major part of the work of SIL and of churches and missions involved in translation has been in developing literacy materials and programs. It has often happened that different groups have developed different orthographies and methods of teaching reading, so that two or three systems may exist in the same language. Increasingly, however, governments have intervened to ensure that there are official orthographies developed.

One of the secondary benefits of these efforts in developing writing systems and literacy programs has been that translators have been responsible for gathering and publishing oral literature such as folktales and family histories. These materials have not only helped in the analysis of the languages but also have helped preserve important aspects of the culture, and heightened people's awareness of their own cultures.

3.2 Translation Problems

Producing understandable translations which are also accurate and faithful to the original presents problems of wide variety of types.

3.2.1 Lexical

One immediate problem translators face is how to handle unfamiliar words. How can one say 'wheat' in an area where it does not grow? How about 'figs'? or 'bread'? Or 'camels'? Should the translators substitute some local terms and render 'wheat' as 'maize,' 'figs' as 'mangoes,' 'bread,' as 'rice' or 'yams,' and 'camels' as 'cows'? Should 'denarius' be rendered as 'dollars' or 'pounds' or 'francs'?

Obviously some kind of adaptation has to be made, but although translators want readers of today to understand the Bible, they also feel that the translation should not sound as if the events took place just recently in the reader's own context. So if 'wheat' is not known, translators might use a word such as 'grain,' 'figs' might be compared to a local fruit in expressions such as a 'fruit like X called "fig,"' or 'bread' in some contexts can be rendered as 'food,' 'camels' might be translated as 'large beasts of burden,' and since money values change so rapidly, a 'denarius' can often be called a 'kind of money (or, coin) called "denarius,"' or 'money worth a laborer's daily wage.'

Certain key theological terms of the Bible are particularly difficult. A common problem concerns the terms for 'Devil' and 'God' and other spirit powers and forces. To give a specific example, translators in the Yala language area in the Cross River State in southeastern Nigeria were shocked to hear local people say that they would never be able to be Christians because Christians said they had to give up the Devil, but the Devil was too important to them. The problem was not that the people were any kind of Devil worshippers but rather that the wrong term had been used in translation. Translators then investigated all the terms in their language related to spirit and other forces. There were many different terms in this general area of meaning, but none of them corresponded exactly to the biblical concepts. For example, for the Yala people the spirit who was the creator and ultimate cause of everything, *Owo*, was now removed and distant from people. The powers which were concerned with the affairs of this world were not this supreme creator, although they owed their strength to that creator. So, if translators used *Owo*, for 'God,' they would then have the task of teaching that according to the Bible, God is not far away but is concerned with the daily lives of people.

One of the important spirit powers among the Yala, *Yapliija*, was the force that was behind all the shrines where people worshiped, and which also gave power to the fetishes they used. It could do mischief, cause diseases, and even kill. This was the term that the translators had chosen for Devil. But *Yapliija* could also do a great deal of good, including causing women and fields to be fertile, and protecting young children and mothers. No wonder he was important.

So the translators has to find an alternative way to render 'Devil.' The eventually chose *yapliija odwobi*, bad *yapliija* for 'demon' or 'devil,' and translated 'the Devil' as the leader of these bad spirits.

There are many similar problems. How should a language gauge distinguish between 'prophet,' 'angel,' 'apostle,' and 'messenger'? Many translations had rendered 'prophet' as 'future-teller,' but borrowed the words 'apostle' and 'angel' from English or Greek, as English has done. But in the case of 'Prophet' the translation would be wrong, and in the others the meaning would be zero, so that in both cases there is a failure to translate. It would be better to consider a 'prophet' as a 'spokesperson for God,' an 'angel' as a 'messenger from God,' and an 'apostle' as 'someone who is sent with a particular commission.'

3.2.2 Grammatical

Many problems relate to the differences in the syntax of the source languages and of the languages in which the translations are being prepared, the receptor languages. An example concerns the custom in the Bible of employing the passive construction to avoid using the name for God, as for example in the expression 'Your sins are forgiven' or 'Judge not that you be not judged.' Many West African languages do not have passive voice at all, and must supply an agent and an active verb. Other languages such as Thai do have a passive but usually use it for negative events as in 'I was beaten' (but not for 'I was rewarded').

So translators are forced by their language to supply an agent. In the case of judging, it is clear in the biblical context that it is God who judges, so that it would be acceptable to say. 'Don't judge other people so that God will not judge you.' However, in the story in Mark, chapter 2, where Jesus tells the paralytic 'Your sins are forgiven,' the problem is more delicate. If translators have Jesus say what is perhaps theologically correct, 'God forgives yours sins,' it may not account for the negative reaction of the scribes who were sitting there. They felt Jesus was blaspheming. But if a translation were 'I forgive your sins,' it would have Jesus making a claim for the authority to do something that only God could do. Some translators have solved this by saying 'I tell you God has forgiven your sins,' so that Jesus is still claiming the type of authority which accounts for the reaction of the scribes.

Each language uses direct and indirect speech in different ways. That is, in some languages one can say 'Jesus said, "I am the way, the truth, and the life,"' but in other languages the more natural way would be 'Jesus said that he was the way, the truth and the life.' And yet linguists and theologians alike would feel that possibly some of the force of the claim being made by Jesus is lost in this way. So translators must then look carefully at the best way in their language to be at once natural and yet capture the force and impact of what Jesus is claiming, as in 'Jesus claimed that he himself, he is the way, he is the truth, and he is the life.'

3.2.3 Discourse

Languages construct narratives and expositions and descriptions in different ways, and failure to understand this can result in translations that not only sound strange, but possibly also have the wrong meaning.

In the Fulfulde Bible in Cameroon different sets of pronouns are used depending on whether participants in the story are in the foreground and in focus, or are part of the background. This is a distinction of which even the translators were not really conscious. But careful analysis of the discourse and of this feature made it clear that in the translation of the Prodigal Son in Luke 15, the sets of pronouns had been mixed so that readers could not tell whether the father or one of the sons was in focus at any one place in the parable.

Problems with a translation prepared in the Bwamu language of Burkina Faso serve to illustrate several types of problems which arise if discourse is not studied carefully. Although the translation was a careful and grammatically correct rendering of the Greek text of the New Testament, speakers of Bwamu were simply not able to understand it, so that after some testing of drafts, that New Testament was never published.

There were primarily four reasons for this, all having to do with differences between Bwamu discourse and that of the koine Greek. In Bwamu, for example, it is common to maintain cohesion in a text by repeating certain verbs. A narration might read something like this: 'The man decided to goto the next village. After he decided, he went on the road until he arrived at the village. After he arrived at the village...' This technique is not a feature of New Testament Greek discourse, and therefore the translator had not used it, so the readers, deprived of the expected repetitions, found the translation unnatural.

A second problem had to do with sequence of tense. Essentially, the tense for a narration in Bwamu is established in the first sentence. After that, an unmarked or narrative tense form is used throughout. If another form such as a past or a future is used, it means past or future with reference to the time that was established in the first sentence. Thus if there were a simple past at the beginning of the narration, any subsequent past tense forms would in fact be understood as pluperfects. The translator had not realized this, and had simply employed Bwamu tense forms as in the Greek. The result was that readers thought they were getting a series of pluperfects and were quite confused as they read the translation.

Flashback is another feature used differently in the Greek New Testament and in Bwamu. A number of cases where it occurs in the New Testament are better rendered in Bwamu by reordering the passage so as to have a more chronological sequence. Secondary information or events only needed at particularly points in the narrative can be marked in Bwamu in other ways.

Bwamu also handled reported speech differently from koine Greek. In fact, direct reported speech is quite unusual in Bwamu, being used only to give a heightened emotional content, usually negative, to a particular statement. The use of first person in such cases is normally interpreted not to refer to the speaker in the text, but to the person who is reading aloud, or possibly to the translator! 'Jesus said "I am the light of the world"' would not mean in Bwamu that Jesus is the light of the world, but that the translator or reader is.

3.2.4 Cultural Context

Perhaps the greatest barrier to producing translations that are understandable is the very different ways that cultures interpret things that are said and done. For example, in Job 2: 7–9, after Job is severely afflicted to the point of almost dying, he laments his unfortunate life. However, in cultures such as the Tonga in Central Africa where the causes of such woes would normally lie with some evil spirit or spirits, this behavior would not be understood. People would wonder why Job did not make supplication to his ancestral spirits instead, and why his whole family did not join him in this, for the family's role would be important in Tonga society. But Job queries why his parents brought him into this world, and his wife rebukes him. As a result of this 'odd' behavior, readers in Tonga would decide that Job is bewitched, probably by his wife.

Translators cannot change a story, of course, but they must realize how a passage will be understood by readers, and consider what can be done to avoid misunderstanding. Vocabulary might be carefully selected (for example, to avoid expressions in this account that would seem to insult his mother), or notes provided for the readers.

Another example would be in a Buddhist culture such as in Thailand where correct behavior is believed to lead to a series of reincarnations. The assurance of life eternal in a verse such as John 3: 16 ('... so that everyone who believes in him may not die but have eternal life') is seen as a condemnation, so translators must look for a rendering which puts the emphasis on the quality of new life, not on its unending nature.

Even simple terms can pose complex problems. If the only cross people know is a crucifix, then Jesus' call to take up one's cross, meaning being prepared to die, might be misunderstood. And if a particular group practices circumcision only at the time of puberty when children are initiated into adulthood, then the account of Jesus' circumcision on the eighth day could well be understood as a mark of his wonderful power that made him an adult after only a week. In fact, this is exactly what did happen with one group in Cameroon. And if in a language 'to have a hard heart' means 'to be courageous,' or possibly 'to be miserly,' then people may not understand that in the Bible people with hard hearts are stubborn.

3.3 Theory Development

A common criticism of the method is that it is contradictory to have a translation which attempts to render the meaning naturally and yet is limited to common language. Essentially, it is argued, for a translation to be functionally equivalent, to aim at the closest natural equivalent, it must use the full resources of the language, so that attempts to make one translation serve a wide linguistic area are seriously handicapped.

Another criticism is that such translations lose certain aspects of the meaning of texts which are in fact part of the form of the texts. For example, features such as plays on words are going to be lost, as well as the element of the meaning of poetry which is conveyed in the very form itself.

'Word play' is used somewhat loosely here to include not only aesthetically pleasing literary devices, but those cases where a common theme or topic is maintained through word play. An example would be the Hebrew word *yada'* and its cognates in the early chapters of Genesis. The word is most commonly glossed as 'to know' or 'knowledge.' Thus in Genesis 2 there is the tree of *knowledge* of good and evil; in 3: 5, the serpent uses it twice: 'For God *knows* that on the day when you eat of it, your eyes will be opened and you shall be as gods, *knowing* good and evil'; after the humans eat the fruit, their eyes were opened, 'and they *knew* they were naked'; in 3: 22, God says that people are like 'one of us, *knowing* good and evil'; and in 4: 1, one finds 'And Adam *knew* Eve his wife, and she became pregnant.' Thus in the passage *yada* is used for knowing, understanding, and having sexual relations. But translations that strive for functional equivalence often render these in quite different ways, using words such as 'discovered' or 'realize' and 'to sleep with' or 'to have intercourse with.' Linked together are the ideas of the tree of knowledge and shame, the knowledge of God, and sexuality. All of this linkage is lost in functional equivalence translation in which context takes precedence over form (see Hammond 1987).

Underlying the theory of translation put forward by Nida, and indeed underlying most theories of communication, is a code model. According to this model, communication is achieved by encoding and decoding messages. However, experienced translators often find that there is a gap between the semantic representations of sentences and the actual meaning that is communicated by them. This leaves open problems such as the degree to which implicit material in the text should be made explicit, and how figurative language and irony are to be handled. Such matters are often better dealt with through models of communication based on inference. In this approach, translators see themselves as having an informative intention, which their translation conveys to an audience in the receptor language. Success or failure depends not on the theory of translation followed but on how well the translator has considered the assumptions available to the audience, and how well the text stimulates a particular interpretation by them.

4 Future Directions

One of the basic assumptions of translators has always been that the Bible is best communicated through written translation. However, in much of the Third World the level of illiteracy is very high, and translators have begun to use other media to communicate the Bible.

4.1 Audio Media

In many cases, translators have simply recorded a reading of the written translation, and distributed this on cassettes or used it in radio broadcasts. Increasingly, however, translations are prepared which are designed for the audio media. Such translations incorporate features of oral discourse from the receptor language, such as certain kinds of redundancy and repetition, and avoid grammatical forms which are used only in writing. Clearly, careful attention must be paid to problems that arise from homonyms. For example, 'prophesy with lyres' in I Chronicles 25: 1, could easily be misunderstood when read aloud. In addition, dialogue is often created, and different voices are then used in the recording.

One of the interesting things about preparing the Scriptures for audio media is that the use of these oral features brings to completion a full circle. Much of the material in the Bible was originally communicated orally, and many of the oral discourse features were retained when the text was written down, even if they were not natural in a written text. For example, the heroic tales of Jesus in Mark's Gospel are in their very content similar to oral literature. Moreover, there are many stylistic and rhetorical features of oral literature in the book. Folkloristic triads are pervasive (three disciples are separated from within the twelve, three times Jesus predicts his passion and resurrection, three times he enters Jerusalem, and so on), the third person plural is used instead of the passive for narration, again a feature of oral literature. Pleonasms ('birds of the air'), repetitions, double imperatives, double negatives, constructions which restate in positive terms a preceding negative—all of these are common in oral speech and occur frequently in the Gospel of Mark.

Yet the translator of written texts often finds them awkward and unnatural.

4.2 Visual Media

In a large number of languages of Asia and Africa, parts of the Bible have been produced in a comic strip format. For these to be legitimate translations, however, great care has to be given to what must be made explicit in a picture. Does the biblical text indicate if the background should be desert or forest? Who in the dialogue should have the most prominent position? Should that person be in the foreground or in the background? Should the other figures in the picture be smiling, frowning or looking shocked? With care such adaptations can legitimately be called translations.

Translating parts of the Bible for video is another development being seriously considered by many translators. Many of the questions that are raised about comics are the same as those for video. Obviously in the written text there are few directions as to things such as at what speed people are walking, how many of them there are, or how close they are to each other. Yet the video medium requires that such details be made explicit. Even the choice of background music influences the understanding an audience has of a text, and must therefore be considered by the translator.

4.3 Other Audiences

In general most translation has been aimed at a literate, adult, Christian population. Increasingly, however, translation is aimed at other, often narrowly defined, audiences. In areas where there are many newly literate people, translations are often prepared at a level which will help them develop their reading skills. Translations are being prepared for children in a number of languages, such as Indonesian, and the Spanish of Latin America. These are translations from the Greek and Hebrew but they are done in a way that children perhaps nine years old can read and understand them. Other translations are prepared for people who have limited usage of a particular language, such as when two translations in Hausa are prepared, one for native speakers and one for those who use it as a second language. In Lingala from Congo one translation serves traditional monolingual users, and another has been prepared for those who live in the city of Kinshasa, who speak the language extensively but yet for whom it is not their first language.

4.4 Computers

Machine-assisted translation for Bible translators is still a far-off dream. The complexities involved in understanding the biblical texts are such that it is still considerably more efficient to train native speakers to work in their own languages than it is to attempt to develop a computer program which can handle factors such as cultural and historical background, the way a culture processes information, or the experience of the readers with interpreting texts. However, computers have become standard tools for translators, being used particularly in two ways (see *Computers and Religion*).

4.4.1 Computer-assisted Dialect Adaptation

In cases where it is deemed useful to have the Bible published in two or more closely related dialects, a common technique is to use programs which makes certain automatic conversions, so that the material translated in one dialect area is adapted into the second with the assistance of the computer, for example, in different Quechua groups of Peru and Ecuador, and in several closely related Bantu languages of Congo.

4.4.2 Computer-assisted Text Processing

There are a number of programs available to translators so that if they key in their texts, it is possible to use the computer to prepare word lists, conduct morphological, syntactical, and lexical searches, develop concordances, and do checks for punctuation, consistency of orthography, and completeness of verses and chapters. In addition, desktop publishing has now become a widespread feature. Translators who have keyed in their texts can publish their materials quickly and easily, and can more easily than ever before obtain crucial feedback from their intended audiences.

See also: English Bible; African Traditional Religions; Missionaries; Summer Institute of Linguistics.

Bibliography

Beekman J, Callow J 1974 *Translating the World of God.* Zonder-van Publishing House, Grand Rapids, MI

de Waard J, Nida E A 1986. *From One Language to Another: Functional Equivalence in Bible Translating.* Thomas Nelson Publishers, Nashville, TN

Grimes J E 1975 *The Thread of Discourse.* Mouton, The Hague

Hammond G 1987 English translations of the Bible. In: Alter R, Kermode F (eds.) *The Literary Guide to the Bible.* Belknap Press of Harvard University Press, Cambridge, MA

Larson M L 1984 *Meaning-based Translation: A Guide to Cross-language Equivalence.* University Press of America, Lanham, MD

Longacre R E 1964 *Grammar Discovery Procedures: A Field Manual.* Mouton, The Hague

Longacre R E 1983 *Anatomy of Speech Notions: The Grammar of Discourse.* Plenum Press, New York

Nida E A 1947 *Bible Translating.* American Bible Society, New York

Nida E A 1964 *Toward a Science of Translating*. E J Brill, Leiden
Nida E A, Taber C R 1969 *The Theory and Practice of Translation*. E J Brill, Leiden
Noss P A 1981 The oral story and Bible translation. *The Bible Translator* **32(3)**: 301–18
Pike K L 1947 *Phonemics: A Technique for Reducing Languages to Writing*. University of Michigan Press, Ann Arbor, MI
Pike K L 1967 *Language in Relation to a Unified Theory of the Structure of Human Behavior*. Mouton, The Hague.
Smalley W A 1991 *Translation as Mission: The Role of Bible Translation in the Modern Missionary Movement*. Mercer University Press, Macon, GA
Bulletin 188/189, 2000, United Bible Societies, Reading, UK
Wonderly W L 1968 *Bible Translations for Popular Use*. United Bible Societies, London

Buddhist Canons: Translations

L. R. Lancaster

The Buddhist teachings were from the very beginning the object of some type of translation. The founder of the tradition, Śākyamuni, is believed to have spoken Ardha–Māgadhī or a dialect of it. However, he had a long career of teaching and his travels, as recorded in the texts, took him across linguistic boundaries among such tribal groups as the Kāsīs, Kosalas, Vrjis and Vatsas. In the extant accounts of the history of Indian Buddhism it is told that he changed his language of discourse to communicate with the audience at hand. If this is true then the 'words of the Buddha' were not limited to one regional dialect or language; it is probable that this wandering teacher made his own translations as he moved among a heterogeneous audience.

One of the important features of the language used in Buddhist texts can be seen in a proscription which states that the doctrine is not to be put in *chanda*, that is into either the Sanskrit language of the Vedas or the metric format of the Vedic literature. Since chanting was not limited to the Vedic manner, local dialects could be used with regard to vocabulary and metric considerations.

The diversity of language usage was not followed by the Theravādins of Ceylon, a group that interpreted the passage concerning the presentation of the teaching 'in his own dialect' to mean a reference to Śākyamuni's own dialect, which they understood to be the language of the Māgadhī region of the sixth and fifth centuries BCE. The texts accepted by Theravāda as containing the language and direct words of the Buddha were called '*pāli*' while the commentarial literature was referred to as '*atthakathā*.' Later *pāli* came to have the meaning of a language, and was traditionally held to be the Māgadhī as spoken by the Buddha. The *pāli* texts were not translated into Sinhalese, only in the case of the *atthakathā* was translation permitted. While Māgadhī or Ardha–Māgadhī may be the basis for much of what is seen in Pāli, there is sufficient evidence to suggest that these texts are in a composite language showing influences from a number of dialects, with Sanskrit, Dravidian, and even Sinhalese elements included.

There does not seem to have been a defined canon of texts written in one language spoken by the Buddha from which all other canons have emerged. Buddhist texts exist not only in the Prakrits, such as Pāli, but also in mixed or hybrid Sanskrit, where Classical Sanskrit forms are mixed with Prakrit ones. The texts of Buddhism reflect the changes that were occurring in language. The oldest layer is found in Middle Indic Prakrits, and was followed during the first three centuries CE by a mixed Sanskrit, and finally by Buddhist Sanskrit which is quite close to the Classical form, but still exhibits some of the older Prakrit. Sanskrit was becoming the common language of India, and Buddhism followed the trend by putting its texts into this language rather than the Prakrits which were more locally fixed. Thus, the Sarvāstivādins of the north finally came to compose their texts in pure Sanskrit while transposing many of the older texts into a form of Sanskrit that was close to the Classical formulations. This process of transposition from Prakrit into Classical Sanskrit may not be a true translation, but it was one way in which the language used in the texts underwent changes over time.

When Buddhism was carried by mercantile groups from India through Central Asia into China, the texts of the religion followed. Excavations at sites along the trade routes have recovered a number of manuscripts, many of them Buddhist in content. They were written in Indian languages, some in Chinese, and a number in four languages of the Central Asian region. The Iranian languages of Sogdian and Khotanese are represented as well as two other languages not known before the archaeological discoveries. These latter two types were first called 'Tocharian A' and 'Tocharian B,' but scholars have raised questions about such designations and have suggested instead the names of 'Agnean' and

'Kuchean.' While these Central Asian documents come from a region that had Buddhism prior to its introduction to China, the manuscripts in the four languages of the trade route states are later in data than the existing Chinese translations of Buddhist texts. It is not known when the process of making translations started in those oasis cities.

The Buddhist texts that first came to China along the trade routes were in a variety of language forms, each one some mixture of Sanskrit and Prakrit formulations. These Indic texts represented a major challenge to the missionary monks in China, who conceived the plan to make translations of them into Chinese. The first identified center for translation was in the capital Ch'ang-an under the leadership of An Shih-kao, a Central Asian monk. Here in 150 CE, the Buddhist Indic texts in whatever linguistic form, were translated by a laborious method. The work of making translations was quite difficult because of the essential differences between the languages. Sanskrit is highly inflected with person, number, gender, mood, tense, while Chinese characters can be used as nouns, verbs, adjectives, adverbs, grammatical markers depending upon placement and context. The missionary monks from Central Asia and India did not read and write Chinese and thus had to rely on some translation technique that required intermediary assistance by those who could use languages known to both the missionaries and the Chinese learned group. This meant that the translations had to be done in a kind of committee structure with discussions in at least three languages. There were at first no dictionaries, no grammars, no word lists, and no rules for the establishment of equivalence. The vocabulary of the translations finally came to be drawn from the existing literature and it is said that Chu Fa-ya developed the method known as '*ke-yi*' for finding appropriate equivalent words. Using the philosophical texts, Chu tried to find words close in meaning to the technical terms from the Buddhist sutras. While this approach is only partially successful, the texts that remain from the first three centuries of translation work in China are still readable and can be compared with existing Sanskrit manuscripts of India and Nepal showing that at least the basic meaning was being communicated through these versions.

There were distinct periods in the translation process. The first one started with the second-century workshop of An Shih-kao and continued until the early part of the eighth century. In this set of translations, there are more than 1,000 texts still preserved and it is in the transliterated words of these documents that Prakrit and Middle Indic pronunciations can be identified. A second translation effort in the eight century followed directly on this, with 139 Tantric texts included in this project; and while there are many transliteration none exhibit the older sounds of Prakrit, since the texts coming into China from India had by this time been transposed or written in Classical Sanskrit. The political problems faced by the T'ang dynasty directly affected the translation process and there was a period from 790 until 983 when no translations were made. A new translation bureau was established by the Northern Sung court in the capital of Kaifeng and it is from this bureau that a steady stream of translations appeared from 983 until the middle of the eleventh century. With the fall of the Northern Sung, the translation of Indian texts into Chinese came to an end.

The next culture to accept Buddhism and to devote time to the translation of the texts into their own language were the Tibetans. Having no written language, they had the added task of having to invent a script. In addition to the alphabet, it was necessary to construct a form of language in which the grammar, including long compounds and the Sanskrit word order, could be translated. This linguistic development started in the first half of the seventh century when the king sent a group of students to India to learn the alphabet and to secure the written form of language. The script which was copied by the Tibetans was not *devanāgarī*, the best known one in India; it was the script of the Kashmir region that was taken as a model.

A text with a dated colophon of 655 supplies the first extant account of a document written in the Tibetan script. From this seventh-century development of the script, grammar, and vocabulary, translation of the canon went forward under the direction of missionaries. Those monks who participated in this work came to Tibet in part because of the impact of non-Buddhist peoples in areas that had once been important parts of the Buddhist sphere of influence. From Northern India, learned monks who fled centers such as Nalanda came under non-Buddhist influence, and from the oasis centers of Central Asia, monks pushed out of their monastic sites by the Islamic takeover of Khotan in 1006 moved into the Amdo region. While the majority of the translations were made from Sanskrit into Tibetan, some of the texts were taken from the Chinese Buddhist canon. The translation of the Buddhist texts continued from the late seventh century until the twelfth century, a task which dominated Tibetan intellectual life for those centuries.

The Mongol court, a strong supporter of Tibetan Buddhism, made the first printed version of the canon in the thirteenth century, and began the translation of this canon into their own language. This was the largest project of making a secondary translation from a set of translations, that is, the Tibetan was a translation of the Sanskrit, and the Mongolian was in turn a translation of the Tibetan.

Under the patronage of Kublai Khan, Lama Phagspa invented a Mongol script based on the Tibetan and this was used for Buddhist translations as well as official documents. Later, the Uighur alphabet was use as model for producing a new script which is still used in Mongolia in the late twentieth century. By the seventeenth century, the translation work of the canon was complete and the first edition of the Mongol canon was published in 1628–1629. Under the support of the Yuan dynasty, the Hsi Hsia people also made a version of the Chinese canon using their own Tangut script in place of the characters.

The peoples of Northeast Asia accepted the Chinese-language version of the Buddhist canon and did not attempt to translate it into their own vernaculars. Printed versions of the Chinese were produced as royal projects among the Khitan, Jurchen, and Korean kingdoms from the eleventh to the thirteenth centuries. Japan at first relied solely on copies of the canon from the mainland and for some centuries did not make its own national copy. Since these people had taken the Chinese characters as their own written method, translation was not considered necessary. The Koreans developed their alphabet in the fifteenth century and while this was a great achievement, the new form of writing did not have the prestige of the Chinese characters and was slow in being accepted. The attempt to translate the Chinese Buddhist canon into Korean using the *han'gŭl* alphabet has only been undertaken during the twentieth century and is not yet complete. The Japanese also developed their own alphabet and have made a translation of a major part of the canon into a classical form of Japanese using a mixture of Chinese characters and their syllabary *hiragana*. The results of the this type of translation is a hybrid, part mere reproduction of the Chinese vocabulary in characters, with *hiragana* used to mark Japanese grammatical elements. In many ways this is a rearrangement of the Chinese characters in the order of Japanese grammar for the benefit of scholars who do not read Chinese with ease.

European translations of Buddhist texts were first undertaken beginning in the mid-nineteenth century. The first Pāli grammar was published in 1824 by a missionary in Ceylon. Eugene Burnouf and Christian Lassen wrote a description of Pāli language in 1826 and, after this, a succession of studies, dictionaries, and grammars of Pāli, Sanskrit, and later of the other canonic languages of Buddhism, which stimulated and assisted scholars in the task of translation into European languages. The largest project for the translation of Buddhist texts was started in the latter part of the nineteenth century when the Pāli Text Society of London began to make editions and translations from manuscripts found mainly in Ceylon. This work on the canon has been completed, but additional commentarial and extracanonic texts are still to be translated. In 1991, the first three volumes of a project to translate the Chinese Buddhist canon into English appeared, sponsored by the Numata Translation Center of Tokyo and Berkeley. Scholarly editions and translations for many of the important Mahayana texts have appeared in published form over the last century, but no attempt has been made to have one complete version in Western languages.

The artifacts of Buddhist texts exist in a number of places and a variety of materials. Manuscripts are found on palm leaves, birch bark, silk, paper, and wood. Early translations into Chinese dating from the fifth century or even earlier, exist in the fragments uncovered in Central Asia and the caves at Dunhuang. A rock-cut version of the Chinese canon, the earliest carvings data in the seventh century, is a collection of more than 15,000 stone slabs housed at Fang Shan. The oldest complete set of printing blocks, made in the thirteenth century, is at Hae-in Monastery in South Korea. Single volumes and fragments are preserved from more than nine of the printing block editions that were prepared in China starting in the tenth century. Sanskrit manuscripts are scattered throughout India, but the most important center for Buddhist texts has been the Kathmandu Valley in Nepal where many Mahayana texts have survived. Only one of the old Tibetan printing block sets still exist: the Derge Monastery edition carved in the eighteenth century. It is from this array of manuscripts, xylograph copies, and carvings that a full understanding of the process of translations of the Buddhist canons can be known.

See also: Pali; Pali Canon; Apocrypha, Buddhist; Buddhism, Tibetan; Kumarajiva.

Bibliography

Bechert H (ed.) 1980 *The Language of the Earliest Buddhist Tradition*. Symposien zur Buddhismusforschung II, Vandenhoeck & Ruprecht, Göttingen

'Butsugo' 1929 *Hōbōgirin Dictionnaire encyclopédique du Bouddhisme d'après les sources chinoises et japonaises* III: 207–09. Maison Franco–Japonaise, Tokyo

Edgerton F 1953 *Buddhist Hybrid Sanskrit Grammar and Dictionary*, vol. I: Grammar. Yale University Press, New Haven, CT

de Jung J W 1968, 1979 Buddha's Word in China. In: *Buddhist Studies*. Asian Humanities Press, Berkeley, CA

Lamotte E 1988 *History of Indian Buddhism*, transl. by Sara Webb-Boin. Publications de L'Institut Orientaliste de Louvain 36, Louvain

Röhrborn K, Veenker W 1983 *Sprachen des Buddhismus in Zentralasien*. Veröffentlichungen der Societas Uralo–Altaica, vol. 16. Harrassowitz, Wiesbaden

T'ang Yung-t'ung 1938 *Han Wei Liang-Chin Nan-pei ch'ao Fo chiao shih*. Shanghai

Zürcher E Late Han vernacular elements in the earliest Buddhist translations. *Journal of the Chinese Language Teachers Association* **12**: 177–203

Cairo Genizah

S. C. Reif

According to Jewish religious law, texts containing sacred language and literature that are no longer used are not destroyed but consigned to a *genizah*, or depository (Hebrew *gnz*, 'hide', 'bury') to await natural disintegration. Archives were thus inadvertently amassed, the most famous being that of the Ben Ezra Synagogue in Old Cairo, from which some 210,000 items were obtained in the late nineteenth century. These are now housed and researched in academic institutions around the world, some two-thirds of them at Cambridge University Library. Although generally fragmentary, Genizah manuscripts have greatly increased knowledge of the medieval Near East (tenth–thirteenth centuries) and include not only religious literature but also mundane writings. Such writings were reverentially treated because they might mention sacred matters or even because of a respect for anything written, especially in what the Jews regarded as the 'sacred language' of Hebrew. They testify to a remarkable degree of literacy and linguistic competence.

The subjects, contents, religions and languages represented in the Genizah texts are surprisingly varied. The most common items relate to the recitation, translation, and interpretation of the Hebrew Bible; the transmission of rabbinic works containing talmudic, midrashic, legal, liturgical, and poetic texts; and the daily activities of the Jews and their neighbors. More unexpectedly, however, there are versions of works that the Rabbinic authorities had long regarded as heretical and that also appear among the Dead Sea Scrolls, as well as some Muslim and Christian religious literature.

Although the Jews used Hebrew and Aramaic for their standard religious texts, there are many items in Judeo–Arabic, the medieval Arabic dialect that they wrote in Hebrew characters, as well as other 'Jewish languages' such as Judeo–Greek, Judeo–Spanish, Judeo–German, and Judeo–Persian. The Genizah demonstrates that Rabbanite and Karaite Jews adjusted their linguistic norms for theological purposes and that the latter were particularly prominent in Hebrew language and philology, substantially advancing the work of Muslim and Jewish predecessors.

See also: Judaism; Hebrew, Biblical and Jewish; Aramaic, Jewish; Hebrew Grammarians.

Bibliography

Goitein S D 2000 *A Mediterranean Society: An Abridgement*, Lassner J (ed.) University of California, Berkeley, CA

Lambert P (ed.) 1994 *Fortifications and the Synagogue*. Weidenfeld & Nicolson, London

Reif S C 2000 *A Jewish Archive from Old Cairo*. Curzon, Richmond, Surrey

Chinese: Translation of Theological Terms

L. Pfister

When monotheistic religious traditions entered China, they were confronted with a radically different cultural and linguistic context in which to express their faiths. Largely unaware of each other until the eighteenth century, they developed different strategies in the translating ideas of the One God into an apparently polytheistic culture. Both Roman Catholic and Protestant Christian missionaries felt these problems profoundly, since they came to propagate their faith rather than remain culturally distinct, as was generally the case with Jews and Muslims.

By the mid-nineteenth century, a proliferation of translation for theological terms had spread confusion among Chinese audiences. This prompted a thorough analysis of the linguistic and cultural backgrounds of various terms, raising a host of fairly complex logical and comparative religious problems.

During the past century, despite modernization, linguistic popularization, and writing system reforms, the effects of these translation problems, in particular the controversy over naming God, are still evident and largely unresolved. All the monotheistic traditions have attempted to standardize their own terms, but the Christian communities have faced some particular difficulties.

1. Ambiguities in Contemporary Chinese Religious Language

The idea of a unique and transcendent God, who reveals universal truth and abundant mercy to save humankind, remains largely foreign to most Chinese persons. Sometimes this is due to the theological translations themselves. The Islamic title for Allah, *zhenzhu*, 'True Lord,' for example, might refer to a human ruler as well as to a divine being. Several generic terms for God used by Chinese Christians have unexpected associations as well. One classical term for God, *Tian*, for example, also means 'sky,' and another major term, *shen*, is used currently in the phrase, *shenhua* (lit. 'god(s) talk') to denote 'myths.' Even the term for Christmas, *Shengdan jie*, is not exclusively Christian. It may also refers to holidays celebrating the births of Master Kong ('Confucius'), the Buddha, and the modern revolutionary, Sun Yat-Sen.

Sometimes even the translations of the names of scriptures misled Chinese readers. While the Qu'rān is known by several unique translations into Chinese, the Bible, in spite of its unique status in many African, European, and North and South American contexts, was given more general name, *shengjing*, 'Holy Scripture'. The term *jing* occurs in the titles of hundreds of Buddhist sutras and Daoist scriptures, while *shengjing* itself did also refer to the whole of the Ruist ('Confucian') canon even until the end of the nineteenth century. Thus, the uniqueness of both God and the Bible is difficult to portray in Chinese.

After the Maoist revolution, theological criticism seemed to herald the death of all religions. Nevertheless, religions have survived and, in some situations, prospered. Consequently, the question of the conceptual clarification of theological terms in Chinese remains a living concern.

2. The Term Controversy

When the major public debate regarding terms for God commenced among Protestant missionaries in China and Hong Kong in 1846, the tools available for translation were not always reliable. The first Chinese dictionary for Europeans, published in Latin in 1735, chose to represent the Chinese characters in a phonetic system amenable to educated Europeans, and effectively prevented students from learning how to use regular Chinese dictionaries. Chinese grammars, taking the case systems of nouns in some Mediterranean and Germanic languages as their standard, were often incorrect. Transliteration systems had not been standardized. Protestant missionaries who sought to translate the biblical texts in the early part of the century were reliant on native informants, but had little access to linguistic training and very few adequate translation tools. By the middle of the nineteenth century, however, some of the second generation missionaries were capable scholars, well versed in classical Latin, Greek and Hebrew languages and students of the first Chinese language teachers in the English-speaking world. The major question confronting them was imbedded in the problem of identifying the best translation terms of 'God' and 'spirit,' so that they could convey the Christian message without confusion to Chinese audiences.

2.1 Linguistic Hindrances and Semantic Obstacles

In Classical Chinese, terms depend much more on their context for their meaning than in modern Chinese. For example, apart from numbers and some stylizations reserved for the emperor and highly respected persons, the language gave no clues in declensions or conjugations about whether a term out of context was singular or plural, masculine or feminine, a noun or a verb or an adjective. Proper names were often composed from common terms, so that one had to be careful to make important foreign names obvious by employing a loosely standardized set of transliteration characters. For example, translators discovered clever ways to render Yahweh (*Yehehua*) and Jesus (*Yesu*) so that both began with the same character (suggesting familial ties) and the former included the sense of 'bringing peace to Chinese.'

These personal names became meaningless, however, if generic terms for 'God' and 'spirit' were not available. Earlier translators, relying heavily on the original meaning of the biblical terms, were sometimes too literal in their renditions. Since both *rūah* (Hebrew) and *pneuma* (Greek), 'spirit,' could refer to 'wind,' for example, the Chinese term for 'wind,' *feng*, was adopted to translate 'spirit.' This style of translation led to some very awkward results, leaving Chinese readers puzzled. Second generation missionaries suggested a number of terms to translate 'God(s)' and 'spirit(s),' but none of them was a perfect synonym, and all were largely dependent on the translation strategies they assumed.

2.2 Strategies in Theological Translation

Some translators, fearing the inevitable problems involved in using any normal Chinese terms, advocated the mere transliteration of proper names. Muslims presented Allah as *Ala* or *Anal*. Jesus and Yahweh could be handled similarly. The discovery of an eighth-century monument which preserved a Christian treatise written by Syrian monks supported some of their claims: transliteration terms for *'ĕlōah* (a cognate of *'ĕlōhim*) and *mashiaḥ* (Hebrew 'Anointed One,' i.e., Christ) were discovered on it, along with some unusual phrases for the Trinity and Incarnation which were previously unknown (see *Christianity in East Asia*).

Others argued that transliterations were insufficiently clear in meaning, but then only offered coined terms in their place. One of the most radical was the introduction of the Greek letter *theta* as a symbol for *theos*, 'God.' This was an insufficient option because the symbol was not known by Chinese readers, and it was, even after being learned, phonetically inexpressible. Roman Catholics had settled for *Tianzhu*, 'Lord of Heaven,' as a result of a papal decision in 1704. This was much more meaningful to the Chinese listener, but was not easily accepted because of its foreignness.

A third group chose terms from religious language currently used both ordinary people and scholars, such as the term for 'god,' *shen*. This is the broadest generic term denoting 'spirit(s),' 'god(s),' and in certain cases, 'intelligent men,' and by it all spiritual beings which were worshiped could be identified and gradually be distinguished from the true God, the one 'true *shen*'.

Arguing that *shen* was too intimately connected with a throng of strange spiritual beings in Daoism and Buddhism, a final group of translators located a set of Ruist ('Confucian') terms to serve for God. In the ancient Ruist scriptures the term *Tian*, 'Heaven,' was identified with another shadowy figure of great significance, the 'Lord on High,' or 'Supreme Lord,' *Shangdi*. This term carried with it the ring of classical authority, but it too was not unproblematical. The Chinese emperor divinized his ancestors as *Di*, 'Lords,' worshiping them in the state cult, and three important Daoist deities, historically much younger than their Ruist namesake, took the name *Shangdi* along with other titles. Therefore none of the strategies offered an unquestionable solution, although the latter two were preferable to most Protestants.

2.3 Logical Debates

The conceptual unclarity hindering different strategies, particularly in those opting for *shen* or *Shangdi*, required purification. Key advocates of *shen* argued that *'ĕlōhim* (He) and *theos* (Greek), 'God(s),' were absolute generic terms: words applied generally to 'god,' whether false or true, standing completely independent of all other terms or realities. Thus *shen* was in their minds the best term to portray this range of meanings, once it itself was purified of its unsalutary denotations. Advocates of *Shangdi* disagreed, claiming that the biblical terms were relative, mirroring the relationship of creator to creature. *Shangdi* or simply *Di* manifestly relayed this image in the classical texts, and so could be employed generically for 'god.' The *shen* party countered that *Shangdi* was in fact a proper name, like Jupiter or Zeus. The *Shangdi* group claimed that the fundamental meaning of *shen* was 'spirit,' not 'god,' explaining on that basis why some *shen* were not objects of worship. Many other tangential issues followed these debates, polarizing the two parties.

3. Theological Facts Influencing Linguistic Frameworks

In the late twentieth century, most language theorists argue that meaning is not located in single terms or phrases, but is dependent on sentences and larger units of meaning. Sentences themselves rely on the whole system of language symbols for their determinate significance (Quine 1960). Thus a number of the problems raised by the terminological question depend on the larger linguistic framework which translators determine as critical to their projects. Believers in specific divine revelations in human history, monotheists were not expecting to identify a term for 'God' in ancient or contemporary Chinese texts. Yet some of the *Shangdi* party claimed they had done just this in discovering *Shangdi* and identifying him with the God of the Bible. The translators identified two fundamental theological facts: God is the creator; God is self-existent. These two factors became increasingly important in determining which term was most appropriate in Chinese, and in particular prompted new reflection on the original Greek, Latin, and Hebrew contexts in which biblical and theological terms were grounded.

3.1 Original Monotheism

In order to support the claim that *Shangdi* is the true God, it was pointed out that in *Shangdi*, ancient Chinese scriptures confirmed the reliance of all life on "God", but did not refer to the notion of self-existence. Just as Yahweh was not known in this aspect until the time of Moses, so like the biblical patriarchs, the ancient Chinese sages knew of God's existence, but little of God's nature. Furthermore, the presence of *Shangdi* in these ancient Ruist scriptures showed that an originally pure monotheism must have existed in early Chinese tradition.

3.2 Incarnational Theology

Early literalists had translated the Greek term *logos*, 'Word', as *yan*, 'a word, saying'. This was thought to be a grave reduction of the philosophical importance of the original biblical term, and alternatives were sought. Jews, who had migrated to northern China in the seventeenth or eighteenth century and were discovered by Protestant missionaries, had translated the term *'ĕlōhim* by *Dao*, a term pregnant with meanings ranging from 'path' or 'way', to 'speech' and 'truth'. Adopting this for *logos*, translators gained an equivalently evocative Chinese term. In spite of this change, skeptics complained that it gave a Daoist flavor to the whole biblical message. The term rested on a broad linguistic framework of popular culture as well as being rooted in classical Ruist and Daoist scriptures.

All the options of these Chinese translations left the Trinity, a theological term full of complexities and dependent on classical Greek and Latin metaphysical assumptions, in an even more beclouded linguistic framework. It placed the uninformed Chinese listener in a very awkward position, since the connotations of the terms suggested different cosmological and metaphysical frameworks. For example, how could such a Chinese listener intuit that the same being was referred to by terms which suggested the God worshiped only by the emperor (*Shangdi*), the impersonal principle in Daoism from which all reality emanated (*Dao*), and a plurality of immortal beings or spirits (a very possible rendering of *Shengshem*, 'Holy spirits(s)')? These labyrinthine misunderstandings could only be overcome by laborious explanations and educated Chinese Christian commentaries on these terms in the Chinese biblical context.

3.3 Transformative Possibilities

Although the debate lasted well into the twentieth century, the major figures involved all admitted that language does change and so terms and their meanings could also be guided in their future developments. New teachings can transform the content and associations of various terms. The impact of terms can also change: the average Chinese responded to the term *shen* with fear, and the use of the term *Shangdi* caused apprehension, because it was the imperial privilege alone to worship that being in its purity in Beijing. The political implications were made all the more obvious when the Taiping Heavenly Kingdom arose (1851–1864) claiming to follow *Shangdi*'s revelations in its revolt against the Manchu emperor.

The demise of traditional China in 1911 accompanied harsh reactions before and afterwards against foreigners and foreign religions, but the transformation of China and its language did proceed. Language reform initiated in 1919 followed on the heels of a new openness to liberal conceptions of education, politics and scientific development. These consequently made possible new adaptations in general religious terminology and the relative acceptability of those debated terms, full of all their Chinese suggestiveness.

4. Contemporary Compromises

In a typically pragmatic manner, Chinese publishers have continued to publish Islamic, Jewish, and Christian literature using all the standardized terms. In editions of the Chinese Bible published in the 1990's in Nanjing, the Chinese reader finds on the back of the title page: 'One may substitute *Shangdi* whenever *shen* appears'. An international effort at an ecumenically translated Chinese Bible using another term for "God", *Shangzhu* or 'Lord on High', has been initiated in the 1990s, and new Chinese translations of the Qu'rān have also appeared, but remain commited to *Zhenzhu* or 'True Lord' as their distinctive reference for Allah.

Conceptual clarification of theological terms still proceeds in China, although in completely different contexts from those in which the terminological question arose. Well established tertiary institutions of Christian learning and numerous Islamic schools continue to exist and grow in China. Increased critical awareness of non-Chinese civilizations, gradually accumulated over the past century, is beginning to generate new scholarship which will extend and refine the problems attending theological reflection in Chinese.

See also: Bible Translations, Modern Period; Christianity in East Asia; Missionaries; Translation: History.

Bibliography

Broomhall M *Islam in China: A Neglected Problem* (London: Morgan and Scott, Ltd., 1910)

Covell R 1986 *Confucius, the Buddha and Christ: A History of the Gospel in Chinese*. Orbis, Maryknoll

Eber I 1999 *The Jewish Bishop and the Chinese Bible: S.I. Schereschewesky (1831–1906)*. Brill, Leiden

Goldstein J (ed.) *The Jews of China–Volume One: Historical and Comparative Perspectives* (Armonk: M. E. Sharpe, 1999)

Legge J 1880 *A Letter to F. Max Müller Chiefly on The Translation into English of the Chinese Terms Tî and Shangtî...* Trübner, London

Leslie D D *Islam in Traditional China: A Short History to 1800* (Canberra: College of Advanced Education, 1986)

Minamiki G 1985 *The Chinese Rites Controversy from Its Beginning to Modern Times*. Loyola University Press, Chicago, IL

Mungello D E 1994 *The Chinese Rites Controversy: Its History and Meaning*. Steyler Verlag, Nettatal

Pfister L "Nineteenth Century Ruist Metaphysical Terminology and the Sino-Scottish Connection: Evaluating the Hermeneutic Relevance of this Connection in James Legge's *Chinese Classics*" in Michael Lackner, Natascha Vittinghoff, eds., *Translating Western Knowledge into Late Qing China* (Leiden: E. J. Brill, forthcoming 2001)

Quine W V O 1960 *Word and Object*. MIT Press, Cambridge MA

Ricci M 1985 *The True Meaning of the Lord of Heaven (T'ienchu Shih-i)*. Ricci Institute, Taipei

Strandenaes T 1987 *Principles of Chinese Bible Translation as Expressed in Five Selected Versions of the New Testament...* Almqvist and Wiksell International, Stockholm

Williams S W 1878 The conflict among the Protestant missionaries on the proper translation of the words God and Spirit into Chinese. *Bibliotheca Sacra* **35**: 732–78

Wong Man-Kong. "The Rendering of God in Chinese by the Chinese: A Preliminary Study of the Chinese Reponses to the Term Question as Seen in the *Wanguo gongbao*" in Michael Lackner,

Natascha Vittingoff, eds., *Translating Western Knowledge into Late Qing China* (Leiden: E. J. Brill, forthcoming 2001)

Zetzsche J O 1999 *The Bible in China: History of the Union Version or the Culmination of Protestant Missionary Bible Translation in China.* Steyler Verlag, Nettatal

Dead Sea Scrolls

T. H. Lim

Eight hundred or so ancient Hebrew, Aramaic, and Greek scrolls were discovered between 1947 and 1962 in the caves along the northwestern shore of the Dead Sea by the archeological site of Khirbet Qumran. Widely believed to have originally belonged to the library of a Jewish sectarian group known as the Essenes, these two thousand year old manuscripts have revolutionized the study of nascent Judaism and early Christianity. Some scholars argue, however, that the scrolls do not belong to the Qumran community, but were treasured writings of the libraries in Jerusalem, hidden in the Judean Wilderness and away from the advancing Roman army in CE 68.

Some one quarter of the mostly fragmentary scrolls are copies of all the books of the Hebrew Bible or Old Testament, except for Esther and Nehemiah. The biblical manuscripts date to a period in history before the standardization of the text and the closing of the canon. The Qumran community considered as authoritative scriptures that were textually pluriform and their 'canon' included the books of Jubilees and 1 Enoch, which are not part of the traditional Jewish, Protestant and Catholic scriptures.

Of the six hundred non-biblical scrolls many reflect the beliefs and practices of the sect that lived at the site. The sect had two branches, the stricter celibate community of men who lived in the inhospitable environment by the Dead Sea and another married group who lived in camps and towns. Sectarian texts include the Community Rule, the Damascus Document, and biblical commentaries known as the Pesharim. These documents describe a community that punctiliously held to the commandments of the law and that hoped for the coming of the end time, led by their leader known only as 'The Teacher of Righteousness.'

The remaining scrolls are copies of previously known works (e.g. Tobit) and other hitherto unknown literature (e.g. the Temple Scroll, Moses Apocryphon). Since 1991, all the remaining unpublished scrolls from Cave 4 have been published in microfiche, CD ROM and facsimile editions.

See also: Bible; Judaism; Hebrew, Biblical and Jewish; Cairo Genizah.

Bibliography

Abegg M Flint P Ulrich E 2000 *The Dead Sea Scrolls Bible.* T & T Clark, Edinburgh

Golb N 1995 *Who Wrote the Dead Sea Scrolls? The Search for the Secret of Qumran.* Michael O'Mara, London

Schiffman L H VanderKam C 2000 *Encyclopedia of the Dead Sea Scrolls.* Oxford University Press, Oxford

VanderKam J C 1994 *The Dead Sea Scrolls Today.* Eerdmans, Grand Rapids, MI

Vermes G 1994 *The Complete Dead Sea Scrolls.* Penguin, London

English Bible

G. Hammond

In an increasingly fundamentalist world the linguistic integrity of the English Bible is a matter of importance. When a US president declares that he has been reading, and is much moved by, apocalyptic verses in Isaiah, anxious citizens will want to know which version he has been reading and what are the alternative translations. Unlike the Qur'ān, whose interpreters stick closely to the original Arabic (see *Qur'an*), the great majority of the Bible's readers and expositors do not know its original languages, and even scholars of biblical Hebrew and Greek can have only a limited appreciation of the senses of the words, phrases, and syntactic structures of the original languages (see *Bible*). The idea that an English translation makes the Bible misleadingly accessible has always worried the Church. Nowadays this is overcome by sponsoring versions so bland that they are virtually unreadable; in earlier times more strenuous methods of prohibiting or controlling translations were employed.

1. The Medieval Bible

There had been 'Englishings' of parts of the Bible in Anglo–Saxon times, but the first complete English Bible, a translation of the Vulgate, was undertaken towards the end of the fourteenth century by Lollard followers of John Wyclif. This Wyclif Bible exists in two major versions, one very literal, the other much freer. Its preface, by one of the translators, has a surprisingly sophisticated discussion of the problems involved in translating the Latin of the Vulgate, in particular its verb system, into English. Suppressed by the authorities, this version had only a limited influence upon later translations, but some of its phrasing became part of the common English biblical stock. Examples from the New Testament include 'perish by the sword,' 'sounding brass,' 'tinkling cymbal,' 'wise master carpenter,' 'strait gate.'

2. The Tudor Bible

Printed Bibles in English appeared first just before the Reformation: William Tyndale's New Testament (1525) and Pentateuch (1530), followed by Miles Coverdale's Bible, the first complete printed English Bible (1535); the 'Matthew' Bible (1537), containing more of Tyndale's Old Testament translation; the Great Bible (1539), mainly by Coverdale, with claims to being the first English 'authorized version'; the Geneva Bible (1560), translated by Marian exiles and strongly associated with the emerging Puritan movement; the Bishops' Bible (1568), an establishment rival to the Geneva version; the Catholic Rheims–Douai Bible (completed 1609); and, finally, the Authorized Version (AV) (1611), also known as the 'King James Bible.' Each of these is a distinct version, with its own contribution to English biblical style and language, but each builds upon its predecessors' work. As the AV preface puts it, their idea was not to make a new translation but 'to make a good one better, or, out of many good ones one principal good one'.

This developing tradition means that by far the most important contribution to English Bible language was Tyndale's. In the New Testament, for instance, his work makes up three-quarters of the AV text. Unlike other European vernacular translators in the first half of the sixteenth century, Tyndale knew Hebrew and Greek well enough to translate from the original languages and not be dependent upon the Vulgate and Luther's German version. His one emphatic comment on translating from Hebrew into English was the claim that the two languages paralleled each other in their word-order much more naturally than did Hebrew and Latin. So, Tyndale's Old Testament stamps on to the English Bible, and therefore on to English prose and the spoken language, forms which are imitative of some of the basic structures of Classical Hebrew. The most striking elements, in narrative passages, are a paratactic syntax, with clause linked to clause by the simple conjunction 'and,' equivalent to the Hebrew *waw*; the formula '*x*-of-*x*' for genitival and adjectival phrases, matching the Hebrew construct form; a simple, uncluttered vocabulary; and a phrase by phrase, often word by word, following of the Hebrew, as in this verse from Genesis 3: 14:

> And the Lord God said unto the serpent because thou hast so done most cursed be thou of all cattle and of all beasts of the field: upon thy belly shalt thou go: and earth shalt thou eat all days of thy life.

In his New Testament translation, Tyndale virtually invented modern English prose, turning what was largely an unwieldy medium into something graceful and controlled. Fitting Tyndale's aim, to make the Bible accessible to all, to be sung by a plowboy at his plow, the style is simple and direct. He trusted the native, spoken tradition at a time when other writers of English were larding their prose with Latinisms in syntax and vocabulary. In a passage like this one, from 1 Corinthians, he produced so controlled a rendering that it has gone almost word for word into the AV:

> Though I spake with the tongues of men and angels, and yet had no love, I were even as sounding brass: or as a tinkling cymbal. And though I could prophesy, and understood all secrets, all knowledge: yea, if I had all faith so that I could move mountains out of their places, and yet had no love, I were nothing. And though I bestowed all my goods to feed the poor, and though I gave my body even that I burned, and yet had no love, it profiteth me nothing.

Thomas More who led the intellectual opposition to a vernacular Bible, attacked Tyndale for his 'mischievous' renderings, aimed at undermining religious and secular authority: using 'senior' instead of 'priest,' 'congregation' instead of 'church,' and so on. But More had a wider point to make about the impossibility of making any responsible English version when he criticized Tyndale's use of 'love' here, because 'love' has too many secular implications for it to stand as a fitting equivalent to the Greek *agapē*. Tyndale replied that under this reasoning, if one word were to mean exactly what the word it translates means, then it would be impossible to translate at all. In the case of other texts this would be merely a problem, but the Bible, as the inspired word of God, requires total fidelity. More and Tyndale knew that this is an impossible ideal.

3. The Authorized Version

Because it was so reliant upon Tyndale and the mid-sixteenth-century versions, particularly the Geneva Bible (the version which Shakespeare knew best), the AV already had an 'archaic' element when it appeared: hence, for example, its failure to use the possessive form 'its' which had come into common use in the last quarter of the century. But in many ways it remains a very modern version, not least in its vocabulary. A comparison with Shakespeare is revealing. Where an editor of the dramatist needs repeatedly to gloss words whose meanings have shifted, or which have gone out of use, the reader of the AV is only seldom inconvenienced by such changes. Of course, this is partly testimony to the influence of this version upon English usage. No other book has been so widely read, or heard, and its formulations have remained part of our common idiom.

One difficulty which exercises all Bible translators, and which the AV only partly overcame, lies in the rendering of parallelism, the underlying form of most Hebrew poetry and much of its prose. Parallelism depends upon the finding of synonyms, and because the target-language does not share the cultural concerns of the source-language, such synonyms may not exist. Accordingly, the AV repeatedly uses the word 'destroy' as an equivalent for the dozens of Hebrew words whose semantic range covers some small area of inflicting harm. A verse like Joel 2: 2 illustrates the difficulty of finding enough English words to represent four Hebrew words for 'darkness':

> A day of *darkness* and of *gloominess*, a day of *clouds* and of *thick darkness*. . .

Other untranslatable forms include word-play. Isaiah 21: 2, for example, contains a tightly bound series of puns which are impossible to render adequately into English:

> A grievous vision is declared unto me; the treacherous dealer dealeth treacherously, and the spoiler spoileth.

And even at a very simple level the effect of word-play is lost, as in the case of Eve, whose name in Hebrew is a play on the word meaning 'life' (Genesis 3: 20):

> And Adam called his wife's name Eve (*hawwā*); because she was the mother of all living (*ḥāy*).

Similarly, no English translation can get the connection between 'Adam' and the Hebrew words for 'man' and 'ground' (Genesis 2: 7):

> And the Lord God formed man (*hā'ădhām*) of the dust of the ground (*hā'ădhāmā*).

One modern translator felt compelled to coin the ungainly compound 'earth-creature' for Hebrew *'adham*.

More positively, the AV stamped onto English, for the next 350 years, a vocabulary and syntax which influenced all parts of the national culture, from the revolutionaries, who established the first republic in the 1650s, to poets and novelists like Blake and Lawrence. Forms which the translators developed to render the grammatical peculiarities of the original languages include the use of adverbs like 'surely'—as in 'you will surely die'—to translate the Hebrew infinite absolute; 'come to pass' as an equivalent for the Hebrew use of the verb 'to be' to introduce a new element in the narrative; and 'cause' to render the *hiphil* form, 'and cause his face to shine upon us.' As influential as any other element was the translators' great rhythmic facility, their cadenced prose, which made the AV most effective when read aloud in church services:

> And the Gentiles shall come to thy light, and kings to the brightness of thy rising (Isaiah 60: 3).

4. Modern Translations

In the second half of the twentieth century a spate of new translations appeared, many of them having 'new' in their titles. Some, like the Good News Bible, are very free. Others, like the American New International Version, remain in the literal line of the Revised and Revised Standard versions, themselves revisions of the AV. Most contentious has been the New English Bible because of its general use in religious services. Its inadequacy for such a function led to much criticism and, eventually, in 1989, to a revised version, the Revised English Bible (REB), whose preface affirms its purpose to combine the most advanced scholarship with an English style suitable for reading aloud to a congregation. Such aims are difficult to reconcile, for a narrow semantic accuracy constantly gets in the way of a lucid style. In Psalm 23, 'your shepherd's staff and crook afford me comfort' shows a translator too concerned with registering the exact meanings of the parallel nouns, rather than leave them as the simple 'rod' and 'staff' of the AV (the Psalm begins by telling us that the Lord is a shepherd), and adopting a clumsy verb phrase, 'afford comfort,' to convey the Hebrew *piel* form, rather than the natural and direct 'they comfort me.'

As well as dropping all 'thou' language in such contexts as prayers to God (see *Prayer*), as in the verse quoted above, the REB is the first attempt, in any major Bible version, to achieve a gender neutral translation as in Genesis 1: 26 ('Let us make human beings in our image') and the opening verse of Psalm 41: 'Happy is anyone who has a concern for the helpless!' The AV had rendered this, following the Hebrew, 'Blessed is he that considereth the poor.' However, the REB is not consistent in this practice, for, in spite of their claims to modernity, the translators did not feel able to use 'they' and 'their' as singular forms. In their version Psalm 41: 1 continues 'the Lord will save him in time of trouble' rather than 'will save them.'

Other features which the REB shares with the majority of modern versions include a reluctance to reproduce the more earthy elements of Biblical language, as when it gives 'every mother's son' instead of the AV's literal 'him that pisseth against a wall' (1 Kings 14: 10); or 'dribbling down his beard,' where the AV has 'let his spittle fall down upon his beard' (1 Samuel 21: 13). In spite of claims to be in 'natural' English, it also frequently offers a highly academic prose: 'God took thought for Noah' (Genesis 8: 1); 'they are to wear linen turbans, and must have linen drawers on their loins' (Ezekiel 44: 18); 'These people are a danger at your love-feasts with their shameless carousals' (Jude 12). Figurative language is constantly literalized: 'For you know very well' (Ecclesiastes 7: 22), where the Hebrew has *yāda' libbĕkhā,* 'your heart knows'; 'so Pharaoh still remained obstinate' (Exodus 7: 22) for Hebrew *yeḥĕzaq lēbh*, '(his) heart was strong'; 'and has no inward doubts' (Mark 11: 23; Greek *en tēı kardiāi*, 'in your heart'). It frequently avoids reproducing the verbal repetition of the original. The AV translators, in their preface, disclaimed an automatic word for word translation as a slavish literalism, savoring 'more of curiosity than wisdom,' but there are many places where ignoring verbal repetition prevents the reader from understanding the text's rhetorical and narrative purposes. An example is in 1 Samuel 15, where the Hebrew uses the same verb three times. In verse 11 God tells Samuel that he repents *(niḥam)* having made Saul king, and in verse 35 the narrator recapitulates this by saying that God repented (*niḥam*) having made him king. Between the two, in verse 29, Samuel tells Saul that God is not a man and does not repent (*niḥam*) his actions. The reader of the AV will easily perceive this contradiction since 'repent' is used in all three places, but not the reader of the REB, which has 'repent... change his mind... repented.'

A major consequence of modern English Bible translation, partly because of its variety, but more because its translators do not always appreciate that they are dealing with great literary works rather than historical documents, is that the Bible's influence on our language will dwindle to nothing. This will severely handicap understanding and appreciation of our literary culture, but may have a positive effect if it thwarts those who try to take literally words which are only the misleading things which all translations must be.

See also: Tyndale, W; Coverdale, M.; Driver, G. R.; Fundamentalism; Bible.

Bibliography

Benjamin W 1973 (transl. Zohn H) The task of the translator. In: Arendt H (ed.) *Illuminations.* Fontana, London

Butterworth C C 1941 *The Literary Lineage of the King James Bible 1340–1611.* University of Philadelphia Press, Philadelphia, PA

Hammond G 1982 *The Making of the English Bible.* Carcanet New Press, Manchester

Granth

C. Shackle

The Granth is the Sikh scripture. Written in the Gurmukhi script, it is a large collection of hymns, comprising 1,430 pages in standardized editions of the modern *textus receptus*. It is often specified as the *Ādi Granth* ('the primal Book') in distinction from the later *Dasam Granth* (see *Panjabi (Gurmukhi) Sacred Texts*), while the Sikh preference for the honorific *Gurū Granth Sāhib* reflects the exceptional status of the scripture in Sikhism.

The bulk of the Granth consists of verse compositions by the earlier Sikh Gurus: Nānak (1469–1539), the formative and most creative contributor (McLeod 1968), followed by Angad (d.1552), Amar Dās (d.1574), Rām Dās (d.1581), and Arjan (d.1606). While the Granth's sacred status has inhibited the investigation of the process of canon formation and the establishment of a critical text (Deol 2001), it is accepted that the crucial figure in its formation was the fifth Guru, Arjan, who installed the scripture in the Golden Temple at Amritsar in 1604. Himself the largest single contributor, Guru Arjan drew upon earlier collections containing not only hymns by the earlier Gurus but also compositions by like-minded medieval Indian teachers called Bhagats ('devotees'), including figures from the Sant tradition like Nāmdev or Kabīr and Sufis like Farīd.

While certainly considerable, the linguistic variety of the Granth can be exaggerated, and the fundamental components of this mixed sacred language of the Sikhs (see *Sikhism*) are drawn from Old Panjabi and Old Hindi. With the increased use of Braj bhāṣā forms, the Hindi component, already more marked in much of Guru Arjan's oeuvre, dominates the final additions to the Granth, the compositions by the ninth Guru Tegh Bahādur (d.1675). Reflecting their respective areas of origin, the main deviations from the standard mixture are naturally found in the hymns of the Bhagats, with e.g. forms from Marathi in Nāmdev, from Avadhi in Kabīr and from Siraiki in Farīd. Further variety is introduced by the Gurus' occasional deliberate exploitation of alternative poetic idioms (Shackle 1978).

Full contemporary understanding of the condensed and archaic scriptural language is dependent upon modern Panjabi commentaries, or in the diaspora, upon English translations (McLeod 1984, Singh 1995).

See also: Panjabi; Sikhism; Gurmukhi; Panjabi (Gurmukhi) Sacred Texts.

Bibliography

Deol J S 2001 Text and Lineage in Early Sikh History: Issues in the Study of the Adi Granth. *Bulletin of the School of Oriental and African Studies* **65**: 34–58

McLeod W H 1968 *Gurū Nānak and the Sikh Religion*. Clarendon Press, Oxford

McLeod W H 1984 (ed.) *Textual Sources for the Study of Sikhism*. Manchester University Press, Manchester

Shackle C 1978 The Sahaskritī Poetic Idiom in the *Ādi Granth*. *Bulletin of the School of Oriental and African Studies* **41**: 297–313

Singh N G K 1995 *The Name of My Beloved, Verses of the Sikh Gurus*. HarperCollins, San Francisco

Hindu Sacred Texts

J. L. Brockington

Hinduism (itself a contested term) has a rather different relationship to its major texts from that of many religions. Most who classify themselves as Hindus regard acceptance of the authority of the Vedas as basic but in terms of their day-to-day practice turn to a range of religious texts in modern Indian languages (for example, for Hindi speakers, the Kṛṣṇa poetry of Sūrdās or the *Rāmcaritmānas* of Tulsīdās), which are regarded as authoritative only by the particular group concerned. In between lie the *Bhagavadgītā* (the best known of Hindu religious texts outside India), or more generally the *Mahābhārata* and the *Rāmāyaṇa*, the *Purāṇas* and a few other traditional texts that enjoy a substantial measure of authority. The orthodox view, though, is that the Vedas alone are revelation—as is shown by two of the terms often used for them: *śruti*, meaning literally 'hearing,' and *śabda*, 'word'—and they will be treated here.

1. Extent of the Vedas

Within the Indian tradition, the term Veda designates four groups of texts, each consisting of four categories of material: the four groups are the *Ṛgveda*, *Sāmaveda*, *Yajurveda*, and *Atharvaveda*, while the four categories are the *Saṃhitās* ('collections of hymns'), *Brāhmaṇas* ('texts relating to *brahman*'), *Āraṇyakas* ('belonging to the forest') and *Upaniṣads* (probably 'sitting around a teacher'). Confusingly and inaccurately, the term Veda and the four individual names are often used in Western writings to refer only to the first category of the hymn collections, the *saṃhitās*, which are implicitly assigned greater significance as being earlier (the four categories in fact represent in broad terms a chronological progression). However, to Hindus all four categories are equally authoritative, timeless and—on some views—authorless.

2. Saṃhitās

The oldest of the hymn collections, compiled around 1200 BCE to judge by its language, is that of the *Ṛgveda*, consisting of 1028 hymns, divided into ten books, of which the last is rather different in style and content. Next comes the *Sāmaveda* collection, followed closely by the *Yajurveda* collection, and finally the *Atharvaveda* collection. The hymns in most books of the *Ṛgveda* collection are grouped according to the deity invoked, beginning with Agni, the god of fire, because of his importance in the sacrifice, continuing with Indra, the most prominent of the deities, and then the other deities in descending order of importance. The ninth book is addressed to Soma, the other major deity of the sacrificial ritual, while in the tenth book some of the older gods disappear, to be replaced by more abstract deities, and several hymns are speculative in character.

The *Sāmaveda* and the *Yajurveda* draw to a considerable extent on the *Ṛgveda* collection (often using just one or two verses at a time), forming distinct collections to serve the needs of the chanting priest and the officiant respectively and supplemented appropriately. The *Atharvaveda saṃhitā* is again a collection of complete hymns but addressed to a more popular pantheon, including spells and incantations for every purpose, as well as a few more speculative hymns.

3. Brāhmaṇas (and Āraṇyakas)

As the ritual became more elaborate, the need was felt—first in the *Yajurveda* tradition—for texts relating more directly to such concerns: the *Brāhmaṇas*, the texts 'relating to *brahman*' the sacred power above all manifested in sacrificial ritual. They are enormous prose works linked to the requirements of various priests, with for example the Brāhmaṇas of the *Ṛgveda*, the *Aitareya* and *Kauṣītaki Brāhmaṇas*, intended for use by the invoking priest. They include a large amount of other material incidental to their main purpose of describing and explaining the ritual, including full narrations of myths only alluded to in the hymns; their contents are usually divided later into the commands (which are obligatory) and the explanations (whose only function is to encourage the performance of the commands).

Each Brāhmaṇa usually includes an Āraṇyaka of the same name, the generic term indicating that their subject matter was considered esoteric; only to be studied outside the gaze of society at large, in the forest; in practice, most Āraṇyakas are transitional texts, containing varying blends of hymn, Brāhmaṇa and proto-Upaniṣadic material.

4. Upaniṣads

The early Upaniṣads are similarly incorporated within Brāhmaṇas but later Upaniṣads have an increasingly tenuous link with the rest of the Vedic literature. Their concerns are now not so much with the ritual as with the nature of the universe, and especially with Brahman, the sacred power of the ritual which, on the basis that ritual sustains everything, comes to be seen as the power underlying the universe. Brahman is thus the inner essence of the cosmos, just as the *ātman*, the true, unchanging self, is the essence of the empirical individual, the microcosm; the ultimate identity of Brahman and *ātman* is indeed the most significant new idea expounded among the ferment of speculation included in the Upaniṣads.

5. The Vedas in Hinduism

Although the Vedas are regarded as revealed, they are not in fact studied by the vast majority of Hindus, most of whom (the lower castes and all women) were in due course forbidden to learn or study them. Nevertheless, certain Vedic hymns are still employed in many forms of major life-cycle rituals, despite their incomprehensibility to participants in the rituals. Two later schools of Hindu thought base themselves on the Vedas. The Mīmāṃsā system concentrates on the ritual commands of the Brāhmaṇas, in the process jettisoning the concept of deities (except as nominal recipients of the sacrifices), while the Vedānta system concerns itself almost exclusively with the Upaniṣads, seeking in its various schools to construct a consistent system from their varied speculations but identifying this as monism (Advaita, literally 'nondualism'), a qualified monism or dualism. The survival and employment of the Vedas within later Hinduism is limited but far from insignificant.

See also: Hinduism.

Bibliography

Elizarenkova T J 1995 *Language and Style of the Vedic Ṛṣis* (SUNY Series in Hindu Studies). State University of New York Press, Albany, NY

Gonda J 1975 *Vedic Literature: Saṃhitās and Brāhmaṇas* (History of Indian Literature, vol. I, fasc. 1). Harrassowitz, Wiesbaden

Maurer W H 1986 *Pinnacles of India's Past: Selections from the Ṛgveda*. John Benjamin, Amsterdam

Oberlies T 1998 *Die Religion des Ṛgveda* (Publications of the de Nobili Research Library 26), 3 vols. Institut für Indologie der Universität Wien, Vienna

O'Flaherty W D 1981 *The Rig Veda: an Anthology*. Penguin, Harmondsworth

Mormon, Book of

A. Cunningham

The Church of Jesus Christ of the Latter-day Saints provides the most impressive example of a religious organization based upon a secondary myth of language (see *Myths About Language*). In Manchester, Ontario County, New York, on September 21–22, 1824, Joseph Smith (1805–44) received the promise of a new religious dispensation. An angel appeared to him telling of certain gold plates hidden near his home recording, in a 'reformed Egyptian' script, Christ's revelation to the ancient inhabitants of America. On September 22, 1827 Smith recovered the tablets and a key for interpreting them. His transcription of the plates appeared as the *Book of Mormon* in 1830. The nature of the original gold plates, and even their existence, has been a controversial issue in Mormonism.

The plates were a condensed record of the history, faith, and prophecies of America's ancient inhabitants. Three migrations are described: (a) of Jared after the Flood and the dispersion of peoples at the Tower of Babel (see *Babel*); (b) of Lehi, of the tribe of Manasseh, from Jerusalem in 600 BCE; (c) of further Israelites some 11 years later. From Lehi descended two groups, the now extinct Nephites and the Lamanites, ancestors of the Native Americans. Mormon was the last Nephite prophet, inscribing the plates at the end of the fourth century CE. His son, Moroni, survived a Lamanite massacre in 420 and 'hid up' the plates at the hill of Cumarah, site of the final battle. The *Book of Mormon* also describes the coming of Jesus Christ to America ca. 34–35 CE, shortly after his ascension from Judaea; his repeating of the Sermon on the Mount, appointing of 12 American apostles and instructing them in baptism by immersion.

Smith's claims for his text in their detailed and systematic nature differed from anything that had gone before, such as the odd macaronic fragments of Hebrew, Greek, Arabic, or Coptic that occur in late medieval and Renaissance magic or the apparently grammatical structure of the Enochian language for the invocation of spirits communicated to the seventeenth century magus John Dee (see *Magic*). They also differ from many later nineteenth- and twentieth-century claims to have received extensive revelations of ancient wisdom, which do not have the problems of any physical evidence for the original text, or any issues of translation from an unknown language, since the messages are received from hidden masters or extraterrestrial sources able to communicate in any human language. Interesting linguistic questions are raised by claims of telepathic communication between people of different languages.

To point to the way in which motifs familiar from other sources are present in the transmission claimed by Joseph Smith does not mean that he had to have detailed knowledge of such sources; the motifs may simply be likely combinations of possibilities in the general configuration of biblical/Old World/New World problems. Smith's imagination may have been fired by the finding of brass plates in the excavation of the Erie Canal in 1821. It may also be interesting that Champollion's deciphering of the Egyptian of the Rosetta Stone (by allowing for a phonetic as well as pictographic element in the hieroglyphs) occurred in 1822, the year before Smith's vision of the angel, and was generally accepted by 1827. Given the military and scholarly rivalry and France and England over Egypt and Egyptian antiquities, Champollion's discovery was very extensively publicized (see *Rosetta Stone*).

Bibliography

Jackson K P 1988 The sacred literature of the Latter-day Saints. In: Frerichs E S (ed.) *The Bible and Bibles in America*. Scholars Press, Atlanta, GA

Stott G St J 1988 Joseph Smith's 1823 vision: uncovering the angel message. *Religion* **18(4)**: 347–62

Nag Hammadi Texts

A. Crislip

The *Nag Hammadi Texts* comprise 13 papyrus books (codexes) manufactured in the fourth century CE. These books were discovered in 1945 by farmers working opposite the modern Egyptian city of Nag Hammadi. The books had been buried in a large clay jar in the fourth or fifth century CE, probably as a result of doctrinal persecution. These manuscripts include a variety of religious texts, including many Gnostic texts, as well as other Christian apocrypha and several philosophical texts. The manuscripts are also referred to as the Nag Hammadi Library and the Coptic Gnostic Library. The *Nag Hammadi Texts* are written in Coptic, although they are all translated from Greek originals. They document two Coptic dialects, Sahidic (with numerous deviations from what would become standard biblical Sahidic) and Lycopolitan L6, a dialect of Middle Egypt. Even within these two basic dialects, the scribes of the manuscripts vary significantly in their orthography and lexicon.

The owners of these manuscripts remain unknown. Scholarly debate has centered on their possible association with a nearby Pachomian monastery, but no association with any particular group has been convincingly proven. Along with the *Dead Sea Scrolls*, the *Nag Hammadi Texts* are among the most important manuscript discoveries of the twentieth century. They have augmented and altered our understanding of early Christianity and provided the impetus for important research in a number of areas of early Christian history, including Gnosticism, gospel traditions, gender studies, and later Platonism, as well as providing abundant data for Coptic dialectology.

See also: Apocrypha, Christian; Ancient Egyptian and Coptic; Gnosticism.

Bibliography

Robinson J (ed.) 1978 *The Nag Hammadi Library in English.* Harper Collins, San Francisco

Scholer D 1971 *Nag Hammadi Bibliography 1948–1969.* Leiden, Brill

Scholer D 1997 *Nag Hammadi Bibliography 1970–1994.* Brill, Leiden

Pali Canon

I. Onians

The *Pali Canon* is a collection of scripture (*buddhavacana* 'the word of the Buddha') preserved by the *Theravada* tradition of Buddhism, active in Sri Lanka, Burma, Cambodia, Laos, and Thailand.

The term itself is somewhat tautologous, since *pali* originally referred to 'canonical text' (as opposed to 'commentary' *atthakatha*). Pali as the name of the Middle Indo-Aryan Prakrit language of canon, commentaries, and chronicles, was not attested before the seventeenth century. That language had previously been known as *Magadhi*. Moreover, there was no such a thing as a closed corpus until the first known writing down of the canon in Sri Lanka in the first century BCE.

Pali is a literary language, based on a Western Prakrit close to that of third century BCE Ashokan inscriptions from the West of North India. But by the time of the canon's closure the Buddhists had begun to Sankritize their texts, under the influence of brahmanical high culture. Dravidian and Sinhalese elements are included in the language of the postcanonical chronicles and commentaries composed in South India and Sri Lanka.

The Theravadins of Sri Lanka were alone in the Buddhist community to understand a passage in the canon as prohibiting the translation of the Buddha's words. Only the commentaries could be translated from Pali into Sinhalese.

There are several different recensions of the canon, published in local scripts in India, Sri Lanka, Burma, and Thailand. A complete canon has been published in Roman script by the Pali Text Society in London, as well as very nearly the whole in English translation. There are still many manuscripts to be published and collated.

See also: Pali; Buddhism and Language; Buddhist Hybrid Sanskrit; Buddhist Canons: Translations.

Bibliography

Collins S 1990 On the very idea of the Pali Canon. *Journal of the Pali Text Society* **15**: 89–126

Hinüber O von 1996 *A Handbook of Pali Literature.* Walter de Gruyter, Berlin

Norman K R 1983 *Pali Literature.* Harrassowitz, Wiesbaden

Panjabi (Gurmukhi) Sacred Texts

C. Shackle

While modern Sikh orthodoxy accords a unique canonical status to the *Gurū Granth Sāhib* (see Granth), Sikh sacred literature embraces numerous other texts dating from between the sixteenth and early nineteenth centuries. All were composed and transmitted in the Gurmukhi script, although they are diverse in language and in genre.

Three generic types of supplemental sacred texts may be distinguished: the *Dasam Granth*; the *rahit-nāmā* literature; and the *janam-sākhī* and other hagiographic literature.

Of comparable size to the *Ādi Granth* whose last contributor was the ninth Sikh Guru, the *Dasam Granth* ('The Book of the Tenth One') contains writings associated with the tenth and last Guru Gobind Singh (1666–1708). Composed mostly in Braj bhāṣā verse, the *Dasam Granth* (Loehlin 1971) once enjoyed comparable canonical rank, but the prominence therein of apparently Hindu or secular themes has latterly caused more reserved treatment to be given to all but those few compositions believed to be by Guru Gobind Singh himself: for example, the liturgical *Jāpu*, a long doxology invoking Islamicate as well as Sanskritic divine names, and the *Zafarnāmā*, a Persian verse epistle addressed to the Mughal emperor Aurangzeb.

The absence from both Granths of rules of conduct was made good in the eighteenth century by the texts called *rahit-nāmā* ('conduct book'). Generally naive in content and style, these are in a mixed Panjabi-Hindi prose (McLeod 1987).

Greater interest attaches to the hagiographic literature, especially the *janam-sākhī* ('birth-witness') collections assembled from the early seventeenth century (McLeod 1980). These hagiographies of the first Guru Nānak are also in Panjabi-Hindi prose, with scriptural quotations. The Gurmukhi hagiographic literature culminates in the Braj bhāṣā works of Santokh Singh (1787–1843), later edited in 14 volumes by the Sikh reformer Vīr Singh.

See also: Gurmukhi; Sikhism.

Bibliography

Loehlin C H 1971 *The Granth of Guru Gobind Singh and the Khalsa Brotherhood.* Lucknow Publishing House, Lucknow

McLeod W H 1980 *Early Sikh Tradition, a Study of the Janam-sākhis.* Clarendon Press, Oxford

McLeod W H 1987 (ed.) *The Chaupa Singh Rahit-nama.* University of Otago Press, Dunedin

Peshitta

A. G. Salvesen

The Peshitta is the standard Syriac version of the Bible, used for centuries by Syrian Christian communities in Asia as far as South India and China, and still read today in the Syrian Orthodox Church and the Assyrian Church of the East (see *Christianity in Iran and Central Asia*; *Christianity in the Near East*).

The term Peshitta is not found in reference to the Syriac biblical text until the ninth century CE: it means either 'simple' or 'widespread.' 'Simple' would perhaps distinguish it from later, very literal translations of the Greek Bible, or it may refer to the straightforward nature of its rendering. 'Widespread' would refer to the Peshitta's status as the authoritative version of the Bible in every branch of the Syriac-speaking church, receiving acceptance long before the fifth century when disagreements about the nature of Christ caused serious rifts. The oldest extant manuscripts of the Peshitta in fact date from the fifth century CE.

The Peshitta version of the Old Testament is a collection of books translated separately and at different times. For the Hebrew canon, Jewish, or Jewish Christian translators generally worked directly from a Hebrew text without vowels which closely resembled the later standard text of the rabbis known as the Masoretic Text (see *Hebrew Grammarians*; *Masoretic Tradition*). Sometimes there are parallels with Targum tradition (see *Targum*), and occasionally there is evidence of consultation of the Septuagint (see *Septuagint*). The books of the Apocrypha (see *Apocrypha, Christian*) render from Greek, though Sirach is based on the Hebrew Ben Sira. Dating is problematic, but it is likely that the various parts of the Peshitta Old Testament were translated during the first and second centuries CE. Chronicles, Esther and Ezra-Nehemiah, which may have been translated at the very end of this period, were not considered fully canonical by the Syriac churches. The place of translation is debated: the conversion to Judaism of the royal family of Adiabene (Northern Mesopotamia) in the mid-first century CE has led some to suggest that this is the origin of the Peshitta Old Testament, while others prefer the city of Edessa (modern Urfa in Turkey), since the language of the Peshitta, Syriac, is essentially the dialect of Aramaic used there.

The Peshitta New Testament is based on a revision of the existing Old Syriac Gospel tradition (dating from the second or third century CE) along with new translations of other New Testament books. It gradually superseded both these Old Syriac Gospels and the influential gospel harmony known as the Diatessaron (composed c. 160 CE by Tatian). However, the Peshitta New Testament did not include the book of Revelation or the Catholic Epistles (2 Peter, 2 and 3 John, and Jude). Although the exact date and provenance of the New Testament Peshitta translation is unknown, it was being cited regularly by authors of the mid-fourth century CE, so must have originated in the previous century.

See also: Syriac, Christian; Bible Translations, Ancient Versions.

Bibliography

Brock S P 1992. Versions, Ancient (Syriac). In: Freedman D N et al. (eds.) *The Anchor Bible Dictionary.* Doubleday, New York, VI, pp. 794–796

Weitzman M P 1999. *The Syriac Version of the Old Testament: An Introduction.* University of Cambridge Oriental Publications 56. Cambridge University Press, Cambridge

Pseudepigrapha

J. F. A. Sawyer

The term is applied in modern times to a large and amorphous group of texts, mostly of Jewish origin, composed between c. 250 BCE and 200 CE. They are mainly expansions of biblical stories, written in familiar literary genres including visions, journeys to heaven and testaments, but often containing ancient material not attested elsewhere. They were probably given canonical status of a kind in some ancient contexts, but, unlike the Apocrypha, were never included in either the Hebrew or the Greek Bible. The pseudonymity suggested by the term applies to some of the Pseudepigrapha including the Book of Enoch, the Odes of Solomon, the Testaments of the Twelve Patriarchs, the Sibylline Oracles, and Pseudo-Philo's Biblical Antiquities, falsely attributed to individuals from the past, but not to others such as Joseph and Aseneth, Jubilees and the Life of Adam and Eve. Some of these works were originally composed in Hebrew or Aramaic, as fragments of Jubilees in Hebrew and of Enoch in Aramaic discovered at Qumran show (see *Dead Sea Scrolls*). Others were probably Greek compositions and it was certainly in Greek that the Pseudepigrapha were used by the early Church. The influence on Christian origins of some of these writings, especially the Book of Enoch, has been significant, while Christians interpolations are evident in others such as the Martyrdom and Ascension of Isaiah. Eventually rejected both by the rabbis and by the Church Fathers, the most complete or most reliable surviving manuscripts of many of the Pseudepigrapha are those written in Ethiopic, Syriac, Armenian, Coptic, or Slavonic.

See also: Apocrypha, Christian; Bible; Christianity in the Near East; Gnosticism; Nag Hammadi Texts.

Bibliography

Charles R H 1913 *The Apocrypha and Pseudepigrapha of the Old Testament in English*, Vol. 2. Oxford University Press, Oxford

Charlesworth J H 1985 *The Old Testament Pseudepigrapha*, 2 Vols. Darton, Longman and Todd, London

Kraft R A, Nickelsberg G W E (eds.) 1986 *Early Judaism and its Modern Interpreters*. Scholars Press, Atlanta, GA/ Fortress Press, Philadelphia, PA

Qur'ān

I. R. Netton

Muslims believe that the Qur'ān, the most sacred text of the Islamic religion, is the uncreated word of God. Since God is eternal, so is His word. The text was revealed, according to Islam, via the Angel Gabriel to the Prophet Muḥammad (ca. 570–632 CE), and thence to mankind. Muḥammad received his first revelation of the Qur'ān in his hill cave above Mecca in about 610; the revelations continued throughout his life in both Mecca and Medina. These revelations, which were frequently exhortatory or eschatological in content were memorized by Muḥammad's followers or preserved in writing on a variety of materials. After Muḥammad's death in 632, orthodox Muslim opinion holds that the final text of the Qur'ān, as known in modern times, was collected and edited during the caliphate of the third ruler over the Islamic community, 'Uthmān (ruled 644–656).

The text comprises 114 chapters, called in Arabic '*sūras*,' of unequal length, with the longest chapters appearing first. These are further divided into verses of varying length, called '*āyāt*,' a word which occurs a number of times in the Qur'ān with the meaning 'signs,' 'miracles.' It is believed that the Arabic dialect in which the scripture is couched was akin to that of the dominant tribe in Mecca at the time of Muḥammad, the Quraysh, and also has considerable affinities with that of pre-Islamic poetry, a notable corpus of which still survives. The language of pre-Islamic poetry indeed, could be used to clarify the language of the Qur'ān. In a strange but very real way, the language of the pre-Islamic bards prefigured the superior language of the Qur'ān: a human linguistic prototype, as it were, of the divine articulation. Thus, when the great Egyptian scholar, Ṭāhā Ḥusayn (1889–1973), alleged that most of the corpus of pre-Islamic poetry was in fact of later provenance, he was anathematized by orthodox theologians as if he had attacked the language of the Qur'ān itself.

A fundamental doctrine associated with the Qur'ān is that it possesses the quality of *i'jāz* or inimitability. Indeed, the Qur'ān challenges its opponents to produce a facsimile of some of its verses, which is of equal merit and quality. There are a number of other features which particularly characterize the language of the Qur'ānic text: much of it is written in the rhymed prose called in Arabic '*saj*'' and the entire text may be said to have an, albeit disjointed, poetic quality and style which set it apart from later Arabic prose. The principal feature, however, is assonance rather than strict rhyme, though constraints of rhyme or assonance may sometimes appear to dictate the grammatical form of the Arabic. The overall effect of the language of the Qur'ān is often one of great lyricism and beauty, and this is perhaps enhanced by the variety of rhythms to be found in the text, rather than the presence of a single dominant meter.

Twenty-nine of the *sūras* begin with small groups of letters of the Arabic alphabet and both Muslim and Western scholars have put forward diverse explanations of these 'mysterious letters of the Qur'ān.' These include the idea that the letters were the initials of Arabic epithets for God, the initials of the people responsible for collecting and memorizing the words uttered by the Prophet, the remnants of original titles which some *sūras* bore, and mysterious symbols whose very unintelligibility to human minds is itself proof of divine authorship.

Against the traditional view that the Arabic of the Qur'ān was in some way pure (16: 103; 26: 195), it is noteworthy that it contains non-Arabic foreign vocabulary. Mecca was a trading city and the Qur'ān was revealed in the Arabic language of the age which must have absorbed a quantity of foreign words. The majority of 'loanwords' derive from Syriac, but there are also words of Ethiopic, Hebrew, Aramaic, Greek, and Persian origin. Examples claimed by scholars include *sakīna* 'divine immanence or peace' from the Hebrew *Shĕkhīnā*, and *ḥanīf* 'monotheist' from the Syriac *ḥanpo* (which has, however, the reverse meaning!). It has been also noted that the vocabulary and imagery of the Qur'ān drew heavily on the language of commerce and bookkeeping.

The above features—and, in particular, the poetic qualities—of the text have combined to give the Qur'ān, in the Muslim mind, a unique quality which they firmly believe is inimitable and, indeed, untranslatable, despite the existence of many 'translations' for those unable to read the Arabic original. In some countries, parts of the Arabic text are memorized (because of the intrinsic merit in such a religious activity) but without real understanding. There is no doubt that the syntax and vocabulary of the Qur'ān has had a profound effect on the later development of the Arabic language—despite obvious points of difference the modern literary language has much in common with Qur'ānic language—as well as on the other languages of the Islamic world, notably Persian, Turkish, Urdu, Malay, Hausa, and Swahili.

Theology and language are inextricably linked in many aspects of Qur'ānic studies. From early times it was rapidly realized that the sacred text of the Qur'ān, like that of the Holy Bible, required interpretation, in order to identify the real *meaning* behind the written words. As with the Bible, various modes of exegesis were espoused, including the allegorical and the symbolic. The problems of apparent contradiction, and of verses which are culturally or temporally conditioned, were solved by endowing one verse (revealed later) with the capacity to abrogate an earlier (apparently contradictory) one. Islamic textual exegesis has never, however, gone to the extremes of the 'demythologizing' of a Bultmann. Classical Islamic exegesis of the Qur'ān, for example, by al-Ṭabarī, al-Zamakhsharī, and al-Bayḍāwī, is language-based but it operates within strict parameters, concentrating on highlighting apparent obscurities in the text, commenting at length on the grammar, and elaborating brief Qur'ānic references to historical figures.

The Qur'ānic text as the eternal uncreated word of God is fundamental Muslim doctrine. However, a school of thought arose in medieval Islam called the 'Mu'tazila,' which believed that the Qur'ān was created (admittedly by God, but at a certain time) rather than uncreated. The contrast, in a nutshell, was that of an *uncreated* body of divine language, as supreme arbiter of man's actions, versus a *created* body of (still) divine language in which a ruler's exegesis might act as a subtle or not-so-subtle counterpoise to that of the orthodox custodians of sacred knowledge, the theologians (see Watt 1985: 49). In Shī'ite Islam, both now and then, the orthodox custodian of the faith is the '*mujtahid*' who may be of Ayatollah rank and who may interpret the law in the absence of the awaited Imam. Elsewhere, in Sunnī Islam, interpretation of the text is in the hands of the orthodox '*ulamā*' from such citadels of learning as the Azhar University in Cairo.

See also: Arabic; Arabic Linguistic Tradition; Islam in the Near East; Arabic Script: Adaptation for Other Languages; Qur'ān, Translations.

Bibliography

Bell R, Watt W M 1977 *Bell's Introduction to the Qur'ān*, Islamic Surveys No. 8. Edinburgh University Press, Edinburgh

Gätje H 1976 *The Qur'ān and its Exegesis: Selected Texts with Classical and Modern Muslim Interpretations.* Routledge and Kegan Paul, London

Hussein Abdul Raof 2000 *Qur'ān Translation Discourse, Texture and Exegesis.* Curzon Press, Richmond

Jeffery A 1938 *The Foreign Vocabulary of the Qur'ān*. Oriental Institute, Baroda
Muhammad Abdel Haleem 1999 *Understanding the Qur'ān Themes and Style*. Tauris, London
Qur'ān 1986 transl. with commentary by M M Khatib *The Bounteous Kor'an* [Arabic text of the Royal Cairo edition with facing English Translation; authorized by al-Azhar]. Macmillan, London
Robinson N 1996 *Discovering the Qur'ān: A Contemporary Approach to a Veiled Text*. SCM, London
Wansbrough J 1977 *Qur'ānic Studies: Sources and Methods of Scriptural Interpretation*, London Oriental Series No. XXXI. Oxford University Press, Oxford
Watt W M 1985 *Islamic Philosophy and Theology: An Extended Survey*. Edinburgh University Press, Edinburgh

Qur'ān: Translations

T. J. Winter

The geographical spread and missionary logic of Islam have prompted translations of its most sacred scripture into several hundred languages. This process has often been hampered however, by theological hesitations about the translatability of God's word. Three such hesitations may be identified. First, for the theologians, the Qur'ān is *mu'jiz*, inimitable, thus serving as the religion's indispensable and supreme evidentiary miracle. Since this quality pertains to its Arabic diction as well as to its meaning, no translation can be said adequately to represent the original. Second, the Muslim belief that earlier scriptures had been compromised by interpolation and distortion (*taḥrīf*) led many to defend God's Book from the *traduttore* who might turn *traditore*. Thirdly, twentieth-century Arab theologians sometimes feared that translation into European languages would entail a diminution of the religion's perceived Arab particularity, leading to its symbolic conquest by the colonialist Other.

The prohibition has been upheld with great success in the case of the text's liturgical use. Probably every mosque in the world currently uses the Arabic Qur'ān for congregational prayer. The Ḥanafīs alone, among the four rites of Sunnī law, permit the use of translations in the canonical worship (*ṣalāt*), but this dispensation is granted only to new proselytes who have yet to master the Arabic pronunciation.

Translations have, however, been regarded as permissible as study aids, examples being reported from as early as the second and third centuries of the religion. The dozens of extant medieval Persian and Turkish renderings often present themselves as paraphrases or glosses, or as disconnected explications of individual Qur'ānic words and phrases. Interlinear translations often emphasize the lack of continuity and literary equivalence by writing each translated section at an angle (for illustrations see Meredith-Owens 1957). In other cases, however, a continuously flowing text was produced, which could itself initiate an autonomous vernacular tradition, as is seen from the archaisms present in some Ottoman versions made from earlier Turkic translations.

Almost by definition such translations were made for readers of modest education, and therefore present a valuable cache of colloquialisms that may not otherwise have been preserved. Where the target language is already Islamized, the translations typically avert difficulty by exploiting Qur'ānic lexis already integrated into the religious registers of the reader's language. Where only partial Islamization has taken place (as with the seventeenth-century translations for communities in Poland and Belorussia), marginalia may gloss a word of Arabic origin used in the translation. When Muslims have translated the scripture into languages with little or no Arabic vocabulary (Japanese, Czech, Creole) the process may become a fascinating and revealing exercise in cultural relocation.

From the early Muslim centuries translations have also been composed by Christians (beginning with Syriac, and then Latin and Armenian), primarily for purposes of refutation. These are characterized by polemical annotation, and by the absence of the use of Arabic script.

See also: Qur'ān; Islamic Calligraphy; Islam in Africa.

Bibliography

Johns A H 1978 Qur'ānic translation: some remarks and experiments. *Milla wa-Milla* **18**: 37–51
Ma'ayergi H 1986 *World Bibliography of Translations of the Meaning of the Holy Qur'an (Printed translations from 1515–1980)*. IRCICA, Istanbul
Meredith-Owens G M 1957 Notes on an old Ottoman translation of the Ḳur'ān. *Oriens* **10**: 258–76
Shakir M 1926 On the translation of the Koran into foreign languages. *Moslem World* **16**: 161–5

Qur'ān: Versions

T. J. Winter

Irrespective of sect or region, Muslims today use a standard Qur'ānic text. This striking unanimity masks a complex history of redaction, which is only partially discernible to modern scholarship.

Qur'ānic specialists customarily accept that no complete physical copy existed in the lifetime of the Prophet Muḥammad (d. 632), but that Qur'ānic revelations were first gathered, and perhaps bound together as a codex (*muṣḥaf*), by the first caliph, Abū Bakr (regn. 632–4). It is likely that this innovation, which may not have been completed until the time of his successor 'Umar (634–44), was intended to safeguard the integrity of the text rather than to establish an authorized version; but the caliph 'Uthmān (644–56) is credited with convening a redaction committee under the Prophet's scribe Zayd ibn Thābit, which, consulting senior disciples of the Prophet, established an official codex, copies of which were sent to provincial capitals with orders that alternative versions were to be destroyed.

No complete copy of such a rival version exists today. Standard Qur'ānic commentaries, and works in a specialized literature treating of Qur'ānic variants, in which the best surviving early example is the *Kitāb al-Maṣāḥif* of Ibn Abī Dāūd (d.928), nonetheless preserve abundant evidence that several disciples of the Prophet possessed their own Qur'ānic codices which differed materially from the 'Uthmānic *textus receptus*. Probably the most important such variant was that of Ibn Mas'ūd, which appears to have omitted sūras 1, 113 and 114, while ordering the remaining sūras differently and including numerous minor lexical departures from the 'Uthmānic canon, such as 17:93, where *dhahab* (gold) becomes *zukhruf* (adornment). Also significant was the *muṣḥaf* of Ubayy ibn Ka'b, which may have lacked approximately 10 of the 'Uthmānic sūras, and which included two new sūras, al-Khal' and al-Ḥafd, whose style is clearly redolent of the Hadīth literature rather than the Qur'ān. The additional sūras also appear in a third important early version, that of Abū Mūsā al-Ash'arī. These variants, associated with Kūfa, Syria and Baṣra respectively, probably reflect, and in some cases prolonged, regional memories which developed as the Prophet's disciples settled in the conquered provinces. This may account for the unanimity with which the Islamic world finally acquiesced in the imposition of 'Uthmān's text, which could boast the authority of the Prophet's own city of Madīna and its resident scholars.

The 'Uthmānic text is nonetheless not uniform. Dialectal differences, and the absence of diacritical marks in early Arabic orthography, produced minor variations, almost invariably pertaining to vocalisation or the use of the glottal stop, until the reform of Ibn Mujāhid (d.936) permanently fixed the number of vocalisation systems at seven, each of which was associated, quite legitimately, with the name of a leading regional Qur'ānic expert of the second Muslim century. These Seven Readings (*qirā'āt*), sometimes increased to ten or fourteen, are taught to this day in Muslim universities.

See also: Qur'ān; Islamic Calligraphy.

Bibliography

Jeffery A 1937 *Materials for the History of the Text of the Qur'ān*. E.J. Brill, Leiden, The Netherlands

Watt W M 1970 *Bell's Introduction to the Qur'ān*. University Press, Edinburgh

Rosetta Stone

J. D. Ray

The Rosetta Stone is the key to ancient Egyptian civilization (see *Egyptian Hieroglyphs*). It was discovered, built into a fortress at the Rosetta mouth of the Nile, in July 1799 by officers of Napoleon's expedition to Egypt, and it was quickly realized that the text, written in Egyptian hieroglyphics and demotic, but also in Greek—a known language—might provide the long-lost clue to the decipherment of Egyptian. After the surrender of French forces in Egypt to the British in 1801, the black basalt Stone was given, along with other antiquities, to the British Museum, where it is now exhibited. A translation of the Greek text of the Stone was soon in circulation throughout Europe, and it attracted the attention of Orientalists such as Åkerblad and Silvestre de Sacy. In England, the problems of the Rosetta Stone were tackled by Thomas Young, physicist, linguist, and optician. Young made important contributions to the

Figure 1. The Rosetta Stone. By courtesy of the British Museum, London.

study of the hieroglyphic text, and achieved even more progress with the central (demotic) section of the Stone, which is the best preserved.

The decipherment of the hieroglyphic was essentially the work of the French scholar, Jean-François Champollion (1790–1832). Champollion's method was outlined in his *Lettre à M. Dacier*, which was completed in September, 1822. He began by reading Greek names such as Ptolemy and Cleopatra, which he knew from the Stone and from another, shorter, bilingual text. The fortunate fact that these names contained the same sounds in different positions helped Champollion to draw up a hieroglyphic alphabet, on the lines already suggested by Young. However, the French Egyptologist went far beyond this, proceeding rapidly to decipher the names of earlier Pharaohs discovered on other monuments. A knowledge of Coptic grammar and vocabulary, and a list of kings' names preserved in classical sources, greatly aided his efforts (see *Ancient Egyptian and Coptic*). By the end of his short life, Champollion was able to read ancient Egyptian, and was well on the way to reconstructing Pharaonic history, religion, and civilization.

The text of the Rosetta Stone records a decree set up in the temples of Egypt in 196 BCE, during the region of the Greek Pharaoh, Ptolemy V Epiphanes. The generosity of the ruler toward the Egyptian temples is emphasized, and the best possible light put on the fact that he had just suppressed an Egyptian revolt. In return, the Egyptian priesthood agree to celebrate the royal cult with renewed splendor. The concessions made by the crown are far greater than the cosmetic actions of the native priesthood, and the whole text gives a valuable insight into the realities of Hellenistic politics. Other copies of this inscription are now known.

Ancient Egyptian would have been deciphered sooner or later, as the number of texts on stone or papyrus constantly increased throughout the nineteenth century, but the Rosetta Stone gave a dramatic birth to the new science of Egyptology. It is certainly a major landmark in the history of linguistics, and it is also an important symbol of the modern world's need to understand its origins (see Fig. 1).

See also: Silvestre de Sacy, Baron Antoine-Isaac; Young, Thomas; Champollion, Jean-François.

Bibliography

Andrews C A R 1981 *The Rosetta Stone*. British Museum Publications, London

Pope M 1975 *The Story of Decipherment*. Thames and Hudson, London

Quirke S, Andrews C A R 1988 *The Rosetta Stone; Facsimile Drawing, with an Introduction and Translations*. British Museum Publications, London

Septuagint

T. Muraoka

The Septuagint is a Greek document representing a translation of the Jewish Bible in Hebrew and Aramaic and also containing a number of texts partly translated from Hebrew (or possibly Aramaic) texts originally written in Greek. This latter group of texts is referred to as Apocrypha (see *Apocrypha, Christian*). The name 'Septuagint,' derived from a Latin word meaning 'seventy,' is taken as a reference to the legendary 72 scholars reputed to have produced this translation. The character of the translation varies from book to book, fluctuating between the two extremes of literalness and freedom. Hundreds of Septuagint manuscripts testify to a long history of textual evolution, in most cases an original translation undergoing various degrees and kinds of revision and only rarely a completely fresh translation.

Of competing theories on the origin of the Septuagint two are worthy of mention. There exists an ancient document of uncertain date (probably second century BCE), the so-called Letter of Aristeas, which purports to inform the reader precisely on this matter. According to this document, the translation was officially commissioned by the king, Ptolemy II Philadelphus (285–246 BCE) on a recommendation from the librarian of the famed library in Alexandria, who wished to fill the striking gap in its collection. This would seem to imply that the Greek Old Testament or the Pentateuch owes its origin to the intellectual curiosity of the pagan world. This information as well as other details in the document are dismissed by most scholars as historically unreliable. They conjecture, instead, that a more plausible reason for the production of the translation was the internal need of the Hellenized Jewish community in Alexandria and other parts of the Diaspora where the knowledge of Hebrew had sunk to a very low level. The first legend, however, may contain a grain of truth.

The Septuagint may be read without reference to its Semitic original, as was done by those who had little or no Hebrew/Aramaic. This may be called a reader-orientated approach. Modern examples of this include an ongoing series *La Bible d'Alexandrie* (1986–), M. Harl (ed.). An attempt to produce a modern Septuagint lexicon (Muraoka) is another expression of the same interest. The Septuagint embodies the oldest exegesis of the Jewish Bible.

Others, however, study the Septuagint in relation to its Semitic original, establishing characteristics and techniques of translation or identifying agreements and disagreements between it and its putative Semitic original, and tracing the evolution of the latter in relation to the standard text of the Jewish Bible. This latter approach may be called translator-orientated. Notwithstanding a significant number of calques due to the influence of the source language, the Septuagint is a rich source of major importance for those interested in Hellenistic (Koiné) Greek. Furthermore, the Septuagint continues to throw light on the meaning of obscure Hebrew/Aramaic words and forms in the Bible.

See also: Byzantine Greek; Bible Translations, Ancient Versions.

Bibliography

Brock S P, Fritsch C T, Jellicoe S A 1973 *A Classified Bibliography of the Septuagint*. E J Brill, Leiden

Dogniez C 1995 *Bibliography of the Septuagint: Bibliographie de la Septante (1970–1993)*. E J Brill, Leiden/New York/Köln

Dorival G, Harl M, Munnich O 1988 *La Bible grecque des Septante: Du Judaïsme au Christianisme ancien*. Edition du Cerf, Paris

Fernández Marcos N (trans. Watson W G E) 2000 *The Septuagint in Context. Introduction to the Greek Version of the Bible*. E J Brill, Leiden/New York/Köln

Jellicoe S 1968 *The Septuagint and Modern Study*. Oxford University Press, Oxford

Swete H B 1914 *An Introduction to the Old Testament in Greek*, 2nd edn. Cambridge University Press, Cambridge

Tov E 1981 *The Text-critical Use of the Septuagint in Biblical Research*, 2nd edn. Simor, Jerusalem

Talmud

G. Khan

The term 'Talmud,' a Hebrew word that literally means 'teaching,' or 'learning,' refers to a Jewish corpus of learning that was composed in the first half of the first millennium CE (approximately between 200 to 500 CE). This tradition of learning arose in Babylonia and Palestine and gave rise to the two written corpora known as the Babylonian Talmud and the Palestinian Talmud, respectively. The Talmudic tradition originated as an interpretation and elaboration of the postbiblical Jewish legal corpus known as the Mishnah. Throughout most of the period of its development it existed only in an orally transmitted form and was not committed to writing until around the middle of the first millennium. The written text was recited aloud in a reading tradition that was transmitted orally throughout the Middle Ages and has survived in some Jewish communities down to the present day. The existence of the reading tradition in the Middle Ages is demonstrated by the existence of manuscripts with vocalization.

The Babylonian Talmud (Bavli) was composed mainly in a form of Aramaic known as Jewish Babylonian Aramaic. It also contains many passages in a form of post-biblical Hebrew, which was considerably influenced by Aramaic. Jewish Babylonian Aramaic belongs to the eastern group of Aramaic dialects. The other major dialects in this group that were roughly contemporary with it are Syriac and Mandaic. Aramaic was spoken by Jewish communities throughout Babylonia until the Arab conquest in the seventh century CE, after which most Jews in the region adopted Arabic as their vernacular. Aramaic continued to be spoken in the mountains areas of the north down to the middle of the twentieth century. The Aramaic that is recorded in most of the Babylonian Talmud appears to be close to the vernacular form of the language that was being spoken in the Jewish rabbinic schools at the time of its composition. In some parts of the work, a typologically more archaic form of Aramaic is used, which is likely to be a literary language that differed from the spoken vernacular.

The Palestinian Talmud (Yerushalmi) was composed in Jewish Palestinian Aramaic, which was spoken by the Jewish communities in Palestine in the Byzantine period. This belongs to the western group of Aramaic dialects. Other contemporary dialects of the group include Christian Palestinian Aramaic and Samaritan Aramaic. Very few of the surviving manuscripts of the Palestinian Talmud have preserved the language accurately. In most cases the scribes adapted many aspects of the language to that of the Babylonian Talmud, which had become the more authoritative of the two Talmuds by the Middle Ages.

See also: Aramaic, Jewish; Judaism.

Bibliography

Dalman G 1894. *Grammatik des Jüdisch-Palästinischen Aramäisch*. Hinrichs, Leipzig

Kutscher E Y 1976 *Studies in Galilean Aramaic* (translated by M. Sokoloff). Bar-Ilan University, Ramat-Gan

Margolis M L 1910 *A Manual of the Aramaic Language of the Babylonian Talmud*. C.H. Beck, Munich

Targum

G. Khan

The term 'Targum' refers to a Jewish translation of the Hebrew Bible (Old Testament) into Aramaic. Various Targums of the Bible were made in the first millennium CE. The need for such translations arose at the beginning of the Common Era, after Hebrew had ceased to be a spoken language. They were recited orally in the synagogue in conjunction with the liturgical reading of the Hebrew scriptures.

The Targums that became most authoritative in Judaism and were most widely known are Targum Onqelos to the Pentateuch and Targum Jonathan to the Prophets. The Aramaic of both of these texts is close in form to the type of literary Aramaic that was used in Palestine at the end of the first millennium CE, which suggests that they were composed in Palestine. During the first millennium, however, they appear to have been transmitted only in Babylonia. The vocalization that they have in the medieval manuscripts reflects some features that are likely to have been adopted from the Aramaic dialects of Babylonia. In general, however, their language is very different from the Aramaic of the Babylonian Talmud, which is closer to the vernacular of Babylonia. The majority of the earliest manuscripts of Onqelos and Jonathan have Babylonian vocalization. Numerous manuscripts exist, however, with Tiberian vocalization, some of which are likely to emanate from medieval Palestine.

Various other Aramaic Targums were produced in Palestine, all of which appear to have emerged later than those of Onqelos and Jonathan. These Palestinian Targums were only transmitted in Palestine and never attained the same authority as Targum Onqelos and Jonathan. They include texts known as Targum Pseudo-Jonathan (Pentateuch), Targum Neofiti (Pentateuch), Fragmentary Targum (selected passages from the Pentateuch), and Genizah fragments of Targums to the Pentateuch. These translations are written in a dialect known as Jewish Palestinian Aramaic, which is similar to that of the Palestinian Talmud. It was the vernacular language of the Jews in Palestine during the Byzantine period. Of particular importance linguistically are the Genizah fragments, which have been dated to as early as the eighth century CE and are vocalized.

Targums to the Hagiographa are also extant. Most of these have a complicated textual history and the form in which we find them in the extant manuscripts is often written in an Aramaic that is an amalgam of Jewish Palestinian Aramaic and the Aramaic of Targums Onqelos and Jonathan. The Targum to Proverbs is unusual in that it exhibits some linguistic features that are characteristic of Syriac (an eastern Christian Aramaic dialect). It appears that it was largely derived from the Syriac version of the Bible (Peshitta).

See also: Judaism, Aramaic, Jewish; Cairo Genizah; Syriac, Christian; Peshitta.

Bibliography

Dalman G 1894 *Grammatik des Jüdisch-Palästinischen Aramäisch.* Hinrichs, Leipzig

Fassberg S 1991 *A Grammar of the Palestinian Targum Fragments from the Cairo Genizah.* Scholars Press, Atlanta

Tal A 1975 *The Language of the Targum of the Former Prophets and its Position within the Aramaic Dialects.* Tel-Aviv University, Tel-Aviv

Translation: History

L. G. Kelly

From Roman times to the present, Europe has been a civilization of translations, every aspect of its culture, literature, administration, trade, religion, and science having been deeply influenced by translators. Modern thought on translation derives ultimately from the Jews of Alexandria in the first century BCE who translated literally, and the Romans of the Classical Age, who did just the opposite. Two short passages have had an inordinate influence on translation theory: *De optimo genere oratorum* (v. 14) by Marcus Tullius Cicero (106–43 BCE), which insisted on the necessity of 'weighing' words rather than 'counting them,' and the famous condemnation of literal translation by the poet Horace (65–8 BCE) in his *Ars poetica* 131–35 (ca. 19 BCE).

1. The Classical Period

1.1 Jewish Translation

Translation was a constant of ancient civilizations—there are bilingual inscriptions from Assyria and

Mesopotamia (3000 BCE) and the Rosetta stone from Egypt (196 BCE). Most of these translations dealt with administrative and commercial matters. The Jewish translators of the Old Testament were based in Alexandria, then one of the most important Greek-speaking cities in the Mediterranean. By 200 BCE they were facing a dilemma. On the one hand most Jews living outside Palestine could not understand Hebrew well enough to read the Scriptures. On the other, translation of the Scriptures was tampering with the Word of God. Both Jewish theology and Neoplatonist philosophy agreed that the Divine Word illuminated the human soul and mind, and that names directly reflected natures. One could only avoid negating the creative power of the Scriptures by strict word-for-word translation. The Greek version of the Hebrew Scriptures, the *Septuagint* (q.v.), was complete by about 150 BCE. The persistent legend that the 70 translators were left in solitary confinement each with a Hebrew text and in 70 days each produced identical texts shows that literal translation was accorded mystical value (see *Judaism*).

1.2 Roman Translation

In ancient Rome, translation was always done from Greek texts normally as a rhetorical or creative task. Roman thought on the craft was summed up by the first-century rhetorician, Quintilian, who repeated the ideas of Cicero and Horace, seeing translation as 'rivalry' of the original author. The one dissenting voice was the philosopher, Seneca the Younger, who demanded that if truth was to be kept, translation should be strictly literal.

In about 250 BCE, Livius Andronicus, a Greek slave captured at Tarentum in southern Italy in 272 BCE, produced a Latin version of the *Odyssey*, which was still being used as a textbook in Roman schools a couple of centuries later. In the meantime soldiers and other administrators were coming back to Rome with a taste for Greek amusements, particularly theater. Enterprising writers supplied the need by free translation and even adaptation from Greek dramatists. The two most famous of these Roman dramatists of the generation after Livius Andronicus, Plautus (d. 184 BCE) and Terence (190–159 BCE), were regarded as authorities on translation until the end of the western Roman Empire.

The greatest age of Roman literary translation lasted from the first century BCE to the middle of the first century CE. The Roman Golden Age set the custom, which lasted until well into the twentieth century, of treating translation as a literary apprenticeship and constant exercise. Most of the extant poets have some translation in their corpus; for example, Cicero's major contribution was to create scientific terminology through his versions of Greek philosophy. Translation remained common in the centuries following, one notable translator being the philosopher Apuleius (120–155), the author of *The Golden Ass*.

The importance of literary translation has obscured the immense amount of Roman technical and scientific translation. There was a small corpus of medical translators whose adherence to the originals by Hippocrates, Galen, and some minor Greek medical writers is typical of technical work in all ages. Drawing on the talent at his disposal the Emperor Augustus set up a translation office as part of the imperial household to assist in administering the Empire. Its most prominent piece of work is the *Monumentum ancyranum*, Emperor Augustus's own statement of his achievements, translated as a blatant piece of propaganda. This translation office remained active until after the fall of Rome in the fifth century.

1.3 Christian Translation

Christian translation, from Greek into Latin (except for Wulfila's fourth-century Gothic version of the Bible (see *Wulfila*)) began in the second century CE with the *Shepherd of Hermas* and parts of the Bible (see *Bible Translations, Ancient Versions*). The Jewish Platonist ideas on the relationship between language and the divine flourished in their assiduously literal style. Translation of Greek Christian liturgies for Latin-Speakers began soon after. The Christian tradition culminated in the work of St Jerome (348–420) (q.v.), famous for his Latin version of the Bible, the Vulgate (383–406) (q.v.), and for a huge number of miscellaneous translations covering Church administration, monastic rules, and theology. However, he was only one of a very skilled band of translators, which included his former friend, Rufinus (345–410), the philosopher, Marius Mercator (ca. 400–450), and a large number of anonymous churchmen.

Roman translation came to an end with Boethius (480–524). He had meant to stave off the tide of barbarism attendant on the collapse of the Roman Empire by producing Latin versions of the complete corpus of Plato and Aristotle, but was executed for treason in 524 with only a small part of the work done. His versions revert to the strict type of translation thought proper by Biblical translators. His preface to Porphyry's Isagoge, which castigates elegance as inimical to 'truth,' may owe as much to Seneca as to the Judeo–Christian tradition.

2. The Middle Ages

2.1 Translation from Greek to Latin

Although Jerome was revered and quoted right through the Middle Ages and the Renaissance as the main model for translation, the medieval tone was set by Boethius. His methods were followed by

Cassiodorus (ca. 490–583). Between 550 and 560 Cassiodorus assembled a stable of translators in a monastery in Calabria called the Vivarium, dedicated to preserving Classical culture. He, like Boethius, had the ambition to translate the whole of Greek philosophy and theology into Latin. Though he did not succeed in this aim, he put translation on a sound administrative footing which kept cultural lines open with the Greek East. From the sixth until the sixteenth century there was a flourishing traffic of religious translations between East and West.

Among the most significant translation centers were the schools of the Muslim world at Baghdad, Seville, Toledo, and Cordova, where Greek philosophy and science were translated into Arabic. From the tenth to the early twelth centuries these centers, in particular Toledo, played host to a number of Christian philosophers who translated Arab texts into Latin and brought back to the West Greek texts that had been lost. Another important center for this work was the Kingdom of the Two Sicilies where scientific, diplomatic, and religious translators worked between Latin, Arab, and Greek. But even there can be found flashes of the ancient rhetorical theories of translation. Henricus Aristippus, Archdeacon of Catania (fl. 1100–70), supported illuminist arguments for literal translation by quoting Horace's *Ars poetica* 361–62, which compares poetry to a picture that is different according to the angle from which you view it. Between the ninth the sixteenth centuries there were Latin communities in Constantinople and Greek ones in the West which kept up a steady flow of translation between Latin and Greek in an effort to heal the breach between Eastern and Western Christianity.

The thirteenth-century controversy at the University of Paris over translating Greek philosophers from Arabic versions caused a fierce discussion of translation. Roger Bacon, arguing from lexical and terminological evidence, condemned it out of hand in his *Opus tertium*, while other philosophers, notably Thomas Aquinas, speculated on the nature of translation, seeing it almost as a barter transaction in which fair value must be paid. Following attempts to condemn Aristotle as corrupt and corrupting, his works were retranslated from the Greek texts to rid them of Arab accretions. The greatest of these translators were William of Moerbeke (1215–86), a Dominican friar, and Robert Grosseteste (1168–1253), Bishop of Lincoln.

2.2 Towards the Vernaculars

St Cyril and St Methodius (early ninth century) Christianized the Slavs and translated the Greek liturgy and Bible into Slavonic (see *Old Church Slavonic*). In England the first Bible translation was the verse rendering of Caedmon (seventh century). A century and a half later, Alfred the Great (848–99) ordered Pope Gregory the Great's *Pastoral Care* and other important ecclesiastical documents to be translated into Anglo-Saxon to counteract a certain laxness in the English church. In Germany, the English missionary, St Boniface (673–754), produced one of the early versions of the Scriptures. During the eighth century there was much legal translation between the vernaculars and Latin, as new codes were evolved from Roman Law.

After the Christian conquest of Spain, the kings, particularly Alfonso el Sabio, commissioned technical translations from Arab and Latin into the vernacular. By the fourteenth century there existed a full corpus of medical works in Spanish and Catalan. In France, Charles V founded a similar cultural center in his court. His translators included men of letters, administrators, and scientists. The most important was Nicole Oresme (1320–82), reputed to be the first to translate Aristotle into a vernacular language. London too was an important center of royal patronage, and gained dramatically in importance after William Caxton (1422–91), a skilled translator, set up his printing press.

Literary translation into vernacular languages, either from Latin or from other vernaculars, begins around the tenth century. The first translations of Classical rhetoric date from this period—vernacular writers saw such translation in the same light as Livius Andronicus had seen it twelve hundred years before: it was a way of bringing the language to maturity. For the general public there were versions of Ovid and Virgil, very often taken from medieval Latin reworkings. Epic poetry, like the *Chanson de Roland*, was also translated widely, so that most of this great medieval epic exists in a large number of dialects and languages. Much of the really important translation was in the hands of the troubadours, who translated very freely between the vernacular languages, often extempore and as part of a performance.

The laity benefited from translation of popular devotional books, much of it anonymous (see *Prayer*). Boethius's *Consolation of Philosophy* was very popular, and was normally taken from a French version, for example, Chaucer's translation. Many countries produced versions of the Epistles and Gospels used at Mass, and it seems that these were often read while the celebrant read the Latin.

Where a technical translation remains very close to its original, literary translation is extremely free. The first attempts to apply linguistics to translation seem to be the orthodox attacks on the fourteenth-century Lollard Bibles: the claim is that translation from Latin to the vernaculars is impossible because the lack of formal identity between language resources (see *Wycliffe, J.*). The Lollard reply turns on functional arguments—if one can do the same or similar things in English (i.e., construct sentences, show the line of argument) one does not need formal identity.

3. Renaissance and Humanism

3.1 Philosophy and Science

As the Turks were increasing the pressure on the Byzantine Empire in the fourteenth century, Greek scholars began moving west. Once established they made their living by setting up schools. Major schools were set up at Florence and Venice, both powerful trading republics with ruling families interested in scholarship, by Manuel Chrysoloras (1355–1415) and Constantine Lascaris (fl. 1450–90), who soon distinguished themselves as translators from Greek into Latin, and put translation at the center of the educated person's skills. Among their pupils were Marsilio Ficino (1433–99), who translated Plato into Latin, and Aeneas Silvius Piccolomini (1450–64), later Pope Pius II. In these schools translation reverted to the manner and principles of the Classical rhetoricians, and thus dethroned the translation model of Boethius. An early pupil of the Florentine schools, Leonardo Bruni Aretino (1369–1444), translated Aristotle into Latin (ca. 1420) and wrote a rather pugnacious preface on the necessity of translating works in a style consonant with their elegance.

Because the basic training of a scientist was Classical and philological, noted translators like Thomas Linacre (1465–1524), Professor of Medicine at Oxford, and Janus Cornarius (1500–88), first Dean of Medicine at Jena, scoured European libraries for Greek medical and scientific manuscripts, edited them, and translated them into Latin. By 1600 practically every important Greek work on science and philosophy had its humanist Latin version for use in the medical schools, and in many cases a vernacular version as well. Alongside these were translations from texts on alchemy, both works ascribed to the thirteenth-century scholastics like Roger Bacon and Albert the Great, and books by later alchemists like Basil Valentine and Nicholas of Cusa. Contemporary alchemists like P. A. Paracelsus (1493–1541) who wrote in their own languages (in the case of Paracelsus, German), were translated into Latin, and then from there into the local vernaculars. Gerhard Dorn (fl. 1570–90) was the most prominent Latin translator of alchemy.

3.2 Religion

Sixteenth-century humanism was essentially religious, and translators were essential to Reformation and Counter-Reformation. They treated religious material no differently from other writings, assessing the worth of manuscripts, interpreting readings against parallel texts, etc. Translators first sought to produce Latin Bibles of humanist standard; and there were a large number of them. The most influential was the Greek–Latin New Testament (1523) of Desiderius Erasmus (1466–1536), the *texus receptus*, which studiously tried to be doctrinally neutral. But other Latin translators like Théodore de Bèze (1519–1605) and Sebastian Castalio (1515–63) produced Bibles in fairly Classical Latin, but with strong doctrinal leanings.

Of the vernacular Bibles, *Luther's* (1534) is preeminent (see *Luther, M.*). Other German versions were produced by reformers in Switzerland. Luther influenced the Dutch version of 1537, the Swedish of 1541, and the Danish of 1550. Other important Protestant Bibles were the 1641 Italian version by the Calvinist, Giovanni Diodati (1576–1649), which he himself turned into French in 1644, and the French Bibles of Jacques Lefevre d'Etaples (1455–1537), Pierre Olivétan (d. 1538), and de Bèze's 'Geneva Bible' which came out in 1528, 1535, and 1556, respectively. In Spain the first complete version of Scripture was published in 1569 by Cassiodoro de Reina (1520–94), a follower of Jean Calvin; and in Italy the first complete Bible was by Antonio Brucioli (ca. 1495–1566) in 1532. In England there was a long progression from the *Tyndale* Bible of 1526–30 (see *Tyndale, W.*) to the Authorized Version of 1611, which is an excellent example of teamwork. The work was divided between six 'companies,' which included theologians as well as experts in Classical languages (see *English Bible*).

Catholic countries tended to lag in Biblical translation. Spain continued the medieval custom of translating the Epistles and Gospels used at Mass. France often readapted Protestant or doubtful Bibles; for example, the Catholic *Bible de Louvain* (1550) was Lefevre d'Etaples's edition brought up to date. Likewise in Germany: Hieronymus Emser's version (1523) tried to 'correct' those parts of Luther's Bible already circulating. In 1548 Nicolaus van Winghe produced a Dutch Catholic Bible which remained standard until 1926. In England the Douay–Rheims version, translated from the Vulgate, appeared in 1588 as an emergency measure to counter Protestant accusations, partially justified, that the Catholics were afraid of the Bible. Most of the Protestant Bibles were taken from the original Hebrew and Greek, the only major exception being *Miles Coverdale's* (1535), taken from the Vulgate. Until Ronald Knox's Bible in 1949, Catholic Bibles were almost exclusively taken from the Vulgate.

Developing vernacular liturgies was essential to the Reformation. Partial translations of the Catholic liturgy already existed in the 'Primers' (see *Prayer*). In England the *Book of Common Prayer* (1549) rose out of English versions from the 'Primers' and translations from the Sarum Missal and Breviary. The translation committee was headed by Thomas Cranmer (1489–1566), Archbishop of Canterbury.

For the next two hundred years, the *Book of Common Prayer* was translated into other European languages to serve Anglicans living overseas and missionary congregations. Other Reformers who created similar works of liturgical adaptation mixed with translation were Martin Luther (q.r.) and Jean Calvin (1509–56). As the Reformation spread there were translations of Luther's liturgy into Scandinavian languages, which were adopted for the normal worship. Translators also entered with gusto into religious controversy. Luther's and Calvin's polemical works were translated into most European languages and rebuttals, both Catholic and Protestant, were translated and circulated just as vigorously. Luther's works were translated into English by Richard Taverner (1505–75), who was responsible for Taverner's Bible (1539); and Thomas Norton (1532–84), a noted scourge of both Catholics and Lutherans, translated Calvin's *Lens Institutions de la Religion Chrestienne* which Calvin himself had translated into French from his own Latin version. There was also some translation of Jewish prayer books and synagogue liturgies into vernacular languages, but as yet no Biblical work.

3.3 Literary and Educational Translation

The rise of the vernaculars as standard languages slowly shifted the focus of translation towards literature. However, what could be termed a 'modern language' changed subtly. The standard languages of political and cultural centers—English, French, Spanish, and Italian—moved in to replace those like Catalan and Provençal which were losing ground. In the recognized languages, literary translation brought to fruition what the Romans from the preclassical dramatists to Jerome had to teach. The Italians were in the forefront, one of the most important names being Petrarch (1304–74). The humanist printing presses, like those of Aldus Manutius (1455–1515), himself a fine translator, and Frobenius in Antwerp, commissioned vernacular translations and sold them widely.

In the rest of Europe, literary translation arrived late in the sixteenth century, though there were some earlier pioneers like (Gavin Douhlas (1474–1522), Bishop of Dunkeld, whose Scots version of Virgil's *Aeneid* is particularly interesting. The major inspiration was Classical, within an Italian cultural dominance, although Jean Baudoin (1564–1650), Lecteur to Marguerite of Navarre, translated a number of English books, including Sir Philip Sydney's *Arcadia*, into French. Poetry predominated, but by 1600 most of the common Latin and Greek prose writers had been translated into modern languages. In France, among the important translators were the group of poets centered around Pierre Ronsard (1524–85), known as the *Pléiade*, whose interest lay in the latest from Italy as well as Greek and Latin literature; and Jacques Amyot (1513–93), whose French version of Plutarch's *Lives* was translated into English by Sir Thomas North (1535–1601). In England, Henry Howard, the Earl of Surrey (1517–47) was known for his translations of Petrarch and the Classics, and, the most famous of all, George Chapman (1559–1634) for his Homer. In Spain the Franciscan poet, Fray Luis de Leon (1520–91), was also renowned for his translations from Classical literature.

Though the center of their intellectual world was in the Classics, the humanists saw popular education as a priority. Educational works by Erasmus (particularly the *Colloquia*) and Luis Vivès were widely translated. One of the most characteristic manifestations of this interest was concern for the education of the 'Prince,' that idealized Renaissance figure who embodied all possible human virtues. The tone was set by works such as *Doctrinall of Princes* (1533), translated by Sir Thomas Elyot (1490–1546) from the Greek of Isocrates, and the versions of Castinglione's *Il cortegiano* by Thomas Hoby (1424–1585; English), Juan Boscan (d. 1542; Spanish), and Bartholomew Clerke (1537–90; Latin). Machiavelli's work was translated but feared, and the English version of *Il principe* by Thomas Bedingfield (d. 1613) was unfavorably noticed by Queen Elizabeth I and remained in manuscript until after 1960.

4. The Age of Reason

4.1 Literary Translation

During the seventeenth and eighteenth centuries literary translation was dominated by French models, the notorious *belles infidèles*, which judged a translation according to contemporary norms of taste. In France the salon, in Britain the coffeehouse, and everywhere in Europe the learned society, were essential to the development of translation at this time. The influence of the Royal Society and the Académie française were seconded by periodicals like the *Gentleman's Magazine* and *L'année littéraire*. In France the dominant figure was Nicholas Perrot d'Ablancourt (1600–43) whose ruling principle was to 'remove everything that could wound our sensibilities.' The same principle was followed by Anne Dacier (1651–1720) in her Homer, which is a classic of the style. The dominant figure in Britain was John Dryden, who took his famous typology of 'metaphrase,' 'paraphrase,' and 'imitation' from French practice. He opted for paraphrase as ideal but, in practice, his poetic translation leans more towards 'imitation.' German translators, like Bodmer (1698–1783), Breitinger (1701–76), and Gottsched (1700–76) followed the same line.

Though Classical works were still the staple of the literary translator, there was also work from modern languages, much of it for recreational reading. This work included Latin versions of contemporary poets, the version of *Paradise Lost* by William Hogg adding to John Milton's international reputation. From the end of the seventeenth century, translators begin to demand authenticity and close translation. T. R. Steiner traces this change to the influence of Pierre-Daniel Huet (1630–1721), who championed literal translation. Among English translators affected by him were Sir Edward Sherburne (1616–1702). The new manner became standard later in the eighteenth century, as in the translations ascribed to Tobias Smollet (1721–71) in England, and taught in France by Charles Batteux (1713–80), a noted translator from Latin and Greek; in Spain, in Antonio Capmany Suris y Montpalau (1742–1813), who translated from French; and in Russia, in Vasily Trediskovsky (1703–79), who worked from Classical languages. The eighteenth century is discussed at length in Tytler's 1791 *Essay on Translation*. But the old manner persisted—L'Abbé Prévost, one of the few who kept away from Classical translation, and specialized in translation from English, published a version of Richardson's *Clarissa Harlowe* that followed *les belles infidèles* to the point of wounding the author. And Jacques Delille (1783–1813) was still translating like this during the French Revolution.

4.2 Religious Translation

The Dutch Protestants produced their standard *Statenbijbel* in 1637 (see *Bible Translations, Modern Period*). Luther's German Bible was kept constantly up to date, and the Douay–Rheims Bible was updated by Bishop Richard Challoner (1691–1781) in 1763. The Bishop of Florence, Martini, translated the Bible into Italian between 1769 and 1781, and the official Spanish version of 1793 was also from the Vulgate. If attempts like the Bible of Lemaistre de Saci (1613–84) taken from the Vulgate are set aside, in France translation was merely an incidental part of Biblical scholarship. This gathered pace during the eighteenth century with the work of Richard Simon (1638–1712), the author of a huge Biblical encyclopedia, and Charles Houbigant (1686–1783), whose Latin version of the Hebrew Old Testament has an important preface on translation. This work came into its own in Britain at the end of the eighteenth century among those who were trying to replace the Authorized Version. The greatest translator of the period was George Campbell (1719–96), principal of Marischal College in Aberdeen; his *Four Gospels* (1789) was meant to be an ecumenical version. At the beginning of the nineteenth century, it was frequently published with the Epistles by James MacKnight (1721–1800) and the Books of Acts and Revelation by Philip Doddridge (1739–86). Campbell's work is notable for its voluminous notes and introduction, which is a summing-up of eighteenth-century thought on translation in general.

Strangely enough French Catholicism provided Protestant Europe with much devotional literature, Fénélon, the Archbishop of Cambrai, being a popular author. As Catholicism became more sure of itself, there was a great deal of translation of traditional devotional literature, like *The Imitation of Christ* ascribed to Thomas à Kempis (ca. 1379–1471), into vernaculars—even in England after the break with Rome. There was a fair amount of polemical translation as well, the most virulent occasioned by the 1643 quarrel between Port-Royal and the Jesuits, and centering round Pascal's *Lettres provinciales*, though the fallout from the Reformation kept translators going for the whole century. Translators tried to temper the acrimony by translating works on religious tolerance, like the religious writings of the great Dutch jurist, Hugo Grotius.

4.3 Technical Translation

At the beginning of the seventeenth century three scientific paradigms were fighting for supremacy, and for the warring scientists translation was a professional responsibility. First there was the scientific paradigm, of which Thomas Linacre, the founder of the Royal College of Physicians, had been typical; the second was the alchemist paradigm; and the third was the new philosophy of science taught by Francis Bacon and René Descartes. There was still a little translation from Classical writers, but the humanist versions remained standard.

Not only were the latest medical sources translated, but also medievals with a reputation like Albertus Magnus, Roger Bacon, and Ramon Lull. Alchemists and surgeons often wrote in their own languages. The most famous of these authors, Paracelsus and Glauber, were still translated into Latin for international consumption. In Britain in particular both vernacular and Latin translation had its political side, as is quite clear from noted Puritan apothecaries like Nicholas Culpeper (1616–54), and Royalist translators like Elias Ashmole (1617–92). The fight continued all over Europe until about 1680.

Between 1660 and 1700 there was a staggering amount of translation of the writings of Bacon, Descartes, and, at the end of the century, Isaac Newton's works. This was a time when scientists were beginning to write in their native languages, with consequent difficulties for readers in other countries. Robert Boyle and Isaac Newton commissioned their own Latin translations, and sat on the translators' shoulders. Descartes was well served by his French translator, le Duc de Luynes, and badly by the Dutch mathematician, Frans van Schooten (1615–60). In the rare cases where scientists were incapable of writing Latin (e.g., A van Leeuwenhoek), they found anonymous Latin translators. Scientific translation was largely in the hands of the medical profession, encouraged by publication subsidies. The demand was so high that entrepreneurs made use of unemployed university graduates as translators, usually without acknowledging their help. The peak of this activity was in the period 1700–45, and coincided with the general acceptance of the scientific ideas of Desecrates and Newton. Indeed it is doubtful whether Linnaeus, the famous biologist, Albrecht von Haller, the founder of physiology, or T. O. Bergman, the noted Swedish chemist, would have had the effect they did if they had not written in Latin and been translated into the vernaculars.

By the early eighteenth century vernacular work on medicine was usually translated directly into modern languages. By the late eighteenth century the center of scientific translation in Britain was moving north to the scientific communities of the Midlands and Scotland, who were in contact with France, Germany, and Sweden. In France the center was still Paris, where Louis-Bernard Guyton de Morveau (1737–1816) was particularly active in both translation and research. Creative physicians like William Lewis (1714–81) of Edinburgh, de Rusieux of Paris, and J. H. Ziegler of Germany were both translators and translated.

The seventeenth century had produced a lot of 'gentlemanly' translation, on gardening, building, and architecture, much of it from French and Italian sources; for example, the translations by John Evelyn (1620–1706), on gardening and art, and translations of important Italian architects like Giacomo da Vignola and Andrea Palladio. The eighteenth century too was also marked by the translation of applied science, much of it from French, Swedish, and German. A good part of it dealt with agriculture—the concentration of population in the new towns demanded intensive agriculture if they were to be fed. There was also much on the manufacture and use of weapons, the French being in the forefront. Navigation and traditional crafts like dyeing also benefited from translators. However, the most radical changes came in pharmacy, which followed the 'new chemistry' so closely that its practice was reformed.

Education was an important issue and authors translated into most European languages, including Latin, ranged from Jan Amos Comenius to John Locke. Much translation of history, education, and the like was commissioned for political purposes. In Britain, Cromwell's Parliament commissioned legal and historical translation in an effort to legitimize the regime. On his return to power (1660), Charles II used translators like Dryden to translate political, if not polemical, works in support of the Royalist cause. In the following century, Adam Smith's *The Wealth of Nations* was translated into Spanish for the financial guidance of the government (1794) and in France there were at least four translations of Smith's work between 1793 and 1815, each coinciding with a change of regime. T. R. Malthus's work on population was also translated. As usual a good deal of this translation was anonymous, and done to meet specific scientific needs.

5. The Nineteenth Century

5.1 Romanticism and Literature

It was not until the rise of Romanticism that 'translation' became popularly identified with literary translation. The precursor of the movement, Johann Gottfried von Herder (1744–1803) (see *Herder, J. G.*), left to it a thorough-going Platonism that saw man and his society as creatures of the language spoken. For Herder, translators were the 'morning star' of a literature, because they introduced a literature to the great things in other literatures. His own contribution to German was a collection of translations from European poetry, the *Volkslieder* (1778–79), which imitated the original meters as the appropriate dress for the verse. Classical meters were acclimatized in German by Friedrich Klopstock (1724–1803): English experimentations, even by the poet Tennyson, were never successful.

Herder's view of translation as a hermeneutics of text was refined by Friedrich Daniel Ernst Schleiermacher (1768–1834). Romantic translators took on two interlinked tasks: the first was penetration to 'pure speech' supposed by Friedrich Hölderlin (1770–1843) to underlie all languages; the second was to present author and text unadorned to the reading public in the second language. Hence the famous classification by Johann Wolfgang von Goethe (1748–1832): literal, 'parody,' and interlinear version. The first was word-for-word, and to be used if no other was possible; in 'parody' translation the translator imposed himself and his society on the original; and the interlinear version was the penetration to the very essence of the original.

All of these theorists were practical translators as well; Hölderlin and Schleiermacher translating from Greek poetry, and Goethe and Wilhelm von Humboldt from both modern and ancient languages. In France, Goethe's ideas were taken up by Madame de Stael whose *Esprit des traductions* (1816) is one of the seminal statements of Romantic idealogy. Such ideas were also illustrated by the version of *Paradise Lost* (1836) by René de Chateaubriand, who boasted that he had kept both the virtues and faults of the original. On a more pedestrain level, Amadée Pichot (1795–1877) publicized English literature with assiduous but extremely literal translations of contemporary writers. In Britain, after a much-reviled translation of *The Sorrows of Young Werther* from a French version, Goethe's most prominent publicist was Thomas Carlyle (1795–1881); in America, Bayard Taylor (1825–78), and, in Italy, Michele Leone di Parma (1776–1858). But Goethe's ideas had special impact in Russia and other parts of Eastern Europe, where translation still had the creative status it had enjoyed in the Western Renaissance. Romantic poets, English, German, and French, were translated by Zhukovsky (1783–1852). Dickens was a favorite subject: both his French translator, Pichot, and his Russian, Vvedensky (1813–55), wrote to him. Shakespeare was another favorite, the German Tieck-Schlegel version being almost a national monument, unmatched by any other version. Romanticism also occasioned the midcentury vogue of Eastern literature. Eastern languages were taken up in France by Emile-Louis Burnouf (1821–1907), and in Germany by the Romantics, in particular von Humboldt (see *Humboldt, W. von*). The most famous English translation of Eastern poetry is probably *The Rubaiyat of Omar Khayyam* (1859) from the Persian by Edward Fitzgerald (1809–83).

The crux of the Romantic legacy was the nature of authenticity. It was given public airing in the famous quarrel between Matthew Arnold (1822–88) and F. W. Newman (1805–97) over translating Homer. Newman believed that the archaic and antique in Homer should be presented to the reader of English by conscious archaism, while Arnold insisted on presenting Homer as poetry that conformed to the contemporary experience of poetry. Probably the greatest of Newman's partisans were John Conington (1825–69), Professor of Latin at Oxford, and Sir Richard Jebb (1841–1905) of Cambridge. Robert Browning's *Agamemnon* (1877) is an excellent example of the Newman style, and his preface recalls that of Chateaubriand to Milton's *Paradise Lost*. Arnold's approach culminated in the translations of Dante and his circle by Dante Gabriel Rossetti (1828–82). His cardinal principle was that 'a good poem should not be turned into a bad.' In other countries, particularly France, translation showed much influence of contemporary literary movements. Charles Baudelaire (1821–67) changed Poe from a very good second-rate American writer into a first-class French one, and Leconte de Lisle (1818–94), a true Parnassian, went back to the Classics. In Germany the development of literary translation followed much the same lines as in England, with conflict between the antiquarian and the authentic in the Romantic sensibility.

Romantic ideas on translation also had their political side. The subject peoples of the Austro-Hungarian Empire, particularly in what became Czechoslovakia, were strongly influenced by the nationalism inherent in Romanticism and plotted revolution. Elsewhere, for example, in Canada where English and French were in close contact, Romantic ideas on the teaching role of the translator affected the problems of preserving the identity of the minority; interpreting the two cultural groups to each other; and the French minority had to decide whether to absorb material from the dominant culture or to stand aloof. The Canadian situation is interesting for the critical role played by newspapers in fostering translation between the two languages, especially by serializing translated novels.

There was also some translation of libretti; this practice continued into the twentieth century. Gilbert and Sullivan operas were presented in German in Germany, and French and Viennese operettas (e.g., the Strauss family and Offenbach) in London in English. There was also some translation of French, Italian, and German operas into other European languages, though nowhere near the twentieth-century scale of such translation. German *Lieder* and the French art song were also translated, often very badly, for the drawing-room soprano and tenor.

5.2 Religious Translation

The issue of updating the Bible did not go away. In 1836 a Catholic historian, Dr John Lingard (1771–1851), published a Bible with the New Testament translated from the Greek (see *Bible Translations, Modern Period*). Among Protestant efforts was the modernized King James Bible (1833) produced by the American lexicographer, Noah Webster. During the 1850s pressure began to mount in England for a revision of the Authorized Version, if not a completely new translation, for Biblical scholarship had advanced considerably. In 1870 the Convocation of the Anglican Province of Canterbury set up a committee to revise the Authorized Version. Other Protestant churches joined in. In 1881 the English New Testament was published, and in 1885 the whole Bible (the Revised Version). The American Bible Union (ABU) had been established in 1864, and sent observers to keep an eye on what the English Anglicans were doing. The American Standard Version was published in 1901.

Spain was still nervous of Bible translation, however, the British and Foreign Bible Society was happily supplying Protestant versions of the Bible in European languages—for example, a revision of Valera's 1625 Spanish version was reprinted many times between 1806 and 1817, and a Catalan New Testament was produced by J. M. Prat (1832). At the end of the nineteenth century, l'Abbé Augustin Crampon (1826–94) produced what was to become the standard French Catholic Bible of the early twentieth century. For French Protestants, the most important Bible was the version of Louis Ségond (1810–85) whose Old Testament came out in 1874; the New Testament followed in 1880.

The Jews were once again facing the ancient problem: a religiously vital social group which could read but not understand the sacred books (see *Judaism*). In America, Rabbi Isaac Leeser (1806–68) published his English version of the Old Testament in the Masoretic text in 1853. The Jewish Publication Society, founded in 1892, produced an official Jewish version in English in 1901. Other Jewish communities followed suit.

The Oxford Movement in the Anglican Church sought to prove its essential Catholicism by returning as far as possible to early Christian practices. There was much interest in the Fathers of the Church, in both doctrine and hymnody (see *Hymns*). The movement's search for ancient Christian hymns began with the Roman Breviary, then passed to the Paris Breviary, and finally to pre-Reformation rites like the Sarum (from Salisbury) and the York. The leading translator was John Mason Neale (1818–66), whose hymn versions took into account the traditional melodies of medieval service books. Most of his work appeared in *Hymns Ancient and Modern* (1861), edited by Reverend Sir H. W. Baker (1821–77). Another important contributor to this famous hymnbook was Catherine Winkworth (1827–78), an early feminist, whose speciality was translation from German, and particularly the Lutheran hymns.

5.3 Technical Translation

Technical translation in the nineteenth century did not benefit at all from the Romantic revolution; indeed its practice had continued in the same manner since the early seventeenth century. The work of Michael Faraday, J. J. Berzelius, the Swedish chemist, and other scientific pioneers were widely translated. The quantity of translations increased as the century went on, though now the scientist was no longer his own translator. In the humanities, by contrast, the task of translation was still regarded as the professional responsibility of contemporary philosophers and social scientists.

Less is known of the translation that went on in the bureaucracies of the Ottoman, Austro–Hungarian, or Russian empires, than of the work carried out in the empires outside Europe. European colonial expansion gathered pace during the nineteenth century. Training local people as interpreters was the first step: colonists then learned the native languages. Soon colonial administrators benefited from a loosely organized translation profession. In most places a system of professional certification had slowly developed. For example, in the previous century Sir William Jones (1746–94), though most famous for demonstrating that Sanskrit was an Indo-European language, was an assiduous translator from Eastern languages, specializing in law. His ideas had considerable influence on later British colonial policy.

Tensions between French and English, and English and Spanish antedated British expansion in North America. The resulting warfare occasioned a fair amount of translation. Bilingual officers worked as volunteer translators between English and French or Spanish. Apart from this there is very little on record of anything beyond ad hoc translation before the British takeover of Canada in 1759, the Louisiana Purchase of 1803, and American expansion into the Spanish territories that now make up parts of Florida, Texas, and California. The press played a very important role. It was to it that the various Canadian governments (and also the government of Louisiana) later turned when they needed translators.

6. Missionary Translation

During the eighteenth century, European expansion into the New World revived ancient problems entailed in translating between sophisticated and unsophisticated languages. Little is known of how early Christian missionaries, like St Boniface (d. 755), had faced the problems of creating literacy before being able to translate the Bible into languages previously unwritten. Until the sixteenth century it was trade not colonization, that usually went with the missionary. A new pattern developed in the Americas, where in the British, French, Spanish, and Portuguese dominions, missionary and colonist often arrived together, and at times cooperated. The practice of the New England and the Jesuit missionaries with Native American languages was typical: translation of the Bible and the introduction of Christian worship, for example, by Thomas Mayhew (d. 1657) and John Eliot (d. 1690) were preceded by and prepared for, the production of grammars and lexicons: literacy as well as conservation was an objective.

Missionary translation was first given direction by the formation of the *Congregatio pro Propaganda Fide* in Rome in 1662. There are reports of translations of the Bible into Eastern languages mainly form Catholics like St Francis Xavier (1506–52), and the Congregation has continued active translation. On the Protestant side, the Society for the Propagation of Christian Knowledge (1698), the Society for the Propagation of the Gospel in Foreign Parts (1701), and the Moravian Brotherhood (founded 1722) took a vital part in Bible translation into non-Indo-European languages. Perhaps the most important development was the foundation of the interdenominational British and Foreign Bible Society in 1804, which had as its sole aim the production and distribution of vernacular scriptures all over the world, including England and and Wales. Early in the nineteenth century the Church Missionary Society of the Anglican Church entered into an agreement about cooperation. Parallel Bible societies were founded in Scotland and the United States. In many parts of the world Catholic and Protestant Bibles were in competition. There are extensive records of Protestant liturgical translation into the languages of the mission fields: the Tamil translation of the Lutheran liturgy published in Ceylon in 1781 is far from unusual. Indeed, Anglican translation of the *Book of Common Prayer* into the languages of the Indian subcontinent helped lay the foundations for the development of eastern forms of Christianity. During the nineteenth century most of the vernacular scriptures published by these bodies were translated in the field, often with the help of native speakers (see *Prayer*; *Hymns*; *Bible*; *Missionaries*).

In the USA in particular, linguists began to take a large hand in the Bible translation in the mid-twentieth century. After World War II American Bible Societies merged into the United Bible Societies (UBS) with its own periodical, *The Bible Translator*. On the evangelical side the work of UBS was grouped around the Summer Institute of Linguistics, also known as the 'Wycliffe Bible Translators.' One of its leaders was Eugene Nida (q. v.), whose work on the theory of translation focused specifically on the Bible. The linguistics of the mid-twentieth century, with its strong anthropological bias, suited this work.

The Qu'rān was also translated early into European languages. There is a 'curiosity-oriented' translation into Latin dating from the twelfth century ascribed to Robertus Ketenensis and Hermannus Dalmata. This was republished in 1543 by Theodore Bibliander (1504–64). There are also a few sixteenth-century Latin versions of the Qu'rān for the information of Christian missionaries. It was a popular book among European translators during the nineteenth century, versions being made in all the important European languages. Because Muslims have the same attitude to the Word of God as Jews, translation of the Qu'rān for religious purposes is suspect. Nevertheless, a number of modern translations into European languages have been tolerated by the authorities for use by European Muslims. The Western interest in Eastern religions has also occasioned much translation and commentary on the Hindu scriptures (see *Qu'rān*; *Qu'rān*: *Translations*; *Hindu Sacred Texts*).

7. The Twentieth Century

7.1 Religious Translation

7.1.1 Christian

The dominant motivation was the increasingly urgent need to replace the great European language translations of the past by up-to-date versions. This coincided with two contradictory movements—the centripetal force of ecumenism which increased pressures towards a Bible common to all Christian churches, and the centrifugal forces created by new types of Christian and Jewish fundamentalism (see *Fundamentalism*). In English there is a huge number of Bibles, the best known early twentieth-century ones being *The New Testament*: *A New Translation* by James Moffat in 1913, with the Old Testament following in 1924, and *The New Testament*: *An American Translation* by Edgar J. Goodspeed (1923). In 1931 a version of the Old Testament by Powis Smith and others was published with Goodspeed's, the whole being known as *The Bible*: *An American Translation*.

Among 'official versions' in English the most notable Protestant versions are the American *Revised Standard Version* (1952) from the International Council for Religious Education, and the British *New English Bible* (1961) which was initiated by the Church of Scotland but which eventually became a joint effort by most of the mainstream Protestant denominations. Later on a printing of the *New English Bible* was authorized by the Catholic Church. The Catholic Church first published the *Westminster Bible* (1913), Monsignor Ronald Knox's version was published in its entirety in 1949, but was superseded by the *Jerusalem Bible* in 1966. The Knox is the last important version from the Vulgate, and it was done with a close eye on the Greek and the Hebrew texts.

Probably the best of the modern versions is the French *Bible de Jérusalem* (1948–54) from the Ecole biblique de Jérusalem. The English *Jerusalem Bible* (1966) comes from the same team, and they also produced a Spanish translation (1987).

Other important modern Bibles are the Spanish versions by Nalcar-Colunga (1944), and Bover-Cantera (1957). The Catalan version, from the Benedictine Monastery at Montserrat, began publication in 1926, but the work was suspended between 1936 and 1950 by the anti-Catalan policies of the Franco government.

The Roman Catholic and various Orthodox churches produced bilingual service books. Liturgical reforms instituted by Pope Pius X (1903–14) encouraged the production of a very large number of missals of various states of completeness for the laity. There were also a few translations of the Divine Office for the laity and certain religious communities. One of the most interesting of these is *Byzantine Daily Worship* (1969) translated from the Greek *Horologion* (Breviary) and the ancient liturgy of St John Chrysostom for the Greek Uniate community worldwide. The Anglican Church continued translating the *Book of Common Prayer* into the languages of the British Empire and Commonwealth. Following Vatican II (1962–65) national commissions were set up throughout the Catholic world to organize the translation of the entire Roman Catholic liturgy into the vernaculars. For international languages like English, French, and German, there were international commissions that came to agreement on language standards and other matters. In the name of ecumenism the various churches cooperated in versions of common texts like the Creeds and the *Gloria in excelsis Deo* (see *Prayer*).

7.1.2 Jewish

The most notable Jewish Bible translators, mainly because of their very telling and coherent arguments for literal translation were the philosopher-theologian, Martin Buber (1878–1965), and Franz Rosenzweig (1886–1929), whose German Bible, with a preface, was published 1926–1938 (see *Judaism*). Their principles were taken up by Henri Meschonnic (1932) in France, and applied to secular translation as well. Jewish bilingual versions of the synagogue liturgies and private prayers go back a considerable time, at least to the sixteenth century. However, as Reform Jews began to worship in the local vernaculars, unilingual service books were produced from the middle of the twentieth century onwards. Among the Jewish Bibles in English, *The Holy Scriptures* by the Jewish Publication Society was published in 1917.

7.2 Technical Translation

The twentieth century saw the rise of the translating profession, centered on technical work. The trigger seems to have been the founding of the League of Nations in 1918. By that time many governments had translation offices for administrative purposes. After World War II these expanded quickly, following the postwar political and trade patterns. Private firms began to follow the lead of governments and created their own translation sections to translate everything from technical reports and instruction manuals to publicity. It was only a matter of time before freelance translators began organizing themselves as commercial operations and into societies like FIT (la Fédération Internationale des Traducteurs). Specialized training is a twentieth-century phenomenon, and it gained pace in the 1960s with courses being established in universities and specialized schools. There continued to be a lot of inhouse translator training; one of the finest translation schools in the world being run by the electronics firm, Philips, in The Netherlands.

There has been a growing body of theory of technical translation, with some attempt to relate it to be mainstream literary and religious work. One obvious result has been the creation of specialities like terminologist and documentalist. The great expansion of translation in the first half of the twentieth century occasioned experimentation in machine translation (MT), which stemmed from a memo from an American founder of the field, Warren Weaver, in 1947 on applying code-breaking techniques to languages. Results have proved limited. Its most useful spinoff has been the development of automated dictionaries.

7.3 Literary Translation

At the beginning of the twentieth century literary translation remained what it had traditionally been, a searching apprenticeship for the creative writer. Nineteenth-century manners of translation spilled over into the first half of the twentieth with the vaguely Swinburnesque manner of the translations from Greek by Gilbert Murray (1866–1957), and the versions of modern and Classical literature from Valéry Larbaud (1881–1957), Paul Valéry (1871–1945), André Gide (1928–45), and the English version of Proust by Scott Moncrieff. In Germany figures like Ulrich von Wilamovitz-Moellendorf (1848–1931) carried the Romantic tradition to its limits. Reaction against the tradition started at the beginning of the century with Rudolf Borchardt (1877–1945), and continued in Symbolists like Walter Benjamin (1892–1940). In Slavic Europe, translation has remained an activity central to the work of creative writers without excluding specialist translators of literature.

The decisive break in the tradition came with Symbolist writers and writers under Symbolist influence like Ezra Pound (1888–1972), Yves Bonnefoy (1923–), the Russian, Balmont (1867–1943), and the German, Walter Benjamin, who developed the Romantic idea of the language shape having its own meaning (see *Benjamin, W.*). Attitudes and practice range from Benjamin's attempts to get rid of meaning altogether, to Pound and Henri Meschonnic who successfully walk the tightrope between sound and sense, with some striking results. Bonnefoy, in particular, comes very close to some of the twentieth-century theorizing on the linguistic element in translation in his Shakespeare translations.

Under the pressure of changes in education, translation from Classical languages diversified: beside translations for the reader's recreation grew up translations to help students, for example, in English-speaking countries the Loeb editions from Harvard University Press, and in French the Editions Budé. Translation began to acquire its own impressarios: one of the most important was Betty Radice (1912–85), a Classical scholar and excellent translator in her own right, who was editor of the Penguin Classics series.

It is in the translation of modern languages that there has been the most change. Theater has taken the interest of many translators, even if at times they chafe against what producers do to their texts. Translation of libretti has continued, some of it anonymous, and opera has attracted people of the caliber of W. H. Auden (1907–73). As had happened during the Middle Ages, hitherto unimportant languages and literatures have gained worldwide recognition through translation. Eastern European work has become influential, and smaller European countries important, as they appreciate that translation provides access to a greater audience for their literatures. Indeed at times, translation into the languages of non-Communist Europe was the only way in which dissident writers like Milan Kundera in Czechoslovakia, and Alexander Solzhenitsyn in the former Soviet Union could be published at all. As well, former European colonies developed their own distinctive literary voice; they attracted the notice of translators, and produced translators themselves, for example, Octavio Paz from Mexico. The number of translators from the former European colonies in Africa and Asia has been growing. Many bilingual countries have attempted to foster literary translation for the sake of national cohesion: Canada, for instance, subsidizes translation of Canadian French writers into English, and vice versa. At times translation has been used as it had been in nineteenth-century Europe, as a nationalist rallying-point in Quebec, Scotland, and Wales.

Interest has grown in hitherto unconsidered literatures. Many Classical translators, for instance, Peter Green, have taken up translation of modern Greek literature. There has also been increased interest in Eastern literatures by translators like I. A. Richards and Achilles Fang. The twentieth-century literary prizes have had an important influence on the extent of translation: Nobel prize-winners like Patrick White, the Australian, and Alexander Solzhenitsyn, himself a fine translator, have been translated worldwide.

New areas of translation have developed, including popular fiction for the mass market (e.g., the works of detective writers Georges Simenon and Agatha Christie) and film-dubbing, which reconciles the sense of what is said with the observable features of lip and face movement.

Theories of translation have followed changes in linguistic and literary theory. Symbolist theories of literature have been most prominent in the translation theories of people like Ezra Pound and Yves Bonnefoy. In Eastern Europe, translation theory has been of vital interest, for example, the Prague School, whose linguistic theories did not prevent them from producing extremely perceptive work on poetics and translation. Linguistic theories of translation have been a feature of the twentieth century, though usually in complete isolation from the more traditional literary stream. In the English-speaking world, American structuralism gave rise to the theories and practice of the Summer Institute of Linguistics (see *Summer Institute of Linguistics*), typified by the work of Eugene Nida; and English translation theory has risen out of the work of J. R. Firth and M. A. K. Halliday. In the French-speaking world a contrastive linguistics applied to translation was developed from the Geneva School, chiefly from the theories of Charles Bally. Its first manifestation was the stylistique comparée of Malblanc, and Vinay and Darbelnet; it was further developed by reference to the theories of Gustave Guillaume and Culioli's theories on enunciation. Like the linguistics of Prague, contrastive linguistics takes account of discourse phenomena. The end of the 1980s saw some attempt to combine both linguistic and literary theories of translation by absorbing the idea of linguistic transfer into a concept of translation as a communicative act whose source and target texts are embedded in differing cultural matrices.

See also: Missionaries.

Bibliography

Bassnett-McGuire S 1981 *Translation Studies.* Methuen, London

Blake N F 1969 *Caxton and his World.* Andre Deutsch, London

Beer J (ed.) 1988 *Medieval Translators and their Craft.* Medieval Institute, Kalamazoo

Cambridge History of the Bible 1963–70, 3 vols. Cambridge University Press, Cambridge

Cary E 1956 *La traduction dans le monde moderne.* Georg, Geneva

Cohen J M 1962 *English Translators and Translations.* Longmans for the British Council, London

Conley C H 1927 *The First English Translators of the Classics.* Yale University Press, New Haven, CT

Courcelle P 1943 *Les lettres grecques en occident de Macrobe à Cassiodore.* de Boccard, Paris

Delisle J 1987 *La traduction au Canada 1534–1984.* Les Presses de l'Université d'Ottawa, Ottawa

Dunlop D M 1960 The work of translation at Toledo. *Babel* **6:** 55–99

Ellis R (ed.) 1989 *The Medieval Translator.* Boydell and Brewer, Woodbridge

Firth C H (ed.) 1939 *Lives of the English Poets.* Clarendon Press, Oxford

Horguelin P 1975 *Histoire de la traduction: Domaine français.* Linguatech, Montreal

Jourdain A M M B 1843 *Recherches critiques sur l'âge et l'origine des traductions latines d'Aristote.* Joubert, Paris

Kelly J N D 1975 *Jerome: His Life, Writings and Controversies.* Duckworth, London

Kelly L G 1979 *The True Interpreter.* Basil Blackwell, Oxford

Knox R A 1957 *On English Translation.* Romanes Lecture, Oxford

Kushner E, Chavy P (eds.) 1981 Translation in the Renaissance/Traduction à la renaissance. *Canadian Review of Comparative Literature* **8(2)** (whole issue)

Ladborough R W (1938–39) Translation from the Ancients in seventeenth-century France. *Journal of the Warburg Institute* **2**: 85–104

Lathrop H B 1967 *Translations from the Classics into English from Caxton to Chapman 1477–1620.* Octagon Books, New York

Lefevere A 1977 *Translating Literature: The German Tradition from Luther to Rosenzweig*. van Gorcum, Assen and Amsterdam

Leighton L G 1984 *The Art of Translation: Kornei Chukovsky's A High Art*. University of Tennessee Press, Knoxville, TN

Matthiessen F O 1931 *Translation: An Elizabethan Art*. Harvard University Press, Cambridge, MA

Mohrmann C 1957 *Liturgical Latin: Its Origin and Character*. Burns and Oates, London

Mukherjee P 1981 *Translation as Discovery and Other Essays on Indian Literature in Translation*. Allied Publishers, New Delhi

Newman M, Stratford P 1975 *Bibliography of Canadian Books in Translation: French to English, English to French*. HRCC, Ottawa

Norton G P 1984 *Ideology and Language of Translation in Renaissance France*. Droz, Geneva

Piercy L T 1984 *The Mediated Muse: English Translators of Ovid 1560–1700*. Archon Books, Hamden, CT

Pound E 1954 *Literary Essays of Ezra Pound*. New Directions, Norfolk, CT

Rener F M 1989 *Interpretatio: Language and Translation from Cicero to Tytler*. Rodopi, Amsterdam and Atlanta, GA

Santoyo J-C 1987 *Teoría y crítica de la traducción: Antología*. Universitat Autònoma de Barcelona, Bellaterra

Scott M A 1916 *Elizabethan translators from the Italian*. Houghton Mifflin, Boston, MA and New York

Selver P 1966 *The Art of Translating Poetry*. Baker, London

Setton K M 1956 The Byzantine background to the Italian Renaissance. *Proceedings of the American Philosophical Society* **100**: 1–76

Steiner G 1975 *After Babel*. Oxford University Press, Oxford

Steiner T R 1975 *English Translation Theory, 1650–1800*. van Gorcum, Assen and Amsterdam

Strand K A 1961 *Reformation Bibles in the Crossfire*. University of Michigan Press, Ann Arbor, MI

Thorndike L 1923–58 *A History of Magic and Experimental Science*, 8 vols. Columbia University Press, New York

Weiss R 1950 Translators from the Greek of the Angevin Court of Naples, *Rinascimento* **1**: 194–226

Zuber O 1980 *The Languages of Theatre*. Pergamon, Oxford

Zuber R 1968 *Les belles infidèles et la formation du goût classique*. Armand Colin, Paris

Vulgate

T. O'Loughlin

Vulgate refers to the Latin translation of the Christian scriptures used in western Europe from the fifth to the sixteenth centuries. Traditionally claimed as St Jerome's fresh translation from Hebrew and Greek, its history is far more complicated.

By the late fourth century several Latin translations were in use among Latin-speaking Christians in Europe and North Africa. In order to produce a better and common text, especially of the gospels, Pope Damasus employed Jerome to produce a fresh translation in 382. Initially, Jerome translated afresh, but as he progressed he increasingly left the existing translation (now labelled the *Vetus Latina* 'Old Latin') where it was not faulty either textually or in meaning. He finished the gospels within a year, and moved to the Old Testament. Initially he revised against the Septuagint, but later came to the doctrinal conclusion that only the Hebrew text could be trusted for pre-Christian texts. This left a muddle: for some texts there were only the older versions, for others there were Jerome's revisions (but in some cases these were hard to spot), and in some cases wholly new translations. It took several centuries for a 'standard' Latin bible to emerge—and even then there was considerable variation in manuscript families in terms of which selection of versions (Jerome, *Vetus Latina*, or some mixture) they contained. However, with this standardization developed the myth of it being solely Jerome's work and having some intrinsic authority such that its style—with many mimics of Greek and Latin constructions—accounts for many features of medieval Latinity. The term 'Vulgate' (from *Biblia vulgata* 'commonly used bible') arose in the twelfth century.

As with any complex, much-copied work, corruptions and variations entered the text, especially the New Testament, and it was subject to constant substrate interference from older versions. Hence, there were many attempts to correct it (e.g. by Alcuin of York: late eighth century) prior to printing, and a critical text was a desideratum since the Renaissance but was only finished in the later twentieth century. The Vulgate continues to be a valuable versional witness in editing the scriptures, especially the New Testament, and to a lesser extent the Septuagint and Hebrew texts; and as a key to distinctive western or medieval approaches to religious questions wherever its slant is notably different to the original texts. It was the authorized text of the Roman Catholic Church until 1979 when replaced by a new Latin translation.

See also: Bible; Bible Translations: Ancient Versions; Church Latin; Jerome; Septuagint; Translation: History.

Bibliography

Metzger B M 1977 *The Early Versions of the New Testament*. Oxford University Press, Oxford, pp. 285–374

O'Loughlin T 1995 The Controversy over Methuselah's Death: Proto-Chronology and the Origins of the Western Concept of Inerrancy. *Recherches de Théologie ancienne et médiévale* **62**: 182–225

Plater W E, White H J 1926 *A Grammar of the Vulgate*. Clarendon Press, Oxford

Weber R 1983 *Biblia Sacra iuxta Vulgatam Versionem*, 3rd edn. Württembergische Bibelanstalt, Stuttgart

SECTION III

Religious Languages and Scripts

Introduction

J. F. A. Sawyer

The close relationship between religion and language is illustrated by the existence of special languages or scripts used only or primarily in a religious context. Avestan, Sanskrit, and Pali are obvious examples of such languages, no longer used for everyday speech. In Jewish tradition Hebrew is so closely associated with religious beliefs and practices that in modern times, when it came to be used as a normal everyday language, there was fierce opposition from ultra-orthodox groups to such debasing of the 'sacred language.' Jewish Aramaic survived in religious academies in Babylonia and elsewhere long after the Muslim conquests. In Islam so important are the original Arabic words of the Qur'an that translation is officially forbidden, and the use of the Qur'an, as a text for studying Classical Arabic, frowned upon. The distinctive variety of Arabic in which the Qur'an is written is further separated from common use by the Muslim doctrine of *i'jāz* 'inimitability.'

The global spread of the world's alphabetical scripts, including the Hebrew, Greek, and Roman alphabets, from the Sinai peninsula where the so-called 'Proto-Sinaitic' system is first documented, was due less to religious factors than to its vastly superior efficiency, compared with Mesopotamian cuneiform and Egyptian hieroglyphics. But the spread of the Arabic script was due primarily to the close relationship from the very beginning between Islam and the Arabic language. Arabic is a Semitic script, perfectly designed to represent a Semitic language, yet despite the difficulties involved, Muslim writers adapted it for use with Persian, Turkish, Spanish, Malay, Swahili, Hausa, Tamil, and many other languages. Under modern cultural and political pressures, some of these, Turkish and Swahili, for example, gave up the sacred script of Islam, and switched to the Roman script. But the established use of the right-to-left Perso–Arabic script to write Urdu and Pashto, despite the fact that the Devanagari script in which Sanskrit is written is a far superior writing system for such Indo–Aryan languages, illustrates what a powerful cultural symbol of religious identity scripts can be. Another illustration from the Sub-continent is the case of Punjabi which is written in the Perso–Arabic script by Muslims in Pakistan, while Sikhs in India write the same language in Gurmukhi.

The impact of religious conservatism on the history of writing can also be illustrated from Jewish history. While by c. 500 BCE most Jews had adopted Aramaic as their spoken language and the square Aramaic script even for writing Hebrew, 'the sacred language,' the Old Hebrew script continued to be used occasionally in special contexts as for example on coins, and in the writing of the unpronounceable name of God, YHWH, in some of the Essene manuscripts found at Qumran. Another small ultra-conservative sect, the Samaritans, also clung to the old Hebrew script, no doubt to dissociate themselves as sharply as possible from the Jews.

The spread of the Syriac script and its adaptation by certain Christian communities for use with other languages, to some extent parallels the spread of the Arabic script. Garshuni, for example, is a form of the Syriac script used for writing in Arabic. Greek, Latin, Armenian, Turkish, Kurdish, and Malayalam were also at times written in the Syriac script. Indeed the Arabic script itself may have been derived from Christian Syriac. The many scripts invented by Christian scholars and missionaries down the centuries, Armenian, Georgian, Slavonic, Gothic, for example, were originally used primarily to write religious texts, for the first time in many cases, although later they came to be used for general purposes as well. The Tibetan script invented by Buddhist missionaries shows that this was not only an exclusively Christian contribution to the development of language.

Christian tradition has produced many special languages and language varieties. They include Ge'ez, the language of the Ethiopian Church, and Christian Syriac, the language of the Syrian Orthodox Church, as well as Church Latin, Old Church Slavonic, Church Slavonic and Byzantine (Church)

Greek. The language of the Authorized Version of the Bible (1611) acquired a special status among some Protestant groups, similar to that of Church Latin in the Catholic Church; and Biblical English, full of Hebraisms and other biblical expressions coined or popularized in the 1611 Version, has played a fundamental role in the history of English literature, both religious and secular.

Akkadian

J. G. Macqueen

Akkadian is the name given to a language used in ancient Mesopotamia (roughly modern Iraq) from the early third millennium BCE to the beginning of the Christian era. There are two main dialects, Assyrian and Babylonian, each divided into Old (ca. 2000–1500), Middle (ca. 1500–1000), and Neo- (ca. 1000–500), which are preceded by Old Akkadian (ca. 2500–2000) and followed by Late Babylonian (ca. 500 BCE to CE 75). A literary form based on Old Babylonian was current in the later second and first millennia BCE, and varied local forms were in use at scribal centers in Syria, Iran, Anatolia, and Egypt, where for a long period Akkadian was the accepted language of international correspondence and diplomacy.

Akkadian is a member of the Semitic group (see *Semitic Languages*), and retains many of that group's characteristic features, such as a morphologic system based on the patterned interweaving of consonantal roots (mostly triliteral) and infixed vowels together with a limited number of affixes, and the 'construct' state of a noun before a dependent genitive. But there are significant innovations. The phonological system is simplified, with the loss of most laryngeals and pharyngeals. Nouns have three case-forms (nominative, accusative, genitive) in the singular, but only two in the plural, and after ca. 1000 BCE case-endings are further simplified, with loss of mimation. As well as these forms, and the 'construct' state mentioned above, there is an 'absolute' state without case-ending used mainly in number-phrases. Dual forms are attested, but are usually confined to hands, feet, etc. The verbal system includes a stative (permansive) form indicating a state or condition without regard to time, as well as those which indicate present (imperfective, durative), preterite (perfective, punctual), and 'perfect' (expressing an action anterior to the future of the main verb, or posterior to its past) actions. There are also subjunctive, ventive ('goal of motion'), and imperative forms, as well as a participle and a verbal adjective. Syntax is on the whole simple and straightforward, with a tendency toward parataxis rather than hypotaxis.

A sentence illustrating some of the above features is (in syllabic transcription):

šum-ma a-wi-lum mâr a-wi-lim ṣi-iḫ-ra-am iš-ta-riq, id-da-ak
'If a man has kidnapped a man's infant son, he will be put to death.'

Here *awilum* is nominative, while *awilim* is genitive following *mâr*, the construct state of *mârum*, 'son.' Then, *ṣiḫram* ('young') is accusative, agreeing with *mâr*, or rather with the accusative that *mâr* would have been had it not been followed by a genitive. Finally, *ištariq* (with infixed -ta-) is 3sg prf indic or *šarāqu*, 'to steal' (*šumma*, 'if,' though introducing a subordinate clause, does not take the subjunctive), and *iddak* (<*indak* with infixed -n-) is 3sg pres/fut pass of *dâku* (root *dwk*), 'to kill.'

See also: Semantic Languages.

Bibliography

Caplice R 1980 *Introduction to Akkadian*. Biblical Institute Press, Rome
von Soden W 1952 *Grundriss der akkadischen Grammatik*. Biblical Institute Press, Rome

Alphabet: Development

J. F. Healy

This article is concerned specifically with the origin and early development of alphabetic writing in the Near East. This development, which most scholars would date to the earlier part of the second millennium BCE, was a significant departure from such forms of writing as existed already, such as the

Sumero–Akkadian cuneiform and the Egyptian hieroglyphic systems. These had been in use since before 3000 BCE and were pictographic in origin (the signs being pictures of objects), though in due course they developed into systems for representing syllabic sound-combinations.

1. The Consonantal Alphabet: General Notions

An alphabet uses single signs to represent individual sounds and the development of the first alphabets created the possibility of a dramatic simplification of writing, since the number of phonemes in any language is relatively small by contrast with the number of possible syllables. For example, the syllabic writing of Akkadian required hundreds of separate syllable signs and continued to use stylized pictographs. Modern scholars should not overlook the originality of linguistic thought behind the first devising of the alphabet—the isolation of individual distinctive and contrasting sounds and the representation of each such sound by a single sign.

It may be noted, however, that I. J. Gelb (Gelb 1963) took the view that the early alphabets are not in fact true alphabets but should be regarded as syllabaries in which each sign stands for a consonant followed by any vowel. The reason for taking this view is the fact that the inventor or inventors of the first alphabet only isolated consonantal sounds and made no allowance for vowels. All the ancient Near Eastern alphabets dealt with here are 'consonantal' alphabets. The true alphabet in the modern sense came into existence when the Greeks, who adopted the consonantal alphabet from the Phoenicians, began to use certain signs which they did not need in Greek, to represent vowels (see *Semitic Scripts*).

It is possible that the nonrepresentation of vowels in early alphabets used for the writing of Semitic languages is a reflection of the separation of the roles of vowels and consonants in those languages (see *Semitic Languages*), but the failure of the newly invented alphabet to deal with the vowels was an intrinsic weakness which was later rectified for languages like Arabic, Syriac, Ethiopic, and Hebrew by the introduction of additional signs. There were, however, some early attempts in the Semitic sphere to represent vowels, since in early Aramaic and then in Hebrew script certain signs for consonants (h, w, and y) came to be used in limited circumstances also to represent vowels. Consonants used in this way as vowels are called 'vowel-letters' (see *Semitic Scripts*).

One other aspect of the study of the early alphabet needs a brief mention, the development and fixing of the order of the letters. There is a considerable amount of evidence on this even from the earliest times in the form of texts which simply list the letters in the alphabetic order. Such texts, usually practice or school texts, are called 'abecedaries,' though the actual ordering was not the same as in the modern ABC (and the letter C has no real equivalent in these old alphabets). The very ordering of alphabets like the Ugaritic and the Greek alphabets reveals that certain letters were added secondarily.

2. Proto-Sinaitic and Proto-Canaanite Scripts

The Egyptian writing system is essentially syllabic, though the vowel in any syllable is not defined. Thus there were in Egyptian signs representing /b/ followed by any vowel, /d/ followed by any vowel, etc. It appears that ultimately the signs used for these single-consonant syllables derived from pictographs, though through the course of time the sign came to represent not the object pictured but the first consonant of the Egyptian word for this object. Thus the sign for 'mouth,' 𓂋, originally pronounced as the word for 'mouth,' *r*3 or *rt* came to be used for /r/ followed by any vowel or none. This principle of using a sign to represent the first letter of the word it stands for is called acrophony ('initial sound'). It gave the Egyptians the ready possibility of alphabetic writing, since they had all the ingredients to hand. Indeed in the Middle Kingdom period, scribes used single-consonant signs and vowel-letters to transcribe foreign names (Sass 1991). However, the Egyptians generally continued to use multiconsonant signs as the basis of the script and the single-consonant signs were only used in special circumstances.

It was in the early to middle second millennium BCE that the first steps towards (consonantal) alphabetic writing were taken. Since the early years of the twentieth century a number of inscriptions have been discovered in Sinai and Palestine (and hence called Proto-Sinaitic or Proto-Canaanite) in which it appears that the Egyptian way of writing has been converted into an alphabetic system.

The inscriptions in question date to ca. 1500 BCE, number several dozens (full discussion in Sass 1988, who dates the material to the eighteenth century BCE) and were carved by miners at the turquoise mines at Serabit el-Khadim in Sinai. Because the number of signs in these inscriptions was so small (less than 30) it became clear to scholars working on them that the script was alphabetic, not syllabic.

Other examples have been found in Palestine (Shechem, Gezer, Lachish), which are slightly earlier in date. These show that the phenomenon was fairly widespread. While one can never hope to know who invented this new alphabetic way of writing, two things seem clear. First, there is Egyptian inspiration behind the invention, since there are some similarities between the Proto-Sinaitic and Egyptian signs and the basic acrophonic principle must have come from knowledge of the Egyptian script (being unknown in the Sumero–Akkadian system). It is on the other hand surprising that the use of vowel-letters was not taken up also, since this was part of Middle Kingdom practice (above). Second, the texts, though not well understood, are in a Canaanite, West–Semitic language, not Egyptian. This and the geographical distribution of the inscriptions imply that the script must have had its origin in a Semitic-speaking area which had strong cultural contacts with Egypt. Palestine is currently the strongest candidate, though the Phoenician coast with its close contact with Egypt was long the focus of inventiveness in scripts and further discoveries might shift the focus to that region.

The Proto-Sinaitic or Proto-Canaanite script, which has been deciphered to some extent, though the texts are not always understood, uses the Semitic (rather than the Egyptian) word for the object of the original pictograph as the starting point. It is to this word that the acrophonic principle was applied and the first letter of the Semitic word gave the value of the particular sign. Thus the drawing of a house stood for 'house.' 'House' in West Semitic was *bētu*. Hence the house-pictograph was used for the consonant b. The acrophonic principle may not explain all the signs but Fig. 1 shows examples which are fairly secure.

While there are great difficulties with the Proto-Sinaitic inscriptions, some later Proto-Canaanite

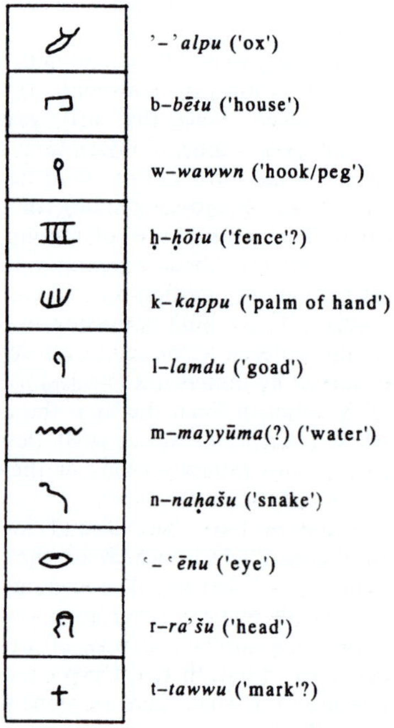
'–'*alpu* ('ox')
b–*bētu* ('house')
w–*wawwn* ('hook/peg')
ḥ–*ḥōtu* ('fence'?)
k–*kappu* ('palm of hand')
l–*lamdu* ('goad')
m–*mayyūma*(?) ('water')
n–*naḥašu* ('snake')
ʿ–ʿ*ēnu* ('eye')
r–*raʾšu* ('head')
t–*tawwu* ('mark'?)

Figure 1. Examples of Proto-Sinaitic characters with acrophonic derivation (after J. F. Healey 1990 *The Early Alphabet*. © British Museum Press, London. Reproduced with permission).

texts are less obscure (e.g., the thirteenth and twelfth century BCE material from Lachish, Beth Shemesh, and Izbet Sartah) and, although the material in this type of writing is very limited, it is clear from comparison of many of the letters with the much better known Phoenician script that the Phoenician is the direct descendant of the Proto-Sinaitic/Proto-Canaanite. There are transitional forms found in a variety of small inscriptions from Palestine (the el-Khader arrowheads, twelfth century BCE) and Lebanon (two in Proto-Canaanite and two in Phoenician). There are even fragments from as far away as Crete and Sardinia (eleventh century), which should be especially noted in connection with the spread of the Semitic alphabet to the Greeks.

3. Varieties of the Early Alphabet and its Spread

Other experiments in alphabet creation were going on at roughly the same time in northern Syria and Palestine, as is clear from a number of finds, but principally from the archives of the ancient city of Ugarit (modern Ras Shamra) recovered since 1929. These are dated to ca. 1400–1200 BCE and while many were written in the familiar syllabic cuneiform of Akkadian and Hittite, some were written in a previously unknown cuneiform script (i.e., based, like the Sumero–Akkadian script, on wedge-shapes pressed in wet clay) written from left to right.

The decipherers quickly realized that the new script, despite being cuneiform, was alphabetic, since it had only 30 signs in all. They assumed that the language was probably West Semitic, akin to Phoenician and Hebrew, using like them a consonantal alphabet. With little delay all the signs were identified and the language was confirmed to be a West Semitic one related to the later languages Phoenician and Hebrew. In 1955 a new tablet was found at Ugarit which, though broken, listed the majority of the letters and gave alongside each one the consonantal equivalent as represented in the Akkadian cuneiform script (with vowel attached, since the Sumero–Akkadian system cannot express consonants alone).

The remarkable thing about the Ugaritic alphabet apart from its early date was the fact that it was a 'cuneiform' alphabet, as opposed to the linear scripts of Egypt and Proto-Sinaitic/Canaanite. This makes it look superficially like Akkadian cuneiform, but the individual signs are different from the Akkadian signs. No doubt the basic technology of writing followed a Mesopotamian model (Akkadian texts were well known in the West at this time), but the actual forms of the letters (see Fig. 2) seem to have been inspired at least in part by the linear alphabet of the Proto-Canaanite/Proto-Sinaitic inscriptions.

Ugarit also provides the first glimpse of an established ordering of the letters of the alphabet, since an abecedary was found in 1948 which simply

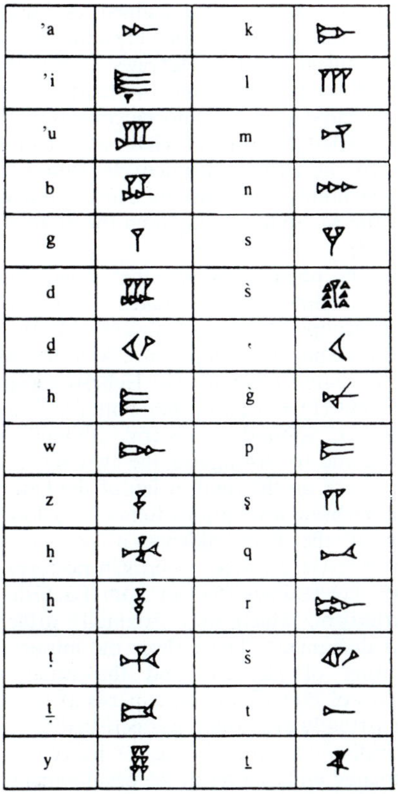

Figure 2. The Ugaritic Cuneiform Alphabet (after J. F. Healey 1990 *The Early Alphabet*. © British Museum Press, London. Reproduced with permission).

lists the letters in order: 'a, b, g, ḫ, d, h, w, z, ḥ, ṭ, y, k, š, l, m, ḏ, n, ẓ, s, ʿ, p, ṣ, q, r, ṯ, ǵ, t, 'i, 'u, s̀. The last three appear to be additional, so it appears to have been a basic 27-letter system which has been expanded by the addition of 'i, 'u, and ś, a special s-sound used in words of Hurrian origin. This cuneiform alphabet is regarded as a 'long' alphabet, by comparison with the 'short,' 22-letter alphabet used later (first millennium BCE) for Phoenician and Hebrew.

It may be noted that in the Ugaritic script there are signs to represent three varieties of the glottal stop: 'a, 'i, 'u, (called *aleph* in Hebrew). Apparently the three forms of *aleph* were devised as aids to help indicate the vowel following the *aleph* (or sometimes in front of it), though without any distinction in vowel length. Occasionally, though not regularly, these signs seem to be used as pure vowel signs. The three *alephs* are, in fact, an intrusion of syllabic writing into an otherwise consonantal system. The Ugaritic scribes who developed the long cuneiform alphabet may have been inspired in this regard by the existence of certain syllabic cuneiform signs which were sometimes used simply to indicate a vowel. The Ugaritic signs for /'i/ and /'u/ may actually be derived from the Akkadian i and ú signs. Like the letter s̀, they may have been devised initially to assist with the writing of non-Semitic words.

There are a number of other cuneiform alphabetic inscriptions of similar or slightly later date from the area to the south of Ugarit. These come from various sites such as Ta'anach, Nahal Tabor, and Beth Shemesh in Palestine, Tell Nebi Mend in Syria, and Sarepta in Lebanon. There is also a Ugaritic-type inscription from Cyprus (Hala Sultan Tekke), though it is uncertain whether the silver dish on which it is found is an import from the Levantine coast. Some of these inscriptions, as well as a small number of texts from Ugarit itself, are in a shorter version of the cuneiform alphabet, representing a smaller range of phonemes. The shorter alphabet was more or less adequate for the later languages of the area like Phoenician and Hebrew, since some phonemes had merged.

3.1 *The Plurality of Alphabets in the Second Millennium* BCE

It is not easy to explain the complex history of the alphabet in this period. According to a widespread view the alphabet was in the process of being shortened because linguistic changes were taking place which involved the loss of certain sounds. Thus Hebrew did not need to represent /ḫ/, /ḏ/, /ẓ/, /ǵ/, or /ṯ/. While a sign to represent /š/ was needed, it came to be represented by the otherwise unwanted sign for /ṯ/, so that the old letter š was dropped. The shorter cuneiform alphabet is usually seen as a step in this direction, though the sporadic nature of the finds suggests that the idea of a cuneiform alphabet never became popular. It depends upon the local availability of suitable clay, while the southern area of Syria–Palestine was under Egyptian cultural influence at this time and writing there, using a descendant of the linear Proto-Sinaitic/Proto-Canaanite script, was normally carried out on papyrus, which unfortunately rarely survives.

However, a variation on this view has recently been put forward (Dietrich and Loretz 1988), suggesting that the normal (longer) Ugaritic cuneiform alphabet was created to allow for extra sounds which were needed as a result of southern Semitic—Arabian—influence involving an expanded phonemic repertoire. Key evidence for this view would be the cuneiform alphabetic abecedaries from Ugarit (discovered 1988) and Beth Shemesh in Palestine, which, instead of following the established northwest Semitic order (beginning ', b, g, d ...), follow the South Arabian order (h, l, ḥ, m ...). This would suggest that what is known as the South Arabian letter-order (though only from a later date) already existed in the second millennium BCE and may have been brought to Palestine with an incoming ethnic group at a very early date.

Ugaritic cuneiform is the only alphabetic cuneiform that is well known. The cuneiform alphabets disappeared and the other branch of alphabetic tradition, that of the linear forms descended from the Proto-Sinaitic/Proto-Canaanite script, replaced it. Ugarit itself was destroyed ca. 1200 BCE.

3.2 Variable Direction of Writing

West Semitic texts before the emergence of the Phoenician script are not uniform in their direction of writing. The Ugaritic alphabet is written left to right, but there are a few right to left Ugaritic texts. The earlier Proto-Sinaitic/Proto-Canaanite scripts are very irregular. Writing could be in either direction or vertical. Some early Greek and South Arabian texts are written *boustrophedón* (Gk)—reversing direction at the end of a line like on ox ploughing a field. In such inscriptions the letters are often reversed to face the direction of writing.

With the settling down of the Phoenician alphabet (ca. 1100–1050 BCE) the right to left order became fixed. It may be noted that this is of some significance in the discussion of the date at which the Greeks received the alphabet from the Phoenicians, since in the earliest Greek inscriptions the direction is still not fixed.

4. The Settling of the Alphabet

Although the main evidence of the Proto-Sinaitic/Proto-Canaanite and even cuneiform alphabets is in the south—Palestine, Sinai, etc. (with Ugarit an outpost of the cuneiform alphabet in the north)—Byblos may have been a major focus of script development. The 22-letter Byblian alphabet, the early Phoenician alphabet, evolved ca. 1050 BCE in a direct line of descent from the earlier linear alphabets (see Fig. 3). The right to left orientation of writing and the stylized linear character of the letters became fixed about this time. The inscription of the Ahiram sarcophagus, dated ca. 1000 BCE, finds the script already in a classic form. Other inscriptions follow soon after, also from Byblos.

This Phoenician script spread and came to be used also by kingdoms to the north, as is evidenced by inscriptions from Zincirli and Karatepe (Turkey, ninth and eighth centuries BCE) and to the south, where the Phoenician alphabet spread to the Hebrews. To the east it was adopted by the Aramaeans. Both the Hebrews and Aramaeans were at this time establishing kingdoms. The Aramaeans have left a number of monumental inscriptions, while the Hebrew material is mostly of a less formal kind, though it is very extensive (letters, seals, etc.), partly because of the intensive archaeological exploration of Palestine.

The Phoenician script remained essentially unchanged during most of its long life and it was used at first unchanged by the Hebrews. Thus the very earliest 'Hebrew' inscription, the tenth century BCE Gezer Calendar is in the Phoenician script, but it is uncertain whether this text is Hebrew. In fact the best witness to the earliest distinctively Hebrew script-form is the ninth century Moabite inscription of King Mesha, the Moabites having used the Hebrew script (see Fig. 3).

It may be noted, however, that when the short, Phoenician alphabet was taken over by other language-groups, it was not always able to express distinctions which were important. At least one of the Phoenician letters taken over by Hebrew was used for two different Hebrew phonemes, both for /š/ and also for another s-sound (a lateral sibilant?). Later Hebrew came to distinguish the two by placing a diacritic mark on the right or left of the letter.

Other Hebrew inscriptions follow in a long series throughout the first millennium BCE, frequently written on ostraca (pieces of broken pottery). There are also clay sealings (*bullae*) from Lachish, Arad, and Jerusalem, which were originally attached to papyrus documents. These show the importance of the writing of Hebrew, and the other related derivatives of Phoenician, on papyrus at this period, though virtually everything has perished.

Politically and culturally ancient Israel was somewhat isolated and as a result the developments in the script during this long period are limited. There are certain tendencies to a more cursive style, but almost all available sources are inscribed on stone and pot and only very limited evidence is extant on soft materials. There may have been no Hebrew tradition of royal inscriptions requiring a monumental script.

Having been in decline from the time of the Babylonian exile (sixth century BCE) when the Aramaic language was in the ascendant, the Hebrew script was eventually abandoned by the Jewish community. The old script, called in later Jewish tradition *kĕtāb 'ibrī* 'the Hebrew script,' did not, however, disappear immediately. Among the Dead Sea Scrolls there are Bible fragments in the old script and there are also coins from the Hasmonaean period (135–37 BCE) and coins and ostraca from the first and second Jewish Revolts (66–70 CE and 132–35 CE). The retention of the old script may have had an element of nationalism about it. It was also favored by certain Jewish sects, certainly by the Samaritans who retained the old script throughout the ages.

The Aramaic script, derived from Phoenician ca. the eleventh and tenth centuries BCE, was the most flourishing and long-lived of the three scripts (see Fig. 3). Not only did it ultimately supplant the other two, it also spread far beyond the area of the Aramaean people and became a script of convenience for Assyrians, Persians, and others and was used in

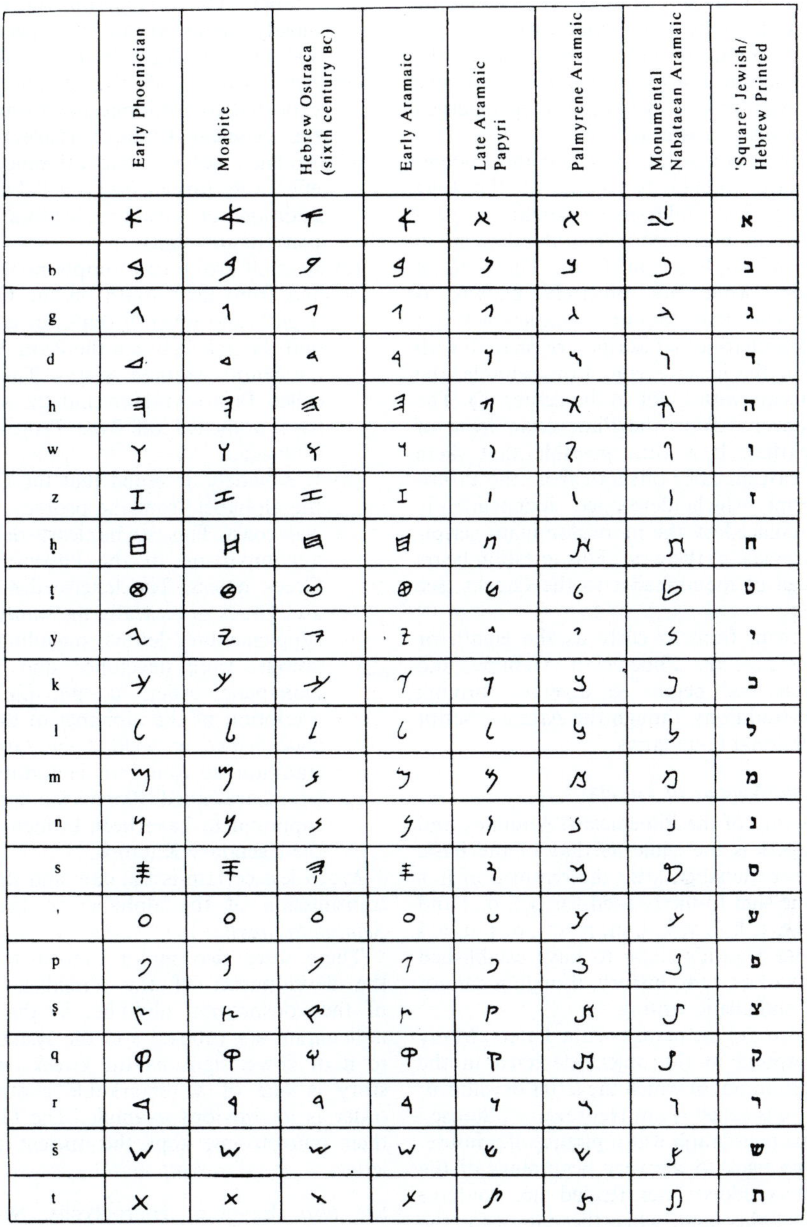
Early Phoenician
Moabite
Hebrew Ostraca (sixth century BC)
Early Aramaic
Late Aramaic Papyri
Palmyrene Aramaic
Monumental Nabataean Aramaic
'Square' Jewish/ Hebrew Printed
ʾ
b
g
d
h
w
z
ḥ
ṭ
y
k
l
m
n
s
ʿ
p
ṣ
q
r
š
t
א
ב
ג
ד
ה
ו
ז
ח
ט
י
כ
ל
מ
נ
ס
ע
פ
צ
ק
ר
ש
ת

Figure 3. The Phoenician script and its major derivatives (after J. F. Healey 1990 *The Early Alphabet*. © British Museum Press, London. Reproduced with permission).

Egypt, Arabia, Cilicia, Anatolia, Afghanistan, etc. At first Aramaic simply used the Phoenician script (as in Aramaic inscriptions from Zincirli, Hamath and Damascus in the ninth and eighth centuries BCE), but as a result of its international currency under the Assyrians and the powers which succeeded them it developed extremely rapidly, diverging from Phoenician from the eighth century BCE onwards and becoming increasingly cursive and simplified. There developed a difference between formal and cursive styles. The cursive is better known and is attested mainly on papyrus and leather from Egypt and

Palestine (sixth to third centuries BCE—including papyri from Hermopolis and Elephantine), but the Aramaic script retained homogeneity until the collapse of the Persian Empire, which was a cohesive force. Local variations of the script then emerged (Palmyrene, Jewish, Nabataean, etc.).

On the relation between the Aramaic and Phoenician scripts, note should be made of the long inscription from Tell Fakhariyah found in 1979 near Tell Halaf in northeast Syria, a bilingual in Aramaic and in Assyrian cuneiform. The date of this inscription, while not precisely known, is certainly not earlier than the ninth century BCE, yet some of the peculiarities of script are shared with earlier forms of the linear script. For example, the letter *'ayin* appears with a dot in the center: ⊙. The dot had disappeared from the Phoenician form of *'ayin* much earlier. It is thus possible that there existed in the east an early offshoot from the Proto-Canaanite script which developed independently before being replaced by the more dominant script-form of the Aramaic of the west. This question bears upon the spread of the alphabet to the Greeks (see Naveh 1987).

Gradually, then, from as early as the eighth or ninth centuries BCE, the Phoenician, Hebrew, and Aramaic scripts had begun to diverge, forming national script-traditions, though the Aramaic script transcended national boundaries.

4.1 Ordering and Naming of Letters

The basic ordering of the Phoenician, Aramaic, and Hebrew alphabets is the same as that of the basic Ugaritic 27-letter alphabet, after the removal of ḫ, š (replaced by the sign formerly used for /ṯ/), ḏ, ẓ and ǵ:', b, g, d, h, w, z, ḥ, ṭ, y, k, l, m, n, s, ', p, ṣ, q, r, š (old ṯ), t. Hence Ugarit's claim to have established the first alphabet known to history, though it cannot claim the first alphabetic writing.

Of interest also are the names of the letters. Many of these correspond to the object depicted in the original pictograph out of which the letter developed. Thus the letter b is called *bēt* in Hebrew, i.e., 'house,' and the original pictograph was a picture of a house. These names go back to the very beginnings of the alphabet. Letters added later tended not to have proper names of this kind, while the names for the main letters were fixed to such a degree that when the Greeks took over the Phoenician alphabet (Sect. 5(d)) they retained the old names, *alpha*, *beta*, etc., despite the fact that these names were absolutely meaningless in Greek.

5. Later Developments

Brief reference may be made to some early offshoots from the newly invented alphabet:

(a) Directly related to the linear proto-alphabet is the alphabetic system adopted in southern Arabia. The inscriptions in this script are mostly assigned to the period from ca. 500 BCE to as late as CE 600.

(b) An offshoot of this southern script was exported to Ethiopia and forms the basis of the classical Ethiopic (Ge'ez) and modern Amharic scripts. The Ethiopic alphabet was effectively turned into a syllabic script by the addition of vowel indicators to the basic consonantal signs.

(c) A small group of inscriptions from Babylonia and from near Elath on the Gulf of Aqaba (eighth and seventh centuries BCE) may represent the link between the Proto-Canaanite and the South Arabian scripts. These are usually called Proto-Arabian and the script seems to have branched off from Proto-Canaanite ca. 1300 BCE.

(d) It is widely accepted that the Greeks learned the alphabet from the peoples of the Phoenician coast. This can be clearly demonstrated by a comparison of the Phoenician and early Greek letters. The letter-order in Phoenician and Greek is basically the same, though some supplementary letters, including some of the vowels, were developed and added to the alphabetic order: u, ph, kh, ps, ō. The ascription of the alphabet to the Phoenicians was firmly embedded in Greek historical tradition as found in Herodotus, where the letters are called 'Phoenician letters,' and were supposed to have been brought to Greece by the legendary Kadmos.

Much less certain is the date and the route of the transmission of the alphabet to the Greeks (see *Semitic Scripts*).

There were two major innovative moments in the development of the alphabet, the first use of the consonantal alphabet in the early second millennium BCE (above) and the systematic addition to it of vowel signs by the Greeks. Otherwise the story is one of a remarkable continuity. Letter-order is an obvious example. The Greeks, despite their innovations, kept the ancient names of the letters.

See also: Egyptian Hieroglyphs; Semitic Scripts; Arabic Script: Adaptation for Other Languages.

Bibliography

Bordreuil P, Pardee D 1995 "Un abécédaire du type sud-sémitique..." *CRAIBL* 1995, 855–60

Dietrich M, Loretz O 1988 *Die Keilalphabete: die phönizischkanaanäischen und altarabischen Alphabete in Ugarit*. UGARIT-Verlag, Münster

Diringer D 1962 *Writing*. Thames and Hudson, London

Diringer D 1968 *The Alphabet: A Key to the History of Mankind*, 3rd edn. Hutchinson, London

Driver G R 1976 *Semitic Writing from Pictograph to Alphabet*, 3rd edn. British Academy/Oxford University Press, London
Gelb I J 1963 *A Study of Writing*, 2nd edn. Chicago University Press, Chicago, IL
Healey J F 1990 *The Early Alphabet*. British Museum Publications, London
Naveh J 1982 *Early History of the Alphabet: An Introduction to West Semitic Epigraphy and Palaeography*. Magnes Press, Jerusalem and E. J. Brill, Leiden
Naveh J 1987 Proto-Canaanite, Archaic Greek, and the script of the Aramaic text on the Tell Fakhariyah statue. In: Miller P-D, et al. (eds.) *Ancient Israelite Religion: Essays in Honor of Frank Moore Cross*. Fortress Press, Philadelphia, PA
Puech E 1986 Origine de l'alphabet. *Revue Biblique* **93**: 161–213
Sass B 1988 *The Genesis of the Alphabet and its Development in the Second Millennium* BC. Otto Harrassowitz, Wiesbaden
Sass B 1991 *Studia Alphabetica: On the Origin and Early History of the Northwest Semitic, South Semitic and Greek Alphabets*. Universitätsverlag, Freiburg and Vandenhoeck & Ruprecht, Göttingen

Ancient Egyptian and Coptic

J. D. Ray

The Ancient Egyptian language is first attested a little before 3000 BCE, when the earliest inscriptions in hieroglyphic make their appearance. Connected texts of some length are found from about 2700 BCE onwards, and these develop into a considerable literature, which forms one of our major sources of information about the ancient Near East. The language survived the downfall of the Roman Empire and the transition to Christianity, and in its latest form, written in a modification of the Greek alphabet, it is known as Coptic. Coptic continued until well after 1000 CE. Egyptian therefore has the longest attested history of any language, and this fact alone makes it important for linguistic study.

The language is a member of the Hamito–Semitic (increasingly referred to as the Afro–Asiatic) family, although its exact place within this family is disputed. The main reason for this is that many of the related languages were not written down until much later, and several 'missing links' may have died out without being recorded at all. Egyptian shares the preference of most of this family for triconsonantal roots, from which whole groups of words may be formed, normally by variations on the internal vowels and with the use of some suffixed endings. This patterning probably encouraged the Egyptians to omit the vowels from their writing-system (see *Egyptian Hieroglyphs*). The language recognizes two genders, masculine and feminine; neuter meanings are expressed in the early stage of the language by the feminine, later by the masculine. Adjectives follow the noun, and agree with it in number and gender. It is possible that case-endings, similar to those in the Semitic languages, existed at a very early stage of Egyptian, but they are not written and soon fell away; traces may remain in the construct state, where a direct genitive relationship is expressed by two nouns in apposition. Strict word-order is used to mark grammatical function. A dual number is recognized alongside singular and plural.

The Egyptian verb has unique features. A stative tense, known in Coptic as the qualitative, seems to be inherited from an early stage of Afro–Asiatic, and has cognates in Semitic. This tense expresses the result of the verbal action, and is often best rendered by an adjective or an adverbial phrase: 'absent, continuous, far away, already knowing,' or the like. The narrative tense system, on the other hand, is peculiar to Egyptian, and seems to consist of various forms of a verbal noun with a possessive suffix as subject ('his hearing' developing into 'he hears'). Other forms include a possessive construction with an interesting parallel to modern perfects ('heard to him' developing into 'he has heard'), and a series which express past, present, and future contingency. There is also a set of so-called participles, which are really nouns of agent ('a hearer'), and a sequence of relative tenses formed from passive participles ('his heard-one' developing into 'the one which he heard'). Participles and relative forms show two aspects, perfective and imperfective, depending on whether the action is regarded as completed or not; there may also be traces of a prospective, referring to future action. Aspect may also feature in the narrative tenses, where a prospective tense certainly occurs. The language is strongly VSO in its structure. A remarkable feature is that three uses of the English verb 'to be'—existential, predicative, and identifying—are rendered by distinct constructions; on the other hand, there is no verb 'to have,' which is conveyed by phrases such as 'there is to me.' A welcome omission is comparison of adjectives: 'she is better than he' is expressed as 'she is good against/in respect to/him.'

This is the form taken in Egyptian in its classic period, Middle Egyptian, which is the language of the early second millennium BCE. This canonical stage was recognized by the Egyptians themselves, and was retained in formal inscriptions until the end of Pharaonic history. However, after about 1400 BCE, pressure from the spoken language, which was constantly changing, begins increasingly to affect the written texts, and the result is Late Egyptian, which takes over most of the functions of its predecessor. Late Egyptian, which is the direct ancestor of Coptic, stands to Middle Egyptian much as Italian does to Latin, although phonetic changes are largely concealed by the continuity of the script. The most obvious innovations are in the verb, where the old patterns are replaced by analytic expressions derived from fossilized verbal forms. The process —which is strikingly similar to the development of modern English—leads to greater emphasis on time-distinction and modal subtleties. The number of compound 'tenses' in such a system is almost limitless, although one useful distinction which is present in Late Egyptian—that between preterite and present perfect—is lost in Coptic. One remarkable feature of Late Egyptian is the existence of a second series of tenses, which throw emphasis on an adverbial adjunct. These bear some relation to the relative forms ('the fact that he went is yesterday' developing into 'it was yesterday that he went'). This system is foreshadowed in Middle Egyptian, although the details are still far from understood. The development of the verbal system makes Coptic appear an SVO language, although this is historically accidental. Coptic also dispenses with most adjectives, preferring paraphrases, with the passive voice, preferring third-person plural constructions, and with most plurals, allowing the prefixed article or possessive to bear the marks of number and gender. Late Egyptian contains many Semitic loanwords; Coptic, on the other hand, is almost as full of Greek words as modern English is of French or Latin.

In all, Egyptian throughout its history well deserves the epithet *lingua geometrica* which was given to it in the nineteenth century, when the regularity and elegance of its constructions were first appreciated. The following examples may illustrate this. (Egyptian is conventionally transliterated into Romanized consonants.)

Middle Egyptian: *'ḥ'.n h3b.n wỉ ḥm.f r*
arise + pa send + pa me embodiment + his to

K3š r sn-nw sp,
Cush for two + ord occasion,

ỉb.f 3w ỉm.ỉ r ḫt nbt
heart + his content + stat in + me against thing any + f/sg

'As a result his majesty sent me to Nubia a second time, his heart being pleased with me more than anything.'

Late Egyptian: *wn.ỉn Pr-'3 ḥr h3b.ỉ*
exist + pa contingency Pharaoh upon sending + me

r p3 t3 Nḥs n
to the + m/sg land Nubian in

p3 sp mḥ-sn, ỉw ḥ3ty.f
the + m/sg time filling + two, situation heart + his

mtry ỉm.ỉ m šsr
content + stat in + me in abundance

Coptic: ⲁϥϫⲟⲟⲥ ⲛ̄ϭⲓ ⲟⲩⲁ ⲛ̄ⲛⲉⲥⲛⲏⲩ ϫⲉ ⲁⲛⲟⲕ ⲛ̄
ϯ ⲙ̄ⲡϣⲁ ⲁⲛ ⲉⲛⲁⲩ ⲉⲡⲁⲅⲅⲉⲗⲟⲥ
ⲉⲁⲓⲱⲛϩ ϩⲛ̄ⲛ̄ⲛⲟⲃⲉ ⲛⲁϩⲟⲟⲩ ⲧⲏⲣⲟⲩ

afjoos nci oua n ne snēu
pa + he + say + it namely one + m/sg of the + pl brother + pl

je anok n ti m p
saying myself not[1] 1/sg in the + m/sg

ša an e nau e p angelos
value not[2] to look at the + m/sg angel,

eai ōnh hn n nobe na hoou tērou
situation + pa + I live in the + pl sin my + pl day entirety + their

'One of the brethren said "For my part, I am not worthy to see the angel, having lived in sin all my days".'

Bibliography

Callender J B 1975 *Middle Egyptian* (= *Afroasiatic Dialects*, vol 2). Undena Publications, Malibu, CA

Gardiner A H 1950 *Egyptian Grammar*, 2nd edn. Griffith Institute/OUP, Oxford

Griffith F Ll 1902 Egyptology (language). In: *Encyclopaedia Britannica*, 9th edn. London

Lambdin T O 1983 *Introduction to Sahidic Coptic*. Mercer University Press, Macon, GA

Polotsky H J 1944 *Etudes de syntaxe copte*. Publications de la société d'Archéologie copte, Cairo

Polotsky H J 1971 Coptic. In: Hodge C T (ed.) *Afroasiatic: A survey*. Mouton, The Hague

Vergote J 1971 Egyptian. In: Hodge C T (ed.) *Afroasiatic: A Survey*. Mouton, The Hague

Vergote J 1973 *Grammaire copte*, 2 vols. Edit Peeters, Louvain

Arabic

C. Holes

Arabic is the sole or joint official language of some 21 independent Middle Eastern and African states, and is the native language of approximately 183 million people. Since January 1, 1974 it has been an official language of the United Nations. As the language in which the holy book of Islam, the Qur'ān (or Koran) was revealed, Arabic is the liturgical language of Muslims worldwide (ca. 1 billion people or 20 percent of the world's population, living in more than 60 countries; see *Qur'an*).

1. History

The early history of Arabic is obscure. Genealogically, it is a member of the southwestern subbranch of the so-called 'Semitic' group (see *Semitic Languages*) of the Afro–Asiatic language family, a term which designates certain languages with a Near Eastern origin which show a sufficient degree of structural similarity for a common origin to be supposed. The earliest extant written evidence for a language unmistakably identifiable as Arabic is an inscription found on a tombstone at Nemara in the Syrian desert, which has been dated to 328 CE.

Arabic does not move into the full light of world history until three and half centuries after this, when, in the space of 80 years from 632 to 710 CE, the conquering armies of Islam emerged from Arabia to occupy (or in some instances establish) the cities of the Levant, Egypt, the Fertile Crescent, North Africa, and Spain. Over the ensuing centuries, several factors conspired to cause Arabic to supplant the indigenous languages—Aramaic, Greek, Coptic, Berber—of the conquered territories: the gradual consolidation of Arab political control; the continuing waves of new Arabic-speaking immigrants from the Arabian peninsula, which provided fresh injections of the language; and, perhaps most important of all, the conviction on the part of the indigenous population that there were political and economic advantages to be gained by adopting the religion, and, a fortiori, the language of their conquerors. The process of Arabicization began in the relatively cosmopolitan atmosphere of the towns with Arabic taking over as the written language of government and administration early on, and subsequently as a spoken lingua franca. In the countryside, it spread much more slowly because of the pattern of early settlement and the nature of rural life, and, although there is little direct evidence in the form of reports to this effect, there must have been a long period of bilingualism in all of what are now thought of as 'Arab' countries. The exact details of this process, and in particular whether there was a phase of pidginization and creolization is disputed (see Versteegh 1984, Holes's 1986, and Hopkins's 1988 critical reviews).

The status of Arabic as the language of Islam has had the most profound effect on its development, and continues to provide one of the major cultural matrices which condition that development. Orthodox Muslims regard the text of the Qur'ān as the literal word of God, revealed through his Prophet, Muhammad. The language and style of the Qur'ān, even though regarded as of, by definition, inimitable excellence, provided for many centuries a literary model in the same way as the meaning of the words provided the model for lawful and righteous behavior. The codification of the language, which began in the eighth century, took the Qur'ān, pre-Islamic poetry, and to some extent the language of contemporary Bedouin untainted by foreign influence, as the sources for the rules of 'correct' morphology and syntax. The description of Arabic written during this period by Sibawayhi (d. 794) remains to this day the basis of indigenous modern grammatical treatments of the language (see *Sibawayhi*).

While the grammarians, starting with Sibawayhi and his contemporaries, and continuing to the present day, have continued to prescribe what is 'correct' (*fasi:ħ* lit. 'pure') according to Qur'ānic and other 'Classical' usage, Arabic as a living spoken language (and more recently as a living written one) has undergone considerable change. The development of the spoken Arabic dialects, at least during the centuries before the present one, is for obvious reasons poorly documented, and a matter of some controversy. What seems clear from their general similarity of structure, when compared to the Classical Arabic of the Qur'ān and the early poetry, is that the spoken dialects probably had a single source (or a number of similar sources) and that this source was not Classical Arabic as it is now known. Although some interdialectal similarities could be explained as the result of natural drift and morphological reduction from a common Classical base, by no means all the interdialectal similarities can be accounted for in this way. A more plausible explanation (on historical as well as linguistic grounds) is that they represent the end point of a continuous process of development from a shared species of spoken Arabic which was never fully identifiable with 'Classical Arabic' although at the beginning of the process the two may have been quite similar, with Classical Arabic perhaps representing an elevated stylistic variant of the common speech (see Ferguson 1959a on the proposal for an Arabic koine as the starting point; for a rebuttal, see Cohen 1962 and Blau 1977). Of course, developments in spoken Arabic occurred in different conditions at different speeds in different places, and the substrate linguistic influences (Coptic, Aramaic, etc.) must also have been local differentiating factors. However, the unchanging, codified rules of Classical Arabic, and the centrality of the document which embodies them, the Qur'ān, to religion (and hence to law and social organization) and learning throughout the Arabic-speaking world over the last thirteen centuries, have provided a constant normative influence on the evolution of the vernaculars and restrained the fragmentation of Arabic into totally separate languages. The result of the development of the vernaculars away from the norms of written Arabic has been a diglossic situation in which the standard (=based on written norms) and nonstandard (=based on spoken norms) are usually allocated to different sets of communicative functions (Ferguson's classic 1959b article provides lists of typical situations where 'standard' or 'nonstandard' forms (in his terms 'H' and 'L') are typically required).

2. The Status and Role of Arabic in the Late Twentieth Century

The view of many Arabs, particularly educated ones, is that Arabic is 'really' Classical Arabic, or its modern descendant Modern Standard Arabic (MSA)—that is, the language of all written Arabic from the seventh century on (see Ferguson 1972 for a discussion of popular myths about Arabic). Vernacular Arabic, which all speakers whatever their level of education use for all speech purposes apart from religious ritual and other forms of 'frozen' formulaic public speaking, is popularly regarded as a mere 'corruption' of Classical or MSA which, some believe, the school system should attempt to eradicate. Nonetheless, the vernaculars continue to flourish, and it is by no means the case that the mutual influence which results from the constant use of the two varieties side-by-side in the modern world is all in the direction standard→ nonstandard.

Views on the educational or cultural value of MSA versus the vernaculars are of course loaded with political significance. The use of the vernaculars in literature and for educational purposes, for example, has at different times been viewed positively as a means of promoting democratic populism (e.g., in Egypt and Syria in the 1950s and 1960s) or negatively as a cunning imperialist ploy to divide the Arabs (by most governments and educational establishments at most times). In practice, the ability to use MSA accurately and flexibly in extempore speech is rare: most native speakers, even highly educated ones, tend even in serious monitored discussion such as might occur in a TV discussion program to begin with a few prepared statements in MSA and then, as soon as the conversation becomes more animated and unpredictable, to resort to a mixed form of Arabic in which the basic syntax and morphology is nonstandard but in which there is strong MSA influence on the choice of lexical items and general phraseology. The wide availability of the media, especially television, has meant that even illiterates living in remote areas now have regular exposure to MSA in the form of news broadcast, 'classical' drama, and documentaries. This influence, reinforced by the massive increase in public education since the 1960s, has tended to exert a leveling influence on regional dialects in the direction of MSA. However, MSA is not the only 'leveling' influence: the increasing economic importance of large urban centers such as Cairo, Damascus, Amman, and Rabat has bestowed on the coloquials of these cities a certain prestige in the eyes of countrymen from outside them, and hence to their elevation to the status of a kind of regional spoken standard (see Ibrahim 1986 on the notion of 'prestige' dialects in Arabic).

3. The Dialect Geography of the Arab World

MSA, the nonnatively spoken pan-Arab variety of Arabic, is to a very high degree the same throughout the Arab world, at least, in its morphology and syntax. There are minor differences of pronunciation in its spoken form, for example in radio and TV broadcasts, and certain stylistic and vocabulary preferences which differentiate MSA as used in North Africa from that used in the rest of the Arab world. But these differences are insignificant compared to those between the regional dialects.

Dialect differences in the Arab world correlate both with geography and, within any given geographical area (such as a modern nation state) with degree of, and recentness of, urbanization.

There is a major division on grounds of vocabulary, morphology, and preferred syllable structure between the Maghreb (Morocco, Algeria, Tunisia, and western Libya) and the Mashriq (the eastern countries of the Arab world) such that a Damascene might claim he is unable to understand the informal, relaxed speech of an Algérois. In practice, however, educated speakers from widely separated areas like these are aware of this problem and capable of adjusting their speech in the direction of MSA to solve it. Within the Mashriq, there are divisions between (a) Egypt/Sudan, (b) Arabia, (c) the Levant (Lebanon/Palestine/Syria/Jordan), (d) Iraq. Between these divisions, however, the differences are much smaller as compared with the Mashriq as a whole versus the Maghreb as a whole. Further regional subdivisions could of course be made within each of (a)–(d).

Cross-cutting these geographical differences are those which correspond to degree of urbanization. In all Arab countries, the dialects of the countryside or the desert differ, sometimes quite sharply, from those of the cities. In the eastern Arab world, for example, the dialects of the descendants of nomads in Jordan, Syria, Iraq, and Arabia have, broadly speaking, more in common with each other than they have with the dialects of the old established cities such as Damascus, Jerusalem, Aleppo, Amman, even though such communities of sedentarized nomads may be living very great distances from each other. Similarly, the dialects of the inhabitants of these cities have much in common. The reasons for this have to do with the original patterns of migration and settlement over many centuries from the Arabian peninsula into the contiguous areas, and, subsequently, the maintenance of quite separate sets of social and speech networks in the cities on one hand and in the countryside on the other. Thus it is still true to say that an unlettered settled Bedouin from eastern Jordan speaks a dialect more akin to that of a settled nomad from Kuwait, some 600 miles away, than to that of a city dweller born and bred in Amman, only 30 miles distant. These age-old urban-rural differences are now, however, beginning to break down as the 'prestige' dialects of the cities, and the leveling influence of MSA become ever stronger.

4. A Sketch of the Structure of Arabic

It is not possible in a survey article of this kind to give anything more than the briefest of sketches of the morphology and syntax of Arabic. For more detailed accounts of MSA accessible to the non-Arabist, see Yushmanov (1961), Bateson (1967), Beeston (1970); for detailed descriptions of individual dialects, see, for example, AbdelMassih (1975) (Cairene), Erwin (1963) (Baghdadi), Cowell (1964) (Damascene), Holes (1990) (Gulf).

Perhaps the most striking feature of Arabic, whether MSA or dialectal, is its interdigitated morphology. By this is meant that the basic morphological resource in word building is a large set of (mostly) triconsonantal roots, and a relatively small set of highly productive fixed consonant–vowel patterns or templates which are applied to these roots to generate various categories of verb and noun stems. Here are a few examples from MSA. From the triconsonantal root *ʕ-l-m*, which has the basic meaning of 'cognition' one can derive the past tense verb stem *ʕalim-* 'to know' by applying the pattern CaCiC- (where C = consonant). If the pattern CaCCaC- is applied, in which the middle radical is doubled, and which (generally) indicates causativity, *ʕallam-* is generated, the past tense verb stem meaning 'to teach' (= 'to cause to know'). If the pattern taCaCCaC- is applied, that is, the causative pattern with a ta- prefix, one usually gets a passivized or reflexive meaning: thus *taʕall-am-* 'to learn' (= 'to teach oneself, to be taught'). In applying the pattern istaCCaC- which (amongst other possibilities) often has desiderative meaning, one gets *istaʕl-am-* 'to enquire' (= 'to want or ask for knowledge'). Nouns are generated on similar principles. Thus Ca: CiC- is the 'agent noun' pattern applied to all verbs which have a CaCvC- past stem, so *ʕa:lim-* means 'one who knows' or 'scientist'; muCaCCiC is the agent noun for causative verbs of the CaCCaC- stem, so *muʕallim-* is 'teacher,' and so on. To these noun and verb stems are added inflections to indicate person, number, gender, and case: thus *ʕalim-tu* 'I knew,' *ʕalim-ta* 'you (masc sg) knew,' etc.; *ʕa:lim-un* 'a scientist (nom),' *ʕa:lim-an* 'a scientist (acc),' *ʕa:lim-in* 'a scientist (gen).'

The root-pattern system of derivation is still highly productive in both MSA and the dialects. In MSA, the Arabic Language Academies have coined huge numbers of words by applying these derivational principles in order to enable the language to keep pace with developments in science and technology. Thus miCCaC, a pattern indicating 'noun of instrument' was applied to the root *s-ʕ-d* with a basic meaning of 'ascent' to generate *misʕad* 'elevator' (= 'device for ascending'). In the dialects, the same process has occurred but in a less controlled, more haphazard fashion and with no concern for language purity. Thus, in Gulf Arabic, the English word 'finish' was borrowed and adapted, as if it were a triconsonantal root, to the CaCCaC- causative pattern exemplified above, to give *fannaš* 'to fire, dismiss.' Secondary derivations followed in the normal way, giving the verbal noun *tafnīš* 'firing, dismissal' (verbal noun pattern taCCi: C) and the plural *tafnīšā* 'redundancies.'

In their inflectional morphology, the dialects as a whole are much simpler than MSA, with fewer categories of number and gender in the verb, a total loss of mood distinctions carried by short final vowels, and the loss of case endings in the noun phrase. These changes all seem to have had a phonological origin, as the loss of final vowels, which seems to have happened in the spoken language soon after the Islamic conquests (seventh century), collapsed many morphological distinctions. In syntax, dialectal word order is generally fixed as SVO in contrast to the rather more flexible ordering which was possible in an inflectional language like Classical Arabic (and remains possible in its modern descendant, MSA). The dialectal systems of negation, and subject-verb and noun-adjective agreement are also simpler (in the sense that they involve a smaller number of distinctions) than in MSA. The dialects also show a tendency toward a more 'analytic' structure: for example, relationships of possession between two nouns in the dialects have a linking particle (usually a decayed lexical item which originally meant something like 'property' or 'belonging') whereas in MSA the two nouns are directly juxtaposed with the relationship indicated by short-vowel case endings; in the expression of modality and aspect, the dialects have all developed similar systems of preverbal particles (again, seemingly decayed lexical items) in contrast to MSA, which preserves the original system of indicating such distinctions by short-vowel endings.

The Arabic writing system goes from right to left. Normally, only the consonants and long vowels of a word are written, the short vowels and other orthographic marks (such as those indicating doubled consonants or a consonant which is syllable-final) being omitted. The only exceptions to this are children's or other learners' primers and the Qur'ān, in which vowels, etc. are written, superscript and subscript. Thus a written Arabic word typically consists of a consonant (and long vowel) skeleton only. Decontextualized graphemes are therefore highly ambiguous, since the quality of the unwritten short vowels, as well as the length of consonants (similarly unmarked in the normal case) is meaning-bearing. Thus the grapheme *y-r-d* could be read, out of context, as *yaridu* 'he arrives,' *yaruddu* 'he answers,' *yuraddu* 'it is returned,' *yurid* 'may he want!' *yarda* 'may he perish!' and in several other ways. Context disambiguates.

Phonologically, all varieties of Arabic are characterized by contrasting sets of 'emphatized' versus 'plain' consonants (which differ slightly from dialect to dialect but which in MSA are /d/-/ᵭ/, /t/-/ᵵ/, /s/-/ᵴ/ and /ð/-/ð̴/); by a pair of velar fricatives /x/ and /ɣ/; and by a pair of pharyngeal fricatives (/ʕ/ and /ħ/). It is these sounds in particular which create the unique auditory impression of spoken Arabic. The Arabs themselves sometimes refer to their language as *luɣat aᵭ-ᵭa:d* 'the language of *ᵭa:d*,' *a:d* being the Arabic name for the sound /ᵭ/, which historically was a voiced emphatized dental plosive with a lateral release (in modern Arabic the lateral release has been lost), apparently in the belief that this sound was unique to Arabic.

See also: Semitic Languages; Arabic Script: Adaptation for Other Languages; Semitic Scripts; Qur'an; Islamic Calligraphy.

Bibliography

Abdel-Massih E T 1975 *An Introduction to Egyptian Arabic*. University of Michigan, Ann Arbor, MI

Bateson M C 1967 *Arabic Language Handbook*. Center for Applied Linguistics, Washington, DC

Beeston A F L 1970 *The Arabic Language Today*. Hutchinson, London

Blau J 1977 The beginnings of Arabic diglossia. *Afroasiatic Linguistics* **4(4)**: 1–28

Cohen D 1962 Koine, languages communes et dialectes arabes. *Arabica* **9**: 119–44

Cowell M W 1964 *A Reference Grammar of Syrian Arabic*. Georgetown University Press, Washington, DC

Erwin W M 1963 *A Short Reference Grammar of Iraqi Arabic*. Georgetown University Press, Washington, DC

Ferguson C A 1959a The Arabic koine. *Language* **35**: 616–30

Ferguson C A 1959b Diglossia. *Word* **15**: 325–40

Ferguson C A 1972 Myths about Arabic. In: Fishman J (ed.) *Readings in the Sociology of Language*. Mouton, The Hague

Holes C D 1986 Review of Versteegh (1984). *Bibliotheca Orientalis* **43(1/2)**: 218–22

Holes C D 1990 *Gulf Arabic*. Croom Helm Descriptive Grammars Series, Routledge, London.

Hopkins S 1988 Review of Versteegh (1984). *Zeitschrift für arabische Linguistik* **18**: 98–99

Ibrahim M H 1986 Standard and prestige language: A problem in Arabic sociolinguistics. *Anthropological Linguistics* **28(1)**: 115–26

Versteegh K 1984 *Pidginization and Creolization. The case of Arabic*. Benjamins, Amsterdam

Yushmanov N V 1961 *The Structure of the Arabic Language*, Perlmann M. (transl.). Center for Applied Linguistics, Washington, DC

Arabic and Spanish: Linguistic Contacts

L. P. Harvey

After the Muslim conquest of the Iberian Peninsula in 711, Arabic rapidly replaced Latin there as the language of administration and of high culture. Latin (with its various Romance vernaculars, as they developed) was relegated, within the Islamic state, to being the language of the large but impotent subject-Christian (*dhimmī*) communities in which Romance dialects, usually known as 'Mozarabic,' were spoken. Latin and Romance also survived in the fringe of small Christian kingdoms to the north. From the eleventh century onwards these kingdoms pushed southwards, until, by the second half of the thirteenth, most of the Peninsula was in Christian hands. Substantial Arabic-speaking Muslim communities thus fell under Christian rule, particularly in Valencia. In the independent Islamic kingdom of Granada, Arabic flourished: it was probably the only language in use there at the end of the Middle Ages, for to this mountain redoubt scholarly and pious Muslims had fled from many other regions. The last Arabic-speakers were eventually expelled to North Africa in 1611.

The Arabic and the Latin/neo-Latin languages thus had 900 years in which to interact, but the nature of that interaction was a complex and unusual one. Where two languages are in contact, it is usually quite clear which is politically and culturally dominant, and that dominance determines the direction in which linguistic influences flow. In the Iberian Peninsula, the balance shifted. Arabic established its ascendancy rapidly, and by the tenth century its dominance was overwhelming. But by the sixteenth it was a decadent tongue surviving with difficulty among a marginalized minority who were subjected to persecution if they were caught using it.

The number of ethnic Arabs who took part in the invasion of 711, or who crossed subsequently as Islamic rule came to be established, is subject to dispute, but was certainly not large: this was no mass migration. Arabic imposed itself because of its unique status among Muslims as the language of the divine revelation; it was also the language of culture, commerce and self-advancement. Although there are references to Arabic-speakers from Spain being recognized by their accent elsewhere in the Arab world, there is no indication that their command of the language was found to be defective, and indeed writers from the Peninsula made many major contributions to Arabic literature. Nevertheless there are some fairly early (eleventh century, perhaps before) examples of a tendency to linguistic hybridism. Scholars do not agree on the nature of the bilingual refrains to some Arabic strophic poetry (*muwashshahāt*): genuine vernacular poetry in which the mixed language reflects the realities of life, or contrived macaronic exercises? An Arabic root may occur with a Romance bound form (*hamrālla* Ar. *hamr* 'red' + a Romance diminutive *-lla*), or a Romance word with an Arabic suffix (*qurajūnī* Romance for 'heart' + Arabic possessive 'my'). Proverbs and other evidence from the thirteenth century (including the Arabic lines on the capture of Valencia in the *Primera crónica general*) show verbal forms by then being calqued on Romance models: e.g., periphrastic pseudo-passives formed with Arabic verbs such as *'ād* or *raja 'a* + an Arabic participle, periphrastic futures, or perhaps inchoatives, with *yurīd* ('will') + *masdar* (verbal noun). However, the great morphological gulf between the languages prevented further merging. As late as the sixteenth century, on the eve of the Expulsion, Valencian Arabic, although modified at the phonemic level by contact (loss of some of the distinctive Semitic emphatic consonants, gain of an unvoiced labial plosive), and above all because it had adopted many Romance loanwords or calqued expressions (*'alā manīra aw 'alā ukhrā* 'in one way or another'), still remained unquestionably Arabic.

In the reverse direction, Arabic linguistic influence on all the Romance vernaculars of the Peninsula was considerable, and the earliest Castilian text, the *Poema de Mio Cid* (early thirteenth century, some place it earlier), already has a large vocabulary of loanwords from Arabic, besides calques of various sorts: *amaneció a Mio Cid* (*asbaha lahu*). Arabic influence on the Latin of the translations of the Toledan school was considerable, again both loanwords and linguistic calques. When translations began to be made directly into Castilian the new prose style incorporated elements of vocabulary and even of morphosyntax of Arabic origin (see Galmés de Fuentes 1956). In the thirteenth century Arabic influence on Castilian reached its peak, but there ensued an irregular but continuing process of de-Arabization which has by now replaced many of the distinctive forms derived from Arabic by the common terminology and structures of the European Latin languages. There still survive in Spanish (and the other Iberian Romance languages) many Arabic elements so deeply embedded that they are in no danger of disappearing altogether.

There is no indication that Arabic contributed to the repertory of the phonemes of Castilian. The assertion that Castilian owes its *jota* to the *khā* of Arabic appears to founder if it is borne in mind that *kh* in words borrowed does not result in *jota*. The sound change in Castilian wereby [ʒ>x] was probably not consummated until after the Moriscos were expelled. The most highly Arabized form of Spanish was the literary language written in Arabic characters (*literatura aljamiada*) exclusively by and for Muslims. It can have had no influence on the wider Spanish-speaking community, who appear to have remained ignorant of its very existence. When, in the fifteenth century, the Muslims of Castile and Aragon (who spoke the same Romance dialects as their Christian neighbours) realized that their ignorance of Arabic was cutting them off from their sacred literature, they had translations made of pious texts, and even of the Qur'an (in spite of the doctrine that the Qur'an is untranslatable). Such texts are closely calqued on the Arabic originals. Loanwords from Arabic abound: *khaleqar* 'to create,' and Spanish words acquire the semantic range of the Arabic word they are made to represent: *descender* (and derivatives) may mean 'to reveal' because in Arabic form IV of *nazala* 'to descend' means 'to reveal' (of a sacred text). *Literatura aljamiada*, which flourished in clandestinity in the sixteenth century, repeated many of the characteristics of the Alphonsine translations from Arabic. There is no evidence that the everyday speech of the Moriscos was affected, but their original writings often do imitate the style of the translations. After their expulsion, 1611, the Moriscos were absorbed into the mass of Arabic speakers in North Africa and elsewhere, and within a few generations the language they had brought from Spain had disappeared.

See also: Arabic; Qur'ān.

Bibliography

Corriente F 1977 *A Grammatical Sketch of the Spanish Arabic Dialect Bundle*. Instituto Hispano-Arabe de Cultura, Madrid

Galmés de Fuentes A 1956 *Influencias sintácticas del árabe en la prosa castellana.* Boletín de la Real Academia Española, Madrid
Huffman H R 1973 Syntactical influences of Arabic on medieval and later Spanish prose. Unpublished University of Wisconsin dissertation
Jones A 1988 *Romance kharjas in Andalusian Arabic Muwaššaḥ Poetry: A Paleographical Analysis.* Ithaca Press for the Board of the Faculty of Oriental Studies, Oxford University, London
Steiger A 1932 *Contribución a la fonética del hispano–árabe y de los arabismos en el ibero–románico y el siciliano.* Junta para Ampliación de Estudios, Madrid
Steiger A 1963 *Origin and Spread of Oriental Words in European Languages.* S. F. Vanni, New York

Arabic Script: Adaptation for Other Languages

J. N. Mattock

Most of the languages associated with Islam have, at some time, been written in the Arabic script, with appropriate modifications. The first language to which it was adapted after the Islamic conquests was the newly emergent form of Persian; there is no solid evidence for this until the tenth century CE, but it must have begun considerably earlier. With the spread of Islam from Iran into Central Asia, the Turkic languages next came to employ the script, during the period from the tenth to the twelfth centuries. It was used for the writing of various Hispanic dialects from at least the thirteenth century. There are indications that Malay and Kurdish were written in it as early as the fourteenth century, and, by the sixteenth century, Urdu and Pashto had adopted it. It is uncertain when it was first used for such languages as Swahili and Hausa; the first definite indications are from the eighteenth century, but it is quite probable that it was used well before that. It has also been used for Malayalam and Tamil.

The modifications that had to be made to the script were largely cumulative, each language retaining those made by that from which it had received it and adding its own. At the same time, the Arabic letters that were redundant, in that they represented no sounds existing in the new language, were retained, principally for loanwords from Arabic, but in a few cases for native words, even when these could be perfectly well represented with other letters; examples are Persian *sad* [صد] 'hundred' (spelt with *ṣ* rather than *s*) and Turkish *dağ* [طاغ] 'mountain,' and *oda* [اوطه] 'room' (where *d* is represented by *ṭ*). The pronunciation, generally speaking, of these redundant letters in all the languages that adopted the script was as follows: *th* [ث] = *s* or *t*; *ḥ* [ح] = *h*; *dh* [ذ] = *z* or *d*; *ṣ* [ص] = *s*; *ḍ* [ض] = *z*; *ṭ* [ط] = *t*; *ẓ* [ظ] = *z*; *q* [ق] = *k*, except in Persian, in which it coalesced with *gh* [غ] as a voiced or voiceless uvular plosive according to phonetic context (*'ayn*) [ع] was more or less disregarded.

The modified letters that Persian added are four: *b* [ب] modified to *p* [پ]; *j* [ج] to *ch* [چ]; *z* [ز] to *zh* [ژ]; and *k* [ك/ک] to *g* [گ]. It should be remarked, however, that in all the languages that adopted the script, modified letters were often written informally as though they were the original letters from which the modifications were made. This, of course, adds a further complication to reading.

No further modifications were necessary for the Turkic languages. The script was able adequately to represent the Turkic consonants, although the representation of *n* in certain circumstances (where it was a voiced velar nasal in some languages, but not in Ottoman Turkish) by *k*/*g* [ک / گ] created a further difficulty. In addition, a factitious distinction was made between the 'hard' (following a back vowel) and 'soft' (following a front vowel) forms of certain consonants, *g*, *h*, *k*, *s*, *t*, and *z*; the 'hard' forms were represented by the redundant Arabic letters, the *gh* [غ] being used for Turkish *ğ*. It was for the Turkic vowels that the script was less serviceable; *i*, *ı*, *o*, *ö*, *u*, *ü* could often not be distinguished from one another.

The adaptation of the script to Urdu again required modifications. The retroflex sounds *ḍ*, *ṛ*, and *ṭ* were represented by the Arabic *d* [د], *r* [ر], and *t* [ت], with a superscript *ṭ* [ط], which displaced the dots of *t*, or alternatively four dots arranged in a square, e.g., [ڐ]. A final/independent *n* [ن] without a dot was adopted to represent the velar nasal, and a modified form of independent *y*/*ī* [ي] to represent *e* [ے].

Pashto has the same retroflex sounds as Urdu, but modified the Arabic letters differently, putting a small ring beneath them [ډ , ړ, ټ], as it did also with the nasal [ڼ]. In addition, it adopted three further modifications: *ḥ* [ح] to [ځ] for *dz*/*ts* (in different dialects), *r* [ر] to [ږ] for *g*/*zh*, and *s* [س] to [ښ] for *sh*/*kh*.

Malay made three further modifications: *gh* [غ] to [ڠ] for *ng*, *n* [ن] to [ڽ] for *ny*, and *f* [ف] to [ڤ] for *p*.

The last indicates that the script (known as *Jāwī*, i.e., of Java) arrived in the peninsula directly from the Arabs, rather than by way of other Asian countries. Malay also modified *k* [ک] rather differently for *g* [ڬ].

Swahili used both modifications for *p* [پ and ڤ], represented *ch* by *sh* [ش] and sometimes *g* [ڠ], and used *gh* [غ] for both *g* and *ng*. Nasals preceding other consonants were mostly not written, but *nd* was often represented by *d* with *tashdīd* (mark of a doubled letter) [دّ]. Swahili in Arabic script was not easy to read, and it was hardly surprising that Latin script was adopted in the twentieth century, as was the case with other African languages that had previously used Arabic script.

Arabic script is reasonably well suited to Persian, Urdu, and Pashto, and there has never been a serious suggestion of adopting any other script. *Jāwī* script is still occasionally used for religious writing in Malay and related languages, but Latin script has proved more generally convenient. Turkey adopted its own version of Latin script in 1928; Arabic script is incapable of rendering the most important elements of Turkic phonology. The principal advantage of the use of the Arabic script by any language in which there is a large amount of Arabic vocabulary is that the recognizable form of this vocabulary is preserved, even though it does not indicate how it should be pronounced in the host language. In Turkish the other advantages conferred by the Latin script certainly outweigh this. It remains to be seen if the Central Asian Turkic languages will revert to the use of Arabic script, after a considerable period of the enforced use of Cyrillic; Tajik almost certainly will do so, in order to facilitate written communication with Persian speakers in Iran and Afghanistan.

One of the most interesting, and little-known, developments of the Arabic script is that now used for Kurdish in Iraq. It is, ideally, an entirely phonetic system of using the script, devised by Taufiq Wahby in the late 1920s and subsequently somewhat modified by the Iraqi Scientific Academy. In practice, it is not uniformly employed, since Arabic elements of vocabulary are frequently written in their conventional form rather than according to the reformed phonetic principles, and a number of diacritics are disregarded. However, it does offer a sensible, if aesthetically rather unpleasing, medium in which a language unrelated to Arabic can be fully represented.

The 'redundant' Arabic letters have been largely eliminated; Arabic words are, in theory, rewritten as they are pronounced in Kurdish. Thus, for example, *muwazẓaf* [موظف] = 'official, employee' appears spelled as مووەزەف (pronounced *muwezef*). All vowels, except for a short *ɨ*, are represented, *e* by a final/independent *h* [ە], the rest by the letters of prolongation appropriately modified: *a* [ا], *u* [و], *ū* [وو], *o* [ۆ], *ö* [وێ], *ē* [ێ], *ī* [ی]. Initial vowels are preceded by *hamzah* on a *y* bearer, e.g., ئێران [*ēran*] 'Iran.' Two consonants are modified: *r* [ر] to [ڕ] for a trilled *r* and *l* [ل] to [ڵ] for a dark *l*.

See also: Islam; Islamic Calligraphy; Persian; Semitic Scripts.

Aramaic, Jewish

M. Sokoloff

The term 'Jewish Aramaic' in the past has been misused as a generic term for a variety of separate Aramaic dialects employed by the Jews as their vernacular and literary language from biblical times until the Middle Ages. This article will describe briefly the various dialects and will also discuss the use of Aramaic in Jewish liturgy.

1. The Emergence of Aramaic and its Earliest Use by the Jews

Aramaic is one of the West Semitic languages and was originally spoken by the Arameans, a people who made their first historical appearance in the eleventh century BCE, and whose center was in the Harran area of present-day Turkey. When Aramaic became a lingua franca in the Near East in the Persian Period (539 BCE onward), it was taken over both as a spoken and written language by the Jews. Contact with this language during the Babylonian captivity (586 BCE onward) and the subsequent need for the Palestinian Jewish community to communicate with the Persian authorities and their coreligionists in Egypt, Babylonia, and other parts of the Persian Empire, were dominant factors in their gradual adoption of Aramaic and the extinction of Hebrew as the vernacular of the Jews by the end of the second century CE.

Evidence for the chancellory use of Aramaic by the Jews during the Persian Period is amply provided by the Elephantine papyri from Egypt (fifth century

BCE), while literature is known both from the Aramaic parts of the Bible (Ezra 4: 8–6: 18; 7: 12–26; Daniel 2: 4–7: 28) and from the literary documents written in Aramaic among the Dead Sea Scrolls. The latter also include our earliest examples of written Targums (Aramaic translations of scripture: see *Bible Translations, Ancient Versions*), providing the first evidence for the use of Aramaic in synagogue ritual.

2. 'Jewish Aramaic'

Following the conquests of Alexander the Great, and the political divisions in their wake, a dialectal split already recognizable in earlier Aramaic became more pronounced and divided Aramaic into eastern and western dialects. Since Jewish communities existed in both areas, each adopted the local dialect as a spoken and literary language. In time, Jewish dialects also became differentiated from non-Jewish ones both in the east (Syriac, Mandaic) and in the west (Samaritan, Christian Palestinian).

While the spoken Jewish Aramaic dialects of late antiquity were probably mutually intelligible to some degree, there is anecdotal evidence in the Talmud to indicate that the speakers themselves were aware of the differences between them. Dialect distinctions are also specifically mentioned. Though mutual intelligibility was somewhat greater in the written language, a distinction should be maintained, on the phonological, morphological, and lexical levels, between the language of the surviving literary Aramaic from the east (the Babylonian Talmud) and that from the west (the Palestinian Talmud, Midrashim, Targumim, and epigraphic material). In the light of this, one should speak of 'Jewish Palestinian Aramaic' and 'Jewish Babylonian Aramaic,' rather than a nonexistent entity called 'Jewish Aramaic.'

3. The Demise of Aramaic as a Jewish Language

Following the Muslim conquest of the Near East, Aramaic gradually ceased to be the spoken language of the Jewish communities and was replaced by Arabic. However, during the Gaonic (i.e., post-Talmudic) period in Babylonia, Aramaic served as the literary language for legal compositions (e.g., *Shĕ'eltot, Hălakhot Păsuqot*) as well as for *Responsa* sent by the Gaonim (heads of religious academies) to the various Jewish communities in the Diaspora. Eventually, Arabic displaced Aramaic even as the language of religious literature. In Europe, however, where the study of the Babylonian Talmud and its exposition became the basis of medieval Jewish culture, literary expression found its linguistic vehicle in a blend of Rabbinic Hebrew and Babylonian Aramaic, the so-called 'Rabbinic language.' This artificial dialect was used by all of the Classical Rabbinic commentators and respondents and is still employed in these literary genres today.

4. Aramaic in the Liturgy

While Aramaic prayers are found already in the Book of Daniel, Aramaic never became a dominating factor in Jewish liturgy, since prayer was always officially recited in the holy tongue, Hebrew, and never in the vernacular. Nevertheless, Aramaic certainly had its place in the synagogue in Palestine as may be attested both by the large number of Aramaic synagogue inscriptions and from the recital of the Targum which accompanied the weekly Pentateuchal reading.

In Babylonia, the evidence begins essentially with the Gaonic period when the Aramaic *Qaddish* prayer, certainly the most famous Jewish Aramaic prayer, became part of the liturgy. From this period also are found a number of penitential hymns (*Sĕliḥot*) as well as legal formulaic prayers composed in Aramaic. Interestingly, the Aramaic dialect of these prayers is not that of Babylonia, but is akin to a more Classical dialect which was comprehensible throughout the Jewish Diaspora.

The modern Jewish prayerbook has retained a number of Aramaic prayers from various periods. Aside from the previously mentioned *Qaddish*, the anachronistic *Yĕqum purqan* prayer for the welfare of the leaders of the Babylonian Gaonic community is still recited on the Sabbath in some European liturgies. A remnant of a more widespread use of Aramaic poetry is the *Aqdamut* prayer recited at Pentecost. Several Aramaic prayers have entered into the prayerbook from the Zohar, a Kabbalistic work of the thirteenth century composed in an artificial Aramaic dialect and attributed traditionally to R. Yoḥanan b. Zakkai (late first century CE). In spite of its linguistically difficult Aramaic vocabulary, the Zohar still remains a popular work among the Jewish communities. However, the weekly recitation of the Targum has now been abandoned by all but the Yemenite community.

The pervasive influence of the Babylonian Talmud on traditional Jewish life has left its imprint in the form of borrowings from Babylonian Aramaic in both Yiddish and Modern Hebrew, e.g., *khutzpah* 'audacity' (Classical *ḥuṣpah*); *klafta* 'a bitch' (Classical *kalbĕtah*).

5. Modern Jewish Aramaic

Modern Aramaic dialects are still spoken by members of the Jewish communities originating in Iraq (e.g., Zakho) but who now all live in Israel. While the indigenous name for this language is *lishanit targum* 'Targumic language,' it is neither connected with the Targum nor is it descended from Jewish Babylonian Aramaic, but in fact is closely related to Modern Syriac. Aside from serving as a vernacular, a literature consisting of a Bible translation, homilies, and folk tales, composed over the last few centuries, has been preserved.

See also: Judaism; Hebrew, Biblical and Jewish; Syriac, Christian; Talmud; Targum.

Bibliography

Greenfield J C 1995 "Aramaic and the Jews," Studia Aramaica, new sources and new approaches. *Journal of Jewish Studies* Suppl. 4, 1–18

Kutscher E Y 1971 Aramaic. In: *Encyclopaedia Judaica*, vol. 2, pp. 259–88. Macmillan, Jerusalem

Naveh J, Greenfield J C 1984 Hebrew and Aramaic in the Persian Period. In: *The Cambridge History of Judaism*, vol. 1, pp. 115–29. Cambridge University Press, Cambridge

Armenian

B. G. Hewitt

Armenians (*Hajk^h* in Armenian) live in the (former Soviet) Republic of Armenia in Transcaucasia and constitute the majority population in the neighboring enclave of Nagorno Karabagh (Azerbaijan). The attempted genocide of the indigenous and Christian Armenians by the Ottoman Turks in 1895 and 1915 led to mass migrations producing a diaspora which created/reinforced Armenian communities all over the Middle East, in France, the UK, USA, etc. The native word for their homeland is *Hajastan*. The term 'Armenians' derives from the Greek '*Arménioi*, which in turn is adapted from Persian.

According to the 1989 Soviet census the total Soviet Armenian population was 4,627,227, of whom 3,081,920 resided in Armenia itself. This made Armenia ethnically the most homogeneous of the then-republics (with a 97.3 percent native population), even though a higher proportion of Armenians also lived outside their home-republic than any other nationality among the union-republics. Since 1989 most of the Armenians living in Azerbaijan (i.e., other than Nagorno Karabagh) have moved to Armenia, whilst most of Armenia's Azerbaijanis have gone to Azerbaijan. In 1989, 437,211 Armenians lived in the third Transcaucasian republic of Georgia, constituting 8.1 percent of Georgia's population.

Armenian is an Indo–European language of the *satəm*-type. For many years it was believed to be an Iranian dialect owing to the large number of Persian loans. Hübschmann in the late nineteenth century finally succeeded in demonstrating its true status as a separate branch of the Indo–European family. It has been suggested that Phrygian may have been a close relative, but it is difficult to prove or disprove this hypothesis because of the paucity of Phrygian data. Modern Armenian is divided into two main dialectal groups: Eastern and Western, which roughly correspond to what is spoken on (formerly) Soviet territory versus the speech of the diaspora-communities respectively. There are many subdialects, whose evidence is crucial in the investigation of, for example, the thorny question of Armenian consonantism. Unfortunately, the loss and/or dislocation of sources for Western Armenian complicates such research.

The classical written language (*Grabar*) dates from the early fifth century CE, and, although Old Armenian was probably extinct as a living form of the language as early as the eleventh century, it continued to exert an influence on literary norms until replaced by the contemporary spoken Modern Armenian (*Ashkharhabar*) in the nineteenth century. The true 'Golden Age' of literature is confined to the fifth century, though works for another two centuries do not differ greatly from their antecedents. The newly devised script permitted the dissemination of the Bible and other ecclesiastical works, mostly translated from Greek or Syriac, in the native language. Among original works Eznik Koγbats^{h}i's *Against the Sects* is regarded as the epitome of the classical style. History made an early appearance with Agat^{h}angeγos and P^{h}awstos Biwzandats^{h}i, followed by Γazar P^{h}arpets^{h}i and Eγishē. The history of Movsēs Khorenats^{h}i is known only in later redactions. Byzantine and Seljuk Turkish incursions interrupted the development of Armenian in the eleventh and twelfth centuries. The creation of an independent kingdom in Cilicia saw a flourishing of poetry, so that Cilician Armenian is the best known of all the Middle Armenian dialects. From the sixteenth century émigré communities in Venice, Constantinople, Rome, Amsterdam, Madras, and Calcutta played an important role particularly in printing Armenian books. The first Armenian book was printed in Venice in 1512, and the first press established in Constantinople in 1567. The great national epic *David of Sassoun* is a cycle of folktales built up over many centuries; it was first written down only in the nineteenth century. Lord

Byron actually composed and published a grammar of Armenian in English. Throughout the Soviet period and subsequently, Armenian has flourished in Armenia as the language of education and literature. Of the Republic's Armenian population 99.6 percent claimed native-speaker fluency in 1989, with 44.3 percent acknowledging command of Russian.

The unique, angular script, which distinguishes upper and lower case forms, is reputed to have been invented by Bishop Mesrob early in the fifth century CE. There are basically 36 characters, though 2 more were added in the eleventh century, and today a further addition represents a contraction of ևւ[(j)ɛw]. The letters were ordered after the pattern of the Greek alphabet, with non-Greek sounds being fitted in where judged appropriate. The last letter of the alphabet with the value [f] was one of the later creations to allow accurate rendition of foreign names with voiceless labio-dental fricative, itself absent from the native Armenian phoneme-inventory. The modern script remains essentially unaltered.

By far the strongest influence on Armenian, essentially in terms of its lexical stock, has come from Persian; other borrowings have occurred from Syriac, Arabic, Greek, French and, in the twentieth century, Russian. Rather than borrow widely used foreign roots, Armenian often likes to create neologisms from its own lexical stock, so that 'university' is *hamalsaran*. The shift from inflexion to agglutination within the nominal system would seem to be the result of Turkish influence. While Classical Armenian was prepositional, the modern forms are predominantly post-positional, as are Turkish and Georgian to the north.

See also: Christianity in the Near East; Mesrob.

Bibliography

Gulian K 1961 *Elementary Modern Armenian Grammar*. Frederick Ungar, New York

Jensen H 1959 *Altarmenische Grammatik*. Carl Winter. Heidelberg

Karst J 1901 *Historische Grammatik des Kilikisch-Armenischen*. K J Trübner, Strasbourg

Pisowicz A 1976 *Le Développement du Consonantisme Arménien*. Polish Academy of Science, Krakow

Shilak'adze I 1971 *Axali somxuri enis gramat'ik'a*. University Press, Tbilisi

Avestan

P. G. Kreyenbroek

Avestan is an Old Iranian language, known only from the sacred texts of the Zoroastrians, the Avesta. Two main forms of the language are attested: Old Avestan, very similar in morphology and idiom to the language of the Indian Vedas, and Younger Avestan, which is probably a later form of a slightly different dialect. The larger part of the Avesta is in the younger dialect; only Zarathustra's own hymns (the *Gāthās*), the text of an ancient liturgy (the *Yasna Haptanghāiti*), and two prayers are in genuine Old Avestan. A few short texts were composed later in imitation of that dialect. Those texts which are preserved in Old Avestan were presumably felt to be especially sacred, and were memorized exactly as they had been pronounced in the early days of the faith, whereas the language of other texts continued to evolve along with the spoken language.

Zarathustra's exact date and place are unknown, and linguistic evidence is insufficient to show exactly where the native speakers of Avestan were living at any given period. There is some evidence, however, that they settled somewhere in the eastern part of the area where Iranian languages are now spoken. At a later stage, the Zoroastrian religion spread to Media and Persia, where it was eventually accepted by the local priesthood, the Magi. These then learned to recite in Avestan, which differed considerably from their own Western Iranian speech. The correct enunciation of the sacred texts is of the utmost importance in Zoroastrianism, and the Magi evidently sought to hand down all Avestan texts exactly as they had been taught to recite them. In the extant written version of the Avesta—which is based on the oral Western Iranian tradition—the Younger Avestan texts are therefore preserved in a form of the language which appears to belong roughly to the Achaemenian period (sixth to fourth centuries BCE), and the influence of Western Iranian pronunciation can be detected there. Writing played no significant part in the transmission of these texts until well into the Sasanian era (third to seventh centuries CE), when an adequate alphabet was devised.

For Zoroastrians, Avestan is the sacred vehicle of communication between the human and divine spheres. Ritual recitations in that language must not be interrupted by an utterance in any other tongue; if this is unavoidable, the profane words must be pronounced in a peculiar muttering tone, with closed lips. As the spoken languages of the various areas evolved to the Middle Iranian stage, however, believers found it more difficult to understand the Avesta. Relatively primitive word-for-word translations (*Zand*) were made into the local languages. As comprehension of Avestan declined further, the meaning of the Avesta was increasingly regarded as being beyond human understanding. When, in the nineteenth century, the Indian Parsis were confronted with early Western translations of the Avesta, this led to a profound crisis. Even in the late twentieth century the Parsis are divided in their attitudes to Avestan. Many regard the language itself as sacred, and some believe that it can only be understood intuitively by the pious. Others would now prefer to pray and worship in their own language.

See also: Zoroastrianism.

Bibliography

Bartholomae C 1883 *Handbuch der altiränischen Dialekte*. Von Breitkopf and Härtel, Leipzig

Boyce M 1984 *Textual Sources for the Study of Zoroastrianism*. Manchester University Press, Manchester

Kellens J 1989 Avestique. In: Schmitt R (ed.) *Compendium Linguarum Iranicarum*. Reichert, Wiesbaden

Buddhist Hybrid Sanskrit

P. Dundas

The medium of the earliest Buddhist teaching in India was both oral and vernacular. However, towards the beginning of the common era many Buddhist monks began to write in Sanskrit, the learned lingua franca, thus reflecting a desire to engage with wider Indian intellectual culture.

Although the majority of Buddhist Sanskrit texts are composed in a standard form of the language, many important early sectarian works, such as the *Mahāvastu*, a vinaya text of the Mahāsāṅghika-Lokottaravādin sect and the verse portions of the Mahāyāna *Saddharmapuṇḍaīkasūtra* (the 'Lotus Sūtra'), are couched in a style of Sanskrit which does not reflect the normative rules enshrined in the grammarian Pāṇini's (c. fifth century BCE) *Aṣṭādhyāyī*. Instead, these texts evince the marked grammatical influence of a vernacular Middle Indo-Āryan base.

The American Indologist Franklin Edgerton coined the expression 'Buddhist Hybrid Sanskrit' to describe this dialect and in 1953 produced a full-scale grammar, along with dictionary, charting its usage. For some scholars, this Buddhist Hybrid Sanskrit was simply incorrect Sanskrit, as much the product of scribal ignorance as of conscious linguistic choice. Current scholarship, however, is more ready to accept the validity of differing, often sectarian varieties of Sanskrit, which need not be stigmatized as grammatically deviant. Buddhist Hybrid Sanskrit in the broadest sense can thus be regarded as a cluster of intersecting dialects influenced by a range of contemporary vernacular usages, and works written in this idiom coexisted for a period within the Buddhist community along with those written in standard Sanskrit.

See also: Sanskrit; Pāṇini.

Bibliography

Edgerton F 1953 *Buddhist Hybrid Sanskrit Grammar and Dictionary*, 2 Vols. Yale University Press, New Haven, CT

Kameshwar Nath Mishra (ed.) 1993 *Aspects of Buddhist Sanskrit. Sarnath*. Central Institute of Higher Tibetan Studies, Varanasi

Oguibénine B 1996 *Initiation Pratique à l'Étude du Sanskrit Bouddhique*. Picard Éditeur, Paris

Byzantine Greek

Archimandrite Ephrem

When, in the middle of the first century CE, Christianity expanded from Palestine into the wider Greco–Roman world, the language of the Church became predominantly Greek. The New Testament was written in the common Greek of the day and the Jewish Greek Septuagint became the Church's Old Testament, and remains that of the Eastern Churches. In the West from the ninth century, except for the Psalter, Jerome's Latin version from the Hebrew prevailed. The Church wrote in Greek and worshipped in Greek, and this was true in the early centuries even of the Church in Rome. As Christianity spread among the educated classes the uncouthness of the Greek Bible and of the New Testament in particular was smoothed out and the Greek 'improved,' notably by Lucian of Antioch († 312), to conform more nearly to proper classical Attic.

By the fourth century, and more particularly after Constantine's edict of toleration and the recognition of the Church as an official part of the imperial system, increasing numbers of Christians, even from devout families like those of Basil of Caesarea and his brother Gregory of Nyssa, studied in the famous pagan schools of Athens, Alexandria, Antioch, and Beirut. This meant that they studied the ancient Greek authors and learned the rhetorical skills necessary for a public career in the ancient world. One of the leading teachers in Athens, Prohaeresios, was an Armenian Christian; and when his contemporary, the great pagan teacher Libanius († 393) was asked who would succeed him as head of his school in Antioch, he is said to have replied, 'John, if the Christians hadn't got him.' He was referring to John Chrysostom. All this meant that the language of the Church had become the fashionable Attic Greek of the educated classes. An old woman is said to have interrupted a sermon of John Chrysostom to complain that she could not understand half of what he was saying. He continued in the vernacular. Diglossy is no new phenomenon in Greek. As an answer to Julian the Apostate's decree on teaching, Apollinarios of Laodicea and his son set about 'hellenizing' the Scriptures, translating the Octateuch into Homeric hexameters in twenty four books, like the Iliad, and the Gospels into Platonic dialogues. A version of John 20: 19–25 in Homeric hexameters is still chanted in many Greek churches on Easter Sunday. Gregory Nazianzen, a fellow student in Athens of Basil and the future Emperor Julian the Apostate, wrote a great deal of poetry in strict classical metre. Although John of Damascus († c. 750) wrote a series of hymns (Canons) in classical iambic metre that are still sung in church, the later hymn writers preferred metres based on stress accents rather than classical quantities. Between the sixth and the ninth centuries a whole series of poets enriched the Church with a great quantity of texts, many of outstanding literary and theological quality. Notable among them are Romanos the Melodist (sixth century), Andrew of Crete (eighth century), Kosmas of Maiouma (eighth century), Theodore the Studite (ninth century), Joseph the Hymnographer (ninth century). Of these only Romanos has been critically edited and the work of the others is still virtually unknown outside the Eastern Churches.

The Greek of the Fathers, though, is very varied in style and the Greek of many authors, particularly among the monastic writers, is more popular than that of the university trained bishops. It is also heavily influenced by the Greek of both the Old and New Testaments and its lexicon much enriched with theological and liturgical matter. Not only that, but the deliberate exclusion of ecclesiastical Greek from Liddell and Scott and the early cut-off point for Lampe mean that many words for quite ordinary things appear as *hapax legomena* in numerous Byzantine texts in both prose and verse. The large number of Latinisms in Byzantine Greek are nearly all concerned with military, commercial and political matters, hardly at all with religious. There is still much linguistic work to be done in the 162 volumes of the *Patrologia Graeca* and the twenty or so volumes of the Byzantine service books.

Bibliography

Browning R 1969 *Medieval and Modern Greek*. London

Marrou H I 1964 *A History of Education in Antiquity*, English translation. New York

Kaster R A 1988 *Guardians of Language: The Grammarian and Society in Late Antiquity*. University of California Press, Berkeley, CA

Trypanis C A 1951 *Penguin Book of Greek Verse*. London

Lash E 1995 *On the Life of Christ: Kontakia by Romanos the Melodist*. Acta Mira, London

Lim R 1995 *Public Disputation, Power, and Social Order in Late Antiquity*. University of California Press, Berkeley, CA

Trapp E 1994 *Lexikon zur Byzantinischen Gräzität*. Vienna

Chinese

B. Arendrup

As a language name, Chinese is an extremely comprehensive term. It is and has been commonly employed in reference to numerous highly disparate written and spoken styles, dialects, and languages flourishing at various times from the middle of the second millennium BCE and down to the late twentieth century, thus including the modern language in both its standard and dialectal forms. In fact, Chinese written sources from the first millennium BCE represent a language which is at least as different from the Chinese standard language of today as Latin is from modern Italian or French; and what are generally known as the modern Chinese dialects are more like a family of languages, some being further apart than Portuguese and Italian. They are not mutually intelligible, neither are major subdivisions within most individual dialects. They have therefore often and with good reason been termed languages rather than dialects—the Chinese or Sinitic languages—especially by foreign linguists.

The notion of a single Chinese language existing at all times and in many forms is all but universal, however, among the Chinese themselves. It has been sustained by an ancient common writing system and an equally persistent common ideal of cultural and political unity. In this article, the Chinese tradition will be followed insofar as the Sinitic languages will generally be referred to as Chinese dialects and subsumed under one broad class, that of Chinese or the Chinese language.

Among the terms with which the Chinese refer to their language and some of its subcategories the most common are: *Hànyǔ* 'the language of the Hàns,' a name referring to the great Hàn dynasty (206 BCE–CE 220) and distinguishing the Chinese language from the minority languages of China as well as from foreign languages in general; *Zhōngwén* 'the language of the Middle (Empire),' mainly employed for Chinese as a philological and literary concept; *Pǔtōnghuà* 'the common language,' i.e., Modern Standard Chinese (MSC), the national standard adopted by the government of the People's Republic in 1956; and *Guóyǔ* 'the national language,' an older term for much the same notion still used by many, especially in Taiwan. Classical and Literary Chinese are known as *wényán* 'written language,' the written vernaculars as *báihuà* 'plain talk,' and the dialects as *fāngyán* 'regional languages.'

Chinese is spoken in continental China, in Taiwan, and by a majority of the population in Singapore. In addition, Chinese is spoken by important minorities in all other countries of Southeast Asia as well as by Chinese immigrants in most parts of the world, especially in Oceania and in North and South America. The total number of speakers amounts to well over a billion people, far more than that of any other language in the world.

Chinese is one part—and in terms of number of speakers by far the most important part—of the Sino-Tibetan language family, the other part being the Tibeto-Burman languages. Some sort of genetic affinity between these language groups has been recognized since the nineteenth century; the hypothesis is based on phonological correspondences found in their lexicons and is still broadly accepted.

Typologically, on the other hand, Chinese occupies an intermediate position between the nontonal, polysyllabic, and agglutinative Altaic languages in north Asia and the tonal, monosyllabic languages of Southeast Asia. Properties which may be due to Altaic influence, for example, are the modifier–noun order, from which a few instances of deviation are found only in the southern variants of Chinese; certain sentence patterns of the subject–object–verb order, the so-called SOV type, in Northern Chinese; and the exclusive/inclusive distinction in the first person plural pronouns of the Běijīng dialect and a few other northern dialects. Among the important characteristics which Chinese shares with Southeast Asian language groups such as Tai, Miao-Yao, and Viet-Muong are monosyllabicity, tonality, and the prevailing SVO sentence pattern.

The traditional Chinese script is the oldest of all the writing systems used in the world today and the only one in common use among the Chinese for everyday written communication. It is a nonalphabetic system of graphs called characters, each representing a syllable. Since most syllables are meaningful, i.e., morphemes, and many characters represent phonetically identical morphemes (homonyms), the script may most accurately be characterized as a basically morphemic writing system.

In addition to the character script, various phonemic writing systems have been devised first by Christian missionaries, beginning soon after 1600 with the Jesuits in Běijīng, then by foreign and Chinese scholars from the late nineteenth century on. The two most widely used transcription systems (romanizations) are that of Wade–Giles (first created by Sir Thomas Francis Wade in 1867 and modified by Herbert A. Giles, 1912) and the official Chinese transcription system known as Pinyin (i.e., *Pīnyīn Zìmu*, 'The Phonetic Alphabet,' adopted in 1958). A third system, created in 1918 from elements and simplified forms of traditional Chinese characters, is the *Guóyǔ Zhùyīn Fúhào* 'National Phonetic Symbols'; like Pinyin, it is used in China mainly for glossing characters in dictionaries.

The Chinese dialects fall into a northern and a southern group (see Fig. 1). A great part of the lexicon, especially at the morphemic level, is common to all dialects, differences among them being most conspicuous in phonology, less remarkable in grammar. Generally, the northern speech forms, also known as the Mandarin dialects, are much closer to each other than the southern ones.

1. Northern Chinese Dialects

The Mandarin dialects are further divided into four subgroups: the northern, the northwestern, the southwestern, and the lower Yangtze River dialects. They are spoken in China north of the Yangtze River; in Sìchuān, Yúnnán, Guìzhōu, and small parts

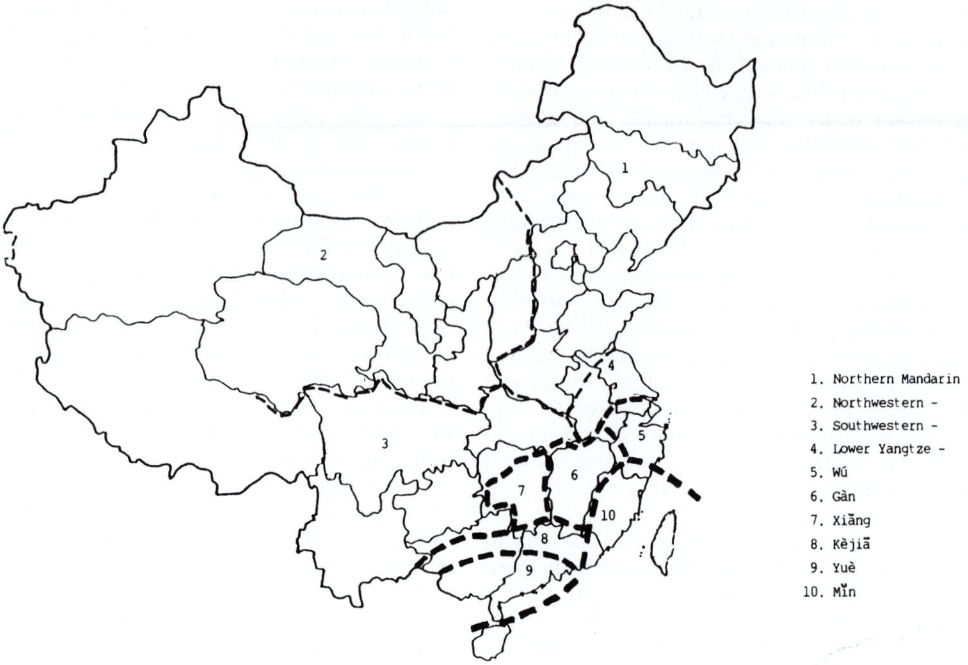

Figure 1.

of Húnán, as well as in a narrow belt south of the Yangtze River in Jiāngxī, Ānhuī, and Jiāngsū. The ratio of speakers of these northern dialects to the total Chinese-speaking population is estimated at 71.5 percent.

On the whole, the Mandarin dialects are remarkably homogenous, a person from northern Manchuria, for instance, having little difficulty in understanding the speech of a native of Yúnnán some 3,000 kilometers away. In fact, the Mandarin dialects of the southwest are the most uniform, the area having been settled or resettled by northerners fairly recently, from the thirteenth century on while the northwestern group, especially in Shānxī province, display the highest degree of diversity among the northern speech forms.

Characteristics common to most Mandarin dialects include the devoicing of all voiced obstruents, i.e., stops, affricates, and fricatives, found in Middle Chinese (the literary pronunciation of the sixth century CE; see Sect. 5) as well as the simplification of Middle Chinese finals, its set of final consonants, *m*, *n*, *ng*, *p*, *t*, *k* for instance, having been drastically reduced, only *n* and *ng* being retained in the 1990s.

The Mandarin dialects are exceptional because of their vast number of speakers, the extensive territory they occupy, and because the present national language, MSC, is based on the phonology of a northern speech form.

2. Southern Chinese Dialects

The southern dialects are usually classified into six major groups: Wú is spoken in southern Jiāngsū (including Shànghǎi), southeastern Ānhuī, and by the majority in Zhèjiāng. An estimated 8.5 percent of the total Chinese-speaking population speak WE dialects. Gàn is spoken in most of Jiāngxī, southern Ānhuī, and southeastern Húbei; Gain speakers are estimated to form 2.4 percent of the total Chinese-speaking population. Xiāng is spoken in the greater part of Húnán; Xiāng speakers are estimated to form 4.8 percent of the total Chinese-speaking population. Like Gàn, the Xiāng dialects are a southern group in transition, the great majority having undergone strong influence from Mandarin-speaking neighbors to the north, west, and southwest. Kèjiā is spoken in widely scattered areas from Sìchuān to Taiwan; it is estimated to be spoken by 3.7 percent of the total Chinese-speaking population.

The MSC word Kèjiā (in English often rendered as Hakka, from its pronunciation in Cantonese) means 'guest' or 'stranger,' a name given to the Kèjiā when they first settled in south China among people speaking Yuè or Mǐn. Traditionally they claim to be of northern origin, which may be partly true; the dialects they speak, however, are of the southern type.

Yuè is spoken in southeastern Guǎngxī and the greater part of Guǎngdōng (including Guǎngzhōu [Canton], Xiānggǎng [Hong Kong], and Àomén [Macao]); it is estimated to be spoken by 5 percent of the total Chinese-speaking population. Cantonese is the prestige or standard language in the area, including Hong Kong and Macao.

Mǐn is spoken in Fújiàn, southern Zhèjiāng, northeastern Guǎngdōng, and also in Hǎinán and Taiwan; it is estimated to be spoken by 4.1 percent of the total Chinese-speaking population. Fújiàn, the homeland of the Mǐn-speaking peoples, is a highly mountainous region lacking major rivers, the only relatively easy access to the province being by sea. The Mǐn dialects all bear the stamp of this geographical isolation, showing numerous archaisms and local innovations lost or unknown elsewhere.

Xiàmén dialect is also known as Hokkien (the local pronunciation of Fújiàn) or Mǐn Nán 'southern Mǐn,' and it is essentially the same dialect as Taiwanese.

3. Non-Chinese Languages in China

There have always been peoples of non-Chinese stock in China, but actual research into their linguistic and cultural characteristics has been undertaken only in the present century, mainly in the 1950s and in the 1980s. Even so, many groups are still little-known. In the early 1990s, the Chinese government recognizes 55 minority nationalities, amounting to 6 percent of the total population, i.e., around 67 million. In some cases, however, groups have been classified according to cultural and political, rather than linguistic, criteria and the official list of minority nationalities therefore comprises only 54 minority languages.

In north China, groups on the list are defined as Mongolian (c. 4 million); Tungus (c. 4.5 million, primarily Manchus of which very few, if any, know the Manchu language); Turkic (c. 7 million, including 6 million Uighurs and almost 1 million Kazakhs); Korean (c. 1.8 million); and Indo–European (c. 30,000, mostly Tajiks, plus a few Russians).

In south China, major groups are Tibeto–Burman (c. 12 million, among which 5.5 million Yí and almost 4 million Tibetans); Tai (c. 19 million, by far the biggest group being the Zhuàg, at well over 13 million); and Miáo-Yáo (c. 7 million). Smaller groups include some Mon-Khmer (c. 400,000) and, in Taiwan, the Gāoshān (10 small Austronesian peoples adding up to c. 450,000); etc.

One relatively large group officially recognized as a minority nationality is the Huí; it is distinguished, however, only by its Muslim religion and customs: the Huí; totaling well over 7 million, speak Chinese; they are found in many parts of China.

4. Historical Survey

The history of the Chinese language can be divided into three major periods, each of them long enough to include several stages of transition and change: preclassical (c. 1500–500 BCE); classical (c. 500 BCE–CE 200); and postclassical Chinese (from CE 200 on).

Preclassical Chinese comprises Oracular Chinese, known only from fairly brief oracle inscriptions on bones and tortoise shells (Shāng dynasty, c. 1600–1066 BCE); and later forms of the language represented by bronze inscriptions, by the oldest parts of *Shūjīng* 'Classic of History,' and by an anthology of 305 poems entitled *Shījīng* 'Classic of Poetry.' From this period on, many important features of the pronunciation of the Chinese characters have been reconstructed (i.e., Old or Archaic Chinese). The grammatical system differed considerably from that of later ages, so much so that attempts at imitating it have been very rare.

The Classical Chinese period spans the centuries from the appearance of the earliest Confucian philosophical writings, (fifth century BCE) to the end of the Hàn dynasty (206 BCE–CE 220). Major prose works are *Lúnyǔ* 'The Analects' (of Confucius), the writings of Mèngzi (Mencius) and Zhuāngzi, the *Dào dé jīng* 'Classic of the Way and Its Power,' and the *Shìjì* 'Records of the Historian' by Sīmā Qiān (c. 145–c. 90 BCE). Linguistic features in these texts indicate that Classical Chinese was a fairly close reflection of the contemporary vernaculars; and although they represent language forms which are by no means uniform, still they were sufficiently similar to be regarded as variations on a common pattern and taken for models by later writers.

In the postclassical period authors of formal works and high literature continued to model their prose and poetry on Classical Chinese, while the spoken languages underwent very different and, by and large independent, developments in phonology and grammatical structure. Soon this emulous style of writing, known as *wényán* 'Literary Chinese,' made little sense when read aloud. As a purely written medium, however, it was largely unaffected by differences in time and location and remarkably successful for administrative, scholarly, and artistic purposes. It was the language in which the poets of the Táng dynasty created some of the greatest masterpieces of all time and in which the Sòng scholars wrote their neo-Confucian philosophical works, later introduced to the West by the early Jesuit missionaries. It survived well into the first half of the twentieth century.

Concurrently with this, but for more popular and homely purposes, writings were also produced in *báihuà*, a style close to the spoken dialects especially of the north. From Táng times on, it is preserved in Buddhist sermons and pious tales, in polemic ideological writings and private letters, as well as in secular stories, drama, and novels.

The notion of a common written and spoken standard language, *Guóyǔ*, regarded as a primary condition of national revival and modernization, took form during the first decades of the twentieth century. Major attacks on the use of Literary Chinese appeared in 1915 and gained further strength during the May Fourth Movement of 1919. About this time, experiments with an updated form of written *báihuà*, in some measure influenced by foreign styles and grammar, began in poetry and fiction, later, and in a less radical form, spreading also to scientific writings. The unification of pronunciation, on the other hand, presented a quite intricate political and practical problem; although Mandarin was commended as the national standard already in 1913, it remained an abstract ideal until the publication in 1932 of *Vocabulary of National Pronunciation for Every day Use*, a dictionary based on the Běijīng dialect. In the 1930s, however, Communist intellectuals and politicians were advocating a plan of separate standards for the various dialect areas, each with its own alphabetical writing system, in order to forestall the possibility of non-Mandarin speakers being consigned to illiteracy and second-class citizenship. This policy was never carried out. After 1949 it was rejected by the newly established Communist government as it had always been by the former Nationalist regimes for fear of stimulating regionalism and impeding national modernization. Since the adoption of MSC in 1956, this one standard has been unwaveringly promoted through the media of education, broadcasting, television, and the press and it is steadily gaining ground.

5. The Reconstruction of the Phonology of Older Stages of Chinese

5.1 Middle, or Ancient, Chinese

The foundation for what is known about Chinese phonological history is represented by a single work, the rhyming and pronouncing dictionary *Qièyùn*, compiled in CE 601 by a small group of scholars aiming at providing a guide to the proper recitation of literary texts. The sound system which it presents does not reflect one particular contemporary dialect but is the outcome of a conscious attempt at balancing the refined literary pronunciation of both northern and southern regions, the variety practiced in the area of present-day Nánjīng, however, being the most important component. The *Qièyùn* soon became a model for elegant, scholarly speech and although it was copied, revised, and expanded in later centuries, its phonological categories were, by and large, faithfully preserved.

In the *Qièyùn*, syllables are classified first according to tones, of which it has four, known as *píng* 'level,' *shǎng* 'rising,' *qù* 'departing,' and *rù* 'entering' or 'checked' tones. The *rù* tone comprised all syllables that ended in a stop (i.e., *p*, *t*, or *k*); the *shǎng* and *qù* tones may still have retained traces of the phonetic segments from which they can most probably be derived, glottal stop and *h*(<*s*), respectively. Next, the dictionary is divided according to rhymes, and finally according to initial consonants. Inside each rhyme the pronunciation of characters is indicated by means of a spelling method known as *fǎnqiè*, a system in which the reading of a character is shown by using two other, presumably known, characters, one alliterating with, the other rhyming with, the word to be glossed. The dictionary employs a total of 61 rhymes, 32 initial consonants, and 136 finals. It gives a great deal of structural information, but in the absence of a phonemic writing system it does not reveal anything concrete about the sound values.

These must be recovered from information sought out elsewhere, a task undertaken only in the twentieth century. Data have been gathered from various modern Chinese dialects; from Chinese loanwords in Korean, Japanese, and Vietnamese, and from Chinese renderings of Indo-Aryan words. It turned out that the *Qièyùn* inventory of initial consonants must have included voiceless aspirated and unaspirated and voiced forms of labial, dental, retroflex, palatal and velar stops and affricates, as well as voiced and voiceless fricatives, and glottal sounds; and that the finals ended in a vowel, a nasal (*m*, *n*, *ng*), or a stop (*p*, *t*, *k*); the number of vowels is not certain, but was probably greater than in either Old (Archaic) Chinese or in MSC.

Much remains to be done before the history of Chinese will be sufficiently well-known and understood. Data are still lacking from a great many places, hindering the reconstruction of major common forms such as Proto-Mandarin, Proto-Wú, etc. In addition, the linguistic complexities within individual dialect areas render the work difficult: most if not all of the major dialects have substrata of non-Chinese origin; and all dialects comprise at least two Chinese layers, an older one representing the original local tongue, antedating the language of the *Qièyùn*, and a younger one that is descended from the *Qièyùn* language or from a slightly later but closely related form, the so-called Táng *koine* (the standard spoken language of the Táng dynasty, 618–907). The degree to which this latter new layer has influenced the modern Chinese dialects varies, being slightest in the north, of greater import in the south. The old layer cannot be the direct ancestor of the new layer, and the division into the northern and southern dialects must be very old.

5.2 Old, or Archaic, Chinese

Unlike the reconstruction of Middle Chinese which to all intents and purposes is the interpretation of the *Qièyùn* and its legacy, that of Old Chinese is based on evidence from several sources, primarily the rhymes and alliteration of the *Shījīng* 'Classic of Poetry' (an anthology from c. 800–600 BCE) and the phonetic components contained in the great majority of Chinese characters, the latter being the main evidence for the nature of the old initials. As in the case of Middle Chinese, both the rhyme groups and the classes of initial consonants are abstract entities needing to be provided with phonological substance. Since so far this has had to be done almost solely by comparing the categories of Old Chinese with those of Middle Chinese, the results are highly hypothetical, and so far many issues (such as the number of tones, if any, and the order of elements in consonant clusters) are matters of considerable controversy among scholars working in the field. Enough is known, however, to determine the typology of Old Chinese and to undertake comparative work with the Tibeto–Burman and Karenic languages. Most scholars agree that as opposed to Middle Chinese which tolerated only simple initial consonants, Old Chinese possessed cluster initials; that it had a rich inventory of final consonants, among which a series of final voiced stops; and that it employed fewer vowels than Middle Chinese, a feature linking the phonology of Old Chinese to that of the modern dialects of north China.

5.3 The Course of Investigation

The pioneering effort in the study of Middle and Old Chinese phonology was accomplished by the Swedish Sinologue, Bernhard Karlgren (1889–1978), who published his complete sets of reconstructions for these protolanguages, which he termed Ancient and Archaic Chinese, in the dictionary *Grammata Serica*, 1940, followed by a revised version, *Grammata Serica Recensa*, 1957. In spite of later contributions from a number of Chinese and foreign specialists such as Li Róng (1952), Dǒng Tónghé (1954), Samuel Martin (1953), Edwin G. Pulleyblank (1962, 1970 etc.), Wáng Lǐ (1957), Sergei Yakhontov (late 1950s, early 1960s), and F.K. Li (Lǐ Fānggui, 1971), *Grammata Serica Recensa* for decades remained the only compilation of reconstructions in dictionary form; it was complemented only in 1991 by Edwin G. Pulleyblank, *Lexicon of Reconstructed Pronunciation in Early Middle Chinese, Late Middle Chinese, and Early Mandarin*.

See also: Tibetan; Chinese Linguistic Tradition.

Bibliography

Benedict P 1972 *Sino–Tibetan: A Conspectus*. Cambridge University Press, Cambridge

Chao Y R 1968 *A Grammar of Spoken Chinese*. University of California Press, Berkeley and Los Angeles, CA

DeFrancis J 1950 *Nationalism and Language Reform in China*. Princeton University Press, Princeton, NJ

DeFrancis J 1984 *The Chinese Language: Fact and Fantasy*. University of Hawaii Press, Honolulu, HI

Egerod S 1967 China: Dialectology. In: Sebeok T A (ed.) *Current Trends in Linguistics*, vol. 2. Mouton, The Hague

Egerod S 1974 Sino–Tibetan languages. In: *Encyclopaedia Britannica*, 15th edn., pp. 796–806

Karlgren B 1954 Compendium of phonetics in Ancient and Archaic Chinese. *Bulletin of the Museum of Far Eastern Antiquities* **26**: 211–367

Karlgren B 1957 Grammata serica recensa. *Bulletin of the Museum of Far Eastern Antiquities* **29**: 1–332

Kratochvíl P 1968 *The Chinese Language Today: Features of an Emerging Standard*. Hutchinson University Library, London

Norman J 1988 *Chinese*. Cambridge University Press, Cambridge

Pulleyblank E G 1991 *Lexicon of Reconstructed Pronunciation in Early Middle Chinese, Late Middle Chinese and Early Mandarin*. UBC Press, Vancouver

Ramsey S R 1987 *The Languages of China*. Princeton University Press, Princeton, NJ

Church Latin

B. I. Knott

Church Latin is the distinctive usage of Latin developed (first century CE onwards) to serve the Latin-speaking Church in the Western Roman Empire and is manifested in a heterogeneous body of texts including official documents, the liturgy (finally Latinized from Greek in the fourth century), hymns, pastoral letters and sermons, devotional works, the Bible, biblical exegesis, theological discussion and controversy, and Christian literature. It is immediately differentiated from Classical (pagan) Latin by numerous special terms for Christian institutions and ideas. Some are loanwords from Christian Greek (*evangelium* 'evangel,' *baptisma* 'baptism') or from Hebrew via Greek (*Pascha* 'Passover') or calques from Greek (*diakonos/minister*, *baptisma/tinctio*). Others are Latin neologisms (*salvare* 'to save,' *trinitas* 'Trinity,' *consubstantialis* 'consubstantial') or existing terms which either had their semantic field extended (*salus* 'well-being'> 'salvation,' *fides* 'trust'> 'Christian faith,' *credere* 'to believe'> 'to believe the Christian message') or acquired a Christian meaning in phrases (*vita temporalis* 'life in this world,' *originale peccatum* 'original sin').

In the early Latin versions of Greek biblical texts (produced probably mid-second century and known collectively as 'Vetus Latina'), the unknown authors, providing for believers mostly of humble status, preferred nonliterary vocabulary (*manducare*, not *edere* 'to eat'), simple paratactic style and colloquial constructions (*dixit quod* in place of accusative with infinitive, infinitive to express purpose) which often corresponded to similar usages in Greek. Reverence towards the source text occasioned syntactic innovation through literal translation of Greek constructions or Hebraisms already incorporated into the Greek: genitive, not ablative, absolute; *sublimius ab* 'higher than'; *percutere in* 'strike with'; *confiteor* 'confess' sins, 'glorify' God (following the change in Greek *ekxomologeisthai*); *dominus gloriae* 'Lord of glory'; *respondens dixit* 'he answered and said.' This assemblage of popular, exotic, and Christian elements, barbarous to educated Romans, was familiarized and sanctified to Christians in teaching and worship, and its style influenced nearly all subsequent Christian writing. St Jerome retained much of the familiar text in his Latin version of the Hebrew Bible, which became part of the Vulgata).

While early Christian writers could employ a style conforming to contemporary pagan literary expectations, a distinctive Christian literary idiom steadily developed marked by Christian semantemes, nonliterary vocabulary and constructions, citation of biblical texts, and pervasive use of biblical style, phraseology, and imagery. A heightened emotional tone was often generated by devices such as wordplay, antithesis, rhythmical, and rhymed prose. (For the theory of a spoken Christian 'special language' widely differentiated from pagan usage, the creation of self-contained Christian groups alienated from pagan society, and the matrix from which Christian writing emerged, see Mohrmann (1961–77). Official and liturgical texts also show the influence of Roman administrative, legal, and sacral styles.

By the fourth century, the Christian prose style was fully developed. At the same time, Christian poetry and the hymn came to maturity. The hymn is characterized by a simple, repeated four-line stanza form; the style is plain, though the imagery may be elaborate; the verses are paired for antiphonal singing.

Christianized Latin, as the language of the Church, everywhere accompanied the spread of Christianity in its Western form. Those committed to the service of the Church, whatever their native language, learned and used it. In the Dark and Middle Ages of Europe, when most educated persons had some connection with the church, this universal language was the natural medium for written communication of all kinds, its characteristics maintained by reading of the Bible, the Church Fathers, and Christian literature (with some fresh input from Classical literature). This Medieval Latin was superseded by classicizing Renaissance Latin and eventually by the vernaculars, but Christian elements such as specialized vocabulary and use of biblical phraseology were transmitted to both. Throughout, Latin has remained the official language of the Western (Roman Catholic) Church, which until recently still used in its worship the ancient Latin liturgical texts.

See also: Christianity in Europe; Bible Translations, Ancient Versions; Roman Religion; Vulgate.

Bibliography

Mohrmann C 1961–77 *Etudes sur le Latin des chrétiens*. Edizioni di Storia e Letteratura, Rome

Church Slavonic

C. M. MacRobert

'Church Slavonic' is a generic term for the closely related, highly conservative varieties of Slavic language used for liturgical purposes by the Eastern Orthodox Slavs, the Romanians until the sixteenth century, the Ukrainian Uniates, and Roman Catholic Croats of the Slavonic rite. In the medieval period, Church Slavonic also had the wider functions of a literary language.

Church Slavonic originated in the translations of Scripture and liturgy made mainly from Greek by SS Cyril and Methodius (see *Cyril and Methodius*) and their associates in the late ninth and early tenth centuries (see *Old Church Slavonic*). The basic vocabulary, grammatical forms and pronunciation of these texts predominantly followed the usage of Slavs in the southeast Balkans, while syntax and word-formation were modeled on Greek.

Two developments signal the transition, by the end of the eleventh century, from Old Church Slavonic to Church Slavonic. One was the emergence of local varieties, such as Russian and Serbian Church Slavonic, which compromised between traditional pronunciation and grammatical forms and the vernacular usage of the area. The other was the revision of syntax and vocabulary, sometimes apparently to aid intelligibility, but often in order to make the texts conform to a received Greek version and to produce a more literal translation. This tendency culminated by the fourteenth century in a comprehensive reform which has been associated with the Bulgarian Patriarch Euthymius, though research indicates that it began rather earlier, perhaps on Mount Athos.

Subsequent revision initiated in the Ukraine in the late sixteenth century, although controversial in its time and rejected by the schismatic Old Believers in Russia, dealt with minor textual discrepancies or the detail of grammatical and orthographic norms. A final standardization was effected in the publications approved by the Synod of the Russian Orthodox Church in the eighteenth century. Thanks to the dissemination of these printed books in the Balkans, the Orthodox Bulgarians, Macedonians, and Serbs now use 'Synodal' Russian Church Slavonic, albeit with their own pronunciations.

Modern Church Slavonic does not stand in a simple genetic relationship to other Slavic languages. Its texts may be understood in different ways and to varying degrees by Slavs of differing linguistic background, and some of them are intelligible only with the help of their Greek originals. It is virtually a closed system, for though new texts can be created if need arises, they are acceptable as Church Slavonic only insofar as they reproduce traditional constructions and phraseology.

Bibliography

Mathiesen R C 1972 *The Inflectional Morphology of the Synodal Church Slavonic Verb*. University Microfilms, Ann Arbor, MI

Mathiesen R 1984 The Church Slavonic language question: An overview (IX–XX centuries). In: Picchio R, Goldblatt H (eds.) *Aspects of the Slavic Language Question*, vol. I. Yale Concilium on International and Area Studies, New Haven, CT

Picchio R 1980 Church Slavonic. In: Schenker A M, Stankiewicz E (eds.) *The Slavic Literary Languages*. Yale Concilium on International and Area Studies, New Haven, CT

Plähn J 1978 *Der Gebrauch des Modernen Russischen Kirchenslavisch in der Russischen Kirche*. Buske, Hamburg

Devanagari

C. Shackle

Devanagari (also called Nagari) is the leading member of the family of North Indian scripts. It is the script nowadays normally used for writing Sanskrit and Hindi (Snell 2000).

Because of the primacy of oral transmission in the Indian tradition (see *Hindu Views on Language*), the details of script development are less clearly attested in India than in the Middle East or Europe. The essential characteristics of all North Indian scripts are nevertheless already clearly present in their phonetically highly sophisticated common ancestor, the classical Indian Brahmi script (Dani 1963) used to write the Prakrits of the Ashokan inscriptions of the third century BCE: above all the principle of syllabic writing with the distinctive feature that vowels following a consonant are differentiated by the use of graphically subordinate vowel signs. The more immediate ancestor of the North Indian scripts is the imperial Gupta script of the fourth–sixth centuries CE which by the eleventh century CE had developed into the left-to-right Devanagari script whose characteristic square-shaped forms reflect writing by pen or brush with Indian ink (Masica 1991).

दृष्ट्वा तु पाण्डवानीकं व्यूढं दुर्योधनस्तदा ।
आचार्यमुपसंगम्य राजा वचनमब्रवीत् ॥

dṛṣṭvā tu pāṇḍavānīkaṃ vyūḍhaṃ duryodhanastadā

ācāryamupasaṅgamya rājā vacanamabrāvīt

Having seen the Pandava army arrayed, King Duryodhana then approached his teacher and spoke these words:

Figure 1. Bhagavadgītā 1:2 in Sanskrit.

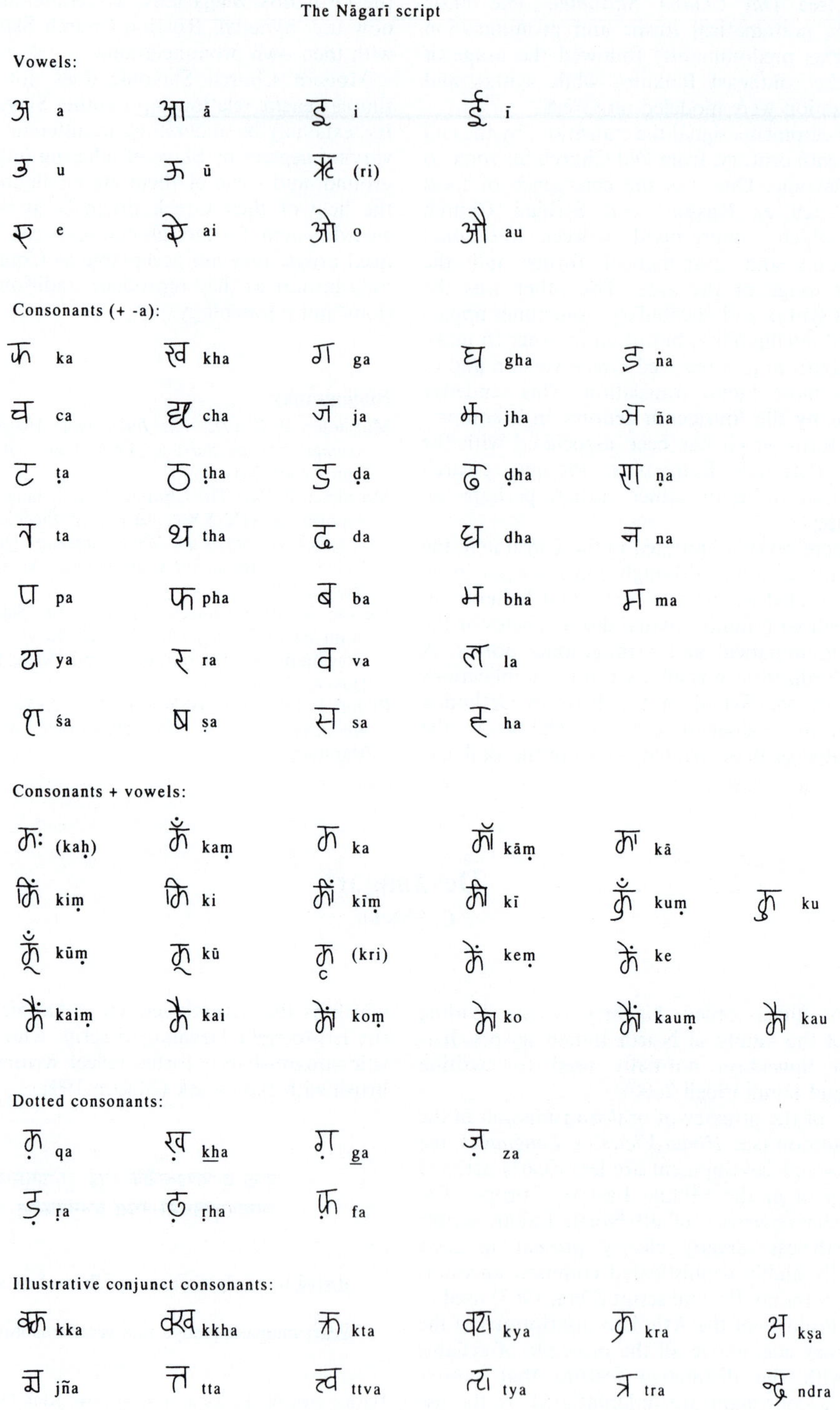

The Nāgarī script

Vowels:

अ a आ ā इ i ई ī

उ u ऊ ū ऋ (ri)

ए e ऐ ai ओ o औ au

Consonants (+ -a):

क ka ख kha ग ga घ gha ङ ṅa

च ca छ cha ज ja झ jha ञ ña

ट ṭa ठ ṭha ड ḍa ढ ḍha ण ṇa

त ta थ tha द da ध dha न na

प pa फ pha ब ba भ bha म ma

य ya र ra व va ल la

श śa ष ṣa स sa ह ha

Consonants + vowels:

कः (kaḥ) कँ kaṃ का ka काँ kāṃ का kā

किं kiṃ कि ki कीं kīṃ की kī कुँ kuṃ कु ku

कूँ kūṃ कू kū कृ (kri) कें keṃ के ke

कैं kaiṃ कै kai कों koṃ को ko कौं kauṃ कौ kau

Dotted consonants:

क़ qa ख़ k͟ha ग़ g͟a ज़ za

ड़ ṛa ढ़ ṛha फ़ fa

Illustrative conjunct consonants:

क्क kka क्ख kkha क्त kta क्य kya क्र kra क्ष kṣa

ज्ञ jña त्त tta त्त्व ttva त्य tya त्र tra न्द्र ndra

Figure 2.

Numerals:

१ 1	२ 2	३ 3	४ 4	५ 5
६ 6	७ 7	८ 8	९ 9	० 0

Illustrative spellings:

आई [āī]	गए [gae]	सोई [soī]
कर [kar(a)]	करना [kar(a)nā]	कर्ता [kartā]
हिंदी [himdī]	हिन्दी [hindī]	

John 3:16 in Hindi:

क्योंकि परमेश्वर ने संसार से ऐसा प्रेम रखा कि अपना एकलौता
पुत्र दे दिया, कि जो कोई उस पर विश्वास करे, नष्ट न हो, परंतु शाश्वत
जीवन पाए।

[kyoṃki parameśvara ne saṃsāra se aisā prema rakhā ki apanā] *kyomke parmeśvar ne sansār se aisā prem rakhā ke apnā* [ekalautā putra de diyā, ki jo koī usa para viśvāsa kare,] *eklautā putr de diyā, ke jo koī us par viśvās kare,* [naṣṭa na ho, paraṃtu śāśvata jīvana pāya.] *naṣṭ na ho, parantu śāśvat jīvan pāe.*

Figure 2. (continued)

The name Devanagari ('Script of the City of the Gods') indicates a particular sacred association with Sanskrit (Bright 1996). Arranged in a sophisticated phonetic order beginning with the vowels, then proceeding systematically through the different phonetic classes of consonants, the letters of the Devanagari alphabet indicate open V or CV syllables, with all unmarked consonants assumed to have the inherent vowel *-a*. Sanskrit, however, has many closed CVC or CCVC syllables. In order to accommodate the resulting sequences of two (rarely three) consonants, some 170 conjunct clusters were developed, in which a part of the first consonant is typically joined to the second, with special conventions for e.g. writing the very common combinations with *-r-*. The difficulty of reading Sanskrit is further increased by the conventions of word sandhi, where the final letter of one word is combined with the initial letter of the next.

The religious associations of the Devanagari script with Hinduism were successfully exploited by the nineteenth century protagonists of modern standard Hindi, now the official language of India, in their struggle against Urdu, written in Perso–Arabic script and increasingly identified with South Asian Islam (Shackle and Snell 1990). While simplifications and other modifications are used in writing Hindi words, the full set of classical rules is carefully observed in writing the numerous *tatsama* loans from Sanskrit which are so important a feature of all formal registers of Hindi.

See also: Gurmukhi; Hinduism; Sanskrit.

Bibliography

Bright W 1996 The Devanagari Script. In: Daniels P T, Bright W (eds.) *The World's Writing Systems*. Oxford University Press, New York and Oxford, pp. 384–90

Dani A H 1963 *Indian Palaeography*. Oxford University Press, Oxford

Masica C P 1991 *The Indo–Aryan Languages*. Cambridge University Press, Cambridge

Shackle C, Snell R 1990 *Hindi and Urdu since 1800*. School of African & Asian Studies, London

Snell R 2000 *Teach Yourself Hindi Script*. Hodder, London

Egyptian Hieroglyphs

J. D. Ray

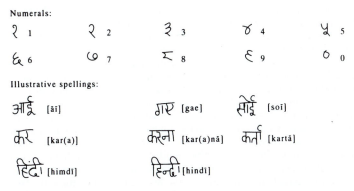

It is likely that all writing began with pictures: certainly all known early scripts start as a series of natural representations. The next stage is to employ picture-writing to express ideas which cannot be

shown pictorially. In China, the answer was sometimes found by combining pictures in a way reminiscent of a modern cartoon ('reliability,' for example, can be illustrated by the sign for 'man' next to the sign for 'speech': a man standing by his word). However, the ancient Near East had recourse to a very different system. According to this approach, which seems to have been invented in Mesopotamia towards the end of the fourth millennium BCE, pictures were used to represent abstract ideas which had identical or similar sounds to the pictures chosen; in other words, the principle of the rebus, or pun. The same principle is adopted shortly afterwards in Egypt, where the first inscriptions are dated to around 3100 BCE. It is possible that this was a separate invention, but such an idea would be bound to travel quickly, and other Mesopotamian influences are found in Egypt at this time. However, there is no doubt that the forms of Egyptian picture-writing are essentially an Egyptian creation, owing nothing to Mesopotamian canons of art. The suddenness of its appearance in the Nile Valley suggests that the hieroglyphic script developed extremely rapidly, and may even be an invention of the royal court. Nevertheless, whatever its origins, the result is one of the most decorative scripts ever devised. In its developed form, which was reached about 2000 BCE, some 2,500 signs can be recognized, although in practice much fewer need to be committed to memory, and the script is easier to learn than many others in the ancient world.

1. Hieroglyphic

Hieroglyphs (from the Greek words for 'sacred carving') are a mixed script. Some, which are known as ideograms, represent tangible or natural objects; these occur commonly, although they are not the largest category of sign. Many more represent phonetic elements, whose values are probably derived from the rebus-priniciple mentioned above. The Egyptian language, in common with the Semitic languages to which it is related, consists largely of triconsonantal roots, each carrying a basic meaning (see *Ancient Egyptian and Coptic*). Variations on this meaning were generally obtained by altering the vowels. Thus the root *nfr*, which means something like 'complete,' gives rise to words meaning 'be good, beautiful,' 'there is an end to,' and 'final room of a house,' while the root *ḥtr* ('yoke') can produce words meaning 'twin,' 'team of oxen' (later 'horse'), 'necessity,' 'taxation,' and so on. This property of the language may have encouraged the Egyptians to omit vowels from their script; while this creates difficulties for modern scholars, it greatly simplified the task for its originators. Some phonetic signs are triliterals, which embody all three consonants of a root, but many more are biliterals, used to express combinations such as *mn*, *ḥs*, *mr*, *qb*, etc. (see Fig. 1). The system therefore contains most of the elements of a syllabary. Even more remarkable is the existence of some 25 uniliteral signs; in other words, an alphabet. These are normally embedded among combinations of other signs, and often do duty for grammatical elements which could hardly be expressed otherwise. They are also used in the writing of proper names, especially foreign ones which made no sense in Egyptian and therefore suggested no other signs. Obviously several alternative spellings could exist for the same word, but there is a noticeable tendency for words from a family to prefer a particular arrangement of signs; this may, however, have been largely unconscious. Ambiguity, which was a hazard of the script, was largely avoided by the use of so-called 'determinatives.' These may be seen as displaced ideograms, positioned at the end of a word to indicate the class to which it belonged: human being, wooden object, place-name, etc. The system may seem cumbersome, but it was not designed as a medium for universal use; and paradoxically enough, when Egyptian first appears written in the Greek alphabet, without determinatives and other aids, the result is remarkably difficult to follow. Hieroglyphs suited the Egyptian language well.

There are very few regional variants in hieroglyphic, which suggests that its use was controlled to considerable extent by central authority, and most early inscriptions record the achievements of the ruling élite. Nevertheless, the script develops steadily throughout Egyptian history, and most texts can be dated by their outward form to a particular period or dynasty. The principles remain constant throughout three millennia, although there is a tendency to lead to fuller writings with more determinatives. In the temples of the Ptolemaic period (after 300 BCE) a system is used which represents the application of lateral thinking to hieroglyphic; reading such texts can be more like solving crossword-puzzle clues (a picture of a cat, for example, looking at itself in a mirror, turns out to be the word for 'like, similar,' while a man hitting the rump of a hippopotamus can signify 'lapis-lazuli,' for reasons which are partly phonetic, partly connotational). Although rooted in the normal script, this system is essentially an aberration, and is confined to sacred areas. The usual direction for most hieroglyphic is from right to left; the signs are intended to be read against the way that they are facing, so that the individual signs normally face right. However, since the script is also a medium for decoration, texts may run from left to right (often as a mirror-image of a right-to-left text), or in vertical columns. In some religious compositions, signs are arranged to be read in retrograde, but these cases are rare. The cursive Egyptian scripts (see below) all run from right to left, like the Semitic alphabets but

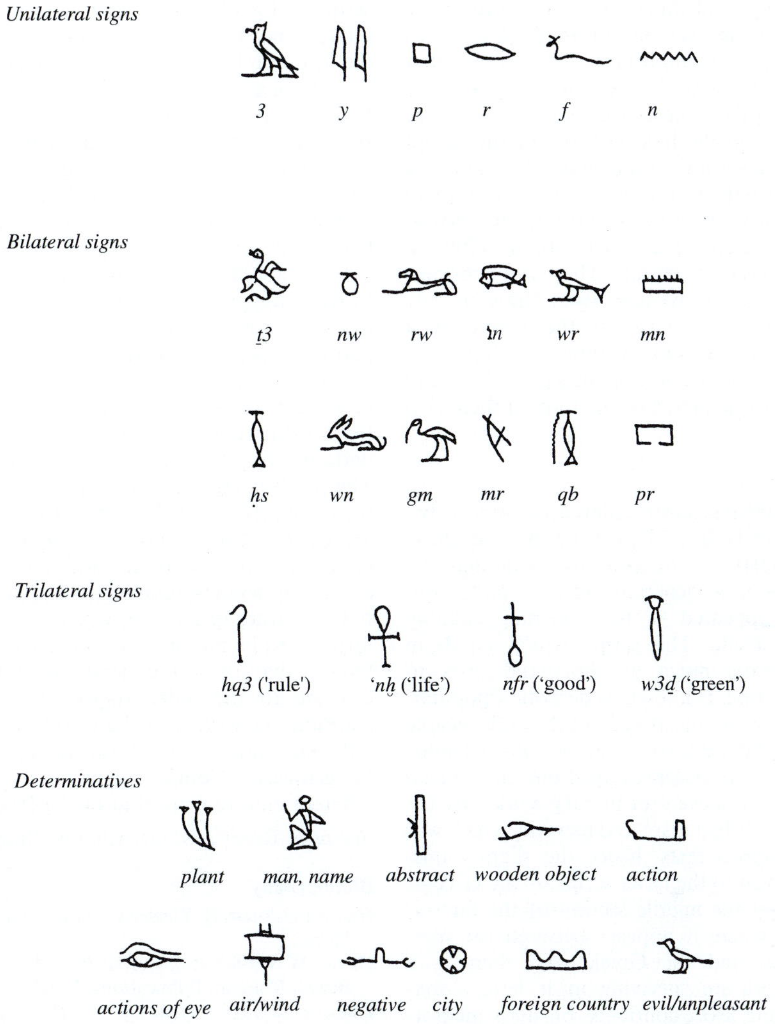

Figure 1.

unlike cuneiform, and this appears to be the natural direction for Egyptian writing.

The language of the Middle Kingdom (ca. 2100–1700 BCE) was felt by the Egyptians to be canonical, and much of Egyptian literature survives in this medium, although the later vernacular language, generally known as Late Egyptian, also became a literary idiom. The rich literature which survives is extremely varied, with some surprising features, such as the short story of novella, and lyric poetry, both of which can be claimed as Egyptian inventions. However, the corpus is dominated by the didactic texts known as 'Instructions'; these are normally pseudonymous. It is interesting that while the names of many sages are preserved to us, most of the rest of Egyptian literature is anonymous. Estimates of the percentage of ancient Egyptians who were literate vary from a generous 10 percent down to 2 percent or less, and the public letter-writer must have been a familiar figure in an Egyptian village.

2. Hieratic

Although Egyptian survives on stone, wood, leather and metal, most writing was intended for rolls of papyrus, using a thin brush for a pen. This in itself altered the nature of hieroglyphic writing, which rapidly became more impressionistic. Ligatures of signs became easier to make, and considerable speed could be maintained. Thus hieroglyphs became a cursive script, in which most of the day-to-day records of society, and much of its literature, were recorded. This script is conventionally known as hieratic, although it is important to remember that there is no real boundary between hieroglyphic and hieratic; the Egyptians themselves did not recognize this distinction, and the link with the picture-script was never lost. Modern Egyptologists, when editing a hieratic text, normally transcribe it into conventional hieroglyphs. Early hieratic is written in vertical columns facing right, but after about 1700 BCE horizontal lines become the rule. There is a considerable variety of hieratic writing, from the elaborate calligraphy of a literary scribe to the jottings of a workman. There are also many apprentice hands, of varying degrees of proficiency. Some kinds of text are so cursive as to form a specialized study in their own right.

3. Demotic

After about 1100 BCE, clear differences appear between hieratic texts from Upper Egypt and those from further north in the country. Although the details are lost, it is generally agreed that about 650 BCE there appeared a new script, probably invented in the Delta. This script, which stands in relation to hieratic much as shorthand does to modern handwriting, is known as demotic ('popular' writing). The new script spread south, and became the medium for most everyday transactions. At some point it became the accepted medium for official pronouncements, and even for literary works. By the Hellenistic period it had displaced hieratic, which was confined to religious texts; hence the slightly misleading name given to the latter script by the Greeks. Demotic occupies the middle section of the famous Rosetta Stone, where it appears between the hieroglyphic version and the Greek, and there is a considerable literature surviving in it letters, tax-receipts, economic texts, contracts, business memoranda, as well as literary, medical, religious, and scientific writings. After the Roman occupation of Egypt in 30 CE demotic continues, and the old brush-pen is sometimes replaced by a split reed, which gives a thin line like a modern nib. The result was probably easier to write, although it is not an aesthetic improvement. However, demotic as an everyday script in Egypt was fighting a losing battle against Greek, and, like hieratic before it, disappeared into the field of religious literature. The last demotic texts, like the last hieroglyphs, come from the island of Philae in the First Cataract, and date from about sixty years after the establishment of Christianity throughout the Roman Empire. Thereafter knowledge of Egyptian writing was lost until the arrival of Napoleon in Egypt and the decipherment by Champollion in 1822.

From about 200 BCE onwards, attempts were made to write Egyptian in the Greek alphabet. Spasmodic examples appear throughout the Graeco–Roman period, especially in the realm of religious and magical literature, where the correct pronunciation of words was important. However, the impetus which led to the abandonment of the old script was undoubtedly the spread of Christianity in Egypt. The result is known as Coptic, after a corruption of the Greek *Aigyptios* 'Egyptian' (see *Ancient Egyptian and Coptic*). Coptic, which is written in the Byzantine Greek alphabet with the addition of seven letters expressing sounds peculiar to Egyptian, possesses a rich literature of its own, which owes little to pagan forms, and its importance to the Egyptologist lies in the fact that it is well understood, and can be used as a guide to the older stages of the language. In addition, the writing of the vowels means that dialect differences appear, which the older scripts concealed. Nevertheless, Coptic Egypt is in many ways a different culture from that of the Pharaohs.

See also: Rosetta Stone; Champollion, J.-F.

Bibliography

André-Leicknam B, Ziegler C 1982 *Naissance de l'Écriture*. Paris

Davies W V 1987 *Reading the Past: Egyptian Hieroglyphs*. British Museum Publications, London

Hussein M 1970 *Origins of the Book: From Papyrus to Codex*. Leipzig

Ray J D 1986 The emergence of writing in Egypt. *World Archaology* **17(3)**: 307–16

Sauneron S (ed.) 1972 *Textes et languages de l'Egypte pharaonique*. 3 vols. Institut français d'archéologie orientale, Cairo

Schlott A 1989 *Schrift und Schreiber im Alten Ägypten*. Munich

Garshuni

J. F. Coakley

Garshuni is Arabic written in Syriac letters. The forms *garšuni* and *karšuni* are both found, and since no convincing etymology has been proposed for either one, it remains unclear which is original. With the rise of Islam, Christian literature began to be produced in Arabic, but the earliest manuscripts, from the eighth century on, are in the Arabic script. The use of the Syriac script alongside the Arabic seems to have begun in the thirteenth century, and there are dated manuscripts from the fourteenth century. The Syriac alphabet of 22 letters was adapted with diacritical points on certain consonants to make up the extra six letters in Arabic.

Garshuni writing arose perhaps as an attempt to distinguish Christian texts at sight, or to limit them to Christian readers, or simply to serve those educated within the community who were unpracticed with the Arabic script. Almost all garshuni manuscripts are West Syriac, that is, originating in the Syriac Orthodox and Maronite churches. They include many kinds of literature: the Bible, commentaries, liturgy, theology, saints' lives, and other popular texts. A particularly wide range of these is represented in the Mingana collection in Selly Oak Colleges Library (Mingana 1933; as here, garshuni manuscripts in libraries tend to be classified as Syriac rather than Arabic). The first book to use Syriac type (Theseus Ambrosius, *Introductio in Chaldaicam linguam*, 1539) prints a passage (Luke 3.23–38) in garshuni. The Propaganda Fide published the New Testament in parallel columns of Syriac and garshuni (2 vols., 1702–3), and many other Maronite printed books of the sixteenth to nineteenth centuries are at least partly in garshuni.

The term garshuni is also used to refer to other languages written in Syriac characters. Most common is 'Turkish garshuni,' found in manuscripts as early as the seventeenth century and as late as a newspaper *Lišono d-Umto* (Beirut, 1927–)

See also: Christianity in the Near East; Peshitta.

Bibliography

Assfalg J 1982 Arabische Handschriften in syrischer Schrift (Karšūni). In: Fischer W (ed.) *Grundriss der arabischen Philologie I: Sprachwissenschaft*. Reichert, Wiesbaden, pp. 297–302

Mingana A 1933 *Catalogue of the Mingana Collection of Manuscripts. I. Syriac and Garshuni manuscripts*. Heffer, Cambridge

Ge'ez

S. Uhlig

Ge'ez *(lesānā ge'ez)* is the old Ethiopic language which originated from the South Arabian languages. The term goes back to a South Arabian tribe which settled in Aksum, the Ag'azi (from *g'z* 'to be free, to emigrate'). The term 'Abyssinian' probably comes from another tribe, the Habašat. 'Ethiopian' is from Greek *Aithiops* 'blackfaced.'

In pre-Christian times, South Arabian settlers founded colonies in today's Eritrea and Tigre and brought their culture, religion, script, and languages with them. In the 'Sabean' or 'pre-Aksumitic' epoch (first century BCE to third century CE), they expanded southwards and developed a new language, clearly distinguished from South Arabian and known as 'Ge'ez.'

At the same time, the Sabean script increasingly disappeared, and in its place a new writing system evolved. At first it consisted of 26 'letters,' or rather (in the case of syllables) 'symbols,' with the elimination of interdentals and the Arabic /ɣ/, the appearance of a second /p/ phoneme, and the emergence of a labio-velar. The script, apart from a short period in the earliest stages of its development when it runs from right to left or *boustrophedon*, is always written from left to right. Eventually a syllabary of about 200 characters, in seven 'orders' (a, u, i, ā, ē, ĕ/0, ō) was created.

The first Aksumitic period (fourth to seventh century) is marked by strong Greek influence in the Red Sea area due to the fact that the Aksumitic kings used Greek for diplomatic and commercial purposes. This was also a time of political and economic consolidation, involving tributes from Meroë and Somalia and expeditions against kingdoms to the southwest. With the conversion of King Ezāna to Christianity in the fourth century and the foundation of the Church of Aksum, an independent Christian culture was established in Africa and with it the proselytization of that kingdom and adjoining regions. For about 1,000 years Ge'ez was the medium for the spread of all kinds of literature, culture, trade, and economy. Its main function was in the church, but it was also used for historical, juridical, and chronological works.

From the fourteenth century onwards, under Cushitic influence, Amharic became the colloquial language of Christian Ethiopia (after intermediate stages known as *lesānā negus* 'the language of the king' and *lesānā tārik* 'the chronicle language'). But Ge'ez remained the language of the Bible, the Anaphoras, and some parts of the 'classical' literature. Most of the literature in Ge'ez consists of translations from Greek, Arabic, and, to a small extent, Coptic, but very free use is made of the foreign *Vorlage* and, in the process, a new literature is actually created. Bible translation, in particular, is characterized by a very open understanding of the Canon, which means, on the one hand, that the Ethiopians included a number of pseudepigraphical books, and on the other, made numerous additions to the text, resulting in a paraphrase very different from the scriptures of the Western, Catholic, and Eastern Orthodox Churches.

Manuscripts written in Ge'ez show no influence from the neighboring Coptic culture with the exception of such features as the use of the *crux ansata* (derived from Egyptian *ankh* 'life') in early codices. There are also some special ligatures in the biblical and ecclesiastical books for frequently used words. Although Ge'ez is a dead language in the late twentieth century, like Latin and Sanskrit, it survives in the liturgy and the scriptures of the Ethiopian Church.

Bibliography

Littman E, Krencker D, Lüpke T von, Zahn R 1913 *Deutsche Aksum-Expedition*, vols. I–IV. Generalverwaltung der Königlichen Museen zu Berlin

Grohmann A 1914–18 Über den Ursprung und die Entwicklung der äthiopischen Schrift. *Archiv für Schriftkunde*, vol. I. Deutsches Schriftmuseum, Leipzig

Ullendorff E 1955 *The Semitic Languages of Ethiopia: A Comparative Phonology*. Taylor's (Foreign) Press, London

Georgian

B. G. Hewitt

Georgian is spoken in the (now former Soviet) Republic of Georgia, in the Ingilo district of Azerbaydzhan, by residents of former Georgian territories now within Turkey, by descendants of Georgians transplanted to Fereydan in Iran by Shan Abbas (seventeenth century), and by small émigré communities in some Western countries (France, America).

The 1989 Soviet census counts 3,983,115 'Georgians' for the whole Soviet Union, 98.2 percent of whom claimed native-speaker command of the language (99.7 percent of those within Georgia itself). This, however, is misleading, for those here styled 'Georgians' include Georgians proper plus the related Mingrelians, Svans, and the relatively few Laz resident inside the USSR; additionally included are the circa 6,000 speakers of the obsolescent North Central Caucasian Bats (Ts'ova-Tush), who inhabit one east Georgian village and represent the entire tribe. All of the perhaps 80,000 Svans and most of the maybe one million Mingrelians will have Georgian as their second language through receiving their education in Georgian-language schools during the (post-) Soviet period.

Georgian belong to the Kartvelian (South Caucasian) family, whose other members are Mingrelian, Laz, and Svan, the most divergent. The first two are close enough to be regarded by (former-)Soviet linguists as mere dialects of a single language (Zan). No genetic link with any other language(-family) even within the Caucasus has yet been demonstrated.

With 15 centuries of texts it is customary to periodize thus: Old Georgian (fifth–eleventh centuries) => Mediæval (twelfth–eighteenth centuries) => Modern (post-1800). Iranian and, latterly, Russian lexical influences are marked; Greek, Armenian, Arabic, and Turkish loans are also noticeable.

The oldest inscription dates from c. 430 CE at a site near Bethlehem. Within Georgia the oldest inscription (494) belongs to the Bolnisi church. Iak'ob Tsurt'aveli's *Martyrdom of Shushanik*, apparently composed between 476 and 483, represents the first native work of literature, while the oldest dated manuscript hails from 864. The earliest manuscripts and inscriptions exhibit peculiarities in the marking of third-person indirect objects, from which they are named *xanmet'i* 'with extra *x*' or *haemet'i* 'with extra *h*'; the nature of this distinction (diachronic vs. dialectal) has been hotly debated. Little seems to have been written during the centuries of Mongol and Tatar depredations.

Georgian is written in a unique, wholly phonemic alphabet with 33 characters from left to right without any upper vs. lower case distinction. The modern script *mxedruli* 'military; secular' evolved in the eleventh century from its precursor *k'utxovani* 'angular,' which in turn developed in the ninth century from the oldest variant *mrg(v)lovani* 'rounded,' which was probably devised in the fourth century AD on the model of Greek to aid the spread of Christianity, adopted as the state-religion c. 330. Even after the eleventh century religious texts continued to be written in a combination of the two earliest scripts, called *xutsuri* 'ecclesiastical,' such that the oldest served as majuscule (*asomtavruli*) to the miniscule (*nusxuri*) of its successor.

Georgian possesses a number of dialects, which can differ sharply from both one another (e.g., western Gurian vs. north-eastern Khevsurian) and the literary standard, which is based on the norms of the central region of Kartli, wherein lies the capital, Tbilisi. Georgian is the only literary language within Kartvelian: early Soviet attempts to turn Mingrelian and (amazingly) Laz into literary languages failed. With a general choice between education in Russian or Georgian following the introduction of universal schooling to eradicate illiteracy by the Soviets, most Georgians and Mingrelians have tended to choose Georgian schools for their children, particularly in rural areas; the absence of Russians in Svaneti(a) meant that only Georgian schools were established here. No widespread knowledge of Georgian among Svans or even Mingrelians can be automatically assumed for the pre-Soviet period despite Georgian's role as the language of worship. Georgian has been making inroads at the expense of Mingrelian, especially in eastern Mingrelia, for over a century, and the migration of thousands of Svans to lowland Georgia after the tragic winter of 1986–87 must raise fears for their retention of Svan when no longer living in compact, isolated communities; while Mingrelian itself tended to gain at the expense of Abkhaz in the north-west from the mid to late nineteenth century, the demographic and thus linguistic situation in Abkhazia (*de facto* independent at the moment of writing) altered with the flight of the bulk of Mingrelian speakers from Abkhazia at the end of the Georgian-Abkhazian war of 1992–93, though up to 100,000 are reported to have returned to Abkhazia's south-eastern Gal Region. The designation 'Georgian' became obligatory for Mingrelians and Svans c. 1930, since when there have been no accurate data for either ethnic numbers or first vs. second vs. third language knowledge with respect to the Kartvelian peoples and their languages.

The languages to have undergone Georgian influence the most are naturally its congeners, Mingrelian and Svan, plus other languages spoken within Georgia such as Bats, (North West Caucasian) Abkhaz, and (Iranian) Ossetic. As a feudal power throughout the Caucasus and source for the spread of Christianity to the north Caucasus before the coming of Islam Georgia has left some lexical traces here too.

See also: Christianity in the Near East.

Bibliography

Hewitt B G 1995 *Georgian. A Structural Reference Grammar*. Benjamins, Amsterdam

Hewitt B G 1996 *Georgian. A Learner's Grammar. Routledge*, London

Tschenkéli K 1958 *Einführung in die georgische Sprache*, 2 vols. Amirani Verlag Zürich

Vogt H 1971 *Grammaire de la langue géorgienne*. Universitetsforlaget, Oslo

Gothic

J. M. Y. Simpson

Gothic is the only documented member of the East Germanic group of Germanic languages.

1. Early History and Wulfila's Gothic

From the late first century BCE onwards, various Gothic tribes migrated from southern Scandinavia to eastern and southeastern Europe (following the rivers Vistula and Danube), reaching the Black Sea by the middle of the third century CE. To the east of the River Dniestr were tribes of Ostrogoths, to the west Visigoths. In the fourth century, in modern Bulgaria, a translation of most of the Bible was made by the Visigoth Bishop Wulfila; parts of this have survived and, since it is the earliest text of any length in a Germanic language, these are documents of outstanding importance for Germanic and Indo-European linguistic history. Wulfila designed an alphabet clearly based on the Greek, but with some characters from Latin and one or two that may be runic in origin. It appears in Fig. 1 with a widely use transliteration. (The two untransliterated symbols were used only to form numerals.) ⟨q⟩ is taken to be /kw/, ⟨þ⟩ to be /θ/, ⟨ƕ⟩ to be /ʍ/ or /hw/. It may be assumed that this system is phonemic though the following digraphs have the probable values: ⟨ei⟩=/i/, ⟨au⟩=/ɔ/, ⟨ai⟩=/ɛ/, and ⟨gg⟩=/ŋg/. It is possible that intervocalically the letters ⟨b⟩, ⟨d⟩, and ⟨g⟩ denote fricative allophones.

The Gothic of Wulfila shows the typically Germanic features of (a) the 'First Sound Shift' development; (b) strong verbs versus weak verbs (respectively with vowel-change ('Ablaut') versus a dental suffix in the past tense); (c) a 'weak' declension of adjectives

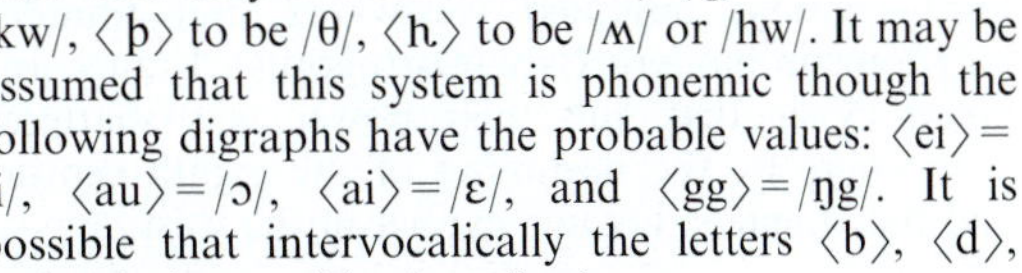

Figure 1.

(used after a demonstrative) versus a 'strong' (used elsewhere). Among various archaic features, the most striking is perhaps the retention of a nominative ⟨-s⟩ in such forms as *fisks* 'fish', *akrs* 'field'.

Morphologically, Gothic is conservative. Verbs show inflections for (a) past and non-past tenses; (b) indicative, subjunctive, and imperative moods, plus an infinitive form; (c) active and passive voices; (d) first, second, and third persons; (e) singular, dual, and plural numbers. There are not, however, distinct forms for every possible combination of these. Nouns, adjectives, and pronouns show inflections for (a) singular and plural numbers; (b) masculine, feminine, and neuter genders; (c) nominative, accusative, genitive and dative cases. Pronouns in addition have distinct forms for the dual number.

2. Sample Text

Jah	þan	bidjaiþ	ni	sijaiþ
AND	WHEN	PRAY + 2/pl/press/indic	NOT	BE + 2/pl/pres/subj

swaswe	þai	liutans,	unte
LIKE	THE + m/pl/nom	HYPOCRITE + m/pl/nom	FOR

frijond	in	gaqumþim
LOVE + 3/pl/pres/indic	IN	SYNAGOGUE + f/pl/dat

jah	waihstam	plapjo
AND	CORNER + m/pl/dat	STREET + f/pl/gen

standandans	bidjan	ei
STAND + pres.pr/m/pl/nom	PRAY + infin	SO-THAT

gaumjaindau	mannam.
SEE + 3/pl/pres/subj/pass	MAN + m/pl/dat.

'And when you pray, do not be like the hypocrites, for they like to pray in synagogues and on street corners standing up, so that they may be seen by people.'

3. Later History and Crimean Gothic

Some Goths, forced out by the invading Huns in the third century, migrated westwards and founded kingdoms in modern Italy (Ostrogoths), France and Spain (Visigoths); but their power was shattered everywhere by the beginning of the eighth century and the language became extinct in the west.

Gothic lived on longer in the east, surviving in present day northern Bulgaria until the ninth century and in the Crimea until the sixteenth century, according to accounts by travelers. The last of these was by Ogier Ghiselin de Busbecq in 1560–62, the Imperial ambassador to the Ottoman court at Constantinople, who recorded a list of some hundred Crimean Gothic words. This is of rather limited value, for it was published without his permission and may contain misprints; more importantly, his two informants were dubious, one being a native Greek-speaker. One great lack is that of any indication of morphological variation and syntax. But it seems likely that Crimean Gothic was a descendant of a somewhat different variety from that of Wulfila. Busbecq also notated a 'Gothic' song (the 'Cantilena'); but he gives no translation and it has been variously claimed to be not Gothic but Turkish, Swedish, or Italian. Gothic had died out by the end of the eighteenth century.

Related East Germanic languages are those of the Vandals (who established themselves in North Africa) and the Burgundians (who set up a kingdom in Gaul); both languages became extinct in the sixth and seventh centuries and little is known of them except personal and place names.

See also: Wulfila (Ulfilas) (311?–382?).

Bibliography

Braune W 1961 *Gotische Grammatik* 16. Auflage neu bearbeitet von Ernst A. Ebbinghaus. Tübingen

Friedrichsen G W S 1961 *Gothic Studies*. Blackwell, Oxford

Heinemeyer W 1961 *Studien zur Geschichte der gotischen Urkundenschrift*. Bohlau, Cologne

Stearns M 1978 *Crimean Gothic: Analysis and Etymology of the Corpus*. Anma Libri, Saratoga, CA

Voyles J B 1981 *Gothic, Germanic, and Northwest Germanic*. Steiner, Wiesbaden

Wright J 1954 *Grammar of the Gothic Language* [with selected texts]. 2nd edn. with supplement by Sayce O L. Clarendon Press, Oxford

Gurmukhi

C. Shackle

Gurmukhi ('guided by the Guru') is the script of the Sikh scriptures, which has also become the standard script for writing modern Panjabi by Sikhs and others in India.

Although it is visually similar to Devanagari, the Gurmukhi script is typologically somewhat distinct, having proved to be the sturdiest survivor of a formerly very widespread subgroup which might be

A verse by Guru Nānak (*Ādi Granth* 83):

ਦਾਤੀ ਸਾਹਿਬ ਸੰਦੀਆ ਕਿਆ ਚਲੈ ਤਿਸੁ ਨਾਲਿ।
ਇਕਿ ਜਾਗੰਦੇ ਨ ਲਹੰਨਿ੍ ਇਕਨਾ ਸੁਤਿਆ ਦੇਇ ਉਠਾਲਿ।

dātī[ṃ] sāhib(a) sandīā[ṃ] kiā calai tis(u) nāl(i)

ik(i) jāgande na lahannh(i) ikan[h]ā[ṃ] sut[t]iā[ṃ] dei uṭhāl(i)

Gifts are the Lord's, what prevails with Him?

Some get none though awake, others He wakes up to give to.

Figure 1.

termed 'semi-learned' in view of its intermediate position between learned full scripts of the Devanagari type and abbreviated commercial shorthands. Now mostly obsolete, other exemplars of this type include the Khojki script of the Ismaili Muslims of western India (see *Islam in South Asia*).

These semi-learned scripts contrast with Devanagari in having a reduced syllabary, which eliminates some distinctive vowel graphemes as well as signs for consonants found only in Sanskrit. The 35 letters of the Gurmukhi alphabet begin with the three vowel letters [u], [a], [i] where the reversal from the usual Indian order reflects the primacy of the sacred syllable *oṃ*. They also follow the Brahmi model more closely in largely eliminating the conjunct consonants of the learned scripts. The doubled consonants so generally retained in Panjabi from Middle Indo–Aryan are indicated as in Brahmi by a single consonant in Gurmukhi, which has only a few subscripts to indicate e.g., *-r-* and *-h-* in place of the numerous Devanagari conjunct clusters.

The sacred associations with Gurmukhi as the vehicle for recording the *gurbāṇī* ('the Word of the Guru') were successfully drawn upon by the twentieth century Sikh protagonists of modern standard Panjabi in opposition to the Hindi written in Devanagari favored by Panjabi Hindus. There are however a number of significant divergences between scriptural and modern conventions in writing and reading the script. While orthographic rules have been systematized for writing the modern language, the printed scriptural *textus receptus* (see *Granth*) carefully continues to reflect looser medieval usage, e.g., in frequent omissions of superscript or subscript features (indicated in square brackets in the transcription in Fig. 1). Conversely, the modern reading pronunciation of the Granth omits the final postconsonantal short vowels (indicated in round brackets) which were essential grammatical markers in the older language (see *Sikhism*).

See also: Devanagari; Panjabi (Gurmukhi) Sacred Texts; Panjabi.

Bibliography

Dani A H 1963 *Indian Palaeography*. Oxford University Press, Oxford

Gill H S 1996 The Gurmukhi Script. In: Daniels P T, Bright W (eds.) *The World's Writing Systems*. Oxford University Press, New York and Oxford, pp. 395–8

Masica C P 1991 *The Indo–Aryan Languages*. Cambridge University Press, Cambridge

Shackle C 1983 *An Introduction to the Sacred Language of the Sikhs*. School of Oriental and African Studies, London

Hebrew, Biblical and Jewish

J. F. Elwolde

Hebrew is the language of the people who, throughout the first millennium BCE, comprised a major part of the population of the territory broadly coterminous with that of the modern State of Israel. Members of this people stopped living in most of its ancient lands in any significant numbers following the Roman suppression of the BarKochba revolt in 135 CE. Indeed, for some 500 years previously Jews (from Judah/Judea, in the south of Israel) had settled in large numbers throughout the Persian and Greco-Roman world. Even though they retained a high level of ethnic exclusivity, Jews became identified, and tended to identify themselves, as being more a 'religious' than a 'national' group, and this has been of enormous significance for the survival of Hebrew over three millennia.

1. A Holy Language

From the early centuries CE, Hebrew is frequently referred to as '*lēshōn ha-qōdesh*' 'the sacred language' (an expression also found in the Dead Sea Scrolls) in contrast to other languages spoken by Jews—particularly Greek, Aramaic, and, much later, Yiddish. In addition, the Hebrew of the Bible was sometimes regarded (by certain medieval writers, for example) as 'purer' than later varieties. It is possible that this view is attested as early as the second century BCE, when the Qumran community derided their religious adversaries as speaking an 'uncircumcized tongue' (Rabbinic Hebrew perhaps; see Sect. 3 below). Jewish traditions claim that Hebrew was the language spoken at the creation, that the letters of the Hebrew alphabet were active in the creation (see *Alphabet*: *Religious Beliefs*), and that it is the only language understood by the angels and efficacious in prayer.

2. Biblical Hebrew

The main corpus of ancient Hebrew is the Bible (minus its Aramaic portions), consisting of some 451,000 running words distributed over slightly fewer than 10,000 items of vocabulary (including proper nouns). The consonantal text of this corpus had achieved roughly its current state by the second century BCE, after ongoing revision of its different parts. A point to be stressed is that Biblical Hebrew, as it has been handed down, comprises a literary, rather than an oral or 'colloquial,' corpus. The Bible is not a straightforward record of spoken utterances from biblical times, but is better viewed as a collection of written compositions, including literary versions of conversations, orally transmitted stories, etc.

The language of those parts of the Bible composed after the Jews' return from exile in Babylonia (538 BCE) is usually called 'Late Biblical Hebrew,' and it differs from the 'Classical' literary language of before the exile (586 BCE). Partly it appears to represent a consciously 'archaizing' imitation of the earlier language and partly, like Rabbinic Hebrew (see Sect. 3 below), a distinct, naturally developed, stage in the history of Hebrew.

When the Bible is viewed as a single work, albeit a composite of different works, it is clear that it has been written, or at least edited, from a religious perspective and with religious motives. Even so, it contains relatively little material that was composed in order to express feelings of a specifically religious character. Far more representative are historical or epic narratives, historical fiction, social polemic ('prophecy'), and detailed regulations about law, the cult, and city planning. It has been claimed that Biblical Hebrew is particularly rich in vocabulary related to, for example, farming and water-sources. But unlike the Arabic of the Qur'ān created in a state of religious fervor, Biblical Hebrew is restrained in its descriptions of and vocabulary for the divine. In short, the corpus is more concerned with a people whose religion was of major importance to it rather than with that religion itself.

Hebrew is not the only language used in the great documents of Judaism. The Palestinian and Babylonian versions of the Talmud (fifth to sixth centuries CE), excluding the Mishnah (ca. 200–225 CE), are both written mostly in Aramaic, as is the Zohar (late thirteenth century CE). Aramaic is also used for parts of the prayer book and even the Bible itself. Arabic (albeit often written in Hebrew characters) was the language of most of the great works of Jewish theology/philosophy written in territories under Muslim domination, especially Spain. Elsewhere in Europe, with the introduction of printing, Yiddish was widely employed from the sixteenth century onward for devotional, ethical, popular midrashic, and homiletic literature.

Moreover, even in biblical times, the use of Hebrew for secular (and nonliterary) purposes is attested on hundreds of inscriptions (usually very short but occasionally extensive) on seals, ostraca, graves, etc. (These provide a further corpus of 'pre-Rabbinic' Hebrew along with various manuscripts of Ecclesiasticus and the majority of the Dead Sea Scrolls.)

3. The Decline of Hebrew

The Hebrew represented by the Mishnah and other early rabbinic works (Tannaitic, or early Rabbinic, Hebrew) is generally thought to be the literary crystallization of a vernacular form of Hebrew that had existed perhaps even in pre-exilic times as a northern spoken counterpart to literary 'Biblical' Hebrew, and had already vitrually died out as a spoken language when the Mishnah was compiled in the third century CE. Rabbinic Hebrew survived for another seven centuries as a literary and scholarly dialect (Amoraic Hebrew). However, during even its early phase, Rabbinic Hebrew had to vie with Aramaic and Greek, and it is known that large Jewish communities in Egypt apparently spoke Aramaic (Elephantine) or Greek (Alexandria) exclusively. Although the testimony of Jerome in the late fourth century CE indicates a good knowledge of Hebrew among his Jewish informants, the emergence, from the third century BCE onward, of Greek and Aramaic translations/interpretations of the Bible (see *Septuagint*, *Targum*) is a sign of Hebrew's decline. Moreover, because written Hebrew gives relatively few indications of vocalization, there was a danger that unlearned Jews would forget even how to read their Scriptures properly let alone understand them. The situation was made yet more difficult by the existence of versions of the Bible containing different readings of the consonantal text and contentious interpretations of passages by the emerging Christian movement.

4. The Masoretes

The sixth to eighth centuries saw a flowering of activity among various schools of Masoretes ('bearers of tradition'), who can perhaps be regarded as religiously motivated linguistic theorists (see *Masoretic Tradition*). Their aim was to safeguard against corruption of the consonantal text and to provide a system of 'pointing' the basically consonantal Hebrew script to represent how it was to be pronounced at both segmental and suprasegmental levels. One of the systems developed by the Masoretes of Tiberias became dominant and is used in the oldest surviving undamaged manuscript of the whole Hebrew Bible. This document, *Codex Leningradensis* (*Firkowitsch I*) *B19*^{A} from 1008–09, is standardly reproduced in critical editions of the Hebrew Bible. Much earlier texts of parts of the Bible also exist, most notably the second century BCE Isaiah Scroll from Qumran Cave 1 (unpointed). Texts employing other Masoretic traditions have also survived, and different pronunciations of Hebrew, as well as different trends in morphology, etc., are represented by the various communities of the diaspora (e.g., Ashkenazic, Sephardic, Yemenite).

5. Hebrew in the Diaspora

After its complete demise as the day-to-day spoken language of the Jewish people and until its twentieth-century revitalization as the principal language of the modern State of Israel, Hebrew survived as a language spoken and written by Jews in most diaspora communities in synagogue worship and religious texts. Hebrew was used, for example, in ceremonial documents, such as Torah scrolls, Passover *haggādōt*, and texts inside phylacteries and *mĕzūzōt*, as well as in synagogue and grave inscriptions. With the exception of the sermon and the prayer for the Royal Family (in the UK), Orthodox synagogue services are conducted throughout the world in Hebrew. Elementary Hebrew is traditionally taught to children in a *heder* or 'synagogue-school.' All orthodox Jewish males have to be sufficiently competent in Hebrew to read out loud a portion of Scripture at the age of *bar-mitzvā* (13 years), and, thereafter, when called upon, at ordinary synagogue services. Note as well that Hebrew is imparted within the family in the context of festivals like Passover and *Hanukkah*. At a much more advanced level, Hebrew is also used for instruction within rabbinic academies (*yĕshībhōt*).

5.1 Literature

The use of Hebrew by Jewish writers never died out, even though its geographical center shifted through time in accordance with the fate of Jewish communities in different countries. For example, in France, Rashi, the great eleventh-century Bible and Talmud commentator, wrote in Hebrew. Indeed, the 'dynamic' of Hebrew—the cause of its internal developments and its ability to adapt to new circumstances, most notably the need to provide a language for what would become the State of Israel—has been one of literature, not speech. In the twelfth to thirteenth centuries CE, for example, the Ibn Tibbon family, through their translations of Arabic works, accommodated Hebrew to the expression of a wide range of philosophical and scientific topics. Although medieval and earlier literature is frequently religious (including material written at relatively short notice, such as *responsa* to problems arising within particular communities), there is also a wealth of Hebrew poetry, especially from Andalusia, on profane themes.

5.2. Secular Contexts

To a limited extent, Hebrew was also used as a lingua franca for Jews from different parts of the world, as well as in correspondence and in credit notes, contracts, and other commercial and legal documents within Jewish communities. Records of the Spanish Inquisition attest to the use of Hebrew in oaths, etc., by forced converts to Christianity. From the late eighteenth century, the widespread use of Hebrew for secular composition developed with the *Haśkālā* or Jewish 'Enlightenment.' This had less to do with Hebrew's status as a lingua franca than with the Enlightenment's negative view of the Yiddish dialects of European Jewry, associated by the reformers with the socially disadvantaged status of Jews and their allegedly low level of cultural achievement. It has also been claimed that Hebrew was in daily use in Palestine during the nineteenth century.

6. Hebrew in Other Languages

Jews have normally spoken the dominant language of their host community, although in pre-modern times specifically Jewish vernaculars have usually emerged (Yiddish, Ladino, etc.), with varying degrees of literary, educational, and formal social functions, and with significant influence from Hebrew not only in vocabulary and phraseology but also in morphology and syntax. Where such a development has not taken place, or where a Jewish language/dialect has been superseded by the dominant language, it is in most cases misleading to speak of a Jewish dialect (or sociolect) of a non-Jewish language. But in this situation, Jews continue to use a number of Hebrew expressions for items of Jewish culture (e.g., *siddūr* 'prayer book,' *tĕphillīn* 'phylacteries,' *tallīt* 'prayer-shawl') and in particular contexts (e.g., *mazzāl tōbh* 'congratulations'). The Israeli pronunciation given here represents that used by younger members of

Jewish communities, who also tend to use more Hebrew expressions. But the Hebrew pronunciation of older Jews and their vocabulary often reflects that of the Jewish language/dialect once used by themselves or their parents (e.g., Ashkenazic/kōshēr/for Israeli/kāsh' ēr/'kosher,' Yiddish *shul* for Hebrew *bēt-kĕneset* 'synagogue').

Classical Hebrew has left a few direct traces in the religious vocabulary of other languages, although this has been through the medium of Bible translations rather than that of Jewish communities (e.g., *hallelujah, amen, behemoth, shibboleth*). In the occult, various terms, for example, names for God and other supernatural beings, have been taken over, often in garbled form, from Hebrew. More significantly, the vocabulary and phraseology of the languages of Christian countries have been influenced in a variety of ways by loan-translations from Hebrew via prestigious early, fairly literal, vernacular translations of the Bible. Hebrew also underlies many 'Christian' names (e.g., *Isabel, David, John, Jeremy, Sarah*), and is encountered in some Jewish surnames (e.g., *Cohen, Levi, Rabinowitz*).

7. The study of Hebrew Within Christianity

Historically, Hebrew has gained the scholarly attention of Christians wanting to gain a better understanding of the Old Testament or to facilitate attempts at conversion of the Jews. Until the beginning of modern 'scientific' analysis of the Bible, few non-Jewish scholars could have claimed a familiarity with Hebrew or the ability to contribute to its linguistic analysis on anything approaching the scale of the medieval Jewish grammarians. But it is possible that their efforts aided the long survival of Hebrew, and it is in large measure due to them that Hebrew, elementary Biblical Hebrew at least, still finds a place in the curricula of many universities.

See also: Judaism; Hebrew Grammarians; Hebrew.

Bibliography

Aronoff M 1985 Orthography and linguistic theory: The syntactic basis of Masoretic Hebrew punctuation. *Lg* **61**: 28–72

Caird G B 1980 *The Language and Imagery of the Bible*. Duckworth, London

Davis M D 1888 *Hebrew Deeds of English Jews before 1290*. Jewish Chronicle, London

Horbury W (ed.) 1999 *Hebrew Study from Ezra to Ben-Yehuda*. T & T Clark, Edinburgh

Joüon P 1993 *A Grammar of Biblical Hebrew* (Corrected rev. ed.; trans. and ed. by T. Muraoka). Editrice Pontificio Istituto Biblico, Roma

Koehler L, Baumgartner W 1994–2000 *The Hebrew and Aramaic Lexicon of the Old Testament*. E.J. Brill, Leiden

Kutscher E Y 1982 *A History of the Hebrew Language*. Magnes Press, Jerusalem

Parfitt T V 1972 The use of Hebrew in Palestine 1800–1882. *Journal of Semitic Studies* **17**: 237–52

Sáenz-Badillos Á 1993 *History of the Hebrew Language*. Cambridge University Press, Cambridge

Pérez Fernández M 1997 *An Introductory Grammar of Rabbinic Hebrew*. E.J. Brill, Leiden

Korean

J. H. Grayson

The Korean language, a member of the Altaic family of languages, is spoken as a native language by peoples of Korean ethnic derivation living in the Korean peninsula, southern and eastern Manchuria, the Russian Far East (eastern Siberia), Kazakhstan, Japan, North America, and in other communities scattered throughout the world. The total number of speakers of the Korean language now numbers over 69 million persons, more than 67 million of whom live on the Korean peninsula. Based upon the subcultural regions of the Korean peninsula, there are six principal dialects, the dialects of the northeastern, northwestern, central, southeastern, and southwestern regions plus the dialect spoken on the island of Cheju. The latter dialect shows marked differences from the language spoken on the Korean mainland. As the language spoken by a people of a culture stretching back for nearly two millennia, the Korean language possesses a rich body of literature.

The Korean language is a nontonal, polysyllabic, agglutinative language belonging to the Altaic family and probably closely related to the Manchu and Tungus members of that language family. The only modern, major language to which Korean would appear to be related is Japanese, but the two languages—although similar in most respects grammatically—are significantly different phonologically. Korean and Japanese are therefore linguistic isolates because of the lack of source material to demonstrate the precise linguistic connections between themselves, and with the members of the Altaic family.

Throughout the vocabulary of Korean, there exists a parallel set of Korean and Sino-Korean vocabulary. Mention must be made of the existence of two systems of counting. This feature carries throughout the entirety of the Korean lexicon. Often, but not exclusively by any means, Sino–Korean words are used to name objects or subjects of discourse, whilst Korean words have a descriptive function. On some occasions, there is no preference in the use of one or the other type of vocabulary, in other instances it is a matter of honorific or nonhonorific usage. With regard to time, hours are given in Sino–Korean numbers, whilst minutes are given in Korean numbers. Again, duration of time (i.e., 'it took one hour to go home') is given using Korean numerals.

Notwithstanding the enormous impact which Sinitic vocabulary has had on enriching the vocabulary of the Korean language, there has been virtually no influence from Chinese on the grammar of Korean. This is possibly because Chinese and Korean derive from two radically different language families.

Although Korea is a full member of the Chinese cultural sphere, the language spoken in modern Korea and its ancient antecedents spoken in the early states of Koguryŏ, Paekche, and Silla are significantly distinct from both ancient and modern Chinese. Whereas ancient and modern Chinese are tonal, monosyllabic languages with a comparatively simple syntax, ancient and modern Korean are highly agglutinative, polysyllabic languages with an extraordinarily complex syntax. Two languages could hardly be more different than Chinese and Korean. Because of the prestige of Chinese civilization, when the ancient Korean states accepted the culture of their great neighbor, the canons of written Chinese and the Chinese writing system were both adopted. It was obvious from the first that considerable adaptations would have to be made to the Chinese writing system to make it suitable for transcribing the structure of Korean. The history of writing in Korea is essentially the attempt to write Korean using a script designed for a radically different language.

Three systems were used for writing Korean before the development of a true alphabet in the fifteenth century. These were the *idu*, *hyangch'al*, and *kugyŏl* scripts. These scripts were not, however, the first attempt to write Korean words. One of the oldest Korean historical sources before the advent of the early writing systems was the great stele erected in 414 to King Kwanggaet'o of Koguryŏ (reigned 391–412) which is written with Chinese characters and uses Chinese syntax. What distinguishes this monument from Chinese monuments of the period is the occurrence of a set of more than 100 Chinese characters which are used to represent phonologically the sounds of personal names, place names, and official titles. Using Chinese characters in this way was not unique to Koguryŏ, as the Chinese themselves used a certain set or sets of characters for the purpose of transcribing foreign words and names. This type of system, however, is not a true transcription system for the Korean language. Significantly, the same set of characters used for transcription purposes on the Kwanggaet'o monument was used for the same purpose at a later date in Paekche, Silla, and Japan.

The earliest writing system for which there is firm evidence is *idu*. This system was used primarily for the purpose of prose transcription, whereas *hyangch'al* and *kugyŏl* were used for poetic transcription and transcription for translation and interpretative functions, respectively.

The twelfth-century historical work, the *Samguk sagi* ('History of the Three Kingdoms'), indicates that the *hyangch'al* writing system was used from at least the ninth century, and it is entirely probable that it may have been used much earlier. Nonetheless, the earliest extant examples of this system of writing occur in an eleventh-century eulogy of a Buddhist monk, the *Kyunyŏ-jŏn*.

The *kugyŏl* system attempted to give a complete and accurate representation of the underlying Korean sentence and as such this system of transcription was used especially for the elucidation and interpretation of Buddhist scriptures and Confucian philosophical works. As with *hyangch'al*, there is no extant documentation for the early use of this transcription system, although its use as far back as the seventh century has been postulated by some authorities. The earliest records of *kugyŏl* are marginal notes in a copy of the Buddhist scripture, the *Inwang-gyŏng* (Chinese, *Jênwang Ching*, 'Sutra of the Benevolent King'), dated to the fifteenth century.

A text which is rendered in the *kugyŏl* system has two elements: the Chinese character textual material itself and a marginal system of annotation to transform the textual material into a piece of Korean prose. The latter element is the *kugyŏl* system proper. In this system of writing, parts of Chinese characters are used for phonetic purposes to transcribe Korean morphemes and to annotate a given text. This is obviously a development from the original use of Chinese characters to provide the phonetic values of Korean words, but in this case the characters have been abbreviated to provide a set of phonetic symbols. This system resembles the Japanese *kana* syllabaries both in function and in form and, indeed, the *kanbun kundoku* system of annotation in Japanese for which there is documentary evidence from 828, is very similar to the Korean *kugyŏl* writing system.

See also: Ross, J.; Christianity in East Asia.

Bibliography

Buzo A 1980 Early Korean writing systems. *Transactions of the Royal Asiatic Society, Korea Branch* **55**
Ch'oe H 1942 *Han'gŭl kal.* Seoŭl

Cho S B 1967 *A Phonological Study of Korean With a Historical Analysis*. Uppsala
Hulbert H B 1905 *A Comparative Grammar of the Korean Language and the Dravidian Dialects of India*. The Methodist Publishing House, Seoul
Kanazawa S 1910 *The Common Origin of the Japanese and Korean Languages*. Sanseido, Tokyo
Kim C-W 1965 On the autonomy of the tensity feature in stop classification: With special reference to Korean stops. *Word* **21**: 339–59
Kim C-W 1968 The vowel system of Korean. *Language* **44**: 516–27
Kim C-W 1972 Regularity of the so-called irregular verbs in Korean. In: Kisserberth C W (ed.) *Studies in Generative Phonology*. Linguistic Research Inc, Edmonton
Kim C-W 1974 The making of the Korean language. *Korea Journal* **14(8)**: 4–17
Kim K 1961 Idu yŏn'gu *Asea yŏn'gu* **4(1)**
Kim M 1957 *Chuhae Hunmin chŏngŭm*. Seoul
Konsevič L R 1965 Pervyi pamjatnik koreiskoi pis'mennosti. *Narody Asii i Afriki* **4**
Lee H H B 1989 *Korean Grammar*. Oxford University Press, Oxford
Lee K 1971 Formation of the Korean language. *Korea Journal* **11(12)**
Lee S B 1957 *The Origins of the Korean Alphabet*. National Museum of Korea, Seoul
Martin S E 1951 Korean phonemics. *Lg* **27**: 519–33
Martin S E 1954 *Korean Morphophonemics*. Linguistic Society of America, Baltimore, MD
Martin S E 1966 Lexical evidence relating Korean to Japanese. *Language* **42**: 185–251
Martin S E 1968 Grammatical evidence relating Korean to Japanese. In: *Proceedings of the 8th Congress of Anthropological and Ethnological Sciences*
Mazur I N 1960 *Koreiskii iazyk*. Izd. vostočnoj literary, Moscow
Nam P 1975 Hanja ch'ayong p'yogibŏp ŭi paltal. *Kungmun hangnon-jip* **7–8**
Ramstedt G J 1933 The nominal post-positions in Korean. In: *Mémoires de la Société Finno–Ougrienne* **67**
Ramstedt G J 1939 *A Korean Grammar*. Suomalais–ugrilainen seurs, Helsinki
Ramstedt G J 1949–53 *Studies in Korean Etymology*, Mémoires de la Société Finno–Ougrienne, no. 95, 2 vols. Helsinki
Rosén S 1974 *A Study on Tones and Tonemarks in Middle Korean*. Orientaliska Institute Stockholm University, Stockholm
Yi K 1972 *Kugŏ-sa kaesŏl kaejŏng p'an*. Seoul

Ogam

J. M. Y. Simpson

Ogam or Ogham is an encoding of the roman alphabet by means of notches cut on stone slabs. It was principally used for writing Old Irish. Some 300 Old Irish inscriptions in Ogam are to be found in Ireland (principally in the southwest), but an additional 57 are outside Ireland, 40 being in Wales and the remainder in England, the Isle of Man, and Scotland. The majority probably date from the fifth and sixth centuries CE, though some may be from a century or more later. The existence of such inscriptions outside Ireland makes it possible to argue for the continuing presence of Irish-speaking colonies in western southern Britain until the sixth or even the seventh centuries (Jackson 1953: 171).

These inscriptions are in general very short and the language is purely funerary, being limited usually to a personal name; they are therefore of limited philological value.

Ogam is also used in some two dozen inscriptions in Pictish, all in Scotland. None of these is intelligible. However, it has recently been claimed (Cox 1999) that the language of these is not Pictish, but Norse.

The system was also used for divination.

The basis of encoding is highly uneconomical, consisting in numbers of straight or diagonal lines incised across one edge of a slab, or to one or other side of it. In the case of Pictish Ogam this baseline was sometimes drawn across the face of the slab. Twenty letters could be encoded in this way; they were divided into four groups, each containing from one to five similar notches (see Fig. 1).

Each letter had some kind of divinatory connotation and was associated with a tree and an animal or bird, for example, <B> with the color white, *beithe* 'birch' and *besan* 'pheasant'; <L> with light grey,

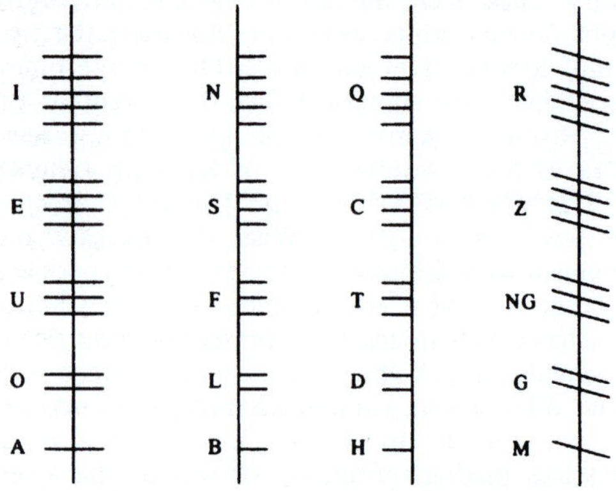

luis 'rowan' and *lacha* 'duck'. (The alphabet was, in fact, sometimes known as the *Beithe-Luis* after these two letters.) The system is reputedly named after its inventor Ogma, son of the God of Eloquence, whose name appears in Gaul as Ogmios and whose tasks included that of taking souls to the Other World.

See also: Celtic Religion.

Bibliography

Cox R A V 1999 *The Language of the Ogam Inscriptions of Scotland: Contributions to the Study of Ogam, Runic and Roman Alphabet Inscriptions in Scotland*. Department of Celtic, University of Aberdeen

Henderson I 1967 *The Picts*. Thames and Hudson, London

Jackson K H 1950 Notes on the Ogam inscriptions of southern Britain. In: Fox C, Dickins B (eds.) *The Early Cultures of North-West Europe*. Cambridge University Press, Cambridge

Jackson K H 1953 *Language and History in Early Britain: A Chronological Survey of the Brittonic Languages, 1st to 12th C.* CE. Edinburgh University Press, Edinburgh

Jackson K H 1955 The Pictish language. In: Wainwright F T (ed.) 1955

McManus D 1990 *A Guide to Ogam*. An Sagart, Maynooth

Marstrander C J et al. 1913–76 (4 vols) *Dictionary of the Irish Language*. Dublin

Price G 1984 *The Languages of Britain*. Edward Arnold, London

Wainwright F T (ed.) 1955 *The Problem of the Picts*. Nelson, Edinburgh

Old Church Slavonic

C. M. MacRobert

Old Church Slavonic is the earliest Slavonic literary language. It was first used in the ninth century as the vehicle of translations and original compositions by SS Cyril and Methodius (see *Cyril and Methodius*) and their associates for the benefit of the Slav peoples who had recently accepted Christianity. Some of these texts have survived in copies of the late tenth and eleventh centuries, which are the prime source of information about the language.

The sound system implied by the two alphabets, Glagolitic and Cyrillic, in which Old Church Slavonic was written, antedates certain radical changes in the phonology of the Slavonic languages which took place between the tenth and twelfth centuries. Many grammatical forms used in Old Church Slavonic manuscripts are also highly conservative. The evidence of Old Church Slavonic therefore has considerable weight in attempts to reconstruct the Common Slavonic proto-language and to elucidate the relationship between Slavonic and other Indo-European languages.

Old Church Slavonic is the main source of information about the early history of the South-East Slavonic languages. As natives of Saloniki, SS Cyril and Methodius doubtless spoke the local variety of Slavonic. There is some ground for supposing that during their work in Moravia (863–885 CE) they may have adopted some West Slavonic linguistic features; but the manuscripts of South Slavonic origin from which the information about Old Church Slavonic is largely derived at best preserve only traces of such a hybrid usage, for the most part reflecting the Slavonic dialects of the Southeast Balkans.

From its inception, however, Old Church Slavonic must have differed from contemporary spoken varieties of Slavonic, as it was used primarily to translate Scriptural, liturgical and patristic texts from Greek and, sometimes, from Latin and Old High German. Comparison with Greek shows that the translations aimed at faithfulness: while the grammatical forms and most of the words and semantic distinctions were Slavonic, the syntax mirrored Greek constructions, apart from a specific range of exceptions where imitation of Greek would presumably have led to unacceptable results. The compound word-formations of Greek were also frequently reproduced in Old Church Slavonic, and even pronunciation may have been modified to accommodate Greek loan-words. Texts believed to be original Old Church Slavonic compositions display the same type of language, which can be characterized as a compromise between early Slavonic idiom and Greek literary usage in a balance so delicate that it was not subsequently maintained (see *Church Slavonic*).

See also: Christianity in Europe; Cyril and Methodius.

Bibliography

Aitzetmüller R 1978 *Altbulgarische Grammatik als Einführung in die slavische Sprachwissenschaft*. U. W. Weiher, Freiburg

Grünenthal O 1910–1911 Die Übersetzungstechnik der altkirchenslavischen Evangelienübersetzung. *Archiv für slavische Philologie* **31**: 321–66, 507–29; **32**: 1–48

Lunt H G 1974 *Old Church Slavonic Grammar*, 6th edn. Mouton, The Hague

Vlasto A P 1970 *The Entry of the Slavs into Christendom*. Cambridge University Press, Cambridge

Pahlavi

A. V. Williams

Pahlavi is generally synonymous with the term 'Middle Persian,' i.e., the language of the Sasanians (224–651 CE) and their subjects in the province of Fars in southwest Iran. It was imposed by the Sasanian authorities as the sole official language of Iran and consequently it became the living language of the state religion, Zoroastrianism. More specifically, 'Pahlavi' (Book Pahlavi) is the name given to the medieval language in which Zoroastrian religious texts were written down in the Sasanian and early Islamic periods until the tenth century. It may be compared with the other main Middle Iranian dialects: Parthian, Sogdian, Khwarazmian, and Khotanese Saka. The earliest examples of Pahlavi script are found in rock inscriptions and on coins from the Parthian and early Sasanian periods. The orthographical system was derived from the western semitic consonantal script of Aramaic, the court language of the Achaemenian Empire. The cursive script of Book Pahlavi is full of ambiguities and corrupt forms, having only 14 letters (as compared with the 22 letters of Imperial Aramaic). For example *gimel* represents the letters *dâleṯh*, and *yôḏh*, but also the corrupt forms of *bēṯh*, *zayin*, and *kap̄h*. Combinations of these letters, accidental reduplications, and the fact that two *yôḏh* resemble both *'ālep̄h* and *sâmeḵh*, create further difficulties.

The chief characteristic of Pahlavi is that, in spite of its being phonetically purely Iranian, it mixes Semitic and Iranian words in its orthography. From an early period, writers of Pahlavi used Aramaic words as ideograms, that is, they no longer pronounced or even thought of them as Semitic words but as familiar shapes or signs only, written to convey Iranian equivalents. The Semitic words are not ideograms in the sense of Sumeric or Chinese symbolic characters, but are written with a consonantal alphabet, and so may be better termed 'heterograms,' and Iranian phonetic spellings 'eteograms' (Klíma 1968: 28). By convention, modern scholars transliterate ideograms in upper case type, phonetic spellings in lower case. Book Pahlavi is written in an almost equal mixture of Iranian eteograms (e.g., *pyt'k'* = *paydāg* 'revealed,' *gwpt'* = *guft* 'said,'—but cf. also *YMRRWNt* = *guft*) and Aramaic heterograms (e.g., *GBRA* 'man' was read and pronounced as Iranian *mard*, and *YWM* 'day' renders Iranian *rōz*). Usually verbal stems are written heterogrammatically, with Iranian phonetic inflexional endings, e.g., *YHWWNyt'* = *bawēd* 'it is.' Occasionally a word can be read as both an ideogram or as a phonetic spelling, e.g., *TWB*/*did* is like *tang*, and *LHYK*/*dūr* is identical to *lhyk*/*rahīg*. Problems of haplography and dittography blemish the manuscripts and make reading difficult: since Pahlavi was no longer a vernacular language in Islamicized Iran, nor was its script used outside the Zoroastrian religious texts after about 700 CE, copyists often did not understand what they were writing.

The greater part of Sasanian literature in Pahlavi was in fact secular poetry, but this has not survived in its original form, having been translated to suit Islamic tastes into New Persian, notably in the *Shāhnāna* of Ferdausi (c. 935–c. 1020), in Arabic script. Those who remained faithful to Zoroastrianism after the Islamic conquest (seventh century CE) continued to use Pahlavi to preserve their scriptures and religious lore in the archaic orthography which kept them obscure to all except Zoroastrians. They are of interest to the historian of religions because of the richness of their theological and mythological content, but, with a few exceptions, they are of limited literary merit. Pahlavi was a sonorous and robust language, which is recognizably the source of the characteristic mellifluous qualities of New Persian, even after centuries of arabicization.

See also: Avestan; Zoroastrianism.

Bibliography

Boyce M 1968 Middle Persian literature. In: Spuler B (ed.) *Iranistik*. E J Brill, Leiden

de Menasce J P 1983 Zoroastrian Pahlavi writings. In: Yarshater E (ed.) *Cambridge History of Iran*, vol. 3. Cambridge University Press, Cambridge

Klima O 1968 The Middle Persian era. In: Rypka J (ed.) *History of Iranian Literature*. D. Reidel, Dordrecht

MacKenzie D N 1967 Notes on the transcription of Pahlavi. *Bulletin of the School of Oriental and African Studies* **XXX**: 17–29

MacKenzie D N 1983 *A Concise Pahlavi Dictionary*. Oxford University Press, Oxford.

West E W 1904 Pahlavi literature. In: Geiger W, Kuhn E (eds.) *Grundriß der Iranischen Philologie*, vol. II, Strasbourg

Palaeography

K. A. Lowe

Palaeography (literally 'old writing') is the study of ancient and medieval handwriting. The term is generally used to refer to Greek and Latin scripts and their derivatives (all western European and American scripts), although some include Chinese and Arabic in the study.

The term 'palaeography' does not seem to have come into common use until 1708, with the publication of *Palaeographica Graeca* by Bernard de Montfaucon. First attempts to study manuscripts systematically by date and script had, however, begun at the end of the previous century with Jean Mabillon's *De Re Diplomatica* (1681), which included a section on Latin palaeography. It was not until the invention of photography in the mid-nineteenth century that the study of palaeography attracted wide interest. Photography has allowed basic materials of research to be easily reproduced, collected together from different repositories, and circulated to scholars all over the world.

Palaeography involves the study of writings on papyrus, animal skins, paper, and wax tablets (see Sect. 3.1 below). Inscriptions on other writing materials, including stone, metal, wood, clay, and slate are also of interest, especially for periods where there is no other available evidence. For example, up to the beginning of the first century BCE, the development of Latin script can be established only through inscriptions. Usually, however, inscriptions are considered to be the province of the related discipline of *epigraphy*. The technique of cutting individual letters with a chisel onto a hard surface results in a different style from writing on a flexible material such as papyrus.

The basic task of palaeography is to provide the means of dating and localizing manuscripts by establishing patterns in the development of characteristic letter-forms and abbreviations. Its study has developed as a result of work on other disciplines, most notably *diplomatics*, the investigation of the form, structure, and authenticity of charter material. Palaeography is therefore generally regarded as an auxiliary historical science, although it is now increasingly studied in its own right.

Palaeography is closely associated with *codicology*, the study of the physical manufacture of the book, for example, the nature and preparation of the material it has been written on, the ruling for script, the make-up of the material into booklets (known as *quires* or *gatherings*), and the binding. These practices vary with the time and place of production. Together with codicology, palaeography can reveal much about the methods by which a manuscript book was produced and the audience for which it was made, and even about the changing role and function of writing itself.

This article concentrates on the development of Latin script in the Middle Ages, the principles and problems underlying the study of palaeography during this period, and the value of the science to other disciplines. Space does not permit more than a brief survey of scripts. Those interested in Greek palaeography should consult Barbour (1981) or Metzger (1981). Discussion of Roman script in antiquity can be found in Ullman (1980) and Mallon (1952). Boyle (1984) provides a comprehensive bibliography on specific subjects, including a section on post-Humanistic scripts.

1. Terminology

Palaeographers have various terms for the strokes which go to make up a letter, as well as for the types of scripts themselves. The nomenclature has not been standardized, and there is still some disagreement about terminology. For example, the term *provenance* (*provenience* in America) is generally applied to a manuscript's earliest known place of preservation. Some, however, use it to designate the manuscript's place of origin (where this can be ascertained). Occasionally the term refers instead to the place where a manuscript is preserved (such as the British Library in London).

1.1 Letter-forms

The most basic stroke of a letter is the simple upright stroke, known as a *minim*. In later medieval scripts, such as Gothic, a word such as *minim* would be formed as 10 virtually identical i-strokes. This causes obvious problems for transcribers and editors, as a group of letters such as *min* could be read variously as *ium*, *vim*, *nun*, *miu*, and *uni*, among other possibilities. It is not uncommon for the scribe himself to miscount the numbers of minims in a word. An *ascender* is a letter-stroke which extends above the top of other letters, such as *l* or the upright stroke of *b*. A *descender* projects below the level of the shortest letters, such as the tail of *g* or *p*. A letter such as *p* is composed of a *stem* (the name given to a minim when it supports another part of a letter) and a *bow*, or *lobe*. A *serif* or *finial* is the name given to the fine stroke which is sometimes used to finish the main strokes of letters. A *ligature* is where two or more letters are joined together in a way which changes the appearance of either or both of them. Ligatures are often used at the end of a line where space is confined.

The script's *ductus* refers to the way in which it has been written, for example, how the letters have been formed or how carefully they have been executed. The general appearance of a hand is known as its *aspect*.

1.2 Abbreviations

Abbreviations are often of great value in ascertaining when and where a text has been written. There are many thousands of different abbreviations, and it is often very difficult to know how to expand them. They fall into three major categories or types: suspensions, contractions, and abbreviations symbols.

A *suspension* is where one or more letters at the end of a word have been omitted. A *contraction* is where a letter or letters have been omitted from elsewhere in the word. *Abbreviation symbols* are often used to replace whole words, such as ⁊ for *and* or *et*, and ÷ for *est*. Some scripts are much more heavily abbreviated than others.

1.3 Dating Conventions

Palaeographers usually employ a system for indicating the approximate date of a script based on the word *saeculo*, abbreviated to *s.*, followed by the century in lower-case Roman numerals (thus s.ix for ninth century). Where more specific dating limits can be arrived at, the conventions are generally as follows: s.ix^{1} (first half of the ninth century); s.ix^{2} (second half of the ninth century); s.ix^{in} (for *ineunte*: beginning of the ninth century); s.ix^{ex} (for *exeunte*: end of the ninth century); s.ix^{med} (for *medio*: middle of the ninth century); s.ix/s.x (indicates the turn of the century). Dating information such as s.ix–s.x indicates no more than that the text was written at some stage during the ninth or tenth centuries.

1.3.1 Dated and Datable Texts

A distinction should also be made between dated and datable texts. Few medieval manuscripts are reliably dated. This is particularly the case in the early medieval period. A *datable* text is one in which the date (or, more frequently, dating limits) can be reliably established by external information. For example, a royal *diploma* (a document recording grants of land or of privileges to religious foundations or individuals) can often be dated quite closely, first by the regnal dates of the monarch in whose name it is written, and second by the persons cited in the witness-list. A later medieval manuscript may similarly contain references within the text to known individuals, or name the person for whom the manuscript was written. An inscription which records details in the manuscript such as the name of the scribe and the date or place of production is known as a *colophon*. As colophons are sometimes later additions to a manuscript, they cannot be relied upon to provide accurate information.

1.4 Grades of Script

Palaeographers make initial distinctions between scripts based on their aspect. Scripts can, for example, be broadly described as *calligraphic* or *cursive*, *majuscule* or *minuscule*.

1.4.1 Calligraphic and Cursive

In *calligraphic* script, individual letters or parts of a letter are formed separately. The sequence of strokes making up each letter is rigorously followed and executed. It is thus a *constructed* script. Examples of calligraphic scripts are Uncial (see Sect. 2.2 below), Caroline minuscule (Sect. 2.5), and Textualis (Sect. 2.6.1). These scripts are written with a broad quill and are known generically as *bookhands*, formal scripts which are deliberately and carefully produced. A *cursive* script is one in which more than one part of a letter is made in a single stroke. Letters are joined together without the writing instrument (generally a finer quill) being lifted from the writing surface. Cursive scripts are generally informal and utilitarian. They are sometimes known as *charter-hands*. Such a distinction can, however, be misleading, as some charters are written in bookhand, and some books in a more cursive script. There are many intermediate grades between the extremes of calligraphic and cursive.

1.4.2 Majuscule and Minuscule

The Latin alphabet existed originally in majuscule script, in which the letters are all of the same height. *Majuscule* scripts are those which correspond to the printer's uppercase letters, that is, confined between two parallel lines. A majuscule script is therefore a *bilinear* script. Capitalis (see Sect. 2.1 below) and Uncial (Sect. 2.2) are examples of majuscule script. A *minuscule* script is one which corresponds to the printer's lower-case letters, and includes ascenders and descenders. It is thus a *quattrolinear* script.

2. Latin Script in the Middle Ages

By the third century CE, formal bookhands existed alongside cursive forms of both majuscule and minuscule script. From these scripts were developed the new bookhands of Uncial and Half-Uncial during the late Antique period and the Continental minuscule scripts of the Middle Ages.

2.1 Capitalis

The most highly revered script during the late Antique period was that of Capitalis, which had two basic varieties. Square Capitals (*Capitalis Quadrata*) was originally used for monumental inscriptions and was restricted in use to very high-grade manuscripts. Canonical Capitals (also known, rather misleadingly, as Rustic Capitals or *Capitalis Rustica*) was more fluidly written and therefore more suitable for the pen (see Fig. 1). From the fifth century onward, Capitalis seems to have been reserved as a distinguishing script used for running titles and where special emphasis was required. It was still used in this way into the twelfth century.

2.2 Uncial

Capitalis seems to have been superseded in popularity as a text hand by Uncial, a broader, more rounded script which became widely diffused after the fourth century (see Fig. 2). The term itself is attributed to St Jerome, who criticized the script for its luxury status and waste of space, with letters as much as an inch high ('uncial') written on expensive material. Uncial appears to have been the most popular script for copying a text from about the fifth until well into the eighth century, although its use was generally confined to gospel and some liturgical books. Elsewhere it was used, like Capitalis and often in conjunction with it, as a display script. Although in many cases the ascenders and descenders in Uncial extend beyond the head and baseline, early examples show the script to be virtually confined between two lines. The script may therefore be considered majuscule. Abbreviations are rare.

2.3 Half-Uncial

Despite its name, Half-Uncial is no longer believed to have developed from Uncial, but from a common ancestor, the Roman cursive minuscule. During the Middle Ages, it rivaled Uncial in popularity in some centers, especially in Anglo–Saxon England, where Insular Half-Uncial became a characteristic and influential script. *Insular* is the name given jointly to the Irish and Anglo–Saxon system of scripts in the early Middle Ages, emphasizing the close interaction between the two countries during this period. Opinions vary as to whether Half-Uncial should be considered a majuscule or minuscule script. Half-Uncial is very important in the development of national scripts (see Fig. 3).

2.4 National Scripts

After the disintegration of the Roman Empire, various regional minuscule scripts were developed in western Europe from Roman cursive minuscule as well as distinct forms of the Half-Uncial scripts. In many cases, one can distinguish between scripts of various centers (such as Corbie, St Gall, Fleurie,

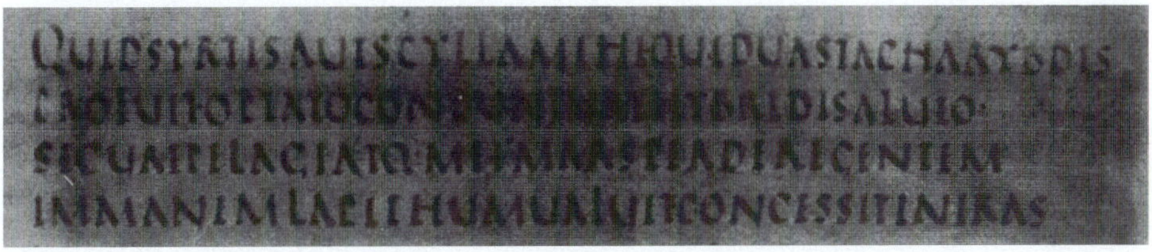

Figure 1. Canonical Capitalis (from Vatican City, Biblioteca Apostolica Vaticana, Vat. Lat. 3225, fo. 64).

Figure 2. Uncial (from London, British Library, Harley 1775, fo. 193), s. vi.

Bobbio, and Luxeuil) and phases of development within these centers. These scripts evolved during the fifth and sixth centuries and lasted until the development of Caroline minuscule in the ninth century. Some national hands lasted longer: Visigothic minuscule (in Spain) survived until the twelfth century, and Anglo–Saxon minuscule until the middle of that century, and Beneventan minuscule survived in parts of southern Italy into the fifteenth century. The endurance of these scripts may be attributed to a greater measure of political independence.

2.5 Caroline Minuscule

By the beginning of the ninth century, there were many regional minuscule scripts. From the ninth to the twelfth century, however, an international script was developed and eventually predominated over regional scripts. Caroline minuscule takes its name from the Emperor Charlemagne (771–814). Its development is closely associated with his extensive educational and ecclesiastical reforms, which led to a wider dissemination of texts. There is considerable debate about the precise origins of Caroline minuscule, but its obvious advantages over many of the regional scripts—it was clear, regular, and balanced—led to the gradual adoption of this disciplined and elegant script across Europe. In England, Caroline minuscule script was generally reserved for Latin texts. Old English texts continued to be written in Anglo–Saxon minuscule. Elsewhere, the script was used for both book and documentary purposes. Caroline minuscule was a calligraphic script and was therefore comparatively slow to write and hard to execute (see Fig. 4).

2.6 Gothic Scripts

From the tenth to the twelfth century, Caroline minuscule underwent gradual changes, with the script becoming more angular, compact, and vertical in appearance. These changes became marked during the twelfth century, and a new type of script, Gothic, evolved at the end of that century which was uniform and consciously systematic in character. Both calligraphic and cursive forms were evolved. Gothic

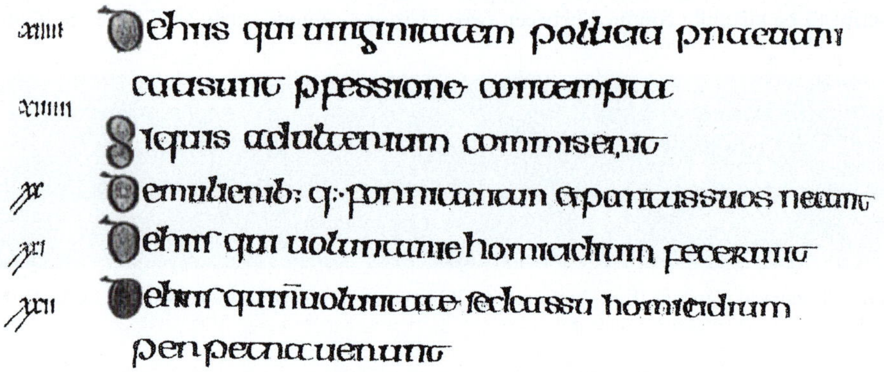

Figure 3. Half-Uncial (from Cologne, Diözesan- u. Dombibliothek, 213, fo. 19v), s. viii.

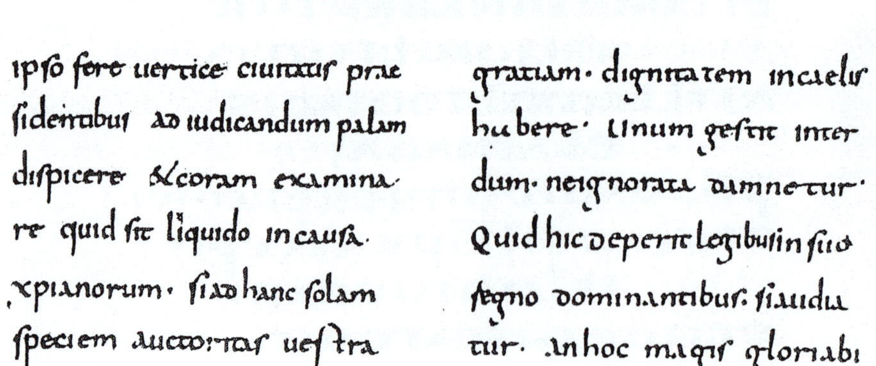

Figure 4. Caroline minuscule (from Leningrad, Publichnaya Biblioteka im. M.E. Saltikova-Shchedrina, Q.v.1.40, fo. 1), s. viii–ix.

scripts were used throughout much of Europe into the sixteenth century.

2.6.1 Textualis

The calligraphic range of Gothic scripts is known as *textualis*, with four grades of script: *prescissa* (used only in the most luxurious manuscripts), *quadrata* (see Fig. 5), *semiquadrata*, and *rotunda* (the lowest grade). This hierarchy of scripts was carefully observed. Differences between these grades consisted mainly in the addition of approach and finishing strokes to the letters and the treatment of minims. Textualis was adopted as a font by early printers, and in the twentieth century is known as black letter. As a calligraphic script, it was painstakingly slow and difficult to write, and increasingly became more artificial. It was used for liturgical volumes and other high-quality manuscripts.

2.6.2 Gothic Cursive and Bastard Scripts

From the end of the twelfth century in England, a cursive Gothic script (*Anglicana cursive*) used for documents was developed, and other areas soon developed their own forms of cursive script. From the end of the thirteenth century, cursive Gothic scripts were also used for books. They were often highly compressed and abbreviated, making them suitable for texts which had to be produced quickly and cheaply. Gradually, *bastard* scripts (less picturesquely known as *hybrid*) were introduced. These combined aspects of both Textualis and the cursive varieties, thus narrowing the gap between the two categories of Gothic script. The Textualis series of scripts, which seems to have become too difficult for anyone other than the best scribes to execute well, was supplanted by these compromise scripts from the end of the fourteenth century. Its use thereafter was restricted to display purposes.

2.7 Humanistic Scripts

At the beginning of the fifteenth century, a new script was invented in Florence by scholars closely associated with the Humanist movement. This script arose from a dissatisfaction with the Gothic series of scripts, which had become hard to read and cramped. The result, a range of Humanistic scripts, is clearer and more legible than Gothic and is a development from a twelfth-century Italian variant of Caroline minuscule. The range of scripts includes a formal and modified cursive book script and a cursive form initially intended for documentary use. The system spread from Italy into the rest of Europe from the later fifteenth century, and was adopted by early printers. The late twentieth-century Roman font is derived from the Humanistic book-hand, and the cursive variety was the model for modern *Italic* fonts.

3. Literacy and the Development of Script

Changes in script, copying practice, and book production reflect changes in demand for manuscripts. The system of scripts adopted by the Romans suggests a wide variety of written forms and widespread literacy, from inscriptions and deluxe manuscripts to the informal and cursive handwriting used for administrative and business purposes. The choice of script in the post-Antique period was similarly dictated by the nature of the text to be copied, with formal, calligraphic scripts being reserved for biblical and liturgical volumes, and more cursive versions for library or schoolbooks.

The period from around 1200 constitutes something of a watershed in the history of palaeography during the Middle Ages, with secular scribes taking

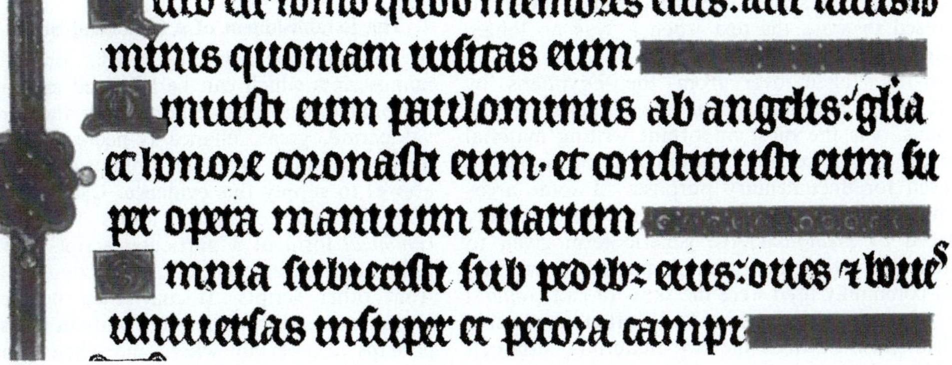

Figure 5. Textualis quadrata (from London, British Library, Additional 24686. fo. 14v), s. xiii^{ex}.

over much of the professional production of books from the religious communities. This was the result of a substantial growth in the numbers of schools and universities and the spread of lay literacy. The development of the system of cursive Gothic scripts can be seen as a response to the increased desire for the written word. Writing became part of everyday life, used for the purposes of trade and administration. From the end of the fourteenth century, there was a demand from all classes for cheap books such as romances and popular texts.

From the educational revival of the twelfth and thirteenth centuries came a more efficient method of book production alongside the new cursive Gothic scripts, devised to cater for the needs of the increased numbers of university students. In order to facilitate quick and controlled production of texts, a standard copy of a particular work would be produced by the university and deposited at a central stationer's. From there, sections (*peciae*) could be borrowed and recopied, normally by professional scribes who would be paid for their work. This would speed up the copying process, as different scribes could copy different sections of the same text at the same time. These various parts would later be assembled for distribution to the students. The *pecia* system went into decline from the fifteenth century, when university students copied much of the materials by dictation from their teachers.

3.1 Changes in Codicological Practice

The cost of production, both in the time spent executing the script and in the physical space that it occupied on the page, as has been seen, was often influential in the development and adoption of new scripts. The choice of writing material and layout used is also affected by this consideration.

Wax tablets were probably the most commonly used material for writing on during antiquity, and were used as part of daily life during the Middle Ages for correspondence, accounts, and other ephemeral documents. Letters were scratched on the surface of these tablets by a stylus. The broad end of the stylus was used to erase the text when it was no longer required.

Papyrus, taken over from the Egyptians by the Greeks and then from the Greeks by the Romans, was the most important writing material until the fourth century. Although it continued to be used for documentary purposes in some areas during the early Middle Ages, it was generally replaced by *membrane*, the generic term given to animal skin which has been prepared for writing. Most commonly used were the skins of calf (*vellum*) and of sheep (*parchment*). It is often impossible to distinguish between the two materials, although calfskins, larger in size than sheepskins, were generally reserved for deluxe manuscripts, such as liturgical and the more important service books. Such manuscripts, featuring large display scripts, wide margins, and few abbreviations, used enormous quantities of membrane. It has been estimated that the Lindisfarne Gospels, written around 700 CE in Insular Half-Uncial, would have taken 127 calfskins to produce.

As membrane was very expensive, scribes were reluctant to waste such valuable material. A text which was no longer required or considered important could be erased by washing or scraping. The manuscript could then be reused. The resulting text is known as a *palimpsest*.

Paper was introduced in the west from the thirteenth century, although it was not commonly used until after 1400. Even after the invention of printing, the use of paper was still treated with some suspicion, and the canon of the mass was often printed on membrane with the rest of the text on paper. One detractor exhorted his scribes to copy out printed texts onto membrane, remarking that the latter could survive for 1,000 years, but paper would barely last 200! Entire books were occasionally printed directly onto membrane, but the practice proved extremely costly. A copy of the Gutenberg Bible produced in this way would have used up to 300 sheepskins.

The voracious demand for texts by universities from the twelfth century onward led to a design of a book which could be more cheaply and quickly produced and which was easier to use. Manuscripts were more commonly *foliated* (in which the leaves of a manuscript are consecutively numbered), facilitating reference. *Pagination* (in which separate sides of a page are numbered, as in the modern practice) is found from the thirteenth century onward, and manuscripts first appear with indices during this period. At the same time, the space between lines narrowed, abbreviations became more frequent, and the accompanying commentary would be written in a very small glossing hand.

4. The Establishment of a Canonical Script

A palaeographer initially works on a body of manuscripts which can be localized and dated to a reasonable degree of certainty. For the early medieval period, great reliance is necessarily placed on documents such as royal diplomas (see Sect. 1.3.1 above) to supply this evidence. Using this information, the palaeographer hopes to establish the *canonical* form of a particular script, one which is fully mature, standardized, and recognizably distinct from other scripts. It may then be possible to recognize trends and developments in the script and perhaps to ascertain where and when a manuscript which cannot be dated or localized by any other means was written.

5. Survival

The principal problem facing the palaeographer is one of survival: a vast amount of evidence has been lost through historical accident. This makes it particularly difficult to assess the value of what remains.

Much material has perished through natural deterioration. Few papyrus manuscripts dating from the medieval period have survived the European climate. Many texts were not designed to be permanent: for example, the ephemera recorded on wax tablets.

Still more has been lost as a result of civil unrest. Many Anglo–Saxon churches were looted during the Danish invasions of the eighth and ninth centuries. Many manuscripts were stolen, largely because of their beautiful and costly bindings, which were often decorated with gold, silver, and gems. One (minus its binding) was sold back to an Anglo–Saxon by a unusually entrepreneurial Viking; most were never recovered.

By far the greatest disaster to befall manuscripts in England was the dissolution of the monasteries in the sixteenth century. In 1500 CE, the monastic library of Christ Church at Canterbury possessed some 2,100 volumes. Only 300 have survived to the late twentieth century. The evidence from other foundations suggests that Christ Church escaped comparatively lightly. Some manuscripts were saved due to the zeal of early antiquaries keen to find some affirmation of the Protestant faith in ancient texts. Many others, however, suffered the ignominious fate of being used to fuel bakers' ovens or wrap soap and butter. It is no exaggeration to say that many thousands of manuscripts were lost during this period.

Although ecclesiastical records were not destroyed on anything like the same scale as service books and literary manuscripts during the dissolution, few early documents are preserved in their contemporary form. Of the 1,500 or so charters dating (or purporting to date) from the Anglo–Saxon period, only about 300 survive in single-sheet form copied before the end of the eleventh century. The majority of the rest are preserved only as post-Conquest copies in *cartularies*, collections of title-deeds and documents relating to a monastery's possessions. In contrast, the majority of the 839 charters from St Gall dating from before 920 CE survive in contemporary form, thus allowing the palaeographer an opportunity to study the script of the region in depth.

6. The Value of Palaeography to Other Disciplines

The study of palaeography, of course, primarily enables one to read and approximately date a manuscript. Although it was first developed as an aid for diplomatists, the science has become extremely valuable in the wider field of cultural and ecclesiastical history. Palaeography is also an important tool in the study of textual transmission.

6.1 Palaeography and Diplomatics

The palaeographer can play a useful, if limited, role in assessing whether a single-sheet charter is likely to be an original, a contemporary, or a later copy.

The fact that a charter survives in single-sheet form is no evidence that it is original, that is, believed to have been produced at approximately the same time as the oral grant itself was made. A palaeographer cannot prove that a charter was actually written in a certain year, but can only say whether the appearance of the script is roughly consonant with the date of the charter in which it occurs. It is, however, sometimes possible to establish that a document is *not* original if the script is clearly much later than the date of the text. Caution is necessary here, as two pieces of writing produced in the same year can look generations apart, due either to the respective ages of their scribes or whether they are the output of an active monastic center or some rural backwater.

6.2 Palaeography and History

It has already been seen how new scripts can be developed in response to changing requirements. The cursive forms of the Gothic series of scripts evolved from a necessity to produce texts economically and quickly. The enormous influence of its predecessor, Caroline minuscule, reflects the power and prestige of Charlemagne's kingdom. On a smaller scale, conservatively or poorly executed scripts from a single scriptorium can reveal much about the relative importance of the foundation responsible for their production at that time. If the archive is large enough to permit identification of individual scribes, much can be deduced about the organization, efficiency, and development of monastic scriptoria in the earlier Middle Ages. In the later period, a greater amount of material survives, allowing one to trace the interests and activities of many individual scribes engaged in secular book production.

6.3 Palaeography and Textual Tradition

A knowledge of palaeography is also important in establishing a textual tradition for a particular work. A scribe copying a text which has been written in an unfamiliar language and script is likely to confuse similar letter-forms in that hand. Modern editors will sympathize with this tendency. It is also possible that he will expand abbreviations incorrectly, either making nonsense of his exemplar, or (more alarmingly) changing the sense of it completely. A palaeographer may be able to determine the script and approximate date of the copy-text used by the scribe from the errors made in transcription, and thus assess the probability that the scribe used a surviving manuscript as his direct exemplar. Similarly, errors such as *homoeoteleuton* (where a group of letters or words is omitted) or *dittography* (where a group of letters or words is repeated by accident) can also determine the relationship of one manuscript to another. Attention to the relative positions of words on a line or lines can again help to determine whether a scribe used a particular manuscript as his direct exemplar, for eye-skip is easily explained if the words omitted lie in a similar position on different lines.

The study of palaeography and codicology necessitates a return to the manuscript itself. The wise observation that records 'only speak when they are spoken to, and they will not speak to strangers' (Cheney 1973: 8) can equally well be applied to manuscripts in general, for much is lost in translation from manuscript to printed edition. Those scholars prepared and equipped to ask questions from a manuscript directly can find out a great deal about the scribe and institution responsible for its production, the interests of those for whom it was made, and the age in which it was written.

See also: Islamic Calligraphy.

Bibliography

Barbour R 1981 *Greek Literary Hands* AD *400–1600*. Clarendon Press, Oxford.

Bischoff B (transl. O Cróinín D, Ganz D) 1990 *Latin Paleography: Antiquity and the Middle Ages*. Cambridge University Press, Cambridge

Boyle L E 1984 *Medieval Latin Palaeography: A Bibliographical Introduction*. University of Toronto Press, Toronto

Brown M P 1990 *A Guide to Western Historical Scripts from Antiquity to 1600*. British Library, London

Cheney C R 1973 *Medieval Texts and Studies*. Clarendon Press, Oxford

Jackson D 1981 *The Story of Writing*. Studio Vista, London

John J J 1976 Latin palaeography. In: Powell J M (ed.) *Medieval Studies: An Introduction*. Syracuse University Press, Syracuse, NY

Mallon J 1952 *Paléographie romaine*. Instituto Antonio de Filología, Madrid

Metzger B 1981 *Manuscripts of the Greek Bible: An Introduction to Greek Palaeography*. Oxford University Press, Oxford

Reynolds L D 1974 *Scribes and Scholars: A Guide to the Transmission of Greek and Latin Literature*, 2nd edn. Clarendon Press, Oxford

Ullman B L 1980 *Ancient Writing and Its Influence*, 2nd edn. Reprinted by Toronto University Press, Toronto

Pāli

K. R. Norman

Pāli is the language of the Theravādin Buddhist canon. The original meaning of the word '*pāli*' was '(canonical) text,' as opposed to 'commentary' (*aṭṭhakathā*). Its use as the name of a particular language, attested in Thailand before the end of the seventeenth century (Pruitt 1987: 124–25), probably arose from the compound *pāli-bhāsā* being misunderstood as meaning 'Pāli language' instead of 'language of the (canonical) text.'

Pāli is a Middle Indo–Aryan dialect, or 'Prakrit.' The Theravādin commentarial tradition wrongly states that Pāli was the language spoken by the Buddha, and identifies it as the language of Magadha. Although the Buddha probably used at times an early form of that language, Māgadhī is an eastern Prakrit, whereas Pāli is predominantly western, closely resembling the language of the western versions of the Aśokan inscriptions (third century BCE).

Pāli cannot be identified with any one spoken vernacular dialect, and must be classified as a literary language. It is not of uniform structure, showing a number of archaisms, especially in verse texts where the meter prevented innovation (Geiger 1994: 1), and also anomalous morphological and phonological features. Some of these are probably traces of earlier dialects through which Buddhist teachings were transmitted, and result from shortcomings in the translation procedures employed as Buddhism spread westwards from Magadha (Norman 1989).

Following the reassertion of Sanskrit as the language of religion after Aśoka's death, the Buddhists began to transpose their texts into a variety of Sanskritized Prakrits ('Buddhist Hybrid Sanskrit'). When the Theravādin canon was written down in Ceylon (first century BCE), a number of Pāli forms had already been replaced by Sanskritizations, including some incorrect backformations (Norman 1983: 5). The wholesale restoration of Sanskrit forms ceased after the writing down of the canon.

The use of the name 'Pāli' has been extended to include the language of the chronicles and commentaries, which were written in Ceylon from the fourth century CE onwards. Sinhalese and Dravidian words appear in these and other works which were composed in Ceylon or South India, and a Dravidian origin has been postulated for certain Pāli grammatical and syntactical features (de Vreese 1980).

In Ceylon in medieval times, Pāli was influenced by Sinhalese and Sanskrit. Some works dating from that period are translations from Sinhalese, and include borrowings from that language. Lexical borrowings from Sanskrit are numerous, since the Pāli lexicons are based upon Sanskrit works. The Pāli grammarians' descriptions of the language, written in imitation of the Sanskrit grammarians, were taken as normative by scribes, who tended to 'correct' their manuscripts accordingly. Some scribes had a knowledge of Sanskrit, which led them to insert Sanskritisms into canonical texts (von Hinüber 1983: 74–75).

The introduction of Theravādin Buddhism into Southeast Asia led to the adoption of the canonical language for the writing of commentaries and chronicles there. The language of these works is also called 'Pāli' despite peculiarities in spelling and syntax, which are due to the influence of the underlying languages (Norman 1983: 6–7).

See also: Buddhist Canons: Translations; Buddhism, Indian; Buddhist Hybrid Sanskrit; Pali Canon.

Bibliography

Geiger W 1994 *Pāli Grammar*. Pali Text Society, Oxford

Hinüber O von 1983 *Beiträge zur Überlieferungsgeschichte des Buddhismus in Birma*, I, (Nachrichten der Akademie der Wissenschaften in Göttingen). Vandenhoek und Ruprecht, Göttingen

Norman K R 1983 *Pāli Literature*. Harrassowitz, Wiesbaden

Norman K R 1989 Dialect forms in Pāli. In: Caillat C (ed.) *Dialectes dans les littératures indo-aryennes*. Institut de Civilisation Indienne, Paris

Pruitt W 1987 References to Pāli in 17th-century French books. *Journal of the Pali Text Society* **XI**: 121–31.

Vreese K de 1980 Dravidian idioms in later Pali. *Orientalia Lovaniensia Periodica* **11**: 179–222.

Panjabi

C. Shackle

Panjabi (also spelt 'Punjabi') is the Indo–Aryan (IA) language spoken to the northwest of the Hindi area, in the plains of the Panjab traversed by the five great tributaries of the Indus (Persian *panj āb* 'five rivers'), divided since 1947 between India and Pakistan. Within IA, many shared features align Panjabi (Pj) with Hindi (H), while its uncertain western boundary is with the awkwardly distinguished 'Lahnda' dialect-group. Numbers of speakers must be extrapolated from census statistics with unusual caution, given the artificial reduction of the Indian figures by Hindu Panjabi-speakers opting for Hindi, and inflation of Pakistani returns by inclusion of 'Lahnda'-speakers. Rough estimates (1981) indicate some 20,000,000 for India and 25,000,000 for Pakistan, besides a substantial diaspora, perhaps approaching 1,000,000 in the UK.

Panjabi is first recorded in the *Ādi Granth* (1604), the Sikh scripture written in the Gurmukhi script, which includes material dating from at least the fifteenth century. Many of the archaic features of the 'Old Panjabi' which forms but one element of its mixed language are no longer apparent in the Panjabi literature of the classic period (1650–1800), mostly written by Muslim authors and recorded in the Perso–Urdu script.

1. Distinctive Characteristics

Panjabi (Shackle 2001) is notably distinguished within IA by its phonology. It shares only with some other northwestern languages the conservative retention of Middle IA geminates after short vowels, e.g., Pj *uccā* 'high,' *miṭṭhā* 'sweet' (Sans *ucca-*, *mṛṣṭa-* > Pkt *miṭṭhā-*), elsewhere simplified with compensatory vowel-lengthening as in H *ūṃcā*, *mīṭhā*.

Panjabi is best known to linguists for its system of tones (Sandhu 1968). As in the neighboring 'West Pahari' Himalayan dialects, these tones result from the loss of historical IA voiced aspirates (still written in both the Gurmukhi and Perso–Urdu scripts). Post-tonic voiced aspirates are replaced by the high-falling tone, hence written *koṛhā* 'leper,' *bāhar* 'outside,' but phonetic /koˊɽa, baˊr/. Pretonic voiced aspirates are replaced by the low-rising tone, involving a devoicing of the consonant only partially obscured by glottal constriction, so written *ghoṛā* 'horse,' *bhār* 'load' represent phonetic /k‘oˋɽa, p‘aˋr/. Three-way contrasts are completed by words with the simple stress, e.g., written *koṛā* 'whip,' *bār* 'upland,' *pār* 'across,' phonetically /ˈkoɽa, bar, par/. This stress (sometimes called the 'mid-tone') is notably heavier than in Hindi, and when non-initial frequently results in weakening or loss of pretonic vowels, e.g., Pj /bəˈmar/ 'ill,' /ˈkəʈʈha/ 'together,' versus H /biˈmar, ɪˈkəʈʈha/.

Other conservative features of Panjabi, now lost in Hindi, include the maintained distinction between /n/ and /—ɳ/, e.g., *man* 'mind,' *maṇ* 'mound'; the survival of numerous locative-instrumentals, e.g., *hatthe* 'in the hand,' PL *hatthīṃ* 'with the hands,' besides many irregular past participles, e.g., *khādhā* 'ate,' *pītā* 'drunk'; and the preservation of full feminine concord for modifiers and verbs. The consequent prevalence of the feminine plural marker -*āṃ* (also marking all oblique plurals) is shown in /o´nã dıã t'i 'ã tʊ'a `ḍe nal t'ʊ`ppe 'kədõ tək ræ´ ɳgıã/ 'How long will their daughters stay in the sun with you?' ('their-daughters your-with sun-in when-till remain-will'), whose written form *uhnāṃ dīāṃ dhīāṃ tuhāḍe nāl dhuppe kadoṃ tak rahiṇgīāṃ* may be compared with the syntactically identical H *unkī beṭiyāṃ āpke sāth dhūp meṃ kab tak raheṃgī.*

2. Modern Panjabi

The official language of the Panjab throughout the British period (1849–1947) was Urdu. From the 1870s Sikh reformists began to promulgate a standard Panjabi written in Gurmukhi script as the appropriate language for modern Sikhism. Effectively confined to the Sikhs, since Panjabi-speaking Hindus came increasingly to identify their cultural language as Hindi, this modern standard Panjabi (Gill and Gleason 1969) is one of the official languages of India, and was finally recognized as the state language of the truncated Sikh-majority Indian Panjab which emerged in 1966 after its uneasy partition from the Hindu-majority 'Hindi' state of Haryana. In Jammu to the north, the Dogri dialect written in Nagari is being promoted as an independent standard.

In Pakistan Panjab, Urdu remains the official language in spite of efforts to replace it by a standard Panjabi (Shackle 1970), which differs from Indian Panjabi both in using the Perso–Urdu script and in its preference for Perso–Arabic over Sanskritic loans, but is similarly based on the central Majhi dialect of Lahore and Amritsar. Its appeal is therefore restricted in the western areas of Pakistan Panjab, where rival 'Lahnda' standards are now being promulgated.

While most descriptions of Panjabi are based on the Indian standard, it therefore seems more appropriate to postulate a 'Panjabi language-group' including several actual and incipient standards, characterized throughout by extensive diglossia with Hindi/Urdu (Shackle 1979).

See also: Granth; Gurmukhi; Panjabi (Gurmukhi) Sacred Texts; Sikhism.

Bibliography

Gill H S, Gleason H A 1969 *A Reference Grammar of Punjabi*, 2nd edn. Punjabi University, Patiala

Koul O N, Bala M 1992 *Panjabi Language and Linguistics, an Annotated Bibliography*. Indian Institute of Language Studies, Patiala

Sandhu B S 1968 The tonal system of the Panjabi language. *Parkh* 2

Shackle C 1970 Punjabi in Lahore. *Modern Asian Studies* **4**: 239–67

Shackle C 1979 Problems of classification in Pakistan Punjab. *TPLS*: 191–210

Shackle C 2001 Panjabi. In: Cardona G, Jain D (eds.) *Indo–Aryan Languages*. Curzon, Richmond

Pashto

P. G. Kreyenbroek

Pashto, the language of the Pashtun or Pathan people, belongs to the northeastern group of Iranian languages. It is spoken by approximately 50 percent of the population of Afghanistan—where, together with Dari Persian, it has been recognized as the national language—and by a large majority of the inhabitants of Pakistan's Northwest Frontier Province; there is also an important community of Pashto speakers in the Pakistani province of Baluchistan. Conservative estimates give the number of native speakers of the language as at least 10 million people (MacKenzie 1987: 547).

A written form of Pashto is widely held to have emerged when, in the sixteenth century CE, Bāyazīd Anṣārī (also known as Pīr Raušan), a heterodox religious leader, claimed to have received a divine command to write down an inspired text in Pashto. Whether this is correct or not, the work in question is probably the earliest extant written text in Pashto.

The main groups of dialects of Pashto are the western or southwestern one, whose most prestigious subdialect is the speech of Qandahar; and the eastern or northeastern (Yusufzay) group, whose center is Peshawar in Pakistan. These forms of the language are sometimes referred to as 'Pashto' and 'Pakhto' respectively. Pashto has always been written in an adapted form of the Arabic script, in which special signs were used for phonemes which are realized differently in the various dialects. In the southwestern dialects, for example, the phonemes usually transcribed x̌ and ǧ are realized as retroflex spirants (ş̂, ẑ), and distinguished from the postalveolar š, ž; in southeastern dialects, there is no difference between the two pairs of sounds; in central dialects, the former pair is realized as medio–palatal fricatives (x̌, γ̌); while in northeastern ones it coincides with velar, x, g. Separate letters were invented for each of such problematic phonemes; this masked the characteristic differences between dialects, which are mainly phonological, and strengthened a sense of linguistic unity among speakers of Pashto. In Pakistan, where Pashto has seldom been taught in schools, there is in the early 1990s a tendency toward 'phonetic' spelling (with x̌ and ğ in some cases represented by x, g in the north, and by š, ž in the south), whereas in Afghanistan a refined orthography is used. The main variants of written Pashto, therefore, are the Afghan and the Pakistani ones, although traces of authors' local speech can often be discerned.

Bibliography

MacKenzie D N 1959 A standard Pashto. *BSOAS* **22**: 231–35

MacKenzie D N 1987 Pashto. In: Comrie B (ed.) *The World's Major Languages*. Routledge, London

Morgenstierne G 1927 *An Etymological Vocabulary of Pashto*. J. Dybwad, Oslo

Skjærvø P O 1989 Pashto. In: Schmitt R (ed.) *Compendium Linguarum Iranicarum*. Ludwig Reiner, Wiesbaden

Persian

J. Ardehali

Persian is the language of several Muslim nations and is also spoken by some Christians and Jews as well as Zoroastrians, who are historically the original speakers of this language.

Persian has three main dialects: Farsi (the Persian word for this variety), written in a modified Arabic alphabet, is the official language of present-day Iran and spoken by at least 90 percent of the 67 million population, although it is the native language of only about half of it; Dari, also written in modified Arabic script, is one of the two official languages of Afghanistan (alongside Pashto); Tajiki is the language of the former Soviet Republic of Tajikistan in Central Asia. These varieties are sometimes reckoned to be separate languages.

The history of Persian as an official language dates back to the sixth century BCE, when Old Persian was the official language of the Achaemenid dynasty. Among the numerous inscriptions in cuneiform from this period. King Darius I's huge monument in the rock at Bisotun (in Iran) is most notable. Middle Persian was the official language of the Sassanids (ca. 225–651 CE). The epigraphic texts of kings, written in the Pahlavi (developed from the Aramaic) alphabet, are the surviving evidence from this period (see *Pahlavi*). Following the Islamic conquest of Iran, resulting in the Iranians' conversion to Islam, the evolution of Modern Persian started in the seventh century as a koiné and it was flourishing as a standard language, written in a modified Arabic alphabet, by the end of the twelfth century (see *Arabic Script: Adaptation for Other Languages*). Ferdowsi's great epic poem *Shahnameh* (*The Book of Kings*) was written in this period. Modern Persian is considered to have '...one of the most glorious literatures of the world' Rypka (1968: viii).

1. Characteristics

Persian is a member of the Iranian group of the Indo–Iranian branch of the Indo–European languages. Since the Old Persian period there have been many changes in Persian, increasing its differences from its siblings. In terms of morphology, unlike Pashto and some other Iranian languages, it has lost the Old Persian synthetic nominal and verbal inflection, although person, number, and human and nonhuman gender are still distinguished. So are the present and past tenses and the past participle form of verbs. Persian can be said to be among the least 'sexist' languages in the world: there is no masculine–feminine gender distinction in the entire grammar and lexis. The third person singular pronoun /u/ means 'she/he,' and the possessive suffix /aʃ/ means 'her/his.' It follows that one can talk in a normal way about somebody for as long as one wishes, without the addressee knowing the natural gender of the person talked about, for example, (1):

هنرپیشه‌ای گفت اوهمیشه بهترین لباسهایش را باخودش میبرد.

/honarpiʃei goft u hamiʃe behtarin lebɑshajɑʃ rɑ bɑ χodaʃ mibarad/ (1)

$$\text{An}\left\{\begin{matrix}\text{actor}\\\text{actress}\end{matrix}\right\}\text{said}\left\{\begin{matrix}\text{he}\\\text{she}\end{matrix}\right\}\text{always takes}\left\{\begin{matrix}\text{his}\\\text{her}\end{matrix}\right\}\text{best}\left\{\begin{matrix}\text{clothes}\\\text{dresses}\end{matrix}\right\}\text{with}\left\{\begin{matrix}\text{him}\\\text{her}\end{matrix}\right\}.$$

Although Persian has the nominal plural marker /-hɑ/ (and in formal registers /ɑn/ for human beings), the singular form of the noun is used with numerals. Definiteness is not marked, but in colloquial Farsi the ending /-e/ is used as a singular definite marker. The indefinite marker is /-i/, as in (2):

	Indefinite		*Definite*	(2)
SG	/deraχti/	'a tree'	/deraχt/	'the tree'
			/deraχte/	'the tree' (col Farsi)
PL	/deraχthai/	'some trees'	/deraχtha/	'the trees'

The simple (without a relative clause) noun phrase has the structure (3):

$$\text{numeral} + \text{N}\begin{Bmatrix} \text{/-je//V-} \\ \text{/-e//C-} \end{Bmatrix} + \left(\text{modifier}\begin{Bmatrix} \text{/-je//V-} \\ \text{/-e//C-} \end{Bmatrix}\right)^n + \text{modifier} \quad (3)$$

(*n* signifies any number); for example, /do ketabe bozorg/ 'two large books,' /paje tʃape man/ 'my left foot,' /zane parviz/ 'Parviz's wife.' The kernel clause structure is SO^dO^i ACV; however, as in English, the position of the adverbial is variable.

Arabic 'loanwords' constitute about 50 percent of the lexicon, although only about half of them are in everyday use. There are also a number of words from Turkish, French, and other languages. Although almost the entire loan component is nominal, other word classes are derived from them by Persian processes of lexical morphology, in particular verbalization by suffixation (adding /-idan/) or by compounding with a small number of Persian verbs, mainly /kardan/ 'to do' and /ʃodan/ 'to become.' There are many lexical and semantic differences between Farsi and Dari: many Arabic and native forms have different meanings in the two dialects; some ordinary words in Dari occur only in the formal, written, and even archaic registers of Farsi; and there are more French words in Farsi than in Dari.

The inventory of consonants consists of /p, b, f, v, m, t, d, s, z, n, r, l, tʃ, dʒ, ʃ, ʒ, j, k, g, χ, ɢ, h, ʔ/. Contrasted with English, the absence of /w, θ, ð / and the presence of /ɢ, χ/ are the most noticeable distinctive features of Persian phonology. The vowels are /i, e, a, ɑ, o, u/ in Farsi, and /ɪ, e, eː, a, ɑ, o, oː, ʊ/ in Dari; and the diphthongs are /eɪ, aɪ, ɑɪ, uɪ, ou/ (the last one is /ɑʊ/ in Dari).

2. Influences and Changes

Following the Ghaznavids' conquest in the eleventh century, Persian entered India, where Urdu developed under its powerful influence. Persian was the official language of the Mogul empire until 1857. Furthermore, a variety of Persian developed and flourished in India; this was finally abolished as an official language only in 1837 by the East India Company. Persian has as great a share, if not greater, in the development of literary Ottoman Turkish (Osmanli) as Turkish itself.

In turn, Persian itself has been influenced and, as a result, undergone changes. Modernization and Westernization of Iran during the reign of the Pahlavi dynasty (1925–79) had enormous effects on Farsi, so much so that a new period can be considered to have started in the early decades of the twentieth century, referred to by some as 'New Farsi.' In this period official attempts were made to purge Farsi of Arabic words as much as possible, and to introduce from the native stock appropriate equivalents for the European terminology pouring into Iran from the West. Many foreign forms, however, entered the language and, particularly in later years, even the grammar and idioms were affected, through the literal translation and use of English and French expressions. Contact with the West resulted also in a great change in literature. Western-style fiction was introduced as a literary genre into Farsi, with a wider effect on prose style in general, relieving it from the straitjacket of stilted ornate conventions. Similarly, in poetry, traditional Persian metrics, rhyme schemes, and poetic diction underwent a revolution and much less rigid 'New Poetry' (/ʃeʔre nou/) was founded by the poet Nimayushij (1895–1960).

Since the Revolution of 1979, Islamic fundamentalism has had some effects on Farsi. Many new Arabic terms, emanating from the ruling clergy, are current in mass media, bureaucracy, and even every day ordinary usage. In addition, there is a kind of implied indignation on the part of the regime for any linguistic fervor for Persian, since it is associated with nationalism (as opposed to pan-Islamism), and this has had an adverse effect on grammar and style.

See also: Pashto; Semitic Scripts: Dissemination and Influence; Arabic Script: Adaptation for Other Languages; Islamic Calligraphy.

Bibliography

Lambton A K S 1967 *Persian Grammar*. Cambridge University Press, Cambridge

Rypka J 1968 *History of Iranian Literature*. Reidel, Dordrecht

Windfuhr G L 1979 *Persian Grammar: History and State of its Study*. Mouton, The Hague

Phoenician/Punic

W. G. E. Watson

Phoenician was the language of the coastal region of what is now Lebanon and Syria, used in the cities of Byblos, Tyre, and Sidon, and on the island of Cyprus. Each city probably had its own dialect but the official language of inscriptions was a type of standard Phoenician. The earliest Phoenician inscription, which is from Byblos, dates to the tenth century BCE, and the language was still being used as late as the second century CE, chiefly by merchants.

'Punic', a term derived from the Latin sources, refers to the language of the Phoenician colonies, spread over the Western Mediterranean. After the Fall of Carthage in 146 BCE, scholars refer to it as 'Neo-Punic.' Subject to the influence of African languages such as Berber, Neo-Punic survived right up to the sixth century CE, probably spoken by peasants.

Phoenician/Punic is a Northwest Semitic language most closely related to Ugaritic (see *Ugaritic*) with some affinity to Hebrew and Aramaic. The alphabetic script, which was exported to Greece by the eighth century BCE (see *Semitic Scripts*) runs from right to left as in Hebrew. Vowel-letters are used in late Phoenician and Neo-Punic (e.g., *b't*/bat/ for *bt* 'daughter'). The shift of stressed [ā] to [ō] always occurs, as does the loss of a final short vowel (retained in Ugaritic): e.g., [maqāmu] becomes [maqōm] 'place.' Punic is also marked by the gradual weakening and disappearance of laryngeals (e.g., *phl'* for *p'l'* 'he made it') and the loss of inner alef (e.g., *mlkt* for *ml'kt* 'work'). Characteristic of Phoenician grammar is the yifil (causative) form of the verb, corresponding to Hebrew *hifil* and Ugaritic *shafel.*

See also: Hebrew, Biblical and Jewish; Ugaritic.

Bibliography

Cunchillos J-L, Zamora J A 1997 *Gramática Fenicia Elemental.* Consejo Superior de Investgaciones Científicas, Madrid

Gibson J C L 1982 *Textbook of Syrian Semitic Inscriptions*, vol. 3: *Phoenician Inscriptions.* Clarendon Press, Oxford

Hoftijzer J, Jongeling K *Dictionary of the North–West Semitic Inscriptions*, 2 vols. Brill, Leiden

Segert S 1976 *A Grammar of Phoenician and Punic.* C. M. Beck, Munich

Segert S 1997 Phoenician and the Eastern Canaanite languages. In: Hetzron R (ed.) *The Semitic Languages.* Routledge, London

Tomback R S 1978 *A Comparative Semitic Lexicon of the Phoenician and Punic Languages.* Scholars Press, Missoula, MT

Runes

A. King

Runes are the letters of the first alphabet or script used by the Germanic peoples which, over time, developed several variant types. The script was used primarily for epigraphic purposes. Extant, known runic inscriptions, the earliest of which date from about the second century CE, number 5,000 or so in total. The great majority of objects (portable and nonportable) inscribed with runes by Germanic-speaking people originated and survive in Sweden; the remainder are to be found in Norway, Denmark, Iceland, England, Lowland Scotland, the Orkney and Shetland Islands, the Western Isles, Greenland, the Faroes, Ireland, and the Isle of Man. There are also a few from Germany, Poland, Hungary, and the former Soviet Union. By the twelfth century, runes had been more or less superseded by Roman letters everywhere except in the Scandinavian countries where runes continued to be used occasionally until about the seventeenth century. Though runic inscriptions are generally brief, those predating the twelfth century are of immense value since they constitute the earliest, and sometimes only, linguistic evidence of several of the Germanic languages.

1. The Origins and Uses of Runes

1.1 Origins

It is not known for certain when, where, and by whom runes were invented. Three theories exist (see Page 1987: 9). Moltke (1985) holds that runes were created by one of the Germanic tribes of Denmark, probably of southern Jutland. For several reasons, this is credible. Many of the earliest known inscriptions come from there. Two scripts: the Etruscan (from southern Switzerland and northern Italy) and the Roman-letter (itself influenced by the Etruscan and Greek scripts). seem, from a comparison of character shapes, to have formed the basis of the runic one. Of Nordic Germanic areas, southern Jutland was geographically closest to Switzerland and Rome. Also, Denmark, though independent of Imperial Rome, traded with its trading posts and military camps on the Rhine—circumstances facilitating adoption and adaptation of the mixed-origin Roman-letter script. The maturity of epigraphic and rune-using skills apparent in the earliest inscriptions supports an invention date of around the beginning of the Christian era.

1.2 Uses

Runes were incised on free-standing boulders, living rock, stone crosses, and a variety of moveable objects like brooches, buckles, neck-rings, and medallions in precious or semiprecious metals, bone combs, spear-heads, scabbards, boxes made of wood, ivory, or whalebone, urns, coins, and even tweezers. The inscriptions most often name owners or makers, e.g., the famous one on the fabulous golden horn, made ca. 400 CE and known as the 'Gallehus Horn' after the place in Denmark where it was found: (tr. = transliterated) *ekhlewagastiR|holtijaR|horna|tawido* 'I, Hlewagastir, son of Holti, made the horn.' Sometimes they merely name the object they are carved on. Many are memorial inscriptions. A few give the complete runic alphabet; fewer still are verse texts like that on the 'Ruthwell Cross.'

It is often claimed that runes had ritualistic or magical significance in Germanic society. Their mention in this connection in later Germanic

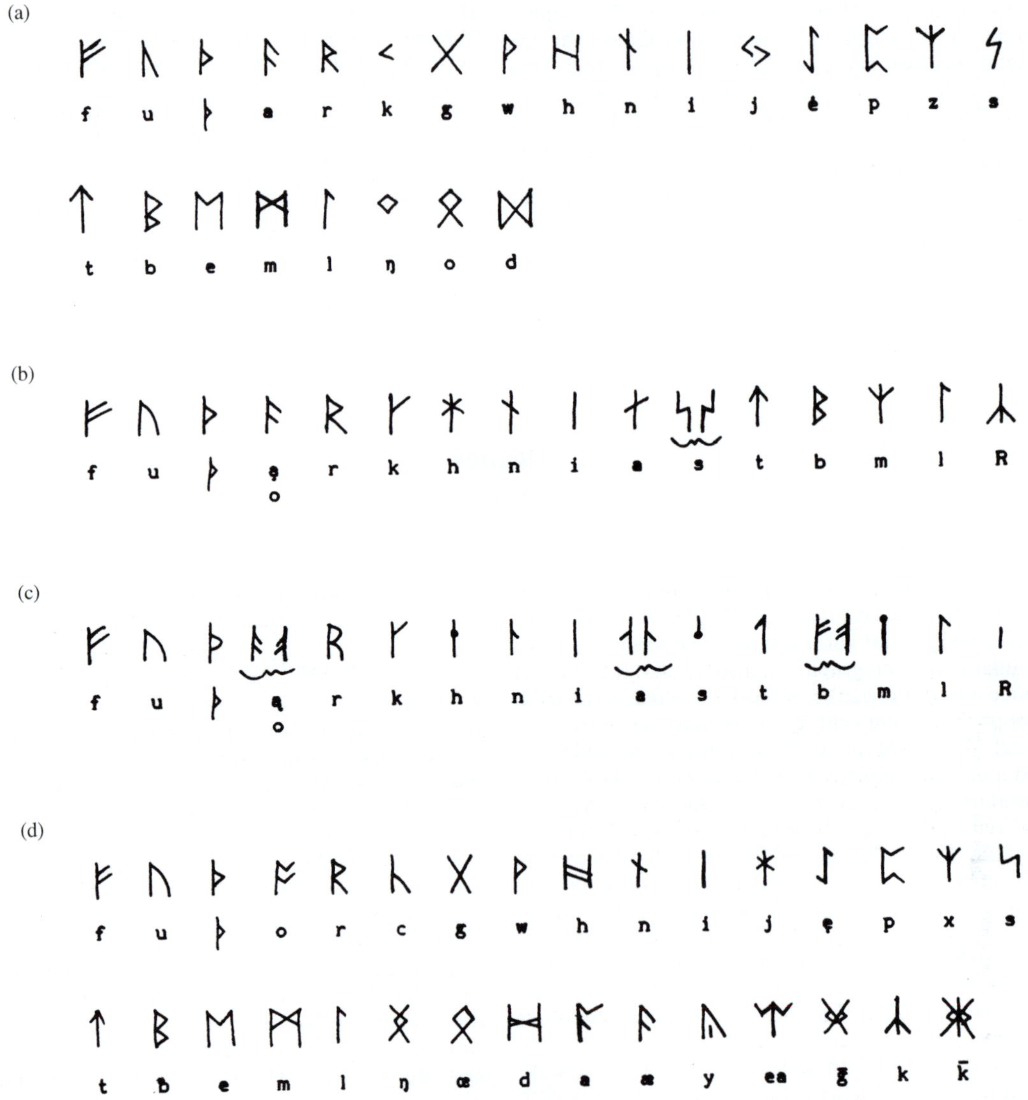

Figure 1. Runic alphabets.

literature, together with the existence of largely uninterpretable inscriptions, such as (tr.) *aaaaaaa RRRnnn?bmuttt:alu* where only the last three characters read as a recognizable word (reputed to mean 'good luck'), as well as the historical definition of the word 'rune' itself ('secret/mystery/whispering') do point to this conclusion. It should, however, be borne in mind that the ability to write and read any script, runic or not, would seem secret and mysterious anyway to the majority of the Germanic population who would be unable to do either. Additionally, the runic script was the only one known to Germanic peoples, except the Goths, until into the seventh century; consequently it had, perforce, to be used for all writing purposes—magic ones as well as everyday ones.

2. The Runic Script and its Development

2.1 Characteristics

The angular shape of the runes in the original Common Germanic alphabet, along with their vertical and slanting, not horizontal, strokes, attest their original epigraphic purpose and the material—wood—on which they were cut at first. The direction of writing of runes is variable; some times they read from left to right, sometimes vice versa and sometimes boustrophedon (left to right, and right to left, with the runes reversed, in alternate lines). Runic script is always what one would think of as upper case. Mirror image and upside-down runes sometimes occur and the rune shapes themselves can show some minor variation in form within each alphabet.

2.2 Runic Alphabets

The Common Germanic runic alphabet had 24 letters arranged in the order depicted in Fig. 1(a). It is known, from the first six letters of this traditional sequence, as the *fuþark*. From ca. 800 CE this fuþark was reduced in number from 24 to 16 runes in Scandinavian (especially Swedish) usage and some of the rune shapes changed quite significantly (Fig. 1(b)). These two fuþarks are normally referred to respectively as the older and the younger. The younger fuþark had a major—short-twig—variant type in which the runes were slightly more cursive as shown in Fig. 1(c). Some inscriptions mixed both younger fuþark types. Several other minor Scandinavian variants developed, for instance, the dotted fuþark (after ca. 1000 CE), in which a system of dots was used to point up some of the vowel and consonant distinctions missing since the ninth century, or the Hälsinge runes, which lack vertical strokes and were in use from the tenth to the twelfth century in the Hälsingland region of Sweden. The runes used in Anglo-Saxon England resemble fairly closely those of the older fuþark, but some rune shapes were changed (becoming diagnostic of source) and new ones were invented (bringing the final total to 34) thus reflecting diachronic phonological differences between the two branches of Germanic (Fig. 1(d)).

3. Deciphering Runes

Each rune symbol had a name, usually a common noun of the language. The runic system worked on an acrophonic principle whereby each rune represented a broad phonetic value derived from the initial sould segment of its name. These sound values can be reconstructed, for Proto-Germanic and its individual offshoots, with the help of the rune names and the alliterative schemes given in the 'Rune Poem' which survives in Old Norwegian, Old Norse, and Old English manuscript versions. So, for instance, the rune ᛚ has the name *lagu* 'water' in Old English and, with the same meaning, *lǫgr* in Old Norse. The defining line accompanying the rune in the Old English 'Rune Poem': *Lagu byð leodum langsum geðuht* 'water (ocean) to people interminable seems' has the initial letter of *lagu* alliterating with those of *leodum* and *langsum* and so the sound value /l/ can be assigned to this rune.

Conventionally, runes are transliterated into Roman letters or, for Old English ones, a mixed system of Roman letters, untransliterated runes and IPA symbols devised by Bruce Dickins (1932).

4. Runes as Linguistic Evidence

4.1 Drawbacks

These consist of the peculiarities described in Sect. 3 above. These may sometimes be put down to carvers, who cannot be assumed in all cases to have composed the inscriptions, being semiliterate or not literate, and might be increased if an unsatisfactory transliteration system is employed to present the linguistic information contained in the inscriptions. Other drawbacks center on the shortness of inscriptions generally and the fact that only a small proportion of what must have been a sizable corpus of them survives. Among other things, many inscriptions on materials like wood will have perished, ones on nonprecious metals are subject to corrosion and become unreadable, and precious metal objects whether or not they have runes on them are likely to be melted down (as was the 'Gallehus Horn') as bullion. The extant corpus may, too, be only partially representative of the whole. Nothing can be done about these latter problems, except for respecting the existing runic data as they stand. The first ones, however, can be considerably lessened with knowledge of the spelling characteristics of runic usage, combined with use of a good transliterating system.

4.2 Advantages

Rune names were predominantly common nouns so they, like the nouns, were subject to diachronic and diatopic linguistic developments (i.e., changes over time and according to geographical situation). Rune names were changed in accord with these developments, so through the name changes the linguistic developments themselves can be traced. For example, the twelfth rune in the fuþark, had the name **jára* in Primitive Norse. By the Old Norse period, the rune name is changed to *ár* and so it can be deduced from this evidence and that of the inscriptions' data that some time around 600 CE, word initial /j/ was lost in Norse.

Not only the rune names, but also the data of the inscriptions themselves are useful in this respect. The runic spellings on Old English coins of the personal names of moneyers and kings (whose reign dates are known) can, for instance, be of especial value in dating Old English sound changes fairly precisely. The data themselves record the very earliest known details of Proto-Germanic phonology, inflectional morphology, syntax, lexis (both lexical stock and information on derivational morphology), and onomastics—otherwise there would be no evidence of these until the fourth century when the first manuscript in Gothic was written. Developments affecting inflectional morphology, etc. from Proto-Germanic and into the individual Germanic languages can be traced by comparing the earlier with later runic inscriptions (see Antonsen 1975; Haugen 1982). This information is precious with regard to the Scandinavian languages—were it not for inscriptions in runes, no record of Old Norse, for instance, would exist until the eleventh century when Roman-letter writing was introduced.

See also: Gothic.

Bibliography

Antonsen E H 1975 *A Concise Grammar of the Older Runic Inscriptions*. Niemeyer, Tübingen

Dickins B 1932 A system of transliteration for Old English runic inscriptions. *Leeds Studies in English* **I**: 15–9

Elliott R W V 1959 *Runes: An Introduction*. Manchester University Press, Manchester

Haugen E 1982 *Scandinavian Language Structures*. University of Minnesota Press, Minneapolis, MN

King A 1986 The Ruthwell Cross: A linguistic monument (Runes as evidence for Old English). *FoLH* **VII(1)**: 43–79

Moltke E 1985 *Runes and their Origin: Denmark and Elsewhere*. Nationalmuseets Forlag, Copenhagen

Page R I 1973 *An Introduction to English Runes*. Methuen, London

Page R I 1987 *Runes*. British Museum Publications, London

Samaritan

A. D. Crown

Samaritan is the name given to the language and script used by the Samaritan sect for their sacred literature.

The traditions of the origins of the Samaritans and their version of the Pentateuch go back to at least the second century BCE. The Bible regards them as the offshoot of alien immigrants to Israel (2 Kings 17): by Samaritan accounts they are true Israelites, *bnai Yisrael*. They regard themselves as *shomrim*, the preservers of the true Law and indeed, the Samaritan Pentateuch preserves their orthography and script, and, as is now becoming clear from Zeev Ben-Hayyim's researches, their ancient pronunciation of Hebrew. The Samaritan Pentateuch is anticipated in many ways in the Qumran manuscripts, the Dead Sea scrolls, so that it can be seen there is an ancient connection between the Samaritans, the sacred writ and the Hebrew language.

Scholars from the eighteenth century and onwards were convinced that Samaritan was a thoroughly debased mixture of Hebrew, Aramaic, and Arabic, which languages were spoken and written by the Samaritans successively. To this language they gave the name Cuthean, after the pejorative term applied in Rabbinic literature to the Samaritans. The Hebrew of the Samaritan Pentateuch, like their textual tradition, was regarded as late and secondary. It is still customary to use the term Samaritan for the hybrid Hebrew and Aramaic of the Samaritan liturgy, particularly that dating from the fourteenth century and onwards.

Recent studies of Samaritan Hebrew by Ben-Hayyim, starting with a description of their contemporary reading of the Biblical text, show its antiquity and continuity. In the area of pronunciation there is no difference between the language of the Pentateuch and the Hebrew language outside it, nor is there any difference between them and the Aramaic to be heard in Samaritan prayers. Though there are written indications that a number of changes in pronunciation have taken place since Aramaic ceased being spoken by the Samaritans (at the end of the tenth century and the onset of the eleventh), there is no reason to doubt that the Hebrew pronunciation heard today, on the whole, corresponds to what was heard when Aramaic was spoken. This pronunciation probably represents Samaritan Hebrew speech towards the end of the first century CE and for a few generations after. Some of the features of this Hebrew are manifest in the Samaritan Pentateuch and the antiquity of these textual features has been supported in our days by the Qumran scrolls. In phonology as well as textually, there exists a continuity stretching back to a Hebrew dialect. Ben-Hayyim observes that its chronology and geography are not definable in precise terms in the present state of research.

The script in which Samaritan Hebrew and Aramaic is written is known in two forms, the first is the *mujallas* = well-set, or majuscule (as in the table below), which developed from the old Hebrew script and the Samaritan lapidary form. The second, the *taris* = rapid or minuscule script, developed under the influence of Arabic and is first found in Pentateuch scrolls of the thirteenth century but may well be older. It developed into a full cursive script for use in secular documents and the prayer book. The alphabet, like Hebrew, read from right to left, is as follows:

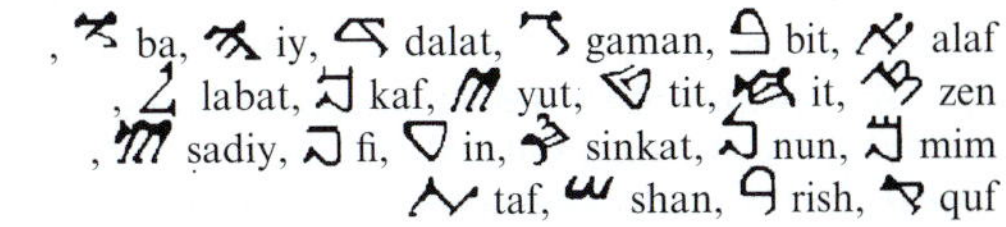
, ba, iy, dalat, gaman, bit, alaf
, labat, kaf, yut, tit, it, zen
, ṣadiy, fi, in, sinkat, nun, mim
taf, shan, rish, quf

See also: Hebrew, Biblical and Jewish; Judaism; Aramaic, Jewish.

Bibliography

Ben Hayyim Z 2000 *A Grammar of Samaritan Hebrew*. Hebrew University, Magnes Press, Jerusalem//Eisenbrauns, Winona Lake, Indiana, IN

Ben Hayyim Z 1989 Samaritan Hebrew—an evaluation. In: Crown A D (ed.) *The Samaritans*. J C B Mohr, Tubingen, pp. 517–30

Crown A D 2001 *Samaritan Scribes and Manuscripts*. J C B Mohr, Tubingen

Macuch R 1989 Samaritan Languages: Samaritan Hebrew, Samaritan Aramaic. In: Crown A D (ed.) *The Samaritans*. J. C. B. Mohr, Tubingen, pp. 531–584

Sanskrit

J. L. Brockington

The Sanskrit language—one of the oldest of the Indo–European group to possess a substantial literature—has particular interest for linguists from the circumstances of its becoming known to western scholars and the stimulus so given to historical linguistics. It has also been of enormous and continuing importance as the classical language of Indian culture and the sacred language of Hinduism.

1. Origin and History

Sanskrit, in its older form of Vedic Sanskrit (or simply Vedic), was brought into the northwest of India by the Āryans some time in the second half of the second millennium BCE and was at that period relatively little differentiated from its nearest relation within the Indo–European group, Avestan in the Iranian family of languages (these two being the oldest recorded within the Indo–Iranian branch of Indo–European). From there, it spread to the rest of North India as the Āryans enlarged the area that they occupied, developing into the classical form of the language, which subsequently became fixed as the learned language of culture and religion throughout the subcontinent, while the spoken language developed into the various Prākrits. There is ample evidence of rapid evolution during the Vedic period, with the language of the latest phase, attested for example in the Upaniṣads, showing considerable grammatical simplification from that of the earliest hymns. The later Vedic is, in broad terms, the form of the language that Pāṇini described with such exactness in his grammar around the fourth century BCE, thereby creating—no doubt unintentionally—an absolute standard for the language thereafter; his work is clearly the culmination of a long grammatical tradition, based on concern to preserve the Vedas unaltered (hence the stress on phonetics), and is itself intended for memorization and oral transmission, as its brevity indicates.

This standardization was not as universal as has sometimes been represented (nor was the preceding Vedic a unified language, for it exhibits features only explicable as coming from slightly differing dialects, while classical Sanskrit is based on a more eastern dialect than the one attested in the *Ṛgveda*) and it has come to be recognized that, for example, the two Sanskrit epics exhibit systematic divergences from the language described by Pāṇini and represent a distinct epic dialect. However, with the growth of classical Sanskrit literature (mainly within the period from the fourth to the tenth centuries CE, when Sanskrit was clearly no longer a natural language), Pāṇini's description was regarded as prescriptive and followed to the letter, although the spirit was less closely observed (as shown by the tendency to longer and longer compounds, to nominal constructions and the like).

The earliest record of the language is contained in the hymns of the *Ṛgveda*, which belong to around 1200–1000 BCE, but they were not committed to writing until a much later period because of their sacred character, for the Indian tradition has always placed greater emphasis on oral tradition than on written texts. In fact the earliest dated record in Sanskrit is an inscription of 150 CE, significantly later than the use of Prākrit by the Buddhist ruler Aśoka for his inscriptions in the third century BCE. Early inscriptions used one of two scripts: the Kharoṣṭhī, deriving from the Aramaic script used in Achaemenid Iran, and the Brāhmī, less certainly deriving from a North Semitic script. The latter evolved into the Nāgarī family of scripts, to which the Devanāgarī script now usually used for Sanskrit belongs, although before the twentieth century manuscripts were normally written in the local script.

2. Characteristics

Any analysis of Sanskrit syntax must take account of the shift from the natural language of the Vedic and epic forms of Sanskrit to the learned language of the classical literature, which selectively exploits certain features of Pāṇini's description. Whereas the older forms of the language show frequent use of nominal compounds of two or three members and Pāṇini's grammar describes their formation in great detail (but in terms of their analysis into types: *dvandva*, *bahuvrīhi*, *tatpuruṣa*), classical literature is marked by a predilection for longer compounds, consisting in some styles of writing of twenty or more members. Another common feature, inherited from the Indo–European background but found much more extensively in the classical language, is the use of nominal sentences involving the juxtaposition of the subject and a nonverbal predicate. The frequent use of the past participle passive as a verbal equivalent leads to a preference for passive constructions, in a way typical of the Prākrits. Use of the absolutive becomes in the classical language a common means to form complex sentences by indicating actions occurring prior to that of the main verb; again the effect is a reduction in finite verbal forms. The usual sentence order is subject, object, verb; however, this is so commonly modified for emphasis (with initial and final positions in the sentence or verse-line carrying most emphasis) that Sanskrit word order is often regarded as being free. In vocabulary, the freeing from the affective connotations of a natural language brought a striking enlargement of the range of synonyms, skillfully exploited in much of the classical literature to produce rich sound effects.

In its morphology, Sanskrit is broadly comparable to Greek or Latin, though somewhat more complex. In both the nominal and verbal systems the dual is obligatory for all twos, not just pairs. The nominal system employs eight cases (seven according to the Indian reckoning, which regards the vocative as a form of the stem), three numbers and three genders (masculine, feminine, neuter). Unlike other Indo–European languages, Sanskrit lacks a developed series of prepositions and the relatively few adverbial formations used to define case relationships more exactly tend to be placed after the noun. The use of *vṛddhi* (IE strengthened grade) to form derivatives from nominal stems is a notable feature. The verb has two voices, active and middle, their functions well distinguished by the Sanskrit terms for them: *parasmaipada* 'word for another' and *ātmanepada* 'word for oneself'; it also has five moods (injunctive, imperative, subjunctive, optative, and precative) in the Vedic, somewhat simplified in the classical language. Prepositional affixes to the verb may in Vedic be separated from the verb but in the classical language must be prefixed to it (there is a comparable development between Homeric and classical Greek). There is both an ordinary sigmatic future and a periphrastic future (formed through a specialized use of the agent noun), several aorist formations (principally a sigmatic aorist and a root aorist), and a perfect normally formed with a reduplicated stem; these are comparable to the equivalent tenses in Greek or Latin. The augment is prefixed to several past tenses: imperfect, aorist, pluperfect, and conditional. Verbal roots are divided by the Sanskrit grammarians into ten classes: six athematic and four thematic. A distinctive feature of the verbal system is the employment of secondary conjugations with specific meanings: causative, intensive, and desiderative. Historically, the passive is also such a secondary conjugation, formed by adding the middle endings to a modified root. The Vedic language is marked by rather greater grammatical complexity with, most notably, a whole range of case forms from nouns functioning as infinitives, which are reduced to a single infinitive in the classical language. It also possessed a pitch accent which had died out by the time of the classical language.

Phonetically Sanskrit is marked by a number of innovations by comparison with other Indo–European languages of comparable age. It is also notable for the concern with phonetics of its own grammarians (exemplified by the fact that the alphabet is arranged according to the organ of articulation, with vowels preceding consonants) and the precision of their descriptions. On the one hand Sanskrit has collapsed the three Indo-European vowels, *a*, *e*, and *o* into *a*, and on the other it has introduced a complete new class of consonants, that of the retroflex consonants, mainly under the influence of one of the other language groups already present in India, either Dravidian or Munda, although in some instances the retroflex consonants probably arose through internal phonetic developments in relation to *ṣ* and *r*. The most widely known feature is that of *saṃdhi* 'junction,' the process of phonetic assimilation of contiguous sounds at the junctures between both words and their component parts (external and internal *saṃdhi*).

3. Sample Sentence

teṣāṃ khalv eṣāṃ bhūṭānāṃ trīṇy eva bījāni bhavanty
/teʂa:ŋ khəlv eʂa:ŋ bhu:ta:na:ŋ tri:ŋy evə bi:ja:ni bhəvənty
aṇḍajaṃ jīvajam udbhijjam iti‖
əŋɖəjəŋ ji:vəjəm udbhijəm iti/

'Living beings here have just three origins [literally 'Assuredly of these living beings are/come into being indeed three seeds']: being born from an egg or live-born or produced from a sprout.'

This simple sentence (from *Chāndogya Upaniṣad* 6.3.1) nonetheless exemplifies already several of the features which are taken to extremes in the classical language. There is the avoidance of a transitive construction (although here the verb, *bhavanti*, is expressed, whereas later such a copula is normally suppressed), the employment of compounds and the liking for etymological figures (the latter two combined in the three compounds ending in the adjectival form *-ja*, coming from $\sqrt{}$*jan* 'to be born,' while the use of cognates is exemplified by *bhavanti* 3rd pl present indicative and *bhūta* past participle passive from $\sqrt{}$*bhū* 'to become'). The use of *iti* may also be noted—here to function as the equivalent of the colon in the translation, more usually to perform the function of quotation marks, to mark off a passage in direct speech from the sentence in which it is embedded (an idiom probably calqued on the Dravidian); Sanskrit has no method of indicating indirect speech.

4. Role and Influence in Indian Culture

As is implicit in some of the statements above, it is clear that throughout the main period of its use as a literary language Sanskrit was not the first language of its users, who in North India would have been native speakers of one of the Prākrits deriving from Sanskrit (used here in its widest sense of the group of OIA dialects) or even of the next stage of MIA, the Apabhraṃśas, and in South India were speakers of one of the Dravidian languages (which have been influenced to varying degrees in their vocabulary by Sanskrit). The prestige attaching to its use for the Vedas, the authoritative scriptures for Hindus, resulted in its being regarded as the only language fit for use in the major rituals of brahmanical Hinduism, a role that to a limited extent it retains to the present day. This was undoubtedly the reason why the Purāṇas and the many popular texts related to them were composed (from the fourth century to as late as the nineteenth century) in a form of Sanskrit which is greatly indebted to the epics for its linguistic and metrical expression, while similarly Mahāyāna Buddhism employed the so-called Buddhist Hybrid Sanskrit (essentially a Sanskritization of MIA). Sanskrit has therefore been a dominant influence on the development of the languages in both the MIA and NIA phases, supplying much of the religious vocabulary in the form of direct loans, over and above the large proportion of the vocabulary descended from Sanskrit.

5. Sanskrit and the West

First acquaintance with Sanskrit by Western scholars came even before the period of British rule. Sir William Jones's famous discourse in 1786 to the Asiatick Society in Calcutta on the affinity of Sanskrit with Greek, Latin, and the other languages now known as Indo-European was not the first notice of such connection, which had been proposed two centuries earlier by Thomas Stevens (in 1583) and Fillipo Sassetti (in 1585). However, his eminence ensured it a much wider audience than before and this was in a significant sense the start of the discipline of comparative philology, while the appreciation before long of the achievements of the early Indian grammarians was an important stimulant to the development of modern linguistics, which has paid them the compliment of borrowing a number of their terms, such as *saṃdhi*.

See also: Hinduism; Sanskrit: Discovery by Europeans; Buddhist Hybrid Sanskrit; Hindu Views on Language; Devanagari.

Bibliography

Burrow T 1973 *The Sanskrit Language*, 3rd edn. Faber and Faber, London

Cardona G 1988 *Pāṇini: His Work and its Traditions*, vol. 1. Motilal Banarsidass, Delhi

Coulson M 1992 *Sanskrit: An Introduction to the Classical Language*, 2nd edn. Hodder and Stoughton, London

Gonda J 1971 *Old Indian*, Handbuch der Orientalistik, 2. Abt., 1. Bd., 1. Abschnitt. E J Brill, Leiden-Cologne

Scharfe H 1977 *Grammatical Literature*, History of Indian Literature, vol. V, fasc. 2. Harrassowitz, Wiesbaden

Semitic Languages

W. G. E. Watson

The term 'Semitic,' derived from the Hebrew name Shem (Genesis 10: 21–31; 11: 10–26) and originally applied to Arabic, Aramaic, and Hebrew by A. L. Schlözer in 1781, now also includes several other languages, some only discovered in the late twentieth century. Although inaccurate it is a convenient label for a set of languages sharing common features within the larger family of Hamito–Semitic, or Afroasiatic as it is now commonly called. General issues such as dialect geography, connections with very early non-Semitic languages and the defining characteristics of a Semitic language are now to the fore in scholarly debate. The tendency for scholars to study better known and better attested languages to the neglect of others considered less important or peripheral has contributed to the difficulty in making statements of general application to the Semitic language group.

1. The Semitic Language Group

Among the two dozen or so languages or dialects which can be identified as Semitic are Akkadian, Amharic, Arabic (see *Arabic*), Aramaic, Assyrian, Babylonian, Eblaic, Epigraphic South Arabian, Ethiopic, Ge'ez (see *Ge'ez*), Hebrew, Maltese Mandaic, Nabataean, Palmyrene, Phoenician, Punic (see *Phoenician/Punic*), Syriac, Ugaritic (see *Ugaritic*), and Ya'udic. For some of these languages the evidence is very meagre. For example, Amorite is known almost entirely from personal names in texts from Mari on the Upper Euphrates and the glosses to the El-Amarna Letters (written predominantly in Babylonian) are the only vestiges of the Canaanite dialect used by the scribes. Others, such as Linear A (from Crete), have been classed as Semitic but may not be and the Proto-Sinaitic and Proto-Canaanite inscriptions remain difficult to read. For yet other languages, such as Hebrew and Arabic, there exist relatively large written corpora developed over a very long and continuous time span and a wide range of geographical locations, which display clear differences connected with historical period, region, and register.

2. Contact with Non-Semitic Languages

The area covered by Semitic languages includes Mesopotamia (modern Iraq), parts of Turkey, Syria and the Levant, the Arabian Peninsula as well as coastlands and islands of the Mediterranean. Not only was there influence on the Semitic-speaking world from outside but even within the same area speakers of Semitic and non-Semitic languages coexisted. Thus, in Mesopotamia, both Sumerian and Akkadian were used and in the kingdom of Ugarit, Anatolian influence, particularly from Hurrian and Hittite, was strong. Similarly, Cushitic influenced Ethiopic, and the European languages have affected modern Arabic and Hebrew. To take a concrete example, it has been suggested that although other Semitic languages developed from SOV (Subject-Object-Verb) to VSO, Akkadian remained an SOV language. The determining factor was interference from Sumerian which prevented this evolution. There was also mutual influence between languages within the Semitic family. For example, the verb forms of the Akkadian used at ancient Ugarit (Ras Shamra) were subject to Ugaritic grammar and Aramaic words were borrowed into Akkadian and Hebrew.

3. The Characteristics of Semitic

Typical of the Semitic languages are verbless clauses, in which no verb equivalent to 'to be' is expressed, for example, Akkadian *awâtum dannâ* 'affairs are pressing.' The verbal system, which appears historically to have expressed 'aspect' more than 'tense,' employs an extensive series of inflections of a consonantal 'root' (typically comprising three consonants) in order to express in a regular and productive manner modalities such as passive, causative, intensive, reflexive, passive-reflexive, etc. for example, (from the root *ṢBT* in Akkadian) *iṣbat* 'he will seize,' *iṣṣabit* 'he was seized,' *taṣṣabbata* 'you will grasp one another,' *tiṣbut* 'it is joined to,' *uṣabbit* 'he captured,' *ušaṣbit* 'he caused to seize,' *ittaṣbatā* 'they were gripped together.' Lists of common lexical items or isoglosses have also been compiled, e.g., Akkadian *bītu*, Arabic *bayt*, Aramaic *baytā*, Ethiopic *bēt*, Hebrew *bāyit*, Phoenician and Ugaritic *bt* (vocalization uncertain) all meaning 'house,' and the verb *bky* 'to weep,' found in all these languages and also in Eblaic. Only two genders are well-attested, masculine and feminine, although there are also traces of a common gender. In general there are extremely few compound nouns in Semitic.

Other features are sometimes claimed to be typical of, although not necessarily exclusive to, the Semitic languages.

(a) Emphatic consonants (often held to be velarized) are used in phonemic opposition to nonemphatic (non-velarized ones) and the pharyngeal consonants are common.

(b) Typically, a triconsonantal lexical root/or a lexical root comprising three consonants/(or 'archilexeme') is employed from which words are derived by incorporating vowels and affixes (e.g., from Arabic *'LN* 'evident,' *'alana* 'to become known,' *'alin* 'overt' *mu'lin* 'announcer' *'alāniya* 'publicity'): however, many roots are apparently biconsonantal or appear to have only two consonants (e.g., *'ḥ* 'brother'), others have just one consonant (e.g., *p* 'mouth'), and a few four or even five consonants (e.g., *'qrb* 'scorpion,' *sprd'* 'frog'). In fact, it is now generally accepted that many verbal roots were originally biconsonantal, later expanded by the affixing of another consonant or the insertion of a root vowel.

(c) Following on from (b) it has been asserted that the root meaning is carried by the (three) consonants with the vowels as modifiers. However, the same phenomenon of grammatical inflexion by vowel change is attested in non-Semitic languages, e.g., 'fall,' 'fell.' Further, as just mentioned, not all roots comprise three consonants and even where that is the case words can have identical consonants but distinct meanings, e.g., *RGM* 'to call' in Akkadian and Ugaritic but 'to stone' in Hebrew and Arabic.

(d) In syntax, coordinated main clauses predominate over the use of subordinate clauses.

4. Proto-Semitic

The fact that Semitic languages share so many characteristics has led historically to the search for a common ancestor usually termed 'Proto-Semitic.' Although scholars now would hesitate to posit development from an unattested proto-language, the clear existence of elements common to many recorded Semitic languages makes the concept of Proto-Semitic, or at least of 'Common Semitic', a useful one. Various theories have been put forward concerning the alleged homeland of the earliest Semites and their spread over the area where Semitic is found. A series of migrations in waves, all stemming from the Arabian desert, notably an Amorite migration in the second millennium BCE followed by a migration of Aramaeans in the first, has long been the accepted explanation. A refinement of this thesis prefers to speak of 'infiltration' rather than 'invasion.' The use of a lingua franca, for example, Akkadian in the second millennium BCE or Aramaic in the first may have played a part in the spread of different dialects.

Geographical linguistics has also been employed to help explain the evolution of the Semitic languages. Generally one can speak of a 'center' producing linguistic innovations which spread out to 'marginal' areas. In this case, the central area, the Arabian Peninsula, underwent less change than the two marginal regions, which comprised Syria to Mesopotamia to the north and Ethiopia to the south. In fact, the first of these 'peripheral' regions, especially in the northwest corner, itself became a major center of innovation through its special contacts with the non-Semitic world and with other Semitic-speaking areas. Examples of innovation are broken plurals and both the passive and the causative in the verbal system. It is also possible that instead of a single origin, there was a convergence of the various Semitic languages followed by a later divergence.

5. Semitic with Afroasiatic

The Hamito–Semitic phylum, now commonly referred to as Afrasian or Afroasiatic, has six branches: Berbero–Libyan (or Libyan–Guanche), Chadic, Cushitic, Egyptian, Omotic, and Semitic. After Egyptian, Semitic is the oldest recorded language group. These languages cover a very wide area (for maps see Diakonoff 1965) and their origin is very ancient. Broadly speaking they fall into two groups: the northern group, more open to change, with the great civilizations of Egypt, Syria, and Mesopotamia as its center, and the southern group, far removed from the center and therefore more traditional in character.

6. Subdivisions within Semitic

Although no overall consensus exists regarding allocation of languages within the family tree, it is generally accepted that there are two main branches: East Semitic (i.e., Akkadian, from about 3000 BCE) and West Semitic (ca. 2000 BCE). Further subdivision is into northwest (Ugaritic, Hebrew, Aramaic) and southwest (Arabic and South Arabic with Ethiopic). Diakonoff groups these languages as follows: northern peripheral (Akkadian), northern central (Eblaic, Canaanite, Amorite, Ugaritic, Hebrew, Phoenician–Punic, Aramaic, etc.), south central (Arabic), south peripheral (Early South Arabic), and Ethiosemitic both north and south. The disagreements involve the subbranches due, in part, to the discovery of languages such as Eblaic and Ugaritic. A new subbranch of the western branch, called 'Central Semitic' embracing Aramaic, Canaanite and, unexpectedly, Arabic has been proposed. The morphology of the verb, though, seems to suggest, instead, that Central Semitic has two further branches: Northwest Semitic (Ugaritic and the El-Amarna glosses; Arabic, Aramaic, and Canaanite) and Southwest Semitic (Egigraphic South Arabian). The different Semitic languages use a variety of scripts but this is of no significance for classification.

7. Modern Semitic Languages

The following languages survive among speakers in the 1990s: Amharic, Tigre, etc. in Ethiopia; Arabic in the Arabic-speaking world; Modern Western Aramaic dialects in Syria (notably the village of Malūla), Central Aramaic in Turkey, and Eastern Aramaic dialects (in the mountains of Kurdistan, the shores of Lake Urmia and elsewhere); Neo-Mandaic in Iran, and Modern Hebrew in Israel. Syriac is still in liturgical use.

8. Future Work

Future research needs to take into account languages only discovered in the late twentieth century (e.g., Eblaic, Ugaritic), and dialects (e.g., the Akkadian dialect used at Emar), and integrate them within the larger group of Afroasiatic languages. Certain languages or dialects such as Ya'udic (used in Northern Syria) remain unclassified. Detailed syntactic, as opposed to morphological analyses are rather sparse in certain of the Semitic languages. Onomastics, reflecting to some degree the correlation between a population and its language(s) is a further important area of future study. A synchronic approach, which examines a Semitic language or a group of related languages as it presents itself at a particular period, needs to be complemented by a diachronic approach which takes account of the historical evolution of the language or languages. Furthermore, scholars usually stress similarities (for example, between Ugaritic and Phoenician) but it is equally important to determine the individual characteristics of each language and establish, for instance, what makes Hebrew different from Akkadian. It also remains to be determined whether some languages are really dialects (e.g., Moabite may be a dialect of ancient Hebrew) or even pidgins (e.g., the glosses to the El-Amarna Letters). The interactions between such dialects and standard languages also require study.

Bibliography

Bennet P R 1998 *Comparative Semitic Linguistics. A Manual*. Eisenbrauns, Winona Lake, IN

Bergsträsser G 1983 *Introduction to the Semitic Languages: Text Specimens and Grammatical Sketches*. Eisenbrauns, Winona Lake, IN

Blau J 1970 *On Pseudo-Corrections in Some Semitic Languages*. Israel Academy of Sciences and Humanities, Jerusalem

Cohen D 1973–79 Qu'est-ce qu'une langue semitique? *Comptes rendues du groupe linguistique d'etudes chamito-semitique* **18–23**: 431–61

Diakonoff I M 1965 *Semito–Hamitic Languages: An Essay in Classification*. Nauka, Moscow

Edzard L 1998 *Polygenesis, Convergence, and Entropy: An Alternative Model of Linguistic Evolution Applied to Semitic Linguistics*. Harrassowitz, Wiesbaden

Garr W R 1985 *Dialect Geography of Syria–Palestine, 100–586* BC. University of Pennsylvania, Philadelphia, PA

Haayer G 1986 Languages in contact: the case of Sumerian and Akkadian. In: Vanstiphout H L J, Jongeling K, Leemhuis F, Reinink G J (eds.) *Scripta Signa Vocis: Studies about Scripts, Scriptures, Scribes and Languages in the Near East, presented to J. H. Hospers by his pupils, colleagues and friends*. Egbert Gorsten, Groningen

Hetzron R (ed.) 1997 *the Semitic Languages*. Routledge, London

Hospers J H 1973 *A Basic Bibliography for the Study of the Semitic Languages*. Brill, Leiden

Khan G 1988 *Studies in Semitic Syntax*. Oxford University Press, Oxford

Lipiński E 1997 *Semitic Languages. Outline of a Comparative Grammar*. Peeters, Leuven

Moscati S et al. (eds.) 1964 *An Introduction to the Comparative Grammar of the Semitic Lang-uages: Phonology and Morphology*. Harrassowitz, Wiesbaden

Rabin C 1963 The origin of the subdivisions of Semitic. In: Thomas D W, McHardy W D (eds.) *Hebrew and Semitic Studies: Presented to Godfrey Rolles Driver*. Clarendon, Oxford

Retsö J 1989 *Diathesis in the Semitic Languages: A Comparative Morphological Study*, Studies in Semitic Languages and Linguistics, 14, Brill, Leiden

Sekine M 1973 The subdivisions of the north-west Semitic languages. *Journal of Semitic Studies* **18**: 205–21

Ullendorff E 1958 What is a Semitic language? *Orientalia* **27**: 66–75

Voigt R M 1987 The classification of Central Semitic. *Journal of Semitic Studies* **32**: 1–21

Semitic Scripts

A. Gaur

Semitic scripts go back to a purely phonetic form of writing which originated in the Near Middle East between 1800–1500 BCE. They are generally divided into two, considerably different main branches, a northern and a southern one, with the latter being of less importance. In the course of time Semitic scripts became the most powerful instruments for the storage and dissemination of knowledge, stimulating the development and growth of a large number of new and highly effective writing systems in Europe and Asia—some extinct, some still in use (see *Alphabet: Development*).

1. Characteristics

The term 'Semitic' was first used in the eighteenth century in relation to a group of languages of which Hebrew and Arabic were the most prominent constituents, and referred to an imaginary connection with Shem, the son of Noah. The characteristics of Semitic scripts are that of the Semitic language: the root meaning of a word is born by the consonants (usually three in number), vowels serve mainly to fashion grammatical forms. Thus the Arabic root k-t-b, depending on the interpolated vowels, can stand for *kātib* 'writer,' *kataba* 'he wrote,' *kitāb* 'book,' *kutub* 'books' *kutubī* 'bookseller,' *kitāba* 'writing,' *maktab* 'office,' and *maktaba* 'library, book shop'; which vowels have to be interpolated depends on the context and on the grammatical construction of the sentence. This absence of vowel signs was to some extent remitted, at quite an early stage, by the use of consonant signs, such as *j* and *w*, for the representation of long vowels ī (ē) and ū (ō), and by using the sign for the glottal stop (*aleph*) for ā. Though this convention has been retained up to the present, it was never used consistently. Only relatively late, by the middle of the first millennium CE, languages such as Arabic, Hebrew, and Syriac developed additional systems by which vowels could be indicated through the use of diacritical marks, but such conventions were always strictly optional.

One of the advantages Semitic scripts offer is the small number of characters necessary for writing: twenty-two for North Semitic, twenty-nine in the case of South Semitic scripts. Compared to the large amount of signs used by other pre-Christian scripts of the Near Middle East (see *Egyptian Hieroglyphs*), and the even larger number of characters required for writing some of the contemporary scripts of the Far East, Semitic scripts are more economic, more easily accessible, and in consequence more flexible. The reason for this lies in the fact that Semitic scripts are purely phonetic in character: individual signs are meant to represent, not ideas or concepts, but the smallest possible sound unit (phoneme) of a particular language, and though phonetic elements played an important role in almost all ancient writing systems, in the case of Semitic scripts this element was for the first time used in an exclusive and consistent manner.

Other characteristics Semitic scripts share are the names given to many (though not all) individual letters, and (except for Arabic) the basic order in which those letters are represented; the direction of writing, somewhat ambivalent at first, has since c. 1100 BCE been consistently from right to left.

2. Origin

The question of the origin of the Semitic script is one of the most debated subjects in the history of writing and has occupied scholars and amateurs from antiquity to the present day. Was it an independent, unique invention of the Semitic people, an adapted borrowing from one of the prevailing scripts of antiquity—Egyptian, Cuneiform, Cretan, Cypriote, or Hittite, or did it originate in Crete from a set of prehistoric geometric signs (Evans 1909)? The theory still most widely accepted is that of an, at least tentative, connection with Egyptian role models which is to a large extent based on a series of short inscriptions found in Sinai and subsequently also in Palestine, which have (roughly) been dated to a period between ca. 1730–1580. This proto-Sinaitic script is thought to use Semitic words for pictorial signs which some scholars (Gardiner and Peet 1955) equate with carelessly executed Egyptian hieroglyphs (see *Egyptian Hieroglyphs*); the Semitic word used provides, by the acrophonic principle, the new value for this particular sign; e.g., the Egyptian sign for 'house' (p-r) stands, when translated into Western Semitic, for *bet*; the first letter of this word can then be used to represent the consonant *b*, and so forth. Adherent to this theory point out that to this day languages like for example, Greek or Hebrew name some of their letters in a fashion which seems to hark back to the object depicted by an original (Egyptian) pictorial sign (hieroglyph); despite the fact that those words are meaningless in either language. This theory is not universally accepted and much does indeed rest on guesswork. Some scholars (Sethe 1917), while agreeing to Egyptian influence, see this influence less in the outward appearance of the characters but in the concept of single consonant signs which indeed formed part of the Egyptian system (see *Egyptian Hieroglyphs*). It has been argued that the letters may just be conventional signs with no direct relation to original pictorial signs, and the names given to them nothing but mnemonic devices.

Another question still under discussion is: who invented the Semitic script? One single inventor (Schmitt 1938) or a group of people? The latter theory, which has generally more credence, has again been answered differently by different scholars, one theory naming the Hyskos, a Semitic pastoral people who used a Canaanite language (Sethe 1917) and conquered lower Egypt in about 1670 BC. Another possibility is that of a series of parallel developments in the Syro–Palestinian area which does, however, not exclude variations of mutual influence (Jensen 1970).

Attempts at cuneiform phonetic scripts were made, at around the same time, in northern Syria and Palestine. Inscribed clay tablets found at the site of the ancient city of Ugarit (ca. 1400–1200 BCE) document a system which uses some thirty different cuneiform signs (twenty-seven for consonants and three for vowels). The order of the letters is more or less the same as that used in the Phoenician and the

Hebrew system. Various theories have been put forward as to the relationship between the cuneiform and the linear forms of phonetic writing. In the opinion of some scholars (Diringer 1968) cuneiform phonetic scripts presuppose the existence of North Semitic but much is still speculative.

3. North Semitic Scripts

North Semitic scripts are generally thought to have emerged from the above proto–Sinaitic/proto–Semitic/proto–Canaanite. They are divided into various branches; the two most important ones, which are directly or indirectly responsible for the development of most contemporary forms of writing, are Phoenician and Aramaic (see *Masoretic Tradition*).

3.1 The Phoenician Script

The Phoenician script, which became stabilized ca. 1050 BCE, can claim the distinction of being the direct ancestor of the Greek alphabet (see *Alphabet: Development*); it seems to have evolved in a direct line of descent from early North Semitic consonantal script forms. During the long period of its existence (thirteenth/eleventh–third centuries BCE) it remained remarkably consistent, any development, even in its many colonial subdivisions—Cypro–Phoenician (ca. tenth–second centuries BCE) and the Cathargininan or punic script with its secondary branches (the last discovered Punic inscription dates from the third century CE)—being purely external. The number of letters (twenty-two) and their phonetic value stayed unchanged, as did the direction of writing which remained horizontal, with the script running from right to left.

3.2 The Aramaic Script

The most vigorous offshoot of the Phoenician script was Aramaic, which came into existence around the eleventh/tenth century BCE. Whereas the Phoenician script, despite its wide use among trading communities, had basically been a national script, Aramaic soon acquired a truly international character. In the seventh century BCE, after the Aramaic city states had lost their independence to the Assyrians, the Aramaic language, written in the Aramaic script, became the lingua franca of the Assyrian empire. In the period of the Persian Empire (ca. 550–323 BCE) Aramaic was the official language and the principal script of diplomats and traders between Egypt and northern India; its introduction to India had far-reaching consequences and led to the development of a large number of scripts in South and Southeast Asia. From the eighth century BCE onward Aramaic became progressively more cursive and simplified: the tops of certain letters such as *b*, *d*, and *r* (originally closed) became open, a tendency toward a reduction of strokes in certain letters appeared, final angles became more rounded, and ligature were introduced. After the collapse of the Persian empire the Aramaic language, and the Aramaic script, both up to then fairly homogenous, split into several local dialects, and corresponding scripts developed. The main variants being Jewish (Square Hebrew), Palmyrene, Nabataean (Arabic), and Syriac; there was in addition also the Mandaic script used by the Mandaeans, a gnostic Jewish–Christian sect. The continued tendency toward cursiveness in some of those scripts (notably Syriac and Nabataean) led to the emergence of final forms of letters, and of definite conventions about how individual letters should be joined.

3.3 Hebrew, Syriac, and Arabic

At first the Hebrews simply used the Phoenician script unaltered but by the ninth century BC a distinct script form appeared in an inscription found in the Moab. This early (paleo)–Hebrew script was however a purely national form of writing, more or less restricted to the people of Judea; in the course of time it was also favored by certain Jewish sects such as the Samaritans who retained it for their (handwritten) literature.

After the sixth century BCE this script was abandoned in favor of Aramaic. To give legitimacy to the new convention, its introduction was ascribed to Ezra, who is supposed to have brought it back from the Babylonian exile, and by the second century BCE a somewhat modified form of Aramaic was used by most Jewish communities. This script, which became known as Square Hebrew, spread eventually through-out the Jewish Diaspora and is still the standard Jewish book hand. Square Hebrew letters are bold and well proportioned, nearly all of them have a top bar or head, some have a base as well. Out of the twenty-two Hebrew letters five (*kaf*, *mem*, *nun*, *pe*, *tzade*) have dual form, one when standing initially or medially, and another in the final position. During the Middle Ages two cursive hands developed alongside Square Hebrew: the rabbinical (after the scholar Rashi d. 1105) used by medieval Jewish savants, and another cursive script which became responsible for the creation of many local variations in the Levant, Morocco, Spain, and Italy.

Like all Semitic scripts, Hebrew is purely consonantal, though some letters (*āleph*, *hē*, *vāv*, and *yodh*), generally referred to as *matres lectiones*, can be used for the representation of long vowels. But with Hebrew being replaced by Aramaic as the language of daily use, and the knowledge of Biblical Hebrew in

א ב ג ד ה ו ז ח ט י כ ל מ נ ס ע פ צ ק ר ש ת

t š r q ṣ p ʻ s n m l k y ṭ ḥ z w h d g b ʼ

Figure 1. The Hebrew script (order of letters from right to left).

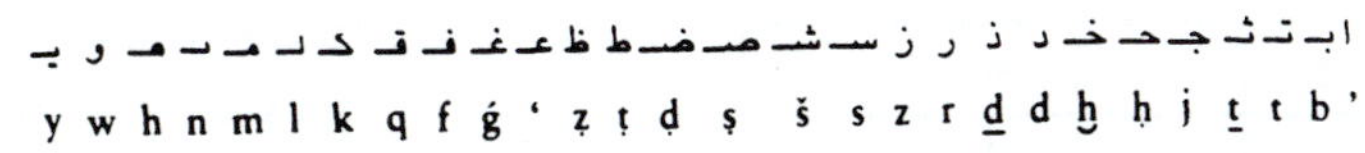

Figure 2. The Arabic script (order of letters from right to left).

decline, the need arose for a system of vocalization which would ensure the correct pronunciation of the Biblical texts. Vocalization by means of punctuation marks, consisting of little dots and dashes placed above or below a consonant, was probably introduced in the fifth or sixth century CE, with the older Syrian vowel indication system acting as model. The three main systems of vocalization are the Palestinian and the Babylonian (both supralinear) and (after the eighth/ninth century) the Tiberian (sublinear) which eventually superseded the others and is still in use today.

Syriac, another offshoot of Aramaic, developed in Edessa in the first century AD. In its early stage, it showed a strong resemblance to Palmyrene; both scripts have a tendency to join letters together, and most letters are written differently according to whether they stand alone, at the beginning of a word, at the end of it, or whether they are joined on both sides to another letter. An important event, which encouraged the maturing of the Syriac script, was the fact that Edessa became the focus for the spread of Christianity to Semitic-speaking countries. When in the third century the Bible was translated from Greek into Syriac (the local Aramaic dialect) the difficulty of transcribing Greek words written in the alphabet into Semitic consonant script encouraged moves toward a reasonably consistent and effective vocalization. The three main systems eventually used are: Nestorian, the earliest, which consists of a combination of the consonants *w* and *y* and a dot placed above or below them, and of one or two dots placed above below or above the consonant to be vocalized; the Jacobite system created c. 700 CE, which uses small Greek letters placed below or above the line, and the later Syriac system consisting of a combination of diacritical vowel marks and small Greek letters.

Over the centuries variations of Syriac, mainly based on the choice of the vocalization system, came into being.

The three most important ones being Estrangela (the earliest extant manuscript is dated 411 CE), Nestorian, and Jacobite; the two latter scripts developed as a result of a heretical split between Syrian Christians. As the Nestorian church grew in importance, Nestorian missionary monks traveled westward along the old trading routes and brought the knowledge of their script to central Asia and India.

Arabic, the final offshoot from Aramaic, is today the most prominent Semitic script, and, after the Latin alphabet, more widely used than any other form of writing. It is generally accepted that it originated in the fourth/fifth century CE from the script of the Nabataeans, the people of the first well-defined (northern) Arab kingdom around Petra (now Jordan). The Nabataeans employed two script variations, one monumental for inscriptions, and another, more cursive, which developed into a cursive forerunner of modern Arabic. Before the coming of Islam in the seventh century, the Arabs relied to a large extent on oral traditions for the transmission of their rich literature, but the revelation of the Qu'rān created the need for more widespread literacy.

The Arabic script consists of twenty-nine letters made up of the original twenty-two Semitic consonant signs, plus seven additional characters designed to represent the finer shades of pronunciation required by the Arabic language. Graphically those letters are made up of seventeen basic outlines plus diacritical points to distinguish otherwise identical character signs. Short vowels can be indicated by vowel marks written above or below the consonant preceding the vowel. Some Arab traditions name al-Khalil (d. 786) the inventor of this vocalization system which gained prominence in the eighth century, but its roots go back to much earlier, probably Syriac models. Vocalization is to some extent less important since Arabic has remained a living language. But the sacred nature of the Qu'rān requires exactness of transmission and to this day vocalization is employed consistently in Qu'rānic texts.

Already in the early Islamic period two distinct styles of writing existed: Kufic, a bold monumental script which became the favored script for the writing of the Qu'rān; and Naskhi, a more rounded and cursive form which served as model for a number of different styles that developed at the courts of non-Arab rulers—it is also the parent of the modern Arabic script.

4. South Semitic Scripts

South Semitic scripts remained confined within Arabia where they were used by the Minaens and Sabaens; there are also some inscriptions written in Himyaritic, Qatabanic, and Hadhramautic. Despite much effort, those inscriptions are still difficult to date, the earliest is thought to get back to c. 500 BCE

Figure 3. The South Semitic (or south Arabian) script.

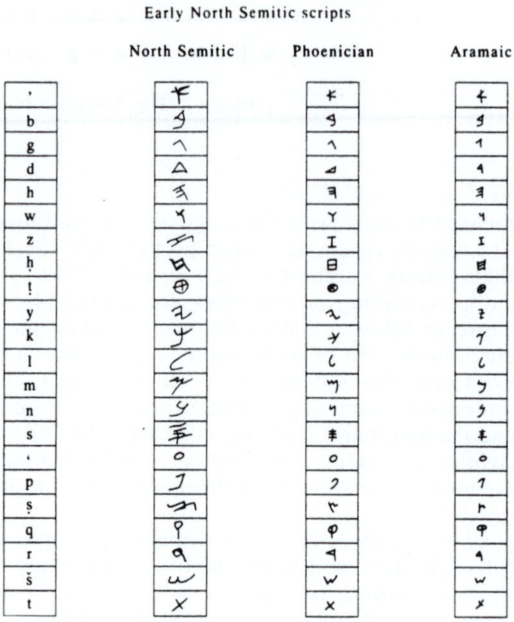

Figure 4. Early North Semitic scripts.

and the script(s) became extinct at around 600 CE; with the exception of Sabaen which spread into Africa and became the direct ancestor of the classical Ethiopic and the modern Amharic scripts. Sabaean (or south Arabian) inscriptions are written in a beautifully proportioned, elegant script, individual letters are carefully arranged and executed, often—especially after 300 BCE—in hollow relief. During the same period related forms of writing were used in northern Arabia for Thalmudene, Liyanite, and Safaitic. Inscriptions in those scripts are mostly irregular, cursive, stone graffiti; they too are difficult to date and may have existed down to the Islamic period.

The question of the origin of the South Semitic scripts, and their exact connection with North Semitic, is still under discussion. Some seventh/eighth century BCE inscriptions seem to indicate a line between proto–Canaanite and South Arabian (Healey 1990), but on the whole it is doubtful that South Semitic descended directly from North Semitic; e.g., the South Arabian/Sabaen *b*, *d*, *h*, and *p* have a more archaic appearance and are closer to Sinaitic; also, like Ugaritic, South Semitic, with its twenty-nine letters employs symbols for phonemes no longer presented in North Semitic languages. One view (Diringer 1968) sees in proto–Sinaitic a possible link between proto–Simitic/Canaanite and South Semitic.

5. Dissemination and Influence

The revolutionary achievement of Semitic scripts lie less in their (linear) appearance than in the applied ability to isolate individual basic sounds of a particular language and represent each sound by one distinct sign. The question about their exact origin will probably remain speculative. The reasons for their emergence, however, were geographical and historical: the cosmopolitan nature of the coastal towns, and changes in the old hieratic/theocratic Egyptian and Mesopotamian order which created the need for a more 'democratic' (Diringer 1968) form of writing.

All contemporary writing systems, with the exception of those based on the Chinese script can be traced back to Semitic prototypes which developed in the near Middle East between 1800–1500 BCE. Semitic scripts are consonantal in character; this means that words are primarily represented by their consonants which carry the root meaning. One of the advantages of Semitic scripts over previous systems (see *Egyptian Hieroglyphs*) is the small number of signs required which in turn promotes greater flexibility. When adapted for the use of non-Semitic languages Semitic scripts developed into alphabets in Europe (see *Alphabet: Development*), and into syllabic scripts in south and southeast Asia (see *Akkadian*); with variants along the old trade routes which connected Central Asia and China to the west.

5.1 Europe and the Alphabet

Around 1000 BCE the Greeks came into contact with the Phoenician form of writing and by using some of the Semitic consonant signs to represent vowels, they adapted it successfully to the use of their own (Indo–European) language. In the eighth century Greek settlers took the Greek alphabet to Italy where it was used, first by the Etruscans, and from around the

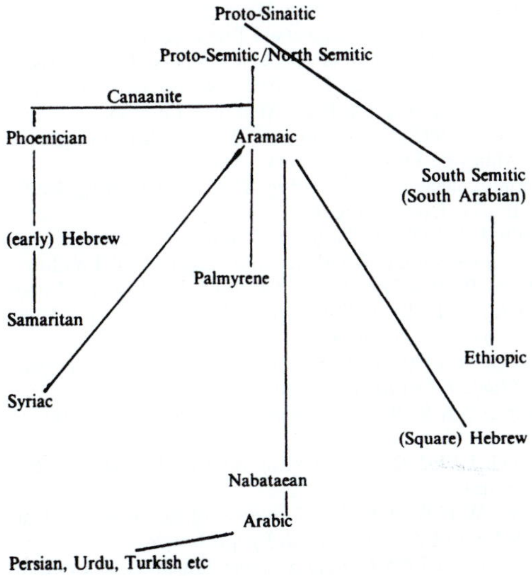

Figure 5. Relationship between main scripts.

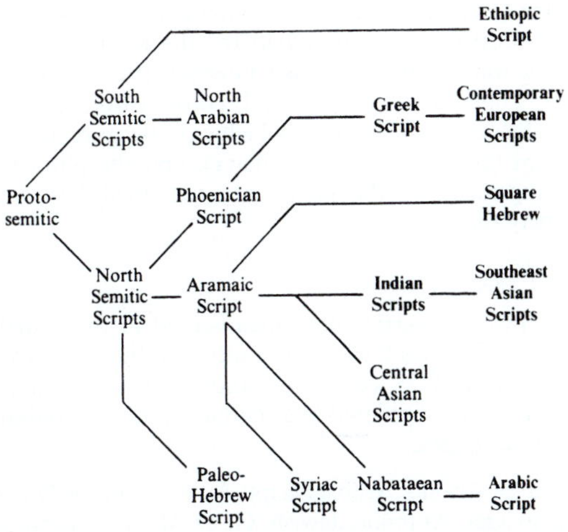

Figure 6. (After A. Gaur *A History of Writing*, reproduced with permission.)

seventh and sixth century BC on, by the Romans (see *Alphabet: Development*).

5.2 Iranian and Central Asian Scripts

Semitic traders and Christian (Manichaean and Nestorian) missionaries brought writing to Iran and Central Asia. The scripts which consequently evolved to serve, with varying degrees of success, a large number of local languages go directly or indirectly (via Syriac) back to Aramaic.

Decisive for the development of writing in Central Asia was the script used from 500 AD for Sogdian (a Middle Iranian language). It was a basically consonantal script, consisting of seventeen letters plus two special signs. At first letters were written separately but in the seventh century a more cursive hand developed which linked individual signs by a continuous baseline. In the eighth century the Uighur script evolved from a later form of Sogdian among the Buddhists in Turkestan. It was not a good instrument for writing Turkish, especially when the dots meant to distinguish certain letters were omitted. In 1206 Genghis Khan chose the Uighur script (and language) for the Mongol chancellery. Efforts to use the Mongolian vernacular as the official language led to a remodeling of Uighur; in 1272 the so-called Passepa script, an adaptation of the Tibetan seal script added some (Indian) syllabic elements; a hybrid and still cumbersome script called Kalika developed to become the forerunner of modern Mongolian.

5.3 Syllabic Scripts in Asia and Ethiopia

5.3.1 The Indian Subcontinent

Around the seventh century BCE Semitic traders and Persian administrators brought Aramaic to the northwestern part of India. Two scripts developed: Kharoshthi (third century BCE–seventh century CE), a short-lived and historically less important cursive business script, and Brahmi, first documented in the inscriptions of the Emperor Asoka (272–31 BCE); both of them syllabic. Since the correct pronunciation of the Vedic hymns had always been an essential aspect of ceremonial Hinduism, an orally transmitted knowledge of phonetics existed prior to the use of writing, and Brahmi was perfectly adapted to the sounds of Indian languages. All contemporary Indian scripts including those used in the Himalayan countries and in Sri Lanka, can be traced back to Brahmi. They consist basically of about 48 to 54 signs with vowels written in their full form only if used on their own or in an intial position; in conjunction with a consonant they are abbreviated to auxiliary signs before, after, below, or above the consonant sign.

5.3.2 Southeast Asia

During the first Christian millennium Indian traders colonists, military adventures, and Buddhist missionaries brought their scripts (mostly a South Indian grantha variation of Brahmi) to Southeast Asia. Designed to fit the linguistic peculiarities of Indian languages they now had to accommodate four entirely different language groups: Sino–Tibetan, Malayo–Polynesian, Austro–Asiatic, and Thai. This was achieved by a number of compromises (some more, some less effective), mostly restricted to the usage and the number of characters; sometimes diacritical marks were added for the representation of the tonal range. The basic internal structure of the script, the arrangement and construction of the syllabic unit, the way in which vowels were represented (either initial or auxiliary), and the phonetic arrangement of the characters remained however largely the same.

5.3.3 Ethiopia

The Ethiopic script, first documented in the fourth century CE, goes back to a South Semitic prototype. It consists of 27 consonant and seven vowel signs which are manipulated in a manner similar to Indian syllabic scripts.

See also: Arabic; Arabic Script: Adaptation for Other Languages; Aramaic, Jewish; Ge'ez; Hebrew, Biblical and Jewish; Islamic Calligraphy; Phoenician/Punic; Semitic Languages; Samaritan; Syriac, Christian; Ugaritic.

Bibliography

Diringer D 1968 *The Alphabet—a Key to the History of Mankind*, 3rd edn. Thames and Hudson, London

Driver G R 1948 *Semitic Writing: from Pictography to Alphabet*. Oxford University Press, London

Evans A J 1909 *Scripta Minoa*. Clarendon Press, Oxford

Gardiner A H, Peet T E 1955 *The Inscriptions of Sinai*. Egypt Exploration Fund Memoirs, London

Gaur A 1992 *The History of Writing*, 3rd enlarged edn. Abbeville Press, New York/London

Gaur A 2000 *Literacy and the Politics of Writing*. Intellect Books, Exeter/Oregon

Gelb I J 1952 *A Study of Writing: The Foundations of Grammatology*. Routledge and Kegan Paul, London

Harris R 1986 *The Origin of Writing*. Duckworth, London

Healey J F 1990 *The Early Alphabet*. British Museum Publication, London

Jensen H 1970 *Signs, Symbols and Cripts: An Account of Man's Effort to Write*. Hutchinson, London

Mercer S A B 1959 *The Origin of Writing and Our Alphabet*. Luzac, London

Naveh J 1982 *Early History of the Alphabet*. Magnes Press, Jerusalem

Petrie W F W 1908 *The Formation of the Alphabet*. British School of Archaeology in Egypt, London

Sampson G 1985 *Writing Systems*. Hutchinson, London

Schmitt A 1938 *Die Erfindung der Schrift*. Academia Fridericiana, Erlangen

Sethe K 1917 *Die neuentdeckte Sinaischrift und die Entstehung der Semitischen Schrift*. Nachrichten der Goettingen Gesellschaft der Wissenschaften, Goettingen

Syriac, Christian

S. P. Brock

Syriac is a dialect of Aramaic, itself one of the main northwest Semitic languages (Hebrew being another). Originally the local Aramaic dialect of Edessa (modern Urfa, southeast Turkey), Syriac is first attested in an inscription of 6 CE. Probably by the mid-second century CE it had already been adopted as the literary dialect employed by Aramaic-speaking Christians in north Mesopotamia. The first attested Christian writer to use Syriac, Bardaiṣan of Edessa, died in 222.

1. Spread and Use of Syriac

By the end of the fourth century, Syriac had become a literary language which straddled the eastern provinces of the Roman Empire (approximately modern Syria and southeast Turkey to the east of the Euphrates) and the western part of the Persian (Sasanid) Empire (approximately modern Iraq); in the following two or three centuries its use spread further both to east and west.

The theological controversies of the fifth and sixth centuries brought about a three-way split in the Christian communities using Syriac, out of which three separate Churches emerged: (a) the Church of the East (sometimes misleadingly called 'Nestorian'), mainly in the Persian Empire; (b) the Syrian Orthodox (sometimes misleadingly called 'Monophysite' or, after its sixth-century organizer, 'Jacobite'), in the eastern provinces of the Roman Empire and to a lesser extent in the Persian; and (c) the Melkites (from *malkā*, 'emperor'), designating those who followed the imperial theological policy of the Roman Empire, especially in the bilingual (Greek–Aramaic/Syriac) areas of Syria and Palestine (the Maronites are a subsequent offshoot from the Melkites).

Although the Arab invasions in the seventh century led to the gradual demise of Aramaic dialects as spoken languages, the literary dialects, including Syriac, continued in active use for several centuries more. In the Syrian Orthodox Church and the Church of the East a great deal of literature was produced in Syriac right up to the end of the thirteenth century, but since then its active use as a literary language has greatly diminished, though it has not even entirely disappeared in the late twentieth century, especially in Syrian Orthodox circles. By contrast, the Melkite and Maronite Churches soon dropped Syriac in favor of Arabic as a literary language, though it survived in a passive role as a liturgical language among some Melkite communities in south Syria and Lebanon until the sixteenth century, and among the Maronites until the present day (though it is rapidly being replaced by Arabic). In Middle Eastern (and a few diaspora) communities of the Syrian Orthodox and the Church of the East, Syriac still continues in use as a liturgical language, and many clergy can converse in it.

2. Cultural Role

Syriac has much the largest surviving body of Aramaic literature (much of it remains unpublished). Since Syriac has been transmitted largely through monastic or ecclesiastical circles, the vast majority of this literature is specifically Christian, though philosophy, medicine, and science are also represented to some extent. There must, however, once have existed a considerable Manichaean literature in Syriac (and perhaps also a pagan one, centred on Harran), but of this only minute scraps survive. The Golden Age of Christian Syriac literature was from the fourth to the seventh century. The finest literature is undoubtedly to be found in the field of poetry, and Ephrem (d. 373) ranks as one of the great Christian poet–theologians of all time. Much of the literature of the Arab period tends to be encyclopedic in character. In the ninth century, many of the translations into Arabic of Greek philosophical, medical, and scientific literature were made by way of Syriac intermediaries, since a long tradition of skilled translation from that Indo-European language into Syriac had already been built up. Syriac theological vocabulary has exercised a strong influence on Christian Arabic.

According to some scholars, the Syriac script may have played some role, alongside the Nabataean script, in the early development of the North Arabian script. Syriac script was adopted for writing Christian Sogdian and it has also been widely used in certain Christian communities for writing in other languages, notably Arabic (known as 'Garshuni' or 'Carshuni'), but also Armenian, Malayalam, and, occasionally, Greek, Latin, Kurdish, and Turkish.

3. Development

Once adopted as a literary language, Syriac has been extremely stable as far as morphology is concerned (though there were evidently certain developments in the first centuries of its use, prior to the emergence of standard Syriac, probably in the third century). By the fifth century two different reading traditions had already developed, largely as a result of the shift $\bar{a} > \bar{o}$ in the more westerly area (e.g., *yawnāyā* > *yawnōyō* 'Greek'); the original *ā* was thus preserved only within the Church of the East. In subsequent centuries two different vocalization systems grew up (c. seventh century) and the older *estrangela* (or 'rounded') script developed in two different ways in the two main Syriac Churches. None of these developments, however, prevented texts traveling from one community to the other.

The only development in Syriac over the course of some seventeen centuries has been in the fields of word-formation, lexicon, and syntax. In the pre-Arab period, when enormous numbers of translations from Greek were made, Syriac took in a large stock of Greek loanwords (e.g., Greek *poros* > *pursā* 'device,' whence *etparras* 'devise'), and many new adjectival and adverbial forms came into being (e.g., *ṣebyānāyā* 'voluntary' and *ṣebyānā'īt* 'voluntarily' < *ṣebyānā* 'will'). Syntax and style too came under strong Greek influence, especially in the sixth and seventh centuries. Arabic, by contrast, was never to have anything like the same influence on Syriac as Greek.

4. Modern Developments

Surprisingly, a number of new developments are taking place as a result of increasing ethnic awareness among some members of the Syriac Churches (primarily Syrian Orthodox), especially in the diaspora which now covers all five continents. Also important was the proclamation in Iraq in 1972 of cultural rights for 'speakers of Syriac' (which was intended to refer to speakers of Modern Syriac dialects). Some even have hopes of reviving Classical Syriac as a spoken language (it is in fact used as such in some church schools), and so seek to equip its lexical stock to meet the requirements of the modern world. As a consequence, many neologisms and calques on Western European languages have made their appearance—at a time when many Western scholars had considered Syriac to have been long defunct.

See also: Aramaic, Jewish; Christianity in the Near East; Garshuni; Peshitta.

Bibliography

Brock S P 1980 An introduction to Syriac studies. In: Eaton J H (ed.) *Horizons in Semitic Studies*. University of Birmingham, Birmingham

Brock S P 1989 Some observations on the use of Classical Syriac in the late twentieth century. *Journal of Semitic Studies* **34(2)**: 363–75

Drijvers H J W 1973 Syriac and Aramaic. In: Hospers J H (ed.) *A Basic Bibliography for the Study of the Semitic Languages*, vol. I. Brill, Leiden

Tamil

R. E. Asher

Tamil is one of the small number of the world's languages which have a continuous recorded history of more than two millennia. The earliest records date from 200 BCE and are of two sorts, namely a set of inscriptions in Ashokan Brahmi script and a unique body of poetry, the so-called Sangam works (see Rajam 1992). The language of this classical period is described in the earliest extant Tamil grammar, *Tolkāppiyam*. The main home of Tamil is still very close to what it was at the beginning of this history, and the greatest numbers of speakers live in the south Indian state of Tamil Nadu (91 percent of the 53,006,369 speakers recorded for the whole of India in 1991). There are substantial numbers of Tamil speakers in Sri Lanka (more than 4,000,000 in 1981) and Malaysia, and significant minorities in Singapore, Fiji, Mauritius, and (from more recent immigration) in the UK, the USA, and Canada. Tamil has been the vehicle for sacred and other texts of most of the major religions of India—Hinduism, Islam, Christianity, Buddhism and Jainism. Islamic texts have been published in Tamil written in the Arabic script.

1. Phonology

Tamil has a special place in the Dravidian family not only because of its long history but also because, being in many respects the most conservative member of the group, it has retained a number of features that were present 2,000 years ago. Thus, if loanwords are ignored (and there is a good case as far as the phonology of Tamil is concerned for treating native and nonnative vocabulary separately), the set of distinctive segments is very similar for the two periods.

For both classical Tamil (CT) and modern Tamil (MT), it is necessary to recognize five long and five short vowels: *a ā i ī u ū e ē o ō* (examples in italics, except where noted, follow the transliteration of the Tamil script used in the University of Madras *Tamil Lexicon* (*TL*); see Vaiyapuri Pillai 1924–39). Two further units in the script, *ai* and *au*, represent closing diphthongs, but it is not necessary for either period to set up separate vowel phonemes to account for these.

Among consonants, though there are voiced and voiceless segments, voice is not distinctive. In CT, there is a six-term set of plosives: velar *k*, palatal *c*, retroflex *ṭ*, alveolar *ṯ* (*TL ṟ*), dental *t*, and bilabial *p*; a similar analysis is justifiable for MT. In MT, the range of phones is considerably greater than this might suggest. Word-initial stops and medial geminate stops are voiceless; postnasal stops are voiced; intervocalically, the same units are realized by a more lax sound—voiced or voiceless fricative, or voiced stop. It is this complex allophony (as described by Firth in Arden 1934) that led Trubetzkoy (1939) and Jones (1967) to cite Tamil as an example of complex allophonic variation. CT nasals comprise a five-term set; that is, [ŋ] is not phonemic. If marginal cases are ignored, MT distinguishes only three nasals; retroflex, dental/alveolar, and bilabial. There are six other consonants in CT and MT: *y r l v ḻ* (a voiced retroflex continuant) *ḷ*. Alveolar and retroflex consonants occur initially in neither CT nor MT.

Over the centuries, borrowings have had a considerable impact on the phonology of Tamil, particularly those from Sanskrit and, later, from English. Linguistic purism has, however, always tended to have a stronger effect on Tamil than on the other major Dravidian languages, and loans in Tamil tend therefore to be assimilated to the native system to a greater degree. The result is that the four-way distinction among plosives in Sanskrit (the effect of the two independent binary features of voice and aspiration) is reduced to a maximum of two (voiced vs. voiceless) in Tamil, and the voice distinction too is lost in some dialects. It is nevertheless overwhelmingly the case that voiced and voiceless plosives contrast in word-initial position in most varieties of MT. This is not, however, reflected in the writing system. Word-initial consonant clusters, absent from CT, are found in later periods, and examples in MT are frequent (though they may be avoided in formal speech). The inventory of vowels has also been extended under the influence of English, the commonest of the additional vowels being /æ/.

2. Morphology

Tamil is appropriately described as an agglutinating language, in that: (a) morphologically complex word forms are usually readily segmentable into morphs; (b) the phonological realization of morphemes is in most cases relatively invariable; and (c) the correspondence between morph and morpheme approaches one-to-one. This can be illustrated by examples of the two major word classes, noun and verb. It will be noted that in both cases the first element is the root, that is to say that word forms are built up by suffixation.

A nominal form has the following structure: root (+plural) +case (+particle). The two most common particles in this position are interrogative *-ā* and emphatic *-ē*. For example:

ppṭṭi- kaḷ- il (1)
box PL LOC
'in the boxes'

Some case forms may be followed by postpositions. Depending on the stance taken on the question of the definition of case ending and of postposition, the number of cases proposed by different scholars varies. The most frequently listed set is: nominative, accusative, dative, comitative, genitive, instrumental/agentive, locative, ablative.

A finite verbal form typically has the following structure: root (+causative suffix) (+aspect) +tense +person (+particle). The causative suffix (*-vi*/*-pi*/*-ppi*) is less frequently used in MT than in earlier periods, and it is difficult to regard it as productive. the following is a representative example of a verb form (note that aspectual forms, whatever their tense, are attached to a past-tense stem, here marked by *-tt-*):

etu-tt- iru- kkiṟ- āṉ- ā (2)
pìck up PERF PRES 3SM INTER
'Has he picked [it] up?'

There are three first-person pronouns: singular, plural inclusive (i.e., of addressee), and plural exclusive; three second-person: singular, singular honorific (in formal Tamil), plural; six third-person: masculine singular, feminine singular, honorific singular, neuter singular, human plural, and nonhuman plural. Second- and third-person plurals are also used as honorifics. One personal ending on verbs serves for first-person plural inclusive or exclusive; all other pronouns each have their individual marker of concord. The selection of a personal ending for a noun subject depends on gender, which in Tamil is 'natural.' Nouns in Tamil fall into two classes—'high' and 'low'. 'High' includes humans (apart from very young children), gods, and demons. Within this set, nouns denoting male beings are masculine, and those denoting females are feminine.

3. Syntax

Tamil syntactic structures are head-final. The basic word order of a simple sentence is SOV. Adpositional phrases have postpositions. Modifiers (including relative clauses) and genitives precede nouns. Subordinate clauses precede main clauses.

Sentences, however complex, normally contain only one finite verb (and finite verb forms cannot be coordinated). Sequences of events involving the same individual as subject are normally expressed by a sequence of past participles ('pp' below), with only the last verb in the sequence being finite. There are, nevertheless, some exceptions to this generalization about the number of finite verbs in a sentence, the main one being that in the case of reported speech the embedded clause can, and most commonly does, contain a finite verb. Examples (3) and (4) illustrate some of these points. Segments in parentheses are linking consonants required by orthographic (and phonological) rules:

pārvati pai(y)- ai eṭu- ttu, vaṇṭi(y)- ai viṭ- ṭu (3)
parvati bag ACC pick up PP carriage ACC leave PP
iraṅk- i, ōṭṭal- ukku(p) pō- ṉ- āḷ
descend PP hotel DAT go PAST 3SF

'Parvati picked up her bag, got down from the train and went to the hotel.'

appoḻutu paiyaṉ ōṭ- i va- ntu 'ammā, 'ammā, (4)
then boy run PP come PP mother mother
nāṉ- um akkā(v)- ōṭu pō- kiṟ- ēṉ', ēṉ ṟ- āṉ
I also elder sister COM go PRES ls say PAST 3SM
'Then the boy ran up and said, "Mummy, Mummy, I'm going with elder sister too." '

4. Varieties of Tamil

Tamil is often, and rightly, cited as a paradigm case of diglossia (see Britto 1986). The variety used for most forms of writing, for public speaking, for news broadcasts, etc. exhibits clear differences at all levels from the language of informal conversation (for a summary of these differences, see Asher 1985: 254–62). Within colloquial Tamil, there is a wide range of dialects. Variation is along two parameters, namely regional (there being a wide divergence, for instance, between the Tamil of north Arcot and of Nagercoil) and social (different castes having their own distinct forms of speech). Partly through the influence of radio and films, a sort of standard colloquial is tending to develop, and it is this variety which is the basis for such works as Schiffman 1999 and Asher and Annamalai 2001.

5. Writing System

The Tamil writing system is alphasyllabic, in that it shares features both of a syllabary and of an alphabet. Word-initial vowels are written by independent letters, while vowel signs of different form

		a	ā	i	ī	u	ū	e	ē	ai	o	ō	au
		அ	ஆ	இ	ஈ	உ	ஊ	எ	ஏ	ஐ	ஒ	ஓ	ஔ
k	க்	க	கா	கி	கீ	கு	கூ	கெ	கே	கை	கொ	கோ	கௌ
ŋ	ங்	ங	[ஙா	ஙி	ஙீ	ஙு	ஙூ	ஙெ	ஙே	ஙை	ஙொ	ஙோ	ஙௌ]
c	ச்	ச	சா	சி	சீ	சு	சூ	செ	சே	சை	சொ	சோ	சௌ
ñ	ஞ்	ஞ	ஞா	[ஞி	ஞீ	ஞு	ஞூ	ஞெ	ஞே	ஞை	ஞொ	ஞோ	ஞௌ]
ṭ	ட்	ட	டா	டி	டீ	டு	டூ	டெ	டே	டை	டொ	டோ	[டௌ]
ṇ	ண்	ண	ணா	ணி	ணீ	ணு	ணூ	ணெ	ணே	ணை	ணொ	ணோ	ணௌ
t	த்	த	தா	தி	தீ	து	தூ	தெ	தே	தை	தொ	தோ	[நௌ]
n	ந்	ந	நா	நி	நீ	நு	நூ	நெ	நே	நை	நொ	நோ	[நௌ]
p	ப்	ப	பா	பி	பீ	பு	பூ	பெ	பே	பை	பொ	போ	பௌ
m	ம்	ம	மா	மி	மீ	மு	மூ	மெ	மே	மை	மொ	மோ	மௌ
y	ய்	ய	யா	யி	யீ	யு	யூ	யெ	யே	யை	யொ	யோ	யௌ
r	ர்	ர	ரா	ரி	ரீ	ரு	ரூ	ரெ	ரே	ரை	ரொ	ரோ	[ரௌ]
l	ல்	ல	லா	லி	லீ	லு	லூ	லெ	லே	லை	லொ	லோ	[லௌ]
v	வ்	வ	வா	வி	வீ	வு	வூ	வெ	வே	வை	வொ	வோ	வௌ
ḻ	ழ்	ழ	ழா	ழி	ழீ	ழு	ழூ	ழெ	ழே	ழை	ழொ	ழோ	[ழௌ]
ḷ	ள்	ள	ளா	ளி	ளீ	ளு	ளூ	ளெ	ளே	ளை	ளொ	ளோ	[ளௌ]
ṟ	ற்	ற	றா	றி	றீ	று	றூ	றெ	றே	றை	றொ	றோ	[றௌ]
ṉ	ன்	ன	னா	னி	னீ	னு	னூ	னெ	னே	னை	னொ	னோ	[னௌ]
j	ஜ்	ஜ	ஜா	ஜி	ஜீ	ஜு	ஜூ	ஜெ	ஜே	ஜை	ஜொ	ஜோ	[ஜௌ]
ṣ	ஷ்	ஷ	ஷா	ஷி	ஷீ	ஷு	ஷூ	[ஷெ]	ஷே	ஷை	[ஷொ]	ஷோ	[ஷௌ]
s	ஸ்	ஸ	ஸ	ஸி	ஸீ	ஸு	ஸூ	ஸெ	ஸே	ஸை	[ஸொ]	ஸோ	[ஸௌ]
h	ஹ்	ஹ	ஹ	ஹி	ஹீ	ஹு	ஹூ	[ஹெ]	ஹே	ஹை	[ஹொ]	ஹோ	[ஹௌ]
kṣ		க்ஷ		க்ஷி	க்ஷீ				க்ஷே				
śrī					ஸ்ரீ								

Figure 1. The Tamil writing system.

from these are used when a vowel occurs medially in a word after a consonant. The script is syllabic in the sense that sequences of consonant + vowel have to be read as a single unit, since the vowel sign may occur above, below, before, after, or both before and after the consonant (as two discontinuous components). It is alphabetic in the sense that in a CV symbol it is possible to identify which part represents the consonant and which the vowel. As in most South Asian scripts, there is no separate sign for a postconsonantal *a*, which is said to be 'inherent' in the consonant symbol. To indicate a consonant that is not followed by a vowel, a dot is placed above the consonant. The basic Tamil script is adequate to represent all phonological distinctions in the Dravidian part of the lexicon. To go some way towards the representation of new sounds introduced by the borrowing of words from Sanskrit, letters were added to this basic script some centuries ago from the Grantha script used in South India for the writing of Sanskrit texts. In Figure 1, the Grantha letters are in the last section. The last two are unusual, for Tamil, in representing CC(V) structures. The writing system was slightly simplified in the 1960s, and it is this reformed script that is presented below. Items between square brackets are theoretical constructs, in that none occurs in any Tamil word.

See also: Tamil Linguistic Tradition.

Bibliography

Andronov M S 1989 *A Grammar of Modern and Classical Tamil*, 2nd edn. New Century Book House, Madras

Arden A H 1934 *A Progressive Grammar of Common Tamil*. Church Missionary Society, Madras

Asher R E 1985 *Tamil*, 3rd impression. Routledge, London

Asher R E, Annamalai E 2001 *Colloquial Tamil*, Routledge, London & New York

Britto F 1986 *Diglossia: A Study of the Theory with Application to Tamil*. Georgetown University Press, Washington, DC

Jones D 1967 *The Phoneme: Its Nature and Use*, 3rd edn. Heffer, Cambridge, UK

Lehmann T 1989 *A Grammar of Modern Tamil*. Pondicherry Institute of Linguistics and Culture, Pondicherry

Meenakshisundaram T P 1965 *A History of Tamil Language*. Deccan College Postgraduate and Research Institute, Poona

Rajam V S 1992 *A Reference Grammar of Classical Tamil Poetry (150 BC to pre-fifth/sixth century AD)*. American Philosophical Society, Philadelphia, PA

Schiffman H S 1999 *A Reference Grammar of Spoken Tamil*. Cambridge University Press, Cambridge

Trubetzkoy N S 1939 *Grundzüge der Phonologie*, TCLP 7. Jednota Ceskoslovenských Matematiků a Fysiků, Prague

Vaiyapuri Pillai S 1924–39 *Tamil Lexicon*, 6 vols and Supplement. University of Madras, Madras

Tibetan

P. Denwood

Tibetan comprises a multiplicity of spoken dialects, and a standardized written language which is the vehicle of a major civilization whose main religion is Buddhism.

1. Geography, Affiliation and History

Tibetan is spoken in the Tibetan Autonomous Region of China, and in adjoining high-altitude parts of Bhutan, India, Pakistan, Nepal, Burma, and the Chinese provinces of Yunnan, Szechwan, Kansu, and Chinghai. Estimates of the number of speakers range from about three to seven million. It is also used as a religious language by the Mongols and some ethnic groups in Nepal.

It is usually reckoned to be a member of the Tibeto–Burman group which, with the Karen and Chinese groups, forms the Sino–Tibetan family.

The Tibetans and their language emerge into history in the seventh century CE, It is from that time also that their alphabetic writing system, based on a model of Indian origin, is alleged to date. Since then the written language has been closely associated with Buddhism, having been used to translate a vast range of literature, mostly from Sanskrit. There is also an indigenous literature (much of this also religious); and now also journalism and other 'nonfiction.' The spoken dialects, poorly recorded from premodern times, have often developed separately from the written language.

2. Grammar

Tibetan clauses are of SOV (subject–object–verb) type, with OSV order also possible. The main clause is the last in the sentence. Nouns may be polysyllabic; verbs, adjectives, and particles are monosyllabic. Many verbs have variant forms or 'roots' corresponding to tense/aspect differences; other parts of speech are invariable, apart from sandhi variation with suffixed or prefixed particles. Particles express noun case categories and adjectival degree, mark the ends of subordinate clauses, and establish verb tense/mood/aspect categories. Most are suffixed, though a few negative, dubitative, or interrogative ones are prefixed. Past tense and often present tense clauses are syntactically ergative, the subject of a transitive clause being marked with a particle identical in form to the 'instrumental' noun particle. Subjects and objects are normally omitted unless they are 'new.'

3. Phonology

Central, southern, and eastern dialects have well-developed lexical tone which has been analyzed in various ways, the simplest being as a two tone system (high and low). These dialects mostly have few word-initial consonant clusters, and often a system of vowel harmony. In western (and some northeastern) dialects tone is usually less well-developed or absent, with a richer variety of consonant clusters and less vowel harmony. The writing system, whose spellings are full of consonant clusters and give little evidence of vowel harmony, would suggest that the dialect it was based on may have been pronounced somewhat like the modern western dialects. The most 'archaic' of these to have been investigated is Balti, spoken by a Muslim population in northern Pakistan.

4. Honorifics

The written language and most of the dialects have a well-developed honorific system, in which choice of verb is determined by the social status of the person acting as its grammatical subject or, in some cases, direct or indirect object. Nouns, adjectives, and verb particles are also affected.

5. Sample Sentence (Lhasa dialect: tones unmarked)

ɂalɛɛ . raŋgi sejala tʃa ʃaana, ɬɛsɛ namʃi ni guŋga tropo taŋ jaaga siipo jøbədra.

'Well! To believe what you say, the climate of Lhasa seems to be warm in winter and cool in summer!'

ɂalɛɛ (exclamation). raŋ (noun) 'you.' gii (ergative subject-marking particle). se (transitive verb) 'say.' ja (nominalizing particle). la (dative-locative particle). tʃa (noun) 'belief.' ʃaa (verb) 'place.' na (subordinate clause-final particle) 'if.' ɬɛsɛ (noun + genitive particle) 'Lhasa.' namʃi (noun) 'climate.' ni (topic-marking particle). guŋga (noun) 'winter.' tro (adjective) 'warm.' po (adjective particle). taŋ (particle) 'and.' jaaga (noun) 'summer.' sii (adjective) 'cool.' po (adjective particle). jø (verb) 'is.' bədra (verb particles) 'seem.'

6. Tibetan Script

The maintenance of the Tibetan writing system in a remarkably standardized form over almost the whole Tibetan-speaking area since about the seventh century CE has been vital to the unity and success which Tibetan civilization has been able to achieve over vast areas of thinly populated and inhospitable territory. The script is used to write classical Tibetan, modern literary Tibetan, Dzongkha (Bhutanese), Ladakhi, Sikkimese, and, rarely, other Tibetan dialects. In its early days it was occasionally used in Central Asia for writing other languages, while a development of it, the 'Phags-pa script,' was used for writing Mongolian during the thirteenth and fourteenth centuries. Apart from the occasional use of the Perso–Arabic script in Baltistan and Ladakh, it is the only script which has been regularly employed for the Tibetan language.

7. History

The earliest securely datable example of its use is on the stone pillar at Zhol, Lhasa, from about 764 CE. Native historical tradition dating the adoption of writing to shortly before 650 may be not far wide of the mark. Tradition credits the invention of the script to one Thonmi Sambhota, a Tibetan of noble birth who traveled to some part of India, Nepal, or possibly Khotan under royal sponsorship. However, this attribution has been seriously questioned by some modern scholars.

Many of the letters of the script were clearly modeled on those from some version of the Brahmi alphabet as used to write Sanskrit, Prakrit, and other languages in India and Central Asia. Scholars are not in agreement as to the precise alphabet, region, and period of origin. A number of the letters required for Sanskrit were not taken over; conversely, some new ones were devised. Although Tibetan writing generally follows the principles of the Indian system, its strongly syllabic emphasis and invariable nature, well suited to the language, might owe something to the example of Chinese characters. Considerable care evidently went into the development of the writing system; once created, the normative attitude of Tibetan culture ensured a high degree of standardization and conservatism, though a few early spelling conventions became obsolete between the ninth and thirteenth centuries. Local attempts at script reform have mostly come to nothing, though a few modifications have been made in Bhutan.

8. Alphabet and Syllable

The script runs from left to right and comprises a string of separate syllables with no indication of word division. There are 30 consonant letters and 4 vowel letters, 2 common punctuation marks and several rarer ones, and 10 numbers. A syllable consists minimally of: (1) a consonant (the 'radical'); (2) an inherent, unmarked vowel transliterated as *a*; and (3) a following punctuation mark (dot or vertical stroke). In addition there may be: (4) a letter inserted before the radical ('prefix'); and/or (5) a letter above the radical ('head letter'); (6) a letter below the radical ('subjoined letter'); (7) a vowel letter above or below the radical, displacing the inherent vowel; (8) a

ཀ་ཁ་ག་ང་། (ka, kha, ga, nga) ཅ་ཆ་ཇ་ཉ། (ca, cha, ja, nya)

ཏ་ཐ་ད་ན། (ta, tha, da, na) པ་ཕ་བ་མ། (pa, pha, ba, ma)

ཙ་ཚ་ཛ་ཝ། (tsa, tsha, dza, wa) ཞ་ཟ་འ་ཡ། (zha, za, 'a, ya)

ར་ལ་ཤ་ས། (ra, la, sha, sa) ཧ་ཨ། (ha, a)

ཨ་ཨི་ཨུ་ཨེ་ཨོ། (a, i, u, e, o)

Figure 1.

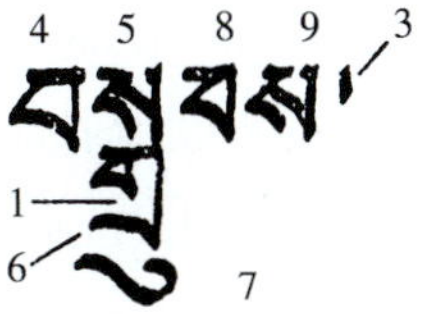

Figure 2.

letter after the radical ('final') (sometimes with a second vowel letter); and (9) a letter after the final ('second final'). Thus the graphic form of a syllable can be complex. Since it usually exists as a standardized and unchanging entity, the rules for deriving the pronunciations of the different modern dialects and reading styles, though on the whole consistent, can also be complex to the point of bizarreness (the syllable in Fig. 2, which can be transliterated as *bsgrubs*, is pronounced 'drup' in the modern Lhasa dialect). As with Chinese characters, however, the persistence of a single form for a written syllable which is still relatable to varying spoken forms is a distinct advantage.

Twenty of the consonants are also used reversed when transliterating Sanskrit words (mainly in book titles). In addition to the printing style of the letters as shown in Fig. 1 and used for carving wooden printing blocks and stone inscriptions, there is a variety of cursive manuscript styles, and a rectilinear style used for seals.

9. Recent History

Developments since World War II have led to the political fragmentation of the Tibetan speaking world and the increasing influence of other languages, particularly Chinese, English, Urdu, and Nepali. However, the same period has also seen the development of Modern Literary Tibetan (in Tibet and among refugees), Dzongkha (in Bhutan), and Ladakhi (in Kashmir) as written languages. It has also witnessed a Tibetan diaspora which has led to vastly increased interest in the language and culture, centered on a numerically small but culturally active refugee community in India and Nepal. In the late twentieth century, there has also been a marked revival of Tibetan in the Mongolian People's Republic. Despite the problems experienced by its speakers, Tibetan remains a living, vigorous, and developing language.

See also: Sanskrit; Buddhism, Tibetan.

Bibliography

Goldstein M C 1973 *Modern Literary Tibetan*. University of Illinois Press, Urbana, IL

Miller R A 1956 *The Tibetan System of Writing*. ACLS, Washington, WA

Ugaritic

W. G. E. Watson

Ugaritic was discovered in 1929 when tablets in a previously unknown script were unearthed at Ras Shamra in North Syria. Once deciphered it was quickly realized that the language was close to Phoenician, Hebrew, and other Northwest Semitic languages. The users of Ugaritic were principally the inhabitants of the city of ancient Ugarit (Ras Shamra) and its environs (notably Ras Ibn Hani) on the coast of Syria. But clay tablets with Ugaritic writing have been found as far afield as Hala Sultan Tekke in Cyprus and Beth Shemesh in Israel. The city of Ugarit flourished in the Late Bronze Age, from 1400 to 1200 BCE when it was sacked by the 'Sea Peoples.' It is conceivable that the language survived as Phoenician (see *Phoenician/Punic*) although this is not certain.

The texts in Ugaritic found at Ras Shamra and elsewhere include letters, literary texts (mythological texts, epics), interstate treaties, lists of personal names (e.g., ration lists, allocations of equipment), commercial and administrative documents, scribal exercises (chiefly abecedaries), rituals, incantations, a set of equine medical texts, and inscribed clay models of lungs. There are also a number of multilingual vocabularies which are of particular importance since they provide equivalents in Hurrian, Sumerian, and Babylonian for many Ugaritic words.

The script is cuneiform but instead of representing syllables, as in other cuneiform scripts, the 30 signs stand for letters of the alphabet. It has 27 letters with the addition of two vowel letters *'i*, *'u* and the Hurrian consonant *ś*, making a total of 30 in contrast to the 22-letter alphabets of Phoenician and Hebrew. Word-dividers are used, but not consistently. Like syllabic cuneiform and unlike Hebrew and Phoenician, Ugaritic was usually written from left to right.

As in Phoenician the simple uninflected verb form (*qtl*) can also be used with any subject including the first person singular (*ank*). So, *ngš ank* means 'I approached' (*ngšt* would be expected). Ugarit was a cosmopolitan city and Ugaritic vocabulary includes many loanwords. Typical examples are *śśw*, 'horse' (Indo–European); *grbz*, 'type of armor' (Hurrian); *ḥtṯ*, 'silver' (Hittite); *snnt*, 'swallow' (Akkadian). The personal names also reflect the polyglot character of Ugarit, e.g., *urǵtṯb*, '(The god) Teshub is faithful' (Hurrian); *alḫn*, 'miller' (Akkadian); *snb*, 'healthy' (Egyptian).

See also: Phoenician/Punic; Semitic Languages.

Bibliography

Caquot A et al. 1974, 1989 *Textes ougaritiques. vol. 1: Mythes et Légendes. vol. 2: Textes Religieux, Rituels, Correspondance.* Les Editions du Cerf, Paris

Gordon C H 1965 *Ugaritic Textbook.* Pontifical Biblical Institute, Rome

Pardee D 1997 Ugaritic. In: Hetzron R (ed.) 1997 *The Semitic Languages.* Routledge, London

Watson W G E, Wyatt N (eds.) 1999 *Handbook of Ugaritic Studies.* Brill, Leiden

Wyatt N 1998 *Religious Texts from Ugarit. The Words of Ilimilku and his Colleagues.* Sheffield Academic Press, Sheffield

Xella P 1981 *I testi rituali di Ugarit I.* Consiglio Nazionale delle Ricerche, Rome

Yiddish

D. Katz

Yiddish is spoken on all the world's continents by East-European-born Jews and some of their descendants. Most estimates place the number of speakers at four million, the (rapidly declining) majority of whom are elderly East Europeans (whose children do not speak the language), and a (steadily growing) minority of whom are members of traditionalist Hasidic communities, where the language continues to serve as principle vernacular.

Yiddish consists of an intricate fusion of diverse stocks. The most ancient component is Semitic (postclassical Hebrew and Aramaic). Most of the lexicon and grammatical machinery are derived from medieval Bavarian and east central German urban dialects. In the Baltic and Slavonic lands, the language acquired a Slavic component. There is a trickle of medieval Romance.

Yiddish arose on the banks of the Danube about a thousand years ago as the vernacular of the nascent civilization of Ashkenaz, the traditional Jewish name for central and east European Jewry and their progeny. Semitic vocabulary and sound patterns brought from the Near East fused with local German dialects, but close ties with Jews elsewhere led to a Germanic component not identifiable with any one German dialect. A number of catastrophes, including the Crusades from 1096 and the massacres following the Black Death of 1348–49, led to extensive geographic expansion. Many Ashkenazim, motivated also by the promise of religious freedom and economic opportunity offered by some Eastern European rulers, made their way to Lithuania and Poland, forming the nucleus of the Eastern Yiddish speech community. At its geographic apex in the sixteenth century, Yiddish territory stretched from Holland in the northwest and Italy in the southwest to deep into Russia.

As a result of assimilation to German and other central European languages, the western dialects, known as 'Western Yiddish,' declined sharply in the eighteenth century. By about 1500, the center of gravity of the language was shifting to Eastern Europe, which eventually became the new center of Ashkenaz. The key cultural center was Vilna (now Vilnius), known as the 'Jerusalem of Lithuania.'

The earliest dated records are late-eleventh-century proper names in martyrs' lists from the First Crusade; a single sentence from 1272; and a continuous literary work from 1382.

Yiddish is written in the Hebrew alphabet and the evolution of its spelling system entails the adaptation of a Semitic alphabet to a European language, accomplished by recycling as vowels the letters for old Semitic pharyngeal consonants that had disappeared in the European phonetic environment (Semitic alphabets are strictly consonantal). The modern spelling system, dating to the early twentieth century, boasts a perfect one-to-one relationship between the graphemes and the phonemes of the standard language (which is based on the Lithuanian dialect).

By abolishing the preterite tense of verbs, weak–strong opposition of nominal declensions, and 'dangling verbs,' Yiddish has streamlined its syntax vis-à-vis German. Its Germanic-type phonology (minus front rounded vowels and the voiceless palatal fricative or 'ich'-Laut), coexists with Semitic features which survive in the Semitic component of the language, e.g., boundary-triggered penultimate stress (which shifted from ultimate but did not merge with Germanic root-bound stress). Phonetics have been profoundly impacted by the Slavonic component, which provided a series of palatalized consonants and regressive voice assimilation. The unique Yiddish intonational pattern has been the subject of much speculation, including the impact of the traditional chant of Talmudic study.

The following is a sample sentence in standard pronunciation (words not of German origin are marked HA = Hebrew or Aramaic, Sl = Slavonic):

lexatxíə [HA] hɔt dɛr zéjdə [Sl] gɪzɔ́kt nejn, nɔr ibəraxtɔ́g hɔt ɛr xarɔ́tə [HA] gɪhát.

To start with, grandfather said no, but a week later he changed his mind.

In traditional Ashkenazic society, Yiddish participated in a system of internal trilingualism which comprised two sacred languages, the 'more prestigious' Hebrew used for communal documents and much of rabbinic literature, and the 'most prestigious' Aramaic, written only by leading scholars of the Talmud and Kabbalah. In addition, most Ashkenazim had working knowledge of one or more 'external' (i.e., coterritorial, non-Jewish) languages.

At least from the fourteenth century onward, a secular Yiddish literature developed, featuring knightly romances modelled on, e.g., King Arthur or Dukus Horant. A popular religious literature arose, too, and both strands fed into the European-wide launch of Yiddish printing in the 1530s and 1540s, which made for a standard literary language modeled broadly on the Western Yiddish of Italy, Germany, and Holland.

In the eighteenth century, the Hasidic movement in the Ukraine, and latter Poland, elevated Yiddish to the status of sanctity as part of its religious philosophy of reaching out to the masses. The very same secularizing 'enlightenment' movement that helped to eradicate Western Yiddish served to develop a modern Yiddish literature in Eastern Europe, where its proponents had to use the language to reach the majority of the population.

Both strands, Hasidism and Enlightenment, promoted the abandonment of the old Western-based standard and the rise of a new standard written language based on the major Eastern European dialects: Northeastern (popularly 'Lithuanian'), Mideastern ('Polish'), and Southeastern ('Ukrainian'). By the mid-nineteenth century, didactic and polemic works gave way to masters of prose. They were followed by the first modern poets by the turn of the century. Pro-Yiddish forces in Eastern Europe organized a conference at Chernowitz in 1908 which proclaimed Yiddish to be 'a national language of the Jewish people' thereby marking the transition from folk language to modern national language (albeit one without a country of its own). Some 5.5 million Yiddish speakers were murdered by the Nazis and their collaborators in World War II. The Holocaust forever obliterated the native eastern European Yiddish speech territory.

During the twentieth century, many Jews in Western countries shunned Yiddish as the reminder of oppression in the 'old country,' while the Zionist movement and the State of Israel in its early years pursued a harsh campaign to eradicate the language as a purported threat to the revival of modern Hebrew. In the Soviet Union, Lenin's pro-Yiddish policies, which enabled a major literature to arise in the 1920s, were reversed by Stalin who eventually purged nearly all major writers in a campaign culminating in the murder, on August 12, 1952, of 24 major Yiddish writers and cultural leaders.

Nevertheless, Yiddish and its literature have thrived in the hands of groups of devotees in many lands, and have of late enjoyed the prestige of Isaac Bashevis Singer's Nobel prize (1978) and inclusion into the curricula of many leading universities (including Harvard, Oxford and the Sorbonne). Several thousand young devotees, Jewish and non-Jewish, are taking over the mantle from the disappearing last generation of East-European-born speakers, and pursue the modern secular language, in total separation from the hundreds of thousands of young Hasidim who speak the language as a vernacular but have no interest in modern secular literature.

During the mid-1990s, the last generation of East-European-born writers and editors were still producing an impressive, and even astounding number of quality books and journals, in Israel (more than anywhere), the United States (the second major center), and on a smaller scale in Argentina, Australia, Canada, France, Russia, and other countries.

The history of Yiddish linguistics dates back to early sixteenth century Christians, who studied

Hebrew and Aramaic in the humanist tradition, and investigated Yiddish as an adjunct to their study. They were followed by numerous schools of Yiddish scholars driven by myriad motivations, including the selling of dictionaries and grammars to Christian businessmen who wanted to learn the language of Jewish colleagues; theologians who wanted to train missionaries in the language of the targeted population; criminologists who needed to decipher the Hebrew and Yiddish elements in Rotwelsch, the German underworld language; anti-semites who purported to reveal 'secrets of the Jews,' and, in the late nineteenth century, Germanists trained in the comparative method. In the wake of the Chernowitz Conference of 1908, young East-European scholars, themselves native speakers of Yiddish who partook in the Yiddish culture movement, began a tradition of Yiddish linguistics as a field in its own right. In 1913, Ber Borokhov (1881–1917) founded modern Yiddish linguistics by publishing two seminal works: 'The Aims of Yiddish Philology' and a bibliography covering 400 years of writings on the language. In 1925, the Yivo Institute for Jewish Research was founded in Vilna, and produced a prodigious number of linguistic volumes. Its founder, Max Weinreich (1884–1969), escaped to America where he spent the rest of his life completing his monumental *History of the Yiddish Language*.

Bibliography

Birnbaum S A 1979 *Yiddish: A Survey and a Grammar*. University of Toronto Press, Toronto

Weinreich M 1980 (trans. Noble S) *History of the Yiddish Language*. University of Chicago Press, Chicago, IL

SECTION IV

Special Language Uses

Introduction

J. F. A. Sawyer

In addition to the languages of their sacred texts, religious communities frequently employ special languages or language varieties in other contexts. Glossolalia or 'speaking in tongues' is a conspicuous example where utterances in a language unintelligible to virtually everybody present add a prophetic dimension to public worship. Another is hwyl, where the voice of the Welsh preacher transcends ordinary modes of expression. Untranslateable or 'nonsense' languages are a feature of particular religious rites among the Australian aborigines of northern Arnhem land, while some American Indian medicine men use an incomprehensible language when talking to each other or to supernatural powers. Probably more for social than spiritual reasons, Rastafarians have evolved a distinctive mode of speech among themselves, unintelligible to the outsider, substituting, for example, the morpheme *I* for the first syllable in such terms as *Idrin* 'brethren' and *Ital* 'vital,' and transforming words like *dread* into terms of approbation. A similar phenomenon can be observed in the cargo cults and several new religious movements.

Examples of the belief that everyday language is not sacred enough for religious purposes are the use of Sumerian in ancient near eastern rituals long after it had ceased to be a living language, Sanskrit in Hindu worship, and Hebrew in Judaism. Other examples are Ge'ez in Ethiopian Christianity, and Syriac in Eastern Christianity (in Kerala in South India, for example). The notion that no human language at all, ancient or modern, natural or artificial, is adequate, appears both in the well-known Quaker predilection for silent worship and in the 'language-transcendent' meditation techniques of some varieties of Christianity and Buddhism, for example, 'nothing but sitting meditation' (*shikan-za*) in Zen. Theologians, like Thomas Aquinas, have sought alternative ways of tackling the problem of finding language adequate to speak of a deity who is by definition beyond human understanding. One is by reference to the distinction between apophatic and cataphatic ways of describing things; another by adducing the notions of symbolism, allegory, metaphor, and analogy whereby it may be possible to speak of one thing, and by so doing convey to the believer some idea of another.

Within the context of a religious community meeting regularly for worship, special languages or language varieties are often used for public prayer, hymn-singing, preaching and the like, partly to heighten people's awareness of the sacredness of the moment, and partly to highlight the continuity of what they are doing with the worship of other communities elsewhere. Thus, for example, by using precisely the same Hebrew words as their ancestors have used for generations, as they celebrate Passover or Yom Kippur ('the Day of Atonement'), Jews all over the world experience a sense of solidarity as 'God's people' which would not be possible in any other language. The same applied until the twentieth century to the use of Church Latin in the Catholic Mass, and the distinctive English of the 1661 Book of Common Prayer in the Church of England. A similar phenomenon can be observed in Brazilian Candomblé and Cuban Santeria where the more solemn rituals are marked by a greater use of African languages than Portuguese or Spanish. The introduction of the vernacular into worship places the emphasis more on communication and the fuller participation of the people, although the precise wording of the modern Catholic 'Missal' and the Anglican 'Alternative Service Book' must still be officially authorized. Conservatism, intended to maintain continuity with tradition, is a major factor operating in many if not all religious communities, which consequently often show a tendency to use archaic language (e.g., *thou* and *thee*) in worship.

A special type of communication with a transcendent reality through a human being is known as Channeling, a term derived from Spiritualism. Well-known published examples of channeled material include *Oahspe: the New Age Bible* (1881) and *A Course in Miracles* (1975). There is also the widespread use of set words and formulae, sometimes in a special language, for curses, blessings, incantations, oracles and other performative utterances, where what language does is more important than what it means. Personal names, especially divine names, are particularly common in this context, as in the case of the repetition of the name of Allah by Muslims and the frequent use of the tetragrammaton, the divine name too sacred to pronounce, on Jewish amulets.

Allegory

J. F. A. Sawyer

It is in the nature of language that words can have symbolic or metaphorical meanings as well as a literal meaning, and an allegory, in its most general sense, is a text understood to have a meaning other than its literal meaning. Influenced by the Platonic notion of a timeless world of ideas beyond the material world of sense perception, Jewish and Christian scholars, notably Philo (first century CE) and Origen (third century CE), developed at Alexandria an allegorical method of interpretation, in opposition to more literal and historical approaches to biblical exegesis practiced elsewhere. It provided a means whereby interpreters could find deeper spiritual or moral meanings in such texts, making them relevant to their own situation. There are some allegories in the Bible (*Ezek*.17:2; 24:3 RSV) and some passages have been regularly interpreted allegorically, notably 'the allegory of old age' (*Eccl*.12:1–7) and the Song of Songs, interpreted by the rabbis as an allegory of God's love for Israel, and by Christians as an allegory of Christ's love for his Church. An early Christian example, used to give scriptural authority to the method, is Paul's allegorical interpretation of the story of the sons of Sarah and Hagar in *Gal*. 4:21–31.

In the Latin West, particularly under the influence of Jerome and Isidore, allegory comes to be understood as the dominant method whereby believers can arrive at the true, mystical meaning of scripture. One of its most common uses was in apologetic or polemical discourse, directed by Christians against Jews and heretics. The reformers and humanists, and the succeeding two centuries of higher criticism, biblical archaeology and semitic philology, rejected allegorical interpretation as arbitrary, artificial and far-fetched, confident that the literal meaning of the text and the author's intention were sufficient goals for biblical exegesis. More recently disillusionment with the historical critical quest for a single original meaning along with a new appreciation of the fact that texts can and do have more than one meaning, has led to a reassessment of the value of allegorical interpretations, ancient, mediaeval and modern.

See also: Metaphor; Christian Views on Language; Religious Symbols.

Bibliography

Bloomfield M W (ed.) 1992 *Allegory, Myth and Symbol*. Harvard University Press, Cambridge, MA

Dawson D 1992 *Allegorical Readers and Cultural Reasoning in Ancient Alexandria*. University of California Press, Berkeley, CA

Soskice J 1985 *Metaphor and Religious Language*. Oxford University Press, Oxford

American Spirituals

W. Best

American Spirituals are an indigenous folk musical tradition rooted in the slave experience. Expressions of sorrow, faith, and the hope for deliverance, spirituals reflect the cosmology of Christian slaves in words rich with Biblical imagery and metaphor. 'Exodus,' 'Land of Canaan,' 'Judgment Day,' and 'Gabriel's trumpet' are recurrent themes. Though essentially sacred in content, American Spirituals also contain a double and more subversive social meaning. 'Go down Moses' and 'Didn't my Lord deliver Daniel' have as much to do with rebellion and the desire for freedom as with the epic stories of Ancient Israel. Slave Christians often used the spirituals to warn of impending danger, as well as to shepherd escaping slaves to freedom. Runaway slaves understood that the way was safe when they heard 'Steal away to Jesus' or 'Get on board, little children.'

In addition to African musical styles, there have been several influences upon American Spirituals, including eighteenth century evangelical hymns, revival 'shout songs,' and slave 'work songs.' The Methodist revivals of the early nineteenth century brought wide attention to American Spirituals. These meetings, which often comprised large numbers of slaves and free blacks, welcomed the musical form, and revivalists incorporated it into their worship. By the 1850s American Spirituals had become associated as much with evangelicalism as with slave Christianity.

During the late nineteenth century American Spirituals underwent a process of professionalization. White American composers restyled the spirituals to conform to European classical music. What had been emotionally charged songs of spiritual yearning became highly structured, sentimental chorals, sung by classically trained voices. And, what had been the exclusive domain of Protestant churches and the lower classes became top billing at concert halls, often attended entirely by elite whites.

The process of professionalization did have some positive effects. Many of the songs were written down for the first time and thus preserved for posterity. This process also drew attention to, and raised financial support for many black colleges in the South that had been founded after the Civil War. Most of these institutions had established choral groups that specialized in American Spirituals. The most famous of these groups was the Fisk Jubilee Singers, formed in 1871.

Bibliography

Cone J H 1992 *The Spirituals and the Blues.* Orbis Books, New York

Thurman H 1975 *Deep River and the Negro Spiritual Speaks of Life and Death.* Friends United Press, Indiana

Work J W 1940 *American Negro Songs.* Crown Publishers, New York

Archaism

K. Wales

'Archaism' has two main senses, one of particular importance to philologists and lexicographers, the other to literary critics and stylisticians.

In one sense archaism (and its appropriate adjective 'archaic') refers to the retention or survival in language of linguistic features no longer in general circulation. These are not yet obsolete, but are outside the common core. Archaisms tend also to be associated with varieties that are themselves marked: such as regional dialect (e.g., *drouth* 'thirst' and *oxter* 'armpit' in Scots and Hiberno–English); or registers of ancient or conservative tradition, such as legal language (*witnesseth*; *thereto*) and the liturgy. It is in this register that the archaic 2sg pres. forms of pronoun and verb (as in '*thou* who *takest* away…') survive; although the remoteness of these forms and others from everyday usage had led controversially to the 'modernization' of liturgical language. The pressure towards comprehensibility is matched by the strong association of religious archaisms with a special elevated ceremonial language appropriate for its use: hence the resistance to change.

Until the early twentieth century archaism was also an accepted feature of poetic language, reflecting a similar idea that poetic diction was in some way special, different from everyday usage, and that it reflected a common inherited tradition. In the poems of Robert Bridges (d. 1930), archaisms are still as prominent as other traditional poetic devices of personification, apostrophe, etc.: e.g.,

> Beautiful must be the mountains *whence ye* come,
> And bright in the fruitful valleys the streams, *wherefrom*
> *Ye* learn your song…
>
> (*Nightingales*)

Archaism in poetry can also be of a different kind, difficult sometimes for readers to identify without some knowledge of the history of the language, but reflecting the second sense of the term. For archaism can mean not only the survival of older forms, but the revival: words can have dropped out of the language completely, but be deliberately revived; or an older state of the language can be artfully recreated or 'imitated.' This kind of archaism Leech (1969) usefully terms 'linguistic anachronism'; and the appropriate adjective for this distinction is 'archaistic.' The poetry of Spenser provides an excellent illustration of archaistic forms, because of the consistency of use in his poems *The Shepherds Calendar* and *The Faerie Queene*, and the variety of his motivations: his admiration for Chaucer, his desire to create a 'Doric dialect' suggestive of antiquity and rusticity for pastoral; and a chivalric bygone age for epic. So the 'April' Eclogue of *The Shepherds Calendar* begins:

> Tell me, good Hobbinoll, what *garres* thee *greete*?
> ('makes'; 'weep')

Archaisms of this kind are also a distinctive feature of historical novels, where writers like Sir Walter Scott in the nineteenth century and Georgette Heyer in the twentieth century try to give a period flavor to dialogue. In some cases, anachronism in the usual sense of the word is the result: the archaism may not be placed in its accurate temporal setting, however obsolete in modern usage.

Bibliography

Leech G N 1969 *A Linguistic Guide to English Poetry*. Longman, London

Blasphemy

W. S. F. Pickering

The word 'blasphemy' is derived from Middle English *blasfemie*, but its deeper roots are in the Greek *blasphēmia*. Primarily it refers to verbal irreverence towards God, or to sacred persons or objects. By extension it becomes the verbal defamation of people, as individuals or collectively. The word has come into the Western world mainly through Christian ideas and through many references to blasphemy in the Bible, which are related to or derived from Jewish religious thought.

For the Jews, blasphemy is associated with the fear of offending God. If people speak evil of God, retribution will follow, either against the individual offender, or just as likely against society itself. One way of placating a potentially wrathful God is to take measures against offenders by casting them outside the bounds of society or more generally through execution, often by stoning. Blasphemy thus stands within the province of religious penal law.

Whereas blasphemy can only have meaning within a religious society, the form of the religion has to be one where the deity is conceived as a spiritual being having personal qualities and such anthropomorphism implies that the deity is offended by blasphemy. Blasphemy is more prominent in monotheistic societies—Judaism, Christianity, and Islam—than polytheistic ones, such as Hinduism, where the multiplicity of gods tends to fudge the issue.

Blasphemy is closely associated with cursing. That Job was tempted to 'curse God and die' means an open rejection of God's majesty and creative power and a realization that such a rejection incurs death. To hate God is the worst of all crimes.

In the West, blasphemy became a criminal offence through the establishment of Christianity as the official religion and through the code of Justinian I in the sixth century. After the Reformation in England, it was moved out of the ecclesiastical courts and became part of common law. The law was rigorously applied until the 1920s. Owing to the growth of humanism and religious pluralism, it has been less frequently used and the punishment for offenders diminished from execution to a minimal fine. It was revived or appealed to in UK legal cases involving *Gay News* (1977) and *The Satanic Verses* written by Salman Rushdie (1989). A movement exists in the UK for the abolition of the law without replacement. Originally the law grew out of laws against heresy. It was defended by Sir Matthew Hale in the seventeenth century as being a threat to the state and liable to give rise to social disorder. In the late twentieth century, in the West, such reasons are said to be no longer applicable and its retention is a violation of the notion of freedom.

That blasphemy as a criminal offence is rarely appealed to nowadays stands as a clear indication of secularizing influences in society. Some, for example, the French sociologist, Emile Durkheim (1858–1917), have argued that the existence and application of laws against sacrilege and blasphemy are an indicator of the religious character of the society. An absence of such laws reflects the absence of a religious component within society.

The word is now only rarely used even within the churches themselves. Whereas the Authorized Version of the Bible (1611) invariably translated Hebrew or Greek words with the English word 'blasphemy,' modern translations tend to employ less strong or offensive words, for example, 'slander,' 'words against,' 'speak against.'

See also: Names: Religious Beliefs.

Bibliography

Encyclopaedia of Religion and Ethics 1908. T and T Clark, Edinburgh
Levy L W 1981 *Treason Against God: A History of the Offense of Blasphemy*. Schocken Books, New York
Nokes G D 1928 *A History of the Crime of Blasphemy*. Sweet and Maxwell, London

Blessings

B. G. Szuchewycz

Blessings are utterances associated primarily with the sphere of religious activity, but they also appear with varying frequency in the politeness formulas and parenthetical expressions of everyday conversation. In both contexts the dominant linguistic feature is the use of formal and/or formulaic language. Blessings, particularly in religious ritual, may also be accompanied by specific nonlinguistic features including gestures (e.g., laying on of hands, the sign of the cross) and the use of special objects (e.g., a crucifix) or substances (e.g., water, oil). Concern with such patterned relationships between linguistic form, on the one hand, and social context and function, on the other, is central to the study of the role of language in social life.

Linguistically, blessings (and their opposite, curses) are marked by the use of a special language which may be either a highly formal or archaic variety of the dominant language (e.g., Classical Arabic) or a different code entirely (e.g., Latin). In addition to their specific content, linguistic features such as repetition, special form (e.g., parallel couplets), special prosody (e.g., chant), and fixity of pattern distinguish blessings from other types of speech and contribute to their formal and formulaic character.

The concept of blessing in Jewish, Christian, and Muslim thought, as in many other traditions, is concerned with the bestowal of divine favor or benediction through the utterance of prescribed words. As such, blessings represent an example of the belief in the magical power of words, other manifestations of which include the use of spells, incantations, and curses.

As an aspect of religious behavior, blessings are associated with essential components of public and private ritual activity. They are performed by religious specialists in situations of communal worship as, for example, in rituals where a general blessings of those present marks the end of the event. Blessings are also used by nonspecialists to solemnize, sacralize, and/or mark the boundaries of social events. In traditional Judaism, for example, *brokhe* 'blessings' include short formulaic expressions used in a wide variety of situations as well as longer texts associated with domestic ceremonies (e.g., a grace after a meal) and specific occasions or rites (e.g., Passover, weddings, funerals). Common to all is a fixity of form and the strict association of specific texts to specific occasions.

In the Bible, the Hebrew root *brk* 'blessing' is associated with a number of meanings. A blessing may be an expression of praise or adoration of God, a divine bestowal of spiritual, material, or social prosperity, or an act of consecration which renders objects holy. The Greek *eulogia* of the New Testament stresses the spiritual benefits which are obtainable through Christ, the gospels, and the institution of the church (e.g., liturgical blessings). Each instance—praise, benediction, and consecration—represents a social and religious act accomplished through the use of a highly conventionalized form of language.

Blessings often function as 'performatives.' A performative is a speech act which when uttered alters some state of affairs in the world. Under the appropriate conditions, if a minister states, 'I pronounce you man and wife,' then a marriage has been socially established. If someone says, 'I promise,' then a promise has been made. Similarly, blessings function as religious performatives, in that the utterance of the requisite expression precipitates a change in spiritual state.

Mastery of the linguistic formulas, however, is not sufficient for the successful realization of blessings (and other performatives). The existence of an extralinguistic institution (e.g., family, descent group, religious institution, etc.) with differentiated social roles and statuses for the blessor and blessee(s) is a necessary precondition to an authentic and valid performance of the act. Only certain individuals may pronounce a couple man and wife and create a legally binding marriage. The same is true of blessings.

Catholicism, for example, distinguishes those blessings exchanged between lay persons, the spiritual value of which depends on the personal sanctity of the blessor, from liturgical blessings, which carry the force of the ecclesiastical institution. As the institution itself is hierarchically organized, so too is the right to confer particular blessings. Some may be performed by the pontiff alone, some only by a bishop, others by a parish priest, and yet others by a member of a religious order. Similarly, and in a very different ethnographic context, among the Merina of Madagascar the *tsodrano* is a ritual blessing in which seniors act as intermediaries between ancestors and those being blessed, their juniors. A father bestows fertility and wealth on his son through a ceremonial public blessing which transfers to the son the power of the ancestors in a ritual stressing the continuity and reproduction of the descent group.

Like other performatives, blessings operate properly only within a context of social and cultural norms and institutions, which are necessary for their realization and to legitimate and maintain their force.

Much of human face-to-face interaction is ritualistic in nature, and it has been argued that the use of formalized and prepatterned linguistic and nonlinguistic behavior in everyday life is evidence of a link between interpersonal rituals of politeness on the one hand, and ritual behavior in the sacred sphere on the other (Brown and Levinson 1987). Blessings are an example of a specific linguistic routine common to both.

In nonreligious contexts, blessings are evident in the politeness formulas and parenthetical expressions of everyday conversation: for example, the English 'Bless you!' as a conventional response to a sneeze. Similarly, in greetings, thanks, and leave-takings, blessings are exchanged between interlocutors and, although they may literally express a wish for supernatural benefits, their primary communicative function is as highly conventionalized markers of social and/or interactional status. In both their religious and secular uses blessings thus function as expressions of solidarity, approval, and good will.

When embedded parenthetically within larger sentences or longer texts, blessings may also function as semantically and interactionally significant units. In oral narratives the use of a blessing (or curse) serves to communicate directly the emotional state or attitude of the speaker towards the topic, providing a means of internal evaluation and signaling speaker involvement in the text. Yiddish speakers, for example, make extensive use of a large set of fixed expressions, many of which are blessings, for just such a purpose (Matisoff 1979).

See also: Cursing; Magic; Performative Utterances.

Bibliography

Brown P, Levinson S C 1987 *Politeness: Some Universals in Language Usage*. Cambridge University Press, Cambridge

Matisoff J A 1979 *Blessings, Curses, Hopes and Fears: Psycho-Ostensive Expressions in Yiddish*. Institute for the Study of Human Issues, Philadelphia, PA

Ries J 1987 Blessing. In: Eliade M (ed.) *The Encyclopedia of Religion*. Macmillan, New York

Westermann C 1978 *Blessing: In the Bible and the Life of the Church*. Fortress Press, Philadelphia, PA

Channeling

J. Algeo

Channeling is communicating messages through a human being (the *channeler* or *channel*) from an entity on another level of reality. It is a phenomenon that grew out of Spiritualism and is similar to the latter in that it purports to convey messages to the living from disembodied entities. Channeled messages, however, are more likely to be philosophical or theological in content than personal; they are directed to the channeler or to the world at large rather than to specific persons who consult the channeler; and they are likely to come from entities of unidentified or extraterrestrial origin rather than from dead relatives or friends. Channeling shows less indication of becoming institutionalized into associations or churches than Spiritualism did, although it may be used by institutions as a method of transmitting messages and directions to their members and organizations have grown up around channeled material.

Well-known channeled material includes *Oahspe: The New Age Bible* (1881), *The Aquarian Gospel of Jesus the Christ* (1907), *The Urantia Book* (1955), *The Seth Material* (1970) followed by other Seth books, and *A Course in Miracles* (1975). Channeling entities and their channelers include 'Uvani' by Eileen Garrett (generally thought of as a medium), 'Ramtha' by J. Z. Knight, 'Lazarus' by Jach Pursel, and 'Li Sung' by Alan Vaughan. Although contemporary channeling may seem to be a new phenomenon, like Spiritualism it has ancient roots. The speaking in tongues (or glossolalia) reported in the Acts of the Apostles and practiced by Pentecostal Christians is, except for its unknown language, similar to much channeling. Christian mystics and saints, such as Hildegarde of Bingen and Joan of Arc, have heard interior voices. Andrew Jackson Davis, the first proponent of Spiritualism, received channeled messages before the Fox sisters inaugurated modern Spiritualism.

A number of physical, nonsupernatural explanations have been offered for channeling. Some channeled messages are 'heard' by the channeler, although no sound waves are perceptible in the environment. It has been proposed that such messages are auditory hallucinations generated by the right hemisphere of the brain and perceived by the left hemisphere. Some channeled messages are spoken by the channeler without that person's conscious awareness of the message or even the fact of communication. It has been proposed that such messages are the product of multiple personalities, only one of which can be dominant and communicative at a time. Because some channeling experiences are similar to those of altered states of consciousness induced by mind-altering drugs like LSD or in cases of schizophrenia or by electrical stimulation of the left temporal lobe of the brain (the language area), it has been proposed that channeling is a spontaneous abnormal functioning of the brain. All such explanations assume the need for a reductionist physical explanation, and none provide evidence.

Channeling is of several kinds. *Classic channeling* is the reception of information from an identified (or self-identified) source. *Open channeling* is the reception of information from an unidentifiable source. *Trance channeling* is the reception of information while the channeler is in an unconscious state. Except for the term *channel* and its derivatives, the vocabulary of channeling is derived mainly from Spiritualism, psychology, and the New Age lexicon.

See also: Glossolalia; Spiritualism; Ecstatic Religion.

Bibliography

Brown M F 1997 *The Channeling Zone: American Spirituality in an Anxious Age.* Harvard University Press, Cambridge, MA

Klimo J 1987 *Channeling: Investigations on Receiving Information from Paranormal Sources.* Tarcher, Los Angeles

Copying

I. Reader

Copying religious texts by hand is a practice found in many religious cultures, and many of the important themes of this practice can be illustrated by examining it within the context of one tradition, Buddhism, and especially in its East Asian and Japanese contexts. The tradition of copying Buddhist sutras by hand—normally using ink and a calligraphy brush—has been especially prominent in the Buddhist world, and particularly in China and Japan, whose ideogram-based scripts have lent themselves to the development of calligraphy as an artistic and spiritual practice.

The transcription of the scripts of the Buddhist canon fulfils a number of purposes and meanings. Its origins were clearly pragmatic: prior to the development of printing blocks it was the only means of producing new copies of the texts which were needed to assist in the propagation of the faith. To copy the sutras was therefore transformed into an act of immense merit since it aided in this process. The practice was also based on the belief that the written script—since it both expresses the literal meanings of the sutras and articulates the sacred sounds believed in many Asian cultures to be inherent in the words of sacred texts—contained an inherent sacrality, and that as written representations of the words and meanings of Buddhism, the sutras themselves were inherently holy objects. To copy them was therefore to create anew the spiritual power of the texts, and it was an act that thus brought virtue and merit to the practitioner.

Because sutra copying was believed to be a merit-making activity, it often accompanied the presentation of petitions to Buddhist figures of worship, either at collective or individual levels. Projects to make large numbers of copies of sutras to be stored in specially built pagodas or storehouses, in furtherance of mass prayers (for example, for rain, for good harvests or for the protection of the state) were common in East Asia in the first millennium CE, especially in Japan, where the Imperial government during the Heian (794–1185) period established an Office of Sutra Copying.

The practice of *shakyô* (sutra copying in Japanese) also became highly popular in Japan as part of the act of making individual petitions or prayers to the Buddhas: the petitioner would make a copy of a sutra and use this as an offering while making a request for some form of benefit or boon from the Buddhas. Copies of sutras offered in this way can frequently be seen at Buddhist temples, having been left there by ardent petitioners. This is especially common at important pilgrimage temples. Pilgrims on the 88 temple pilgrimage in Shikoku, Japan, for example, may make 88 copies of the *Hannya Shingyô* 'Shorter Heart Sutra' prior to departing on pilgrimage, so as to leave one copy at each temple on the route. This is the most commonly copied sutra in Japan since it is just 262 ideograms long and can be copied in around an hour and chanted as a prayer in a few minutes. Copying sutras such as the *Hannya Shingyô* in Japan is often treated and promoted by the Buddhist clergy as a form of meditative exercise, and many temples hold *shakyô* meetings in which participants silently copy the *Hannya Shingyô* while meditating together under the guidance of a priest. Numerous *shakyô* manuals, usually expounding the spiritual virtues of the practice and of the *Hannya Shingyô* itself, as well as explaining the calligraphic techniques needed to copy the sutras in an appropriate manner, can be found in bookshops in Japan. Thus, although the pragmatic need for copying sutras by hand has long disappeared with the advent of printing presses and the like, the spiritual values of the practice retain an appeal in contemporary Japan and testify to the enduring belief in the inherently sacred nature of the written text in Buddhism.

See also: Sutra; Mantra; Islamic Calligraphy.

Bibliography

Abe R 1999 *The Weaving of Mantra*. Columbia University Press, New York

Stevens J 1993 *Sacred Calligraphy of the East*. Shambala Publications, Boston

Cursing

P. Collins

A curse is a solemn act, spoken or otherwise, intended to invoke a supernatural power to inflict harm on a person, group or thing. Cursing is the opposite of *blessing*. Many, if not most, religions facilitate cursing by legitimizing the punishment, by supernatural as well as natural means, of perceived wrongdoers. Cursing involves three main elements: the source of the curse (the cursing), the object or target of the curse (the cursed), and the curse itself, generally but not always spoken. Biblical curses sometimes issue directly from God (e.g. Deut 28:20), sometimes from one acting on God's authority (e.g. Noah, Gen 9:25). Among the Dinka of the Sudan, Prophets may curse, as may the priestly caste called spear-masters (Lienhardt 1961). In any case, the cursing rarely act on their own behalf, claiming authority from divine and/or secular sources. Among the Fang, elders are allowed to curse on account of their place in the lineage (Fernandez 1982: 182). The cursed may be animate or inanimate, singular or plural and may or may not be made aware of the curse. The curse itself may be in the common language or in an esoteric tongue known only to the cursing and may include a non-discursive form such as the construction of some material object, a doll in the likeness of the cursed for instance or the snuffing of candles in medieval ecclesiastical curses (Little 1993: 9).

A curse is often composed of several parts. First, the person cursing will cite his or her authorities which in Christian cursing will probably be a hierarchical process commencing with God the Father, the Son, the Holy Spirit, the Virgin Mary Mother of Jesus, the Saints, the Apostles, the Martyrs, and so on. In other traditions, authority might derive from a wholly evil source such as the devil or one of his minions. After establishing their legitimate authority and simultaneously making explicit the seriousness of the curse, the next task is to clarify the punishment to be inflicted on the cursed. Traditionally, excommunication has been the most dire punishment in the Christian church, but then there are many horrible alternatives: death, illness, maiming, the annihilation of family, friends and property. The curse continues with the naming of the person, group or thing cursed. The motivating intention is generally revenge against someone who or something which has wronged the Supreme Being(s), the cursing, the religious community, or society in general. There is often a short coda allowing for the curse to be lifted should the cursed repent. Curses may be revoked for various reasons: the cursed might appease the cursing by giving them gifts or by compensating those they have wronged.

See also: Blessings; Incantations; Magic; Performative Utterances; Religious Symbols; Taboo Words.

Bibliography

Fernandez J 1982 *Bwiti, an Ethnography of the Religious Imagination in Africa*. Princeton University Press, Princeton, NJ

Lienhardt G 1961 *Divinity and Experience*. Clarendon Press, Oxford

Little L K 1993 *Benedictine Maledictions. Liturgical Cursing in Romanesque France*. Cornell University Press, Ithaca, NY

Dhāraṇī (root dhṛ, 'to hold')

I. Astley

Originally mnemonic devices for retaining long sacred texts, *dhāraṇī* came to be regarded as possessing the same efficacy as the texts themselves and developed into magical formulae, very often used, by lay and ordained alike, as protective devices as well as aids to concentration. Distinguish *mantra*, which generally are shorter and have no discursive basis, and *bīja*, which are monosyllabic *mantra*.

In orthodox Indian traditions, *dhāraṇī* and *mantra* are an integral part of life's religious dimension, their correct utterance being ensured by conferring them personally in a clearly defined ritual context, a contributing factor in the rise of esoteric cults in both orthodox and unorthodox Indian traditions. The magical aspect of *dhāraṇī* was also a major factor in the lay, ordained, and sociopolitical propagation of Buddhism. Protection (individual and collective) against natural disasters, danger, ill health, evil influences, and psychic phenomena has been paramount in Buddhism from a very early stage. In the Theravāda traditions of South and South-East Asia such protective rites have traditionally taken the form of *parittā*, chanted at public gatherings, though the *dhāraṇī* and *mantra* of the Mahāyāna and Vajrayāna traditions are also historically important.

In the Vajrayāna a highly elaborate system of rituals and their doctrinal (mainly Yogācāra and Madhyamaka) interpretation was developed, incorporating *dhāraṇī* (and *mantra* and *bīja* in particular). The combination of complex ritual, doctrinal sophistication and mysterious efficacy ensured the widespread success of the Vajrayāna in China, Korea and, especially, Japan, where the Shingon and Tendai traditions flourish to this day. They in turn have influenced indigenous Shintō and other beliefs, which have adopted Buddhist *dhāraṇī* and *mantra*. Tibet developed similar traditions and though much was destroyed in the Chinese invasion of Tibet from 1950 onwards, refugee communities maintain them.

See also: Sūtra; Mantra.

Bibliography

Bharati A 1965 *The Tantric Tradition*. Rider, London

Chou Yi-liang 1945 Tantrism in China. *Harvard Journal of Asiatic Studies* **8**: 241–332

Euphemism

W. D. Redfern

'Euphemism' means 'sounding good.' Instead of blunt or coarse words, euphemizers prefer bland or enhancing terms. The ancient Greeks propitiated the implacable Furies by calling them *Eumenides* 'the good-tempered ones,' as they feared invoking them by their right name, *Erinyes*. Euphemism recognizes the magical and dangerous potentialities of words.

Some experiences are too vulnerable to be discussed without safeguards. The prime subjects of anxiety or shame are: death, the supernatural, sexuality, the body, illness. The precise areas of taboo are culture- and era-specific, but the urge to vet or veto is timeless. There is an etymological kinship between the Greek verb *phanai* 'to speak' and the English word 'ban.' Speech is not only for communication, but also for hushing up. Euphemism provides a way of speaking about the unspeakable. It falls midway between transparent discourse and total prohibition. It is the would-be safe area of language, constrained by decorum.

Tact in everyday circumstances, and diplomacy on the international stage, are inhibitors reducing tension. Social discretion can generate genteelisms. One of the many nineteenth-century substitutes for 'trousers' was 'ineffables.' A down-to-earth article was made to sound other-worldly. Dickens satirized this practice by jokingly referring to trousers as 'ethereals.' Thus, euphemisms often seek to prettify common reality, e.g., calling a coffin a 'casket.' Euphemism turns its nose up. The term 'handkerchief' is preferred to the more precise 'snot-rag' (a perfect example of the opposite tendency, dysphemism—the full frontal assault). Jokes are made about linguistic squeamishness. In the French Revolution, being guillotined was rechristened 'looking through the republican window.' A British government spokesman in the 1980s admitted to having been 'economical with the truth.' Euphemism always takes such evading action with the plain facts.

Much euphemism is undeniably well-intentioned, and designed to protect the weak. A Jules Feiffer cartoon of 1965 captures perfectly the misleading nature of such solicitous double-talk. A man in rags says: 'I used to think I was poor. Then they told me I wasn't poor, I was needy. They told me it was self-defeating to think of myself as needy, I was deprived.' He works his way through 'under-privileged' and 'disadvantaged.' He concludes: 'I still don't have a dime. But I have a great vocabulary.' This is the reverse side of the argument which holds that euphemizers, despite their prim sins, introduce variety and range into the national word-hoard.

The extreme form of euphemism consists in leaving out the offending word(s) altogether, and inserting blanks, dots, asterisks (or, on screen or radio, beeps). This is clearly counterproductive. Dots are also used to indicate suspense. In novels or memoirs, asterisks positively beg the reader to divine the real identity of the unnamed person. In these ways, like circumlocution, a euphemism erects a puzzle. The expression 'a four-letter man,' used to denote a person so repellent that he deserves only obscenities, summons up the very forbidden words that it seeks to hold at bay. Of course, in heavily policed societies, veiled allusions are all that citizens dare allow themselves. In freer societies, some of the world's finest minds have protested at the widespread refusal to name what is both natural and lawful. 'If you chase nature away,' warned a French poet, 'it comes back at full gallop.'

Euphemism backfires. A replacement term gradually becomes loaded with the same associations as the word displaced. One of the coarsest of Yiddish words for the sexual act, *yentz*, came from the mild German pronoun *jenes* 'that (thing), the other.' As with all codes, the receiver of the euphemism wants to unscramble the message. Prurience is built into euphemism. Via innuendo, any word(s) can be made to serve a suggestive function in a helpful context. George Orwell's *Nineteen Eighty-Four* shows how even plain, 'Anglo-Saxon,' words can be pressganged for brainwashing. 'Goodsex' is not what couples hope for in their lovemaking, but sex stripped of pleasure and performed solely for procreation. This is a propagandist attempt to hijack language.

Verbal disguise does not invariably protect, then; it also endangers. It can be murderous, as in military jargon (e.g., the CIA phrase 'to terminate with extreme prejudice'). This is language literally dressed to kill. Like cosmetic surgery, political euphemism tries to hide the ugly face of political deeds, and seeks to be a major means of reality-control. Understatement may appear to be the opposite of escalation, but it remains a rhetorical ploy in a different key, the soft pedal still serving the ends of the hard peddle. In sophisticated advertisements, mock euphemism is often exploited to boost a product. Like periphrasis or litotes, euphemism sneaks around taboos while apparently respecting them.

However hard they try, words cannot keep things incognito. Even the most secretive language blows the gaff to someone. Euphemism wants to talk about things without mentioning them, or at least without granting them their common-or-garden names. Yet, in the very act of alluding indirectly, it calls those things to mind; it tips the wink. In trying to censor reality, it triggers off what it wants to suppress. Behind euphemism lies the much larger question of censorship. Can there be good censorship? Antiracists certainly think so. Can any power on earth silence language, for do people not go on talking in their heads? And so euphemisms have a very high mortality rate, for they are always engaged in a losing battle. Above all, euphemisms serve as a reminder that mankind cannot bear too much reality.

See also: Taboo Words; Taboo Religious.

Bibliography

Enright D J (ed.) 1985 *Fair of Speech: The Uses of Euphemism.* Oxford University Press, Oxford

Lawrence J 1973 *Unmentionables and Other Euphemisms.* Gentry Books, London

Evangelism

W. S. Bainbridge

In the Christian tradition, great emphasis is placed on the winning and revival of personal commitment to Christ, and such evangelism is typically made through impassioned verbal appeals. But religious evangelism is more than simple fulfillment of a tradition, and among its more interesting linguistic functions is raising the social status of the evangelist. If one speaks of God, then one must be a very special person, deserving of great honor, while those who do not accept the message are contemptible. As a rhetoric, evangelism manipulates the religious sentiments of the community to the advantage of the evangelists and their most fervent followers, who can plausibly claim to be members of the elect.

1. Social Roots

Modern evangelism is more common among nonconformist religious group than within the conventional denominations, and sociologists often distinguish two kinds of religious organization that serve different publics in different ways: the church (or ecclesia) and the sect. The established modern church accepts the surrounding social environment, finds its recruits primarily among the children of members, and generally fails to proselytize actively among nonmembers. The sect largely rejects the social environment in which it exists, recruits many of its members from outside, and undertakes often strenuous campaigns of evangelical conversion.

Because a sect's members tend to suffer significant socio-economic deprivations, relative to the members of an ecclesia, many of its beliefs and practices seem designed to assuage members' frustrations and resentments, and its political structure tends to be egalitarian, placing more emphasis upon the laity than upon the clergy. In principle, each member can be a preacher, and each potential convert must be preached to personally.

2. The Message and its Medium

Although the rhetoric of evangelism assumes that the evangelist is filled with the Holy Spirit, and extreme emotionality surrounds the communication of faith, in fact great skill and planning go into each campaign of revival and conversion. In the second half of the nineteenth century Charles Finney offered detailed instructions on how to do this, and the charisma of the most successful modern evangelists is packaged by a bureaucratic organization that knows how to manipulate communication media.

The most visible form is often called 'televangelism.' Although many assume this practice is quite new, in fact a religious service was first broadcast by radio in 1919 and by television in 1940. While such programs are fairly popular among people who are already religiously involved, there is some question whether they are capable of converting anyone. Much research indicates that people do not adopt a set of religious beliefs and practices until they become committed members of an intimate social group that accepts them, usually a strong local congregation. Disembodied appeals such as television or books appear quite ineffective as recruitment and conversion techniques, however attractive they may be to the already converted. Thus, evangelism is far more than transmission of the Word; it is a process of interpersonal influence in which a creed is communicated via the medium of powerful social relationships.

Evangelism stresses the transformation of the individual through a conversion process believed to be so total that it is like being born again. In fact, research on religious converts indicates that few really change markedly in personality or behavior, and thus social–scientific analysis has tended to focus on the functions that this rhetoric serves for believers. Persons who are ashamed of themselves, perhaps despising their own low social status and seeking an alchemy that will transmute them, will be especially open to such appeals. The evangelist usually appears to be a highly confident and attractive person, filled with qualities that engender respect, and the implied promise is that acceptance of the evangelist's message will confer the same virtues upon the convert.

Perhaps because personal transformation is so difficult, sectarian religions typically employ the tactic of symbolic transvaluation. The poor and dispossessed know they are unlikely to gain the material wealth and social influence of the dominant groups in society, and so they redefine these worldly glories as sinful and accept the compensatory belief that the tables will be turned in Heaven. Defining their deprivations as a self-chosen austerity, blessed by God, they claim honor for the social characteristics they possess rather than for those valued by secular society. The motivator is social inequality, not objective poverty, so even groups that are materially quite comfortable may be open to evangelistic appeals, so long as they feel that other groups have more honor and influence than they. Individuals and categories of person with low self-esteem are susceptible to evangelism, regardless of their objective social status, because they long to redefine themselves in more positive terms.

Despite its rhetorical claim to the contrary, most evangelism consists of preaching to the converted. The people who join particular religious groups tend already to share their general assumptions, to which they were usually socialized in childhood. Many of the conversions that take place in Protestant revivals, such as the Billy Graham crusades, are ritual experiences repeated numerous times by the same individuals. As they come forward to be reborn in Christ, these longtime Christians symbolically reaffirm their enduring faith and provide the audience of fellow believers with concrete expression of their shared hopes.

3. Consequences of Religious Populism

Because it holds that every believer should personally know the Word, evangelistic religion has contributed significantly to the growth of literacy. McLeish (1969) has documented that religious motives contributed to the establishment of many schools in Wales and England in the eighteenth and nineteenth century, and in populist American denominations great stress was laid on each individual reading the Bible for himself. Religious movements that gave preaching responsibilities to lay members incidentally trained them in public speaking skills.

Evangelism often gives a political voice to people previously excluded from debates concerning secular power and policies. In the 1960s, for example, the American Civil Rights Movement used the methods of religious evangelism to spread from the pulpit its liberal message among disadvantaged minorities. In the 1980s, a conservative Evangelical message was promulgated through churches, movements, and electronic media. The religion of the deprived and dispossessed frequently expresses their social grievances. Depending upon the particular issue, the message may appear either left-wing or right-wing, and the one constant is that evangelism is populist, using religious language to assert the rights and values of common people against those of secular elites.

See also: Glossolalia; New Religious Movements; Preaching.

Bibliography

Finney C G 1960 *Lectures on Revivals of Religion*. Harvard University Press, Cambridge, MA

Hadden J K, Shupe A 1988 *Televangelism: Power and Politics on God's Frontier*. Henry Holt, New York

Hadden J K, Swann C W 1981 *Prime Time Preachers: The Rising Power of Televangelism*. Addison-Wesley, Reading, MA

McLeish J 1969 *Evangelical Religion and Popular Education*. Methuen, London

Stark R, Bainbridge W S 1985 *The Future of Religion*. University of California Press, Berkeley, CA

Stark R, Bainbridge W S 1987 *A Theory of Religion*. Lang, New York

Feminism

D. Sawyer

Feminism has been a key source for the critique of religion in modern times, most explicitly from the mid-sixties of the twentieth century. Feminist theology, as it grew out of second-wave feminism, was born and nurtured in academic environments and concerned itself primarily with Christianity and Judaism in North American and European contexts and was encapsulated in the 1970s and 1980s by work of such scholars as Rosemary Radford Ruether and Letty M. Russell. Many scholars involved in this movement were biblical scholars, producing exegesis from feminist hermeneutical standpoints. Two key vanguard figures from this period are Elisabeth Schüssler Fiorenza and Phyllis Trible. The call for equality and inclusivity in religious structures and language mirrored many of the features of Liberation Theology. Feminist theologians and biblical scholars engaged in reforming traditional religion, recognized that the exclusive use of male language and images for the deity, articulated from a male perspective, meant that religion was not simply a reflection of patriarch societies, but played a major role in perpetuating male hierarchical structures with societies, both ancient and modern. Feminist responses to traditional religion can be mapped onto a wide spectrum, including reformist attempts to use feminine nouns and pronouns for the divine, as well as radical rejection of male language and symbols.

Since feminism began as a Western and middle-class movement, usually restricted to the academic elite, its universal application has been problematic. This critique, voiced by North American women of colour, or 'womanists' coined by Alice Walker in her introduction to *In Search of Our Mothers' Gardens* (1983), is apparent in the interaction between feminism and religion. For women with the dimensions of 'low' class and 'non-white' colour as indicators of oppression, the focus of their critique would not necessarily be exclusively men, but would include women whose liberation had been bought at their expense—epitomized in the collection of essays entitled, *This Bridge Called My Back*. Male language and images are not necessarily at the forefront: for example, the maleness of Jesus Christ is not problematic for women who can identify with him in terms of his poverty and race (Jacquelyn Grant).

Relativizing women's experience through such critique has led to the identification of many feminisms engaged with a variety of religions and spiritualities throughout the world. These include the Mujerista movement in Latin America, Minjung women in Korea, and many feminist theologies that engage with a plurality of religious traditions in postcolonial contexts. In these contexts religious language is being appropriated and re-articulated by women and for women, drawing on the richness of their experiences. In South East Asia new spiritualites can be syncretistic, women-centered reconfigurations of indigenous religions with traditions that have been imported by waves of colonial domination down the centuries: Buddhist, Confucian, Christian, Muslim. Such processes highlight the transition in the post-modern world from monolithic notions of transcendent religion with its particular language, to immanent notions of the divine that delight in fragmentation and re-construction, and that create and renew religious language and images through a multiplicity of experiences.

See also: Daly, M.; Christianity in Europe.

Bibliography

Russell L M, Shannon C J (eds.) 1996 *Dictionary of Feminist Theologies*. Mowbray, London

Grant J 1989 *White Women's Christ and Black Women's Jesus: Feminist Christology and Womanist Response*. Scholars Press, Atlanta

Moraga C, Anzaldua G (eds.) 1981 *This Bridge Called My Back: Writings By Radical Women of Color*. Kitchen Table Women of Color Press, New York

Walker A 1983 *In Search of Our Mothers' Gardens*. Harcourt Brace, New York

Glossolalia

C. G. Williams

The term glossolalia derives from the Greek words *glôssa* 'tongue' and *lalein* 'to speak' as used in the Bible (I Corinthians 14; Acts 10: 46) and has been employed to indicate the phenomenon known as 'speaking in tongues.' It has been dismissed as gibberish by some, while others describe it as the language of angels.

Since the first century CE it has occurred only sporadically in the Christian church but at no previous time has it been as pronounced as in the Pentecostalism of the twentieth century and in the charismatic renewal which has crossed denominational boundaries. These regard it as an exclusively Christian phenomenon, a divinely inspired manifestation identical to that which occurred in the early days of Christianity. However, studies of glossolalia refer to similar phenomena in other cultures, for example, in various forms of shamanism, in spirit possession, in Zulu prophetism and certain rites among Buddhists of north Thailand (see *Buddhism in Southeast Asia*).

Its medium is sound and not the printed page, auditory rather than visual. There are no transcripts of the earliest examples of glossolalia and samples are not abundant even in this age of recordings. Studies of the phenomenon in Pentecostal settings show that it is characterized by rapid vocalization, strong rhythm, and a discernible intonation pattern. There is also a lowering of volume and an abating of discharge of energy towards the end of an occurrence. A distinct development in a speaker's 'tongue' is not unusual as it progresses from inarticulate utterances to more structured forms with word-like and even sentence-like constructions. Generally glossolalic speech is unintelligible both to the speaker, who in fact cannot recall what has been uttered, and the listener, but interspersed among the nonsense syllables identifiable words from the speaker's inventory may occur.

In glossolalia, invariably one finds a recurrence of basic sounds, but different 'tongues' have their own peculiarities such as a propensity to favor certain clusters of consonantal alliterations. However, 'tongues' from within the same group can show a family resemblance suggesting learned behavior in undesigned emulation of a leader. A speaker may develop more than one 'tongue' but certain features seem to be common to them.

Glossolalia manifests itself also in group 'singing in the Spirit' when the vocalizing of each participant seems to blend harmoniously in chorus with telling effect. In Afro–American worshiping groups glossolalia produced in a trance state is often integrated in the music of gospel songs.

While glossolalia is lexically noncommunicative, in Christian groups the meaning is conveyed to the group by an interpreter whose ability to 'translate' is considered to be as charismatic as that of the speaker, and described as one of the vocal gifts of the Spirit. The 'translation' may not correspond in length to the original glossolalia and is not to be regarded as a word by word 'translation.' It would seem rather that the interpreter is, so to speak, on the same 'wavelength' as the speaker and conveys the mood or the inner mental processes of the speaker. The message or prophecy imparted is usually couched in general terms of warning or consolation but delivered in sublime scriptural language and not in the interpreter's vernacular. It is meant for the edification of the group, but glossolalia can also be practiced in private when it is deemed to be addressed to and a means of communing with the deity. There are instances in other cultural contexts of interpreters of unintelligible 'inspired' talk speaking in trance in an unfamiliar voice and in rhythmic fashion.

Some forms of glossolalia are held to be actual foreign languages unlearned by the speaker. Believers maintain this phenomenon is described in the biblical account of Pentecost (Acts 2). In modern studies it is referred to as 'xenoglossy' and the ability to respond in the unlearned language as 'responsive xenoglossy,' but investigators have been cautiously skeptical of such claims, and offer other tentative explanations.

Earlier research was predominantly psychological but more recently greater attention has been paid to the form and structure of glossolalia. Two of the more important investigations arrive at differing conclusions. For W. J. Samarin (1972), glossolalia is a pseudolanguage which may show development in the skill with which it is produced. Felicitas Goodman (1972), on the other hand, regards it as the artifact of a state of hyperarousal. For her, it is a speech automatism produced in an altered state of consciousness whose processes are reflected in its external structures. The fact that the speaker has no conscious control of what is uttered would seem to support this view, but since the speaker can usually exercise choice whether to speak or not, this could be adduced as evidence to the contrary. Part of the problem lies in the ambiguity in use of terms like 'trance' and 'dissociation.'

Another line of enquiry concerns the function of glossolalia. It serves to strengthen the bond between the individual and the group, and to bolster belief. It has also been employed in faith-healing sessions and in exorcisms.

Future research may develop diachronic and comparative studies as well as linguistic analyses of glossolalia in bilingual communities. Diachronic studies will observe likely subjects before as well as after they become glossolaliacs. Comparative studies will extend cross-cultural investigations particularly of seemingly related phenomena such as the use of mantras (see *Mantra*) and sacred chants and lend support, or otherwise, to the view that there is a configuration of pattern for glossolalic utterance. Linguistic studies may continue to explore the extent to which a person's normal inventory determines the content and nature of glossolalic vocalizing. It may also extend the search for recurring segmental similarities in vocal expression drawn from geographically widely separated areas.

Theological evaluation will continue to have a place especially for the believer who is not content to restrict examinations to the formal properties of glossolalia to the neglect of the contextual setting.

See also: Ecstatic Religion; Channeling; Shamanism; Hwyl.

Bibliography

Goodman F D 1972 *Speaking in Tongues: A Cross Cultural Study of Glossolalia.* Chicago University Press, Chicago, IL

Samarin W J 1972 *Tongues of Men and Angels.* Collier-Macmillan, New York

Williams C G 1981 *Tongues of the Spirit.* University of Wales Press, Cardiff

Zaretsky I I, Leone M P (eds.) 1974 *Religious Movements in Contemporary America.* Princeton University Press, Princeton, NJ

Hwyl

D. D. Morgan

The hwyl is a particular intonation of the voice used in nineteenth and early twentieth century Welsh preaching indicating the emotional and sometimes ecstatic climax of a sermon. Rhythmic and musical in character, it comprised the raising of the preacher's voice towards a melodic crescendo in successive phrases or sentences indicating his having been imbued with an anointing or afflatus of the Spirit. Such inspiration tended to transcend ordinary powers of expression and enhanced normal pulpit delivery in the service of the divine. Although reminiscent of glossolalia and perhaps related to it, ordinary language (in this case Welsh) was not abandoned but heightened, dramatized, and transformed.

The Welsh word hwyl has three principal meanings. First it is the word used for a ship or yacht's sail. Its second meaning in both medieval and modern Welsh referred to a hearty physical disposition or mental condition or being, as it were, at the top of one's form. Its third meaning in modern Welsh is mirth, fun, or gaiety. Its use in the religious context is probably a combination of the first and second senses: the image of the Spirit as a breeze or wind (Hebrew *rūaḥ* or Greek *pneuma*) filling the sail and propelling the vessel onwards with speed and excitement, is metaphorically both apposite and arresting. How these two meanings coalesced to express the fervent musical intonation of the Welsh pulpit is not clear, though the hymnist William

Williams of Pantycelyn in *Ateb Philo-Evangelius*, a prose work of 1763, refers to 'the heavenly hwyl of their [sc. believers'] spirits' whereafter the description becomes commonplace in Welsh religious literature.

The first apparent reference to the hwyl as a characteristic of a preacher's sermonic delivery occurs in the periodical *Seren Gomer* (1819), and by mid-century it was remarked upon extensively. Owen Thomas in his 1874 biography of the popular Calvinistic Methodist preacher John Jones Tal-y-sarn describes it thus: 'When he ascended to his highest hwyl his voice would take on a particular tone similar to the musical form called recitatio—a sort of declaratory song—somewhere between speaking and singing, though much nearer speaking. He would also vary his pitch according to the point which he desired to make' (*Cofiant John Jones Tal-y-sarn*. Hughes a'i fab, Wrecsam, pp. 988–9).

When spontaneous and sincere the hwyl would often have been a powerful means of conviction and uplift though through a stylized over use by the earlier part of the twentieth century it tended to lose its potency and effect. It is now very rare indeed.

See also: Glossolalia; Ecstatic Religion; Preaching.

Bibliography

Williams C G 1981 *Tongues of the Spirit: A Study of Pentecostal Glossolalia and Related Phenomena*. University of Wales Press, Cardiff

Hymns

J. F. S Sawyer

In most religious traditions public worship involves the singing of hymns, either with musical accompaniment as in the case of most forms of Christianity (where a special musical instrument, the church organ, has evolved), or without, as in the case of orthodox Judaism. Hymn-singing groups (*bhajan-mandali*) are a familiar feature of the devotional life of many Hindu communities. Islam is an exception: hymn-singing is not part of public worship in the mosque, although hymns in the vernacular, sometimes accompanied by music and dancing, are sung in certain Sufi rituals.

It is therefore only to be expected that much of the religious literature of the world consists of hymns. The 'Psalms of David' make up the largest book in the Bible, for example, and the Rigveda, the oldest part of Hindu scripture, consists entirely of hymns. Hymns are often composed by, or attributed to famous leaders, saints, and poets of the past such as St Gregory, Martin Luther, John Milton, William Blake, and John Henry Newman among Christian examples, and Shankara, Namdev, and Ramakrishna in Hindu tradition.

The language of hymns is affected by a number of factors common to most religions. The popularity of a traditional melody may be a constraint on the production of new translations of ancient words. Thus, for example, Christian congregations continue to sing bizarre theological terms such as *sempiternal* and *triune* because they are required by the meter, not to mention Hebraisms like *Adonai* and *Sabaoth*, which would rarely be heard outside that special context. Musical and liturgical considerations often take precedence over intelligibility, so that in many religious communities hymns are sung in a language totally unknown to the vast majority of the worshipers. Hymns were still being sung in Sumerian, for example, in ancient Babylon long after it had become a dead language (see *Ancient Near Eastern Religions*), and Japanese Buddhist priests intone texts written in Chinese (see *Buddhism, Japanese*), while the use of Latin in Christian worship and Hebrew in Jewish worship is well-known.

Tension between these two considerations, intelligibility, on the one hand, and the desire or religious duty to uphold ancient liturgical tradition, on the other, is nicely illustrated by the emergence in fifteenth-century Europe of 'macaronic carols,' a compromise in which short lines of Latin alternate with phrases in the vernacular. A century later the reformer Martin Luther (see *Luther, Martin*), as well as composing many hymns in German himself, went to considerable lengths to incorporate existing hymns in the vernacular into public worship, as an alternative to the traditional Latin hymns of the Church he was rebelling against.

His younger contemporary John Calvin went further and prohibited all singing, as irredeemably associated with the Latin Mass, except for the Psalms and a metrical setting of the Ten Commandments. This led to the production of metrical versions of the Psalms, together with English paraphrases of many other passages of scripture. Some of these are contrived in the extreme and descend to the level of doggerel, while others, such as 'The Lord's my shepherd,' set to specially commissioned tunes, are still among the most familiar in Christian worship. At the opposite pole, Latin hymns are still being composed at the ecumenical Taizé community in France, and widely used by both Catholics and Protestants.

See also: Christianity in Europe; American Spirituals; Metrical Psalms and Paraphrases.

Bibliography

Ellingson T 1987 Music and religion. In: Eliade M (ed.) *Encyclopedia of Religion*, vol. 10, pp. 163–72. Macmillan, New York

Hymns. In: Hastings J (ed.) 1914 *Encyclopedia of Religion and Ethics*, vol. 7, pp. 1–58. T and T Clark, Edinburgh

Routley E 1952 *Hymns and Human Life*. J. Murray, London

Watson J R 1997 *The English Hymn*. Oxford University Press, Oxford

Incantations

J. Pearson

An incantation generally consists of a formula of words which are repeated in a chant, usually as part of the performance of ritual, to produce a magical effect. It includes spoken spells (see *Magic*) or charms, and is linked to such other words as *chant* and *enchant*. The repeated chanting of a psalm, for example, or Gregorian chants, might be regarded as incantations because of their musical quality and the effects they produce, rather than because they are inherently magical. However, whilst the chanting of psalms may be practised for the purposes of worship, making a link to God through words and song, incantation in occult practice generally takes this further: the purpose is not only to make a link with spirits or deities but to summon or placate them. Based on the belief in the creative power of sound, incantations enable the exaltation of consciousness through rhythm and repetition in order that the practitioner might address the gods, experience revelations of a mystical nature, or release magical energies in a spell or charm. An incantation can take the form of a prolonged piece of poetry or it can be based on the repetition of names, such as the Kabbalistic names of God (e.g., Adonai, Elohim). Alternatively, incantations consisting wholly of nonsense, foreign, ancient, or forgotten languages to achieve a mental state in which consciousness is altered or attuned have been argued to be efficacious.

See also: Magic; Judaism; Mantra; Performative Utterances; Hindu Views on Language; Names; Gematria.

Bibliography

Luhrmann T M 1994 *Persuasions of the Witches' Craft: Ritual Magic in Contemporary England.* Picador, London, pp. 246–248

Regardie I 1994 *The Tree of Life: A Study in Magic*. Samuel Weiser Inc., Maine, pp. 139–152

Yates F A 1991 *Giordano Bruno and the Hermetic Tradition*. Chicago University Press, Chicago, pp. 78–79

Islamic Calligraphy

S. Auld

The opening words of God's revelation to the Prophet Muhammad, recorded in Chapter 96: 3–5 of the Qur'ān, include 'Recite in the name of thy lord/Who taught by the pen/Taught man what he knew not.' This conjunction of God and the pen have given a sanctity to the written word in Islam from its earliest days, and, by association, a high status to the writer. The earliest standing monument of Islam, the Dome of the Rock in Jerusalem built in AH 72/CE 692, bears witness to this importance. Two long mosaic bands of gold calligraphy on a blue ground (the colors invoking the heavens) encircle the inner and outer faces of the interior octagonal arcade of the building. Containing Qur'ānic and pious passages as well as identifying the patron and date of construction, by their position they act as a link between heaven (the dome) and earth. Throughout the Islamic world up to the present day, information is given by monumental inscriptions on buildings' foundation and restoration, patrons, dates, and endowments, details of administrative decrees, commemoration, and craftsmen. Through them, individuals receive not only benediction by association with God's word, but also a degree of immortality.

The key elements of public inscriptions—piety and propaganda—were widely used before Islam by the Romans and by the Christians. Allied to the ban on the depiction of the Holy in Judaism, the concentration on the written word as both message and decoration within Islam was almost inevitable, although its prevalence in the medieval period raises interesting questions on the rate of literacy among early Muslims.

The creative brilliance achieved by Islamic calligraphy is unique. Arabic, like its Semitic predecessors, reads from right to left; it is usually only the consonants which are represented by horizontal and vertical strokes and hooks. The Arabs took over the alphabet of 22 letters from the Nabateans, making a distinction between similar letter forms by the addition of dots. In calligraphy (literally 'beautiful writing'; in Arabic *al-khaṭṭ* pl. *khuṭūṭ*, 'penmanship') the spacing and length of these individual letters, based on the cut nib of the reed pen (referred to in Sura **96**: 3–5), is strictly proportional. The earliest proper reference to Arabic script is by the term *jasm*, and its stiff formality doubtless influenced the development of the best-known early script known somewhat confusingly as *kufic*, the pre-eminence of which lasted for more than 300 years to become the sole hieratic form for copying the Qur'ān. At first severe and unadorned, it was later embellished by floral, foliate, and geometric flourishes. Its horizontal format is perfectly adapted for monumental inscriptions, the strict proportions giving a freedom within its constraints, allowing its accommodation to say, the swell of a dome, or the curve of a portal. Later, forms of cursive calligraphy were developed, often used in conjunction with *kufic*. There are traditionally six cursive styles (*thuluth, naskhī, muḥaqqaq, rayḥānī, tawqī'* and *riqa'*), in additional to more localized scripts such as *maghribi* (Western), and *nasta'liq*, which became the national script of Iran. Ottoman calligraphists perfected images in zoomorphic and architectural forms, often with religious significance.

The facility of calligraphy to adapt to different surfaces allowed its use not only as a large-scale embellishment on buildings but also on mosque 'furniture' such as the *minbar* (pulpit), *miḥrab* (prayer-niche), Qur'ān stand and lamp, and also in miniature, for example, in a tiny Qur'an whose text is no more than 1 3/4 inch wide. To this day, every year a specially woven cover for the Ka'ba (*kiswa*) is traditionally decorated with panels and bands of calligraphy in gold and silver. Sometimes with talismanic or benedictory messages, secular objects too frequently depend on writing to add elegance and information—metalwork, stone, textiles, ceramics, woodwork, glass, coinage, gemstones all use calligraphy to stunning effect, while the beauty of the Qur'āns themselves, whether illuminated or not, do

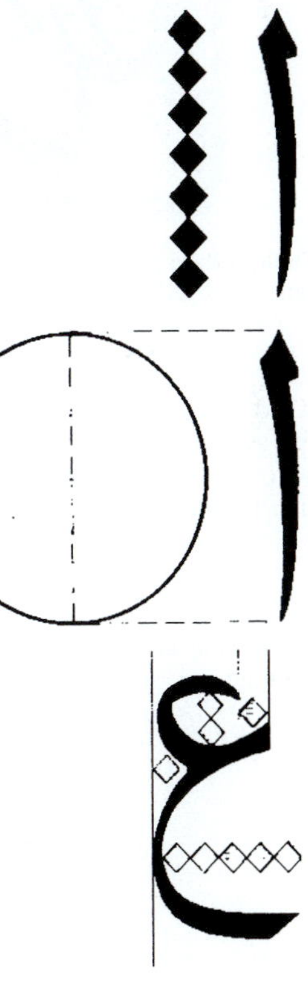

Figure 1. Ibn Muqlah's system. Top: *Alif* scaled to the seven rhombic dots placed vertex to vertex; centre: standard *Alif* and standard circle; *above*: proportional measurements the letter '*Ayn* (from Safadi Y H 1978 *Islamic Calligraphy*. Thames & Hudson, London)

Figure 2. Thuluth Basmalah (in the lower section) with the added words 'My trust in Him', on a tile, probably from Persia late seventeeth century. (from Safadi Y H 1978 *Islamic Calligraphy*. Thames & Hudson, London).

justice to God's revelation. No other religion has perfected the art of calligraphy to such a degree as Islam, and no other religion has used its achievements to such telling effect.

Bibliography

Blair SS 1998 *Islamic Inscriptions*. Edinburgh University Press, Edinburgh

Minorski T 1959 *Calligraphers and Painters. A Treatise by Qadi Ahmad, son of Mir-Munshi (c. A.H. 1015/A.D. 1606)*, trans. from the Persian. Washington, DC

Pedersen J 1984 *The Arabic Book*, trans. by G. French. Princeton University Press, Princeton, NJ

Safadi YH 1978 *Islamic Calligraphy*. Thames and Hudson, London

Sourdel-Thomine J et al. 1978 In: Khaṭṭ (ed.) Encyclopedia of Islam, 2nd edn. E J Brill, Leiden, The Netherlands, Vol. IV, pp. 1113–28

Language and Power

N. Fairclough

For the most part, questions of power have either been ignored in language studies, or dealt with at a rather superficial level. The richest insights into the relationship between language and power have come from increasing attention to language in social theory (its so-called 'linguistic turn'), in the work of Louis Althusser, Pierre Bourdieu, Michel Foucault (see *Foucault, M.*), Jurgen Habermas, and others. But in the 1980s and early 1990s, there were attempts to operationalize these insights in language analysis, within 'critical linguistics', and within more critical work in discourse analysis and pragmatics. A major problem for such work is that there are many divergent theories of power, which can lead to different approaches to language. There are also different levels at which the language–power relationship can be investigated: one could focus upon how power relations are enacted in discourse, or alternatively upon power asymmetries associated with unequal access to certain languages or language varieties (including questions of language politics and language planning). This article concentrates mainly upon the former. It discusses, first, meanings of 'power.' It then moves from a rather static view of domination in discourse to a more dynamic view of discourse as embedded within power struggles, discussing in turn power in discourse, power 'behind' discourse, and power struggle in and over discourse.

1. The Concept of 'Power'

Theories of power differ on fundamental issues; for example, whether power belongs to individuals or collectivities or systems, whether it necessarily involves conflict, whether it presupposes resistance, whether it is just repressive and negative (a matter of domination) or also enabling and positive. Within the bewildering divergences, it is possible to differentiate two major contrasting conceptions of power. The first and more general sense is power as transformative capacity, the capacity of agents to affect the course of events. Power in this sense may be enabling and positive as well as repressive, and it is a capacity possessed in some degree by any actor, dominant or dominated. Power in the second sense is a relational concept 'power over,' and is linked to domination by individuals or collectivities. In critical language studies as in other spheres, there has tended to be a one-sided emphasis upon the latter, giving an overly pessimistic view of the sociolinguistic and discourse practices of a society as simply an apparatus of domination. This article begins with domination and 'power over,' looking first in the section 'power in discourse' at the power of one participant over another in particular interactions, and then in the section 'power behind discourse' at the power of certain collectivities over others arising from their control over the sociolinguistic practices of a community. But in the section 'power struggle in and over discourse,' the more general sense of power is brought in, in the process of arguing that power in language is not simply domination.

2. Power in Discourse

Perhaps the most obvious instances of 'power over' and domination are cases where using language is a way of directly policing or mobilizing people. One example is the orders, threats, or diatribes parents sometimes use to control their children; a more institutionally regulated example is the discourse of military command (e.g. *Attention! From the left, quick march!*).

Domination takes a more indirect form in what are sometimes called 'unequal encounters'—types of discourse such as job interviews or medical consultations or lessons, where participants have unequal institutional status and authority. In such cases, higher-status participants (such as doctors or teachers) may control the development of the discourse, and the contributions of other participants to it, in various ways. For example, a medical consultation may consist largely of questions from the doctor, with the patient being limited to providing answers. This gives the doctor control over the content of the discourse (what topics are raised and how they are dealt with), as well as positioning the patient as a particular sort of medical subject (a passive participant in medical practice, a body worked upon by the doctor), in a particular sort of relationship (subordination and dependency) to the doctor. Generalizing from this example, one can say that power in discourse is exercised over content, relations between participants, and the identities of participants as social subjects.

Higher-status participants may also control the contributions of others by treating them as performances to be evaluated. In classroom discourse, for example, teachers systematically evaluate what learners say (e.g., Teacher: *What's the capital of France*? Pupil: *Paris, Miss*. Teacher: *Yes, Paris*). And there are various other ways of controlling contributions: by interrupting and curtailing them when they are judged to be irrelevant, by providing authoritative summaries or 'formulations' which impose particular interpretations upon them, by asking for them to be reformulated in different words which may force participants to be more explicit than they would wish to be, and so forth.

Power asymmetries between participants of different status may be evident in their orientation to what some pragmaticists call the 'face' of coparticipants. Participants may differ in how polite they are to each other, or in how directly or indirectly they say or write things which may be intrusive or offensive or threatening (compare, for example, two ways of asking a question which might be asked in a medical consultation: *How's your sex life?* versus *Are there any aspects of your personal life that might have a bearing on these problems?*). Participants may also differ in the extent to which they try to be accommodating to other participants, for example, by modifying their own usual linguistic practices toward those of others.

But it is not just differences in the institutional status of participants that give rise to discoursal inequality and domination; so too do differences in age, gender, cultural identity, and so forth. One aspect of unequal gender relations is that men sometimes dominate in female–male interactions. A study of the discourse of married couples in the USA, for example, (by Pamela Fishman, reported in Graddol and Swann 1989) showed that men gave women much less supportive feedback when they were talking than vice-versa, and that topics introduced by men were much more likely to be taken up than those introduced by women. Such inequalities are aggravated in institutional interactions, where the higher-status participants are men, or members of cultural majorities, and the lower-status participants are women, or members of cultural minorities. Some research has suggested that, in such situations, higher-status participants systematically misinterpret cultural differences in discourse practices (e.g., between the majority white community in the UK or the USA and black or Asian minority groups), as evidence of lack of cooperation, incompetence, etc., on the part of lower-status participants (Gumperz 1982).

So far 'face-to-face' discourse has been considered, where participants are interacting together at a particular time and place, and conjointly producing the discourse (though with different degrees of influence on it, as indicated above). But in the case of written discourse, and the discourse of the mass media (radio, television, film), there is a separation between participants who produce the discourse and those who constitute its audience (be they readers, listeners, or viewers). Producers have power over audiences in that they can determine what is included or excluded, and how people, objects, and events are represented. And since mass audiences are so potentially diverse, producers have to build into their discourse 'ideal' readers or listeners or viewers, which may significantly contribute to the social shaping of real readers, listeners, or viewers. Of course, audiences sometimes have means of counteracting the power of producers: they may stop reading or turn the television off, or be hostile audiences that contest producers' discourse in some way or other.

One section of the mass media whose power has been widely debated is the news media, and there is much controversy over the extent to which, and ways in which, news discourse shapes the beliefs and actions of audiences, but broad agreement that it has some significant effect. The central issue is what might be called 'signifying power': if it is assumed that there is no neutral or objective way of representing events, then all reports signify them in particular ways, perhaps according to the strategies (economic, political) and ideologies (see Sect. 3.1 below) of the reporter. For example, the headline *Police shoot 100 in riot* is quite explicit about the agency of, and responsibility for, the violence reported, whereas the headline *100 die in riot* is quite inexplicit, and there may be good strategic or ideological motivations for one rather than the other. What is not entirely obvious is who exercises signifying power in the media: behind the journalists and editors are the powerful sections of society (government, industry, the professions, etc.) that constitute the major sources of news, and it is arguable that events are often signified in ways which accord with their interest, strategies, and ideologies. Their power is a hidden power, which might be related to a 'hidden agenda' for the media: to mediate between those who hold power and the mass of the population. Signifying power in the media may be used to consciously manipulate audiences and readerships. A more general and perhaps more insidious effect of signifying power is that particular signifying practices with particular ideological investments become naturalized for media professionals.

3. Power Behind Discourse

'Power in discourse' draws attention to discourse as one site where domination takes place and power relations are enacted; whereas 'power behind discourse' identifies discourse itself as a target for domination and hegemony. Societies and their constituent institutions (e.g., education, health care, law) have 'orders of discourse'—sets of codes, conventions, and norms which are structured in relation to each other in particular ways, and which are open to restructuring. Orders of discourse can be regarded as one domain of cultural hegemony: dominant groups in societies and institutions seek to win consent for particular structurings of orders of discourse, as part of their attempt to achieve hegemony in the sphere of culture (complementing economic and political hegemony).

One dimension of a society's order of discourse is the structuring of relationships between different languages, and different varieties (social dialects) of one language. Certain languages or varieties are typically attributed high prestige and designated as appropriate for prestigious functions in law, government, education, and so forth, whereas other languages or varieties may be marginalized by being designated as appropriate only for functions in the private and domestic spheres, or indeed may be excluded through bans or ideological offensives.

'Language standardization' is the process through which one variety of a language becomes the 'standard language' of a society, or even a broader international community —'Standard English' is an example. Standard English developed from the East Midland dialect of the late medieval period, which became the language of the merchant class of London, the class which was to achieve dominance in the transition from feudalism to capitalism. This link between the standard and social class is still there, although its form has changed: it is upper-class and middle-class children who learn Standard English as their mother tongue in the home, and for whom it constitutes the most efficacious 'cultural capital'—a passport to positions of influence and power. The claims of Standard English to be a national language are, it is true, recognized by all sections of British or American society, but it tends to be a forced and superficial recognition on the part of working-class people and cultural minorities, who still adhere strongly in practice to their own varieties and languages. Standard English is universally taught in the school system, yet a substantial proportion of children fail to achieve high levels of competence in it. The process of language standardization does not merely elevate one variety, it simultaneously demotes others, and imposes a structuring upon the societal order of discourse which marginalizes 'nonstandard' varieties and other languages. Standardization belongs to the era of the modern nation-state with its centralization of national economies, political systems, and cultures. As this era comes to an end, nation-states are simultaneously under pressure from larger international entities and smaller local entities, and so too is the position of standard languages within orders of discourse.

As the last paragraph suggests, power behind discourse is not only a question of securing hegemonic structuring of orders of discourse, it is also a question of controlling access to languages, varieties, and codes which are ascribed prestige within orders of discourse. The educational system is of considerable importance in controlling access, being as Foucault put it 'a political way of maintaining or modifying the appropriation of discourses, along with the knowledges and powers which they carry' (1984: 123). Whatever the political rhetoric of education, the effect of the schools in Britain, for example, has been to consolidate class differences in 'linguistic capital' established in the family, rather than ironing them out. Access to prestigious functional varieties or 'registers' such as varieties of writing (literary, scientific), professional varieties such as legal English, or genres such as interview or public speaking, is similarly filtered by the education system. This is not to say that working-class or cultural minority children do not acquire them, but that the development of high degrees of competence in them is disproportionately weighted toward upper-class and middle-class children.

Another important aspect of power over orders of discourse is the shaping, imposition, and naturalization of particular variants of the functional varieties just referred to. For example, there are various ways in which medical consultations might be and indeed are conducted, but there has tended to be approved way of conducting them which has been institutionally 'policed' through inducements, pressures, and sanctions. A particular way of conducting a medical consultation will involve a given distribution of discourse 'rights' and 'obligations' between doctor and patient, such as rights and obligations to take turns at talking, respond to the other's turns in particular ways, develop and change topic, probe into aspects of the other's private life through direct or more tentative questioning, provide summaries of what has been said, give accounts of illnesses and problems, and so forth. What participants are allowed or required to do, and inequalities between participants in this regard, point to implicit assumptions—ideologies—about the nature of medicine, what it means to be a doctor or a patient, what relationship there ought to be between doctor and patient, and so on.

One may say that particular practices of medical consultation, classroom teaching, or interaction between managers and workers, carry particular ideological investments. That is, they embody sets of assumptions which correspond to the interests and points of view of particular social groups, but are made to look like mere common sense. This is why the imposition of particular practices is an objective for power holders: they can progressively naturalize ideological assumptions which help reproduce existing social relations and structures. Ideology is one modality of power, which uses control of meaning and definition of common sense as a means of producing and reproducing domination, positioning people as 'social subjects' of various sorts, and underpinning the interpretation of language texts as 'coherent' (see Sect. 3.1). The other major modality of power is the use of force, which may have more immediate effects than ideology, but is less effective in the longerterm in maintaining relations of domination. Modern societies, in which domination takes the form of hegemony (i.e., rule through the generation of consent), have become increasingly reliant upon the modality of ideology. They have therefore become increasingly reliant upon discourse, because it is in discourse that ideological processes mainly take place.

3.1 Ideology

Ideology, like power, is a complex and contested concept. It is central element of Marxism, where ideologies have traditionally been seen as misrepresentations of reality through which the ruling class dominates other classes. Outside Marxism, more general definitions have emerged which see different ideologies as merely different perspectives or points of view. But the power of ideology as a concept is the connection it makes between domination and points of view, meanings, and representations. This link between ideology and domination has been maintained and developed in more recent Marxist theory. One influential tradition, based upon the theories of

Antonio Gramsci and Louis Althusser, sees ideologies as: (a) generally implicit or 'commonsense' assumptions about the nature of the world, social relationships, and social identities, which (b) invest and shape social practices, including discourse practices, that constitute their material form, and which (c) contribute to reproducing or restructuring relation of domination ('power over'). Most studies of language and ideology have adopted a view of ideology along these lines.

Language texts, written or spoken, may be ideologically 'invested' in various ways and at various levels—that is, choices of vocabulary, grammar, organization of turn-taking, and so forth, may come to be ideologically significant. Words and their meanings have received most attention, on the assumption that contrasting ways of 'wording' a particular domain of experience may embody different ideologies. An example would be the contrast between more traditional wordings of educational practices, and current 'commodified' wordings (e.g., *we can offer our customers a range of purpose-built packages to choose between*). But aspects of grammar may also be ideologically invested—compare, for example, the sentences *Thousands are out of work* and *Company directors have sacked thousands of workers* as different ways of reporting the same event (e.g., redundancies in the car industry). The former is an intransitive sentence without an agent which represents a state, the latter is a transitive sentence with an agent which represents an action. Systematic selection among such alternative sentence types may be connected with representations of unemployment as a condition which nobody is responsible for, or alternatively as caused by the actions of specific agents. On a different level of analysis, the turn-taking system operative in a classroom, or the politeness conventions operating in interaction between managers and workers, may be invested with particular ideologies of education and work. Other features of texts are also ideologically important, including the sorts of metaphor (see *Metaphor*) that are used, and the sorts of presupposition that are made.

To understand fully the ideological effects of discourse, however, it is necessary to consider the processes of producing and interpreting texts as well as texts themselves. In this connection, Althusser's emphasis on the relationship between ideology and the constitution of social subjects is important. He claims that ideologies 'interpellate' individuals as subjects of particular sorts, placing them in particular subject 'positions.' Discourse plays a major part in such processes of interpellation. For example, one effect of a set of conventions for medical consultations or classroom teaching is to cumulatively construct definite identities and 'positions' for doctors, patients, teachers, and pupils. If such a set of conventions comes to be dominant and naturalized (a matter of common sense), individuals who wish to become doctors or teachers have to compliantly occupy the positions provided. When a doctor addresses a patient drawing upon such conventions, (s)he implicitly positions the patient through the way (s)he speaks, and the same is true vice-versa. Those so positioned may resist these positionings, but it is often extremely difficult to do so. Compliance does not however entail acceptance: people may 'go through the motions' of adhering to conventions, while at the same time privately distancing themselves from them. In favorable circumstances, they may challenge and try to restructure them (see Sect. 4).

At the end of Sect. 3, a connection between ideology and the production of coherent interpretations for texts was referred to. 'Coherence' has been a major concern of discourse analysts, because a central question about discourse is how interpreters can make sense of written or spoken texts which on the surface are highly disjointed and incoherent. However, from the perspective of ideology and the subject, the production of coherent interpretations can be seen as a key moment in the positioning of subjects. In order to establish coherence, interpreters need to draw upon the sort of implicit assumptions and knowledge structures which cognitive psychologists and specialists in artificial intelligence have called 'scripts,' 'frames,' and 'schemata.' Suppose, for instance, that a text contains this sequence of sentences: *She's giving up her job next week. She's pregnant.* To link the sentences coherently, an interpreter needs a 'bridging' assumption, that women who are about to have children stop working. It is an ideological assumption, tied to particular (now contentious) views of gender relations in the family. The point is that in achieving a coherent reading of the text, the interpreter is simultaneously being positioned, or repositioned, within a particular ideology of gender relations which (s)he needs to take for granted in making the text coherent. Similar comments apply to text producers: producing a text is an achievement which rests upon the mobilization of ideological assumptions and knowledge structures, thus ideologically positioning the producer.

4. Power Struggle in and Over Discourse

The view of power in and over discourse which has been presented so far is too static, and overemphasizes the imposition of domination from above. It neglects ways in which power may be contested. This section will adopt a more dynamic conception of power in and over discourse, centered around the concept of power struggle.

4.1 Struggle is Discourse

The exercise of power in discourse frequently meets with resistance, though only under particular subjective and social conditions. In terms of the former, resistance presupposes participants who have the motivation, resources, and confidence to resist. These subjective conditions are often discussed in terms of the 'empowerment' of members of dominated social groups (be it workers, women, or members of cultural minorities). Empowerment can be thought of as educative action to equip people to make use of the power they have—using 'power' now in the more general sense of transformative capacity—to resist in circumstances of domination. But empowerment can be effective only under favorable social conditions: resistance in discourse is more likely to occur, and more likely to take active forms, in institutional locations where the domination of one group over others is partial, precarious, or contested.

Struggle and resistance in discourse take a variety of forms, some of which are more active than others. It was suggested earlier that compliance with dominant discourse practices may amount to no more that 'going through the motions,' a form of passive resistance which may be as much as is possible in certain circumstances. Participants may also resist by fully exploiting the rights made available to them within dominant discourse practices, rather than challenging those practices (e.g., the right of interviewees to question interviewers, which is often offered to them at the end of an interview in the expectation that they will make at most token use of it). Or participants may overtly question the practices themselves; I could, for example, under certain circumstances tell my doctor that he might learn more about my problems if he sat back and listened to me for a while, rather than submitting me to a battery of diagnostic questions. A more covert and more pervasive form of resistance is not conforming with the rights and obligations imposed by dominant discourse practices, and drawing instead upon other practices. For example, provided (s)he has the resources to bring it off and provided the social conditions are favourable, a lower-status participant may be able to prevent a higher-status participant from conducting an interaction as a formal interview by talking (and more generally acting) as if it were a friendly chat.

4.2 Struggle Over Discourse

Such forms of struggle in discourse may be manifestations of longer-term processes of contestation between social groups in which the structuring of societal and institutional orders of discourse is at stake. In Sect. 3 the imposition of hegemonies from above was referred to, but hegemonies are also open to challenge from below, and must constantly be reproduced and redefined under conditions of struggle. An example of the challenging of hegemonies from below is the attack by feminists upon what are seen as sexist and male-dominated discourse practices across a range of institutional orders of discourse—in the family, politics, trade unions, the media, education, social services, and so forth. One focus of this attack has been the forms of female–male interaction referred to in Sect. 2, which constitute modes of male domination: forms of conversation, for example, in which women are kept in the marginal and passive roles of listener and respondent, where their contributions are interrupted, where they are expected to talk to men's topics without being able to introduce their own, and so forth. The feminist challenge has made hitherto hegemonic practices problematical for many men as well as women, and led to some restructuring of practices.

Another example is the widespread tendency for institutional discourse (e.g., interviews of various kinds) to become more informal and conversational, less directive and judgmental and more empathetic, sometimes drawing upon the discourse of counseling as a model. This tendency is associated with struggle against traditional authoritarianism and bureaucratic impersonality in relationships between professionals and their clients or publics, and the late twentieth-century ascendancy of values of individualism and consumerism. But this tendency illustrates how challenges from below may be contained and appropriated from above: these now forms of institutional discourse are now widely cultivated by professionals and managers as strategies for attracting clients and consumers, or in personnel contexts for increasing the commitment of employees to the firms they work for, and making a greater range of their skills and talents available for exploitation by the firm. This can be seen as a shift in ideological investment (see Sect. 3.1): the concept of ideological investment implies that a given set of discourse practices or linguistic features does not have one inherent and permanent ideological value, but may come to be differently invested in different contexts, in the course of ideological struggle.

This example points to a basic feature of power struggle over orders of discourse in late twentieth-century society. On the one hand, there are centrifugal tendencies. Modern industrial society has been associated with the imposition of homogeneous and unitary dominant practices for such types of institutional interaction as medical consultations, job interviews, teacher–pupil interactions, or the discourse of managers and workers. There is now a shift away from this, associated with what some see as a 'postmodern' fragmentation of the modern structuring of society into discrete institutional and professional domains. Discourse practices are becoming more heterogeneous, partly because there are more opportunities for challenges from below to have effects. So the practices of medical consultation or classroom teaching are now highly variable, allowing the preferences and dispositions of doctors and teachers, patients and learners, to find some expression.

On the other hand, however, there are centripetal tendencies. These may be partly in response to the above centrifugal tendencies, but they also give them fresh impetus. Thus centripetal and centrifugal tendencies are tied into a single dialectic. Late twentieth-century centripetal tendencies involve a process of 'technologization' of discourse: the subjection of discourse practices (e.g., various types of interview) to systematic and institutionalized processes of research, redesign, and training. The technologization of discourse is a form of linguistic manipulation. But as suggested above, these impositions from above may generate resistance and moves toward further diversity.

5. Conclusion

Absence of serious attention to the relationship between language and power is a major weakness of linguistic theory in the late twentieth century, including much of the work that has been done in sociolinguistics. In the 1960s, a distinction was often drawn between two branches of language study which link language and the rest of society in different ways: sociolinguistics, which places the focus upon language; and 'sociology of language,' which starts from society and social theory. This distinction has dropped out of fashion, and sociology of language has not really developed. The time has come for 'mainstream' linguistics to take note of recent critical work on language and power, perhaps in the form of resurrecting the sociology of language. But work on language and power may have a deeper significance for mainstream linguistics in the longer term: it may lead to new, more socially realistic theories of language which displace currently dominant asocial theories in the center of the discipline.

Bibliography

Bourdieu P 1991 (ed. Thomson J B) *Language and Symbolic Power*. Polity Press in association with Basil Blackwell, Cambridge

Dijk T A van 1987 *News as Discourse*. Erlbaum, Hillsdale, NJ

Fairclough N 1989 *Language and Power*. Longman, London

Foucault M 1984 The order of discourse. In: Shapiro M J (ed.) *Language and Politics*. Basil Blackwell, Oxford

Fowler R, Hodge B, Kress G, Trew T 1979 *Language and Control*. Routledge & Kegan Paul, London

Graddol D, Swann J 1989 *Gender Voices*. Basil Blackwell, Oxford

Gumperz J J 1982 *Discourse Strategies*. Cambridge University Press, Cambridge

Hodge B, Kress G 1988 *Social Semiotics*. Polity Press, Cambridge

Mey J L 1985 *Whose Language? A Study in Linguistic Pragmatics*. John Benjamins, Amsterdam

Mishler E G 1984 *The Discourse of Medicine: Dialectics of Medical Interviews*. Ablex, Norwood, NJ

Thompson J B 1984 *Studies in the Theory of Ideology*. Polity Press, Cambridge

Magic

C. McIntosh

The word 'magic' is derived from the Greek *mageia* and the Latin *magia*. In its original meaning, this referred to the set of beliefs and ritual practices of the ancient Persian magi, or priests of Zoroaster. In the late twentieth century, the word has a variety of applications, but in the most general sense, to use the definition given in *The New Encyclopaedia Britannica* (1985), it refers to any 'ritual performance or activity believed to influence human or natural events through access to an external mystical force beyond the ordinary human sphere.'

The subject of magic is intimately linked with that of language and linguistics in a number of ways. Underlying the practice of magic is a Platonic as opposed to an Aristotelian view of language. For the Aristotelian, language is merely a set of conventions to facilitate communication, and is totally separate from the world it represents. For the Platonist, on the other hand, there is a direct connection between the world of names and the world of things. Names therefore have the power to influence reality.

The belief in the connection between names and things is often linked with the idea that language itself is divine. Language as sound has often been given a primary role in the very creation of the world, as in the opening of St John's Gospel: 'In the beginning was the Word...' A similar notion is found in the Jewish Kabbalistic tradition which has formed the basis of much magical practice in the West. In his study *Major Trends in Jewish Mysticism*

(1961), Gershom Scholem, discussing the major Kabbalistic text known as the 'Zohar,' writes, 'The action and development of that mysterious force which is the seed of all creation is, according to the Zohar's interpretation of scriptural testimony, none other than speech.' From this belief it is only a short step to the idea that it is possible to influence events by uttering certain potent words and sounds, a notion that is found in virtually every magical tradition.

As Sir James Frazer pointed out in his classic study of magic, *The Golden Bough* (1913), an essential element of magic is the belief in a law of sympathy. This posits an occult link between things and their symbols. Thus, by manipulating the symbol one can supposedly manipulate the thing itself. In many magical systems, such symbols are arranged into whole chains of correspondence, in which one link can affect any other link. The symbols used can include gestures, movements, substances, colors, sounds, foods, species of plant or animal, and, of course, words and letters. In a sense, all of these symbols can be seen as components in a language of magic.

Written language, as well as spoken, has frequently played a role in magic. The *Kabbalah*, for example, attaches great importance to the Hebrew script. In the Kabbalistic text known as the '*Sefer Yetsirah*' (Book of Creation) appears an account of how God created the universe using the 22 letters of the Hebrew alphabet in different combinations. Again, this belief is reflected in magical practice. An example of the occult significance attached to the alphabet can be found in the Hebrew legends about the Golem, a humanoid creature fashioned out of clay and brought to life by magical rituals. Scholem quotes the following passage about the Golem from the seventeenth-century writer Christoph Arnold:

> On the forehead of the image, they write *emeth*, that is, truth . . . . In order to take away his strength, which ultimately becomes a threat to all those in the house, they quickly erase the first letter *aleph* from the word *emeth* on his forehead, so that there remains only the word *meth*, that is, dead.

The Nordic runic system is another case where letters are considered to possess a primal force that can be used magically. Although there has been some dispute among scholars as to the extent to which runes were used for magical purposes, Stephen Flowers convincingly argues in his study *Runes and Magic* (1986) that runes do constitute a magical system. As he points out, the runic system has an unusual feature in common with Hebrew, namely 'the use of lexes as *names* for the various graphs or letters.' For example, the first letter of the Hebrew alphabet has the name *aleph*, while that of the runic alphabet, in its older form, is called *fehu*. In both languages, the letters have an iconic value over and above their function of representing sounds.

Although it is not possible to determine precisely how the runes were used in magical or occult workings, the fact that they were so used is indicated by a number of textual references. The tenth chapter of Tacitus's *Germania*, for example, describes what appears to be a runic divination practice which involved throwing slips of wood carved with certain signs (*notae*) onto a white cloth. Later references, from the Norse sagas, describe how the runic magician would carve the characters, color them with blood, and then speak a magical formula over them. An echo of this tradition is found in M. R. James's story *Casting the Runes*.

Other traditions also ascribe an iconic value to letters or characters. In Taoism, for example, the Chinese characters are given a talismanic function and are used in communication with the spirit world.

In ancient Egyptian mythology, the mystique of written language is reflected in the figure of the ancient Egyptian diety Thoth, inventor of writing, who doubles as the patron of the occult arts when he merges in the Hellenic era with the Greek god Hermes to become Hermes Trismegistos, the 'Thrice-Great.' From him is derived the word 'Hermetic,' referring to a distinct body of esoteric lore and practice that has been transmitted through Western culture to the present day.

On the stylistic level, magic and religion use a variety of linguistic devices, such as mood-altering speech rhythms, to create a sense of exaltation or solemnity. The type of language used for the casting of spells and other magical practices also frequently shares with religious language the quality of deliberate archaism. This serves to give magical rituals an aura of tradition and to emphasize their separateness from everyday life. The same purpose is served by the use of a language other than the vernacular. As with the use of Latin in the traditional Catholic mass, so Western ritual magic has often made liberal use of Hebrew names and terms.

Often magic goes even further and uses utterances that have no obvious meaning but possess a resonant quality and convey a feeling of mystery. The word *abracadabra* is a popularized example that has passed into the language of stage conjurers. Many of the spells given in the grimoires (books of magical formulae) are made up of mangled Latin, Hebrew, or other linguistic elements, combined with unidentifiable words. Here, for example, is a passage from a spell to make oneself invisible, taken from a manuscript in the Bibliothèque de l'Arsenal in Paris, dating from about the late seventeenth century and entitled 'Le Secret des Secrets, ou le Véritable Grimoire':

> Athal Bathel nothe yhorum Asey elyungit gabellin semenei mecheno Bal habenentior mero meclab

> Halalerly Balnein Tigimiel pligas peneme Fruora Hean Ha Ararna Avira Ayla Ayes soye heremies survey levezo Haay Beruchata Acath turab Buchare Caralin per misericordiam habebit et go mortales perficiat hoc corpus ut invisibiliter ire passim.

The use of exotic language in magic is often accompanied by a preoccupation with extracting hidden meanings by means of special knowledge or through the understanding of cryptography, the science of codes and ciphers. One of the most famous figures in the history of cryptography is Johannes Trithemius (1462–1516), a German Benedictine whose best known work is the *Steganographia*, a sort of combined grimoire and cipher manual. Trithemius uses a number of different modes of encipherment, each of which is governed by the angel Pamersiel. When a message in this mode is received, the recipient chants the following conjuration: 'Lamarton anoyr bulon madriel traschon ebrasothea panthenon nabrulges Camery itrasbier rubanthy nadres Calmosy ormen ulan, ytules demy rabion hamorphyn.' When this is deciphered by taking every alternate letter of every alternate word (considering 'ie' as one letter), it yields a message in a mixture of German and Latin: 'Nym die ersten bugstaben de omni verbo (take the first letter of each word).'

Cryptography, magic and the notion of a divine language are themes that come together in the work of John Dee (1527–1607), the mathematician, geographer, and confidant of Queen Elizabeth. Dee and his collaborator Edward Kelley claimed to have rediscovered the angelic language of Enochian (so named because of the references to angelic magic in the apocryphal *Book of Enoch*). They believed that the language was a powerful medium for conjuration and enabled them to communicate with angels and spirits. A thorough investigation into Enochian was carried out by the philologist Donald Laycock in his *Enochian Dictionary*. Laycock found that Enochian had a grammer of its own and that certain roots could be identified. The letters *om*, for example, meant 'understand' or 'know.' Derived from this root were the words *oma* ('understanding'), *omax* ('knowest'), and *ixomaxip* ('let it be known').

One theory regarding Enochian is that it was invented by Dee and Kelley to transmit secret messages, but, as Laycock points out, it would be very difficult to write a text in an invented language in such a way that there could be both a straightforward translation and an enciphered message. Enochian therefore remains an enigma. Two centuries after Dee, Enochian was taken up by the English occult society, the Hermetic Order of the Golden Dawn, whose members played what was called 'Enochian chess,' both a game and a divinatory device.

Magic and language therefore have many connections. While the Aristotelian view of language has predominated since the Scientific Revolution, the Platonic view still has its protagonists. By the same token, the belief that a special power resides in the spoken or written word seems likely to survive as long as language itself.

See also: Alphabet: Religious Beliefs; Gematria; Ogam; Runes.

Bibliography

Flowers S E 1986 *Runes and Magic*. Peter Lang, New York
Frazer Sir J G 1913 *The Golden Bough*, Vol. I. Repr. 1990. Macmillan Press, London
Laycock D C 1978 *The Complete Enochian Dictionary*. Askin, London
McIntosh C 1985 *The Devil's Bookshelf. A History of the Written Word in Western Magic from Ancient Egypt to the Present Day*. Aquarian Press, Wellingborough
Merkel I, Debus A C (eds.) 1988 *Hermeticism and the Renaissance*. Folger Books, Washington, DC
The New Encyclopaedia Britannica 1985 Magic. In: 15th edn., Vol. 7, p. 671. Encyclopaedia Britannica, Chicago, IL
Scholem G G 1961 *Major Trends in Jewish Mysticism*. Schocken Books, New York
Scholem G G 1969 *On the Kabbalah and its Symbolism*. Schocken Books, New York
Tosgraec (undated) *Le Secret des Secrets, ou le Véritable Grimoire*. Manuscript 2493, Bibliothèque de l'Arsenal, Paris
Trithemius J 1982 *The Steganographia of Johannes Trithemius*. McLean A (ed.) Magnum Opus Hermetic Sourceworks, Edinburgh

Mantra

D. Smith

'Mantra' is the Sanskrit word for a sacred formula addressed to a deity, a magical formula, an instrument of thought (from *man* 'to think'). It is a key element in religions of South Asian origin from early times to the present day. The traditional etymological definition (see *Hinduism*) is 'that which protects (*-tra*) by being meditated upon (*man-*).' Believed to be of supernatural origin, mantras range from a single syllable (e.g., an utterance *om*) to an utterance hundreds of words in length. They may or may not have translatable meaning, and may vary in function from being a simple spell (for instance, against snake venom) (see *Magic*), to constituting an essential part of one of various complex mystical theologies. The sacred quality of a mantra is generally maintained by its verbal and secret transmission from teacher to pupil. The body of knowledge constituted by mantras and the details of their application is known as '*mantra-śāstra*.'

Mantras feature in Buddhism, Sikhism, and Jainism, but are particularly important in Hinduism. Mantras accompany the rituals of daily life and of the life-stages in Hinduism: a Hindu can be said to live and die in mantra, from the mother's womb to the funeral pyre. Manuals of mantras are published all over India.

1. Vedic Origins

The earliest meaning of mantra is 'a verse [of the Vedas].' Traditional Vedic exegesis divides the Vedic texts into *mantra* (the words uttered in the ritual), *vidhi* 'injunction' (telling how the ritual is to be performed), and *artha-vāda* 'statement of purpose.' The older parts of the Veda, consisting of texts spoken or sung in the ritual, are therefore sometimes called the 'mantra' portion. Excerpted verses came to be used in rituals, thus beginning the process of abbreviation that culminates in mantra as subsequently understood. The best-known mantra is the syllable *oṃ*, which is uttered frequently in Vedic ritual along with other syllables such as *o*, *śoṃ*, *hūṃ*. Being also used to precede and conclude any recitation of a Vedic text, it came to mean the totality of the Vedas, and consequently of all truth. Phonetically a single nasal vowel [õ:], *oṃ* can be divided phonologically into three sounds, $a+u+m$; it is therefore sometimes romanized as *aum*.

One verse of the Vedas became a particularly important mantra: the Gāyatrī or Sāvitrī mantra, which is daily recited by orthodox brahmin men: 'May we obtain that desirable radiance of the god Savitṛ who is to impel our visions' (*Ṛg-Veda* 3, 62, 10).

2. Mantra and Worship

Already in the Vedic hymns, mantras are regarded as having special power. They not only please or implore the gods, but strengthen them: 'For you thrive on praise, Indra, you thrive on hymns' (*Ṛg-Veda* 8, 14, 11). In post-Vedic times, mantras are treated as sacred objects: they must not be heard except by those who have become entitled to hear them through initiation. They play an important part in worship, being spell, prayer, and point of meditational focus combined. Besides the Vedic mantras, other forms of words are called mantras. Often these are quite simple, a common form being *oṃ* + *namaḥ* 'bowing, reverential salutation' + the name of the deity in the dative case. Thus among worshippers of Śiva the most sacred expression is the mantra *oṃ namaḥ śivāya* 'Om reverential salutation to Śiva.' Even such simple mantras are considered powerful, both as spells and as objects of meditation. Particular mantras are taught to initiates of different cults; they embody the god or goddess of the cult in verbal form, much as an image embodies him or her in visible form. The esoteric tradition of Tantrism sets great importance on mantras, including the monosyllabic mantras, often ending in a nasal vowel, known as *bījas* ('seeds'), such as *hūṃ*, *hrīṃ*, *krīṃ*, *phaṭ*, and the much more widely used *oṃ*. Two of these occur in the well-known Buddhist mantra *oṃ maṇipadme hūṃ* 'Om O lady with the jeweled lotus! Hūṃ.'

Such sounds are not part of language in the usual sense, since they are uttered only in particular ritual contexts and are not syntactically related to ordinary words. The same may be said of mantras in general, and some ancient Indian ritual theorists state that mantras are meaningless. The meaning of a mantra lies not in the words it comprises or their arrangement, but in its power, which is only available to the initiate, and in the correct ritual context. Staal (1989) argues that mantras, like many other mystical phenomena, are archaic; so archaic in fact that they are the predecessors of language in the process of human evolution. The traditional Indian view is that the mantra constitutes a higher plane of reality, beyond conceptual thought.

3. Complex Systems

From about 500 CE there developed theologies of sound, which identified the Indian alphabet (see *Alphabet: Religious Beliefs*) with the phonic origin of the universe, and gave a crucial role to mantras, understood as vibrations of the Ultimate. The earliest known system is Buddhist, but thereafter the main divisions of Hinduism developed their own speculations; so too the Jains. In these systems, the macrocosm of mantras is identified with the microcosm of the body, and particular mantras are placed on parts of the participant's body in a process called '*nyāsa*.' Ritual gestures (*mudrā*) accompany the repetition, audible or inaudible (*japa*) of mantras. The original literature is extensive, but has been little studied. For a full account of mantra within one theological system (Śaiva–Siddhānta), see Brunner-Lachaux 1963–77.

See also: Dhārāni; Hinduism; Ritual; Prayer; Hindu Views on Language.

Bibliography

Alper H P (ed.) 1989 *Mantra*. State University of New York Press, Albany, NY

Bharati A 1965 *The Tantric Tradition*. Rider, London

Brunner-Lachaux H 1963–77 *Somaśambhupaddhati*, 3 vols. Institut Français d'Indologie, Pondichéry

Gonda J 1963 The Indian Mantra. *Oriens* **16**: 244–97
Padoux A 1975 *Recherches sur la symbolique et l'energie de la parole dans certains textes tantriques*. Paris Institut de Civilisation indienne, Paris
Staal F 1989 Vedic Mantras. In: Alper H P (ed.) *Mantra*. State University of New York Press, Albany, NY
Gupta S, Hoens D J, Goudriaan T 1979 *Hindu Tantrism*. E J Brill, Leiden

Masoretic Tradition

G. Khan

The term 'Masoretic Tradition' or simply 'Masora' (which is a Hebrew word meaning 'tradition') refers to the activity of scholars known as Masoretes in the first millennium CE, the purpose of which was to transmit the Hebrew Bible (Old Testament) accurately in both its written and orally recited form.

After the destruction of the Temple in Jerusalem in 70 CE particular efforts were made to preserve the Jewish Scriptures. Already before this time attempts had been made by the Jewish religious authorities to fix one particular form of the text. After 70 CE this authoritative form of the text replaced all other variant forms and was the exclusive written form of the Biblical text that was transmitted in Judaism. From antiquity the transmission of the written text was accompanied by a tradition of oral recitation. Whereas there was only one written form of Jewish Scripture in the first millennium CE, there were several different forms of oral recitation, known as reading traditions. All of these had a certain amount of independence from the written tradition, as is shown by the fact that in many places the way that the text was read did not correspond exactly to the traditional written form. The reading traditions consisted of two components, viz. pronunciation and musical cantillation.

One of the reading traditions was regarded as the authoritative one throughout the first millennium. This was transmitted by a circle of Masoretes in the town of Tiberias in Galilee and so became known as the Tiberian reading tradition. It was restricted largely to learned scholars and does not seem to have been used extensively by the common people. Some time in the early Middle Ages, the Tiberian Masoretes devised a means of graphically representing the reading tradition (pronunciation and cantillation). They did so by a series of signs and diacritical marks that were in the written codices of the Bible. These are generally referred to as vocalization and accent signs. In the Bible codices they also wrote a series of marginal notes and appendices that recorded data concerning the occurrence of words in the Biblical corpus. The purpose of these notes was to guard against copyists' errors in the transmission of the written text. All the aforementioned components of the medieval Bible codices, namely the written text, vocalization, accents, marginal notes and appendices, formed the 'Tiberian Masora,' which is generally referred to simply as the 'Masora.'

At about the same period other reading traditions that were current during the Middle Ages were recorded by similar systems of written signs. These include the Palestinian and Babylonian sign systems, which represented traditions of reading that were widely used in the Jewish communities of Palestine and Babylonia, respectively.

By the early second millennium CE, the Tiberian reading tradition became defunct. The Tiberian vocalization and accent signs, however, soon became the standard in written manuscript codices of the Bible. The result was that the Tiberian signs were read with a pronunciation that did not correspond to the one that the signs were originally designed to represent.

See also: Judaism.

Bibliography

Dotan A Masorah. *Encyclopaedia Judaica*. vol. XVI, 1401–1482
Morag S 1972 *The Vocalization Systems of Arabic, Hebrew and Aramaic*. Gravenhage, Mouton
Khan G 1996 The Tiberian pronunciation tradition of Biblical Hebrew. *Zeitschrift für Althebraistik*. **9**: 1–23

Meditation

G. Houtman

Meditation aims to suspend ordinary discursive thought to achieve a goal, which may be either: (a) the realization of particular truths as formulated within the context of particular religions or philosophies; or (b) any goal conceived freely by an individual irrespective of heritage. There are many different religions with different meditation practices, including Islam, Christianity, and Hinduism. However, it is in Buddhism that meditation is the core activity, and its techniques have sometimes been adapted by other religions. This entry will concentrate on Burmese Buddhist meditation in particular.

1. Language-supported versus Language-transcendent Meditation

Language-supported meditation includes casual prayer and reciting a mantra. By using language to communicate with other (supernatural) entities, as in the four conventional methods of Christian discursive meditation and affective prayer (see Keating 1986), or in the formulae of Buddhist loving-kindness meditation, an elevated onepointed sense of consciousness is brought into existence for a particular goal. In language-transcendent meditation not only is ordinary linguistic discourse suspended, but as language itself is held to be incapable of communicating truth directly, there is an attempt to uproot conceptual techniques. In Theravāda Buddhist *vipassanā* complete silence is required, no reading or writing is allowed, and all conceptualization is avoided, emphasizing instead the experience of the inevitable forces of change, insubstantiality, and nonself.

Particularly useful to this distinction is the overlap with instrumental vs. salvation meditation. Instrumental meditation aims to achieve a particular, often secular, goal conceived as desirable by a practitioner (which may or may not be sanctioned in a religious sense), such as meditating to relax, improve one's finances, acquire psychic powers, pass an examination, or get promotion. Here the aim is to achieve control over the world outside interactively using language and other man-made symbolism. Salvation meditation, by contrast, aims for intuitive realization of particular truths formulated and sanctioned within the context of a particular religion or philosophy, such as to 'extinguish the flame of desire' in Buddhism, or to 'achieve union with God' in Christianity. Here the meditational goals are often held to be beyond language. If the first is about controlling the world, the second is to know oneself to be controlled by truth (God or Impermanence).

Language-supported techniques are sometimes identified with theistic, and language-transcendent techniques with nontheistic religion. In religions where gods and their truths can be reached through language, language-supported meditation will play a more important role than in religions where this is not the case. However, this association is not always valid. In Christianity contemplative prayer is based on 'direct feeding of the soul by God' without the instrument of language and, conversely, there are language-supported meditation techniques in Buddhism. Indeed, in both theistic and nontheistic religions language-transcendent techniques of meditation often follow the language-supported type. In Catholic monasticism centering prayer is used before contemplative prayer, in Theravāda Buddhism concentration before insight meditation, and in Zen *koan* paradoxes are used before 'nothing but sitting meditation' (*shikan-taza*).

2. Language as a Perceived Hindrance to Meditation

Though meditation may take place in groups, it often does so in withdrawal from society as a whole. This helps meditators achieve separation from the obligations of regular social and linguistic intercourse. This is sometimes reflected in terminology. Burmese sometimes refer to the 40 objects of meditation as the '40 forests,' and 'to meditate' as 'to go out into the forest.'

The study of books is known in Burmese Buddhism as one of the Ten Impediments to Meditation. Language is held to threaten to overpower meditation as a practical skill based on personal experience. With the revival of meditation in Theravāda Southeast Asia, it is now common for Buddhists to trace two lineages: a scriptural learning lineage, based on monastic ordination and teaching of scriptural learning, and a practice lineage, based on teaching of meditation. The dilemmas of the monastic teachers are, on the one hand, to fulfil the demanding duty of scriptural learning—i.e., to research the scriptures and commentaries and to fulfil their duties to pass this knowledge to their students as incumbents of a monastery—and, on the other hand, to practice meditation and teach it to people generally. This tension between scriptural learning and meditation, often put in terms of the tension between village and forest monasteries, is a major theme in teachers' biographies.

3. Discourse by Meditators

Meditation traditions flourish at times of fast change in society, as happened during the period of colonization and subsequent national independence of Burma; by appealing to personal experience *vipassanā* allows the reinterpretation of inherited values in ways appropriate to a new age. Prolonged meditation affects the way meditators perceive things. In particular, by suspending or transcending the ordinary discursive nature of thought the relationship between I and the world is altered.

First, the whole of the religion may be in for a redefinition. For example, some *vipassanā* meditators have come to interpret the most commonly used Burmese term for Buddhism (*bok-da'ba-tha*) as a term of recent invention by an American Baptist missionary signifying inherited tradition contaminated with 'foreign' influences. A more scriptural and purer term is reserved for the Buddhism they seek (*bok-da' tha-tha-na*). A parallel development has taken place regarding terms for 'Buddhist,' where meditators feel they are 'inside true Buddhism' (*tha-tha-na win*) as opposed to merely a 'member of Buddhendom' (*bok-da' ba-tha win*).

Second, the above emphasis is symptomatic of a complete reordering of a whole range of concepts in Buddhism. In this way, Burmese *vipassanā* meditators will not only emphasize true Buddhism over foreign and cultural Buddhendom, but also emphasize practice against scriptural learning, meditation against charity and morality, and insight against concentration. This emphasis on particular concepts is replicated in infinite ways in meditators' discourse. *Vipassanā* meditators insist doctrinalists and concentration meditators confuse meditation with verbalism, textualism, and conceptual imagery. The popular term for *vipassanā* meditation is no longer 'to sit and apply oneself to the meditation object,' which is ambiguous as to whether it means concentration or insight meditation, but 'to sit and apply oneself to the *dhamma*,' a term specifically about insight meditation.

Third, meditation may sanction an individual to use language to claim an entirely different status in the world than is attributed to him/her by conventional tradition. Some secretive Burmese concentration meditation cults adopt royal regalia and use royal language. Some unordained meditators in the more public *vipassanā* traditions have adopted monastic language normally reserved for monks. Also, some meditators use the numerative *ba''* to count lay meditators, normally used for counting members of royalty, monks, and spirits, instead of the more usual *yauk* for normal mortals. These are considered quite inappropriate in wider society.

Fourth, meditators often claim that through meditation a profound knowledge can arise, which is better and more accurate than knowledge generated by scriptural learning. Some proficient meditators with little knowledge of the scriptures are thought capable of giving more erudite answers than the most capable scholars.

4. Language Supports Meditation History

Despite their anti-language attitude, meditation traditions are, like all ancient historical traditions, inevitably tied up with language and text. A degree of language-based scholarship is crucial for meditation teachers as: (a) meditation knowledge needs to be recorded, transmitted, and preserved historically; (b) studied; and (c) disseminated and made relevant by interpretation and illustration. The authoritative scriptures and commentaries are often in a different language from the vernacular (e.g., Sanskrit or Pāli), so that scholarship is a time-consuming and technical vocation in itself. Conversely, the experiences by meditation teachers are recorded in biographies and testaments to be studied by their pupils. The meditation–language dialectic is thereby guaranteed to continuously evolve historically.

See also: Mantra.

Bibliography

Houtman G 1990 How a foreigner invented Buddhendom in Burmese. *Journal of the Anthropological Society at Oxford* **21**(**2**): 113–28

Keating T 1986 *Open Mind Open Heart*. Amity House, New York

Metaphor

V. Sage

Metaphor (from the ancient Greek verb *metapherein*, to 'carry over, transfer') means 'to speak about X in terms of Y'—e.g., 'The moon is a sickle.' Aristotle (384–322 BCE) defines it in his *Poetics* (ca. 339 BCE) thus:

> Metaphor consists in applying to a thing a word that belongs to something else; the transference being either from genus to species or from species to genus or from species to species or on grounds of analogy.
>
> (1965: 61)

Aristotle's distinction between 'simple replacement' and 'analogy' governs, effectively, the difference between simple and complex 'metaphor.' Discussion of metaphor varies along an axis of assumptions about what Aristotle terms here 'analogy' as to whether it is conceived of as including the mental act of perceiving analogy—the idea-content—or whether it is a strictly and exclusively linguistic operation—the language level. Writers vary significantly, but most—though certainly not all—lie between these two extremes. Thus puzzles about metaphor may, at the one end of the scale, raise problems in psychology and philosophy and, at the other, problems in the study of language. In between these extremes lie the problems the subject raises for literary criticism, both traditional and modern. Metaphor is also an index of the power relations between literary genres and what is said about metaphor often indicates what the assumptions of a period or a critic are about these matters: what is sayable microcosmically about metaphor is often sayable macrocosmically about literature.

1. The Classical View: Aristotle

Metaphor is treated by Classical writers as a desirable rhetorical means, not an end in itself. This does not mean, however, as is often assumed, that it is treated as a simple ornament.

Most rhetorics of the ancient world contain an account of metaphor which places it firmly as a figure of speech (trope, paradigmatic) rather than a figure of thought (schema, syntagmatic). The strongest version of this distinction is Quintilian's in the *Institutio Oratoria* (ca. 75 CE) but he derives it from Greek sources. However, most rhetorical treatises are written not about poetry and poetics, but about speaking and prose writing. They are a set of written instructions, to train the reader in the art of persuasion, either forensically—as was first the case with Corax of Syracuse (467 CE)—or epideictically (decoratively, publicly in a more general sense than simply advocacy). Aristotle's is the only *Poetics* surviving from the ancient world, even including Longinus' treatise *On the Sublime* of the second century CE, which is a general rhetorical manual. It is characteristic of this split between the genres that Aristotle should separate his remarks about poetry from his other discussion of metaphor in the *Rhetoric* (337 BCE). Thus the use of metaphor in poetry and in prose is formally separated, though it is noticeable that Aristotle and Quintilian both choose their examples of metaphor from poetry—the former from Hesiod, Homer, and the dramatists, and the latter from Virgil and Ovid.

The development from fifth-century Greece to Augustan Rome seems to be that of a progressive pragmatism. Aristotle always takes an empirical approach, but he believes rhetoric to be an art of the possible whereas for Quintilian it is a set of exercises to commit to memory. For Aristotle in the *Rhetoric*, metaphor is a part of the larger topic of the enthymeme (from Greek *en thumō* 'in the mind'), a kind of rhetorical syllogism, looser than the strictly logical forms but vital to the art of manipulating the 'probable.' For both of them, metaphor gives *energeia* which means 'force, vigor,' or, as the Loeb edition interestingly translates it, 'actuality.' But Aristotle makes an important distinction between metaphor and simile:

> For the simile, as we have said, is a metaphor differing only by the addition of a word, wherefore it is less pleasant because it is longer, it does not say this *is* that, *so that the mind does not even examine this.*
>
> [Author's italics]

It follows that the characteristic compression and enigma of metaphor makes the mind of the beholder entertain something not immediately understandable and thus 'a kind of knowledge (*oion mathesis*) results.' Metaphor, says Aristotle, is proportionate or analogical (*kat'analogian*), and sets things 'before the eyes.' But he insists that the analogy should be between things that are unlike or resistant to an extent, 'just as, for instance, in philosophy it needs sagacity to grasp the similarity in things that are apart...' And he goes on to link this *energeia* to the defeat of expectations:

> Most smart sayings are derived from metaphor, and also from misleading the hearer beforehand. For it becomes evident to him that he has learnt something, when the conclusion turns out contrary to his expectation, and the mind seems to say, 'How true it is ! but I missed it.'

Metaphors are like jokes and philosophical paradoxes. This is not an assimilation of metaphor to simile, nor is it a simple view of metaphor as comparison. Aristotle's more famous structural insistence in the *Poetics* on the analogical proportion idea in metaphor—B is to A as D is to C—needs to be put in the context of the above remarks because they show that analogy has plenty of room to include the idea of implicit meaning (the distance of the elements one from another and the suppressed aspects of analogy) and is a source of wit, or a contrast between appearance and reality. This is a more mentalistic view of metaphor than the Roman Quintilian's recipe-book approach to the store of ornamental figures.

2. The Platonic Tradition: Metaphor and the Paradox of Representation

Plato (429–347 BCE) does not have a 'view' of metaphor stated in any one place like Aristotle. Nevertheless his dialogues abound in examples and ideas about the significance of metaphor and figurative language which—deeply ambiguous as they are—have proved enormously influential, especially on the practice of poetry. There are two lines of thought in Plato, both of which are sometimes found within the same dialogue. One is that all language originates in metaphor and figuration. The *Cratylus*, for example, represents an often playful and obscure enquiry into the origins of language in which Socrates mounts a critique of representation—the names for abstractions like 'truth' and 'necessity' are broken down into their earlier elements which point (figuratively) towards the 'true' elements (by metaphor) of our current speech, which we have forgotten—hence the word for 'truth,' for example, i.e., *aletheia*, 'really' means 'a divine wandering' because it is made up of the elements *ale* and *theia*, or necessity means 'walking through a ravine' because 'necessary' (*anangkaion*) is made up of *an angke ion* meaning literally 'going through a ravine.' In this way, argues Socrates, perhaps abstract language itself—and therefore the very language of definition—contains hidden figuration and is an extended metaphor whose origins perpetually threaten its ability to represent abstractly.

However, metaphor reveals the traces of its divine origin, for 'speech' says Socrates, punning on the Greek words for 'they speak' and 'everything' (*pan*), 'signifies all things':

> *Socrates* You are aware that speech signifies all things (*pan*) and is always turning them round and round, and has two forms, true and false.
> *Hermogenes* Certainly.
> *Socrates* Is not the truth that is in him the smooth or sacred form which dwells above among the Gods, whereas falsehood dwells among men below, and is rough like the goat of tragedy, for tales and falsehoods have generally to do with the tragic or goatish life, and tragedy is the place of them?
> *Hermogenes* Very true.
> *Socrates* Then surely, Pan, who is the declarer of all things (*pan*) and the perpetual mover *(aei polon*) of all things, is rightly called *aipolos* (goatherd), he being the two-formed son of Hermes, smooth in his upper part, and rough and goat-like in his lower regions. And, as the son of Hermes, he is speech or the brother of speech, and that brother should be like brother is no marvel.

Language is portrayed, metaphorically, as a satyr: through a grasp of its perpetually dual form—i.e., analogy—one can get glimpses of the truth it can offer. The other view playfully expressed here is that language is perpetually unstable, untrustworthy, and quite unsatisfactory for reasoning with, because it can never identify absolutely with what it seeks to picture and therefore can only be, at best, an approximation to an inner truth. Skepticism about representation in language is thus inseparable from a self-consciousness about the figurative. But Plato, the enemy of poets in the *Republic*, give the grounds here for a profound defense of metaphor as a positive instrument of thought.

Later, in the Medieval and Renaissance periods, Nature becomes a book written by God, and, in a common extension of the metaphor, language is again thought of as a repository of hidden analogies and correspondences which form—to use the usual sub- or associated metaphor—the signatures or traces of God's presence. This view also uses the technique of 'poetic etymology' which purports to uncover the original metaphors of language itself. So Sir Philip Sidney (1554–86), who claimed in his *Apologie For Poetrie* (1595) that only the poets can recreate the 'golden world,' is borrowing the technique of Socrates in the *Cratylus*.

This self-conscious view of the conceptual paradox posed by metaphor in representation was systematized by one continental eighteenth-century philosopher. One can see the Platonist influence in the *The New Science* (1725) of the Italian protostructuralist thinker, Vico (1668–1744)—particularly in the important place given to metaphor in Vico's inquires into the origin of languages. Vico proposes a universal fourfold development for every national culture; and to every phase he gives a rhetorical master trope, beginning with the original of all perception: 'metaphor.' Then follow 'metonymy,' 'synecdoche,' 'irony.' Language originates in metaphor in this tradition; and culture, in epic.

3. Empiricism

In the latter half of the seventeenth century, a new hostility to metaphor emerged. The English empiricist Thomas Hobbes (1588–1679) in his treatise *Leviathan* (1651), classified metaphor as an 'abuse of speech': '... when they [men] use words metaphorically; that is, in other sense than they are ordained for; and thereby deceive others' (1651: 102). Hobbes conceives of language as a kind of 'naming' and the problem he seeks, as a result, to solve is the problem of 'inconstant signification':

> For one man calleth Wisdome, what another calleth *feare*; and one *cruelty*, what another *justice*; one *gravity*, what another *stupidity*, etc... And therefore such names can never be true grounds of any ratiocination. No more can metaphors, and tropes of speech: but these are less dangerous, because they profess their inconstancy; which the other do not.

Here one sees graphically the decline of rhetoric: Hobbes has a profound distrust of metaphor, but his 'realism' contradicts what Aristotle has to say by suggesting that metaphor always declares itself as deceptive. This view initiated the cult of the plain style.

Later, John Locke (1632–1704), in his *Essay Concerning Human Understanding* (1690), also tackled the problem of the 'unsteady uses of words.' He regards language as a process of labeling, and the 'reform of language'—i.e., the precedence of the 'literal' over all figuration is explicitly a part of the age's antirhetorical project. Like the Puritan side of Plato, Locke is deeply suspicious of abstractions but also equally so of metaphor and simile. Metaphor is thus not distinguished from any other form of figuration—all of which for Locke are ruled by one prior law; the association of ideas. The satire of Laurence Sterne (1713–68) in *Tristram Shandy* (1760–67) employs metaphor directly at the expense of Locke's association of ideas principle, obeying it and yet triumphantly violating it at the same moment:

> —My young Master in London is dead! said Obadiah.
> —A green satin night-gown of my mother's, which had been twice scoured, was the first idea which Obadiah's exclamation brought into Susannah's head.—Well might Locke write a chapter upon the imperfections of words.—
> —Then, quoth Susannah, we must all go into mourning—But note a second time: the word *mourning* notwithstanding Susannah made use of it herself—failed also of doing its office; it excited not one single idea, tinged either with grey or black,—all was green,—The green satin night-gown *hung there* still.
> [Author's italics]

This passage is a perfect illustration of Locke's theory that thought and language are ruled by the association of ideas, except that the association is not the conventional one between mourning and black which it should universally be, according to Locke, but a private one, based on a combination of desire and habit which is so dominant that Susannah's mind is transformed, comically, by metaphor, into a wardrobe. The separation, vital for Locke's whole theory, between the idea in the mind and the thing being thought of, is eroded. It is Sterne's metaphor 'hung there' which creates this satirical refutation: this metaphor will not unpack properly into idea and thing, and therefore is not replaceable by a 'concrete,' 'simple,' or 'literal' paraphrase without loss of significance.

4. Neoclassicism

'As to metaphorical expression,' said Samuel Johnson (1709–84), 'that is a great excellence in style, when it is used with propriety, for it gives you two ideas for one.' Neoclassical attitudes to metaphor are founded on the linguistic pragmatism of the Roman, as opposed to the psychological subtlety of the Greek writers. Horace's (65–8 BCE) highly pragmatic update of parts of Aristotle's thinking in the *Ars Poetica* (ca. 17 BCE) is mainly concerned with such things as appropriateness, decorum, and consistency: significantly, it does not mention metaphor.

An example of what Johnson means is in his famous emendation of the speech of Shakespeare's Macbeth at v, iii, 27–8; 'My way of life/Is fall'n into the sere, the yellow Leafe,' which Johnson amended to 'My May of Life' on the grounds of metaphorical propriety. The result, which reveals the prejudices of the age, is a rococo prettification, in the name of consistency, of something that strikes the ear as massive and rugged. It is likely that Shakespeare felt 'way of life' to be a metaphorical expression, but if Johnson thought of it as a metaphor at all, then it was an inconsistent one which made the whole line metaphorically mixed. He reconstructed the phrase on the assumption of a compositor's error, thus restoring the stylistic consistency which he felt that Shakespeare would not have missed.

It is from this strain of thought that the familiar idea of the inappropriateness of mixed metaphor, which survived until the Edwardian period in manuals of composition, is derived.

5. The Romantic View

In the Romantic period, poetry gained a new ascendancy as the paradigm of literature itself. The Romantics, reacting against the rhetoric of Augustan Rome and reaching back to Aristotle and Plato, as Vico had done, gave an enormous impetus to metaphor as the dynamic founding trope of poetry and literary culture.

Two views are to be distinguished here, which ultimately influence the modern tradition in different ways; the Organicism of Samuel Taylor Coleridge (1772–1834) and the Romantic Platonism of Percy Bysshe Shelley (1792–1822), both of which make equally far-reaching claims for metaphor but by different routes.

Metaphor for Coleridge is part of the 'interinanimation of words' and his view is neither that of 'simple replacement' nor 'substitution' nor 'comparison,' but of 'organic unity.' In his 'Lectures on Shakespeare' (1808, publ. 1836), Coleridge closely analyses how metaphors reveal an inexhaustible mutual reactiveness amongst their elements, which creates an unparaphraseable richness of meaning. This approach depends on Coleridge's notion of the 'imagination' as a separate and dynamic faculty. Coleridge's view of metaphor is deeply antiempiricist. A metaphor has the form of a duality but is always surmounted by a unity in the mind of the perceiver. Coleridge's main distinction is to have isolated and stressed this drive towards unity-in-difference in metaphor.

Shelley's *Defence of Poetry* (1821) again uses the argument from the origins of language, but gives it a new, optimistic twist. Language, it is argued, was in its beginning not a set of atomic labels, of names, as the empiricists would argue, but 'the chaos of a cyclic poem'; and 'In the infancy of society every author is necessarily a poet, because language itself is poetry...' A defense of poetry amounts to a defense of metaphor, which is the agent by which language produces new meaning. 'Their language [i.e., the poets'] is vitally metaphorical; it marks the before unapprehended relations of things...' Metaphor, for Shelley, is the Ur-perception of analogy and hence the governing trope of language and poetic art.

'Language,' he claims in the *Defence*, 'is arbitrarily produced by the imagination, and has relation to thoughts alone.' Shelley's poetic practice is ruled by perpetually dispensible analogy, as in his triply metaphorical description of Plato as '*kindling harmony* in thoughts *divested* of shape and action'—a phrase in which the reader is required to shift lightly from music, to fire, to clothing, without pausing or isolating these single elements, in order to apprehend fully Shelley's notion of the entirely conceptual nature of Plato's art.

6. Post-Romantic Views

Coleridge's view of 'organic form' has been heavily influential in the modern period, developed, transformed, and hardened into the loose collection of doctrines known as Anglo–American Formalism. This movement is a continuation of the Romantic opposition between Poetry and Science, which crystallizes in the early statements of I. A. Richards (1893–1975). In 'Science and Poetry' (1926), Richards proposed to reduce meaning to two types—the 'emotive' and the 'referential,' in which metaphor belongs to the former not the latter category. There is a residue of 'empiricism' and utilitarianism in the early Richards which he later came to change.

The notion that a metaphor is a vital part of language's power to generate new meanings, is an assumption which underlies three or four different movements in poetry and criticism in the modern period, and in this tradition the romantic view of metaphor is preserved but renamed and assimilated into certain related terms, for example, 'image' and 'symbol,' which seem to many writers in this period exclusive features of lyric poetry itself, not of discourse in general, but which can be regarded as reducible to metaphors with one term suppressed, and which no longer display explicitly their analogical character.

There is a general movement in both theory and practice towards the autonomy of figurative language. Poetic theory, in Symbolist France and Imagist England up to the 1920s, turns inward. Despite the rise of the novel, the ascendancy of lyric poetry—and the corresponding demand for a theory of the lyric moment in language—is unbroken from the Romantic to the Modern Periods and the modulation from high Romanticism into Symbolism which has been exhaustively documented, yields a high concentration on the autonomy of symbolic—in reality, metaphoric—language as part of the general conception of what Eliot called the 'autotelic' nature of poetic language.

This attitude is reified in the obsession with 'imagery' in the Anglo–American criticism of the post-war period, which began in Shakespeare criticism and spread into general critical vocabulary under this rather misleading name, and which later writers, notably P. N. Furbank, in his book *Reflections on the Word 'Image'* (1970), have again reduced to metaphor. I. A. Richards, however, shifted his viewpoint radically and went on to write one of the most influential modern accounts of how metaphor works based on a significant re-reading of Coleridge, which pushes him much more towards the anti-Empiricist and Platonist tradition—the so-called Interaction theory of metaphor. In his later book *The Philosophy of Rhetoric* (1930) Richards attacks the empiricist account of metaphor quite explicitly as 'The Proper Meaning Superstition' and calls for a new rhetoric which can clarify the confusion inherited from the Lockeian tradition. Richards identifies the confusion as lying in the distinction between the 'metaphorical' and the 'literal' meaning of expressions and demonstrates convincingly that the so-called literal meaning is not equivalent to the meaning of the whole expression. Instead, he invents the terms 'tenor' and 'vehicle' for the two parts of a metaphor—which correspond, in empiricist language, to the 'literal' and the 'figurative' parts—e.g., in the 'moon is a sickle,' the tenor is the 'moon' and the vehicle is the 'sickle'—and he then shows how in complex metaphors the tenor and the vehicle can change places—for example he quotes the Sufi apothegm: 'I am the child whose father is his son and the vine whose wine is its jar' and asks his reader to entertain the deliberate chain of exchanges, designed, for the purposes of spiritual meditation, to defeat a 'literal' paraphrase.

Richard's theory is a modified, nonmystical version of the interaction view of metaphor which resists the tautology involved in supposing that there is such a thing as the 'literal meaning' which can replace the 'metaphorical meaning.' A development of this attitude can be found in William Empson's theory of Mutual Comparison elaborated in *Some Versions of Pastoral* (1936). Another effective analysis of metaphor in this tradition is W. Nowottny's *The Language Poets Use* (1962).

7. Structuralism

The most persuasive and influential Structuralist account of metaphor is contained in Roman Jakobson's classic essay. 'Two Types of Aphasia' (1956). In this essay, Jakobson examines the evidence from the records of the speech of aphasics, and from this evidence he classifies speech defects into two types—failures of vocabulary (lexis, paradigmatic axis of selection) and failures of grammar (syntagmatic axis of combination). From there he goes on to show that both types of patients make substitutions which correspond to metaphor and metonymy. He then maps this point on to the Saussurean binary distinctions between linguistic axes (see also *Saussure, Ferdinand(-Mongin) de*). The two tropes then become, in his classic 'Closing Statement: Linguistics and Poetics' (1960), the master tropes governing different literary genres, and this can yield a complete definition of what poetry characteristically does.

This view of the relations between the tropes explicitly changes again the center of gravity for the literary genres. Metaphor is firmly and explicitly consigned to the paradigmatic axis of discourse and associated with poetry, and opposed in a binary fashion to the trope of metonymy, which becomes syntagmatic, and which generates prose narrative. The account is in some ways reductive—metaphor is a form of substitution of in absentia particles of lexis from the paradigm (selection axis), and there is no way in this account for metaphor to enter the syntagm and become a combinative factor. By definition it is held in a certain position by its mutual opposition with metonymy's chain of linear substitutions.

In some ways this idea ought to be merely a relativistic instrument of analysis: both poetry and prose narrative may contain both metaphor and metonymy. On the macro-level, genre and form are generated by the extent to which each text foregrounds metaphor or metonymy: a text which is all metaphor will be a lyric poem and one which is all metonymy will be a realistic novel. (However, Jakobson does suggest that metonymy, not metaphor, is the method of surrealism, which is sometimes conveniently forgotten.)

In Jakobson's own critical practice, however, the oppositional method works to minimize the cognitive content of metaphor and yield a formalist analysis of poetry. In general, the structuralist analysis of poetry, compared with its insights into prose narrative, has been disappointing—precisely because of the reductive account of metaphor which its taxonomic grid relies upon.

The structuralist account has the advantage of getting rid at a stroke of the old-fashioned and rather Cartesian confusion between 'figures of thought' and 'figures of speech'—metaphors can coexist on the linguistic and the conceptual levels without any problem; but it does not add to the traditional understanding of metaphor (as opposed to metonymy which becomes a more important concept than ever before), except in rearranging its relations with other tropes.

However, the very stabilizing of this taxonomic grid itself presents further difficult problems in relation to the concept of metaphor.

8. Poststructuralism

Nietzsche's remarks about metaphor in his 1873 essay *Über Wahrheit und Lüge im außermoralischen Sinn* 'On truth and falsity in their ultramoral sense'), form an important reference point for the poststructuralist account of metaphor. Nietzsche argues, in a hostile, but also dependent, parody of Socrates, that we necessarily and often unknowingly use metaphors when we discuss the question of truth, taking them to be the original things themselves:

> When we talk about trees, colors, snow, and flowers, we believe we know something about the things themselves, and yet we only possess metaphors of the things, and these metaphors do not in the least correspond to the original essentials.

This is another version of the argument-from-origins, used to attack the worn-out humanist tradition. Nietzsche attacks our confidence in our representations, arguing that language itself is metaphorical and that when we seek definitions of things, we deceive ourselves unknowingly and take for truths those things which are merely our own anthropomorphic fictions:

> What therefore is truth? A mobile army of metaphors, metonymies, anthropomorphisms: in short a sum of human relations which became poetically and rhetorically intensified, metamorphosed, adorned, and after long usage seem to a nation fixed, canonic and binding...

In a manner reminiscent of the Socrates of the *Cratylus*, he self-consciously uses the metaphor, for our notions of truth, of coins whose obverses have become effaced, and which have lost their value as a result. Perception of nature can only be, originally, metaphorical but man, argues Nietzsche, 'forgets that the original metaphors of perception *are* metaphors, and takes them for things themselves.'

There are two main areas in which this argument has been influential.

First, some of the most eloquent writing about literature in the immediate postwar period takes up this antihumanist posture and attacks anthropomorphic fictions in literary language. This leads to experiments in a new form of writing in the Paris-based group, the Nouveau Roman, led by Alain Robbe-Grillet. Robbe-Grillet's explicit hostility to figurative language, including metaphor in particular, as a literary 'consolation,' is recorded in a number of brilliant essays, of which perhaps the most notable is 'Nature, humanism and tragedy' (1958) which uses the same argument as seen in Nietzsche (i.e., that 'nature knows no forms') to make a plea for a new kind of literature which will not 'take refuge' in tropes. Robbe-Grillet himself experiments in writing which agonizingly prolongs the act of meticulous description without figuration, notably in the opening of his novel *Le Voyeur* (1958). This posture is echoed in the early critical work of Roland Barthes, particularly in *Writing Degree Zero* (1953, transl. 1967) which argues for a neural 'zero' style in prose fiction which rejects the bourgeois compromise of 'style.'

Second, explicitly indebted to Nietzsche for its central metaphor of worn-out coins, stands the elaborate discussion of metaphor by Jacques Derrida, 'White mythology' (1974) (see *Derrida, J.*). The basic point which Derrida seeks to demonstrate is that it is impossible to arrive at a 'metaphorology' because metaphor cannot be eradicated from any meta-language which would stabilize itself as non-metaphorical. This is because the nature of metaphor is such that it leaves its mark upon concepts—in a passage of almost Socratic bravura, Derrida reveals the metaphorical element in the Greek term 'trope' which means 'a turning,' and which is used, as shown above, as a stable instrument of taxonomy, to confine metaphor to a linguistic level only and remove it from the domain of the conceptual. Thus he argues that anything that claimed to be a metalanguage would have to have a meta-metalanguage which would 'lead to classifying metaphors by their source'; but the self-defeating nature of such a tropology is obvious:

> If we wanted to conceive and classify all the metaphorical possibilities of philosophy, there would always be at least one metaphor which would be extended and remain outside the system: that one, at least, which was needed to construct the concept of metaphor or,... the metaphor of metaphor.

Thus metaphor is assimilated to *aporia* and *mis-en-abyme* and made the instrument of an infinite regress at the heart of any empirical effort to separate the defining from the defined.

Paradoxically, in the realm of literary criticism, metaphor has once again assumed a position of tremendous power and is cultivated, by the Yale group of poststructuralists who follow Derrida, in particular Paul de Man and Hillis Miller , as a critical instrument for revealing the *aporia* of largely romantic, lyric poetry. Deconstruction, as it has come to be known, is in practice a secondary wave of Anglo-American formalism, using self-conscious metaphors of infinite regress to draw a charmed circle around literariness, largely in the genre of lyric poetry. Deconstruction—because of its obsession with the 'tropical'—is not a method which can be readily used in the discussion of extended narrative or prose fiction.

However, the discussion of metaphor has recently begun to use more representational assumptions. These are even evident in the earlier Derrida of *Dissemination* (transl. 1972). The tour de force of this volume is the essay called 'Plato's *Pharmakon*' in which, drawing on the work of J.P. Vernant, he exposes the complexities of hidden metaphor in the Greek text of Plato's *Phaedrus*, using the technique triumphantly to draw attention to the metaphor used by Socrates, at the climactic point of his exposition, in claiming that truth is 'written upon the soul' and thus ostensibly to defeat his argument that 'writing,' and indeed rhetoric, is logically secondary to the spoken dialectic. The claim that Socrates is contradicting himself rests upon the presence of what Derrida takes to be unacknowledged metaphor in this text.

The implication here is that the use of a metaphor for Derrida, is not only conceptual, but also representational: the metaphor can drag along with it, it is implied, the whole of a belief system:

> But it is not any less remarkable here that the so-called living discourse should suddenly be described by a 'metaphor' borrowed from the order of the very thing one is trying to exclude from it, the order of its simulacrum. *Yet this borrowing is rendered necessary by that which structurally links the intelligible to its copy*, and the language describing dialectics cannot fail to call upon it.
>
> [Author's italics]

Derrida is using, ironically, against Plato, the Platonic argument of the *Cratylus*. But: 'that which *structurally* links the intelligible to its copy,' is in fact an old argument about metaphors in some sense representing domains of thought, or *topoi*.

However, a more pragmatic version of this representational notion of metaphor, which locates its source in a whole ideological complex of often unconscious beliefs, forms an important part of the more mainstream contemporary analysis of metaphor in discourse. It is consistent, of course, with the Freudian analysis of metaphor as a revelation of unconscious meaning. A version of it is also employed in more eclectic linguistic analyses of discourse such as the influential *Metaphors We Live By* (1980) by George Lakoff and Mark Johnson. Political analysis of the racist and feminist bias in much contemporary rhetoric uses this assumption about metaphor—i.e., that it has a mimetic or representational relationship to the subconscious or, more often, unconscious beliefs of a speaker or writer, or a society. The metaphors it uses are symptomatic of the state of a culture. For example, the recent writings of Susan Sontag—e.g., *Illness as Metaphor* (1978)—tend to use similar assumptions.

See also: Analogy; Christian Views on Language; Postmodernism; Romanticism.

Bibliography

Aristotle 1926 (337 BCE) (transl. Treece H) *The Art of Rhetoric*. Loeb Classical Library, Cambridge, MA

Aristotle 1965 *Poetics*. In: Dorsch T R (ed. and trans.) *Classical Literary Criticism*. Penguin, Harmondsworth

Barthes R 1988 The old rhetoric: An aide-memoire. In: Barthes R *The Semiotic Adventure*. Basil Blackwell, Oxford

Booth W C 1978 Metaphor as rhetoric. *Critical Inquiry* **5**: 49–72

Brooke-Rose C 1958 *A Grammar of Metaphor*. Secker and Warburg, London
Burke K 1941 Four master tropes. *Kenyon Review* **3**: 421–38
Derrida J 1972 Johnson B (ed.) *Dissemination*. University of Chicago Press, Chicago, IL
Derrida J 1974 White mythology: Metaphor in the text of philosophy. *New Literary History* **6**: 5–74
Furbank P N 1970 *Reflections On The Word 'Image'*. Secker and Warburg, London
Hawkes T 1972 *Metaphor*. Methuen, London
Jakobson R 1956 Two types of aphasic disturbance. In: Jakobson R, Halle M (eds.) *Fundamentals of Language*. Mouton, The Hague
Jakobson R 1960 Closing statement: Linguistics and poetics. In: Sebeok T A (ed.) *Style in Language*. MIT Press, Cambridge, MA
Lakoff G , Johnson M 1980 *Metaphors We Live By*. University of Chicago Press, Chicago, IL
Lodge D 1970 *The Modes of Modern Writing*. Edward Arnold, London
Nowottny W 1962 *The Language Poets Use*. Athlone Press, London
Ong W J Metaphor and the twinned vision. *The Sewanee Review* **63**: 193–201
Quintilian M F 1920–2 (ca. 75 CE) (trans. Butter H E) *Institutio Oratoria*. Heinemann, London
Richards I A 1965 (orig. 1936) *The Philosophy of Rhetoric*. Oxford University Press, London
Ricoeur P 1977 *The Rule of Metaphor*. Routledge & Kegan Paul, London
Shelley P B 1953 (orig. 1821) Brett-Smith (ed.) *The Defence of Poetry*. Oxford University Press, London
Sontag S 1978 *Illness as Metaphor*. Farrar, Strauss and Giroux, New York
Vico G 1984 (orig. 1725) *The New Science*. Cornell University Press, Ithaca, NY

Metrical Psalms and Paraphrases

J. M. Y. Simpson

Metrical psalms and paraphrases are portions of the Old and New Testaments of the Christian Bible translated into vernacular languages and cast in regular, usually rhyming, stanzas.

From the singing of Psalms during worship in the early Christian church there evolved various traditions of chanting; for various reasons (rhythmic subtlety and the fact that the texts were not in the vernacular), by the later Middle Ages performance of these had become confined to trained choirs. In the sixteenth century in various Reformed churches congregational singing was introduced with simple, strongly accented melodies. At first, however, the singing of non-Biblical texts was not permitted, except in the Lutheran tradition. This meant that vernacular Biblical texts, crucially the Psalms, had to be converted into metrical and strophic forms that could fit such melodies.

The first notable collection of these metrical psalms was the Genevan Psalter of 1562, prepared at the behest of John Calvin. An English Psalter also appeared in 1562 followed by more than half a dozen others before the end of the seventeenth century, an important one being Thomas Ravenscroft's *Whole Booke of Psalms* of 1621 which contained more than one hundred metrical psalm tunes. The 'Bay Psalm Book' (*The Whole Booke of Psalms Faithfully Translated into English Metre*), perhaps the first book to be printed in the New World, was published in Cambridge, Massachusetts, in 1640. Nahum Tate, the Poet Laureate, and Nicholas Grady produced *A New Version of the Psalms of David* in England in 1696; many of these found their way into later collections. (Later, metrical psalms became particularly associated with Scottish Presbyterian churches, but their texts had originated in England.) The predominant English meter used in these psalters was a form of ballad stanza, a quatrain containing successive lines of 8, 6, 8, and 6 syllables.

The writers had a difficult task, in that they had to compose rhyming lines of a given number of syllables to a pre-existing tune. However, an additional and supremely important constraint was that the original text itself was sacred, hence nothing of substance could be omitted or added. The consequence, at least as far as English versions are concerned, was that the linguistic style became exaggeratedly different from that of prose or even secular verse: in particular, 'normal' word order was virtually unknown. Thus meaning, though paramount, was sometimes not immediately obvious, for example *The barren woman house to keep/he maketh, and to be/Of sons a mother full of joy/Praise to the Lord give ye* (Psalm 113, 9). Indeed, so ubiquitous was abnormal word-order, not to say perverse, that it is difficult to avoid the conclusion that it had become a deliberate stylistic marker of this genre.

The distance between the concise original Hebrew and a verbose metrical version can be illustrated from Psalm 133, 1.

Hebrew	Literal meaning	Metrical Version
hinnē mā-tōv	'behold how good	*Behold, how good a thing it is,*
umā-na'īm	and how pleasant	*and how becoming well,*
shevet aḥīm	to live brothers	*Together such as brethern are*
gam-yaḥad	like one'	*in unity to dwell*

In some traditions, various prose passages of the Old and New Testaments (for example, the story of Creation, the parable of the Prodigal Son, and the vision of New Jerusalem in the Book of Revelation) were similarly converted into stanzas that could be sung, appearing as *Translations and Paraphrases in Verse, of Several Passages of Sacred Scripture*; these became popularly known simply as 'Paraphrases.'

The texts of metrical psalms themselves became regarded as so sacred in some Scottish Presbyterian traditions that they came under a taboo and could be sung only during actual services. Therefore, so that the tunes could be practiced, secular texts fitting their meter and rhyme scheme had to be written: for example, for Psalm 23, of which the first line in a metrical version is *The Lord's my shepherd, I'll not want*, there was substituted a text beginning *There was an auld Seceder cat*.

See also: Hymns.

Bibliography

Chibbett M 1988 Sung Psalms in Scottish Worship. In: Wright D F (ed.) *The Bible in Scottish Life and Literature*. Saint Andrews Press, Edinburgh

Davie D 1993 Psalmody as Translation. In: *The Eighteenth-Century Hymn in England*. Cambridge University Press, Cambridge

le Huray P 1967 *Music and the Reformation in England, 1549–1660*, 2nd ed. 1978. Cambridge University Press, London

Leaver R 1990 English Metrical Psalmody. In: Glover R (ed.) *The Hymnal Companion*. The Church Hymnal Corporation, New York

Louden R S 1979 Psalmody in the Church. In: *Handbook to the Church Hymnary*, 3rd edn. Barkley J M. Oxford University Press, London

Miller R J 1971 *John Calvin and the Reformation of Church Music in the Sixteenth Century*. University of Michigan Press, Ann Arbor, MI

Patrick M 1949 *Four Centuries of Scottish Psalmody*. Oxford University Press, London

Mysticism

R. W. Perrett

The term 'mysticism' is commonly taken to describe a special set of conscious experiences found in many different religious traditions, though the doctrines in terms of which mystics describe their experiences differ. The primary marks of a mystical experience, according to an influential suggestion of William James, are its ineffability and a noetic character (James 1902). But the conjunction of the ubiquity claim with the ineffability and noetic theses is problematic.

Consider first the ineffability thesis. Mystics typically claim that the contents of their experiences are inexpressible in language. However, the strong version of the ineffability thesis is self-contradictory, since it simultaneously denies that anything can be predicated of the mystical experience and predicates something of it, viz. ineffability. Weak versions of the ineffability thesis claim only that mystical experiences are ineffable relative to a particular language (or set of languages). But then it is unclear what evidence the mystic might offer for such claims.

Conjoining the ineffability thesis with the noetic thesis leads to further difficulties. If mystical experiences are ineffable then they cannot be knowledge-that states, since such knowledge is propositional and propositions are expressible in language.

Finally, the ubiquity of mystical experience is sometimes appealed to as evidence for its revelatory character. This assumes that there is a core mystical experience which can be differentiated from the interpretations placed upon it in various religious traditions. However, 'constructivists' about mystical experience argue that all such experiences are shaped by the concepts which the mystic brings to the experience: there are no pure, unmediated experiences (Katz 1978, Proudfoot 1985). Hence there is a diverse plurality of mystical experiences, many of which are noetically incompatible. Moreover, since the conceptual mediation of such experiences inevitably involves language, mystical experiences cannot be ineffable.

Respondents to these charges urge at least two lines of reply. First, they argue that the notion of ineffability is to be understood less literally, emphasizing instead the great variety of functions performed by mystical language (Katz 1992). Such language may often be less descriptive than expressive or transformative, showing something that cannot be said in language.

Second, some argue that constructivism is mistaken and there is no reason to believe that unmediated, pure consciousness events do not occur (Forman 1990, 1999). But then perhaps what mystics mean when they describe their experiences as ineffable is just that their experiences are non-intentional conscious states. Since such states have no objects, their contents are indeed inexpressible in any intentional language.

See also: Ecstatic Religion; Glossolia; Meditation; Shamanism.

Bibliography

Forman R K C (ed.) 1990 *The Problem of Pure Consciousness*. Oxford University Press, New York

Forman R K C 1999 *Mysticism, Mind, Consciousness*. State University of New York Press, Albany

James W 1902 *The Varieties of Religious Experience*. Longman, Green & Co., New York

Katz S T (ed.) 1978 *Mysticism and Philosophical Analysis*. Sheldon Press, London

Katz S T (ed.) 1992 *Mysticism and Language*. Oxford University Press, New York

Proudfoot W 1985 *Religious Experience*. University of California Press, Berkeley

Myth

J. W. Rogerson

Is myth a particular way of experiencing the world, with corresponding ways of experiencing time, space, number, and logic (Hübner 1994), or is it simply a word used in various ways in different scholarly accounts and analyses of aspects of culture (Strenski 1987)? The truth probably lies in between these extremes; but the fact that such radically divergent explanations of myth can be maintained is an indication of the complexity of the subject and a warning against simplistic answers. A brief sketch of the ways in which myth has been understood in the past two hundred years shows how divergent views of its meaning and nature can arise. For the eighteenth century classicist C. G. Heyne, the myths of the ancient world and of modern so-called primitive peoples arose from their attempts to explain the natural world on the basis of inadequate scientific knowledge, whereas for writers such as Schelling, Goethe, and Schiller myths expressed metaphysical and aesthetic truths. Social anthropologists in the late nineteenth and early twentieth centuries linked myth with rituals, and suggested that both had a performative role, providing communal rites and stories that enabled ancient and modern 'primitive' peoples to cope with and seek to control the harsh realities of daily life. The rise of psychology, on the other hand, directed the search for the meaning of myth into the human psyche, whether into its sexual frustrations (Freud) or its alleged archetypes (Jung).

The French structuralist Claude Lévi-Strauss combined aspects of the performative and psychological approaches to suggest that myths were a product of the need for the unconscious mind to resolve the binary oppositions of reality, especially that between nature and culture. Mircea Eliade and his followers believed that myths arose from encounters with 'the sacred.' This sketch indicates that the understanding of myth has gone hand-in-hand with changes of intellectual fashion and interest. This has led to the view that myth is such an ill-defined and imprecise term that it can be used in almost any context, and that it is virtually meaningless. However, if an affirmative answer is given to the question whether there are any constant factors in the varying uses of the concept of myth over the past two hundred years, this will lead to attempts to construct a typology of myth as a distinct way of experiencing reality.

A pragmatic way of approaching the subject is to work from modern myths back to ancient ones. The sixtieth anniversary of the Battle of Britain has produced studies that indicate that Germany did not have an overwhelming superiority of aircraft in the August of 1940 and that British aircraft production matched its losses during the battle (Overy 2000). Yet the belief has become widespread that Britain was saved by the bravery of 'a few' who faced overwhelming odds. This is an example of a believable story that articulates national pride, explains historical events, symbolizes the triumph of good over evil and, for some people with religious convictions, provides evidence for divine intervention in human affairs. Many ancient myths, which are not believable for modern readers, functioned in the same way. There are accounts of battles in the Old Testament that attribute Israel's deliverance from superior enemies to the actions of 'a few,' assisted by God (e.g. the story of Gideon in Judges 7; and there are many instances in the books of Chronicles). Other believable stories accounted for the origin of nations (e.g. the story of the Exodus in the Old Testament) or of cities (e.g. David's capture of Jerusalem). Such texts are often called charter myths. Other texts have been called myths of origins. These account for the origin of the world and of the human race; and they also seek to account for the injustices of human life, which they contrast with a lost, idyllic original state of existence. Myths of origins contain themes that could not have been believed by those for whom they were intended, precisely because they portray a lost world. Another feature of myths of origins is the presence of sexual license among gods, of adultery, incest, rape and murder. These elements are best seen as human attempts to struggle free from the inscrutable forces, such as fate, that controlled their lives, by showing the gods to be worse than humans.

If the question of how myths arose and arise is posed, the answer is that all the theories of the nineteenth and twentieth centuries probably contain an element of truth. Humans have a fundamental need to explain things and provide scientific or historical accounts where vacuums exist. Where these accounts are based upon rudimentary science or history they will be unconvincing to modern readers. But humans also need to answer philosophical questions such as the origin and nature of evil, and the liminal problems presented especially by death. Resources for answering these questions are likely to come from within the human psyche, from fantasies caused by sexual longings, from intimations of transcendence mediated by cultural or natural beauty, by liberating experiences of love and passion; and it is not difficult to see why myth has often been linked to poetry.

Myths, then, can be said to arise from attempts to understand the world of human experience, but no single account of their origin, whether in terms of rudimentary science or sexual fantasies can do full justice to their origin. These origins are as varied and complex as humanity itself. Neither must it be forgotten that, as literary products, oral as well as written, myths possess narrative power and artistry which, especially in the case of the myths of ancient Greece, have inspired poetry, drama and visual art, creations which in many cases have also made a contribution to attempts to understand the origin, nature and destiny of humanity.

Bibliography

Cancik H 1995 Mythos. In: *Neues Bibel-Lexikon* fascicle 10, Benzinger Verlag, Solothurn, pp. 864–76

Dundes A 1984 *Sacred Narrative. Readings in the Theory of Myth.* University of California Press, Berkeley

Hübner K 1994 Mythos I. In: *Theologische Realenzyklopädie* vol. XXIII, W. de Gruyter, Berlin, pp. 597–608

Feldman B, Richardson R D 1972 *The Rise of Modern Mythology 1680-1860.* University of Indiana Press, Bloomington, IN

Kirk G S 1970 *Myth. Its Meaning and Functions in Ancient and Other Cultures.* Cambridge University Press, Cambridge; University of California Press, Berkeley

Oden R A Jr 1992 Myth and Mythology. In: *Anchor Bible Dictionary*, Vol. 4, Doubleday, New York, pp. 946–56

Overy R 2000 *The Battle.* Penguin Books, London

Segal R 1998 *The Myth and Ritual Theory.* Blackwell, Oxford

Segal R 1998 *Jung on Mythology.* Routledge, London

Segal R 1999 *Theorizing About Myth.* University of Massachusetts Press, Amherst

Stolz F 1994 Mythos II. In: *Theologische Realenzyklopädie* vol. XXIII, W. de Gruyter, Berlin, pp. 608–25

Strenski I 1987 *Four Theories of Myth in Twentieth-Century History. Cassirer, Eliade, Lévi-Strauss and Malinowski.* Macmillan, Basingstoke

Oracle

J. F. A. Sawyer

The custom of consulting an oracle in times of danger or doubt is well documented from many parts of the world in ancient and modern times. Two of the best-known examples are those of Apollo at Delphi and of Zeus at Dodona in ancient Greece. Most enquiries at such institutions came from individuals with the same concerns as those consulting horoscopes today, although often they were controlled by the state, and officially consulted when divine sanction is required for some military or political action. Oracular responses come in various forms. The most spectacular is through the inspired words of a prophet or priest, usually female, speaking perhaps in a trance-like state. This led to the term 'oracle' being applied to the utterances of the biblical prophets, conventionally introduced by the formula

'Thus saith the Lord.' But other techniques were common too, including casting lots, as in the case of the Urim and Thummim of biblical tradition (Num.27:21), prophetic dreams experienced while spending a night at an oracular site, like Jacob at Bethel (Gen.28), and other means of divination.

Another method involved consulting a sacred text of some kind such as the Sibylline Oracles, an ancient Greek text used officially by the Roman government. The works of Virgil and the Bible could be used as a means of divination too, by opening them at random, as St Augustine is said to have done, and finding there a text appropriate to the occasion. The notion that 'oracular' answers are normally ambiguous or enigmatic is a popular misconception arising from the legendary experience of Croesus, king of Lydia, who discovered too late that the 'great army' which would be destroyed if he went to war, was his own.

See also: Etruscan Religion; Greek Religion; Roman Religion.

Bibliography

Parke H W 1967 *The Oracles of Zeus*. Blackwell, Oxford
Potter D S 1994 *Prophets and Emperors*. Harvard University Press, Cambridge, MA
Wilson R R 1980 *Prophecy and Society in Ancient Israel*. Fortress Press, Philadelphia, PA

Performative Utterances

P. Collins

J. L. Austin argued that because of our obsession with truth/falsity we often fail to understand that in saying something we might also be doing something and not merely stating or describing. He called statements that do things 'performative utterances' (Austin 1975). For example, when a minister in the Seventh Day Adventist Church raises his hand and utters the words 'I now baptise you in the name of the Father, and the Son, and of the Holy Ghost...' he is not merely talking about baptism: he is actually baptising the candidate about to be submerged. By saying the words 'I do' in response to the priest's questions, the bride and bridegroom at the altar marry one another. In appropriate circumstances to say 'I do' is not so much to say something that is true or false about marriage, but rather to engage in the act of marriage itself.

The analysis of speaking as doing, 'speech-act theory,' is founded on three features of utterances. The 'locutionary' concerns the truth/falsity of an utterance, the 'illocutionary' describes what the utterance does (marries, blesses, curses, promises, denies, vows, etc.) and the 'perlocutionary' produces effects upon the actions, thoughts or feelings of the listener (convinces, deceives, inspires, bores, etc.). These are not mutually exclusive characteristics however and an utterance may display one, two or all three of them.

Performative utterances abound in religious faith and practice. When the Pope says 'Bless you,' he is not only saying something but also carrying out the act of blessing. Traditionally, when a witch begins to recite a spell, those who are listening do not quibble over its truth or falsity but hope that it is not they who will turn into a frog. However, this example raises the issue of validity in relation to performative utterances. Although we do not judge them in terms of truth/falsity, does that mean we cannot judge them at all? If the spell is recited wrongly then surely no one is going to turn into a frog. A performative utterance can 'fail' due to one or more of a wide variety of 'infelicities' (Austin 1975: Chaps. 2 and 3). For instance if at the critical moment I say 'I do,' but am already married, or if the person conducting the ceremony is not a priest but actually someone who wandered in off the street, then the act of marriage does not take place.

The nature of performative utterances has been debated and developed by philosophers and linguists alike (Holdcroft 1978; Searle 1979). Perhaps Austin's most profound legacy has been the increased interest shown in talk as performance, depending not only on what is said but also on the circumstances in which words are uttered.

See also: Analogy; Blessings; Cursing; Incantations; Magic; Mantra; Naming; Prayer; Religious Symbols.

Bibliography

Austin J L 1975 *How to do Things with Words*, 2nd edn. Clarendon Press, Oxford
Holdcroft D 1978 *Words and Deeds*. Oxford University Press, Oxford
Searle J R 1979 *Expression and Meaning*. Cambridge University Press, Cambridge

Prayer

J. F. A. Sawyer

Special languages or language varieties are often used in public prayer, partly to heighten people's awareness of the sacredness of the moment, and partly to highlight the continuity of what they are doing with the worship of other communities elsewhere. Until recently, for example, archaic forms like *thou*, *thee*, and *ye* were used in most English-speaking varieties of Christian worship. The custom is now much less widespread, except, significantly, in the case of the 'Lord's Prayer' and the 'Hail Mary.' The popularity of these two prayers, in particular their use by individuals outside the context of priest-led public worship, distinguishes them from others and explains the survival of the traditional forms. A similar situation exists in Judaism where several short prayers, notably the Qaddish, are still recited in Aramaic, instead of Hebrew (see *Judaism*).

The dynamics of prayer in which human individuals believe they are engaged in dialogue with a deity or saint, may also determine the variety of language adopted. In most cases the relationship is considered to be one of servant to master ('Lord, lettest now thy servant depart in peace') or children to parent ('Our Father, who art in heaven'). Mystics, by contrast, in many religious traditions use erotic language, often quite explicit, to express their desire for, or experience of, union with the person they are praying to. The colloquial importuning and complaining of Jewish hasidic prayer illustrate another form of close, intimate relationship, as do the 'prayers' in *Fiddler on the Roof* and the comic altercations between the priest Don Camillo and his God in the novels of Giovanni Guareschi.

Many prayers are not actually in language addressed directly to the deity at all, so that communication between the human and the divine is achieved as much by the ritual act of praying as by the words used. Thus the *sh̲ĕma'*, one of the main Jewish prayers, recited daily morning and evening, begins 'Hear, O Israel,' and is in fact a statement of faith, taken verbatim from the Bible, rather than a prayer literally addressed to God. Similarly, the Muslim prayer, known as *ṣalāt*, performed five times a day, consists mainly of prescribed physical movements together with the recital of the *s̲hahāda* (a summary creed) and passages from the Qur'ān. The recital of set formulas, like the Sanskrit syllable *Om* or the names of God, often accompanied by gestures and in an ancient language unknown to the worshiper, creates an atmosphere which leads to the most intimate kind of relationship with the divine, and even mystical union itself.

See also: Dhāranī; Mantra; Meditation; Names: Religious Beliefs.

Bibliography

Alhonsaari A 1973 *Prayer: An Analysis of Theological Terminology*. Luther-Agricola Society, Helsinki

Gill S D 1987 Prayer. In: *Encyclopedia of Religion*, vol. 11, pp. 489–94. Macmillan, New York

Heiler F 1932 *Prayer: A Study in the History and Psychology of Religion*. Oxford University Press, New York

Preaching

T. G. Addington

Preaching is used by many religions as a vehicle through which doctrine is conveyed (cf. the Friday sermon, *k̲huṭba*, in the mosque, and Jewish vernacular sermons in the synagogue). But the history and theory of preaching are most highly developed in the Christian tradition because of its pivotal role in church life.

1. Definition

The Biblical Greek word for preaching (*kērygma*) means 'the act of proclaiming,' and carries with it the concept of a herald who goes before the king announcing the ruler's approach. Thus in the Christian context, the Kingdom of God is proclaimed by the herald/preacher. The goal of the proclamation is faith on the part of the hearer, not simply intellectual assent (I Corinthians 2: 4–5). Preaching is inherently persuasive, and biblical references to preaching encompass both the content of the message and the act of proclamation. As such, the content of truth is presented by the preacher from a biblical text in such a way 'that the hearers may discern how God teacheth it from thence' (*Westminster Directory for Public Worship*). The preacher's purpose is to elicit an appropriate response from the audience, a reaction which Paul commends in Romans 6: 17:

'But thanks be to God that, though you used to be slaves to sin, you wholeheartedly obeyed the form of teaching to which you were entrusted.'

2. Theoretical Development

Biblical addresses evidence the use of some rhetorical strategies common to formal systems of communication. For example, the prophet Ezekiel used illustrative parallel to warn residents of Jerusalem of impending disaster (Ezekiel 5: 1–6). Paul displays a knowledge of both Greek and Roman rhetorical theory in his address on Mars Hill (Acts 17: 16–31). However, no theory with specific application to pulpit rhetoric existed until Augustine's *On Christian Doctrine*, written between 397 and 427.

Augustine, who was a professor of rhetoric prior to his conversion to Christianity, used Cicero to fashion communication strategies relevant to the church. Until then the church had resisted the use of pagan Greek and Roman rhetoric. But Augustine, who was searching for an effective way for priests to teach the Gospel to illiterate parishioners, argued that all truth—whether discovered by pagan or Christian—is God's truth.

His adaptation of mainstream rhetorical theory to Christian preaching began a process of pulpit theory development which continued into the early nineteenth century. Clergymen like François Fénelon in France, and George Campbell, Hugh Blair, and Richard Whately in Britain, wrote texts which were used to teach preaching in Europe and the USA. Campbell's *The Philosophy of Rhetoric* was reprinted over forty times following its initial publication in 1776, while *Lectures on Rhetoric and Belles Lettres* by Blair saw over twenty reprintings. Although a proliferation of preaching texts appeared in the USA during the late nineteenth century, Richard Whately's *Elements of Rhetoric* (1828) marked the end of significant pulpit rhetorical theory. Most preaching texts in the late twentieth century center on the logistics of sermon preparation, and take either a structural 'how-to' approach or emphasize the hermeneutical task of exegesis.

3. Trends in the 1990s

Preaching in the 1990s shows a shift from even that of a generation ago. Sermons in the past typically seek to answer the question: 'what does the text say?' The central focus of the sermon is on the content of scripture and implicit is the assumption that the scripture itself is enough to draw the audience's interest, as well as motivate to action. For example, John Chrysostom in the fourth century begins his sermon *Excessive Grief at the Death of Friends* with an immediate explication of the text: 'We have occupied four days in explaining to you the parable of Lazarus, bringing out the treasure that we found in a body covered with sores; a treasure, not of gold and silver and precious stones, but of wisdom and fortitude, or patience and endurance.' Likewise, Charles Spurgeon's nineteenth-century sermon, *Songs in the Night*, launches straightaway into the biblical material: 'Elihu was a wise man, exceeding wise, tho' not as wise as the all-wise Jehovah, who sees light in the clouds, and finds order in confusion…'

Late twentieth-century preaching, however, shows a trend away from that exclusive focus on the text. Along with the question regarding the Scripture's content are two others: 'Why should I listen?' and 'Why should I obey?' The first is addressed in the introductory portion of the sermon, and the second is considered in the conclusion. This tendency toward more ethnocentric sermons can be illustrated by the preaching of Charles Swindoll, one of the most popular of American pulpit teachers. His introductions are usually quite lengthy, often consisting of stories and other captivating verbal imagery which is designed to strike the audience's imagination and finally lead them into the biblical text. Then the exposition of the text is followed by another discrete section which shows how the hearers will benefit by obedience to the principles just discussed. This section often includes personal accounts and compelling testimony similar to the introductory part of the sermon. Although the sermon may be equally biblical, the result is that far less time is spent on the content of Scripture than was true in the past.

4. Language Varieties

Sermons such as those of John Donne, John Henry Newman and other celebrated personalities in the history of Christian preaching, were prepared in writing beforehand, almost as an art form and often with a view to subsequent publication, and the styles in which they were written are accordingly formal and literary. In sixteenth-century England, official collections of sermons known as 'Books of Homilies' were published and preachers were encouraged to use these in preference to their own compositions. A notable feature of such formal preaching is that congregations are expected to sit in silence and to display none of the responses considered normal in the case of most other types of rhetoric (e.g., clapping, heckling, cheering).

There are other less literary language varieties, however, such as those used in Black Pentecostal preaching. Black preaching, like Black rhetorical style in general, is more interpersonal than White. It is characterized by active listener response (*Amen*, *Praise the Lord*, *Hallelujah*, *Preach it preacher*, etc.), often spontaneous but frequently elicited by prompts or questions from the preacher. Simultaneous speech tends to become increasingly frequent as the sermon proceeds, and a major function of this type of discourse is the affirmantion of group solidarity.

Research on Tlingit oratory has shown that this is also one of the functions of similar types of utterance among American Indians.

Pentecostals also place great value on impassioned discourse as evidence that the preacher is being moved by the Spirit, a feature that may result in disordered sentence structure (see also *Glossolalia*). Repetition, both between preacher and congregation and within the preacher's own discourse, is also typical. A distinctive form of rhythmic speech may be used where the preacher times his words to fit the beat of his clapping. Gestures and movements are also frequent: for example, as the preacher says *God put running in my feet*, he does a kind of slow run across the floor.

Another feature of Black Pentecostal preaching is 'talk-singing,' a style of communication used also in Black soul music and some forms of contemporary Black poetry. It is usually associated with the dramatic high point of the sermon, and is characterized by the elongated articulation of single words, long pauses, and the frequent interjection of expressions like *ha* and *aha*. A specific use of stress and pitch known as 'intonational contouring' to exaggerate the pronunciation of important words like *God* or *possessed* is another feature of Black preaching style, the resulting singsong effect being associated by Pentecostals with 'getting into the spirit.'

In an interesting parallel from the Welsh preaching tradition, speaking and singing merge in a very powerful form of rhetorical utterance known as *hwyl*, literally, 'sail (of a ship or windmill),' hence 'fervor (especially religious), ecstasy, gusto.' Preachers developed their own patterns of *hwyl* or 'sing-song cadence,' which started low as a sort of undercurrent in their intonation and then grew stronger and stronger as they warmed to their subject (*mynd i hwyl*), until it was a full chant that really could overpower the hearer. The origin of this passionate and eloquent mode of preaching, which was still widely practised in the early twentieth century, is unknown, but may possibly go back to the chanting of the Church.

See also: Evangelism; Hwyl.

Bibliography

Callendar C, Cameron D 1990 Responsive listening as part of religious rhetoric: The case of Black Pentecostal preaching. In: McGregor G, White R S (eds.) *Reception and Response: Hearer Creativity and the Analysis of Spoken and Written Texts*. Routledge, London

Dauenhauer N M, Dauenhauer R 1990 *Haa Tuwunaagu Yis. For Healing the Spirit: Tlingit Oratory*, vol. 2. University of Washington Press, Seattle, WA

Geiriadur Prifysgol Cymru (A Dictionary of the Welsh language). University of Wales, Cardiff

Holland D T 1980 *The Preaching Tradition*. Abingdon, Nashville, TN

Lischer R 1981 *A Theology of Preaching*. Abingdon, Nashville, TN

Logan S T (ed.) 1986 *The Preacher and Preaching*. Presbyterian and Reformed Publishing Co., Phillipsburg, NY

Smitheman G 1986 *Talkin and Testifyin: The Language of Black America*. Wayne State University Press, Detroit, MI

Wiersbe W W 1980 *Listening to the Giants*. Baker Book House, Grand Rapids, MI

Wiersbe W, Perry L M 1984 *The Wycliffe Handbook of Preaching and Preachers*. Moody Press, Chicago, IL

Religious Symbols

M. Douglas

One can 'do things with symbols' so as to have results in the everyday world, as one can 'do things with words.' John Austin's original instances of performative utterances include, 'I name this ship...,' 'I bet...,' 'I thee wed.' The words not only refer, as words normally do, but they actually change situations by the fact of having been spoken. Likewise, religious symbols may do more than say something about (stand for, signify) transcendent reality: they can manipulate it. Religion conceives the known universe as part of a transcendent cosmos replete with other intelligent beings, and more or less controlled by one or more deities. Religious symbols may be performative in a fuller sense than Austin's examples because they interact with transcendent powers. The deity invoked in a spoken curse or a blessing guarantees that the cursed person does not prosper or that the subject of the blessing does well.

Symbolic actions are on a level with symbolic words, gestures such as sprinkling holy water to chase away the devil are supposed to work, like magic. And the same for symbolic objects, holy places, relics of saints, consecrated things, fetishes, they can be credited with power. 'Doing things' with religious symbols unleashes transcendental powers, but note that any religion institutes the power of religious symbols, restricting it, more or less. Divine grace flowing through the seven sacraments was instituted once and for all in the history of the Catholic Church. In other religions grace is available to individuals either by divinely instituted selection or special merit.

It is possible to believe in a transcendental cosmos without believing in a god, still less believing in a comprehensive divine organization of the universe and its people. A pressure to treat religious symbols as having power corresponds to non-religious ideas about magic. Superstition describes an indiscriminate bundle of ideas about how to contact and control transcendental power. Lucky colors, lucky numbers, words, animals, or persons of ill omen, illustrate free-floating beliefs in performative symbols. Only a thin line divides superstition from sacrament and efficacious symbols tend to fall periodically into disrepute. At some point in history a doctrine about automatically effective symbolic action will seem obnoxious, as if the deity could be put under constraint. To suppose that the universe responds to symbolic action like a machine answering to levers and buttons suggests blasphemy (see *Blasphemy*). Furthermore, religious symbols usually have a pictorial element. The very idea that the invisible can be pictured, or that the all-powerful can be located in a carved or painted image, becomes highly controversial: piety to some is sacrilege to another. Aniconic religion is not new, controversies about religious symbolism probably go back to the beginning of thinking about God.

See also: Analogy; Magic; Performative Utterances; Taboo.

Bibliography

Austin J L 1975 *How to Do Things with Words*, 2nd edn. Clarendon Press, Oxford

Barasch M 1992 *Ikon*. New York University Press

Douglas M 1970 *Natural Symbols*. Routledge, London

Turner V W 1970 *The Forest of Symbols, Aspects of Ndembu Ritual*. Cornell University Press, New York

Valeri V 2000 *The Forest of Taboos. Morality, Hunting and Identity among the Huaulu of the Moluccas*. University of Wisconsin Press

Silence

M. Saville-Troike

Silence, perhaps because it seems that antithesis of linguistic form, has long been neglected in the study of language. Nevertheless, it forms an essential part of communication, and speech communities differ as much in the uses and interpretations they give to silence as they do in regard to the linguistic forms that they use. Silence is thus better seen as the complement to sound; an awareness of its potential functions, structures, and meaning therefore necessarily becomes as relevant to the study of linguistic communication as the recognition of clauses, lexical networks, and intonation is now.

1. Societal Patterning of Silence

At a societal level, patterning in the use of silence generally relates to dimensions of social organization, to community attitudes, and to such macrofunctions as social control, ritual interaction with the supernatural, and establishment or reinforcement of group identity. In part this patterning is determined by the institutions of a specific society, and the functional meaning of silence can only be understood in relation to particular institutional contexts. These contexts may be as various as physical locations, ritual performances, or the enactment of social roles/relationships. Communication may be proscribed, for example, between a commoner and a chief, or a man and his mother-in-law, while membership in certain religious groups may require a vow of silence.

Where institutionally determined power is accorded voice, silence is often indicative of passivity and powerlessness. Thus women may keep silent in the presence of men, or children in the presence of adults. The opposite is the case in settings where self-exposure is required, however, and where the listener sits in silent judgment: e.g., religious confession, psychotherapy, bureaucratic interviews, and jury trials (Gal 1989).

In some cases, the interpretation of silence may be institutionally defined by a society's covenants and laws. In the USA, for instance, suspected legal offenders must be explicitly informed that they have the 'right to remain silent' to avoid self-incrimination, while instances of implicit silence (i.e., nondisclosure) in business transactions have been ruled to constitute active concealment and fraud. In some societies, silence in interpersonal interaction may be invoked as a powerful instrument of social control (e.g., 'shunning' among the Inuit, the Igbo, or the Amish).

Many societal patterns of silence are also determined by members of a group in relation to dynamics of social organization. Patterns may be situational, as when access to speaking privilege in public forums is allocated by group decision and others must remain silent or normative, as when differential speaking privileges are allocated to individuals or classes of individuals.

The amount of talk versus silence that is prescribed is closely tied to social values and norms. The relative value of talk or silence in a society may be partly inferred from whether one or the other is ascribed to its rulers, priests, and sages. The value of silence may also be found in proverbs: e.g., 'Silence is golden' (English); 'Because of the mouth the fish dies' (Spanish); 'The way your eyes look can say more than your mouth' (Japanese); and 'Man becomes wise through the ear' (Persian).

Additionally, cultural understandings regarding the contextual or interactional interpretation of silence may be made explicit in the choice of adjectives coupled with the term 'silence' itself (e.g., 'ominous silence,' 'worshipful silence,' 'eerie silence,' 'smug silence,' 'thoughtful silence,' 'pregnant silence') or may be implied by terms used to describe people who exhibit relatively silent behavior (e.g., 'taciturn,' 'reserved,' 'secretive,' 'circumspect'). Differing group norms of appropriateness for speaking versus maintaining silence can give rise to cross-cultural misunderstanding, as when 'friendliness' is equated differently with one or the other in a conversation, or 'sincerity' and 'politeness' in a business or political encounter.

Societal norms for the use and interpretation of silence inevitably influence artistic expression, with painters, poets, authors, composers, and playwrights using pauses and silences, or their visual and orthographic counterparts, for aesthetic effect. Silence, like other components of communication, may also serve amusement functions, often as a key element of joke and story telling. One of the most successful jokes performed on radio by Jack Benny (a USA comedian who cultivated the image of being miserly) was his long silence in response to a robber's directive, 'Your money or your life!'

2. Individual and Small Group Patterning of Silence

At the level of individuals and small interacting groups within a society, patterning of silence occurs in relation to expression and interpretation of personality, and to micro-functions related to participants' purposes and needs. Bruneau (1973) terms these 'psycholinguistic' and 'interactive' silences, which include an array of functions ranging from defining the role of auditor in a communicative exchange, to providing social control, to demonstrating deference, to indicating emotional closeness, to managing personal interaction. Jensen (1973) presents a similar array, categorizing functions as 'linkage,' 'affecting,' 'revelational,' 'judgmental,' and 'activating'.

Some interactional functions of silence may be viewed as primarily sociocontextual in nature: defining (e.g., status and role), structuring (e.g., situations), tactical (e.g., non-participation, avoidance, disapproval, mitigation, image manipulation), and phatic (emotional sharing); some as primarily linguistic: discursive (e.g., prayer, fantasizing, rehearsing) or propositional (e.g., negation, affirmation, refusal, acknowledgment); and some as primarily psychological (e.g., expression of anger, sorrow, embarrassment, joy, or fear). Some noninteractional functions of silence involve contemplative/meditative states, while others are inactive in nature.

While none of these listings is entirely comprehensive, such taxonomies provide a basis for recognizing and contrasting many potential functions of silence in relation to situational contexts of use.

3. Structures of Silence

A basic distinction should be made between silences which carry meaning, but not propositional content, and silent communicative acts which carry their own illocutionary force. The former include the pauses and hesitations that occur within and between turns of talking —the prosodic dimension of silence. Such nonpropositional silences may be volitional or nonvolitional, and may convey a wide variety of meanings. The meanings carried by pauses and hesitations are generally affective in nature, and connotative rather than denotative. Their meanings are nonetheless symbolic and conventional, as is seen in the various patterns of use and norms of interpretation in different speech communities (see examples in Tannen and Saville-Troike 1985).

Silent communicative acts conveying either emotional or propositional content may be accompanied by meaningful facial expressions or gestures, but they may consist of silence unaccompanied by any visual cues. Even in a telephone conversation where no visual signals are possible, silence in response to a greeting, query, or request which anticipates verbal response is fraught with propositional meaning in its own right. Silence as part of communicative interaction can be one of the forms a 'speech' act may take—filling many of the same functions and discourse slots—and should be considered along with the production of sentence tokens as a basic formational unit of linguistic communication. Thus, silence on the part of an Arabic or Japanese woman in response to a proposal of marriage implies consent, while in many speech communities a silent response to a request to borrow money or for a favor would be interpreted as a refusal.

Silence may even carry grammatical and lexical meaning within the sentence. One form of the *wh*-question in English, for instance, is a fill-in-the-blank structure, e.g., 'And your name is...?' (said with nonterminal intonation), meaning 'What is your name?' Utterances may be completed in silence when the topic is a particularly delicate one or the word which would be used is taboo, or when the situation is emotionally loaded and the speaker is 'at a loss' for words. The Japanese term *haragei* 'wordless communication' captures the essence of this latter type of silence.

Silence over longer segments of communication may convey a more generalized meaning, as in 'sulking' to express disapproval of others' behavior, or silent attentiveness during relatively long stretches of speaking to convey listener interest and respect. (The same absence of conversational backchannel noise in some speech communities (e.g., African–American) would convey disinterest or hostility.)

Entire communicative events without sound are also common. Especially in ritual contexts, silence may be conventionally mandated as the only form which could achieve the event's communicative goals. Thus we find the invocation in Christian ritual: 'The Lord is in His holy temple; let all the earth keep silence before Him.'

4. Interpretation and Production of Silence in Communicative Events

Appropriate participation in communicative events requires recognition of the components which are likely to be salient to members of the speech community within which the event occurs (Saville-Troike 1989). Each component that can call for a different form of speech can also permit or prescribe silence. These include the extrapersonal context, as well as the status and role-relationships of the participants: the genre, topic, or setting (time and place) may be designated as inappropriate for vocal interaction. The sequence of communicative acts in an event includes turn-taking and overlap phenomena, which include silence on the prosodic dimension. Maintaining silence between turns may be an indication of politeness (e.g., among the Navajo), or a violation of norms of interaction. Rules for appropriate interpretation and production of speech include knowing the properties relating to silence which should be observed in different types of speech situations, as well as the potential significance of silence in negotiating meaning within any specific interaction. Finally, as an overarching consideration, successful communication requires shared knowledge and cultural presuppositions which allow inferences to be drawn about the unsaid as well as the said.

Almost all research on child-language development has focused on how children learn to speak. But an essential part of children's acquisition of communicative competence is learning when not to talk, and what silence means in their speech community. Because cultural beliefs, values, and practices are integrally involved in the process, socializing young children to the use of silence may be considered part of the transmission of world view. This question remains largely unexplored, but constitutes a promising direction for future cross-cultural studies of silence.

See also: Meditation; Quakerism; Performative Utterances.

Bibliography

Bruneau T J 1973 Communicative silences: Forms and functions. *Journal of Communication* **23**: 17–46

Dauenhauer B P 1980 *Silence: The Phenomenon and Its Ontological Significance*. Indiana University Press, Bloomington, IN

Gal S 1989 Between speech and silence: The problematics of research on language and gender. *Papers in Pragmatics* **3(1)**: 1–38

Jensen J V 1973 Communicative functions of silence. *ETC: A Review of General Semantics* **30**: 249–57

Saville-Troike M 1989 *The Ethnography of Communication*, 2nd edn. Basil Blackwell, Oxford

Tannen D, Saville-Troike M (eds.) 1985 *Perspectives on Silence*. Ablex, Norwood, NJ

Traber M (ed.) 1982 *Media Development* **29**(4) [Issue devoted to Silence in Communication.]

Sūtra

I. Astley

A *sūtra* is a technical text which pertained originally to the correct performance of Vedic rituals. The basic meaning of 'thread' is reflected in the *sūtra*'s pithy, aphoristic nature. The first date to the end of the Vedic period proper; they were classed as *vedāṅga* ('ancillary to the *veda*').

The importance of liturgy and the sacred role of language meant that *sūtra* became an essential ancillary genre to the *veda*. They developed into six further types: *śikṣā* (the correct articulation of the Vedic texts); *chandas* (metre); *vyākaraṇa* (grammatical analysis); *nirukta* (the lexical explanation of obscure items); *jyotiṣa* (the fixing of the correct times for rituals by astronomical means); and *kalpa* (the correct performance of the ritual). The *kalpasūtra* date from c. 600 BCE and include the *śrautasūtra* (rules for the more complex Vedic rituals) and the *gṛhyasūtra* and *dharmasūtra* (rules for domestic rituals and customs), which in time together formed the basis of the books of Hindu law, the *Dharmaśāstra*. The Jaina tradition incorporates *śūtra* in the *dṛṣṭivāda*.

In Buddhism, the *sūtra*, being *buddhavacana* (the Buddha's words, his teaching), is the scriptural basis of all traditions. The form of the earliest texts, as preserved in the *suttā* sections of the Pāli Canons or the Sanskrit and Chinese *āgama*, implies a prior oral tradition. They are prolix compared to the orthodox tradition, being intent on recording the Buddha's actual words. The range of types of Buddhist *sūtra* is broad, particularly in the Mahāyāna and the Vajrayāna, as the genre was extended to encompass *inter alia* fantastic myths and ritual instructions in addition to doctrinal expositions. There also arose the concept of the ideal existence of a *sūtra*, the physical book being an imperfect reflection thereof. In East Asia the genre became extended to teachings of indigenous deities, recluses, etc.

See also: Dhāranī; Mantra; Copying.

Bibliography

Sangharakshita B S 1985 *The Eternal Legacy*. Tharpa Press, London

SECTION V
Beliefs About Language

Introduction

J. F. A. Sawyer

One of the most widespread beliefs about language is the conviction that one's own language is the original one or directly derived from it. Hebrew, for example, was the language spoken by Adam and Eve in the Garden of Eden. It was the language of the angels so that prayers in any other language would not be understood in heaven. It was the language by which God created the universe, the language in which the Torah was written before anything else was created. According to one tradition God used the 22 letters of the Hebrew alphabet to create the universe, arranging them in patterns of 3, 7 and 12, that is, the three elements (wind, water, fire), the seven planets and the twelve signs of the Zodiac. Syrian Orthodox Christians, on the other hand, believed that Syriac was the original language, while from mediaeval times there have been claims that Adam and Eve spoke a 'Teutonic language.' Martin Luther derived German from Ashkenaz, the eldest grandson of Japheth, and claimed that it was, next to Hebrew, the earliest (and thus the best) of all the languages of the world as we know them. Subsequent scientific research into the origins of language was employed to support the belief that Teutonic retained more of the Adamic original than the greatly distorted forms of Hebrew and Arabic. With the discovery of Sanskrit by the Europeans, attention shifted to theories of an Indo–Aryan origin for most of the known languages of the civilized world, and the superiority of the Aryan race from which the Teutonic peoples are descended. According to Hindu tradition Sanskrit was the original language.

Discussion of the meaning and power of the 'word of God' is a recurring theme in many religions. In Egyptian mythology the god Ptah uses words to create the world. In Biblical tradition God creates by his command (e.g., 'let there be light!'); in the Qur'ān he says 'Be!' (Arabic *kun*) and the world is created. In Hindu mythology the creator God Prajapati produces earth, atmosphere and heaven by uttering syllables, and his spoken word is often personified as *Vac* (Sanskrit 'speech'), his female consort. Other personifications include *Memra* (Aramaic 'word'), who is identified with God in some Jewish texts, *Logos* (Greek), incarnate in Jesus Christ according to the beginning of St John's Gospel, and Arabic *kalimat Allah* 'word of God' which is used as an epithet of Jesus. The 'word of God' (Arabic *kalam Allah*) is identified with scripture in some forms of Christianity and Islam.

The power of the sacred syllable *Om* can be seen in the belief that it encapsulates and symbolizes the whole essence and goal of the Vedas, a belief similar in some respects to the Muslim belief that the whole essence of the Qur'ān is contained in the point in the first letter of the first word of the first Sura, *bismillahi*. Intense concentration on such a focal point became an important element in meditation, as did the mystics' repetition of a single syllable like *om* or a word or name. In Islam Sufi mystics repeated the 99 'Most Beautiful Names of Allah' over and over again in a ritual known as *dhikr*, and similar practices appear in Sikhism (*nam japan*), Hinduism (*nama vali*) and Buddhism (Japanese *nembutsu*; Chinese *nien-fo*). The awesome power of the Tetragrammaton, which can be both life-giving and destructive, features prominently in Jewish legend. In Jewish tradition the divine name is too sacred ever to be pronounced by ordinary human beings: only the High Priest can utter it in special circumstances once a year. Similar taboos surround the names of Jesus ('our Lord') and Mary ('our Lady') in some forms of Christianity, while in West Africa the Igbo refer to their god as 'the One whose name cannot be spoken.'

The challenge posed by modernity to all religious traditions, particularly in Europe, resulted in rich and powerful innovations in the history of language and religion. From Romanticism came a new awareness of the expressive fecundity of language, not simply its utility, and the suggestion that divine truth can after all be revealed in human language. While evangelical scholarship continued to defend various forms of fundamentalism, radical new approaches to understanding scripture and religious language in general emerged in the twentieth century. Influenced by new insights from psychology (Freud), political theory (Karl Marx), general linguistics (Saussure) and elsewhere, Heidegger and Gadamer pointed towards new horizons in the search for meaning in religious language, as did liberation theology and feminism. More recently from French postmodernism have come Derrida's assertion of the complexity and indeterminacy of textuality, and the focus on female symbolism in the revolutionary writings of Julia Kristeva and Luce Irigaray. Characteristic of the language of postmodernism is the use of agenda-setting neologisms like alterity, circumfession, *différance*, linguisticality, and phallogocentrism.

Alphabet: Religious Beliefs

A. P. Hayman

In the ancient Near East, where the alphabet originated, writing, along with all other cultural artifacts, was regarded as a gift from the gods. It could, therefore, be regarded as a clue to the divine mind(s). It was also perceived as a source of power—originally, perhaps, social and economic power. Like magicians the gods effected things by using words. Hence the endless speculation in religions deriving from, or influenced by, the ancient Near East, on the source of the power inherent in the alphabet. Did the power lie in the sounds the letters represented, in their number or shape, their divisions into consonants and vowels, their position in the sequence of letters in the alphabet, or the numerical values attributed to each of them?

The Greeks used the letters of the alphabet both as numerals and to depict musical notes. Combined with the Pythagorean notion of 'the harmony of the spheres' and their discovery of the numerical ratios on which music is based, this gave rise to elaborate schemes which correlated letters, numbers, the planets, the zodiac, and the parts of the human body. In Greek, the same word *stoikheion* was used for the letters of the alphabet, the signs of the zodiac the planets, and the basic elements of matter. The Pythagoreans had seen number as the integrating principle of the universe. It was easy for others (using the numbers = letters principle) to locate this unity in the alphabet.

As in Greek, so in Hebrew the word for a letter of the alphabet (*'ōt*) also had a wider range of meaning ('sign, miracle') which left the way open for speculations of all kinds, while the Hebrew letters were similarly used also as numerals. This latter fact was used with great skill as an interpretative tool (see *Gematria*). In the rabbinic writings the very physical shape of the letters and their sequence in the alphabet were believed to have been designed by God in order to teach moral and religious lessons. For example: R. Jonah said in the name of R. Levi, 'The world was created by the letter *Bēṯ h* (B). As *Bēṯh* is closed on all sides except one, so you have no right to investigate what is above, what is below, what went before or shall happen afterwards, only what has happened since the world and its inhabitants were created' (*Jerusalem Talmud, Hagigah*, 2.1).

The Hebrew book *Sēphēr Yĕṣīrā* 'the Book of Creation,' drawing probably on the Pythagorean legacy, has an elaborate system describing how God created the World using the letters of the Hebrew alphabet. The 22 letters of this alphabet are divided into groups of three, seven and twelve letters, and these correspond to the three primeval elements (wind, water, and fire), the seven planets and the seven days of the week, the twelve signs of the zodiac, and the twelve months of the year. Many other correspondences are described. Each letter creates the reality to which it corresponds. It is clear that the roots of this system lie in the ancient Near Eastern perception that, by the actions of the gods, language and its physical expression, the letters of the alphabet, create reality.

See also: Hebrew, Biblical and Jewish; Gematria; Judaism; Magic.

Bibliography

Billigmeier J-C 1987 Alphabets. In: Eliade M (ed.) The *Encyclopaedia of Religion*, vol. 1. Macmillan, New York

Dornseiff F 1922 *Das Alphabet in Mystik und Magie*. B. G. Teubner, Leipzig

Hayman A P 1989 Was God a magician? *Sefer Yeṣira* and Jewish magic. *Journal of Jewish Studies* **40**: 225–37

Analogy

D. B. Hart

An analogy, defined simply, is a common proportion or inherent similitude between two things, which allows the use of a single term in reference to both. As a purely semantic issue, analogy concerns the question of how a word or concept can be used of two disparate realities without being reduced either to a meaning identical in both cases (to, that is, a 'univocal' predicate), or to two entirely different meanings (an 'equivocal' predicate): a properly analogous predication must comprise within itself kindred but distinct meanings. Thus one may speak either of a tributary of a river or of a text cited in a book as a 'source,' on account of a strictly structural proportion between the cases. In this sense, analogy subsists upon a sign's 'polysemous' capacity to refer, and its logic is the logic of metaphor. Inevitably the question must be raised of how the sign preserves its integrity, as more than a mere nominative unity, across the spectrum of its related meanings. The traditional answer to this is that each analogous term has both a prior (or most proper) meaning and various posterior (or derivative) meanings. Thus one can speak of the health both of a man and of his diet, because the prior meaning of health (more properly applied to the man) renders the posterior reference intelligible.

The problems of analogy, however, are not only linguistic, but ontological: that is, does the propriety of an analogical predication rest upon some essential likeness within the separate objects? As an issue of religious language, this question becomes especially acute in regard to how language appropriate to finite and immanent truths can be applied meaningfully to the transcendent, the infinite, or the divine. Every religious philosophy that recognizes both a cataphatic and an apophatic dimension in its language must, at least implicitly, confront the issue of analogy, especially in regard to that supreme analogand 'being': can one speak meaningfully of both finite ontic realities and infinite ontological reality in terms of 'being' or its attributes? Christian theology, in particular, has wrestled with this issue, in its patristic, medieval, and modern periods, and the classic (if by no means uncontroversial) answer to the question is that predications may be shared between creatures and God on the basis of a fundamental *analogia entis*, or analogy of being, sustained by a metaphysics of participation. The being and perfections of God are wholly convertible with his essence, which is simple and infinite, and thus infinitely transcend thought and language; but creaturely being participates in and reflects divine being, and all its perfections have their 'supereminent' source in God. Thus we can speak truly of God, though the meaning of what we say infinitely exceeds our limited understanding. As Thomas Aquinas says, a theological analogy refers properly to God, and only derivatively to creatures (even in the case of seemingly anthropomorphic terms like 'father'). As the Fourth Lateran Council (1215) asserts, within every similitude between creatures and God one finds an always greater dissimilitude. All of which means that, in the context of religious language, analogy is that liminal interval mediating the transition from cataphatic to apophatic language: a moment of conceptual conversion, in which a sign's meaning is at once preserved and superseded, as thought and language strive towards a fullness greater than either.

See also: Aquinas, Thomas; Christian Views on Language.

Bibliography

Burrell D 1973 *Analogy and Philosophical Language.* Yale University Press, New Haven, CT

Gilson E 1952 *Being and Some Philosophers.* Pontifical Institute of Medieval Studies, Toronto

Mascall E L 1949 *Existence and Analogy.* Longmans, Green and Co., London

Przywara E 1962 *Analogia Entis: Metaphysik.* Johannes-Verlag, Einsiedeln

Babel

J. F. A. Sawyer

The biblical story of the Tower of Babel reached its present form probably in the sixth to fifth century BCE, and has played a not insignificant role both in the history of linguistics and in popular perceptions of language. It is in two parts. The first describes a family tree in which all the peoples of the world are descended from Noah's three sons, Ham, Shem, and Japheth (Genesis 10). It is clearly motivated, not by linguistic curiosity, but by the desire to separate the author and his people who are descended from Shem (Greek *Sēm*), from the Egyptians, Canaanites, Babylonians, Assyrians, and Philistines descended from Ham, and the Persians, Greeks, and Romans (as *kittīm* was later interpreted) who are descended from Japheth.

Modern scholars noted a rough correspondence between two of the three branches and what they recognized as major language groups, and coined the widely used linguistic terms 'Hamitic languages' and 'Semitic languages.' The term 'Hamito–Semitic' was also used to denote a larger grouping comprising what are nowadays more often known as the 'Afroasiatic' languages. The term 'Japhetic' has also occasionally been applied to the Indo–European languages of Western Asia and Europe.

The second part of the story begins with the statement that at one time 'the whole earth had one language and the same (or few) words (Hebrew *dĕbhārīm 'ăhādīm*)' (Genesis 11: 1). The story of the Tower of Babel is then told to explain why the current language situation in the world is so complicated. Men 'from the east' attempt to build a city with a tower that will reach the heavens. As a punishment for this sin of pride, the languages, of the world are 'confused' (Hebrew *bālal*), and the sinful city is given the Hebrew name *Bābēl* 'Babylon,' henceforth a symbol of linguistic confusion (cf. Steiner 1975).

Here too there is no suggestion that languages can be a source of fascination or intellectual curiosity. Instead the story provides a mythical context for wistful visions of a world with one language, and early Christian traditions about Pentecost envisage a reversal of the Babel story in which people speaking many different languages are all miraculously able to understand one another (Acts 2) (see *Glossolalia*).

See also: Myths About Language; Semitic Languages.

Bibliography

Babel, Tower of 1971 In: *Encyclopedia Judaica*, 2nd edn., vol. 4, pp. 22–27. Keter, Jerusalem

Borst A 1957–60 *Der Turmbau von Babel: Geschichte der Meinungen über Ursprung und Vielfalt der Sprachen und Völker*. 3 vol. A. Hiersemann, Stuttgart

Steiner G 1975 *After Babel: Aspects of Language and Translation*. Oxford University Press, London

Westermann C 1984 *Genesis 1–11: A Commentary* (transl. by Scullion J J). Fortress Press, Philadelphia, PA/SCM Press, London

Buddhism and Language

I. Onians

Language, its ontological status and grammatical analysis, are central concerns in Indian culture. Brahmins, the creators and support of orthodox religious practice, agreed that Sanskrit is the original language, of which the world is a reflection. The Buddha is traditionally presented as a kshatriya (the royal and warrior caste), not a brahmin, and was a religious innovator of the fifth century BCE. A heterodox teacher, he redefined brahmanical concepts in showing a new path to a new liberation. Understanding the conventions of the educated, he was able to undermine them.

When the founder of the teaching was gone his followers settled down to the task of perpetuating the community's growth. Through a perhaps inevitable circularity ensured by a brahmin majority of converts (40 percent of those named in the Pali *Theragatha* '*Verses of the Elders*'), through their direct competition with brahmanical orthodoxy, and through the resultant coincidence of concerns, the Buddhist attitude to language became brahmanized.

The following is an exposition of language and Buddhism in the sense of what can be reconstructed through textual study as closest to the historical Buddha Shakyamuni's own ideas about language. The primary corpus for such study is the Pāli canon, the *Tipitaka* 'the three baskets [of the Buddha's words],' the scripture of *Theravada* 'the teaching of the Elders' Buddhism. Most of the texts contained therein also exist in Chinese versions, and some in Tibetan translations of the canon from Indian originals of other contemporary early schools of Buddhism. Thus what will here be attributed to the Buddha can be assumed to be common to all Buddhist traditions, however different their later developments are, as will be discussed below. Because of the oral transmission and late redaction (29–17 BCE) of the Pāli canon it can be difficult—some would say impossible—to extrapolate definite distinctions between what the Buddha said himself and what compilers adapted or inserted. True to a core doctrine of the Buddha's, the emphasis here is on what can be inferred to be the spirit of his teaching since it is impossible to be certain about its letter.

1. Language, Impermanence and Suffering

The first Noble Truth of Buddhism is suffering, or dissatisfaction. The cause of this torment is desire, or attachment. The impermanence, or conventional conditioning, of phenomena means that attachment inevitably ends in dissatisfaction. These truths apply equally to language, for it is as impermanent, or conventional, as everything else. The Buddha taught that the first Noble Truth is absolutely true, but immeasurable are the ways of describing it. He showed in his teachings that different words may share an identical reference which would be unacceptable to brahmanical authors. For them the relationship between a word and its referent is a beginningless natural connection. The Buddha repeatedly stressed the overriding importance of content, meaning and understanding rather than attachment to formulae or expressions. He feared the strife that such formal dogmatism could engender. There are many examples in the sutras of the confusion created by the misunderstanding of a particular word, especially words for 'self.' The Buddha stressed that '*I* speak' (or think), does not imply 'therefore *I am*.' In the end it is bondage to the impermanent, that is everything including language, which must be cut off for the realisation of enlightenment (see *Hindu Views on Language*).

2. Buddhism and Hieratic Language

No particular language had, for the Buddha, a privileged status, as Sanskrit certainly had for brahmins. Early sources show that the Buddha did not want such a hieratic language, particularly because he knew that the consequences for understanding, and therefore conversion, would be dire. This view of his intention has been controversial, in both the tradition and Western scholarship, but is based on the sound analysis of a scriptural passage permitting the learning of the Buddha's words 'in one's own dialect.' The transmission of Buddhism across Asia and beyond has been both the cause and result of a vast number of translations (see *Hindu Sacred Texts*; *Pāli Canon*; *Buddhist Canons: Translations*).

Tibetan Mahayana Buddhism, for example, produced a huge number of more or less accurate translations from Indian originals. Yet that achievement is a long way from contemporary transmission of the tradition in the West, which often prescribes chanting of whole texts, not just mantras, in Tibetan, as though that language has a sacred status. Similarly, in Japan monks have long recited texts in Chinese that they cannot understand. And both Tibet and Japan developed a writing system derived from that of the geographical source of their Buddhism, respectively India and China (see *Buddhism, Japanese*; *Buddhism, Tibetan*; *Buddhism in the West*; *Tibetan*).

3. The Language of the Buddha

The canon nowhere specifies what language[s] the Buddha spoke, which indicates that the question was at that time of little interest to him and his disciples. The geographical location of his audiences means that he was a speaker of a relatively narrow group of dialects in North-East India. That Middle Indo–Aryan language-group, *Magadhi* '[the language] of Magadha,' became associated with his own supreme status, and was in turn identified in the post-canonical *Theravada* tradition with Pāli, the Middle Indo–Aryan language of their canon. These steps are understandable, although incongruent with the Buddha's insistence that language is conventional and that the message should be able to travel freely, as it in fact did. *Magadhi* was also said to be the 'root language of all people,' natural in that a child would learn it even if 'born in an uninhabited forest,' easiest to learn, and even required in religious matters. Each of these propositions closely parallels the arguments of Sanskrit grammarians and exegetes of ritual. (See *Sanskrit*; *Pāli*.)

The adoption of one language, and one no longer in common use, for the teachings of *Theravada* Buddhism meant that they could be transported and studied in a limited unchanging corpus to create a *Theravadin* identity across South-East Asia. Sanskrit and Latin have had much the same useful functions as lingua francas. Whereas in India Buddhist texts were originally composed in Prakrits, local Middle Indo–Aryan languages like Pāli and Magadhi, later authors adopted the lingua franca of Indian intellectual life and began to write in a combination of Prakrit and Sanskrit (Old Indo–Aryan) which Western scholarship has called Buddhist Hybrid Sanskrit. (See *Buddhism in Southeast Asia*; *Buddhist Hybrid Sanskrit*.)

4. The Buddha as Omniglot

Other texts describe the Buddha's wonderful ability to speak with audiences human and divine, 'having first adopted their speech, whatever it might be.' This gift of tongues is part of the attribution to the Buddha of omniscience, and as such is qualified by not being simultaneous and only availed of when appropriate. Later Buddhists became dogmatic about their founder's omniglottism, proclaiming that he could pronounce all at the same time. Thus a Mahasamghika doctrine describes a linguistic reductionism, the use of a single sound to utter all, like the monotone *divyadhvani* 'divine sound' attributed by Digambara Jains to Mahavira. (See *Jainism*.)

5. Language as the Medium for Religious Truths

The Buddha did consider language sufficient to express the essence of his experience, as the canon itself testifies. Yet straight after his enlightenment he was reluctant to preach, for fear of frustration in the effort to get his message across to the world. His words are scripture, the revelation of absolute truths in the same way as Vedic *Shruti* 'that which has been heard' is; but unlike *Shruti* its author was an historical figure. Many texts teach the lesson that talk without experience is just hot air. There is negative language in Buddhism, so that enlightenment is named apophatically as the extinction (Skt *nirvana*), cessation or absence of passion, hatred and delusion, but it is equally positively described as *bodhi* 'awakening,' the root of the word Buddha.

6. Language as a Style of Expression

The form and method of preservation of the teachings are also different from those of brahmanical sacred literature. The form of a Buddhist *sutra*, with its lengthy prosaic self-explanatory nature, is the opposite of the aphoristic verses (*sutra*) of brahmanical culture. Its preservation is unusual in that it was not by metrical chanting but by self-conscious memorisation, within a community who shared the mammoth task. Canonical passages prohibiting the chanting of texts warn that such emphasis on form will distract one from the content, as well as possibly encouraging aesthetic self-congratulation. (See *Sutra*.)

7. Language as the Use of Words

Language is also speech and speech in action was something the Buddha often spoke about. The required correctness and kindness of what one may say must always finally be judged on the potential impact of the words. Thus the spiritual condition of the recipient must be considered, and even abuse can be appropriate. Nevertheless, the Buddha did teach the moral that sticks and stones can only break bones, and how could words ever hurt you. The moment is to be carefully timed, and only what is essential should be taught. Rather than the homogenised mass of *Shruti* and ancillary texts and sciences that a brahmin was compelled to respect, the Buddha's style of dialectic was ad hominem.

8. Language and Silence

This skillful technique extended to silence in debate, a sure symptom of defeat in the brahmanical context. The Buddha repeatedly left unanswered 14 questions, not because he did not know the answers, but because they were irrelevant on the religious path. He nevertheless also condemned silence as a practice, which was already that of other dumb sects. Speech and silence have, for him, each their moment. The brahmanical contest between ascetic silence and the powerful true utterance was repeated in the canon, both ideals finding acceptance there. Silence is of course a necessary condition of meditation. Truth statements are effective when one has an impeccable moral status; then one's true assertion can, for example, cause a river to flow upstream. A different kind of silence is the withholding of teachings from certain people. The Buddha's words are said to be open to all, but certain topics were withheld from a major early banker patron of his community, as being inappropriate for a householder. But anyone could become a monk or nun. This contrasts with the brahmin prohibition on a person of low caste even hearing the *Veda*. (See *Silence*; *Performative Utterances*.)

9. Word Magic

Finally, the fact that words could themselves be magically efficient is because of loving-kindness, according to the Buddha. The making of a snake charm *paritta* 'protection' is permitted, because by pervading the world with compassion one can transform it. But that form of word-magic was less rigorously applied in other texts. Thus first mountains are shown to have had different names in the past, which is a lesson in impermanence, and then permanence and protective power are attributed to the name of a particular mountain. The Buddha openly solicited lay approval for the monastic community through the endorsement of superstitious expressions, such as 'Bless you' (lit. 'Live long') when someone sneezes; but he ruled that monks should always remember that such expressions are meaningless in terms of one's health. The early *paritta* charms should be contrasted with his philosophy that language is not mysteriously efficacious in the way that brahmins and Mahayana Buddhists believed it to be. (See *Dharani*; *Mantra*; *Names*: *Religious Beliefs*.)

Bibliography

Bechert H (ed.) *Sprache der Ältesten Buddhistischen Überlieferung*. Symposien zur Buddhismusforschung II. Vandenhoek & Ruprecht, Göttingen

Gomez L O 1987 Buddhist Views of Language. In: Eliade M (ed.) *Encyclopedia of Religion*. Macmillan, New York, vol. 8, 446–451

Lamotte E 1988 *History of Indian Buddhism* (trans. S. Webb-Boin; French original 1958). Publications de l'Institut Orientaliste de Louvain 36, Louvain

Onians I C R 1996 *Language, Speech and Words in Early Buddhism*. Thesis, University of Oxford

Christian Views on Language

J. Martin Soskice

Already in their myths of origin one can detect in Jewish and Christian traditions a concern with words and language. In the book of Genesis, God is represented as 'speaking' words of creation and the human being, made in the image of God, is given the task of naming the animals. In the same book, the arrogance of the human architects of the tower of Babel is punished by confusing the human languages and scattering the people across the earth. In Christian mythopoetic language, God incarnate in Jesus the Christ is also the Incarnate 'Word' of God. The words of Jesus and those of the early Christian communities are preserved in the Bible, which itself has become, in some Christian contexts, the 'Word' of God almost on a par with the Incarnate Word.

The article will address two clusters of interest in Christian religious language; the first concerns the elementary but profoundly religious question of how it is that God can be spoken of at all given God's transcendence. That is, can God be 'named' by us? The second concerns the critical interpretation of texts received as sacred within the Christian tradition.

1. How can God be 'Named?'

The unnameability of the deity within Judaism and Christianity follows from God's holiness. God is represented in the Book of Exodus as too holy to be named or imaged by human beings, revealing himself to Moses as 'I AM who I AM.' While it would be anachronistic to attribute to the authors of this early text the concern with metaphysical ultimacy that was to preoccupy later thinkers, scripture evidences changes in the conception of God from a polytheism in which the God of Israel is the greatest of the gods towards a heightened and radical monotheism. God, as creator of all that is, is in a strict sense incomparable with any 'thing.'

A pure and late Christian expression of this insight can be found in Anselm's Proslogion, a text which continues to impress modern writers, if not for its success in demonstrating the existence of God, then for the subtlety of the means by which Anselm (ca. 1033–1109) tries to name God, His designation of the God he addresses as 'that than which nothing greater can be conceived' avoids the pitfalls of saying either that God is the greatest of all things or of suggesting one could adequately conceive (comprehend) the deity. God for Anselm could not be so conceived because God is God and not a creature to which human language could adequately apply. Similar reflections are found in the work of Anselm's Jewish near contemporary, Moses Maimonides (1135–1204), who writes of the Tetragrammaton (the divine name) that 'the majesty of the name and the dread of uttering it, are connected with the fact that it denotes God Himself, without including in its meaning any names of the things created by Him' (*A Guide for the Perplexed*).

Thomas Aquinas (1224–74) (see *Aquinas, T.*) made use of a variety of sources in his deliberations on the knowledge of God and the speaking of God: Aristotle, of course, but also Augustine and neo-Platonist thinkers like Denys the Areopagite. Aquinas argued that God could be known and named principally as creator. This is the basis of his so-called 'proofs' for the existence of God, but also for his discussion of the language adequate to God. In the *Summa Theologiae* (Ia. 13) Aquinas discusses the inadequacy of human words for speaking of God, but suggests that there may be very few terms which might be predicated of God literally by means of what he calls 'analogy'. Analogy for Aquinas is not the crude proportionality suggested by some later writers but rests on his conviction that some terms like 'good' and 'wise' signify perfections which inhere perfectly in God and flow from God to creatures. By analogy, human beings could say, for instance, that God is wise, without being able fully to grasp what wisdom in the Godhead might be. While Aquinas employs a theory of meaning which one would be unlikely to advance in the early 1990s, he nonetheless stands in an ancient tradition of reflection on religious language which, in its linking of the theological and the mystical and its sensitivity to the limitations of human language of the Divine, continues to be of importance.

A quite different sensibility is apparent following the Enlightenment in the British philosophers who, in the course of their writings, readdressed questions of the meaningfulness of religious language. David Hume (1711–76) in *The Dialogues Concerning Natural Religion* proceeds like a Ciceronian skeptic, demonstrating the poverty of the then popular arguments for God's existence from evidence of design in the world. No arguments from natural circumstances could, to Hume's mind, give any idea of the divine nature. Such 'analogies' (here meaning something like 'comparisons' and thus used in a different sense from that of Aquinas) could as easily prove the world to be the product of an immature or senile deity as of a good and powerful one. Natural knowledge of God, it is argued, is useless and humans must rest on the revealed. But since Hume elsewhere makes it clear that the gravest doubts must be cast on any claims to revelation, one is left with the position that, when speaking of God, a truly agnostic silence is best. Hume's *Dialogues* set an agenda for English-language philosophy of religion which is still being addressed. One of the most strident twentieth-century offspring of this debate is A. J. Ayer's *Language, Truth and Logic*, one of whose stated objectives was to show that religious language was 'literally' meaningless.

In this century religious language has become a more explicit topic for theologians and philosophers of religion. As Ayer's logical positivism disintegrated under the weight of its own contradictions, theists found the emphasis on diversity of linguistic tasks and modes favored by ordinary language philosophy to be useful. Ian Ramsey's *Religious Language* (1957) pioneered an interest in models in religious language, and subsequently metaphor, too, has emerged as an important topic, with parallels drawn between the use of models and metaphors in religious language and in the language of scientific theory construction. Wittgenstein (see *Wittgenstein, L.*) has had an important and lasting influence. His notion of the diversity of linguistic tasks and functions ('language-games') has been much used, and even abused; its most extreme variant being forms of a 'Wittgensteinian fideism' wherein religious language is meaningful to religious adherents but not to others. Paul Ricoeur has shown a sustained interest in religious language running from his early book on *The Symbolism of Evil*, through works on metaphor, narrative, and biblical interpretation. Ricoeur's work is useful in bringing together continental and analytical philosophical concerns, for instance, with reference and narrative. More recent philosophy of religious language in the analytic tradition has been interested in questions of reference and realism, conceptual and linguistic relativism, and the status of 'God' as a proper name.

2. Religious Language and the Interpretation of Texts

The books which make up the Hebrew scriptures, written and compiled over many centuries, are already works of theological interpretation with later writings glossing and building upon the earlier, a tradition continued in Rabbinic exegesis. The early Christians, after some debate, retained the holy books of the Jews but set about providing Christian rereadings of them, a task which guaranteed from the outset that Christian theology must concern itself with the interpretation of religious language. Already in the letters of St Paul, new Christian interpretations are being given of books like Genesis. Early interpretation assumed the texts to be oracular and this, in conjunction with the conviction that the books of the 'Old Testament' must be read as pointing to Christ, led to the view that all scripture must have some edifying meaning. Typological and allegorical methods of interpretation were employed to discern this and it was widely held that all scriptures had two senses, literal and spiritual. By the fourth century CE, Augustine was already cautioning against overly allegorical readings of scripture. By medieval times exegetes looked for four senses of scripture: literal or historical, allegorical, moral, and anagogical or prophetic. Many of the early theologians were also students of rhetoric and, while their interpretations may at times seem odd to the modern reader, their works displayed considerable sensitivity to the specific natures of the texts before them.

Modern biblical interpretation might be said to begin with the Renaissance and Reformation. Reformers like John Calvin (1509–64) were skilled in the new tools of literary analysis and eager to get behind the accretion of church teachings to the texts themselves in the original languages. Yet while consensus could be reached on the desirability of straightforward readings of the Biblical texts, it proved more difficult and indeed impossible to achieve uniformity in the interpretation of the Biblical texts.

The Romantic philosopher–theologian Friedrich Schleiermacher (1768–1834) is credited with elevating the study of interpretation to a science, which he called 'hermeneutics.' Schleiermacher's own concern was psychological and concerned with the gap between the reader and the mind of the author, but later nineteenth-century writers like Wilhelm Dilthey emphasized historical and cultural dimensions of the interpretive task, subjects of note to the then rapidly developing discipline of Biblical studies.

In the twentieth century, the works of Martin Heidegger (see *Heidegger, M.*) and Hans-Georg Gadamer (see *Gadamer, H.-G.*) while not themselves addressed directly to religious matters, have been influential for theological hermeneutics, especially in studies dealing with parable, narrative, text, and rhetorical criticism.

3. Questions

While questions of truth and reference will always be of importance, work on religious language in the late twentieth century shows a movement away from straightforward interest in the justification of religious claims towards the literary particularities of religious texts. Biblical rhetoric is enjoying renewed attention and narrative has emerged as an important if elusive analytic category. Questions familiar to secular literary criticism arise inevitably when considering the biblical texts: what constitutes a text? who is the reader? how do texts inform texts? It is not surprising that literary critics like Northrop Frye, Frank Kermode, and Robert Alter continue to find the biblical literature of interest.

Questions about the validity of received interpretations of canonical literature have led naturally to study of the link between power, ideology, and language. As Paul Ricoeur has said, 'to narrate is already to explain.' Arguing that interpretations of religious language themselves are never neutral, liberation and feminist theologies propose new interpretive strategies that challenge reigning views on texts and meanings. New ways of naming and knowing God are being sought by theologians.

It also appears that nontheologians, especially those influenced by French philosophy, are taking a renewed interest in religious language. Following Heidegger's essay on 'The Onto-Theological Constitution of Metaphysics' some of this interest was initially hostile to the theological and metaphysical presence in language. However, writings show that religious language may be once more recommending itself to nonreligious critics, with special interest being shown in the task, native to traditional negative theology, of 'saying the unsayable.' Noteworthy, too, is the work on female symbolics and the language of love which has drawn French postmodernist critics like Julia Kristeva (see *Kristeva, J.*) and Luce Irigaray (see *Irigaray, L.*) to reconsider Christian religious language.

See also: Analogy, Aquinas, T.; Metaphor; Feminism; Postmodernism; Romanticism; Heidegger, M.; Gadamer, H. G.

Bibliography

Ackroyd P R, Evans C F (eds.) 1970 *The Cambridge History of the Bible: From the Beginnings to Jerome*. Cambridge University Press, Cambridge

Burrell D B 1986 *Knowing the Unknowable God: Ibn-Sina, Maimonides, Aquinas*. Notre Dame University Press, Notre Dame, IN

Kerr F 1986 *Theology After Wittgenstein*. Basil Blackwell, Oxford

Palmer R E 1969 *Hermeneutics*. Northwestern University Press, Evanston, IL

Ramsey I T 1957 *Religious Language*. SCM Press, London

Ricoeur P 1984 *Time and Narrative*. University of Chicago Press, Chicago, IL

Soskice J 1985 *Metaphor and Religious Language*. Oxford University Press, Oxford

Fundamentalism

J. Barr

In its original and most common sense, 'fundamentalism' is a form of conservative evangelical Protestantism, which considers the infallibility of the Bible, not only in its theological authority but also in its historical inerrancy, to be absolute. More recently the term has been extended to refer to some other aspects within Christianity, and also in Judaism, Islam, and other religions.

Christian fundamentalism is heavily dependent on language and words, for ritual and ceremony are minimal. Scripture is divinely inspired, both as a whole and in every word and detail. Meanings, on the other hand, are commonly derived from modern common-sense awareness plus evangelical tradition. Though some religions insist on the original language (so Judaism, and especially Islam), Christianity has worked mainly with translations. Many fundamentalists have regarded the King James Version as final and quoted it verbally, even though its diction is often far removed from modern usage. This means the retention of archaic English usages, and also the reproduction of features of the original languages: thus calques on Hebrew such as 'take captivity captive.' Recently, however, many fundamentalists have accepted a modern translation, provided that it has evangelical scholarship behind it.

Many think of fundamentalists that they 'take the Bible literally'; this however is misleading. They are perfectly able to perceive the presence of metaphor: if God is described as a 'rock,' they do not think that he is an actual stone. Over both theological values and historical statements, however, they commonly insist on a reference in reality: hell may not be physically a burning fire, but there must be some reality which is well conveyed by the term 'burning fire.' If Israel is said to have dwelt in Egypt for 430 years (*Exodus* 12: 40), this may not state all the facts but it must be an accurate, even if a partial, reflection of a real event. It would be illegitimate to think of Jesus' ascension into heaven as a metaphor for something in the consciousness of the nascent Christian community.

Such interpretation of biblical language leads to potential clashes with both science and history. The biblical picture of a world some six thousand years old is seen as irreconcilable with geology and evolution: hence the modern development of 'creationism' or 'creation science.' Creationism does not necessarily take the biblical dating as entirely precise, but nevertheless insists on a world of vastly shorter duration than that implied by common scientific opinion.

Devotionally, however, fundamentalism enjoys the Bible as something like a kind of poetry: its words and sentences create a world of peace, justice and bliss, within which the believer feels himself close to God.

Used in contexts other than Protestant Christianity, 'fundamentalism' may refer not to a written document but to an institution like the papacy, a political tradition like Marxism, or a national historical consciousness. Each of these may show some analogies in the use of language to the root example of Protestant fundamentalism.

See also: Bible; Christian Views on Language.

Bibliography

Barr J 1977 *Fundamentalism*. London, SCM

Harris H A 1998 *Fundamentalism and Evangelicals*. Clarendon Press, Oxford

Marty M E, Appleby R S 1991–1995 *The Fundamentalism Project*, 5 vols. Chicago University Press, Chicago

Gematria

M. Idel

Semitic languages use characters, not figures, in order to point to numerical values. Thus, it is possible to calculate the numeral equivalent(s) for each and every word and consequently to propose distinct values for each of them. There are several types of calculation under the generic name 'gematria,' most of them described in manuscript manuals. In most cases implicitly, but sometimes also explicitly, the use of gematria presupposes the divine, or at least a nonconventional, nature of the Hebrew language, which ensures the significance or the numerical relations. The Hebrew consonants of the name of the Emperor Nero (*nrwn qysr*), for example, add up to 666, the number of the 'Beast' in Revelation, and for Jesus (*yshw*) to the same total as 'the alien god' (*elohei nekhar*) in Deuteronomy 21: 16 and elsewhere.

There are two different explanations as to the origin of the gematria device in Judaism: that of Saul Lieberman, which attributed it to Greek sources and that of Stephen J. Lieberman, which makes a strong case for the importance of Mesopotamian sources which could have eventually influenced also the Greek texts.

Though found in many instances in the earlier strata of Jewish writings. Midrashic and Talmudic literatures, gematria was not allowed a decisive role in the hermeneutics of their authors. In medieval Jewish speculative writings, however, especially those belonging to mystical corpora, the use of gematria is widespread and conspicuous. Occurrences of gematria are especially evident in the extensive literature dealing with calculations of the date of the advent of the Messiah. Though there were a few important authors opposed to too great a reliance on mathematical calculations, like Rabbi Abraham ibn Ezra and Rabbi Moses ben Nahman (Nahmanides), in general, medieval, Renaissance, and even later Jewish authors display sympathy toward this technique. The first systematic exposition of a wide spectrum of gematria techniques is found in the Ḥasidē Ashkenaz literature, written in Germany, especially that written by Rabbi Yehudah he-Hasid and Rabbi Eleazar of Worms (twelfth to thirteenth centuries), who not only explained them in detail, but also used them extensively in their exegetical writings. Especially famous is the Commentary on the Pentateuch, written at the beginning of the fourteenth century by Rabbi Jacob ben Asher, which is entirely based on numerological speculation.

In medieval texts, 'gematria' became a generic term referring not only to the calculation of the numerical values of each letter of a word, but also for other linguistic components like the value of the letters which make up the name of each letter, and their vocalization. Gematria is also crucial for the understanding of the dense *Commentary on Sepher Yetṣirah* of Rabbi Barukh Togarmi (ca. 1260). Under their influence, the ecstatic Kabbalah, founded by Rabbi Abraham Abulafia (1240–ca. 1292), adopted gematria as a major vehicle for expressing its views. The device became an integral part of their conception of *kabbalah*, and it was used, together with other linguistic devices like *notariqon* (anagram) and *temura* (metathesis) as part of the creative process of word association characteristic of this kind of *kabbalah*. Sometimes, *kabbalah* was defined as including the technique of gematria. In this school, the device is applied not only as part of the interpretation of the canonical texts but of any text at all, and even in cases of non-Hebrew words, as part of the effort to extract new insights, rather than to reinforce the accepted views, as is often the case in the previous types of literature. Thirteenth-century kabbalists observed that in gematria 'Satan' (=359) was equivalent to the Hebrew for 'the evil body' (*guf ra'*), and therefore to be understood not as an external, independent power, but rather as an integral part of the human constitution.

Very rare in Catalan *kabbalah*, gematria played a more important role in Castilian mystical writings from the second part of the thirteenth century. It was then that this kind of numerology combined with kabbalistic theosophy. Gematria played an important role in Lurianic kabbalistic literature, especially in its European versions, such as Polish *kabbalah* at the beginning of the seventeenth century, and likewise in some of the Sabbatean literature of the following century. A well-known Sabbatean example of gematria relates the Hebrew form of the name of their founder, Shabbatai Zevi, whose numerical value is 814, to the divine name *shaddai* 'the Almightly,' which has the same value. In the Hasidic literature of the eighteenth and nineteenth centuries as a whole, there was a decline in its popularity, though in the Viznitz line of Hasidism it is still prominent. A number of computer-assisted gematria programs are available on the Internet.

Due to a deep interest among Christian kabbalists in Jewish exegetical techniques, Renaissance Christian kabbalistic literature is replete with explanations based on gematria. This is peculiarly evident in the writings of the influential German humanist, Johannes Reuchlin (1455–1522), and in the work of Francesco Giorgio of Venice.

See also: Alphabet: Religious Beliefs; Hebrew, Biblical and Jewish.

Bibliography

Dan J 1980 The Ashkenazi Hasidic 'Gates of Wisdom.' In: Nahon G, Touati Ch (eds.) *Hommage à Georges Vajda*. Peeters, Louvain

Dornzeiff F 1925 *Das Alphabet in Mystik und Magie*. B. G. Teubner, Leipzig

Idel M 1989 *Language, Torah and Hermeneutics in Abraham Abulafia*. State University of New York Press, Albany, NY

Lieberman S 1962 *Hellenism in Jewish Palestine*. Theological Seminary of America, New York

Lieberman S J 1987 A Mesopotamian background for so-called Aggadic 'measures' of biblical hermeneutics. *Hebrew Union College Annual* LVIII: 157–225

Sambursky S 1976 The origin and the meaning of the term *Gematria*. *Tarbitz* **45**: 268–71 [Hebrew]

Scholem G 1971 *Kabbalah*. Keter Publishing House, Jerusalem

Hindu Views on Language

J. J. Lipner

Hinduism in its roots and in its history is fundamentally an oral phenomenon. This means that traditionally saving knowledge, viz., the knowledge that brings about the ultimate welfare of the human being, has been transmitted par excellence by the spoken rather than the written word. In the Brahminic Hinduism that has regulated the majority of religious Hindus down the ages, the repository of saving knowledge has been the Vedas, Hinduism's original scriptures (ca. 1500 BCE to the first and second centuries CE). In this context, the Vedas are regarded as *śruti* 'hearing,' the hearing, that is, in the mind's ear by primeval sages of a precise sequence and accenting of a large body of verbal utterances. The language of these utterances is a form of Sanskrit; as a result for traditional, orthodox Hinduism the Sanskrit of the Vedas had always had a mystique of its own, an inner efficacy and power which can be controlled and implemented in certain circumstances. Even in the present day, there is a residual deference in the educated Hindu mind to the sacred use of Sanskrit. This stems from the earliest form of Vedic religion, which revolved around the solemn sacrificial ritual at the heart of which lay the Sanskritic utterance of the Vedas. The idea was that if the ritualistic utterance was performed aright its variously designated 'fruit' (*phala*) must result. This gave rise to the tradition of transmitting the *śruti* word-perfect, from generation to generation, in numerous schools of Vedic recitation and study, in accordance with the traditional recitative usages of each school. Thus the Sanskrit of the Vedas was sacred speech par excellence, the model for all language, and in Hindu tradition philosophical issues which have traditionally hinged on the nature of the Sanskritic language in the context of *śruti*, have either no counterpart or only derivative relevance in the use of Sanskrit outside the *śruti*, or in the vernaculars.

In the earliest portion of the Vedic scriptures, consisting of hymns (see *Mantra*), the word for sacred speech is *vāc*. Though there is no philosophy proper in the Vedas about the nature of religious language, one can inquire philosophically into the Vedic view of *vāc*. This view is implicit in verses such as the following: 'By sacrifice [the priests] walked the track of Speech [*vāc*]. They found her entered within the sages. Having fetched her, they distribute her manifoldly. Seven celebrants chant her together' (*Ṛg*

Veda 10.71.3). Here *vāc* is likened to a cow in whose track priests and sages walk. In essence and origin, *vāc* is not an artifact, a human construct; she is discovered and then implemented for human well-being (through the sacrifice). Other texts imply that *vāc* exists essentially as an inexhaustible and unmanifest reservoir, like a river dammed up and unflowing (*akṣara*), which then streams forth (*kṣarati*), via various promulgators, its power and purity intact, in the form of the Vedic syllables (*akṣara*: a play on the word here; see Killingley 1986). It is through the sacrifice that humans benefit from *vāc* in manifest form. It is from this original conception of sacred speech that key philosophical views and debates about the nature of language stem in Hindu tradition, often with the help of controversy with Buddhists and Jains.

In later Vedic texts (from at least the time of the Upanishads, beginning about 800 BCE), the word par excellence which encapsulates and symbolizes the essence of the Vedas and their goal is *Om* (see *Mantra*). A whole short Upanishad—the Māṇḍūkya—is devoted to opening up the different levels of spiritual experience encapsulated by this syllable. Subsequently, from time to time, mainly but not exclusively Vedantic thinkers, beginning with Gauḍapādā (fifth or sixth century CE), philosophize on the religious implications of *Om*. Thus the Vedāntin, Rāmānuja (eleventh to twelfth century CE), enhances his theory that there is a structural correspondence between Vedic language and reality (including ultimate reality) by an analysis of *Om*. According to the theory, which is developed in the context of Rāmānuja's opposition to monism, language in its normative form (i.e., Sanskrit as the language of the Vedas) cannot be interpreted to reveal an undifferentiated Brahman or Absolute. This is because there is a structural correspondence between Vedic Sanskrit which is differentiated by way of inflection, sentence-formation, predication, etc. and its ultimate referent, Brahman (on which the whole corpus of the Vedas converges).

The conclusion is that Brahman is also differentiated internally (by way of being the possessor of various attributes and modes of being) as well as from finite being. Implied here is a particular theory of denotation, viz., that (Vedic) substantives signifying material things (e.g., '*gau*'), have besides their explicit empirical referents (e.g., 'the cow'), also an implied, metaempirical referent (which only the eyes of faith can perceive), namely Brahman (see Lipner 1986). In contrast, the monists, drawing their inspiration from Śaṃkara, the great theologian who established the monist tradition around the eighth century CE, were arguing that the ultimate import of both literal and figurative scriptural language is an undifferentiated Brahman, undifferentiated internally and existing ultimately as the only reality (see Lipner 1989). Part of Rāmānuja's argument consists in analyzing *Om* as the (somewhat mystical) consummation of the Vedas and denotative, as such, of their ultimate referent, Brahman, the source of all intelligibility and being. Even today, *Om* is the sacred sound, par excellence, for most upper-caste Hindus.

Though the language of the Vedas was a subject of intense systematic concern—phonetically, etymologically, grammatically, and exegetically—from very early on (about the beginning of the first millenium BCE), this concern was not philosophical in any strict sense of the term. Sustained philosophical attention to language first appears in the Mīmāṃsā Sūtras, attributed to Jaimini (about the beginning of the Christian era). In general, in philosophical contexts in Hinduism, traditionally the term used for 'language,' 'word,' or even 'verbal testimony' as a valid source (*pramāṇa*) of true cognition (*pramā*), has been *śabda*. Jaimini contends (to some extent by implication) that those words of the Veda which denote (material) substantial entities (e.g., *gau* 'cow,' *aśva* 'horse') have a natural (*autpattika*) and eternal (*nitya*) relationship, not directly with the objects they denote, but with a sort of concrete-universal (*ākṛti*) of each denoted object, and that it is through its *ākṛti* that such a word's object is instantiated.

This view of the natural and eternal relationship of (Vedic) naming-words to objects, known in general as the 'Mīmāṃsā' view (to which the Vedāntins also subscribed), was directly challenged and debated upon in due course by the Nyāya–Vaiśeṣika school. The Nyāya–Vaiśeṣikas argued that the relationship in question is conventional in the sense that it has been determined by God whose nature is personal (*pauruṣeya*), and passed on among humans by general consent. The debate as to the *pauruṣeya* or *apauruṣeya* (viz., nonpersonal, that is, eternally preestablished) nature of the Vedic text was a central one in the history of Hindu philosophical debate about the nature of language. By and large, the Mīmāṃsā view prevailed in orthodox circles till well into the nineteenth century, after which, with the rise of a Western rationalist critique among the Hindu intelligentsia, it rapidly declined. But even at the beginning of the twenty-first century, there is a strong residual sympathy for the traditional view not only in the popular mind but also among traditional-minded pundits. This view has interesting correlations with some modern Western philosophical theories about language as an innate capacity.

Jaimini also argues that the unit of *referential* meaning or of the judgment is the sentence (*vākya*), a view with which most Sanskritic philosophers of language agreed though there was disagreement concerning the most basic units (or 'building blocks') of meaning (here some form or other of atomism tended to prevail), and as to whether Vedic language is primarily injunctive or fact-assertive in nature. Though the Vedāntins, who were also Mīmāṃsakas in the broad sense (Vedānta was also known as Uttara Mīmāṃsā or the Later School of Exegesis in contrast to the Pūrva Mīmāṃsā or Prior School of Exegesis which showed greater dependence on Jaimini's work and outlook), agreed about the *autpattika*, *nitya*, and *apauruṣeya* character of Vedic words, they argued that Vedic language is basically fact-assertive (*yathābhūtavādi*—it 'states what is the case'). It was only in this way that they could derive *information* from scripture about the existence and nature of the supreme metaempirical reality, Brahman, attaining which was the goal of human existence for them. For the theologically agnostic Pūrva Mīmāṃsakas, however, human fulfilment was bound up not in the attainment of some ultimate Being but in the proper performance of the sacrificial ritual and the various kinds of *phala* or fruit this engendered. This is why, for the Pūrva Mīmāṃsakas, Vedic language was essentially injunctive (*kāryārtha*), that is, concerned with how the ritual was to be performed. A modern Western counterpart of this debate is that between the cognitivists and noncognitivists about the nature of religious language.

But Pūrva Mīmāṃsaka and Vedāntin alike opposed the *sphoṭa* theory of the Grammarians (for whom the philosophy of grammar was of particular heuristic importance). A leading light in the articulation of this view was Bhartṛhari (sixth-seventh century CE), according to whom there is no cognition without some form of verbal expression. In fact, for Bhartṛhari the source of all being and intelligibility is a metaphysical reality which may be described as an original 'Word' (*Śabda*) which has an inherent power (*śakti*) to burst forth (*sphuṭ*) into creative expression. The aim of his complex theory is to explain not only the production of being, but also true and false cognition and final release by way of different forms of the *sphoṭa*, 'the word burst forth.' The ultimate form of the *sphoṭa* in fact is Brahman (called *Śabdabrahman*, a view which can be derived from the Upanishads, e.g., *Bṛhadāraṇyaka Upanishad 4.1.2*). For many subsequent Hindu thinkers this view was religiously too impersonal or realist to commend itself. Abhinavagupta, however (seventh century), a noted philosopher of northern Saivism, expresses a view with similar features (see Sastri 1959).

As may have been noted, Hindu speculation about the nature of religious language recurrently concerns metaphysical implications of *śabda* or 'Word' as in some sense creative. During the passage of time this idea has been translated into iconographic form (of which a fine example is the famous representation of Śiva Naṭarāja or Śiva as Lord of the Dance (of existence), in which Śiva is depicted as producing the sound which creates, sustains, and destroys the world) and into various (sometimes implicit) theories of aesthetics.

The idea that the Vedic naming-word (*nāmaśabda*) has an inherent efficacious power has some affinity with a pervasive popular view which is current even today. This is the view popularized in the vernacular by poet–mystics from the fifteenth century on, the Sants. According to Sant teachings, the divine exists in the form of an eternal sound, *śabd*, *śabad*, or *nād* (<Sanskrit *śabda* 'sound, word'; *nāda* 'sound'), having an intrinsic salvific efficacy, which can be heard by advanced initiates and is also manifest in the poems of the Sants. This doctrine can be found in the Hindi poems of Kabīr, Sur Dās, and others, and among the Sikhs. Its affinity with the Vedic concept of the transcendent syllable is corroborated by the Sikhs' use of *ekoṅkār* (<Sanskrit *eka oṃkāraḥ* 'the one *oṃ* sound') as a name of God. However there is no noteworthy philosophical treatment of this aspect of Sant doctrine, nor did it generate a trend of philosophizing in the vernacular.

There were a number of other schools and thinkers, more or less close to the Vedic pale, who gave philosophical consideration to the nature of religious language, but generally within the framework of the kinds of issues and views mentioned hitherto. Thus in the variegated and scripturally somewhat independent tradition of Tantra, which to some extent sought to coexist with Vedic authority, the role of language is important. Speech here is conceived of as an expression of divine power and in appropriate ritual context can help control those forces through which liberation (especially in this life) can be achieved.

Modern Hindu thinkers, influenced by the West, who have given philosophical attention to religious language, fall into two camps: those who have, for all practical purposes, severed intellectual links with their ancestral faith (by far the majority—these need not concern us further since there is nothing distinctively Hindu here), and those who philosophize at least in the penumbra of tradition. Even here notable thinkers have been directly concerned with the status of the Vedas for modern society and only by implication with the language in which they have been transmitted (e.g., S Radhakrishnan, 1888–1975, who repudiates the traditional sacrosanct nature of Sanskrit but who bases his philosophy on a monistic interpretation of the Upanishads). In fact there has been disappointingly little effort made by moderns to articulate an original, systematic, distinctively Hindu account of religious language (whether of Sanskrit or otherwise). Possible exceptions would include Aurobindo Ghose (1872–1950) who maintained (but hardly with philosophical rigor) that Vedic utterances if properly interpreted were revelatory of structures of reality and the path to ultimate fulfilment. In fact, the enormous wealth of traditional

Hindu philosophizing about the nature of religious language has only just begun to be unearthed, whether by way of critical exposition or of incorporation into modern debate, and awaits fuller study.

See also: Hinduism; Mantra; Sanskrit; Matilal, B. K.

Bibliography

D'Sa F X 1980 *Śabdaprāmāṇyam in Śabara and Kumārila: Towards a Study of the Mīmāṃsā Experience of Language*. De Nobili Research Library, Vienna

Ganeri J 1999 *Semantic Powers: Meaning and the Means of Knowing in Classical Indian Philosophy*. Clarendon Press, Oxford

Houben Jan E M 1996 *Ideology and Status of Sanskrit: Contributions to the History of the Sanskrit Language*. E J Brill, Leiden

Killingley D H 1986 Oṃ: The sacred syllable in the Veda. In: Lipner J J, Killingley D H (eds.) *A Net Cast Wide: Investigations into Indian Thought in Memory of David Friedman*. Grevatt & Grevatt, Newcastle upon Tyne.

Lipner J J 1986 *The Face of Truth: A Study of Meaning and Metaphysics in the Vedantic Theology of Rāmānuja*. Macmillan, London, especially Chaps 1 and 2

Lipner J J 1989 Śaṃkara on metaphor with reference to Gītā 13.12–18. In: Perrett R W (ed.) *Indian Philosophy of Religion*. Kluwer, Dordrecht

Matilal B K *The Word and the World: India's Contribution to the Study of Language*. Oxford University Press, Delhi

Padoux A 1990 *Vāc: The Concept of the Word in Selected Hindu Tantras* (transl. Gontier J). State University of New York Press, Albany, NY

Sastri G B 1959 *The Philosophy of Word and Meaning: Some Indian Approaches with Special Reference to the Philosophy of Bhartṛhari*. Sanskrit College, Calcutta

Myths About Language

A. Cunningham

In the primary sense myths about language include traditional narratives concerned with the origin and diversity of language, more particularly of speech and utterance. Vedic 'vāc' and Christian 'logos' in their different ways take speech as an image or expression of a transcendental creativity which utters and sustains the universe. Religious practices may be prescribed for attuning to this originating utterance, the word which speaks, or the sound which reverberates, in the soul. At a different level, and far more common, are stories concerned with the loss of an original language common to all human beings, whether this loss be through an accidental error, or as punishment for some deviation from divine order.

In a wider context one might also need to examine what could be called *secondary* myths of language, using the term in the pejorative sense of fallacious beliefs, i.e., claims about primary myths of language which appeal to unwarrantable historical or linguistic evidence. Thus the biblical story of Babel is a primary myth accounting for the diversity of languages; nineteenth-century attempts to show scientifically that Aryan languages preserve more of the pre-Babel Ur-language are secondary myths.

1. Primary Myths

In defining themselves human beings distinguish themselves from other human groups and, generically, from other animate beings—animals and gods—marking the similarities and the differences. In many myths there is a common language in the time of the beginnings. In the Bible God talks with the primal pair, Adam and Eve, and brings the animals before Adam to see what he will call them. It is through the speech of the most subtle of creatures, the serpent, that the pair are expelled from the paradise; and later traditions have speculated on a loss of a level of communication with animals at this point.

The Emergence story of the Pueblo has a more extended view of primal communication: long ago when the earth was soft and all relations with spirits were more intimate, everything could talk, animals, plants, even wood and stone.

There are many such stories of an original language common to animals and humans, many too accounting for the diversity of languages today (see *Babel*), or giving reasons for the names of particular people or places. By contrast there are surprisingly few significant myths in which language is itself discussed in any detail. The first chapter of the Bible is clearly organized around the utterances of the creator, but the detailed exploration and elaboration of this pattern is the work of centuries of Jewish and Christian interpretation and speculation.

Elsewhere one may find striking connections between language and divinity, as in the following Pygmy example:

> In the beginning was God.
> Today is God,
> Tomorrow will be God.
> Who can make an image of God?
> He has no body.
> He is as a word which comes out of your mouth.

That word! It is no more,
It is past, and still it lives!
So is God.

In Greek myths the role of language or reflection on language is not heavily marked. In a beautifully penetrating phrase Aeschylus attributes to Prometheus, the creator of mankind as such, the origin of setting down words in writing, 'the all-remembering skill, mother of many arts' (*Prometheus Bound*, line 457). But this does not seem privileged among the useful arts Athene transmits to him: architecture, mathematics, medicine, navigation, metallurgy. In this respect the Prometheus story overlaps that of the hero Palamedes who (along with musical notation and dice, checkers and calendars) is credited with adding eleven consonants to the five vowels and B and T ascribed to Io, or to the three Fates. The rendering of these sounds into the characters of a first alphabet is the work of Hermes, the messenger, who is also the inventor of the lyre and, sometimes, numbers too. In Hindu mythology, the creator God Prajapati utters the primal syllables which produce earth, atmosphere, and heaven. *Vāc* 'speech,' becomes personified as his consort with some of the creative ordering functions comparable to the later Greek Logos. Although she is the key to all human knowledge by the time of the Upaniṣads (the latest Vedic texts), speech has a decidedly secondary role. In the development of Brahminism as Saravasti she is the goddess of wisdom and music; in the development of Buddhism she becomes Prajna, the personification of the Buddha's doctrine.

But there seem to be only a few instances in the mythologies of the world where a narrative of creation through language, or of the origin of language, plays a central role. Origin myths are necessarily paradoxical, attempting some classification of what lay before classification. Perhaps language, as the presupposition of any account, is a limiting case in talk of origins and it is only in societies with a long *written* tradition that one might expect some mythic account of this. The absence, however, of a significant Greek myth of this kind, as we have seen, and the central importance of a Dogon one do not support so general a view.

The Dogon of Mali, as recorded by Marcel Griaule in 1946, have a cosmology, metaphysics, and religion of exceptional complexity and sophistication in which the Word is a primary focus. God creates Earth and by her produces two twin primal spirits, the Nummo—a term interchangeable with water, or with life-force. Born perfect, with speech, looking down and seeing their mother naked and speechless, they cover her genitals with fibers full of water and words. Thus clothed, earth had a rudimentary language with basic syntax, few verbs, and words barely distinguishable one from another. By incestuous pursuit of Earth the jackal also obtains speech and the world requires reorganization.

The male Nummo, speaking to himself, fertilizes himself and regenerates the world. He grants the seventh, the most perfect, of the eight original ancestors, mastery of language—associated with weaving as the first word was with plaiting. The self-sacrifice of this ancestral master of speech is part of a final reorganization of the world in which it receives its present structure and systems of classification, symbolized by the various levels and compartments of a Dogon granary. The third word is also associated with drumming: the stretching and tying of the skins follow the image of weaving as does the action of drumming, as the sound reverberates between the skins at either end. As each drum has its own sound, so today there are different languages.

In this remarkable dense and subtle system there is a development from the one-dimensional plaiting of the Earth's skirt and inchoate language, through the two-dimensional weaving of the warp and the woof in the mastery of language, of the dialectic of verbal exchange, to the three-dimensional imagery of granary and drum. The difference between nature and culture is marked by language: 'to be naked is to be speechless.' And various kinds of oscillation and exchange—linguistic, woven, sexual—are correlated. '... the craft of weaving is the tomb of resurrection, the marriage bed and the fruitful womb.' As Griaule remarks, Dogon beliefs are on a par with those of the people of antiquity and something that Western thinkers might study with profit.

The lack of many primal myths of language may suggest that modern focus on language as key to the understanding of human worlds does not have a charter-myth of its own as it tries to make a metastatement about myths and language. Thus Lévi-Strauss's conclusion is that there is no meaning to myth but that what myths say is beautifully said. If language is *the* human factor then why are there so few stories about this? Can it be that such reflection, such pondering on the puzzle, comes only sporadically and relatively late in a few societies? Is twentieth-century Western investigation into language then both privileged and cut off from any founding model? Whether this is taken as scientific liberation or loss will depend upon one's veiw of myth.

2. Secondary Myths

The reworking of diverse myths of origins and claims about language in a secondary mythology can be seen in the efforts at different times to provide a contemporarily acceptable account of the English people, their speech and institutions. Geoffrey of Monmouth in the twelfth century managed, for example, to link Noahic origins, the Trojan war (the naming of Britain, previously Albion, from Aeneas's grandson Brutus), and stories of King Arthur's conquest of Aquitaine and Normandy to accommodate the expansionist ambitions of the Norman occupiers. In the English Reformation scholarly doubts about Geoffrey's version, combined with desires to demonstrate an essential authentic continuity of belief and practice, provided new accounts of origins. It was a principal aim of Foxe's *Actes and Monuments* (1534, later retitled *The Book of Martyrs*) to show the key role of the historically proven Saxon King Alfred over that of Arthur, the Normans, and the Roman church. Camden in his study of the languages of Britain underscored the primacy of Germanic origins, while Richard Verstegen (1605) concluded: 'if Teutonick be not taken for the first language of the world, it cannot be denied to be one of the most ancientist of the world.'

The seeking of mythic antecedents for national identity, and later nationalism, in the antiquity of a language's pedigree are strikingly exemplified in the case of Germany. As early as the twelfth century the unmixed character of the language had been taken to qualify it as the language of Adam and Eve themselves. 'Adam et Eve Teutonica lingua loquebantur, quae in diversa non dividitur ut Romana.' As a manuscript of ca. 1500 (published in 1893) has it 'allemand' equals 'alle-Mann.' Luther's claim was pitched only slightly lower: it was Ashkenaz, eldest son of Gomer, eldest son of Japheth, who taught his language to the Germans. It was thus only bettered by the Hebrew spoken by the children of Adam before the flood. Leibniz (following Becanus, 1518–72, and Böhme who saw its monosyllabic form as most accurately expressing the true nature of things) took German as the original language of the Bible and traced Germanic root words in names, places, towns, and rivers throughout Europe. The radical primitive language may be lost, but Teutonic was taken to retain more of the Adamic original than the greatly distorted forms of Hebrew and Arabic. Towards the end of the eighteenth century, as linguistic and historical evidence shifted the site of human origins from the Holy Lands towards Northern Asia (Kant suggested a link between the names Abraham and Brahma), the Noahic origin of German was transposed into a comparably primeval Sanskrit one.

The discovery of the New World provided a major spur for theories of linguistic and cultural diffusion. Landa, for example, in 1566 attempted to show the Semitic origin of the Mayan script and Francis Bacon's 'New Atlantis' is located in the Pacific west of America. Here, as with the pentecostal gift of tongues in the Acts of the Apostles reversing the confusion of tongues at Babel, the original natives together with the Hebrews, Persians and Indians who also happened to be there at the time, were able to read the Christian scriptures at first sight, as if they had been written in their own language. The most impressive example of a religious organization based upon a secondary myth of language, is that of the Mormons, the Church of Jesus Christ of the Latter-Day Saints (see *Mormon, Book of*).

Atlantis has had various possible locations—Heligoland, Scotland, the North and South Poles among others—but Ignatius Donnelly's *Atlantis The Antediluvian World* (1882) placed it firmly in the Atlantic opposite the mouth of the Mediterranean. Donnelly's Atlantis was the original Garden of Eden, Elysian Fields, and Asgard; its kings, queens and heroes the originals of Phoenician, parent of all European alphabets, and of the Mayan script. Finally James Churchward's once fashionable *The Lost Continent of Mu* (1926) was situated in the Pacific. Churchward claimed to have been taught the original language of mankind, 'Nacal' in India in the 1870s, and was thus able to decipher ancient stone tablets providing the history of Mu (from whose Gobi colony the Aryans derived), the Great Pyramid, white supremacy, and other matters.

Among the last of the schematic attempts in general studies of myth to maintain the Noahic thesis, deriving all pagan beliefs (taken as primarily focused upon sunworship) from the descendants of Ham, was Jacob Bryant's *New System* of 1774. Root words for names of gods, sacred animals and places are used to show that all mythologies are, ultimately, mistaken versions of pre-flood beliefs. It is instructive to note that whilst Bryant's linguistic methods are rejected, his aims and conclusions are shared by one of the founders of modern Oriental studies, William Jones, whose essays show the conflict of loyalties between the Noahic model and the evidence of an even older civilization recorded in Sanskrit and other non-Semitic sources.

In 1788 Jones had put Coeurdoux's observations (1767) on resemblances between European languages and Sanskrit on a systematic philological basis and 6 years later in his *Asiatick Researches* concluded that the Hindu 'Laws of Manu' could be dated around 1580 BCE, considerably earlier than the date then assigned to the Laws of Moses. Yet, if the Genesis account was not true then 'the whole fabric of our national religion is false.' Jones retains a primordial monotheism and a single original geographical center. After the flood 'the Hindu race' expanded in three branches from Iran (Jones was originally a Persian specialist). He found no evidence for the Mosaic stories deriving from Egyptian let alone Indian sources, older though these may be. Rather, his researches confirmed the autonomous nature of Genesis 1–10, the revealed nature of which, as it were, retrospectively orders the disparate remnants of the diluvian heritage found elsewhere. Herder does not seem to have had to face this particular question of historical priority in his work on the origins of language(s), and thus Jones is probably the first person with the relevant linguistic and historical skills to try to retain the revelatory and ultimate truth of the Genesis stories in an historical context but without giving them historical priority as the source of all else.

As late as 1884 as respected biblical commentator, F. C. Cook, editor of the ten-volume *Speaker's Commentary* would use an extensive collection of all the great families of languages and their ultimate derivation from the sons of Noah (the soma of Indian tradition coming from Noah's accidental discovery of wine). Cook's *Origins of Religion and Language* has its own variations upon the pervasive turning of the Orient into a theatre for representations of the Orient, so powerfully outlined by Edward Said. The weird, uncouth and repulsive feature of shamanism, orgiastic ritual, and devil-worship of Turanian peoples (variously Asiatic/Scythian/Tartar/Dravidian/Akkadian, coming from the line of Magog and primordially expelled from the Japhetic stock) are linked to their deteriorated, unruly, proletarian and revolutionary propensities. His passing observation that the Japanese upper classes are mostly of Aryan descent and the lower of Turanian (with Negro and Papuan elements) evidences the fusion or confusion of linguistic, racial, and social class categories common in nineteenth-century philological work. Cook also has elements of the old degenerationist arguments, for the difficulty experienced in tracing the origins of Chinese resides not in the lack of skills of the scholarly investigator but in the degeneration of the beautiful Ur-language into the agglutinative languages through the migration across wild and dreary deserts. And, 'as in Eastern Asia the language sinks into the most helpless and formless condition, so too does the religious instinct find new expression in dreary superstitions.' The world of infantile monosyllabic spoken Chinese in Cook's account is not far removed from the Bushmen and Arapahos cited by Herbert Spencer (1882) whose primitively restricted language was so dependent upon being helped out with gestures that the speakers became virtually unintelligible to one another after dark.

Although it lingered on in some biblical commentaries, nineteenth-century academic philology for the most part simply abandoned the Noahic framework. It did not, however, so easily abandon the search for an original source for all language and culture inherent in the traditional scheme. Indeed, the precision offered by scientific philology and the frequent alliance between it and the rise of nationalism, study and celebration of national languages and folk traditions (the work of the Grimms and Lönnrot's *Kalevala* compilation are outstanding examples) produced more powerfully atavistic language myths than ever before. Linguistic paleontology is part of that search for origins and development which characterizes almost every field of nineteenth-century inquiry. It was basically an intralinguistic enterprise generating a virtually baseless pre-history for the Europeans.

In general, language came to be seen as the organizing focus of human development and as an entirely human phenomenon. In particular, Biblical Hebrew lost its privileged sacred position of primordiality and divine provenance. This rejection of a divinely authorized original and therefore perfect language complicated the preceding assumptions of degeneration before the impact of evolutionary thinking. There is not a simple or clear shift, for the differences between a fall from original perfection and development towards increased communicative subtlety and analytical power, are woven into a set of powerfully tendentious analogies between the biographical growth of individuals and the history of human groups or of humanity as a whole—the idea of the family being the crucial link between the two registers. Thus the families of languages into which the new comparative philology had reclassified the data, could be taken as if they were actual families or races and the children placed at various levels of age, intelligence, social standing, physical and mental health, granted always the superiority of the observer's own antecedents. Oriental civilizations, for instance, could be seen to have had a high even precocious classical period in the long distant past compared with their degenerate present, whilst European cultures (especially English, French and German ones) represented steady development into maturity. Other significant dualisms cross cut these basic schemes: monotheism versus polytheism; monogenetic versus polygenetic claims for human origins; historical diffusion (the origin of all the world's civilizations in the 'Fertile Crescent' was axiomatic in English schools until well into the 1950s) versus separate spontaneous development to account for apparently universal motifs in different mythologies. But the elision between concepts of language, race, and social class was so fateful because the new linguistic methods were so exact and fruitful.

The principles of comparative linguistics, their very rapid development and scale of achievement, were, for at least the first half of the twentieth century, far in advance of any other form of investigation into human origins and human variation. Comparison in language studies often came to be synonymous with an apparent 'ontological inequality' (Edward Said) of Occident and Orient, let alone sub-Saharan Africa or Australia. Later physical anthropology can perhaps be more striking in the crudity of its assumptions and methods of measurement but nowhere else was racism so close to the root of scientific subject matter as in comparative linguistics and philology. The two often most direct sources of European civilization,

Greek and Hebrew, are handled in different ways. The landscape of Greece remains with an abiding nostalgia of Classical times, whilst the present-day Greeks inhabiting this stable mystical landscape are seen as if puzzlingly transient, at best picturesque, figures. The Hebrew inheritance and its less picturesque setting could be both attested and rejected as a case of arrested development. The Semites, according to Renan, fully flowering in their first age, 'have never been able to attain full maturity.' There is nothing further for them to do, so 'let us remain Germans and Celts; let us keep our "eternal gospel," Christianity... only Christianity has a future.'

The classificatory terms change: 'Indo–European' (1813, Thomas Young); 'Indo–Germanic' in the 1830s with Bopp and others; 'Aryan' (1861, Müller). Claims for the original home of the Aryans shift as constantly as the location of Atlantis: Central Asia, the Hindu Kush, the Black Sea, between the North Sea and the Urals, south of the Baltic, even in one instance West Africa. The basic strategy, however, remains fairly constant: the reconstruction of an Indo–European *Ursprache* through which the location and civilization of its speakers prior to dispersal can be traced. Double counting of evidence spirals, and the reconstructed or invented civilization, are by turns expressed in the linguistic forms and folk-lore 'remnants,' 'vestiges' or 'survivals' from which they were deduced in the first place.

With or without assumptions of racial superiority, the fundamental characteristic of all these enterprises was the attempt to generate patterns of complex historical change from wholly linguistic models. Apart from the now easily recognized flaws, errors and prejudices involved, it may be that this fundamental strategy is a methodologically impossible one. In recent decades many of these old arguments have been rehearsed in debates over Georges Dumézil's work on the structure, myths and religion of Indo–European societies.

Many of the motifs touched on here in the interaction of myth and language still have their contemporary echoes on and beyond the margins of academic study. Debate continues as to whether the Davenport stele found in 1877 is, as Professor Fell of Harvard argues, an authentic trilingual text in Egyptian, Ibero–Punic, and Libyan languages or a fraud taken from a page of Webster's *Unabridged Dictionary* of 1872. Semitic hieroglyphs are found in a Peruvian jungle in 1989. The sexual origins of the alphabet are traced. The British represent a lost tribe of Israel (see *British Israelites*). Hebrew was a language invented by the Romans for political purposes. Hebrew is really Greek. What James Barr calls 'language superstition' and 'text superstition' deserve further study. Many such modern transpositions of mythical motifs have a considerable audience and a fascination which endures beyond the exposure of any particular instance.

See also: Alphabet: Religious Beliefs; Names: Religious Beliefs; Babel; Word of God; Hindu Views on Language; British Israelites; Buddhism and Language.

Bibliography

Feldman B, Richardson R D 1972 *The Rise of Modern Mythology 1680–1860*. Indiana University Press, Bloomington, IN

Griaule M 1965 *Conversations with Ogotemmêli: An Introduction to Dogon Religious Ideas*. Oxford University Press, Oxford

Haller W 1963 *The Elect Nation: The Meaning and Relevance of Foxe's 'Book of Martyrs'*. Harper and Row, New York

Poliakov L 1974 *The Aryan Myth, A History of Racist and Nationalist Ideas in Europe*. Chatto/Heinemann, London

Said E W 1978 *Orientalism*. Pantheon Books, New York

Names: Religious Beliefs

J. F. A. Sawyer

Belief in the power of names is documented in most cultures: to know people's names is to have power over them. In the story of the Garden of Eden at the beginning of the Bible, for example, Adam achieves dominion over the animals by giving them names (Genesis 2: 19), and in another biblical legend the deity refuses to reveal his name as this would be tantamount to putting himself under Jacob's control (Genesis 32: 24–32). In Chinese Taoist tradition the ultimate creative power, over which nothing can have control, is thus not named: 'the nameless was the beginning of heaven and earth' (see *Taoism*).

1. Naming

There is often a perceived connection between bearing a name and existing. The ancient Akkadian creation epic *Enuma elish*, for instance, begins with the words 'When the heavens were not yet named [i.e., created]...' There may thus be more involved in the naming of children than merely labeling them: it ensures their very existence as well as their identity. While Christian baptism may not always be associated with such crude beliefs about the importance of naming, it is connected with salvation, and the giving of 'Christian names,' frequently names associated with characters in the Bible (Adam, Deborah, Mary, Paul) or saints (Theresa, Francis, Denis, Margaret), must certainly be viewed in this light. The Council of Trent (1545–63) decreed that all baptized Catholics should be given the names of saints.

Changes of name are likewise often motivated by religious factors. Converts to a religion are given new names: the heavyweight boxer Cassius Clay, who took the name Muhammad Ali when he became a Muslim, must be one of the best-known examples. Again this is not merely a matter of changed identity, but part of a highly charged religious ritual in which a change of name symbolizes the convert's new relationship both to the people he or she is joining and to their God. A new name is likewise in many religions an integral part of becoming a monk or a nun.

There are dangers involved in having the wrong name or uttering a name at the wrong moment. According to ancient Jewish sources, for example, children's names were occasionally changed to deceive the angel of death. Among Native Americans and Australian aborigines there is a ban on uttering the names of the recently dead, and in some cases even on uttering everyday words that resemble them (see *Native American Religions, North*; *Australian Aboriginal Religions*). In some cultures, deliberately unpleasant or unappealing names are given to babies to make them less attractive to the evil spirits who might abduct them.

Many names have a religious or theological meaning. But the original meaning of such names, even such transparent ones as Spanish Catholic *Asunción* 'Assumption (of the Virgin Mary)' and *Corazón* '(Sacred) Heart,' or Hebrew *Michael* 'who is like God?,' is normally less significant than their association with traditional religious role models or their effectiveness as symbols of religious truth or affiliation.

According to the Confucian doctrine of the 'rectification of names' (*Cheng-ming*) there is a correspondence between names and things, which implies that if a person changed behavior in such a way that they could no longer be called by the name they assume (e.g., 'father,' 'ruler'), then they should not be permitted to employ the name with its associated tasks and responsibilities. This is in direct opposition to Taoist thought which takes all names as arbitrary and artificial (see *Confucianism*).

2. The Name of God

The name of a deity is believed to have special significance in many religious traditions. In ancient Judaism, the name of God (probably 'Yahweh') was believed to be so sacred that it could not be pronounced except by a priest, and then only once a year, on the Day of Atonement, when the High Priest emerged from the Temple at Jerusalem, surrounded by the smoke of incense, and uttered the Holy Name in the context of a blessing. In Jewish scripture only the four consonants of the name were written, sometimes (as in some of the Dead Sea Scrolls) in a special, archaic script different from the rest of the text, and the name, known for that reason as the 'Tetragrammaton' ('four letters'), read as *Ădōnāi* 'the Lord' or *Ĕlōhīm* 'God' or *hashēm* 'the Name.' One of the Ten Commandments forbids 'taking the Lord's name in vain,' and Jews and Christians use euphemisms to avoid the word 'God' as in *Heaven forbid*!, and Hebrew *bārūkh ha-shēm!* 'Blessed be the Name!,' which is roughly equivalent to 'Thank goodness!' In some Christian traditions, the name of 'Jesus' is surrounded by a similar taboo and avoided except in the context of the liturgy, where the pronunciation of the name is accompanied by a bow of the head, a tradition claiming Pauline authority (Philippians 2: 10). In West Africa, the Igbo similarly avoid the name of their god who is referred to as 'The one whose name is not spoken.' Similarly, the name for the mother of Jesus Christ, Mary, was long felt to be too sacred for general use as a Christian forename, and it did not become popular in Europe until about the twelfth century.

In Muslim tradition the first words of the Qur'ān, *Bismillah* 'In the name of God (the Merciful and Compassionate),' have a number of important functions, notably as an invocatory blessing before many acts such as eating or studying or writing a letter. They are also frequently used as a motif in Islamic calligraphy and on talismans and amulets of many kinds. Sufi mystics practice a liturgical ritual known as *dhikr* (literally 'remembering': cf. Qur'ān 33: 41), which involves repeating the 'Ninety Nine most beautiful names of Allah' over and over again. Sikhs also practice a meditation technique, known as '*nām japan*' or '*nām simaran*' 'repeating the divine Name,' and in Hinduism there is a bhakti ritual involving the repetition of the name of Krishna, and another known as '*nāma vali*' 'necklace of names.' In such cases, the Name of God is believed to embody his whole being and nature, and so to provide a path to salvation. Similar practices, termed '*nembutsu*' in Japanese and '*Nien-fo*' in Chinese, involving the ritual repetition of the Buddha's name, occur in Mahayana Buddhism.

Belief in the magical power of divine names is wide-spread. They were often written on amulets in the belief that they would frighten off evil spirits. Muslim amulets are often inscribed with one or more of the 99 names of God, while popular Christian examples are those with the monogram XP (the first two letters of the Greek for 'Christ'), and the Latin words *Pater Noster* 'our Father' written in the following intriguing cryptic form:

R	O	T	A	S
O	P	E	R	A
T	E	N	E	T
A	R	E	P	O
S	A	T	O	R

Jewish traditions about the life-giving power of the name of God include the legend of the Golem, an artificial human being created out of dust by the letters of the Tetragrammaton (see *Magic*), and the belief that resurrection could be assured by placing a scroll inscribed with the Tetragrammaton on the lips of the dead. There is also the bizarre legend of the martyrdom of Isaiah according to which the prophet, in a vain attempt to escape from his persecutors, dared to pronounce the forbidden name of God and was instantly swallowed up by a cedar tree, which they promptly sawed in half.

See also: Gematria; Magic.

Bibliography

Denny F M 1987 Names and naming. In: Eliade M (ed.) *Encyclopedia of Religion*. Macmillan, New York, vol. 10, pp. 300–7.

Eisenstein J D 1905 Names of God. In: *Jewish Encyclopedia*, vol. 9, pp. 160–65. Funk and Wagnall, New York

Levi-Strauss C 1966 *The Savage Mind*. Weidenfeld and Nicolson, London

Sawyer J F A 1999 *Sacred Languages and Sacred Texts*. Routledge, London, pp. 112–126

Naming

A. P. Cohen

The naming of individuals is a universal practice. However, the superficial truth of this assertion masks the diversity of naming conventions and the very different kinds of significance which naming has in different societies and cultures. Indeed, the single category 'naming' hardly seems adequate to encompass the variety of phenomena to which the English word 'name' is applied, and the disparate tasks it is required to perform: to signify respect; address and/or refer to someone; to denigrate, greet, or associate a person with his forebears (see Zabeeh 1968: 65).

1. What Does Naming Accomplish?

The difficulty, then, is not just that naming conventions vary among societies; but also, that the purposes served by naming and by different kinds of naming vary widely. In the UK, it is generally the case that the choice of a person's name is made by the parents who are unconstrained in their choice of name by anything other than their own preferences and, possibly, by family tradition. The name both serves a bureaucratic requirement as an official means of identification which will remain with the person throughout his/her life and will be used both as a term of reference and of address to that person. It may be complemented by a 'nickname'; but it can only be discarded or changed through a legal procedure which, though routine, is rarely used. The personal name—that is, the combination of forename and surname—is taken for granted, and would generally not be regarded as very meaningful. In some other societies, distinctions may be made between terms of address and of reference, and the use of the personal name as a mode of address is forbidden; a person's name may change at various points of the life-cycle; the name may be a miniature sociological index of the person's status and history; the name may be a *social* rather than a personal possession, and be so valued that it becomes the object of warfare between different groups of people (cf. Harrison 1990). At its most general, one may say, with Lévi-Strauss, that naming is a form of classification (1966); but, quite what it is that is thus classified cannot be the subject of useful generalization.

Like other classificatory devices, names are symbolic. As such, it is appropriate that they are commonly bestowed through the essentially symbolic medium of ritual, whether religious or secular (Alford 1987; 47ff), dramatic or anodyne (Charles 1951). So notwithstanding its routine character, naming is given special significance. Why should this be so? Anthropologists who have been schooled in Van Gennep's and Turner's analyses of *rites de passage*, and in the cross-cultural study of classification systems, may well be inclined to answer that the ritual of naming terminates the dangerously ambiguous condition of liminality—of being, in Turner's phrase, 'betwixt and between,' neither one thing nor the other: biologically, but not yet socially, constituted; a presence, but not yet a member. For Lévi-Strauss classification is a precondition of possession (1966). Following his logic, naming is required for a society to possess a person, that is, to make that person a member. It does not often confer *full* membership; that remains a task for future rites of initiation. Rather, it confers socialness (Alford 1987: 29), possibly in a way which signals some of the conventions of social organization. One aspect of this minimal socialness may be the propitiation of ancestors or spirits who are themselves integral elements of the society; or of a God, gods, or religious precepts which, similarly, are major referents of the society's identity.

The evidence for this kind of interpretation is very powerful. It suggests that the point of ritual naming is to confer socialness, rather than selfhood; that is to say, the performance of ritual which sacralizes the conferment of a *social* identity also minimizes the mystery of the self, either by concealing it, or by making the self in a social image, or both.

2. Cultural Practices in Naming

This dialectic of the individual as (a) socially constituted, and (b) self-conscious and self-directing lies behind most dilemmas of identity and their analysis in social science. It is manifest in many discussions of naming although a great and obvious lacuna in the literature on naming is work which deals substantially and descriptively with people's experience of being named and with the meanings they impute to their names as symbols or icons of themselves. Many writers have drawn attention to the light shed by conventions of naming upon the nature of the societies in which they occur. For example, there is ubiquitously the use of local ancestors' names to stress continuity and the primacy of affiliation to a descent group; or, conversely, of the parent's choice of an affinal forebear's name to express the importance of the child's *bi*lateral descent (Rossi 1965); there is the French requirement to use an officially approved saint's name, not to indicate allegiance to the saint nor even to the Church but, according to the sociolinguist Monique Léon, to France herself (Léon 1976). Segalen has shown that the practical importance of godparenthood in nineteenth-century Brittany was expressed in name-sharing (1980: 69). This 'spiritual' or 'mystical' bond which is held to inhere in name-sharing has been noted in such other widely dispersed instances as the *Saunik* system of Qiqiktamuit Inuit (Guemple 1965), and in the Hispanic *compadrazgo* tradition.

Anthropologists have looked extensively at the putative meanings of names: at whether these are descriptive, predictive, both, or are merely arbitrary. They have also raised the paradox that while the name is, in a sense, the individual's possession (although it is often the case that names are claimed as the property of a group), a hook for the individual's identity, it is usually bestowed by others and obligates the individual in its use (Zonabend 1980: 7, 15). Naming is coercive, and not just in its obviously extreme forms, such as that which obligates the Sarakatsani bride to adopt *every* element of her husband's name in place of her own (Campbell 1964). The confrontation between individual and society, alluded to above, is implicit in many of these issues, and sometimes raised explicitly.

In order to pursue this subject, the biases which are present in cultural practices with regard to the nature and function of names must be acknowledged. As suggested above, it seems that in the UK naming is regarded as unproblematic. People are given names and are required to use names. They may dislike them, they select among their forenames those they will use and discard the others, they may even take the legal step of inventing a new name. But they have to be consistent: normally, they do not change their names at will, they cannot require others to classify them in a different way, and they cannot reasonably claim not to know their names or those of their children.

By contrast, the anthropologist David Maybury-Lewis recalls the sheer consternation he caused by almost the first question he put as a nervous neophyte ethnographer to the headman of the Akwe-Xavánte village in which he had just arrived to do his fieldwork. Making polite conversation, he asked, 'What is your daughter's name?' (Tooker 1984). Frantic consultations ensued, prompted first, by the multiplicity of possible answers to the question; and, second, by its impolite nature. Work on other Amazonian peoples confirms that they too find such direct questioning about names unacceptable (e.g., Bamberger on the Kayapó (1974: 364); and Ramos on the Sanumá (1974: 172)). Names are not used universally as means of addressing people. In very many cultures, such address is avoided. Among the Muslim Kandayan of North-west Borneo, and the Nigerian Oru–Igbo, the impoliteness of addressing people by their given names is avoided by the use of 'greeting-names.' These may be descriptive, often slightingly so. For example, there is the freckled-faced Kandayan boy addressed as *silalat* (*tay-lalat*, excrement of flies) (Maxwell, in Tooker 1984: 35–36); and the less than assiduous Igbo man greeted as, 'he eats while the others farm' (Jell-Bahlsen 1989: 203). Or they may constitute a kind of formulaic word-game in which the greeting name elicits a congruent response, exchanges which, according to Jell-Bahlsen, serve to confirm a person's identity. For example, greeting name: 'if sickness kills somebody...'; answer '...it goes to the grave with the corpse' (ibid.: 204). Evans-Pritchard (1964) described the variety of greeting terms used by Nuer, of which the best known is the ox-name, after the person's favorite ox which, in the case of a male, would usually be the beast given to him on his initiation. Richard Antoun (1968) observes that the use of proper names as modes of address, rather than of reference, in the Jordanian village of Kufr al-Ma is deprecated since it ignores the several forms of address available as a means of indicating respect. Nuttall (1992) shows that Inuit of North-west Greenland insist on the use of kin terms rather than of personal names as means of address; both forms of appellation reflect the relationship between the speaker and the person spoken of/to, as is commonly the case elsewhere with pronouns.

There are other, perhaps less exotic circumstances in which formal names are not used. In two Scottish cases in the literature, the coincidence of given names, patronymic, and surname is so frequent in Lewis (Mewett 1982) and in East Sutherland (Dorian 1970) that other means are required to distinguish among individuals. Segalen (1980) finds a similar issue of homonymy in Bigouden-sud. Hence we find 'substitute naming systems' (Dorian 1970) or nick-names, 'by-names,' popular names or *surnorms*, perhaps referring to physical characteristics, place of birth or residence, personal idiosyncrasy or whatever. For similar reasons, in Barbados and Bermuda nicknames appear to be in widespread use among all but the elect and the elite, and are supplemented by the owner's car registration number, even in public announcements of marriage or death (Manning 1974). In many societies, these descriptive 'informal' names were formalized in due course into family names, as was the case among Kurdistani Jews on emigration (Sabar 1974) and for Mexican Indians in Zinacantan in a process linked to lineage segmentation (Collier and Bricker 1970).

To add to these complications is another, also ubiquitous, in which the name of the individual changes at various moments during his/her life. According to Needham, the Borneo Penan change and/or add names as their children are born or as significant kin die (1954, 1965, 1971). Writing about the Philippine Ilongot, Rosaldo argues that such name changes should be regarded as indicative of social relationships (in Tooker 1984). Through them the individual's identity is manipulated by his/her significant others, as in the Moroccan *nisbah*, the identity tag affixed to a person by others which refers to what *they* regard as the person's salient associations. For example, one may refer to a friend as 'The Glaswegian,' as if his provenance is all that is pertinent about him. As with Oru–Igbo greeting terms, Ilongot names often have the quality of play and teasing about them, the bestowing of names being tantamount to a process of initiation, and Rosaldo argues that such jousting is a fundamental means of constituting the person (p. 22). Yet again views of naming are seen as a means by which society attempts to make the self.

In similar theoretical vein, Brewer shows how the naming system of Bimanese islanders encodes information about individuals and their social relationships. All given names are modulated by 'common' and 'respect' forms, the use of which depends on the relative seniority of the person addressing and the person addressed. They also connote the primacy of kinship since, on becoming a parent, a person assumes a teknonym (the father/mother of...), referring to his/her eldest child. Of course this is not uncommon elsewhere. But the Bimanese go further: on becoming grandparents, people replace their teknonyms with 'paidonyms,' referring to the name of the first grandchild (Brewer 1981: 206). Lopes da Silva reports that after initiation, a Xavánte boy is given the name of his mother's brother; but since adult homonymy is proscribed, the uncle has simultaneously to divest himself of his old name and take a new one (1989: 384). For the Xavánte, names may be 'individual identifiers,' but they are also public and corporate property, intended for distribution rather than for private hoarding (ibid.: 336).

All of this is customarily explained as a means of imprinting society on the initiate's blank consciousness. Even when this is done through ostensibly supernatural devices, the ritual is nevertheless given *social* reference to the exclusion of the personal. Here are some examples. The Sanumá Indians, Brazilian hunter-gatherers, name their children after forest animals. An animal of the chosen species is ritually hunted and killed by the father after he has observed appropriate taboos (Ramos 1974). It is not a random choice, for the child will be invested with the spirit of the animal which will enter through its lumbar spine. However, this does not betoken an ideology of human–animal symbiosis, nor even a form of totemic belief. Grafted on to it through the ritual sequences of naming are practical and pragmatic statements of social balance: between kinship and affinity; between agnatic and nonagnatic kinship, statements which correct the biases of formal social organization. So the child who is supposedly named for an eponymous coccyx spirit is actually an ambulant depiction of the Sanumá ideal of social normality.

As a second example, Jewish naming in the pre-exilic biblical era strictly avoided the repetition of forebears' names, since not to do so would have traduced the uniqueness of the original holder and questioned 'the absolute identity of the person with the name' (Lauterbach 1970: 30). In *post*-exilic times, such repetition, referring to grandparents, became normal. In the post-Talmudic period, conventions changed again. Sephardic Jews established the practice which they still routinely follow of naming children after living relatives: Ashkenazim were more squeamish. Tormented by the suspicion that the spirits—not least among them the Angel of Death—were fallible, they assiduously avoided repeating the name of a living relative, for fear that the spirit might mistakenly take the wrong person (pp. 52–3). There is also here an echo of the mystical belief which associates the name with the soul, so that to give the name of one person to another would cause the soul of the first to migrate, thus killing him or her. Rabbi Jacob Lauterbach found no theological rationale either in any of these practices nor in their transformations. They were circumstantial. It does not take much ingenuity to see why, historically, Jewish emphasis on the uniqueness of the individual might give way to stressing continuity—to the extent—that individuality becomes so masked that even the Angel of Death can be misled.

A final example is one of the most noted in the literature, Goodenough's famous comparison of naming in two Oceanic societies, Truk (in the Caroline Islands) and Lakalai (on the north coast of New Britain). On Truk, personal names rather than kin terms are used as modes of address, and there is virtually no duplication of personal names among the 793 inhabitants. On Lakalai, by contrast, almost everyone shares one or more names with others; the use of teknonyms and kin terms is common, and names do not even discriminate gender. Naming is strictly regulated and codified.

So, while Truk naming clearly emphasizes individuality Lakalai naming stresses the social order (p. 271). The apparently obvious inferences to be drawn about the relative rights to individuality in each society would, however, be quite wrong. Truk social organization is firmly based on matrilineal descent groups whose lineage elders exercise near-absolute authority over the decisions of their juniors and sustain the primacy of solidarity within the lineage, even to the extent of obliging a woman to take her brother's side in any dispute he might have with her husband. Lineage ideology and authority thus frustrates a desire for individuality (p. 272). According to Goodenough, one of the more prosaic ways in which Truk islanders relieve their frustration is in naming. Individuality exists, quite literally, in nothing more than name (p. 273).

Lakalai presents the obverse case. Public values emphasize *individual* achievement; lineages have few corporate functions; and leadership, like that of the Melanesian Big Man, is sustained tactically rather than based on seniority. While in Truk, personal virtue elicits nothing, in Lakalai it is everything. The Lakalai are rugged individualists, and their apparently contradictory naming conventions are to be understood as 'continual reminders that people are, after all, part of a social order' (p. 274).

3. Naming and Identity

Goodenough concludes that names communicate ideas of the self and of self–other relationships (p. 275). His account reveals with the greatest clarity the conventional *modus operandi* in the anthropology of naming and, more generally, of identity: the assumption of an isomorphism between the logic of a particular anthropological interpretation, and the ways in which the persons thus named made sense of and supplied meaning to their selfhood and their experience of being named. If naming is a means of claiming possession, then the study of naming has tended to be an instance of the possessive ways in which people have constructed cultures in the images of their own intellectual consciousness, and then derived selves from them.

Names are applied *to* persons; they are social identifiers. They do not necessarily form part of the person's self-concept, and thus should not be confused *with* the person. There is therefore raised the intriguing philosophical question of the nature of the relationship between a person and her/his name. The person is not knowable without a name (and a 'name' here has to be understood as any conventional identifier—even as a number); and yet, the name is not intrinsic to the person. The confusion is frequently made in colloquial English usage. For example, instead of asking, 'What is your name?' one may ask, 'Who are you?' and expect the same kind of answer. The widely varying cultural conventions of naming sketched above clearly reveal that the assumption that 'I am my name' is ethnocentric and/or the consequence of linguistic imprecision.

See also: Names, Religious Beliefs; Magic.

Bibliography

Alford R A 1987 *Naming and Identity: A Cross-cultural Study of Personal Naming Practices*. HRAF Press, New Haven, CT

Antoun R 1968 On the significance of names in an Arab village. *Ethnology* **7**: 158–70

Bamberger J 1974 Naming and the transmission of status in a central Brazilian society. *Ethnology* **13**: 368–78

Brewer J D 1981 Bimanese personal names: meaning and use. *Ethnology* **20**: 203–21

Campbell J K 1964 *Honour, Family and Patronage*. Oxford University Press, Oxford

Charles L H 1951 Drama in first-naming ceremonies. *Journal of American Folklore* **64**: 11–65

Collier G A, Bricker V R 1970 Nicknames and social structure in Zincantan. *American Anthropologist* **72**: 289–302

Dorian N C 1970 A substitute name system in the Scottish Highlands. *American Anthropologist* **72**: 303–19
Evans-Pritchard E E 1964 Nuer modes of address. In: Hymes D (ed.) *Language in Culture and Society: A Reader in Linguistics and Anthropology*. Harper and Row, New York
Goodenough W H 1965 Personal names and modes of address in two Oceanic societies. In: Spiro M E (ed.) *Context and Meaning in Cultural Anthropology*. Free Press, New York
Guemple D L 1965 Saunik name sharing as a factor governing Eskimo kinship terms. *Ethnology* **4**: 323–35
Harrison S J 1990 *Stealing People's Names: History and Politics in a Sepik River Cosmology*. Cambridge Univeristy Press, Cambridge
Jell-Bahlsen S 1988 Names and naming: instances from the Oru–Igbo. *Dialectical Anthropology* **13(2)**: 199–207
Lauterbach J R 1970 The naming of children in Jewish folkore, ritual and practice. In: Bamberger B J (ed.) *Studies in Jewish Law, Custom and Folkore*. KTAV Publishing House Inc., New York
Léon M 1976 Of names and first names in a small rural community: linguistic and sociological approaches. *Semiotica* **17(3)**: 211–31
Lévi-Strauss C 1966 *The Savage Mind*. Weidenfeld and Nicolson, London
Lopes Da Silva A 1989 Social practice and ontology in Akwe–Xavánte naming and myth. *Ethnology* **28(4)**: 331–41
Manning F G 1974 Nicknames and numberplates in the British West Indies. *Journal of American Folkore* **87(2)**: 123–32
Mewett P G 1982 Exiles, nicknames, social identities and the production of local consciousness in a Lewis crofting community. In: Cohen A P (ed.) *Belonging: Identity and Social Organisation in British Rural Cultures*. Manchester University Press, Manchester
Needham R 1954 The system of teknonyms and death-names among the Penan. *South-western Journal of Anthropology* **10**: 416–31
Needham R 1965 Death-names and solidarity in Penan society. *Bijdragen Tot de Taal-, Land- en Volkenkunde*. **121**: 58–76
Needham R 1971 Penan friendship names. In: Beidelman T (ed.) *The Translation of Culture*. Tavistock, London
Nuttall M 1992 *Artic Homeland: Kinship, Community and Development in North-west Greenland*. Belhaven Press, London
Ramos A R 1974 How the Sanumá acquire their names. *Ethnology* **13(2)**: 171–85
Rossi A S 1965 Naming children in middle-class families. *American Sociological Review* **30**: 499–513
Sabar Y 1974 First names, nicknames and family names among the Jews of Kurdistan. *Jewish Quarterly Review* **65(1)**: 43–53
Segalen M 1980 Le nom caché. *L'Homme* **20(4)**: 63–76
Tooker E (ed.) 1984 *Naming Systems: The 1980 Proceedings of the American Ethnological Society*. American Ethnological Society, Washington, DC
Zabeeh F 1968 *What is in a Name? An Enquiry into the Semantics and Pragmatics of Proper Names*. Martinus Nijhoff, The Hague
Zonabend F 1980 Le nom de personne. *L'Homme* **20(4)**: 7–23

Postmodernism

G. Hyman

No contemporary study of either language or religion can be undertaken without some understanding of the influence and impact of postmodernism. That being said, however, the importance of postmodernism can by no means be restricted to either the linguistic or the religious. It has been variously and extensively analysed as a cultural phenomenon, a mode of thought, a philosophical 'sensibility', a style of art and architecture, an economic logic and a genre of literature, as well as approach to language and to theology. There is, however, no postmodern 'essence' that is common to all of these various instances of its manifestation. Consequently, an encyclopedic account or simple 'definition' of postmodernism are precluded. In this article, therefore, I shall address the question of the meaning and implications of postmodernism for language and religion.

1. Postmodernism and Modernity

As the very term suggests, postmodernism is parasitically dependent upon modernity for its definition. In which case, it is clear that in order to understand postmodernism, one must have some understanding of what is meant by modernity. Definitions and characterizations of modernity vary, but it is often said that modernity seeks 'presence' and in its pursuit of this desire, it seeks clarity, precision, certainty, and totality. At the same time, it excludes that which is not conducive to this pursuit. Thus, Stephen Toulmin has argued that the advent of modernity is marked by a repression of the literary and the humanistic in favor of the philosophic and scientific. Linguistic forms pertaining to the literary and humanistic, such as poetry, fiction, rhetoric, and narrative are downgraded. In their place, scientific, logical, and representational languages are in the ascendancy. Science and reason thereby become the arbiters of truth, and language is said to be true in so far as it accurately 'represents' reality.

It is obvious that such a modernist sensibility is hardly conducive to theological thought. Theological language is, for the most part, constituted by the very poetry, fiction, and narrative that modernity seeks to exclude. Furthermore, orthodox theologians, most notably St Thomas Aquinas, had always emphasized that language can never 'represent' God univocally. The most that we can expect is to attain some limited understanding of God indirectly through the use of analogy. It may be said, therefore, that the advent of modernity sounded the death knell for theology. Although Descartes, Locke and Kant attempted to provide a space for God within their rationalist, empiricist, and transcendentalist frameworks, these efforts gave rise to contradictions and inconsistencies that could be resolved only by dispensing with God altogether. Indeed, Hume did precisely that, and was later followed in this move by Marx, Durkheim, Freud, and especially Nietzsche.

2. Nietzsche and his Legacy

Nietzsche's relationship to both modernity and postmodernism is highly ambivalent. On the one hand, he appears to embody the apotheosis of modernity, with his open hostility to Christianity and his explicit declaration that 'God is dead.' On the other hand, however, he also appears to subvert the very modernist sensibility that he initially seems to embody. He sets himself against the normative status of reason and science and jettisons the modernist conception of truth as representation. He declares that truth itself is a fiction, and that so-called facts should be seen as 'interpretations.' His writings themselves embody the genres of language that modernity sought to repress—aphorisms, rhetoric, narrative. In these ways, therefore, it may be said that Nietzsche was bringing to light modernity's 'other;' his writings may be regarded as a performative enactment of that which modernity sought to exclude. He thereby called modernity's pretensions into question, particularly its obsessions with absoluteness, mastery, and certainty. Ironically, however, Nietzsche's narrativist turn also prepared the way for the return of that most narrativist of all languages—theology. After modernity, the modern prohibition of religion, founded as it was on the tyranny of secular reason, is overcome. If religion was one of the things that modernity excluded, then postmodernism provides a space within which religion can return. Nietzsche, the 'death of God' philosopher and self-styled 'anti-Christ' finds himself the unwitting friend of that which he most despised.

3. Theological Responses

Theology has recognized that postmodernism provides much more fertile ground within which it can flourish than did modernity, and has responded in a multiplicity of ways. Of these various responses, however, two in particular stand out.

The first is that of Mark C. Taylor, who was one of the first theologians to confront the implications of postmodern thought. In 1984, he published what has become a landmark book, *Erring: A Postmodern A/Theology*, in which he argued that theology must confront and respond to four particular challenges presented by postmodern thought. These are the death of God, the disappearance of the self, the end of history and the closure of the book. For Taylor, the 'death of God' does not constitute an atheistic confession (hence the neologism a/theology), but is rather a metonym for the eradication of a whole mode of thought. A/theology must now proceed without foundations, without a secure anchor, without a transcendental signified. In effect, this means the end of the traditional enterprise of theology. In his most recent work, he has insisted that 'religion is most interesting where it is least obvious.' He elucidates the various ways in which religious language, themes, tropes, and images, which usually go undetected, actually saturate ostensibly 'secular' culture. He finds religious language to be 'hiding' in art, literature, science, economics and technology. He thus illustrates the more and less distorted ways in which religion 'returns' in postmodern culture.

The second response is that of John Milbank, for whom Taylor's a/theology is itself a religiously disguised species of nihilism. Milbank argues that the end of modernity means the end of a universal rational truth and the coming of nihilism, which now constitutes the most severe threat to Christianity. Milbank accepts the postmodern primacy of the linguistic genre of narrative, and insists that Christianity can only overcome nihilism by 'out-narrating' it, by showing that it tells a 'much better story,' that it is a story of peace, harmony and love, rather than a story of violence and arbitrary conflict. The Christian 'story' that Milbank promotes is specifically a patristic and medieval form of Christianity prior to the corrupting distortions inflicted upon it by modernity. Postmodernism (understood as the 'end of modernity') allows one to make a 'half-turn' back to the pre-modern. This is not a simple restoration of the pre-modern (which would be as impossible as it is undesirable), but a re-reading of the pre-modern theological texts in the context of contemporary culture. For Milbank, therefore, postmodernism opens the space for a recuperation of a theological orthodoxy which, because it is so rooted, can radically challenge contemporary secular culture. Thus it is that this form of postmodern theology has come to be known as 'radical orthodoxy.'

It is illustrative of the heterogeneity of postmodernism that it should give rise to two such contrasting and, indeed, antithetical theological responses. Both Taylor and Milbank agree that postmodernism entails a linguistic turn that has fundamental implications for the place of religion and/or theology in contemporary society. But whereas for Taylor, this linguistic turn arrives as a consequence of the 'death of God,' Milbank argues that such 'linguisticality' was already promoted within theology itself, and particularly by the doctrine of the Trinity. It was Trinitarian doctrine, he claims, that had already called into question the modernist, prior and 'substantial' God, whom Nietzsche declared to be dead. Through the work of Taylor and Milbank, therefore, one can see how postmodernism gives rise to both the 'end' and the 'return' of theology. Always at hand without ever being 'present,' postmodernism opens a space within which theological language is as impossible as it is unavoidable.

See also: Analogy; Barthes, R.; Bataille, G.; Christian Views on Language; Derrida, J.; Feminism; Foucault, M.; Heidegger, M.; Irigaray, L.; Kristeva, J.; Lacan, J.; Levinas, E.; Metaphor; Mysticism; New Religious Movements; Performative Utterances; Wittgenstein, L.

Bibliography

Anderson P 1998 *The Origins of Postmodernity*. Verso, London

Griffin D R 1989 *Varieties of Postmodern Theology*. State University of New York Press, Albany

Hyman G 2001 *The Predicament of Postmodern Theology: Radical Orthodoxy or Nihilist Textualism?* Westminster/John Knox Press, Louisville

Milbank J 1990 *Theology and Social Theory: Beyond Secular Reason*. Blackwell, Oxford

Milbank J 1997 *The Word Made Strange: Theology, Language, Culture*. Blackwell, Oxford

Taylor M C 1984 *Erring: A Postmodern A/Theology*. University of Chicago Press, Chicago

Taylor M C 1999 *About Religion: Economies of Faith in Virtual Culture*. University of Chicago Press, Chicago

Toulmin S 1990 *Cosmopolis: The Hidden Agenda of Modernity*. University of Chicago Press, Chicago

Ritual

F. Staal

There is no generally agreed definition or concept of 'ritual.' In this article, data from Vedic ritual will be used to characterize a concept of ritual in terms that display similarities and dissimilarities between ritual and language and between the science of ritual and linguistics.

Both ritual and language are rule-governed activities that may be characterized in terms of the rules that govern their use and that are made explicit in their description and analysis. In ritual, these rules have rarely been studied, but in language, they fall within several domains that provide the methodology adopted here in order to find out where ritual belongs.

If a distinction is made between phonology, syntax, semantics, and pragmatics, it should be observed first that there is no clearly demarcated domain in ritual that corresponds to phonology, not because there could not be such a domain but because it is not clearly demarcated since ritual activities (which include, for example, starting a fire, killing an animal, crossing a bridge, producing sound, meditating silently, sprinkling, bathing, lifting one or both hands) range over almost the entire realm of human activities and have not, so far, been the subject of a generally accepted scientific treatment.

Adopting a logical terminology, the three remaining linguistic domains are defined roughly as follows: syntax is concerned with the relations between linguistic expressions, semantics with the relations between those expressions and meanings, and pragmatics with the relations between expressions, meanings, and users or contexts of use. If in these definitions 'linguistic expressions' are replaced by 'ritual activities' then it will be possible to explore to what extent there are corresponding ritual domains, which may be referred to provisionally as 'ritual syntax,' 'ritual semantics,' and 'ritual pragmatics.'

1. Ritual Syntax

Vedic rituals constitute a hierarchy of many levels in which, for example, D (*darśapûrṇamāsa*, 'full and new moon ceremonies') occupies a lower rank than P (*paśubandha*, 'animal sacrifice'). Thus, D may be embedded in P, but P cannot be embedded in D. The embedding mechanisms involve rules that are recursive, a feature discovered by the ancient Indian grammarians who also noted that the recursiveness of ritual is similar to the recursiveness of grammar.

Rituals consist of sequences of smaller units, namely 'rites.' If rituals are referred to by capital letters and rites by small letters, rituals may be defined by phrase structure rules where sequential order is expressed by concatenation, e.g.:

$$D \rightarrow d_1 \cdots d_m$$

If D is embedded in P, the rites of D will occur, generally in the same sequence, between the rites of P, e.g., as follows:

$$p_1 \cdots p_j d_1 \cdots d_m p_{j+1} \cdots p_n,$$

where $1 \leqslant j < n$. In general, in such an embedding, at least one of the rites that are embedded will be modified. For example, D involves a recitation of 15 *samidheni* ('kindling') verses, but when D is embedded in P, 17 such verses are recited. Assuming that the rite with 15 verses is $d_k (1 \leqslant k \leqslant m)$ and the rite with 17 verses is d_k^*, a rule can be postulated that operates within the described context, that is, a transformational rule between the trees shown in Fig. 1. In whatever way these regularities are described—here they are described by transformations, Chomsky has since used 'binding theory,' and others have used other mechanisms—it is clear that these structures in ritual syntax and in the syntax of natural languages are the same.

The same cannot be said for self-embedding structures that are generated by rules of the type:

$$A \rightarrow BAB$$

which lead by repeated application to structures such as:

$$\cdots BBBBBABBBBB \cdots$$

that are common in ritual but rare to nonexistent in language. For example, each layer of the brick altar of the Agnicayana ritual is laid down after an Upasad rite is performed, and another Upasad rite is performed immediately afterwards; the initial Upasad is preceded by the Pravargya rite, and the final Upasad is followed by another performance of the Pravargya. Similarly, at the beginning and end of each consecration of such a layer, the Adhvaryu recites the same mantras. Again, the well-known Aśvamedha horse sacrifice is preceded and followed by the Odana rite of preparing a rice stew. These structures exhibit self-embedding because when such sequences consist of more than one step they occur in the opposite order at the beginning and at the end.

From these examples of transformational rules (with their implied phrase structure rules) and self-embedding rules it may be concluded that ritual syntax is in some respects similar and in others dissimilar to the syntax of language.

2. Ritual Semantics

Neither rituals nor rites refer to meanings in the manner in which linguistic expressions refer to meanings or in any other systematic manner. Philosophers or theologians (rather than ritualists) frequently provide rituals with interpretations which may be regarded as 'meanings' although many of them are obvious rationalizations. In India and in Asia generally, these interpretations change constantly whereas the rituals remain the same. Thus fire rites which originally were part of the Vedic ritual have been incorporated in Hindu and Buddhist rituals and provided with interpretations that have nothing to do with whatever interpretations, if any, were assigned to them originally. Moreover, there is no function that assigns meanings to rituals on the basis of the alleged meanings of their constituent rites.

In general, Indologists (e.g., Louis Renou) have observed that there are no close connections between mythology and ritual in Vedic religion, Hinduism or Tantrism, and anthropologists (e.g., A. van Gennep) have noted that such rites as sprinkling may indicate fecundity, repulsion, or something else. Since semantic rules, which are an essential part of language, do

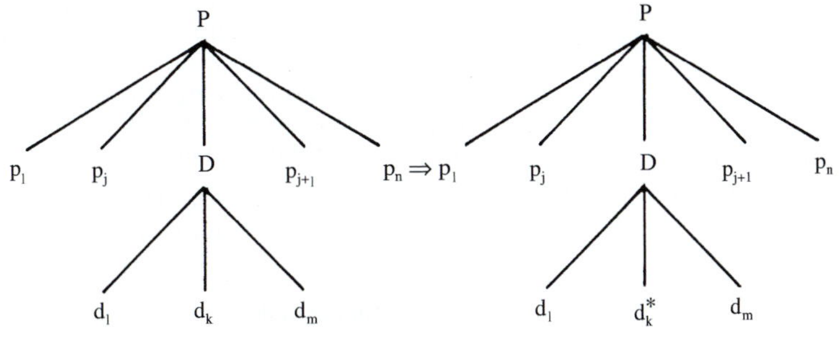

Figure 1.

not occur in ritual, ritual has no semantics and should not be referred to, even in metaphorical terms, as a language or be conceived of in linguistic terms.

3. Ritual Pragmatics

Austin (1962: 14–15) formulated conditions for the felicity of performatives which may be regarded as falling within pragmatics. The use of rites, and especially of mantras, is governed by similar conditions: they can only be used by the appropriate person and at the appropriate time and place; they have to be executed correctly; and mantras have to be recited with the correct degree of loudness, at the correct pitch, and at the correct pace. Most of these conditions are more extensive and more stringent than anything that applies to the normal use of a natural language such as English or Sanskrit.

4. Mantras

Rites are often accompanied by mantras, that is, ritual chants or recitations. According to the Indian science of ritual, there is a one-to-one correspondence between rites and mantras (e.g., *ekamantrāṇi karmāṇi* 'each act is accompanied by one mantra': *Āpastamba Śrauta Sūtra* 24.1.38). The properties of ritual syntax are therefore also properties of the syntax of mantras which are similarly, like the rites to which they are attached, devoid of meaning. This was recognized by the ancient Indian ritualist Kautsa: *anarthakā mantrāḥ* 'mantras are without meaning.'

Mantras possess other syntactic properties that are not found in language. For example, they abound in three-, four-, or fivefold repetitions that may be recursively combined, as, for example, in:

$$A^3(BC^5)^3A^3$$

where X^3 means: X X X. Such structures are closer, in form and function, to musical structures or configurations found in bird songs than to anything found in the syntax of natural languages.

When linguistic utterances containing mantras are translated from one language into another, the mantras are not translated but quoted: they do not change although they may be adapted (like geographical names) to the phonology of the receiving language. Like rituals and individual rites, mantras remain invariant over long stretches of time and space, even when crossing linguistic, social, geographical, cultural, or religious boundaries—traveling, for example, from India to East and Southeast Asia as far as Japan or Bali. Rites and mantras are accordingly attributed to an *Urzeit*:

yajñena yajñam ayajanta devās
tāni dharmāṇi prathamāny āsan

'with ritual the gods performed ritual;
these were the first ordinances' *(Ṛgveda 1.164.50)*

and mantras assigned to a primordial realm beyond language:

yato vāco nivartante
aprāpya manasā saha

'from which words return,
beyond the reach of mind' *(Taittirīya Upaniṣad 8.4.1)*

Mantras are always archaic. The most celebrated Indian mantra, *om*, typifies what Jakobson called 'the most natural order of sound production,' an opening of the mouth followed by its closure.

Since ritualization and mantra-like sound production are common among animal species, these and other facts combine to suggest that, in the course of evolution, language developed from ritual through the intermediary of mantras. Language originated when meanings were attached to mantras, which must have happened by chance, perhaps playfully. It was selected because of its almost miraculous power to communicate and deal with the world. That the syntax of natural languages came from ritual before there was any semantics explains, amongst other things, why syntax is, from the semantic point of view, so illogical, inefficient, and roundabout. This independence from semantics accounts likewise for the need to go beyond 'natural' language and construct the rational but artificial languages of mathematics, logic, computers, and whatever else the future may have in store.

Ritual and mantras are found among many animals but religion, like language, is confined to humans. That ritual and mantras came to be connected with religion is due to the latter's intrinsic nature. For religion is not merely archaic, it is also characterized by an urge to find meaning which is an extrapolation from the systematic reference to meanings that characterizes language. After language had begun to attach meanings to mantras and then to words, sentences and other linguistic utterances that linguists and philosophers are still in the process of dissecting, religion went on to make sense of trees, animals, and mountains, then ritual, the universe, and man himself. More truly human than the attribution of life to everything that is referred to as 'animism,' this impulse to make sense must also have come into being by chance. It was selected because it was so reassuring, probably at a point in time not very long after the origin of language, on all counts the most bewildering event in the development of the human animal.

See also: Mantra; Hinduism; Australian Aboriginal Religions; Performative Utterances; Shamanism.

Bibliography

Austin JL 1962 *How to do Things with Words*. Oxford University Press, Oxford

Gennep A van 1911 De la méthode à suivre dans l'étude des rites et des mythes. *Revue de l' Université de Bruxelles*, pp. 502–23

Renou L 1953 *Religions of Ancient India.* Athlone Press, London

Staal F 1985 Mantras and bird songs. *Journal of the American Oriental Society* **105**: 549–58

Staal F 1989 (Paper back 1993) *Rules without Meaning: Ritual, Mantras and the Human Sciences.* Peter Lang, New York

Romanticism

P. Fletcher

The term 'Romanticism' has come to signify an epoch that incorporated a variety of expressionist movements—principally in Germany, England, and France—which reacted to the arid, purely conceptual temper of the Enlightenment: Beethoven and Chopin's transformation of the very texture of music; Blake and Goethe's redefinition of the poem and the novel; Friedrich Schlegel and La Rochefoucauld's redemption and reconstitution of the fragment, to name but a few. While there is a notable commonality in the diverse projects of these major figures, the range of aesthetic, philosophical, and theological creations of the European Romantics warns against any easy assimilation of a complex set of movements and characters into a single 'movement.' Nevertheless, the emphasis on creativity, spontaneity, and sentiment is most certainly warranted. From Romantic philosophy to musical composition, and especially in religious and theological writings, language is treated as expansive rather than mimetic: the word is centrifugal in its movement of the individual and social imagination rather than a diminished mirror of nature to be utilized in logical propositions and inferences.

The expressive fecundity of language (and not simply its utility) in Romanticism is evident from the start of the careers of the so-called 'early' or Jena Romantics. This fertile and precocious group, that included the brothers Schlegel (see *Schlegel, F.* and *Schlegel, A. W.*), Friedrich Schleiermacher and Novalis, was the architect of many genres, themes and tropes that became central to Romanticsm in its wider contexts. In the main, it was the short-lived but revolutionary journal, the *Athenaeum*, which served as the organ of dissemination for their ideas. Put simply, they suggested that language mediates—indeed, incarnates—given truths and so the work of art is a way of realizing the Divine in the immediacy of experience. On this basis, Friedrich Schlegel boasts, in a fragment that attempts to define Romantic poetry, that 'It can be exhausted by no theory and only a divinatory criticism would dare try to characterize its ideal.' Romantic poetry alone is free and above all laws because it carries and transmits the infinite.

The groundwork for such an aesthetic revolution was provided by J. G. Hamann who, in his attack on the pretensions of Enlightenment rationality, stressed the priority of the sensual over the conceptual in any apprehension of knowledge. Yet Hamann's originality arises in his contention that it is in language (rather than a strict empiricism) where this bodily epistemology is to be examined and understood. This linguistic viscerality, in turn, has been impregnated by the divine Word. The seed will come to fruition through the imagination of the one who allows the spirit in the letter to live.

One of the surprising factors in the development of European Romanticism is the lack of systematic and critical exchange between leading figures of different nationalities. In France, for example, F.-R. Vicomte de Chateaubriand constructed in his *Génie du Christianisme* a project that was not dissimilar to the retrieval of religious discourse undertaken by Schleiermacher in Germany. Yet there is little evidence that Chateaubriand read his German neighbor, let alone was influenced by him. Where French Romanticism converges with Schleiermacher is in the need to construe the sacred in terms that might be acceptable to a skeptical audience, for whom religion is related to superstition and irrationality. In France, however, the adversarial public was not made up of enlightened and cultured 'despisers' but a post-Revolutionary audience who saw religion as unacceptably conservative. Where Chateaubriand differs from Schleiermacher is in his argument (at the beginning of *Génie*) that the creation of the world must be seen as the portrayal of the Divine imagination. Consequently, Christianity's beauty and excellence comes not from its procession from God. Rather it comes from God because it is excellent. Its excellence is revealed, contends Chateaubriand, in the aesthetic, imaginative and symbolic power of language in religion.

The status of language and its supernatural fecundity is primarily perceived in the medium of poetry and poetic diction in English Romanticism of the early nineteenth century. Without doubt, there is little of the rebellious—almost violent—enthusiasm of their continental cousins in the Romantic movement that was dominated by Coleridge, Blake, Byron and Wordsworth. Yet there is one striking similarity: the poetic imagination is the storehouse and progenitor of the power of the imagination. Thus Blake, in *Visions of the Last Judgement*, replying to the question, 'When the sun rises, do you not see a round disc of fire somewhat like a Guinea?' answers unequivocally, 'O no, no. I see an Innumerable company of the Heavenly host crying, "Holy, Holy, Holy is the Lord God Almighty".' The poet sees with the imaginative eye and the language of the poem creates a world of imagination that transcends the transient, mundane world of appearances and reveals, in its stead, the infinite realm of beauty and truth.

In many respects, the emphasis on the poetic and the (somewhat) gnomic aphorism or fragment in Romantic considerations of religious experience is dependent on a thorough-going Idealism in which the imagination of the aesthete reconstitutes and recreates the world in which we live. Intuition is given priority over reason in that the latter refuses to see the immanence of the ideal in the concrete medium of language. Thus, the transcendent, according to A. W. Schlegel, can become apparent 'only symbolically, in images and signs.' In many ways, this might stand as a suitable prēcis of the Romantic understanding of the transcendent status of language.

See also: Metaphor; Christian Views on Language.

Bibliography

Blake W 1966 *Complete Writings*. Keynes G (ed.) Oxford University Press, Oxford

Chateaubriand F-R de 1948 *Génie du Christianisme*. Flammarion, Paris. 2 vols

Schlegel F 1991 *Philosophical Fragments* [trans. P. Firchow]. Minnesota University Press, Minneapolis, MN

Schleiermacher F 1988 *On Religion: Speeches to its Cultured Despisers* [trans. R. Crouter]. Cambridge University Press, Cambridge

Berlin I 1999 *The Roots of Romanticism*. Chatto & Windus, London

Prickett S 1976 *Romanticism and Religion*. Cambridge University Press, Cambridge

Reardon B M G 1985 *Religion in the Age of Romanticism*. Cambridge University Press, Cambridge

Taboo, Religious

M. Douglas

In common usage a taboo word only means a solecism, a breach of etiquette. But this is quite remote from the meaning of taboo in religion. To understand the latter it must first be recognized that a word can have efficacy to change things. The idea of taboo is the other side of the idea of the magic spell, it is a word with power to affect events. In the case of magic, pronouncing the spell brings success; in the case of taboo, speaking the taboo word brings on disaster.

Religions recognize several kinds of words of power: oaths, curses, and blessings as well as spells. Curses and blessings in Christian doctrine depend on God to ensure their efficacy. An insulted father or elder, or a debtor or poor man treated unjustly, may utter a curse, and when misfortune later falls on the cursed one it is taken for granted that God made the words efficacious. Likewise for prophecy, the seer who foretells a good or bad event is enabled to look into the future by virtue of a divine calling: what he says is backed by God. The theistic background to these beliefs gives them an easy explanation: there is a watching, intelligent being who guarantees blessings and curses. Taboos and spells are different in that they work automatically, less like an expression of anger or promise and more like a handle, or a lever, or a keg of dynamite. Their efficacy lies in the action of reciting the spell or saying, or doing the tabooed thing. Taboo is different again from magic in that the magic rite or spell interrupts regular events. It is a way of deliberately engineering a change, while the taboo's effects are just as much part of the regular order of the universe as the effects of gravity or water.

The idea of sin in Christian terms is an offence against God, who may forgive it, or may be angry enough to punish it. In many religions sin is negatively efficacious: if God is offended, disaster will surely follow, but it is generally assumed that it follows because God will take action to see that it does. Taboo is different: as a belief in disaster which follows inevitably on a breach of specified rules; it works within the physical world like the belief that fire burns and water wets. There is no call for God's specific intervention each time: taboo works automatically because that is how the world is. In fact, it is often thought that God can do nothing to avert the consequences of a breach of taboo. Thought it has different nuances in each religion, its automatic action makes taboo into a word that is not specially connected with religious discourse. In the usage of anthropologists it has more to do with medicine and diet. Breach of taboo is invoked to explain bad health or other misfortune.

The surface structure of taboo involves two things, the infraction of a rule, witting or unwitting, and the certain punishment that will follow. This simple scheme depends on a third assumption, that the world was made to behave in this way and is sustained in its efficacy by God. The rules whose breach constitutes taboo are sometimes morally neutral, sometimes seem to be neutral but in fact have a burden of moral implication, and quite often have an important function for maintaining the community's customs. Thus three separate orders may be combined in the system of taboo, the natural order, the divine order, and the social order. However, for most of the religions which anthropologists study, such a division of life between three separate orders does not apply.

God made the people; He also made the rules by which they should deal with one another; and He made the rules of ritual for dealing with the cult: the word taboo articulates the interactions of persons in all these contexts. Some things are forbidden and disasters will ensue if they are said or done. Seen in this light taboo is not an irrational belief.

The world may be seen as controled, not by one God but by many spirits. Then each of them is likely to have a set of taboos which have to be observed. There may be so many spirits in the universe that it is beyond human capacity to know all the taboos that they have imposed. The spirits themselves may be under their own taboos which they have no choice but to observe. The taboos may be completely severed from moral purposes, serving only to demonstrate the power of capricious spiritual beings. It may be that only the members of a cult need to observe the taboos of the deity whom they worship, or it may be that each spirit's power extends unpredictably over everyone coming within its range. In that case, no one knows when they may have broken a taboo, only the misfortune will suggest that one has been broken, and a course of divination may be needed to find out how to cancel the ill effects.

In a secular culture, taboos that connect illness directly to immorality sound either like failure of scientific reasoning or an absurd attempt to use misfortune to coerce behavior. Why should anyone believe that incest produces skin disease, or adultery a perilous childbirth? Or that eating swine's flesh presages doom? Outsiders to the culture can see no connection. Ridicule used to be poured on beliefs associating death with breach of dietary taboos, as if they were based on primitive, mistaken nutritional science. Such interpretations fall beside the point when taboos is classed, as it should be, along with prophecy, curses, and blessings.

Just as it makes sense for a worshiper to believe in the real power of curses, sins, and blessings, so it makes sense for the worshiper to believe that God set up a human society and protected it by making real dangers attend on breach of His laws. Imagine a universe built as an abstract model of all approved moral values and religious meanings, fully sensitized to human behavior. In this responsive universe the whole conceivable range of good deeds and acts of respect and piety would automatically bring down blessings and all injustices, insults, and disregard for symbolic distinctions would bring down punishments. In some religions the automatic operation of taboo is expected to be intelligible if one has broken taboo unwittingly: one could and should have known the offense. In other religions there are so many taboos and their connection with social life is so tenuous that no one can be expected to look out for them in advance. Only when tripped by a misfortune, and after consulting a diviner, does the normal person discover that a taboo has been breached, for example, finding that one has unwittingly walked on a dog's grave, or touched a corpse.

See also: Names: Religious Beliefs; Magic; Blessings; Performative Utterances.

Bibliography

Douglas M 1996 *Purity and Danger: An Analysis of Concepts of Pollution and Taboo.* Routledge, London

Steiner F 1956 *Taboo.* Cohen and West

Turner V 1975 *Revelation and Divination in Ndembu Ritual.* Cornell University Press, Ithaca, NY

Valeri V 2000 *The Forest of Taboos, Morality, Hunting, and Identity Among the Huaulu of the Moluccas.* University of Wisconsin Press, Madison

Wagner R 1987 Taboo. In: Eliade M (ed.) *Encyclopedia of Religion*, vol. 14, pp. 233–36. Macmillan, New York

Taboo Words

M. L. Apte

The word 'taboo' (also spelled 'tabu') was introduced into English from Polynesian cultures where it played a significant part in the religious belief systems. The concept of taboo has been discussed in the writings of the anthropologists Frazer, Van Gennep, Wundt, Radcliffe-Brown and Mead. Freud has also discussed it extensively in his book *Totem and Taboo*. Steiner (1967) provides the full history of the origin of the word, its various cognates and their meanings in Polynesian languages, its significance and functions in the religious belief systems of Polynesian cultures, and its relevance to anthropological and psychoanalytic theories. Under the entry 'Tabu' in the *Encyclopedia of Social Sciences*, Margaret Mead (1937: 502–05) defined the concept as 'a negative sanction whose infringement results in an automatic penalty without human or super-human mediation.' According to her, one of the several meanings of the Polynesian concept of taboo is 'any prohibitions which carry no penalties beyond the anxiety and embarrassment arising from a breach of strongly entrenched custom' (quoted in Steiner 1967: 143).

1. Taboo Words Defined

The primary semantic attribute of the concept of taboo in English seems to be the same as the meaning by Mead quoted above. Prohibition or avoidance is socially determined and its breach results in anxiety, embarrassment, and public shame. This seems to be the primary aspect of the notion of linguistic taboo. Taboo words are those that are to be avoided because they are deemed unfit for normal linguistic usage and by community consensus are banned in everyday language in the public domain. In Webster's *Ninth New Collegiate Dictionary* (1990) the second meaning of taboo as an adjective is 'banned on grounds of morality or taste.' As a noun its secondary meaning is 'a prohibition imposed by social custom or as a protective measure' and as a verb 'to avoid or ban as taboo.'

Much of the discussion of taboo words in popular and scholarly literature has been based on the assumption that certain words are offending, dangerous, or sacred. Thus, underlying the avoidance of taboo words are cultural values and belief systems according to which attitudes are formed and judgments are made regarding the offending, dangerous, or sacred nature of certain words. Since there are cross-cultural variations in attitudes and belief systems, there are also differences concerning the semantic range and topical nature of taboo words. Despite such differences, it appears that in many societies words pertaining to objects, actions, and phenomena within the following domains are considered taboo.

In general, words referring to processes and states of human biological existence appear to be taboo because of their association with danger and their anxiety-provoking nature. Words referring to birth, death, pregnancy, various illnesses and diseases, menstruation, sexual and excretary activities, feces, urine, blood, and semen are considered taboo in many societies. Another taboo domain is that of deceased persons, animals considered to have special powers, ancestors, and benevolent and malevolent supernatural beings and their activities. In many cultures, referring to dead persons, sacred objects, and animals and deities is considered taboo except when done by those endowed with special powers in situations of ritual significance.

One underlying belief regarding taboo words is the magical power of the spoken word. It is as if uttering a taboo word may bring about the occurrence of the object, action, or phenomenon it refers to. Words that refer to supernatural beings are also taboo because they, too, can invoke dangerous phenomena beyond the control of human beings. Taboo words are to be avoided because they are powerful and cause unforeseen consequences. It needs to be noted that there are degrees of tabooness and some words are much more strongly tabooed than others.

Whatever the taboo words, all societies have ways of obliquely expressing their meanings using paraphrases, synonyms, euphemisms, and code words. These linguistic processes are universal. In English, for example, many speakers will use the expression 'to pass away' instead of 'to die,' or instead of saying that a woman is pregnant an expression such as 'she is carrying' is used. Use of code words is quite common. Some are phonetically similar to the taboo words, e.g., 'shoot' for 'shit' or 'fudge' for 'fuck' or they are phonetically similar nonsense syllables, e.g., 'frig' for 'fuck,' 'heck' for 'hell.' Occasionally, abbreviations are also used, e.g., 's.o.b.' for 'son of a bitch' (Saporta 1988–89: 164–65). In English language cartoons in the USA, the established convention to indicate a character's use of taboo words is to use punctuation and diacritical marks as well as other symbols commonly found on typewriter keys, e.g., '!?#%@.'

2. Other Related Concepts and Words

Terms such as 'swear words,' 'curse words,' 'obscene words,' 'four-letter words' and 'dirty words' are often used interchangeably with the expression 'taboo words' in popular and scholarly writings. Although avoidance or prohibition is the semantic attribute shared by all of them, the range of each is slightly different. Swear and/or curse words are those which invoke damnation, misfortune or degradation of the targeted person or object. Swearing and/or cursing reflect a speaker's wrath or frustration towards a person or an object. In English 'hell,' 'damn,' 'Jesus' and 'Christ' are commonly used curse words and 'damn it,' 'God damn it,' 'damn you' and 'go to hell' are frequently used swearing/cursing expressions. Swearing and cursing are thus ways of venting a strong emotion.

Defining the semantic range of obscene words is difficult because notions of obscenity vary across cultures, over a period of time within a culture, and from one person to another. It appears that words that refer to sexual organs and acts are obscene. Words referring to the same organs and activity in physicians' usage and in scientific writings, however, are not considered obscene. Words that refer to the various body elimination processes and excretary substances—'shit' is the most commonly used word—are also considered by many to be obscene though they are generally labeled 'scatological' in scholarly writing. The use of obscene and scatological words evokes disgust or repugnance in many listeners. In this respect obscenity is determined by the hearer of a linguistic utterance, in contrast to tabooness which is determined by the speaker. It is the hearer who is affected by obscene words while it is the speaker who decides which words are to be avoided because s/he considers them taboo. Not all taboo words are obscene from a speaker's point of view. Obscene words and phrases are also used for swearing and thus can belong to the category of swearing/cursing expressions. In English, a common swearing expression, for example, is 'fuck you.'

The expression 'four-letter words' is restricted because it is language specific. It is valid only for English in which many so-called obscene words, e.g., 'cock,' 'cunt,' 'fuck,' 'ball,' and 'shit' have only four letters in their spelling. It is quite possible that comparable words in other languages may also be spelled or written with four characters. No systematic comparative linguistic studies focusing on this issue exist.

The label 'dirty words' indicates a very personal and subjective attitude. For many individuals dirty words are those that refer to sexual organs and acts, body elimination processes such as defecation and urination, and excretary substances. In cultures where such acts are considered defiling and where an attitude of repugnance towards them exists, the mere use of such words arouses a strong reaction of disgust.

Whether or not a word used in speech belongs to any of the above categories depends on the sociocultural context. Generally, the use of taboo, obscene, swear/curse, four-letter, and dirty words is determined on the basis of whether the situation falls in the public or the private domain and whether the linguistic discourse is formal or informal. Words designated by any of the above labels are usually avoided in formal language in the public domain. The greater the aura of respectability in any social situation, the stricter the ban on using words that may be viewed as even mildly taboo. On the other hand, taboo words are likely to be used in social interactions among friends in a private domain where an informal speech style prevails. The use of slang among members of a close-knit group encourages the use of taboo words. According to popular belief persons in certain occupations such as the army, the navy, or construction work tend to use taboo words frequently. Their speech is considered 'colorful' by some.

3. Cross-cultural Differences in Attitudes Towards Taboo Words

The domain of taboo words varies cross-culturally. The inclusion of vocabulary items for particular phenomena, acts, objects, etc., in the taboo word category depends on sociocultural values and attitudes. It can be hypothesized that in societies where sexual and excretary acts are generally accepted as necessary and natural, and attitudes towards them are casual and/or relaxed, there is less likelihood that words referring to sexual and excretory organs and acts will be treated as taboo. On the other hand, in societies with attitudes of disgust or repugnance towards sexual and excretary organs and acts, there is greater likelihood that words referring to them will be considered taboo.

Even in individual cultures attitudes towards sexual and excretary acts are likely to change over a period of time so that words once considered taboo may be used in speech. In nineteenth-century England and America, the puritanical ethics of communities and society at large resulted in an almost total ban on using words that referred to sexual and excretary organs, acts, and bodily excretions. Until the 1960s, these words were not used in print in the USA. In their place only the first letter, an empty space, or dashes were used. Even with liberalized attitudes, in the USA and other English-speaking communities from the mid-1960s onward, sexual and scatological words do not routinely occur in newspapers and magazines though they are now used in fictional writing. In a mass medium such as television, taboo, obscene, and swear/curse words are still not used. If they occur in real-life interview situations, they are beeped out. In the published transcripts of the taped conversations between US president Richard Nixon and his White House associates, which were full of taboo and obscene words, the expression 'expletives deleted' was used rather than the verbatim conservations.

To a large extent the sociocultural context of speech and the backgrounds of the participants in social interaction determine the use of taboo words. Such factors as enculturation and socialization, age, gender, social status, degree of religiosity, and educational level influence the use of taboo words in speech. Children and adults in agricultural rural communities have many opportunities of observing animal sexual behavior. Children growing up in poor families who lack privacy because of limited living space have many occasions to observe adult sexual activities. In such an environment references to sexual and excretory organs and activities may be common and casual. No sense of disgust or repugnance may be associated with the use of taboo or obscene words. On the other hand, a rural community may be strongly religious and hence is likely to avoid using blasphemous and swear/curse words. Much depends upon the socialization and enculturation processes which determine an individual's attitude regarding the taboo quality of words. An individual brought up in a religious and orthodox household with puritanical values is likely to consider many more words taboo than one brought up in a nonreligious atmosphere which may treat body-waste elimination processes and sexual and procreation acts as natural, not shameful or repugnant. Therefore, even within a specific culture, words that may be shocking to one individual and/or a particular group of people may not necessarily be so to others of a different background.

In general it appears that women, old persons, educated individuals, urbanites, and elites are less likely to use taboo, obscene, and swear words in public domains than men, young people, uneducated persons, rural folks, and the proletariat. Cultural notions of modesty and politeness often constrain individuals, especially women, from using taboo words in the public domain. In many societies such language is not permitted in social settings where both men and women are present.

Although women generally abstain from using taboo words in the public domain, in some cultures old women beyond menopause are known to compete with men in freely using such words (Apte 1985: 79–80). Even those who normally avoid taboo words in their routine use of language are given to using them on special occasions such as specific festivals and rituals. There is ethnographic evidence which indicates that in many societies saturnalian celebrations create an atmosphere where the use of taboo words and lewd and lascivious behavior on the part of participants is quite common. Such occasions have been labeled 'Rites of Reversal' (Apte 1985: 152–53).

4. Functions of and Responses to Taboo Words

The use of taboo words is generally associated with strong emotions. Therefore, speakers use them to express strong feelings and listeners respond with equally strong feelings and reactions. Speakers who are aware of the potential of taboo words to arouse strong reactions may deliberately use them to shock their listeners. The use of taboo words gives an individual a feeling of momentary freedom from social conventions and constraints. Individuals may also use taboo words as a protest against what they consider antiquated values regarding speech because using these words will make their listeners uncomfortable. The use of taboo words in such a context can also be considered a form of verbal aggression since those who believe in avoiding such words in their speech will be forced to hear them. In a way, then, one function of taboo words is to degrade listeners, especially women who are much less likely to use them because of the ideas of modesty that dominate women's actions and speech in many cultures (Apte 1985: 74–75). For the same reason the use of taboo words is common in ethnic slurs since such words reflect the strong aggressive and hostile feelings a speaker may have towards certain ethnic groups. Their use is meant to insult and offend the targeted group.

In some contexts the use of taboo and obscene words may serve an opposite function, namely to show affection. Verbal encounters among close friends may be full of taboo and obscene words as terms of endearment (Bloomfield 1933: 155, 401; Cameron 1969: 101) and occasionally may even be accompanied by insults and horseplay, all of which is seen as joking. This usually results in loud laughter (Apte 1985: 259).

Individuals may use taboo words to express pent-up emotions such as anger or frustration. Persons who have occupations that are stressful also tend to use taboo words since using them relieves tension. Anthropologist W. W. Pilcher (1972) who studied a community of longshoremen in the city of Portland, Oregon, USA, observed that there was a high degree of taboo word use among these men when they were working on board the ship since such work was quite hazardous and stressful. Once they were off the ship and engaged in leisure activities, the use of taboo words declined significantly. The longshoremen were also very careful in totally avoiding swearing, obscenities, and the use of taboo words in family surroundings.

The repeated use of taboo words diminishes their tabooness since the prohibition on their use is the crucial attribute of such a designation. Individuals who use taboo words excessively in their speech may become insensitive of both the socially determined taboo nature of these words and the fact that such words are offensive to listeners. Individuals known for their excessive use of taboo words may be avoided by others who do not wish to be offended.

5. Taboo Words and Linguistic Differentiation and Change

Linguistic research has shown that in many societies the speech of men and women differs and that the degree of such difference can vary from one society to another. One explanation put forward for this is that the phenomenon of taboo causes these gender speech-differences since men in many linguistic communities use words in several contexts that woman never use. However, linguistic differences attributed to gender differences occur not only with regard to vocabulary, but also with regard to phonology, morphology, and syntax (Trudgill 1983: 78–99). The extensive research done on the topic of language and gender (see references in McConnell-Ginet 1988) since the mid-1970s reflects the complexity of the problem.

To what extent language change is due to the existence of taboo words has not been systematically investigated. It is common for speakers of a language to avoid not only taboo words but other phonetically similar words which consequently may fall out of use and become extinct. An explanation for the replacement of the old word 'coney' (pronounced [kʌni]) by the word 'rabbit' is that the former sounds very similar to a taboo word (Trudgill 1983: 31). No quantitative studies exist, however, to test such a hypothesis.

Bibliography

Apte M L 1985 *Humor and Laughter: An Anthropological Approach*. Cornell University Press, Ithaca, NY

Baudhuin E S 1973 Obscene language and evaluative response. *Psychological Reports* **32**: 399–402

Bloomfield L 1933 *Language*. George Allen and Unwin, London

Cameron P 1969 Frequency and kinds of words in various social settings or what the hell's going on? *Pacific Sociological Review* **12(2)**: 101–04

Eckler A R 1986–87 A taxonomy for taboo-word studies. *Maledicta* **9**: 201–03

Fleming M 1977 Analysis of a four-letter word. *Maledicta* **1, 2**: 173–84

Hartogs R, Fantel H 1967 *Four-letter Word Games: The Psychology of Obscenity*. M Evans and Co. Delacorte Press, New York

Jay T B 1977 Doing research with dirty words. *Maledicta* **1, 2**: 234–56

McConnel-Ginet S 1988 Language and gender. In: Newmeyer F J (ed.) *Linguistics: The Cambridge Survey IV, Language: The Socio-cultural Context*. Cambridge University Press, Cambridge

Mead M 1937 Tabu. In: Seligman E R A (ed.) *Encyclopaedia of Social Sciences*, vol 14. Macmillan, New York

Montagu A 1967 *The Anatomy of Swearing*. Macmillan, New York

Partridge E 1947 *Usage and Abusage: A Guide to Good English*. Hamish Hamilton, London

Pilcher W W 1972 *The Portland Longshoremen: A Dispersed Urban Community*. Holt, Rinehart and Winston, New York

Sagarin E 1962 *The Anatomy of Dirty Words*. Lyle Stuart, New York

Saporta S 1988–89 Linguistic taboos, code-words and women's use of sexist language. *Maledicta* **10**: 163–66

Steiner F 1967 *Taboo*. Penguin Books, Harmondsworth

Trudgill P 1983 *Sociolinguistics: An Introduction to Language and Society*. Penguin Books, Harmondsworth

Wentworth H, Flexner S B 1967 *Dictionary of American Slang*. Crowell, New York

Word of God

J. F. A. Sawyer

'The Word of God' or 'the Word' (Greek *ho logos*; Aramaic *memra*) is a theological term widely applied to means of communication, not all of them purely linguistic, between the divine and the human. At its simplest, it refers to the word of command by which a deity, like an all-powerful king, imposes his will on chaos and creates the world. The creative 'Word' in Islam, for example, is the divine imperative *kun* 'be!' (Qur'ān 2: 117; 6: 73; 36: 82). Like the Arabic *kun*, Biblical Hebrew *dĕbhar YHWH* 'the word of the Lord' is used in the context of other acts of divine intervention as well: thus 'He sent his word and healed them' (Psalm 107: 20; cf. Qur'ān 3: 47, 59). The utterances of the prophets are frequently introduced by the formula 'Hear the word of the Lord!' Occasionally the term denotes more than speech or words as in the statement 'the word which Isaiah the son of Amoz *saw* concerning Judah and Jerusalem' (Isaiah 2: 1). (For a discussion of Hindu theories of an original creative word (*śabda*), see *Hindu Views on Language*.)

The centrality of this notion leads in various religious traditions, especially Judaism and Christianity, to the personification of this divine 'Word.' In ancient Jewish literature, the Aramaic term *Memra* 'the Word (of God)' occurs in place of the divine name, sometimes where the predicate was considered to be in some way theologically inappropriate (e.g., 'the Memra repented ...' Genesis 6: 6), but also as a divine agent or mediator in his own right and distinct from God.

The introduction into Jewish tradition of the Greek term *logos* 'word, reason,' with its metaphysical meaning, given it by the Stoics, of divine wisdom immanent in the universe, paved the way for the 'Logos Christology' first described in St John's Gospel: *ho logos sarx egeneto* 'The Word became flesh' (John 1: 14). The unique identification of Christ as 'the Word incarnate' (preferred to 'Wisdom' perhaps because both Hebrew *ḥokhmā* and Greek *sophia* are feminine) concentrates the whole range of methods of divine–human communication in one person, and the precise doctrinal, liturgical, and ecclesiastical implications of this are still disputed. Jesus is described as *kalimat allah* 'the Word of God' in Muslim tradition as well, but this is explained by reference to his miraculous birth, rather than his divine nature (cf. Qur'ān 4: 171; 19: 35).

The term 'Word of God' is frequently also applied to sacred texts. Public readings from scripture are accompanied in many churches by the formula 'This is the Word of God' (see also *Bible*; *Granth*; *Qur'ān*; *Baha'ism*; *Mormon, Book of*). In Christian theology, especially, for reasons mentioned above, there has been much debate about the nature of Scripture. For those who believe that there is no other authority equal to the Bible, divine inspiration implies the verbal inerrancy of 'the Word of God' (identified on occasion with King James's Authorized Version). For others, on the analogy of the person of Christ, true God and true man, it is at the same time wholly divine (in terms of authority) and wholly human (in terms of authorship, verbal accuracy). More authority then rests with the Church, who must then, with the guidance of the Holy Spirit, seek to interpret it correctly. Similar divisions exist in Islam between those who believe that the Qur'ān is the uncreated 'word' or 'speech of God' (*kalam allah*) and therefore the only source of divine authority, and those who believe that human leaders, like the ayatollahs, have divine authority as well (see *Islam in the Near East*).

See also: Qur'ān; Christian Views on Language.

Bibliography

Brown R E 1966 *The Gospel according to John, 1–12*. Anchor Bible, Doubleday, Garden City, NY

Köhler K 1904 Memra. In: *Jewish Encyclopedia*, vol. 8, pp. 464–65. Funk and Wagnall, New York

McKim D K (ed.) 1983 *The Authoritative Word: Essays on the Nature of Scripture*. Eerdmans, Grand Rapids, MI

SECTION VI

Religion and the Study of Language

Introduction

J. F. A. Sawyer

Religion has had an enormous influence on the history of the study of language. One only has to glance at the syllabus of any rabbinical college or theological seminary to appreciate this. Serious students of the Hebrew Bible have always been required to study at least two languages, Hebrew and Aramaic, and the ability to handle the uniquely difficult text of the Talmud in its original language, remains a central aim of Jewish religious education. With advances in comparative semitic linguistics since the eighteenth century, it has been quite normal for students of Christian theology to study Arabic, Ethiopic, Babylonian, Ugaritic, and other Semitic languages as well as the biblical languages themselves, in the belief that these may often hold the key to discovering the lost original meaning of biblical words. The Dutch scholar Albert Schultens (1686–1750), whose book *Hebrew Origins or the Most Ancient Nature and Character of the Hebrew Language Recovered from the Interior of Arabia* (1761), was an early example of this method, studied theology and began life as a Christian pastor. In Scotland it is no coincidence that many of the best-known names in Biblical language research, like A. B. Davidson, Matthew Black, and James Barr, also began their semitic studies as divinity students.

Powerful religious factors influenced the history of language and linguistics in other ways too. A passionate concern to ensure the accurate pronunciation and transmission of liturgical texts led to the production of such masterpieces of conciseness and theoretical consistency as Pāṇini's Sanskrit Grammar (c. 350 BCE), and the birth of a linguistic tradition in the mediaeval Islamic world as well as in China and Japan. The same religious concerns led to the invention of sophisticated Masoretic vocalization systems applied to the text of the Hebrew Bible and the development of the mediaeval Hebrew linguistic tradition. In the Later Middle Ages, under the influence of Aristotle, philosophical speculation about language among the theologians, notably Thomas Aquinas, produced its own distinctive linguistic theory.

Probably the most conspicuous example of religion and language interacting is the impetus of missionary activity, particularly Buddhist and Christian, to record vernacular languages, some of them for the first time, and translate their sacred texts into them. It is probable that the Buddha himself made his own translations as he addressed different audiences, and similarly Jesus almost certainly spoke more than one language in cosmopolitan first century Judaea. Thus from the very beginning there has been in Buddhism and Christianity a tradition of openness to translation, in sharp contrast to Islam, for example, where translation of the Qur'ān is officially prohibited. Buddhist missionaries did pioneering work on the languages of India, China, Japan, and South East Asia. A striking example from China is the Translations Bureau set up by Kumarajiva (344–412 CE) with a staff of between 500 and 800 people. It was the Buddhists who invented the Tibetan script, just as it was Bishop Mesrop who invented the Armenian script, Bishop Wulfila the Gothic script, and Cyril and Methodios the script known as Cyrillic used for writing Old Church Slavonic and later Russian, Bulgarian, Serbian, and other languages.

The influence of the Christian reformers including Jan Huss in Czechoslovakia, Martin Luther in Germany, John Wycliffe and others in England, who first translated the Bible into the vernacular, just at the time of the invention of printing, was enormous. Since those early publications, the Churches have invested a vast amount of energy and resources in translating the Bible into every language in the world: it is reckoned that by the 1990s the Bible or parts of it had been translated into over 2000 new languages. To achieve this Christian organizations and institutions, like the Bible Societies and the Summer Institute of Linguistics, have been set up to give translators specialist linguistic training. From these came some of the greatest names in the history of language and linguistics, from professional missionaries like William Carey, Roberto de Nobili, and Matteo Ricci from earlier centuries, to those in our own day who, like Eugene Nida and Kenneth Pike, are better known to the wider public as theoretical linguists than as evangelists.

Arab and Persian Phonetics

M. H. Bakalla

The first half of the seventh century CE witnessed the birth of the religion of Islam in the Arabian Peninsula. By the mid-eighth century the Arab expansion was being felt throughout the Ancient World. The new Islamic Empire had already been established in Damascus and later spread to the cities of Anbar and Baghdad. It was to flourish for the following four or five centuries. The Empire reached, at times, the ancient borders of China in the east and the Atlantic Ocean in the west and its achievement was that it was able to unify both mentally and intellectually the diverse structures of its peoples. The Persian states, the Byzantine colonies, the Iberian Kingdoms, the Turkic Emirates, and the Arab tribes and communities were all destined to build this new Empire and to serve its religion, Islam, and its language, Arabic (see *Arabic*). Charmed by the eloquence and the challenge of the Qur'ān, scores of newly emerging Muslim scholars competed to study Arabic intensively in order to unravel the secrets of the Holy Book. These zealous and diligent scholars of Arab, Persian, Greek, Andalusian, and Turkish descent paved the way for the establishment of new Arabic sciences, such as grammar, semantics, stylistics, and phonetics. Thus they helped sow the seeds of Islamic Culture.

Under the Caliphate's patronage and encouragement, the scholars of the Empire, Arabs, Persians, Turks, Christians, and Jews, translated into, and/or wrote in, Arabic books and treatises on all subjects. For centuries they produced abundant works dealing not only with Arabic, but also with medicine, philosophy, anatomy, physics, geography, and mathematics.

1. The Beginning

1.1 Writing

With the advent of Islam the need arose for recording the Qur'ān in writing. The Prophet Muhammad was greatly interested in employing the system of writing used by the Nabateans of northwest Arabia, which went back to the Phoenicians. The system was not without shortcomings and it was not until later that the partial syllabic system was improved upon in order to meet the needs of writing the Arabic consonantal and vocalic phonemes.

There must have been a kind of a phonemic principle (one grapheme for each phoneme) behind the development of the writing system into an alphabetical one (see *Alphabet: Development*). The Arab grammarian and statesman, Abū al-Aswad al-Du'alī (d. 688), together with contemporaries and disciples, introduced symbols for short vowels and differentiated between otherwise identical or similar letters by means of dots.

The symbols for the short vowels now known were devised in the eighth century by the Arab lexicographer and grammarian al-Khalīl ibn Aḥmad (718–87).

1.2 Grammar

Tradition attributes to al-Du'alī the initiation or invention of Arabic grammar, in response to the need then felt to correct the errors in Arabic pronunciation and grammar. He introduced for the first time some phonetic terms which are still in common vogue: for example, the terms, *fatḥa*, *ḍamma*, *kasra*, and *ghunna*, to stand for the short open vowel a, rounded vowel *u*, short high close vowel *i*, and nasal *n*, respectively.

From the beginning the word *ḥarf* was used to mean either the basic sound or *ṣawt* (phoneme), the letter name, or the written symbol of a certain consonant or vowel.

2. Development

2.1 Al-Khalīl's Lexicon

Al-Khalīl was reputed, among other things, for his lexicographical work, particularly his Arabic lexicon *al-'Ayn*, whose entries were arranged according to phonetic order of the phonemes rather than the already well-known alphabetical order. Apart from a few exceptions, the phonemes were arranged according to an ascending order: starting with the laryngeal consonants, followed by the pharyngeals, and ending with the bilabials. He attempted to classify Arabic consonants according to certain phonetic categories: guttural, uvular, liquid, palatal, alveolar, dental, interdental, and labial. This system was later criticized by the Arab–Greek phonologist Ibn Jinnī (932–1001; see Sect. 4.2.1) in the introduction of his book, *Sirr Sinā'at al-I'rāb* (*SS*), (*Secret of the Art of Grammar*). Although the criticism is theoretically justified, al-Khalīl's classification was only meant for practical use in the arrangement of the entries of his lexicon.

2.2 Sībawayhi's Grammar

The Persian Muslim grammarian Sībawayhi (died 795 or 809) is considered the father of Arabic grammar (see *Sibawayhi*). His book, *al-Kitāb*, contains the complete grammatical rules of the Arabic language. Its chapters are arranged in such a way as to give the syntactic rules first, followed by morphology, and then phonology. The phonological section is considered here.

Sībawayhi laid down all the basic ideas concerning the classification, description, and analysis of Arabic phonology. Many of his ideas are still valid and used by modern Arabic scholars. Certainly, his statements and terminology are definitive.

2.2.1 Classification by articulation

Although he knew that there are 29 letters in the writing system of Arabic, Sībawayhi recognized other phonemes which had no written symbols. After stating the basic phonemes of standard Arabic, he discussed some nonbasic speech sounds, dividing them into two groups. First, the allophonic variants of the standard phonemes such as the homorganic nasals [ŋ, ɴ, ɳ, ɱ]; Alif Imāla or the umlaut [ē]; and back quality of [ā] or Alif Tafkhīm [ā]. Second, the dialectal variants which are not accepted in standard Arabic, e.g., [g] and [v].

Sībawayhi recognized 16 points of articulation in the vocal tract, starting with the larynx where [ʔ] and [h] are articulated and ending with the bilabials [b, m, w]. The sixteenth point is the nasal cavity which produces nasals and nasalization. In dealing with the articulatory points, he divided speech organs into smaller parts, giving their names and stating their function in a detailed and accurate way. He conveniently divided the throat into three parts; the extreme back of the throat (larynx), the middle of the throat (pharynx), and the extreme front of the throat (uvula). Other parts of the speech organs were also mentioned: back of tongue, palate, midtongue, midpalate, apex of the tongue, lateral part of tongue, canine, bicuspid, lateral incisor, front incisor, etc.

2.2.2 Manner of articulation

After classification by place of articulation, Sībawayhi went on to give a detailed analysis of the manner of articulation. His description included a wide spectrum of terminology with definitions and exemplification.

(a) *majhūr* and *mahmūs*—This binary category included voiced and voiceless phonemes of Arabic. The discrepancy between Sībawayhi's and modern descriptions of some phonemes suggests the possibility of slight changes or modification in the pronunciation of some speech sounds at a certain time in the history of the language.
(b) *shadīd* and *rikhw*—In this category Sībawayhi divided the phonemes into either stops or continuants. In this analysis [ʕ] stands out as neither stop [ʕ] nor continuant. In modern investigations, [ʕ] has more constriction in the pharynx than its cognate [ḥ] and the remaining consonants.
(c) Other subclassifications in Sībawayhi's description are nasal [n] and [m], trill [r], semivowels [y] and [w], and velarized or emphatic consonants.
(d) There was a kind of 'distinctive feature approach' in Sībawayhi's classification of the Arabic phonemes. A single concept or feature was utilized which is either present or absent from the phoneme or phonemes it characterizes. Note for instance, his statement concerning velarization or emphaticness: 'without *ʔiṭbāq* or the feature of emphaticness, [ṭ] would become [d], [ṣ] would become [s], [ð̣] would become [ð].'
(e) As a phonetician and grammarian, Sībawayhi employed his phonetic analysis in order to explain the intricate morphophonemic changes, rules of assimilation, dissimilation, substitution, and mutation, deletion, metathesis, and phonotactics.

Like al-Du'alī and al-Khalīl, Sībawayhi belonged to the Basrite school of Arabic linguistics. His book has remained the milestone in its field. Arabic linguistics is still indebted to this master of the art.

3. Growth

3.1 The Ninth Century

The ninth century witnessed slight development in the field. The impact of the great masters like al-Khalīl and Sībawayhi was strong and lasting in different linguistic domains such as phonotactics, defects of speech. Among the renowned Basrite scholars and authors are al-Jāḥiẓ (773–869), al-Mubarrad (826–99), Ibn-Durayd (837–934); the Persian, Abū Sa'īd al-Sīrāfī (897–979), and his son

Yūsuf (941–95), both of whom wrote commentaries on the Book of Sībawayhi.

3.1.1 Defects of speech

Al-Jāḥiẓ's encyclopedic book, al-*Bayān wal-Tabyīn*, on stylistics and rhetoric, discussed subjects ranging from method of translation, to language acquisition, bilingualism, phonotactics, and speech and language disorders. He not only cited some cases of lisping, misarticulation, and stuttering, but also attempted to cure them.

This subject of speech defects was later given special attention, and a number of independent works were written with detailed analysis. The Andalusian Arab, Ibn Sīda from Murcia (d. 1066), devoted a chapter to this subject in his book *al-Mukhaṣṣaṣ*. Al-Kindī (died c. 870) and Ibn al-Bannā' (986–1078) each wrote a treatise on the subject. The Persian grammarian, Abū 'Alī al-Fārisī from Baghdad (920–87), was said to have attempted to cure a person who could not pronounce [r]:

> Ibn Jarw could not articulate [r] and pronounced it as uvular ([ʁ]). Abū 'Alī said to him: insert the nib of your pen under your tongue and push your tongue up with it and do it frequently while repeating a word containing [r]. He did as his professor advised and the [r] came forth faultlessly from his mouth.

3.1.2 Phonotactics

Ibn Durayd in his book *Jamharat al-Lugha* and al-Mubarad in *al-Muqtaḍab*, both influenced by al-Khalīl and Sībawayhi, drew many phonetic statements, terms, concepts, and rules from *al-'Ayn and al-Kitāb*.

Phonotactics was further developed in books dealing with oratory, eloquence, and morphophonemics. Ibn Sinān al-Khafājī of Aleppo (1032–73) devoted his book *Sirr al-Faṣāḥa* (*the Art of Eloquence*) to phonotactics and related issues. He discussed acceptable and nonacceptable sequences of all phonemes in Arabic, giving reasons and examples in all cases.

3.2 The Tenth and Eleventh Centuries

This period is considered by historians to be the golden age of Islamic scholarship. Scores of learned people and researchers, individually and in teams, produced hundreds of books and treatises on all known subjects of the time; formalizing ideas and methodology in ways which were much more advanced than ever before.

Ibn Jinnī, or IJ, of Mosul was a prolific author on morphology, phonology and philosophy of language. His book, *SS* (see Sect. 2.1 above), on the secret of the arts of grammar drew most of its phonetic statements from Sībawayhi. However, in his phonological and morphophonemic analysis he went beyond his predecessors. He formalized their ideas and rules and presented them in a more definitive manner. He emphasized the 'binary feature analysis' of the phonemes. He clearly and succinctly developed further the descriptive techniques of the Arabic vowel system and reformulated its definitions, rules, and frequencies.

Ibn Jinnī introduced for the first time the term for Arabic phonology *'Ilm al-Aṣwāt wal-Ḥurūf*, which is still used. This book, out of more than 50 of his, applied the general phonological principles which were laid down in the introduction to *SS*. He demonstrated the function of each phoneme and its potential occurrence and frequency.

Ibn Jinnī was of the opinion that the production of speech and voice is similar to note-making in music. He compared the speech apparatus to both the flute and lute, on the grounds that they all produced sounds and melodies. He also dealt briefly with prosodic features such as pause, juncture, and prominence.

It is an open question whether or not Ibn Jinnī was influenced by the scholastic society Ikhwān al-Ṣafā' and their work *al-Rasā'il* (the *Treatises*). There are areas where their works seem to meet. This group of learned men also made very intelligent statements concerning speech mechanism, physics of speech, articulatory, auditory, pulmonic, and mental processes.

Ibn Jinnī was also influenced by his mentor Abū 'Alī al-Fārisī with whom he was associated for more than 40 years. He seems to have influenced later scholars, such as: Ibn Sinān al-Khafājī; Ibn Ya'īsh (1161–1254), the Persian master al-Zamakhsharī (1075–1144); the Persian encyclopedist al-Sakkākī (1160–1228); and al-Suyūṭī (d. 1505). Each of them contributed greatly to Arabic linguistics but only slightly to Arabic phonetics. Al-Sakkākī, from Khwarizm in Persia, in his compendium *Miftāḥ al-'Ulūm* (*Key to Arabic Sciences*) described briefly the phonetics of Arabic and included, for the first time, a diagram of the speech apparatus displaying the different organs responsible for the articulation of Arabic sounds (see Fig. 1).

3.3 Other Contributions to Arabic Phonetics

Other factors contributing to the advancement of Arabic phonetics came from outside the discipline itself, with inter-disciplinary activities emanating from the caliph's courts and scholars' circles. The ancient scholars possessed encyclopedic knowledge and, as a result, wrote on diverse subjects and numerous disciplines.

3.3.1 Anatomical works

The Arabic terms which are related to speech organs are common in both linguistic and anatomical works. The Arab lexicographer and grammarian al-Aṣma'ī

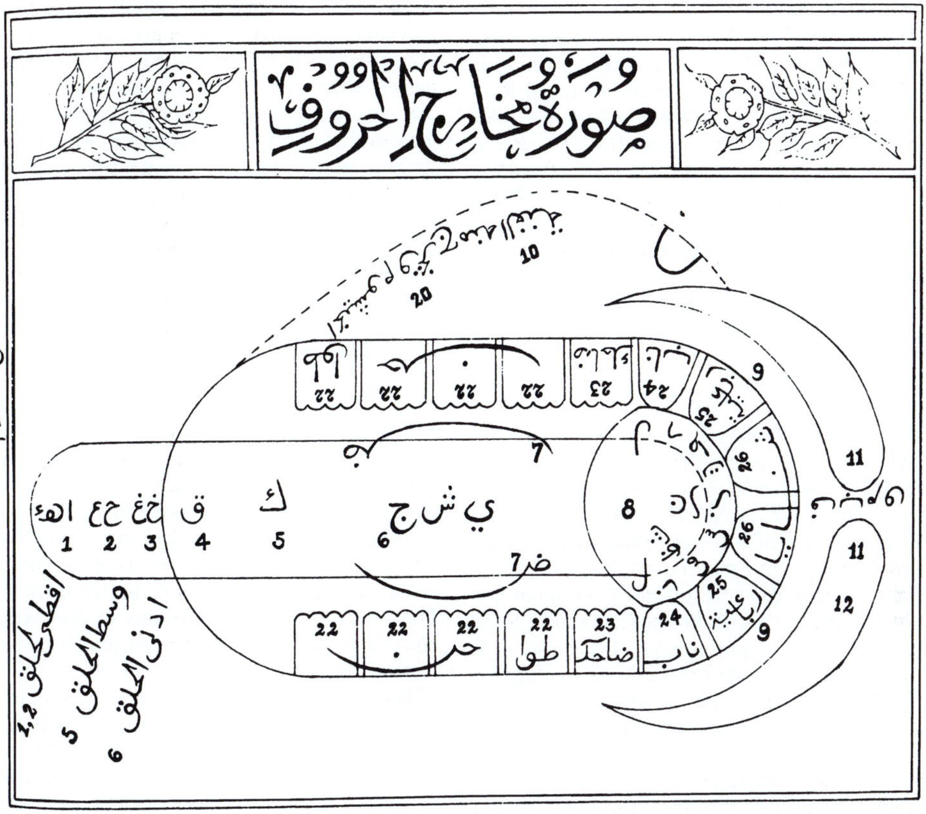

Figure 1. An early Arabic illustration of the vocal organs. This is apparently the earliest ever recorded diagram of the organs of speech and points of articulation which was made for phonetic analysis. (From *Miftāḥ al-ᶜUlūm*, [*Key to Arabic Sciences*], by Yūsuf Al-Sakkākī (1159–1228 CE, published in a modern edition in Cairo, 1937.) Key (note: numbers added in modern times and those skipped refer to vocal structures not represented in this figure): 1: vocal cords, 2: larynx, 3: epiglottis, 4: root of the tongue, 5: pharynx, 6: uvula, 7: palate, 8: hard palate, 9: alveolae, 10: nose, 11: lips, 12: lower lip, 20: nasal cavity, 22: molars, 23: bicuspids, 24: canines, 25: lateral incisors, 26: central incisors.

(740–831) compiled the first extant book, in which he listed and discussed all human anatomical terms related to the human body such as the names of its parts, their definitions, and functions. Naturally, parts of the speech organ were also given. This was later followed by more comprehensive works on the subject such as those by the versatile author, al-Zajjāj (d. 922) and the Persian lexicographer, Aḥmad Ibn Fāris (d. 1000).

3.3.2 Recitation of the Qur'ān

Tajwīd, or the science of proper recitation of the Qur'ān, is considered one of the main sources in Arabic phonetics. It goes back to the early beginning of Islamic scholarship. It was kept as an oral tradition for a long time until canonized and codified by later scholars. Such works gave phonetic details of Arabic sounds, and followed strict scientific methodology, which has parallels in general Arabic phonetic scholarship.

Books on Tajwīd are abundant; some are written in verse and probably intended for teaching purposes. Important authors include the Andalucian al-Dānī from Cordova (981–1053), Ibn al-Ṭaḥḥān of Seville (1104–64), and Ibn al-Jazarī of Damascus (died 1429).

Ibn al-Taḥḥān wrote a treatise, *Makhārij al-Ḥurūf wa Ṣifātuhā* (*The Places and Manner of Articulation* [of Arabic]), in which he listed 33 speech sounds relevant to the recitation of the Qur'ān. Another four chapters cover place and articulation, manner of articulation, definition of the phonetic features, and, finally, the speech sounds which are weakly articulated. Ibn al-Ṭaḥḥān followed the same principles, description methodology, and terminology which had been employed previously in grammar, Tajwīd, and related disciplines.

3.3.3 Medical research

Works on anatomy, physiology and medicine were not uncommon in Arabic Scholarship. The three renowned Persian medical scholars were al-Rāzī (864–932), with his book *al-Ṭibb al-Manṣūrī*, 'Alī ibn 'Abbās al-Majūsī (d. 1010), with his book *Kāmil al-Sinā'a al-Ṭibbiyya*, and Ibn Sīnā (980–1037), with his celebrated work *al-Qānūn fil-Ṭibb*. These books gave detailed medical analysis of the human body and the functions of each part, as well as diagnosis and treatment. There were very close parallels between medical and grammatical works (Bakalla 1982b: 137) in terminology, description, and definition.

3.3.4 Ibn Sīnā

Ibn Sīnā, or Avicenna, was a scholar of many talents. Besides his work as a physician, he was also a mathematician, philosopher, man of letters, and phonetician. His book, *Asbāb Ḥudūth al-Ḥurūf* is a very interesting piece of work on phonetics. Avicenna's objective was to give an account of the physical, anatomical, physiological, respiratory, articulatory, and synthetical properties of the speech sounds. Such information about the physiology and physics of speech was not uncommon in this era, particularly in such linguistic and philosophical circles as that of Ikhwān al-Ṣafā'. The treatise is divided into six chapters (Semaan 1963: 19):

(a) on the cause of generation of sound;
(b) on the cause of the formation of speech sounds;
(c) on the anatomy of the larynx and of the tongue;
(d) on the particular causes of the production of each of the Arabic speech sounds;
(e) on speech sounds similar to these *ḥurūf*; and
(f) on (how) these speech sounds can be heard (as a result of activities other than speech articulation).

The sixth chapter of *Asbāb Ḥudūth al-Ḥurūf* appeared to be a new contribution to phonetics. The treatment is reminiscent of modern work in speech synthesis. Note his reconstruction of the consonants [t] and [d]: '[t] is generated from striking the hand forcibly with the finger; [d] from a similar striking that is weaker than the previous one.'

Avicenna also described speech sounds which are not found in standard Arabic; e.g., the Persian [ʒ], [v], [t]ʃ, and [p]. A comparison with other languages was not uncommon in Arabic linguistics and is a practice which can be traced in the works of Sībawayhi, Ibn Jinnī, al-Jawālīqī (1073–1144), al-Khafājī (1571–1659), and many others.

4. Conclusion

Arab and Persian phonetics in the Middle Ages seem to have had the same origin right from the start. They merged and developed as a single entity working together in order to serve the language of the Qur'ān. The Persian Muslim scholars were pioneers in some areas of Arabic scholarship, particularly phonetics. The unity among the Muslims in the Middle Ages kindled the lights of the Arabic and Islamic learning and research.

The contribution of Muslims to phonetics has been underestimated in modern times. There is a wealth of observations and data in this body of literature that deserves careful study by the modern researcher.

Bibliography

Bakalla M H 1982a *Arabic Linguistics: An Introduction and Bibliography*. Mansell, London

Bakalla M H 1982b *Ibn Jinnī: An Arab Muslim Phonetician*. European Language Publications, London

al-Nassir A A 1993 *Sībawaihi the Phonologist*. Kegan Paul International, London

Semaan K I 1968 *Linguistics in the Middle Ages: Phonetics Studies in Early Islam*. Brill, Leiden

Arabic Linguistic Tradition

M. Y. I. H. Suleiman

The Arabic linguistic tradition spans centuries of intellectual activity and covers a wide range of topics, all pertaining to the Arabic language (see *Arabic*) in its capacity as, primarily, the medium of religious expression (in the form of the Qu'rān; see *Qur'ān*) as well as a vast body of poetry. Participants in this tradition came from a variety of ethnic backgrounds; for example, al-Khalīl (d. 791); Sībawayhi (d. 804) and Ibn Jinnī (d. 1002), the three most important scholars in the core disciplines of this tradition, were Arab, Persian, and Byzantine by origin respectively. But they all engaged in their work from a position which recognizes the centrality of Arabic and Islam in the life of the community of which they were a part.

In addition to the ethnic diversity of the major participants in the Arabic linguistic tradition, this tradition was not shaped just by scholars whose expertise lay only in the field of linguistic studies, but extended to include contributors from outside the strict confines of this domain. Ibn Sīnā's

Treatise (*Risāla*) on the points of articulation of the Arabic speech sounds (Semaan 1963) shows that linguistic science was not the exclusive preserve of linguists, but that a philosopher and medical scholar could contribute to aspects of this field, drawing, obviously, on his expertise in his primary field of research.

As understood here, the Arabic linguistic tradition covers two major areas: grammar in the wide sense (including phonetics/phonology, morphology, and syntax) and lexicography which deals with the compilation of lexica. Serious research in these two areas dates back to the eighth century. It was al-Khalīl who, together with his student Sībawayhi, laid down the foundations of grammar; but the credit in the development of lexicographic work is al-Khalīl's alone.

This article will concentrate on grammar—minus phonetics/phonology which will be dealt with elsewhere in this encyclopedia (see *Arab and Persian Phonetics*)—and lexicography. Also, aspects of semantics and pragmatics will be dealt with. But first the beginnings and fundamental principles (*uṣūl*) of Arabic grammatical thinking will be outlined.

1. The Beginnings of Arabic Grammar

The beginnings of Arabic grammatical thinking are universally attributed in the sources to the emergence of the phenomenon called *laḥn* (solecism) in early Muslim society. As explained in these sources, *laḥn* is a socially induced phenomenon which primarily emerged from the events and conditions set in train by the rapid spread of Islam and the conversion to it by large numbers of speakers of languages other than Arabic. New converts to Islam had to familiarize themselves with their adopted religion, especially its primary text, the Qu'rān, which prides itself on being revealed in 'clear Arabic.' Not unexpectedly, their speech was faulty, and, if what the sources say is accepted, faulty speech later spread to the Arabs themselves who mixed with these new converts in the newly conquered lands.

Broadly speaking, the term *laḥn* initially referred to the deviations from the pre-descriptive patterns of Arabic, as those patterns were assumed to be intuitively grasped by authentic speakers of the language in its pure and uncontaminated form, the ultimate repositories of which being the Qu'rān and early poetry. Various reports in the literature show that *laḥn* obtained not only in ordinary speech, but also in recitations of the Qu'rān. The occurrence of *laḥn* in the latter domain was viewed with alarm by those who were in a position to do something about it, as it represented a dangerous interference in the total veracity of the message of the Qu'rān in its capacity as the revealed word of God *verbatim*. It is in this context that Abū al-Aswad al-Du'alī was entrusted with the task of placing the hitherto untranscribed short vowels in the text of the Qu'rān. However, contrary to what the Arabic sources say, this undeniably important contribution cannot be seriously regarded as the 'official' beginning of grammar, simply because it does not amount to any publicly formulated descriptive statement of the structure of Arabic.

The above discussion is important because it throws serious doubt on the almost universal claim in the Arabic sources that Abū al-Aswad was the originator of Arabic grammar. It is also important because it points to two main considerations which played a significant role in the rise and development of Arabic grammar. The first consideration pertains to the importance of grammar as an indispensable tool in the promotion of the full range of scholarly activities which revolve around the Qu'rān, for example exegesis (*tafsīr*) and jurisprudence (*fiqh*). The second consideration is the role of grammar as a pedagogic instrument in the teaching of Arabic to, primarily, non-Arab converts to Islam, as well as to those Arabs whose speech was, or might have been, affected by *laḥn*. Clearly, in its inception, Arabic grammar was not an end in itself, but a means to something else. This, however, did not prevent it from being largely built on premises, or from utilizing notions and techniques, which are germane to providing immanent descriptions of the language.

2. The Foundation of Arabic Grammar

Most of the seminal work on Arabic grammar was carried out by al-Khalīl and his student Sībawayhi, whose *Kitāb* constitutes the most original and full-fledged description of the Arabic language of the Qu'rān and poetry (see *Sībawayhi*). Al-Khalīl and Sībawayhi set the tone for Arabic grammatical thinking by offering an approach which was largely synchronic in character, albeit that Arabic grammar contains copious, but unsystematic, references to phenomena of a diachronic nature. Furthermore, by primarily concentrating on the supradialectal form of the language, al-Khalīl and Sībawayhi relegated dialect studies to a secondary place in the totality of the Arabic grammatical tradition. In addition, description in the *Kitāb* is largely anchored in relation to the written forms of the language, even with respect to phonological processes, in spite of the fact that Sībawayhi, building on the work of al-Khalīl, gives a thorough phonetic analysis of the Arabic speech sounds in, chiefly, articulatory terms. The existence of all three features as defining properties of the Arabic grammatical studies is clear testimony of the strength of the legacy bequeathed by these two linguists.

2.1 The Fundamentals (uṣūl) of Arabic Grammar

Attested data (*samā'*) and analogy (*qiyās*) are the two most important fundamentals of Arabic grammatical thinking. A third, less important, fundamental is presumption of continuity (*istiṣḥāb al-ḥāl*). As will become clear from the discussion below, these fundamentals cover three different, albeit related, dimensions of Arabic grammatical thinking.

2.1.1 Attested Data (samāʿ)

Attested data fall into two categories: transmitted data, mainly constituting the Qu'rān and poetry, and elicited data. Briefly, each one of these categories of data will be dealt with below. First the reasons offered by the grammarians for excluding the Prophet's Traditions (*ḥadīth*) from the scope of transmitted data will be set out.

The first argument in this connection concerns the fact that the majority of Traditions were not verbatim records of what the Prophet had said, but that they represented the gist of what was said, moulded in the language of the transmitter. The second consideration pertains to the problem of *laḥn*, the general assumption being that since many non-Arab Muslims participated in the transmission of the Traditions, and since *laḥn* was regarded as a property of the speech of speakers from this background, there was no guarantee that the Traditions were not contaminated by *laḥn*.

However, these arguments seem to have been discounted in the work of the thirteenth-century grammarian Ibn Mālik (d. 1273).

3. Transmitted Data

3.1 The Qu'rān

The Qu'rān is universally regarded as the primary source of linguistic data in the Arabic grammatical tradition on two grounds. On the one hand, it is thought to represent God's revealed word verbatim and, as such, it is regarded as the most eloquent/clear (*faṣīḥ*) text there is in the whole of the Arabic language. On the other hand, it is revealed to the Arabs through the medium of Muhammad, who was considered as one of the most eloquent members of his community on account of the fact that he combined the eloquence of the Meccans, his own people, with that of the tribe of Banū Sa'd, among whom he was brought up.

However, the Qu'rān is not a totally uniform linguistic text, as is evident from the existence of the variant readings (*qirāʾāt*) which represent phonological, morphological and, to a lesser extent, syntactic variations in the Qu'rān. Arab grammarians adopt the position that all attested variant readings of the Qu'rān are valid data for analysis and description. But they split into, roughly, two camps with regard to the validity of these readings as bases for generating new utterances through analogy. On the one hand, the Baṣrans insist that only those readings of the Qu'rān which conform to the general patterns of the language can serve as models of analogical derivation. On the other hand, the Kūfans hold the view that all variant readings, including the ones which represent rare features of the language, are eligible to serve as models for generating new items in the language. The Kūfan–inclined grammarians argue that rare variant readings of the Qu'rān are as much a part of the language as the rest.

3.2 Poetry

The utilization of poetry as a source of transmitted data reflects the importance of this literary genre in the life of the Arabs. The general position held by the Arabic grammarians vis-à-vis the validity of poetry as data source favors its restriction to specimens prior to the Abbāsid period. However, it is not unknown for later grammarians to use the poetry of Abbāsid poets as a source of data. Clearly, the attitude of the Arabic grammarians toward poetry was not totally uniform, and the best one can hope to do here is to outline some of the considerations which were applied in the selection of poetry of the early period of Islam as data source.

The first consideration is the remoteness of the poet from urban life, the underlying assumption here being that contact with speakers from the urban centers endangers the linguistic competence of the poet through *laḥn*. A second consideration is the excellence of the poetry from the thematic and stylistic points of view. A third consideration is the lexical and grammatical robustness of the poetry. Obviously, different selections were made depending upon which considerations were applied. However, the subjectivity of these considerations, particularly the latter two, led to a great deal of uncertainty in the reliance on poetry as linguistic data.

3.3 Elicited Data

The transmitted data of the Qu'rān and poetry were augmented by data directly elicited from speakers whose speech was judged to be eloquent/clear (*faṣīḥ*). As understood in this context, the concept of eloquence/clarity (*faṣāḥa*) applies to speakers whose linguistic behavior was judged to be devoid of *laḥn*. Speakers of this type were generally believed to be members of Quraysh, the Prophet's tribe, or any of the tribes which continued to live in the heart of Arabia (*ahl al-wabar*) and, thus, had no, or very little, contact with the urban population (*ahl al-madar*). However, this theoretical position was not always totally respected in practice.

Two types of setting were resorted to in eliciting data from native speakers. In the first setting, the grammarians traveled deep into the desert to meet members of the tribes which shunned contact with the urban world. In the second setting, the grammarians elicited data from speakers who visited the markets which sprang up around the urban centers on the edge of the desert, notably al-Mirbad outside Baṣra. These settings are mentioned here to emphasize the point that the Arabic grammarians took data collection very seriously in the work.

However, the data elicited by the grammarians were defective in at least three important ways. First, the reliance of the grammarians on memory and their utilization of a less than phonetically adequate script to record their observations adversely affected the accuracy of their data. Second, the concentration of the grammarians on the segmental dimension of speech meant that the paratactic aspects of the language were largely excluded from the data. Third, the data were almost exclusively restricted to male speechs, thus, there is very little indication of the type of language employed by females. Grammar was the preserve of males who concentrated on male speech.

4. Analogy (Qiyās)

Analogy is the soul of Arabic grammar. According to one famous definition in the literature 'grammar is nothing but analogy which is to be followed' (Suyūṭī: *Iqtirāḥ*: 94). Anbāri (d. 1181) specifies grammar as 'knowledge of the analogical patterns which are extracted from the speech of the Arabs by means of induction' (*Luma*': 44). He further declares that 'it is not possible to deny the existence of analogy in grammar because the whole of grammar [is based on] analogy' (ibid). This view of grammar is sanctioned by Sībawayhi and Ibn Jinnī.

Analogy is used in a variety of senses in the literature. In the predescriptive sense, it is used to refer to the intuitively conceived patterns of the language which underlie the speaker's ability to encode and decode utterances in the language concerned, in this case Arabic. In the postdescriptive sense, analogy incorporates the general patterns of the language which the grammarians established by, inter alia, applying the inductive method to the attested data. Analogy also refers to the use of the general postdescriptive patterns of the language to generate novel data. It is also used to designate the generation of what might be called hypothetical data in morphology, a process the purpose of which is to inculcate in the learners a conscious knowledge of the patterns of the language. In the latter senses analogy acquires a pedagogic dimension, which is different from the primarily structural dimension implicit in the other senses of analogy above.

Analogy in grammar serves a variety of functions, the most important of which is the rationalization of the descriptive facts of the language by means of *ta'līl* (explanation). In this sense analogy breaks down to four components: the base (*aṣl* or *maqīs 'alaihi*), the subsidiary (*far'* or *maqīs*), the *'illa* (rationalization, cause, reason, or norm) and the verdict (*ḥukum*). To illustrate how analogy works here, the well-known example in the literature involving '*inna* and its sisters' will be considered.

A characteristic feature of '*inna* and its sisters' is their occurrence with a subject (*ism*) in the accusative and a predicate (*khabar*) in the nominative, as the following example illustrates:

inna akhāka *Muḥammadun* (1)
subj (acc) pred (nom)
'Your brother is Muhammad.'

This property of '*inna* and its sisters' is explained in Arabic grammar by invoking their similarity to transitive verbs in sentences exhibiting the linear order Verb–Object–Subject, instead of the normal Verb–Subject–Object in which the object (*maf'ūl bihj*) appears in the accusative and the subject (*fā'il*) in the nominative, for example:

ḍaraba akhāka *Muḥammadun* (2)
V Obj (acc) Sub (nom)
'Muhammad hit your brother.'

The constituent components of the analogy invoked to systematize/rationalize the afore-mentioned property of '*inna* and its sisters' may be specified as follows:

(a) base: the transitive verb in V–O–S sentence types;
(b) subsidiary: *inna* and its sisters;
(c) verdict: the occurrence of the accusative with the object and the nominative with the subject in sentences of the above type; and
(d) *'illa*: *inna* and its sisters govern a subject (*ism*) in the accusative and a predicate (*khabar*) in the nominative by virtue of resembling the base (a) which is characterized by the verdict (c).

4.1 The 'illa

The concept of *'illa* is one of the most important concepts in Arabic grammatical thinking. This concept has received a variety of classifications, and an article of this type can but outline the major senses in which it has been used in the literature.

An important sense of the *'illa* is that of grammatical pattern, rule, or norm, particularly when viewed from the perspective of pedagogical grammar. Seen from this perspective the *'illa* serves the function of helping the learners acquire the correct linguistic habits, thus enabling them to encode and decode utterances in the language accurately. Used in this sense, the *'illa* is labeled pedagogical (*ta'līmiyya*) by Zajjājī (d. 948), primary (*ūlā*) by Ibn Maḍā' (d. 1196; see *Ibn Maḍā' al Qurṭubi*) and just *'illa* by Ibn al-Sarraj (d. 929), although it is viewed as being equally descriptive in function by the latter linguist.

Another important sense of *'illa* is that of a rationalization whose aim is to explain a significant feature of the language. *'illas* of this type are called analogical *'illas* by Zajjājī when applied in the fashion set out in the example at the end of the preceding section. Ibn Maḍā' refers to *illas* of this type as secondary (*thawānī*), but he does not accept them all. He only accepts a subtype of the secondary *'illas* which he calls the absolutely necessary *'illas*.

A third sense of *'illa* is that of a rationalization used in debates about the nature of the language as a medium of communication, conducted in a cultural context dominated by the principle of the wisdom of the Arabs (*ḥikmatu al-'Arab*) as native speakers of the language. Zajjājī refers to *'illas* of this type as *naẓariyya-jadaliyya*) reflective/theoretical-argumentative), while Ibn Maḍā' refers to them as tertiary *'illas*. The latter linguist, however, rejects this type of *'illas* because they often violate the empiricism of grammar which, in terms of his Ẓāhirite views on the nature of linguistic inquiry, is interpreted in relation to what may be called observable surface structure phenomena. Ibn al-Sarrāj does not distinguish between the latter two types of *'illa*, treating them as just one type. These different views and classifications of *'illa* serve to show the complexity of this concept.

Another important classification of the *'illa*, albeit less known than Zajjāji's, is provided by Ibn Jinnī in his famous work *al-khaṣā'iṣ*. Ibn Jinni distinguishes between what he calls obligatory/mandatory *'illa* (*mūjiba*) and optional *'illa* (*mujawwiza*), the latter he also calls reason (*sabab*) to indicate that it is not a full-fledged *'illa*. Broadly speaking, the difference between these two types of *'illa* may be stated by saying that the former offers causal explanations of linguistic data while the latter generally offers teleological ones.

4.2 Presumption of Continuity (istiṣḥāb al-ḥāl)

This is the least studied fundamental in the foundations of the Arabic grammatical tradition. It is invariably relegated to a marginal status in treatises on the *uṣūl* (fundamentals) of Arabic grammar. This attitude is best represented in the work of Anbāri, although this linguist invokes it in a few places in his famous *Inṣāf*. The status of this fundamental as set out above reflects its status in jurisprudence whence it was borrowed.

Broadly speaking, the presumption of continuity fundamental is framed in terms of the view that linguistic features, whether items or patterns/rules, have two dimensions an 'emic' dimension, which represents their abstract aspect, and an 'etic' or concrete one, which pertains to variations in the realization of the emic elements. This boils down to saying that the etic elements are exponents of the emic ones which, that is the latter, have priority in description.

In Arabic grammar the etic features represent deviations from the norms, these being the emic elements. Deviations of this type are anchored in description in relation to their emic sources by the two processes of interpretation (*ta'wīl*) and explanation (*ta'līl*). Within this overall framework, the presumption of continuity fundamental boils down to saying that features in the language are treated as emic unless they can be shown to be different. In instances where the tentative emic elements turn out to be emic proper, the processes of interpretation and explanation do not apply.

4.3 The Schools of Grammar

Arabic grammar does not constitute a totally uniform set of theoretical and procedural principles, yielding universally acceptable descriptive results. Differences between the grammarians existed, resulting in the recognition of two major trends (*madhhab*) named after the two centers in which they had originally developed: Baṣra and Kūfa in modern Iraq.

The term *madrasa* (school), used in place of what was called *madhhab* in the preceding sentence, was given currency mainly by modern scholars, particularly Shawqī Ḍaif in his now famous book *al-Madāris al-Naḥwiyya* (The Schools of Grammar). What is interesting to point out here is that this shift in nomenclature has generated heated, but perhaps unnecessary, debate as to whether the above schools warrant this label, in the sense of their being coherent models with sufficiently irreconcilable differences between them in theoretical and methodological orientation. Had the modern grammarians continued to apply the term *madhhab*, instead of the ill-fitting *madrasa*, to designate each group of grammarians, the Baṣran's and the Kūfans, much of the heat would have been taken out of the debate, thus creating a more balanced perspective to assess the differences between them. A sober look of this kind would have shown that the differences between the Baṣrans and the Kūfans were differences of degree not kind.

The main differences between the Baṣrans and the Kūfans concern the two fundamentals of attested data (2.1.1) and analogy (4). As far as the former is concerned, the Kūfans did not apply the same rigid considerations which their Baṣran counterparts used in the selection of informants for the elicitation of data. Unlike the Baṣrans, the Kūfans sanctioned the use of bedouin speakers as informants, even when they were known to have had extensive contact with the urban population whose speech was judged to be grammatically suspect from the point of view of correctness. Although this is generally true, preference was always given by the Kūfans to informants who had very little or no contact with the urban population. With respect to the second fundamental, the Kūfans, unlike the Baṣrans, sanctioned the use of 'rare data' as bases for analogical creations of new utterances. The Baṣrans accepted attested rare data as part of the language, but they were extremely hesitant to use such data as the base or models for the analogical creation of new utterances.

Other differences existed between the Baṣrans and the Kūfans, but these are largely limited to the provision of different descriptive solutions to the same data and, in certain instances, to the employment of different terminologies.

The above differences between the Baṣrans and the Kūfans are best treated as variations on the same themes, or as divergences in degree, not kind. This conclusion is supported by the fact that differences existed in each group, creating fuzziness in theoretical orientations and tastes whose ultimate effect is to blur whatever flimsy boundaries existed between the two overarching groups. Furthermore, differences exist in the literature as to the total number of schools, in addition to the Baṣrans and the Kūfans, which obtained in the Arabic grammatical tradition. If this indicates anything, it shows that the theoretical and procedural grounds upon which the various schools are established are not rigorously defined. As a matter of fact, it seems that the chief consideration in attaching the label 'school' to a group of grammarians is primarily the fact that they operated in the same center in the Arabic and Muslim worlds, whence the labels the 'Andalusian School,' the 'Baghdad School,' the 'Egyptian School,' the 'Maghreb School,' and the 'Syrian School.' With Modern Arabic scholars, grammatical schools became like national airlines in modern times: each country/area must have one as a sign of its own identity and progress.

5. The Organization of Arabic Grammar

What must be avoided here is the temptation to force Arabic grammar into the all too prevalent orientation in modern linguistics to view models or theories as constructs consisting of fairly well-defined components which interact with each other in a (specified) manner. The Arabic grammarians viewed grammar as a coherent totality, but within this totality they recognized two major portions: morphology and syntax, the former often not easily distinguishable from what some modern linguists would call morphophonology. Arabic grammar also deals with issues of semantics and pragmatics as well as with phonology and phonetics.

5.1 Morphology

As has been mentioned in the preceding section, morphology is very closely linked with morphophonology in Arabic grammar. The primary notion in this portion of grammar is the *kalima*, which primarily designates a unit of the language similar to the word in structuralist and other approaches. But the same notion is also used to designate discrete morphemes which stand in a relation of prefixation or suffixation to the word in its capacity as a stem, for example the definite article and the sound masculine plural morphemes respectively.

It is clear from this brief presentation that the word in Arabic grammar is regarded as the central notion in morphology, and that it is viewed as an uninterruptable unit of the language. The latter feature of the word may be regarded as a reflection of an implicit bias in Arabic grammar toward treating linearity as a relevant feature of grammatical constructions.

Morphology is dealt with extensively by Sībawayhi in his *Kitāb*. The foundations laid down by this grammarian were later extensively developed by Ibn Jinnī in his two books *al-Khaṣā' iṣ* and, especially, *al-Munṣif* which is almost totally devoted to the task of expounding this area of linguistic description in relation to Arabic. The major notions in this area will be outlined in this section (for a fuller treatment see Bohas 1984 and Owens 1988).

A basic concept in morphology is the distinction between simple, unanalyzable or aplastic words (*jāmid*) and complex, derived or analyzable ones (*mushtaqq*). Considered from the perspective of the tripartite classification of words (*kalim*) into word classes, simple words are typically represented by members of the particle word class, for example prepositions, while substantives (*asmā'*) and verbs (*af'āl*) typically represent complex words. Morphology is restricted to words of the second category only, i.e., complex or derived words. However, complex here is not synonymous with polymorphemic (as the following discussion will show) although certain words are recognized as polymorphemic.

Take the derived word *kātib* which is usually glossed as 'writer (m.).' The morphological complexity of this word is explained in terms of its composition of a triliteral root *k-t-b*, which is given a vocalic pattern—represented by the vowels *ā-i* after the first and second consonants respectively—to create the structure or form (*binā'*, *wazn*) *kātib*. The meaning of the derived word *kātib* emerges from the interaction of the abstract lexical meaning of the root, which may be stated as 'something to do with writing,' and the equally abstract notional/functional meaning of the vocalic pattern visualized in relation to the root, which may be stated as 'agentive.' Clearly, in Arabic grammar the complexity of derived words is conceived in terms of their composition of consonantal roots and vocalic patterns which, together as a totality, may be further expanded by utilizing the sounds of augmentation (*ḥurūf al-ziyādah*): (*s*, ', *l*, *t*, *m*, *n*, *w*, *y*, *h*, *ā*). It should be added here that the majority of the derived words in

Arabic are reduced to triliteral roots. However, there is a minority of derived words in the language which consist of 4 or 5 root consonants.

This mode of generating words in Arabic is called minor derivation (*ishtiqāq asghar/ saghīr*) and is often taken to mean the same thing as *tasrīf* (a term that is better left untranslated to avoid confusion). Ibn Jinnī recognizes a second type of derivation which he calls major derivation (*ishtiqāq akbar*). Major derivation refers to the observation that the set of permutations of a triliteral root all share the same semantic import. Ibn Jinnī illustrates this type of derivation by the six permutations of the root *k-l-m* which share the overall arching meaning of 'power and strength.' The idea of major derivation was not original with Ibn Jinnī, as it was already present in the work of his mentor Abū 'Ali al-Fārisī (d. 978). However, the genesis of this type of derivation may be traced all the way back to the process of factorization which al-Khalīl applied in his lexicon *al-'Ayn* to calculate the lexical stock of the Arabic language (see Sect. 7).

Major derivation has a marginal status in Arabic morphology as does the process of blending (*naht*) which is used to produce new words by concatenating parts of two or more words to create a new word, in very much the same way as the English word 'smog' is created from the underlined elements in smoke and fog. A typical example of a blended word in Arabic is *basmalah* which is formed from the constituent parts of the religious formula: *bismillāhi al-rahmāni al-rahīm* (In the Name of God, the Compassionate, The Merciful). Blending has the status of being a marginal word-formation process in Arabic because it involves a very small number of items in the language.

The phenomenon of *i'rāb* (desinential inflection) covers the two categories of case and mode, and is treated in Arabic grammar as a morphosyntactic phenomenon, with the main emphasis being placed on its syntactic dimension. In a similar fashion, certain entities which would be treated as bound morphemes from the point of view of modern linguistic theory, for example the attached personal pronouns, are treated as primarily syntactic in nature in Arabic grammar. These two examples show that the delineation of morphology and syntax in Arabic grammar is based on grounds that are different from those which would be set up for this language in terms of modern linguistic theory. It is also clear from the earlier discussion in this section that what is called derivation in Arabic grammar is significantly different from derivation in modern linguistic theory. This is why it is important to avoid the recent tendency in the literature of hastily casting Arabic grammar in the light of this or that linguistic theory, often on the basis of facile comparisons.

5.2 Syntax (nahw)

Syntax is the other major area of Arabic grammar. The principal concern of syntax is the analysis of sentences into, ultimately, words, and the assignment of grammatical functions to these words, with special emphasis on the way these functions are formally marked by the desinential inflections in substantives and verbs (*i'rāb*) The Arabic grammarians recognize a type of entity approaching in status the phrase in modern linguistic theory. However, this entity is not established as a fully functioning unit on a full-fledged level of analysis between the sentence and the word.

Syntax in Arabic is dominated by the principle of governance or, more traditionally, regency (*'amal*), whose primary purpose is to account for the occurrence of desinential inflections (*i'rāb*) in words in their capacity as components of larger units. The principle of governance (regency) revolves around a triad of notions: the governing entity (*'āmil*), the governed entity (*ma'mūl bihi*) and the effect of the former on the latter (*'amal*), this being the occurrence of the syntactically appropriate desinential inflection in substantives and verbs. The following example will be used to illustrate these notions:

daraba Muhammad-un 'Aliyy-an (3)
Lit: hit Muhammad-nom 'Ali-acc
'Muhammad hit Ali'

In this example the verb *daraba* is said to be the governing entity (*'āmil*) of the two governed entities (*ma'mūl bihi*) *Muhammadun* and *'Aliyyan*, producing the effect (*'amal*) of controlling the former in the nominative and the latter in the accusative.

The governing entity in the above example is said to be overt/expressed in the sense that it is formally marked as an entity in the body of the sentence. In other instances, the governing entity may be covert/semantic in the sense that it is not formally marked as a unit in the sentence. Thus, in the following nonverbal sentence:

al-walad-u nashītu-un (4)
the boy nom industrious nom
'The boy is industrious.'

the subject/topic (*mubtada'*) *al-walad-u* is said to be in the nominative by virtue of its being the inceptive element in the sentence. Here, the governing entity is inception or topicalization (*ibtidā'*) and the governed entity is the subject *alwalad-u* which is in the nominative, this morphosyntactic category being the effect of the former on the latter.

An important feature in the discussion of the principle of governance is the set of conditions that are placed on the governing and governed entity. It would be impossible to state all these conditions here. The following are given for illustrative purposes only:

(a) the governing entity precedes the entity it governs;
(b) no entity can be governed by more than one governing entity; and
(c) the entities which govern the substantives are 'stronger' than those which govern the verbs.

The uncompromizing application of the governance principle in Arabic grammar gives rise to a number of notions whose purpose is to ensure that governance applies uniformly throughout the language. Chief among these notions are *iḍmār* (deletion or ellipsis) and *taqdīr* (paraphrase). To illustrate the former notion, consider the following examples.

In the sentence:

qāma *Muḥammad-un* (5)
stood up Muhammad-nom
'Muhammad stood up.'

the governing entity *qāma* precedes the governed subject/agent (condition (a) above) which is in the nominative. However, if the order of these two entities is reversed as in:

Muḥammad-un qāma (6)

then *Muḥammad-un* ceases to be treated as a governed entity of the verb because it precedes it, with the result that the occurrence of the nominative with this substantive is attributed to topicalization/inception in its capacity as the governing entity. But this leaves the governing verb without a formally expressed governed subject. To deal with this situation in terms of the governance principle, the verb is said to govern a deleted/ellipted subject *huwa* (he). Clearly, deletion, at least in contexts of this type, is a corrective strategy whose main purpose is to iron out awkward situations which emerge from the application of the governance principle throughout the grammatical portion of the language.

The recoverability of the deleted element in (6) above is determined by the structural properties of the sentence. In other instances, the recoverability of a deleted element may be determined only by reference to contextual or pragmatic factors: see the following well-known example:

al-hilāl-u *wallāhi* (7)
def-crescent-nom by God

is said to correspond to the sentence:

hadhā al-hilālu wallāhi (8)
'This is the crescent by God.'

in which the deleted element *hadhā* is recovered by reference to factors pertaining to the situational context.

One of the topics dealt with in discussions of the principle of governance is whether the governing entity/governor is a component of linguistic structure or the speaker himself. The predominant view in the literature is that it is the former, although grammarians like al-Fārisī, Ibn Jinnī, Ibn Maḍā', and al-Astrabādhhī consider the possibility that the speaker is the ultimate governor of the elements which occur in his linguistic utterances. At least as far as Ibn Jinnī is concerned, the adoption of this view—peripheral though it may be in his approach—represents his *mu'tazilite* predilections which, in scholastic theology, decree that man is the ultimate creator of his own actions, including speech.

The influence of scholastic theology on the principle of governance is, however, more pervasive. To a certain extent the governance principle in grammar echoes some of the salient properties of *ta'līl* (explanation) by means of causes (*'illas*) in scholastic theology. Thus in the same way as every governed entity must be controlled by a governor in grammar, every effect must be governed by a cause in scholastic theology. Similarly, in the same way as no governed entity can be controlled by two governors, no effect can be produced by two or more causes in scholastic theology.

The principle of governance held full sway in syntax, the only dissenting voice being that of the Andulusian grammarian Ibn Maḍā' al-Qurṭubī. This grammarian argued against the application of this principle in grammar because its descriptive consequences transcend the surface, observable structure of utterances in the language, thus leading to an unacceptable degree of speculation. He also opposed this principle because its application requires the setting up of corrective methods, for example deletion/ellipsis which distort the language by introducing into its utterances extraneous elements. In this, Ibn Maḍā' based his approach on the literalist Ẓāhirite views of Ibn Ḥazm in jurisprudence who rejected all attempts to tamper with the surface forms of the Qur'ān because that would amount to the falsification or fabrication of this text.

5.3 Semantics and Pragmatics

Arabic grammar adopts a predominantly formal approach to the setting up of its grammatical categories, including word classes, in the sense that it relies, inter alia, on properties of form—as opposed to meaning—and the distributional properties of entities in the language. However, semantic observations are not totally excluded from the scope of grammar. For example, Sībawaihi's classification of sentences into *mustaqīm ḥasan* (syntactically and semantically well-formed), *muḥāl* (ungrammatical), *mustaqīm kadhib* (syntactically well-formed but semantically unacceptable in terms of our knowledge of the world as it is), *mustaqīm qabīḥ* (awkward, albeit grammatically well-formed) and *muḥāl kadhib* (ungrammatical and semantically unacceptable in terms of our knowledge of the world as it is) shows an awareness of the importance of semantic consideration in grammar, particularly with regard to the question of the acceptability of sentences by native speakers.

Arab grammarians also deal with the semantically based notions of synonymy and antonymy, as well as with homonymy which is partly semantically anchored. They also deal with portions of the lexicon of the language utilizing concepts which correspond to hyponymy and hyperonymy in modern semantic theory. Furthermore, the Arabic grammarians invoke meaning as a consideration to iron out grammatical discrepancies in sentences, as, for example, when a masculine substantive is made to agree with a feminine verb, in verbal sentences, against the established grammatical rules of the language. The main method in dealing with this situation is *al-ḥamlu ʿalā al-maʿnā* (semantic correspondence) which interprets one of the entities, in this case the substantive, as being a legitimate constituent of the verbal sentence concerned by virtue of its semantic correspondence to another substantive which fits the context from the point of view of gender concord.

In later stages of Arabic grammar, the grammarians developed the disciplines of *ʿilm al-bayān* and *ʿilm al-maʿānī*, utilizing in this regard the views of earlier scholars. Broadly speaking, the main objective of *ʿilm al-bayān* is to deal with issues of metaphor and metaphorical meanings. *ʿilm al-maʿānī* deals with a variety of issues, chief among which is the correlation of sentential meanings with the variations in their constituent arrangements, in the light of the different pragmatic functions served by these permutations of constituents. Clearly, *ʿilm al-maʿānī* starts from the assumption that the main function of language is communication and that, within this framework, meaning assumes primary importance. Jurjāni (d. 1078) is the leading grammarian in the development of this branch of Arabic linguistic studies. Central to his approach is the importance of context as a factor in the proper analysis of language as a communication tool, with textual and situational contexts being given pride of place in this respect.

Jurjāni's work has attracted scholarly attention because it revolves around notions which are closely akin to some principal ideas in discourse analysis, particularly with respect to the organization of information in sentences. One of the main notions in this regard is that of placing important items before less important ones with respect to the pragmatic force of the message to be conveyed. Another important notion is that of treating the organization of constituents in sentences in terms of the parameter of new/old information.

6. Lexicography

The compilation of lexica started at a very early stage in the Arabic linguistic tradition. It is generally agreed in the sources that the impetus behind the emergence of this activity was the overriding one of providing an aid to the study of the meaning of the Qu'rān, as well as the preservation of its message as understood by the early Muslims before their language was affected by *laḥn*. The primacy of this objective imposed its limitations on the type of materials which were regarded as valid data for lexicographic work. Broadly speaking, lexical materials were culled from the Qu'rān and the poetry of the pre-Islamic and Islamic eras up to around the middle of the second century Hegira. Furthermore, in the elicitation of data from subjects the lexicographers tended to rely on informants who were judged to have had little or no contact with the urban population to guard against the inclusion of materials affected by *laḥn*.

Lexicographic work in the Arabic linguistic tradition is very diverse in nature. With respect to their organization, lexica may be based on a phonetic/phonological classificatory principle (as in *al-ʿAyn* by Al-Khalīl) or on the essentially graphologically-based alphabetical principle of letter arrangement (as in Ibn Duraid's *al-Jamhara*). Notional lexica group items together on the basis of their membership in lexical domains, for example *al-Mukhaṣṣaṣ* by Ibn Sīdah (d. 1066). There are also specialized lexica which list the items relevant to a particular field of inquiry, for example *al-Tadhkira* by al-Anṭāki (d. 1405) which deals with medical treatments. In all these lexica items which share the same root are grouped together into one principal entry headed by the root in question (see Sect. 5 for 'root'). Thus, all the items which share the root *k-t-b*, for example *kātib* (writer), *maktaba* (library), would be listed under the root concerned. However, this general organization principle is sometimes modified by the introduction of other classificatory principles. To illustrate this point, the Arabic lexicographic practice will be looked at in more detail by considering four different lexica, each representing a fairly well-defined trend in this domain.

The first lexicon is the famous *al-ʿAyn* by al-Khalīl which has the distinction of being the oldest lexicon, in the full sense of the term, in the Arabic linguistic tradition. Al-Khalīl organized the root entries in his lexicon in terms of the mode of articulation of the first element in each root, starting from the back of the vocal tract and moving forward to the front of the mouth. Another important feature of *al-ʿAyn* is the fact that it lists all the permutations of a root under the same entry, with the choice of entry being subsumed under the permutation which contains the letter with the highest order in the phonetic/

phonological spectrum established in terms of the first principle above. Thus, in terms of this principle, the set of root permutations *k-t-b*, *k-b-t*, *b-k-t*, *b-t-k*, *t-b-k*, *t-k-b*, would be listed under the letter *k* because its phonetic reflex is produced further back in the mouth than the reflexes of *t* or *b*. Furthermore, of the two *k* initial roots *k-t-b* and *k-b-t*, the former would take precedence over the latter because the phonetic reflex of the second radical letter *t* is produced further back in the mouth than that of *b*. However, since not all the permutations of a root may be lexically active, al-Khalīl distinguishes between root permutations which correspond to actual words in the language and those which represent what may be called phonological, or potential, words.

The second lexicon is *al-Jamhara* by Ibn Duraid (d. 933). This lexicographer arranges the entries in this lexicon first in terms of the number of radicals in the root, starting with biliteral roots and ending with roots which consist of five radicals. The entries within each root class are then arranged serially by reference to the position of the first letter in the root in the overall alphabetical hierarchy of the letters. Entries under each letter subclass are then subjected to a further listing principle whereby they are arranged on the basis of the serial ordering of the letters of the alphabet, starting with the letter of the subclass concerned, and moving down the hierarchy of letters until the roots are exhausted. Thus, under the letter (ج = *j*) in, say, triliteral roots, Ibn Duraid would first list all the roots beginning with this letter followed by (ح = *h*), followed by those beginning with (ج = *j*) and (خ = kh) and so on down the alphabetical hierarchy until all the roots are exhausted. Ibn Duraid also incorporates the root permutations principle first employed by al-Khalīl. The cumulation of all these principles in the compilation of this lexicon inevitably leads to overloading in its organization which, in turn, makes it rather unwieldy and user unfriendly.

The third lexicon considered is *al-ṣiḥāḥ* by al-Jawharī (d. 1003). Entries in this lexicon are based on the root concept, following the alphabetical system of subclassification in two ways. First, roots are serially subclassified in terms of the alphabetical order of their last radical; thus roots which end with letter (ب = *b*) would be listed before ones ending with (ت = *t*) or (ج = *j*). Second, within each subclass entries are arranged serially in terms of the position of their first letter in the alphabetical hierarchy. Thus, within the entries subsumed under the letter (ب = *b*) in the triliteral root class, the root *sh-r-b* would be listed before *k-t-b* because *sh* precedes *k* in the alphabetical hierarchy. Obviously, this lexicon is rather unwieldy to use, but it is extremely useful in poetry because of its bias toward the rhyme (*qāfiya*) which is a characteristic feature of poetry. It seems also to be directed at those engaged in the art of alliterative prose.

The fourth lexicon is the one by the nineteenth-century lexicographer and educationist al-Bustānī (d. 1883): *Muḥīṭ al-Muḥīṭ*. The main classificatory principle in this lexicon is that of listing roots according to the alphabetical order of their first radicals. Thus, roots which begin with (ب = *b*) precede those which begin with (ت = *t*) and so on until the end of the alphabet, regardless of the number of radicals involved. However, this classificatory principle is not original with Bustānī, as it was employed earlier in different types of lexica. An interesting feature of this lexicon is its utilization of data which fall outside the scope of the 'principles' of selection outlined at the beginning of this section. For example, Bustānī cites late poets from the Abbasid period, a practice more or less outlawed in the standard lexical works, although this restriction was relaxed by some later lexicographers.

Bustānī's lexicon shows that Arabic lexicography continued well into the nineteenth century, and that the process of development was generally one of simplification for the user, but without relinquishing the central notion of the root owing to its semantic and derivational significance in the language. However, Arabic lexicography in the twentieth century has moved away from this long-standing commitment to the root as a primary classification principle, preferring to arrange entries alphabetically by reference to actual word shapes. Thus, whereas all the words which are built on the root *k-t-b* are all listed under this root, in, say, Bustānī's *Muḥīṭ al-Muḥīṭ*, in al-ʿAlāylī's *Marjiʿ* they are listed under different entries according to their first letters, with the result that the words *kātib* (male writer) and *maktaba* (library), for example, are listed under the letters *k* and *m* respectively. It must be pointed out, however, that this mode of listing items in modern lexica is not totally foreign to the Arabic lexicographic tradition, although the immediate impetus seems to have come from western lexicography. A major factor in this shift of focus in modern lexicographic practice is undoubtedly the desire on the part of the lexicographers to facilitate the task of looking up words in the language, by reducing the reliance on the grammatical information needed in this connection. Finally, the twentieth century has also seen an explosion in bilingual, mainly Arabic–English/French, and specialized dictionaries to meet the demands of foreign language learners and to keep pace with the development of specialized terminologies.

7. Conclusion

The preceding discussion barely scratches the surface of the rich and varied terrain of the Arabic linguistic tradition. Within this tradition, Arabic grammar developed in the light of insights from the neighboring disciplines of jurisprudence and scholastic theology. The influence of the former is present in the treatment of the fundamentals of the Arabic grammar (Sect. 2.1), whereas the influence of the latter is clear in the development of the principle of governance. Arabic grammar was also influenced by external grammatical traditions, for example Greek and Sanskrit grammars. However, the channels of influence are not always easy to trace. Consequently, one must be careful before one pronounces affirmatively on the possible external sources which are assumed to have fed into the Arabic grammatical tradition.

The Arabic linguistic tradition is not a hybrid of disparate external influences. Rather, it is developed on foundations which are primarily directed by the principal objective of providing a framework for the analysis of the text of the Qu'rān, Arabic poetry, and other types of data. Other objectives do exist, but they are nowhere near this one in their centrality within the Arabic linguistic tradition.

See also: Arab and Persian Phonetics.

Bibliography

Al-'Alāyhī, Abd al-Alla (n.d.) *Al-Marji'*. Dār al-Mu'jam al-'Arabī, Beirut

Baalbaki R 1983 The relation between *Naḥw and Balāgha*: A comparative study of the methods of Sībawayhi and Jurjānī. *Zeitschrift für Arabische Linguistik* II: 7–23

El-Badry N 1986 The development of the bilingual English Arabic dictionary from the middle of the 19th century to the present. In: Hartmann R R K (ed.) *The History of Lexicography*. Benjamins, Amsterdam

Blanc H 1957 Linguistics among the Arabs. *Current Trends in Linguistics* **13**: 265–83

Blau H 1963 The role of the Bedouins as arbiters in linguistic questions and the *Mas'ala Zanbūriyya*. *Journal of Semitic Studies* **8**: 42–51

Bloch A 1986 *Studies* in *Arabic Syntax and Semantics*. Otto Harrassowitz, Wiesbaden

Bohas G 1984 *Etudes des Théories des Grammairiens Arabes*. Institut Francais de Domas, Damascus

Al-Bustānī B 1979 *Muḥīṭ al-Muḥīṭ* Librairie du Liban, Beirut

Carter M 1981 *Arabic Linguistics*. Benjamins, Amsterdam

Ḍaif S (n.d.) *Al-Madāris al-Naḥwiyya*. Dār al-Ma'ārif bi Miṣr, Cairo

Al-Farāhīdī, al-Khalīl Ibn Aḥmad 1914 *Kitābu al-'Ayn*. Anstās al-Karmalī, Baghdad

Al-Fārisī, Abū 'Alī 1978 *'Aqsāmu al-'Akhbār*. *Al-Mawrid* **7(3)**: 201–20

Haywood J A 1986 The entry in medieval Arabic monolingual dictionary. In: Hartmann R R K (ed.) *The History of Lexicography*. Benjamins, Amsterdam

Ibn al-Anbārī, Abū al-Barakāt 1957 *Asrāru al-'Arabiyya*. al-Majma' al-'il'mī al-'Arabī, Damascus

Ibn al-Anbārī, Abū al-Barakāt (n.d.) *Luma' al-Adilla fī Uṣūl al-Naḥw*. Almqvist and Wiksell, Stockholm

Ibn al-Anbārī, Abū al-Barakāt (n.d.) *Kitābu al-Inṣāfī fī Masā'il al-Khilāf bayna al-Naḥwiyyīna al-Basriyyīn wa al-Kūfiyyīn*. Muḥammad Muḥyī al-Dīn 'Abd al-Ḥamīd, Dār al-Fikr. Beirut

Ibn Duraid, Abū Bakr Muḥammad Ibn al-Ḥasan 1344 A H *Jamharatu al-Lugha*. Haydar Abad, India

Ibn Jinnī, Abū al-Fatḥ 'Uthmā'n 1954 *al-Munṣif*. Idārat'Ihyā' al-Turāth al-Qadīm, Cairo

Ibn Jinnī, Abū al-Fatḥ 'Uthmān 1952–56 *al-Khaṣā'iṣ*. Cairo 1952–56. (Reproduced by Dār al-Kitāb al-'Arabī, Beirut, n.d.)

Ibn Maḍā', Abū 'Abbās 1982 *Kitāb al-Radd 'alā al-Nuḥāt*. Shawqī Ḍaif, Dār al-Ma'ārifa, Cairo

Ibn al-Sarrāj, Abū Bakr 1973 *Al-Uṣūl fī al-Naḥw*. 'Abd al-Ḥusayn al-Fatḥ, Maṭba'at al-Nu'mān, Najaf

Al-Jawharī, Ismā'īl Ibn Ḥammād 1979 *Al-Ṣiḥāḥ*. Dār al-'llm li al-Malāyīn, Beirut

Al-Jurjānī, 'Abd al-Qāhir 1978 *Dalā'il al-'I'jāz*. Muḥammad Riḍā, Dār al-Ma'ārifa, Beirut

Al-Jurjānī, 'Abd al-Qāhir 1981 *'Asrār al-Balāgha*. Muḥammad Riḍā, Dār al-Ma'ārifa, Beirut

Owens J 1988 *The Foundations of Grammar: An Introduction to Medieval Arabic Grammatical Theory*. Benjamins, Amsterdam

Peterson D 1972 Some explanatory methods of the Arab grammarians. Papers from the Eighth Regional Meeting: Chicago Linguistic Society. Chicago, IL

Semaan K I 1963 *Arabic Phonetics. Ibn Sīnā's Risāla on the Points of Articulation of the Speech Sounds*. Sheikh Muhammad Ashraf, Lahore

Sībawayhi, Abū Bish 'Amr Ibn 'Uthmān Ibn Qanbar 1983 *Al-Kitāb*, 3rd edn. 'Abdu al-Salām Muḥammad Hārūn, Al-Hay'a al-Miṣriyya, Cairo

Al-Suyuṭī, Jalāl al-Dīn 1976 *Kitāb al-'Iqtirāḥ*. Aḥmad Qāsim, Maktabat al-Sa'āda, Cairo

Versteegh C 1977 *Greek Elements in Arabic Linguistic Thinking*. E J Brill, Leiden

Aristotle and the Stoics on Language

F. W. Householder

The period from about 350 BCE to 150 BCE was perhaps the most productive for Greek linguistics. In the case of Aristotle, there exists a substantial portion of his writings preserved in manuscript; for all the others, including the Academy, Epicurus, and the Stoics, as well as the various scholarly writers associated with Alexandria and Pergamon, there remain only fragments, summaries, and comments preserved in later writings (often in two or more steps: 'Sextus Empiricus quotes Chares quoting Crates,' for instance). But, fortunately, the fragments of the Stoics are sufficient to give an excellent idea of their linguistic teachings. And, like Aristotle, they approach language from a philosophical, logical perspective.

1. Aristotle

Aristotle's linguistic output falls into two parts, one represented especially by chapters 19–22 of the *Poetics* (1456a–1459a), but also four paragraphs elsewhere (*Rhetoric* III, 5, 1407b; *Prior Analytics* I, 36, 48b–49a; and *Sophistical Refutations* 14, 173b–174a and 32, 182a–b); the other by the *Categories* and the *de Interpretatione*. The former items seems to contain substantially the standard analysis presented in the *grammatikē* of the fifth and fourth centuries BCE, much like what is seen in Plato, while the latter represent Aristotle's own original research.

In the *Poetics* are three of the recurring linguistics topics of antiquity: (a) sentence-types or illocutionary forces (question, command, statement, etc.); (b) parts of speech (Aristotle does not here use the expression *meros tou logou*, but lists *sundesmos, onoma, rhēma, arthron*); and (c) the four transformations (addition, deletion, substitution, and transposition—here used for the derivation of poetic words from ordinary ones). There is also a clear anticipation of the pattern of later *technai* (grammatical sketches like Dionysius Thrax's): first a list of some technical terms (providing a table of contents), then definitions, subclassification, and discussion of each in turn, then, in the *Poetics*, a further subclassification of nouns and their inflections. The most interesting additions to Plato's treatment of phonology is the mention of voiced stops, shapes of the mouth, places (of articulation), and aspiration (a brief treatment, but basically better than in Dionysius Thrax). He treats tense, mood, case, and number on 1457a 17–22 (all called *ptōsis*), but gender in 1458a 8–17, since it is not an inflection (for nouns, at least), but an inherent property, partly signaled, in the nominative, by the final consonant or vowel. His only way of naming the cases is with the forms of *houtos* ('this'): *toutou* means 'genitive case,' *toutōi* 'dative', etc. This usage recurs in *Prior Analytics* 4–9a 1–5 and *Soph. Refut.* 182a 32–b3 and 173b 26–37. It is interesting that Pāṇini sometimes uses the same device. Aristotle in some of these places uses it to indicate gender, though he knows the three Protagorean names also, and sometimes uses *metaxu* 'between' for the neuter.

The interesting addition in these last three passages and in the *Rhetoric* one (1407b) is what seems to be standard fifth-century treatment of syntax. It is introduced under the heading of solecism (a word first attested in this sense in Herodotus 4.117.1). While there is only one word for correct Greek, 'hellenism,' there are two for errors: 'barbarism,' which includes all errors of pronunciation, spelling, inflectional morphology, and vocabulary choice, and 'solecism,' which means any error in syntax. In particular it refers to errors of agreement in gender, number (or case), of case government, and apparently certain instances of word-order and semantics (*Rhetoric* 1407b 6–7). The rules implied in these four passages are the following:

(a) correlative conjunctions (like *men* and *de*) should be made to correspond (and at a reasonable distance);
(b) each word should be placed so that its syntactical connection is unambiguous (remember the hyperbaton in Plato's *Protagoras* 343F);
(c) participles and adjectives must agree with the nouns they modify in case, gender, and number;
(d) the subject of a finite verb is in the nominative;
(e) the subject of an infinitive (unless identical with the subject of its governing verb) is in the accusative;
(f) the gender of a noun (as opposed to interrogative and sometimes relative and demonstrative pronouns) need not be the same as the sex or animacy of its referent;
(g) a relative pronoun must agree in gender and number with its antecedent;
(h) a predicate noun or adjective with a verb like *einai* 'to be' agrees in case with its subject;
(i) words like *isos* 'equal to' govern the dative;
(j) words like *diplasios* 'double' govern a genitive; and
(k) transitive verbs (like *tuptō* 'hit' and *horō* 'see') govern the accusative.

All of these passages, except the one in *Rhetoric*, also include a technical term for 'nominative singular' (besides *houtos*) or, sometimes, 'nominative singular masculine,' or, perhaps, in one passage, 'the termination of the nominative singular,' *klēsis*. This is opposed, of course, to the *ptōseis*, which are all the other forms (case, number, and gender) of a noun, pronoun, or adjective (which are all *onoma* to Aristotle).

The reason why syntax is discussed in all these passages is the same, to show how some *soloikismoi* may either be used to deceive your interlocutor or audience, or else be analyzed to avoid being deceived or to refute an opponent. (Since the sixth century, when an educated man need only be able to discuss and analyze poems at a dinner party or drinking party, a new recreation had arisen in Athens, to which Plato's dialogues give literary life, the disputation on philosophical or technical points.)

To sum up, the grammar sketched in the *Poetics* and used in Aristotle's discussions of solecism may be said to summarize the linguistic achievements of the fifth century, and thus, in a sense, represent the earliest grammatical treatment of Greek that can be reconstructed.

The *Categories*, by contrast, contain a great deal that is new. In spite of the vague similarity of Plato's *onoma* and *rhēma* to 'subject' and 'predicate,' it is only in Aristotle that the notion of 'predicate' is really developed. And even he does not provide a perfect expression for 'subject': *hupokeimenon* is indeed the source of our term calqued into Latin—*hupo* = *sub*, *keimenon* = *jectum*—but none of the later grammarians made such use of it. For Apollonius Dyscolus it is almost as often used for the object as for the subject, and he often flounders around for lack of such a term. But after the rediscovery of Aristotle, the term does come into grammatical use. The *Categories* (the term means 'predicates' or 'predicate-types') does, however, provide the only elaborated classification of predicates outside of the Stoics. Essentially Aristotle envisages a formula S = X + (is/are) + Predicate in which the 'is/are' may sometimes be swallowed up in the Predicate (see *De Interpretatione* 21b *badizei* 'walks' equals *badizōn esti* 'is walking') and lists 10 different types of Predicate, which he may or may not have meant to be an exhaustive list, based, apparently, on a mixture of semantic and formal (morphological or syntactic) criteria, but which certainly comes close to being exhaustive. The traditional names of these predicate-types can be matched up with grammatical classes as follows:

(a) Substance (including particulars, species, and genera) = noun phrases, including proper nouns and definite NPs as particulars, simple NPs as species and genera.
(b) Quantity (including size) = adjectival expressions of size and number (but excluding words like 'big' and 'little,' 'many' and 'few,' which are really *relative* terms (*pros ti*)), hence numbers and numerical phrases.
(c) Quality = nonquantitative, nonrelative (although Aristotle suggests that some adjectives are both qualitative and relative), adjectives, and adjective phrases.
(d) Relation (*pros ti*) = adjectives which may be compared (or modified by 'more,' 'very,' 'so,' etc.) and nouns which require or imply a dependent genitive (like *father*, inalienably possessed, or like *knowledge*, nominalizations of transitive verbs).
(e) Place = adverbs and prepositional phrases of place.
(f) Time = adverbs and phrases of time.
(g) Position (*keisthai*) seems to include stative verbs of sitting, standing, lying down, and the like, though it probably is not limited to human subjects.
(h) State (*echein*) appears to mean perfect passive verbs other than any included in Position.
(i) Action (*poiein*) seems to include both transitive and intransitive verbs (in the present or aorist especially).
(j) Affection (*paschein*) includes verbs in the passive voice plus other verbs of sensation or emotion.

Though a few of the same terms will be met later in Dionysius Thrax's lists of verb voices, noun types, and adverb types, most of these notions do not appear in later grammarians.

The *De Interpretatione* (*peri hermēneias*) starts out with some more precise definitions of terms seen before, like 'noun' and 'verb' and 'sentence,' plus some new ones like 'proposition.' The opening paragraph, however, contains an interesting refinement of the innateness assumption used by Psammetichus: 'What occurs in speech are symbols of feelings in the mind, and what is written are symbols of what is spoken. Speech is not the same for all men, any more than writing is, but the mental feelings of which spoken words are signs, *are* the same for all, and likewise the things (*pragmata*) of which those feelings are symbols.' This defines four layers: 'things' in the outside world are symbolized by 'feelings' (*pathēmata*) in the mind (and both the things and the feelings are the same for all men), which are, in turn, symbolized by speech, spoken words (*phōnē*), which, in their turn, are represented by writing (*grammata*). This layer of *pathēmata*, then, constitutes a universal mental language common to all men. This view is, of course, more a matter of psychology than linguistics, but it seems to occur again in the Stoics, and to be presupposed by some modern linguistic and semantic theories.

Here again are met not all six of the illocutionary forces listed in the *Poetics* (command, wish/hope/prayer, statement, threat, question, and answer), but at least one of them, statement or proposition (*apophansis*), which is the only one capable of truth or falsity (this must also include 'answer,' as he says in 17a, which does not really belong on the same list as the others). All through the *De Interpretatione* Aristotle emphasizes the arbitrariness of the sign (*katasunthēkēn*), as in the initial paragraph quoted above.

The improved definitions of noun and verb include the notions of tense (verb is [+tense], noun is [– tense]) and minimality (no fully significant parts). The Greek negatives (*ouk*/*ou* and *mē*) are treated as prefixes, and negatived nouns or verbs (remember adjectives are also nouns) are called indefinite (*aorista*) nouns and verbs. The name *ptōsis* is given to the oblique cases of nouns (genitive, dative, etc., is the order, though no names are used); subjecthood possibility is made the criterion for nouns in the strict sense (i.e., nominatives). The same name (*ptōsis*) applies to verbs for all tenses (he mentions past and future) except the present indicative; nothing is said here about subjunctives, optatives, infinitives, and participles. Unlike nouns and verbs, sentences (*logoi*) have meaningful parts, but not parts capable of being true or false (this clearly excludes complex and compound sentences, which he alludes to later). Incidentally, though this discussion of propositions or simple sentences makes much reference to subjects, neither *hupokeimenon* nor any other term for subject is used.

Numerous small references to linguistic matters (including phonetics) occur elsewhere in Aristotle, but these are the main passages of interest.

2. The Stoics

It is the work of the Stoics, which clearly establishes most of the framework for later grammatical writing. Though Zeno (at least to some extent) and Chrysippus (see the numerous titles listed in Diogenes Laertius VII. 191–2, and also for syntax, VII.63) did the basic work, much of our knowledge (for phonology and morphology) comes from Diogenes the Babylonian as quoted in Diogenes Laertius VII.55–60 (though there are many other sources). It is possible, of course, that if the complete works of Aristarchus had survived, the Alexandrians might be assigned more importance than the Stoics. Diogenes of Babylon's treatise was not called 'Grammar' (*Technē grammatikē*) but *Peri Phōnēs*, which is hard to translate; *phōnē* is a very widely used word meaning, in grammarians, most often 'word' or 'phonological word,' but also 'voice' (of animals or man), 'speech,' 'utterance,' or even sometimes 'style' or 'sound' (though noises made by inanimate objects are sometimes excluded). Among the Stoics *phōnē* is sometimes restricted to the concrete *aisthēton* 'perceptible,' which is the *sēmainon* 'signifier' (as opposed to the *sēmainomenon* 'signified' which is *noēton* 'thinkable' or abstract), but Diogenes clearly includes more. Similar variation applies also in the case of other words for 'word,' e.g., *dialektos* (so used by Plato and Aristotle, though Diogenes narrows it down to 'other Greek dialect word') and *lexis*, 'significant word' or 'spellable word' for the Stoics, but often also, 'speech,' 'expression,' 'style,' and, of course, *onoma* and *rhēma*, which may both be simply 'word' in Plato and Aristotle, though not in the Stoics. *Logos*, which always means 'sentence' or 'proposition' in grammar and logic, never means 'word,' though occasionally it means 'prose work' and, of course, 'reason' and related ideas.

Though the Stoics add only one new 'part of speech' (which should, of course, have been rendered 'part of the sentence' from Plato on) to Aristotle's list, the *prosēgoria* ('common noun,' *onoma* being now restricted to 'proper noun'), they give new definitions. This involves, in part, the incorporation of Aristotle's 'substance' into 'quality,' so that proper nouns signify an 'individual quality,' and the use of a feature [$\pm$case] for verb, conjunction, and article (now apparently restricted to the definite article, though later the simple relative pronoun is also included). And, though Antipater's proposed adverb (*mesotēs*) does not catch on, a new term *morion* ('particle') does come into use, without being defined, entailing not a new part of speech, but a new classification of words, roughly into full words and empty words, to use modern terms. Examples are: Diogenes Laertius VII.64 referring to the preposition *hupo*, 70 referring to the negative *ou*/*ouk*, the negative prefix *a-*/*an-*, the indefinite pronoun *tis*—cf. Sextus Empiricus *Math.* 8.96—and the demonstrative *ekeinos*. It is often used for words which do not clearly come under any of the official parts of speech. Neither Plato nor Aristotle used the word in this way, nor does Dionysius Thrax, but Apollonius Dyscolus does. Schneider (in his index, *Grammatici Graeci* II, 3) thinks it is merely a synonym of *meros logou* or *lexis*, 'word,' but no two of these three are used in exactly the same way. Both *morion* and *lexis* (but not *meros logou*) may be used with adjectives like 'verbal,' 'pronominal,' but only *morion* occurs with a whole bunch of adjectives ('uninflected,' 'meaningless,' 'interrogative,' 'enclitic,' 'indefinite,' 'underlying,' etc.) and only *meros logou* is used with 'one,' 'two,' 'the same' and 'different' ('one m.l.' is a [compound] word, while 'two m.l.' is a phrase). Nouns and verbs are only rarely called *morion*, most of the examples being pronouns, small adverbs, interrogatives, indefinites, conjunctions, and prepositions. The Latin equivalent *particula* is used once by Priscian (*Inst.* XVII, IV, 29) for the Greek relative pronoun (here *infinita particula* 'indefinite particle'), though Portus in his translation of Apollonius uses it several times, with similar adjectives ('enclitic,' 'interrogative'), referring to various pronouns, conjunctions, interrogatives, articles, enclitics, and the comparative word 'more.' Aulus Gellius almost restricts his use to prepositions and verbal prefixes, but applies the word also to *saltem* ('at least') which is used like such Greek enclitic monosyllables as *ge*, a use which is almost the only one for modern grammarians. By Stoic definitions most of these 'particles' would be either adverbs or conjunctions.

Description of the major Stoic contributions to grammar, must start with the *lekta* ('sayables'), as expounded by Diocles Magnes (in Diogenes Laertius 7.66) and in Sextus Empiricus *Math.* 8.70. These are of two kinds, complete or sufficient (*autotelē*) and deficient or incomplete (*ellipē*). All *lekta* are said to be abstract (thoughts, in some sense, or meanings), though much that is said about them sounds to us like talk about the *expression* of thoughts. A complete *lekton* is a *logos* ('sentence') and these may be of several kinds (illocutions, sentence-types), as follows:

(a) statement or assertion (*axiōma, apophantikon lekton*), which alone can be true of false (this follows Aristotle), e.g., 'Dion is walking';
(b) yes/no question (*erotēma*), e.g., 'Is Dion walking?';
(c) *wh*-question (*pusma*), e.g., 'where does Dion live?';
(d) command (*prostaktikon),* e.g., 'Come here,' requiring the imperative mood;
(e) address or vocative (*prosagoreutikon, klētikon*), e.g., 'O King Agamemnon';
(f) superassertion or exclamation (*pleion ē axiōma,* or *homoion axiōmati* or *thaumastikon*), e.g., 'How that boy resembles the princes!'—(*psektikon* apparently is a variant of this with derogatory content);
(g) rhetorical question (i.e., a question not requiring an answer—*epaporētikon*), e.g., 'I wonder if life and sadness are interrelated';
(h) wish/prayer/curse (*euktikon*, or, if bad, *aratikon*), e.g., 'Zeus give victory to Ajax' or 'May his brain spill like wine,' requiring the optative mood (unreal wishes are ignored);
(i) oath (*omotikon*), e.g., 'I swear by Zeus to do that!'; and, finally,
(j) hypothesis or assumption (*ekthetikon* and *hupothetikon*, treated as different by our source), e.g., 'Let X be the center of a circle' or 'Assume that the earth goes around the sun,' with verbs in the third person singular imperative.

Those of these ten which do not require specific morphology often allow special conjunctions or adverbs. These are all real types, all syntactically distinguished in Greek (as well as English), but not all possible types or all that are distinguished in Greek. The omissions are potential/unreal 'statements' and questions, as well as questions expecting an imperative reply ('Shall I go?'). But no modern grammarian has done any better. In the case of *axiōmata* (falsifiable sentences, i.e., those which are capable of being judged true or false), Chrysippus also allowed (in building a kind of logical calculus) for compound/complex sentences of five basic types, with three or more subtypes. Though the expressions themselves are more logical than grammatical, the conjunctions involved are assigned related names, which appear again in Dionysius Thrax and other grammarians. The types are:

(a.1) real, indicative condition (*sunēmmenon axiōma*, conjunction 'if'—*ei*—, *sunaptikos*);
(a.2) subtype inferential, 'since'—clause (*parasunēmmenon*, conjunction 'since—*epei*—, *parasunaptikos*);
(b) compound sentence (*sumpeplēgmenon*, conjunction 'both–and'—*kai–kai*—, *sumplektikos*);
(c.1) disjunctive sentence (*diezeugmenon*, conjunction exclusive 'either–or'—*ētoi–ē*—, *diazeuktikos*);
(c.2) subtype nonexclusive disjunction (*paradiezeugmenon*, conjunction nonexclusive 'or'—*ē*—, *paradiazeuktikos*);
(d) causal sentence (*aitiōdes*, conjunction 'because'—*dihoti*—, *aitiōdēs, aitiologikos*);
(e) comparative sentence (*diasaphoun to mallon/hētton*, conjunction '(more/less...) than' —*ē, ēper*—, *diasaphētikos*).

All of these conjunctions appear on Dionysius Thrax's list and Apollonius Dyscolus' list; most appear in Latinized form in Priscian, who also uses some of the Greek names.

Before considering Stoic contributions to verb-classification and inflectional categories, first the modern view of the standard analysis of the Greek verb must be laid out. Greek verb forms are all assigned to one or another of four tense/aspect systems and three voices; this makes only 10, instead of 12 aspect-voice categories, because in two aspects (imperfective and stative/perfect) the forms for passive and middle are the same. The other two tense/aspects are the perfective (aorist) and the future, which is not really an aspect, and lacks two moods that all the others have: imperative and subjunctive. All 10 voice-aspect systems have an optative, an infinitive, a participle, and at least one indicative: the future has no forms with augment (i.e., a prefixed vowel) and past tense endings, the aorist (perfective) none without augment and with present endings, but the other two have both. Later grammarians (e.g., Dionysius Thrax and Apollonius Dyscolus) detached the participles entirely from the verb (because they satisfied both the [+tense] and the [+case] requirements which otherwise distinguish verbs from nouns). Two other forms are nowadays associated with verbs, the verbal adjectives or 'verbals' in *-tos, -tē, -ton* (like *lekton, aisthēton, noēton*, favorite Stoic terms) which more or less resemble adjectives in *-able* (*sayable, perceivable, thinkable*), and *-teos, -tea, -teon*, (more or less like the Latin passive periphrastic, 'which must be said, perceived, thought'). All of the ancients, if they mention these at all, treat them as derivatives, not part of the conjugation. In each of the regular moods and tenses, most verbs have eight forms (first, second, and third person singular and plural, second, and third person dual), but imperatives lack a first person (for which the subjunctive is used). Some verbs are impersonal, and have only a third person singular (and it cannot have a nominative subject), meaning things like 'it is necessary,' 'it is best,' 'it is of interest,' etc.

Now can be considered which of these things the Stoics dealt with, and how. The treatment of predicates (*ellipē lekta*, 'incomplete sayables') or *katēgorēmata* (instead of *katēgoriai*) differs sharply from Aristotle's, most of whose predicates required a verb 'is,' in that they count verbs only, separated into four classes by the features [± __ nom] and [± __ oblique]. Verbs which are personal and intransitive (requiring no oblique case) are called *sumbama*. If they need an object of some kind, they are *hētton/elatton ē sumbama* (less than *sumbama*). If they are impersonal, i.e., do not allow a nominative case (i.e., subject) or more than one oblique case (usually dative), they are *parasumbama*. And if they occur with two obliques but no nominative, they are *elatton/hētton ē parasumbama* ('less than p'). But if they occur with two nominatives, but require no obliques (like 'is,' 'becomes,' etc.), the Stoics had no known name for them. These types continued to be distinguished, but new names were adopted for them.

The Stoics also introduced names for the voices: *sumbamata* in the active (governing accusative, dative, or genitive) are *ortha* (upright), a term which is sometimes mentioned by later grammarians, but is normally replaced (by *energētika* or *drastika* 'active'); the same verbs in the passive, capable of taking *hupo* (by) with a genitive ('of agent') are called *huptia* (prone), again normally replaced later by another word (*pathētika*, 'passive'); and verbs which take neither of those two constructions, being intransitive, whether active or middle in form, are called *oudetera* (neither). Dionysius Thrax includes both *epoiēsamēn* (aorist middle for us) and *pepoitha* (second perfect active) in his category *mesotēs* (middleness), and Apollonius also treats second perfect actives as middle, but apparently no other intransitive actives are called that; so the later 'middle' is not the same as Stoic *oudetera*. Nor is it equal to the Stoic *antipeponthota* (reflexively influenced), which are middle verbs with some reference back to the subject, as *keiretai* 'he gets a haircut' (not 'he cut his own hair') from *keirei* 'he cuts (someone's hair).'

Turning to the treatment of tense by the Stoics, there is a curious passage in the Scholia to Dionysius Thrax (on a passage where Dionysius speaks of the three kinships—*sungeneiai*—present to imperfect [*paratatikos*], future to aorist, and perfect to pluperfect):

> The Stoics say the present should be called 'present imperfect' (*paratatikos*, 'extended' which in Dionysius and later means simply the imperfect tense) for when you say *poiō* 'I am doing,' you imply that you were doing it before and will be doing it after the moment of speaking; and the imperfect should be 'past imperfect' for similar reasons.... And the perfect tense (*parakeimenos*) is called [sc. 'by the Stoics'?] 'present *suntelikon*,' and its past is the pluperfect.

But *suntelikon* cannot be translated here as 'perfect' (to give a neat match 'present perfect' and 'past perfect' corresponding to 'present imperfect' and 'past imperfect') because everywhere that *suntelikos* or *sunteleia* is used to refer to an aspect (four or five times, in all) it refers to the aorist, not the perfect (some of these are infinitives, others imperfectives, and one, *hixon*, is indicative). A possible conclusion is that the perfect is 'present perfective,' the aorist is 'indefinite perfective' [*aoristos* means 'indefinite'] and the pluperfect is 'past perfective,' while *suntelikos* by itself includes all forms of the aorist system; but it is not known what the nonindicative forms of the perfect system were called by the Stoics. As for the generic term for aspect, it is clearly *diathesis* (which also serves for *mood* and *voice*). The effects of this analysis are evident in Apollonius Dyscolusas well as Quintilian and Varro (for Latin, which has no distinction like the Greek one between aorist and perfect).

It is difficult to summarize the contribution of the Stoics to linguistic theory, but it appears enormous, both in the way they raise new grammatical questions and in providing solutions for older ones.

Bibliography

Arens H 1984 *Aristotle's Theory of Language and its Tradition: Texts from 500 to 1750*, Studies in the History of Linguistics **29**. Benjamins, Amsterdam

Arnim H von 1902 *Stoicorum veterum fragmenta*, vol. II, *Chrysippi fragmenta logica et physica*. Teubner, Leipzig; repr. 1923

Ax W 1986 Quadripartita Ratio, etc. *Historiographia Linguistica* **13**: 191–214; also in: Taylor (1987)

Baratin M 1978 Sur l'absence de l'expression des notions de sujet et de prédicat, etc. In: Collart J (ed.) *Varron, grammaire antique et stylistique latine*. Les Belles Lettres, Paris

Baratin M, Desbordes F 1986 La 'Troisième partie' de *l'ars grammatica*. *Historiographia Linguistica* **13**: 215–40; also in: Taylor (1987)

Barwick K 1957 *Probleme der Stoischen Sprachlehre und Rhetorik*. ASAW **49(3)**

Collart J (ed.) 1978 *Varron, grammaire antique et stylistique latine*. Les Belles Lettres, Paris

De Mauro T 1965 Il nome del dativo e la teoria dei casi greci. *Atti della accademia nazionale dei lincei, serie ottova, rendiconti, classe di scienti morali, storiche e filologiche* **20**: 151–211

Desbordes F 1983 Le schéma 'addition, soustraction, mutation, métathèse' dans les textes anciens. *Histoire—Epistémologie—Langage* **5**: 23–30

Donnet D 1967 La place de la syntaxe dans les traités de grammaire grecque, des origines au XII siècle. *L'Antiquité Classique* **36**: 22–48

Egli U 1970 Zwei Aufsätze zum Vergleich der stoischen Sprachtheorie mit modernen Theorien. *Arbeitspapier* Nr. 2, Universität Bern, Institute für Sprachwissenschaft

Egli U 1986 Stoic syntax and semantics. *Historiographia Linguistica* **13**: 281–306; also in: Taylor (1987)
Frede M 1978 Principles of Stoic grammar. In: Rist J M (ed.) *The Stoics*. University of California Press, Berkeley, CA
Gentinetta P M 1961 *Zur Sprachbetrachtung bei den Sophisten und in der stoisch–hellenistischen Zeit*. Verlag P G Keller, Winterthur
Householder F W 1989 Review of Taylor 1987. *Historiographia Linguistica* **16**: 131–48
Koller H 1958 Die Anfänge der griechischen Grammatik. *Glotta* **37**: 5–40
Pfeiffer R 1968 *History of Classical Scholarship*. Clarendon Press, Oxford
Pinborg J 1974 Classical antiquity: Greece. In: Sebeok T A (ed.) *Current Trends in Linguistics*, vol 13. Mouton, The Hague
Pohlenz M 1939 Die Begründung der abendländischen Sprachlehre durch die Stoa. In: Pohlenz M 1965 *Kleine Schriften*, vol. 1. Georg Olm, Hildesheim
Pohlenz M 1965 *Kleine Schriften*, vol. 1. Georg Olm, Hildesheim
Priscian (Priscianus) *Institutiones Grammaticae*, Hertz M (ed.) In: 1859 Keil H (ed.) *Grammatici Latini*, vol. III. Teubner, Leipzig
Rist J M (ed.) 1978 *The Stoics*. University of California Press, Berkeley, CA
Robins R H 1990 *A Short History of Linguistics*, 3rd edn. Longman, London
Schenkeveld D M 1984 Studies in the history of Ancient Linguistics, II. *Mnemosyne* **37**: 291–353
Steinthal H 1890–1 *Geschichte der Sprachwissenschaft bei den Griechen und Römern*, 2nd edn. Berlin; repr. 1961, Olms, Hildesheim
Swiggers P, Wouters A 1989a Langues, situations linguistiques et réflexion sur le langage dans l'Antiquité. In: Swiggers P, Wouters A 1989b *Le langage dans l'antiquité*. La pensée linguistique, vol. 3. Leuven University Press (Peeters), Leuven
Swiggers P, Wouters A 1989b *Le langage dans l'antiquité*, La pensée linguistique, vol 3. Leuven University Press (Peeters), Leuven
Taylor D J 1986 Rethinking the history of language science in classical antiquity. *Historiographia Linguistica* **13**: 175–90; also in: Taylor (1987)
Taylor D J (ed.) 1987 *The History of Linguistics in the Classical Period*. Benjamins, Amsterdam
Telegdi Zs 1982 On the formation of the concept of 'linguistic sign' and on Stoic language doctrine. In: Keifer F (ed.) *Hungarian General Linguistics*. Benjamins, Amsterdam

Chinese Linguistic Tradition

W. S.-Y. Wang and R. E. Asher

Of all the living languages of the world Chinese has the longest unbroken recorded history, with texts in the language dating from as long ago as 35 centuries, and there is reason to believe that the art of writing in China may go many centuries further back than this. During the greater part of this history Chinese scholars and thinkers have shown an interest in the nature of language. The nature of the development of this interest, however, has been somewhat different from the way in which the linguistic tradition developed in, for instance, India and Europe. The cause of these differences can be seen to lie largely in the typology of the languages involved, and to some extent in the way they were written. Unlike the languages of India, be they Indo–Aryan or Dravidian, and of Europe of two thousand years ago, Chinese grammar made (and still makes) little use of inflectional morphology. In addition, where the writing systems of India and Europe are all essentially alphabetic, Chinese is written with morphosyllabic graphs. These two factors—the nature of the language and the nature of the linguistic tradition—are probably not unrelated. As will be seen in what follows, where much early linguistic speculation in both India and Europe has to do with grammar, the systematic study of grammar tended to play a minor role in China and did not begin in a serious way there until the nineteenth century, and then only as a consequence of European influence.

Over a period of two and a half millenia one can identify a succession of different foci of linguistic scholars' attention. If a certain amount of simplification is allowed and if overlaps are ignored, one can trace a progression from metalinguistic speculation, through lexicography and dialect geography, phonology, the study of tone, work on language change, and psycholinguistics. It is, of course, from the work of some of these scholars that, in spite of the phonetic and phonological opaqueness of the Chinese writing system, it is possible to reconstruct forms from earlier periods of Chinese as, for example, Karlgren has done (Karlgren 1954).

1. Metalinguistic Speculation

The earliest known linguistic thinker of major importance is the philosopher Xun Zi, the date of whose birth is variously estimated as falling at different points within the period 335–313 BCE. His best known work is *Zheng ming* (most usually translated as 'The rectification of names'), which goes back to a group of several sentences in the *Analects* of Confucius (Kongzi) of two centuries earlier. Kongzi was concerned with the regulatory function of language, the need to ensure that words are used appropriately. Xun Zi starts from the position that words have 'no intrinsic content' and 'no intrinsic correctness.' It is convention which establishes correctness. So, 'When the convention is established and the custom formed, the words then have content'; and 'When the convention is established and the custom formed, the words are then correct. If they are different from convention, they are then incorrect.' A naturalist stance is nevertheless allowed for up to a point, for Xun Zi states that 'words have intrinsic appropriateness. Those which are direct and not misleading are appropriate words.'

2. Lexicography

During the early centuries of the use of the Chinese writing system there was no standard for the use of characters. It is traditionally held that it was above all the achievement of a disciple of Xun Zi, Li Si, who was chief minister under the emperor Qin Shi Huang Di, to unify the use of the characters. This was done by standardizing their varied shapes into a single format, that of the *xiao zhuan* or 'small seal' (the 'seal script' being so called because of its frequent use on seals). This did not, however, make large numbers of them readily available for those who needed them. For this a dictionary was needed. Such a work was produced in the first century CE by Hsü Shen under the title of *Shuo wen jie zi* ('Explanations of simple characters and analyses of composite characters'). This pioneering work remains one of the most important in the history of Chinese lexicography. Taking the *xiao zhuan* as its foundation, it deals comprehensively with 9,353 characters. Hsü Shen's major difficulty, as has inevitably been the case for all Chinese lexicographers, was that of presenting such a mass of material in a sufficiently systematic way for each individual item to be as accessible as possible. The method he chose was to order them in accordance with a system of 540 radicals (*bu shou*). Because of the correspondence that existed between meaning and shape in the radicals—a correspondence which was closer than in the case of modern characters—he chose to base his ordering of radicals on the basis of semantic criteria. The same type of criterion was used for the ordering of the set of characters based on a given radical. One such set, for example, is that relating to the radical 'wood.' Within this set in Hsü Shen's dictionary the names of trees come first, then parts of trees, and then products made from wood. The effect is partially that of a thesaurus. It follows that one of the problems in using a thesaurus, as well as its benefits, is present in a dictionary organized in accordance with these principles. That is to say that a knowledge of a meaning of a character is needed before the user can look it up with a view to finding the meaning. It is with a view to serving the purpose of making readily available the meaning of a character whose shape is already known that modern dictionaries have moved away from the listing of characters in an order based on meaning and followed instead a system based on the number of strokes used in the writing of a character. The concept of the radical of a character as presented by Hsü Shen is nevertheless still a familiar one.

The primary purpose of the *Shuo wen jie zi* is clearly a practical one. It does, however, contain important significant theoretical statements, in that it codifies the *liu shu*, or the six principles according to which the characters are formed. One of these principles is particularly important in a discussion of the nature of the Chinese writing system in the sense that it is a corrective to a widespread but erroneous view that this is entirely nonphonetic. The Chinese characters have been contrasted earlier in this article with writing systems which are basically alphabetic. It is the fact that alphabets in their use relate closely, if not always entirely systematically, to the sequence of phonological segments in the languages for which they are used which has led to the mistaken view that a writing system which has been described in such terms as 'pictographic' or 'logographic' can have no link with phonetic or phonological features of utterance. The *liu shu* principle in question is the third of the six as presented by Hsü Shen, namely that of the *xing sheng* or 'shape-sound.' As the name implies, characters which can be analyzed in terms of this principle are made up of two components, namely *xing*—the 'signific' (which is often the radical)—and sheng —'the phonetic.' The phonetic can be used, when a new character is formed, to provide information about the pronunciation of the composite character, while the signific part provides information about the essential semantic features. In presenting such a character in his dictionary Hsü Shen gives first of all the *xiao zhuan* form of the character, followed by a statement of its meaning, with this followed by an explanation of how it relates to a combination of the signific and the phonetic.

It has been calculated that over 90 percent of modern Chinese characters are of this type, a proportion that has increased significantly since Hsü Shen's time. By contrast, of the characters on the oracle bones of 3,500 years ago which provide the first extant examples of Chinese writing, the proportion was 27 percent. It is the fact of the existence of these 'phonograms' that facilitates the transcription into Chinese of foreign words.

The total number of available characters did not remain constant through time. With extensions in the use of the writing system new characters were added to it—partly to avoid the sort of ambiguity that results when a single character is used with more than one meaning. As can be expected, with the increase in the number of characters, the total included in dictionaries increased with the passage of time. Further increases no doubt resulted also from the fact that lexicographers the world over tend to build on the work of their predecessors. Thus the sixth-century *Yu pian* records 12,158 characters, the *Qie yun* of 601 contains 16,917, and the *Guang yun* of 1011 has 26,194 (statistics taken from Norman 1988: 72). In 1039 Ding Du (990–1053) produced the *Ji yun*, which at 53,525 has the highest count of any dictionary up to the late twentieth century.

3. Dialect Geography

Where Hsü Shen can be considered to have based his lexicographical work on the standard, other scholars of comparable antiquity concerned themselves with geographical variations in language, in other words with the diverse dialects spoken in various parts of the Chinese empire. It is known that such work was done in the later part of the Zhou period, which ended in 221 BCE with the beginning of the Qin dynasty, but the earliest extant work of this sort is that of Yang Xiong who lived from 53 BCE to 18 CE.

Yang Xiong's data were not gathered in the course of what would now be called 'field trips' to different regions of China but in Chang'an, the Han capital, where he would ask questions of soldiers and officials from distant parts whose duties took them to the capital. His findings were reputedly set down (there is some uncertainty with regard to the work's authorship) in *You xuan shi zhe jue dai yu shi bie guo fang yan*, which is usually referred to by the abbreviated form *Fang yan*. Though this work, because of the nature of the Chinese writing system and the way in which the material is presented, provides no direct indication of the nature of phonetic differences, it contains much valuable sociolinguistic information. The author notes not only the different words used to denote given entities in the various regions but also words that were common to a number of areas. Standard forms, or 'elegant speech' (*ya yan*) are also presented and there is mention of words which have gone or are going out of use, the author thus making clear that language varies along two dimensions, the historical and the geographical.

The nature of the regional variations presented by Yang Xiong is not entirely clear. The expression *fang yan*, whose component parts mean respectively 'region' and 'speech' is used in modern times in the sense of 'dialect.' Given the wide extent of the Han empire at the time and the fact that much of the population in regions towards the periphery was not Han, it could well be the case that Yang Xiong was describing different languages as much as different Han dialects. This would partially explain why many of the words he lists are not found in modern Chinese.

4. Phonological Studies

Though Yang Xiong's work provides no phonetic or phonological information about the language of his day, there was in ancient China sophisticated knowledge both of acoustics and of the physiology of speech production. That the former is the case became clear in 1978 with the discovery of a set of 65 bronze bells which were cast 2,500 years ago. These bells can be struck at two different points to produce two distinct musical tones. Clear evidence for the claim relating to speech production is to be found in the second-century BCE *Ling shu jing*, a work on anatomy which contains an account of the function of the various organs of speech, including the epiglottis, the uvula, the tongue, and the lips. The description is, however, in very general terms, these particular parts of the vocal tract being described respectively as the door for speech sounds, a pass (perhaps because of the uvula's capacity to open or close off the nasal passage), the engine of speech, and the fan of speech. Nothing is said by way of relating to particular speech sounds the positions that these organs of speech can adopt. This development in Chinese linguistics came much later, and the earliest known instance of an account of places of articulation of speech sound appears towards the end of the *Yu pian* (mentioned above in Sect. 2).

The procedure adopted two thousand years ago to indicate the pronunciation associated with a given character is known as the *du ruo*, or 'read as,' method. That is to say that character X is said to be read as character Y. This method is clearly far from ideal, in that the ability to understand from this how X is to be pronounced is clearly dependent of prior knowledge of the pronunciation of Y. It is an approach to the indication of pronunciation which has a family likeness to *xing sheng* (see Sect. 2 above), the difference being that in *xing sheng* the standard of comparison is not a different character but an element within the same character. That is to say that a formula for *du ruo* would be of the type X = Y, whereas *xing sheng* could be satisfactorily represented by $X = s+p$, the formula indicating that the character X has the signific of s and the phonetic of p, the components that make up X.

It seems likely that the impetus for a new approach was provided by knowledge of a nonindigenous tradition, namely that of India. The phonetic description of speech sounds in India goes back several centuries before the Christian era. With the spread of Buddhism to China came knowledge of some of the ancient Sanskrit sutras. Just as the knowledge of Asian writing systems has over the centuries stimulated the rethinking of approaches to phonetics and phonology in Europe, so the need to translate and transliterate the Sanskrit sutras led to the development in China of new ideas in these areas.

One of these ideas was *fan qie* ('reverse cut'), of which an early instance is to be found in the *Qie yun*, a dictionary compiled in 601 CE by Lu Fa-yan and his fellow-poets. The aim of *fan qie* was to overcome one of the major difficulties inherent in the *du ruo* approach, which could only work if another word existed which was homophonous with the word whose pronunciation it was intended to indicate. Clearly, where no homophone existed, no such indication could be given. The novelty of the *fan qie* method was to break down the syllable represented by a character into two component parts, namely (a) the initial consonant and (b) the syllable final element(s) and the tone. The appropriate formula in this case is $X = A+B$, where A is a word with the same initial consonant as X, and B is a word with the same final and the same tone. Just as it would be in most cases a simpler matter as far as English is concerned to indicate the pronunciation of, say, *song* by stating that it begins in the same way as *sob* and ends in the same way as *gong*, rather than by searching for a homonym, so it is easier in the case of Chinese to find a suitable 'A' and 'B' than to find a 'Y' which is homophonous with 'X.' It is an interesting fact that, because of the regularity of the phonetic changes in the history of a language and because of the regularity of the phonetic correspondences in sets of cognate words in related languages or dialects, the *fan qie* method works both across different periods of a Chinese dialect and across different dialects.

It seems certain that another characteristic of the phonology of Chinese existed for some centuries before it was discussed by scholars interested in language. This characteristic is the tonal features found in all Chinese dialects. It is generally believed that the language was not always tonal and that it acquired tones approximately 3,000 years ago. The first explicit discussion of tones that is known, however, goes back only half as long and is found in the work of Shen Yue (late fifth century CE). The four distinctive tones in the Chinese of his time are described as *ping* 'level,' *shang* 'rising,' *qu* 'departing,' and *ru* 'entering.' Though the number of distinctions is thus clear, the actual phonetic interpretation of each term remains somewhat obscure.

Modern scholarship, in Europe and America as well as in China, has endeavored to reconstruct the phonology, both segmental and suprasegmental, of early periods of Chinese. Such efforts, however, have not been confined to the twentieth century, for they began in China some four centuries ago during the Ming dynasty. An early historical phonologist was Chen Di (1540–1620). Fully aware of the fact that languages change over time, he attempted to reconstruct the pronunciation of the poems of the *Shi jing*, an anthology of 305 poems by different (but unknown) poets compiled in the sixth century BCE. The poems themselves cover a period of perhaps as much as 500 years but share a common pattern of rhyming. This latter fact is important in that Chen Di's study of the historical development of Chinese focused on rhyming practices. As is evident from the brief discussion of the *Qie yun* above, this work makes use of the fact that different words rhyme. It was an awareness of the fact that the rhyming patterns and the rhyming groups of the *Shi jing* and the *Qie yun* exhibited significant difference that led Chen Di to state unequivocally, perhaps for the first time in China, that the phonological structure of a language changes over time.

Chen Di's work was built on to good effect by his successors during the Qing dynasty (1644–1912), most particularly during the late eighteenth and early nineteenth centuries, with the work of Duan Yucai (1735–1815) being outstanding. An important part of his work was to expand on the studies of the *Shi jing* collection. These studies had been able to indicate which words in the *Shi jing* could be classified together on the basis of rhyme. They said nothing, however, about the large number of words which did not occur in the collection in a rhyming position. It was Duan Yucai's discovery that, in the majority of cases, the 'phonetic' element in a character allowed almost all characters to be classified on the basis of rhyme. His work on rhyme was further developed by Wang Niansun (1744–1832) and Kong Guangsen (1752–86). Before Duan Yucai the foundations laid by Chen Di had been strengthened by studies of rhyme and tone by Gu Yanwu (1613–82) and Jiang Yong (1681–1726), the former of whom made a comparative study of the rhymes in the *Shi jing* and in the early eleventh-century lexicon *Guang yun* (see above, Sect. 2).

5. Twentieth-century Developments

During the twentieth century, the Chinese linguistic tradition has largely merged into the international community of linguistic scholarship. While attempts to apply models based on European languages to the study of Chinese grammar led to obvious failures during the early 1900s, efforts to investigate Chinese syntax using more sophisticated theories developed in the West promise more useful results. At the same time, such efforts have a reciprocal effect of extending as well as refining and enriching such theories by confronting them with typological features found chiefly in the languages of China.

One example of such enrichment is the incorporation into theories of phonology of the features and methods which are necessary for the analysis of tones (Wang 1967). Previously, phonological theories typically were restricted to the analysis of consonants and vowels, even though they were intended for application to all languages. A more subtle, and perhaps more significant, example of such enrichment is the development of concepts of lexical diffusion, which originally grew out of studies of tonal changes in Chinese dialects. These concepts have stimulated a great deal of innovative work and have significantly deepened the basis of historical linguistics.

The first linguists who could move freely between the Chinese linguistic tradition and that of the West were trained either in America, or in Europe. Since the 1950s, however, research institutes in Beijing and in Taiwan have trained many young scholars who are expert in their indigenous tradition and at the same time can contribute to the international scholarly activities in linguistics. These developments led to the formation in Singapore of the first International Association of Chinese Linguistics in 1991.

See also: Buddhism, Chinese; Chinese: Translation of Theological Terms; Kumarajiva.

Bibliography

Bloom A H 1981 *The Linguistic Shaping of Thought: A study in the Impact of Language on Thinking in China and the West*. Erlbaum, Hillsdale, NJ

Forrest R A D 1965 *The Chinese Language*, 2nd edn. Faber and Faber, London.

Gough K 1968 Implications of literacy in traditional China and India. In: Goody J R (ed.) *Literature in Traditional Societies*. Cambridge University Press, Cambridge

Guo Jin-Fu 1984 Woguo gudai yanjiu yinyunde shengli he wuli texingde lishi chengjiu. *Yuyan Lunji* **2**: 223–43

Hansen C 1983 *Language and Logic in Ancient China*. University of Michigan Press, Ann Arbor, MI

He Jiu-Ying 1982 Xianqin zhuzide yuyan lilun. *Yuyan Wenzixue* **10**

Hong Cheng (ed.) 1982 *Zhongguo lidai yuyan wenzixue wenxuan*. Renmin Chubanshe, Jiangsu

Hu Shih 1934 *The Chinese Renaissance*. University of Chicago Press, Chicago, IL

Karlgren B 1954 Compendium of phonetics in Ancient Chinese. *Bulletin of the Museum of Far Eastern Antiquities* **22**: 211–367

Lehmann W P 1975 *Language and Linguistics in the People's Republic of China*. University of Texas Press, Austin, TX

Malmqvist G 1990 La linguistica cinese. In: Lepschy G C (ed.) *Storia Della Linguistica*. Il Mulino, Bologna

Norman J 1988 *Chinese*. Cambridge University Press, Cambridge

Wang Li 1981 *Zhongguo Yuyanxueshi*. Shanxi Renmin Chubanshe

Wang W S-Y 1967 Phonological features of tone. *International Journal of American Linguisitics* **33**: 93–105

Wang W S-Y 1991 *Explorations in Language*. Pyramid Press, Taipei

Zhang Jianmu 1956 Fojiao duiyu zhongguo yinyunxue de yingxiang. *Zhongguo Yuwen* **11**: 23–25

Computers and Religious Studies

J. F. Elwolde

1. Introduction

The emergence of affordable, powerful, and easy-to-use personal computers in the late 1980s and of the widespread use of electronic communications in the following decade, has had an enormous impact on study and research in the humanities. Although the developments presented below employ examples from the field of Religious Studies, they will in general be shared with other disciplines. Having said that, the study of the Hebrew and Greek texts of the Bible has long been at the forefront of computerized study and has generated numerous electronic tools. Religious Studies has also, of course, participated in general changes brought about by widespread computer use in the academic world, which has, notably, greatly speeded up and eased communication among colleagues (and indeed has helped make colleagues of scholars one rarely, if ever, sees) and publishing, in particular the production of material in nonroman scripts.

2. Specialist Web-sites

Well-established and numerous web-sites dedicated to particular areas within a discipline, e.g., Dead Sea Scrolls or Hebrew language, will often give information about forthcoming scholarly events, new publications, and even academic posts, as well as providing a forum for exchange of views and links to related sites. Indeed, some of the most useful sites are those that simply provide a list of links to sites relevant to a particular subject area: for example, the quite selective 'Links for Orientalists' page of the

Cambridge (UK) University Faculty of Oriental Studies web-site, or the much more comprehensive 'ABZU' ('Guide to Resources for the Study of the Ancient Near East Available on the Internet') of the University of Chicago Oriental Institute, or the 'Islamic Studies Resources' site offered by the University of Lampeter's Centre for Islamic Studies, which in November 2000 listed 100 links to other sites.

Quality assurance is largely incompatible with the nature of the internet. However, on the one hand, internet authors are sometimes refreshingly honest about their lack of formal qualifications; on the other hand, web-sites of respected academic institutions should have an interest in the intellectual and moral respectability of material to which they give access, for example, the 'midrash bibliography' pages of the Hebrew Union College web-site or the Septuagint material on the University of Pennsylvania web-site.

3. Distance Learning and the Internet

By its very nature, the internet lends itself to 'distance learning' and some web-sites are directed not so much to the research scholar as to students from a particular discipline, for example the 'Virtual Beit Midrash,' which subsumes a large number of introductory lectures on rabbinic themes.

4. On-line Publications

A relatively recent development is that of on-line journals, internet sites where, after browsing through a list of articles and abstracts, the user can then, either for free or on payment of a subscription, download a word-processed file containing an article of interest. Examples are *Journal of Hebrew Scriptures* and *Journal of Buddhist Ethics*, two of the on-line journals accessible via the ATLAS (American Theological Library Association Serials) service. Note that the *Journal of Hebrew Scriptures* is unusual in that it is only available on the internet; in general, on-line journals are simply electronic versions of print publications, although this situation is likely to change, perhaps in conjunction with the development of rewritable e-books. Newsletters are also available via the internet, for example *Tic Talk*, on the United Bible Societies web-site, which provides information about bibliography (and web-sites) on Bible translation, or the newsletter of the *Comprehensive Aramaic Lexicon* (on the Hebrew Union College web-site), which provides, for example, detailed reports on new readings of Aramaic Dead Sea Scrolls.

Apart from facilitating the presentation of text archives in, for example, ancient languages (e.g., Oxford University's *Electronic Text Corpus of Sumerian Literature*), where a restricted readership might make conventional publishing prohibitively expensive, 'internet publishing' also enables, for example, multiple, international, contributions to a particular work; searches for words or word combinations often not covered by, or difficult to extract from, conventional concordances; easy access to the work by even the nonspecialist; and continual updating of the work; in other words, an 'internet publication' is an open book not a closed one. Despite these advantages, until easy and efficient access to the internet becomes much more widespread, market and academic forces are likely to continue to prefer conventional publishing, and there will be a tendency for material from high-quality internet projects to appear in print as well (this has happened, for example, with the *Ancient Hebrew Semantic Database* project, a venture supported by a variety of European universities).

5. Text Analysis

Within Religious Studies, text- and language-based biblical studies has long been at the forefront in the use and development of computerized tools. In connection with the analysis of sacred texts, packages based on the compact-disk (CD) medium remain most efficient for intensive use. Outside of the purely academic environment such tools have found a special place among Bible translators, who often work in environments where a laptop computer and CD-ROM is their only source of technical information. For occasional consultation, numerous editions of religious texts (Bible, rabbinics, Qur'ān, etc.), in original languages or translated, also exist on the internet. Often these have search facilities, so that, for example, at a Brown University site one can check that *Elisha* occurs twice in the Qur'ān (in M. M. Pickthall's translation) and at the American Bible Society site one can find, by searching the *CEV*, that *Adam* and *Eve* occur together once in the Hebrew Bible, twice in the New Testament, and once in the Deuterocanon.

6. Confessional Web-sites

A different kind of internet site is the explicitly confessional. However, the distinction between 'confessional' and 'academic' is often irrelevant in practice, for example when accessing a sacred text, and confessional sites will frequently contain much of interest to Religious Studies scholars (e.g., a site dedicated to Edith Stein/Santa Teresa Benedicta de la Cruz and the Brooklyn-based website of the Lubavitcher Hasidism) or to a wider audience, for example the 'Latin Language' links of the *Una Voce* (traditionalist Roman Catholic) web-site.

Finally, the numerous web-sites that provide a kind of 'virtual church,' either mainstream or 'cult,' employing sound and video to encourage a particular form of religious behavior, illustrate how the internet cannot only provide scholarly tools and data but also generate entirely new fields of study.

Hebrew Grammarians

D. Téné

Biblical Hebrew (= BH) became an independent subject of investigation around 900 CE at the latest. It is commonly held that Saadya ben Joseph al-Fayyūmī (882–942), known as Saadya Gaon, is the first to have composed a Hebrew grammar and a Hebrew dictionary (See *Saadya Gaon*).

Until the middle of the sixteenth century, for more than 600 years the study of BH had been pursued almost exclusively by Jewish scholars for an almost exclusively Jewish audience. Therefore, early Hebrew linguistics should be considered as a branch of Jewish expository writing. In the sixteenth century, the situation gradually changed as Christian scholars made substantial attempts to write grammars for non-Jewish students of BH (e.g., Johann Reuchlin 1506; Sebastian Münster 1524) (see *Reuchlin, J.*). Thereafter, Hebrew linguistics became part of European linguistics and will not be dealt with here. Nor will this article cover modern grammars of BH composed in Hebrew in the nineteenth and twentieth centuries, since these works, although they continue the early Hebrew linguistic tradition, in the main reflect modern scholarship.

1. A Late Beginning and a Quick Development

It is rather astonishing that Hebrew linguistics emerged so late, that until the beginning of the tenth century there had been no explicit attempts to produce a systematic grammatical and lexical description of BH. The answer to this may be sought in two reasons. (a) Until the end of the first millenium, Jews had expressed their encyclopedic knowledge in pre-disciplinary and nonterminological discourse in the *Midrash* (lit. 'examination,' or 'investigation,' a particular genre of early Rabbinic literature (second century CE onwards) constituting a compilation of homilies, biblical exegesis and sermons delivered in public). Jews did not yet write treatises on mathematics and geometry, astronomy and medicine, nor did they write systematic grammars and dictionaries. (b) In semitic languages a word is structurally the point of intersection of a lexical root (a sequence of usually three consonants) and a grammatical pattern (a sequence of vowels with or without affixes). The intersection is by way of staggering. Semantically, roots signify the lexical, patterns the grammatical meaning of the word. In writing, letters represent consonants only. For centuries, the BH text was made of letters only. Hence, only consonants were represented graphically. Consequently, the grammatical meaning was not (and could not be) represented at all. It follows that before the introduction of the vowel signs, a grammatical description of BH was an impossible task. In the third quarter of the first millenium CE, generations of *Masoretes* (*Masora* being a branch of Rabbinical literature that dealt with the transmission of the BH text: the rules of its exact copying and correct recitation) both in Palestine and in Babylon made great efforts to provide the Hebrew biblical text with vowel signs. By the end of the ninth century, the *Masoretic* school of Ben Asher (a family of *Masoretes* that flourished in Tiberias for six generations from the second half of the eighth century) finally produced a copy of a fully vocalized BH including cantilation signs. This vocalized text became the officially received version of the BH text, and would later serve as a corpus for the description of BH (except for the Samaritan grammarians and lexicographers) (see *Samaritan*).

Despite its late and modest beginning, Hebrew Linguistics developed quickly and by 1050 it reached its culmination in the words of Yehuda Ḥayyūj (see *Ḥayyūj, Judan*), Yonah ben Janāḥ, (see Ibn Janāḥ) and Samuel ha-Nagid. Once the BH text had been fully and finally vocalized, Hebrew linguistics did not embark on the painstaking route of inventing a descriptive method. Instead, they borrowed it wholesale from the Arab Grammarians. As BH and Classical Arabic are cognate languages, these early grammarians only had to adapt the Arabic descriptive method to the specific features of BH and to the linguistic situation of the Arabic-speaking Jews.

The borrowing of the Arabic descriptive method is linked with the personality of Saadya Gaon (882–942; born in Pithon, Egypt, he lived in Tiberias and became head of the Rabbinical academy of Sura near Baghdād) (see *Saadya Gaon*). A man deeply sensitive to the spiritual needs of his time, he ushered in a new epoch in almost every area of Jewish culture, integrating it into Arabic–Islamic civilization. He was a pioneer in philosophy; he systematized Talmudic law; he translated the Bible into Arabic; he wrote commentaries on many Biblical books, formulating new principles of interpretation modeled upon the rules of Greco–Arabic rhetoric. He was also the first to compose a Hebrew Grammar and he understood that as his contemporary co-religionists, scholars and students, studied Arabic Grammar as part of their education and formation, it would be appropriate to follow in the first grammar of BH the descriptive method of Arabic grammarians known in his time.

2. The Development of Hebrew Linguistics

The period 900–1550 should be considered as one well-defined and well-delimited unit in the history of the scientific study of BH. We know of altogether 91 authors who composed 145 works. This unit can be divided into four major periods:

(a) The period of the first attempts which extends until the end of the tenth century: 10 authors—14 works.
(b) The creative ('classical') period which reaches the middle of the twelfth century: 23 authors—37 works.
(c) The period of popularization ending in the middle of the thirteenth century: 17 authors—30 works.
(d) The period of stagnation until the middle of the sixteenth century: 41 authors—64 works.

A chronological list of the authors and their works has been published in the *Encyclopedia Judaica*, Vol. 16 (1971), pp. 1352–90, with a bibliography *ibidem*, pp. 1400–01, and may be consulted there.

2.1 Period I: First Attempts (Tenth Century)

Except for the Grammar composed by Saadya Gaon, no other work composed in this period dealt with grammar, but instead there were lexical works containing grammatical excurses. In the East and in North Africa, authors used Middle Arabic with Hebrew characters. In Spain, they wrote in Hebrew. David b. Abraham Alfāsī (in Arabic, Abū Suleimān Dā'ud ibn Ibrāhīm al-Fāṣī) (mid-tenth century; born in Fez, Morocco, lived in Jerusalem) a *Karaite* (member of a Jewish sect—founded in Babylonia between 754 and 775—that recognized the Scriptures as the sole and direct source of religious law to the exclusion of the Rabbinical oral tradition), composed in Jerusalem the first comprehensive Hebrew-Arabic lexicon of the Bible: *Kitāb Jāmiʿ Al-Alfāẓ* ('Book of Words'). The second half of the century was dominated by a controversy surrounding a dictionary of the Bible composed in Hebrew in Cordoba around 960 by Menaḥem ben Saruḳ (mid-tenth century) titled Maḥberet ('Book [of Solutions]'). His opponent Dunash ben Labrat (mid-tenth century; born in Baghdād, lived in Fez and afterwards in Cordoba) raised 160 criticisms, most of them well-founded. Three of Menaḥem's pupils defended their master and wrote some 50 replies to the objections raised by Dunash and a pupil of the latter wrote 41 replies to the objections of Menaḥem's pupils. The controversy continued into the twelfth century outside the borders of Spain, in France, Provence and even reached England. Jacob b. Meir Tam (ca. 1100–71: of Ramerupt, Champagne) in his *Sefer Ha-Hakhraʿot* ('Book of Decisions') defended Menahem and mostly decided in his favor. Joseph b. Isaak Ḳimḥi (ca. 1105–ca.1170; born in Spain, died in Narbonne, Provence) wrote his *Sefer Ha-Galuy* in answer to Tam's 'Decisions' justifying the criticisms of Dunash. And finally, Benjamin of Cambridge (twelfth–thirteenth centuries) defended Tam's 'Decision' against Ḳimḥi's criticisms. The scientific achievements of Period I are rather meagre.

2.2 Period II: The Creative ('Classical') Period (1000–1140)

In this period, all works were written in Arabic with Hebrew letters, mostly in Spain. In the East authors of the first half of the eleventh century continued to produce works that do not differ theoretically or methodologically from that of Period I. Abū al-Faraj Harūn ibn al-Faraj (in Hebrew: Aaron b. Jeshua) (first half of eleventh century; lived in Jerusalem), wrote in Arabic three works, the most important being *Al-Kitāb Al-Mushtamil 'ala Al-Uṣūl Wa Al-Fuṣūl fī Al-Lugha Al-Ibrāniyya* ('The Comprehensive Book on the Roots and Branches of the Hebrew Language') a vast and prolix grammar of nearly 600 pages. Ḥay ben Sherira (939–1038; Pumbedita near Baghdād) composed in Arabic an anagrammatic dictionary of Biblical and Mishnaic Hebrew as well as Aramaic. It is a vast and rudimentary work probably planned as a means of memorizing Hebrew and Aramaic words, their Arabic translation and their immediate contexts.

Around 1000 CE, Yehudah b. David known as Ḥayyuj (Arabic, Abū Zakariyyā Yaḥyā Ibn Dāwud) (ca. 945–ca.1000; born in Fez, lived in Cordoba) wrote inter alia his two works on the hollow and geminate verbs in BH: (a) *Kitāb Al-Afʿāl Dhawāt Ḥurūf Al-Līn* ('The Book on Hollow Verbs'), an essay on the morphology of verbs which contain *'alef, waw* or *yod* as one of their radicals or *he* as third radical; (b) *Kitāb Al-Afʿ'āl Dhawāt Al-Mithlayn ('The Book on Geminate Verbs')*, an essay on the morphology of verbs whose second and third radicals are identical. Each of these books has two parts; theoretical introductions and alphabetically arranged lexical entries. The book on the hollow verbs contains a general introduction and four introductions to the four groups of weak verbs: one to *prima alef*, one to *prima yod*, one to verbs with a medial weak radical and one to verbs with a final *he*. In the general introduction, Ḥayyūj formulated two basic rules: (a) Following Arab Grammarians, the rule that every Hebrew verbal root consists of at least three letters. Hence, if a verbal form contains less than three radicals, it is defective and its trilateral root can be figured out by analogy (*qiyyāṣ*) to the strong verbal root. (b) The rule of 'hidden' quiescent letters: the letters *'alef, waw, yod* and final *he* in contrast with all other consonants (letters) can be 'hidden' quiescents i.e., not-pronounced but written, and sometimes not-written. They nevertheless function in the structure of the root of the verbal form.

The rule of triliterality was known to Arab Grammarians already in the eighth century. In Arabic, because of its schematic structure due to analogy, triliterality is quite conspicuous and the triliteral root, especially in verbs, prevalent. In Hebrew, due to prehistorical evolution, triliterality is somewhat obfuscated. Linguists of the tenth century—Saadya, Alfāsī, Menaḥem—failed to recognize it, and when faced with verbal forms which contained less than three radicals, they established biradical or even uniradical verbal roots. The verbal forms derived from these roots were recalcitrant to any morphological analysis and the roots themselves were unreasonably overloaded with homonymy. Hence any progress in the morphological study of the Hebrew verb was hampered all throughout the tenth century. It is by the means of the ingenious notion of those 'hidden' letters that Ḥayyūj established 467 weak triliteral roots (17 *prima 'alef*, 46 *prima yod*, 125 medial quiescent, 164 final *he* and 115 geminate roots) and described the derivation and inflection of their verbal forms by analogy to the strong triliteral verb. He succeeded in founding the morphology of the Hebrew verb, thus providing a new basis for the study of Hebrew grammar.

Ḥayyūj's two books raised a controversy that dominated the first half of the eleventh century: by the second decade of the century Ibn Janāḥ (Arabic, Abūal-Walīd Marwān, known as Rabbi Yonah) (first half of the eleventh century: Cordoba and Saragossa) had written his *Kitāb Al-Mustalhaq* ('The Book of Critical Addition') in which he completed what Ḥayyūj had 'overlooked': more than 50 roots not mentioned by Ḥayyūj, some additional 50 meanings of roots, more than 100 verbal forms (conjugations, tenses), 50 different interpretations and some 40 theoretical points (see *Ibn Jañah*). In a few instances he even rejected the analysis of Ḥayyūj, suggesting his own solutions. Samuel ha-Nagid (Ar. Ismail ibn Nagrel'a) (933–1055/56; Granada) wrote *Rasā'il Al-Rifāq* ('The Epistles of the Companions') in which he objected to some of the comments made by Ibn Janāḥ in his *Kitāb Al-Mustalhaq*. To this, Ibn Janāḥ replied in his *Kitāb Al-Tashwīr* ('The Book of Shaming') which Ibn Janāḥ often mentioned with pride (only a few small fragments of it reached us). Samuel ha-Nagid replied in turn in his *Kitāb Al-Ḥujja* ('The Book of Evidence'). Yonah ibn Janāḥ again replied in *Kitāb Al-Taswī'a* ('The Book of Rebuke') to other objections that ha-Nagid and his associates had voiced against *Kitāb Al-Mustalhaq*. A work entitled *Kitāb Al-Istifā'* ('The Book of Exhaustive Treatment' that Ibn Janāḥ disparagingly called *Kitāb Al-Istikhfā'*–'The Hidden Book') was written in Saragossa, adding criticism on the works of Ḥayyūj which Ibn Janāḥ had not dealt with in *Kitāb Al-Mustalhaq*. Ibn Janāḥ replied to this work in *Risālat Al-Tanbīh* ('The Book of Admonition'). *Risālat Al-Taqrīb Wa-Al-Tashīl* ('The Epistle of Bringing Near and Making Easy') is another work of Ibn Janāḥ in which he explained difficult passages in the introductions of Ḥayyūj. However the controversy did not deal with the principles and rules exposed by Ḥayyūj in the theoretical introductions. On this, agreement was unanimous and without reservations. The controversy was on details exposed in the lexical entries. Even in the second half of the thirteenth century a late-developing echo of the dispute surrounding the works of Ḥayyūj was heard in Meir b. David's *Hassagat Ha-Hassagah* in which he defends Ḥayyūj against the criticism of Ibn Janāḥ in *Kitāb Al-Mustalhaq*. This literature of 'objections' and 'replies' is the written expression of penetrating seminary discussions which took place orally among intellectuals in Spain during the first half of the eleventh century. In these disputes the study of language was ever increasing in depth and refinement, and linguistic tradition became more and more consolidated. Indeed, the investigation of the language never again attained such fine and sharp distinctions as those in the controversy which developed around the works of Ḥayyūj in the generation of Ibn Janāḥ and ha-Nagid.

In the 1040s, far from the noise of the dispute, Ibn Janāḥ and ha-Nagid settled down to summarize their teachings. Ha-Nagid wrote his *Kitāb Al-Istighnā'* ('Book of Amplitude'), a large dictionary of BH, which in many ways (such as scope, arrangement of entries wealth of references, and the precise mention of earlier authors) is perhaps the zenith of BH lexicography. It was lost however, and only a few small remnants have survived. Ibn Janāḥ set down with the wisdom of age a complete description of BH in his work *Kitāb Al-Tanqīḥ* ('The Book of Minute Research'), which consists of two parts: *Kitāb Al-Luma* ('The Book of Variegated Flowerbeds'), a grammar, and *Kitāb Al-Uṣūl* ('Book of [Hebrew] Roots'), a dictionary. The grammar consists of an introduction and 45 chapters. One can get some idea of the scope of the work by classifying its chapters according to the pattern of traditional grammar accepted today.

Ibn Janāḥ's work begins with the division of parts of speech, with which his predecessors had already dealt, but he improves on the definitions of Saadya Gaon and their logical foundation. The difficult types of 'expressions' (sentences) are also classified in this chapter. Matters of pronunciation are considered in 13 chapters: the 'letters', each one's articulation, and its position in the word, whether as base or supplemental letter. The meanings of the supplemental letters are given the most detailed discussion extant. Interchange of letters is also treated, as well as assimilation. Vocalization, too, is discussed: interchange of vowels, the changes which occur in vocalization in the vicinity of the laryngeals, the vocalization of the conjunctive *waw* (including *waw* conversive), and of the interrogative *he*. This concludes the issues of pronunciation.

The grammar of the word—derivation and accidence—is treated in 13 chapters; the formation of the word, i.e., the derivation and the accidence of the verb and the noun, is treated in a unit which runs for five chapters. Pronominal suffixes, relation (*nisba*), plural and dual forms, determination and indefiniteness, genders, and numbers are also discussed.

The other chapters of the work deal with topics which are today included under syntax and rhetoric. Seven chapters are devoted to syntactical topics, including apposition, government of the verb, the construct case, and agreement in gender. Five chapters cover rhetoric: ellipsis, pleonasm, repetitio, inverse order—forward or backward. Five of the six remaining chapters discuss classified groups of exceptional occurrences which the grammarian cannot include under any of the rules which he formulated. Therefore, Ibn Janāḥ uses an astute operative device called *taqdir* ('surmise'), by means of which he formulates in Hebrew the intention of the written expression, thus removing its exceptional character. He now analyzes the surmise instead of the exceptional expression.

This attempt to present the subjects of the work according to the main topics of grammatical description today is likely to distort Ibn Janāḥ's division of the material and the methodological principles underlying it. Ibn Janāḥ—following in this the Arab Grammarians—did not divide grammar into the accepted sections of today, such as phonology, morphology, and syntax.

In his dictionary, Ibn Janāḥ stabilized the internal arrangement of the lexical entry. In general, at the start of an entry he lists the meaning which he considers the main one and then gives its derivative forms in which this meaning is found. He defines the biblical citations grammatically. For the verb, he notes conjugation paradigms, tense and so on, and for the noun its pattern, its forms in *status absolutus* and *constructus*, gender, and number. After listing the other meanings, he draws attention to the relation between the various meanings of the entry. Not intending to make an exhaustive list of the forms, he offers a small selection of illustrations which are to suffice for the explanation of the meanings of the root and for an understanding of the forms derived from it. He does not, however, discuss grammatical issues extensively, but instead refers the reader to his *Kitab Al-Luma'* and to his other works. He is very brief with weak roots since he does not intend to repeat the statements of Ḥayyūj or those statements he already made in his *Kitāb Al-Mustalhaq*, but he does treat in detail strong roots, particles, nouns from which no verbs are derived, nouns of size and weight, plants and animals, Thus in the work of Ibn Janāḥ a balance is established within each entry between the semantic definitions of the root and the grammatical definition of the forms derived from it.

This two part work, together with the writings of Ḥayyūj and the shorter works of Ibn Janāḥ mentioned above, constitute the first complete description of biblical Hebrew, and no similar study comparable in scope, depth, and precision was made before modern times. This description constitutes the high point of linguistic thought in all the literature under discussion.

We know of 20 works composed between 1050 and 1140, mainly monographs on specific linguistic topics in which their authors tried to go more profoundly into the works of their great teachers of the first half of the eleventh century. Moshe b. Samuel ibn Giḳaṭilla (second half of eleventh century; Cordoba and Saragossa) wrote a monograph on gender; Yehudah ben Bal'ām (Arabic, Abū Zakariyyā Yahyā ibn Bal'ām) (second half of eleventh century; Toledo and Seville) wrote three monographs: one on particles, one on denominative verbs and one on homonymy. Isaac ibn Barun (fl. ca.1100; Saragossa and Malaga) wrote his *Kitāb Al-Muwāzana Bayna Al-Lugha Al-'Ibrāniyya Wa Al-'Arabiyya* (Book on Comparison between Hebrew and Arabic), which is a monograph on the similarities and differences between Hebrew and Arabic written in Spain around 1100 CE. It contains a short grammatical chapter and a long lexical part, of which about two-thirds—789 dictionary entries—have been preserved and published. From the beginning of the twelfth century the first comprehensive dictionary of the Talmuds reached us as well as the Midrashim and the Gaonic literature composed by Nathan b. Yeḥiel (1035–ca. 1110) in Rome, and from the first half of the same century we have the first grammar of Samaritan Hebrew *Kitāb Al-Tawṭi'a* ('Book of Introduction') by Abū Ishaq Ibrāhīm b. Faraj b. Marūth (Damascus, Syria).

2.3 Period III: The Popularization of Hebrew Linguistics (1140–1250)

In the wake of the 1148 Almohad invasion and persecutions, Jewish scholars emigrated from Spain mainly to Provence and Italy taking with them their Arabic libraries. They began to teach their contents to students who did not understand Arabic but knew Hebrew. This was accomplished in two ways, by producing Hebrew summaries and Hebrew translations. Abraham Ibn Ezra (See Ibn Ezra) (1089–1164; born in Toledo, a wandering scholar in the East and in the West as well) wrote during his wanderings in Italy and France between 1140–1164 eight books which are nothing more than summaries of the works of Ḥayyūj, Ibn Janāḥ and ha-Nagid. In 1161 Salomon Ibn Parḥon (twelfth century; born in Qal'a, Spain, emigrated to Salerno, Italy) wrote his *Maḥberet He-'Arukh*. It is so faithful a representation of the works of Ḥayyūj and Ibn Janāḥ that it was once mistaken for a condensed translation of them. Joseph Ḳimḥi wrote his *Sefer Zikkaron* in Narbonne.

Meanwhile, Spanish exiles began to translate into Hebrew the most important works that had been written in Spain. Moshe ben Samuel ibn Gikatilla had already translated the two important works of Ḥayyūj by the third quarter of the eleventh century, thus being the first to render grammatical works from Arabic into Hebrew. Abraham ibn Ezra translated the works of Ḥayyūj again, apparently in Rome in 1140. Judah ibn Tibbon (ca. 1120–ca. 1190; born in Granada, Spain, emigrated to Lunel, Provence) completed his translation of *Kitāb Al-Tanqīḥ* of Ibn Janāḥ in 1171 at Lunel (Provence), calling it *Sefer Ha-Dikduk*: the first part of it, *Kitāb Al-Lumaʿ*, under the title *Sefer Ha-Riqmah*; and *Kitāb Al-Uṣūl* under the name *Sefer Ha-Shorashim*. There is also an anonymous translation of the three monographs of Yehudah ben Bal'ām. Outstanding in this work of popularization was the Ḳimḥi family which emigrated to Narbonne, Joseph and his two sons, Moshe (d. ca. 1190, in Narbonne, Provence) and David, known as 'Radaḳ' (ca. 1160–ca. 1235) (see *Ḳimḥi, D*). They wrote five books, the most important being *Sefer Mikhlol*, a complete description of BH by David Ḳimḥi (not later than 1235). This work is shaped in the same way as the *Kitāb Al-Tanqīḥ* of Ibn Janāḥ. It also consists of two parts: a grammar, *Mikhlol*, and a lexicon, *Sefer Ha-Shorashim*. For the content he drew upon the works of Ḥayyūj and Ibn Janāḥ, apparently in their Hebrew translations, and upon the works of popularizers who preceded him. In the *Mikhlol* the theoretical foundations, the methodological clarifications, the substantiations and explanations were reduced and the mechanical, technical, paradigmatic side prevailed. The author give prominence to the verb, devoting much space to it. This work of David Ḳimḥi, did more than any other to spread the ideas of Ibn Janāḥ among the Hebrew reading intellectuals. It is the one which helped cause Ibn Janāḥ's own works to be forgotten. While the two parts of *Sefer Mikhlol* were printed many times (*Sefer Ha-Shorashim* from 1480, and *Mikhlol* from 1532–34), the works of Ibn Janāḥ himself were not published, even in their Hebrew translations, until the second half of the nineteenth century. At the end of the period under discussion, Moses b. Isaac (ben Hanesi'ah) (thirteenth century; England) wrote *Sefer Ha-Shoham*, the first linguistic work written by a Franco-German Jew upon the basis of the linguistic theory of the eleventh century grammars, as found in the writings of Abraham ibn Ezra, Ibn Parḥon, and Joseph Ḳimḥi, and in the translation of the works of Ḥayyūj and of *al-Mustalhaq*.

Although these works of adaptation and translation obviously made but a slight original contribution to linguistic thought, it would be difficult to exaggerate the importance of this scholarly activity. It was the translators and adaptors who saved Hebrew linguistics from oblivion in the West and made it a permanent branch of the history of Jewish literature. They translated into Hebrew the Arabic grammatical terms used in the works of Ḥayyūj and Ibn Janāḥ and established a Hebrew expository style for linguistic description that has existed until today in the study and teaching of the Hebrew language and in Hebrew Bible exegesis.

2.4 Period IV: Stagnation (1250–1550)

This period in the West bears the stamp of the almost exclusive influence of the works of Period III, primarily that of David Ḳimḥi's *Mikhlol*. Since the works of Period II were written in Arabic, they fell into oblivion in the West and *Mikhlol* became *the* formulation of Hebrew linguistics, the authoritative source for grammarians and lexicographers. The unshakable prestige of *Mikhlol* was further strengthened by the widespread distribution of David Ḳimḥi's Bible commentary. Science progresses through controversy and the unshakable authority of *Mikhlol* proved detrimental to Hebrew linguistic thought. Most of the books of this period are of a practical nature, such as introductions, text books or learning aids to punctuators of the biblical text. However, attempts were made sporadically at widening the scope of linguistics: a short work on meter, works on poetics based on Aristotle, a long work on rhetoric based on Cicero and Quintilian, a few dictionaries on postbiblical Hebrew, two thesauri of synonyms, rhyme dictionaries, a Hebrew–Persian dictionary, a Hebrew(–Aramaic)–Italian–Arabic dictionary, a first concordance of BH, Bible Glossaries with Romance (Provençal, French, Italian) translations, etc.

A small number of works are concerned with theoretical issues. First, the demand for basing linguistics upon logic began to make itself felt. This tendency is already felt in *RĕtuḲot Kesef* ('Chains of Silver') by Joseph Ibn Kaspi (1279–1340; Provence). It is prominent in *Maʿaseh Efod* composed in 1403 by Profiat Duran (d. ca.1414; born in Perpignan, lived in Catalonia) which also contains criticism of *Mikhlol*. This reaction against the mechanical nature of *Mikhlol* is in a way a dialectical return to the theoretical nature of *Kitāb Al-Lumaʿ*. Secondly, contact with Latin linguistics increased. This influence is especially noticeable at the very end of the period. In 1523 at Venice, Abraham de Balmes (ca. 1440–1523) composed a Hebrew grammar, *Miqneh Avram*, together with a Latin translation, *Peculium Abramae*. In it he tries to apply the ideas of Latin grammar to the description of the Hebrew language. Thus he devotes the seventh chapter, entitled Harkavah ('composition') to the syntax of the Hebrew word. This work, together with *Maʿaseh*

Efod of Profiat Duran, constitutes the most important theoretical contribution of the period. At the very end of this period, Eliyah Levita, known as Eliyahu Bahur (1468/9–1542; born in Neustadt, near Nuremberg, spent most of his life in Italy) wrote Hebrew grammars, Hebrew and Aramaic dictionaries, and Masoretic research. In 1506 Johann Reuchlin (1455–1522; born in Pforzheim, Baden) published his *De Rudimentis Linguae Hebraicis*. (see *Reuchlin, J.*) Based on David Ḳimḥi, it is the first noteworthy Christian work for the instruction of Hebrew to non-Jews. In Basle in 1524, Sebastian Münster (1489–1552; born in Ingelheim, lived in Heidelberg and Basle) wrote *Institutiones Grammaticae in Hebraeam Linguam* (in Hebrew: *Mĕlekhet Hadiqduq Hashalem*) which is based on the work of Eliyah Levita (see *Levita, E.*). Thus, research into the Hebrew language ceased being exclusively Jewish and became part of European culture: with this too, a new period in the history of Hebrew linguistics began.

3. Selected Topics

3.1 The Status of Biblical and Post-Biblical Hebrew

Around the year 1000 CE, writing about linguistic issues was a new phenomenon in Jewish literature. It was considered by many important people as a vain, senseless activity. Therefore in their introductions the authors discuss the motivating factors which stimulated them to write their linguistic works. They seek to prove to their readers that it is incumbent upon Jews to take up the investigation of their language. Hebrew linguistics had a twofold purpose: to increase the knowledge of the language and thereby aid the understanding of the written word, and to provide Hebrew writers with a suitable literary tool, preventing them from deviating from the rules of the exemplary language of the Bible.

Hebrew linguistics dealt mainly with the language of the Bible. This language is considered complete and ideal. There is harmony and balance in its structure; it has been measured in the scales of justice and law; its rules are logical and its expressions clear. It is free of error and contradiction; everything in it can be explained and substantiated. Yet these characteristics are not obvious from the actual text, rather being hidden in it, so that it is the main task of grammar to reveal them after detailed investigation. Such investigation thus becomes the main object of the grammarian. This self-imposed limitation to biblical Hebrew is already noticeable in Saadya Gaon's grammar, *Kutub al-Lugha*, in which he discusses nothing but the grammar of the Bible. This attitude prevailed among the authors who followed him, and lasted for centuries.

All types of postbiblical Hebrew, including *mishnaic* Hebrew (*Mishnah* is a Hebrew collection of six tomes dealing with religious law redacted, arranged and revised at 220 CE), were marked as inferior, for the fate of the language supposedly resembled that of the people. During the entire period under discussion, not even one grammar on *mishnaic* Hebrew was written, nor any one work which described BH and *mishnaic* as one language. Still, *mishnaic* Hebrew was granted a special status; since the sages lived and worked at a time closer to the prophets, it was assumed that details of language which were not included in BH remained in the *Mishnah*. Therefore, they used the *Mishnah* for their works, especially for understanding difficult works, such as *hapax legomena*. This comparison, mostly lexical, was already begun by Saadya Gaon in *Al-Sab'īn Lafẓa Al-Mufrada* ('The Seventy Hapax Legomena'). Yehuda Ibn Quraysh (second half of the tenth century; Tahert, Algeria) followed him in his *Risāla* ('Epistle'), and all others continued it. Ibn Janāḥ in *Kitāb Al-Luma'* compares BH to *mishnaic* 28 times, and in *Kitāb Al-Uṣūl* 307 times. Needless to say, it never occurred to these grammarians to describe the Hebrew used in post-*mishnaic* texts, such as *piyyuṭim* (Hebrew liturgical poetry from the first centuries CE onwards). They neither listed their forms nor explained their words. They did not even deal with the Hebrew used in the writings of their contemporary Hebrew poets. Only infrequently did they cite a verse of poetry, and then it was not because they were interested in a practical description of its language, but rather to criticize or invalidate it, or to endorse it in accordance with usage found (whether frequently or rarely) in the Bible, or according to a virtually possible form of BH.

3.2 The Dependence of Early Hebrew Linguists on Arab Grammarians

As stated earlier (see Sect. 2.2), authors of the creative period (1000–1140) drew amply upon Arab grammarians for theory and methodology, expository devices and terminology. Ibn Janāḥ in his grammar used extensively though tacitly the works of Arab linguists: Sībawayhi (d. 796) (see *Sībawayhi*), al-Mubarrad (d. 898), Ibn Al-Sarrāj (d. 928), al-Zajjāji (d. 949) and Ibn Jinnī (d. 1002). But he did not use them slavishly:

(a) Arab grammarians centered their attention on *i'rāb*, i.e., the final vowels of the noun and the prefix conjugation of the verb and on their syntactical function. BH had lost the vocalic endings in its far prehistory and therefore Hebrew linguistics could not use this dominant part in the works of Arab grammarians.

(b) BH and Classical Arabic differ in many parts of their structure (number of vocalic qualities, the shewa, the 'hidden' quiescent, etc.). Therefore, Hebrew linguistics could not imitate Arab grammatical theory and methodology slavishly, they adapted it to the structure of BH and to the operative needs of the Hebrew linguists.

(c) Arab Grammarians were not the only metalinguistic source of Hebrew linguistics. For parts of the description they drew on the *Masora* literature (see Sect. 1) and even on earlier sources (*Sefer Yetzira*, third century CE, Talmudic and Midrashic sources) and they used Hebrew and Aramaic terms in their Arabic exposition. Hayyūj used 21 Hebrew and Aramic terms and their derivations, Ibn Janāḥ used 27. Arab grammarians derived from the Arabic root *fa-'ayn-lam* terms to designate the conjugation forms of the verb. Ḥayyūj, following in this his Arab teachers, forged 67 Hebrew terms from the Hebrew corresponding root *pe-'ayin-lamed* and used them for the same purpose in his Arabic exposition, e.g., instead of using the Arabic term *infiʿāl* he forged a Hebrew term *mifʿal*, etc. He was followed by all other Hebrew linguists who wrote in Arabic. Of course, the newer the topic, the heavier the dependence on Arab grammarians, e.g., for numerals, pronouns, *status constructus* etc.

(d) Jewish linguists being well-versed in three semitic languages (Hebrew, Judeo-Aramaic, and Arabic) made constantly explicit comparisons of Hebrew with its two cognate languages, especially with Arabic.

3.3 Comparisons with Aramaic and Arabic

It was in one field only that Hebrew linguistics surpassed their Arab teachers, namely in comparing explicitly and systematically Semitic languages. Whereas Arab authors, such as Ibn-Ḥazm (b. 994; born at Cordoba) had at best some inkling of the relationship between Arabic and Hebrew, Hebrew linguists, by their plurilingual experience and traditional education were well-versed in three Semitic languages: they spoke some Arabic vernacular, and before the age of 13, Jewish boys read and understood (via translation) BH, Post-BH, and Jewish Aramaic. They lived in *diglossia* with bi–trilingualism. These three languages being cognate, knowing them implies being aware of their structural similarities and differences on all levels. Small wonder that early Hebrew linguists quatrilinguals specified these basic parallels explicitly in their comparative statements.

Yehuda Ibn Quraysh and Dunash ibn Tamīm (ca. 890–after 955/56; died in Kairuwan, Tunisia) were the founders of this branch in Hebrew linguistics. Ibn Janāḥ compares Hebrew to Aramaic 10 times in his grammar and 266 times in his dictionary. He also compares Hebrew with Arabic 56 times and 254 times respectively. The comparison reached its climax with Ibn Barun's monograph. In the Hebrew linguistics between Saadya (900) and Ibn Barun (1100) we have 2291 comparisons, 568 with Aramaic (25 percent) and 1723 with Arabic.

Thus Early Hebrew linguists not only made a complete description of BH but also dealt objectively with their interlingual associations apropos BH and produced a coherent body of systematic comparative statements. With the transfer of the center of Hebrew linguistics from Arabic-speaking lands to Europe, this branch of Hebrew linguistics, its most original contribution, fell into oblivion.

See also: Bible; Judaism; Hebrew; Masoretic Tradition; Arabic Linguistic Tradition.

Bibliography

Bacher W 1892 *Die hebräische Sprachwissenschaft vom 10. bis zum 16. Jahrhundert*. S Meyer, Trier. Repr. Benjamins, Amsterdam 1974

Bacher W 1895 Die *Anfänge der hebräischen Grammatik*. Deutsche Morgenländische Gesellschaft, Leipzig. Repr. Benjamins, Amsterdam 1974

Becker D 1995 Ibn Janāḥ's Arabic Sources. *Rubinstein Festschrift*: 143–68. Tel-Aviv (In Hebrew)

Chomsky W 1952 *David Ḳimḥi's Hebrew Grammar*. Bloch, New York

Dotan A 1971 Masorah. In: *Encyclopaedia Judaica* (English). Vol. 8. pp. 1401–82. Macmillan, Jerusalem

Dotan A 1977 Wilhelm Bacher's place in the history of Hebrew Linguistics. *Historiographia Linguistica* **4(2)**: 135–157

Hirschfeld H 1926 *Literary History of Hebrew Grammarians and Lexicographers*. Milford, London

Hirschfeld H 1931 Hebräische Sprache, grammatische Literatur bei den Juden. a) von den Anfängen bis zur Mitte des 16 Jhts. In: *Encyclopaedia Judaica* (German), Vol. 7. pp. 1066–75. Eschkol, Berlin

Maman A 1984 *The Comparison of the Hebrew Lexicon with Arabic and Aramaic in the Linguistic Literature of the Jews from Rav Saadia Gaon (10th cent.) to Ibn Barun (12th cent.)* (Hebrew). PhD thesis. Hebrew University, Jerusalem

Téné D 1971 Linguistic literature. Hebrew. In: *Encyclopaedia Judaica* (English). Vol. 16. pp. 1352–90. 1399–1401

Téné D 1972 Ibn Janāḥ. Jonah. In: *Encyclopaedia Judaica* (English). Vol. 8, Keter. Jerusalem. pp. 1181–86

Téné D 1980 The earliest comparisons of Hebrew with Aramaic and Arabic. In: Koerner E F K (ed.) 1980 *Progress in Linguistic Historiography*, pp. 355–77. Benjamins, Amsterdam

Téné D 1983 Linguistic comparison and linguistic competence (of the Arabic speaking Jews in the 10th–11th centuries). In: *Ben Ḥayyim Festschrift*, pp. 237–87. Magnes Press, Jerusalem (In Hebrew)

Wilensky M 1930 Chajjudsch Jehuda. In: *Encyclopaedia Judaica* (German), Vol. 5. pp. 190–98. Eschkol, Berlin

Japanese Linguistic Thought

S. Kaiser

Japan has a long and proud tradition of scholarship in many areas, but lacks an early systematic thinker of the status of a Pāṇini, even though some influence from Sanskrit studies on early Japanese scholarship can be documented. A systematic approach to language studies was not adopted until the early modern *kokugaku* ('national learning') movement, which emphasized inductive reasoning but also shows some interesting parallels to the mentalistic approaches to language by German philologists in the nineteenth century. It has a still flourishing offshoot in the *kokugogaku* school of Japanese language studies, which has absorbed some western influence but can be characterized as an example of a linguistic tradition outside the western mould. It still shows no signs of attempting to merge with mainstream linguistics as introduced from the west in the twentieth century.

1. Linguistic Tradition

1.1 Periods of Language Research History

It is not clear when research into language first began in Japan, but it seems likely that the introduction of the Chinese writing system with its subsequent adaptation to Japanese and the arrival of Buddhism (largely in Chinese translation) in the early centuries CE provided major stimuli. Scholars distinguish an early and medieval period (to 1600 CE), followed by an early modern (1601–1867) and a modern period (since 1868).

1.2 Groups of Linguistic Thinkers in Japan

The perpetrators of linguistic thought in Japan can be divided into a number of groups, which will be accorded different weighting in this article.

(a) Japanese philologists to the early modern period, when language studies were an offshoot of other forms of scholarship such as Buddhist studies, classical Chinese, and Japanese literature;
(b) Non-Japanese philologists of the early modern and modern periods working in Japan, whose interest in language again tended to be a by-product of other scholarship;
(c) Japanese researchers of the *kokugogaku* school of Japanese linguistics;
(d) Japanese linguists trained in western linguistic methodology, working on Japanese and other languages.

This article will concentrate on the Japanese tradition of linguistic thought as seen in (a) and (c), but will make mention of (b) and (d) insofar as they have cross-fertilized the thinking of the earlier groups.

2. The Early and Medieval Period

2.1 Development of the Writing System and Styles of Writing

The Japanese, lacking a writing system of their own, adopted Chinese characters (*kanji*) from about the third or fourth century CE, initially for writing in (classical) Chinese. *Kanji* were soon used phonetically for Japanese proper names, a function that was developed further for expressing the complex inflectional morphology of Japanese, giving rise to the development of the *kana* syllabaries from simplified forms of *kanji*. *Kanji* were also used as translation equivalents for Japanese words and morphemes. As a result of these developments, it became possible to write Japanese freely, and a rich literature emerged from about the eighth century. However, classical Chinese remained the medium of scholarly writing for many centuries to come.

Owing to this dichotomy between language for private and literary use (native Japanese) and official and scholarly use (classical Chinese and its offshoots, characterized by containing Japanese elements such as honorifics to varying degrees), the study of matters relating to the Japanese language was accorded low prestige and took place largely in the context of Buddhist and Chinese studies and Japanese poetics, until the national learning movement (*kokugaku*) advocated a return to the values of ancient Japan before Chinese influence, thereby validating the study of things Japanese.

2.2 Chinese and Indian Influences

Early language studies were carried out by Buddhist monks in the temples and by scholars of the Chinese classics at the Confucian academy in Kyoto from about the ninth century. Buddhist-related studies were triggered by the study of the Sanskrit script and sounds (so-called Siddhaṃ studies), which entered Japan with the introduction of Buddhism, and were accorded special attention in the newly established esoteric sects. Buddhist sutras circulated in Japan in Chinese translation, and, as many monks were sent to study in China, there were strong influences from Chinese scholarship in Buddhist-related studies and textual/philological scholarship. Sanskrit and Chinese studies centered on phonetic and phonological descriptions; thus Ennin's (794–864, Tendai sect) *Zaitôki*, a record of his studies in Tang China from 840–842 including an account of how he was taught the Sanskrit script and sounds, uses traditional Chinese terminology equivalent to 'dental,' 'nasal,' and 'labial' to explain the sounds of the Sanskrit alphabet. Annen's (841–89 or after, Tendai sect) *Shittanzô* (880) compares the phonology of Chinese with Sanskrit, and *Myôgaku* (1056–1122 or after, Tendai sect) uses examples from Japanese to explain the Sanskrit sandhi.

Scholarship at the Confucian academy, which conducted examinations for aspiring officials on the Chinese model, was mainly concerned with Chinese Confucian classics and poetry. Concordances focused on the correct readings of Chinese characters, initially by quoting Chinese dictionaries and rime dictionaries, and later often by using the *kana* syllabary.

A by-product of Chinese and Buddhist textual study was the beginning of a long tradition of dictionaries and glossaries of Buddhist and Chinese texts, starting with the eighth-century *Shinyaku Kegonkyô ongi shiki*, an extension of a Chinese glossary on the Avataṃsaka (Kegon) sutra, and the ninth-century *Tenrei banshô meigi*, a Chinese–Japanese dictionary by Kukaiü (774–835), the founder of the Shingon sect.

2.3 The 50-sound Chart

Chinese and Sanskrit influences are thought to account for the development of the so-called 50-sound chart. This table is a phonological arrangement of the Japanese *kana* syllabary, listing syllables with the same vowel in horizontal rows and syllables with an identical or related initial consonant in vertical columns. Table 1 is an adaptation in romanized form of a sound chart from Myôgaku's *Hannon-sahô* (1093).

Table 1. An eleventh-century '50-sound chart.'

a	ka	ya	sa	ta	na	ra	ha	ma	wa
i	ki	i	si	ti	ni	ri	hi	mi	wi
u	ku	yu	su	tu	nu	ru	hu	mu	u
e	ke	e	se	te	ne	re	he	me	we
o	ko	yo	so	to	no	ro	ho	mo	wo

The Kuneri system of romanization is used for this table.

As phonemic forms of writing were unavailable in China and Japan (for some reason, the Sanskrit script was not used for this purpose), it was impossible to analyze the typical consonant–vowel combinations of the Japanese syllabary into their constituents. The 50-sound chart arrangement manages to overcome this problem in a way similar to the traditional Chinese *fan-qie* system.

In the *fan-qie* system, two known Chinese characters are used to indicate the initial and 'rime' (the remainder, including the tone) of an unknown third. For instance, tun^1 is induced from $t\partial k^4$ and $hu\eta^1$ by taking the initial *t-* from the former and the rime-$u\eta^1$ from the latter.

The 50-sound table can be used in a similar way; Myôgaku's *Hannon-sahô* (from which Table 1 is adapted) explains how to work out the reading of the same *kanji*, *tou* in its Sino–Japanese reading, by locating the intersection of the initials of the Sino–Japanese readings of the two known *kanji*, that is, *toku* (vertical *t-* column) and *kou* (horizontal *-o* row), retaining the ending *-u* of the second. It is thought that the 50-sound chart was devised for working out Sino–Japanese readings from the information given in Chinese rime dictionaries.

For that purpose, the order of vowels and consonants did not necessarily have to follow the above order, and indeed many different orders are found in earlier examples of the chart; the arrangement in Table 1 follows the order of Sanskrit vowels insofar as they can be equated with Japanese sounds, while the consonants are arranged by point of articulation, that is, laryngeal (i.e., glottal and velar) [ʔ, k, j (y)], lingual [s, t, n, r], and labial [ɸ (h), m, w], an arrangement that diverges from traditional Chinese phonology. Later versions settle on the consonant order [k, s, t, n, h, m, y, r, w] which parallels the order found in works on the Sanskrit alphabet.

Siddhaṃ studies continued in Japan for some 1,000 years and influenced the phonological studies of the early modern *kokugaku* scholars such as Motoori Norinaga; however, the rare occasions when attempts were made at grammatical studies, as in the 1338 *Hachitenjôshô*, which explains the eight cases of Sanskrit correctly with Japanese postpositions (but also erroneously by assigning Japanese verb forms to them), appear to have exerted no influence on later studies. Siddhaṃ studies were eventually replaced by Sanskrit studies under influence from the west, in the nineteenth century.

2.4 Influences from Poetics and Japanese Classics

The study of poetics was initially influenced by Chinese poetic theory, but soon developed into an area of scholarship in its own right from about the tenth century. It was instrumental in raising the linguistic awareness, notably concerning the correct use of postpositions and inflectional endings, that paved the way for the emergence of figures like Fujitani in the early modern period.

3. The Early Modern Period

3.1 The Kokugaku *Movement*

Until the introduction of western linguistics in the twentieth century, the achievements of language studies by Japanese in Japan were largely in the areas of grammar (especially morphology), and to a lesser degree in phonology. There was, however, an important period in the eighteenth and nineteenth centuries when Japan developed its own approaches to the study of grammar and morphology, which influenced generations of linguists in the *kokugogaku* ('national language studies') mould in the modern period.

Research in medieval Japan was hampered by a tradition of secrecy in which scholarly achievements were passed down from teacher to student orally or in manuscript form. In the early modern period, work gradually came to be published and accessible to all. This coincided with a veritable explosion in the arts and sciences from about the mid-eighteenth century, one aspect of which was the development of objective and inductive ways of reasoning to replace the authoritarian and secretive ways of medieval times.

One of the central concerns of the *kokugaku* movement, which advocated a return to the values of ancient Japan prior to Chinese influence, was research into early Japanese thought and culture through textual study of literary works. This philological approach produced a great body of work on language-related matters.

3.1.1 Some Early Results

The first major result of this approach was the commentary by the monk Keichû (1640–1701 Shingon sect) on the eighth-century collection of poems, the *Manyôshû*, and its offshoot, the *Waji shôranshô* (1693), which re-established the correct usage of the *kana* groups i/hi/wi/, e/he/we and o/ho/wo, whose sounds had coalesced into [i], [ye] and [wo] in noninitial position from about the twelfth century, and established the base for a system of 'historical orthography' which was to become standard until 1946.

3.1.2 The First Systematic Grammar by a Japanese

Fujitani Nariakira (1738–79) was the first Japanese scholar (see Sect. 3.3.2 for earlier Portuguese work) to develop a systematic grammar for the Japanese literary language, although his work was left unfinished due to his early death. His celebrated *Ayuishô* has an introduction setting out a part-of-speech theory that was to have a profound impact on *kokugogaku* grammar well over a century later, whereas his idiosyncratic terminology and the fact that he did not found a school limited his influence during the early modern period.

The (1778) *Ayuishô* is a work of great originality and deep insights into the workings of the Japanese language, amazingly free from influence from earlier research except for the work on Chinese particles by Fujitani's elder brother, the Confucian philosopher and Chinese grammarian Minagawa Kien.

Fujitani's main word classes are *na* (nouns), *yosoi* (verbs and adjectives), *kazashi* (adverbs, etc), and *ayui* (postpositions and verbal/adjectival suffixes). The criterion for distinguishing the former two is the presence or absence of inflection, and for the latter whether they precede or follow the item which they modify. The *Ayuishô*, Fujitani's only mature work dedicated to one of his word classes, subcategorizes *ayui* on functional and semantic criteria, and explains their usage with plentiful examples from Japanese classical poetry but, unusually for his time, also with colloquial equivalents. The *Ayuishô* is also the first work that deals systematically with historical change, and introduces a six-part division of the history of Japanese.

3.1.3 The Motoori School

Motoori Norinaga (1730–1801), influenced by earlier *kokugaku* scholars such as Keichû, consolidated the inductive reasoning approach that distinguished the national learning movement from earlier scholarship, although his tendency to emphasize the superiority of Japanese grammar and phonology over Chinese occasionally distorted his otherwise methodical and logical approach. Motoori Norinaga's greatest linguistic achievement was the codiscovery (with Fujitani) of the *kakari–musubi* agreement principle and his attempt to treat this principle as triggering predication.

He also re-established the correct position of the *kana o* and *wo* in the 50-sound chart by examining internal sound correspondences in early Japanese and comparing Chinese rime-dictionary arrangements with equivalent sounds in Sino–Japanese.

Motoori Norinaga established his own influential school of *kokugaku*, which produced noted disciples such as Suzuki Akira and his own son, Haruniwa.

Suzuki Akira (1764–1837) was initially trained as a Confucianist scholar of classical Chinese and was thereby in a position to synthesize earlier work. The widely alleged influence of Fujitani is, however, not documentable: Suzuki did not possess any of Fujitani's works, nor does he mention his name anywhere.

Like Fujitani, Suzuki divides words into four basic classes, but his categorization differs in many respects, and is clearly influenced in content and terminology by classical Chinese scholarship. His most original contribution was his distinction between concept words (nouns) and relational elements (postpositions and verbal/adjectival suffixes, etc), and his theory that predication using adjectives, verbs, and noun-particle combines the two. His characterization of concept words as 'tools' and relational elements as 'the hand that operates them' has captured the imagination of generations of Japanese grammarians, but also shows similarities to the approach to language by nineteenth-century German linguists, notably his contemporary Wilhelm von Humboldt.

Parallels to von Humboldt's characterization of Chinese as lacking surface representation of the category of words that have conceptualized meaning are also found in Suzuki's occasional comparisons with Chinese: word classes are universal, and therefore found in Chinese as well, but their surface representations differ from language to language. Whereas Japanese is unrivaled in the purity of grammatical representation of functional elements, Chinese particles lack such refinement.

Motoori Haruniwa (1763–1828) continued and systematized his father Norinaga's work, especially in the area of verbal inflection. Together with Tôjô Gimon (1786–1843), whose work he influenced, he brought the language studies of the *kokugaku* (national learning) movement to a state beyond which no major results were obtained.

Motoori Haruniwa distinguished regular and irregular inflectional paradigms, and established transitive/intransitive and passive/causative groupings. The names which he assigned to inflectional paradigms, based on the position of the changing vowels in the 50-sound chart, are essentially the same as those still used in the *kokugogaku* school. Motoori Haruniwa also drew diagrams illustrating the structure of poems, including modificational relationships, which may be seen as an attempt to go beyond the morphology-centered approach of national learning language studies toward syntax.

3.1.4 Nationalist Offshoots

In parts, the national learning movement subsequently took on a mantle of nationalist fervor, especially in the person of Hirata Atsutane (1776–1843) and his followers, interfering with the inductive reasoning attitude that had produced such remarkable results earlier. Hirata resurrected the claim made by some medieval Shinto scholars that Japan had its own indigenous writing system, the so-called 'script of the age of gods,' and even went so far as to produce lists of characters. Some contemporaries were, however, quick to recognize that these were imitations of cursive Chinese characters and Korean *hangul* letters.

3.2 Characteristics of Kokugaku Linguistic Research

When attempting to summarize the results of *kokugaku* linguistic research, a number of facts stand out.

Like most nineteenth-century linguistic research in Europe, the work of Japanese researchers was historical and prescriptive, dealing almost exclusively with the classical literary style. This emphasis on historical research over the spoken language also characterizes much of the twentieth-century *kokugogaku* school.

Unlike work in nineteenth-century Europe, comparisons with other languages were minimal and superficial, going little further than asserting the superiority of Japanese over Chinese on account of its inflectional regularity (changes quite neatly follow the vertical columns of the 50-sound chart). Partly, this can be attributed to the geographical and political isolation of Japan at the time.

Grammatical analyses were largely restricted to morphology and parts-of-speech analysis, although attention was accorded to a number of phenomena that stand out in classical Japanese sentence structure: the distinction between sentence-final (*kire*) and continuing or modifying (*tsuzuki*), for which there were distinct inflectional forms, and the *kakari–musubi* phenomenon, a form of grammatical agreement where sets of certain modal particles require specific forms for predication.

Besides functional and positional criteria, meaning formed an important part of the *kokugaku* approach; for instance, Fujitani established inflectional endings as semantic categories, and semantic judgements were used to explain surface linguistic forms, as in Motoori Norinaga's treatment of the modal particles *wa* and *mo* as a separate group triggering predication, even though unlike his other two groups they agree with unmarked forms.

There is also the claim, as in Suzuki's work, that some aspects of language are universal but do not necessarily have representation in a particular language.

There is great attention to factual detail, but generalizations tend to be speculations on psychological processes rather than attempts to abstract rules.

There is little attempt to apply methodology from other areas of scholarship, such as the logical traditions that are found in Buddhist studies, to the study of language. This tendency, too, continues in *kokugogaku*.

3.3 Other Work, and Two Western Interludes

3.3.1 Work Outside the Kokugaku *Movement*

Other work on language took place outside the *kokugaku* movement. This included work in the Siddham tradition and in Chinese phonology, but also produced a proliferation of dictionaries on the spoken language, including the *Butsurui shôko* (1775), a dictionary of dialects by a *haiku* poet, and the unpublished *Rigen shûran*, a work on colloquial expressions and dialects by Ôta Zensai (1749–1829), a scholar of classical Chinese.

3.3.2 An Early Portuguese Interlude

Portuguese missionaries, who had come to Japan from the middle of the sixteenth century onward, were the first to engage in systematic study of the Japanese language. The Jesuit press in Nagasaki produced a variety of books to this end, culminating in João Rodriguez's *Arte da Lingoa de Iapam*

(1604–08) and its more concise sister volume *Arte breve da lingoa Japoa* (1620). These are systematic surveys of standard colloquial Japanese modeled on Latin grammars, with attention to features such as honorifics and regional varieties; however, these works were written in Portuguese and had no discernible influence on language studies by Japanese (Christianity and western books were proscribed in 1614). They did, however, influence western scholars of the Japanese language, such as Hoffmann (*Japansche spraakleer* 1868), who in turn influenced western scholars working in Japan, such as Aston and Chamberlain (see Sect. 4.1) (see *Jesuit Missionaries to Sixteenth Century Japan*).

3.3.3 The Dutch Interlude

During the period of national seclusion (1639–1854), the Dutch were the only westerners who were allowed to maintain a small trading post off Nagasaki, from where a tradition of Dutch studies developed in Japan, initially through the hereditary Japanese interpreters.

Fujibayashi Fuzan's *Waran gohôge* (1815), the first Dutch grammar to appear in printed form, introduced European parts of speech to Japan, including items quite alien to Japanese such as the article, and Tsurumine Shigenobu's *Gogaku Shinsho* (1833) applied Dutch concepts of case and tense to Japanese.

From the mid-nineteenth century, Dutch studies began to be replaced by the study of other European languages, through which European linguistics began to be absorbed from about the 1880s.

4. The Modern Period

4.1 Beginnings, and the Comparative Method

In 1886, a department of linguistics was established at Tokyo Imperial University, initially largely staffed by foreigners, who were hired to train a generation of Japanese scholars. B. H. Chamberlain, an Englishman whose work includes a comparative study linking Okinawan with Japanese, lectured there on linguistics and Japanese from 1886–90, and produced many students who were to be major players in the development of western linguistics as well as *kokugogaku*. One of them was Kazutoshi Ueda (1867–1937), who is sometimes claimed as the father of both Japanese linguistics and the *kokugogaku* school of Japanese language studies. Having studied in Leipzig from 1890–94, he brought the comparative method to Japan and established the long-lasting popularity of Hermann Paul's *Prinzipien* in Japan through his lectures.

Chamberlain and the resident British diplomat W. G. Aston had made some use of the comparative method in their work on the genetic relationship of Japanese, but it was not until Shirô Hattori (born 1908) that the comparative method was applied in Japan in the early 1930s in his work on the pitch accent of the eastern and western groups of Japanese dialects. Hattori, a structuralist, is one of a number of trained linguists who contributed to *kokugogaku* in various ways; but the genetic relationship between these major dialect groups is in the early 1990s still an unresolved issue in Japan (see Ramsey (1982) for details and an assessment of *kokugogaku* research attitudes).

4.2 Kokugogaku Grammars

After a number of attempts at describing Japanese grammar largely on the European model, culminating in Ôtsuki Fumihiko's *Kônihon bunten* (1897), Yoshio Yamada (1873–1958) was the first major modern grammarian to propose a system of its own for Japanese (albeit using ideas from the west), especially in his predication theory (*chinjutsuron*), a mentalistic attempt to capture sentence formation in Japanese that was partly inspired by the early modern grammarians and partly by the European experimental psychologist Wundt. Yamada holds that sentences are formed by 'apperception,' a unification in the mind of its individual components such as words, and argues that this unification is expressed in language by predication. The predication issue has been one of the major issues in *kokugogaku*, with modifications still being proposed.

Like Yamada, Tokieda drew renewed attention to traditional Japanese linguistic thought as the ideal vehicle for dealing with the Japanese language. In contrast, Mikami Akira (1930–71) was a scholar who argued against the uncritical application of western linguistics based on his analysis of modern Japanese. Rejecting the Indo-European subject-predicate matrix as unsuitable for Japanese, he devoted a series of works to demonstrating the advantages of a topic-comment approach, such as *Gendai gohô josetsu* (1953).

Motoki Tokieda (1900–67), who is best known for his 'language as a process' theory which claims that language is not static but a dynamic process that takes place in the mind of the speaker, was also strongly influenced by early modern grammarians, especially Suzuki Akira's distinction between concept words and relational elements. Tokieda extended this distinction into items that do (*shi*) and do not (*ji*) undergo the conceptualization process, claiming that *shi* express the objective world, whereas *ji* express the feelings, etc., which the language user directs toward the objective world. He goes on to say that the basic *shi*/*ji* distinction, which is universal, is encoded in the Japanese language in such a way as to make it particularly noticeable, being often expressed as a combination of two items (e.g., noun + particle), whereas it is much less obvious in fusional languages such as Latin.

4.3 Dialect Geography and Other Western Influences

Ueda may also be said to be the father of modern dialectology in Japan; under his chairmanship, the Investigative Committee of the National Language carried out a nation-wide investigation into the vocabulary, grammar, and phonology of Japanese dialects in the early years of the twentieth century, under influence from Wenker's dialect geography. Dialect geography has been widely practiced in Japan since the 1950s, influenced by Father Willem Grootaers's work there, culminating in the monumental *Nihon gengo chizu* ('Linguistic Atlas of Japan') published from 1967–75 by the Dialect Bureau of the National Language Research Institute.

Phonetics and phonology is another area that has absorbed much influence from the west, initially from the Prague school, later from American phonemics.

Especially since World War II, western influences have been strong in linguistics and foreign language university departments all over Japan, many having become staffed by Japanese returning from study overseas, especially in the USA, armed with the latest methodology.

See also: Buddhism; Japanese; Shinto; Chinese Linguistic Tradition.

Bibliography

Bedell G D 1968 *Kokugaku* grammatical theory (Doctoral dissertation, Massachusetts Institute of Technology)

Doi T 1976 *The Study of Language in Japan: A Historical Survey*. Shinozaki Shorin, Tokyo

Grootaers W A 1967 Dialectology. In: Sebeok T A (ed.) 1967

Hattori S 1967 Descriptive linguistics in Japan. In: Sebeok T A (ed.) 1967

Kaiser S (ed.) 1995 *Introduction: The Western Rediscovery of the Japanese Language*, vol. 1, pp. 1–89

Kaiser S 1996 Translations of Christian terminology into Japanese, 16–19th centuries: problems and solutions. In: Breen J, Williams M (eds.) *Japan and Christianity: Impacts and Responses*. Macmillan Press, London pp. 8–29

Ramsey S R 1982 Language change in Japan and the Odyssey of a *Teisetsu*. *The Journal of Japanese Studies* **8(1)**: 97–131

Sebeok T A (ed.) 1967 *Current Trends in Linguistics. Vol. 2: Linguistics in East Asia and South East Asia. Part 1: Japan*. Mouton, The Hague

Shibatani M 1978 Mikami Akira and the notion of 'subject' in Japanese grammar. In: Hinds J, Howard I (eds.) *Problems in Japanese Syntax and Semantics*. Kaitakusha, Tokyo

Wenck G 1957 Japanese language studies since Chamberlain. *The Transactions of the Asiatic Society of Japan*, 3rd series **5**: 36–55

Jesuit Missionaries to Sixteenth Century Japan

J. Moran

The Society of Jesus, generally known as the Jesuits, was founded by Ignatius Loyola, and was formally approved by Pope Paul III in 1540 as a religious order within the Catholic Church. Francis Xavier, the first Jesuit sent to preach the Gospel to the world beyond Europe, reached India in 1542 and Japan seven years later. Europeans traveled to Japan in the sixteenth century under the Portuguese flag, with Portuguese their common language. They were almost totally dependent on interpreters at first, but good ones were rare, and there was no common culture to help bridge the language gap. The best-known example of the problem of translating the Christian message in Xavier's time is the difficulty of finding an equivalent, in Japanese, of the European words for God. When Xavier began to appreciate how unlikely it was that any Buddhist term would be satisfactory as a translation of 'God' he resolved to use the Latin word 'Deus,' which would have the negative virtue of having no connotations in Japanese.

The director of Jesuit activity in Japan in the late sixteenth century, the Italian Alessandro Valignano, insisted that newly-arrived European Jesuits must be given the time, teachers, and books needed for serious language study, and in 1580 he founded a college of studies for them in Japan. (He also had Japanese studying Latin, without which they could not aspire to become Catholic priests, as 14 of them eventually did.) When he returned to Japan in 1590 Valignano brought with him a European printing press, the first press in Japan to use movable metal types. As well as in Portuguese and Latin it was used to publish books in Japanese transcribed in romanization, but also in the Japanese *hiragana* and *katakana* syllabaries, and, a little later, in Chinese characters. The books included works of devotion and of more general interest, for example Japanese translations of the *Imitatio Christi* and of *Aesop's Fables*, but also grammars, dictionaries, and other textbooks for the study of the Japanese and Latin languages. Among these are the *Arte da Lingoa de Japam* (1604–8) and the *Arte Breve da Lingoa Japoa* (1620), both grammars of Japanese by João Rodrigues, and the *Vocabulario da Lingoa de Japam* (1603), a Japanese–Portuguese dictionary of quite astonishing comprehensiveness, accuracy, and sophistication.

There were some 300,000 Japanese Christians around 1600, but in 1614 the missionaries were expelled, and Christianity was suppressed and persecuted for over 250 years. Their end was frustrated, but works which the Jesuits had produced as means to the propagation of Christianity in Japan are now essential materials for the study of the history of the Japanese language.

See also: Christianity in East Asia; Japanese Linguistic Thought.

Bibliography

Moran J F 1993 *The Japanese and the Jesuits*. Routledge, London

Rodrigues J 1976 *Arte de Lingoa de Japam*. Nagasaki 1604–8. Copy in Bodleian Library, Oxford. Facsimile edition Benseisha, Tokyo

Rodrigues J 1993 *Arte Breve da Lingoa Japoa*. Macao 1620. Copy in Library of School of Oriental and African Studies, London. Facsimile edition Shin-Jinbutsu-Ôraisha, Tokyo

Vocabulario da Lingoa de Japam 1973/75 Nagasaki 1603. Copy in Bodleian Library, Oxford. Facsimile edition Iwanami Shoten, Tokyo

Linguistic Theory in the Later Middle Ages

G. L. Bursill-Hall

The period 1150–1400 is regarded as one of the golden periods in the history of linguistics, a period when the study of language increased considerably, as a result not only of the general increase in learning and literacy, but of the incorporation of the Aristotelian Organon into the university syllabus, especially in the northern schools. As the first subject of the Seven Liberal Arts, grammar enjoyed a privileged position and developed along with logic into the creation for the first time of a linguistic theory which sought to explain the formation and meaning of words and the structure and meanings of sentences. The Schoolmen saw this as necessary if they were to have on hand an instrument sufficiently well honed to enable them to talk about their world, their universe, and God with any degree of success.

1. Grammar in the Later Middle Ages

The term *grammatica* was used in the Middle Ages in different ways and one encounters at least three distinct uses of the term: (a) to represent the teaching of elementary Latin to beginners, (b) to represent the teaching of more advanced Latin, and (c) the study of grammatical theory. There is an additional aspect which was the training of masters for the newly formed grammar schools; this led to the creation at Oxford and Cambridge of the Master of Grammar degree. Grammar, particularly during the high Middle Ages, enjoyed different applications in the northern schools from those in the southern schools. In the former, especially during the twelfth and thirteenth centuries, *grammatica* was closely associated with *logica*, whereas in the latter, above all in Italy, *grammatica* was more closely associated with the *Ars dictaminis*, or *rhetorica*, the study of 'belles-lettres.' These distinctions have often been misunderstood and overlooked. The closer interrelationship between *grammatica* and *logica* is a later development, the result of the incorporation of the Aristotelian Organon (Prior and Posterior Analytics); the earlier Middle Ages had been more concerned with the preservation of the Greco–Latin tradition and with the development of literacy in Latin. It was from such a base that later developments in theoretical and pedagogical practice were to develop and this aspect of their work should not be ignored or neglected. It is quite clear that scholars of the Middle Ages had always practical matters in mind and indeed there was throughout an unbroken tradition of Latin pedagogy.

2. Premodistic Grammar

Grammar was taught in the medieval university in the form of commentaries on the work of the Late Latin grammarians, Donatus and Priscian; such is the conventional statement. The requirements of the Universities of Paris and Oxford, according to statutes dating from 1252, stipulated the required reading of Priscian (but not Donatus). The change in attitude to grammar or, to be more precise, the division of grammar into pedagogical and speculative started in the early twelfth century; it was the study of Priscian only that provided the basis for the new scientific grammar. Grammars based on Donatus however were prolific and 'humanist' grammars (what might be called *grammatica practica*) were written throughout this period, but grammars of the scientific kind were based on Priscian (according to the Aristotelian definition of science) and derived from the 'ordinarie' reading under the guidance of a master. A large number of these are still extant.

Attempts were made to replace Priscian as the required text but these do not appear to have succeeded to any great extent, or at least not until the late fourteenth century. The Statutes of Oxford dated 1431 still called for the reading of Priscian but this seems to have been 'more honour'd in the breach than in the observance.' Two works in particular, i.e., the *Doctrinale* (1199) of Alexander de Villa-Dei and the *Graecismus* of Eberhardus Bethuniensis (fl. 1212) along with the works of John of Garland (fl. 1235) were very popular—many copies of these have survived. Nevertheless, commentaries on Priscian (sometimes described as Doctrinale commentary of *Quaestiones*/ or *Tractatus*/ or *Summa de grammatica*) formed the basis of medieval speculative grammar. There are over 200 such commentaries still extant; few have been edited.

The changes in direction that characterize the scientific study of grammar in the twelfth and thirteenth centuries appear to have started with the teaching of William of Conches (ca. 1080–ca. 1154) who taught at Chartres, and of his pupil Petrus Helias who taught in Paris ca. 1140, though it is probable that the movement actually started in the late eleventh century; details are to be found in marginal commentaries of Priscian of the time, written in what has been described as *écriture microscopique* 'microscopic hand.' William's Priscian commentary has not yet been edited, but it can be said that his importance rests on two facts: his criticism of the adequacy of Priscian's criteria and his invention of the *causae inventionis* 'theoretical bases,' and the teaching of his pupil Petrus Helias in mid-twelfth century. The implications of this were enormous, i.e., it led to the establishment of grammar as an autonomous discipline along with the incorporation and refinement of older definitions, the fusion of grammatical and logical terminology, and subsequently, the introduction and refinement of the idea of universal grammar and the extension of the *modus significandi* 'mode of signifying.'

The thirteenth century can be conveniently divided into two parts, premodistic and modistic (see Sect. 3). This was the period of the Schoolmen par excellence, of some of the greatest logicians, philosophers, and theologians, e.g., Petrus Hispanus (d. 1277), Lambert of Auxerre (fl. 1250), William of Sherwood (fl. ca. 1250), Albertus Magnus (ca. 1200–80); Duns Scotus (ca. 1265–1308), St Bonaventure (ca. 1217–74), and Thomas Aquinas (ca. 1225–94). It was at this time that Aristotelian philosophy was fully absorbed into Western thought, the period when logic and grammar became most closely associated. The names of three grammarians stand out—Jordan of Saxony, Robert Kilwardby, and Roger Bacon.

Jordan (fl. ca. 1210), the earliest of the three, wrote a commentary on the Priscian Minor in which he proposed the idea of universal grammar, which was necessary if grammar was to be recognized as a science. The implications of this suggest a shift of emphasis away from surface features; he also taught that grammar should be more concerned with meaning which is common to all men.

Two Englishmen, Robert Kilwardby (d. 1279; see *Kilwardby, Robert*) and Roger Bacon (ca. 1214–ca.1294), both of whom taught in Paris, were scholars of great originality, but their position in terms of developments in the thirteenth century cannot yet be defined with any accuracy. This is not intended to diminish their importance. Roger has long been famous for his proposition regarding universal grammar, i.e., 'Grammatica una et eadem est secundum substantiam in omnibus linguis licet accidentaliter varietur' (grammar is substantially one and the same in all languages, although it may vary accidentally), but there is clearly much more to his views on language than that; his was a more practical approach to the study of language and languages without diminishing the scientific approach that he advocated in all his work. Robert Kilwardby was one of the leading English thinkers of the thirteenth century and the leading English Dominican of the period; he wrote extensively on logic, theology, and grammar. His work can be divided into two parts, i.e., his logical and grammatical treatises written while teaching as a Master at Paris and his theological work after his entry into the Dominican Order. In the present context, he wrote an extensive commentary on the Priscian Minor, a commentary on the *Barbarismus* of Donatus, a commentary on the *De Accentu* of the pseudo-Priscian; a collection of grammatical sophismata has been ascribed to him and he also wrote a collection of *Errores condemnati* and a very important *De Ortu Scientiarum*. A commentary on the Priscian Major has been ascribed to him but there is a general consensus that this is an erroneous ascription. Kilwardby was a grammarian of great distinction and importance, but his Priscian Minor commentary is not an account of Latin sentence composition but rather an account of what might be called sentential semantics. If one compares the statement of Petrus Helias on the nature of grammar, i.e., 'grammatica est scientia gnara recte scribendi et recte loquendi' (grammar is the learned science of writing and speaking correctly) and Kilwardby's 'sermo significativus prout abstrahitur ab omni lingua speciali' (significant speech inasmuch as it is abstracted from every individual language), likening grammar to geometry, i.e., irrespective of the superficial differences between languages or the shapes and sizes of different diagrams, one can get some idea of the progress that had been made in grammatical theory in the 100 years that separated Peter from Kilwardby.

Until quite recently there was a gap in knowledge of developments in grammatical thought for a period of about a hundred years, i.e., 1150–1250. Apart from a few names, little more was known: Ralph of Beauvais (fl. ca. 1170) was well known as a grammarian but Petrus Hispanus (nonPapa) (fl. ca. 1175), for instance, author of the treatise *Absoluta*, was little more than a name—indeed, there was much confusion since both Peter Helias and Petrus Hispanus are often referred to in contemporary grammatical manuscripts as P. H.

Such statements are now invalid and more recent work, especially by a small number of younger scholars, has shown that medieval grammarians of the later twelfth and early thirteenth centuries were fully representative of the richness of the intellectual achievements of this period of medieval scholasticism. For example, K. M. Fredburg (Copenhagen) has clarified the status of William of Conches and Peter Halias; C. H. Kneepkens (Nijmegen) has produced texts of late twelfth-century grammarians, e.g., Ralph of Beauvais; Petrus Hispanus; Robert of Paris (fl. ca. 1175), Robert Blund (fl. ca. 1180), as well as a collection of Quaestiones grammaticales from an Oxford (Corpus Christi College 250) manuscript, and a series of studies on various termini technici (cf., biography of Ralph of Beauvais); M. Sirridge (Louisiana) has edited Jordan of Saxony's Priscian Minor commentary and produced studies on Robert Kilwardby (Rosier 1990b); and Irène Rosier (Paris) has written extensively on Roger Bacon, Robert Kilwardby, speculative grammar, and other aspects of medieval grammatical thought (Rosier 1990b).

All the works mentioned in the previous paragraphs are in fact treatises on syntax, and when the Kilwardby Minor and the works of Michel de Marbais (including his commentary on Priscian Minor recently come to light) become available, it will be much easier to justify the claim that the study of syntax made great advances in the Middle Ages; it is certainly quite wrong, as Covington (1984; 126) points out, to ascribe all this progress to the Modistae.

Medieval grammarians introduced and refined certain *termini technici*. It is well known that the idea of *regimen* (rection) was a medieval development, but so also was the refinement of terms and concepts such as *absolutio* (absolute, Kneepkens in Rosier 1988: 155–69), *compositio* (composition, Kelly in Bursill-Hall, et al. 1990: 147–59), *constructio* and *transitio* (Kneepkens in Bursill-Hall et al. 1990: 161–89), *dependentia* (dependency, Covington 1984), *congruitas* (congruity, Kneepkens, cf. biography of Roger Bacon), and *relatio* (relative, cf. Rosier 1990b). Some of these terms can be traced back to Prisician, e.g., *absolutio*, and to Greek linguistic scholarship, e.g., *transitio*, but they did not acquire the precision necessary for a technical term until used by the later medieval grammarians. Some seem to have been medieval creations, viz. *compositio*; Thomas of Erfurt established 'composition' as an accidental mode of the verb to express the relations between the verb and its *suppositum* (subject) in contrast to 'signification' which expressed relations between the verb and postposed nominal (cf. Kelly in Bursill-Hall et al. 1990: 147–59). The Modistae in particular originated the idea of the separate techniques of *Prohemium* (metalanguage), *Etymologia* (word classes), and *Diasynthetica* (syntax); these must be regarded as separate techniques but with the necessary 'mixing' to produce a coordinated statement and without a separate semantic technique.

3. The Modistae

By 1270 there had emerged a new framework used to account for the facts of language and to create a grammatical statement which embodied the philosophy and logic of language which Scholastic philosophers had been developing. This literature was stated in the form of treatises on the *modi significandi* 'modes of signifying' and the authors came to be known as Modistae. This somewhat amorphous group of grammarians dominated the grammatical scene for the next 50 years.

Viewed in terms of the grammatical literature written between 1100 and 1450 and which has survived, modistic grammars represent a rather small proportion of the material available, but their importance is beyond dispute. The names of about 30 authors are known; there are about 100 treatises which are either modistic commentaries or anonymous treatises labeled 'Modus significandi' as well as many others, modistic in tenor, labeled indiscriminately Priscian/Donatus/Doctrinale commentaries. There are seven grammarians who stand out above the others, i.e., Boethius of Dacia (fl. ca. 1270); Martin of Dacia (fl. ca. 1270); Michel de Marabais (fl. ca. 1280); Albertus (fl. ca. 1285); Siger de Courtrai (fl. ca. 1300); Radulphus Brito (fl. ca. 1300); and Thomas of Erfurt (fl. ca. 1310). They separate into three convenient groups; Boethius (who was especially severe in his criticism of the adequacy of Priscian's theoretical base) and Martin were the initiators and gave the theoretical thrust to the whole program; Michel, Albertus, and Siger are the middle group serving to consolidate the proposals of their predecessors (Siger seems to have been most conscious of the pedagogical problems involved with this type of grammatical literature); Radulphus and Thomas represent the completion of the program, with Radulphus providing the theoretical basis for their approach to syntax and Thomas a manual which sets out in an orderly fashion the rudiments of a complete modistic grammar. The result is a full picture of the development of a grammatical theory, especially the refinement of descriptive criteria used to establish the word classes and sentences of Latin, which was for the Modistae a more 'perfect' language than any of the vernaculars. That this was so requires no further comment. If manuscript distribution is any guide, these grammars are to be found in libraries all over Europe which suggests that modistic grammar was quite widespread. Most Modistae had some connection with the University of Paris; Thomas of Erfurt studied in Paris but returned to Erfurt which seems to have been an important center for grammatical studies in the fourteenth century (cf. Pinborg 1967: 139–51). Indeed, some of the earliest and strongest attacks on modistic theory came from Erfurt masters, in particular Johannes Aurifaber (fl. ca. 1330).

Thomas of Erfurt's *Grammatica Speculativa* 'Speculative Grammar' will be used for this account of modistic grammar since his work represents the culmination of modistic doctrine. His terminology and system do vary in relation to other Modistae, but his grammar is the ultimate modistic textbook (for details see Bursill-Hall 1990). A very readable survey of modistic grammar and its intellectual premises is to be found in Rosier (1983) and in Robins (1990); a good albeit brief account of the Modistae linking their grammars to medieval logic and semantics was written by Pinborg just before his death in 1982 (Kretzmann et al. 1982: 254–69) as well as his *Entwicklung* (1967), and an excellent account of modistic syntax can be found in Covington (1984).

For the Modistae, the grammarian expresses in language his understanding of the world and its contents; he does this by means of the *modus significandi* (mode of signifying), but it is in fact by means of the active mode of signifying that the grammarian is able to use language as his mode of expression. His other tool is the *pars orationis* 'word class'; this is a grammatical expression and should be considered the correlative of things. The medieval grammarians argued that any thing or any being which the intelligence can understand can also be indicated by language. A thing may have many properties; a *pars orationis* may therefore have many modes of signifying, each of which will be used to signify some aspect or property of the thing. Its essential mode will describe its essence, and the accidental modes the external variations that may occur to its essence; these external variations allow the *pars orationis* to function at a higher level, i.e., syntactic level. The grammarian's concern is with these various modes of signifying and thus he is tied into the medieval philosopher's view of reality.

A modistic grammar consists of three parts or techniques; Proemium, Etymologia, and Diasynthetica. The Proemium was used to set out their technical vocabulary and/or analytical processes, or in the case of Thomas of Erfurt, to discuss the *modus significandi* which was for him and other Modistae the starting point of grammar. The Proemium can be divided into two parts, one of which has been labeled (Bursill-Hall 1971: 72–88) 'elements,' which consisted of *vox* 'expression,' *signum* 'sign,' *dictio* 'word,' and *pars orationis* 'word class,' and 'categories,' which consisted of *modus essendi* 'mode of being,' and *modus intelligendi* 'mode of understanding' (divided into active and passive), the *modus significandi* 'mode of signifying' (divided into active and passive), and the *modus consignificandi* 'mode of cosignifying,' i.e., syntactically. The first series should be considered linguistic terms and the second (with the exception of the last one) as philosophical; the grammarian steps into the process making it linguistic with the *pars orationis*, the *modus significandi activus*, and the *modus consignificandi*.

The mode of signifying is divided into essential and accidental, the essential being divided further into general and specific, and the accidental into the various traditional accidents of grammatical analysis; a further division was into absolute and respective modes, the latter implying a syntactic function and the former has no such implication, e.g., *species* 'type' is an absolute mode but *casus* 'case' is a respective mode of the noun. The essential mode of signifying is the key to each *pars orationis* and the vital part of their grammatical system; it is here that there is the greatest apparent difference of organization among the Modistae. Siger de Courtrai, for example, divides his essential mode into general and specific, the general containing features which a particular word class shares with another, e.g., the *nomen* has the same general feature *ens* (being) as the *pronomen*, but the specific essential mode is peculiar to that particular class. In contrast, Thomas of Erfurt starts, so to speak, a little 'later'; he has no general essential mode to be shared with another word class. He divides his essential mode into *generalissimus*, *subalternus*, and *specialissimus*, so that his *modus significandi generalissimus* is roughly equivalent to Siger's *generalis* and *specificus*; he uses the *subalternus* 'subaltern' and *specialissimus* to refine his statements and, indeed, the *specialissimus* becomes in fact the inventory of the divisions into which the members of the class can be slotted.

Using the terminology and procedures just outlined, etymologia is that portion of the descriptive process that deals with the definitions of the word classes and their accidents. The Modistae retained the eight word classes of Latin as set out by Donatus and Priscian but, as can well be imagined, their criteria changed. The word classes were divided into declinables, i.e., *nomen*, *pronomen*, *verbum*, and *participium*; and indeclinables, i.e., *adverbium*, *coniunctio*, *praepositio*, and *interiectio*, the division being justified on the grounds that the indeclinable *partes orationes* had fewer modes of signifying, i.e., fewer formal features and hence their meaning rested on fewer properties, fewer modes of being (*modi essendi*) than the declinable classes. A mode of signifying is the means of expressing a mental concept, and a *pars orationis* is such by virtue of its modes of signifying; the mental concept derives its importance from the importance of the object under consideration, i.e., from the properties of the thing itself, and therefore the relative importance of the modes of signifying is a direct result of the relative importance of the things to be signified. As Boethius of Dacia stated (see 11–107), 'omnes modi significandi essentiales, et accidentales, generales et speciales accepti sunt a proprietatibus rerum' (All essential and accidental modes of signifying, both general and particular, are received from the properties of things). It is not surprising that *ens* (entity) and *esse* (being) became the most important properties and therefore the criteria for the noun and verb.

A brief look at the description of the *nomen* at Thomas of Erfurt will reveal a great deal about modistic practice. Thomas set up first of all the *modus essentialis generalissimus* which he defined as the mode of an entity and determinate understanding (*modus entis vel determinatae apprehensionis*). The noun shares the feature of *ens* with the pronoun; they are rendered discrete by virtue of the feature of *determinata apprehensio* in the noun in contrast to the *indeterminata apprehensio* of the pronoun. This is a good example of the way that the Modistae exploited the matter/form contrast adapted from contemporary hylomorphic theory. The *modus entis* represents the matter that the noun and pronoun share; the noun, however, is informed (*determinata apprehensio*) whereas the pronoun is only informable (*indeterminata apprehensio*). Siger used the feature of *ens* to describe the general mode which the noun and pronoun have in common and *apprehensio determinata* to describe the specific mode of the noun which is opposed to the specific mode of *apprehensio indeterminata* of the pronoun, i.e., in Siger's terms the noun and pronoun share the same general mode but are differentiated by the specific mode. Thomas was not concerned to exploit the opposition of matter and form so emphatically as Siger. His *modus generalissimus* combines the criteria of Siger's general and specific modes so that in Thomas's terms the *modus generalissimus* of the noun consists of the *modus entis et determinatae apprehensionis* and the *modus generalissimus* of the pronoun consists of the *modus entis et indeterminatae apprehensionis*.

The *modus genralissimus* of the noun is then subdivided into *modi subalterni*, i.e., the *modus communis* (mode of commonness) which is the common or appellative noun and the *modus appropriati* or the proper noun; the common mode is further divided into two subalternate modes of signifying, i.e., *modus per se stantis* (mode of independence), the characteristic mark of the noun-substantive, and the *modus adiacentis* (mode of adherence), the characteristic mark of the adjective. The *modus per se stantis* is then divided into five *modi specialissimi* to produce five different types of substantives; the *modus adiacentis* is divided into 24 *modi specialissimi*, i.e., 24 different types of adjectives, and the *modus appropriati* is divided into four *modi specialissimi*, i.e., four different types of name—*nomen proprium*, *praenomen*, *cognomen*, *agnomen* (cf. Bursill-Hall 1971: 358). Thomas then describes the accidental modes of signifying of the nomen. Reference has already been made to the use of matter and form, terms taken from hylomorphic theory and incorporated into modistic technical language; the division of *essentialis* and *accidentalis* is one such pair of terms (one can add to these, pairs such as *actus* 'act' and *potentia* 'potentiality,' *ens* 'entity' and *esse* 'being,' the latter pair being the distinguishing criterion between the noun and verb). The accidental modes serve to express variations that can occur to the essence of the word class but which originate from without its essence. Thomas established six accidental modes: *species* (type), *figura* (form), *genus* (gender), *numerus* (number), *casus* (case), and *persona* (person), the first two being absolute modes and the others respective modes. These accidental modes are further subdivided and thus are found the accidents of traditional grammar.

One factor often overlooked in the account of the *partes orationis* is what appears to be an undue amount of attention to the analysis of the *nomen*. More than half of John of Dacia's *Summa grammatica* is devoted to an account of the *nomen*: Thomas of Erfurt devoted 12 pages (in the 1972 edition) to the general modes of signifying of the *nomen* compared to four pages for the *pronomen*, five pages for the *verbum*, and three for the *participium*, i.e., as much for the *nomen* as for the other three declinable *partes orationis*. For the Modistae, nomenclature, i.e., the property of naming, was a necessary part of a grammatical theory that was designed to talk about, classify, and categorize successfully the things of the world, e.g., the sacraments (Rosier 1990a).

The third stage of modistic description was diasynthetica (syntax), and here the Modistae were at their most original. One of the problems that the Schoolmen grammarians encountered in their commentaries on the Priscian Minor was that of putting order into the disorder of Priscian's account; not even Radulphus Brito could do this. Thomas did not attempt an account of Priscian's syntax; instead he established a framework which presents the rudiments of a formal model of sentence structure. Martin has a separate section for syntax in his treatise, Michel de Marbais wrote a Priscian Minor commentary which has recently come to light; Albertus and Gentilis de Cingulo both discuss syntactic problems but the most important treatise on syntax is that of Radulphus Brito. It is probably the most extensive discussion not only of Priscian's syntax but of syntactic problems and difficulties which had not previously yielded to analysis; this treatise itself awaits systematic exegesis. The edition of Radulphus also contains in the introduction a lengthy discussion of the logical and semantic theses of Radulphus Briot current among the Modistae.

Thomas's syntactic model can be divided into two parts: the principles of construing based on Aristotle's four causes (Metaphysics V,2) of material, formal, efficient (subdivided into intrinsic and extrinsic), and final; and the application of these principles to an analysis of the three stages in the construction of a complete sentence. The three stages are *constructio* (construction), *congruitas* (congruity), divided into internal (according to the rules of rection) and external (according to the rules of collocational propriety), *perfectio* (completion) (divided into *propinquus* (primary) and *remotus* (secondary)), where *propinquus* requires the presence of a verb in a complete construction, and *remotus* that of generating perfect understanding in the mind of the hearer by means of a congruent combination of constructibles, one of which must be a verb.

This theory of syntax is an interesting example of the application of the binary principle. Just as *congruitas* and *perfectio* express a certain type of polarity, so too *constructio* can be divided into *transitivus* and *intransitivus*; each of these can be further divided into *actuum* (acts) and *personarum* (persons). Constructions which are of the *actuum* type are concerned with relations of the verb either to the subject or object and constructions *personarum* are not; therefore constructions of the NV type and of the VN type are *actuum* while relationships such as Nm (modifier) as in *homo albus* (the white man) or Va (adjunct) as in *currit bene* (runs well) would be *personarum*. A complete and perfect sentence must have all its syntactic dependencies complete; a sentence such as *si puer currit* (if the boy runs) would not be perfect because *si* adds a new dependency which is not completed. Thomas established the key terms *dependentia* and *determinatio* to express the relationship between members of a construction: the terminant (T) states the specific nature of the relationship and the dependent (D) specifies the type of relationship, so that *homo albus* is an intransitive *personarum* construction, T D; *legit bene* (reads well) would also be an intransitive *personarum*, T D; *puer currit* would be intransitive *actuum*, T D, so that *puer stultus legit lente* (the stupid boy reads slowly) would be analyzed as *puer stultus* = intransitive *personarum* + *legit lente* = intransitive *personarum*, and the whole sentence is intransitive *actuum*. A sentence such as *Socrates videt Platonem* 'Socrates sees Plato' (the Modistae were not very exciting in their choice of illustrations) would be analyzed:

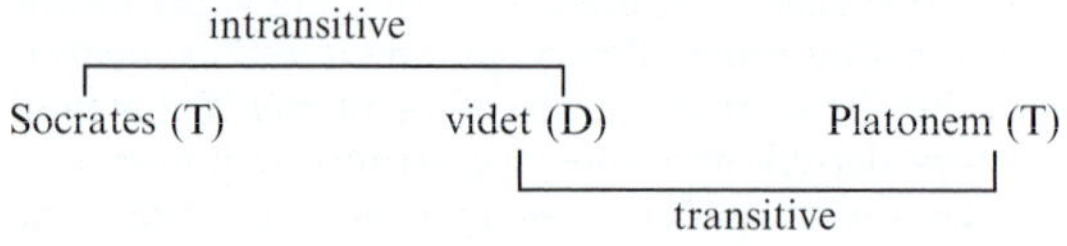

If this were expanded to *Socrates felix videt Platonem tristem* ('Happy Socrates sees sad Plato'), this would mean that both *Socrates felix* and *Platonem tristem* would be intransitive *personarum* constructions. Covington (1984: 83) has properly called the modistic syntactic model a dependency grammar rather than a constituency grammar; for more details of their syntactic theory consult the edition of Thomas of Erfurt, and Robins (Koerner et al. 1980: 231–47).

The Modistae were the last in a long line of medieval grammarians. They were succeeded chronologically by the nominalist grammarians who, however, continued to use much of the technical terminology developed in the earlier period. Modistic grammars continued to be written but they added nothing new to grammatical or modistic theory. The demise of modistic grammar can be accounted for in part by the fact that modistic and nominalist grammarians (it is difficult to say if the latter added anything significantly new to grammatical theory) had nothing to say to each other, but this is not a sufficient explanation, nor is it sufficient to say that the humanist grammarians filled the gap, because their grammars did not appear until the fifteenth century. In fact very little is known about grammatical work in the northern schools in the later fourteenth and early fifteenth centuries. It is however safe to say that philosophers of this period, especially the Oxford Calculators, were not interested in grammar, and as E. J. Ashworth has pointed out (Kretzmann et al. 1982; 787), the fifteenth century did not produce much logical writing of importance, and by this time medieval scholasticism had lost much of its intellectual vigor. As W. K. Percival points out (Kretzmann et al. 1982: 816), it is not yet possible to claim an unbroken tradition between the grammars of the Modistae and those of the universalist grammarians of the seventeenth century.

It would be foolish to make too much of modistic and medieval theory. Their weaknesses are often obvious, e.g., their apparent inability to go beyond the simple declarative type of sentence. This is the wrong way to look at them. It is better to say that medieval grammar in general and modistic grammar in particular is a very important step taken quite a long time ago along the road towards the goal of an 'overall' theory of language, which has not yet been achieved.

4. Conclusion

The *Grammatica Speculativa* of Thomas of Erfurt was the last original treatise written in the modistic vein; 1300 may be taken as the probable date of composition. Thereafter, nothing of significance was produced. Yet, modistic texts continued to be read for some time, their terminology dominated, and even the humanist grammarians did not completely abandon modistic theory. There is in the monastic library of El Escorial a beautifully written version dating from the seventeenth century of the *Grammatica Speculativa* of Thomas of Erfurt. From 1300 onward different approaches to language description are to be found; these have been designated 'nominalist,' but the attacks on the Modistae came from scholars of different philosophical backgrounds. Two names stand out, Johannes Aurifaber (fl. ca. 1330), a Master at Erfurt and an Averroist, and Petrus Alliacus (Pierre d'Ailly, 1350–ca. 1421), an Ockhamist and author of *Destructiones Modorum Significandi*. Were they the *Junggrammatiker* of the Middle Ages?

There are external reasons for the failure of the Modistae; there were internal reasons too. A linguistic theory without a phonological technique cannot succeed. The Modistae did not realize that giving a language such as Latin a privileged status could not alter the fact that a natural language is totally inadequate as a model for universal grammar; this separated the Modistae from Roger Bacon who argued for a much wider study of other languages. Part of the problem for the Modistae was their reliance on Priscian as their model; their criteria for describing the word classes of Latin were an improvement, but they (like their predecessors) could not cope with Priscian's unsystematic account of Latin syntax. There are other reasons, not the least of which was the rigor of their method and their requirement of clear definitions.

Historians of medieval linguistics have tended to overlook the purpose of much medieval grammatical thought; this is no animadversion of their work which has concentrated on the developments in grammatical theory (and there is still much more to be done to clarify developments between 1150 and 1250). The Schoolmen grammarians knew that natural language was sufficient to express their experience of the physical world as they knew it, but they also recognized that something more finely honed was needed if they were to be successful in talking about theological problems, the nature of God, or the meaning of the sacraments. In this context, the work of a number of historians of linguistics, e.g., F. P. Dinneen, SJ (Georgetown), L. G. Kelly (Ottawa), and especially Irène Rosier (Paris), is important. They have been examining the way that medieval theologians used grammatical analysis as taught by the speculative grammarians to analyze, interpret, and explicate fundamental liturgical and theological problems. Much more knowledge is needed about the way that the ideas of medieval grammarians were used in medieval everyday life.

Medieval grammatical thought has its own intrinsic interest, but it offers something else of importance to the modern linguist and historian of ideas. The Modistae were convinced that theirs was a coherent linguistic theory. It was the first attempt in Western Europe to create a fully fledged linguistic theory; it was not a theory of language, although speculative grammar, on which the Modistae constructed their grammatical theory, was, by virtue of its name, a theory of language. They both eventually failed. There is much for the intellectual world of the late twentieth century to learn from this.

See also: Aquinas, Thomas; Kilwardby, Robert; Petrus Hispanus.

Bibliography

Medieval grammatical literature

There are texts for a number of medieval grammarians in addition to those listed below. Of the pre-modistic grammarians, there is a text of Jordan of Saxony, of the Modistae texts of John of Dacia, Simon of Dacia, (Pseudo-) Albertus, Gentilis de Cingulo, Godfrey de Fontaines; of the post-Modistic grammarians texts of Johannes Aurifaber, John Buridan, John Gerson, and Marsilius of Inghen. Editions of teaching grammars have not been included.

Bursill-Hall G L 1971 *Speculative Grammars of the Middle Ages: The Doctrine of partes orationis of the Modistae.* Mouton, The Hague

Bursill-Hall G L 1975 The Middle Ages. In: Sebeok T A (ed.) *Current Trends in Linguistics.* Mouton, The Hague

Bursill-Hall G L, Ebbesen S, Koerner E F K (eds.) 1990 *De Ortu Grammaticae: Studies in Medieval Grammar and Linguistic Theory in memory of Jan Pinborg.* John Benjamins, Amsterdam

Covington M A 1984 *Syntactic Theory in the High Middle Ages: Modistic Models of Sentence Structure.* Cambridge University Press, Cambridge

Hunt R W 1980 (ed. Bursill-Hall G L) *The History of Grammar in the Middle Ages: Collected Papers.* Benjamins, Amsterdam

Kelly L G 1979 Modus significandi: an interdisciplinary concept. *HL* **VI**: 159–80

Kneepkens C H 1988 'Suppositio' and 'Supponere' in the 12th century grammar. In: Jolivet J, de Libera A (eds.) *Gilbert de Poitiers et ses contemporains,* Actes du 7me symposium européen d'histoire de la logique et de la sémantique médiévale. Bibliopolis, Rome

Knowles D 1988 (1st edn. 1962) *The Evolution of Medieval Thought.* Longman, London

Koerner E F K, Niederehe H-J, Robins R H (eds.) 1980 *Studies in Medieval Linguistic Thought: Dedicated to Geoffrey L Bursill-Hall*, Benjamins, Amsterdam
Kretzmann N, Kenny A, Pinborg J (eds.) 1982. *The Cambridge History of Later Medieval Philosophy*. Cambridge University Press, Cambridge
Leader D R 1988 *A History of the University of Cambridge*, vol. I, *The University to 1546*. Cambridge University Press, Cambridge
Leff G 1975 *Paris and Oxford Universities in the Thirteenth and Fourteenth Centuries*. Krieger, Huntington, NY
Pinborg J 1967 *Die Entwicklung der Sprachtheorie im Mittelalter*. *BGPTMA*, 42: 0. Aschendorff/Frost-Hansen
Pinborg J 1984 (ed. Ebbesen S) *Medieval Semantics: Medieval Logic and Grammar*. Variorum, London
Robins R H 1990 *A Short History of Linguistics*, 3rd edn. Longman, London
Rosier I 1983 *La grammaire speculative des Modistes*, Presses Universitaires de Lille, Lille
Rosier I (ed.) 1988 *L'héritage des grammairiens latins de l'Antiquité aux Lumières*, Actes du colloque de Chantilly 2–4 Septembre 1987. Peeters, Louvain
Rosier I 1990a Signes et sacrements. Thomas d'Aquin et la grammaire spéculative. *Revue des sciences philosophiques et théologiques* **74**: 392–436
Rosier I 1990b Grammaire (1971–88). *Contemporary Philosophy. A New Survey* **6(2)**: 783–803

Missionaries

A. F. Walls

1. Introduction

In the developing interaction between Europe and the non-Western world from ca. 1500 CE, missionaries had greater reason than any other definable group to devote themselves to language issues. They wished to communicate a message, and its translation was commonly not straightforward, since its expression had been shaped by centuries of Greek, Latin, and north European intellectual processes. They intended to stay, and thus needed understanding of their host societies. They planned a continuing institutional presence, so tended to give the fruits of their linguistic activity permanent form in grammars, dictionaries, and word lists for their successors, scriptures, liturgies and instructional works for the emerging churches, literature designed to interest people outside the churches, and materials to service the educational and health care work that commonly accompanied missions. These concerns required them to grapple with language at a more fundamental level than most of their secular contemporaries. Not all missionaries had the concern or the skill to go far; even the eminent T. B. Freeman was preaching through an interpreter after many years in Ghana. Missionaries varied greatly in cultural sensitivity, aural sensibility, and in education and the quality of their linguistic training. Taken as a whole, however, the missionary movement provided new depth to the Western engagement with the major literary languages of Asia, supplying many of the pioneer lexical and grammatical tools, and many of the earliest extended translations out of as well as into them. For countless languages in Africa, the Americas, and the Pacific, as well as some parts of Asia, missions designed the first writing systems and supplied the first (in some cases the only) literature. Since they translated into and out of the languages in which they worked, missionaries became intercultural intellectual brokers. Academic study profited immeasurably from their work. Above all, though many translations, especially early ones, were unusable, and others languished unread, missions provided a readership for the materials they produced, and their churches and schools formed communities of mother-tongue speakers who took elements of the translated material into their languages, domesticated them in the wider community, and influenced the subsequent development of those languages.

2. Explaining Christian Faith

Until the early eighteenth century missions and missionaries with few exceptions originated from Catholic southern Europe. In these early missions, translation of the Bible was not usually a priority; the first concern was to produce intelligible and acceptable explanations of what Christian faith was.

In the Spanish conquests in America, where Christianity was largely imposed, and the former official cults had collapsed or been destroyed, large numbers of people with no previous acquaintance with Christianity were required to receive instruction in it. There was no precedent, and no machinery, for a teaching operation on this scale. Catechisms—summaries of Christian teaching—were devised locally and reproduced by hand. They differed widely in content, length, and approach. Some of the earliest known are in pictographic script following the models of Aztec Mexico. A Flemish Franciscan,

Pedro de Gante (1486–1572) designed materials that seem to have been particularly effective. Printing was introduced in the mid-sixteenth century, and was used principally for church purposes. The first catechism printed for America, in Nahuatl, dates from 1546; the first in the Andean languages, Quechua and Aymara, from 1584. Even such elementary materials raised unprecedented semantic problems; how, for instance, should the indigenous names or titles of divinities, be used to designate the Christian God? Official ecclesiastical policy was to use loan words from Spanish or Latin; but loan words had to be explained in the vernacular, and it is clear that at the pastoral level the interaction produced both a Christianized Andes and an Andeanized Christianity.

In Asia, where conquest was not usually at issue, catechisms were needed too. The best known early missionary, Francis Xavier (1506–52), produced them for Christian converts in south India, seeking to employ local musical forms to render them more memorable. But missionaries also wanted to present Christianity within the dominant cultures of India, China, and Japan, and at the highest level. The policy of the Jesuits, in particular, who had invested heavily in intellectual preparation, was to seek to influence the ruling classes towards Christianity. This required a high degree of linguistic competence and deep absorption in the literary culture and tradition. Matteo Ricci (see *Ricci, M.*) was accepted as a member of the Confucian literati, Roberto de Nobili (see *Nobili R. de*) as a Roman raja and Brahmin using both Sanskrit and Tamil. In Vietnam, Alexandre de Rhodes (1593–1660) developed a similar approach to Ricci's. His Vietnamese–Latin catechism is a substantial and sophisticated document. All three avoided loan words where possible, and were adventurous in adopting religious terms from Asian languages, frequently drawing controversy and sometimes ecclesiastical censure.

A few later missionaries penetrated still more deeply into the old traditions. Another Jesuit, Giuseppe Beschi (1680–1747) became a major Tamil poet, composing epics on Christian themes, and earning the title V*ram ~ munivar, '*The Heroic Sage*.' Some nineteenth century Protestants entered the Sanskrit field. W. H. Mill (1792–1853), who began by trying to translate the historic Christian creeds, turned instead to poetic presentation of the life of Christ. A Christian Sanskrit literature grew up, with Indian Christians such as Krishna Mohun Banerjea (1813–85) contributing substantially, while later poets such as H. A. Krishna Pillai and N. V. Tilak produced Christian lyric poetry in Indian vernaculars.

But nineteenth century missionaries aimed more often at a mass audience, particularly in China, where missionaries were effectively excluded until 1842. The press in the overseas Chinese settlement in Malacca was producing Christian literature in Chinese long before such operations were possible in China. Some tracts, intended to get a hearing for Christianity, had a long life, notably *Good Words to Admonish the Age* by the convert Liang A-Fa, and *The Two Friends* by the missionary William Milne.

3. Translation of the Bible

For Protestants, especially the evangelical Protestants who spearheaded the missionary movement, translation of the Bible was an imperative. The Puritan John Eliot designed a writing system for the Massachuset language and in 1663 published the complete Bible in it. In one of the earliest overseas missions, Bartolomäus Ziegenbalg (see *Ziegenbalg, B.*) completed the Tamil New Testament in 1715. By the early nineteenth century, new translations were in progress in many parts of the world. William Carey (see *Carey, W.*) and his colleagues in Serampore produced by far the most ambitious program including versions for languages in which there was no missionary activity. Robert Morrison (1782–1834) was appointed to translate the Bible into Chinese despite conditions designed to prevent foreigners learning the language. Early missions in the Middle East gave high priority to making the Bible available in the spoken, rather than the liturgical, languages of the ancient churches. Literate populations emerged surprisingly quickly where missions saw a response; in New Zealand there was a Maori New Testament in circulation for every two Maori within 20 years of the first conversions, and the Maori Bible continued in use even among Maori who had rejected the white churches. In at least one important instance, Korea, the translated Bible precipitated the formation of churches before missionaries arrived (see *Ross, John*).

The first movement to Protestant Christianity among Africans occurred among slaves in North and Caribbean America, who were already speaking English. The first in Africa itself occurred in Sierra Leone, among uprooted people from over West and Central Africa. With no single dominant language, English was used for preaching and education, with such effect that some predicted the demise of African languages. The Quaker Hannah Kilham (1774–1852) launched West Africa's first vernacular literary program. One of her assistants, the Yoruba Samuel Ajayi Crowther (1806–1898) (see *Crowther, S. A.*) and some missionaries who had given serious attention to the languages, saw that the spread of Christianity in inland Africa would depend on African missionaries using African languages. In the 1840s Crowther became one of the leaders of a mission to his native Yorubaland, and a key translator of the Yoruba Bible. This translation was significant as the first in Africa where a mother tongue speaker played a major role, and for the care taken to obtain the best international advice on orthography, tone marking and other questions.

The British and Foreign Bible Society (BFBS), founded in 1804, and the American Bible Society, founded in 1816 (with the involvement in some areas of Netherlands and Scottish societies), set new standards in Bible translation. They helped translators with the Biblical languages, and, as experience built up, with wider linguistic issues. They coordinated work where several translators were involved, and financed and oversaw printing and delivery. From the 1930s, especially under the influence of the anthropologically aware E. W. Smith (1876–1967), BFBS's attention turned to the nature of the receptor languages as well as to classical and Biblical scholarship. Such ideas were taken further by Maurice Leenhardt, missionary in New Caledonia, who saw translation in terms of a conversation between cultures, and accelerated by the rise of descriptive linguistics in America. Kenneth Pike (see *Pike, K.*) and Eugene Nida (see *Nida, E.*) of the Summer Institute of Linguistics (SIL) (see *Summer Institute of Linguistics*) applied the new linguistics energetically to Bible translation. Nida, moving to the American Bible Society in 1943, brought linguistic analysis to the center of its work, with professional guidance for translators by consultants and a body of technical publications. The United Bible Societies emerged in 1947 to coordinate the work of national Bible societies and took over the function of professional linguistic consultancy to translators. The principle of 'dynamic' or 'functional' equivalence was common in missionary translations before it was applied to modern English versions of the Bible.

The Summer Institute of Linguistics, founded in 1934 as a training program, continued to develop its academic expertise and to undertake research into minority languages and conduct literacy programs, often sponsored by national governments. But, with its sister organization the Wycliffe Bible Translators, it also acts as a mission agency, concentrating on Bible translation, particularly in minority languages.

Bible translation in most areas is now a matter of regular review, usually by committees of mother tongue speakers, and Catholics and Protestants are equally involved. Earlier translations have been successively revised.

Bible translation, accompanied by translation of the liturgy, was also a feature of Russian Orthodox missionary expansion across Siberia and into Alaska. A central figure was Loann Veniaminov (1797–1879), later Patriarch of Moscow.

4. The Study of Languages

All these activities made the production of grammar, dictionaries, and similar tools a feature of missionary work from the beginning. These varied in quality as much as the translations did, but many were landmarks. De Rhodes' Vietnamese Dictionary (which used an earlier model now lost) marked the sixfold tone system of the language, and made possible the alphabetic script used by de Rhodes' successors. Morrison's vast Chinese Dictionary (1815–23) is an encyclopedia of China. The list of foundational missionary grammars and dictionaries in Africa is endless.

Missionaries (often after a generation or so to acquire the skills and lose prejudices) sometimes assisted in the preservation or recovery of indigenous literary heritage, or in introducing it to Western audiences. Examples are George Pope's editions of the Tamil Classics, James Legge's 50-year program of translating Chinese classics, and John Nicol Farquhar's studies of the religious literature of India.

Missionary linguists preceded, and then helped to shape, the Western academy's treatment of many languages. Missionaries pioneered the study of Chinese in Britain. Robert Morrison's Anglo–Chinese College carried it on in Malacca. In Britain, Morrison established an institute for the study of all Asian languages and he canvassed the idea of a Philological Society. A former missionary filled the first chair of Chinese established in Britain (University College, London, 1837); another, James Legge, first professor at Oxford, was the nineteenth century's most significant sinologist. African languages took still longer to gain academic recognition as a subject. By common consent S. W. Koelle (see *Koelle, S. W.*) missionary in Sierra Leone, whose *Polyglotta Africana* (1854) lists specimens of over a hundred languages, is the father of comparative African linguistics. As new sciences developed in European and American universities, missionaries became important informants, as Max Müller's (see *Müller, F. M.*) and J. G. Frazer's (see *Frazer, J. G.*) acknowledgments testify. Alexander Duff, who initiated Europe's first chair of mission studies in Edinburgh in 1868, wanted to establish an associated institute for the study of all languages and cultures. The impetus for the School of Oriental and African Studies (originally 'Languages' rather than 'Studies') came from a perceived need for a trained colonial service, but many of its early language teachers were missionaries.

5. Some Consequences of Missionary Linguistics

There were unplanned, as well as intended, outcomes from missionary linguistic activity. Occasionally the host society claimed it as a cultural monument. In Chennai (Madras), statues commemorate significant figures in Tamil literature: two are missionaries, Beschi and Pope. The Twi Bible, basically translated by J. G. Christaller in the high style of the royal court of Akuapem, Ghana, has become the standard of reference for the language today. Another effect is shown in the way the influence of Robert Caldwell's

Comparative Grammar of the Dravidian or South India Family of Languages (1856) helped to solidify a regional, South Indian identity (see *Caldwell, R.*) Sharpened ethnic or national identity has often followed missionary translation and the consequent provision of a vernacular literature. This has occurred in south Sudan, southern Ethiopia, and among some forest and mountain peoples in Latin America, despite official centralizing pressures for Arabic, Amharic, or Spanish. Sometimes mission translation gave hegemony to one form of a language among variants; for instance, in developing a 'Union' lgbo from the many local dialects. Vernacular church activities often opened the way for cultural innovations in music or speech; thus Afua Kuma, a barely literate Ghanaian woman, adapted traditional Twi praise songs for ecstatic praises of Christ. A link has been posited between the availability of the whole Bible in an African vernacular, and the emergence of new independent churches.

Initially missionaries perceived language as principally an obstacle to be overcome, then, commonly as a vehicle for their message; and then in E. W. Smith's words, as 'The shrine of a people's soul.'

See also: Bible Translations, Modern Period.

Bibliography

Bediako K 1995 *Christianity in Africa: the Recovery of a Non-Western Religion.* Edinburgh University Press, Edinburgh

Clifford J 1982 *Person and Myth: Maurice Leenhardt in the Melanesian World.* University of California Press, Berkeley, CA

Grimes B 1988 *Ethnologue: Languages of the World.* Summer Institute of Linguistics, Dallas, TX

Hair P E H 1961 *The Early Study of Nigerian Languages.* Cambridge University Press, Cambridge

Jaye B H, Mitchell W P 2000 *Picturing Faith—The Pictographic Quechua Catechism.* Huntington Library, New York

Larson M L 1984 *Meaning-Based Translation: a Guide to Cross-Cultural Equivalence.* University Press of America, Lanham, MD

Nida E A 1961 *Bible Translating: an Analysis of Principles and Procedures,* 2nd edn. United Bible Societies, New York

Nida E A, Taber C R 1969 *The Theory and Practice of Translation.* Brill, Leiden

Phillips G E 1942 *The Old Testament in the World Church.* Lutterworth Press, London

Pike K L 1967 *Language in Relation to a Unified Theory of Human Behavior,* 2n edn. Mouton, The Hague

Sanneh L 1989 *Translating the Message. The Missionary Impact on Culture.* Orbis, MaryKnoll, NY

Smalley W A 1991 *Translation as Mission: Bible Translation in the Modern Missionary movement.* Mercer University Press, Macon, GA

Smith E W 1929 *The Shrine of a People's Soul.* Friendship Press, New York

Stine P C (ed.) 1990 *Bible Translation and the Spread of the Church in the Last 200 years.* Brill, Leiden

Walls A F 1996 *The Missionary Movement in Christian History.* Orbis, Maryknoll, NY

Wendland E R 1987 *The Cultural Factor in Bible Translation.* United Bible Society, London

Young R F, Amaladass A 1995 *The Indian Christian: a Concise Anthology of Didactic and Devotional Literature in Early Church Sanskrit.* Gujarat Sahitya Prakash. Anand

Philology and History

D. R. Kelley

Philology here refers to the critical study of literary texts with regard to style, structure, and historical meaning. In this connection it has been associated for centuries with the study of history, understood especially in the sense of the past of western (and by extension non-western) culture through its written remains, and with the human sciences more generally.

1. Ancient Origins

Philology and history were both born of poetry, and they both entailed particular views of language and conceptions of the world. They were 'logocentric' in the most fundamental sense—philology *ante litteram* being the study of *logoi* in the sense of words and 'history' (as designated and initiated by Herodotus) being a recital of *logoi* in the sense of true stories. Textual self-awareness is already apparent in Homer, but it was the Alexandrine 'grammarians' and 'critics' who defined a scholarly field of textual study. Eratosthenes in particular coined the term *Philologus* to indicate the encyclopedic student of literature (rather than the loquacious, disputatious *philologus* of Plato) and called his discipline 'many-sided philologia' (Pfeiffer 1968: 170). From the beginning, too, especially from the feud between Plato and the

the Christian tradition, which at once rejected the corrupt heritage of the Roman papacy and exalted the spiritual truth of evangelical and patristic Christianity. The religious conflicts of the sixteenth century, which increasingly adopted a historical mode, focused attention on human truth, the critical techniques of pursuing it, and the criteria for accepting it. It was in this connection that the humanist art of history (*ars historica*), based on ancient sources, became a scientific 'method,' expressed most famously in Jean Bodin's *Method for the Easy Comprehension of History* (1566).

In this same age of confessional conflict and the printed book classical scholarship also advanced to higher levels of insight and emendation, especially in the work of such masters of the Renaissance 'art of criticism' (*ars critica*) as Henri Estienne, Joseph Justus Scaliger (see *Scaliger , Joseph Justus*), Justus Lipsius, and Isaac Casaubon, who carried Erasmus' and Budé's enterprise of 'restitution' beyond the limits of the western tradition (Jehasse 1976). The greatest of the post-Erasmian 'Critics' was Scaliger, son of the Latin scholar Julius Caesar Scaliger, who added oriental languages to his classicist arsenal and who, besides his many pioneering editions of classical works and studies of early Latin, established the foundations of chronology in his famous *De emendatione temporum* (1583), a work fundamental to the alignment of classical and biblical traditions and thus to the critical reconstruction of universal history (Grafton 1983). Lipsius was best known for his work on Tacitus and especially for his promotion of ancient Stoic philosophy. Estienne, member of the great French printing dynasty who moved to Geneva and wrote, edited, and published voluminously, drew on Budé's commentaries on Greek for his own monumental *Thesaurus graecae linguae* (1572). Casaubon wrote extensive commentaries on Latin and Greek texts and applied his acumen to such later fabrications as the writings of (pseudo) Dionysius the Areopagite. As Ulrich von Wilamowitz-Moellendorf wrote of the last two, 'We are still living on the capital accumulated by the industry of Casaubon and Stephanus' (Wilamowitz-Moellendorf 1982: 54).

The advancement of historical learning took place in a concomitant and often complementary fashion, drawing on the textual riches made available by philologists. Two centuries before Gibbon, Carlo Sigonio, himself following the lead of the fifteenth-century humanist historian Flavio Biondo, provided a critical survey of ancient Roman history (McCuaig 1988); and other scholars continued the exploration of classical antiquity. Even more fascinating to many European scholars were the medieval traditions, that is, the 'antiquities,' of their own nations; and in the sixteenth century the study of national history—after the fashion of Leonardo Bruni, or rather Livy, who was Bruni's model—was pursued by a growing tribe of more or less professional historiographers. What Bruni had done for Florence and Flavio Biondo for Italy as a whole, Paolo Emilio tried to do for France, Polydore Vergil for England, Beatus Rhenanus for Germany, and other followers of Flavio Biondo for the rest of the 'barbarian' nations established on the ruins of the ancient Roman Empire.

In this way the foundations were laid for the achievements of the following century—which was not only a period of 'scientific revolution' but also the 'age of erudition,' when philology and historical scholarship produced monuments of learning and criticism. 'Great historical enterprises' (Knowles 1964)—including Charles Du Cange's great dictionary of medieval Latin, Muratori's collections of medieval Italian sources, and the publications of the French Benedictines, especially Dom Mabillon's *De re diplomatica* (1681)—established medieval scholarship on a par with the classical tradition, while Richard Simon advanced the critical study of the Old and New Testaments beyond the pioneering but less well-founded ventures of Erasmus.

The continuing partnership between philology and history is also suggested in the career of the polyhistor Gerard Vossius, who held a chair of both eloquence and history at the University of Leiden. With the work of Richard Bentley—'the Newton of European philological and literary studies' (Brink 1985: 4)—English scholarship could claim parity with that of Italy, France, and The Netherlands. This was the age of the famous 'quarrel between the ancients and the moderns,' when history and philology were regarded by the philosophical avant garde, especially the Cartesians, as part of the cultural impedimenta obstructing the progress of reason. Yet in the Enlightenment of the following century 'erudition' and the critical study of history came to play a significant role, especially in ideas of intellectual and cultural progress and in the emergence of the human sciences.

5. A New Science

The great champion both of history and of philology in this period was Giambattista Vico, for whom *philologia* indeed was the first form of his 'new science.' For Vico, playing on the ancient res–verba *topos*, the link with history was quite direct: 'Philology is the study of speech,' he wrote in a section of his work on universal law entitled *De constantia philologiae*, 'and it treats words and their history, then shows their origin and progress, and so determines the ages of languages, thus revealing their properties, changes, and conventions. But since the ideas of things are represented by words, philology must first treat the history of things. Whence it appears that philologists study human governments, customs, laws, institutions, intellectual disciplines, and the mechanical arts' (Vico 1974: 387). Applying this first to the legal tradition and then to the 'search for the true Homer,' Vico transformed philology, especially in the form of learned but largely speculative etymology, into a philosophy of history.

The Homeric Question, which constituted a scholarly parallel to biblical problems, had been central to the tradition of classical scholarship since the time of the ancient rhapsodes, and (in a work not extant) Aristotle had himself contributed to Homeric criticism. In the eighteenth century it again captured scholarly attention, and the debate culminated in Friedrich August Wolf's controversial *Prolegomena ad Homerum* of 1795. Like Vico, but with a more orthodox approach to textual interpretation, Wolf tried to probe the recesses of antiquity and oral culture by reconstructing the history of a preclassical text from the time of the ancient rhapsodes through the Alexandrine scholiasts down to his own, even more 'critical' age.

The upshot was that the methods of Wolf — another version of the humanist alliance between philology and history—dominated debates over philological methods for the rest of the century, paralleled as usual by the historically grounded 'higher criticism' of the Bible and the 'quest for the historical Jesus.' It was Wolf's pupil August Boeckh who extended his master's ideas by a formal theory of philology and its relation to the larger tradition of hermeneutics, beginning with grammatical and historical interpretation before moving to broader vistas of understanding; and it was Wolf's patron Wilhelm von Humboldt who defined the 'task of the historian' largely on the basis of his ideas of linguistic structure and change (see Mueller-Vollmer 1985: 105, 132).

In many ways the so-called 'historical schools' of the nineteenth century were founded on the philological investigations of Wolf, the historian of Rome B. G. Niebuhr, the historian of Roman law K. F. von Savigny, the theologian Friedrich Schleiermacher, the Germanist Jakob Grimm, and other scholars who joined the faculty of the new University of Berlin, which was founded in 1807 by Humboldt. Here, in the context of a Romantic fascination with the past and the emergence of comparative linguistics, the partnership between history and philology was reconfirmed. 'O how would philology be cherished,' declared Niebuhr in 1840, 'if people knew the magical delight of living and moving amid the most beautiful scenes of the past!'—and his own *Römische Geschichte* was the product of such enthusiasm (Niebuhr 1852: 240; see *Romanticism*).

Among the leading products of this school in the next generation were Leopold von Ranke, founder of—or at least prime defender and practitioner of—the modern concept of *Geschichtswissenschaft*, and Theodor Mommsen, who applied his philological training to the history of Roman institutions. In a still more rigorous and assertive fashion than in the Renaissance, history and philology both laid claim to a 'critical' and a 'scientific' status in the nineteenth century. As a consequence the modern study of history was professionalized and to some extent divorced from the larger cultural concerns of its humanist founders. Such was already the condition of philology, and in general classical scholarship came under the control of academic scholars like Wilamowitz-Moellendorf and in effect exiled talented amateurs like Friedrich Nietzsche, whose early work, *The Birth of Tragedy*, he panned. Yet until the twentieth century the alliance between philology and history fashioned by Renaissance humanism and confirmed by the historical schools of the nineteenth century was maintained.

In the twentieth century the process of professionalization and specialization continued, producing a divergence between philology and history, in the sense at least that historical linguistics, or linguistic historicism, has fallen out of fashion. Popular as well as professional historians have survived, but philologists have been marginalized in the academy. To this tendency, however, there are two notable exceptions. One is modern philosophical hermeneutics, which according to its chief exponent, Hans Georg Gadamer (see *Gradmer, H-G*) reveals a conceptual as well as historical link between the humanist tradition and the human sciences, especially via Schleiermacher's efforts to establish a 'general hermeneutics.' The other is suggested by the so-called 'linguistic turn' of recent times, which has a critical impact not only on philosophy but also on the study of history and the human sciences more generally. In these contexts the ancient alliance between philology and history seems once again to reassert itself, and for inquiry into the more remote phases of the human past this connection will no doubt continue to be significant.

See also: Aristotle and the Stoics on Language; English Bible; Linguistic Theory in the Later Middle Ages; Plato and His Predecessors; Translation; History.

Bibliography

Billanovich G 1951 Petrarch and the textual tradition of Livy. *Journal of the Warburg and Courtauld Institutes* **14**: 137–208

Brink C O 1985 *English Classical Scholarship*. Clarke, Cambridge

Budé G 1532 *De Philologia libri* II. Badius, Paris

Curtius E R 1953 (transl. Trask W) *European Literature and the Latin Middle Ages*. Pantheon, New York

D'Arnico J 1986 *Theory and Practice in Renaissance Textual Criticism: Beatus Rhenanus between Conjecture and History*. University of California Press, Berkeley, CA

Gadamer H G 1975 (transl. Barden G, Cumming J) *Truth and Method*. Crossroad, New York

Grafton A 1983 *Joseph Scaliger: A Study in the History of Classical Scholarship.* Clarendon Press, Oxford
Grafton A 1990 *Forgers and Critics: Creativity and Duplicity in Western Scholarship.* Princeton University Press, Princeton, NJ
Jehasse J 1976 *La Renaissance de la critique.* Publications de l'Université de Saint-Etienne, Saint-Etienne
Kelley D R 1970 *Foundations of Modern Historical Scholarship: Language, Law, and History in the French Renaissance.* Columbia University Press, New York.
Kelley D R 1988 Humanism and History. In: Rabil A (ed.) *Renaissance Humanism,* vol. III. University of Pennsylvania Press, Philadelphia, PA
Knowles D 1964 *Great Historical Enterprises.* Nelson, London
Levine J 1991 *Ancients and Moderns.* Cornell University Press, Ithaca, NY
McCuaig W 1988 *Carlo Sigonio: The Changing World of the Late Renaissance.* Princeton University Press, Princeton, NJ
Martianus Capella 1971–77 (transl. Stahl W, Johnson R) *Martianus Capella and the Seven Liberal Arts.* Columbia University Press, New York
Momigliano A 1990 *The Classical Foundations of Modern Historiography.* University of California Press, Berkeley, CA
Mueller-Vollmer K (ed.) 1985 *The Hermeneutical Reader.* Blackwell, Oxford
Niebuhr B G 1852 (transl. Winkworth S) *Life and Letters.* Harper, New York
Padley G A 1976 *Grammatical Theory in Western Europe 1500–1800: The Latin Tradition.* Cambridge University Press, Cambridge
Padley G A 1985 *Grammatical Theory in Western Europe 1500–1800: Trends in Vernacular Grammar* I. Cambridge University Press, Cambridge
Pfeiffer R 1968 *History of Classical Scholarship from the Beginnings to the End of the Hellenistic Age.* Clarendon Press, Oxford
Pfeiffer R 1976 *History of Classical Scholarship from 1300 to 1850.* Clarendon Press, Oxford
Sandys J E 1903-08 *A History of Classical Scholarship.* Cambridge University Press, Cambridge
Schwarz W 1970 *Principles and Problems of Biblical Translation.* Cambridge University Press, Cambridge
Smalley B 1952 *The Study of Bible in the Middle Ages.* Blackwell, Oxford
Smalley B 1960 *English Friars and Antiquity in the Early Fourteenth Century.* Blackwell, Oxford
Vico G 1974 *Il Diritto Universale.* Sansoni, Florence
Wilamowitz-Moellendorf U von 1982 (trans. Harris A) *History of Classical Scholarship.* Duckworth, London
Wolf F A 1985 (transl. Grafton A, Most G, Zetzel J) *Prolegomena to Homer.* Princeton University Press, Princeton, NJ

Plato and His Predecessors

F. W. Householder

The basic notion of grammar on which all later Greeks built (see *Aristotle and the Stoics on Language*) was developed by various nameless people between Homer and Socrates. The few whose names are still known (other than mythical ones like Cadmus, the bringer of the Phoenician alphabet to Thebes) are all of the fifth century, some called 'sophists,' others 'philosophers,' and it is mainly from Plato that one learns of them.

1. The Beginnings

In the second book of the *Iliad,* at the beginning of the Trojan catalog (2.804), the goddess Iris offers a comment on the variety of languages spoken by the allies of the Trojans, and near the end (2.867) the poet mentions in particular the 'barbarity' (i.e., non-Greekness) of the speech of the Carians. But nowhere in the *Iliad* does a Greek warrior have any difficulty communicating with a Trojan (or Lycian or Carian, for that matter), nor are interpreters ever needed or mentioned. (The first Greek to mention them [ca. 430 BCE] is Herodotus, 2.154, 4.24.) In the *Odyssey,* Odysseus sails all around the known world, and never meets anyone who speaks a language other than Greek (including Polyphemus, the Laestrygonians, Circe, and the Sirens). True, several words used by the gods are mentioned as distinct from human (i.e., Greek) words, but the difference is scarcely enough even to make divine speech a special dialect of Greek.

In the sixth book of the *Iliad* (6.119–236) Diomedes has a confrontation with the Lycian King, Glaucus in which the latter traces his ancestry back to Bellerophon, a Greek from Argos who came to Lycia with some sort of message ('Kill the bearer' written in Linear B, perhaps) to the king. But the king, instead of killing him, puts him through a number of tests and then gives him his daughter's hand. This passage (6.169) is the only possible reference to writing in Homer, and even it is not unambiguous. Yet it cannot be doubted that some Greeks, namely those on Cyprus, could write at the time of Homer, since in Classical times (seventh to fourth centuries BCE) they wrote in a syllabary closely related to Linear B, which was used by Greeks in Crete, Pylos, Mycenae, and Thebes (at least) around the thirteenth century BCE. It cannot be doubted that some form of this syllabary was used continuously in the intervening centuries, though no specimens from those centuries survive, and hence there must have been teachers and schools throughout the period, apparently teaching both syllabary and alphabet by the fourth century BCE.

The signs of the Cypriote syllabary are by no means all identical to corresponding signs of Linear B; 10 of them are, and another 20 are easily derived. Linear B was mainly written on wet clay (making curves easy); Cypriote on stones or metal (yielding a preference for straight lines), but, in addition, Cyprus dropped the separate set of *d* syllables (*da*, *de*, *di*, *do*, *du*), fusing them with *t*, but distinguished *l* syllables from *r* syllables. The first of these changes has occurred in other syllabaries (e.g., Cherokee, some Southeast Asian) and some alphabets, at least as an option (e.g., Gregg shorthand). It is not true that if a language once acquires a phonemically accurate script it never later drops any distinctions. But this particular case, in which voiced, voiceless, and aspirated stops are written alike, is very common in independently developed syllabaries all over the world: evidently the grouping of all labial stops is an easy piece of phonological analysis, and the Mycenaean and Cypriote Greeks certainly made it. The Semitic alphabet as adopted by the Greeks implies a grouping of voiced stops in the alphabetic order (B, G, D) and also the nasals (M, N).

But the remarkable contribution of the Greeks, apparently unique in the history of writing systems, was the obligatory writing of vowels as letters of the same size and type as those used for consonants. This does not come naturally; syllabaries do. In the Greek alphabet the only grouping or nonwriting of a distinction appears in the case of vowel length, normally unmarked in Linear B, the Cypriote syllabary, most Greek alphabets, Italian alphabets, and their descendants. The Greeks did eventually have two long vowel characters (*eta* and *omega*) opposed to two short ones (*epsilon* and *omicron*), but vowel length was just as contrastive for A, I, U (*alpha*, *iota*, *upsilon*). No doubt the whole development was, in part, a fluke, but no other independent system did the same things. One other distinctive feature, which was not at first completely indicated by the Greek alphabet, was aspiration in stops, but *chi* and *phi* were soon provided.

As noted above, there is good reason to believe that schools existed in Mycenaean times, and that they continued right through into Classical times, with two possible modifications. It is likely that Linear B was used and maintained by a special class of scribes, and that the schools were scribal schools. And some authors hint that the Dorians were illiterate for a few centuries, though it is known that there were lyric poets in Sparta by 675 BCE or so (Terpander). But certainly almost everywhere in the Greek world, by around 700 BCE there were schools for boys, and quite often also schools for girls (Sappho ran one such school), in which the students spent much of the day from the age of 6 or 7 years to 16 or 17. Thucydides mentions (7.29) a school in a smallish town (Mycalessus) in Euboea, 'The largest one there.' The town must then have had at least three or four such schools, but it is hard to guess how many students there were, though the context does indicate that school started early in the morning, something that is also known from Aeschines (*Against Timarchus* 8–12), who cites a law of Solon forbidding (in essence) schools to open before sunrise or close after sunset. Summer vacation is not mentioned, but seems likely.

What the teachers and pupils did during a decade of schooling is not known. A year might conceivably be spent on elementary reading and writing; there is evidence of syllable sequences like *ar*, *bar*, *gar*, *dar*, *er*, *ber*, *ger*, *der*, etc., and beta, alpha, *ba*; beta, epsilon, *be*; beta, ēta, *bē*; etc. (see Callias' *Grammatical Tragedy* cited in Athenaeus 7.276A, 10.448B, 10.453C), but it seems unlikely that this went on 10 hours a day for more than a year. After the elementary lessons, all the evidence is that they read, studied, copied, memorized, recited, and sang (or chanted) the works of poets, principally lyric and epic, but also iambic and elegiac. Here it must be noted that none of these poets wrote in the Attic dialect or confined themselves to familiar Attic vocabulary. Aristotle (who probably provides the best evidence for the traditional lore of the schools in the *Poetics*, ch. 19–22: 1437a–59a) lists seven different kinds of poetic words, three of which involve the four 'transformations,' whose importance for Greek linguistics continues as one moves from Plato through to Apollonius Dyscolus. And as for dialects, all choral lyric poems were written in some form of Doric, solo lyrics in Aeolic, hexameter and elegiac poems in a kind of old Ionic with some Aeolic admixture. Choral lyric, in addition, often has a quite complex syntactic and metrical structure and unusual word order. It is improbable that the teachers have refrained for two or three hundred years from helping the students to understand the words and structures of these poems. Bear in mind what Protagoras says about education (Plato, *Prot*: 338e–39a) 'I think the greatest part of a man's education is to be expert on poetry, i.e., to be able to understand what is said by the poets, to tell whether or not it is properly written, and to know how to discriminate among poems and give an explanation when asked.' This is surely a fifth-century belief; and, as he says earlier, 'if you should advertize for a teacher of Greek (*hellēnizein*), not one would show up.' Of course, that is exactly what teachers did claim to teach in the days of Sextus Empiricus, six centuries later. But in the sixth, fifth, and fourth centuries, they taught what Protagoras wanted; when the students grew up, as gentlemen of leisure, they had to put up a good show of being experts on poets and poetry. Nevertheless, the two basic sins, *barbarizein* and *soloikizein*, are mentioned early, the latter in Herodotus 4.117.1, and both in Aristotle *Soph.El.* 165b2.

2. The Sophists

Besides the schools of the grammarians, the fifth century BCE saw the rise of higher education, the schools of the sophists. What they taught was mainly what later became rhetoric, essentially the principles of writing good prose. While the Greek of the grammarians' schools was unlike their students' native dialect, that dealt with by most of the sophists was that very native dialect. But they rarely considered this from a grammatical or linguistic viewpoint. And, while the grammarians dealt with the rhythms of poetry, sophists might dispute about the appropriate rhythms for prose, especially at the ends of sentences (*clausulae*, to use the Latin name). In vocabulary they did not need to interpret rare or dialect words, but they did assign great importance to discriminating synonyms, and (in general) defining abstract words.

One sophist stands out above the rest for his interest in grammar, Protagoras, about whom tantalizing bits of information come from Plato and Aristotle, as well as Diogenes Laertius. He first distinguished four types of sentence—wish/prayer, question, answer, command (Diogenes Laertius 9.53; Quintilian, *Inst.* 3.4.10)—and reprehended Homer (Aristotle *Poetics* 1456b, 15–18) for using the imperative ('command') in prayer to a goddess instead of the optative ('prayer'). This criticism of course depends on the pre-existence of the name *euktikē* (from *euchomai*, 'I pray') for what one calls the 'optative mood.' In fact, Homer's use is the correct one: second-person prayers to divinities normally are in the imperative. And one can be reasonably sure that Protagoras used the four transformations (see Sect. 3), from Socrates' use of the term *hyperbaton* (transposition) in Plato's *Protagoras* (343F).

But the main contribution of Protagoras seems to have been in syntax, where a passage on solecism in Aristotle's *Rhetoric* (1407b) combined with one in his *Sophistic Refutations* (173b) seems to suggest that Protagoras discussed errors of agreement (solecisms) in gender, for which he used (possibly from the tradition of the *didaskaloi)* the names 'males' 'females,' and 'things,' (in that order); and also in number (Aristotle says 'many and few and one,' probably for 'many and two and one').

3. Plato

It is primarily from Plato (especially the *Theatetus*, *Cratylus*, *Protagoras*, and *Sophist*) that an idea of fifth-century state-of-the-art grammatical science is gained (with additional evidence from Aristotle's *Poetics* and other works). There are several reasons for believing that Plato is not proposing innovative ideas and terms of his own, but merely avoiding anachronism in presenting the conversations of Socrates and his friends.

Clearly, several features of later grammatical art must have been introduced in the fifth century or before.

(a) the four *pathē* or transformations (addition—also known as pleonasm, redundancy, insertion, epenthesis, etc.; subtraction—deletion, ellipsis, elision, apheresis, etc.; substitution—enallage, hypallage, commutation, etc.; and permutation—transposition, metathesis, hyperbaton, anastrophe, etc.—in Plato *Cratylus* 394B, 414C–D, 426C, 432A, etc.) used for etymology, but also for morphology (in treating irregular inflexion) and syntax (as in *Protagoras* 343F).

(b) The terms '*onoma*' and '*rhēma*,' whether for 'noun' and 'verb' or 'subject' and 'predicate' (as often in Plato), and possibly '*arthron*' and '*sundesmos*' (later meaning 'article' and 'conjunction,' but at first including prepositions and some other function words).

(c) The word *ptōsis*, at first meaning any inflected form (as in Aristotle), but later 'case,' and some names for the cases—either the later *eutheia* for the nominative (or perhaps Aristotle's *klēsis*), *genikē* for the genitive, etc., or perhaps more likely the names used by Aristotle (*to toutou* 'the of-this,' i.e., 'genitive'; *to toutōi* 'the for-this,' i.e., 'dative,' etc.).

(d) The traditional order of the cases (nom, gen, dat, acc, voc) may have existed in the fifth century, though a clear example does not appear until Cleochares (ca. 300 BCE), as quoted in pseudo-Herodian's *Peri schēmatōn*, produces an instance of *poluptōton*, the use of a particular noun or pronoun (in this case 'Demosthenes') in the same position in five successive phrases, in a different case each time, with the cases in the traditional order. The traditional order of genders (masc, fem, neut) appears already in Protagoras (quoted above) and several times in Aristotle, but the order of numbers (singular, dual, plural), though perhaps natural (since the *klēsis* or basic form is always nom, sing, masc) is not attested early.

(e) The notion of dual patterning (Hockett) or double articulation (Martinet), that, essentially, the rules for correctness of sequences of vowels and consonants are unrelated to those for sequences of nouns, verbs, etc., appears first in Democritus (565, as cited in Isidore's *Etym.* 13.2.4. 108) and then in Plato (*Theaet.* 202–04, *Cratylus* 424–25, 431–32), though until Apollonius Dyscolus (*Synt.* 1.1–2) it often appears as a merely hierarchical arrangement: letters make syllables, syllables make words, words make sentences, and (in Plato's *Cratylus* 432A–C) sentences make discourses. But Apollonius clearly makes letters and syllables concrete, perceptible entities (Stoic *aisthēta*), while words and sentences are abstract, thinkable entities (*noēta*), so the Stoics should be given credit for the correct form of 'dual' patterning.'

The amount of phonology current in the fifth century BCE is probably reflected in Plato, who (in *Crat.* 431–32) assigns the topic to the science of *grammatikē*, and in Aristotle's *Poetics* (ch. 20, 1456b 25–31). Here (and in Plato's *Theaet.*), the distinction between vowels and consonants is clear, and among consonants there is a distinction between *psophoi* (noises: presumably *s*, *ksi*, and *psi*) and *phōnai* (voices: *m*, *n*, *r*, *l*) and consonants which are *aphōna* (all the stops—*ptkbdg*, *phi*, *theta*, *chi*); Aristotle's *sumphōna* (latinized as 'consonants' but much narrower here) include both *s* and the liquids and nasals, i.e., our 'continuants.' Though words like 'labial' and 'dental' do not appear until much later, there is a curious inscription (*IG* II.5.4321) of about 350 BCE which describes some sort of special notation (interpreted by some as shorthand) for just those two classes. There is no evidence of categories like 'aspirated,' 'voiced,' or 'voiceless' until much later, though the relation between [h] (for initial aspiration) and the aspirated stops must have been learned before students could spell correctly.

Another recurrent theme of Greek grammatical thought is the listing of sentence types, i.e., illocutionary forces (in the sense of John Austin; see *Performative Utterances*) or (in a few instances) moods, which begins in Protagoras, as mentioned above, and culminates with the lists discussed in *Aristotle and the Stoics on Language*.

Finally, the notion to which Saussure gave the name 'arbitrariness of the sign should be considered,' i.e., whether or not there is some rational basis for the association of any given phonological sequence (of a word or morpheme) with a particular meaning or function. As conceived by the Greeks, the question was this: is the sound–meaning relation of all or some Greek words inevitable and natural? This is the main topic of discussion in Plato's *Cratylus*, but Aristotle, the Stoics, and Epicurus all also discussed the question, generally agreeing that all words are now arbitrary, though some suggest that there was once a time when they were not. Democritus (as quoted in Proclus' commentary on the *Cratylus* 16) offered four arguments (with four specially coined names) in favor of arbitrariness: (a) 'homonymy' or 'polysemy,' i.e., the same sequence of phonemes may be associated with two or more unrelated meanings; (b) 'polyonymy' or 'isorrophy,' i.e., the existence of synonyms; (c) 'metonymy,' i.e., the fact that words and meanings change; (d) 'nonymy,' i.e., the nonexistence of single words for simple or familiar ideas. Elsewhere (in Diodorus Siculus 1.8.3) Democritus argues for the 'polygenesis' of language—in other words, that there was no single proto-human language.

But a stronger claim than that of nonarbitrariness is the one implied by the famous experiment of Psammetichus as narrated by Herodotus (2.1–2), not just that some Greek words have a natural origin, but that some existing language really is the single proto-human tongue. This entails monogenesis, of course, plus the notion that only some languages undergo linguistic change. Psammetichus arranged for a child to be raised in such a way that it never heard anyone speak. When, at last, the child spontaneously uttered a word, it was *bekos*, which Herodotus tells us is Phrygian for 'bread.' This belief in a single original language comes into later European thought from the biblical tale of the Tower of Babel (see *Babel*).

Plato thus gives a good idea of what might be called 'normal linguistics,' the kind of grammar that every man knew who had been to school as a boy in the fifth and early fourth centuries BCE. This information can be supplemented by what can be read in Aristotle's *Poetics*, and one or two other places.

See also: Aristotle and the Stoics on Language; Myths About Language.

Bibliography

Ax W 1986 Quadripartita ratio: Bemerkungen zur Geschichte eines aktuellen Kategoriensystems (adiecto—detractio—transmutatio—immutatio). *HL* **13**: 191–214

Baratin M 1978 Sur l'absence de l'expression des notions de sujet et de prédicat etc. In: Collart J 1978

Collart J 1978 *Varron, grammaire antique et stylistique latine*. Les Belles Lettres, Paris

De Mauro T 1965 Il nome del dativo e la teoria dei casi greci. *Atti della accademia nazionale dei lincei, serie ottava, rendiconti, classe di scienze morali, storiche e filologiche* **20**: 151–211

Desbordes F 1983 Le Schéma 'addition, soustraction, mutation, métathèse' dans les textes anciens. *Histoire—Epistémologie—Langage* **5**: 23–30

Donnet D 1967 La place de la syntaxe dans les traités de grammaire grecque, des origines au XII siècle. *L'antiquité classique* **36**: 22–48

Gentinetta P M 1961 *Zur Sprachbetrachtung bei den Sophisten und in der stoisch–hellenistischen Zeit*. Verlag P. G. Keller, Winterthur
Girard P 1889. *L'éducation anthénienne*. Hachette, Paris
Householder F W 1989 Review of Taylor 1987. *HL* **16**: 131–48
Koller H 1958. Die Anfänge der griechischen Grammatik. *Glotta* **37**: 5–40
Pfeiffer R 1968 *History of Classical Scholarship: From the Beginnings to the End of the Hellenistic Age*. Clarendon Press, Oxford
Pinborg J 1974 Classical Antiquity: Greece. In: Sebeok, T A (ed.) *Current Trends in Linguistics*, vol. 13, pp. 69–126. Mouton, The Hague
Robins R H 1967 *A Short History of Linguistics*. Longman, London
Steinthal H 1890–91 *Geschichte der Sprachwissenschsaft bei den Griechen und Römern*, 2nd edn. F Dümmlers Verlagsbuchhandlung, Berlin
Taylor D J 1986 Rethinking the history of language science in classical antiquity. *HL* **13**: 175–90
Taylor D J (ed.) 1987 *The History of Linguistics in the Classical Period*. Benjamins, Amsterdam

Sanskrit, Discovery by Europeans

R. Rocher

The discovery of Sanskrit by Europeans played a determinant role in the development of comparative Indo-European linguistics. Yet this process was neither rapid nor linear. The observation, recording, and transmission of data, the methods according to which they were analyzed and interpreted within existing theories of language, and the purposes which they were made to serve, were largely independent variables. This complex history has been further muddied by the tendency of later generations to read their predecessors' statements anachronistically.

1. Pioneers: Missionaries and Travelers in India (1583–1768)

Though the ancient Greeks have left records, some accurate, most fantastic, of their travels to India, their linguistic slate is blank. Mercantile contacts between Rome and India also failed to prompt linguistic observations. The first known linguistic comment was made in a letter of 1583 by an English Jesuit in Goa, Thomas Stephens (Stevens), who does not mention Sanskrit, but points to a structural similarity between Indian languages and Greek and Latin. It remained unpublished until 1957. In 1586, the Florentine litterateur and merchant Filippo Sassetti wrote from Cochin of Sanskrit's status as the learned language of India, of its high antiquity and complexity, and of lexical similarities with Italian, notably in numerals 6 to 9 and words for 'god' and 'snake.' His letters were only published in 1855.

Europeans began to study Indian languages in a sustained manner in the seventeenth century, with evangelical efforts primarily in South India. Jesuits played a leading role in the discovery of Sanskrit. Since, following Roberto (de) Nobili (1577–1656) (see *Nobilili, R. de*), they targeted the upper castes and accommodated existing cultural and social norms—the controversial issue of the Malabar rites—they tended to devote great attention to the language of the high Brahmanical tradition. Nobili's works attest to his knowledge of Sanskrit, yet contain no linguistic observations. The first-known European grammar of Sanskrit was composed in Agra between 1660 and 1662 by Heinrich Roth. Written in Latin and on a Western pattern, it followed traditional Indian terminology and analysis. Brought to Rome and long thought lost, it was only published in 1988. Roth also contributed the tables of Devanāgarī script and the transliterations of the Latin texts of the Lord's Prayer and of the Hail Mary for Athanasius Kircher's *China Illustrata* (1667). The transliteration of the Lord's Prayer entered polyglot compilations from Andreas Müller (1680) to John Chamberlayne (1715). A grammar written in Kerala in the first third of the eighteenth century by Johann Ernst Hanxleden, and later brought to Rome, described, and used by Paulinus a Sancto Bartholomaeo, appears to have been lost since.

Protestant missionaries in Danish Tranquebar, reports from whom were published in Germany from 1718 on, also contributed information on Sanskrit. In 1717, Bartholomaeus Ziegenbalg (see *Ziegenbalg, Bartholomaeus*), primarily a scholar of Tamil, provided Christian Benedict Michaelis with a syllabary for Sanskrit. In a letter of 1725, published in 1729, Benjamin Schul(t)ze, provoked by a remark by Veyssière de La Croze to the effect that numerals in Malabar are 'pure Latin,' listed the Sanskrit numerals 1 to 20, 30, and 40, with equivalents in Latin for all, and in other European languages for some. He also offered in the *Orientalisch- und Occidentalischer Sprachmeister* (1748), translations of the Lord's Prayer in Sanskrit and other Indian languages, which still recur in Adelung's *Mithridates* (1, 1806).

French Jesuits had the greatest impact on scholarship with the publication of their *Lettres Edifiantes et Curieuses* (1707–) in multiple editions and translations. Most important was a survey of Sanskrit literature by Jean François Pons (1740), which described Sanskrit as 'admirable for its harmony, copiousness, and energy' and reported on the analysis by which native grammarians had reduced 'the richest language in the world' to a small number of primitive elements to which derivational suffixes and inflectional endings are added according to rules, the application of which generates 'several thousand correct Sanskrit words.' Published in 1743, it informed the works of de Brosses, Dow, Sinner, Voltaire, Monboddo, Halhed, Beauzée, and Hervás, and was plagiarized by John Cleland (1778). Of less immediate, yet momentous impact, was a request issued by the Abbé Bignon upon assuming the direction of the French Royal Library in 1718, that French missionaries in Asia send manuscripts according to a list of desiderata drawn up by the orientalist Etienne Fourmont. In 1732–33, Pons sent from Bengal 168 Sanskrit manuscripts which included the first five chapters of a grammar in Latin with Sanskrit words in Bengali script. A sixth chapter on syntax, completed in South India, in French with Sanskrit words partly in Telugu, partly in Roman script, was forwarded in 1772 by Gaston-Laurent Coeurdoux. Pons's grammar was the source of the table of Bengali script in the *Encyclopédie* and the primer used by the first students of Sanskrit in Europe, which Anquetil-Duperron came close to publishing in 1804. Coeurdoux was the author of a memoir that included, besides a basic Sanskrit vocabulary, lists of Sanskrit words that have equivalents in Latin, Greek, or both, notably the numerals 1 to 21, 30, 40, and 100, pronouns, and a partial paradigm of *as-* 'to be.' Solicited in 1767 by the Abbé Barthélémy of the Académie des Inscriptions et Belles-Lettres, who gave it to Anquetil-Duperron, it was only read in 1786 and published in 1808, the same year as Schlegel's *Ueber die Sprache und Weisheit der Indier*, which rendered it obsolete (see *Schlegel, (Carl Wilhem) Friedrich von*).

These pioneers' sometimes faulty data—muddled by erratic transliterations that reflected different local pronunciations and the recorders' various native tongues, and subject to misreadings—were interpreted according to, or used to bolster, divergent linguistic theories. Gottfried Siegfried Bayer (1738) explained similarities by contact and borrowing, pointing to the Indo–Greek kingdoms after Alexander's campaigns as the source of commonalities between Greek, Persian, and Sanskrit, yet the memoir of the Tranquebar missionary Christian Theodor Walther (1733) which he appended attributed them to the common 'Scythian' origin propounded by Boxhorn, Saumaise, Jäger, Leibniz, and others. La Flotte (1768) also posited a 'North Asian' origin for the Brahmans, while Sinner (1771) thought exclusively in terms of borrowing from Greek and Latin into Sanskrit, yet wondered how it could have taken place. The emphasis on numerals and other basic vocabulary, i.e., vocabulary unlikely to have been borrowed, which De Laet, Grotius, Leibniz, and others had pioneered, did not necessarily lead to the conclusion of a common origin. Schul(t)ze was inclined to credit similarities between Latin and Sanskrit to borrowing from Portuguese, yet wondered how Brahmans could have done without counting for so long, while Coeurdoux favored the biblical myth of Babel, making of Sanskrit one of the primitive languages which preserved elements that antedated separation. Scholars in Europe eagerly awaited more information, which they hoped would further their particular lines of enquiry, from the 'language mechanics' of de Brosses (1765), fascinated by Pons's report of Sanskrit's derivation from a handful of primitive elements, to the Celtomania of Le Brigant (1767).

2. Breakthrough: British Colonials in Bengal (1768–94)

When, in 1765, the East India Company obtained the administrative rights to Bengal, Bihar, and Orissa, knowledge of India's culture became a colonial necessity. The reluctance of pandits to instruct foreigners in their sacred language and Sanskrit's reputation for being 'amazingly copious' and for showing a 'regularity of etymology and grammatical order,' induced Alexander Dow (1768) to suspect that it had been invented by Brahmans 'upon rational principles' to be 'a mysterious repository for their religion and philosophy.' This led Christoph Meiners (1780) to explain similarities by assuming that the Brahmans had patterned their artificial language after Greek, a notion Dugald Stewart and Charles William Wall still held in the nineteenth century.

Governor Warren Hastings' decision in 1772 to apply native laws in courts and his patronage of both pandits and orientalists caused a breakthrough. In the introduction to the translation (1776) of the code of Hindu law commissioned by Hastings, which underwent several editions and translations, Nathaniel Brassey Halhed gave an account of Sanskrit that interested Beauzée and Monboddo among others. In his grammar of Bengali (1778) he digressed on features of Sanskrit, spelling out the importance of similarities in basic vocabulary, i.e., 'not in technical and metaphorical terms, which the mutuation of refined arts and improved manners might have occasionally introduced; but in the main groundwork of language, in monosyllables, in the names of numbers, and the appellation of such things as would be first discriminated on the immediate dawn of civilization,' and noting similarities in morphology, such as the conjugation in *-mi* in Sanskrit and Greek. In a letter of 1779 (only published in 1983), he articulated a method built on Monboddo's view that Latin was a dialect more ancient than Greek: Sanskrit, closer to Latin than to Greek, had to be even more ancient, yet, what of 'the existence of the dual number and the middle voice in this tongue and in the Greek, which are totally absent from the Latin'? Holding, after Monboddo, that 'it is one of the last gradations of art to simplify a complex machine,' he mentioned 'in favour of the pretensions to priority of original in the Shanscrit [sic] language, that it contains every part of speech, and every distinction which is to be found in Greek or in Latin, and that in some particulars it is more copious than either.'

Sanskrit's 'copiousness,' noted by Pons, Dow, and Halhed, was emphasized again in a statement (1786) by Sir William Jones, a scholar of Persian and one of the most accomplished men of his day, who, as a judge of the Supreme Court in Calcutta, began to study Sanskrit to check the authenticity of legal opinions given by pandit assistants to the courts:

> The Sanskrit language, whatever be its antiquity, is of a wonderful structure; more perfect than the Greek, more copious than the Latin, and more exquisitely refined than either, yet bearing to both of them a stronger affinity, both in the roots of verbs and in the forms of grammar, than could possibly have been produced by accident; so strong indeed, that no philologer could examine them all three, without believing them to have sprung from some common source, which, perhaps, no longer exists: there is a similar reason, though not quite so forcible, for supposing that both the Gothic and the Celtic, though blended with a very different idiom, had the same origin as the Sanskrit; and that the old Persian might be added to the same family.

Taken out of context, this was elevated later to the rank of a charter of comparative Indo-European linguistics. For Jones, and in keeping with the monogeneticism of his times, it was part of a search for the cradle of civilization from which arts, letters, science, religion, and philosophy might have spread, and which linked the Indians not only to the Persians, Goths, and Celts, but also to the Ethiopians, Egyptians, Chinese, Japanese, and even Peruvians. Less famous, yet of lasting importance, was Jones's 'Dissertation on the Orthography of Asiatick Words in Roman Letters' (1786), informed by the Indian tradition of phonetics, which set a standard for the transliteration of Sanskrit in Roman script.

Most noticed was the unveiling in rapid succession of Sanskrit literary masterpieces with translations by Charles Wilkins of the religiophilosophical poem *Bhagavadgītā* and the moral fables *Hitopadeśa* (1785, 1787), and by Jones of the play *Śakuntalā*, the erotic-mystical songs *Gītagovinda*, and the 'Laws of Manu' (1789, 1792, 1794). These underwent multiple editions and translations and drew enthusiastic comments: the *Bhagavadgītā* from Schopenhauer, *Śakuntalā*, from Herder and Goethe. By founding the Asiatic Society in Calcutta (1784) and its organ, the *Asiatick Researches* (1788–), Jones provided a forum for further advances and a channel to broadcast them to Europe, where they were republished and translated into French and German.

3. Taking Stock in Europe (1780–1806)

European curiosity about Sanskrit was piqued, yet interpretations remained scattered. Summing up the evidence provided by Pons, Dow, and Halhed, Michael Hissmann (1780) still attributed similarities to borrowing into Sanskrit. Drawing from the same sources, Beauzée's five page article in the *Encyclopédie méthodique* (1786)—up from a few lines in Diderot's original *Encyclopédie* (1765)—sought to provide a model for an international scholarly language.

The discalced Carmelite, Paulinus a Sancto Bartholomaeo (born Philip(p) Wessdin (Vesdin)), returned in 1789 from Malabar and undertook to catalogue oriental collections in Rome and to publish in Latin for the use of future missionaries encyclopedic, if polemical, works that incorporated the sum of current knowledge on India. These included a description of Indian scripts (1791) based on the *Alphabetum Brammhanicum* and the *Alphabetum Grandonico-Malabaricum* edited by Amaduzzi (1771, 1772); two grammars—the first grammars of Sanskrit to be printed (1790, 1804)—based on manuscripts of Hanxleden; an edition of the first section of Amarasiṃha's dictionary (1798); and dissertations on the relationship of Zend (Avestan), Sanskrit, and German, and of Latin, Zend, and Sanskrit (1798, 1802). They encapsulate traits of the eighteenth century: the authority still granted to testimonies of classical antiquity; an emphasis on basic vocabulary presented in tabular form for comparison; and, particularly for clerics, a wish to match linguistic evidence with biblical accounts. Explanations by contact and borrowing, however, were discarded, and common origin affirmed. The connection of German and Iranian was accepted, yet, with Sanskrit added, a northern, Scythian origin was rejected in favour of an oriental cradle. Puzzlement persisted on whether to consider Sanskrit closer to Latin or to Greek, with preference for the former, yet with an acknowledgement that morphological similarities such as the augment and the reduplicated perfect, point to the latter. Franz Carl Alter (1799) published the Sanskrit words in the St. Petersburg vocabularies corrected by Paulinus, and Paulinus's and his comparisons of these with other oriental languages. Hervás (1801) and Adelung (1, 1806) drew heavily on Paulinus's work.

4. A New Beginning: Sanskrit in Paris (1802–8)

Paulinus's first printed grammar provided a means to learn Sanskrit, which the publications from Calcutta made a subject of literary, philosophical, and linguistic interest, not just of evangelical or colonial necessity. In 1802 the Paris collections, the richest in Europe, attracted at the same time European scholars eager to learn Sanskrit and a member of the Asiatic Society returned from Calcutta eager to teach it. Detained in Paris by war between Britain and France, Alexander Hamilton catalogued anew the Sanskrit manuscripts in the French National/Imperial Library with their keeper, Louis-Matthieu Langlès, and introduced all those who were interested to Sanskrit. Of the first consequence was his daily tutoring of Friedrich Schlegel, which provided a foundation for Schlegel's *Ueber die Sprache und Weisheit der Indier* (1808). In this complex, sometimes paradoxical book, which blends linguistic, literary, historical, philosophical, and theological themes, Schlegel was already retreating from the first enthusiasm that had him exclaim that Sanskrit is 'the actual source of all languages, of all thoughts and poetry of the human spirit; everything, everything without exception stems form India,' yet he still viewed Sanskrit as the most perfect, spiritual, quasidivine language, the oldest, and possibly the parent of, 'organic' inflectional languages, which he considered superior to the 'mechanical' agglutinative languages. Deeming lexical similarities inherently inconclusive, he focused on morphological similarities as the determining criterion for establishing genealogy.

5. Mainstream (1808–)

Schlegel's example demonstrated that Sanskrit could be learned in Europe. It inspired Antoine-Léonard de Chézy, who, self-taught with the grammars of Paulinus and Pons and other manuscripts in the French National/Imperial Library, became in 1814 the first incumbent of a chair of Sanskrit, at the Collège de France. August Wilhelm Schlegel (see *Schlegel, August Wilhelm*) followed in the footsteps of his younger brother, learning Sanskrit in Paris before initiating its teaching in Germany (Bonn 1818). Franz Bopp, Othmar Frank, and others went on from Paris to London to consult manuscripts in the East India Company Library founded in 1801 according to a plan proposed by Charles Wilkins, who became its first librarian. Thanks to collections made in India by the likes of Colin Mackenzie and Henry Thomas Colebrooke (the first author of a Sanskrit grammar in English, which remained incomplete, and the first Sanskrit scholar some of whose works are still read for other than antiquarian purposes), the London holdings soon eclipsed those in Paris; however, Britain was slow in recognizing Sanskrit as more than a colonial necessity. Hamilton, upon his release from France in 1806, taught Sanskrit at the East India College, but no mainstream British university offered it until 1832, when the Boden chair was created at Oxford thanks to a bequest by a former military officer of the East India Company. The chair's first incumbent, Horace Hayman Wilson, who had learned Sanskrit from pandits in India, was embroiled in a dispute with A.W. Schlegel, who had learned Sanskrit in Europe, about the qualifications required of a Sanskrit scholar, so epitomizing the extent to which Sanskrit had become appropriated by Europeans, particularly on the Continent.

More than joining the academic mainstream, Sanskrit took pride of place in the development of comparative Indo-European grammar. Though, unlike Friedrich Schlegel, Bopp never referred to Sanskrit as the parent language, he made it the centerpiece of his comparative studies of conjugational and other grammatical systems, and, although he did not share Schlegel's Romantic enthusiasm but bore down on matters purely linguistic, he likewise appended translations of Sanskrit texts to his *Conjugationssytem* (1816). Sanskritocentrism remained the norm for generations of comparatirists. So significant was the discovery of Sanskrit in the development of comparative Indo-European linguistics that it has been felt necessary of late to voice reminders that it was not a prerequisite—as the works of Rask, Grimm, and others demonstrate. Accounting in part for the magnitude of this impact are the quality, quantity, antiquity, and longevity of Sanskrit literature, yet more important was the fact that Sanskrit was first taught to Europeans—directly or mediately—according to the enduring tradition of rigorous analysis by Pāṇini (see *Pāṇini*) and other Indian grammarians and phoneticians. The identification of the root as the smallest common denominator of derived forms, vocalic alternation, derivational and inflectional suffixes, substitution rules, zeroing, etc., and the description of articulatory processes were the procedures according to which Europeans learned Sanskrit from pandits. While this created an illusion that Sanskrit is more regular and transparent than other languages, the fact that the same procedures could serve to analyze cognate languages provided a framework that facilitated comparison.

See also: Hindu Views on Language; Hinduism; Sanskrit.

Bibliography

Benfey T 1869 *Geschichte der Sprachwissenschaft und orientalischen Philologie in Deutschland.* Cotta, Munich

Camps A, Muller J-C 1988 *The Sanskrit Grammar and Manuscripts of Father Heinrich Roth S J (1620–68)*. Brill, Leiden

Mayrhofer M 1983 Sanskrit und die Sprachen Alteuropas: Zwei Jahrhunderte von Entdeckungen und Irrtümern. *Nachrichten der Akademie der Wissenschaften in Göttingen 5*

Muller J-C 1985 Recherches sur les premières grammaires manuscrites du sanskrit. *Bulletin d' Études Indiennes* **3**: 125–44

Rocher L 1977 *Paulinus a S Bartholomaeo: Dissertation on the Sanskrit Language*. Benjamins, Amsterdam

Rocher R 1968 *Alexander Hamilton (1762–1824): A Chapter in the Early History of Sanskrit Philology*. American Oriental Society, New Haven, CT

Rocher R 1983 *Orientalism, Poetry, and the Millennium: The Checkered Life of Nathaniel Brassey Halhed 1751–1830*. Motilal Banarsidass, Delhi

Schlegel F 1808 *Ueber die Sprache und Weisheit der Indier*. Mohr & Zimmer, Heidelberg (New edn. by E F K Koerner, Benjamins, Amsterdam, 1977)

Schwab R 1950 *La Renaissance orientale*. Payot, Paris (Transl. *The Oriental Renaissance: Europe's Rediscovery of India and the East, 1680–1880*, Columbia University Press, 1984)

Windisch E W O 1917 *Geschichte der Sanskrit-Philologie und indischen Altertumskunde*. Trübner, Strasbourg

Wüst W 1929 Indisch. In: Streitburg W A (ed.) *Die Erforschung der indogermanischen Sprachen: Indisch, Iransich, Armenisch*. de Gruyter, Leipzig

Sanskrit (Pāṇinian) Linguistics

P. Kiparsky

1. Pāṇini's Grammar

Pāṇini's grammar (ca. 350 BCE) seeks to provide a complete, maximally concise, and theoretically consistent analysis of Sanskrit grammatical structure. It is the foundation of all traditional and modern analyses of Sanskrit, as well as having great historical and theoretical interest in its own right. Western grammatical theory has been influenced by it at every stage of its development for the last two centuries. The early nineteenth-century comparativists learned from it the principles of morphological analysis. Bloomfield modeled both his classic Algonquian grammars and the logical-positivist axiomatization of his *Postulates* on it. Modern linguistics acknowledges it as the most complete generative grammar of any language yet written, and continues to adopt technical ideas from it.

The grammar is based on the spoken language (*bhāṣā*) of Pāṇini's time, and also gives rules on Vedic usage and on regional variants. Its optional rules distinguish between preferable and marginal forms, and a few rules even have sociolinguistic conditions. It is entirely synchronic: variants are simply treated as alternate forms, indeed, the very concept of linguistic change is foreign to the tradition. The grammar consists of four components:

(a) *Aṣṭādhyāyī:* a system of about 4000 grammatical rules.
(b) *Śivasūtras:* the inventory of phonological segments, partitioned by markers (*anubandhas*) to allow abbreviations for classes of segments to be formed by a technique described below (*pratyāhāras*).
(c) *Dhātupāṭha:* a list of about 2000 verbal roots, with subclassification and diacritic markers encoding their morphological and syntactic properties.
(d) *Gaṇapāṭha*: an inventory of classes of lexical items idiosyncratically subject to various rules.

The rules of the *Aṣṭādhyāyī* make reference to classes defined on the elements in the other three components by means of conventions spelled out in the *Aṣṭādhyāyī* itself. Thus, while none of the components is intelligible in isolation, together they constitute a complete integrated system of grammar.

There are also various peripheral adjuncts to the system. The most important of these are the *Uṇādisūtras*, which extend the Pāṇinian technique to analyze unproductive and irregularly formed derivatives from roots. Though mentioned in a few rules of the *Aṣṭādhyāyī*, many of the words they derive are treated as underived there, and they are probably post-Pāṇinian at least in their present form.

2. The Indian Grammatical Tradition

The science of language in India probably has its ultimate intellectual roots in the richly developed science of ritual (Staal 1988) (see *Ritual*). The *sūtra* style of analysis and some of the technical concepts of grammatical description originated in the methods developed for codifying complex Vedic sacrifices. On a philosophical level, ritual is probably also the origin of a leading idea behind grammar as well as other disciplines such as yoga in ancient India: that human activities, even those normally carried out in an unconscious or unselfconscious way, can be analyzed by explicit rule systems, and that performing those activities in awareness of the rules that govern them brings religious merit.

The predecessors of Pāṇini's grammar and its compositional history are largely unknown. The *Aṣṭādhyāyī* itself cites a number of earlier grammarians, whose works have not survived. It has been suggested that its first redaction dealt with root derivation and inflection, and that rules for compounds and denominal (*taddhita*) formations were incorporated into it later from another source (Joshi and Roodbergen 1983). The early grammatical tradition appears to have had ties to the editorial activity which led to the standardization of Vedic texts (Bronkhorst 1981; Thieme 1935), and the technique of grammatical analysis probably evolved from related but less sophisticated methods like those used in the *Prātiśākhyas*, treatises that give the phonological rules relating the word-by-word (*padapātha*) version of Vedic works to their connected text (*saṃhitā*). These works share the goal of providing explicit and general rules for linguistic regularities, but they do not deal with morphology and syntax, and are confined to accounting for the data in a single Vedic text. By dealing with all levels of structure and not being bound to a particular corpus, Pāṇini's grammar attains an incomparably greater depth of analysis, and does justice to the unbounded nature of language.

The text of the *Aṣṭādhyāyī* is rather accurately preserved. It came quite early to be regarded as canonical, and probably only relatively minor changes were later made in its wording. The problems lie in its interpretation. Even though Pāṇini's grammar is a complete, self-contained system of rules, some of the principles that determine how those rules are to be applied are not stated, and must be inferred. A massive commentatorial tradition is concerned with just this. By far the most important work is Patañjali's *Mahābhāṣya*, the 'Great Commentary', which incorporates and discusses Kātyāyana's earlier notes (*vārttikas*) on Pāṇini. It broaches topics ranging from minutiae to major philosophical questions, and attempts to remedy apparent lapses of the grammar by reinterpreting its rules, or, if that is not possible, by rephrasing them. It is one of the great works of Sanskrit literature, remarkable for its elegant dialectic structure and luminous style. Its conclusions are adopted in all later works. Pāṇini, Kātyāyana, and Patañjali's are referred to as the 'three sages' (*munitraya*) and considered authoritative by later grammarians.

The *Kāśikā* provides an explicit rule-by-rule paraphrase of the *Aṣṭādhyāyī*, and explains the wording of each rule with appropriate examples. Its simplicity, like that of the modern translations of Pāṇini which are largely based on it, can be deceptive: the interpretation which it states apodictically for a rule may just be the tip of the *Mahābhāṣya's* enormous iceberg of (sometimes inconclusive) argumentation about it.

The text most commonly used to teach the system in India is Bhaṭṭoji Dīkṣita's *Siddhānta-Kaumudī*, which reorganizes the rules according to grammatical topics and takes the student through Pāṇini's whole system in an orderly way. Since the rules that come into play in any particular derivation are likely to be scattered all through the *Aṣṭādhyāyī*, this reorganization is a great help to the learner. The drawback of this method is that the architecture of the system is obscured. For example, the wording of a rule must usually be completed in context from the rules preceding it according to certain conventions, but this context is lost when the rules are rearranged as in the *Siddhānta-Kaumudī*.

The standard treatise on the principles and metarules (*paribhāṣās*) of the system is the *Paribhāṣenduśekhara* of the great eighteenth-century grammarian Nāgojībhaṭṭa (a.k.a. Nāgeśa). At an even higher level of generalization, Bhartṛhari's *Vākyapadīya* deals with topics in the philosophy of language from a grammatically sophisticated point of view (see *Bhartṛhari*).

These later works in the Pāṇinian tradition make important contributions in their own right. The innovations they come up with are prompted by several circumstances: (a) careful analysis of Pāṇini's grammar reveals occasional gaps and inconsistencies in its formulations, both at a descriptive level and in matters of theory; (b) after Pāṇini's time, new words and forms not covered by his rules appeared in the Sanskrit language; (c) the original intent of some rules had been forgotten because of discontinuities in the early grammatical tradition. Increasingly reluctant to tamper with the wording of the rules, grammarians after Pāṇini prefer to fix the problems by devising ingenious reinterpretations. These reinterpretations, while extending the coverage of the grammar in the intended ways, can also cause considerable overgeneration, and sometimes obscure the original rigorous simplicity and beauty of the *Aṣṭādhyāyī*. One of the urgent tasks of Pāṇini research at the moment is to reconstruct the original design of the system and the evolution of the interpretive apparatus later built on top of it. This can be done by a combination of philological and analytic research. It is often possible to recover the intent of a doubtful rule by examining the relevant usage in actual Sanskrit literature, especially the surviving works of Pāṇini's time (Brāhmaṇas and early Upaniṣads). Analysis of the internal structure of the system has even revealed underlying principles in the *Aṣṭādhyāyī* of which the commentators and the earlier Western scholars who followed them were wholly unaware (Kiparsky 1979; 1982).

3. The Method of Grammatical Analysis

The *Aṣṭādhyāyī* is formulated in a morphologically, syntactically, and lexically regimented form of Sanskrit. To maximize concision with a minimum of ambiguity, rules are compressed by systematically omitting repeated expressions from them, according to a procedure modeled on natural language syntax (*anuvṛtti*). Coordination and certain types of compounding are assigned standardized interpretations; and the nominal cases of the language are used in a conventional way to designate the elements of grammatical rules.

From the viewpoint of their role in the system, rules can be divided into four types: (a) definitions (*saṃjñā*), (b) metarules (*paribhāṣā*), (c) headings (*adhikāra*), and (d) operational rules (*vṛtti*).

Definitional rules introduce the technical terms of the grammar. Metarules constrain the application of other rules throughout the grammar. Headings supply a common element for a group of rules. A heading must be read into every rule in the domain over which it is valid unless it is semantically incompatible with its wording. Headings can extend over large stretches of the grammar (over 1,000 rules in some cases), dividing it into overlapping topical sections.

Operational rules are the workhorses of the system. Subject to the applicable definitions, metarules, and headings, they carry out four basic types of operations on strings: replacement, affixation, augmentation, and compounding. The basic format of an operational rule is (la), represented in the grammatical system by the case frame shown in (lb).

A→B/C_D ('in the context between C and D, A is replaced by B') (1a)

$A_{\text{Genitive}}B_{\text{Nominative}}C_{\text{Ablative}}D_{\text{Locative}}$ (1b)

This use of the cases to mark the elements of rules is absolutely consistent. However, the same cases are also used in their ordinary language meanings; (in general, Pāṇini's metalanguage allows ambiguity but not inconsistency). For example, the locative case, in addition to its technical use in marking a right-hand context in (1), figures in conditions limiting processes to certain meanings, dialects, genres, and connotations, such as *in the meaning 'action,' in the country of the Easterners, in Vedic literature, in a derogatory sense*.

The format in (1) covers most operational rules in the system. This includes not only standard replacement operations, but also deletion, which is treated as replacement by a null element (defined as invisibility). Several types of replacement processes, however, require a formally richer type of structural change. Certain phonological coalescence rules (*ekādeśa* 'single substitute' rules) effect replacement operations of the form (2a), and reduplication requires 'doubling' operations of the form (2b):

AB→C (2a)

A→AA (2b)

Insertion of affixes (only suffixes actually occur, prefixation being treated as compounding) is done by rules of the same format as replacement (see (1)), except that since nothing is replaced there is no genitive. Augments, which differ from suffixes in that they become part of the element they are added to, are also inserted by such rules but with a different interpretation ('A gets the augment B in the environment C_D'). A diacritic marker on the augment shows whether it is to be put before, after, or inside the base. The fourth type of operation on strings is the combination of two or more words to form a *samāsa* (compound). The format is

$A_{\text{Nominative}}B_{\text{Instrumental}}$ = 'A is compounded with B' (3)

where A is the governed member of the compound (*upasarjana*).

Lexically, the grammar makes a fundamental distinction between technical terms and ordinary language expressions. The convention on their respective interpretations is that *ordinary language expressions denote their own form and technical terms denote their referents*. Thus, the expression *gauḥ* (cow) in a grammatical rule refers only to the word *gauḥ* (not, for example, to a cow, or to words meaning 'cow,' or to words denoting particular kinds of cows), whereas the technical term *pada* (word) refers to any element that meets its definition in the system.

Two kinds of technical terms are used: 'primitive' and 'theoretical' (*śāstrīya*). The meaning of primitive terms is assumed to be known from outside grammar, partly from other sciences and partly from ordinary language. For example, the technical terms of phonetics (*śikṣā*) and of ritual and Vedic studies, and certain semantic and logical terms, are taken as primitive terms within grammar. Also primitive are the notion of a rule (*vidhi*) and such associated notions as *ādeśa* (substitute, replacement), *sthānin* (substituendum, item to be replaced), (*a*) *siddha* ((not) effected), *vipratiṣedha* (conflict (between rules)). Theoretical terms are defined by a network of rules in the *Aṣṭādhyāyī* on the basis of these primitive terms and lists of linguistic primes (sounds, roots, etc.). Expressions which have both an ordinary meaning and a theoretical meaning may be used in the grammar in both meanings. On the other hand, if a theoretical term is defined in the grammar, no other term, theoretical or primitive, is ever used in that meaning. In other words, ambiguity is permitted but inconsistency is not.

A large number of technical terms denote classes of linguistic elements. Some rules must apply not just to specific segments, morphemes, stems, etc., but to whole classes of them, and since the same or related classes tend to reappear in many different rules, listing all the individual members of these classes in each rule would be unnecessarily complicated. Indeed, it would be impossible, because some of these classes have no upper bound, there being no limit on the length of derived words, stems, or even roots. Providing terms for each of these classes makes it possible to refer to them in rules in a simple way. In accord with the economy requirement (*lāghava*) that governs Pāṇini's entire grammatical system, all and only the theoretical terms that can be defined within grammar are defined, and each term is defined as simply as possible and without redundancy.

Many lists of grammatical elements are divided into grammatically relevant subclasses. Instead of defining terms ad hoc for each subclass, Pāṇini provides standardized procedures for generating them from the lists themselves. In this way, the theoretical terminology includes several kinds of expressions freely generated and defined by conventional procedures specified in the grammar.

A key technique of generalization used by Pāṇini is to organize rules into hierarchies of generality. There is always an 'elsewhere' case, covered by the maximally general applicable rule (*sāmānya*), and where necessary it is restricted by special rules (*viśeṣa*), each of which can itself be restricted by still more special rules, and so on. If the set of forms to which rule A is applicable is properly included in the set of forms to which rule B is applicable, then A is automatically interpreted as superseding B in the shared domain (a convention which has been taken over in modern linguistics). This blocking relation between special and general rules can be generalized from pairs of rules to sets of arbitrary size. A special rule S can be considered to block a set $G = G_1, G_2, \ldots, G_n$ of general rules if the environments of S are properly included in the combined environments of G. Because of this convention, as well as *anuvṛtti* and other devices, the import of a rule does not come just from its wording but from its relation to other rules in the system.

The order in which the rules of the *Aṣṭādhyāyī* are to be applied is determined in the following way. In general, any applicable rule, no matter where it occurs in the grammar, is to be applied to a form, and the resulting form is again subjected to any applicable rules, until no more rules are applicable. This procedure goes a surprisingly long way. Additional constraints are, however, required for those cases where this procedure allows or even forces wrong derivations. Pāṇini clearly assumes such constraints, but he does not state them explicitly, and they must be inferred from the way he phrases his rules. Traditionally, they are assumed to be the following (see, for example, Buiskool 1939):

Rule A has priority over rule B if A is:

ordered after B (*para*) (4a)

applicable whether or not B applies (*nitya*) (4b)

conditioned internally to B (*antaraṅga*) (4c)

applicable in a proper subset of the cases to which B is applicable (*apavāda*) (4d)

These principles form a hierarchy of increasing strength, so that the last is strongest of all. All cases of 'conflict' between simultaneously applicable rules are assumed to be resolved by them. Not included in this list, but tacitly assumed by the tradition, is the 'feeding' principle, that when a rule can apply to the output of another, it does, unless this is blocked by some other constraint or rule.

The *para*-principle (4a) and the *antaraṅga*-principle (4c) have probably been overgeneralized by the tradition, though both have a valid kernel. Modern scholars agree that the former is intended to apply only in the section which provides definitions (1.4–2.3). More controversial is the claim (5) that the latter should be restricted to give priority to word phonology over sentence phonology,

The *Word-integrity Principle*: rules apply first within words and then to combinations of words. (5)

and that the *nitya* and feeding principles are to be unified into the *siddha*-principle (6), which, with the *apavāda*-principle, is solely responsible for the ordering of rules within words:

The *siddha-principle*: when any rule is applied, the rules pertinent to its application should be 'effected' (*siddha*). (6)

Here, A is defined as 'pertinent' to the application of rule B with respect to a form F if the result of applying A and B to F in that order is different from the result of applying A and B to F simultaneously.

The advocates of the revised system (5, 6) note that it unifies the basic ordering principles, eliminates a series of subsidiary *paribhāṣās* posited to deal with the unwanted side-effects of the *antaraṅga-paribhāṣā*, and explains the wording of many of its rules. In particular, exactly in those cases where these principles would yield the wrong result for some rule, Pāṇini imposes special conditions on it to contravene them (Joshi and Kiparsky 1979). For example, a block of rules at the end of the grammar must be applied exactly in the order listed (technically, this is achieved by the condition that each rule is *asiddha* (not effected) with respect to all rules that precede it). This block of strictly ordered rules contains only rules whose relationship to the other rules of the system is not determined by (5) and (6), and rules which they in turn feed.

4. Morphology/Syntax

The *Aṣṭādhyāyī* is not rigidly divided into subcomponents, and one should beware of mechanically imposing categories of Western linguistics on it. However, there is some basis for a distinction between the rules which build up words ('morphology') and determine how they can be combined with each other ('syntax'), which form one subsystem (roughly, the rules of chs. 1–5), and the rules which determine how morphemes and words are modified in combination with each other ('phonology,' chs. 6–8).

The two types of word-formation in the *Aṣṭādhyāyī* are compounding and suffixation. Suffixation consists of adding a *pratyaya* (suffix) either to a (verbal) root (*dhātu*), or to a (nominal) stem (*prātipadika*), or to a word (*pada*). The resulting form itself belongs to one of these three categories. The following seven subtypes of word-formation occur:

(a) $[\text{Root+Suffix}]_{\text{Root}}$: desideratives, intensives, causatives
(b) $[\text{Word+Suffix}]_{\text{Root}}$: denominal verbs
(c) $[\text{Root+Suffix}]_{\text{Stem}}$: primary (*kṛt*) suffixes
(d) $[\text{Word+Suffix}]_{\text{Stem}}$: secondary (*taddhita*) suffixes
(e) $[\text{Word+Word}]_{\text{Stem}}$: compounding
(f) $[\text{Root+Suffix}]_{\text{Word}}$: verb inflection
(g) $[\text{Stem+Suffix}]_{\text{Word}}$: noun inflection

A 'word' is defined as anything that ends in an inflectional suffix. The definition covers indeclinable words too, for they are all assigned nominal inflectional endings, which are then deleted. Similarly, each member of a compound is a word because it contains a later deleted case ending. The reason for this procedure is that it simplifies the morphological derivation of compounds and automatically accounts for certain phonological phenomena. For example, in *rājapuruṣa* (king's servant) the first member *rājan-*, being a word, gets its correct form by an independently motivated phonological rule which deletes word-final *-n*.

A general constraint of the grammar restricts word-formation rules to semantically connected (*samartha*) elements. Hence, in a string such as *bhāryā rājñaḥ, puruṣo devadattasya* (the wife of the king, the servant of Devadatta), the semantically unrelated words 'of the king' and 'servant' cannot be compounded with each other, which would yield the incoherent **bhāryā rājapuruṣo devadattasya* (*the wife the king-servant of Devadatta).

Morphological alternants can be handled both with the replacement technique and with the blocking technique described above. In either case, one form in a set of alternating forms is chosen as basic, in such a way as to allow the simplest overall description. Unless other considerations intervene, the simplest description results if one of its actually occurring forms is chosen, and among those the one with the widest distribution. If replacement is used, the basic form is introduced by a general rule everywhere and then replaced by the other alternants in specific contexts. If blocking is used, the basic form is introduced by a general rule and the alternants by special rules which block the general rule in specific contexts. (The grammarians were well aware of the conceptual relationship between replacement and blocking; indeed Kātyāyana uses the term '*utsarga*' for the basic form in both senses, the substituendum and the 'elsewhere' form.) Pāṇini typically uses blocking in derivational morphology and replacement in inflectional morphology. There are several interesting reasons for this. The most important is that, by convention, replacements inherit the morphological properties of the elements they replace (for example, they have the same effects on the vowel shape and accent of the stem to which they are added as the original morphemes do). These properties are typically invariant in inflectional alternants, but vary in derivational alternants.

More complex relationships can be represented by a combination of the replacement and blocking techniques. This method involves setting up a wholly abstract underlying form, and a rule replacing it by the basic alternant, which in turn is blocked by the special alternant.

A descriptive problem which arises in especially acute form in dealing with *taddhita* suffixes (denominal 'secondary derivation') is that most suffixes have a range of different meanings with different stems and most meanings are expressed by several suffixes, with considerable semantic overlap between them. Modern linguistics has not found the right tools for dealing with the intricate web of polysemy and synonymy that such systems constitute. Pāṇini achieves this by organizing the *taddhita* section in an ingenious way. He separates the affixation rules from the rules assigning meanings to the affixes, which allows concurrent blocking at both the morphological and semantic level.

Unlike the phonology and morphology of the *Aṣṭādhyāyī*, the syntax is strictly structure-building. There are no rules that replace words and no rules that delete them. Passive sentences are not derived from actives, and nominalizations are not derived from sentences. They are in fact generated in parallel by the same rules in a way which permits their structural parallelism to be captured to the fullest extent. Pāṇini does assume an extragrammatical process of ellipsis, by which words which are obvious from the context can be omitted. Although ellipsis is not a rule of grammar, Pāṇini has carefully considered its consequences for his grammatical system, and explicitly taken account of them in several syntactic rules of his system. Not surprisingly since Sanskrit is a 'free word order language,' the grammar says nothing about word order, even though in fact not every permutation of words in a sentence is equally felicitous and there do exist constraints.

Pāṇini accounts for sentence structure by a set of grammatical categories which allow syntactic relationship to be represented as identity at the appropriate level of abstraction. The pivotal syntactico-semantic categories which do this are roles assigned to nominal expressions in relation to a verbal root, called '*kārakas*.' A sentence is seen as a little drama played out by an Agent and a set of other actors, which may include Goal, Recipient, Instrument, Location, and Source. These roles are systematically related to semantic categories, but the correspondence is not ont-to-one. One *kāraka* can correspond to several semantic relations and one semantic relation can correspond to several *kārakas*, in ways duly stated in the grammar. *kārakas* in turn are the categories in terms of which the assignment of case and other morphological elements is formulated. They are essential to accounting for the active and passive diatheses (including impersonal passives), for the syntax of finite verbs and nominals, for the use of the cases, and for the identification of the understood agent of infinitives and participles (control). The use of *kārakas* eliminates the need for deletion or designated null elements as in many modern treatments of these constructions, and makes the category of 'subject' unnecessary.

The key principle is that every *kāraka* must be 'expressed' (*abhihita*) by a morphological element, and none can be expressed by more than one. For example, the Agent can be expressed by the active endings and by Instrumental case, but because every role must be expressed exactly once, Instrumental case must mark the Agent if the verb is passive, and it cannot mark the Agent if the verb is active.

Another principle ensures that any given argument gets only one role. For example, in *dhanuṣā vidhyati* ('he pierces by means of a bow'—that is, with arrows shot from a bow), *dhanuṣ* (bow) satisfies both the definition of the instrument role (*karaṇa*) and the definition of the source role (*apādāna*), since it is both the 'means' for launching the arrows and the 'fixed point' from which the arrows move off, but in fact it only gets the former role, hence 'with,' not 'from' a bow (Instrumental case).

5. Phonology and Phonetics

When morphemes and words are combined, they may undergo contextual phonological modifications. Many phonological rules have morphological conditions on their operation. Some are restricted to word-final position, some to a stem-suffix boundary, some to compounds. If such a condition is shared by several rules, they can be grouped together under a heading which supplies it for the lot. Other rules apply to specific morphemes, or to classes of morphemes, ranging from general classes such as roots to utterly idiosyncratic classes whose members must be listed or identified by markers. Those phonological rules which apply across the board, both inside and across words, appear in several blocks under the heading *saṃhitāyām* (in close contact). These are the *sandhi* rules proper.

Pāṇini's grammar does not define phonetic categories but presupposes them, nor does it deal with purely phonetic combinatory processes. This is assumed to be the province of *śikṣā*. According to this remarkably sophisticated theory of phonetics, resonance (*dhvani*) in the vocal tract is produced either by tone (*nāda*), if the throat aperture is closed, or by noise (*śvāsa*), if it is open; the results are respectively voicing (*ghoṣa*) and voicelessness (*aghoṣa*). Aspiration is considered to depend on the degree of air flow (*vāyu*). High pitch (*udātta*) is ascribed to tenseness of the articulatory organs, resulting in constriction of the glottis (*kaṇṭhabila*); low pitch (*anudātta*) to relaxation of articulatory effort with consequent widening of the glottis. Pāṇini's grammar makes important use of certain phonetic notions, such as *savarṇa* ('having the same oral articulation'—but possibly differing in length, nasality, and in the laryngeal features of voicing, aspiration, and pitch).

Not all grammatically relevant categories, however, can be defined purely by their phonetic properties. A number of special conventions specify terms for purely phonological categories, which can be used in rules in exactly the same way as designations of individual sounds or morphemes. Most importantly, the underlying segments of the language are enumerated and grouped into classes in the *akṣarasamāmnāya*, popularly called the '*Śivasūtras*':

1.	a	i	u			Ṇ	(7)
2.				ṛ	ḷ	Ḳ	
3.		e	o			N̄	
4.		ai	au			C	
5.	h	y	v	r		Ṭ	
6.					l	Ṇ	
7.	n̄	m	n̄	ṇ	n	Ṃ	
8.	jh	bh				Ñ	

9.			gh	ḍh	dh	Ṣ
10.	j	b	g	ḍ	d	Ś
11.	kh	ph	ch	ṭh	th	
12.			c	ṭ	t	V
13.		ś	ṣ	s		R
14.	h					L

The consonants at the end of each group (here capitalized for easy reference) are markers. Abbreviations (*pratyāhāras*) are defined on the *Śivasūtras* and other similarly organized lists in the following way. If a list contains the sequence of elements ... x_p, x_{p+1}, ... x_qQ ... , where Q is a marker, then x_pQ denotes the set x_p, x_{p+1}, ... x_q. (Similar lists and abbreviations are used to organize morphological paradigms.) Some examples of *pratyāhāras* defined on the *Śivasūtras* by this procedure are:

iK = i, u, ṛ, ḷ (8a)

aC = a, i, u, ṛ, ḷ, e, o, ai, au (8b)

yaṆ = y, v, r, l (8c)

jhaL = obstruent (8d)

haL = consonant (8e)

aL = segment (8f)

Of the 292 *pratyāhāras* of two or more segments which can be formed from the *Śivasūtras*, 42 are used in the rules of the *Aṣṭādhyāyī*. The *Śivasūtras* form an indispensable part of the grammar, and the phonological classes defined by them are referred to in hundreds of rules. It is said that god Śiva revealed these 14 classes of sounds to Pāṇini to get him started on the *Aṣṭādhyāyī*. The deeper point behind this legend is that the structure of the *Śivasūtras* is thoroughly intertwined with, and determined by, that of the *Aṣṭādhyāyī*. Indeed, if one did not have the text of the *Aṣṭādhyāyī*, but merely a pretheoretical description of Sanskrit phonology, the main properties of Pāṇini's grammar could be inferred just from the way the phonemes of Sanskrit are organized in the *Śivasūtras*. In particular, their structure is determined in large part by the requirement of economy. To be grouped together in a *pratyāhāra*, sounds must make up a continuous segment of the list. Economy requires the shortest possible list: no repetitions of sounds if possible, and as few markers as possible. Consequently, if class A properly includes class B, the elements shared with B should be listed last in A; the marker that follows can then be used to form *pratyāhāras* for both A and B. In this way economy, qua brevity, determines both the ordering of sounds and the placement of markers among them (Staal 1962). Together with the logic of the special case and the general case (*sāmānya/viśeṣa*), it fixes the structure of the *Śivasūtras* completely (Kiparsky 1991b).

As an example of how the classes so defined enter into phonological rules, consider the process which replaces *i, u, ṛ, ḷ* by their nonsyllabic counterparts *y, v, r, l* before a vowel. As the reader can verify from (7) and (8), this is the replacement of *iK* by *yaṆ* before *aC*. To get Pāṇini's formulation of the rule, combine *ikaḥ* (genitive), *yaṇ* (nominative), and *aci* (locative), in accord with the schema in (1), and apply *sandhi* to the combination:

6.1.77 iko yaṇ aci (9)

This rule replaces an entire *class* of vowels by the *class* of their nonsyllabic counterparts. The proper pairings *i*→*y*, *u*→*v*, *ṛ*→*r*, *ḷ*→*l* (rather than, for example, *i*→*r*) are ensured by a further general condition: among alternative possible replacements, the *closest* must be chosen. The closest of the replacements which the rule allows are precisely *y* for *i*, *v* for *u*, *r* for *ṛ*, and *l* for *ḷ*, as desired.

6. Outlook

'One of the greatest monuments of human intelligence' (Bloomfield) is only beginning to claim its rightful position in linguistics. Many of the insights of Pāṇini's grammar still remain to be recaptured, but those that are already understood constitute a major theoretical contribution. Its impact on generative grammar was felt first in phonology (the Elsewhere Condition, unmarked rule ordering), and more recently in syntax (Linking Theory). The rewards for the currently burgeoning study of morphology promise to be richer still.

Bibliography

Bronkhorst J 1981 The orthoepic diaskeuasis of the Ṛgveda and the date of Pāṇini. *Indo-Iranian Journal* **24**: 273–82

Bronkhorst J 1983 On the history of Pāṇinian grammar in the early centuries following Patañjali. *Jounral of Indian Philosophy* **11**: 357–412

Buiskool J 1939 *The Tripādī*. Brill, Leiden

Cardona G 1976 *Pāṇini, a Survey of Research*. Motilal Banarsidass, New Delhi

Cardona G 1988 *Pāṇini: His Work and its Traditions*, vol. I, Motilal Banarsidass, New Delhi

Cardona G 1990 Pāṇinian studies. In: Jha V N (ed.) *New Horizons of Research in Indology*. Pune

Deshpande M 1980 *Evolution of Syntactic Theory in Sanskrit Grammar*. Karoma, Ann Arbor, MI

Joshi S D, Kiparsky P 1979 *Siddha and asiddha* in Pāṇinian phonology. In: Dinnsen D (ed.) *Current Approaches to Phonological Theory*. Indiana University Press, Bloomington, IN

Joshi S D, Roodbergen J A F 1983 The structure of the *Aṣṭādhyāyī*. In: Joshi S D, Laddu S D (eds.) *Proceedings of the International Seminar on Studies in the Aṣṭādhyāyī of Pāṇini*. University of Poona, Pune

Kiparsky P 1979 *Pāṇini as a Variationist*. MIT Press, Cambridge, MA/Poona University Press, Poona

Kiparsky P 1982 *Some Theoretical Problems in Pāṇini's Grammar*. Bhandarkar Oriental Research Institute, Poona

Kiparsky P 1991a On Pāṇinian studies: A reply to Cardona. *Journal of Indian Philosophy* **19**: 331–67

Kiparsky P 1991b Economy and the construction of the Śivasūtras. In: Deshpande M D, Bhate S (eds.) *Pāṇinian Studies: Professor S D Joshi Felicitation Volume.* Center for South and Southeast Asian Studies, University of Michigan, Ann Arbor, MI

Scharfe H 1971 *Pāṇini's Metalanguage.* American Philosophical Society, Philadelphia, PA

Sharma R N 1987 *The Aṣṭādhyāyī of Pāṇini.* Munshiram Manoharlal, New Delhi

Staal J F 1962 A method of linguistic description the order of consonants according to Pāṇini. *Language* **38**: 1–10

Staal J F 1972 *A Reader on the Sanskrit Grammarians.* MIT Press, Cambridge, MA

Staal J F 1988 *Universals: Studies in Indian Logic and Linguistics.* University of Chicago Press, Chicago, IL

Thieme P 1935 *Pāṇini and the Veda: Studies in the Early History of Linguistic Science in India.* Globe Press, Allahabad

Summer Institute of Linguistics

J. Bendor-Samuel

The Summer Institute of Linguistics (recently renamed SIL International) is an educational and humanitarian organization involved in linguistic research and its application in literacy and translation programs in over 1,000 languages. Its research has concentrated on the languages of minority peoples where little previous study has been undertaken, and is focused on assisting in the development of those languages with a view to a body of written materials being published in them and descriptive materials about them (grammars and dictionaries, etc.) being compiled. It has developed training programs in many parts of the world to facilitate this.

1. Purpose

The SIL's statement of goals reads: 'The primary purpose for the existence of the Summer Institute of Linguistics is to:

(a) provide training in language learning and linguistic analysis, carry on linguistic investigation of minority group languages wherever they may be found, and

(b) provide a writing system for such languages and a literature which will be of educational, cultural, moral, and spiritual value.'

In working to achieve this purpose, SIL's activities vary in response to local situations but can be summarized as having the following elements.

1.1 Linguistic Research

Most SIL Language programs involve personnel learning to speak the local language and to record, both in oral and written forms, substantial quantities of language data, including oral literature (traditional accounts of the origin and history of the people, their beliefs and customs) and informal conversational material. Linguistic analysis covering the phonology, morphology, syntax, and discourse structure of the language concerned is carried out. The collection of a lexicon and a body of interlinear text is also made. Local colleagues are trained to participate fully in this research. A significant part of this material is published either in print, or in computer-readable or microfiche form. The need for dictionaries and grammars usable by the local people has also been recognized.

1.2 Translation

In accordance with its aim of providing literature of educational, moral, and spiritual value, SIL works with local speakers to facilitate the translation and publication of the Bible, but does not normally become involved in the translation of other religious material. Usually the New Testament is translated, but increasingly in some parts of the world there is a demand for most or all of the Old Testament in addition. The Institute also assists local government and private agencies in the translation of other materials, for example, health and hygiene booklets, agricultural and other technological and developmental materials.

1.3 Literacy

The aim of SIL is to assist the local communities in establishing ongoing literacy programs which are suited to local conditions and needs. This frequently includes the drafting and testing of reading primers and easy reading materials. Attention is also given to the skills of writing and of numeracy. The training of local people to serve as literacy teachers and supervisors for literacy programs is usually undertaken.

Recognizing the need that exists for the writing and production of new materials in the local language, SIL frequently holds new writers' workshops. In such workshops, those from the local community who have an interest and show some ability in writing are trained to become authors. Frequently, material of considerable cultural value, such as the traditions of the group preserved in their oral literature, is published.

In its literacy work, SIL seeks to cooperate with other government and non-government agencies, and indeed endeavors to ensure that its efforts are fully integrated into local institutions.

In countries where this has been desired by the government and by the communities concerned, SIL has assisted the government to establish a system of bilingual schools. In these schools, students are taught to acquire the skills of reading and writing in their own language and to master the national language. In this way, after the early years of instruction in their own language, they become competent to continue their education with the national language as the language of instruction.

1.4 Training and Transfer of Technology

High priority is given to the transference of language-related skills to the citizens of the countries where projects are undertaken. Training covers a wide range of activities from teaching linguistics, translation, and literacy courses at local universities to on-the-job training as personnel work alongside local translators and literacy personnel. In an increasing number of language programs, SIL personnel serve as advisors or consultants to local personnel.

1.5 Cultural Awareness

In carrying out linguistic, translation, and literacy work, a knowledge of the local culture is acquired. Normally a significant amount of ethnographic material is gathered, to do with the social organization and relationships in the community and the world-view of the language group concerned.

1.6 Practical Community Assistance

Personnel from the SIL normally reside in the language communities for substantial periods of time. Six months of the year over a 15-year period is not uncommon. They seek to be sensitive to the desires of the local community, and are often involved in community development projects of various kinds.

2. Historical Origins

The Summer Institute of Linguistics began modestly enough in 1934 with a summer school to teach young people aboriginal languages. There were two students when it started out. W. Cameron Townsend, who organized the school and taught the grammar and literacy lessons, learned the Cakchiquel language of Guatemala the hard way—without any training. He was convinced that a knowledge of phonetics and some introduction to the structure of non-Indo–European languages would make a big difference. He deliberately chose a rustic setting in Arkansas where nail kegs substituted for chairs as good training for life among aboriginal peoples.

The next summer, there were five students; one of them was Kenneth L. Pike (see *Pike, Kenneth Lee*). After the course, the students accompanied Townsend to Mexico to study some of the Native American languages. This pattern was repeated the next summer, and by the end of 1936 students were studying Aztec, Maya, Tarascan, Mazatec, Otomi, Mixe, Tarahumara, Mixtec, and Totonac. The linguistic schools and the fieldwork of SIL were under way.

The Schools of the SIL International have a pragmatic purpose. They aim to provide the student with the background and skills which will enable him or her to learn a language, usually unwritten, for which pedagogical and descriptive materials are nonexistent or inadequate. The student learns basic linguistic theory and acquires techniques not only to learn to speak but also to analyse a new language and to provide a written form for that language.

A strong emphasis from the very beginning of the Institute has been that linguistic theory and its practical application should continuously interact and reinforce each other. Thus, Pike, who studied under Townsend in 1935 and carried out initial linguistic fieldwork the following winter, came back as one of the teachers for the 1936 session. Similarly, Eugene Nida (see *Nida, Eugene Albert*), who was a student in 1936, subsequently alternated practical fieldwork and regular teaching at the Summer Institutes.

At Townsend's insistence, Pike began to write a textbook on phonetics in the summer of 1936 and continued to work on that manuscript during the winter months when a broken leg kept him out of the Mixtec area. The following summer, 1937, Pike attended the Linguistic Institute of the Linguistic Society of America at the University of Michigan. Professors Charles Fries and Edward Sapir encouraged him to continue his studies, and these led eventually to his Ph.D. in 1942 at the University of Michigan, with the phonetics book as his dissertation.

This pattern of summer teaching followed by practical fieldwork gave the courses and the textbooks that developed from those courses a strong practical emphasis. All the courses utilized extensive language material drawn from the fieldwork that was being carried out, and these served to familiarize the students with diverse linguistic structures and to give them the opportunity of analyzing short language problems. Many of those who were called upon to teach were encouraged to continue their studies in general linguistics so that their teaching could be soundly based as well as practically oriented.

3. Expansion of Activities

The pattern of annual summer schools and linguistic fieldwork in Mexico continued for a number of years. Growth was steady but unspectacular. By the end of 1941, SIL had 44 members and was involved in 17 indigenous languages in Mexico.

A significant year was 1942, when, at the invitation of the University of Oklahoma, SIL moved its summer school to that university. From that summer and for more than 40 years following, SIL offered courses each summer at Norman, Oklahoma, as part of the summer program at the university.

In 1942, for the first time, enrolment reached 100 students. At the end of the summer, 51 of these students joined the SIL organization with the intention of carrying out long-term language work, thus doubling SIL's membership.

Growth made it necessary to put SIL on a legal basis, and in 1942 SIL was formally incorporated. At the same time, a sister organization, the Wycliffe Bible Translators (WBT), was set up to represent the aims of SIL, and particularly its translation work, to friends and churches who did not fully understand an educational and scientific organization such as SIL. Over the years since, the two organizations have worked together in a symbiotic relationship. While SIL carries out the linguistic training, and is responsible for the linguistic, translation, and literacy work, WBT represents SIL's work and seeks to encourage interest, personal involvement, and funding among friends and churches in the countries from which members come.

The next major development occurred in 1946. Until then linguistic fieldwork had been limited to Mexico and the USA. In that year, SIL began work in Peru among the language groups of the Amazon jungle. Within a year, members had begun research in six different languages.

Amazonia posed new challenges. The language groups lived in remote and difficult-to-reach places. Communications were nonexistent and travel slow, dangerous, and exhausting. Not untypical was the experience of one team who had two weeks on a dangerous river, followed by a four-day walk, to reach the language group which they were studying. Cameron Townsend realized that small planes could transform the situation. That same journey could be made in a flight of one hour and 45 minutes. He saw too, that small planes could not only provide much safer communication but also make it possible to reach some language groups which would otherwise be inaccessible. His vision and insistence led to the formation of the Jungle Aviation and Radio Service to provide this service to the linguists.

Another innovation in Peru was the establishment of a system of bilingual schools, to serve the educational needs of the jungle peoples who were outside the normal educational system. Potential teachers in the various jungle villages were selected to come to the SIL center at Yarinacocha to be trained to teach their own people the skills of reading, writing, and numeracy, and the first stages of elementary education, using their own languages as the medium of instruction. At the same time, they were able to acquire a good grasp of the national language, Spanish, so as to be able to teach the national language to their own people.

These new teachers returned to their villages after three months' training and passed on to their people what they had learned. The next year, they came back to Yarinacocha to learn more, and once again returned to their jungle schoolrooms. This cycle of three months' training and the rest of the year in the village was repeated until the normal elementary syllabus had been covered. Successful teachers were given recognition by the government and commissioned as bilingual teachers.

Monolingual pupils who learn to read in their own language, in the first year read with understanding. They also begin to learn Spanish, at first orally, but in the second year they are introduced to reading Spanish. Thereafter their education continues to be bilingual at least through the first three primary grades. Beyond that, materials in Spanish can be used effectively.

Instead of having to use teachers from outside the communities who are alien to the local culture, this system results in teachers who know the local language and culture and in pupils learning to read with comprehension.

This combination of linguistic research with its application in literacy programs and the establishment of bilingual schools, together with the use of the modern technology, of small planes and radios, was seen by many educators and government officials as a very practical way to meet the needs of language groups in remote areas.

Soon, SIL was invited to extend its work to other countries in Latin America; Guatemala (1952), Ecuador (1953), Bolivia (1955), Brazil (1957), Colombia (1962), and Suriname (1967).

Another landmark year for SIL was 1953. Up to that year, SIL's work was limited to the Americas. In 1953, at the invitation of the Department of Education, Culture, and Sport of the Philippine government, SIL began a program of linguistic research with its practical applications in literacy and translation in the Philippines. This was followed by new work in Papua New Guinea in 1956. Work spread to other countries around the Pacific (Vietnam 1957, Australian Aborigines 1961, Indonesia 1971, Solomon Islands 1980, Vanuatu 1981, and New Caledonia 1984) and to other parts of Asia (Nepal and India 1966, Thailand 1977).

It was in 1962 that SIL began work in Africa, under a cooperative agreement with the Institute of African Studies of the University of Ghana. The next year, similar work began in Nigeria in cooperation with the University of Nigeria (Nsukka). Subsequently, linguistic work has begun in some 25 African countries.

Work has also been undertaken in some of the languages spoken in the Commonwealth of Independent States. Some of the textbooks developed by SIL have been translated into Russian and training courses in translation principles have been carried out in response to local requests.

4. Current Activities

4.1 Language Programs

Work is being undertaken in some 1,050 languages, and SIL has been involved in various ways in a further 450 languages. These languages are found in all parts of the world in more than 50 countries, approximately as follows:

Africa	300 active programs
Americas	300 active programs
Asia	220 active programs
Pacific	230 active programs

In addition to research in the individual languages included in these figures, SIL is involved in a number of linguistic and sociolinguistic surveys, covering many other languages. In many parts of the world, scholars recognize extensive chains of related speech forms. SIL has been engaged in collecting wordlists, making comparisons between such wordlists, recording and transcribing oral texts, and then using these to assess the intelligibility of spoken forms among speakers of divergent dialects/languages. Information has also been gathered through interviews and orally administered questionnaires with speakers of these various speech forms, covering their ethnic self-identification, their dialect group contacts, and their perception of linguistic similarities and differences. Groupings of relatively similar speech forms which can be labeled 'languages' can be established on the basis of the criteria of lexical similarity, a high degree of intelligibility, patterns of contact, and the perceptions of the speakers themselves. Casad (1974) describes in detail the fieldwork involved in such research.

In the many areas of linguistic diversity, there is also considerable multilingualism. Where there are so many languages in close proximity, people frequently acquire some degree of proficiency in a national or regional language or in one or more of the neighboring languages. The sociolinguistic surveys being carried out also gather data regarding the patterns of use and acquisition of second languages as well as data on proficiency in these languages. In doing this, SIL has been developing several methods of assessing the degree of proficiency that speakers have in second languages such as a sentence repetition test and a second language oral proficiency evaluation (SLOPE) which adapts the procedures that are used in the FSI second language proficiency testing to make them appropriate for use in nonliterate communities.

SIL's linguistic and sociolinguistic surveys are usually carried out in close cooperation with local academic institutions. An illustration of this and of the nature and scope of SIL's activities in this type of research can be seen in the five volumes of the *Sociolinguistic Survey of Northern Pakistan* amounting to some 1,400 pages and published jointly by the National Institute of Pakistan Studies of the Quaid-i-Azam University and SIL (O'Leary 1992).

4.2 Publications

Less than two years after the start of fieldwork in Mexico, in 1937, SIL published the first results of its linguistic research—12 papers in *Investigaciones Lingüísticas*, the organ of the Mexican Institute of Linguistic Investigations. Since then, SIL has continued to publish its research.

Publications so far are listed in its *Bibliography* (1992) and can be grouped into four categories:

(a) Approximately 5,000 articles and books on general linguistic topics. This includes the various textbooks used in SIL schools.

(b) Some 7,000 linguistic articles and books about specific languages and groups of languages. This includes both descriptive and comparative works. While the majority of these have been in English, there are a number in Spanish and French.

(c) Approximately 8,500 books and articles written in minority languages. This category includes a wide range of educational, literacy, and cultural books.

(d) Biblical material. Up to the time of writing, SIL has been involved in the translation of the New Testament into over 500 languages and of portions of the Bible (e.g. a gospel) into a further 400 languages. The Institute does not normally publish these books, but leaves this to the various Bible Societies and similar agencies. One of the most widely used books published by SIL is the *Ethnologue*, edited by Barbara F.

Grimes. This is a listing of all the languages of the world arranged alphabetically within each country. Each entry includes the name of the language, alternative names, a three-letter language code, the number of speakers, the location of the speakers, its linguistic classification, a list of known dialects, information regarding the degree of bilingualism, and what Scriptures have been translated, with their date. In addition, the existence of Braille materials, some ecological information, and linguistic typological information is included where available. Maps showing the location of each language are included. The 13th edition (1996) has entries for over 6,700 languages. The Ethnologue is updated with a new edition published every four years. It is available on the World Wide Web at http://www.sil.org/ethnologue.

A companion volume is an Index with over 33,000 entries which identifies all language names, their alternative names, and dialects, and refers these to the main language names and codes.

4.3 Training Programs

From Oklahoma, the summer schools spread to other universities in the USA (North Dakota, Oregon, and Texas), and to Australia, Canada, England, Germany, France, and Singapore. Combined enrollment since the early 1970s has averaged around 1,200 students each year. Most of these students take introductory courses in various aspects of linguistics and also in ethnography, but since the late 1970s around 300 enroll each year for the advanced courses at the various schools.

These advanced courses, besides covering various theoretical approaches to phonological and syntactic analysis, include topics such as 'Language Use in Multilingual Societies,' 'The Constituent Structure of Discourse,' 'Semantics and Pragmatics,' 'Historical and Comparative Linguistics', and 'Teaching English as a Second Language'

Linked to the development of these advanced courses has been the expansion of some of the original summer schools into all-year-round institutes which can offer a wider range of linguistic and applied linguistic courses than the summer schools are able to. In Dallas, an affiliation to the University of Texas at Arlington (UTA) provides for the sharing of faculty and a joint program in linguistics leading to advanced degrees. All-year-round training is also offered in England (in association with the University of Reading) and in Australia.

Overall, SIL schools have used a wide variety of theoretical approaches to linguistic analysis. Some schools have used the theoretical approach developed by Pike known as Tagmemics, but never to the exclusion of other linguistic theories. Generally, SIL schools have tended to reflect the theoretical orientation of the universities in which its members studied. Thus, the British School was strongly influenced by J. R. Firth's prosodic analysis, and the North Dakota School has used a generative approach. At Oregon, a functional-typological approach is used, while at Texas, generative, stratificational, and tagmemic courses are offered.

5. Information Processing

In the 1960s and early 1970s, SIL began using computers to facilitate linguistic analysis and typesetting of documents. Since small computers were not yet available at that time, work had to be done on mainframe computers. In the most notable project of that era, text collections in over 300 languages were turned into concordances in a process developed by Dr Joseph F. Grimes, first at the Universidad Nacional Autónoma in Mexico, and then at the University of Oklahoma with the assistance of a grant from the National Science Foundation. Each field linguist sent in up to 200 typed pages of texts which were entered by keypunch operators at the university and submitted to the program, which generated a printed concordance of every word form and morpheme.

In the mid-1970s, with the advent of microcomputer technology, pioneering work began to investigate the feasibility of such information-processing technology being used in field locations. By the early 1980s, when portable personal computers became commercially available, SIL had already developed some basic software tools for supporting field linguistics. By 1990, the use of personal computers by field workers of SIL was virtually universal. Particularly popular are battery-operated laptop computers. Programmers within the organization have developed a full range of programs for both MS-DOS and Macintosh platforms that support the work of field linguistics.

SIL has developed programs that are now in use for many linguistic tasks, including: acoustic analysis of speech; automatic glossing and interlinear alignment of text; compilation of dictionaries; generation of concordances; morphological parsing; analysis of comparative wordlists of related dialects and languages; automatic adaptation of written texts among related dialects and languages; and editing and printing of documents using non-Roman characters. Throughout, SIL's policy has been to share these programs freely with others, provided they are not used for commercial gain.

Of particular interest to field linguists because of its ability to be used in field situations anywhere in the world is the development of a hardware interface which connects a tape recorder or microphone to a computer and so provides an acoustic phonetics field laboratory. This system, labeled CECIL, and the accompanying Spectrum program, produces a display on the computer screen giving an analysis of loudness/intensity, fundamental frequency, and changes in sound quality with numerical and graphical readouts for frequency and intensity. The Spectrum program uses the files produced by CECIL and calculates spectrograms and spectra. The program has the very useful facility of being able to play back stretches of speech at one-third or one-fifth of the original speed of the utterance while maintaining the frequency level. Many linguists have found CECIL to be of real assistance in their analysis of pitch features and other difficult phonetic parameters.

Attempting to produce similar written materials in hundreds of languages, SIL has developed a program which enables it to adapt materials from one language into a related language or dialect. Such computer-assisted related language adaptation has exciting possibilities for the production of written materials in many languages where the comparatively small number of speakers had previously made the inevitably small number of copies of a book relatively uneconomic.

In the 1990s, attention turned to developing a new generation of integrated application programs built on object-oriented and knowledge-based technologies. At the heart of this endeavor is a system called CELLAR (Computing Environment for Linguistic, Literary, and Anthropological Research) which has been developed by a team of programmers at SIL's international headquarters. CELLAR is the data management 'engine' for SIL's LinguaLinks CD-ROM, which was released initially in 1996 and is updated at least once a year. Technical information about CELLAR, and about LinguaLinks, is available at http://www.sil.org on the Internet.

6. Personnel

SIL is set up as a member organization, that is, those who carry out its activities become members of SIL and control its work. Members in a given geographical area, frequently a specific country, form an entity of SIL and set the policies in that country and elect their own leadership. Every three years, delegates from all these entities meet in conference to determine the general policies of the organization and to elect its Board of Directors.

The original members of SIL were Americans, but, since the 1990s, personnel come from over 40 countries. While over half its members come from USA, substantial numbers, over 300 from each country, come from the Canada, the UK, and Australia, and significant numbers (over 100 from each country) from Germany, Switzerland, and the Netherlands. The Institute increasingly has an international flavor, with some 50 members from Japan, 100 from Korea, 80 from New Zealand, and 60 from Finland, to name but a few countries.

Approximately half the members are engaged in language-related activities while the other half provide services which enable the language work to be carried out, often in remote areas—pilots and mechanics for the planes, radio technicians, computer specialists, accountants and other business people, teachers for members' children, and so on. All share the same motivation—service to minority people and, in particular, the provision of Scripture for them.

7. Finances

The bulk of the funding for SIL's activities comes from individuals and churches who are interested in SIL's services to minority peoples. They are drawn from a wide spectrum of Christendom; for the most part, they are evangelicals from many different denominations who share a strong desire to see the Bible made available to all the peoples of the earth and who have a keen interest in the educational and humanitarian aspects of SIL's work.

Specific projects such as major literacy programs and some linguistic research projects have benefited from government funding grants and from non-government funding agencies, such as private foundations.

8. Future Prospects

With the number of distinct languages in the world standing at over 6,500 and bearing in mind that more than half of these have not been described in any detail, SIL is not likely to run out of work in the near future! The organization is aiming to be involved in a further 1,000 languages.

The pattern of its work will continue to evolve. The increased focus already being given to the transference of language-related skills to local scholars will certainly continue with growing impetus. The higher priority being given by governments in many parts of the world to the eradication of illiteracy, coupled with the recognition that literateness in local languages is vital for economic and social development, will impact on SIL and lead to an increase in all aspects of its literacy-related activities.

The harnessing of modern technology will remain another priority. An example of this is LinguaLinks, an 'electronic encyclopedia' produced by SIL with a new generation of tools, helps, and training for the field researcher in anthropology, sociolinguistics, linguistics, and applied linguistics, including literacy and language learning activities. LinguaLinks is a Knowledge Support System (KSS) designed to provide whatever is necessary to generate performance and learning at the moment of need. The goal is to provide a field researcher with information, training, and expert advice at any time and place through the use of the personal computer. This system combines the use of hypertext documents, 'smart' computer programs, experts systems and computer-based training. LinguaLinks contains a set of electronic field manuals, with resources for the field language worker in five subject domains: anthropology, language learning, linguistics, literacy, and sociolinguistics. These electronic resources assist the language researcher to observe, collect, organize, analyze, and publish language and culture data. The initial version of LinguaLinks was released in 1996 and incorporates the work of SIL and non-SIL scholars. LinguaLinks is updated at least once a year as new material and functionality is added. The research agenda for LinguaLinks is multidisciplinary, requiring knowledge from a constellation of disciplines. SIL hopes that LinguaLinks will be seen as a contribution to academic excellence in all of its knowledge domains, and invites contributions by SIL and non-SIL scholars. The researchers developing LinguaLinks are committed to close consultation both with those involved in doing field research and with theoreticians. This makes LinguaLinks reference materials and data management tools useful to a broad range of researchers.

9. Further Information

For more information on SIL worldwide, consult the World Wide Web: http://www.sil.org/

See also: Missionaries; Bible Translations, Modern Period.

Bibliography

Brend R M, Pike K L (eds.) 1977 *The Summer Institute of Linguistics*. Mouton, The Hague, TX

Casad E H 1974 *Dialect Intelligibility Testing*. SIL, Dallas, TX

Grimes B F (ed.) 1996 *Ethnologue, Languages of the World*, 13th edn. SIL, Dallas, TX

O'Leary C F (ed.) 1992 *Sociolinguistic Survey of Northern Pakistan*. Quaid-i-Azam University and SIL, Islamabad

SIL 1992 *Bibliography*. SIL, Dallas, TX

Tamil Linguistic Tradition

K. V. Zvelebil

The beginnings of Tamil (see *Tamil*) linguistic tradition are lost in the legendary accounts of the semimythical sage Akattiyan (Sans Agastya) who is said to have composed, in 'hoary antiquity,' a huge fivefold grammar of Tamil, *Akattiyam*. The fragments of this treatise which are available today are almost certainly forgeries.

From very early times, there must have been enormous learned activity in the field of grammatical description of Tamil including the related fields of prosody, rhetoric, and poetics, reaching back at least to the third century BCE. Only a fragment of the actual output has survived. Apparently, at least three or four different linguistic traditions existed even at that early stage: one was definitely that of *Tolkāppiyam*, the earliest grammar extant; another was probably that of the lost *Akattiyam*, connected with the Aintiram (Sans *aindra-*) grammatical school.

The two characteristic conceptual features of indigenous Tamil linguistic tradition are the vision of Tamil language as a threefold manifestation (*muttamiḻ*) of textual (*iyal*), musical (*icai*), and representational (*kūttu, nāṭakam*) performance, and the notion of grammar as fivefold discipline (*aintu ilakkaṇam*) of *eḻuttu* (sound and symbol), *col* (word and its forms), *poruḷ* (meaning and subject-matter), *yāppu* (metrics), and *aṇi* (rhetoric). The term for grammar, '*ilakkaṇam*' (Sans *lakṣaṇa-*) can be rendered as 'marker'; 'literature' is not 'words written' (Latin *litera*) but 'words marked,' *ilakkiyam* (Sans *lakṣya-*) by the markers of grammar; but 'grammar' is 'squeezed out' of literature like 'oil from sesamum seeds.'

The earliest grammar, *Tolkāppiyam* (The Ancient Book) is probably the result of protracted (possibly collective) composition from the first century BCE up to about 450–500 CE; in its three books (1,611 aphorisms) on *eḻuttu*, *col*, and *poruḷ*, it is one of the finest monuments of human intelligence, the first literary expression of pre-Aryan south Indian civilization, representing the essence of classical Tamil culture. Among later grammars one must mention at least two: Puttamittiraṉ's five-fold *Vīracōḻiyam* (eleventh century CE) and Pavaṇanti's *Naṉṉūl* ('The Good Book,' about 1200 CE) which is still of much influence as the norm of literary language. Besides, there exists a wealth of specialized grammars of the literature of love (*akam*) and of heroism (*puṟam*), as well as dozens of *pāṭṭiyal* grammars—descriptive treatises of more than 1200 literary genres, and handbooks of poetics and rhetoric. In later medieval and early modern periods two main trends in Tamil linguistic thought may be discerned: one is based on the indigenous Tamil tradition; another is closer to Sanskritic models.

See also: Sanskrit (Paninian) Linguistics; Tamil.

Bibliography

Albert D 1985 *Tolkāppiyam—Phonology and Morphology (An English Translation)*. International Institute of Tamil Studies, Madras

Meenakshisundaran T P 1965 *A History of Tamil Language*. Deccan College, Poona

Subrahmanya Sastri P S 1934 *History of Grammatical Theories in Tamil and Their Relation to the Grammatical Literature in Sanskrit*. Journal of Oriental Research, Madras

Vijayavenugopal G 1968 *A Modern Evaluation of Nannul* (eḻuttatikāram). Annamalai University, Annamalainagar

SECTION VII

Biographies

Ælfric (fl. 987–1010)

C. Robinson

Ælfric, homilist and grammarian, was a leading figure in the English literary movement brought about by the Benedictine reforms of the tenth century. He studied at Winchester and in 987 was sent as novice master to the monastery at Cernel, now Cerne Abbas, in Dorset. He had already been ordained by this time and therefore must have been at least 30 years old. His years at Cerne Abbas were his most productive. In 1005 he became the first abbot of the monastery at Eynsham near Oxford. The date of his death is not known.

Ælfric's grammatical works include his *Grammar*, which is of interest because it is the first Latin grammar book to be written in English and moreover because of the evidence it provides for Old English grammar; a Latin glossary; and the *Colloquy* written to provide his pupils with model Latin dialogues, lively, imaginary conversations, full of insights into the everyday lives of ordinary people. The interlinear gloss found in one of the two extant manuscripts of the *Colloquy* is not by Ælfric.

Among his many homiletic works are the *Catholic Homilies* (991–92) consisting of two books intended to be read in alternate years and each consisting of 40 readings. These readings are expositions of the gospels and the passions and lives of those saints whose festivals were observed by the laity. The *Catholic Homilies* were followed by the *Lives of Saints* which include the passions and lives of saints whose feast days were celebrated in the services of monks rather than by the laity. Some of the second series of *Catholic Homilies*, the *Lives of Saints*, and all his later homilies are written in a distinctive rhythmical prose consisting of pairs of phrases each usually with two stressed syllables and often linked by alliteration.

A number of Ælfric's letters survive. Three of the best known constitute the *Epistola de Canonibus*: a letter to Wulfige (Bishop of Sherborne 992–1002) and two letters to Wulfstan (Archbishop of York) originally in Latin but translated at the Archbishop's request and expanded. These three letters were worded so that they could be read out to the clergy instructing them in canonical, liturgical and other matters. He wrote another such letter for his own clergy at Eynsham.

De Temporibus Anni was also intended for the edification of the clergy. It is a treatise in Latin on astrology and chronology explaining the calculation of the date of Easter.

Ælfric's other works include a Life of Æthelwold, his former mentor at Winchester.

In his many translations from Latin, he aimed to convey meaning rather than provide an exact literal translation. He felt strongly that the clergy had a duty to instruct but at the same time he had doubts about the wisdom of translating the Bible and was selective about the passages he translated. Nonetheless he translated or paraphrased many passages from the Old and New Testaments.

A full bibliography of his writings may be found in Clemoes (1959). Reinsma (1987) gives a comprehensive bibliography of scholarship of Ælfric from early times to 1982.

See also: Translation: History.

Bibliography

Clemoes P A M 1959 The chronology of Ælfric's works. In: Clemoes P A M (ed.) *The Anglo-Saxons: Studies in Some Aspects of their History and Culture presented to Bruce Dickins*. Bowes and Bowes, London

Clemoes P A M 1966 Ælfric. In: Stanley E G (ed.) *Continuations and Beginnings*. Nelson, London

Reinsma L M 1987 Ælfric: *An Annotated Bibliography*. Garland, New York

Agamben, Giorgio (1942–)

P. Fletcher

Polymathic in his interests and in the subjects that he has brought to print, Giorgio Agamben, Professor of Aesthetics at the University of Verona, works at the intersection of philosophy, theology, law, literary studies, and political theory. Something of a celebrity in Italy, Agamben starred as Saint Philip in Pier Paolo Pasolini's cinematic version of *The Gospel According to St. Matthew* in 1964. It is for his academic output, however, that Agamben is best known, particularly for his directorship of the Italian edition of the complete works of Walter Benjamin (see *Benjamin, Walter*).

Born in 1942, Giorgio Agamben studied law in Rome until 1965. His interest in the conjunction of language, politics, and religion seems to have commenced at this stage of his academic career with a dissertation on the political thought of Simone Weil. On various occasions between 1966 and 1968 Agamben studied under Martin Heidegger (see *Heidegger, Martin*) and in 1974 he worked at the Warburg Institute on the relation between language and phantasm in the medieval notion of melancholia. Agamben's interest in language and experience has developed since those early years and has resulted in a number of academic appointments in Italy, France, and the USA.

Much of Agamben's analysis of politics, law, and religious texts and traditions begins from an interrogation of the medium in which assemblages of propositions, discourses and concepts take place. In some respects, his task is a simple one: simply to reveal the existence of language *itself*. The exposure of the *factum loquendi*—which is itself the condition of the possibility of community and tradition—makes possible an analysis of the potential of language and what it might become in actuality. But this *factum* itself cannot be stated because if an utterance attempts to define its status it has already become a saying, a proposition, and has elided the condition of its sayability. Nonetheless, the singularity of this 'experience' of language *itself* is found in the theological and philosophical writings of Judaism, Christianity, and Islam. These traditions look to the redemption of that which has been said and understand only too well that such an 'experience' is always one at the threshold and can never be captured in propositional or logical terms.

The religious traditions of the west, then, in their Cabilistic, mystical, apophatic and symbolic reflections on language, the creative word and the singularity of divine discourse, expose the 'pure' existence of language freed from the conformation of any presupposition, and, in doing so, conceive of a community which is beyond any representational condition of belonging. Agamben gives this community the name of 'the coming community.' It has no definable identity—other than its existence in language without identity—and, as such, is irreducible and absolute potential. In forging this politics of potential, Agamben takes the deliberations on the intractable status of language that is gestured towards in religious language and, on that basis, challenges contemporary political and juridical ideologies.

Bibliography

Agamben G 1993 *Stanzas: Word and Phantasm in Western Culture* [trans. R.L. Martinez]. University of Minnesota Press, Minneapolis, MN

Agamben G 1993 *The Coming Community* [trans. M. Hardt]. University of Minnesota Press, Minneapolis, MN

Agamben G 1998 *Homo Sacer* [trans. D. Heller-Roazen]. Stanford University Press, Stanford, CA

Agamben G 1999 *Potentialities: Collected Essays in Philosophy* [trans. D. Heller-Roazen]. Stanford University Press, Stanford, CA

Wall T C 1999 *Radical Passivity: Levinas, Blanchot, and Agamben*. SUNY Press, Albany, NY

Albright, William Foxwell (1891–1971)

K. J. Cathcart

William Foxwell Albright was one of the most influential figures in twentieth-century biblical studies and in the development of so-called biblical archaeology. A scholar who combined considerable philological gifts and great intellectual curiosity, he was a prolific writer and published 20 books and more than a thousand articles. He was born in Coquimbo, Chile, 24 May 1891, the eldest son of the Reverend William Finley Albright and Zephine Viola, née Foxwell, who were Methodist missionaries. He graduated from Upper Iowa University in 1912 and spent one year as principal of a high school in Menno, South Dakota. In 1913 he went to the Oriental Seminary at Johns Hopkins University, where he studied under Paul Haupt. After he was awarded a Ph.D. in 1916 for his dissertation on 'The Assyrian Deluge Epic,' he taught at the Oriental Seminary for some years, with a break of five months doing limited service in the US army. In 1919 he was able to take up a Thayer Fellowship at the American School of Oriental Research in Jerusalem, where he spent the next ten years. During this period in Palestine he conducted archaeological digs at Tell el-Ful and Tell Beit Mirsim. Later on he excavated at Bethel and Beth-Zur. From 1929 to his retirement in 1958, Albright was chairman of the Oriental Seminary at Johns Hopkins. He died on 19 September 1971 in Baltimore.

There has been much scholarly debate about Albright's work. He believed passionately that archaeology provided objective external evidence to confirm the biblical story and was convinced that his archaeological research and discoveries in Palestine demonstrated the value of the Bible as a source of history. He was sure that he had discredited the views of Wellhausen and his followers. However, his arguments in favour of the substantial historicity of the Mosaic tradition, the patriarchal narratives and the antiquity of Israelite monotheism have not stood the test of time. Albright had learned much about Semitic philology from Haupt, his teacher at Johns Hopkins, and he knew the civilizations of Mesopotamia, Canaan and Egypt intimately. Quite rightly, he promoted the integration of textual and archaeological data, but he was an historian rather than an archaeologist. His published works show that he was an historian preoccupied with Israelite religion and with the historicity of the Bible. A master of synthesis, he wrote his works with great enthusiasm, though often with rather naïve claims for archaeological data.

Bibliography

Dever W G 1993 What remains of the house that Albright Built? *Biblical Archaeologist* **56(1)**: 25–35

Freedman D N, Mattson D L (eds.) 1975 *The Published Works of William Foxwell Albright: A Comprehensive Bibliography*. American Schools of Oriental Research, Cambridge, MA

Long B O 1993 Mythic trope in the autobiography of William Foxwell Albright. *Biblical Archaeologist* **56(1)**: 36–45

Machinist P 1996 William Foxwell Albright: the Man and his Work. In: Cooper J S, Schwartz G M (eds.) *The Study of the Ancient Near East in the Twenty-First Century*. Eisenbrauns, Winona Lake, IN, pp. 385–403

Andrew of St. Victor

W. McKane

At the Abbey of St. Victor in Paris, Andrew was a pupil of 'Master Hugh' who was resident at St. Victor from about 1118 until his death in 1141. According to later information Andrew was born in England of English parents, and he was abbot of Wigmore in Herefordshire from 1147 to about 1155, when he returned to St. Victor. The Abbey of St. Victor was a house of Augustinian canons regular whose rule was founded on that drawn up by Augustine for secular clergy. The canon regular was cloistered and was especially devoted to sacred learning. St. Victor had a splendid library, donated by the French royal family, and was a center of vigorous intellectual life. Andrew's scholarship is founded essentially on Jerome's Vulgate and his grasp of Hebrew should not be exaggerated—he conversed with Jews in French. Such evidence as there is suggests that he did not know Greek. He produces a few Hebrew words (not always accurately), but he was principally dependent on Jerome's Vulgate for his access to the Hebrew Bible. He was a scholar of independent mind who clashed with patristic exegesis in general and Jerome in particular.

Andrew of St. Victor is interesting and significant not because of the excellence of his biblical scholarship, but because of the novelty of his exegetical stance in the theological context of the twelfth century and because of the lively way in which he expressed it. Andrew by his uncompromising pursuit of the literal (Jewish) sense pushed into the foreground an exegesis of the Old Testament which did not have a Christian content and ruffled feathers in doing so. He is an important figure in connection with the history of the Old Testament in the Christian Church. Isaiah 7.14 was a text on which patristic and mediaeval exegetes concentrated in connection with the Virgin Birth and it was over this that Andrew fell foul of perhaps his leading adversary, Richard of St. Victor. Richard's complaint was, 'He (Andrew) gives the Jewish objections or questions without answering them; he seems to award the palm to them, since he leaves these questions unsolved.' Richard's outburst is an indication that Andrew has stepped out of line in crucial respects and has made a departure which is intolerable to Catholic exegetical orthodoxy. The 'literal' (Jewish) sense of the Old Testament is not to be granted such ill-considered freedom: it must be leashed to the pursuit of Christian truth and not rise above its lowly station in the exegetical system. Andrew's pupil, who springs to his master's defense, cuts little ice with Richard: 'Do not call it my master's opinion but the Jews', for he advances it not as his own but as theirs.' This makes no impression on Richard and his rejoinder is that Andrew ought to have made it clear when he was formulating a true exegesis, which was his own, and a false one which was Jewish. It is because Richard accepts Jerome's 'literal' (Christian) interpretation of Isaiah 7.14 that he is so vexed by Andrew's exegesis of it.

Bibliography

McKane W 1989 *Selected Christian Hebraists.* Cambridge University Press, Cambridge, pp. 42–75

Smalley B 1983 *The Study of the Bible in the Middle Ages*, 3rd edn. Basil Blackwell, Oxford, pp. 112–95

Aquinas, Thomas (1224/5–74)

D. Hart

Theologian, philosopher, hymnode, exegete, patristic scholar, avid trencherman, and mystic, St Thomas Aquinas produced the most majestic theological synthesis of the Latin Middle Ages, especially in his two compendious masterpieces the *Summa Contra Gentiles* and the *Summa Theologiae*. Certainly no one was more daring or deft in his adoption of the Aristotelian learning emanating from Islamic philosophy in the thirteenth century, nor better able to reconcile its uses with scripture, the Christian platonist writings of the fathers (especially the Pseudo-Dionysius), and the doctrinal deposit of the Catholic Church. More germane here, no one in the mediaeval Church did more to advance coherently—both in theory and in practice—an understanding of the use of human language in regard to the nature and acts of God, and so of the relation between natural reason and the science of divine revelation. Though he devoted a very small portion of his writings to the issue of analogy, he is credited with many of the formulae largely preferred by later generations of Catholic philosophers, especially as regards the primacy of the divine pole of any analogical predication, the apophatic stricture against any attempt to construct a univocal predication of God, and the underlying structure of ontological participation of the creature in God (however this language is tempered by the austere Aristotelian terminology of causation) that certifies the truth of our analogies despite their ultimate transcendence of our powers of thought. Born in Roccasecca in 1224/5, into the landed gentry of the Kingdom of Sicily, Thomas was placed as an oblate in the monastery of Monte Cassino as a small child, where for nine years he was housed and educated, till the expulsion of the monks by the Emperor in 1239; thereafter he went to the University of Naples, where he encountered the impressive scholarly and pedagogical disciplines of the still young Dominican order. Had he persevered in the vocation his family had chosen for him, he could quite plausibly have ascended to the abbacy, adding the monastic estates, informally, to their freehold; so, when he elected instead to become a Dominican, they even resorted to abduction and a year's incarceration to dissuade him. But, when his will proved intractable, he was released, and in 1245 he went to Paris, where he studied under Albert the Great.

From 1248 to 1252 he served under Albert as a Master of Students at the new *Studium Generale* in Cologne, but then returned to Paris to complete his studies. In 1256, possessed now of his baccalaureate and *licentia docendi* (soon to be followed by full certification as a *Magister*), he began teaching at the University of Paris. From 1259 to 1268, he served as an advisor of the papal curia, under three popes (from 1265 to 1267, he lectured at the Santa Sabina convent in Rome). In 1268 he returned to Paris, where he became embroiled in the 'Averroist' controversy. Caught between the Scylla of the rigid Augustinians (who held to a strict illuminationist understanding of knowledge, natural or graced) and the Charybdis of the Averroist rationalists (who presumed an irresoluble heterogeneity between philosophic reason and religious faith, and so an autonomous sphere peculiar to each), Thomas (who scandalized one camp with his defense of empirical reason, and the other with his insistence on natural reason's compatibility with and subordination to revelation) could not emerge with his reputation unscathed. The condemnation of the Averroists in 1270 redounded (unjustly) to his discredit. In 1272, he repaired again to the University of Naples to establish a Dominican house; in 1273 he became involved in a new dispute with the greatest of the pure Augustinians, Bonaventure; and in January of 1274 Pope Gregory X appointed him to the Council of Lyons. This last commission he could not discharge; on his way to the council, he fell ill and had to stop in Fossanova, at the Cistercian abbey. There, on 7 March, he died.

Canonized in 1323, made a *doctor ecclesiae* in 1567, he now wears the lovely title *doctor angelicus*. It is perhaps somewhat ironic that a man who contributed so much to theological language, and to the elucidation of its fundamental rationality, chose to end his days in virtual silence: given to spiritual ecstasies, he experienced one of extraordinary duration and profundity while celebrating mass on 6 December 1273. Thereafter he wrote not another word, remaining instead in a state of rapt serenity, and confessing that, by comparison to the mysteries of which he had been vouchsafed a glimpse, all he had produced now seemed to him to be just 'so much straw.'

See also: Analogy; Linguistic Theory in the Later Middle Ages; Christian Views on Language.

Bibliography

Aquinas T 1996 *Opera Omnia*. Editoria Elettronica Editel, Milan

Gilson E 1956 *The Christian Philosophy of Thomas Aquinas*. Random House, New York

Siewerth G 1961 *Der Thomismus als Identitätssystem*. G. Schulte-Bulmke, Frankfurt am Maim

Arnauld, Antoine (1612–94)

P. Swiggers

Antoine Arnauld, called 'le grand Arnauld,' was born in Paris, the son of a court lawyer. He studied philosophy, law, and theology in Paris, and in 1635 he was received as Bachelor at the Sorbonne, and in 1641 as Doctor of Theology. He was ordained priest in 1641, and became a harsh critic of Protestantism and an adherent of the ideas of Cornelius Jansen (Jansenius). In 1643, Arnauld published *De la Fréquente Communion*, a defence of Jansenism directed against the Jesuits. Jansenism was condemned in 1653 by Pope Innocent X. Arnauld, who lived as a 'solitaire' at Port-Royal, where an anti-Jesuit school system had been installed, published two pamphlets (1655) in defense of Jansenism. As a result, he was banned from the rank of Doctor of Theology. He left Port-Royal and pursued his polemical work. In 1656, Pope Alexander VII condemned again the doctrine of Jansen, and the French clergy drew up a formulary to be signed by all ecclesiastics. Arnauld replied with three memoirs, and was instrumental in having Pascal's *Lettres Provinciales* brought out. At the same time, he took part in the French translation of the Bible, and in the redaction of the Port-Royal grammar (*Grammaire Générale et Raisonnée*, 1660), published with Claude Lancelot (see *Lancelot, Claude*). In 1661, Arnauld signed the formulary. Under Pope Clement IX, tensions between Jansenists and Jesuits diminished, and Arnauld became a prominent figure in royal circles. In 1662, he published, with Pierre Nicole, the Port-Royal *Logique* (*La Logique ou l' Art de Penser*), and in 1664 *La Perpetuité de la Foy de l'Eglise Catholique Touchant l'Eucharistie*, a refutation of the Calvinist doctrine. In 1672, Arnauld attacked the Protestants in his book *Le Renversement de la Morale de Jésus-Christ par les Erreurs des Calvinistes Touchant la Justification*. Louis XIV wanted to eradicate the influence of Port-Royal, and persecuted the Jansenists. Arnauld went into voluntary exile to the Low Countries, and established himself in Brussels, where he published some pamphlets against Calvinism (1682, 1688), and against the Jesuits (1689). He continued his philosophical work, often in the form of polemics with Malebranche and Lamy, and of epistolary exchange (e.g., with Leibniz). In 1683, he wrote *Des Vraies et des Fausses Idées*, and in 1693 the *Règles du Bon Sens pour Bien Juger des Ecrits Polémiques dans les Matières de Science*. He died in Brussels in 1694, and was buried in Port-Royal. A bibliography of his writings can be found in Baudrillart (1930), cols. 447–84.

See also: Bayle, Pierre; Lancelot, Claude.

Bibliography

Arnauld A 1775–83 *Œuvres de Messire Antoine Arnauld, Docteur de la Maison et Société de Sorbonne*. 45 vols, Paris/Lausanne

Balteau J 1939 Arnauld, Antoine. *Dictionnaire de Biographie Française*, vol. 3. Letouzey and Ané, Paris

Baudrillart A (ed.) 1930 *Dictionnaire d'Histoire et de Géographie Ecclésiastiques*. D'Arnay, Paris

Bracken H M 1967 Arnauld, Antoine. In: Edwards P (ed.) *Encyclopedia of Philosophy*, Vol. 1. Collier-Macmillan, London
Brekle H E 1964 Semiotik und linguistische Semantik in Port-Royal. *Indogermanische Forschungen* **69**: 103–21
Carré I 1887 *Les Pédagogues de Port-Royal.* Delagrave, Paris
Cognet L 1961 *Le Jansénisme.* Presses Universitaires de France, Paris
Dominicy M 1984 *La Naissance de la Grammaire Moderne. Langage, Logique et Philosophie à Port-Royal.* Mardaga, Brussels
Donzé R 1967 *La Grammaire Générale et Raisonée de Port-Royal.* Francke, Berne
Jacques E 1976 *Les Années d'Exil d'Antoine Arnauld (1679–94).* Nauwelaerts, Louvain
Kunow J von 1926 Sprach- und Literarkritik bei Antoine Arnauld. *Romanische Forschungen* **39**: 123–69
Ndiaye A R, et al. 1991 *La Philosophie d'Antoine Arnauld.* Vrin, Paris
Swiggers P 1987 La sémiotique de Port-Royal: Du savoir au vouloir(-dire). *Semiotica* **66**: 331–44
Verga L 1972 *Il Pensiero Filosofico e Scientifico di Antoine Arnauld.* Vita e Pensiero, Milan

Ascham, Roger (1515–68)

A. P. R. Howatt

Roger Ascham (pronounced ['æskəm]) was born into a North Yorkshire family of yeoman background which had long been settled in the area. His early education took place in the house of a local landowner who succeeded in inspiring an intense love of learning and archery, both of which were to prove significant in Ascham's later work. In 1530 he entered St John's College, Cambridge, and his aptitude for languages, in particular Greek, was so striking that he was asked to act as tutor to the younger students. After gaining his MA in 1537, he accepted the offer of a readership in Greek and settled down to a life of scholarship.

Ascham's health was never good and a period of sickness during a visit to Yorkshire in 1541 depleted his limited resources and he was forced to take up a translator's post with the Archbishop of York. The trip north had, however, revived his love of archery and he set about writing *Toxophilus* (1545) which is both a practical manual on the topic and a conscious attempt to prove that English was an effective medium for serious work of this kind. Dedicating the book to Henry VIII himself, Ascham traveled south to present it in person to the king, an undertaking that was rewarded with warm praise and a pension of £10. Ascham's royal connections were renewed in 1548 when he was hired to teach the Italian hand to the young Edward VI and later when he was appointed tutor to Princess (later Queen) Elizabeth.

After a disagreement with his royal patron in 1550, Ascham traveled abroad where he remained (mainly in Augsburg in south Germany) until after Edward's death in 1553. Given his strong Protestant convictions, his next post as Latin secretary to Queen Mary was unexpected but he fulfilled his duties well and engendered sufficient trust to renew his relationship with Elizabeth who, shortly after her accession in 1558, installed him as a prebendary at York. This gave him the financial security to embark on his major work *The Scholemaster*, but recurrent illness meant that progress was slow and he died in 1568 without having completed it. It was finally published in 1570 by his wife Margaret.

At first sight The *Scholemaster* appears to be merely a method for the teaching of Latin ('a plaine and perfite way of teachying children... the Latin tong'), but in reality it is much more. The primary focus is Ascham's philosophy of a humanist education rooted in the study of the classical languages and their literatures accompanied by a strong emphasis on the development of Christian piety and moral judgment. Aims of this nature were familiar in Renaissance Europe, but they were buried in Latin tracts and had rarely been expressed with such cogency in the vernacular language. The book is famous for promoting the technique of 'double translation' (i.e., translating from Latin into English and, after a pause, recreating the original Latin text) but it is not always realized that the purpose of such exercises was not merely to teach Latin but also to develop confidence and elegance of expression in the mother tongue. In many ways Ascham was ahead of his time—he was a firm opponent of corporal punishment, for instance, and a champion of education for girls—but the broad thrust of his curriculum reflected contemporary concerns in seeking to instill in the young, and particularly the young ruler, both soundness of judgment and a forceful eloquence in the use of language.

See also: Translation: History.

Bibliography

Ryan L V (ed.) 1967 *The Schoolmaster (1570) by Roger Ascham.* Cornell University Press, Ithaca, NY

Barr, James (1924–)

S. Groom

James Barr, biblical scholar and philologist, became renowned in the 1960s for his negative criticisms of the etymological approach to biblical interpretation and the biblical theology movement. He continues to write widely on semitics, biblical studies and theology.

Born in Glasgow in 1924, Barr was raised in the Church of Scotland and attended Edinburgh University. He was ordained and served briefly in Tiberias, Israel. He has taught at various institutions in the UK and North America, receiving numerous honorary degrees, fellowships, and guest lectureships. He is Emeritus Professor of Hebrew at Oxford and Vanderbilt.

In *The Semantics of Biblical Language* (1961), Barr produced a devastating critique of procedures which he believed mishandled and distorted linguistic evidence. The biblical theology movement claimed that the structure of the Hebrew language reflects the particular mode of thinking identified as the Hebrew mindset. Barr demonstrated that this was insufficiently supported by the evidence: neat correspondences between linguistic and thought structures cannot be assumed.

In *Comparative Philology and the Text of the Old Testament* (1968) Barr criticized how scholars turned to other Semitic languages to aid comprehension of Biblical Hebrew. He urged philologists to note their motives and mental processes and to become better acquainted with the Semitic languages. He cautioned against undue reliance on the root in the meaning of Hebrew words and excessive emphasis on a word's origin versus its semantic value in its current context. Barr encouraged scholars to be more rigorous in method, to consider the wider implications of their suggestions, and to remember that philological results are always tentative, never final.

In *Fundamentalism* (1981) Barr challenged those who allowed the principle of inerrancy to dictate the meaning of texts regardless of their linguistic and literary structure. He pointed out that semantic emendation is just as creative as textual emendation and urged that texts be treated with respect. He insisted that semantic analysis and biblical interpretation be allowed adequate freedom from controlling theological assumptions.

In *The Concept of Biblical Theology* (1999) Barr asserted that knowledge of Hebrew grammar is no more a tool in understanding Hebrew texts than prayer is a tool in communication with the deity: language is the means of communication. The Hebrew language is not in itself a theological phenomenon, although statements with theological implications are made through it, hence the need for a command of biblical languages.

Barr's contribution to the study of language and linguistics in the context of biblical studies has been twofold: to summon biblical scholars to modern methods of linguistic analysis; and to call for a more responsible and productive relationship between linguistic analysis and theological discussion.

See also: Fundamentalism.

Bibliography

Barr J 1961 *The Semantics of Biblical Language*. SCM Press, London

Barr J 1968 *Comparative Philology and the Text of the Old Testament*. Oxford University Press, Oxford

Barr J 1981 *Fundamentalism*, 2nd edn. SCM Press, London

Barr J 1999 *The Concept of Biblical Theology: An Old Testament Perspective*. SCM Press, London

Knight D A 1999 Barr, James. In: Hayes J H (ed.) *Dictionary of Biblical Interpretation*. Abingdon Press, Nashville, TN, vol. 1, pp. 98–9

Barthes, Roland (1915–80)

M. Toolan

A French critic and theorist of literature and culture, Barthes came to international prominence in an era of structuralist–semiological analyses of myths and cultural practices (see his *Mythologies*). Semiology was Saussure's (see *Saussure, Ferdinand (-Mongin) de*) term for a broadranging 'science of signs,' which would apply the methods Saussure adumbrated for the study of languages to the study of signifying practices quite generally. Barthes' semiological work, more than anyone else's, seemed to validate Saussure's earlier observation that although 'semiology' did not yet exist, its emergence was guaranteed. But Barthes' cultural criticism, which combined subtle philosophical critique with personal and even confessional individuality of response, moved on to new topics and new methods and anti-methods in the decades that followed. Thus in his later writings, having rejected the idea of the autonomous author as authoritative controller of his or her text and its reception, and having recast characters and readers as shimmering confluences of traces and signs rather than abbreviated denotations of fixed and stable free-standing individuals (the latter view became for him part of an insupportable rationalist, liberal and bourgeois reading of culture), Barthes sought to elaborate a logic of writing and reading which was based on pleasure (*jouissance*), a concept whose erotic or quasi-erotic aspects he sought to bring out. Certainly from *S/Z* onwards, Barthes is no longer (or not merely) a structuralist analyst, but one who puts structuralist principles (of oppositions, binarisms, markedness, and proportionality) to such far-reaching tests that the principles' nonrational roots, in desire and emotion, re-emerge. In such ways Barthes contributed to the poststructuralist and deconstructionist turn.

For stylistics and linguistic criticism Barthes was chiefly influential in three texts: his early essay on structural analysis of narrative, in which his ideas of functions, indices and catalyzers etc. were introduced; his collection of essays, *Mythologies*, which innovatively applied structuralist–anthropological methods to an explication of the overlooked systematicities of aspects of popular culture (e.g., wrestling, restaurant menus) and the mass media; and his 1970 study *S/Z*, on systematic reversals and deceptions in a Balzac story, in which a procedure of detailed analyses of verbal chunks (lexias) in terms of 5 shaping semiotic codes (hermeneutic, proairetic, semic, cultural, and symbolic) is elaborated in a virtuoso demonstration.

See also: Postmodernism; Myth; Romanticism.

Bibliography

Barthes R 1957 *Mythologies*. Editions du Seuil, Paris
Barthes R 1966 Introduction à l'analyse structurale des récits. *Communications* **8**: 1–27 [reprinted in English translation in *Image–music–text*, 1977]
Barthes R 1967 *Elements of Semiology*. Cape, London [transl. from *Eléments de sémiologie*. Seuil, Paris, 1964]
Barthes R 1970 *S/Z*. Seuil, Paris [English transl., 1974]
Barthes R 1977 *Image–music–text*. transl. S Heath. Fontana, London
Barthes R 1980 *New Critical Essays*. Hill and Wang, New York
Culler J 1975 *Structuralist Poetics*. Routledge, London
Jefferson A, Robey D (eds.) 1986 *Modern Literary Theory: A Comparative Introduction*, 2nd edn. Batsford, London

Bataille, Georges (1897–1962)

P. Fletcher

The prominence of such themes as violence, eroticism, excess, and sacrifice have led critics to denounce (or, indeed, celebrate) the work of Georges Bataille as little more than 'pornographic philosophy.' As the co-founder of the Collège de Sociologie, established to consider the manifestations of the sacred in society, and as an economic theorist, renegade Surrealist and the author of scandal-provoking novels, Bataille's influence has been both profound and wide-ranging. Recognized by Martin Heidegger (see *Heidegger, Martin*) as 'one of France's best minds,' Bataille authored numerous books and essays relating to religion, sacrifice and the sacred. Yet his work has always sat uneasily with the beliefs and pretensions of the orthodox. Indeed, his (unfinished) *magnum opus*—consisting of three texts, *Inner Experience* (1943), *The Guilty* (1944) and *On Nietzsche* (1945)—was given a title that placed it in direct confrontation with the Christian tradition (and Roman Catholicism in particular), *La Somme athéologique*.

Georges Bataille was born in Billon, Puy-de Dôme, in central France in 1897. Just prior to the First World War, Bataille converted to Catholicism although he soon lost his faith and abandoned mainstream religion. By 1920, he was heavily involved with the Surrealist movement. This was yet another of Bataille's flirtations with commitment as he was soon excommunicated from the group. From 1922 he served as a librarian and a deputy keeper at the Bibliothèque Nationale in Paris but he resigned in 1944 when he contracted tuberculosis. However, it was his philosophical and literary output which brought Bataille fame and infamy. Indeed, such was his distinction that before his death in 1962 Pablo Picasso, Max Ernst, and Juan Miro arranged an auction of paintings to help alleviate his financial difficulties.

Bataille believed that language, in its everyday and scientific use, represents a flight from truth and reality and a securing of identity (the ego) through the tyranny of words. Language, in this form, creates a discontinuity from the sacred and a chasm between selves. His preoccupation with violence, eroticism and sacrifice point to his quest for a form of communication that is only possible with the loss of the self or ego. At the limits of possible experience the self disintegrates and in the midst of this limit-experience comes an intense fusion with the other. Language is the human attribute that points to the possibility of this experience which Bataille calls the sacred. Linguistic communication is founded on a freedom to connect in networks, with others and the world, that comes prior to our actual speech with another subject. This freedom (or space) in which language is possible depends on the loss of the sovereign position and the destruction of the security of the one who addresses the other. In revealing this loss and the possibility of conjunction, language presages death and opens human beings to the outside—the sacred realm of continuity. Language is therefore dangerous in that is reveals the force of sacred violence and the experience of death which destroys difference and separation.

Bibliography

Bataille G 1987 *Eroticism* [trans. M. Dalwood]. Marion Boyars, London

Bataille G 1988 *Inner Experience* [trans. L.A. Boldt]. SUNY Press, New York

Bataille G 1989 *Theory of Religion* [trans. R. Hurley]. Zone Books, New York

Bataille G 1992 *On Nietzsche* [trans. B. Boone]. Athlone Press, London

Gill C B (ed.) 1994 *Bataille: Writing the Sacred.* Routledge, London

Noys B 2000 *Bataille: A Critical Introduction.* Pluto Press, London

Batchelor, John (1853–1944)

J. C. Maher

John Batchelor, missionary and pioneer in the field of Ainu language studies, was born in Uckfield, Sussex in 1853, the son of a tailor and parish clerk. He left school at the age of 12 and worked as a gardener in Uckfield Parish Church. He decided to become a missionary and after preparatory studies was sent to Hong Kong. For reasons of health he transferred to the colder climate of Hokkaido, the northern island of Japan, and landed in Hakodate on May 1, 1877.

Moved by the miserable plight of the Ainu, the indigenous people of Hokkaido, Batchelor requested permission to minister to them. From 1879 onwards, he spent 60 years with the Ainu people, becoming an acknowledged authority on the language and the author of numerous works including the *Ainu–Japanese–English-Dictionary and Grammar* (Batchelor 1938, first edition 1889). His investigations on place names and speculations regarding the origin of the Ainu people contributed towards a re-interpretation of the Ainu people's role in Japan and particularly in its early history. Batchelor's argument, which subsequent archaeological and anthropological studies have tended to favor, was that the Ainu presence was not limited to the far north only but, in fact, extended to other parts of the mainland and perhaps even the entire archipelago. His suggestion that Ainu possesses genetic affinities with the Indo–European languages of Europe, such as Cornish and Welsh, and even with Basque, has not, however, been substantiated by later generations of scholars.

By means of his *Grammar* and other works, Batchelor emphasized Ainu's independent status as a language different from Japanese. It was Batchelor who devised the system of romanization to write down the language (previously Japanese *kana* had been employed) and with this system translated the Bible and other religious works into Ainu. His fluency in the language as preacher, writer, and member of the Ainu community was well-known and he was particularly delighted to be mistaken, as sometime happened, for an *ekashi* or Ainu elder. During the early part of the twentieth century in Sapporo, when Batchelor met Bronislaw Pilsudski, the Polish scholar of Ainu, they conversed in their only common language—Ainu. Batchelor spoke the Saru dialect of Piratori, the ancient capital of Saru. Batchelor's influence was felt in the fields of linguistics, ethnography, and anthropology. He became an honorary member of the Hokkaido government and was decorated by the Emperor. He returned to Britain in 1940 where he died four years later at the age of 91. His work is displayed in commemorative museums both in Hokkaido and near his birthplace in England.

See also: Japanese Linguistic Thought.

Bibliography

Batchelor J 1882 An Ainu vocabulary. *Transactions of the Asiatic Society of Japan* **20**

Batchelor J 1986 *Ainu Karisia Eiwange Gusu An Inonno-itak Oma Kambi* (*The Book of Common Prayer*). The Church Missionary Society, Tokyo

Batchelor J 1897 *Chikoro Utarapa Ne Yesu Kiristo Ashiri Aeuitaknup (The New Testament)*. Yokohama Bunsha, Yokohama
Batchelor J 1903 *A Grammar of the Ainu Language*. Kelly and Walsh, Yokohama
Batchelor J 1924 '*Uwepekere*' *or Ainu fireside Stories as told by one of themselves*. Kyobunkwan, Tokyo
Batchelor J 1938 *Ainu–Japanese–English-Dictionary and Grammar*, 4th edn. Iwanamin, Tokyo
Batchelor J 1965 *Tegami* (*Letters*). Yamamoto Shoten, Tokyo

Bayle, Pierre (1647–1706)

N. E. Cronk

Bayle, a French Protestant scholar, is now remembered as a powerful champion of religious toleration, as a debunker of human reason, and as a pioneering exponent of modern historical method. Driven from France by religious persecution, he moved to Holland, where he published his most famous work, the *Dictionnaire historique et critique* (1696), translated into English in 1710 (*An Historical and Critical Dictionary*). Originally conceived as a supplement and corrective to the Catholic bias of Louis Moreri's *Grand Dictionnaire historique* (1674), Bayle's *Dictionary* is important both for its breathtaking erudition and for the manner in which this learning is marshaled. Arranged as a biographical dictionary, there are articles on Old Testament and mythological figures alongside others on modern philosophers and theologians. The choice of subject is tantalizingly arbitrary: while there is no article on Plato, for example (because Moreri's treatment was deemed satisfactory), there are numerous articles on obscure heretics. The style of the articles is dry and factual, and copious marginal notes refer to sources. The notes at the foot of each page, often longer and more interesting than the article which is their pretext, are written in a distinctively personal and humorous voice. In the eighteenth century, Bayle was widely—if wrongly—read as a sceptic, and the *Dictionary* was an influential model for the polemical encyclopedias of the Enlightenment.

See also: Arnauld, Antoine; Lancelot, Claude.

Bibliography

Labrousse E (ed.) *Correspondence de Pierre Bayle*. Voltaire Foundation, Oxford
Labrousse E 1983 *Bayle*. Oxford University Press, Oxford
Popkin R H, Brush C (eds.) 1965 *Bayle, Historical and Critical Dictionary—Selections*. Bobbs-Merrill, Indianapolis, IN

Benjamin, Walter (1892–1940)

P. Fletcher

As both a man and a thinker Walter Benjamin is best described as a nomad. He was constantly on the move—*en passant*—both materially and theoretically and never held a professional academic position despite his many efforts. If there is any focus to his *oeuvre*, it can be found in two preoccupations: melancholy, the consequence of what he described in a letter to Gershom Scholem (in 1932) as a life of 'small-scale victories' and 'large-scale defeats,' and an attachment to Jewish thought, particularly its concern with language, law and redemption and its transmutations in a modern context.

Born in Berlin in 1892, Benjamin married Dora Sophie Kellner in 1917. He received his doctorate for a thesis entitled 'Concept of Art Criticism in German Romanticism' in 1919 and began to make a moderate living as a literary critic for newspapers and journals and through the writing and presentation of numerous radio broadcasts. Divorced in 1930, Benjamin moved to Paris and was interned along with other exiles of German nationality as the war began in 1939. He was released two months later and fled (after the German occupation of Paris in 1940) to the south of France with the intention of crossing to Spain. However, the Spanish border guards refused to accept Benjamin's transit visa and, in despair, he took his own life.

The centrality of language in the thought of Benjamin is apparent from the very beginning of his writing career. In his essay *On Language as Such and on the Language of Man* (1916) and his study of the Baroque Mourning Play, *Origin of the German Tragic Drama* (1925), language is presented as the truth content of everything that exists. There is a spiritual essence to all that is and it is this truth that is communicated in language. Nevertheless, this quasi-mystical understanding of language, which is only possible on the basis of the creation of the world *through* language (Genesis 1), is heavily qualified. For Benjamin, *human* language is *not* language *as such*. The original 'Adamic' language before God consisted in *naming* and the status of such language was not the disclosure of facts but the communication of 'communicability as such.' It is obvious that revelation is central to Benjamin's delineation of language 'as such' and that he depends on the thought of the early German Romantic philosopher J. G. Hamann who criticized purely natural explanations for the origin of language (see *Herder, J. G.*) and claimed that language and its use were dependent on the constant and immutable language of God. The fall away from the perfect word of creation (Babel), argues Benjamin, to the imperfections and plurality of human language results in a linguistic being who laments this loss of purity.

These themes are more fully developed in Benjamin's later work on Baroque Tragic Drama in which Benjamin concentrates on the place and status of allegory in the work of seventeenth-century Protestant writers. The use of allegory in this period moves hand in hand with a loss of faith in the proximity of the supernatural. The profuse nature of human utterance conveys the absence of revelation and the loss of salvation. Language as such is lost in the babble of the language of humanity. Human beings in the modern world are marked—as was Benjamin—by the melancholy of this loss.

See also: Allegory.

Bibliography

Benjamin W 1996 In: Bullock M, Jennings M W (eds.) *Selected Writings: Volume 1, 1913–1926*. Harvard University Press, Cambridge, MA

Benjamin W 1996 In: Jennings M W (ed.) *Selected Writings: Volume 2, 1927–1934*. Harvard University Press, Cambridge, MA

Benjamin W 1977 *Origin of the German Tragic Drama* [trans. J. Osborne]. Verso, London

Handelman S A 1991 *Fragments of Redemption*. Indiana University Press, Bloomington, IN

Wolin R 1994 *Walter Benjamin: An Aesthetic of Redemption*. University of California Press, Berkeley, CA

Bergsträsser, Gotthelf (1886–1933)

A. Shivtiel

Bergsträsser was one of the most distinguished Semitic philologists. He was born in Oberlosa, Germany and was killed in an accident while on holiday in the Bavarian mountains. He studied and later taught classical and oriental languages and literatures and in particular was an acknowledged expert on Arabic, Hebrew, and Aramaic. He was a professor at the University of Constantinople, Turkey, and during World War I became a German liaison officer with the Ottoman Army. It was at this time (1915), that Bergsträsser published two of his well-known books, *Sprachatlas von Syrien und Palästina* and *Neuaramäische Märchen und andere Texte aus Ma'lula*. The first work is an atlas of the spoken Arabic dialects in Syria and Palestine, whereas the latter work deals with folktales in the neo-Aramaic dialect used in the village of Ma'lula in Syria. To those he later added a glossary for the neo-aramaic dialects of Ma'lula (1921). He was assigned to the task of preparing the 29th edition of Wilhelm Gesenius's *Hebräische Grammatik* which was first published in 1813 (see also *Gesenius, Wilhelm*). Since this book became one of the most important grammar books of Biblical Hebrew, twenty-eight editions of this work had been re-edited and updated from time to time, first by Gesenius himself and later by E. Rodiger and E. Kautzsch. The latter, who was responsible for its 22nd–28th editions re-edited and enlarged the 28th edition which appeared in 1910 and which was used for the second edition of the English translation, prepared by A. E. Cowley (the first English translation had been published in 1898).

Bergsträsser updated the work and published it in two stages: the first part appeared in 1918 and the second part in 1926, when he was acting as professor of Semitica at the University of Munich. His edition of Gesenius's *Hebrew Grammar* is so different from all previous editions and so much enlarged that it only covers, apart from a short introduction to the Semitic languages, a chapter on Hebrew phonology and a chapter on the verb system, mainly based on the comparative study of grammar. The pronouns, nouns, and particles were planned to follow it together with a new part which was supposed to cover Hebrew syntax, but this was never achieved, because of his other interests, mainly in the field of Arabic, and because of the vicissitudes caused by World War I and his early death.

Bergsträsser's contribution to the study of the Arabic language, Arabic dialectology, Qur'anic studies, and Islamic law won him a worldwide reputation among scholars. Thus, his works *Zum arabischen Dialekt von Damascus* (1924); *hunain Ibn Ishak und seine Schule* (1913), *Hunain Ibn Ishak über die syrischen und arabischen Galen–übersetzungen* (1925–32), and *Grundzüge des islamischen Rechts* (1935), are still regarded as classical sources. His work on *Einführung in die semitischen Sprachen* (1928) is in fact an excellent introduction to the Semitic languages including a synopsis of their grammars and texts in all the major languages. He also prepared translations into Arabic of works originally written in Greek and wrote on various aspects of Qur'ānic studies, including the preparation of Qur'anic manuscripts which were collected for the purpose of comparative analysis of the various versions.

He was well known for his opposition to Nazism and helped many Jewish scholars to escape from Germany and find jobs in other countries.

See also: Arabic; Aramaic, Jewish; Gesenius; Wilhelm; Hebrew, Biblical and Jewish; Qur'ān; Semitic Languages.

Bibliography

Rabin C 1972 Introduction to the Hebrew edition. In: Bergsträsser G (ed.) *Hebräische Grammatik*, translated into Hebrew by Ben Asher M. Magnes Press, The Hebrew University, Jerusalem

Encyclopaedia Judaica 1971 *Bergsträsser, Gotthelf*. Keter Publishing House, Jerusalem

Bhartṛhari (c. 500 CE)

H. Coward

Bhartṛhari is a renowned author of Sanskrit literature and philosophy. His book the *Vākyapadīya* is foundational for the Grammarian School of Indian Philosophy and systematizes speculations about language (vāk) present in Vedas (Hindu scripture). For Bhartṛhari, language is divine in nature. His viewpoint is very similar to The Gospel According to John, Chapter 1, Verse 1, 'In the beginning was the Word, and the Word was with God, and the Word was God.' Bhartṛhari's term for God is *Śabdabrahman*—the intertwined unity of word and consciousness that is ultimate reality and both the material and efficient cause of creation. OM, the sacred syllable, is held by Bhartṛhari to have flashed forth in the mind of *Śabdabrahman* while in deep meditation giving birth first to the Vedas and then to all of language. As a manifestation of divine consciousness, language is the source of all knowledge and provides a spiritual discipline (a word-yoga) by which release or salvation may be realized. This word-yoga involves: (a) correct word use (following the rules of grammar) and (b) the repeated chanting of words or phrases (selected by one's teacher or *guru*) until the obstacles of passion and ignorance, which obscure the divine nature of one's consciousness, are removed.

Exact details about Bhartṛhari's life are not fully known. Tradition dates him around 500 CE in India and suggests that he was a king who gave up his worldly life (due to the inconstancy of women) and became a *sannyāsin* or forest dweller. In addition to establishing himself in the classical Indian tradition as a grammarian and a metaphysician, Bhartṛhari is also well known for his Sanskrit poetry—especially his *Vairāgya-Śataka* or 'Hundred Verses on Renunciation.' Bhartṛhari's life has been dramatized by Harihara in his *Bhartṛharinirveda*. In this story Bhartṛhari is portrayed as a student of Goraksanātha, from whom he learns Yoga and renounces the world. According to I-tsing, the Chinese Buddhist pilgrim, who studied at the Nalunda monastry/University in India, Bhartṛhari was a contemporary of Dharmapāla (CE 530–561). Quotations from Bhartṛhari are frequently found in Buddhist texts of the period.

While Bhartṛhari's poetry may still be found on the lips of Indians today, his most important contribution to modern life is in the field of religious experience. It is Bhartṛhari's understanding of language as revelation of the Divine and as a means of Yoga that has a contemporary fascination. Rather than trusting in the methods of science, reason and historical analysis to take one to the essence of the Divine, Bhartṛhari counsels trust in and deep meditation upon the revealed word itself. In response to the modern fascination for any meditational technique that will raise one beyond empirical or rational consciousness, Bhartṛhari offers a spiritual message. That desired higher state of consciousness is already present within language itself. But the higher levels of language/consciousness are known only through the special words of scriptural revelation. Therefore, meditate on such Divine Words, with no thought for yourself. Let your consciousness be filled with their truth and power, and the ultimate religious experience of knowing God will be yours.

See also: Word of God; Mantra; Hinduism.

Bibliography

Coward H G 1976 *Bhartṛhari.* G K Hall, Boston

Coward H G, Raja K K 1990 *The Philosophy of the Grammarians.* Princeton University Press, Princeton, NJ

Miller B S 1967 *Bhartṛhari: Poems.* Columbia University Press, New York

Subramania Iyer K A (translator) 1965 *The Vākyapadīya of Bhartṛhari.* Deccan College, Poona

Black, Matthew (1908–94)

W. McKane

After a distinguished career at the University of Glasgow, Matthew Black went to the University of Bonn, was a pupil of Paul Kahle and became a doctor in 1937. The influence which Kahle exerted on a young Matthew Black may be gathered from his description of Kahle as 'the doyen of European Orientalists.' Black's Bonn thesis on the text of a Syriac (Melchite) liturgical document was published in 1954. With respect to its linguistic area, his thesis presaged his best known book, *An Aramaic Approach to the Gospels and Acts* (1946), but his interest in the liturgy of the Syrian Church, in the Syriac language and in the New Testament Peshitta is vouched for by publications at different periods of his life.

Black's approach to the *Aramaic of the Gospels and Acts* is both linguistic and textual. The latter betrays an abiding interest in Greek manuscripts and in textual criticism: he was involved with others in the production of the *Greek New Testament* (1966), a project of the Bible Societies. The former led him to review the work of those who had earlier investigated evidences of Aramaic behind the Greek of the New Testament, Wellhausen, Nestlē, Dalman, Torrey, and Burney. His most fundamental quarrel with them was that they had been undiscriminating in their choice of Aramaic and had not identified the Palestinian Aramaic dialect which would have elucidated the Aramaic background of the Gospels. There was a second (1954) and third edition (1967).

Matthew Black's earliest article on the Dead Sea Scrolls shows that he was in the field before September 1953. *The Scrolls and Christian Origins* (1966) is his major book, along with *The Scrolls and Christianity: Historical and Theological Significance* (1969) which he edited and to which he contributed. Otherwise he published several articles. His interest in the Scrolls was that of a New Testament scholar. He identified the Qumran community as Essenes and set it in the context of Jewish sectarianism, discussing the extent of its connections with Christian origins. He states that there is evidence for some kind of link between Qumran and emerging Christianity, but he argues that direct dependence has not been demonstrated.

He agrees with Renan that Christianity was an Essenism which succeeded and the implication of this conclusion would appear to be that Jesus emerged from Jewish sectarianism and not from mainstream Judaism. The 'Son of Man' topic appears as early as 1948 with its emphasis on 'The Similitudes of Enoch' (*I Enoch* 37–71) which he describes as a pre-Christian, Jewish apocalypse. He published a Greek text of Enoch in 1970, but the culmination of his work on the Suffering Servant and the Son of Man, which he developed in articles between 1952 and 1976 was his last book, *The Book of Enoch or I Enoch* (1985), that is, the Ethiopic Enoch. He printed a revised version of the translation done by R. H. Charles and continued to hold that the Son of Man of the Similitudes is the foundation of Son of Man christology in the Gospels.

Bibliography

Black M 1946 *An Aramaic Approach to the Gospels and Acts.* Clarendon Press, Oxford

Brock S 1969 Review of an Aramaic approach to the gospels (1967). *Journal of Theological Studies* **20**: 274–8

McKane W 1995 Matthew Black 1908–1994. *Proceedings of the British Academy* **90**: 283–94

Bovelles, Charles de (1479–1566)

C. Demaizière

Bovelles was born in Saint-Quentin in 1479; he died in Ham (Somme) in 1566. A philosopher, theologian, and mathematician, he also wrote a treatise on his linguistic thoughts in 1533, published by Robert Etienne in Paris: *Liber de differentia vulgarium linguarum et Gallici sermonis varietate*. It is his only book on linguistic matters. He was the disciple of Jacques Lefèvre d'Etaples, then became a professor, possibly of mathematics. After various trips to Switzerland, Germany, Spain, and Italy he lived for some time in Paris before settling in Picardy from where he maintained an important correspondence in Latin with French and foreign scholars. He was appointed canon of the collegiate church in Saint-Quentin, then in Noyon.

In his treatise, he raises the question of the relation between the vernacular languages, French in particular, and Latin. As French grammar books were just beginning to be published, Bovelles wanted to show that the idea of fixing rules for the language is utopian considering the instability of language and the inconsistency of its use. He gives a historical account of the shaping of the French language with its parenthood to Latin; then in a sort of phonetic approach, he studies the pronunciation of the letters of the Latin alphabet and its variations under the influence of heaven (*horoscopus caeli*) and the will of men (*arbitrium hominum*). His conclusion is that the vernacular language shows too many disadvantages for it to be corrected with rules and that none of its dialectal forms could be chosen as a model. Latin only is unalterable, the ideal archetype being the original language, the one used by God when he spoke to Adam and Eve, the one all men will find again on judgment day. This treatise is followed by a sort of etymological dictionary presenting tables of words that are explained and commented upon. It is to be noticed that about 60 percent of the etymologies provided are correct, which is a rather good score at a time when the most fanciful explanations were given as to the origin of the French language. Finally, the book closes on a brief and rather flighty collection of onomastic topography, which constitutes no more than a curiosity.

Bibliography

Bovelles C de 1973 (ed. Dumont-Demaizière C) *Sur les langues vulgaires et la variété de la langue française*. Klincksieck, Paris (Contains facsimile of Latin text of 1533)

Demaizière C 1983 *La grammaire française au XVIème siècle*. Atelier National Reproduction des thèses, Université de Lille III, Paris

Université François Rabelais Centre d'études supérieures de la Renaissance 1982 Colloque international de Noyon. *Charles de Bovelles et son cinquième centenaire (1479–1979)*. Trédaniel, Paris

Caldwell, Robert (1814–91)

R. E. Asher

Born of Scottish parents on May 7, 1814 in County Antrim, Ireland, Robert Caldwell was Bishop of Tinnevelly (modern Tirunelveli) and coadjutor to the Bishop of Madras from 1877 until 7 months before his death on August 28, 1891. After completing his school education, mainly in Glasgow, he was accepted by the London Missionary Society and sent to study at the University of Glasgow, from where he graduated in 1837. While there he developed a passionate interest in comparative philology. Shortly after graduation he left for Madras and had the good fortune during the voyage of receiving advice on linguistic matters from the eminent Telugu scholar Charles Philip Brown (1798–1884).

In 1841 Caldwell began 50 years of missionary service in Tinnevelly. His particular concern was education, and he established numerous schools for boys and girls. Having embarked on the intensive study of Tamil during his first year in India, he had an impressive knowledge of the language. One of the uses he made of this knowledge was in helping with the revision of the Tamil version of the Prayer Book and of the Bible.

Caldwell published widely—works on South Indian history, archaeology and anthropology as well as collections of lectures and sermons—but as far as posterity is concerned, his major achievement is his *Comparative Grammar of the Dravidian or South-Indian Family of Languages* of 1856, which appeared in a considerably revised edition in 1875 and which, further revised by other hands, has been several times republished in English and in a Tamil translation.

Recognition of the existence of the Dravidian languages as a separate family came with E. W. Ellis's (d. 1819) 'Note to the Introduction' in A. D. Campbell's (d. 1857) *Grammar of... Teloogoo* (1816), but it was with the publication of Caldwell's influential work that Dravidian linguistics as a major field of study is seen to begin. Caldwell had come to the conclusion that 'the supposition of the derivation of the Dravidian languages from the Sanskrit... is now known to be entirely destitute of foundation' (1856: 29) before learning of Ellis's pioneer work, and it was he who gave the family the name by which it is known (Caldwell 1894: 150).

For Caldwell there were 11 Dravidian languages—Tamil, Telugu, Canarese (Kannada), Malayâlam, Tulu, Tuda (Toda), Kôta, Gônd(i), Ku(vi), Rajmahal (Malto), and Ûrâon (Kurukh)—with Brahuî containing a significant 'Drâvidian element' (1856: 23). The bulk of his *Grammar* is concerned with a comparison of the forms, mainly phonological and morphological, of the first nine, but there is some discussion of syntax. In the parts that speculate on the wider affinities of Dravidian (Caldwell favoring 'Scythian,' and particularly 'Finnish or Ugrian'), there are statements which would now be seen to fall under the heading of typology.

At the level of detail Caldwell is known for his 'law' of 'the convertibility of surds and sonants' (1875: 21–23). This is intended to encapsulate a feature of Dravidian phonology, as exemplified most notably in Tamil, by which in the plosive system the feature of voice is nondistinctive, surds and sonants (voiceless and voiced sounds respectively) being in complementary distribution.

See also: Gundert, Hermann; Missionaries; Tamil.

Bibliography

Caldwell R 1856 *A comparative Grammar of the Dravidian or South-Indian Family of Languages*. Harrison, London

Caldwell R 1894 *Reminiscences... ed. by J L Wyatt*. Addison, Madras

Day E H 1896 *Mission Heroes. Bishop Caldwell*. Society for Promoting Christian Knowledge, London

Ellis F W 1816 Note to the Introduction. In: Campbell A D 1816 *A Grammar of the Teloogoo Language, commonly called the Gentoo*. College Press, Madras

Carey, William (1761–1834)

A. Mukherjee

William Carey, a cobbler who became a Dissenting minister, founded the Baptist Missionary Society in 1792. He arrived in Calcutta in 1793, found employment in an indigo factory in Malda district and began studying Sanskrit and Bengali. His goal was to translate the Bible into all the major languages of India.

In 1800 Carey moved to Serampore where, with Joshua Marshman (1768–1837) and William Ward (1769–1823), he established the Serampore Mission. The Serampore Press was set up and supervised by Ward with Panchanan Karmakar as punchcutter. Carey's translation of Matthew's Gospel was published in 1800 and his complete Bengali Bible in 1809. Bitter controversy arose over Carey's decision to translate *baptise* with *abagāhan* 'immerse.' Anglicans preferred a transliteration of the Greek.

The Serampore Community Agreement of 1804 included the commitment 'To labour unceasingly in biblical translation.' At one time 30 pandits were employed in translation and by 1837 the Bible, or parts of it, had been printed in around 40 languages or dialects. First drafts were undertaken by pandits and then revised by the missionaries, but in the case of Bengali, Sanskrit, and Marathi, Carey himself did the initial draft. The Press also published the first Bengali periodical *Digdarśan* and weekly paper *Samācār Darpan*, as well as texts translated from English for educational purposes.

From 1801 Carey was employed to teach Sanskrit and Bengali, and later Marathi, at the Government's Fort William College. In order to obtain Bengali prose for use in class, Carey encouraged his pandit colleagues to translate from Sanskrit and write original works. Carey himself compiled *Kathopakathan* (1801) colloquial conversations between country folk, and *Itihāsmālā* (1812) a collection of stories. He has been called the father of modern Bengali literature, but a more balanced assessment sees him as pioneer of a revived interest in the vernacular.

Carey wrote a Sanskrit grammar, a Bengali grammar and dictionary, a Marathi grammar and dictionary, and Panjabi, Kanarese and Telegu grammars. In accordance with the evangelical aim, which underpinned all his language work, these books were intended to help future missionaries acquire the Indian languages. His planned dictionary of all the oriental languages derived from Sanskrit, with corresponding Greek and Hebrew words, was intended to assist Scripture translation. The proofs for this perished in the fire that destroyed the Press in

1812. Carey was elected to the Asiatic Society in 1806 and with that Society's support, he and Marshman began translating the *Rāmāyaṇa*. In addition he developed a keen interest in horticulture and agriculture. In 1807 Brown University USA awarded Carey an honorary DD.

Carey constantly revised his Bengali Bible, the final edition appearing in 1832, but his translations have been criticized for following English syntax. Although his prose is crude and often incomprehensible, Carey strove to preserve Bengali clause order, a principle abandoned by later Baptist translators. His revisions move from colloquial towards sanskritized language. Carey firmly believed that Indians, not Europeans, should undertake future translation work.

See also: Missionaries; Christianity in South Asia.

Bibliography

Carey S P 1934 *William Carey 1761–1834*, 8th edn. Carey Press, London

Potts E D 1967 *British Baptist Missionaries in India 1793–1837*. Cambridge University Press, Cambridge

Sen Gupta, Kanti Prasanna 1971 *The Christian Missionaries in Bengal 1793–1833*. Firma, Calcutta

Cerulli, Enrico (1898–1988)

A. K. Irvine

By profession an administrator and diplomat, Enrico Cerulli's massive contribution to Ethiopian cultural, ethnographic, and language studies reveal him as one of the ablest orientalists of his age. Born in Naples on February 15, 1898, he studied Arabic and Islam at the Oriental Institute there, and at the age of barely 18 produced studies of Amharic popular poetry and Somali customary law which immediately established his scholarly reputation. In 1920 he entered the Italian Colonial Service in Somalia, joining the Ministry of Foreign Affairs in 1925. Largely self-taught in Somali and Oromo, he published several fundamental ethnographic and linguistic studies, notably 'The folk-literature of the Galla of southern Abyssinia' (*Harvard African Studies* **3**: 11–228) in 1922. His direct involvement with Ethiopia began in 1926–9 when he joined the Italian Legation in Addis Ababa and was able to undertake extensive travels in the south and west of Ethiopia, described in his *Etiopia occidentale: dallo Scioa alle frontiere del Sudan* (2 vols., Rome, 1930, 1933). After further service as Secretary-General of the Ministry for Italian Africa and, from 1935 till 1937, in the League of Nations at Geneva, he was in 1938 appointed Governor of the Province of Harar, where he remained until 1940. The fruits of his wide experience of the complex language mosaic of southern and western Ethiopia are contained in his *Studi etiopici*, of which the first volume is devoted to a descriptive study of the Semitic language of the Muslim Hararis (*La lingua e la storia di Harar*, Rome, 1936). Further volumes were concerned with the Cushitic and Omotic languages of the Lake Abaye region of southwest Ethiopia: *La lingua e la storia dei Sidamo* (Rome, 1938); *Il linguaggio dei Giangerò ed alcune lingue Sidama dell'Omo (Basketo, Ciara, Zaissè)* (Rome, 1938); and *La lingua caffina* (Rome, 1951). Other languages on which he provided data are the Hamer, Gidicho, and the Wellamo dialects (Omotic), Arbore and Deresa (Cushitic), and Berta, Majang (Mekeyer), and Tirma (Sudanic).

Cerulli's direct association with the Horn of Africa ended in 1940 when he retired to resume his scholarly interests in Rome. Although his political record in Italian-occupied Ethiopia was impeccable, it was no longer possible for him to work in the newly-liberated country. However, his interest remained undiminished. He resumed his political career in 1944 and from 1950 until 1954 served as Italian Ambassador to Persia. There he concerned himself with medieval Persian religious drama and the Neo-Aramaic dialects of Persian Azerbaijan, of which he published meticulously annotated texts in his *Testi neo-aramaci dell'Iran settentrionale* (Naples, 1971). On his return to Italy he was appointed Counsellor of State from 1955 until 1968 when he finally retired to devote the remainder of his life to scholarship. He died in Rome on September 19, 1988.

After his departure from Ethiopia in 1940 Cerulli continued to write extensively on her societies and languages, but a notable shift took place in his interests. It is to this period that some of his most influential work belongs. Recognizing the significance of monasticism in Ethiopian society, he published a number of important Ethiopic hagiographical texts and perceptive studies of the cultural interchange between medieval European and Oriental Christianity, notably in his magisterial *Il Libro etiopico dei miracoli di Maria e le sue fonti nelle letterature del Medio Evo latino* (Rome, 1943), and his *Etiopi in Palestina: storia della communità etiopica di Gerusalemme* (2 vols., Rome, 1943, 1947). His *La letteratura etiopica* (Milan, 1968) is the only work on the subject to attempt an aesthetic appraisal of classical Ethiopic literature.

See also: Ge'ez.

Bibliography

Ricci L 1988 (1990) Enrico Cerulli. *Rassegna di Studi Etiopici* **32**: 5–19

Champollion, Jean-François (1790–1832)

J. D. Ray

French Egyptologist and the decipherer of hieroglyphs, Champollion was born at Figeac (Lot), December 23, 1790, but was educated and spent most of his early life in Grenoble. Hagiographers have tended to exaggerate Champollion's childhood achievements, but it is clear that from his earliest years he set himself the mission to be the decipherer of Egyptian, and the rest of his short life was a translation of this dream into reality. He published his first full-scale work on Pharaonic Egypt before he was 21, and an incessant stream of publications followed. This constant activity was a factor in his early death, and many of his manuscripts were edited posthumously by his elder brother. At one point overwork led to a breakdown; his way of recuperating was to learn Chinese. The Rosetta Stone (see *Rosetta Stone*) was discovered in 1798, and Champollion soon became acquainted with it. Nevertheless, he was convinced that Ancient Egyptian writing (see *Egyptian Hieroglyphs*) was symbolic, and could not be a rational script; as a result his early work on the language was inconclusive, although he was still able to make remarkable contributions to Egyptian history and the study of its religion. The breakthrough in the study of hieroglyphs was made by Thomas Young (see *Young, Thomas*), and the extent to which Champollion was influenced by Young remains debatable. Probably Champollion would have reached the same conclusions as Young independently, sooner or later. A more important factor was the fundamental difference between the two men: Young was a scientific genius with no interest in Egyptology, while Champollion was a linguistic genius with an obsession with the subject. It was precisely this combination which was necessary for success. Champollion's *Lettre à M. Dacier* of September, 1822 is rightly seen as the birthdate of Egyptology, and the first chair in the subject was created for him at the Collège de France in 1831. In 1828–29 he made a survey of the monuments surviving in Egypt, and the published results of this visit are still of supreme interest.

Champollion played a fringe role in revolutionary politics, and his essays and letters, Egyptology apart, would probably earn him a minor place in nineteenth-century literature. His posthumous reputation is such that he probably has more streets named after him than any other figure in the history of linguistics, but it is impossible to begrudge him this distinction. His decipherment of Egyptian was a considerable moment in the history of Western thought, and in the search for its origins.

Bibliography

Bresciani E (ed.) 1978 *Jean-François Champollion; Letters à Zelmire*. L'Asiathèque, Paris
Dawson W R, Uphill E P 1972 *Who Was Who in Egyptology*, 2nd edn. Egypt Exploration Society, London
Hartleben H 1983 *Champollion; sa vie et son oeuvre 1790–1832*, rev. edn. Pygmalion, Paris

Coverdale, Miles (1487–1569)

G. L. Jones

Coverdale, Miles (1487–1569), Catholic turned Puritan, is remembered chiefly for his translation of the Bible into English. A native of Yorkshire, he studied at Cambridge where he became a priest and an Augustinian friar in 1514. But his enthusiasm for reform led him to leave the order in 1526. He moved to Hamburg in 1528 to escape persecution for preaching against the use of images and the practice of confession. There he assisted Tyndale in translating the Pentateuch. He was in Antwerp when he completed his own translation of the Bible in 1535. In that year he went back to England to prepare the Great Bible of 1539. He spent 1540–48 at Strasbourg where he made the acquaintance of Calvin. After his return to England he played an active part in the reforms of Edward VI and was consecrated Bishop of Exeter in 1551. Exiled again under Mary, he settled in Geneva where he was influenced by John Knox. Though he returned to England in 1559, he did not resume his episcopal duties but chose instead to take a leading role in the Puritan party.

Coverdale's Bible, published on October 4, 1535, probably at Cologne, was the first complete Bible to appear in English. In his dedicatory letter to the king, Coverdale admitted that he knew no Hebrew and had only a smattering of Greek. The 'five sundry interpreters' on whom he claims to have relied have been identified as Jerome, Tyndale, Pagninus, Luther, and the group of Zurich divines led by Zwingli. C. S. Lewis describes him as being a 'translator whose choice of rendering came nearest to being determined by taste.' In other words, since he had no knowledge of the original languages, he had to choose between his 'sundry interpreters.' In this he was guided by his own judgement, which, fortunately, was sound.

Within two years of the publication of Coverdale's Bible another English version appeared. Though prepared by John Rogers, the first of the Marian martyrs, it was known as 'Matthew's Bible.' For different reasons both translations were unsatisfactory. Coverdale's version was based on other translations rather than on the original languages. That of Rogers was doctrinally suspect because of its tendency to support the Reformers in its marginal notes. Thomas Cromwell therefore invited Coverdale to prepare yet another version which was to be based on the original texts. Coverdale complied and in April 1539 produced the Great Bible which claimed on its title-page to be 'truly translated after the verity of the Hebrew and Greek texts by the diligent study of diverse excellent learned men expert in the aforesaid tongues.' For this version Coverdale derived considerable benefit from the Hebrew-Latin version of Sebastian Muenster with its copious explanatory notes on difficult and obscure words in the text of the OT. The translation was a success and immediately became the 'authorized version' of its day, holding its ground until 1560.

Perhaps the most significant characteristic of Coverdale as a translator is his rendering of Hebrew poetry. Two centuries before Lowth's analysis of the parallelism of meaning which is fundamental to Hebrew verse, Coverdale had reproduced the pattern of the original. There is good reason why his version of the Psalter was included in the Book of Common Prayer.

See also: English Bible; Jerome; Tyndale, W.; Luther, M.; Wycliffe, J.

Bibliography

Butterworth C C 1941 *The Literary Lineage of the King James Bible 1340–1611*. Pennsylvania University Press, Philadelphia

Haugaard W P 1984 *The Bible in the Anglican Reformation*. Morehouse Barlow, Wilton, CN

Mozley J F 1953 *Coverdale and his Bibles*. Lutterworth, London

Crowther, Samuel Ajayi (1806/08–91)

J. D. Y. Peel

Bishop Crowther was the first black African to be consecrated an Anglican bishop. Through his work as lexicographer and translator he pioneered the creation of Standard Yoruba, one of the foremost literary languages of West Africa.

He was born as Ajayi ca. 1806/08 in the small town of Osogun, about 150 miles to the interior of Lagos, in the Yoruba kingdom of Oyo. In 1821 he was kidnapped by raiders and sold into slavery; but he was rescued from a Portuguese ship by the British anti-slavery squadron and taken to Sierra Leone. Here in 1825 he was baptized—his 'English' names being taken from a leading clerical backer of the Church Missionary Society—by the Rev. J. Raban, a missionary who compiled some Yoruba vocabularies and for whom Crowther worked as an informant. In 1827 Crowther entered Fourah Bay College as its first student and later worked for several years as a schoolmaster and then as Tutor at the College. His own linguistic interests developed when he was chosen to accompany the Niger Expedition of 1841, of which, with the Rev. J. F. Schön, he published an account. After further training in London, he was ordained priest in 1843, the year in which he published his *Vocabulary of the Yoruba Language*. This also included notes on grammar.

It was the CMS which introduced 'Yoruba'—hitherto a name the Hausa applied to the Oyo—as the common designation for a group of peoples who spoke closely related dialects and shared much common culture, but who in their homeland lacked a common name. (In Freetown they were known as 'Aku.') In 1845 Crowther returned to the Yoruba country as one of the founding members of the CMS Yoruba mission, which soon established its main base at Abeokuta, capital of the Egba. More important than Crowther's directly evangelistic work was his key role as the chief translator of the Bible. The project began in 1847 with the Gospels and continued over the next three decades, with much of the later work being done by other African clergy under Crowther's supervision, until published in its entirety in 1889. The language of this translation—based chiefly on the Oyo and Egba dialects—gained enormous authority among educated and Christian Yoruba. Being also used in primers, catechisms and readers, and (from the 1880s) in a growing vernacular literature, it played a decisive role in the formation of modern Yoruba ethnic identity.

Crowther went on two further Niger Expeditions in 1854 and 1857, and became the focus of the hopes of the CMS Secretary, Henry Venn, to develop an indigenous church under African leadership. Despite opposition from many white missionaries, Crowther was, in 1864, made Bishop of the 'countries of Western Africa beyond [the Queen's] dominions.' In practice this meant, not Yorubaland, but the Lower Niger which was staffed with African mission personnel. Notwithstanding his pioneering labors in this sphere, Crowther's leadership of the Niger Mission came under severe criticism from Europeans in the late 1880s, much of it racially motivated, and he resigned early in 1891. He died in Lagos a few months later. Crowther's humiliation at the hands of his European critics was a major spur to the growth of African nationalist sentiment in both church and state. But his most enduring legacy has been the Bible in the Yoruba language. In its cultural significance for the modern Yoruba, it may justly be compared to Luther's German Bible.

See also: Christianity in Africa; Missionaries.

Bibliography

Ajayi J F A 1960 How Yoruba was reduced to writing. *Odu* **8**: 49–58

Ajayi J F A 1965 *Christian Missions in Nigeria, 1841–91.* Longman, Harlow

Ajayi J F A 1967 Samuel Ajayi Crowther of Oyo. In: Curtin P D (ed.) *Africa Remembered.* University of Wisconsin Press, Madison, WI

Crowther S A 1843 *A Vocabulary of the Yoruba Language.* Church Missionary Society, London

Hair P E H 1967 *The Early Study of Nigerian Languages.* Cambridge University Press, Cambridge

Cyril and Methodios

Archimandrite Ephrem

Constantine, more commonly known by his monastic name Cyril, and his elder brother, who is always known by his monastic name Methodios, were from Thessalonika, which included many Macedonian Slavs. In 840, when Constantine was fourteen, their father died and the boy was sent to Constantinople, where he was taught by Photios, the future patriarch. He was appointed *Chartophylax*, librarian, of the Great Church, and his intellectual qualities earned him the nickname of 'the Philosopher.' His elder brother had abandoned his secular career to become a monk on Mount Olympos in Bithynia. In 863 Prince Rastislav of Greater Moravia sent an embassy to the Emperor Michael III asking him to send a 'bishop and teacher' to preach to the newly converted Slavs in their own language. The Emperor chose Constantine, who was to be accompanied by his brother Methodios, remarking, 'You are both from Thessalonika, and all Thessalonians speak pure Slavonic.' Rastislav's motives were not purely religious; he was also keen to secure ecclesiastical autonomy and political independence from the Franks.

Before leaving Constantine composed an alphabet and began work on the translation of the Gospels into Slavonic. The alphabet was almost certainly not the one now known as Cyrillic, but rather the older Glagolitic. While the Cyrillic alphabet is clearly based on the Greek, the origin of the Glagolitic is quite obscure. It was once widely held that the complex letter forms are based on Greek minuscule script. R. Auty, on the other hand, holds that the letters derive from a number of different sources, such as Greek letters, Christian symbols and possibly Semitic and Coptic sources. Once in Moravia the brothers set to work translating liturgical texts, but were soon involved in controversy with Western clerics who held that the only languages that could be used in the services of the Church were Hebrew, Greek and Latin. Constantine dubbed them 'trilinguists' or 'Pilatians.' In 867 the brothers traveled to Rome, where Pope Adrian II publicly approved the use of Slavonic for the Liturgy. Cyril became a monk in Rome just fifty days before his death in 869. Methodios was sent as legate to Pannonia and made bishop of the revived see of Sirmium. In this way Pannonia and Greater Moravia were withdrawn from Bavarian jurisdiction. This provoked a violent reaction and Methodios went into exile for three years. In 879 John VIII summoned him to Rome to answer charges of heresy and of using Slavonic in services. The Pope defended the 'trilingual' view of liturgical language and specifically forbade the use of Slavonic, except for preaching. However, Methodios defended himself successfully on both counts and in June 880 the Pope sent a bull, *Industriae tuae*, to Rastislav's successor Sventopluk in which he asserts the important principle that there is no objection in faith or doctrine to the use of Slavonic in the services, since God, who made the three principal languages, also created all the others 'ad laudem et gloriam suam.' The Gospel, however, was to be read in Latin first. By the time of Methodios' death in 885 the translation into Slavonic of the whole Bible, except Maccabees, was complete. The next year his disciples were expelled from Moravia, but moved south and worked in Bulgaria, Bohemia and southern Poland with far reaching results.

See also: Old Church Slavonic; Christianity in Europe.

Bibliography

Auty R 1968 *Handbook of Old Church Slavonic*, Part II. London 1968, Athlone Press, London, pp. 1–14

Devos P 1967 Cyril and Methodius. In: *New Catholic Encyclopedia*, vol. 4

Cyril and Methodius. 1997 In: *The Oxford Dictionary of the Christian Church*, 3rd edn. Oxford University Press, Oxford

Parry K 1999 Cyril and Methodius. In: *The Blackwell Dictionary of Eastern Christianity*. Blackwell, Oxford

Daly, Mary (1930s–)

D. Sawyer

At the heart of Mary Daly's critique of patriarchy lies the conviction that male power is made absolute and affirmed through the construction and repetition of the words we think, speak, and write. She constantly reconceptualizes words and phrases in ways that unmask patriarchal bias. In her *Websters' First New Intergalactic Wickedery of the English Language*, written with Jane Caputi, she describes her linguistic task as a 'process of freeing words from the cages and prisons of patriarchal patterns,' prompted by the realization that 'words and women have served the fathers' sentences long enough' (p. 3). Daly was a key figure at the vanguard of second-wave feminist theology and philosophy. Her first book, *The Church and the Second Sex* (1968), presents an extensive critique of Christianity informed by the philosophy of Simone de Beauvoir, and reflecting on her own position as a Catholic woman in the immediate aftermath of the Second Vatican Council. Her disillusionment with the reforms of the Council intensified as it became apparent that they fell far short of the ideals voiced by the growing women's liberation movement in secular contexts, particularly in North America.

Her next book, *Beyond God the Father: Toward a Philosophy of Women's Liberation* (1973), with its intensified intellectual critique of Christianity along with its offer of an alternative feminist spirituality, marked her exit from traditional religion. She named her repositioning 'postchristian,' a term that she defines in the introduction to the 1975 edition of *The Church and the Second Sex*. This term is now used extensively to describe feminist religious writers who have a background in Christianity but through their encounter with feminism have concluded that the two are irreconcilable, and have moved away from a traditional Christian identity. *Beyond God the Father* offers an immanent notion of the divine, the 'Ultimate/Intimate Reality' (*Wickedary*, p. 64), through the use of the term 'be-ing': '(w)hy indeed must 'God' be a noun? Why not a verb—the most active and dynamic of all?' (p. 33). Although 'postchristian' continues to be a term used in the context of feminist spirituality, Daly abandoned it as a self-description when her subsequent ideas and beliefs developed in ways that signified a deliberate lack of engagement with the Christian tradition.

In current feminist thinking, Daly's position remains distinctive in its insistence on speaking for women as a single category in tension with a universal notion of patriarchy. This is at odds with the self-conscious shift made by many feminists, in reaction to criticism voiced by non-white and non-western women, towards the accommodation of difference, and away from the essentialism of 'woman's experience.' Despite her indifference to Christianity, her original critique of that tradition continues to be cited in debate, along with her iconoclastic maxims that encapsulate that critique: 'if god is male, then the male is god'; 'the most unholy trinity: rape, genocide and war' (1973, pp. 19, 114).

See also: Feminism; Irigary, L.; Kristeva, J.

Bibliography

Daly M 1968 *The Church and the Second Sex*. Harper and Row, New York

Daly M 1973 *Beyond God the Father: Toward a Philosophy of Women's Liberation*. Beacon Press, Boston

Daly M 1987 (with J.Caputi) *Websters' First New Intergalactic Wickedery of the English Language*. Beacon Press, Boston

Dante Alighieri (1265–1321)

M. Davie

Dante's *Divine Comedy*, written between c. 1308 and the poet's death in 1321, is not only the founding classic of Italian literature but a uniquely ambitious religious poem. His account of a journey through Hell, Purgatory and Paradise encompasses both a comprehensive judgement of the world of his time and a description of eternity culminating in a direct vision of God. Dante's awareness of the unprecedented nature of this undertaking led him to ask fundamental questions about language, both as a literary medium and as the means by which humanity expresses its understanding of the divine.

Dante was born in Florence in 1265. From 1295 he was actively involved in politics, and in 1300 was one of the city's six ruling Priors. Following a coup in 1301 Dante and other leading members of the governing party were exiled, and from early 1302 he never returned to Florence; after a decade of wandering among the courts of northern Italy he found refuge first in Verona, then in Ravenna. His reflection on his experience during the years of exile led to a growing conviction that the political and social ills of his time were the result of fundamental moral error, in which the Church, especially the papacy, bore a heavy responsibility. Given the Church's failure to provide spiritual leadership, Dante undertook his own urgent call for social and individual reform.

Dante's belief in both the universality and the timelessness of his message produced contrary pressures on his choice of language. On the one hand, his work was too important to be confined to the restricted readership of Latin; on the other, he aspired to write the epic of Christian Rome, comparable and complementary to the *Aeneid* (whose author Virgil is introduced as his guide in the first two parts of the *Comedy*). How should he combine the accessibility of the vernacular with the permanence of Latin? Dante addresses this question in the treatise *De vulgari eloquentia* ('On vernacular eloquence') (c. 1304–5), which first polemically asserts the intrinsic superiority of vernacular to the artificial 'grammar' of the classical languages, then proposes an 'illustrious vernacular' capable of achieving a degree of stability while retaining its contact with the spoken language. He sought to put this ideal into practice in a series of poems on ethical themes accompanied by a prose commentary, in the *Convivio* (c. 1304–8).

Both *De vulgari* and *Convivio* were left unfinished as the *Divine Comedy* took shape in Dante's mind. By calling his poem a comedy ('divine' is a conventional epithet added by later editors) Dante chose the classical genre which allowed the greatest variety of style and subject matter, enabling him to include passages ranging from vehement polemic to lyrical adoration. But Dante also saw his work as 'comic' in the more fundamental sense in which all human language is 'comic,' i.e. inadequate, in the face of ultimate reality. At the climax of the *Paradiso*, expressions of inadequacy alternate with passages of daring invention, and the final canto ends with an admission of defeat. But in the attempt Dante had achieved a work whose linguistic range was unprecedented in any European vernacular, thereby establishing his native Tuscan as the foundation of the language which became standard Italian.

Bibliography

Auerbach E 1965 *Literary Language and its Public in Late Latin Antiquity and in the Middle Ages*. Routledge, London

Curtius E R 1953 *European Literature and the Latin Middle Ages*. Routledge, London

Kirkpatrick R 1987 *Dante: The Divine Comedy*. Cambridge University Press, Cambridge

Davidson, Andrew Bruce (1831–1902)

W. Johnstone

Davidson, Andrew Bruce, a pioneer of biblical criticism, is recognized as the author of one of the first 'scientific' commentaries in English on the Hebrew Bible (Strahan 1917: 89). Davidson himself puts it: 'We in this country have been not unaccustomed to . . . creating Exegesis and Grammar by deduction from Dogmatic, instead of discovering Dogmatic by deduction from Grammar' (*Job* [1862], vi). He was born at Kirkhill, Ellon, Aberdeenshire, on April 25, 1831, the youngest of six children of a quarryman turned tenant farmer, and died in Edinburgh, February 24, 1902. He was educated at Marischal College, Aberdeen, where in 1849 he graduated with a degree in Mathematics. After a short time as a schoolmaster in his native Aberdeenshire, he studied theology from 1852 to 1856 at New College, Edinburgh, one of the three theological colleges set up by the Free Church of Scotland in the wake of the Disruption of the National Church of Scotland in 1843. In 1858 he was appointed first to a tutorship in Hebrew in New College and then in 1863 to the Chair of Hebrew, which he held for the rest of his life.

It was Davidson's achievement in an age of turbulent debate, not least within the church, about the status of the Bible, especially as that was thought to be affected by controversies about authorship and composition, to develop in the English-speaking world an academically disciplined approach to Biblical study that both satisfied the inquiring mind and left open the possibility of faith. That Davidson was able to accomplish this bridging task within one of the most theologically conservative churches while holding a Chair in its gift is testimony to his character and standing, and to his reputation as a commanding figure in the lecture room. By nature retiring and by upbringing reticent, he shunned the more adversarial advocacy of new methods of his brilliant younger contemporary and former student, William Robertson Smith (1846–94), which led to the latter's dismissal from his Aberdeen Hebrew Chair in 1881. The key to Davidson's approach was a linguistically soundly based appreciation and interpretation of the Hebrew Bible in itself. Thus he was able to maintain a certain theological and critical detachment: 'I dislike the old, I distrust the new.' His caution on the latter aspect led at least one Free Church colleague (A. B. Bruce) to remark that, in later life, Davidson had not maintained his place at the vanguard of the critical movement (Riesen 1985: 293, 355).

The purity of Davidson's scholarly approach is well indicated by his early writings, *Outlines of Hebrew Accentuation, Prose and Poetical* (1861), and *Commentary, Grammatical and Exegetical, on the Book of Job* (Vol. 1, 1862). The latter volume, predicated on the historical linguistics developed for the Semitic languages by Wilhelm Gesenius (1786–1842) (see *Gesenius, W.*), with its ready deployment of Arabic (which Davidson had studied while in Göttingen with Ewald) and an impressive array of other Semitic languages, and use of the ancient versions chiefly in the London Polyglot of 1657, covers only the first 14 chapters of *Job.* If academically rigorous, it was not commercially successful and the promised second volume was never published; Davidson did, however, contribute at a more popular level *Job* in the Cambridge Bible for Schools and Colleges (1884), for which series he also provided *Nahum, Habakkuk and Zephaniah* (1866) and *Ezekiel* (1892). Indicative of his interest in the Bible as a whole is his commentary on *Hebrews* (1882).

Davidson's *Introductory Hebrew Grammar*, which became the standard text book for generations of students internationally was first published in 1874: it has since passed through the hands of three successive editors and, almost completely transformed, still remains in print in the 27th edition, a monument to traditional Classics-influenced pedagogy. The companion volume on *Syntax*, published in 1894, was thoroughly revised only in 1994. His other chief literary and theological works (e.g., *Theology of the Old Testament*) were, in the main, edited posthumously: the debate about whether the editors correctly arranged these works and thus faithfully reflected development in Davidson's critical thought is perhaps testimony to an essentially enigmatic element in his make-up and theological outlook.

See also: Gesenius, Wilhelm; Bible; Hebrew, Biblical and Jewish.

Bibliography

Anderson G W 1975 Two Scottish Semitists. *Congress Volume Edinburgh 1974* (Vetus Testament Supplement 27). Brill, Leiden

Riesen R A 1985 *Criticism and Faith in Late Victorian Scotland: A. B. Davidson, William Robertson Smith and George Adam Smith.* University Press of America, Lanham, New York

Strahan J 1917 *Andrew Bruce Davidson.* Hodder and Stoughton, London

Delitzsch, Friedrich Conrad Gerhard (1850–1922)

G. L. Jones

Delitzsch, Friedrich Conrad Gerhard (1850–1922), an accomplished German linguist and one of the founders of modern Assyriology, was the son of the famous Lutheran biblical scholar of Jewish descent, Franz Delitzsch. Born in Erlangen and educated at the university of Berlin, he served as Professor of Assyriology in Leipzig (1877), Breslau (1893), and Berlin (1899).

His scholarly endeavours may be summarized under two main headings. First is the contribution he made to the study of ancient languages. His many textual studies placed the grammar of the Mesopotamian languages on a sound academic basis. His first major work was an investigation of the connection between Hebrew and Akkadian, *The Hebrew Language Viewed in the Light of Assyrian Research* (English translation 1883). This was followed by an Assyrian Grammar in 1889, an Assyrian Dictionary in 1896, and a Sumerian Grammar and Glossary in 1914. He and his pupils dominated Mesopotamian studies until World War I.

Second is the impact he made on biblical studies. As a member of the 'history of religions' school of thought, he traced much of the material found in the OT to Mesopotamian origins. Lectures which he delivered to the German Oriental Society in the presence of the Kaiser in 1902 were published a year later in Leipzig under the title *Babel und Bibel* (English translation Chicago 1903). In them he made public what every Assyriologist already knew, namely that there were obvious similarities between the Bible and the literature of the Ancient Near East. But the significance he saw in these similarities were unacceptable to members of faith communities. By calling into question the uniqueness of the Bible, by maintaining that the sources of Hebrew religion were to be found in Babylon and that Babylonian ideas were superior to those of Israel, he unleashed a fierce debate which became known as the 'Babel-Bible controversy' in which he was castigated by those who defended the antiquity and originality of the OT. The only appreciative result of the debate was that the tendency to treat the history and culture of Israel separately from its oriental environment was curbed.

Though silent for a while, Delitzsch returned to the fray in 1921 with the publication of *Die Grosse Täuschung* (The Great Deception), a highly antagonistic two-volume work in which he seeks to demonstrate that most of the OT is not fit to be regarded as Holy Scripture by Christians. He brands as inadequate the traditional method of regarding the biblical account of Israel's origins as the appropriate model for understanding the nation's history because the OT is essentially propaganda. In his view the Bible was an ancient 'deception,' a word which he applies liberally to the account of the conquest of Canaan, the Sinai revelation, the preaching of the prophets, and the religion of the Psalmists. The Hebrews were nothing but a crowd of 'robbing and murdering nomads' responsible for a book full of errors and exaggerations. His attack is reminiscent of that made by Marcion.

Though some discern an antisemitic motive behind Delitzsch's biblical studies, he must be credited with making his readers aware of the limitations of the OT, and warning them of the difficulties inherent in an uncritical acceptance of the written record.

Bibliography

Huffmon H B 1987 *Babel und Bibel*: the Encounter between Babylon and the Bible. In: O'Connor M P, Freedman D N (eds.) *Backgrounds for the Bible*. Eisenbrauns, Winona Lake, MI, pp. 125–136

Kraeling E G 1955 *The Old Testament since the Reformation*. Lutterworth, London, pp. 147–163

Sweek J 1995 The Monuments, the *Babel-Bible Streit* and Responses to Historical Criticism. In: Holloway S W, Handy L K (eds.) *The Pitcher is Broken*: *Memorial Essays for Gösta W. Ahlström*. Sheffield Academic Press, Sheffield, pp. 401–419

Derrida, Jacques (1930–)

G. Collins

Jacques Derrida is one of the most influential poststructuralist thinkers. His writing has interrogated the status of philosophy and literature by focusing on the ambiguities, contradictions, and aporias within texts. Derrida has always asserted the depth, complexity and indeterminacy of textuality. As a result many of Derrida's key ideas, such as deconstruction and *différance*, purposefully resist definition.

Born in 1930 at El-Biar in Algeria to Jewish parents, he grew up in an occupied and anti-Semitic Algeria. In 'Circumfession' he juxtaposes his religious origins in North Africa with a reading of St. Augustine (Bennington 1993). He moved to France, where he studied in Paris at the École Normale Supérieure (1952–6), before going on to teach philosophy at the Sorbonne between 1960 and 1984. Since then he has been Director of Studies at the École des Hautes Études en Sciences Sociales. As a friend of Paul de Man, and in dialogue with the Tel Quel group that included Julia Kristeva, Derrida's thought has remained at the heart of Continental, and increasingly Anglo–American, intellectual life. His frequent lecturing in the United States has assisted the wider dissemination of his thought.

Derrida's first major work was on the phenomenology of Edmund Husserl, preparing the way for his analysis of the sign *Of Grammatology* and *Speech and Phenomena* in 1967. Over the next five years he produced a series of seminal works in which he explored linguistic *différance*. Derrida's neologism *différance* encapsulates his understanding of the differing and deferring active-passivity of language. This analysis of language makes time and spatiality fundamental categories, and signals his fascination with Martin Heidegger. Derrida calls into question Western attempts to stabilize language and eradicate the 'play' (*jeu*) and inherent undecidability of textuality. In this he implicates Heidegger along with other practitioners of the 'metaphysics of presence.' Derrida pressed this point home, with deconstructive readings of thinkers as diverse as Freud, Hegel, Lévi-Strauss, Rousseau, and Saussure. Derrida problematized the distinctions between the literal and metaphorical, implying instead the endless sign substitutions of metonymy.

Increasingly from the 1980s and throughout the 1990s Derrida's interest in language has broadened to an overt analysis of ethical and religious questions. Part of this reflects his interest in Emmanuel Levinas, for whom ethics is first philosophy. Derrida has also engaged at length with the concept of responsibility, famously analyzing John Searle, Paul de Man, and Martin Heidegger. Derrida has argued for the infinite nature of responsibility and justice, connecting these with demands to respect otherness: every other is wholly other. In turn, Derrida's awareness of a fundamental alterity to language has signalled the possibility that the wholly other might at times be the holy other.

Writing on Kierkegaard and the gift in *The Gift of Death*, Derrida focused on the similarities between the religious paradox and aporia. For Derrida the singularity and scandal of religious paradox is anticipated and mirrored in the fabric of language itself. In *Religion* Derrida enlarged on the similarities between religion and textuality by emphasizing a common—yet different—structure of messianicity that underlies both discourses.

Derrida's understanding of this messianicity has its roots in Marx, and is configured as a sense of promise inherently linked to emancipatory justice. Derrida has also been drawn to questions of law and politics, and how these require deconstructive responses. Aside from his vast impact on literary and critical theory, Derrida has become an important figure for theologians—not least because of his concentration on the infinite demands of justice.

Whilst Derrida refuses to be drawn on his religious commitments, there are significant areas of contact between his work and negative theology. Derrida rejects the God of metaphysics and ontotheology, leaving room instead for a more subtle understanding of the divine. In his relentless questioning of how things are named, there remain deep affinities with theology's own emphasis on the unknowability of the divine. Whilst postmodern theologians differ in their reception of Derrida, his thought remains essentially hospitable to religious language.

See also: Postmodernism; Heidegger, M; Levinas, E; Saussure, F de.

Bibliography

Bennington G (ed.) 1993 *Jacques Derrida*. Chicago University Press, Chicago

Caputo J 1997 *The Prayers and Tears of Jacques Derrida*. Indiana University Press, Indianapolis, IN

Derrida J 1973 *Speech and Phenomena* [trans. David Allison]. Northwestern University Press, Evanston, IL

Derrida J 1995 *The Gift of Death* [trans. David Wills]. Chicago University Press, Chicago

Derrida J, Vattimo G 1998 *Religion*. Polity Press, Oxford

Gasché R 1986 *The Tain of the Mirror: Derrida and the Philosophy of Reflection*. Harvard University Press, Cambridge

Ward G 1995 *Barth, Derrida and the Language of Theology*. Cambridge University Press, Cambridge

Dobrovský, Josef (1753–1829)

V. M. Du Feu

Dobrovský was born in Balassagyarmat, in present-day Hungary. He studied philosophy and theology in Prague and Brno and was ordained in 1786. For a time he was tutor in the home of Count Nostic. He was appointed vice-rector and then rector of the Olomouc seminary. However, he left the seminary to live in the Nostics' house in Prague, and subsequently lived in the houses of other members of the gentry, devoting himself to scholarship. His historical and linguistic works made Prague a center of Slavonic studies. An early work (1777) on the so-called '*Prague Fragments*' (Church Slavonic of the late eleventh century) was published in Frankfurt-am-Main, and in the 1780s and 1790s a number of his articles on Slavonic burial types and place-names came out in Germany. But generally he published in Prague, in German or Latin, although probably his most famous work, on Church Slavonic, including declensions and conjugations (Dobrovský 1822) was published in Vienna.

Dobrovský's work on Old Czech *Über das Alter der böhmischen Bibelübersetzung* (1782) laid the foundations of the grammatical description and cultural revival of Czech at a time when it was despised as fit only for the field or the kitchen. He set the scene for understanding the Moravian activities of Cyril and Methodius, the 'apostles of the Slavs' in the ninth century, and also the role of glagolitic (the alphabet invented by Cyril). Slavonic mythology was another of Dobrovský's interests, and in 1806, 1808, and 1823 he published collections under the title *Slavia*: *Botschaft aus Böhmen an alle slawischen Völker, oder Beiträge zu ihrer Characteristik, zur Kenntnis ihrer Mythologie, ihrer Geschichte und Altertümer, ihrer Literatur und ihrer Sprachlände nach aller Mundarten.*

Dobrovský's works touched on all aspects of Slavonic, not just Czech, history and language; they were a source of information and inspiration for other Slavonic nations, particularly the East and South Slavs whose ancient manuscripts were beginning to come to light, mainly in the monasteries of the Balkans. Because he published in Latin and German he had a wide audience; scholars of this period, engaged in early comparative and historical linguistics, could find in his works the material for an *Ursprache* and also the concrete evidence of the interrelations of the South, East, and West Slavs (the divisions, still in use in the late twentieth century, were Dobrovský's) which could then fit into the Indo–European picture. To Dobrovský goes the title of 'Founder of Slavonic Philology'; he was the first Slavonic linguist of European stature.

See also: Church Slavonic; Cyril and Methodius; Old Church Slavonic.

Bibliography

Dobrovský J 1822 *Institutiones linguae slavicae dialecti veteris quae quum apud Russos, Serbos, aliosque ritus Graeci, tum apud Dalmates glagolitas ritus latini slavos in libris sacris obtinet.* Schmid, Vienna

Driver, Godfrey Rolles (1892–1975)

J. F. A. Sawyer

Son of S. R. Driver, who with Brown and Briggs edited 'BDB,' the most used *Hebrew and English Lexicon of the Old Testament* (1907), Sir Godfrey Rolles Driver (1892–1975) inherited from his father a passion for Hebrew. As he was not a clergyman, he could never have become like his father, Regius Professor of Hebrew at Oxford, but was appointed lecturer in Comparative Semitic Philology there in 1927 and Professor in 1938. During both World Wars he spent time in Palestine where he had the opportunity to study colloquial Arabic and gain some experience of contemporary middle-eastern cultures to which he frequently referred to in his writings. His first books published in 1925 were a grammar of colloquial Arabic, and editions of texts in Babylonian and Syriac. Over the next 40 years he published substantial works on the Hebrew verbal system, Semitic writing, the Assyrian and Babylonian laws, Canaanite myths and legends (see Ugaritic), Aramaic papyri from fifth century BCE Egypt and the Dead Sea Scrolls. In addition he published about 200 articles on all manner of philological and textual problems, for which he regularly proposed a novel solution, and hundreds of reviews. He was a Fellow of the British Academy and played a leading role in the *New English Bible* translation project from 1957 till it was published in 1970. He was awarded a knighthood in 1968.

His knowledge of ancient near-eastern texts, including the Bible, and the Semitic languages in which they were written, was encyclopedic, although his theories and conclusions about them were at times unconvincing. In his initial work on the Dead Sea Scrolls, for example, he alone among the experts of the day argued that they were of an early mediaeval date. From his lifelong study of the texts and from his experiences in Syria and Palestine, he amassed detailed information on every word in the

Hebrew Bible, with a view to compiling a Hebrew dictionary. This never saw the light of day, but his influence on Hebrew lexicography in the middle of the twentieth century, through his publications, his teaching and most notably his contributions to the *New English Bible*, was profound. Following comparative philological methods developed mainly in the nineteenth century, he was convinced that the way to discover the original meaning of a rare or obscure Hebrew word, was to identify a cognate in Arabic, Ugaritic, Babylonian, or another semitic language and apply its meaning to Hebrew. In his enthusiasm for comparative philology he occasionally neglected other semantic issues and produced quite inappropriate meanings, some of which, like *tzanaḥ* 'break wind' in Judges 1:14, found their way into the *New English Bible*. He will be remembered for his sense of humour, his generous nature and tireless energy as well as for his keen intellect and immense erudition.

See also: Barr, J.; English Bible.

Bibliography

Barr J 1968 *Comparative Philology and the Text of the Old Testament*. Oxford University Press, Oxford

Thomas D W, McHardy W D 1963 *Hebrew and Semitic Studies presented to G.R.D.* Oxford University Press, Oxford

Falc'hun, François (1909–91)

P.-Y. Lambert

Canon Falc'hun was born in 1909 in a peasant family of North Finistère—so he was a native speaker of Breton. He went to Lesneven college (or 'petit-séminaire') and prepared for priesthood in the Grand-Séminaire of Quimper. Soon after his ordination, he asked his bishop for authorization to go to Paris to study Phonetics and Celtic studies. Researcher in the Centre National de Recherche Scientifique from 1939 on, he became a lecturer (1944) and Professor of Celtic (1952) in the Arts Faculty of Rennes. When Brest University was founded, he transferred there, close to his own birthplace. From the age of 20 he suffered from tuberculosis, which obliged him to interrupt his work for long periods several times. He died in January 1991.

During his stay in Paris, Falc'hun recorded his own Breton language and studied its sounds with various instruments. He became particularly interested in 'initial mutations' in Breton, together with the exact pronunciation of consonant groups. His phonetic observations were also interpreted phonologically under the influence of M.-L. Sjoestedt-Jonval (Professor of Irish in the Ecole Pratique des Hautes Etudes), who had written a thesis on the phonology of Kerry Irish. According to Falc'hun, Breton consonants are divided into strong (*fortes*) and soft (*douces, lenes*), in twelve pairs. In a stressed syllable (that is, in the penultimate for most of the dialects), a strong consonant always follows a short vowel, and a soft consonant follows a long vowel. The initial mutation, called 'lenition' (voicing of voiceless stops, spirantization of voiced stops, etc.), is based on the opposition between strong and soft consonants: in the case of resonants, the strong variants are softened by the 'lenition.' This mutation occurs in every context where the word would have been originally preceded by a word with a vocalic ending: the following initial consonant has been assimilated to the vowel, resulting in softening. In his phonetic analysis of stops and spirants, Falc'hun also suggested a possible explanation for the Germanic *Lautverschiebung*. His phonetic analysis of Breton consonants was published in 1951 as a part of his thesis.

As a consequence of these observations, Canon Falc'hun planned a reform of Breton orthography, in the years 1954–55. This was later called the 'University spelling.' He felt the need for two different spellings for the velar spirants (the voiced and the voiceless). As the final stops of Breton do not have a voice opposition, he proposed to distribute the corresponding letters (-t/-d, -c/-g) according to morphological classes.

His main thesis was devoted to 'Linguistic Geography'; he maintained that the analysis of dialect maps on its own can enable us to understand the history of a language. Basing his study on the *Atlas Linguistique de la Basse-Bretagne*, by Pierre Le Roux, he drew the different isoglosses, trying to establish the main frontiers between the dialects. Though his historical conclusions were fairly rational (as, for example, an innovating center in Carhaix, and archaizing zones in NW and SE), they sometimes suggested erroneous assumptions about what was archaic and what was not: Jackson later proved that the analysis of isoglosses on its own cannot lead one to differentiate archaisms and innovations.

Towards the end of his career, Canon Falc'hun wrote many articles and books on more popular subjects, most of which are condemned to oblivion. He was unfortunately unable to meet the scientific requirements of linguistic history and comparative grammar. His fantastic etymologies, his idea of a direct filiation between Gaulish and Breton, and his supposed 'Gaulish article' are all to be rejected.

See also: Celtic Religion.

Bibliography

Falc'hun F 1951 *Le systéme consonantique du breton, avec une étude comparative de phonétique expérimentale.* Plihon, Rennes

Falc'hun F 1963 *L'Histoire de la langue bretonne d' après la géographie linguistique*, 2nd edn. 2 vols, Presses Universitaires de France, Paris; enlarged edn. in *Perspectives nouvelles sur i'histoire de la langue bretonne.* Union Générale d'Editions, 1981

Falc'hun F 1982 *Les noms des lieux celtiques, première série, vallées et plaines.* Slatkine, Geneva

Hardie D W F 1948 *A Handbook of Modern Breton*: University of Wales Press, Cardiff, UK

Jackson K H 1963 *Language and History in Early Britain.* Edinburgh University Press, Edinburgh

Foucault, Michel (1926–84)

J. C. Maher

Michel Foucault, philosopher, cultural historian, and sociologist whose critical theory involved influential observations on the role of language in society, was born in Poitiers, France in 1926. He held degrees in philosophy and psychology from the Ecole Normale Supérieure at the Sorbonne and the University of Paris. He also held a diploma in psychopathology and was a student of the Marxist scholar, Louis Althusser. After academic appointments in Sweden and Poland, he returned to France in 1960 as chairman of the Department of Philosophy at the University of Clermont-Ferrand and then as professor at the University of Paris-Vincennes (1968–70). He held the chair as Professor of the History of Systems of Ideas at the Collège de France until his death in 1984.

Foucault's inaugural lecture 'Discourse in Language' at the Collège de France in 1970 established his reputation in France as a leading ethnomethodologist of language. In this treatise, he examined the relation between truth and description in language arguing that if one wants to be heard in society it is not enough simply to 'speak' the truth rather one must be, in some sense, within the truth and embody its regime. The prohibitions surrounding speech inexorably reveal language's links with desire and power. In his investigation of mental illness, Foucault noted how, from the Middle Ages onward, a man was considered mad if his speech could not be said to form 'part of the common discourse of man.' The language of the mentally ill was considered either inadmissible in the authentification of acts or contracts or, alternatively, 'credited with strange powers of revealing some hidden truth, of predicting the future, of revealing... what the wise were unable to perceive' (1976: 216). By examining conventional explanations and understandings of madness (likewise, criminality or homosexuality) one can see how the boundaries of the normal are created as new forms of speech emerge.

Foucault's seminal studies on the religious, therapeutic, and judicial domains emphasized the presence of a 'fellowship of discourse' for each distinct social group. In what way does the dominant discourse of a powerful group, established in an 'institutional site' (e.g., hospital, prison), control those it marginalizes? Does not every speaker, in fact, unconsciously site an interlocutor or object of discourse within a power relation as the 'questioning subject,' the 'listening subject', or the 'seeing subject'? The function of a fellowship is to maintain and reproduce discourse in order that it may circulate within its boundaries according to strict regulations. Foucault stressed that the meanings contained in discourse cannot be based upon an a priori system of signification as if the world is given to people simply to decipher. Discourse is, rather, a violence that people do to things.

See also: Language and Power.

Bibliography

Foucault M 1963 *Naissance de la Clinique*. PUF, Paris

Foucault M 1966. *Les Mots et les Choses: une archéologie des sciences humaines.* Gallimard, Paris

Foucault M 1972 Discourse in language (appendix). In: Foucault M (trans. Sheriden Smith A M) *Archaeology of Knowledge*. Tavistock, London
Foucault M 1976 *Histoire de la Folie à l'Age Classique*. Gallimard, Paris
Foucault M 1977 *Language, Counter-Memory, Practice: Selected Essays and Interviews*. Bouchard D F (ed.) Blackwell, Oxford
Hoy D (ed.) 1986 *Foucault*. Blackwell, Oxford
Smart B 1985 *Michel Foucault*. Ellis Horwood, Chichester

Frazer, James George (1854–1941)

J. W. Rogerson

James George Frazer was born in Glasgow in January 1854 and educated at the universities of Glasgow and Cambridge, concentrating upon classical studies, although to please his father he studied sufficient law to be called to the bar by the Middle Temple. In 1879 he was elected to a fellowship of Trinity College, Cambridge, which he held for the rest of his life and where he wrote the books for which he became renowned. From 1907 to 1922 he held a chair of social anthropology at the University of Liverpool, specially created for him, but undertook no duties in connection with it. He was knighted in 1914 and died in Cambridge in May 1941. He had been afflicted with blindness for the last ten years of his life. Frazer is best known for his monumental *The Golden Bough*, so named after a legend recorded by Servius in his commentary on Virgil, according to which such a bough grew on a tree in a sacred grove of Diana at Aricia. The grove's priesthood was held by anyone who broke off the bough and slew the existing priest in single combat. Frazer's quest to understand the meaning of this legend led him not only to classical sources but to correspondence with informants throughout the world, as he accumulated a vast amount of information about customs, rites and legends which was synthesized into an all-embracing theory that was to extend the third edition of *The Golden Bough* (1911–1915) to 12 volumes. Basically, this theory was that the death of the priest at Aricia was regarded as the death of its god, necessary before he became enfeebled and unable to control the cosmic energies on which humans depended; but in its elaboration the theory assumed various different forms, and touched upon many subjects including the moral and spiritual evolution of humanity through the successive stages of magic, religion and science, and the nature of totemism, taboos, and magic. Living in an age dominated by Darwinism, Frazer believed that all races had evolved through similar moral and spiritual stages, with the evidence from contemporary 'primitive' peoples indicating that they were still a long way back on the path of development. Among the important influences on his theories were E. B. Tylor's *Primitive Culture*, published in 1871, and personal contact with William Robertson Smith and the latter's *Lectures on the Religion of the Semites* (1889). In the preface to the first edition of *The Golden Bough* (1890) Frazer also mentioned the importance for him of the research of the German Wilhelm Mannhardt into the superstitions of German peasants.

From a modern perspective, Frazer's work was compromised by being based upon reports of untrained observers, accounts which he severed from their social settings in order to incorporate them into his grand intellectual scheme. He was, however, a great pioneer of anthropology and comparative religion within his own time.

See also: Myth; Religious Symbols.

Bibliography

Ackerman R 1987 *J. G. Frazer. His Life and Work*. Cambridge University Press, Cambridge
Downie R A 1970 *Frazer and The Golden Bough*. Victor Gollancz, London
Evans-Pritchard E E 1981 *A History of Anthropological Thought*. Faber and Faber, London, pp. 132–152
James E O 1959 Frazer, Sir James George 1854–1941. In: *Dictionary of National Biography 1941–50*. Oxford University Press, Oxford, pp. 272–278
Segal R A 1998 *The Myth and Ritual Theory*. Blackwell, Oxford

Gadamer, Hans-Georg (1900–)

L. P. Hemming

Hans-Georg Gadamer is best known for his major contribution to hermeneutics through his most important work, *Wahrheit und Methode* (*Truth and Method*) which is an exploration of historicity, language and art. He has written numerous other shorter pieces, many of which have been translated, as well as a major evaluation of Martin Heidegger.

Born in Breslau in Germany on 11 February 1900, the son of a Professor of Chemistry, he studied at Marburg under Nicolai Hartman and concluded his doctoral studies in 1922 on Plato under Paul Natorp. After Martin Heidegger's appointment to Marburg in 1923 Gadamer worked as his assistant, a formal appointment, and completed his *Habilitationsschrift* in 1928 under Heidegger. In 1933 he was appointed to teach Aesthetics at Marburg, and then given an appointment at Kiel (1934–35). He returned to Marburg, and was then appointed to a professorial chair at Leipzig in 1939. He remained in Leipzig throughout the Second World War and served as Rector in 1946–47. In the autumn of 1947 he went to Frankfurt, and then on to succeed Karl Jaspers in a Chair of Philosophy at Heidelberg. He became Emeritus Professor in 1968, and has remained, often surrounded by young students, a part of the academic scene at Heidelberg. He has often taught in, and developed extensive links with, North America.

Truth and Method remains by far his most influential work. In it he undertakes a critique of German Idealism and the Romantic and Neo-Kantian schools of interpretation of history and aesthetics (Schleiermacher, Droysen, and Dilthey). Through an engagement with Heidegger's phenomenology he developed an understanding of prejudice as a philosophical category, and finally of language as the 'horizon of a hermeneutic ontology.'

Gadamer's concern with hermeneutics, or the enquiry into how we, as humans, take account of our own self-understanding, has been throughout his life carried out as a concern with language. With the problem of language comes the problem of translation and interpretation across time. In this he has been profoundly influenced by Heidegger, and his argument that language and being are inseparable—indeed that being cannot be understood outside language—closely parallels Heidegger. To be human is to be involved in discourse: oral, written, or in more discreet forms. In this Gadamer shares Heidegger's critique of Husserl and of much of nineteenth-century, particularly German, philosophy, that there is no primordial or uninterpreted level of human experience. Perception and interpretation are the same: to know is to translate.

Gadamer has remained rooted in the Classical tradition, with an effortless and encyclopedic understanding of Aristotle and Plato, while continuing to develop a theory of understanding, or hermeneutics, applicable in contemporary thinking. Of particular note have been his critical engagements with Jürgen Habermas and Jacques Derrida. His work continues to have application in philosophy, theology, religious studies, and literary theory.

See also: Heidegger, Martin; Derrida, Jacques; Romanticism; Postmodernism.

Bibliography

Gadamer H-G 1976 *Philosophical Hermeneutics*. University of California Press, Berkeley

Gadamer H-G 1980 *Dialogue and Dialectic: Eight Hermeneutical Studies on Plato*. Yale University Press, New Haven, CT

Gadamer H-G 1985 *Philosophical Apprenticeships*. MIT Press, Cambridge MA [translation of 1977 *Philosophische Lehrjahre: eine Rückschau*]. Klostermann, Frankfurt

Gadamer H-G 1997 (1975) *Truth and Method*. Sheed & Ward, London [translation of 1975 (1960) *Wahrheit und Methode*]. Mohr Siebeck, Tübingen

Gadamer H-G 1997 *Reflections on My Philosophical Journey*. Open Court, Chicago

Gadamer H-G 2001 *Gesammelte Werke*. Mohr Siebeck, Tübingen

Grondin J 1995 *Introduction to Philosophical Hermeneutics*. Yale University Press, New Haven, CT [translation of *1991 Einführung in die philosophische Hermeneutik*]. Wissenschaftliche Buchgesellschaft, Darmstadt

Grondin J 1999 *Hans-Georg Gadamer: Eine Biographie*. Mohr Siebeck, Tübingen

Palmer R E (ed.) 1989 *Dialogue and Deconstruction: The Gadamer–Derrida Encounter*. State University Press of New York, New York

Silverman H J 1991 *Gadamer and Hermeneutics*. Routledge, New York

Gesenius, Wilhelm (1785–1842)

G. Lloyd Jones

Gesenius began his teaching career as a *privatdozent* at Göttingen, Germany, but moved to Halle in 1810 on being appointed professor of theology. There he remained for the rest of his life, despite the offer of Eichhorn's chair at Göttingen and an invitation to go to Oxford. He was a popular and gifted teacher. His lectures, which unfailingly attracted a large audience, were not only clear and concise, but witty and animated; it is unfortunate that they were never published. His influence on oriental studies may be measured by noting his contribution in the related areas of grammar, exegesis, and lexicography.

Gesenius's *Hebräische Grammatik* (1813), which was based on the empirical method, soon replaced existing grammars and became the most widely used of all his writings. It ran into fourteen editions during his own lifetime. The twenty-eighth edition (1909) was revised by E. Kautzsch and translated into English by A. E. Cowley. To his grammatical works also belongs *Die Geschichte der hebräischen Sprache und Schrift* (1815). While this provides a valuable overview of the contributions of earlier scholars in grammar and lexicography, it was not as successful as his earlier work because he did not have sufficient knowledge of Mishnaic Hebrew. It has been the author's intention to revise it later, but he failed to do so.

The commentary on Isaiah (*Philologisch-kritischer und historischer Commentar über den Jesaia*, 1820–21) demonstrates Gesenius's ability as a biblical exegete. The work, which is moderate and circumspect in its criticism of the text, suggests that the author was a rationalist but with conservative tendencies. His attitude to the Masoretic Text was one of caution; where previous textual scholars had criticized it, he came to its defense. But in matters theological he was no dogmatist. For him the Hebrew Bible was not an inspired book, but a graphic history and great poetry. His tendency to be dismissive of biblical miracles engendered fierce opposition which culminated in an unsuccessful attempt to remove him from office.

Gesenius's contribution to lexicography surpasses all his other scholarly work. The *Hebräisch-deutsches Handwörterbuch* (1812) was the basis for all subsequent lexicons by Gesenius himself and those compiled by other Hebraists. His lexicographical sources were three: the Hebrew of the Old Testament itself, traditional interpretation, and cognate languages. The Hebrew Bible was an important source for determining the meaning of Hebrew words. Rare words, and even *hapax legomena*, can be explained from the context. Traditional interpretation comprised of the ancient Greek, Syriac, and Latin versions of the Scriptures, coupled with the contributions of rabbinic and medieval Jewish commentators, lexicographers, and grammarians. The cognate languages were divided into three groups: Aramaic, Canaanite, and Arabic, pride of place as a philological aid being given to Arabic.

See also: Hebrew, Biblical and Jewish; Hebrew Grammarians; Semitic Languages.

Bibliography

Cheyne T K 1893 *Founders of Old Testament Criticism.* Methuen, London

Miller E F 1927 *The Influence of Gesenius on Hebrew Lexicography*. Columbia University Press, New York

Nyberg H S (ed.) 1972 *Congress Volume: Uppsala 1971.* Leiden. Series: Supplement to V.T. no. 22

Gordon, Cyrus Herzl (1908–2001)

K. J. Cathcart

A scholar with remarkable linguistic talents and a prolific writer, Cyrus Gordon has spent much of his distinguished career proposing provocative interpretations of ancient Near Eastern and Mediterranean cultures.

He was born in New York in 1908 to Lithuanian Jewish parents. After attending high school in Philadelphia, he was admitted to the University of Pennsylvania, where he studied under J. A. Montgomery. In 1930 he was awarded a Ph.D. for his dissertation on 'Rabbinic Exegesis in the Vulgate of Proverbs'. During these years he also attended Dropsie College, taking further courses in Hebrew and Arabic. Gordon reckons that at this time he became 'consciously dedicated to international and interconfessional cooperation in scholarship' (Gordon 2000, p. 19). From 1931 to 1935 he held a fellowship at the American School of Oriental Research in Baghdad and Jerusalem. He excavated at the sites of Tepe Gawra and Tell Billa in Iraq and at Beth-Zur in southern Palestine. It is clear that the young scholar enjoyed travelling around the Middle East, visiting the archaeological sites and learning colloquial Arabic. During the following three years he was a teaching fellow under W. F. Albright (see *Albright, W. F.*) at Johns Hopkins University, where he began to point out the parallels between Greek literature and Near Eastern literatures.

In the summer of 1939, while holding a Scandinavian–American fellowship at the University of Uppsala, Gordon wrote the first draft of his *Ugaritic Grammar*, the first of his many significant contributions to the study of north-west Semitic literatures and civilizations. His publications in Ugaritic studies were particularly important for the study of Canaanite mythology. His academic career was interrupted by World War II during which he worked as a cryptanalyst in Washington and then enlisted in the

Persian Gulf Command. From 1946 to 1956 he taught at Dropsie College, giving courses in Assyriology, Egyptology, Aramaic, and Hebrew. He had a particular interest in Aramaic incantations. Then came one of his most notable contributions to academic life in America. In 1956 he moved to Brandeis University as a professor of Near Eastern and Judaic studies and quickly set up a department of Mediterranean studies. Mentor and teacher par excellence, he attracted many fine doctoral students to this new academic program. Unfortunately, in the early 1970s, Brandeis decided to close the department that he had so energetically built up, so he accepted an appointment at New York University. There he remained until his retirement in 1989, contributing to the new field of Eblaite studies.

Bibliography

Gordon C H 1995 Recovering Canaan and Ancient Israel. In: Sasson J (ed.) *Civilizations of the Ancient Near East*. Charles Scribner's, New York, vol. 4, pp. 2779–89

Gordon C H 2000 *A Scholar's Odyssey*. Society of Biblical Literature, Atlanta, GA

Lubetski M, Gottlieb C 1996 Portrait of a Master Scholar with a Global Perspective. *Biblical Archaeologist* **59(1)**: 2–12

Gundert, Hermann (1814–93)

R. E. Asher

The year 1993 saw celebrations in both Germany and South India to mark the centenary of the death of Hermann Gundert, one of the most distinguished among the many missionaries who, having gone to India to spread the message of Christianity, became scholars in the language of the area in which they found themselves stationed. Gundert, who was born in Stuttgart in 1814, left Germany for South India in 1836, arriving at Madras almost 130 years to the day after Ziegenbalg. His purpose was to act as tutor to the sons of A N Groves, an Englishman who had been a missionary. The two boys proving disinclined to study Greek and Hebrew, Gundert was sent to work with K T E Rhenius (1790–1838), a German member of the Church Missionary Society in Tirunelveli, with whom he studied the Tamil classics. Two years later, by then married to Julie Dubois, a schoolteacher, he accepted an invitation to join the Basel Mission in Mangalore. While there he made a study of Kanarese. In 1838 he went to Illikunnu, Thalassery, in Malabar to set up a new mission station and so began his acquaintance with Malayalam. He is reputed to have learnt sufficient Malayalam to preach in the language within a few months of his arrival. The development of his proficiency in the written language was equally impressive and in the course of his life he produced almost 50 works in Malayalam, including a translation of the Bible. His knowledge of a number of Dravidian languages is no doubt part of the reason for his close friendship with Bishop Caldwell.

Ill health forced his return to Germany in 1859. Steeped in the knowledge not only of Malayalam language, but also in the customs, culture, and legends of the part of India in which he had lived for three decades, he devoted the rest of his life to writing and publishing—the latter as chief editor of the Calwer Verlagsverein from 1862. Much of what he learned is contained in his letters and diaries, which were later published (see Gundert 1983a, 1983b and 1986). Among Gundert's descendants was the poet Hermann Hesse, his grandson.

Extensive and varied though his writings were, Gundert is particularly celebrated for his contributions in the field of Malayalam language. His first major endeavor of this kind was his *Malayāla vyākaraṇam* ('Malayalam grammar') of 1851 (see Gundert 1868). Gundert also contributed to the understanding of the importance of epigraphy in the study of the history of Malayalam language by his decipherment of inscriptions.

Gundert's important grammatical and epigraphical studies, however, can be seen as secondary to his work as a lexicographer. After returning to Germany he concentrated all his intellectual energy on the editing of a Malayalam–English dictionary (Gundert 1872) which was still considered sufficiently commercial ninety years later to justify the publication of a second edition and which remained perhaps the most important landmark in Malayalam lexicography until the appearance of the multi-volume *Malayalam Lexicon* (Kunjan Pillai 1965). Gundert attempted, in the manner of the compilers of the *Oxford English Dictionary*, to produce a work on historical principles. He was the first Malayalam lexicographer to illustrate meanings with quotations from literary sources. He aimed wherever possible to indicate the source of lexemes, noting which words were borrowed from Sanskrit and, in the case of pure Malayalam words, those for which cognates existed in other Dravidian languages, the identity of these languages being indicated in each case. For these reasons, and because of its general reliability, it is not surprising that Gundert's Dictionary has been a major source for work on comparative Dravidian by such scholars as T. Burrow and M. B. Emeneau in the second half of the twentieth century. A further innovation was a roman transcription to indicate the pronunciation of each headword, this going beyond a mere transliteration of the Malayalam script to include such symbols as ɣ. Written sources, which include old letters and official records as well as literary works in both prose and verse, are supplemented by spoken materials from most parts of Kerala. Foreign words in regular use are included, as are '*provincialisms* and *vulgarisms*,' including 'coarse and even obscene modes of speech.' Altogether the work is a worthy forerunner of the great *Malayalam Lexicon*. At the beginning of the twenty-first century, the name of no European is held in as high esteem in Kerala as Gundert's and not only among the large Christian community.

See also: Caldwell, Robert; Ziegenbalg, Bartholomäus; Missionaries.

Bibliography

Frenz A 1991 *Dr Hermann Gundert: Biography*. D C Books, Kottayam

Frenz A, Zacharia S (eds.) 1993 *Dr Hermann Gundert and Malayalam Language*. Centre for Kerala Studies, Changanassery

Gundert H 1868 *A Grammar of the Malayálam Language*, 2nd edn. complete [and edited, with preface, brief headings in English and other additions, by K A E Diez]. Basel Mission Press, Mangalore

Gundert H 1872 *A Malayalam and English Dictionary*. C Stolz, Mangalore, 3rd edn., 1992, with critical introduction by Scaria Zacharia, D C Books, Kottayam

Gundert H 1983a *Schriften und Berichte aus Malabar: mit Meditationen und Studien*, Frenz A (ed.) J F Steinkopf, Stuttgart

Gundert H 1983b *Tagebuch aus Malabar*, 1837–1859, Frenz A (ed.) J F Steinkopf, Stuttgart

Kunjan Pillai S 1965– (in progress) *Malayalam Lexicon*. University of Kerala, Trivandrum

Gundert H 1986 *Calwer Tagebuch, 1859–1893*, Frenz A (ed.) J F Steinkopf, Stuttgart

Kurup K K N, John K J (eds.) 1993 *Legacy of Basel Mission and Hermann Gundert in Malabar*. Gundert Death Centenary Committee, Calicut

Guthrie, Malcolm (1903–72)

M. Mann

Professor Guthrie is known chiefly for his contributions to the comparative study of the Bantu languages of Africa.

Born in 1903 into a strict Baptist family, he studied engineering at Imperial College, London, and theology at Spurgeon's College, and served three years as a pastor in Rochester before leaving for Kinshasa, Zaire, as a Baptist missionary in 1932. Jointly in charge of the mission school, he mastered Lingala, and through its medium started investigating some of the 120 languages represented in the school, notably those of the Teke group, transferring after furlough in 1935 (when he renewed contacts with the School of Oriental and African Studies in London) to Upoto, 600 miles upstream, where he produced a much reprinted *Grammaire et Dictionnaire de Lingala* (1939) and translated the New Testament (published 1942).

Returning to England in 1940, he accepted after some hesitation a senior lectureship at the School of Oriental and African Studies, becoming Reader in 1947, Professor in 1951, and serving as head of the department of Africa 1950–68. He died in 1972, two years after his retirement.

In an eighteen-month study tour (1942–44, including a month in Zanzibar to master Swahili), he amassed firsthand material on a large number of Bantu languages, using carefully constructed grammatical and lexical questionnaires, and made a detailed study of Bemba. His corpus of field data is richly reflected in his *The Classification of the Bantu Languages* (1948), which associates the Bantu languages in 80 groups, and then further into 16 (later 15) zones. This yields a widely used reference system (best known through Bryan 1959) in which each language is identified by a letter (representing the zone) and two digits (group and language). The work itself however is rendered somewhat inaccessible by Guthrie's failure to explain his descriptive categories.

Much of Guthrie's work is clearly argued from first principles, frequently in blind disregard of the contributions of predecessors. *Comparative Bantu* (1967–71) assembles over 2000 series of vocabulary items drawn from over 200 languages, each series with a common meaning and connecting 'starred form,' to which all valid entries are related by regular sound-correspondences ('skewed' entries are clearly distinguished, with a note of the nature of their irregularity); insistence on strict regularity leads to a considerable number of—frequently overlapping—'osculant' series differing slightly in form or meaning. A notable innovation is the attempt to codify the geographical distribution of individual series.

Guthrie insists that the presentation of the comparative series is strictly formal and synchronic; only when it was completed did he attempt historical interpretation, which is set out in a parallel commentary. Few people now accept his conclusion that the first Bantu-speakers were iron-using boat-people who expanded from southeastern Zaire, which would leave unexplained the connection of Bantu with other Niger–Congo languages of West Africa.

See also: Christianity in Africa; Missionaries.

Bibliography

Bryan M A 1959 *The Bantu Languages of Africa.* Oxford University Press, London

Guthrie M 1948 *The Classification of the Bantu Languages.* Oxford University Press, London

Guthrie M 1967–71 *Comparative Bantu: An Introduction to the Comparative Linguistics and Prehistory of the Bantu Languages.* Gregg Press, Farnborough

Guthrie M 1970 *Collected Papers on Bantu Linguistics.* Gregg Press, Farnborough

Ḥayyuj, Judah (ca. 940–1010)

E. Gutwirth

Known as Abu Zakharyah Yahya ibn Dawd or Judah ben David, Ḥayyuj established the principle of the trilateral roots of Hebrew verbs. Medieval writers considered him 'the first of the (Hebrew) grammarians.' He was probably born not later than 940 in Fez and died around 1010 after having spent most of his life in Cordoba.

He wrote his grammatical works in Judeo–Arabic. His *Kitāb al tanqīt* or *Kitāb al-nuqat* was translated into Hebrew by Abraham ibn Ezra as *Sēpher ha-niqqūd* (*The Book of Vocalization*). His *Kitāb al-af'āl dhawāt ḥurūf al-līn* (*The Book of the Quiescent Letters and the Prolonging*) was translated into Hebrew by Moses ha-Kohen ibn Chiquitilla as *Sepher' Ōtiōt ha-naḥ wĕ-ha-meshekh* and by Abraham ibn Ezra as *Sĕpher ha-nūaḥ*. It has also been paraphrased by Isḥaq ha-Levi ben Eleazar in the *Sĕphat Yeter*. Fragments of an anonymous translation have also been found. The book deals with the problem of identifying the roots of verbs when these include 'weak' letters (for example, *'aleph, he, waw, yodh*).

His *Kitāb al-af'al dhawāt al-mithlayn* was translated into Hebrew as *Sēpher po'ale ha-kephel* and by Abraham ibn Ezra as *Sēpher ha-kephel* (*The Book of Geminate Verbs*). His declared purpose is 'to help people... to understand the language of the ancient Hebrews for people... think that when the second consonant is geminate the root has only two letters and the third one repeats the second one...' (*Sēpher Ḥayyuj*: 99). He analyzes these verbs and lists them, making reference to the biblical passages where they occur.

The Hebrew translations by Abraham ibn Ezra were edited by L. Dukes in 1844. Moses ha-Kohen ibn Chiquitilla's translations and ibn Ezra's translation of the *Sēpher ha-niqqūd* were published in 1870 by J. W. Nutt with an English translation. Divided into three parts, the first one attempts to classify roots whose first letter is *aleph* or *yodh*; the second deals with roots whose second letter is *waw* or *yodh*, and the third with those roots whose final letter is *he*.

Ḥayyuj explains that with the help of his book it will be possible to discern the root of the verbs in the Bible and understand the Word of God. He establishes the principle of triliteral roots. His *Kitāb al-natf* seems to be identical with the so-called *Sēpher ha-qorḥāh* (*Book of Baldness*), only known through fragments.

In the Middle Ages his work was mainly known through the *Sēpher Ḥayyuj*, which contained his two main treatises: *Kitāb al-af'al dhawāt al-mithlayn* and *Kitab al-af'al dhawāt ḥurūf al-līn*.

See also: Ibn Ezra, A; Hebrew Linguistic Tradition.

Bibliography

Ḥayyuj J 1870 (ed. and trans. Nutt J W) *Two Treatises on Verbs containing Feeble and Double Letters.* London

Israelsohn I 1889 L'ouvrage perdu de Jehouda Hajjoudj. *Revue des études juives* **19**: 306–10

Heidegger, Martin (1899–1976)

L. P. Hemming

Martin Heidegger was born in the small village of Meßkirch in Germany on September 26, 1899. He died at Freiburg in May 1976. Heidegger is arguably the most influential philosopher in the twentieth century, having a profound effect on the development of philosophy, theology, critical and literary theory, as well as fields far removed from his immediate concerns, like architecture and law. His public works began with the publication of *Being and Time* where he lays out a philosophical and phenomenological analysis of the being (*Sein*) of human existence or *Dasein*. *Being and Time* was the only work he wrote as a book that was published in his lifetime, although he also published several of his lecture courses, notably *An Introduction to Metaphysics* and *Nietzsche by Martin Heidegger*.

Educated through the structures of the Catholic Church and Freiburg University, he undertook his doctorate in 1913 and his *Habilitationsschrift* on a text believed (erroneously) to be by Scotus in 1916. He married Elfride Petri in 1917, and in 1919 broke formal ties with the Catholic Church and transferred to the Freiburg Philosophy Faculty, to begin teaching as a *Privatdozent* at Freiburg. He was for some years a close collaborator with Husserl, working in Freiburg as his assistant, although their friendship later cooled. He went to Marburg in 1923, but returned to Freiburg in 1929 to the chair of philosophy. He remained in Freiburg all his life, retreating periodically to a hut at Todtnauberg to write. Notoriously he joined the Nazi Party in 1933, and was elected Rector of Freiburg at the same time, although he resigned as Rector in 1934. He never formally resigned from the Nazi Party and was banned from teaching between 1946 and 1951, although there is no evidence that he subscribed to the biologism or anti-semitism of National Socialism. He continued to write and teach almost to the end of his life, notably with the philosopher Eugen Fink and psychologist Medard Boss.

Heidegger's innovative use and command of the German language has been compared to Luther's, and his use of word-play makes him very difficult to translate. Heidegger's work is rooted in a deep and sympathetic understanding of ancient Greek thought, and he is a masterful interpreter of Aristotle and Plato. His knowledge of the Western philosophical tradition is breathtaking, with, amongst others, transformative understandings of Descartes, Kant, Schelling, Hegel, and Nietzsche. In his later work he developed the understanding of the 'history of being' (*Seinsgeschichte*) which is an analysis of the whole history of metaphysics from its origins in Parmenides and Heraclitus to its 'fulfilment' in Nietzsche and Hegel, a fulfilment which he suggested would continue to dominate thinking perhaps for centuries to come.

He has had an astonishing effect on numerous thinkers, especially in France. His work is very far from being fully understood, although thinkers as diverse as Jacques Derrida, Michel Foucault, Jean Beaufret, Hanah Arendt, Hans-Georg Gadamer, Jacques Lacan, Luce Irigiray, Emmanuel Lévinas, and John Macquarrie as well as many others have acknowledged their indebtedness to him. Although most of his written texts and lecture courses have now been published, his collected works are as yet incomplete, and less than half of them have been translated into English. The full effect of his philosophy is yet to come.

See also: Gadamer, Hans-Georg; Derrida, Jacques; Kant, Immanuel; Foucault, Michel; Lacan, Jacques; Irigary, Luce.

Bibliography

Gadamer H-G 1994 *Heidegger's Ways*. State University of New York Press, New York [Translation of 1983 *Heideggers Wege: Studien zum Spätwerk*. Mohr Siebeck, Tübingen]

Guignon C 1993 *The Cambridge Companion to Heidegger*. Cambridge University Press, Cambridge

Heidegger M 1976 *Gesamtausgabe Vols. 1–121*. Klostermann, Frankfurt. In press

Heidegger M 1987 *Nietzsche by Martin Heidegger* (4 vols.). Harper Collins, London [Translation of *1961 Nietzsche*. Neske, Pfullingen]

Heidegger M 1993 (1977) *Basic Writings*. Routledge, London

Heidegger M 1997 (1962) *Being and Time*. Blackwell, Oxford [Translation of 1997 (1927) *Sein und Zeit*. Niemeyer, Tübingen]

Heidegger M 2000 *Introduction to Metaphysics*. Yale University Press, New Haven [Translation of 1987 (1953) *Einführung in die Metaphysik*. Niemeyer, Tübingen]

Neske G, Kettering E 1990 *Martin Heidegger and National Socialism: Questions and Answers*. Paragon House, New York [Translation of 1988 *Martin Heidegger im Gespräch*. Neske, Pfullingen]

Petzet H W 1993 *Encounters and Dialogues with Martin Heidegger 1929–1976*. Chicago University Press, Chicago [Edited translation of *1983 Auf einen Stern zugehen: Begegnungen und Gespräch mit Martin Heidegger, 1929–1976*. Frankfurter Societäts, Frankfurt]

Philipse H 1998 *Heidegger's Philosophy of Being: A Critical Interpretation*. Princeton University Press, New Jersey

Safranski R 1998 *Martin Heidegger: Between Good and Evil.* Harvard University Press, Cambridge, MA [Translation of *1997 Ein Meister aus Deutschland: Heidegger und seine Zeit.* Fischer, Frankfurt]

Herder, Johann Gottfried (1744–1803)

P. B. Salmon

Herder, in his early adult years a leading figure in the German Storm and Stress movement of the 1770s, is known to linguists primarily for his essay on the origin of language (*Abhandlung über den Ursprung der Sprache* 1772). His early writings include studies in folk literature and the advocacy of simple language based on the vernacular. Common to these and to later works, such as the *Ideen zur Philosophie der Geschichte der Menschheit* (1784–91), is an interest in continuity and development, which is accompanied throughout his writings by another in origins.

In the *Fragmente* (1766–68) a set of mainly literary essays, he suggests, much as Condillac had done, that language originated from a combination of gesture and natural reflex cries, which developed into irregular utterances, and thence into poetry. In social use language evolved further into oratory, before declining eventually into the dull regularity of 'philosophical' (i.e., scientific) language. His view of a language as a key to the national character of its speakers—also anticipated by Condillac—is often seen as a source of similar ideas expressed by Humboldt (see *Humboldt, Wilhelm von*).

The treatise on the origin of language, unlike other writings of the time, asserts unequivocally that language is not God-given, but man-made. However, instead of Condillac's scheme of development it suggests a specifically human quality of 'reflection' (*Besonnenheit*), nature's compensation for man's weak instinctual endowments, which enables man to identify an object by selecting one of the set of features which characterize it. For example, a lamb is identified by its bleat; the observer bleats mentally on seeing it again; this event alone is sufficient to constitute language, even without a listener. What a listener hears is not a reflex sound, but Herder also denies it is merely imitative. Later passages speak of a gestural component in language, and of the mutual reinforcement of reason and language.

The recognition of an object by a distinguishing mark is also used as the initial stage of identification in the mental processes set up in the *Metacritique to the Critique of Pure Reason* (1799), an empiricist attack on Kant's *Critique*, paralleling the increasingly complex perceptions of identity, quality, and activity by the progressive introduction of nominals, adjectives, and verbs in grammar.

While Herder is best known to linguists for his views on the origin of language, the *Abhandlung* is perhaps more important for its vigor than its views; his most influential contribution may lie rather in his sense of the organic growth and decay of language, in his consciousness of the distinctive national quality of languages, and in his propagating the use of simple unaffected German.

See also: Myths About Language; Kant, I.; Romanticism.

Bibliography

Clark R T 1955 *Herder: His Life and Thought.* University of California Press, Berkeley, CA

Haym R 1958 [1st edn. 1877–85] *Herder.* Aufbau-Verlag, Berlin

Heintel E (ed.) 1964 *J G H Sprachphilosophische Schriften*, 2nd edn. Meiner, Hamburg

Herder J G 1877–1913 (ed. Suphan B) *Sämtliche Werke.* Weidmann, Berlin

Moran J H, Gode A (transl.) 1966 *On the Origin of Language*: Jean-Jacques Rousseau, Essay on the Origin of Languages; *Johann Gottfried Herder*, Essay on the Origin of Language. Ungar, New York

Stam J H 1976 *Inquiries into the Origin of Language. The Fate of a Question.* Harper and Row, New York

Holder, William (1616–98)

J. A. Kemp

Holder was born in Nottinghamshire. Having studied at Pembroke Hall, Cambridge, he took his MA in 1640, and was elected a fellow of his college. He became rector of Bletchington, Oxfordshire in 1642, and in subsequent years moved to other parishes in the south of England. He held the post of canon in Ely Cathedral and later in St Paul's Cathedral and became sub-dean of the Chapel Royal. His wife was the sister of Sir Christopher Wren. Holder graduated DD at Oxford, and was elected FRS in 1663. He died on January 24, 1698.

William Holder was a pioneer in the investigation of speech, and in the teaching of the deaf. In 1659 he taught Alexander Popham, who had been deaf from birth, to speak. He published an article (An Experiment concerning Deafness) in 1668, and in 1669 his book *Elements of Speech* appeared. In it Holder sets out to explain what are the various elements which make up speech. What is particularly striking is his independent approach, clearly based on his personal experience of the problems of the deaf, and not on previous authorities. John Wallis had published his own *Tractatus de Loquela* (Treatise on Speech) in 1653, which contains many interesting observations, but there is no doubt that Holder surpasses him in his analysis.

As Abercrombie (1986) points out, Holder adopts the 'hylomorphic' distinction between 'matter' and 'form.' In his application of it to speech, matter is divided into four kinds: firstly, it may be 'spirital' (i.e., breath) or 'vocal' (i.e., voice), and secondly it may be 'nasal' (involving modification by the nose) or 'oral' (not involving nasal modification). Form is imposed on this matter by the various articulations between movable and other organs, such as tongue, lips, palate, gums, jaw, and teeth, to give specific speech sounds. The most interesting and novel aspect of this is Holder's logical deduction that, as any sound may have spirital (breathed) matter, a place must be allocated in analysis to breathed (i.e., voiceless) nasals and liquids, even though they may be rare or nonexistent in languages. Similarly, nasal matter is not confined to [m n ŋ] but may be at any place of articulation, and may not necessarily involve an oral closure. His attempt to describe the mechanism of voicing comes nearer to a correct understanding than any of his contemporaries did, and also his account of the 'formal' aspect of speech.

Apart from his quarrel with John Wallis over who should take the credit for teaching Alexander Popham to speak, Holder seems to have lived a life free from controversy. John Aubrey called him 'a perfect good man.' Apart from his contribution to speech he was a musician, and an accomplished writer of shorthand. The fact that his contribution to phonetics has not been widely recognized may be due to the fact that he provided little evidence about contemporary English pronunciation.

Bibliography

Abercrombie D 1986 Hylomorphic taxonomy and William Holder. *JIPA* **16**: 4–7

Holder W 1669 *Elements of Speech; An Essay of Inquiry into the Natural Production of Letters*. J. Martyn, London; facsimile reprint, Scolar Press, Menston, 1967

Subbiondo J L 1978 William Holder's 'Elements of Speech' (1669). *Lingua* **46**: 169–84

Humboldt, Wilhelm von (1767–1835)

J. A. Kemp

Wilhelm von Humboldt, elder brother of the famous scientist and explorer Alexander von Humboldt, was born on June 22, 1767 in Potsdam, Prussia, and died in Tegel (now in Berlin) on April 8, 1835. Distinguished as a statesman and diplomat, he is generally regarded as one of the profoundest thinkers on linguistic matters, though the difficulty of his style often makes his meaning hard to interpret.

After private tuition at home Wilhelm attended Göttingen University (1788). Completing his legal studies, he traveled in Europe and pursued further studies in Greek language and civilization, which epitomized for him the versatile and harmonious way of life and remained a strong influence throughout his career.

His marriage into a wealthy family in 1791 meant that he was able to devote his time and energies to developing to the full the individuality and independence of mind which from an early age he had striven for. In Jena from 1794 he enjoyed a close and intellectually stimulating friendship with Schiller and Goethe. During a period in Paris he visited Spain, and contact with the Basque language was an early stimulus to the study of languages in general. In 1801 he reluctantly moved to Berlin and the next year to Rome, as Prussian ambassador to the Vatican from 1802 to 1808. State service claimed his full attention on his recall to Germany in 1808, and he was responsible for important educational reforms. It was not until 1819 that disagreements with other members of the Prussian government led him to retire from public life and to devote himself to his study of languages.

By temperament he was throughout his life reluctant to commit himself to writing, or to complete works he had begun, but he realized that his search for the nature of language, and its importance in the life of man, could only be based on a knowledge of a wide variety of languages. To his knowledge of Greek and Latin and other languages of Europe he added Sanskrit in 1821, which had a powerful influence on his view of language. In the same year he helped to secure the appointment of Franz Bopp, one of the great pioneers of comparative linguistics, to a professorship in Oriental and General Linguistics in Berlin. From grammars of the native languages of America, acquired by his brother, Wilhelm had extended his knowledge to the American continent; and Rémusat's work on Chinese led him to publish in this area also. Searching for a link between languages from different parts of the world he studied the Polynesian languages and the languages of Malaya. The search culminated in his great work, published posthumously, *On the Kawi Language on the Island of Java* (Humboldt 1836–39), with its lengthy introduction entitled 'On the Diversity of Human Language-Structure and its Influence on the Mental Development of Mankind.' What perhaps caused Humboldt to select the Kawi language for such close examination was not only the geographical position of Java, but the mixed nature of the Kawi language, combining a Sanskrit vocabulary with a Malayan structure. Although he believed that vocabulary and grammatical structure are inseparable and interdependent parts of language (except for the linguistic analyst), he thought the differences between languages to be most evident in their grammatical structure.

Greek and Sanskrit were for him the most perfect languages—at one extreme of a typological scale, exemplifying the supreme type of inflecting language. At the other extreme he placed Chinese, as an isolating language, lacking inflections or affixes. In between came the so-called 'agglutinating' languages, which he regarded as having an inferior variety of inflection, involving 'mechanical adding, not a truly organic accretion.' Similar classifications can be found earlier in Friedrich von Schlegel (see *Schlegel, (Carl Wilhelm) Friedrich von*) and his brother August Wilhelm von Schlegel (see *Schlegel, August Wilhelm von*). Humboldt, however, identified in the 'Mexican language' (Nahuatl) a new category of sentence form, called 'incorporating'. In this the main elements in the structure of the sentence are 'incorporated' into a single word. The superiority of languages such as Greek and Sanskrit for Humboldt lay in what he perceived as the organic nature of their grammatical structure, where inner modifications and inflections are welded into the root, which contains the crucial concept; but at the same time the unity of the word is maintained. Languages of very different types, such as Chinese and Mexican, clearly could also express the thoughts of their speakers, but are constrained by their structure to do this less perfectly.

The relationship of language with thought is crucial. Humboldt believed that all languages contain certain universal features, arising from the laws of thinking, shared by all men. But without language, he maintained, thinking is not possible, because only through expression in language is a concept given objectivity. Language, however, is not a fixed object or product (Humboldt uses the Greek word *ergon*) but involves constant creation, or activity (Greek *energeia*). This creativity of language is limited in particular languages by the structure or form they have developed. The creativity is constantly at work, but it can only act on what material is available to the speaker at a particular time. So particular languages acquire their individual character, which may be more or less imperfect, as a result of their being animated by 'a more or less fruitful principle of mental development.' Thus Humboldt ranks languages on a scale, at the top of which are those of the Sanskritic type (i.e., Indo–European). The form of Chinese is accepted as exhibiting perhaps more than any other language 'the power of pure thought,' but falls short in versatility and harmony. Humboldt proceeds to associate the particular national character of each language with a particular out-look of its speakers on the world—a thesis that was later to be developed by Sapir and Whorf (see *Whorf, Benjamin Lee*).

Among nineteenth-century writers, Pott acknowledges his debt to Humboldt, and Steinthal and Wundt were certainly influenced by him in developing the notion of 'national psychology' (*Völkerpsychologie*). However, Humboldt's influence on linguistics has been more apparent in the twentieth century than in the nineteenth, e.g., in so-called 'neo-Humboldtian' trends (see Basilius 1952), and in controversial claims as to the similarities between Humboldt's well-known, but variously interpreted, idea of the 'inner form of language' (*innere Sprachform*) and the rules of generative grammar (see Coseriu 1970). For the influence on Humboldt of earlier linguistic philosophers see Manchester (1985).

See also: Myths About Language; Romanticism.

Bibliography

Basilius H A 1952 Neo-Humboldtian ethnolinguistics. *Word* **8**: 95–105 (repr. in Fishman J A (ed.) 1968 *Readings in the Sociology of Language*. Mouton, The Hague)

Coseriu E 1970 Semantik, innere Sprachform und Tiefenstruktur. *FoL* **4**: 53–63

Humboldt W von 1836–39 *Über die Kawi Sparache auf der Insel Java, nebst einer Einleitung über die Verschiedenheit des menschlichen Sprachbaues und ihren Einfluss auf die geistige Entwickelung des Menschengeschlechts.* Königliche Akademie der Wissenschaften, Berlin. (The introduction is translated by P Heath as *On Language: the Diversity of Human Language Structure and its Influence on the Mental Development of Mankind,* with an introduction by H Aarsleff. Cambridge University Press, Cambridge, 1988)

Humboldt W von 1903–36 *Gesammelte Schriften,* 17 vols. Königlich Akademie der Wissenschaften, Berlin

Koerner E F K 1990 Wilhelm von Humboldt and North American ethnolinguistics: Boas (1894) to Hymes (1961). *HL* **17(1–2)**: 111–28

Manchester M L 1985 *The Philosophical Foundations of Humboldt's Linguistic Doctrines.* Benjamins, Amsterdam

Sweet P R 1978–80 *Wilhelm von Humboldt: A Biography,* 2 vols. Ohio State University Press, Columbus, OH

Hus, Jan (c. 1372–1415)

G. L. Jones

Jan Hus, Czech religious reformer, was born in Husinec, Bohemia, and educated at Prague's Charles University, graduating MA in 1396. After his ordination to the priesthood, he was appointed preacher of Bethlehem Chapel at Prague in 1402, a post which he combined with the deanship of the Philosophy Faculty at the university. Influenced by Wycliffe (see *Wycliffe, J.*), whose writings had become popular in Bohemia during the final decade of the fourteenth century, he protested at the public burning of the latter's books by the Archbishop of Prague in 1410. Having been excommunicated in 1411, he went into voluntary exile the following year, but in 1414 he was summoned to attend the Council of Constance to answer an indictment concerning the Wycliffite nature of his beliefs. Though guaranteed safe conduct, he was imprisoned and put on trial for heresy. His refusal to recant led to his condemnation, and he was burned at the stake on July 6, 1415.

Hus' reforming tendencies first appeared when he became preacher at Bethlehem Chapel. Into what had been no more than a vernacular preaching station he introduced a daily sung mass with hymns, many of which he wrote himself, he preached biblically based sermons on a regular basis, and advocated frequent communion. He revised and improved existing texts of the Czech Bible, wrote several commentaries, and translated some of Wycliffe's work into Czech. (Incidentally, he introduced the use of diacritics or accents into written Czech.) But the reform for which he called was moral and practical, rather than theological. He denounced abuses within the Church, especially amongst the religious orders and the hierarchy. It was his passionate preaching against the immorality of the clergy and his challenge to the authority structure of the mediaeval Church which led to his excommunication; the charge of heresy came later. In spite of his motto 'Search the Scriptures,' he based his authority not on *sola scriptura* but on Scripture, tradition and reason—in that order.

The most important of his 15 books is *De Ecclesia* (1412) in which he critiques the ecclesiastical system, the papacy, and the definition of the Church. The fact that the first ten chapters of this work are taken almost verbatim from Wycliffe has fuelled the debate about his intellectual ancestry. Was he an original thinker and a product of the Czech reform tradition, or was he entirely dependent on Wycliffe? Though he was undoubtedly drawn to the sacramental and social reforms advocated by Jan Milic (d. 1374), the undisputed father of the Bohemian reformation, it seems certain that without Wycliffe's writings he would not have possessed the zeal necessary to demand reform. But he was drawn to Wycliffe as an individual rather than as a theologian. He demonstrated at Constance that he agreed with Wycliffe on matters of morals and ecclesiastical authority, but not theology. When asked by his accusers to comment on 45 of Wycliffe's propositions, which had already been condemned by the university in 1403 and by the Church in 1408, he agreed with only four of them.

Hus has been regarded as a forerunner of the Radical Reformers of the sixteenth century. His followers, the Hussites, were also known as Calixtines or Utraquists because of their insistence that the laity should partake of the chalice (*calix*) at the Mass, or be permitted to take communion in both kinds (*in utraque specie*), though Huss himself never demanded this.

Bibliography

Fudge T A 1998 *The Magnificent Ride*: *The First Reformation in Hussite Bohemia.* Scolar Pres, Chico, CA

Holeton D R 1987 Sacramental and liturgical Reform in late mediaeval Bohemia. *Studia Liturgica* **17**: 87–95

Leff G 1986 Wyclif and Hus: A doctrinal comparison. In: Kenny A (ed.) *Wyclif in his Times.* Clarendon Press, Oxford, pp 105–126

Spinka M 1968, 1983 *Jan Hus: A Biography*. Princeton University Press, Princeton, NJ

Zeman J K 1977 *The Hussite Movement: A Bibliographical, Study Guide*. Michigan University Press, Ann Arbor, MI

Ibn Ezra, Abraham (ca. 1089–1164)

E. Gutwirth

Born in Toledo, Ibn Ezra spent his youth in the south, in Andalusia. In 1140 he left Spain bound for other European countries. From Italy (Rome and Lucca) he went to France in 1148, visiting Provence and later the north, where he met R. Tam. In 1158 he went to London, and subsequently returned to Narbonne, France.

Although not an original linguist, he was able to disseminate and popularize the grammatical work of the Hispano—Jewish grammarians through translations and treatises. In 1140 he wrote his first grammatical work, while in Rome—*Sēpher Moznayim* (*The Book of the Scales*). It includes an introduction on the history of his linguistic predecessors, an explanation of 59 philological terms, and a study of verbal conjugations. Some time later, but before 1145, he wrote the *Critique of Saadya* while in Lucca. His *Sēpher ha-Yĕsōd* was lost. It contained a grammatical and an exegetical section. His *Yĕsōd* ha-diqdūq or *Sĕphat Yeter* (*The Principles of Grammar*), deals with the main questions of Hebrew grammar, while his *Sēpher Saḥot* (*The Book of Clarity*) is his most mature work, and contains, apart from the questions of grammar proper, a section on the meter of Hebrew poetry.

See also: Hebrew Linguistic Tradition.

Bibliography

Díaz F 1990 *Abraham ibn Ezra and his Age*. Madrid

Ibn Janaḥ (ca. 990–1050)

E. Gutwirth

Known as R. Yonah, his Arabic name was Abu-l-Walīd Marwan ibn Janaḥ. He was the first to elaborate a complete and systematic grammar of the language of the Bible. He was probably born between 985 and 90. He left Cordoba for Saragossa around 1010–13. His *Sēpher Ha-riqmā* must have been written after R. Hai Gaon's death in 1039. He studied in Lucena where he heard such masters as R. Isḥaq ha-Levi b. Mar Shaul or Abu Walid ben Ḥasday and he calls Isḥaq ibn Chiquatilla his teacher. But most of his work was written in Saragossa.

His first work, the *Kitāb al-mustalhaq* was written in order to complement the work of Ḥayyuj. It was translated into Hebrew in the twelfth century by Ovadiah ha-Sefardi as *Sēpher ha-hassāgā* (The Book of Criticism). In it he adds some roots and verbal forms to those provided by Ḥayyuj. The *Risālat al-tanbīh* is a response to a work written in Saragossa, 'The Complementary Book,' in which ibn Janaḥ had been attacked. It was translated into Hebrew in the thirteenth century by Solomon b. Joseph ibn Ayub. The *Risālat al-taqrīb wa al-tashīl* 'The Book of Approach' was written for students so that they should understand Ḥayyuj's principles as set forth in the introductions to his treatises but ibn Janah adds comments of his own. It consists of four parts. In the first part he treats the vowels. The rest of the book is devoted to verb roots whose second letter is weak and to verb roots with double letters. The *Kitāb al-taswi'a* (translated into Hebrew by Judah ibn Tibon in the thirteenth century as *Sēpher ha-tōkhāḥā*), 'The Book of Admonition' is another polemic work in which ibn Janaḥ responds to criticisms of his work and attributes them to envy and ignorance. *Kitāb al-tashwīr* 'Book of Confusion' is divided into four parts. The first treats certain weak roots; the second the formation and meaning of conjugations such as niph'al, and hitpa'el; the third the imperative and passive verbs; and the fourth difficult forms.

His main work is the *Kitāb al-tanqīh*, known in Hebrew as *Sēpher ha-diqdūq* 'The Book of Grammar.' This influential work is divided into two parts: *Kitāb al-luma'*: *Sēpher ha-riqmāh* and *Kitāb al-uṣūl*: *Sēpher ha-shŏrāshīm*. *Sēpher ha-shŏrāshīm* 'The Book of Roots' is a synthesis of the knowledge in the field of Hebrew lexicography up to its period. He attempted to collect almost all the Hebrew roots preserved in the Bible. His introduction explains the criteria of his arrangement of the roots and surpasses Sa'adya and Menaḥem's *Maḥberet* in its usefulness, because he not only gives the root but attempts to present the various forms. He cites the Targum, Mishnah, and Talmud, Geonic literature [especially Sa'adya] and compares Hebrew and Arabic. The *Sēpher ha-riqmā* 'Book of the Flourishing Gardens,' is the grammatical part of the 'Book of Grammar.' The motivation for writing it is that God created man and taught him how to speak so that he should be able to recognize Him. Hebrew is the superior language. The knowledge of language is a prerequisite for all knowledge. The study of language includes syntax, morphology but also rhetoric and hermeneutics. He advocates comparative study (i.e., with Arabic). The book consists of 46 chapters in which he deals with parts of the sentence, the Hebrew letters arranged according to the points of articulation, the composition of the roots, the form of nouns, the conjugation of verbs, and the interchanging consonants and vowels.

See also: Sa'adya Gaon; Hebrew Linguistic Tradition.

Bibliography

Bacher W (ed.) 1896 *Sepher Haschoraschim*: *Würzelwörterbuch der hebräischen Sprache von Abulwalid Merwan ibn Ganah* (*R. Jonà*). *Aus dem Arabischen in's Hebräische übersetzt von Jehuda ibn Tibbon*. Berlin

Derenbourg J, Derenbourg H 1880 *Opuscules et traités d'Abou 'l-Walīd Merwān ibn Djanāh* (*Rabbi Jonah*) *de Córdoba*. Imprimerie nationale, Paris

Tene D, Ben-Hayim Z 1964 *Sefer ha-riqmah le-R. Jonah ibn Janah be-tirgumo ha-'ivri shel R. Judah ibn Tibbon*. Jerusalem

Ibn Maḍā' al-Qurṭubī (1120–96)

M. Y. I. H. Suleiman

Ibn Maḍā' al-Qurṭubī, Aḥmad Ibn 'Abd al-Raḥmān Ibn Muḥammad, is best known in the Arabic grammatical tradition for his incisive critique of what he regarded as the speculative elements in the Arabic grammarians' approach as represented by the notions *'āmil* (regent), *qiyās* (analogy), and *'illa* (cause, reason). In offering this critique Ibn Maḍā' relies principally on Ẓāhirite theology which advocates a surface-oriented and literalist interpretation of the text of the Qur'ān as a framework for protecting it against falsification, especially in view of its status as the prime legal document in Islamic juridical thinking. In addition to his reliance on jurisprudence as a theoretical frame of reference, Ibn Maḍā' utilizes his experience as a language teacher to undermine the pedagogic value of what he regards as metaphysical elements in Arabic grammar. It is this dimension of his work which explains his pre-eminent position as an inspirational figure in the various attempts to simplify pedagogic grammar in the twentieth century, particularly the two proposals by Muṣṭafā Ibrāhīm in *Iḥyā' al-Naḥw* (1937), and Shawqī Ḍayf in *Tajdīd al-Naḥw* (1982) and *Taysīr al-Naḥw al-Ta'līmī Qadīman wa Ḥadīthan ma'a Nahji Tajdīdihi*) (1986).

In his slim but now famous *Kitābu al-Raddi 'alā al-Nuḥāt* (*Book in Refutation of the Grammarians*) Ibn Maḍā' rejects the two types of regent *lafẓī* (expressed) and *ma'nawī* (abstract) as well as the notion of *ḥadhf* (deletion), *iḍmār* (suppression), and *taqdīr* (supplettive insertion)—which are closely related to the notion of regency—on the grounds that they presuppose a speculatively oriented approach to the study of language, instead of an empirically based one. In the latter approach, emphasis is placed on what might be called the surface structures of attested data as opposed to reconstructed data which form a necessary component of the former approach. Ibn Maḍā' also criticizes what he regards as the overzealous commitment to the use of analogy in Arabic grammatical thinking, directing his most scathing remarks at the predominant application of this notion to generate what he calls 'hypothetical utterances' which cannot be matched with any legitimate data in the speech of the Arabs. The tendency to apply analogy in this fashion is said to be especially characteristic of pedagogic grammars in, particularly, the formation of the morphophonological bases of surface data at the word level.

In a similar manner, Ibn Maḍā' criticizes the practice of *ta'līl* (explanation) in Arabic grammar because it is not always consistent with his view of this discipline as an empirical enterprise. In outlining his position, Ibn Maḍā' divides the *'illa* into three types: *ūlā* (primary), *thāniya* (secondary), and *thālitha* (tertiary). He accepts the validity of the primary *'illa* on the grounds that it amounts to what may be called 'grammatical rule,' in the sense that it captures what is essentially a significant generalization or irregular feature of the language. In addition to its primary descriptive function, a primary *'illa* may be used prescriptively in pedagogic grammars, thus corresponding in this regard to *'illa ta'līmiyya* (pedagogic *'illa*) in Zajjājī. Ibn Maḍā' divides the secondary *'illa* into three subcategories: *maqṭū'un bihi* (absolutely certain), *fīhi iqnā'un* (generally convincing), and *maqṭū'un bifasādihi* (absolutely corrupt). The difference between these subcategories of *'illa* can be explained by saying that the first refers to an empirically testable explanation, the second to a 'plausible explanation,' and the third to a 'metaphysical' explanation. Ibn Maḍā' rejects the application of the first subcategory of secondary *'illa* in grammar on two grounds: (a) it answers a 'why' question which is not the concern of Arabic grammar as a purely descriptive discipline whose main function is to deal with the 'how' dimension of linguistic data; and (b) it does not serve any relevant purpose in pedagogic grammar. This position on the part of Ibn Maḍā' shows that he adopts a narrow interpretation of empiricism in grammatical theory and, furthermore, that he does not totally separate descriptive from pedagogic grammar. Ibn Maḍā' rejects the second subcategory of the secondary *'illa* on the basis of the fact that: (a) it does not answer the definition of empiricism he advocates; (b) it is not characterized by certainty (*yaqīn*); and (c) it is not directly relevant to pedagogic grammar. He also rejects the third subcategory of the secondary *'illa* mainly because it is totally speculative in nature. It is, however, not clear how the latter subcategory differs from the tertiary *'illa* which is left more or less undefined by Ibn Maḍā', particularly in view of the fact that both seem to be rejected on the same grounds.

See also: Arabic Linguistic Tradition.

Irigaray, Luce (1930s–)

T. Beattie

Luce Irigaray was born in Belgium and has lived in France since the early 1960s. A practising psychoanalyst, she holds doctorates in linguistics and philosophy, and is Director of Research in Philosophy at the Centre National de la Recherche Scientifique in Paris. Her second doctoral thesis, published in 1974 as *Speculum de l'autre femme,* resulted in her dismissal from the Ecole Freudienne de Paris directed by Jacques Lacan (see *Lacan, Jacques*), and from her teaching post at the University of Vincennes. In the 1980s she was active with women's political groups in Italy. She has had a mixed reception among English-speaking feminists, some of whom criticize her for essentialism or elitism.

Irigaray offers a sexually transgressive psycholinguistic philosophy based on Freudian and Lacanian psychoanalysis and Derridean deconstruction. She credits Sigmund Freud with exposing the psychological dynamics by which patriarchy is perpetuated, but criticizes him for not recognizing the historical and political determinants of his theory. Although Jacques Derrida's (see *Derrida, Jacques*) influence is mainly implicit, his desconstructive strategies inform her feminized interventions in the texts of the philosophical canon.

Irigaray argues that since Plato the western tradition has been dominated by a universalized form of masculine subjectivity in which sexual difference is elided, and the primal relationship to the maternal body and nature is repressed in favour of an androcentric and disembodied culture. This hom(m)osexual economy is transmitted through language, and the creation of a culture of sexual difference therefore requires the restructuring of language. The phallogocentrism of a linear logic with a singular masculine subject modelled upon a father God, is relativized through the Feuerbachian projection of a feminine divine, the reclamation of maternal genealogies, and the morphology of a pluralized subjectivity symbolised by the two lips of the female sexual/speaking body. Irigaray seeks to speak as (a) woman, *parler-femme,* through the parodic mimesis of the language of the unconscious, associated with repressed desire for the mother but also with femininity, hysteria, death and, in Lacan, female mysticism.

Irigaray's concept of a feminine divine is balanced by her use of the term *sensible transcendental* to describe a non-linguistic sense of divinity constituting a space of symbolic sexual exchange. Her feminization of religious language appeals to values of fecundity and desire rather than of sacrifice and repression associated with Freud's and René Girard's accounts of religion. She proposes alternative religious paradigms through the reclamation of the mother daughter figures of Greek mythology, and the subversive reinterpretation of Christian incarnational symbolism.

Irigaray's poetic linguistic experiments use psychoanalytic methods of transference and counter-transference to draw the reader into a polysemous exchange. Interpreters sometimes read her too literally, because they fail to recognize her techniques of parody and mimesis.

See also: Christian Views on Language; Postmodernism; Feminism.

Bibliography

Irigaray L 1985 *Speculum of the Other Woman*. Cornell University Press, Ithaca, NY

Irigaray L 1985 *This Sex Which Is Not One*. Cornell University Press, Ithaca, NY

Irigaray L 1993 *An Ethics of Sexual Difference*. The Athlone Press, London

Whitford M 1991 *Luce Irigaray—Philosophy in the Feminine*. Routledge, London and New York

Whitford M (ed.) 1994 *The Irigaray Reader*. Blackwell Publishers, Oxford and Cambridge, MA

Jerome (c. 346–420)

G. L. Jones

St Jerome, linguist and exegete, was one of the greatest minds of the Early Church. Born to Christian parents at Stridon in Dalmatia, he was educated in Rome where he studied under the famous Latin grammarian Aelius Donatus. In 374, after spending some time in Trier and Aquileia, he renounced city life and joined the hermits in the Chalcis desert east of Antioch. In 382 he returned to Rome where he became secretary to Pope Damasus and acted as a spiritual guide to several prominent women. From 386 until his death he lived in Bethlehem as the leader of a monastic community.

Jerome's voluminous correspondence testifies to his role as a fierce opponent of Arianism and Pelagianism, and as a spiritual director renowned for his extreme asceticism. But he is best known as a translator of the Bible and a biblical commentator. In both of these enterprises he was able to make full use of his linguistic expertise, references to which are scattered throughout his writings. Having perfected his Latin style and learned Greek during his student days in Rome, he began studying Hebrew when he was in the Syrian desert. Though he complains of initial difficulties, he persisted, and with the help of a converted Jew became a competent Hebraist. In contrast to the negative assessment of some critics, his proficiency in Hebrew must be stressed. The description of him as a *vir trilinguis* is entirely justified. During his period of seclusion he also made some headway in Aramaic (which he calls Chaldaic) and claims to have become a fluent speaker of Syriac. There is also some evidence that he had a basic knowledge of Arabic. These linguistic attainments made Jerome the exception to the rule in the Early Church and equipped him for the task of translating and expounding the scriptures.

Though encouraged by Damasus to assess critically early Latin versions of the gospels, most of Jerome's biblical work was done during the period he spent in Bethlehem. He insisted that a translation of the Old Testament had to be based on the Hebrew original, which he calls the *hebraica veritas*, not on the LXX (see *Septuagint*). His study of the Hebrew Bible persuaded him that only those books found within it should be regarded as canonical by Christians, thereby excluding what later came to be called The Apocrypha (see *Apocrypha, Christian*). During the period he was involved with the translation (390–404) he was in close contact with Palestinian Jews and sought their assistance in procuring manuscripts and in pursuing further studies in Hebrew. His knowledge of Semitic languages was incorporated into the Vulgate, with the result that it is far closer to the original than was once supposed. His biblical commentaries also contain much exegetical material derived from his Jewish teachers. But in spite of the example which he set, Jerome's immediate successors in the Church's scholarly circles were not such enthusiastic Semiticists with the result that the study of Hebrew and cognate languages by Christians lapsed for centuries during the Dark Ages.

See also: Vulgate; Bible Translations, Ancient Versions; Church Latin; Apocrypha, Christian.

Bibliography

Barr J 1966 St Jerome's Appreciation of Hebrew. *BJRL* **49**: 281–302

Kelly J N D 1975 *Jerome*: *His Life, Writings and Controversies*. Duckworth, London

Rice E F 1985 *St Jerome in the Renaissance*. Johns Hopkins University Press, Baltimore

Sparks H F D 1970 Jerome as a Biblical Scholar. In: Ackroyd P R and Evans C F (eds.) *The Cambridge History of the Bible*. Cambridge University Press, Cambridge, I: 510–540

Sutcliffe E F 1969 Jerome. In: Lampe G W H (ed.) *The Cambridge History of the Bible*. Cambridge University Press, Cambridge, II: 80–102

Kant, Immanuel (1724–1804)

R. C. S. Walker

Immanuel Kant was born on April 22, 1724 in Königsberg, East Prussia (now Kaliningrad, Russia), where he spent his whole life, becoming Professor of Logic and Metaphysics in 1770 and eventually Rector of the University. In his lifetime he achieved a revolution in German philosophical thought, opening the way to the idealism of Fichte, Schelling, and Hegel. Elsewhere his influence was felt more slowly (though Coleridge was an early admirer), but its effect was again profound. He died on February 12, 1804.

1. Transcendental Idealism

The Critique of Pure Reason (1781) is concerned with how knowledge is possible. The rationalist tradition (then dominant in Germany) held that humans possess certain concepts innately, and can recognize as self-evident certain truths from which can be deduced substantial knowledge about the world. The empiricists, in contrast, held that concepts and knowledge of the world could only be derived from experience, though Hume—the most consistent of them—argued that the only way of deriving from experience the concepts of cause and physical object showed them to be inherently confused. Kant believes they are not confused, and not derived from experience. He also holds that humans have substantial knowledge which could not have been derived from experience: in his terminology, synthetic a priori knowledge. It includes mathematical truths, and truths like 'Every event has a cause.'

We can know these truths, Kant thinks, only because we ourselves make them true: i.e., read them into the world. Mathematics he takes to be about space and time, which however are not real independently of us, but forms which our mind imposes upon data it receives. Similarly concepts like those of cause and object are so read by us as to guarantee they will apply within the world as we experience it, and in such a way that principles like 'Every event has a cause' will be true within that world. The world of 'appearances' or 'phenomena' is thus partly the product of our mind's activity. Yet truth in that world (the familiar world of space, time, and causality) is not just a matter of what we happen to believe. The concepts and principles which we ourselves supply provide standards for distinguishing true from false beliefs, and allow us to assign to physical objects a reality distinct from our perceptions of them. Because he treats objects in this way, and not (like Berkeley) as sets of perceptions, Kant calls himself an empirical realist; he calls himself also a transcendental idealist, because the phenomenal world as a whole is partly the product of our minds.

Kant does not simply postulate that our minds supply these elements to the world. He argues that they must, for experience would be impossible otherwise. Perhaps other beings could impose forms different from space and time, but some such forms are required for any experience of sensible particulars. Twelve fundamental concepts or 'categories' he argues to be indispensable, including that of cause, and he claims that principles like 'Every event has a cause' must hold for spatio-temporal experience to be possible. Arguments of this kind, that something must be so if experience is to be possible, are often called transcendental arguments.

The phenomenal world is only partly the product of our minds. Minds work on data supplied by things as they are in themselves (or 'noumena'). Things in themselves are wholly independent of us, and about them we can know nothing. We can know nothing about them empirically, since we do not experience them, nor a priori, for *a priori* knowledge is possible only in virtue of what we read into what is known. The failure to realize these limits to knowledge leads, Kant holds, to the errors of metaphysicians, and to natural mistakes in our thinking about the self, the world as a totality, and God—though the tendencies that lead to these natural mistakes have great heuristic value.

2. Judgment and Truth

Kant regards language as the expression of thought, though he also describes thinking as inner speech. Thought consists in making judgements, and he claims that logic, by revealing that there are twelve fundamental types of judgment, shows there are twelve ways in which the mind can act. It is because concepts also involve mental activity that he thinks there must correspondingly be twelve fundamental concepts, the categories.

Judgments may be either analytic or synthetic. Analytic judgments are those whose truth can be determined 'in accordance with the Principle of Contradiction,' or by means of logical laws and conceptual analysis: such as 'All unmarried men are unmarried,' or, equivalently, 'All bachelors are unmarried.' All other judgments are synthetic. Kant considers mathematical, as well as metaphysical, judgments to be synthetic, though also a priori.

Truth is correspondence: 'the agreement of knowledge with its object.' Judgments about things in themselves may be true, but there is no way for us to know they are. Judgments about the phenomenal world, however, can be shown to 'agree with their objects' by establishing their coherence with what is given to us empirically in sensation, in accordance with those forms and principles which our minds supply.

3. Aesthetics and Moral Philosophy

The appreciation of beauty is a matter of feeling, not reason, but in *The Critique of Judgment* (1790) Kant argues that it can be expected of everyone nonetheless. It arises whenever something appears well-adapted to our cognitive faculties, without our being able fully to capture why. The moral law, in contrast, is purely rational. In *Groundwork of the Metaphysic of Morals* (1785) and *Critique of Practical Reason* (1788), he argues it is an imperative which is 'categorical' in that it must be obeyed for its own sake, not for the sake of any further end to be achieved by it (like the promotion of happiness). Only actions performed out of respect for the moral law have genuine moral worth; actions which accord with the law, but are done for some other motive (e.g., because one feels generous), do not. Being purely rational, the categorical imperative must bind all rational beings universally. It can be formulated, 'Act only on those principles of action which you can rationally will as universal law.'

4. Kant Today

Kant's influence is pervasive, but one or two points may be specially noticed. In moral philosophy his conception of the law as a rational motive has often been dismissed, but in the twentieth century there were interesting attempts to give a greater place to rational motivation along roughly Kantian lines. Transcendental idealism also has its supporters, but since Kant's own day people have often been unconvinced by his retention of things in themselves. Many, also, have been unconvinced by the idealistic aspect—the conception of the phenomenal world as in part a product of our minds. The most trenchant of these has been Strawson, who nevertheless finds the key to metaphysics in Kantian transcendental arguments.

Bibliography

Allison H E 1983 *Kant's Transcendental Idealism.* Yale University Press, New Haven, CT
Kant I 1929 (trans. Kemp Smith N) *The Critique of Pure Reason.* Macmillan, London
Kant I 1984 Groundwork of the metaphysic of morals. In: Paton H J (ed. and trans.) *The Moral Law.* Hutchinson, London
Kemp J 1968 *The Philosophy of Kant.* Oxford University Press, London
Körner S 1955 *Kant.* Penguin, Harmondsworth
Langton R 1998 *Kantian Humility.* Clarendon Press, Oxford
Scruton R 1982 *Kant.* Oxford University Press, Oxford
Strawson P F 1966 *The Bounds of Sense.* Methuen, London
Sullivan R J 1994 *An Introduction to Kant's Ethics.* Cambridge University Press, Cambridge

Kilwardby, Robert (ca. 1215–79)

F. P. Dinneen

Robert Kilwardby was a philosopher, theologian, logician, and Archbishop of Canterbury. He died in 1279. Other dates in his career are less certain. He was probably born in England about 1215 and won his Master of Arts in Paris in 1237. His next 8 years of lecturing there on grammar and logic assured his scholarly repute. His commentaries on Priscian and Donatus may have been written during this period. Discussions in both of these works are more philosophic than grammatical.

Kilwardby's *De ortu et divisione scientiarum* ('On the origin and division of sciences') was a commentary on Avicenna written as a preface to his exposition of Petrus Hispanus' *Summulae Logicales.* It was an extensive partition and evaluation of secular branches of knowledge (mechanics appears as 'active philosophy') and theology and was considered the most important introduction to scholastic philosophy. While contemporary *De modis significandi* (on modes of signifying) tracts mixed logical, grammatical, or philosophic sophistries (see *Linguistic Theory in the Later Middle Ages*), Kilwardby distinguished the grammatical from logical ones.

He returned to England around 1245 and entered the Dominican Order in Oxford. After 8 years of study, he lectured there on theology and scripture until elected Provincial of the English Dominicans in 1261. It was he who divided Augustine's work into chapters, prefixing short analyses to them.

He was made Archbishop of Canterbury in 1273, and in 1277 condemned 30 theses of Averroes taught in Oxford which were considered erroneous in logic, natural philosophy, and grammar. One held that *I runs, you runs,* and *(I) run* (*ego currit, tu currit* and *curro*) are equally perfect and congruous.

Renowned among his contemporaries for the development of syllogistics, his works are models of logical form. Notable publications include his *De Tempore*, *De Universali*, *De Relatione*.

Two manuscripts of his commentary on Priscian's *De Constructione* are preserved in Oxford and an edition of his commentary on Donatus' *Ars Minor* was published in 1984. In that work he says that a logician defines parts of speech in terms of what they mean (formally), while a grammarian defines them in terms of what they are composed of (materially).

In 1278 he was made a cardinal–bishop of Porto in Italy and required to reside in Rome. He resigned his English see, taking all its registers and judicial papers with him. Canterbury's oldest records begin with those of his successor, Peckham. He died and was buried in Viterbo in 1279.

See also: Philology and History.

Bibliography

Schmücker L (ed.) 1984 *Robertus Kilwardby O P In Donati Artem Maiorem*. Weger, Brixen, South Tirol

Weisheipl J A 1967 Robert Kilwardby. In: *New Catholic Encyclopedia*, vol. XII, p. 533. New York

Kimḥi, David (1160–1235?)

J. Weinberg

David Kimḥi (popularly known by his Radak) was probably the most widely read of the Jewish medieval grammarians. His work superseded all previous writings on Hebrew grammar. Born in Narbonne, France, in 1160 into a family of grammarians (both his father Joseph and brother Moses wrote grammatical treatises), Kimḥi regarded the study of Hebrew grammar as a prerequisite for correct use of the language in writing, both prose and verse, as well as an indispensable tool for the interpretation of the plain meaning (*pěshat*) of Scripture. Apart from his Bible commentaries in which he raises many points of grammar, Kimḥi wrote one major grammatical work, the *Mikhlōl* (*Summa*), one section of which contained an exposition of Hebrew grammar, the other a lexicon of the Hebrew Bible. The second section was later taken as a separate work and published first in Rome (1469–72) under the title *Sēpher Ha-Shŏrāshīm* (*Book of Roots*), while the title *Mikhlōl* was exclusively used for the section on grammar (first printed in Constantinople 1532–34). The aim of the *Mikhlōl* was to provide a concise and systematic review of earlier grammatical works, most of which had been written in Arabic, and to synthesize divergent sources. Although Kimḥi does not lay claim to originality—'I come like the gleaner after the reaper'—and makes constant reference to Ḥayyūj, ibn Janaḥ and his father, he does advance some original ideas particularly in the presentation of the material. Thus, for example, while he uses his predecessors' division of Hebrew into nouns, verbs, and particles, he devotes the major part of his work to the verb and begins his discussion with it. He appears to have been the first to have distinguished the '*waw*-consecutive' from the *waw*-copulative. While later Hebrew grammarians were critical of the *Mikhlōl*, it became the standard Hebrew grammar for many centuries. It was extensively used by Christian Hebraists such as Johannes Reuchlin and Sebastian Münster and was translated into Latin. An anonymous grammatical work *Petaḥ Débhārai* (*The Beginning of My Words*), the bulk of which was devoted to the verb, was attributed to Qimḥi, but this attribution was rejected by Bacher, although accepted by Hirschfeld. The *Sēpher Ha-Shŏrāshīm* was based on the lexicon of ibn Janah of the same name, but was more comprehensive. He illustrates the entries with quotations from the Hebrew Bible, explanations of grammatical forms, references to post biblical Hebrew and to Aramaic and Arabic and gives translations into Provençal. The lexicon was also used by Christian Hebraists and translated into Latin with additions by Sebastian Münster in Basel in 1535.

See also: Hebrew Grammarians; Ibn Janaḥ; Ḥayyuj, J.

Bibliography

Bacher W 1974 *Die hebräische Sprachwissenschaft vom 10. bis zum 16. Jahrhundert*. Benjamins, Amsterdam

Kimḥi D 1847 *Sēpher-Ha-Shŏrāshīm, Radicum liber sive hebraeum bibliorum lexicon*. Bethge, Berlin

Kimḥi D 1952 *David Kimḥi's Hebrew Grammar* (*Mikhlōl*). Bloch, New York

Talmage F 1975 *David Kimḥi: The Man and the Commentaries*. Harvard University Press, Cambridge, MA

Tauber J 1867 *Standpunkt und Leistung des R. David Kimchi als Grammatiker*. Selbstverlag des Verfassers, Breslau

Kittel, Gerhard (1888–1948)

G. L. Jones

Gerhard Kittel, German biblical scholar, studied at Leipzig, Tübingen, and Berlin. After gaining his doctorate at Kiel in 1913, he taught at various German universities including Tübingen where he was made professor in 1926. He moved to Vienna in 1939, but returned to Tübingen in 1943. An expert in ancient Judaism and its relationship to Christianity, he enjoyed an international reputation as one of the most distinguished and influential NT scholars of the 1930s. His elucidation of the connection between Christianity and Judaism, and his insistence that Rabbinic Judaism was the proper context for understanding the origin and development of NT Christianity, constitutes, his main contribution to scholarship. On this issue he disagreed fundamentally with W. Bousset who played down the importance of Judaism.

Though his early work earned him Jewish admirers, Kittel was no philosemite. Influenced by Nazi propaganda, he maintained that the revolution of 1933 was God's gift to Germany and immediately became an active member of the National Socialist party. In 1945 he was imprisoned for 17 months because of his political sympathies and did not teach again. His antisemitic leanings appear in the several contributions he made to *Forschungen zur Jüdenfrage*, a journal founded by Walter Frank, president of the National Institute for the History of the New Germany. He became an even more active critic of the Jews in his book *Die Jüdenfrage* (1993) in which he accepted that 'the Jewish question', created by dispersion and emancipation, posed a problem for Germany. For him the authentic symbol of the Jew was that of the homeless wanderer whose status reflected God's judgement on a disobedient people.

Undoubtedly Kittel's best-known work is his monumental *Theological Dictionary of the New Testament* which he edited from 1932 until his death. The work concentrates on those words in the NT which have any theological significance and discusses the close connection between philology and Christian theology. Despite the adverse criticism of scholars such as James Barr, who believes that it contains 'great and sweeping linguistic misconceptions,' and despite the accusation that the editor's negative attitude towards Judaism is reflected in the views of his some of his collaborators, this continues to be an indispensible reference work for those engaged in biblical studies.

See also: Barr, J.; Bible.

Bibliography

Barr J 1961 *The Semantics of Biblical Language*. SCM, London, pp. 206–272

Ericksen R P 1985 *Theologians under Hitler*. Yale, London, pp. 28–78

Ericksen R P 1989 Christians and the Holocaust: the Wartime Writings of Gerhard Kittel. In: Bauer Y et al. (eds.) *Remembering for the Future*. Pergamon, Oxford, Vol. 3, pp. 2400–14

Johnson M D 1986 Power Politics and NT Scholarship in the National Socialist Period. *Journal of Ecumenical Studies* **23**: 1–24

Koelle, Sigismund Wilhelm (1823–1902)

M. Schladt

Koelle, a German missionary and linguist, is considered to be one of the pioneers of the classification and description of African languages.

He was born on July 14, 1823 in Cleebronn (Württemberg). After attending the Basel Missionary Seminary, he was transferred to the CMS (Church Missionary Society) college at Islington, London. In 1847, he was ordained a priest; after a course in Arabic he was sent to Sierra Leone, where since 1807 the British fleet had brought captured slaveships back to the naval base at Freetown. By 1850, some 70,000 released slaves had settled there. In view of this, the CMS chose Freetown as one of their first mission fields in Africa. When Koelle arrived in Freetown there already existed a tradition of research into African languages. Their study had two aims: first, to bring Christianity to the Africans; second, to show the essential humanity of African tongues: 'It has often been observed that the Negro race is not a genuine branch of the human family... The genuine humanity of the Negroes can be proved in a variety of ways: and one of them is the philological' (Koelle 1854b).

Koelle taught English, Greek, theology, pastoral training, mathematics, and Hebrew at the Fourah Bay Institute of the CMS in Freetown. Besides his teaching duties, he undertook a unique linguistic documentation. In 1849, he reported on the indigenous writing system of the Vai. After his return to England in February 1853 he published grammars of Vai and Kanuri and his major work, the *Polyglotta Africana*, which in the 1990s is still regarded as the basic pioneer work of African linguistics. On the basis of 296 terms, Koelle compared 200 vocabularies, which, according to late twentieth-century classification, correspond to about 120 African languages. The carefully selected terms included both basic (e.g., body parts, numerals) and cultural words. The publication showed Koelle's considerable grammatical understanding of African languages. Although he did not mark tones and did not differentiate between voiced and voiceless sounds, his orthography was consistent and based on a standard model. There, in his 'Introductory Remarks,' Koelle attempted a mainly geographical classification of the languages. Many of the terms he proposed—such as Westatlantic, Mande, Kru—were still in use in the 1990s.

In the following years Koelle became an internationally recognized linguist. He contributed to the writing down of languages such as the production of a standard 'universal' orthography and the marking of tone in Chinese. In 1856, the French Academy of Sciences awarded him the first prize of the Volney fund for philological research. He completely turned away from the field of African languages when he was sent by the CMS to the Eastern Mediterranean where his major works—including a translation of the Book of Common Prayer (1883)—were in Turkish. Most of these manuscripts have never been published.

Koelle returned to England in 1883, and died on February 18, 1902 in London.

See also: Christianity in Africa; Missionaries.

Bibliography

Hair P E H 1963 Koelle at Freetown, an historical introduction. In: Koelle S W *Polyglotta Africana*. Akademische Druck-und Verlagsanstalt, Graz

Koelle S W 1854a *Outlines of a Grammar of the Vei Language, together with a Vei–English Vocabulary*. Church Missionary House, London.

Koelle S W 1854b *Grammar of the Bornu or Kanuri Language*. Church Missionary House, London

Koelle S W 1854c *Polyglotta Africana*. Church Missionary House, London–Salisbury

Westermann D 1953/54 Sigismund Wilhelm Koelle: Ein Pionier der afrikanischen Sprachforschung. *Afrika und Übersee* **37**: 49–51

Krapf, Johann Ludwig (1810–81)

E. D. Elderkin

Krapf was one of the pioneer missionary linguists whose work provided basic data on which Western scholars could base their discussions of the structure and classification of African languages.

He was born in Württemburg in 1810. He received missionary training at Basel before becoming associated with the Church Missionary Society, under whose auspices he travelled to Eastern Africa in 1837.

He considered that the key to the conversion of that part of Africa lay in the widespread Oroma (Eastern Cushitic) linguistic group (then referred to as Galla), and he believed that evangelization should be conducted directly in the language of the people, rather than working through interpreters. After travelling in Ethiopia, where the majority of the Oromo lived, it was realized that work there would be impracticable and he turned his attention to the East African coast, in what became Kenya, where the most southerly speakers of Oromo were located. Once there he applied himself to the study of the indigenous Bantu languages. He attempted Bible translations into both Oromo and the East African Bantu languages. Linguistically, his best remembered works are the six-language *Vocabulary* and his Swahili dictionary, which was compiled both during his stay in East Africa and with the assistance of missionaries in the field, especially Johann Rebmann, after his return to Europe in 1855. Between 1855 and his death in 1881, he made only two brief visits to East Africa. His Swahili dictionary, based on the Mombasa dialect, despite its transcription which predates the establishment of a phonemic script (and which Edward Steere working in Zanzibar had called 'confused and inexact') is still valuable for its encyclopaedic entries and for its recordings of words and meanings which escaped later lexicographers working chiefly with Zanzibar Swahili. It was in manuscript form at the time of his death and published posthumously.

See also: Christianity in Africa; Missionaries.

Bibliography

Krapf J L 1850 *Vocabulary of Six East African Languages: Kisuáheli, Kiníka, Kikámba, Kipokómo, Kihiáu, Kigálla.* Tübingen

Krapf J L 1860 *Travels, Researches, and Missionary Labours*. Trübner, London

Krapf J L 1882 *Dictionary of the Suahili Language*. Trübner, London

Kristeva, Julia (1941–)

T. Beattie

Julia Kristeva moved to Paris from her native Bulgaria in 1966, becoming a critical voice in the structuralist and poststructuralist movement associated with the influential *Tel Quel* group through whom she met her husband, Philippe Sollers. Her doctorate in French literature was published in 1974 as *La Révolution du Langage poétique*. Kristeva is Professor of Linguistics at the University of Paris VII and a visiting professor at Columbia University in New York. She has published several novels. Personal events in the 1970s, including the birth of her son and the completion of her psychoanalytic training, led to the depoliticization of her work and a greater emphasis on the individual in psychoanalysis, philosophy and literary and cultural theory.

Drawing on Freudian psychoanalysis and Saussurean (see *Saussure, Ferdinand-(Mongin) de*) linguistics, Kristeva developed the science of *semanalysis*. Meaning is a signifying process in which the symbolic, associated with grammar, structure and subjectivity, develops in creative or disruptive tension with the semiotic, comprising the rhythms, inflections and poetics of speech through which the biological drives are discharged and the body is incorporated into language. The semiotic is sometimes expressed as the *chora*, which in Plato's *Timaeus* suggests a fluctuating primal receptacle with maternal connotations.

Following Melanie Klein, Kristeva argues that the process of self-differentiation from the maternal body precedes the Oedipus complex and the Lacanian (see *Lacan, Jacques*) mirror stage, so that language originates in the bodily relationship to the mother. She questions the psychoanalytic reduction of the father's role to that of a threatening oedipal figure who enforces separation from the mother, and proposes an imaginary, pre-oedipal father as a loving presence who facilitates individuation and socialization.

Kristeva advocates a maternal discourse dissociated from femininity, womanhood, and the socialized mother–child relationship, which might express abjection and love, horror and fascination, associated with the alienated other of language and the psyche. The maternal body, divided between self and other, symbolizes this intrinsic heterogeneity. The unified, masculine subject of post-Enlightenment culture is constructed on the repression of otherness, which is projected in the nationalisms and intolerances of modern society. A transformed ethics entails a recognition that as subjects in process, we are *Strangers to Ourselves* (1991).

Kristeva suggests that religion is a cultural anachronism that has been replaced by psychoanalysis, but her work is deeply influenced by Christianity. She accords central significance to the Christian understanding of love, particularly in the Gospels and the writings of Thomas Aquinas (see *Aquinas, Thomas*).

She is critical of aspects of feminism and is not generally regarded as a feminist thinker, but she has had a far-reaching influence on feminist theory.

See also: Feminism; Christian Views on Language

Bibliography

Fletcher J, Benjamin A (eds.) 1991 *Abjection, Melancholia and Love–the Work of Julia Kristeva.* Routledge, London

Kristeva J 1982 *Powers of Horror—An Essay on Abjection.* Columbia University Press, New York

Kristeva J 1987 *Tales of Love*. Columbia University Press, New York

Kristeva J 1987 *In the Beginning Was Love—Psychoanalysis and Faith*. Columbia University Press, New York

Kristeva J 1991 *Strangers to Ourselves*. Harvester, Hemel Hempstead

Kristeva J 1995 *The Kristeva Reader*. Moi T (ed.). Blackwell, Oxford, UK, Cambridge, MA, USA

Oliver K (ed.) 1997 *The Portable Kristeva*. Columbia University Press, New York

Kuiper, Franciscus Bernardus Jacobus (1907–)

A. G. Menon

Franciscus Kuiper was born on July 7, 1907 to Franciscus Bernardus Jacobus Kuiper Sr, a schoolteacher, and his wife Anna Maria van Dijck, in the Hague, the Netherlands. He pursued his university education at Leiden with classical languages as his main subjects, besides Sanskrit, Old Germanic, Baltic, Slavic, and Old Iranian. His most important teachers were C. C. Uhlenbeck and N. van Wijk. In 1928 he took his first bachelor's degree and in the following year got his second bachelor's degree in Indology, both *cum laude*. In the six months between the last bachelor's degree and the start of his military training he wrote his third long article (116 pp.) which was published in 1934, and studied the Vedic Brāhmaṇas under W. Caland in Utrecht. In 1934 he took his master's degree in the classical languages and Russian. Two weeks after this he got his doctor's degree *cum laude* for his dissertation on *Die Indogermanischen Nasalpräsentia*, a complete edition of which appeared in 1937. At the end of 1939 he was appointed as professor of Sanskrit at Leiden University as successor to J. Ph. Vogel, where he served until 1972.

During the German occupation of the Netherlands (1940–45) the University of Leiden was closed, which gave him the opportunity, besides philological work, such as collating a Sanskrit manuscript, to deepen his knowledge of Tamil (Dravidian), which he had studied with a native speaker in Batavia, and Munda (particularly Korku). On the Indo-European side he published in those years 'Notes on Vedic noun-inflexion' (1942), whereas his later publications particularly dealt with the development of the PIE laryngeals in Indo–Iranian, at that time a novel branch of study. Throughout his academic career Kuiper has shown a keen interest in the influence of and interaction between languages belonging to different language families and his belief in language as a means for cultural studies was strengthened by his findings of foreign loanwords in the *Rigveda*. His publications from 1931 up till 1992 reflect his continuing interest in all the language families mentioned above. The tenor of his research is historical and comparative. His studies are not marked by shifting interest, but by a combination of different viewpoints leading to acceptable solutions to linguistic and cultural diffusion.

His interest in Vedic studies brought him closer to the other language families such as Dravidian and Munda, because he strongly believed in the process of convergence in the Indic area when Indo–Aryan started to develop independently and free from its Iranian cognate. For example, *Proto-Munda words in Sanskrit* (1948), 'Rigvedic loanwords' (1954) and 'the Genesis of a linguistic area' (1967) are clear evidence of his unconventional and daring research directed at finding a suitable explanation for the deviating structure of the Vedic language. He stressed that early Indo–Aryan was not a language spoken in a vacuum. The same holistic approach continues up to his latest publication *Aryans in the Rigveda* (1991). The unexpected structural similarities between the three major language families of the Indian subcontinent lead to the study of the Dravidian origin of the Vedic retroflexion, the similarity of the Dravidian gerunds to the Sanskrit *kṛtvā*, and of the function of the Dravidian verb *eṇa* to the Sanskrit syntactic quotative form *iti* (1967). The two important subjects which formed the center of his research deal with the genesis of the cosmos and the genesis of a linguistic area.

The name of Professor Kuiper is also associated with the International Association for Tamil Research of which he was a President. In addition to his membership of the Royal Dutch Academy of Sciences and Letters he is a foreign or honorary member of Academies and Societies in America, Austria, Denmark, and India. In the 1950s he founded, along with his then colleague Jan Willem de Jong, the *Indo–Iranian Journal*, the first issue of which appeared in December 1957. Up to 1992 Kuiper had published 122 items in the form of books and articles.

Bibliography

Heesterman J C et al. (ed.) 1968 *Pratidānam*. Mouton, The Hague

Jong J W de 1977 F B J Kuiper: Bibliography 1967–76. *Indo–Iranian Journal* **19**: 1–4.

Jong J W de 1987 F B J Kuiper: Bibliography 1978–87. *Indo–Iranian Journal* **30**: 159–60

Kuiper F B J 1967 The Genesis of a linguistic area. *Indo–Iranian Journal* **10**: 81–102

Kuiper F B J 1979 *Varuṇa* and *Vidūṣaka*. On the origin of the Sanskrit drama, Verhandelingen der Koninklijke Nederlandse Akademie van Wetenschappen. North Holland, Amsterdam

Kuiper F B J 1983 *Ancient Indian Cosmogony*. Vikas, New Delhi

Kuiper F B J 1991 *Aryans in the Rigveda*. Rodopi, Amsterdam

Kuiper F B J 1992. *Viṣkali-* name of an accouching deity *Amṛtamahotsava*. Annals of the Bhandarkar Oriental Research Institute, Jubilee Volume, Pune

Kumārajīva

P. Williams

Kumārajīva (probably 344–413 CE) was the single most important translator of Indic Buddhist texts into Chinese.

He was born in Kuchā, an area of Central Asia where Indian and Chinese culture met. He studied in Kashmir, and later at Kashgar in Central Asia. At both these places he would have been thoroughly trained in *Sarvāstivāda* ('The doctrine that all [fundamentally real things (*dharmas*) continue to] exist [in the three times—past, present, and future]'). While in Kashgar Kumārajīva adopted the vision of Buddhism known as *Mahāyāna* (the 'Great Way'). This teaches that the ultimate aspiration should be to attain the superior state of a Perfect Buddha in order better to be able to help others. His ontological position was that of *Madhyamaka* (the 'Middling'), which held that *all* things whatsoever—including so-called 'fundamentally real things' (*dharmas*)—are actually just pragmatic mental constructs. They are completely empty (*śūnya*—void) of any fundamental reality. Kumārajīva's translations, and works such as his correspondence with Hui-yüan, are important sources for how Mahāyāna and Madhyamaka were understood in Central Asia and China at that time. His reputation as a Buddhist monk was sufficiently high for him to be captured by a Chinese expeditionary force that conquered Kuchā in 383. At a time of political turmoil Kumārajīva was held for almost twenty years, during which he learnt Chinese, before being carried-off again in 401 to the Chinese imperial capital of Ch'ang-an.

Under imperial patronage Kumārajīva presided over a great translation bureau, with disciples such as Seng-chao who were to become important in the Chinese interpretation of Madhyamaka. Working with a team of translators, comparing previous translations, Kumārajīva made the definitive Chinese translations of many central Mahāyāna Buddhist texts. It is Kumārajīva's translations that are used of the main 'Perfection of Wisdom' (*Prajñāpāramitā*) and Madhyamaka texts. To the present day his is by far the preferred Chinese version of the 'Lotus (*Saddharmapuṇḍarīka*) Sūtra.'

Kumārajīva revised and immensely improved the translation of technical terms, avoiding terms with e.g. prior Taoist significance. He preferred carefully to transliterate Sanskrit where a Chinese equivalent could not be found. On the other hand he was sometimes willing to omit material in his Chinese translations, and also added glosses to make a text more easily understandable by Chinese. Occasionally the translation team chose or used the wrong Chinese word for a Sanskrit expression. It is possible that Kumārajīva's translation choices may themselves have influenced Chinese understanding of the technicalities of e.g. Madhyamaka philosophy.

Nevertheless while there were later translators who were central in transmitting other Buddhist philosophies to China, and their translations may sometimes be more literal than those of Kumārajīva, Kumārajīva's translations remain very often the preferred ones for both Chinese readers and Western translators.

See also: Apocrypha, Buddhist; Buddhism, Chinese; Buddhism, Indian; Buddhist Canons: Translations; Chinese; Translation: History.

Bibliography

Bagchi P B 1927 *Le canon Bouddhique en Chine*. Librairie Orientaliste Paul Geuthner, Paris

Robinson R H 1967 *Early Mādhyamika in India and China*. Wisconsin University Press, Madison, Milwaukee, and London

Zürcher E 1972 *The Buddhist Conquest of China*. EJ Brill, Leiden

Lacan, Jacques (1901–81)

J. C. Maher

Jacques Marie Emile Lacan, the French psychiatrist, suggested the importance of linguistic awareness in psycho-analytic theory. The son of a businessman, he was born and educated in Paris and received at PhD for this thesis on paranoia (1932) from the Faculté de Médecine. He subsequently worked there from 1934. He underwent psycho-analytic training with Rudolph Loewenstein, joining the staff of St Anne's Hospital in 1953 and later the Ecole Normale Supérieure. Known as the 'French Freud,' Lacan attempted to reinterpret the whole of psychoanalytic theory and practice from the viewpoint of language, in particular that of structural linguistics. Following the ideas of Ferdinand de Saussure (see *Saussure, Ferdinand (-Mongin) de*) and influenced by Roman Jakobson, Lacan excoriated the dominant school of Anglo–American ego-psychology and taught that psychoanalysis revealed the entire structure of language. Lacan argued for a 'return' to Freud's original principle that psychoanalysis is the intersubjective communication between analyst and patient, its sole medium being the language provided by the patient.

Lacan proposed that the unconscious mind operates as a linguistic system, expressed axiomatically as 'the unconscious is structured like a language.' Like the operation of meaning in language, meanings in the unconscious are combined, 'condensed,'or 'displaced' outwards towards the making of new meanings. Experience occurs in the form of three 'registers': 'symbolic,' 'imaginary,' and 'real.' Language encodes experience by means of the symbolic, i.e., through signs. The imaginary sphere of the ego is the realm of fantasy involving an absent 'I.' The real involves the raw experience of events before it is symbolized. Thus, following separation from the mother, the child experiences and becomes constituted by a 'loss.' Now alienated from itself, the self wanders through the unconscious as frustrated infantile desire. Lacan elaborated a dividedness at the heart of the symbolic structure in Saussurean terms: a splitting apart of the sign constituted as signified and signifier. The latter enters the unconscious where it is no longer understood by the individual who possesses it. In psychoanalysis, the sign is once again reconstituted by recognition of the original desire and its destructive historical impact on the self.

Lacan employed a rhetorically complex style of writing intended to show that knowledge about the unconscious is deeply embedded in the medium or metalanguage itself. He emphasized the importance of how to listen and how to intervene. There are affinities between Lacan's call for a proper reading of the 'text' provided by the analysand and the speech act theory of J. L. Austin. Having much in common with the deterministic aspects of Wittgenstein's (see *Wittgenstein, Ludwig*) view of language and the perspectives of Levi-Strauss (see *Lévi-Strauss, Claude*) and Barthes (see *Barthes, Roland*), Lacan brought into focus the crucial influence of pre-existing linguistic structures on behavior as found in the oft-quoted statement: 'it is the world of words that creates the world of things.' Lacan died in Paris in 1981.

See also: Performative Utterances; Religions Symbolism.

Bibliography

Lacan J 1966 *Ecrits*, 2 vols. Editions de Seuil, Paris

Lacan J 1977 *The Four Fundamental Concepts of Psychoanalysis*. Hogarth Press/Institute of Psychoanalysis, London

Lemaire A 1977 *Jacques Lacan*. Routledge & Kegan Paul, London

Turkle S 1979 *Psychoanalytic Politics: Freud's French Revolution*. Burnett/Deutsch, London

Lancelot, Claude (1615/16–95)

P. Swiggers

Born in Paris, Lancelot entered the Saint Nicolas Seminary in 1627 and received tonsure in 1628, thus becoming a member of the clergy without being ordained a priest. Lancelot, who received a formal training in theology, philosophy, patristics, the classical languages (Greek, Latin, Hebrew), and some modern languages (Spanish, Italian), became a follower of Saint-Cyran and took up a career as 'solitaire,' assuming care of the education of noble youngsters. In 1646 the 'Petites écoles' of Port-Royal (near Paris) were created. It was in this privileged environment, very different from that of the Jesuit colleges, that Lancelot conceived and wrote his grammatical works for the instruction of his pupils who, grouped in small classes, benefited from daily contact with their preceptor.

Lancelot wrote manuals for learning the classical languages (*Nouvelle mēthode pour apprendre facilement & en peu de temps la langue latine*, 1644; *Nouvelle methode pour apprendre facilement la langue greque*, 1655; *Le Jardin des racines greques*, 1657) and some modern languages which he taught to his classes (*Nouvelle méthode pour apprendre facilement et en peu de temps la langue italienne*, 1660; *Nouvelle méthode pour apprendre facilement et en peu de temps la langue espagnole*, 1660). His grammatical output is one of the most impressive in modern times. Lancelot had keen ideas on language teaching, which he expounded in the introductions to his works: he preferred to start from the native language of the pupil, and he took care to summarize the grammatical information into synoptic tables. He also laid stress on a clear typographical presentation, on structural progression in grammar teaching, and on acquaintance with high-quality literary texts. His method was based on memorizing the grammatical rules (often given in the form of verses), and on the reading and imitation of classical authors. In 1660 Lancelot and Arnauld published, anonymously, the *Grammaire générale et raisonnée*, a treatise on the 'inner content' of grammatical structure, informed by Lancelot's thorough knowledge of classical and modern languages, and benefiting from Arnauld's logical insights, as applied to the categories of grammar. The work is a landmark in the history of general (or philosophical) grammar in modern times (see *Arnauld, Antoine*).

In 1660 the Port-Royal schools were suppressed by order of Louis XIV. Lancelot then became a preceptor of the princes of Conti, but gave up this position in 1672. He became a Cistercian monk in the abbey of Saint-Cyran, and was ordained subdeacon in 1673. Life was made difficult for him at the abbey, and Lancelot went to Quimperlé in Brittany, to become a Benedictine. He died at Quimperlé in 1695.

See also: Philology and History.

Bibliography

Brekle H E 1967 Die Bedeutung der *Grammaire générale et raisonnée* für die heutige Sprachwissenschaft. *Indogermanische Forschungen* **72**: 1–21

Cognet L 1950 *Claude Lancelot, Solitaire de Port-Royal.* Sulliver, Paris

Donzé R 1967 (2nd edn. 1971) *La Grammaire générale et raisonnée de Port-Royal.* Francke, Bern

Gazier C 1932 *Ces Messieurs de Port-Royal.* Perrin, Paris

Laporte J 1932–52 *La doctrine de Port-Royal*, 4 vols. Presses Universitaires de France, Paris

Mertens F J, Swiggers P 1983 La Grammaire générale et raisonnée de Port-Royal: Notes bibliographiques. *HL* **10**: 357–62

Padley G A 1976–88 *Grammatical Theory in Western Europe: 1500–1700*, 3 vols. Cambridge University Press, Cambridge

Pariente J C 1985 *L'analyse du langage à Port-Royal.* Minuit, Paris

Swiggers P 1984 Grammaire et logique à Port-Royal. A propos des fondements d'une linguistique générale. *Sprachwissenschaft* **9**: 333–52

Weaver E 1978 *The Evolution of the Reform of Port-Royal.* Beauchesne, Paris

Lepsius, Carl Richard (1810–84)

J. A. Kemp

Lepsius was born in Naumburg on the Saale on December 23, 1810, son of the Saxon Finance Procurator for the Thuringian district. His studies at Leipzig and Göttingen Universities (1829–32) included classical philology and archaeology. In 1832 he moved to Berlin University where he was strongly influenced by Franz Bopp's approach to grammatical analysis. His dissertation on the old Umbrian language was highly praised. In 1833 he went to Paris, and determined to concentrate on Egyptian studies. He won the Volney Prize with an essay entitled 'Palaeography as a means of etymological research', exemplifying what was to be an enduring interest in the relation between written and spoken language. He was fortunate to have influential patrons, notably Alexander von Humboldt and Carl Bunsen. Moving to Italy in 1836 he continued work on Oscan and Umbrian, but it was to be in Egyptology that he attained his greatest reputation. In 1842 he was appointed Professor Extraordinarius of Egyptology in the University of Berlin, and in 1846 Professor Ordinarius. In the intervening years he led a highly successful expedition to Egypt. His great twelve-volume account of the monuments of Egypt and Ethiopia was completed in 1856. In 1855 he became co-director of the Egyptian Museum in Berlin, and in 1869 Chief Superintendent.

He continued to pursue linguistic interests, stimulated by his contact with African languages, and his articles include work on Nubian, Chinese and Tibetan, Arabic, and Ethiopian. His *Nubian Grammar* (1880) contains a survey of all African peoples, and a classification of their languages which is well worth attention even today. However, in linguistic circles it is probably for his *Standard Alphabet* that he is best-known. He was conscious from early on in his studies of the problems involved in converting spoken language into writing, and the need for a 'standard' method on which to base orthographies for languages as yet unwritten. This led to his being invited by the Church Missionary Society (CMS) in 1852 to devise a new alphabet for use by Christian missions. In 1854 an Alphabetical Conference was held in London on the initiative of Carl Bunsen, the Prussian Ambassador, precisely to try to agree on a universal alphabet, for both philological and missionary purposes. Competing systems were put forward by Lepsius and Max Müller (see *Müller, Friedrich Max*), among others. Before the conference had reached its final conclusions the CMS had committed itself to Lepsius's scheme, and it was published in both German and English editions (1855). Lepsius was encouraged to produce a revised edition, which was published, in English only, in 1863. The most striking difference is that Part 2, his Collection of Alphabets was enlarged from 19 pages to 222, and from 54 languages to 117, with detailed notes on many of the languages. The *Standard Alphabet* did not become widely established, largely perhaps because of its excessive use of diacritics, which made it expensive to produce and difficult for printers, writers, and readers alike.

Lepsius received numerous honors in his later years. He made two further visits to Egypt (1866 and 1869) and in the second visit witnessed the opening of the Suez Canal. He died on July 10, 1884.

See also: Missionaries.

Bibliography

Lepsius C R 1981 (ed. Kemp J A) (1st edn. 1863) *Standard Alphabet for Reducing Unwritten Languages and Foreign Graphic Systems to a Uniform Orthography in European Letters.* Benjamins, Amsterdam

Lepsius C R 1880 *Nubische Grammatik mit einer Einleitung über die Völker und Sprachen Afrikas.* Berlin

Ebers G M 1966 (1st edn. 1885) *Richard Lepsius: ein Lebensbild.* O. Zeller, Osnabrück

Levinas, Emmanuel (1906–95)

P. Fletcher

It was Emmanuel Levinas who introduced the thought of Edmund Husserl and Martin Heidegger (see *Heidegger, Martin*) to the French-speaking world and, as a consequence, instituted the phenomenological approach that has so dominated twentieth-century French thought. Yet his literary output is split in two. On the one hand, there is a body of dense and elliptical philosophical work, on the other, a series of Talmudic readings and reflections. These two genres were kept apart by Levinas even to the extent that he chose different publishers with which to work on each project.

Emmanuel Levinas was born in 1906 in Kovno, Lithuania. Although his family was not assimilated, he grew up in an atmosphere of liberalism with respect to study and the place of the intellectual life. In 1923 he moved to France where he studied in Strasbourg and from where he would travel to Freiburg to hear the lectures of Husserl and Heidegger. In 1930 he moved to Paris and taught at the Normal School for the Alliance Universelle Israélite, a school network for Jewish communities in Europe. As a member of the French army during World War Two, Levinas was captured in 1940 and spent the rest of the war as a prisoner in Germany. After the publication of his first major work, *Totality and Infinity* (1961), he moved to a University position at Poitiers and then to Paris (Nanterre). His second major work, *Otherwise than Being or Beyond Essence* was published in 1974. Levinas died in Paris on 25 December 1995.

Central to Levinas's concerns is the ethical relation to the other that occurs in what he calls the 'face-to-face' relation. There is a responsibility to respond to the face of the other (which commands in its expression 'Thou shalt not kill!'). Here, the self who experiences the proximity of the other is not an 'I,' an ego, but a 'me.' Before the other one appears in the accusative, *me voici*—'here I am' (with all its biblical overtones). Indeed, language itself, in the ethical relation, is an expression of this 'here I am.' It is evident, then, that Levinas pursues no traditional ethics. Ethics for him is first philosophy—it is prior to logic and ontology and any discourse that authoritatively represents the way things are. This distinction between ethics and thought is further reflected in Levinas's understanding of language.

In *Otherwise than Being or Beyond Essence* (1978), Levinas distinguishes between two forms of language: le Dit (the Said) and le Dire (Saying). 'The Said' concerns those propositions and statements about truth, Being, identity and so forth which deal with verification and falsifiability. Much of our discourse—both academic and non-academic—is related to 'the Said.' But this common discursive practice presupposes 'Saying' which is, according to Levinas, anterior or 'pre-original.' In other words, 'Saying' is the condition of the possibility of 'the Said.' This condition (Saying) is an event in which I am exposed to the face of the other in a place where the infinite (and God) is to be found. The infinite leaves a trace of its transcendence (which is totally other) in the 'Saying' which is the proximity of the other. In 'the Said' I secure my identity before the other; in 'Saying' I am a host for the other and the infinite.

Bibliography

Levinas E 1979 *Totality and Infinity* [trans. A. Lingis]. Martinus Nijhoff, The Hague

Levinas E 1978 *Otherwise than Being or Beyond Essence* [trans. A. Lingis]. Kluwer Academic, Dordrecht, The Netherlands

Levinas E 1985 *Ethics and Infinity* [trans. R.A Cohen]. Duquesne University Press, Pittsburgh, PA

Levinas E 1990 *Nine Talmudic Readings* [trans. A. Aronowicz]. Indiana University Press, Indiana

Peperzak A 1995 *Ethics as First Philosophy*. Routledge, London

Stone I F 1998 *Reading Levinas/Reading Talmud*. Jewish Publication Society, Philadelphia, PA

Lévi-Strauss, Claude (1908–)

A. T. Campbell

Having graduated in law from the Paris Law Faculty and in philosophy from the Sorbonne in 1931, Lévi-Strauss visited Brazil in 1934. During a short spell teaching at the University of São Paulo he took the opportunity to do some fieldwork amongst Brazilian Indians. He returned to Brazil for another field trip in 1938–39. He left France after the German occupation and went to New York where he taught at the New School for Social Research and met Roman Jakobson whose work on phonology was to be one of his main intellectual inspirations. After the War he returned to Paris and held a post at the Musée de l'Homme and in 1950 became *directeur d'études* at the École Pratiques des Hautes Études. In 1959 the Chair of Social Anthropology was created for him at the Collège de France. In 1973 he became a member of the Académie française.

Lévi-Strauss is credited with creating the intellectual movement called 'structuralism.' The massive, technical, *Les Structures élémentaires de la parenté* was published in 1949 but perhaps nothing would have come of structuralism had Lévi-Strauss not published *Tristes Tropiques* in 1955. This was a personal account of his travels, written in a readable, but sophisticated style, and it became a best-seller. That set the stage for the publication of *Anthropologie structurale* (*Structural Anthropology*) in 1958 (a collection of essays written in the 1940s and 1950s). The popularity of the previous work guaranteed intense interest in this one. A new intellectual fashion had arrived. Structuralism replaced 'existentialism,' and Lévi-Strauss challenged Sartre's dominance as the star of Parisian intellectual life.

Lévi-Strauss declared that his three 'intellectual mistresses' were geology, psychoanalysis, and Marxism, the common idea being that in each of these enquiries what appears to be the case on the surface is determined by hidden (unconscious) structures, laws, or determinants. Among his other sources of inspiration were cybernetics, music, and above all linguistics.

The original structuralist charter is set out in Chapter 2 of *Structural Anthropology*, originally published as an article in 1945 in one of the first issues of *Word*. Structural linguistics, through Trubetzkoy's phonology, was set to play a 'renovating role' in the social sciences. Edwin Ardener has pointed out that the specialized terminology of phonemic analysis was a red herring. It was the Saussurian principles lying behind phonology that Lévi-Strauss required: a few simple distinctions (like langue/parole, syntagmatic/paradigmatic), related notions such as 'system' and 'value,' and above all, the idea that the building blocks of human logic and human thinking consist of binary oppositions.

The guiding idea behind Lévi-Strauss's work was to find fundamental structures behind the bewildering disparateness of phenomena. *Elementary Structures* was an attempt to show that a huge array of kinship systems could be seen to be based on two simple structural forms: restricted exchange and generalized exchange. From *Totemism* onwards the search is more explicitly for fundamental structures '*of the mind*,' the idea being that by an examination of the structure of various 'objects of thought' (classifications, myths, designs) one can discover something of the structure of the mind that created them. Just as phonology had shown that language can be reduced to those 'distinctive features' expressed as binary distinctions (tense/lax, grave/acute), so the logic of primitive classification and 'mythologic' can be reduced to endless structures of binary oppositions (wet/dry, honey/tobacco, raw/cooked).

While Lévi-Strauss emphasizes his profound concern with linguistics, Chomsky's generative grammar passed him by. ('Transformation,' a key term in structuralism, is taken from D'Arcy Wentworth Thompson's *On Growth and Form*, 1917, a classic in zoology, and has nothing to do with transformational grammar.) Ironically, a short passage in Chomsky's *Language and Mind* provides an illuminating, terse, 'no nonsense' critique of Lévi-Strauss's use of linguistic models. The work on classification, says Chomsky, reduces to the conclusion 'that humans classify, if they perform any mental acts at all.' Linguistics has long left Lévi-Strauss behind. Structuralism, as a fashion, also looks rather dated, but because of the engrossing nature of the material Lévi-Strauss deals with (myths, masks, exotic names and habits) his writing is still found intriguing and he is still revered as one of the leading *intellectuels* of France.

Bibliography

Ardener E (ed.) 1971 *Social Anthropology and Language*. Tavistock, London

Hayes E N, Hayes T (eds.) 1970 *Claude Lévi-Strauss: The Anthropologist as Hero*. MIT Press, Cambridge, MA

Leach E R 1970 *Lévi-Strauss*. Fontana, London

Lévi-Strauss C 1969 (1st edn. 1949) *The Elementary Structures of Kinship*, 2nd edn. Eyre & Spottiswoode, London

Lévi-Strauss C 1973 (1st edn. 1955) *Tristes Tropiques*. Atheneum, New York

Lévi-Strauss C 1963 (1st edn. 1958) *Structural Anthropology*. Basic Books Inc., New York

Lévi-Strauss C 1963 (1st edn. 1962) *Totemism*. Beacon Press, Boston, MA

Lévi-Strauss C 1972 (1st edn. 1962) *The Savage Mind*, 2nd edn. Weidenfeld & Nicolson, London

Lévi-Strauss C 1970–81 *Mythologiques; Introduction to a Science of Mythology*. English transl. Weightman J, Weightman D, 4 vols. *Vol. 1: The Raw and the Cooked*, 1970 (1st edn. 1964); *Vol. 2: From Honey to Ashes*, 1973 (1st edn. 1967); *Vol. 3: The Origin of Table Manners*, 1978 (1st edn 1968); vol. 4: *The Naked Man*, 1981 (1st edn. 1971). Cape, London

Lévi-Strauss C 1977 (1st edn. 1973) *Structural Anthropology* II. Cape, London

Pace D 1983 *Claude Lévi-Strauss: The Bearer of Ashes*. Routledge & Kegan Paul, London

Levita, Elijah (1469–1549)

J. Weinberg

Elijah, son of Asher Halevi (Levita), also known as Baḥur, was a pioneer in Massoretic studies and lexicology and a fine exponent of Hebrew grammar. Born in Neustadt in Germany in 1469, he spent most of his life in Italy and died in Venice in 1549.

Levita taught Hebrew to Christians including the Cardinal Egidio da Viterbo and his work was adopted and disseminated by the greatest Christian Hebraists of his time such as Sebastian Münster and Paulus Fagius. Levita's grammatical treatises were mainly intended as manuals for beginners. He wrote a commentary on the grammar of Moses Kimḥi, explaining the technical terms used by Kimḥi and adding paradigms. He also wrote notes on the *Mikhlol* (*Summa*) of David Kimḥi (see *Kimḥi, David*) whom he regarded as the best of the Hebrew grammarians. He wrote three grammatical treatises: in the *Bāḥūr* (*Young Man* or *The Choice*), he explains the morphology of the noun and verb; in *Sēpher Ha-Harkab̲ha* (*Book of Grafting*), he discusses irregular forms and hybrid words in the Hebrew Bible; the *Pirqē Eliyāhū* (*Chapters of Elijah*) contains useful rules on phonetics, gender and number of nouns, and particles. Levita's rule regarding the five classes of the *shewa* mobile is accepted today. In his epoch-making study of the Masorah, *Masoret Ha-Masoret*, he discusses the problem of Hebrew phonetics not as a grammatical category, but in relation to the Masoretic system through which it evolved. Following the model of David Kimḥi's Hebrew lexicon *Sēpher Ha-Shŏrāshīm* (*The Book of Roots*), on which he also published his own glosses, Levita wrote a lexicon of Aramaic (he wrongly regarded Aramaic as a debased form of Hebrew), the *Mĕturgeman*, for readers of the Aramaic translations (*Targumim*) of the Bible. It includes quotations from verses and gives translations into German and Italian. Like the eleventh-century lexicon of Nathan ben Yehiel of Rome, Levita's lexicon *Tishbī* (*Tishbite*) is mainly a dictionary of rabbinic Hebrew and Aramaic. It is not a dictionary in the modern sense of the word, but contains notes for each entry, sometimes correcting previous interpretations or adding new explanations.

At the request of Egidio da Viterbo, Levita composed a concordance to the Bible, the *Sēpher Zikhrōnōt* (*The Book of Remembrances*). He ordered the work alphabetically according to root, giving verbal forms and nouns, grammatical explanations, and references to the Massorah. It was intended as a guide to punctuation for scribes and to enable preachers to find appropriate verses as subjects for sermons, to teach the art of writing clear biblical Hebrew, and as a source of scriptural verses for use in polemics. Levita's lexicon, the *Shĕmōt Dĕbhārīm* (*Nomenclature*), was also written at the request of a Christian Hebraist, Paulus Fagius, who wanted a work which could be used by scholars wishing to write and speak Hebrew. The words were presented in four columns alphabetically ordered. The columns in Judeo–Hebrew and Hebrew were written by Levita, those in German and Latin by Fagius.

See also: Hebrew, Biblical and Jewish; Masoretic Tradition.

Bibliography

For a full list of Levita's works, see:
Weil G E 1963 *Elie Lévita Humaniste et Massorète (1469–1549)*. Brill, Leiden

Lowth, Robert (1710–87)

I. Michael

Lowth's *A Short Introduction to English Grammar: with Critical Notes*, published anonymously in 1762, was highly regarded and influential until well into the nineteenth century.

Lowth was born on November 27, 1710, and educated at Winchester and New College, Oxford, of which he was a fellow. He was made Professor of Poetry at Oxford in 1741 and his lectures, delivered in Latin, were published in 1753 as *De Sacra Poesi Hebraeorum Praelectiones*. His Hebrew scholarship was much admired, both in this work and in his translation of Isaiah (1779). In 1752 he married Mary Jackson, by whom he had eight children, only two of whom survived him. Although he was given his first living in 1753 it was as a scholar and churchman, not as a parish priest, that Lowth made his career. In 1767 he was made Bishop of Oxford, in 1777 Bishop of London.

It is not known what led him to write an English grammar, his only work of that kind. It may have been suggested by his brief experience tutoring the sons of the Duke of Devonshire or, later, by the needs of his own children. He describes the work as 'intended merely for a private and domestic use,' but it is clear that he was careful to make it suitable for a wider field: it was 'calculated for the use of the Learner even of the lowest class.' The grammar itself contains nothing new, except for his treatment of the sentence. It was intended, like so many, as a preparation for Latin, but Lowth's good linguistic sense avoided most of the absurdities of the latinate approach to English. The grammar was popular because it was simple, well-written, and authoritative. The preface, in particular, gave clear and weighty support for those opinions which needed it: namely that grammar was badly taught, and syntax neglected, because teachers underestimated the difficulty of controlling a mother tongue; that 'Universal Grammar cannot be taught abstractedly,' only 'with reference to some language already known.' The notes to the grammar illustrated the text by quoting from established authors' expressions which Lowth judged incorrect. These notes have been adversely criticized for being prescriptive, but their prescriptiveness follows from Lowth's acceptance of the generally held belief that there were grammatical principles applying to all languages and that the student of English grammar met, and should respect, these principles 'exemplified in his own Language.'

Bibliography

Alston R C 1974 *A Bibliography of the English Language* **1**: *English Grammars*, corrected reprint of 1965 edn. Janus Press, Ilkley
Anon 1787 (obituary memoir of Lowth.) *Gentleman's Magazine* **57**: 1028–1030; 1123–1124; 1155–1156
Howatt A P R 1984 *A History of English Language Teaching*, corrected impression. Oxford University Press, Oxford
Lowth R 1967 *A Short Introduction to English Grammar*, facsimile of a copy of the first edn. containing the author's manuscript additions and corrections. Scolar Press, Menston
Pullum G K 1974 Lowth's Grammar: A re-evaluation. *Linguistics* **137**: 63–78

Luther, Martin (1483–1546)

C. J. Wells

The Germany of Martin Luther was split by intellectual and political factions, and German itself was regionally and socially diverse. The early phase of printing, if anything, enhanced the chaos, since the first German books sometimes reproduced older manuscripts from different areas: Johannes Mentel's first German Bible (1466), for instance, was based on an 'East Central German' text of some one and a half centuries earlier, refracted through the 'Low Alemannic' linguistic habits of fifteenth-century Strasbourg compositors. No standard language had yet emerged, and through the fluctuating local written/printed norms, only the broader outlines of regional forms of language are discernible.

Luther's output was extensive, and he became the first writer to publish on a modern scale, thanks to the controversial politico–religious scope of his ideas and to his spectacularly successful German Bible translation. Indeed, he used printing for propagandistic, proselytizing purposes, part of his deep conviction that the biblical message should speak directly to the individual Christian unalloyed by doctrine or dogma. Such was the dissemination of his writings, both through 'official' printers and via pirated editions, that Luther's reputation was extended to his very use of language. Contemporaries praised his linguistic purity, and the myth of Luther's German was accepted virtually unquestioned by nineteenth-century German scholars. A distinction should be made between Luther's own German, preserved in his manuscripts, and the 'Luther German' disseminated in printed form. Only the latter could be influential, and it has constantly, if imperceptibly, been changing since Luther's day. In fact, the orthographical and pronunciational codifications which followed the political unification of Germany in the late nineteenth century, achieved relative stability in forms often very different from those used by Luther and his printers.

Nevertheless, Luther's style and vocabulary were and remain influential. Writers from Goethe to Brecht have turned to Luther's German Bible. Its powerful idiom would have been familiar to their audiences from a lifetime of churchgoing, if not from private Bible reading, and one seventeenth-century reader, E. D. Pithan, probably no exception, read it from cover to cover as many as 104 times. The patina of archaism which inevitably built up over the centuries dignified and poeticized it, making it attractive to politicians and occasional speakers in search of a trenchant or proverbial phrase. Intervening centuries have enriched German with philosophical, literacy, technical, and social styles of expression which lie outside the biblical sphere, and the Luther text is now less read and heard than hitherto, competing as it does with clearer yet infinitely less expressive modernized versions. But Luther's influence is still apparent.

Luther was not seeking to create a standard German language, but he appreciated the need to communicate as widely as possible in the most accessible language. Oddly enough, he looked to the Electoral Saxon and Imperial chanceries for a 'koine,' not to the printers. In this he was manifestly out-of-date. The short polemical tract *Ein Sendbrief vom Dolmetschen* (1530) ('On Translation') presents his approach to biblical language. The work was an apology for his translation of the New Testament (1522) and a defense against accusations that he was both a paraphrast and a literalist. Like any competent translator, he was both, always adhering strictly to the original text when the biblical meaning required, but not afraid to bring out the sense idiomatically. Translation was for Luther a religious act, where faith alone permits fidelity. The indispensible equipment of the translator/interpreter of the divine word includes an 'upright, devout, loyal, industrious, reverential, Christian, experienced and practiced heart.'

Luther always went back to the original Greek and Hebrew sources. In this, as in his preference for the Vulgate rather than the old 'Itala' or *Vetus Latina*, he was a humanist for whom textual–critical study formed the basis of translation. The Catholic theologians of his day preferred to elucidate the Bible via the accreted patristic secondary literature, which removed the scholars from the text and the text from the laity who could not equal theologically trained exponents of anagogical, allegorical, and tropological interpretation. Luther sought to prune back theological /scholastic ramification and let the Bible speak for itself, plainly and accessibly to all Germans in their mother tongue.

Although faith and piety furnished the translator with understanding, Luther acknowledged each language's own structure and character ('*der sprachen art*'), and saw that failure to render the message accurately from one language to another might pervert the intention. The Latin *penitentiam agite* 'do penance' appeared to support the abuse of selling pardons, whereas the original Greek meant only 'be penitent.' Philological study of sources helped to discover the sense of the biblical message and to render it precisely into uncluttered, direct, and idiomatic German. On occasion, he did not shrink from adding his own emphasis to the German, as in the famous verse of Romans 3: 28, where he adds the work *allein* '(by faith) alone.' Justification through faith, not works, one of the principal tenets of Lutheranism, may therefore have been reinforced, if not actually suggested to Luther, through the activity of Bible translation.

Luther's acute ear for the inflections of his native German was doubtless sharpened by his early contact with Low German and his total familiarity with Latin. His interest in vocabulary is well attested, from enquiries about German technical terms for cuts of meat, or for the names of animals and birds. He collected proverbs, published a small tract on thieves' cant, speculated about the meaning of old German names, ridiculed some of the more bureaucratic chancery words, and so forth. Much of his table talk and correspondence is in Latin, sometimes mixed with German. A more polemical style, robust and occasionally coarse, as in the *Sendbrief* itself, contrasts with his Bible, which he constantly revised in both phrasing and vocabulary. Even after his death, changes were made in the 1546 version to reflect his last wishes.

As Luther's language has receded into the past, it has become unnatural or 'stylized,' despite its vividness. Attempts to modernize Luther's Bible inevitably fail, not because they result from 'committee-work' (Luther's Old Testament was also the product of a 'sanhedrin,' including Melanchthon, Goldhahn, and others) but because they lack spirit. Luther's striking freshness stems from the unmistakeably spoken rhythms of his text. He gives us speech, apparently close to the colloquial, but in heightened, rhetorical form, captured from the pulpit, not copied from the printed page. His text has a vigor and robustness alien to less oral ages, and more akin to the original Bible.

Luther wanted his Bible to speak 'pure and clear' German accessible to all: 'it's no good asking the letters in the Latin language how one should speak German, as these donkeys [=Catholic translators] do, but instead you have to ask a mother at home, children in the street or ordinary people in the market place about it. Observe their chatter and translate accordingly, and then they'll understand it and realize that you're speaking German to them' (*Sendbrief* p. aiiij b).

See also: English Bible; Christianity in Europe.

Bibliography

Arndt E, Brandt G 1983 *Luther und die deutsche Sprache: wie redet der Deutsche man im solchem fall?* VEB, Bibliographisches Institut, Leipzig

Bach H 1974–1985 *Handbuch der Luthersprache*, 1974 *vol. 1: Vokalismus*, 1985 *vol. 2: Druckschwache silben. Konsonantismus*. G.E.C. Gad, Copenhagen

Bainton R S 1955 *Here I Stand*. Mentor Books, New York

Besch W 1999 *Die Rolle Luthers in der deutschen Sprachgeschichte* [Schriften der Philosophisch–Historischen Klasse der Heidelberger Akademie der Wissenschaften; Bd. 12 (1999)] Universitätsverlag C. Winter, Heidelberg

Besch W et al. (eds.) 1998 *Sprachgeschichte*: *ein Handbuch zur Geschichte der deutschen Sprache und ihrer Erforschung*: 2., vollständig neu bearbeitete und erweiterte Aufl. [Handbücher zur Sprach- und Kommunikationswissenschaft; Bd. 2.1] W. de Gruyter, Berlin (vol. 1)

Bluhm H 1965 *Martin Luther—Creative Translator*. Concordia, St Louis, MI

Reinitzer H (ed.) 1983 *Biblia deutsch, Luthers Bibelübersetzung und ihre Tradition*. Ausstellungskatalog der Herzog-August-Bibliothek, Wolfenbüttel, Nr. 40, Waisenhaus-Buchdruckerei und Verlag, Braunschweig

Schildt J (ed.) 1983–1984 *Luthers Sprachschaffen, Gesellschaftliche Grundlagen, Geschichtliche Wirkungen* [=papers from the Eisenach Conference, 21–25 March, 1983]; AdWdDDR (ZfS), Linguistische Studien Reihe A, Arbeitsberichte 119/1–3, Berlin 1984

Schwarz W 1955 *Principles and Problems of Biblical Translation*. Cambridge University Press, Cambridge

Wells C J 1985 *German: A Linguistic History to 1945*. Oxford University Press, Oxford

Wells C J 1993 Orthography as Legitimation. Christoph Walthers Observations on Luther's German Bible and the Printers of Frankfurt on Main 1560–1577. In: Flood J L, Salmon P, Sayce O, Wells C (eds.) *Das unsichtbare Band der Sprache. Studies in German Language and Linguistic History in Memory of Leslie Seiffert*, Verlag Hans-Dieter Heinz/Akademischer Verlag, Stuttgart, pp. 149–88

Wells C J 1999 Nicht-Lutherisches in der Orthographie der nach-Lutherschen Bibel- und Psalmenausgaben des 16. Jahrhunderts. In: Besch W, Hoffmann W (eds.) *Das Frühneuhochdeutsche als sprachgeschichtliche Epoche: Werner Besch zum 70. Geburtstag*. P. Lang, Frankfurt am Main, pp. 209–40

Wolf H (ed.) 1996 *Luthers Deutsch: sprachliche Leistung und Wirkung*. P. Lang, Frankfurt am Main

Malinowski, Bronislaw Kaspar (1884–1942)

A. T. Campbell

Malinowski was born in Cracow, Poland. He was the son of a well-known Slavic philologist (Lucyan Malinowski). After a PhD in physics and mathematics, he turned to anthropology, inspired, he said, by a reading of Frazer's *Golden Bough*. In 1910 he arrived at the London School of Economics, and in 1914 began anthropological fieldwork in New Guinea. Between 1915 and 1918 he did two years fieldwork on the Trobriand Islands (off Papua New Guinea). After some years teaching at the LSE he was appointed to the first Chair of Anthropology there (1927). In 1938 he went to the USA where he was appointed professor at Yale. He died in New Haven at the age of 58.

In the three great ethnographies of the Trobriand Islands (*Argonauts*, *Sexual Life*, and *Coral Gardens*), Malinowski established the tradition of intensive fieldwork, participating in the life of the society being studied, emphasizing the effort to appreciate a total view of the society and to understand matters 'from the natives' point of view.' He constantly emphasized the importance of learning and working with the indigenous language. The vivid style of writing and the colossal amount of detail have established these ethnographies as classics. The account of the *kula* ring, a complex system of formal gift giving described in *Argonauts*, is one of the most celebrated cases in anthropology.

In terms of sociological theory, Malinowski's functionalism and his ideas about 'basic needs' are pretty banal, and are only of interest as indicating an important shift in anthropology away from questions about origins and evolution which had previously been so dominant. On the other hand, his concern with language is much more fruitful. He was proud of his ability to pick up languages quickly, and, as well as insisting on the importance of conducting field research in the native language, he shows an intense concern with the processes and details of translation (*Coral Gardens*, vol. 2). He laments the lack of sound ethnolinguistic theory. Although his attempt to provide one does little with regard to phonetics, phonology, or grammar, his writing on meaning is original. In a remarkable essay (1923) appended to Ogden and Richards' *The Meaning of Meaning*, he coined the phrase 'phatic communion' (gossip, pleasantries, and so on) to make the point that language should not just be seen as a vehicle for thought through which to communicate ideas, but as a mode of action which, in this example, establishes personal bonds between people. Also in this essay he claims originality for the notion of 'context of situation' in an argument which prefigures Wittgenstein's 'the meaning of words lies in their use', developed in *Philosophical Investigations*.

J. R. Firth wrote: 'I think it is a fair criticism to say that Malinowski's technical linguistic contribution consists of sporadic comments, immersed and perhaps lost in what is properly called his ethnographic analysis' (1957: 117). But beyond a strictly 'technical' contribution, his expertise in translating from Trobriand and his writing on meaning and translation deserve a more generous judgment.

See also: Translation: History.

Bibliography

Malinowski B K 1922 *Argonauts of the Western Pacific*. Routledge, London

Malinowski B K 1923 The problem of meaning in primitive languages. In: Ogden C K, Richards I A (eds.) *The Meaning of Meaning* (suppl. I). Harcourt Brace, New York

Malinowski B K 1929 *The Sexual Life of Savages*. Routledge, London

Malinowski B K 1935 *Coral Gardens and their Magic*, 2 vols. Allen and Unwin, London

Malinowski B K 1948 *Magic, Science and Religion and Other Essays*. Free Press, Glencoe, IL

Malinowski B K 1967 *A Diary in the Strict Sense of the Term*. Routledge and Kegan Paul, London

Firth J R (ed.) 1957 *Man and Culture: An Evaluation of the Work of Bronislaw Malinowski*. Routledge and Kegan Paul, London

Kuper A 1983 *Anthropology and Anthropologists: The Modern British School*. Routledge and Kegan Paul, London

Matilal, Bimal Krishna (1935–91)

J. Ganeri

Bimal Krishna Matilal (1935–1991) is best known as a pioneer of the study of the Indian philosophical and linguistic traditions using the methods and techniques of contemporary analytical philosophy. His life's work was to counter the myths and stereotypes about Indian philosophy, and to bring India's philosophical past and rich linguistic heritage into conversation with contemporary debates.

Matilal was born in Joynagar, West Bengal, leaving for Calcutta at the age of fourteen, where he studied first at the Islamia College and then at the Sanskrit Department of the University of Calcutta. In 1957 he was appointed as lecturer in the Government Sanskrit College. He continued to study Nyåya there with a number of eminent pandits, and under their guidance completed a traditional degree, that of Tarkatīrtha, Master of Logic and Argument, in 1962. For some time prior to this, Matilal had been in correspondence with Daniel Ingalls, who suggested to him the possibility of moving to Harvard in order to acquaint himself with the work being done by W. V. O. Quine in philosophical and mathematical logic and philosophy of language. Breaking with his tradition, Matilal followed this advice, completing his Ph.D. at Harvard in 1965 having taken Quine's classes and continued his studies in mathematical logic with D. Føllesdal. In his doctoral thesis, The Navya-Nyāya Doctrine of Negation, published by Harvard University Press in 1968, he gives voice to his growing conviction that 'India should not, indeed cannot, be left out of any general study of the history of logic and philosophy.' This was to be the first statement of a thesis to the defence of which he devoted his academic life, that our philosophical understanding of fundamental problems is enriched if the ideas of the linguists and philosophers of classical India are brought to bear in the modern discussion. In 1976, he became Spalding Professor of Eastern Religions and Ethics at the University of Oxford and Fellow of All Souls College, positions he held until the end of his life. India's highest honour, the Padma Bhusana, was bestowed on him in 1991.

Matilal's collected essays (*Philosophy, Culture and Religion: The Collected Essays of B. K. Matilal* 2001) reveal the extraordinary depth of his philosophical interest in India. His reputation is as one of the leading exponents of Indian logic and epistemology. His book on Indian philosophy of language, *The Word and the World: India's Contribution to the Study of Language* (1991) dealt with all aspect of India's linguistic traditions. Yet those who know of him through his major books in these areas, *The Navya-Nyāya Doctrine of Negation* (1968), *Epistemology, Logic and Grammar in Indian Philosophical Analysis* (1971), *Perception: An Essay on Classical Indian Theories of Knowledge* (1986; 2nd edition 1991) and *The Character of Logic in India* (1998), may be surprised to discover the range of his other writings. His work deals, in general, with every aspect of the relation between philosophical theory and Indian thought: from analysis of the arguments of the classical philosophers to evaluation of the role of philosophy in classical Indian society; from diagnosis of western perceptions of Indian philosophy to analysis of the thought of past Indian intellectuals like Bankimchandra and Radhakrishnan. Matilal, strikingly, is willing to look in a great range of sources for philosophical theory.

As well as the writings of the classical Indian philosophical schools, he uses material from the linguistic literature, the epics, dharmaśāstras, medical literature, poetics, and literary criticism. This eclecticism is no accident. Matilal argues that it is only in the study of such diversity of literature that one can discover the mechanisms of the internal criticism to which a dynamic culture necessarily subjects itself in the process of revising and reinterpreting its values and the meaning of its fundamental concepts, and to be sure that one's own evaluation and criticism is immersed in, and not detached from, the practices and perceptions of the culture. He also observes that a selective attention to particular aspects of Indian culture is part of what has generated a set of myths and misperceptions about Indian philosophy, most notably the popular idea that Indian philosophy is primarily spiritual and intuitive, in contrast with the 'rational' West.

See also: Hindu Views on Language; Sanskrit (Pāninian) Linguistics; Tamil Linguistic Tradition.

Bibliography

Matilal B K 1968 *The Navya-Nyāya Doctrine of Negation.* Harvard University Press, Cambridge, MA

Matilal B K 1971 *Epistemology, Logic and Grammar in Indian Philosophical Analysis.* Mouton, The Hague

Matilal B K 1985 *Logic, Language and Reality.* Motilal Banarsidass, Delhi (2nd edn. 1990)

Matilal B K 1991 *Perception: An Essay on Classical Indian Theories of Knowledge.* Clarendon Press, Oxford (2nd edn. 1991)

Matilal B K 1998 *The Character of Logic in India.* SUNY Press, Albany, NY

Matilal B K 2001 *Philosophy, Culture and Religion: The Collected Essays of B. K. Matilal.* Oxford University Press, Delhi

Meinhof, Carl Friedrich Michael (1857–1944)

M. Schladt

Meinhof, a German pastor and linguist, is considered to be the founder of comparative African linguistics and the great authority on the analysis and classification of the Bantu languages. He published various language monographs and textbooks and was the first to establish the teaching of African languages in German universities.

He was born on July 23, 1857 in Barzwitz (near Rügenwalde). After studying Theology, Germanic Philology, and Hebrew in Halle, Erlangen, and Greifswald, Meinhof worked as a teacher in Wolgast and Stettin. In 1882, he married Elly Heyer, who died in 1894. In 1895 he married Anna Kloß (died in 1944). He was appointed to the parish of Zizow (near Rügenwalde) in 1886.

Influenced by the neogrammarians' method as applied to the Indo–European languages, Meinhof began working on a comparative grammar of the Bantu languages. His main informants were missionaries on home leave. In 1899, he published *Grundriß einer Lautlehre der Bantusprachen* which brought him a grant from the Kaiser. He spent it on his first field research in East Africa in 1902–03. He was then appointed to the School of Oriental Studies in Berlin as a teacher of African languages. In 1905 he was awarded a professorship. In 1909, he became the director of the *Seminar für Kolonialsprachen* in Hamburg. The following year Meinhof founded the Phonetics Laboratory and the periodical *Zeitschrift für Kolonialsprachen* (1920–55, renamed *Zeitschrift für Eingeborenensprachen*, since 1951–52 published under the name of *Afrika und Übersee*). At that time Meinhof concentrated his efforts on the teaching of languages. Between 1909 and 1912 he wrote textbooks on Nama, Herero, Swahili, and Duala.

In 1912 Meinhof published *Die Sprachen der Hamiten*, his most controversial work. Here he tried to establish a genetic group of Hamitic languages claiming that the African noun class systems were an early stage of these languages. Meinhof partially retracted his statements in later publications.

In 1914 he traveled with his then assistant, Herrmann August Klingenheben, to the Sudan. In 1919 he became the first German to be appointed full professor for African languages at the University of Hamburg. In 1927 Meinhof went to South Africa where he held language courses at various universities.

Meinhof retired in 1935. During his last years he continued with his life's work, the exact description and classification of the Bantu languages. His minor contributions on religion, politics, and legal interpretations in Africa showed Meinhof as an enthusiastic advocate of missionary work and colonial politics. For this reason most postwar African linguists avoid referring specifically to Meinhof's works, although his scientific achievements are beyond doubt.

Meinhof died on February 10, 1944 in Greifswald, working on the second edition of his grammar of the Bantu languages.

See also: African Traditional Religions; Christianity in Africa.

Bibliography

Klingenheben A 1937 Überblick über das literarische Schaffen Meinhofs. In*: Brevier Meinhof*

Lukas J 1943–44 Nachruf Carl Meinhof. *Zeitschrift für Eingeborenensprachen* **34**: 81–93

Meinhof C 1910 (1st edn. 1899) *Grundriß einer Lautlehre der Bantusprachen nebst einer Anleitung zur Aufnahme von Bantusprachen*. Reimer, Leipzig

Meinhof C 1948 (1st edn 1906) *Grundzüge einer vergleichenden Grammatik der Bantusprachen*. Reimer, Berlin

Meinhof C 1912 *Die Sprachen der Hamiten*. Friedrichsen, Hamburg

Mesrob (c. 361–c. 439)

Archimandrite Ephrem

Armenia was the first nation formally to adopt Christianity as its religion under King Trdat, traditionally in 301, but more probably about a decade later with the consecration as bishop of Gregory the Enlightener in 314. In around 387 Armenia was divided into a small Roman-Byzantine sector and a considerably larger Iranian one, in which the patriarchal see was established at Ejmiacin. The details of this early period are obscure because Armenian was not at the time a written language and it was not until the reign of King Vramsapuh at the beginning of the fifth century under the Catholicos Shahak (Isaac) III that the Armenian language was provided with an alphabet of its own. This was the work of a missionary monk named Maštoc', who had studied at Antioch. He knew not only Greek, but also Syriac and Persian. The name Mesrob, or Mesrop, by which he is commonly known is not found in any writings before the eighth century.

The first original work to be composed in Armenian was a life of Maštoc', written by his disciple Koriun. The history of Armenia by Moses Khorenats'i despite its claim to be contemporary, was probably written in the eighth century.

It was during his missionary work in Golt'n that Maštoc' seems to have conceived the idea of composing an alphabet for Armenian. His project received royal approval and he visited Edessa to pursue his researches, finally devising an alphabet with vowels and consonants, which accurately represented the sounds of the language, unlike the purely consonantal systems of Syriac and Hebrew. The King had heard of an Aramaic script that had been adapted for Armenian by a Syrian bishop, Daniel. However, it was realized, 'that it was not possible through these letters to render accurately the syllables of Armenian words in a satisfactory way because the script was a foreign one' (Moses *History of Armenia* III.52). The final forms of the letters were worked out with the help of a well-known calligrapher at Samosata, Rufinus. The motivation for this work was not simply religious; it was also inspired by a desire to defend Armenia from cultural assimilation to either of its powerful neighbours, Byzantium and Persia.

It has been claimed that there was a pre-Christian form of Armenian script using Greek or Syriac letters, but there is no evidence for this. The creation of the alphabet was the spring board for a huge work of translation, of the Scriptures and other Christian literature from Greek and Syriac, undertaken by Maštoc' and a group of collaborators. The Armenian Bible has been called the 'Queen of the versions.' He also wrote homilies and a series of Troparia (hymns) for Lent. One of his disciples, Eznik of Kolb, wrote an important theological treatise, *The Refutation of the Sects*. Later Maštoc' also created alphabets for the Georgians and the Albanians of the Caucasus. He founded monasteries and schools and, as a result of a visit to Constantinople, received the support of the Emperor Theodosios II for his educational work. He died in his late seventies in 439.

See also: Armenian; Christianity in the Near East.

Bibliography

Thomson R W 1999 Armenian Christianity. In: *The Blackwell Dictionary of Eastern Chritianity*

Mesrob 1997 In: *The Oxford Dictionary of the Christian Church*, 3rd edn.

Zekiyan B L 1980 Mesrop. In: *Dictionnaire de Spiritualité*, Vol. 10

Müller, Friedrich Max (1823–1900)

R. Söhnen-Thieme

F. Max Müller, the first professor of Comparative Philology in Oxford, was born in 1823 in Dessau, the son of the poet Wilhelm Müller (1794–1827), well-known on account of the celebrated cycles of songs, set to music by Franz Schubert. 'Die schöne Müllerin' and 'Winterreise.' After taking his final school examinations in 1841, Müller entered Leipzig University, where he studied Classics, philosophy, and Oriental languages, and obtained his PhD in 1843. In 1844 he went to Berlin, attracted by Franz Bopp and Scheling (Philosophy), and also studied Persian with Friedrich Rückert, who helped him with his translation of *Meghadūta* (publ. 1847). In 1845 he migrated to Paris, where he was inspired by Eugene Burnouf to copy and collate manuscripts of the *Ṛgveda* (which, though one of the most ancient and most important texts in an Indo–European language, had not yet been printed anywhere). In order to collect more manuscripts in East India House in London, Müller traveled to Britain in 1846. Here he found the support of the German Ambassador Baron Bunsen, who was able to interest the directors of the East Indian Company in the project of publishing the *Ṛgveda*, together with Sāyaṇa's commentary, at the Oxford University Press; consequently Müller, in order to supervise the publication, moved in 1848 to Oxford, where he lived until his death in 1900. In 1849 the first volume of the *Ṛgveda* appeared, followed by five other volumes in 1854, 1856, 1862, 1872, and 1874 (2nd edn. in 4 vols. 1890–92, repr. Varanasi 1966).

In Oxford, he had been appointed deputy Taylorian professor of Modern European Languages in 1850, and obtained the full professorship in 1854, but had been denied the Boden professorship of Sanskrit in 1860 (since his ideas did not conform to the principles of its founder so well as those of M. Monier-Williams), before he obtained the chair of Comparative Philology, which was created for him in 1868 and which he held until 1875.

Müller not only contributed to the study of Sanskrit language and literature (e.g., with his *Ancient Sanskrit Literature* (1859), and *A Sanskrit Grammar for Beginners* (1866), 2nd edn. by M. Macdonell (1886), and to Indian thought and culture in general (e.g., with his probably best-known book *India: What Can It Teach Us*, London 1883, and his later publications on Indian philosophy), but he also introduced the new disciplines of Comparative Religion and Comparative Mythology. In each of these fields he succeeded in exciting the interest of a broader public, mainly by his lectures on various occasions in the UK, such as the 'Hibbert Lectures on the Origin and Growth of Religion' at Westminster Abbey 1878, and the famous 'Gifford Lectures' at Glasgow 1888–92 (4 vols., London 1889–92) in the field of Comparative Religion. He also advanced this field by initiating and editing the *Sacred Books of the East*, a series of translations, by outstanding scholars, of the most important religious texts in Oriental Classical languages.

So also, for Comparative Philology, which was made attractive to his audience by his lectures on 'The Science of Language,' delivered at the Royal Institution in 1861 and 1863 (second series), the Sir Robert Rede's lecture 'On the Stratification of Language' in Cambridge 1868, the *Three Lectures on the Science of Language and its place in General Education*, at Oxford University 1889, etc. His interest in language was mainly centered on the more theoretical or philosophical aspects such as its origin and 'growth' according to laws similar to the laws of nature, its impact on the development of human thought, etc., but he also discussed the etymology of many words in Indo-European languages and used those common to several of them in establishing a comparative mythology and a 'home of the Aryas,' as he called the ancient Indo-Europeans (insisting, however, on using the term only in the linguistic, not in the racial sense).

See also: Sanskrit, Discovery by Europeans; Myths About Language.

Bibliography

Müller F M 1885a *The Science of Language*, new edn. Lectures delivered at the Royal Institution of Great Britain in April, May, and June 1861 in London. Longman, London

Müller F M 1885b *The Science of Language*, new edn. Lectures delivered in February, March, April, and May 1863, London. Second series, Longman, London

Müller F M 1888 *Biographies of Words and the Home of the Aryas*. Longman, New York

Müller F M 1889 *Three Lectures on the Science of Language*. Longman, London (Repr. 1890 Open Court, Chicago, IL. *Vol. 1: Difference between Man and Animal. No Mystery in Language; vol. 2: Analysis of Language. The Lesson of the Science of Language; vol. 3: Thought Thicker than Blood. The Cradle of the Aryas. The Importance of Sanskrit*)

Chaudhuri N C 1974 *Scholar Extraordinary: The Life of Professor the Rt. Hon. Friedrich Max Müller*. Chatto and Windus, London

Macdonell A A 1901 Max Müller, Friedrich. In: Lee S (ed.) *Dictionary of National Biography*, supplement, vol. III: 151–57

Rau H (ed.) 1974 *F. Max Mueller—What Can He Teach Us?* Bombay

Voigt J H 1967 *F. Max Müller: The Man and his Ideas*. Firma K. L. Mukhopadhyay, Calcutta

Nida, Eugene Albert (1914–)

R. E. Longacre

Nida was born in 1914 in Oklahama City, Oklahoma, USA. He received a BA at the university of California, Los Angeles in 1936, MA in patristics in 1939 at the University of Southern California, and PhD in linguistics in 1943 at the University of Michigan; also numerous honorary degrees and awards from institutions in the USA and other countries. He was professor of Linguistics at the Summer Institute of Linguistics (which eventually located for many years at the University of Oklahoma) 1937–53 (see also *Summer Institute of Linguistics*).

Nida has had a continuing involvement with agencies interested in the translation of the Christian scriptures. Besides his involvement with the early work of the Summer Institute of Linguistics in Mexico he has been Executive Secretary for Translations, American Bible Society (1943–84), consultant for the United Bible Societies (1947–90), and continues as consultant for the American Bible Society 1984 to the present. In these various capacities he has succeeded in lifting translation concerns from those of a specialist group onto the plane of broad linguistic and cultural concerns.

Nida's early linguistic interests centered around grammar, which in the 1940s and 1950s was conceived of largely as morphology. Both Nida's 1946 *Morphology* and his larger 1949 volume of the same title (both University of Michigan Press, Ann Arbor, MI) reflect shifting currents in American structural linguistics—from the process orientation of Edward Sapir—to the flat morphemes-and-their-allomorphs orientation of Zellig Harris and Bernard Bloch. Nida has never lost his interest in *words*; some of his most mature and recent work has been his exploration of the lexical resources of the Greek New Testament (see below).

Perhaps Nida's greatest contribution lies in the field of translation theory and practice. In his role as a teacher of future linguists and translators as well as in his more global role of consultant for missionary translators his influence has been profound—exceeded perhaps only by the influence exerted by the constant flow of his writings. He has done fieldwork in over 85 countries and in over 200 languages. Nida early came to emphasize dynamic and functional equivalence across languages and cultures as the key to successful translation. As linguistics has evolved during his scholarly life he has interacted with and made his own contributions to such developments as discourse analysis (textlinguistics) and sociolinguistics.

From his early 1947 work *Bible Translation* a steady stream of publications has followed. Running rather to books than articles his production has been of two sorts: (a) such general works as those already mentioned and exemplified in the bibliography; and (b) special manuals for translators of given books of the Bible (not indicated in the bibliography). The latter have been variously authored, coauthored, and/or edited by Nida, and cover a dozen or so books of the New Testament as well as the book of Ruth. In these manuals Nida has displayed a fine sensitivity to and uncanny prescience of passages where translators of the scriptures are likely to encounter lexical problems, cultural mismatches, syntactic tangles, and problems in textual cohesion and coherence.

Nida's outstanding achievement latterly has been *The Greek Lexicon of the New Testament based on Semantic Domains* (1988). This embodies a new departure in lexicography. Here words of similar semantic domains are so grouped as to give insight into the lexical structure of the Koine Greek.

Nida has belonged to a number of learned societies which reflect his varied interests. Besides the American Anthropological Association, the Linguistic Society of Canada and the United States, The American Association for Applied Linguistics, and the Society of Biblical Literature, they include the Linguistic Society of America (President 1968) and the Society for Textual Scholarship (President 1987–88).

In addition to the works already mentioned, representative pieces of his work are cited below.

See also: Bible; Bible Translations, Modern Period.

Bibliography

Louw J P, Nida E A (eds.) 1988 *The Greek Lexicon of the New Testament based on Semantic Domains*, 2 vols. United Bible Societies, New York

Nida E A 1947 *Bible Translation.* American Bible Society, New York

Nida E A 1950 *Learning a Foreign Language.* National Council of Churches, New York

Nida E A 1952 *God's Word in Man's Languages.* Harper, New York

Nida E A 1975 *Exploring Semantic Structures.* Wilhelm Fink Verlag, Munich

Nida E A 1975 *Componential Analysis of Meaning.* Mouton, The Hague

Nida E A, Reyburn W 1981 *Meaning Across Cultures.* Orbis, Maryknoll, NY

Nida E A 1983 *Style and Discourse.* United Bible Societies, Cape Town

Waard J de, Nida E A 1986 *From One Language to Another: Functional Equivalence in Bible Translating.* Nelson, Nashville, TN

Nobili, Roberto de (1579–1656)

F. X. Clooney

Roberto de Nobili, a member of the Society of Jesus and a Catholic priest, arrived in India in 1605. Soon thereafter he was sent to the city of Madurai in the interior of Tamil Nadu, an area beyond Portuguese control and in which only one Jesuit was working. Early on de Nobili observed that there were few conversions, particularly among the high class brahmins, recognized as the traditional leaders of society. He decided that the problem was the alien mode in which the Christian message reached the Indian context. Because the missionaries were largely ignorant of Indian culture and clumsy in their characterizations of what they did know, they were unable to approach learned Indians in a way that would be intelligible and persuasive. In response, de Nobili devised a strategy for better communication. He drastically transformed his appearance and lifestyle, adopting as his own the customs of sannyasins, i.e., renunciant figures widely respected for their austerity and spirituality. He also immersed himself in the study of Sanskrit, the classical language of brahmanical religion and culture, and Tamil, the local vernacular language. He seems to have become proficient in both, and possibly in Telugu, another vernacular language, as well. His more specific contributions to the area of religion and language are three.

First, de Nobili authored numerous works in Tamil, including theological treatises and a multi-volume catechism. Though not as famous a stylist as the eighteenth century Jesuit Constantine Beschi, S. J., de Nobili's Tamil prose is clear and straightforward and served well as a tool for communication.

Second, while we have no certain examples of his Sanskrit writings, we can say with certainty that de Nobili was proficient in reading and interpreting Sanskrit. He seems to have read widely in Sanskrit literature, despite the difficulties attendant upon obtaining access to texts. For example, *The Report on Indian Customs* is a Latin treatise in which de Nobili defends his view of Indian culture; in it he closely analyzes portions of the Sanskrit-language texts such as *The Laws of Manu*, and shows himself to be an astute interpreter of the subtleties of the language.

Third, de Nobili saw his linguistic expertise as in the service of his philosophical and religious conviction that truth is universal and objective; cultural and linguistic differences, however large, are always less potent than universally shared realities. Accordingly, de Nobili held that language is a reliable vehicle for cross-cultural communication; properly used, every sophisticated language is a reliable vehicle for explaining reality objectively. Even complex philosophical and theological ideas could be successfully translated from language to language, technical Latin vocabulary rendered in technical Sanskrit.

While we have no independent reports of Hindu reactions to de Nobili's writings, contemporary Christian accounts suggest that he was successful in communicating his ideas, winning the respect of Hindu listeners, and in persuading at least some to accept the truth as he expressed it.

See also: Sanskrit, Discovery by Europeans; Missionaries.

Bibliography

Amaladass A, Clooney F X 2000 *Preaching Wisdom to the Wise: Three Treatises by Roberto de Nobili, S. J., Missionary and Scholar in 17th Century India.* Institute of Jesuit Sources, St. Louis

Saulière A 1995 In: Rajamanickam S (ed.) *His Star in the East.* de Nobili Research Institute, Madras and Gujarat Sahitya Prakash, Anand, Gujarat

Rajamanickam S 1972 *The First Oriental Scholar.* de Nobili Research Institute, Tirunelveli

Zupanov I G 1999 *Disputed Mission: Jesuit Experiments and Brahmanical Knowledge in Seventeenth-Century India.* Oxford University Press, Delhi

Nöldeke, Theodor (1836–1930)

A. Shivtiel

Nöldeke was one of the leading Orientalists and, according to H. J. Polotsky (see *Polotsky, Hans (Hayyim) Jacob*), 'the master of Semitists,' in the world. He was born in Harburg, Germany, and taught Oriental philology first at Kiel University (1864–72) and later at the University of Strasburg (1872–1906). He was awarded, at the age of 23, one of the special prizes of the Académie Française for his important work *Geschichte des Qorâns* (1860) which is still considered one of the fundamental studies on the history of the Qu'rān. Nöldeke is well-known for the 'series' of grammars of the Semitic languages he published, of which the most important are *Grammatik der neu-syrischen Sprache* (1868), *Mandäische Grammatik* (1875), *Kurzgefasste Syrische Grammatik* (1880), *Zur Grammatik des classischen Arabisch* (1897), and also for his monographs *Die semitischen Sprachen* (1887), *Beiträge zur semitischen Sprachwissenschaft* (1904), and *Neue Beiträge zur semitischen Sprachwissenschaft* (1910). His article on the Semitic languages included in the eleventh edition of the *Encyclopaedia Britannica*, though out-of-date, is also regarded as an important introduction to the Semitic languages and literatures known at the time. Ugaritic, Eblaite, and several dialects of the various Semitic languages are not dealt with in this article because they were discovered just before or after Nöldeke's death. He published also a large number of works on Biblical and post-Biblical themes including works on various cultures mentioned in the Old Testament and the history of its peoples. Among those which are worth mentioning are his article on the Moabite Inscription known as the Mesha Stele, which was discovered in Jordan in 1868; *The Old Testament Literature* (1868; French translation 1873); and *Study of the Old Testament Criticism* (1869).

Nöldeke's wide scope of research contains also works on the *History of the Jews in Arabia* (1864);

Sketches from Eastern History (1892), which include articles on Semitic themes (appeared also in English); and the Aramaic documents from Elephantine (1907).

His interest in the Oriental languages, literatures, and cultures had exceeded the limits of Semitica, since among his prolific crop are works on Persian themes (1892), the national Persian epic (1896), and the history of the Persians and the Arabs in the Sasanid period (1879). In addition, he published many book reviews, various translations of texts, mainly from Arabic and Persian, and provided the introductions for several important works published by some of his contemporary scholars.

Nöldeke's contribution to the field of Oriental studies is invaluable and his multifarious and variegated research puts him in the front rank of the world's most famous philologists of the Near East. He was an acknowledged scholar on Semitica whose expertise is reflected by his monumental works, mainly on the languages of the East, which continue to serve as essential tools in the hands of linguists, historians, and scholars dealing with religions and cultures of the Orient. Nöldeke's writings are characterized by their erudition and great precision. This is, as J. Fück (p. 217) says, thanks to his common sense and his ability to say 'I do not know' whenever he was not certain.

Finally, some contemporary Jewish and Israeli scholars, who all acknowledge Nöldeke's scholarly achievements, like to note with *Schadenfreude* his skepticism, expressed in his article on the Semitic languages published in the eleventh edition of the *Encyclopædia* Britannica, regarding the success of the attempts of the revival of Hebrew and the establishment of a Jewish state in Palestine.

See also: Semitic Languages.

Bibliography

Bezold C (ed.) 1906 *Orientalische Studien Theodor Nöldeke zum siebzigsten Geburtstag*, 2 vols. Verlag von A Töperman, Giessen

Encyclopædia Judaica 1971 Nöldeke, Theodor. Keter Publishing House, Jerusalem.

Fück J 1955 *Die arabischen Studien in Europa*. O. Harrassowitz, Leipzig

Oldendorp, Christian Georg Andreas (1721–87)

G. G. Gilbert

Oldendorp was born in Grossenlafferte, Germany, in the bishopric of Hildesheim, the son of the local pastor, and died in Ebersdorf. He attended the Gymnasium in Hildesheim and the University of Jena. In 1743, he joined the Unitas Fratrum in Marienborn, and was sent by them to the Danish Virgin Islands in 1767–68 to prepare a history of the mission there. The only known likeness of him was done by Hamerich in Amsterdam in 1777, an oil painting preserved in the Moravian Archives in Herrnhut, Germany. In the same year, his *Geschichte der Mission* (Virgin Islands) was published, abridged to about one-third of its original length by a Moravian editor. After his return from the Virgin Islands, he married Sister Anna Cornelio Labelingh at Hennersdorf; two sons were born to them. In his later years, he lived and preached at Amsterdam, Kleinwelle, Gnadau, Barby, and Ebersdorf.

Churchman, writer, scholar, naturalist, anthropologist, Africanist, Creolist, and artist, the many-faceted Oldendorp was an astute observer who was both very much a product of his age and yet distinctly in advance of it. He was sent to the Danish Virgin Islands for the sole purpose of preparing a history of the mission there, but in line with his many interests, took the opportunity to prepare a many-sided description of their natural, political, ecclesiastic, and human history, as well as of contemporary life in the islands as he was able to observe it at firsthand. His original 3,273-page handwritten report (the original and a copy are preserved in the Moravian Brethren Archives, Herrnhut) was whittled down to about one-third its former size and finally published in a multilated state. The original work, which is without doubt the finest surviving eighteenth-century description of any part of the West Indies, remains unpublished.

For the history of Creolistics, Oldendorp's insightful account of Negerhollands is nothing short of sensational. Grammatical and sociolinguistic information is provided in a 53-page section of the original manuscript, as well as in a separate German–Negerhollands dictionary (*Criolisches Wörterbuch. Erster zu vermehrender, und, wo nötig, zu verbessernder Versuch*). The four bland pages devoted to Negerhollands that found their way into the published version do no justice to Oldendorp's original. No wonder that neither Schuchardt nor Hesseling was able to detect anything of interest in the book. Oldendorp's numerous sociolinguistic observations, together with the formal grammatical description and what he calls his 'first try' at a dictionary of Negerhollands, are an indication of his importance to the study of pidgins and creoles. More so than Schumann and Magens, and perhaps even Schuchardt, Oldendorp can be seen as the father of Creolistics.

See also: Caribbean Syncretistic Religions 1: Cuban Santeria and Haitian Voodoo; Caribbean Syncretistic Religions 2: Jamaican Cumina and Trinidadian Shango; Macumba; American Spirituals.

Bibliography

Gilbert G G 1986 Oldendorp's *History* and other early Creole materials in the Moravian Brethren Archives, Herrnhut. *The Carrier Pidgin* **14(1)**: 5–7

Highfield A R, Barac V 1987a Translators' introduction. In: Highfield A R, Barac V 1987b

Highfield A R, Barac V 1987b A *Caribbean Mission*. English transl. of Oldendorp 1777. Karoma, Ann Arbor, MI

Markey T 1982 Report on the Moravian Brethren Archives in Herrnhut, and Bethlehem, Pennsylvania. *The Carrier Pidgin* **10(4)**: 4–5

Oldendorp C G A 1752–57 Imanuelsburg (an epic poem of 584 pages). Unpublished ms. Orellan, Livonia

Oldendorp C G A 1767–68 *51 Sketches of Life in the Virgin Islands*. Only 3 were published, in the *Geschichte der Mission* 1777; the remainder are in the collections of the Moravian Brethren Archives, Herrnhut

Oldendorp C G A 1777 *Geschichte der Mission der evangelischen Brüder auf den caraibischen Inseln S. Thomas, S. Croix und S. Jan*, 2 vols. Herausgegeben durch Johan Jakob Bossard. Christian Friedrich Laur, Barby. English transl. Highfield A R, Barac V 1987b

Oldendorp C G A Unpublished poetry, letters, diary (apparently lost), and an 80-page critique of Bossard's revision of his published book. Moravian Brethren Archives, Herrnhut

Oldendorp C G A 1987 *Lebenslauf* (begun by Oldendorp and completed by an unknown person). English transl. in Highfield A R, Barac V 1987b

Pāṇini

F. Staal

Pāṇini, the greatest grammarian of all time, author of the 'Eight Chapters' or *Aṣṭādhyāyī* with its various accessories, was born probably in the fifth or fourth century BCE at Śalātura on the Upper Indus, at that time part of the Achaemenid Empire but now in Pakistan, not far from Kashmir. The information about Pāṇini's birthplace is largely based upon traditional accounts and references of much later date, but the Chinese pilgrim Hsüan Tsang visited Śalātura in the seventh century BCE and saw a statue there erected in his memory.

The date of Pāṇini has been much discussed in the light of the two kinds of evidence that are available. The first is that the state of the Sanskrit language that Pāṇini describes corresponds most closely to late Vedic prose, that is, the Āraṇyakas early Upaniṣads, and sūtras of the domestic ritual (*gṛhyasūtra*). Pāṇini composed his grammar at a time when Vedic prose works were still being composed. This would put him around, or a little after, the middle of the last millennium BCE, not too distant from the date of Buddha (who seems later than the earliest Upaniṣads but earlier than the others).

The second kind of evidence is chronology relative to the date of the commentators. Pāṇini's sūtras were the subject of an analysis by Kātyāyana, which was taken up by Patañjali in his Great Commentary (*Mahābhāṣya*). Patañjali's date is known: he lived around 150 BCE, the date of the king Puṣyamitra, who is quoted in his illustration of the use of the present tense:

> We are now officiating at Puṣyamitra's ritual.

Scholars have doubted the value of this attribution and argued that Patañjali might have taken the illustration from an earlier source, but it is unlikely that a grammarian of his distinction could have done so unthinkingly and without adapting existing examples to the time in which he lived.

The language described by Patañjali has changed in some respects from the language described by Pāṇini, but since it is not known how fast or slowly languages change in general or under specific circumstances, speculation sets in at this point. If the gaps between Pāṇini and Kātyāyana and between Kātyāyana and Patañjali are believed to be each about a century or a century and a half, Pāṇini's date can be set at about the fifth or fourth century BCE, which would support and be supported by the first kind of evidence.

O. von Hinüber (1989: 34) has argued for a later date within that period on the strength of numismatic evidence. Invoking J. Cribb, according to whom punch-marked coins of the Greek–Iranian type appear in northwest India only after 400 BCE, and Pāṇini (5.2.120), which accounts for the formation of *rūpya* in the sense of 'punched, punch-marked,' he has concluded that Pāṇini's date must be later than 400 BCE.

Pāṇini mentions 10 predecessors by name, and the type of linguistic analysis of the *Prātiśākhyas* obviously antedates him. It may also be assumed that he stood on the shoulders of giants whose work was eclipsed by his own.

The most important respects in which the scientific methodology of Pāṇini differs from the particularistic and corpus-oriented approach of the *Prātiśākhyas* are that his grammar applies to the spoken language and indiscriminately to all the Vedic schools, and that it is based upon the insight that language is infinite. At the same time, Pāṇini's method has much in common with that of the Vedic ritualists. Renou (1941–42), who was the first to study in detail the terminological and stylistic similarities between these two sciences, wrote:

> When dealing with a particular term, it is not easy to establish whether it originated with the grammarians or the ritualists: in the absence of a fixed chronology of texts, and with the general parallelism of techniques in ancient India, such a search becomes arbitrary. However, in the majority of cases it is clear that the point of departure lies in the religious texts. Grammar appears as a specialized investigation within the larger domain of explicit ritual science. The extent and importance of the religious literature, the undeniable priority of the *mantras* and of the ritual forms which they presuppose, invite us to look for origins in that domain.

In one important respect, the evidence that confirms Renou's view is very specific: the concepts of *sūtra* and *paribhāṣā*, basic ingredients of Pāṇini's linguistics, were introduced by the Vedic ritualist Baudhāyana, who was earlier than Pāṇini (see *Sūtra*). Baudhāyana's work is known as *pravacana*, which, according to Caland's universally accepted interpretation, refers to 'the fixation of ritual in the oral tradition.'

Pāṇini's work, then, is rooted in two oral traditions: that of the ritual sūtras and that of the *Padapātha* and the *Prātiśākhyas*. Although his *Śivasūtras* intentionally deviate from it, Pāṇini was obviously familiar with the scientific arrangement of sounds in the *Prātiśākhyas*, which, unlike the haphazard ABCs of the west which depend on writing, originated not *in spite of* the absence of writing but *because* of it.

The Vedic and ritual background of Pāṇini's linguistics has led to the idea that Indian linguistics is rooted in religion and magic and is therefore something altogether different from 'modern science.' If this magic approach were correct, comparisons with late twentieth-century linguistics would seem to be anachronistic. The magic view is based, however, upon three misconceptions. First, any effort at understanding a different point of view is unavoidably comparative (Staal 1970). Second, the Indian preoccupation with ritual was not only magical or religious but also scientific. And third, a science is measured by its results and consequences, not by its background or origins. If the hypothesis were adopted that science depends on context and circumstances such as the beliefs of the people who help to create it, then Pythagoras theorem would be rejected because he believed in reincarnation, Kepler's astronomy because of his astrology, Newton's physics because of his theology, and most of chemistry because of alchemy. On the contrary, and in accordance with the principles of selection that govern biological evolution, what people do is remember the science and, unless they are historians, forget about the rest.

Pāṇini adhered to the erroneous belief that Sanskrit was eternal and unchanging. He never imagined that Vedic was older than, or a precursor of, classical Sanskrit or Prakrit. These beliefs did not prevent him from creating the conceptual tools that enabled Western scholars to account for sound laws explaining the vowel shifts between early Indo–European, English, German, and other languages. Pāṇini's beliefs, moreover, led to a grammar that was the very embodiment of the system of synchronic analysis that Saussure envisaged but did not create.

Pāṇini, then, was not an ancient and nebulous precursor of a science in which everything has since been done better, but a distant colleague of genius from whom linguists are still able to learn.

Bibliography

Bronkhorst J 1981 The orthoepic diaskeuasis of the *Rgveda* and the date of Pāṇini. *Indo–Iranian Journal* **23**: 83–95

Cardona G 1969 *Studies in Indian Grammarians I: The Method of Description Reflected in the Śivasūtras*. American Philosophical Society, Philadelphia, PA

Cardona G 1980 *Pāṇini: A Survey of Research*. Motilal Banarsidass, Delhi

Deshpande M M 1994 *Sanskrit and Prakrit: Socio-linguistic Issues*. Motilal Banarsidass, Delhi

Hinüber O von 1989 *Der Beginn der Schrift und frühe Schriftlichkeit in Indien*. Franz Steiner Verlag, Stuttgart

Liebich B 1891 *Pāṇini: Ein Beitrag zur Kenntnis der indischen Literatur und Grammatik*. Haessel, Leipzig

Renou L 1941–42 Les connexions entre le rituel et la grammaire en sanskrit. *Journal asiatique* **233**: 105–65

Renou L 1969 Pāṇini. In: Sebeok T A (ed.) *Current Trends in Linguistics*, vol. 5. Mouton, The Hague

Staal F 1970 Review of Cardona 1969. *Lg* **46**: 502–07

Staal F 1972 *A Reader on the Sanskrit Grammarians*. MIT Press, Cambridge, MA

Staal F 1988 *Universals: Studies in Indian Logic and Linguistics*. Chicago University Press, Chicago, IL

Staal F 1989 The independence of rationality from literacy. *European Journal of Sociology* **30**: 301–10

Petrus Hispanus (c. 1210–76)

F. P. Dinneen

Hispanus was a logician, physician, and churchman of the thirteenth century. Born in Lisbon between 1210 and 1220, Peter Julian did his university studies in Paris (where he acquired 'Hispanus'). He studied logic, Aristotle's Physics and Metaphysics under Albert the Great, and Medicine, as well as Theology under John of Parma. After 1245, he taught Medicine in Siena. As physician to Pope Gregory X from 1272, his *Thesaurus Pauperum* became an authoritative medical text. He became a bishop, a cardinal, then Pope John XXI in 1276. He died 8 months later when a newly built study collapsed on him.

His *Summulae Logicales* was a standard introduction to dialectic's basic rules and sophistical examples for five centuries, in very many editions. Dialecticians assume what is said is to be interpreted literally ('Dogs bark so a seadog must bark') and they exploit language logic to defend their own expressions and expose an opponent's contradictions. The *Summulae* treated logical implications of the grammatical properties of words as a modern addition to the traditional logic of Aristotle's *Organon*. Such properties included 'supposition' (what *men* stands for in *Men are mortal*), 'copulation' (*are* links *men* and *mortal*), 'appellation' (*I* and *you* must exist, *men* may not), and 'ampliation' (*all* adds reference to possible *men* to that of actual ones in *all men are mortal*).

Supposition (reference) varies with linguistic structure while a fixed signification (sense) does not. A categorematic expression (like *men* and *mortal*) is a referring term and can be a logical subject or predicate. Syncategorematics (like *all* and *nearly*) are nonreferring expressions. They are not *terms* as Hispanus defined them for logic, so they cannot function as subjects or predicates.

Syncategorematics vary a term's supposition (as in *nearly tall men*) as do categorematics by mutually determining how many things words refer to when in construction with each other (like *tall blond honest men*).

While the *Summulae*'s dialectic purpose was practical, Hispanus also made metalogical distinctions (like the function of subject versus what is the subject) and stressed that dialectic focuses on nominals and verbals, while the grammarian's data is broader.

His mainly lexical semantics may have been extended by a tract on syncategorematic expressions attributed to him. That included the semantic import of conjunctions like *quin* 'without' in expressions like *It cannot be a man without being an animal.*

See also: Linguistic theory in the Later Middle Ages; Aquinas, T.; Aristotle and the Stoics on Language.

Bibliography

Bochenski I M 1961 (trans. Thomas I) *History of Formal Logic*. Notre Dame University Press, South Bend, IN

Dinneen F P (trans.) 1990 *Peter of Spain: Language in Dispute*. Benjamins, Amsterdam

Mullaly J P 1964 *Peter of Spain Tractatus Syncategorematum*. Marquette, Milwaukee, WI

Rijk L M de 1972 *Petrus Hispanus Portugalensis*. Van Gorcum, Assen

Pike, Kenneth Lee (1912–2000)

R. E. Longacre

Pike was born in 1912 in Woodstock, Connecticut. He graduated BA from Gordon College, Boston, Massachusetts; and PhD in Linguistics 1942 from the University of Michigan. While his immediate mentor was Charles Fries, as a graduate student he studied under Edward Sapir and Leonard Bloomfield at Summer Institutes of the Linguistic Society of America, where he also made the acquaintance of prominent American structuralists, such as Swadesh, Trager, Bloch, Hockett, and Harris. Pike became an associate professor at the University of Michigan in 1948, a full professor in 1955, and continued there until his retirement in 1978 (as professor emeritus), and his subsequently becoming an adjunct professor at the University of Texas in Arlington.

Much of Pike's earlier work was shaped by his experience with native languages of Mexico. He began the study of Mixtec in 1935 as a member of a group which eventually became known as the Summer Institute of Linguistics (SIL) (see *Summer Institute of Linguistics*) and the Wycliffe Bible Translators. Pike not only contributed to the translation of the New Testament into Mixtec, but has served on many occasions as consultant to linguist translators throughout the world. Pike served as President of SIL from 1942 to 1979, and as President of the Linguistic Society of America in 1961.

In the 1940s Pike published four works on phonology, of which *Phonetics* (1943) is the best-known; it remains the most encyclopedic compendium of speech sounds encountered in languages (other works from this decade are Pike 1945, 1947, 1948).

In the 1950s Pike's interests shifted to grammar and human behavior in general, as exemplified in his monumental work *Language in Relation to a Unified Theory of the Structure of Human Behavior*. What is perhaps his most far-ranging contribution was made at this time, i.e., the coining of the terms 'etic'/'emic'—as clips from (phon)etic and (phon)emic. The opposition indicated by the two terms is that between the outside/universalistic/observer-oriented description of a culture trait or complex (including language), versus the inside/particularistic/participant-oriented description. This distinction, as embodied in the terms 'etic'/'emic,' while not having attained wide currency among linguists, has been adopted by scholars in many other disciplines, especially anthropology. The spread of the terms led to a public debate at the AAA meeting in Tucson, 1987 as to their use and significance (Headland et al. 1989).

The variety of grammar theory which Pike has developed since the 1950s has come to be called 'tagmemics'. Pike redefined Bloomfield's *tagmeme* and treated it as a paradigmatic slot-filler unit within a syntagmatic unit (cf. Saussure; see *Saussure, Ferdinand (-Mongin) de*), but the theory has been elaborated considerably beyond its starting points. Pike's wife, Evelyn, coauthored with him *Grammatical Analysis* (1972), based on tagmemics and used as a textbook in various countries. A cogent and brief statement of Pike's linguistic creed is the volume *Linguistic Concepts* (1982).

Such a summary as this gives little evidence of the breadth of Pike's research and publications; the latter total up to some 20 books and 150 articles, some of which are coauthored. 'Grammatical prerequisites for phonemic analysis' (*Word* **3**: 55–72, 1947) came in a day when most linguists insisted on a categorical separation of phonology from grammar. 'A problem in morphology–syntax division' (*Acta Linguistica* **5**: 125–38, 1949) challenged another rigid dichotomy made by many in his day. His volume on rhetoric with Young and Becker (1970) provided a textbook for applying his theory to rhetoric and composition. Further works ranged over into comparative reconstruction, Christian apologetics, theology, ethics, and poetry. Pike's most recent interest is in the field of philosophy and language (see, e.g., Pike 1987).

Bibliography

Brend R 1972 *Selected Writings to Commemorate the 60th Birthday of Kenneth Lee Pike*. Mouton, The Hague

Headland P, Pike K L, Harris M 1989 *Emics and Etics: The Insider/Outsider Debate*. Sage, Beverley Hills, CA

Pike E G 1981 *Ken Pike, Scholar and Christian*. Summer Institute of Linguistics, Dallas, TX

Pike K L 1943 *Phonetics: A Critical Analysis of Phonetic Theory*. University of Michigan Press, Ann Arbor, MI

Pike K L 1945 *The Intonation of American English*. University of Michigan Press, Ann Arbor, MI

Pike K L 1947 *Phonemics: A Technique for Reducing Languages to Writing*. University of Michigan Press, Ann Abor, MI

Pike K L 1948 *Tone Languages*. University of Michigan Press, Ann Abor, MI

Pike K L 1967 *Language in Relation to a Unified Theory of the Structure of Human Behavior*. Mouton, The Hague

Pike K L 1982 *Linguistic Concepts*. University of Nebraska Press, Lincoln, NB

Pike K L 1987 The relation of language to the world. *International Journal of Dravidian Linguistics* **16**: 77–98

Pike K L, Pike E G 1982 *Grammatical Analysis*, rev. edn. Summer Institute of Linguistics, Dallas, TX

Young R E, Becker A L, Pike K L 1970 *Rhetoric: Discovery and Change*. Harcourt, Brace and World, New York

Planudes, Maximus (1260–1310)

R. H. Robins

Planudes was a Byzantine linguistic scholar living in the later years of the Eastern Empire. Like a number of other prominent Byzantines, he served as a teacher, writer, diplomat, and ecclesiastical authority. He was one of the few later Greek scholars having a full command of Latin, and among his writings are several translations of Latin philosophical and literary works.

He was sent to Italy in 1295–96 to present the Greek case in Venice during the period when Byzantium was seeking reconciliation and assistance from the West as the Turkish threat grew ever stronger. On the theological controversy about the nature of the Trinity he appears to have been ambivalent, first taking the Latin position and later moving back to the Eastern Orthodox view.

His publications were numerous on a variety of topics; his *Anthology* is the best-known. But as far as linguistics is concerned his two extant works are the *Dialogue on Grammar* and *On Syntax* (both edited by Bachmann 1828). Like other Byzantine grammarians he saw it as his duty to provide teaching material for those engaged in maintaining and transmitting the traditional Greek language and its Classical literature. But Planudes went further than other Byzantines into the abstraction of some fundamental concepts and relations within the structure of the language. His principal theoretical achievements were a subtle analysis of the semantics of the Greek verbal tense system and a comparable analysis of the meanings of the nominal cases.

The meanings of the Greek tenses involve more than the time references past, present, and future, and, as in many languages, formal expression is given in the verbal morphology to the aspectual distinction of complete and incomplete, as is indicated by the terms 'perfect' and 'imperfect.' The Stoics had made a full analysis of this, but, despite the use of some Stoic terminology, the later grammarians tried to force the distinctions of meaning in every tense into the temporal framework originating in Aristotle. Planudes came as near to an explicit account of the temporal and the aspectual senses as was possible within the unidimensional theory of tense meanings.

Planudes is also considered by some linguists to have made the first coherent formulation of what has come to be known as the localist theory of case, in which the various oblique case meanings are referred back to the locational concepts: *whence*, *where*, and *whither*, ideas that had been treated in a less systematic and coherent form by grammarians of later Antiquity and earlier Byzantine times. Others, who are unwilling to give any credit to Byzantine originality, reject this judgment. Each viewpoint is set out in Murru (1979) and in Blank (1987), with full bibliographies up to their dates of publication. A localist theory has been supported by Wüllner (1827), Bopp (1833: 136), and Anderson (1977). A succinct account of the theory is given in Hjelmslev (1935: 13–32).

There is no biography separately written on Planudes, but reference may be made to the article on him in Pauly-Wissowa's *Realenzyklopädie der Altertumswissenschaft*, where a full bibliography of his works is given.

See also: Byzantine Greek; Linguistic Theory in the Later Middle Ages.

Bibliography

Anderson J M 1977 *The Grammar of Case.* Cambridge University Press, Cambridge

Bachmann L (ed.) 1828 *Anecdota Graeca.* Hinrichs, Leipzig

Blank D L 1987 Apollonius and Maximus on the order and meaning of the oblique cases. In: Taylor D J (ed.) *The History of Linguistics in the Classical Period.* Benjamins, Amsterdam

Bopp F 1833 *Vergleichende Grammatik des Sanskrit, Zend, Griechischen, Lateinischen, Lithauischen, Gotischen und Deutschen.* Dümmler, Berlin

Hjelmslev L 1935 *La Catégorie des Cas.* Universitetsforlaget, Aarhus

Murru F 1979 Sull'origine della teoria localista di Massimo Planude. *L'Antiquité Classique* **48**: 82–97

Wüllner F 1827 *Die Bedeutung der sprachlichen Casus und Modi.* Coppenrath, Münster

Polotsky, Hans (Hayyim) Jacob (1905–91)

A. Shivitiel

Polotsky, an Israeli Orientalist and philologist, was born in Zurich and studied in the universities of Berlin and Göttingen. After his participation in the Septuagint Project in Göttingen and the publication of Manichaean texts, he decided to emigrate to Palestine where he began to teach at the Hebrew University in Jerusalem (1934), and later became a professor of Egyptology and Semitica (1948). His profound knowledge of philology and general linguistics, his 'text analysis ability,' and his amazing mastery of numerous languages made his contribution to many areas invaluable. A rough count of the languages with which he was conversant exceeds 40, from East and West, including dead languages, but not including the scores of various dialects of the languages with which he was familiar. Polotsky published invaluable material on Ancient Egyptian and Coptic, Latin and Greek, Hebrew and Arabic, Syriac and neo-Syriac, Turkish, and other Ural–Altaic languages, and the various languages of Ethiopia. His wide knowledge of all European languages and some of the languages spoken in central Asia and the Far East helped him in his comparative studies, quite often between languages of different origins, such as Amharic and Turkish (1960). He published short monographs such as *Etudes de grammaire gourage* (1938) (an English version entitled *Notes on Gurage Grammar* appeared in 1951) and *Etudes de syntaxe Copte* (1938). His collected papers published in one volume (1971) contain a wide scope of languages and their grammar and syntax.

Polotsky's originality in reaching some of the most remarkable conclusions regarding the structures of the grammars investigated was achieved mainly thanks to the living and up-to-date material he collected assiduously. He was well known for his private collections of data (vocabulary and grammar) on all the languages he studied, as well as those he knew but did not write about. He received the Israel Prize (1965) for his important work in the fields of linguistics and Semitica, and many other tokens of acknowledgment in recognition of his contribution to the development of the disciplines handled by him.

Polotsky's list of publications is relatively small in comparison with the number of areas and disciplines of which he had a firm knowledge, but his writings are characterized by terseness and precision. His descriptions, definitions, and presentation of the problems are always succinct and concise, and the solutions offered are both original and convincing, reflecting his analytical mind and his profound knowledge. These qualities can easily be concluded from general articles such as 'Semitics' (1964), in which he guides the reader through the often unmarked territory of Semitica, or his article 'Aramaic, Syriac and Ge'ez' (1964), in which he establishes precisely the relationship between these three languages and demarcates the unmistakable influence of Aramaic on ecclesiastical Ge'ez (Ullendorff 1973: 134).

Moreover, Polotsky's typical methods of investigation have always linked the past with the present, as the solutions offered were not only concluded from comparative analysis with other languages but also through comparative analysis of the various strata of which the language or the dialect consists. As E. Y. Kutscher (1972: 838) says, '[Polotsky] proved that synchronic problems of certain dialects can be solved by comparative dialectology plus the diachronic approach.'

See also: Semitic Languages; Ullendorff, E.

Bibliography

Kutscher E Y 1872 Polotsky, H. J. In: *Encylopaedia Judaica*, vol. 13. Keter Publishing House, Jerusalem

Rosen H B (ed.) 1964 *Studies in Egyptology and Linguistics in Honour of H J Polotsky*. Israel Exploration Society, Jerusalem

Smith H S, Johnson P V 1973 Review of Polotsky's Collected Papers. *Journal of Semitic Studies* **18**: 129–40

Ullendorff E 1973 *The Ethiopians*, 3rd edn. Oxford University Press, Oxford

Postel, Guillaume (1510–81)

R. E. Asher

Author of numerous books in French and Latin, more than 40 of which were published and many of the rest of which are still extant in manuscript form in the Bibliothèque Nationale in Paris, the British Library in London, and elsewhere, Guillaume Postel was one of the most remarkable figures of the Renaissance. While there is no doubt that he died on September 6, 1581, the date of his birth is less certain. The most widely accepted year is 1510, but stories that he lived well into a second century have led to claims that he was born as early as 1475. This would make him a very late developer as an author, in that his first book was published in or about 1538.

A man of great eccentricity and wild enthusiasms, Postel was not without enemies, both real and imagined, yet he was a much loved personality and a profoundly esteemed scholar who could count among his admirers J. J. Scaliger (see *Scaliger, Joseph Justus*). Because of his ideas—seen variously as visionary, outrageous, and insane—Postel's life was one of constant vicissitudes. He was dismissed from a lectureship at what is now known as the Collège de France in 1542, expelled from the Jesuit order in 1545, forbidden to teach in public 1553, wrongly arrested for murder in 1555, and imprisoned for suspected heresy later the same year. He found being declared mad in this last instance a poor compensation for not being judged a heretic. For the last 19 years of his life he was detained in a monastery with only limited freedom of movement.

One of Postel's lifelong obsessions was his scheme for a universal Christian monarchy with the King of France at its head. This goal he saw as dependent on the defeat of the Turks. Yet he was far from seeing the Turks as barbarians and he had a deep respect for their religion (see Asher 1993: 55–6). His aim was the concord of the world (see Bouwsma 1957) and his preoccupation with this aspect of his plan has led some modern scholars to see his thought as anticipating the ecumenism of the late-twentieth century (see Cousins 1985).

Postel's knowledge of Islam was based on an ability to read Arabic texts, for he was one of the most accomplished linguists of his day. One major project in which he was involved was the Polyglot Bible, following a proposal he made in 1565 that this sacred text should be translated into five languages. Yet when the resulting edition of the Bible in Hebrew, Chaldaic, Greek, and Latin was eventually published by Plantin in Antwerp in 1571, Postel's name did not appear in the preface, the reason being that he was still suspect to the more orthodox elements in the Church. He had, nevertheless, made a major contribution both directly and through the training of those of his students who were involved.

Many of Postel's writings, whatever their subject, display an interest in language and part of his argumentation for a universal Christian monarchy is based on his linguistic theories. He believed that world unity was more likely to be achieved if there was a wider knowledge of languages, and he went so far as to recommend that Arabic should be taught in schools. A number of his earliest publications were devoted exclusively to linguistic matters, for he saw language as being innate in man, God's greatest gift to man, and that which distinguishes mankind from all other living beings. Among languages he was particularly fascinated by Hebrew (1538a) and Arabic (1538c), and he wrote about their particularly close relationship—a fact that has led to his being described as the first comparative linguist. In his book on Hebrew, however, he does take it as the source of *all* languages. His most daring endeavor was a book on 12 different languages (Postel 1538b), in the introduction to which he writes favorably of the study of grammar by such scholars as Lefèvre d'Etaples, Erasmus, and Thomas Linacre.

See also: Myths About Language.

Bibliography

Asher R E 1993 *National Myths in Renaissance France: Francus, Samothes and the Druids*. Edinburgh University Press, Edinburgh

Bouwsma W J 1957 *Concordia Mundi: The Career and Thought of Guillaume Postel (1501–81)*. Harvard University Press, Cambridge, MA

Cousins E H 1985 The principle of plenitude applied to world religions: Bonaventure, Postel and contemporary ecumenism. In: *Guillaume Postel 1581–1981. Actes du Colloque International d'Avranches 5–10 septembre 1981*. Editions de la Maisnie, Paris

Kuntz M L 1981 *Guillaume Postel, Prophet of the Restitution of All Things: His Life and Thought*. Martinus Nijhoff, The Hague

Postel G 1538a *De originibus seu de Hebraicae linguae & gentis antiquitate, deque variarum linguarum affinitate, liber*. Apud Dionysium Lescuier, Parisiis

Postel G 1538b *Linguarum duodecim characteribus differentium alphabetum, introductio, ...* Apud Dionysium Lescuier, Parisiis

Postel G 1538c *Grammatica arabica*. Apud Petrum Gromorsum, Parisiis

Postel G 1543 *Alcorani seu legis Mahometi et evangelistarum concordiæ liber, in quo de calamitatibus orbi Christiano imminentibus tractatur*. Petrus Gromorsus, Parisiis

Priestley, Joseph (1733–1804)

I. Michael

Priestley considered himself a theologian and a scientist, but circumstances required him for a time to teach languages and literature. His elementary English grammar was popular for its simplicity and common sense.

He was born on March 13, 1733, in Yorkshire, but was adopted at the age of 9 years by a prosperous relation. In 1751 he entered Daventry Academy, a nonconformist institution of high standing. After a short time as minister to a congregation in Nantwich he was appointed in 1761 as a tutor at Warrington Academy, where he lectured in belles lettres, languages, history, and other subjects. He was ordained in 1762 and married Mary Wilkinson in the same year. In 1767 he moved to Leeds as minister of Mill Hill Chapel, and in 1773 to Bowood as librarian to Lord Shelburne, with whom he remained until 1780, when he was appointed a minister to the New Meeting in Birmingham. He moved in 1791 to a chapel in Hackney, and in 1794 he emigrated to Pennsylvania, where he died in 1804.

Priestley's enquiring, liberal, and restless mind carried his religious beliefs through a succession of dissenting positions, all reflected in his numerous writings. His final stance was that of Unitarianism. His scientific work, for which he is most famous, showed his imaginative and enquiring qualities but, as did most of his theological writing, it suffered from a restless disinclination to follow through its implications. His liberal political views involved him in a period of active persecution, but he was by nature happy and open, and his scientific work was supported throughout his life by many friends.

Priestley's linguistic works were all composed during a period of a few years. *The Rudiments of English Grammar* (1761) was written for a school in Nantwich; in a second edition, 1768, it was supplemented by more advanced notes derived from his teaching at Warrington. Seven editions followed up to 1798; in two nineteenth-century editions the grammar was combined with other works by him. The book was simple and short. Priestley was ready to question the Latinate tradition, but it was common sense and a respect for the English language rather than linguistic theory which prompted his unorthodox views about, for example, tense. Priestley thought of his lectures on the theory of language and universal grammar, 1762, as being in some degree scientific, but they show the customary preconceptions about the nature of a 'primitive' language: that it had few abstract terms and was spoken loudly and slowly, in short sentences. His speculations about the psychological foundations of various linguistic forms are the most original part of the lectures. The lectures on oratory and criticism, given in 1762 but not printed until 1777, draw on both traditional rhetoric and contemporary belles lettres, influenced especially by his admiration for David Hartley and James Harris.

Bibliography

Crook R E 1966 *A Bibliography of Joseph Priestley 1733–1804*. Library Association, London

Michael I 1970 *English Grammatical Categories and the Tradition to 1880*. Cambridge University Press, Cambridge

Priestley J 1969 [1761] *The Rudiments of English Grammar, Adapted to the Use of School: With Observations on Style*, Facsimile repr., Scolar Press, Menston

Priestley J 1970 [1762] *A Course of Lectures on the Theory of Language and Universal Grammar*. Facsimile repr., Scolar Press, Menston

Priestley J 1968 [1777] *A Course of Lectures on Oratory and Criticism*, Facsimile repr., Scolar Press, Menston

Rājarājavarma, A. R. (1863–1918)

V. R. Prabodhachandran Nayar

Easily the most authoritative of grammarians in Malayalam in his times and after, A. R. Rājarājavarma hailed from a princely family of erstwhile Travancore. He was a pioneer of the renaissance of Malayalam at the beginning of the twentieth century. A gifted poet in both Malayalam and Sanskrit and a skilled translator of Sanskrit poetry and prose into Malayalam, he excelled as a farsighted contributor to the overall planning and development of the Malayalam language. A great teacher who produced distinguished students, he was referred to as the Pāṇini of Kerala after his magnum opus *Kēraḷapāṇinīyam*, which presents a descriptive-cum-historico-comparative treatment of the Malayalam language on the lines of the Pāṇinian tradition and that of western grammarians such as Robert Caldwell (see *Caldwell, Robert*).

The first edition of *Kēraḷapāṇinīyam* (1968) was in sūtravṛtti-bhāṣya (aphorism, gloss, and commentary) style (see *Sūtra*); it contained 357 formulaic rules and their explanation in detail. The work was thoroughly recast in its second edition (1917) in the kārikā-bhāṣya (verse and commentary) style, comprising 194 rules. Statements in the *Kēraḷapāṇinīyam* pertain to sociocultural and historical matters; separation of Malayalam and Tamil; phonology, sandhi, parts of speech, inflectional and derivational morphology, differences between case suffixes and postpositions; nominal and verbal compounds; syntactic relations; and etymology. Rājarājavarma evinces a remarkable insight into fundamental principles of coining technical terms acceptable to the speech community.

His other writings include graded grammars of Malayalam, restatements of Sanskrit grammar, textbooks on literary composition, poetics, and metrics; annotation of a Kathakaḷi play; translations in simple Malayalam of famous Sanskrit poems and plays; and original compositions in Malayalam of varying length from single quatrains to an historic epic.

Born in the Lakshmipuram palace in Changanachery, Rājarājavarma spent his formative years in the Anantapuram palace in Haripad, studying Sanskrit grammar and literature, poetics, astrology, and logic under his illustrious uncle, Kēraḷavarma, reputed as the Kāḷidāsa of Kerala. He was the first from the princely class to attend a public school and have formal education in English. So was he to take a BA degree and to join the government service. A graduate in chemistry, he won the prestigious Ross gold medal for his MA in Sanskrit (1891) from the University of Madras.

He held, successively, the positions of Inspector of the Sanskrit School; Principal, Sanskrit College; Professor of Sanskrit and Dravidian languages and the first Indian Principal of the Maharaja's College, Trivandrum. He also served on various boards and committees, including the one that considered the establishment of the first University in Kerala. His influence in shaping the sensibilities of the Keralite in matters of literary appreciation, education, and culture was considerable.

See also: Sanskrit; Tamil; Pāṇini.

Bibliography

Ezhuthachan K N 1975 *The History of the Grammatical Theories in Malayalam*. Dravidian Linguistics Association, Trivandrum

Sankaranarayanan C[handrika] 1985 *A. R. Rājarājavarma—malayāḷattinṯe rājaśilpi*. State Institute of Languages, Trivandrum

Reinisch, Simon Leo (1832–1919)

D. L. Appleyard

Simon Leo Reinisch has been called the 'father of Egyptology and Africanistics in Vienna' and is still considered as the pioneer and creator of Cushitic linguistics (see *Ancient Egyptian and Coptic*).

He was born on October 26, 1832 in Osterwitz, Styria, the fifth child of Josef Reinisch and his second wife Elisabeth Spieler. At an early age he showed himself to be an especially gifted child and, after completing his schooling at the Gymnasium in Graz, in 1854 he was enrolled at the University of Vienna. There he began his involvement with Oriental languages, and in particular Ancient Egyptian, to which he was to devote the rest of his life. In 1864, three years after graduating, Reinisch was invited by Archduke Ferdinand Maximilian, the younger brother of the Emperor, to catalog his collection of Egyptian artifacts housed at Miramar. Shortly after that, when Maximilian became Emperor of Mexico, he sent Reinisch to Egypt to add to his collection, and then in 1866 called him to Mexico to be his private secretary. During the year that Reinisch spent there in Maximilian's service, he worked on the indigenous languages of Mexico, with a particular interest in pre- and early post-Columbian manuscripts, which he cataloged. He also prepared a number of grammars of Mexican languages, none of which, unfortunately, ever reached publication.

In 1868 he was appointed lecturer in Egyptian archaeology, and in 1873 Professor in Egyptian language and archaeology, at the University of Vienna. During this time he used his profound knowledge of a wide range of languages—Classical European, Ancient Oriental, and now Native American—to embark upon the question of the common origin of human languages. To his lectures on Egyptian and Coptic in Vienna he began to add unofficial classes on African languages, notably those of the Sudan and the Horn of Africa. The first of his African journeys took place in 1875–76, to the Bogos in Eritrea, to which he returned in 1879–80. The linguistic data that he collected during these journeys provided the material for over 20 books and articles, including several grammars, such as those of Bilin, Chamir, Quara, Kunama, Saho, and Beja, some of which are still the most extensive descriptions of these languages to date.

Reinisch had begun his studies at a time when modern linguistic science was in its infancy and much of the methodology that he used is necessarily now out of date. This is true not only in phonological analysis, but also in the fields of language comparison and historical linguistics. Nonetheless, the actual language data that Reinisch recorded are still invaluable.

Reinisch's service to the field of Oriental languages was recognized by his country when, first, in 1884, he was elected a full member of the Academy of Sciences and then, in 1899, he was awarded the title of Hofrat. He retired in 1903 to his estate in his native Styria, where he died on December 24, 1919.

Bibliography

Mukarovsky H G (ed.) 1987 *Leo Reinisch—Werk und Erbe*. Õsterreichische Akadamie der Wissenschaften, Vienna

Zaborski A 1976 Cushitic overview. In: Bender M L (ed.) *The Non-Semitic Languages of Ethiopia*. African Studies Center, Michigan State University, East Lansing, MI

Renou, Louis (1896–1966)

R. E. Asher

A prolific and versatile scholar, Louis Renou was one of the foremost indologists of the twentieth century. Born on October 28, 1896, he took his *agrégation* in 1920, his academic career having been interrupted by service in World War I. His first important publications appeared in 1925. These included two doctoral theses, the main one on the prefect tense in the Vedic hymns (Renou 1925) and the subsidiary one comprising a critical edition and French translation of the section on India in Ptolemy's *Geography*.

Renou's interest in India had been aroused by the Sanskrit scholar Sylvain Lévi and his first important appointment was to the chair of Sanskrit and Comparative Grammar at the University of Lyon (1925–28). In 1929 he became professor at the Ecole des Hautes Etudes and in 1937 in the Faculté des Lettres at the Sorbonne. He was Membre de l'Institut and Chevalier de la Légion d'Honneur.

His doctoral research proved to be an indication of the direction Renou was to take subsequently. In the broad pattern of his work there are two main strands: the study of the Vedas and the study of grammar. His study of the language of the Vedas led to the publication of a grammar of Vedic (Renou 1952). As with his work of a similar sort on classical Sanskrit, this was intended to be purely descriptive and deliberately avoided a discussion of the prehistory of the language or indeed of any questions of historical linguistics. He published several translations of Vedic hymns and conceived as a major task a complete translation of the *Ṛgveda*. Sadly he died before this was completed.

Published work by Renou on classical Sanskrit language is essentially of two sorts. First, there are teaching grammars (e.g., Renou 1930) and monographs on aspects of the grammar of Sanskrit. Second, he produced studies on the work of the Sanskrit grammarians. An important publication emerging from this research was a new translation of Pāṇini's *Aṣṭādhyāyī* (1947–54; see *Pāṇini*). His translation was based on the seventh-century exegetical work, *Kāśikāvṛtti*, and in collaboration with a Japanese scholar, Yutaka Ojihara; he published a translation of this (1960–67), completed after his death. Published over a longer period than either of these was his translation of the twelfth-century grammatical treatise *Durghaṭavṛtti* of Śaraṇadeva (1940–56). One offshoot of these studies was a book on Sanskrit grammatical terminology (Renou 1942). A major combined outcome of his work on Vedic and classical Sanskrit was the series of *Etudes védiques et pāṇinéennes*, which was started in 1955 and the sixteenth volume of which appeared in the year after his death.

The wide range of Renou's other publications includes lexicographical and bibliographical works. There are also important works to which his main contribution was that of editor. Among these are editions of the text of the *Upaniṣads* with a French translation, and general studies of Indian civilization. His interests also extended to Indian religion and this led to his being invited to deliver the Jordan Lectures in Comparative Religion in the University of London in 1951 (Renou 1953).

See also: Indian Linguistic Tradition; Ritual; Sanskrit; Sanskrit, Discovery by Europeans; Sanskrit (Pāninian) Linguistics.

Bibliography

Filliozat J 1967 Louis Renou et son œuvre scientifique. *Journal asiatique* **255**: 1–30

Renou L 1925 *La valeur du parfait dans les hymnes védiques*. Champion, Paris

Renou L 1930 *Grammaire sanscrite*, 2 vols. Adrien-Maisonneuve, Paris

Renou L 1942 *Terminologie grammaticale du sanskrit*, 4 parts. Champion, Paris

Renou L 1947–54 *La grammaire de Pāṇini, traduite du sanskrit avec des extraits des commentaires indigènes*, 3 parts. Klinck-sieck, Paris

Renou L 1952 *Grammaire de la langue védique*. IAC, Lyon and Paris

Renou L 1953 *Religions of Ancient India*, tr. Asher R E, Raeside I M P. University of London, London

Reuchlin, Johann (1455–1522)

G. Lloyd Jones

The three areas of language, literature, and mysticism provide a suitable framework for a brief review of the German savant Johann Reuchlin's lasting contribution to Semitic studies.

First, there is his expertise as a Hebraist. Under the influence of Pico (1463–94), the 'father' of Christian Kabbalah, Reuchlin developed a consuming interest in Jewish mysticism. In order to gain access to the Kabbalah he resolved to perfect his knowledge of Hebrew by employing Jewish teachers. Thanks to his instructors, Reuchlin's passion for all things Hebraic remained undiminished for the rest of his life. He never tired of stressing the importance of Hebrew for a proper understanding of the Bible. 'I assure you,' he wrote in 1508, 'that not one of the Latins can expound the Old Testament unless he first becomes proficient in the language in which it was written. For the mediator between God and man was language, as we read in the Pentateuch; but not any language, only Hebrew through which God wished his secrets to be made known unto man.' To encourage and help students, he published a grammar-cum-dictionary, the *De rudimentis hebraicis* (1506). This was followed in 1512 by the Hebrew text of the seven penitential psalms, with translation and commentary (*in septem psalmos poenitentiales*), likewise intended for beginners. Finally, six years later, he published the *De accentibus et orthographia linguae hebraicae*, a treatise on accents, pronunciation, and synagogue music. Reuchlin's importance for linguistic study is that he established philology as a recognized discipline, independent of theology, an approach which led him to criticize and correct the Vulgate at several points.

Reuchlin's high regard for postbiblical Jewish literature emerged in 'the battle of the books,' a bitter controversy which raged for almost a decade. In 1510, the Emperor Maximilian at the instigation of the Dominicans, ordered the destruction of all Hebrew books inimical to Christianity. Reuchlin was asked to assist by deciding which ones should be condemned. He reacted by coming to the defense of Jewish literature. This concern for the preservation of the Jewish literary heritage sprang not from any philo-Semitic feelings, for he was no friend of the Jews, but from educational and humanitarian motives. He was convinced that the loss of the Hebrew language would harm Christian biblical scholarship. As an ex-lawyer, he also knew that the Jews had rights. Whatever their disabilities, they had received guarantees from popes and emperors that their books would not be destroyed. Though he claimed that he was defending Christian rather than Jewish interests in the action he took, Reuchlin had the satisfaction before he died of knowing that he had won 'the battle of the books,' a victory for Jews and Christian humanists alike.

Pico studied Kabbalah for two reasons: to confirm Christian truth and to confute the Jews from their own literature. When he was prevented by death from pursuing further studies, his mantle fell upon Reuchlin who expressed the hope that he would 'soon accomplish precisely what Pico promised.' His first contribution was the *De verbo mirifico* (1494), where he demonstrates the practical value of Jewish mystical techniques for attaining union with Christ. The 'wonder-working word' of the title is YHSVH, the letters of the Hebrew form of the name 'Jesus.' This was followed by the *De arte cabalistica* (1517), the author's *magnum opus*, which represents the climax of his Kabbalistic studies. Written in dialogue form, it is essentially an apologia for the Christian study of Kabbalah.

Reuchlin's contribution in the three areas of language, literature, and mysticism marks a turning point in the Church's attitude towards Hebrew and Jewish literature.

See also: Hebrew, Biblical and Jewish; Mysticism; Hebrew Grammarians; Semitic Languages.

Bibliography

Geiger L 1871 *Johann Reuchlin: sein Leben und seine Werke*. Duncker and Humbolt, Leipzig.

Goodman M, Goodman S 1983 *Johann Reuchlin: On the Art of the Kabbalaha*. (Eng. transl.). Abaris Books, New York

Herzig, Schoeps, Rohde (eds.) 1993 *Reuchlin und die Juden*. Sigmaringen, Germany. Series: Pforzheimen Reuchlinschriften 3

Overfield J M 1984 *Humanism and Scholasticism in Late Mediaeval Germany*. Princeton University Press, Princeton, NJ

Rhein, King (eds.) 1996 *Tolerance and Intolerance in the European Reformation*. New York

Ricci, Matteo (1552–1610)

J. H. Grayson

Matteo Ricci, the most influential of the early Jesuit missionaries to China, was resident there from 1582 until his death. Born in Macerata in east central Italy, Ricci went to Rome in 1568 originally to study law but instead joined the Society of Jesus in 1571. He came under the tutelage of two key figures in the order—Alessandro Valignano (1539–1606) proponent of Christian accommodation to local culture and Visitor to the East (responsible for all Jesuit missions in Asia), and the renowned scientist and mathematician Christophorus Clavius (Christoph Klau, 1537–1612). Ricci, having asked to serve as a missionary in Asia, was sent to Goa in 1578 where he was ordained in 1580. Sent on to Macao in 1582, he and a colleague Michele Ruggieri (1543–1607) were able to enter China itself in 1583 and established themselves in Chaoch'ing near Canton. Subsequently, Ricci lived in Nanjing and other cities in central China and eventually made his residence in the capital Beijing from 1598.

Ricci's mission policy, which was to gain the support if not the adherence of the élite sector of society in order to obtain tolerance for Christian missions, was successful in gaining the support of many of the Confucian literati class and even of the Emperor himself. His mission method was twofold: to use the concepts of classical Confucianism to explain Christian doctrine, and to use Western scientific and technological developments to demonstrate to the literati class that Europeans were not inferior barbarian peoples.

Ricci's mission methods had a profound impact on Jesuit and subsequent missionary activity in China. His views on the appropriate form of Christian participation in Confucian ancestral memorial rites became the model of a sophisticated Christian approach to Chinese culture. Ricci was a prolific writer and his literary impact was immense. He devised the first system of Romanising the Chinese language, introduced the form 'Confucius' for the name of the founder of Confucianism, and translated the Four Books of the Confucian canon (*The Analects, The Mencius, The Doctrine of the Mean, The Great Learning*) into Latin, thus laying the foundation for European scholarship on China.

Excluding cartographic works, Ricci's writings encompass thirteen works, several of which are in multiple volumes. Among his non-religious writings are, *Chiao-yu lun* (On Friendship, 1595), *Erh-shih-wu yen* (Twenty-Five Sayings, 1604), and a translation of Euclid's *Elements* (1607). Perhaps his most important work was the *T'ien-hsüeh shih-lu* (True Record of the Heavenly Religion) of 1595 which was revised as the *T'ien-chu shih-i* (True Meaning of the Lord of Heaven) in 1601. In its revised form, this work had an immense impact in China, and through a study of the document in the late eighteenth century became the source for the Catholic Church in Korea. Other works introducing religious themes would include the *Ch'i-jen shih-p'ien* (Ten Dialogues with an Eccentric, 1608). Ricci also influenced Chinese language usage. From the 1580s, he began to use the word *T'ien-chu* (Lord of Heaven) as the correct term for God which subsequently became the standard Roman Catholic word for God in China and Korea.

See also: Christianity in East Asia; Missionaries; Chinese Translation of Theological Terms; Confucianism.

Bibliography

Bernard H 1973 (1935) *Matteo Ricci's Scientific Contribution to China.* Hyperion Press, Westport, CT

Gallagher L J 1953 *China in the Sixteenth Century: The Journals of Matthew Ricci, 1583–1610 [trans.].* Random House, New York

Malatesta E J (ed.) 1985 *The True Meaning of the Lord of Heaven (T'ien-chu shih-i).* Institute of Jesuit Sources, St Louis, MI

Spence J 1983 *The Memory Palace of Matteo Ricci.* Faber, London

Ross, John (1842–1915)

J. H. Grayson

Ross, John (1842–1915) was a missionary of the United Presbyterian Church of Scotland to Manchuria who worked there from 1871 to his retirement in 1910. Although not the first Protestant missionary to Manchuria, Ross was the effective father of the Protestant Christian churches in Manchuria and also in Korea. He was born in Balintore on the Moray Firth near Inverness, Scotland. He originally trained for ministry amongst the Gaelic-speaking people of northern Scotland and the Hebrides, serving for a few years in various churches before settling on overseas missions as a vocation. He originally intended to go to India, but was persuaded to go to China. In 1910, he returned to Edinburgh where he died in 1915.

A native speaker of Gaelic, Ross knew 10 other languages including English, French, German, Greek, Hebrew, Latin, spoken Mandarin Chinese, written Chinese, Manchu, and Korean of which he spoke four fluently (Gaelic, English, Mandarin, and Manchu). Ross was a prolific and seminal writer, contributing to the later translation of the Bible in standard Chinese, and commentaries in Chinese on various books of the Bible. Among his books are a two-volume connected history of Northeast Asia, *The Manchus, or the Reigning Dynasty of China* (1880) and *History of Corea, Ancient and Modern* (1881), and *Mission Methods in Manchuria* (1903), *The Original Religion of China* (1909), and *The Origin of the Chinese People* (1916). He wrote a basic textbook for Mandarin Chinese, *Mandarin Primer* (1876), and the first European textbook for the Korean language, *Corean Primer* (1879), which was revised as *Korean Speech with Grammar* and *Vocabulary* (1882).

His most important work, however, was the translation of the Bible into Korean, the first portions of which were published in 1882, the whole New Testament appearing in one volume in 1887. Ross worked with a team of educated Koreans in Manchuria, translating the books of the New Testament from the Chinese version which was then checked with the Greek Bible. The importance of this translation is immense because it simultaneously became the source for the self-propagation of the Protestant Christian church in Korea, and the modern revival of the use of the indigenous Korean alphabet (now called *Han'gŭl*). It was a mission principle for Ross that the Korean translation of the Bible should be written entirely in the Korean alphabet and use where possible pure Korean terms rather than terms borrowed from Chinese. Most of the theological and scriptural terms used in contemporary Korean, especially the choice of the term for God, were selected by Ross. In cases where later usage differed from his work, the most recent translations of the Bible have gone back to using the terms selected by Ross as being the most appropriate, for example the Korean title for the Book of the Revelation of St. John.

See also: Christianity in East Asia; Missionaries; Korean.

Bibliography

Choi Sung-il 1992 *John Ross (1842–1915) and the Korean Protestant Church*. Unpublished doctoral dissertation, University of Edinburgh

Grayson J H 1982 *Na Yohan* (*John Ross*): *Han'gug- ŭi ch'ŏt sŏn'gyo-sa* [John Ross: Korea's First Missionary]. Taegu Kyemyŏng UP. In Korean

Grayson J H 1999 The Legacy of John Ross. *International Bulletin of Missionary Research* **23**: 167–172

Saadya Gaon (882–942)

J. Weinberg

Saadya Gaon, son of Joseph Gaon, was born in Upper Egypt and became the religious leader (Gaon) in Babylon. He was a polymath and innovator in many disciplines including Hebrew grammar, and is generally regarded as the first Hebrew grammarian. His linguistic writings show familiarity with contemporary Arabic philology. He was the author of the first Hebrew lexicon, *Ha-'Egron*, which is only partially extant. Its purpose was to assist poets in constructing acrostics and finding rhymes. To this end, he arranged the dictionary in two lists alphabetically; one according to the initial letters, the other according to the final letters of words. Each word is illustrated with quotations from biblical and rabbinic texts. Under the influence of Arab philologists, he later reissued the dictionary with a new title *Book of Poetics*: *Books of Languages* in a revised form, adding an Arabic preface, translating the Hebrew terms into Arabic, and including a section on the consonants. In an extract from this last section quoted in his commentary to the mystical work *Sēpher Yĕṣirā* (*Book of Creation*), he discusses the 'guttural' letters—Aleph, He, Heth, Ayin. In this commentary, he also suggests the distinction between the eleven unchanging consonants and the other eleven and discusses the pronunciation of the letter Resh in Babylon and Palestine.

His work entitled *Book of Elegance of the Language of the Hebrews* (also known as the *Books on the Language* or simply *Twelve Parts*), which has not been preserved in its entirety, constitutes the first study of Hebrew grammar as a separate discipline independent of Massoretic studies. The first part of the work appears to have included a study of the permutation of the twenty-two consonants according to phonetics and lists the precluded combinations of letters. The extant fragments cover the following subjects: augmentation and contraction of Hebrew stems (i.e., when root letters are doubled or elided—he did not recognize the triliterality of the Hebrew stem); inflection of nouns, verbs, and particles; the *dagesh* (a *dagesh* is a dot in the letter indicating either that the consonant is doubled or the plosive pronunciation of the letters *bgdkpt*);

vowels and phonetics; the quiescent and vocal *shewa*; laryngeal (or 'guttural') letters and the changes in their vocalization; interchangeable letters. This work, despite its rudimentary nature, laid the foundation of the scientific treatment of Hebrew grammar.

Saadya Gaon also wrote a glossary of ninety *hapax legomena* in the Hebrew Bible, bringing analogies from postbiblical Hebrew, as well as a treatise on the obscure words in the *Mishnah* (see *Talmud*).

See also: Hebrew Linguistic Tradition; Masoretic Tradition.

Bibliography

(For a full list of publications of fragments of Saadya Gaon's works, see Tene D 1971.)

Allony N (ed.) 1969 Saadya Gaon *Ha-'Egrōn Kitāb 'Uṣūl 'Al-Shi'r 'al-'Ibrānī*. The Academy of the Hebrew Language, Jerusalem

Hirschfeld H 1920 *Literary History of Hebrew Grammarians and Lexicographers*. Oxford University Press, Oxford

Malter H 1921 *Life and Works of Saadia Gaon*. Jewish Publication Society of America, Philadelphia, PA

Skoss S L 1955 *Saadiah Gaon, the Earliest Hebrew Grammarian*. Dropsie College Press, Philadelphia, PA

Tené D 1971 Linguistic literature, Hebrew In: *Encylopaedia Judaica*, XVI, pp. 1364–65; 1367–69. Keter, Jerusalem

Saussure, Ferdinand(-Mongin) de (1857–1913)

E. F. K. Koerner

Saussure was born on November 26, 1857 in Geneva, and died on February 22, 1913, at Château Vufflens near Geneva. He is best known for the posthumous compilation of his lecture notes on general linguistics, the *Cours de linguistique générale*, edited by his former students and first published in 1916 (since translated into more than a dozen languages, including—in order of their first appearance since 1928—Japanese, German, Russian, Spanish, English, Polish, Italian, Hungarian). However, during his lifetime, Saussure was most widely known for his masterly *Mémoire* of 1879, devoted to an audacious reconstruction of the Proto-Indo-European vowel system. It is generally agreed that his *Cours* ushered in a revolution in linguistic thinking during the 1920s and 1930s which is still felt today in many quarters, even beyond linguistics proper. He is universally regarded as 'the father of structuralism.'

Although from a distinguished Geneva family which—beginning with Horace Bénédict de Saussure, whose portrait adorns the Swiss twenty franc note—can boast of several generations of natural scientists, Ferdinand de Saussure was early drawn to language study, producing an '*Essai pour réduire les mots du grec, du latin et de l'allemand à un petit nombre de racines*' at the age of 14 or 15 (published in *Cahiers Ferdinand de Saussure* **32**: 77–101 [1978]). Following his parents' wishes, he attended classes in chemistry, physics, and mathematics at the University of Geneva during 1875–76, before being allowed to join his slightly older classmates who had left for Leipzig the year before. So in the fall of 1876 Saussure arrived at the university where a number of important works in the field of Indo-European phonology and morphology, including Karl Verner's (1846–1896) epoch-making paper on a series of exceptions to 'Grimm's Law,' had just been published. Saussure took courses with Georg Curtius (1820–1886) the mentor of the '*Junggrammatiker*,' and a number of the younger professors, such as August Leskien, Ernst Windisch, Heinrich Hübschmann, Hermann Osthoff, and others in the fields of Indic studies, Slavic, Baltic, Celtic, and Germanic. During 1878–79 Saussure spent two semesters at the University of Berlin, enrolling in courses with Heinrich Zimmer and Hermann Oldenberg.

After barely six semesters of formal study, when just 21, he published the major work of his lifetime (Saussure 1879). In this 300-page work he assumed the existence, on purely theoretical grounds, of an early Proto-Indo-European sound of unknown phonetic value (designated *A) which would develop into various phonemes of the Indo-European vocalic system depending on its combination with various 'sonantal coefficients.' Saussure was thus able to explain a number of puzzling questions of Indo-European ablaut. But the real proof of Saussure's hypotheses came many years later, after his death, following the decipherment of Hittite and its identification as an Indo-European language, and after the Polish scholar Kuryłowicz in 1927 had pointed to Hittite cognates that contained the sound corresponding to Saussure's *A. These were identified as laryngeals, sounds previously not found in any of the other Indo–European languages.

Having returned to Leipzig, Saussure defended his dissertation on the use of the genitive absolute in Sanskrit in February 1880, leaving for Geneva soon thereafter. Before he arrived in Paris in September of that year, he appears to have conducted fieldwork on Lithuanian, like Schleicher and others before him. In Paris Saussure found a number of receptive students, among them Antoine Meillet, Maurice Grammont, and Paul Passy, but also congenial colleagues such as Gaston Paris, Louis Havet, who had previously written the most detailed review of his *Mémoire*, and Arsène Darmester. Michel Bréal (1832–1915), the doyen of French linguistics, secured him a position as Maître de Conférences at the École des Hautes Études in 1881, a post he held until his departure for Geneva ten years later.

During his lifetime, Saussure was best known for his *Mémoire* and the paper on Lithuanian accentuation (1896). Since the 1920s, however, his influence and fame have been almost exclusively connected with the book he never wrote, the *Cours de linguistique générale*. This was largely based on notes carefully taken down by a number of his students during a series of lectures on the subject that he had given from 1907–11 at the University of Geneva (to which he had returned as a professor of Sanskrit and Comparative Grammar in 1891). One of them was Albert Riedlinger, whose name appears on the title page of the *Cours*, which was put together by Saussure's successors, Charles Bally and Albert Sechehaye, neither of whom had attended these lectures themselves (though it is frequently, but erroneously, stated in the literature that they had). The *Cours* was in fact never published in Geneva and was not published in 1915 but in Lausanne and Paris in 1916, that is, exactly 100 years after Franz Bopp's *Conjugationssystem*, which is usually regarded as the beginning of comparative-historical Indo–European linguistics.

The ideas advanced in the *Cours* produced a veritable revolution in linguistic science; historical–comparative grammar which had dominated linguistic research since the early nineteenth century was soon relegated to a mere province of the field. At least in the manner the *Cours* had been presented by the editors, Saussure's general theory of language was seen as assigning pride of place to the non-historical, descriptive, and 'structural' approach (Saussure himself did not use the last-mentioned term in a technical sense). This led to a tremendous body of work concerned with the analysis of the linguistic system of language and its function, and a neglect of questions of language change and linguistic evolution in general—a situation which remains characteristic of the linguistic scene to this day, in particular the framework associated with the name of Noam Chomsky. From the 1920s onwards a variety of important schools of linguistic thought developed in Europe that can be traced back to proposals made in the *Cours*. These are usually identified with the respective centers from which they emanated, such as Geneva, Prague, Copenhagen, and Paris. In North America too, through the work of Leonard Bloomfield (1887–1949), Saussure's ideas became stock-in-trade among linguists, descriptivists, structuralists, and generativists.

At the core of Saussure's linguistic theory is the assumption that language is a system of interrelated terms which he called 'langue' (in contradistinction to 'parole,' the individual speech act or speaking in general). This 'langue' is the underlying code which ensures that people can speak and understand each other; it has social underpinning and is an operative system embedded in the brain of everyone who has learned a given language. The analysis of this system, Saussure maintains, is the true object of linguistics. The system is a network of relationships which he characterized as being of two kinds: syntagmatic (i.e., items are arranged in a consecutive, linear order) and associative, later termed 'paradigmatic' (i.e., the organization of units in a deeper fashion dealing with grammatical and semantic relations). Saussure's emphasis on language as 'a system of (arbitrary) signs' and his proposal that linguistics is the central part of an overall science of sign relations or 'sémiologie' have led to the development of a field of inquiry more frequently called 'semiotics' (following C. S. Peirce's terminology), which deals with sign systems in literature and other forms of art, including music and architecture.

Many of the ingredients of Saussure's general theory of language have often been taken out of their original context and incorporated into theories outside of linguistics, at times quite arbitrarily, especially in works by French writers engaged in 'structuralist' anthropology (e.g., Claude Lévi-Strauss) and philosophy (e.g., Louis Althusser), literary theory (e.g., Jacques Derrida), psychoanalysis (e.g., Jacques Lacan), and semiotics (e.g., Roland Barthes), and their various associates and followers. The trichotomies (usually reduced to dichotomies) which have become current in twentieth-century thought, far beyond their original application, are: *langage–langue–parole* (i.e., language in all its manifestations or 'speech'; language as the underlying system; and 'speaking'), *signe–signifié–signifiant* (sign, signified, and signifier), synchrony versus diachrony ('panchrony' would be a combination of these two perspectives), and syntagmatic versus paradigmatic relations.

See also: Barthes, R.; Derrida, J.; Lacan, J.; Levi-Strauss, C.

Bibliography

(For a full bibliography of Saussure's writings see Koerner 1972a.)

Engler R 1975 European structuralism: Saussure. In: Sebeok T A (ed.) *Current Trends in Linguistics. Vol. XIII: Historiography of Linguistics.* Mouton, The Hague, pp. 829–886

Engler R 1976–1998 Bibliographie saussurienne. *Cahiers Ferdinand de Saussure* **30**: 99–138; **31**: 279–306; **33**: 79–145; **40**: 131–200; **43**: 149–275; **50**: 247–295 and **51**: 295–297

Godel R 1957 *Les sources du Cours de linguistique générale de F. de Saussure.* Droz, Geneva

Koerner E F K 1972a *Bibliographia Saussureana, 1870–1970: An Annotated, Classified Bibliography on the Background, Development and Actual Relevance of Ferdinand de Saussure's General Theory of Language.* Scarecrow Press, Metuchen, NJ

Koerner E F K 1972b *Contribution au débat post-saussurien sur le signe linguistique: Introduction générale et bibliographie annotée.* Mouton, The Hague

Koerner E F K 1973 *Ferdinand de Saussure: Origin and Development of his Linguistic Thought in Western Studies of Language.* Friedrich Vieweg Sohn, Braunschweig

Koerner E F K 1988 *Saussurean Studies/Études saussuriennes.* Slatkine, Geneva

Saussure F de 1879 *Mémoire sur le systéme primitif des voyelles dans les langues indo-européennes.* B. G. Teubner, Leipzig

Saussure F de 1896 Accentuation lituanienne. *Anzeiger of Indo-germanische Forschungen* **6**: 157–66

Saussure F de 1916 *Cours de linguistique générale.* Payot, Lausanne & Paris. (Harris R 1983 *Course in General Linguistics.* Duckworth, London)

Saussure F de 1922 *Recueil des publications scientifiques.* C. Winter, Heidelberg

Scaliger, Joseph Justus (1540–1609)

R. H. Bremmer Jr

Joseph Scaliger has entered history as one of the greatest Renaissance philologists, especially in the field of the Classical languages.

Born in Agen, Lot-et-Garonne (Southern France) in 1540, a son of the renowned humanist Julius Caesar Scaliger, Scaliger received his Latin training mainly from his much-demanding father. In 1559 he went to Paris where he read Greek and various Semitic languages. In 1562 he embraced the Protestant faith and in the following years he traveled widely. Scaliger actively participated in the religious wars in France and in 1572 he fled from the country to Geneva where he lectured in philosophy at the Calvinist academy. In 1574 he returned to France and lived there until 1593, when he moved to Leiden where the University had offered him an attractive post free from lecturing duties. He remained in Leiden until his death in 1609, and bequeathed his books and invaluable manuscript collection to the University of Leiden.

Scaliger's first book, an edition of Varro's *De lingua Latina* (1565) (included in Varro 1573), was an immediate success. In it he displays the philological methods to which he would thenceforth adhere and which were to exercise a lasting influence on contemporary and later scholars. He brought the method of presenting critical text editions to perfection by insisting on the consultation of as many manuscript versions of a text as possible. Many of his conjectures and emendations still stand nowadays. Scaliger was a very prolific scholar, especially during his period at Leiden. There he also stimulated fellow scholars to explore the disciplines of history, epigraphy, Semitic, Slavonic, and Old Germanic studies, among others.

Scaliger still is today esteemed for his insightful criticism of the many texts he edited, as well as for his major achievement in creating order in the chronology of world history (see Scaliger 1583). Finally, he must be counted as one of the founding fathers of comparative linguistics.

See also: Philology and History.

Bibliography

Bremmer Jr R H 1996 Joseph Justus Scaliger. In: Stammerjohann H (ed.) *Lexicon grammaticorum.* Niemeyer, Tübingen

Bremmer Jr R H 1998 *The correspondence of Johannes de Luet (1581–1649) as a mirror of his life. Lias* **25**: 139–64

Grafton A 1983–93 *Joseph Scaliger: A Study in the History of Classical Scholarship* 2 vols. Oxford

Scaliger J J 1583 *Opus novum de emendatione temporum.* M. Patissonius, Paris

Varro M T 1573 *M. Terentii Varronis opera ... In lib. de ling. Lat. conjecteana J. Scaligeri recognita.* H. Stephanus, Geneva

Schlegel, August Wilhelm von (1767–1845)

K. Grotsch

Schlegel, August Wilhelm [from 1815:] von, writer, literary critic, translator, philologist, and student of the Sanskrit language and its literature, elder brother of Friedrich Schlegel (see *Schlegel, (Carl Wilhelm) Friedrich von*), was born in Hanover (Germany) on September 5, 1767. He studied theology and philosophy at the University of Göttingen, where he was mainly influenced by the philologist C. G. Heyne and the poet G. A. Bürger. Between 1791 and 1795 he was a tutor in Amsterdam. From 1798 he was associate professor at the University of Jena. He moved to Berlin where he delivered courses of private lectures on literary history (1801–04). From 1804 till her death in 1817 he was secretary, traveling companion, and literary adviser to Madame de Staël (Anne Louise Germaine de Staël-Holstein, 1766–1817). In 1818 he was appointed professor of the history of art and literature at the University of Bonn, where he established Indic studies, thus becoming the founder of Indic philology in Germany. He died in Bonn on May 12, 1845.

Schlegel was a prominent member of the Romantic movement in Germany and succeeded in transforming the genuine romantic interest in foreign cultures, languages, and literatures, into a systematic scientific approach. He produced excellent translations of Italian and Spanish authors and of the dramas of Shakespeare (in a project later continued by L. Tieck and Tieck's daughter Dorothea). His most influential contributions to the study of language lay in the fields of language typology and reflections on method. As early as 1798 he pointed out the difference between analytical and synthetic languages (Schlegel 1798: 60ff.; cf. Schlegel 1818: 16). By coining the term '*vergleichende Grammatik*' (Schlegel 1803: 203) he paved the way for the linguistic theories of his brother Friedrich (e.g., Schlegel 1808: 28) and significantly contributed to the theoretical evolution of comparative linguistics. He took up and refined Friedrich's theory of language classification (outlined in Schlegel 1808: 44ff. and elsewhere) by proposing three types of languages: those without any grammatical structure, languages using affixes, and inflectional languages (Schlegel 1818: 14ff.). This theory was much discussed throughout the nineteenth century. With his severe criticism of J. Grimm's early etymologies (Schlegel 1815) he gave a decisive impulse to strict methodological rigor in the study of the history of the Germanic languages. He also set the standards for the study of the Sanskrit language by applying the methods of classical philology to the analysis of its literature and the publication of Sanskrit texts (e.g., in his editions of the Bhagavad-Gītā 1823 and parts of the Rāmāyana 1829–38).

See also: Sanskrit; Indian Linguistic Tradition.

Bibliography

Muncker F 1890 Schlegel. *Allgemeine Deutsche Biographie* **31**: 354–68

Schlegel A W 1798 Die Sprachen; Ein Gespräch über Klopstocks grammatische Gespräche. In: Schlegel A W, Schlegel F (eds.) 1798–1800 *Athenaeum: Eine Zeitschrift 1–3*. Vieweg/Frölich, Berlin

Schlegel A W 1803 Ankündigung: Sprachlehre von A F Bernhardi. *Europa: Eine Zeitschrift* **2**: 193–204

Schlegel A W 1815 Altdeutsche Wälder. *Heidelbergische Jahrbücher der Literatur* **8**: 721–66

Schlegel A W 1818 *Observations sur la langue et la littérature provençales*. Librairie grecque–latine–allemande, Paris

Schlegel A W (ed.) 1820–30 *Indische Bibliothek 1–2.1*. Weber, Bonn

Schlegel F 1808 *Über die Sprache und Weisheit der Indier: Ein Beitrag zur Begründung der Alterthumskunde*. Mohr und Zimmer, Heidelberg

Schlegel, (Carl Wilhelm) Friedrich von (1772–1829)

E. F. K. Koerner

Schlegel was born in Hanover, March 10, 1772, and died in Dresden, January 12, 1829. In the annals of linguistic science he is usually accorded a minor role only. His strong involvement in the Romantic movement and his literary production may explain why he is usually seen as a poet and literary critic, and hardly ever as a linguist. It is true that his interest in Oriental studies had originally been aroused by translations from Sanskrit and Persian literature. The book he wrote during 1805 and 1807 and for which he became famous, *Ueber die Sprache und Weisheit der Indier*, contains chapters of approximately equal length on the philosophy and theology (Schlegel 1808: 89–153) and on the '*historische Ideen*' concerning India (ibid. 157–230), with translations of Indian poetry into German (ibid. 231–324). Yet there is no doubt that the first part on language ('*Von der Sprache*,' 1–86) attracted the most enduring interest among his contemporaries. The fact that the King of Bavaria granted two of his subjects, Othmar Frank and Franz Bopp, scholarships to pursue the study of Persian and Sanskrit in Paris a few years later, may serve as an indication of the importance that was soon attached to Oriental studies, and this largely as a result of Schlegel's book. His importance in the history of linguistic science rests on this one work; it appears, however, that once the year 1816, the date of Bopp's *Conjugationssystem*, had been chosen by historians as marking the beginning of linguistics, Schlegel's book was only mentioned as precursory. It was no longer read, although the so-called founding fathers of comparative-historical philology, Bopp, Rask, and Grimm acknowledged their indebtedness to his work. Schlegel is traditionally credited with the first use of the term '*vergleichende Grammatik*.' However, others, like J. S. Vater, had used it in 1801 and the elder Schlegel, August Wilhelm (see *Schlegel, August Wilhelm von*), used it in 1803 before his brother. But it is clear from Friedrich Schlegel's book (p. 28) that he had been inspired by the example of Blumenbach and Cuvier's Comparative Anatomy. By today's standards, Schlegel had a checkered career; following the study of law in Göttingen and Leipzig, he soon turned to literature as his main occupation, circulating among the Romantics as well as the people at the Court of Weimar, notably Goethe, Schiller, and Herder (see *Herder, Johann Gottfried*), who was largely responsible for creating the general climate of the time that expected new and profound ideas to come from the East ('*ex Oriente lux*'). Schlegel's exposure to the writings of Sir William Jones led him to travel to Paris, where Persian, Arabic, and other Oriental languages were taught. He was introduced to Persian by Antoine Léonard de Chézy soon after his arrival in 1802, and familiarized himself with the ancient language of India through Alexander Hamilton, from whom he took private lessons during 1803 and 1804. He copied Sanskrit manuscripts and translated literary texts; for a living, he gave lectures on German literature and philosophy.

Ueber die Sprache und Weisheit der Indier was important for the development of comparative–historical as well as typological linguistics in the nineteenth century. Schlegel's suggestion of comparing grammatical features in order to establish genetic relationships, though not entirely new, was influential. For instance, his suggestion of investigating the conjugation system of Sanskrit in comparison with all the languages thought to be related to it led Bopp to his first work; his evolutionary view of language paved the way for Grimm's emphasis on the historical treatment of language, and his classification of languages according to morphological structure initiated an entire research program. This went from Wilhelm von Humboldt (see *Humboldt, Wilhelm von*) to Steinthal to Sapir, to Greenberg, and beyond, especially after his brother August had introduced the synthetic/analytic distinction in his 1818 essay on the history of the Romance languages. Timpanaro (1972: 77) has pointed out that, when Schlegel discussed at length questions of change and language mixture, he anticipated substratum theory, usually associated with Ascoli, Schuchardt, and others at the end of the nineteenth century. Schlegel maintained that language contact and the resulting borrowings made it difficult at times to identify all 'Sanskritic' languages, making it necessary to consider what we may call the external history of a given language, in addition to submitting it to close morphological analysis. In discussing linguistic contamination and the question of language descent, Schlegel drew particular attention to Armenian, in which he found many similarities with Latin, Greek, Persian, and German roots, and to agreements in grammatical structure. He was not quite ready to include Armenian among those belonging to the IndoEuropean language family, but in view of the material he had at his disposal, he made a great number of important observations which were borne out by subsequent generations of historical linguists. Schlegel undoubtedly deserves a place among the 'founding fathers' of comparative Indo-European grammar, and not only as an interesting 'philological instigator' (see Klin 1967).

See also: Romanticism; Sanskrit; Sanskrit: Discovery by Europeans.

Bibliography

Klin E 1967 Friedrich Schlegel als philologischer Anreger (1802–08). *Germanica Wratislaviensia* **11**: 83–103

Koerner E F K 1987 Friedrich Schlegel and the emergence of historical–comparative grammar. *Lingua e Stile* **22**: 341–65

Nüsse H 1962 *Die Sprachtheorie Friedrich Schlegels*. C Winter, Heidelberg

Oppenberg U 1965 *Quellenstudien zu Friedrich Schlegels Übersetzungen aus dem Sanskrit*. N G Elwert, Marburg

Plank F 1987a The Smith–Schlegel connection in linguistic typology: forgotten fact or fiction? *ZPhon* **40**: 198–216

Plank F 1987b What Schlegel could have learned from Alexander ('Sanscrit') Hamilton besides Sanscrit. *Lingua e Stile* **22**: 367–84

Schlegel F von 1808 *Ueber die Sprache und Weisheit der Indier*. Mohr and Zimmer, Heidelberg

Schlegel F von 1849 (trans. Millington E J, Bohn H G) *The Aesthetic and Miscellaneous Works of Frederick von Schlegel*

Schlegel F von 1975 (eds. Behler E, Struc-Oppenberg U) *Studien zur Philosophie und Theologie*, Schöningh, München–Paderborn–Wien

Schlegel F von 1977 *Ueber die Sprache und Weisheit der Indier*. New edn. prepared by E F K Koerner. Benjamins, Amsterdam

Struc-Oppenberg U 1980 Friedrich Schlegel and the history of Sanskrit philology and comparative studies. *Canadian Review of Comparative Literature* **7**: 411–37

Timpanaro S 1972 Friedrich Schlegel e gli inizi della linguistica indo-europea in Germania. *Critica Storica* **9**: 72–105

Timpanaro S 1977 Friedrich Schlegel and the beginnings of Indo-European linguistics in Germany. In: Schlegel F von 1977

Twaddell W F 1943 Fr. Schlegel's criteria of linguistic relation. *Monatshefte für deutschen Unterricht* **35**: 151–55

Sen, Sukumar (1900–92)

Pabitra Sarkar

Sukumar Sen was born on January 15, 1900 and died on March 3, 1992. He is probably the last major linguist in India to work within the historical-comparative framework and one of the best. He was the most famous student of Suniti Kumar Chatterji, and the one also on closest terms with his illustrious teacher. Chatterji and Sen first worked together, and then Sen took over the former's mantle to give the department of comparative philology (now department of linguistics) at the University of Calcutta a dignity and distinction that attracted many scholars from India and abroad to study and carry on research there. This eventually led to many excellent works on the histories of various languages of this subcontinent, appropriately modeled after Chatterji's magnum opus *The Origin and Development of the Bengali Language* (or *ODBL* 1926).

Sen's School career was replete with medals and prizes. He was awarded the Asutosh Gold Medal, the University Gold Medal, the Premchand and Roychand Scholarship, the Girish Memorial Prize (three times) and the Sarojini Medal—all from his own alma mater—the University of Calcutta. The Asiatic Society, Calcutta, awarded him the Jadunath Sircar Medal and, in 1984, the Gold Medal of the Royal Asiatic Society of London was bestowed on him as a fitting acknowledgement of his lifelong contribution to linguistics.

His tenure as a teacher was long and distinguished. He served the same department for about 34 years. Early on he was appointed the Khaira scholar attached to the department of comparative philology at the University of Calcutta where he served as an honorary lecturer. He then became a full-time member of faculty and promotions followed naturally and deservedly. He became the chairman of his department in 1953, when he was already a professor, and held the position till he retired in 1964. During his long career as a teacher, he not only did excellent research himself, but also supervised some 100 scholars, including several foreign students, who produced celebrated research works.

Sen's early interest was historical syntax, and he was the first to explore the Old IndoAryan morpho-syntax in his *Use of Cases in Vedic Prose* (1928) and *Buddhist Hybrid Sanskrit* (1928). This preoccupation with syntax continued when he proceeded to analyze Middle IndoAryan in *An Outline of Syntax of Middle Indo-Aryan* (1950). His *Old Persian Inscriptions* (1941) and *A Comparative Grammar of Middle Indo-Aryan* (1960), displayed his strong command of historical-comparative methodology and his meticulous concern for details in which etymological insights came to figure prominently. His *Bhāṣhāra Itivṛtta* (1939) is the first book in Bengali on the historical evolution of the language. Although he acknowledges his debt to Chatterji's *ODBL*, his *Itivṛtta* is not merely a condensed restatement of his teacher's book. Sen ventured beyond what his teacher had covered at several points, for example, in postulating the fifth dialect, i.e., Jharkhandi, for Bengali against Chatterji's four and also in suggesting various alternative etymologies for several lexical items. It is interesting to note that, by publishing the above books, and a number of others, he covered about 3500 years of the history of the Aryan languages.

He also produced some descriptive studies, the most notable among which are *Women's Dialect in Bengali* (1923) and a description of standard colloquial Bengali published in *Language Handbook* (Census of India 1971). His history of Bengali Prose (1934) began and still remains the only example of a systematic stylistic description of the literary prose dialect of his language. Etymology, however, became his preferred area in the later years and his *Etymological Dictionary of Bengali* (2 vols, 1971), probably the largest work on historical etymology of any Indian language, and *Bānglār Sthāna Nāma*

('Place-names of Bengal' 1981) are works that show this concern. He also wrote a large number of English and Bengali articles on linguistic subjects bearing both a historical and descriptive orientation.

Apart from the above, Sen published some 70 books on other subjects showing his wide and varied interests, ranging from the pop literature of Calcutta to an analytical history of crime fiction. He himself wrote five collections of crime stories and an autobiography in two volumes, but the work in Bengali that towers above all his other publications is his four-volume history of Bengali literature, *Bāngālā Sāhityera Itihāsa* (1941–58; now issued in five volumes) which has made him the premier historian of this literature. It probably represents a desire to match his teacher's celebrated work of reconstruction of the history of the language, by a parallel and equally meticulous survey of that of the literature. His eminent success in this area has, however, pushed his excellence as a linguist into the background, at least for his compatriots in Bengal.

See also: Indian Linguistic Tradition.

Sībawayhi (Eighth Century CE)

M. G. Carter

Though not an Arab himself—his mother tongue was Persian—Abū Bishr 'Amr ibn 'Uthmān ibn Qanbar Sībawayhi was the first to compile an exhaustive description of Arabic based on a coherent theory of language. Born in the second half of the eighth century CE, he came to Basra to study religion and law, but is said to have turned to grammar after committing a solecism himself. He died in about 793 CE, just after his great master al-Khalīl ibn Ahmad, aged forty or so.

He left only one work, so singular that it never had a title but came to be known as *Kitāb Sībawayhi* 'Sībawayhi's Book' or simply *al-Kitāb* 'The Book.' Although Sībawayhi reveals a considerable debt to his predecessors, most clearly to al-Khalīl, his originality cannot be doubted: he goes far beyond the speculations even of such a genius as al-Khalīl and his innovative achievement is virtually unchallenged in the Arab tradition, where the *Kitāb* has been called the 'Qur'ān of grammar.'

Drawing on an established technical vocabulary and a somewhat primitive grammatical legacy, as well as al-Khalīl's teachings on phonology (some of which he evidently discarded) and substitutability, Sībawayhi applied the fruits of his own study of the law to produce a descriptive grammar of Arabic which has not yet been superseded. Its underlying assumption is that *kalām* 'speech' is a form of behavior which can be regulated in the same way as the legal system regulates all social behavior. Linguistic acts are thus categorized by the following ethico-legal criteria: *ḥasan/qabīḥ* 'good/bad' for the structurally correct/incorrect, *mustaqīm* 'straight, right' for the semantically successful, and *muḥāl* 'wrong, absurd' for the incomprehensible utterance. Speech need not be 'good' to be 'right': ill-formed utterances can convey meaning and well-formed ones can fail to do so. Every speech element has a 'status' *manzila* which determines its 'place' *mawḍi'*, that is its function in the utterance, exactly as lawyers determine the status and function of legal acts, with analogy *qiyās* as the organizing methodology in both domains. The most impressive development of these principles is unquestionably the theory of *'amal* 'operation,' the idea that each element of an utterance acts upon its neighbor, from which it follows that on the level of surface structure speech falls naturally into binary units, one active 'operator', *'āmil*, the other passive, 'operated on' *ma'mūl fīhi*. This purely horizontal metaphor has no connection at all, scientifically or etymologically, with the Latin *regere* 'to govern,' a misperception which has long obscured the nature of Arabic grammatical theory in the West.

By the same token it is futile to look for Greek or other outside influences in the earliest Arabic grammar; Sībawayhi establishes on the first page of the *Kitāb* that there are only three parts of speech, *ism* 'noun,' *'fi'l'* 'verb' and the semantically and morphologically indeterminate *ḥarf* 'particle'. He has no tripartite tense system, no verbal moods, no passive voice in the modern sense, no adverbs, no prepositions, in short there is hardly a trace of foreign influence on Sībawayhi. For him language was simply one 'way,' of behaving (compare with *Sunna*, the 'Way' of the orthodox 'Sunni' Muslim), and his word for 'way', *naḥw*, in the end became the name for 'grammar' per se. However, the *Kitāb* was too descriptive for the normative demands of Islamic civilization and prescriptive grammar subsequently triumphed: in the eventual displacement of Sībawayhi's key behavioral term *kalām* 'speech' by the logically inspired concept of *jumla* 'sentence,' a completely different approach to language can be perceived.

See also: Arabic Linguistic Tradition.

Bibliography

Carter M G 1973 An Arab grammarian of the eighth century AD *JAOS* **93**: 146–57
Diem W 1983 Bibliographie/Bibliography: Sekundärliteratur zur einheimischen arabischen Grammatikschreibung. In: Versteegh C H M, Koerner K, Niederehe H-J (eds.) *The History of Linguistics in the Near East*. John Benjamins, Amsterdam
Jahn G 1895–1900 *Sībawaihi's Buch über die Grammatik, übersetzt und erklärt*. Reuther and Reichard, Berlin
Troupeau G 1976 *Lexique-index du Kitāb de Sībawayhi*. Klincksieck, Paris

Silvestre de Sacy, Baron Antoine-Isaac (1758–1838)

M. V. McDonald

The French Orientalist, Silvestre de Sacy was born on April 21, 1758, the second son of a Paris notary. His father died when de Sacy was 7 and, because of his delicate health, he was educated at home, acquiring a deep knowledge of Greek and Latin, which latter he wrote fluently in his scholarly works. At the age of 12 he met the Benedictine Dom Berthereau, then engaged on a study of Arab historians of the Crusades, who fired his first enthusiasm for Eastern languages.

De Sacy studied in succession Hebrew, Syriac, Chaldean, Samaritan, Arabic, and Ethiopic, and at the same time learned Italian, Spanish, English, and German. His first scholarly work was done on a Syriac MS, while his first published work was a Latin translation of two Samaritan letters originally written to J. J. Scaliger (1793; see *Scaliger, Joseph Justus*). He was then studying Persian and Turkish. In 1785 he was admitted to the Académie des Inscriptions, where he began work on two major studies on the breaking of the dam of Ma'rib and the earliest Arabic literature, only published much later. He was also given the task of preparing a descriptive catalogue of Arabic and Persian MSS in French libraries. While continuing to work in Samaritan studies, de Sacy was now led to an interest in pre-Islamic Persian antiquities, working on the inscriptions of Naqsh-i Rustam and Bīsutūn (the latter without success) and Pahlavi coinage. Next, he was drawn to what became a lifelong interest, the history and doctrines of the Druze. These years were spent in seclusion in the countryside, his scholarly work alternating with the cultivation of his garden.

In 1795, the Terror was over and de Sacy was appointed Professor of Arabic at the new Ecole des Langues Orientales Vivantes. One of the conditions of the appointment was that he should write an Arabic grammar but the preparatory work led him first to study what was then known as 'universal grammar,' and in 1799 he published his *Principles de Grammaire Générale*, which drew upon the ideas of the Port-Royal grammar and others. In 1806 he was made Professor of Persian at the Collège de France, but despite his new duties he continued with his work on Arabic. The first edition of his three-volume *Chrestomathie arabe* appeared in 1806, followed in 1810 by his *Grammaire arabe*. In the same year he published a translation of 'Abd al-Laṭīf al-Baghdādī's *K. al-Ifāda wa-al-I'tibār* (*Relation d'Egypte*) and began work on a major series of studies on the law of property in Egypt from the Arab conquest.

De Sacy had never hidden his royalist principles, and soon after the Restoration he was made Prefect of the University of Paris, and a series of academic honours followed, culminating in his ennoblement in 1832. Major publications of this period were his editions of *Kalīla wa-Dimna* (1816), 'Afṭṭār's *Pand-Nama* (1819), and Ḥarīrī's *Maqāmāt* (1822), a revised and expanded edition of his *Anthologie* (1829) and *Grammaire* (1831), an edition of the *Alfiyya* (1833), and his last work, the two-volume *Exposé de la religion des Druzes* (1838). A projected third volume was cut short by his death on February 21, 1838.

De Sacy's learned output was vast and varied, and in his youth especially his restless temperament took him from one field to another; his best work was done in later life. More even than this, however, de Sacy's main services to Middle Eastern studies probably lay in his textbooks and the outstanding scholars whom he taught. Among many others, these included Flügel, Kosegarten, Quatremère, de Slane, and Fleischer. The enormous expansion of Arabic studies in the nineteenth century owed almost everything to the groundwork laid by Silvestre de Sacy.

Bibliography

Centenaire de Silvestre de Sacy 1938 *Comptes rendus des séances de l'Académie des Inscriptions et Belles-lettres*

Reinaud J T 1838 Notice historique et littéraire sur le Baron Silvestre de Sacy, lue à la séance générale de la Societé Asiatique, le 25 juin 1838. *Journal Asiatique* **3(6)**: 113–95. (English transl. *Asiatic Journal* **27**: 115–29; 182–97)

Trithemius, Johannes (1462–1516)

R. E. Asher

Johann von Trittenheim, generally known as Trithemius, the name under which all his voluminous writings appeared, would appear to have been a remarkable child, in that he is reputed to have learnt to read German within a month of embarking on reading lessons, after having been illiterate for the first 15 years of his life. A little before reaching the age of 20, in 1482, he entered the Benedictine abbey of Sponheim, of which by the middle of the following year he found himself elected abbot. A most energetic young man, he set about reconstituting what had become a very rundown institution, extending the buildings and building up the library. This and his own scholarly interests made Sponheim a center of attraction for other humanists.

The writings of Trithemius fall into two main categories, concerned with either religious or secular subjects. The former include lives of the saints and senior figures in the church, writings on the training of monks, and sermons. The latter are mainly historical works. Among these were two compendia intended to be the basis of a massive history of the Franks. Disliking gaps in a historical narrative, Trithemius was not above inventing material when available sources proved inadequate in this regard. More than that, he invented entire sources, as when for his Frankish history he claimed to have discovered a manuscript chronicle written by a certain Hunibald. The manuscript conveniently 'disappeared' and Trithemius is now universally believed to have invented Hunibald and other supposed earlier historians he refers to.

One of the purposes of this deception was to provide what could be seen as proof of the widespread belief that the Franks, like a number of peoples of Europe, were descended from Trojans who had fled the city after the sack of Troy. Evidence of another kind to support this belief was to be found in certain linguistic facts, including a great similarity between Greek (the language spoken by the Trojans) and German, a similarity less striking than it had been because of the passage of time (see Brann 1981: 326).

The main results of Trithemius's interest in linguistic matters, however, are two cryptographical handbooks, both published posthumously but widely circulated in manuscript during the author's lifetime. They are the *Polygraphia* (1518; written in 1508) and the *Steganographia* (1606; written in 1500), of which a detailed account is provided by Brann (1999), Shumaker (1982: 91–131), and Arnold (1971: 187–95), and which have given Trithemius the reputation of being the first theoretician of cryptography. *Steganographia*, because of the framework in which coded messages are set, also led to a view that Trithemius involved himself in demonic magic (Walker 1958: 88–89), though this is disputed by Shumaker. The work was on the Index from 1609 to 1900. Some of his inventions were borrowed, if not acknowledged, by later writers (Muller 1971: 11), a circumstance which is by no means surprising, for some of Trithemius's ciphers are extremely complex (for an example of a relatively straightforward one, see *Magic*).

See also: Linguistic Theory in the Later Middle Ages; Myths About Language.

Bibliography

Arnold K 1971 *Johannes Trithemius (1462–1516)*. Kommissionsverlag Ferdinand Schöningh, Würzburg

Brann N L 1981 *The Abbot Trithemius (1462–1516): The Renaissance of Monastic Humanism*. E J Brill, Leiden

Brann N L 1999 *Trithemius and Magical Theory. A Chapter in the Controversy over Occult Studies in Early Modern Europe*. State University of New York Press, Albany, NY

Muller A 1971 *Les Ecritures secrètes Le Chiffre*. Presses Universitaires de France, Paris

Shumaker W 1982 *Renaissance Curiosa: John Dee's Conversations with Angels; Girolamo Cardano's Horoscope of Christ; Johannes Trithemius and Cryptography; George Dalgarno's Universal Language*. Center for Medieval and Early Renaissance Studies, Binghamton, New York

Trithemius J 1518 *Polygraphia libri VI*. M Furter, Basle

Trithemius J 1606 *Steganographia: Hoc est, ars per occultam scripturam animi sui voluntatem absentibus aperiendi certa*. Frankfurt

Trithemius J 1982 *The Steganographia of Johannes Trithemius*. Book I tr. by F Tait and C Upton; Book III... [tr. by J W H Walden]; McLean A (ed.) Magnum Opus Hermetic Sourceworks, Edinburgh

Trithemius J 1987 *De origine gentis Francorum compendium. An Abridged History of the Franks. The Latin Text with an English Translation*. Kuelbs M, Sonkowsky R P (eds.) AQ Verlag, Dudweiler

Walker D P 1958 *Spiritual and Demonic Magic from Ficino to Campanella*. Warburg Institute, London

Tyndale, William (1494–1536)

D. Daniell

The first to translate the Bible into English from the original Hebrew and Greek, William Tyndale was a significant figure in the English Reformation, and in the history of the English language. He was executed in 1536 before he could finish his work; nevertheless it has lived on in successive Renaissance English Bibles, particularly the much-admired Authorized ('King James') Version of 1611, and largely in most modern versions. Tyndale was a scholar of languages at a time when Hebrew was known to few English speakers, and Greek not widely. His greatest work was in giving the English-speaking world a Bible language both accurate to the originals and close to common speech, for everyone—even 'a boy that driveth the plough'—to understand.

After Oxford University he may have been at Cambridge, not long after Erasmus. He hoped to print his intended translations in London, under Cuthbert Tunstall, Bishop of London. Snubbed by him, he left for the continent, never to return. His attempt to print a New Testament in Cologne in 1525 reached only Matthew 22 before he was betrayed. In Worms he printed in 1526 six thousand copies of his New Testament (NT). In England, however, Tunstall organized thorough searches, and publicly burned all the copies he found: only two survive today. Tyndale learned Hebrew and in 1530 printed his Pentateuch, which became the foundation of all later English versions. He went on to complete the Old Testament (OT) historical books, which were not printed until after his death. His 1534 NT is the crown of his endeavor: it makes up ninety percent of the Authorized Version NT.

Tyndale wrote much else. His *Obedience of a Christian Man* (1528), for example, came to the approving notice of Henry VIII: it includes a passionate defense of the English language, remarkable for its time. As Tyndale's pocketbook translations spread in England, Tunstall brought in Henry's Chancellor, Sir Thomas More, to attack Tyndale. More, for all his hundreds of thousands of often intemperate words against Tyndale, comes off worse from their exchanges. Tyndale's constant aim as a translator was clarity. To this end he coined works, like 'Passover' and 'mercy-seat.' Very many of his phrases are still in everyday use: 'the salt of the earth,' 'the signs of the times,' 'to make light of it,' 'the scales fell from his eyes,' 'full of good works,' 'the powers that be,' 'a man after his own heart,' and countless others. Though modern understanding of the Hebrew and Greek originals is greater, no Bible translator since has shown Tyndale's skill in writing an English which addresses the reader so memorably, and speaks so immediately to the heart.

See also: English Bible.

Bibliography

Tyndale W 1848–50 *Doctrinal Treatises*, 3 vols. The Parker Society, Cambridge

Tyndale W 1989 *Tyndale's New Testament in a Modern-spelling Edition*. Yale, London.

Tyndale W 1992 *Tyndale's Old Testament in a Modern-spelling Edition*. Yale, London

Daniell D 1994 *William Tyndale: a Biography*. Yale, London

Tyndale W 2000 *The Obedience of a Christian Man*. Penguin, London

Ullendorff, Edward (1920–)

A. K. Irvine

Born in Switzerland on January 25, 1920, Edward Ullendorff studied Semitic languages at Jerusalem in the late 1930s. Among his teachers was H. J. Polotsky (see *Polotsky, Hans (Hayyim) Jacob*), who was to have a profound influence on his philological method and thinking. During World War II, service from 1942 to 1946 with the British Military Administration in Eritrea enabled him to consolidate his knowledge of the Semitic languages of Ethiopia, particularly of Tigrinya, which was then in the early stages of establishing itself as a literary language and of which he subsequently published a chrestomathy with useful annotations

(*A Tigrinya (Təgrəñña) Chrestomathy*, Stuttgart, 1985). (It was preceded by a comparable work for Amharic, *An Amharic Chrestomathy*, Oxford, 1965.)

After further administrative work in Palestine, he proceeded to Oxford in 1948 to further his researches into the phonology of the Ethiopian Semitic languages, his dissertation being published as *The Semitic Languages of Ethiopia: Comparative Phonology* (London, 1955). Although Ullendorff's conclusion that all the modern Ethiopian Semitic languages share a common descent from classical Ethiopic has subsequently been challenged, his study remains the standard exposition of the subject. After nine years at the University of St Andrews, he proceeded to the Chair of Semitic Languages and Literatures at Manchester, which he occupied from 1959 to 1964, when he took up the first, and only, Professorship of Ethiopian Studies at the School of Oriental and African Studies in the University of London. This he retained until 1979, when he became Professor of Semitic Languages until his retirement in 1982.

Ullendorff's research interests are many and varied, and cover a wide range of linguistic, philological, and historical topics involving Ethiopia, Biblical Hebrew, Aramaic, Ugaritic, and comparative Semitic studies. He made an important contribution to S. Moscati et al. (1964) *An Introduction to the Comparative Grammar of the Semitic Languages: Phonology and Morphology*, and wrote a number of articles on various aspects of comparative Semitics. Frequently, his penetrating insights into linguistic arcana are to be found in the numerous reviews and personal appreciations which he wrote, or in annotations to publications of a more cultural or historical nature.

His major contribution to the field of Semitic and Biblical studies may be felt to lie in the profound influence that he has exercised on the contemporary British approach to these studies generally. In earlier years, theological considerations had been very much at the center of Semitic studies in Britain, and these were heavily influenced by the classical exposition of Biblical Hebrew, being promoted in terms of their usefulness in understanding the text of the Bible. Arabic stood largely independent of this trend, and Ethiopian Semitic languages are hardly known. Ullendorff's profound experience of the complete range of the Semitic languages, together with his wide and eclectic knowledge and application of modern linguistic methods, has left its mark on a generation of British Orientalists and persuaded them to take a more holistic approach to their areas of interest.

See also: Semitic Languages.

Weber, Max (1864–1920)

G. Oakes

Max Weber, the German social theorist generally regarded as one of the seminal figures in the history of the social sciences, was born on April 21, 1864 in Erfurt. Weber, a child of the pre-1914 German upper middle class of culture and property, was raised in a bourgeois villa in the fashionable Charlottenburg district of Berlin. As a schoolboy, he developed the voracious reading habits that were to mark his career as a scholar, plowing through Classical literature and philosophy as well as Spinoza, Schopenhauer, Kant, and the forty-volume Cotta edition of Geothe's works. In 1882, he entered Heidelberg University, where his primary studies in law were supplemented with lectures in economics, history, philosophy, and theology. As a student, Weber followed the usual practice of the time, spending a few semesters at several universities and attending lectures by famous professors before he returned to Berlin to complete his doctorate (1889) and Habilitation (1891), the research monograph required for appointment to a teaching post in a German university. In 1893, he married a distant cousin, Marianne Schnitger, and accepted a professorship in economics at Freiburg University, a position he resigned in 1896 to assume the chair in economics at Heidelberg. By the autumn of 1898, Weber began to suffer from a nervous disorder that left him incapable of teaching and virtually unable to pursue scholarly work. This illness effectively ended his professorial career, which was not resumed until 1918, only two years before his premature death in 1920 due to the complications of a lung inflammation. However, it marked the beginning of the work for which he is remembered.

Weber's mature work elaborates a series of themes, hypotheses, and modes of analysis that frame an agenda and chart a course for sociology in the twentieth century. The main question of Weber's research center on the unique character and development of modern Western rationality, the various conditions and consequences of which he explored in an astonishing range of social formations and cultural configurations: ascetic Protestantism and the genesis of the modern professional ethos; the Western city and its distinctive occupant, the independent burgher; Western law as elaborated by an autonomous status group of jurists; harmonic music, which is tied to the development of Western science and its basis in both mathematical and experimental methods; and the Western state and its distinctive form of domination, the bureaucratic organization that functions according to purely formal and impersonal rules.

In his investigations of rationalization processes, Weber developed a comparative sociology of religion of unprecedented scope and sophistication. In his essays on the sociology of religion, he explored the qualifications of different types of religious elites and virtuosi, the conditions for the development of a religion of the masses, the styles of life and political and economic profiles that differentiate adherents of the major religions of salvation, the role of class constellations and social stratification in general as determinants of religious development, and the relations among economic, political, and religious rationalism in Protestant Christianity, Confucianism, Hinduism and Buddhism, and ancient Judaism.

In his investigations of the various institutional and value spheres of culture—economics, politics, religion, erotics, science, and art—Weber stressed the uneven development of these spheres in the same social formations; the circumstances under which one sphere may penetrate and condition another, and the relative autonomy of value spheres and their corresponding orders of life; the progressive mutual isolation produced by the development of value spheres, the tensions, and conflicts generated by this development, and its effects upon alternative strategies for the rationalization of life.

These inquiries were carried out primarily in Weber's series of studies on the economic ethics of the world religions and in his massive unfinished manuscript posthumously entitled *Economy and Society*, the plan for which he outlined in a letter to his publisher dated December, 1913. Noting that he had worked out a 'complete theory' linking all the major social groups to the economy, a sociology of salvation religions and religious ethics, and a 'comprehensive sociological theory of the state and domination,' Weber concluded by claiming that 'nothing of the kind has ever been written, not even as a "precursor"' (Schluchter 1989: 419–20). Seventy years after the death of Max Weber, this claim still holds true.

Bibliography

Bendix R 1960 *Max Weber: An Intellectual Portrait.* Doubleday, Garden City, NY

Bendix R, Roth G 1971 *Scholarship and Partisanship: Essays on Max Weber.* University of California Press, Berkeley, CA

Gerth H H, Mills C W (eds.) 1946 *From Max Weber: Essays in Sociology.* Oxford University Press, New York

Käsler D 1988 (trans. Hurd P) *Max Weber: An Introduction to his Life and Work.* Polity Press, Cambridge

Schluchter W 1989 *Rationalism, Religion, and Domination: A Weberian Perspective.* University of California Press, Berkeley, CA

Weber M 1958 *The Protestant Ethic and the Spirit of Capitalism.* Scribners, New York

Weber M 1978 Roth G, Wittich C W (eds.) *Economy and Society: An Outline of Interpretive Sociology.* University of California Press, Berkeley, CA

Weinreich, Uriel (1926–67)

T. Hill

When Uriel Weinreich died, aged 41, he left a record of remarkable distinction in three diverse fields: Yiddish studies, linguistic geography and sociology, and semantics. Born in Vilnius, the main center of Ashkenazic Jewish culture, he was the son of the Yiddish scholar Max Weinreich, who in 1940 took the family to the USA, joining the faculty of New York City College. Uriel Weinreich studied, and later taught, at Columbia University, graduating with a PhD in 1951 and going on to become the first Atran Professor of Yiddish studies, chairman of the linguistics department, and joint editor of *Word.*

Weinreich stimulated and contributed to modern Yiddish studies in many ways, beginning early with the textbook *College Yiddish* (1949). He founded and edited the collections of occasional papers entitled *The Field of Yiddish* (1954), and with his wife Beatrice Weinreich published the bibliography *Yiddish Language and Folklore* (1959). In his *Modern English/Yiddish, Yiddish/English Dictionary* (1968) his theories on systematic lexicography found concrete application, including the definition and application of the distinctive Yiddish register system. At the time of his death he was engaged upon the *Language and*

Culture Atlas of Ashkenazic Jewry, based on data on their ancestral communities gathered from American Yiddish speakers.

Weinreich's doctoral thesis was on language contact, supervised by A. Martinet, with guidance during a year's field research in Switzerland from J. Jud and E. Dieth. Published as *Languages in Contact* (1953), it presented a systematic framework for categorizing mutual influence and mixing between languages, and quickly became a recognized basic text. The comparison of (mainly phonological) systems between dialects was already accepted practice in many surveys, though rejected by others. Weinreich's article 'Is a structural dialectology possible?' (1954a) expounded its theoretical basis, and initiated a discussion that received interesting contributions from, among others, W. G. Moulton and R. I. McDavid Jr. In the 1960s, Weinreich's attention turned to the study of linguistic variation and change at the level of idiolect and speech situation, his conclusions being presented in the article, posthumously completed by his pupil W. Labov and M. I. Herzog, 'Empirical foundations for a theory of language change' (Weinreich et al. 1968).

Weinreich's writings on semantics express his conviction that a valid (and necessarily complex) theory of meaning requires close study of how diverse languages meet the communicative demands made on them, within their cultures, in actual situations. Accordingly, though he had enthusiastically embraced TGG as a whole, his lecture 'Explorations in semantic theory' (1964; published 1966 in *Current Trends in Linguistics*) was a critique of inadequacies in the Katz–Fodor model, which led to further debate with Katz. Regarding lexicography, Weinreich endorsed the Soviet linguists' view of it as being a distinct discipline, and contributed to it in theoretical papers, as well as in his Yiddish dictionary. His semantic and lexicographical writings were posthumously edited in Weinreich (1980).

See also: Judaism; Yiddish.

Bibliography

Malkiel Y 1967 Uriel Weinreich. *Lg* **43**: 605–10

Moulton W G 1968 Structural dialectology. *Lg* **44**: 451–66

Schaechter M 1971 Weinreich, Uriel. In: *Encyclopaedia Judaica*, vol. 16, p. 406. Keter, Jerusalem

Weinreich U 1949 *College Yiddish*. YIVO, New York

Weinreich U 1953 *Languages in Contact: Findings and Problems*, Linguistic Circle of New York, **1**. Mouton, The Hague

Weinreich U 1954a Is a structural dialectology possible? *Word* **10**: 2–3

Weinreich U (ed.) 1954b. *The Field of Yiddish*, 1st collection. Linguistic Circle of New York, New York

Weinreich U 1980 *On Semantics*. University of Pennsylvania Press, Philadelphia, PA

Weinreich U, Labov W, Herzog M I 1968 Empirical foundations of a theory of linguistic change. In: Lehmann W P, Malkiel Y (eds.) *Directions for Historical Linguistics*. University of Texas Press, Austin, TX

Welmers, William E. (1916–88)

R. G. Schuh

William Welmers was the preeminent Africanist of the American structuralist school. He underscored the importance of tone in African languages. He was also a pioneer in African language pedagogy.

Welmers was born on April 4, 1916 in Orange City, Iowa and grew up in Holland, Michigan, where he graduated in 1935 from Hope College with a degree in philosophy. He received ThB and ThM degrees at Westminster Theological Seminary, and he entered the University of Pennsylvania intending to pursue study of the languages of the Ancient Near East. However, World War II created the need for specialists in 'lesser known' languages, and supervised by Zellig Harris, he completed his PhD in 1943 with a dissertation 'A descriptive grammar of Fanti.'

Welmers remained at Penn two more years as an instructor in Chinese and Japanese for the Army. In 1946, he went to Liberia with his wife Beatrice, whom he had married in 1940, to do research for the Lutheran Mission. Between 1946 and 1950 he worked on Kpelle, which resulted in several publications and an abiding interest in Mande languages. Supported by an American Council of Learned Societies grant, he traveled overland as far as Ethiopia, doing research on Mande, Gur, Benue-Congo, and Cushitic languages.

In the 1950s he taught at Cornell and the Hartford Seminary Foundation. In 1960 he went to UCLA as the first faculty member specializing in sub-Saharan African languages. He remained there until his retirement in 1982. He died in 1988 in Lakeview, Arkansas.

The range of Welmers's work is best exemplified in his encyclopedic *African Language Structures*. The most detailed chapters of this book involve descriptions of the tonal systems of several languages.

Welmers was particularly attentive to the typology of tonal systems, tonal alternations, and the grammatical role of tone. He appears to have coined the term 'terrace level' to refer to tone systems in which a lowered high tone, as opposed to the mid tone of 'discrete level' systems, establishes a new, lowered tonal register. Welmers stressed the necessity of understanding African language grammars from the internal patterns of the languages rather than Eurocentrically, as exemplified in his chapters on verbal systems and (non)-adjectives.

In addition to *African Languages Structures*, Welmers produced book-length works on Igbo (co-authored with his wife, Bee), Jukun, Efik, and Vai, and he wrote numerous historical and descriptive articles on African languages as well as articles on language pedagogy. (A fuller biography and a complete bibliography of his works up to 1976 can be found in Hyman et al. 1976.)

In addition to his linguistic career, Welmers was an ordained minister in the Orthodox Presbyterian Church.

See also: Christianity in Africa; Missionaries; African Traditional Religions.

Bibliography

Hyman L M, Jacobson L C, Schuh R G (eds.) 1976 *Papers in African Linguistics in Honor of Wm. E. Welmers, Studies in African Linguistics, Supplement 6*. UCLA African Studies Center, Los Angeles, CA

Welmers W E 1973 *African Language Structures*. University of California Press, Berkeley, CA

Westermann, Diedrich Hermann (1875–1956)

M. Schladt

Westermann, a German missionary and linguist, is credited with being one of the founders of modern African linguistics. Besides detailed language studies, his major contribution is the attempt at a historical reconstruction of the Western Sudanic languages.

He was born on June 24, 1875 in Baden (near Bremen). In 1895 he joined the Norddeutsche Missionsgesellschaft (NMG). Until 1899 he studied in Basel and Tübingen. In 1901 he was sent to Togo as a teacher, and it took him only a few months to learn the Ewe language. In addition, he carried out studies on Logba, Ful, Hausa, and Twi (Akan). In 1903 poor health forced Westermann to return to Germany, where Carl Meinhof called him to the School of Oriented Studies in Berlin as a teacher of Ewe. After a second visit to Togo in 1907. Westermann taught Ewe, Hausa, Ful, and Twi in Berlin. In 1908, he left the missionary service. In 1910, Westermann took over Meinhof's position as director of the School of Oriental Studies.

From the time he left the missionary service until his death, Westermann concentrated on various topics of African studies: language documentation, language comparison, anthropological and religious as well as historical studies. In 1911, he published *Die Sudansprachen*, an attempt at a historical classification of the Sudanic languages. Apart from Meinhof's similar endeavor at a classification of the Bantu languages, *Die Sudansprachen* is one of the first genetic classifications of languages covering a large area. In the revised 1927 edition (*Die westlichen Sudansprachen und ihre Beziehungen zum Bantu*), he restricted himself to the Western Sudanic languages.

Various visits to Africa resulted in linguistic and cultural documentation, e.g., on the Shilluk, Gola, and Kpelle. In 1925, Westermann was appointed the first director for African Languages and Cultures at the University of Berlin. In 1926, he became co-director of the newly founded International African Institute (IAI). His *Practical Orthography of African Languages* (1927)—commonly known as the 'Westermann-script'—became the guideline for many conferences on the orthography and writing of languages, e.g., of Shilluk, Dinka, Nuer, Bari, Lotuko, Madi, and Zande.

In 1928, Westermann was one of the founders of *Africa*, the mouthpiece of the IAI, and was its editor until 1940. He inspired the founding of many other periodicals.

His non-linguistic publications of the 1930s and 1940s show that Westermann was at that time strongly influenced by the national socialist Zeitgeist. After World War II, Westermann continued writing on African topics. The *Languages of West Africa* (1952) which he published with M. A. Bryan, was the continuation of Westermann's linguistic life's work, the classification of the Western Sudanic languages. *Geschichte Afrikas* (1952) must be considered to be his main non-linguistic work. Westermann was working on its new edition, when he died on May 31, 1956 in Baden.

See also: Missionaries; African Traditional Religions.

Bibilography

Dammann E 1976 Die Bedeutung von Diedrich Westermann. *Internationales Afrikaforum* **12(2)**: 174–80

Hintze U 1957 Diedrich Westermann. Schriftenverzeichnis und einige biographische Daten. *Mitteilungen des Instituts für Orientforschung* **5**: 45–83

Westermann D H 1902 *Wörterbuch der Ewe-Sprache. Vol. 1: Teil Ewe–Deutsches Wörterbuch. Vol. 2: Teil Deutsch–Ewe Wörterbuch.* Dietrich Reimer, Berlin

Westermann D H 1907 *Grammatik der Ewe-Sprache.* Dietrich Reimer, Berlin

Westermann D H 1927 *Die westlichen Sudansprachen und ihre Beziehungen zum Bantu.* Walter de Gruyter & Co, Berlin

Westermann D H 1952 *Geschichte Afrikas. Staatenbildungen südlich der Sahara.* Greven, Cologne

Whitney, William Dwight (1827–94)

E. F. K. Koerner

Whitney was born in Northampton, Massachusetts, on February 9, 1827, and died in New Haven, Connecticut, on June 7, 1894. He is best known as a general linguist and Sanskrit scholar. He was the brother of the geologist Josiah Dwight Whitney (1819–96), after whom the highest mountain in the USA (excluding Alaska), Mount Whitney, California, is named, and William Whitney's early interests lay in the natural sciences, notably ornithology and geology. It is therefore not surprising that he introduced into linguistic theory and practice notions derived from geology, which he had absorbed from Charles Lyells voluminous *Principles of Geology* (1830–33) and other scientific writings, notably the concept of 'uniformitarianism.' His education included a period at Williams College, New Haven, Connecticut (1842–45), after which he devoted himself for three years to bird- and plant-collecting. Part of his collections subsequently went into the Peabody Museum of New Haven. However, books on comparative philology, especially Sanskrit, which his elder brother has brought back from Europe, attracted his interest, and after another stint in the United States Geological Survey, he enrolled at Yale College in 1849. A year later, he left for Germany, studying at the University of Berlin with Franz Bopp, C. Richard Lepsius (see *Lepsius, Carl Richard*), and Albrecht Weber, and at Tübingen with Rudolf von Roth for almost three years (late 1850–July 1853). Whitney worked in particular with Weber and Roth on Sanskrit texts, which culminated in his editions of several important Atharva-Veda texts between 1860 and the end of his life.

On his return to America he was appointed Professor of Sanskrit at Yale University (1854), and when he was approached by Harvard in 1869, Yale also offered him the professorship of comparative philology. Whitney remained at New Haven for the rest of his life except for several trips to Europe, in particular Germany, where he completed his Sanskrit grammar (1879). He was the most important figure in nineteenth-century American linguistics, dominating the field for almost four decades, both as a scholar and organizationally, for example, as librarian (1855–73), corresponding secretary (1857–84), and finally president (1884–90) of the American Oriental Society. His influence on academic appointments throughout the USA appears to have been enormous; his service as editor-in-chief of the *Century Dictionary* (New York 1889–91) was another means of leaving his imprint on American science. He received many honors during his career, beginning with Doctor of Philosophy from the University of Breslau in 1861, and followed by honorary doctorates from his alma mater (1868), College of William & Mary (1869), St Andrews, Scotland (1874), Harvard (1876), Columbia (1887), Edinburgh (1889), memberships in many scholarly societies and academies, and other distinctions such as the Bopp Prize (1871) and Foreign Knight of the Prussian order 'pour le mérite' for arts and sciences. Whitney's chief claim to distinction came from his work in Indic philology, both text editions and the *Sanskrit Grammar* of 1879, and from his two books on general linguistics (1867; 1875); his ongoing polemic with Max Müller of Oxford may have detracted from his importance as a sound methodologist of linguistic science, but as the testimonies of the greats of nineteenth-century scholarship in the field, delivered at the 1894 Whitney Memorial Meeting, show (Lanman 1897), he was regarded by them as a significant influence on their work (Jakobson 1971). The importance of some of his pronouncements on matters of general linguistic theory for Saussure, notably his emphasis on the social nature of language and the conventional and arbitrary character of the linguistic sign, has become generally recognized (cf. Koerner 1973: 74–100, for details).

See also: Sanskrit; Sanskrit: Discovery by Europeans.

Bibliography

For a full bibliography, see Lanman C R (ed.) 1897

Jakobson R 1971 The world response to Whitney's principles of linguistic science. In: Silverstein M (ed.) 1971

Koerner E F K 1973 *Ferdinand de Saussure: Origin and Development of His Linguistic Thought in Western Studies of Language*. F. Vieweg and Sohn, Braunschweig

Koerner E F K 1992 William Dwight Whitney and the influence of geology on linguistic theory in the 19th century. In: Naumann B, Plank F, Hofbauer G (eds.) *Language and Earth: Elective Affinities Between Linguistics and Geology in the 18th and 19th Centuries*. Benjamins, Amsterdam

Lanman C R (ed.) 1897 The *Whitney Memorial Meeting*. Ginn, Boston, MA

Seymour T D 1894 William Dwight Whitney. *American Journal of Philology* **15**: 271–98

Whitney W D 1867 *Language and the Study of Language: Twelve Lectures on the Principles of Linguistic Science*. Scribner, New York

Whitney W D 1873 *Oriental and Linguistic Studies: The Veda; the Avesta; the Science of Language*. Scribner, Armstrong and Co, New York

Whitney W D 1874 *Oriental and Linguistics Studies*. vol. II. *The East and West; Religion and Mythology*. Scribner, Armstrong and Co., New York

Whitney W D 1875 The *Life and Growth of Language: An Outline of Linguistic Science*. D. Appleton and Co., New York and H. S. King, London

Whitney W D 1879 *Sanskrit Grammar; Including Both the Classical Language and the Other Dialects of Veda and Brahmana*. Breitkopf and Härtel, Leipzig (2nd Revised edn. 1889.)

Whitney W D 1885 William Dwight Whitney. In: Whitney W D (ed.) *Forty Years' Record of the Class of 1845, Williams College, New Haven*. Tuttle, Morehouse and Taylor, New Haven, CT

Whitney W D 1892 *Max Müller and the Science of Language*. D. Appleton and Co., New York

Whitney W D 1971 *Whitney on Language: Selected Writings*, Silverstein M (ed.) MIT Press, Cambridge, MA

Whorf, Benjamin Lee (1897–1941)

J. H. Stam

Benjamin Lee Whorf was an amateur linguist who speculated on the relation of language to culture and thought. He is associated with the so-called 'Principle of Linguistic Relativity' or 'Sapir–Whorf Hypothesis.'

Whorf was born in Winthrop, Massachusetts, April 24, 1897. His parents descended from early American settlers and his father, Harry Church Whorf, was a commercial artist, stage designer–director, and amateur geologist.

Benjamin exhibited a comparable range of curiosity as a youth and graduated from Massachusetts Institute of Technology in 1918 with a BS in Chemical Engineering. In 1919 he was hired by the Hartford Fire Insurance Company as a fire prevention engineer, then a field without academic recognition. Equally new was Hartford's notion that fire inspection and prevention could be a customer service, and Whorf became the recognized expert in this area. He ultimately became assistant secretary of the company, which generously allowed him leaves to follow his linguistic and anthropological interests. He worked there until his death from cancer on July 26, 1941. He and his wife Celia Inez Peckham had three children.

An autodidact in linguistics, Whorf began to study Hebrew in 1924, inspired by Fabre d'Olivet's *La langue hébraïque restituée* (1815–16), a work that revived a kabalistic conceit which saw in Semitic sounds and characters mystical meanings. His original motivation was a desire to reconcile modern science with biblical authority: he was brought up Methodist Episcopal, had questioned the theory of evolution, and completed a lengthy manuscript on science and religion in 1925.

Whorf expanded his interests to study Aztec and then Mayan hieroglyphics. Using the collection at the Watkinson Library in Hartford, Whorf extended his pursuits to anthropology and archeology. By 1928 he was working at many other collections in the northeast; he had begun correspondence with scholars of ancient Mexican language and culture; and he published his first article. 'An Aztec account of the period of the Toltec decline.' Whorf started attending scholarly conferences and delivering papers. Although he did not accurately decipher Mayan ideograms, he correctly proposed that they were a system for writing spoken language. In 1929–30 the Social Science Research Council granted him a fellowship, which allowed him to visit Mexico and do further study of Mexican languages.

In 1931 Whorf began to study with Edward Sapir, the prominent anthropological linguist and student of Franz Boas, who had come to nearby Yale University. Although he remained an amateur, Whorf now worked in the company of leading professional linguists and found particular resonance between his own ideas and those of Sapir. His study of Hopi, begun in 1932, led to his fullest formulations of the theory that different languages express different understandings of the world, the so-called 'Linguistic Relativity Principle,' particularly in 'Some verbal categories of Hopi' (1938) and 'The relation of habitual thought and behavior of language' (1941).

Whorf was a popular lecturer and wrote accessible versions of his thesis in *Technology Review*—'Science and linguistics' (1940), 'Linguistics as an exact science' (1940), 'Languages and logic' (1941)—and in the *The Theosophist*—'Language, mind, and reality' (1942).

Bibliography

Carroll J B 1956 *Language Thought and Reality: Selected Writings of Benjamin Lee Whorf.* Technology Press of Massachusetts Institute of Technology, Cambridge, MA

Wilkins, John (1614–72)

J. Subbiondo

John Wilkins's scholarly interests reflected the panorama of seventeenth-century British thought: in addition to his work in linguistics, he distinguished himself in education, lexicography, oratory, science, theology, and taxonomy. His principle contribution to the intellectual life of seventeenth-century Britain was his role as principal founder of the Royal Society, and his contribution to the history of linguistics was his leadership in developing the most comprehensive universal or philosophical language to date.

Born in 1614, Wilkins was educated at Magdalen Hall, Oxford; and upon graduation, he was appointed tutor there in 1634. He was ordained in 1637 and appointed Vicar of Fawsley, and later served as private chaplain first to Lord Berkeley and then to Prince Elector Palatine Charles Louis. In 1648, he was appointed Warden of Wadham College, Oxford, and there received his Doctorate of Divinity. He was appointed Master of Trinity College, Cambridge in 1659; Bishop of Chester in 1668; and, after his resignation, he held a variety of clerical positions in London until his death in 1672.

A significant promoter of the scientific activities of his day, he led the philosophical or universal language movement which attempted to invent an artificial language to remedy the deficiencies of natural languages. There was considerable concern on the part of seventeenth-century scientists that the imprecision of natural languages threatened the advancement and preservation of science. In his *Mercury* (1641), Wilkins advanced a system of cryptology in which he designed a secret language. Expanding the theoretical construct of that design, Wilkins developed the most extensive philosophical language ever devised in his monumental *Essay towards a Real Character, and a Philosophical Language* (1668). In the initial phase of his project, Wilkins worked closely with George Dalgarno; but soon after, he decided not to collaborate with Dalgarno because their goals grew incompatible.

Wilkins's first task in the development of his philosophical language was to compile detailed charts reflecting the knowledge of the universe shared by his colleagues in the Royal Society. He then designed a graphemic system, a 'real character,' and a phonetic system capable of signifying each element in his charts. The symbols of the elements were formed into words and the words were placed in logical order into sentences. He arranged the elements according to meaning—an approach later adopted by Peter Roget who credited Wilkins in the preface of his famous thesaurus. Wilkins provided a dictionary which served as an alphabetical index for locating elements in his charts. Dolezal (1985) has convincingly pointed out that this dictionary merits recognition in the history to lexicography.

In late-twentieth-century scholarship, Wilkins draws growing attention as a significant thinker of his time and also as a substantive pioneer in semiotic theory.

Bibliography

Dolezal F 1985 *Forgotten but Important Lexicographers: John Wilkins and William Lloyd.* M. Niemeyer, Tübingen

Salmon V 1988 *The Study of Language in Seventeenth-Century England*, 2nd edn. Benjamins. Amsterdam

Shapiro B 1969 *John Wilkins: 1614–1672.* University of California Press, Berkeley, CA

Slaughter M 1982 *Universal Languages and Scientific Taxonomy in the Seventeenth Century.* Cambridge University Press, Cambridge

Subbiondo J 1992 *John Wilkins and 17th-century British Linguistics.* Benjamins, Amsterdam

Wittgenstein, Ludwig (1889–1951)

C. Travis

Ludwig Wittgenstein, arguably the most original and influential philosopher of the twentieth century, took up philosophy as a vocation in 1911, having first studied engineering. His choice was prompted by interest in the philosophy of mathematics, a subject on which he lectured and wrote extensively until the end of his life. He also wrote extensively, over long periods, on philosophy of mind, epistemology, and other areas. This article concentrates on his philosophy of language. No area in Wittgenstein's philosophy can be called the foundation, or core, of all the rest. There are many mutual dependencies. His philosophy of language, for example, cannot get started without the proper epistemology—one that can only be understood completely in the light of the resultant view of language. But in Wittgenstein's treatment of language there are keys to much of the rest.

1. The Influence of Frege and Russell on Wittgenstein's Early Work

In his first years in philosophy, Wittgenstein was greatly influenced by ideas of Gottlob Frege and Bertrand Russell, changing earlier Schopenhauer-inspired views. (On choosing philosophy, he visited Frege, who directed him to Cambridge to study with Russell.) Two leading ideas of Frege and Russell were fundamental to Wittgenstein's early views, as epitomized in *Tractatus Logico–Philosophicus* (completed in 1918), although they also remained important in his later work: the idea of 'logical form' and the idea of an 'ideal' language.

1.1 Logical Form

The idea of 'logical form,' and relatedly 'logical analysis,' is roughly this: for each meaningful proposition (one that actually says something in particular to be so), or thought (one that is actually of things being in some definite way), or any proper component of these, there is a unique true logical form which it really has—a way that is constructed out of some unique stock of constituents, where the rules by which it is thus constructed show the contribution each constituent makes to what the whole says, and to what it requires for truth. Logical form may be discovered by thoroughgoing logical analysis which involves, for each bit of an expression, examining the systematic effect of its presence or absence on the conditions of which the whole would be true. Wittgenstein extended these ideas by arguing that a fully analyzed, simple proposition, if it is meaningful, will picture a possible state of affairs with which it shares a form, and also that all complex meaningful propositions are truth–functions of simple 'atomic' propositions. The paradigm for a successful search for logical form was taken to be Russell's analysis of sentences containing definite description (in Russell 1905), which became a sort of oblique manifesto for those who thought discovering such form to be the main business of philosophy.

1.2 An Ideal Language

The other leading idea, strongly promoted by Frege, was that of an ideal language 'suitable for scientific purposes.' Such a language would, first, be totally without ambiguity. So it would never call for disambiguation. What this seems to mean is: the question whether some bit of it is to be understood in this way or that could never arise as a question to be resolved by some fact outside of the language itself. Any such question would be decided uniquely and effectively by the properties already conferred on the language's bits in setting it up, or in specifying which language it is; all this while for any bit, since it has a semantics, there is such a thing as 'the way in which it *is* to be understood.' (One might see in this Frege's fondness for *tertium non datur* elevated to a creed.)

So an ideal language is a sort of self-propelled linguistic perpetual motion machine: everything it does, it does quite independently of outside help, or of any surroundings in which it might occur. If P is one of its predicates, and V an arbitrary item, then P is true of V or it is not, with no thanks to us, or to anyone; and quite apart from anyone's reactions to P. That is the sort of meaning conferred on P by its place in the ideal language; and it is what having a proper meaning would look like.

One might regard such an ideal language as a 'language of thought(s),' provided one understands that in an appropriately Fregean, nonpsychologistic way. The point is not that the language is realized in the brain, though in fact Frege sometimes seems committed to that too (see Frege 1918: 26). The point is this: consider the maximally expressive ideal language that it is humanly possible to construct, or to grasp. Then each thought that we can think, each thing that we can state, will be said by exactly one item in that language, which, conversely, will say nothing *but* that. (Thoughts here are logical, not psychological, objects; individuated by the situations of which they would be true.) Since an ideal language is completely perspicuous, the item will reveal what the structure and essence of that thought really is.

Natural language, being defective, may fail to be univocal: there may fail to be any one thing fixed by the ideal language which is correctly said to be the thought some natural sentence expresses. Still, Frege insists, we may understand such a sentence in one way or another, as saying this or that. Any of us, on hearing it, may take it to state thus and so, even if, strictly speaking, it does not univocally do that. The maximal ideal language reveals what we do in doing that: it exhibits all the understandings it is possible to have, the ways in which words may be understood, in taking them to say something in particular. To take them to say something specific to be so is always to associate them with an item in that language. That is the sense in which it is a language of thought, or better, of thoughts.

Wittgenstein's early interest centered on the question of what an ideal language would be like, leading him to another early and abiding interest: the bounds of sense, or the distinction between sense and nonsense. Both ideas are prominent in the *Tractatus*. Within the picture just sketched, a sentence of one of our defective natural languages expresses nonsense just in case there is nothing in the maximal ideal language which says what it does, if anything. In that case, there is nothing which it says, or says to be so. To express nonsense is to express, and say, exactly nothing. The interesting sort of nonsense is that where, so to speak, 'syntax outstrips semantics'; we produce words which seem grammatically in order, but they lack the semantic properties they must actually have if they are to say something. That notion is central in Wittgenstein's later, as well as in his early, philosophy. But in the later philosophy he has very different ideas as to the specific causes of such failure.

In 1914, Wittgenstein entered the Austrian army. In 1918 he became a prisoner of war in Italy. Between 1919 and 1929, he remained quasi-retired from the philosophical arena. He returned to Cambridge in 1929 with a new view of philosophy and of language; with ideas in terms of which the old leading ideas may be seen as false ideals. (It is important to keep in mind that, like any philosopher, Wittgenstein had to struggle with, and thereby develop, the new ideas. He did not always see clearly what they were, and certainly did not see the *same* thing in them from 1929 on. Nor did he always have the words, or the uses of them, to state those ideas perspicuously, whether to himself or to others. To think otherwise would be idolatry.)

2. Wittgenstein's Later Work on Language

The old leading ideas remained central to Wittgenstein's later philosophy, though his new concern was to exhibit in detail what is wrong with them. Thus, for example, he aims to show exactly why it is wrong 'to think that if anyone utters a sentence and means or understands it he is operating a calculus according to definite rules' (*Philosophical Investigations*, Sect. 81). Or why it is not 'as if our usual forms of expression were, essentially unanalyzed, as if there were something hidden in them that had to be brought to light... as if we were moving towards a particular state, a state of complete exactness; and as if this were the real goal of our investigation' (Sect. 91). Or exactly what the mistake is in the following:

> *The essence is hidden from us*': is the form our problem now assumes. We ask: '*What is* language?,' '*What is* a proposition?' And the answer to these questions is to be given once and for all; and independent of any future experience.'
>
> (Sect. 92)

Wittgenstein was also guided continuously during his later period by another thought, which G. E. Moore reports as follows:

> One chief view about propositions to which he was opposed was... that a proposition is a sort of 'shadow' intermediate between the expression... and the fact... he said... [this view] was an attempt to make a distinction between a proposition and a sentence.... it regarded the supposed 'shadow' as something 'similar' to the fact in question; and he said that, even if there were such a 'shadow' it would not 'bring us any nearer to the fact,' since 'it would be susceptible of different interpretations...' ... 'No interpolation between a sign and its fulfillment does away with a sign.' He said... 'the expression of an expectation contains a description of the fact that would fulfill it,' pointing out that if I expect *to see a red patch* my expectation is fulfilled if and only if I do *see a red patch*....
>
> (Moore 1959: 260–61) (Compare Sects. 95, 429)

Wittgenstein's rule was thus: do not try to solve a problem by drawing technical distinctions between different types of items that might bear semantic properties, as between 'proposition' and sentence, or between concepts and predicates. He had various reasons for the rule. The one that matters here is that the same sorts of problems which arose for the original items (words, for example, which may bear various understandings) are bound to arise for the newly introduced items as well; fresh items are not the means for solving problems. That rule, combined with his insights about the false Fregean/Russellian ideals just discussed, yielded a truly radical approach to semantics, and to understandings.

2.1 Naming and Meaning

To see what the new view is, we should look at the beginning of the of the *Philosophical Investigations*. Here Wittgenstein's first concern is, ostensibly, with the relation between naming and meaning. (Meaning thus and so is what words of a language do. Though Wittgenstein sometimes uses 'meaning', or a word that so translates, to apply to words as used on a particular occasion, here he does not.) Take the

English word 'blue.' We might say that that names a certain color, namely, blue. What is the relation between its doing that and its meaning what it does? Perhaps, for it to do that just *is* for it to mean what it does; in saying that it names the color blue, one states exactly what it means. (What extra fact should one mention? What fact not determined by that one is determined by what 'blue' means?)

But if that is so, as it seems to be, then Wittgenstein's next question arises. What has all that—either what it means or what it names—got to do with the standards for its correct use or, inter alia, with what it would be true of? Here Wittgenstein uses his notion of a language game to make the point. (A language game is defined by its rules. By contrast with actual words, it is thus explicit which rules set its standards or correctness for words and responses that are moves in it.) A language game is an object of comparison: we may sometimes view some properties of our words as modeled in one or another such game. There is no such thing as 'the language game we are playing' in speaking given words (see Sects. 81, 130). That a word, e.g., 'blue,' names what it does is compatible with its figuring in an indefinite variety of language games, with indefinitely many different, and sometimes conflicting, standards or correctness. So its naming what it does does not settle what it could truly apply to.

Now all of these remarks about what naming does not do apply intact to meaning. That 'blue' means what it does not fix what it would be true of. Take the sky. Is it blue? If you said so, in the wrong surroundings, someone might be very disappointed when he looked at it for the first time from close up, in an airplane. Sometimes it counts as blue—in some surroundings, for some purposes—and it is then true to say that it is blue. Sometimes it does not so count, and it is false to say so. What changes from one case to another is not what 'blue' names, not what it means. Throughout it speaks of the color blue, and does so by and in meaning what it does.

By now, the above point has been widely taken, even by those who, not long ago, still thought that meanings of words could be stated by specifying what they were true of. The most usual way of assimilating the point is to echo J. L. Austin in saying that an English sentence is precisely not what can be true or false (it doesn't say anything), then positing some other item (a thought, a proposition) that may be. The point then becomes: an English sentence expresses different thoughts on different speakings, an English predicate different concepts, etc. But a thought has just the sort of truth condition a sentence was originally supposed to.

2.2 Semantic Properties and Occasion-sensitivity

It is just here that Wittgenstein's second guiding idea—the avoidance of 'shadows' between us and the world—leads to major innovations. The principle is: do not try to solve the problem (accounting for variation in what words with fixed meaning say) by postulating new bearers of semantics, since the same problem will arise for them. They, too, will be governed by difference standards of correctness in different surroundings. (We cannot cancel out the sign.) If we are debarred from this solution, what solution remains? The answer is to treat semantic properties as normal properties, on a par with ground-level ones. Consider the property of being blue. Having it, we have just seen, is, or may be, an occasion-sensitive affair. Sometimes the sky counts as having it, sometimes it does not. Now shift to the property of being true, or true of the sky. If that behaves normally, then having it is an occasion-sensitive affair too. Whatever the semantic item—say, a sentence—if that item may ever count as having that property, then the basic state of affairs is: in some circumstances it would, in others it would not. More generally, the having of a semantics (some set of semantic properties) is an occasion-sensitive affair: which semantics an item counts as having varies with the occasions for counting it as having, or lacking, any.

If an item may count, in different surroundings, as having different semantics, then something more than just the item's occasion-independent nature is required for fixing which semantics it counts as having in any given surroundings. The surroundings must help, of course. But, Wittgenstein points out, there being a result depends also on there being such a thing as the reasonable way of understanding the item, or assigning it a semantics, in those surroundings. Facts as to what is reasonable depend, in some way, on facts about us, beginning with the simple fact that we are very often capable of seeing what is reasonable. Without the right background of facts about users, or treaters, or evaluators, of an item, there would also be no facts as to the semantics it counted, in given surroundings, as having.

If the above sort of sensitivity to occasions or surroundings is intrinsic to semantic properties, thus a feature of any item that has a semantics, then the Fregean ideal language is ruled out. Any language would be, necessarily, dependent on the reactions of us, or its users, for the semantic facts about it, particularly those about its applications, being what they are. Languages cannot, in principle, be self-propelled, as they would be on Frege's view.

Wittgenstein argues for the pervasiveness of semantic occasion-sensitivity in two ways: first in his discussion of rules and what they require (see especially Sects. 84–7); and second in the private language discussion (roughly Sects. 243–72). The first is a direct argument, relying on facts as to the conceivable ways of specifying which rule a given rule is. Any specification leaves at least conceivable doubts as to whether in this case, this, or perhaps rather that, would be in compliance with the rule. ('Can't we imagine a rule determining the application of a rule, and a doubt which *it* removes—and so on?' (Sect. 84).) The private language discussion proceeds by stripping away the background of a user's reactions (except for a degenerate and futile case: the lone private linguist), and examining what happens. The upshot is that a language that got along entirely on its own steam would be no genuine language at all. No intelligible language could, in principle, conform to Frege's ideal.

3. More General Issues

With this outline of a new view, some questions that run persistently through all of Wittgenstein's philosophy will now be addressed. First, perspicuity. Wittgenstein remarks in a different connection: 'It is so difficult to find the beginning, Or better: it is difficult to begin at the beginning. And not try to go further back' (*On Certainty*, Sect. 471). We may always make fresh demands for further perspicuity, pushing the identification of an understanding farther back. But if we do so indefinitely, we will never arrive at anything. We are not en route to the Fregean ideal. So:

> It is not our aim to refine, or complete, the system of rules for the use of our words in unheard-of ways.
>
> For the clarity that we are aiming at is indeed *complete* clarity. But this simply means that the philosophical problems should *completely* disappear.
>
> (Sect. 133)

Within or without philosophy:

> an explanation serves to remove or avert a misunderstanding—one, that is, that would occur but for the explanation; not every one that I can imagine.
>
> (Sect. 87)

Complete perspicuity is achieved by our ordinary explanations (inter alia of meaning or content) when they achieved their goal; that is, when they leave no real or live doubt as to whether what was said/meant is this or that. Perspicuity so conceived is, of course, an occasion-sensitive affair.

Finally, nonsense. Nonsense, on this view, comes in many varieties. The most significant one is this. The view is that words depend on their surroundings, or the facts of their speaking, for bearing the sort of semantics words would bear where they said this or that to be so. Their mere semantics (meaning) as words of such and such language (say, English) is not enough for them to do this. The English sentence, 'The sky is blue,' viewed merely as an English sentence, in total abstraction from surroundings, says nothing in particular to be so. There could be no such thing as isolating those states of affairs which would be: things being as that sentence, so viewed, says things to be. For though 'is blue' speaks of being blue, there are various 'sometimes-correct' ways of counting such things as the sky as being, or failing to be, that. Meaning alone does not show which of these ways to rely on in evaluating the truth of those words. We must rely on surroundings to show this—typically those of a speaking—or the project of evaluation cannot begin.

There is, then, a substantive burden on the surroundings in which words are used. Since it is a substantive one, some surroundings may fail to provide what is needed from them (see Sects. 117, 501, 514, 515). Words spoken in such surroundings may be fully grammatical and meaningful. Their semantics may be perfectly coherent. They will still have said nothing to be so, or at least nothing could count either as their being true or as their being false. This is a new conception of a way in which syntax may outstrip semantics: not by outrunning it entirely, nor by getting words paired with an incoherent or internally contradictory semantics (the English sentence is not incoherent), but rather by outrunning the situations in which words would have an adequate semantics—notably, adequate for evaluating them as to truth. This sort of nonsense is what one produces by ignoring the contribution surroundings must make, or by failing to foresee how surroundings may fail to do so. Since philosophers tend to overlook the ways in which their words depend for their semantics on surroundings, assuming that a meaningful sentence, used any old time, will say something, this is one typical sort of philosophical nonsense. It is epitomized not by patently opaque and turgid metaphysical prose, but rather by a philosopher who, clutching his nose says, 'I know I have a nose,' or, pointing at the ground. 'I am here,' or who, for no reason, remarks. 'Hamburger is red'—or who, for no reason, says of Jones, whose accomplishments he has briefly sketched 'Jones understands the words "Aardvarks live in Africa".'

The profound implications of Wittgenstein's views on language and meaning have been felt in nearly all areas of philosophy from, for example, philosophy of science to ethics and aesthetics. A ceaseless outpouring of commentary and debate followed his death in 1951 and not only his ideas but many of his illustrative terms—'picture' from his early work or later 'game,' 'form of life,' 'family resemblance'—have become common currency in discussions of language.

Bibliography

Cavell S 1979 *The Claim of Reason*. Oxford University Press, Oxford

Kenny A 1973 *Wittgenstein*. Harvard University Press, Cambridge, MA

McGuinness B (ed.) 1967 *Ludwig Wittgenstein und der Wiener Kreis*. Blackwell, Oxford
Pears D 1988 *The False Prison*. Oxford University Press. Oxford
Rhees R (ed.) 1981 *Recollections of Wittgenstein*. Oxford University Press, Oxford
Travis C 1989 *The Uses of Sense*. Oxford University Press, Oxford
Wittgenstein L 1956 (trans. Anscombe G E M) *Remarks on the Foundations of Mathematics*. Blackwell, Oxford
Wittgenstein L 1958 *The Blue and Brown Books*. Blackwell, Oxford
Wittgenstein L 1961 (trans. Pears D, McGuinness B) *Tractatus Logico-Philosophicus*. Routledge and Kegan Paul, London
Wittgenstein L 1967 (trans. Anscombe G E M) *Philospohical Investigations*, 2nd edn. Blackwell, Oxford
Wittgenstein L 1969 (trans. Paul D, Anscombe G E M) *On Certainty*. Blackwell, Oxford
Wittgenstein L 1974 (trans. Kenny A) *Philosophical Grammar*. Blackwell, Oxford
Wright von G H *Wittgenstein*. University of Minnesota Press, Minneapolis, MN

Wulfila (Ulfilas) (311?–382?)

J. M. Y. Simpson

Wulfila (also known by the Greek forms of his name 'Ulfila' and 'Ulfilas') was the translator of the Bible into Gothic. He was born in Dacia, in Visigothic territory (present-day Romania north of the Danube), probably in 311. His forebears had been brought as prisoners from Cappadocia some 50 years earlier by Gothic invaders of Asia Minor and it is possible that these ancestors had already been converted to Christianity. Wulfila went to Constantinople as a young man and in 341 was consecrated bishop of the Gothic Christians by Eusebius of Nicomedia, Bishop of Constantinople, an Arian. He returned to evangelize and minister to his people for the rest of his life, carrying to them the Arian form of Christianity. The first seven years or more were spent in Dacia; thereafter, as a result of persecution Wulfila and his congregation crossed the Danube, settling in Moesia (present-day Bulgaria). Arianism, part of Wulfila's legacy, a national characteristic not only of the Visigoths but of Ostrogoths, Vandals and Burgundians, caused a long-standing rift between these Germanic peoples and the post-Nicene Roman Empire. In 381, the Roman emperor, Theodosius the Great, an upholder of Nicene Trinitarian orthodoxy, summoned Wulfila to Constantinople for discussions; in the course of these he died.

Wulfila reputedly translated the whole of the Bible, except for the Books of Kings, allegedly omitted in order not to incite the bellicose Goths to further deeds of war (Philostorgius *Historia Ecclesiastica* II, 5). The New Testament was translated from the original Greek, the Old Testament from the Septuagint.

In carrying out his translation, Wulfila was inevitably faced with the two problems that have confronted Bible translators down to the present day. The first, peculiar to those translating into a hitherto unwritten language, was that of inventing a suitable writing system. Wulfila carried out a phonemic analysis of Gothic (however he himself might have described this task) and produced an alphabet that appears to be totally appropriate. This was based on the Greek alphabet and certain fourth century Greek spelling conventions were carried over into Gothic, for example the notation of the vowels /ɛ/ and /iː/ as <ai> and <ei> respectively and of the sequence /ŋg/ as <gg>. His other task was that of extending the vocabulary of Gothic so that it could convey the new concepts of Christianity. This he did in the three ways familiar to Bible translators. The first is by borrowing: thus Greek *euaggelion* 'gospel' was simply taken over into Gothic as *aiwaggeljo*. The second is by loan-translation (calque): Greek *synagōgē* 'synagogue' (literally 'gathering together') is formed from *syn* 'together' and *agein* 'to bring' and this compound was reproduced in Gothic dress as *gaqumþs*, made up of *ga*, a prefix that forms a collective noun, and *qiman* 'to come.' The third is by extending the use of an already existing word, thus *naseins* 'rescue' was used to convey the meaning 'salvation'. There is Greek influence in Wulfila's Gothic syntax. These points illustrate the general principle that the receptor or target language may itself be changed by translation.

Unfortunately most of Wulfila's translation has been lost. Just over half of the Gospels are preserved in the surviving pages of the splendid Codex Argenteus, an Ostrogothic manuscript dating probably from the fifth century and now in Uppsala. Other portions of the Gospels and of the Pauline Epistles, together with three chapters of Nehemiah, survive in various other manuscripts, the majority of them in Milan.

See also: Gothic.

Bibliography

Braune W 1961 *Gotische Grammatik* 16. Auflage neu bearbeitet von Ernst A. Ebbinghaus, Tübingen
Ebbinghaus E A 1992 Some remarks on the life of Bishop Wulfila. *General Linguistics* **19**: 15–29

Wycliffe, John (1330–1384)

G. L. Jones

John Wycliffe, described as 'the last of the Schoolmen and the first of the Reformers,' was born in Yorkshire and educated at Oxford. He became a Fellow of Merton (1356), Master of Balliol (1360), and Warden of Canterbury Hall, later incorporated into Christ Church (1365–1367). Though he continued to live at Oxford until 1381, he also held the livings of Fillingham (1361–1368), Ludgershall (1368–1384) and Lutterworth (1374–1384), where he died during a celebration of the Mass on December 31, 1384.

A prolific author, he penned over 40 major works on philosophy, theology, and biblical exegesis. As a philosopher he was a Realist, and therefore opposed the Nominalism of the Schoolmen. As a theologian he was not as radical as some have supposed; he advocated Augustine's doctrines of predestination and grace. His study of the Bible led him to appreciate its significance and to call for a vernacular version so that its message would be accessible to everyone. Four aspects of his teachings aroused the hostility of his superiors: his rejection of the doctrine of transubstantiation, his refusal to acknowledge ecclesiastical authority, his criticism of clerical abuses, and his promotion of an English translation of the Scriptures.

Because he regarded Scripture as the only criterion of Christian teaching, he felt obliged to condemn transubstantiation in favour of a belief closer to Luther's doctrine of consubstantiation. In lengthy arguments against the Scotists and the Thomists in the *De Eucharistia* and the *De Apostasia*, in which he claims that it was unknown in the Church before the twelfth century, he describes transubstantiation as unscriptural, idolatrous, and based on an unsound philosophy. It served no purpose but to encourage superstition among worshippers. His consuming commitment to Scripture and his belief in its sufficiency as a guide for Christian living led him to regard canon law as secondary. He resisted the political power of the hierarchy and challenged the claims of the papacy. The authority of the pope was binding only if it could be demonstrated that he held office in conformity with biblical teaching. The religious orders, especially those of the friars, had no foundation in Scripture.

It was the ignorance of the Bible among the clergy which led to pastoral infidelity and abuse. Because God's law was not known it was not kept. Part of the problem was the clergy's poor command of Latin which meant that the Bible was a closed book. The remedy was a vernacular version of the Vulgate. The first translation appeared in c.1384 and a revision in c.1395. It cannot be stated with certainty that Wycliffe was responsible for translating any part of the original work himself, but it was inspired by him and executed under his guidance. Greeted enthusiastically by his followers, the Lollards, it was rejected by the religious authorities.

Though many of Wycliffe's ideas were adopted by Jan Hus and the Czech reformers, his forthright views eventually led to the charge of heresy. The Lollards were condemned at the Council of Constance in 1415 and in 1428 their mentor's bones were disinterred and burnt.

See also: Hus, J.; English Bible; Linguistic Theory in the later Middle Ages.

Bibliography

Kenny A 1985 *Wyclif Press.* Blackwell, Oxford

Kenny A (ed.) 1986 *Wyclif in his Times.* Clarendon Press, Oxford

Robson J A 1961 *Wyclif and the Oxford Schools.* Cambridge University Press, Cambridge

Young, Thomas (1773–1829)

J. D. Ray

English scientist and pioneer of linguistics, Young was born at Milverton, Somerset, and brought up in the Quaker tradition. Educated at Edinburgh, Göttingen, and Cambridge, he practiced as a physician in London and Worthing until his death. Young was a polymath, and showed exceptional ability even in his earliest years; by the age of 14 years he had mastered the elements of 12 European and Near-Eastern languages, but his main discoveries were to be in the realm of medicine and the physical sciences. He is celebrated as the founder of modern optics, and of the wave-theory of light, as well as making important contributions to the theory of vision and the workings of the human eye. He also worked on navigation, and laid down the principles of life insurance. On the strength of these discoveries he was appointed Professor of Natural Philosophy at the Royal Institution, of which he also became the Foreign Secretary. Young also found time to pursue his interest in languages, and he reviewed some 400 of them for the *Encyclopaedia Britannica*. It was during the course of these researches that he first coined the word 'Indo–European' to describe the language family discovered by William Jones. In a sense he is the last of the universal philosophers of the seventeenth and eighteenth centuries, and the first of the scientists of the nineteenth and twentieth.

Young's main contribution to linguistic knowledge lies in the field of Egyptology. The Rosetta Stone (see *Rosetta Stone*), discovered in 1798, held out the promise of deciphering the lost secrets of the hieroglyphs, and Young was the first scholar to reject the traditional belief that Ancient Egyptian Writing (see *Egyptian Hieroglyphs*) was symbolic and mystical. He went on to show the phonetic nature of the script, and drew up an alphabet which was partially correct. This was published in 1819. Young's work on hieroglyphs was the essential background to the decipherment by Champollion (see *Champollion, Jean-Francois*). In the field of demotic, his achievement was greater, and his last work was *Rudiments of an Egyptian Dictionary*, published after his death. Young was the first person since the Roman Empire who could read a demotic text, and he deserves to be known as the decipherer of this script. His work in linguistics falls into the same pattern as his scientific achievements: Young made the decisive breakthrough, leaving the details to others and moving on to new problems. But even if he did not always develop his ideas, the range of his discoveries is unique.

Bibliography

Dictionary of National Biography, vol. LXIII. Oxford University Press, London

Dawson W R, Uphill E P 1972 *Who was Who in Egyptology*, 2nd edn. Egypt Exploration Society, London

Ray J D 1991 The name of the first: Thomas Young and the decipherment of Egyptian writing. *Journal of the Ancient Chronology Forum* **4**: 49–54

Wood A, Oldham F 1954 *Thomas Young:* A Memoir. Cambridge University Press, Cambridge

Ziegenbalg, Bartholomäus (1682–1719)

R. E. Asher

The contribution of European missionaries to the knowledge in the west of both major and minor languages of India is enormous. Bartholomäus Ziegenbalg was an important figure in the history of this contribution, for his grammar of Tamil in Latin (1716) was the first comprehensive description of Tamil in a European language to appear in print. Jesuit missionaries had written short accounts of aspects of the sounds and grammar of Tamil as early as the sixteenth century. Most of these, however, were never published, though some are still extant in manuscript form.

Ziegenbalg left for India along with another German member of the Danish mission, Heinrich Plütschau, in the autumn of 1705. After an eight-month voyage they landed at Tranquebar on July 9, 1706. One of the many difficulties they immediately faced was that of communicating with the people among whom they wished to propagate the teaching of Christ, for they managed to find no one who knew both Tamil and a language which they themselves understood. Their first lessons are recounted in a letter which Ziegenbalg sent home soon after his arrival in India: they sat with a group of schoolboys tracing letters in the sand. They thus learnt the shapes of the Tamil letters and the sounds associated with each—but without understanding the meaning of the words which they were repeating. It therefore seemed a matter of real good fortune to meet a Tamil who knew not only Portuguese, which by then was by no means a rare circumstance, but also Danish, Dutch, and German. Diligent study, at the level of eight hours of intensive work a day, followed and within a year their proficiency was such that they were able to preach in 'Malabarick' (i.e., Tamil) three times a week.

Ziegenbalg studied the language of poetry as well as colloquial Tamil, and he prepared translations of parts of the corpus of early 'ethical' literature of some 1500 years ago, though these were not published until long after his death (Ziegenbalg 1930). Ziegenbalg's work was very well known in London, where several books under his name were published between 1710 and 1718: translations of letters sent home to Germany, the story of the work of the Danish mission, and books on south Indian customs and religion. His many writings in Tamil include a translation of the New Testament and the part of the Old Testament, a life of Christ, a number of hymns, and translations of sermons by distinguished theologians.

His work on Tamil led to the production of a Tamil primer, a dictionary of more than 40,000 words, a separate dictionary of poetic language, and his grammar. Only the last of these has survived. An earlier version of what was to become the *Grammatica Damulica* was written, not later than 1710, in German, but Ziegenbalg decided to prepare a revision in Latin so that it might be accessible to speakers of other European languages. It was written in 1715, during a return voyage to Europe, and published the following year in Halle, where there was a stock of Tamil type.

One of the most interesting aspects of Ziegenbalg's grammar is his presentation of colloquial forms, for these provide a clear indication that the diglossia which is a feature of modern Tamil was also a characteristic of the language in the early eighteenth century. Many of the forms he uses to illustrate grammatical points (e.g., palatal rather than dental consonants as one of the exponents of past tense) had not traditionally appeared in Tamil grammars and were not to be thought worthy of serious study again for more than two centuries. They provide valuable information about the history of the spoken language.

See also: Tamil; Missionaries.

Bibliography

Beyreuther E 1956 *Bartholomäus Ziegenbalg, Bahnbrecher der Weltmission*, 2nd edn. Evang. Missionsverlag, Stuttgart

Jeyaraj D 1996 *Inkulturation in Tranquebar. Der Beitrag der frühen dänisch-halleschen Mission zum Werden einer indisch-einheimischen Kirche (1706–1730)*. Verlag der Ev. Luth. Mission, Erlangen

Settgast A-C 1986 *Der Mann in Tranquebar: ein Porträt des Bartholomäus Ziegenbalg, gestattet nach alten Urkunden und Briefen*, 2nd edn. Evangelische Verlagsanstatt, Berlin

Singh B 1999 *The First Protestant Missionary to India. Bartholomaeus Ziegenbalg (1683–1719)*. Oxford University Press, New Delhi/Oxford

Ziegenbalg B 1716 *Grammatica Damulica, quæ per varia paradigmata, regulas & necessarium vocabularium apparatum, viam brevissimam monstrat, qua Lingua Damulica seu Malabarica, quæ inter Indos Orientales in usu est, & huiusque in Europa incognita fuit, facile disci possit: in usum eorum qui hoc tempore gentes illas ab idololatria ad cultum veri Dei, salutemque æternam Evangelio Christi perducere cupiunt*:...Litteris & impensis Orphanotrophei, Halæ Saxonum

Ziegenbalg B 1930 *Ziegenbalgs kleinere Schriften*, Verhandelingen der Koninklijke Akademie van Wetenschappen. Afd. Letter-kunde, Nieuwe reeks. dl. 29, no. 2. Amsterdam

Ziegenbalg B 1985 *Grammatica damulica* (Brentjes B, Gallus K (eds.)) Martin-Luther-Universität Halle-Wittenberg, Halle

Ziegenbalg B, Schulze B, Gruendler J E (eds.) *Biblia damulica*, 1714–28, Tranquebariae

SECTION VIII

Glossary

M. Dareau

ablative absolute A type of **absolute construction** (see **absolute clause)** found in some **inflecting** and **agglutinating languages**, e.g., Latin, specif. a phrase consisting of a **noun** in the **ablative** case and a **modifier**, usu. a participle, in **agreement** with it, e.g., ***Regibus exactis***, *consules creati sunt* ('Kings having been abolished, consuls were elected').

ablative In **inflecting** and **agglutinating languages**, the **case** expressing **locative** and **instrumental** meanings, separation, origin, etc.; equivalent to prepositions 'by,' 'with,' 'from.'

ablaut A systematic variation of a root vowel signaling a change in grammatical function, e.g., *sing/sang/song/sung*.

absolute clause (phrase, construction) A nonfinite adverbial clause or other adverbial construction not linked syntactically to the main clause, e.g., ***Other things being equal***, *we leave at nine*. ***However***, *the train was late*. Cf. **ablative absolute**.

absolute state see **status constructus**.

accent 1 Features of pronunciation which, taken together, identify a speaker's regional or social group. Cf. **dialect. 2** The emphasis, due to loudness, pitch, or duration which gives prominence to particular words or syllables in speech. **3** In metrics the regular beats in a line of verse, e.g., *Fair dáffodils we wéep to sée*. **4** also **word accent** The stress on a particular syllable of a word, sometimes signaling a difference in meaning, e.g., *récord* (v) vs *récord* (n). **5** A mark added above or below a letter in written language, e.g., acute (é), grave (è), etc., indicating a particular pronunciation, etc.

accusative, **objective** In **inflecting** and **agglutinating languages**, the **case** of the **noun** when it is the **object** of a verb; trad. applied to the object in English (the inflected pronomial forms *him*, *her*, etc., are now usually said to be in the **objective** case).

accusative-and-infinitive A **construction** such as *Bertie thought Gwen to be intelligent*, because in a Latin translation *Gwen* would be in the **accusative** case and *to be* would be an **infinitive**. (This in fact is the normal Classical Latin way of expressing 'Bertie thought that Gwen was intelligent.')

active In the analysis of **voice**, a sentence or clause in which the **subject** is also the actor, e.g., *Mary drove the car*; the **verb** form in such a sentence or clause. (Contrasts with **passive**.)

adjective A member of the word class whose main function is to specify an attribute of a noun, e.g., a ***fat*** *cat*, *The cat is* ***fat***; in many languages displaying contrasts of degree: *fat*, *fatter*, *fattest*.

advanced Of a **vowel**: pronounced further forward in the mouth than the symbol used to notate the sound would indicate.

adverb A member of the word class whose main function is to specify the mode of action of a **verb**, e.g., *She ate* ***quickly***; other functions include sentence connector, e.g., ***Besides***, *it's blue*, and intensifier, e.g., ***very*** *good*.

adverbial An element of structure functioning like an **adverb**, said esp. of **phrases** or **clauses**, e.g., *He telephoned* ***at once/last year/when he got home***.

affirmative Said of a **sentence** or **verb** which is not negative (see **negation**), i.e., which expresses an assertion, e.g., *It is raining*.

affix A **formative** capable of being added to a **root** or **stem** to make a more complex **word**, e.g., ***un****friend****ly***. See also **infix**, **prefix**, **suffix**.

Afroasiatic, **Afro-Asiatic** The name of an extensive family of languages, spoken in Northern Africa and the Near East, which itself includes the following families; Berber, Chadic, Cushitic, Omotic, and Semitic, as well as Ancient Egyptian.

agglutinating language A language in which words are made up of a sequence of **morphs**, each expressing a separate item of meaning as, **number**, **person**, **tense**, etc. Cf. **inflecting language**, **isolating language**.

agreement also **concord** A formal relationship in which the form of one element requires a corresponding form in another, e.g., between **subject** and **verb**: *the cat sits, the cats sit.*

allative In **inflecting** and **agglutinating languages**, the **case** expressing the meaning of motion 'to' or 'towards' a place.

allegorical Describes a text with more than one level of meaning, e.g., *Pilgrim's Progress* has a religious meaning beside the superficial story of a journey.

alliteration A number of words beginning with the same sound, typically in a line of verse, e.g., *Radio romance.*

allomorph One of a number of alternative realizations of a **morpheme** which are, e.g., conditioned by their phonetic environment, as in the case of the **plural** morpheme in English, realized by the allomorphs /s/, /z/ and /ɪz/.

alphabet A set of symbols representing the sounds of a language; a writing system.

alveolar Of a **consonant**, produced by contact or a close approximation of the tongue with the alveolar or teeth ridge (in English [t, d, l, n, s, z]).

aniconic Symbolizing without aiming at resemblance.

antithesis The contrast of ideas by means of parallel arrangements of words, phrases, etc., e.g., *They gave not bread, but a stone.*

aorist In some **inflecting languages**, the **aspect** of the verb denoting an action without reference to completion, duration, or repetition. (Contrasts with **imperfect** and **perfect**.)

apical Of a **consonant**: pronounced with the **tip** of the tongue against e.g. the **alveolar ridge** or upper teeth or upper lip; often contrasted with **laminal**.

apophatic Describing by means of negatives, that is, by saying what the thing being described is not, e.g. *God is invisible, immortal, intangible, unchanging...* Cf. **cataphatic**.

apposition Two or more noun phrases having the same referent and standing in the same syntactical relation to the rest of the sentence, e.g., *Dylan Thomas, poet, playwright, drunk.*

approximant A **consonant** during which the **articulators** are brought together but without **friction** resulting from the air passing between them.

archaism A word or phrase no longer in general use.

Arian Applied to the doctrine in Christianity that Jesus the Son, though divine, was neither equal with God the Father nor eternal. (From Arius, a presbyter of the church of Alexandria in the fourth century CE.) Cf. **Trinitarian**.

article A **determiner** which differentiates nouns according to their definiteness: *the* is the **definite article** in English, *a*(*n*) the **indefinite**.

articulator One of the organs of speech involved in the production of a speech-sound.

aspect A category of description referring to the way in which the performance of an action, esp. its duration or completion, is denoted by the **verb**, e.g., *I am going/I go.* Other possible aspectual distinctions include **habitual**, **inceptive**, **iterative**, **progressive**, etc.

aspiration The audible breath accompanying the articulation of some sounds, esp. the voiceless **plosive**. [ʰ] as in [pʰat], such sounds are sometimes called **aspirates**.

assimilation The modification of a speech sound by its proximity to another in that it becomes more similar or identical to the influencing sound. See also **progressive assimilation**, **regressive assimilation**.

automatic writing Writing performed without the volition of the writer.

back of tongue That part of the tongue which, when in a position of rest, lies under the **velum**.

back vowel A **vowel** articulated towards the back of the vowel area, that is, in the back of the mouth, i.e. one in which the **back of the tongue** is brought nearer to the **uvula** or in which the tongue is lying more or less flat, e.g. [u], [o], [ɔ], [ɑ] as in *you, rope* (Scottish pronunciation), *awe* and *calm* (Southern English pronunciation).

bhakti Devotion to a god, as a path to salvation.

bilabial A speech-sound in which the **primary articulation** is a narrowing between or a closure of the lips.

bilingualism The use by an individual or speech community of two (or more) languages.

blade of tongue That part of the tongue which, when at rest, lies under the **alveolar ridge**.

borrowing = **loan(word)**

boustrophedon Writing or text having alternate lines written in opposite directions.

breathy voice A type of **phonation** in which the **glottis** is in vibration but air escapes through it in such a way that a murmur is imparted to the resulting **voiced** sound.

calque = **loan translation**

canon The works of an author, literary movement, etc. regarded as authentic and hence authoritative or standard.

canonical Belonging to the **canon**, nondeviant, standard.

cantillation Chanting or intoning, especially of Hebrew scriptures in Jewish liturgical services.

cardinal vowel One of a set of standard reference points, based on articulatory and auditory criteria, used to identify **vowel** sounds; four tongue positions (open, half-open, half-close, close) and three parts of the tongue (front, center, and back), with presence or absence of lip rounding (see **rounded**), produce two sets (primary and secondary) of standard vowel sounds by comparison with which the sounds of a language may be accurately transcribed.

case In **inflecting** and **agglutinating languages**, the inflectional forms of the noun, pronoun or adjective used to identify syntactic relationships within the sentence, e.g., the **nominative** case identifies the **subject**, the **accusative** the **object**, the **genitive** the relation of possession, etc.

cataphatic Describing by affirmation, that is, by stating what the thing being described is Cf. **apophatic**.

central vowel A **vowel** articulated with the highest point of the tongue raised toward the back part of the hard palate or the front of the **velum**, e.g. [ɜ] as in Southern English *bird*.

clause A syntactic unit consisting of **subject** and **predicate** which alone forms a simple **sentence** and in combination with others forms a compound sentence or complex sentence.

click A **consonant** produced on a **velaric ingressive** airstream, e.g. the noise sometimes written as *tut-tut* or *tsk!* used to indicate disapproval in English.

close approximation In the articulation of a **consonant**, the bringing together of the **articulators** so closely that **friction** results when air passes between them.

close vowel A **vowel** in which the highest point of the tongue approaches the roof of the mouth most closely, e.g. [i], [u], as in *see* and *you*; it stands in contrast to **close-mid**, **open-mid**, and **open vowels**.

closed Describes a **syllable** ending in a **consonant**.

close-mid A **vowel** in which the highest point of the tongue approaches the roof of the mouth less closely than in a **close vowel**, but more closely than in an **open-mid** or **open vowel**, e.g. [e], [o] as in *hair* and *hope* in a Scottish pronunciation, or in French, *dé*, *eau*.

cognate Deriving from a common ancestor as, e.g., English and German from Common Germanic or French and Italian from Latin.

cognitive (space) grammar A theory based on a view of language as facet of cognition, **grammar** being the means whereby conceptual content is structured and functioning solely as a link between **phonological** and **semantic** structures.

cohesion The phonological, grammatical, or lexical means of linking **sentences** into larger units, paragraphs, chapters, etc., e.g., ***The girl** went out*. ***She** shut the door*.

comparative method The comparison of forms between **cognate** languages as a means of establishing historical data about one or all of the related languages.

comparative philology see **philology**

comparison = **degree**

complementary distribution Sounds in complementary distribution cannot occur in the same phonetic **context** environment.

componential analysis The analysis of lexical items or lexemes in terms of sense-components (or **semantic**

features), e.g., male/female, young/adult, human/nonhuman, etc.

concord = **agreement**

conjugation In **inflecting** and **agglutinating languages** the set of **verbs** that vary according to the same model of formation or **paradigm**.

conjunction One of the class of words whose main function is to connect **clauses**, **phrases** or **words**; trad. **coordinating conjunctions**, e.g., and, *but*; and **subordinating conjunctions**, e.g., *that*, *when*. see **Subordination**.

consonant A speech sound produced with constriction to a degree where audible friction is produced or closure of the vocal tract, e.g., [s], [r], [k], etc. **2** The unit of sound which occurs at the margin of the syllable, e.g., /***sɪk***/. **3** A letter or group of letters representing a consonant in senses **1** or **2** above, e.g., ⟨***sick***⟩.

construct state see **status constructus**

construction The **syntactic** arrangement or patterning within a grammatical unit.

context 1 The stretch of utterance or text in which a linguistic element occurs, e.g., in [pɪn], [p] and [n] are the phonetic context of [ɪ]. **2** The discourse around a word or expression which clarifies its meaning in that environment, e.g., in *Even foxes have holes in which to lay their heads*, *holes* may be identified as meaning 'lair'. **3** The extralinguistic setting of an utterance or the nonlinguistic information contributing to the meaning, e.g., in the above example, the fact that the reference is biblical.

corpus Written texts, transcriptions, recorded data, etc. used as a basis for any sort of **linguistic** or language related investigation; a computer or computerized corpus is a body of such data in a machine-readable form.

creaky voice A **phonation** in which the glottis is in vibration, but in such a way that a 'creak' or noise like a stick being drawn along railings is imparted to the resulting **voiced** sound.

cuneiform A writing system of the ancient Near East employing symbols composed of wedge shapes (from Latin *cuneus* 'wedge').

dative In **inflecting** and **agglutinating languages**, the **case** expressing the relationship of **indirect object** or the meanings *to* or *for*.

declension A set of **nouns**, **pronouns** or **adjectives** which have the same inflections.

deep structure In transformational grammar, the abstract representation of a **sentence** specifying the **syntactic** facts which govern how the sentence is to be interpreted, disambiguating, e.g., *Flying planes can be dangerous* as between *planes which fly* and *the flying of planes*; or assigning the same underlying form to, e.g., **active** and **passive** sentences such as *John loves Mary* and *Mary is loved by John*. Cf. **surface structure**.

definite article see **article**

degree A grammatical category specifying the level of comparison of an **adjective** or **adverb**, specif. positive, comparative, and superlative, e.g., *hot*, *hotter*, *hottest*, also equative, e.g., *as hot as*.

demonstrative (adjective, pronoun) An **adjective** or **pronoun** which serves to distinguish between members of a class, specif. *this* (*these*), *that* (*those*), e.g., ***This** rose not **that** one, or **these** if you prefer. No I'll have **those**.*

dental Of a **consonant** (sense **1**), produced by contact or close approximation of the tongue with the upper teeth.

determiner A sub-class of **modifiers** cooccurring with **nouns** and **pronouns** to express semantic contrasts such as number or quantity, e.g., specifying count or mass nouns; specif. the articles *a*/*the*, also, items which occur in '**article** position' in the noun phrase, e.g., *some*, *every*, *much*, *this*, etc. In some approaches the term is extended to cover other sorts of modifier.

diachronic (historical) linguistics The study of languages as they change through time.

dialect A variety of language distinguished **1** on geographical, **2** on social grounds by differences of **grammar**, **vocabulary** and **accent**.

diglossia The cooccurrence of two distinct varieties of a language within a speech community, each performing a separate social function on differing levels of formality; a diglossic situation occurs, e.g., in Switzerland between Standard German (Hochdeutsch), the formal or high variety, and Swiss German, the low variety.

discourse analysis A methodological approach to the analysis of **language** above the level of the **sentence**, involving criteria such as **connectivity** (see **cohesion**).

distinctive feature A piece of **phonetic** information distinguishing one sound from another; the minimal unit of a sound system capable of making such distinctions, e.g., **labiality**, **roundness**, etc.

downstep A gradual descent of the pitch of the high-pitched **tones** throughout a stretch of speech.

dual(ity) A contrast of **number** in some languages, referring to 'two'.

egressive Applied to the air moving out from the mouth during the production of a speech-sound.

ejective Of a **consonant** (sense **1**) produced by means of the **glottalic** egressive airstream mechanism, e.g., **glottalized** stops [p', t', k', etc].

elision The omission of sounds (freq. unstressed **vowels** or medial **consonants**) in connected speech or verse, e.g., *bacon 'n' eggs*; o'er.

ellipsis The omission of that part of a linguistic structure which would be repetitive, hence is recoverable from the **context**, e.g., *Where are you going? Home*. (*Home* being an abbreviated form of *I am going home*.)

emphatic consonants A series of **phonemes** in Arabic, very typical of that language; the sounds involved are characterized by **velarization** and/or **pharyngealization** (and perhaps other articulatory phenomena). (See *Arabic*.)

epiglottal Made with the **epiglottis**, that is, the plate of cartilage that closes over the **glottis** during swallowing.

epigraph An engraved inscription.

ergative 1 Said of a **language** (e.g. Basque), **construction**, etc. where the **object** of a **transitive verb** and the **subject** of an **intransitive verb** display the same **case. 2** In such a language, said the subject of a transitive verb. **3** In transferred use, applied to languages not traditionally regarded as 'ergative,' relating **sentences** such as *The glass broke* and *The boy broke the glass* in a similar fashion, the agent of the action being referred to as the 'ergative' subject.

etymology 1 The history of a linguistic form (esp. a word) delineated by tracing its antecedents or etymons recorded in earlier stages of the **language** it is in, or has come from, **cognate** forms in related languages and reconstructed forms (indicated by *, as Gmc **skirmjan*). **2** The branch of **linguistics** concerned with the history of linguistic forms.

euphemism A less unpleasant or direct locution, e.g., *pass away* used in place of *die*.

exegesis A critical interpretation or explanation of a text.

feminine see **gender**

First Sound Shift A historical development affecting **consonants**, and peculiar to the Germanic languages in the Indo-European family; it explains, for example, why the initial sounds (which have remained unshifted) of the Latin *piscis*, *tres*, and *cornu* correspond to those of English *fish*, *three* [θ], and *horn*.

flap A **consonant** made with a flick of the tongue, the **tip** of which strikes the **alveolar ridge** in passing; the movement made is of a greater extent than that used in a **tap**.

foot, group A basic unit in the rhythm of speech, consisting of one **stressed syllable** and subsequent syllables, up to but not including the next stressed syllable.

formalism 1 An artificial **language** whose purpose is the precise characterization of other languages, artificial or natural, specif. in linguistic theory as a method of defining explicitly the **grammatical** properties of individual languages. **2** Applied to various literary movements concerned with the study of literature as formally autonomous works, rather than, say, literary history, e.g., New criticism.

formative 1 A **bound** form which is part of a **word**, e.g., complex Latin verb endings such as *-abat*, *-abit* or minimal forms such as the English **plural** ending *-s*. **2** More generally, a grammatical element not further reducible to other elements, i.e., a **morpheme**.

fortis Sometimes applied to a speech-sound that is said to be pronounced with greater muscular effort and/or tension, e.g. [i] in *seat* or [t^h] in *tar* respectively, as compared with [ɪ] in *sit* and [t] in *star*; the latter are said to be pronounced with less muscular effort and/or tension and are termed **lenis** sounds.

fricative Of a **consonant**, produced with audible friction, e.g., [f], [v], [θ], etc.

friction In the definition of **consonants**, the sound of air passing through a constriction in the vocal tract.

front of tongue That part of the tongue which, when at rest, lies under the palate.

front vowel A vowel articulated toward the front of the vowel area, in which the **tip** or **blade** is raised in the direction of the **alveolar ridge** or the palate, e.g. [i], [ɛ] as in *see* and *head* respectively.

function How a constituent works, its relationship with the other constituents in a larger unit, as a noun or noun phrase in relation to a sentence can work or function as subject, object, complement, modifier, etc., freq. seen in contradistinction to form **1**. **2** A mathematical expression connecting a number of **arguments** in a particular relationship and dependent on the individual values of the arguments for its own value, e.g., $a+b$ is a function whose value is dependent on the values of a and b. **3** The role played by language in the social situation, how it is used to express attitudes, communicate feelings, etc. See also **register**, **variety**. **4** In the analysis of **narrative**, specif. in plot analysis, the sort of action performed by a type of charater, e.g., 'here rescues innocent victim.'

future (tense) see **tense**

geminate verb In Semitic languages, a **verb** with a triliteral **root** in which the second and third **consonants** are the same, e.g. *SBB* 'to encircle'.

gemination The analysis of a sequence of identical segments as the repetition of the segment rather than as an example of length because of the occurrence of a **syllable** division, e.g., Italian *notte* /nɔtte/ rather than */nɔt:e/.

gender A grammatical category in which **nouns** are classified as belonging to a number of subclasses based on properties related to some extent to natural properties: the trad. genders are **masculine**, **feminine**, and **neuter**, others are also required (based, e.g., on shape, edibility, animacy, in, e.g., the Bantu languages). Gender **concord** may be required between noun and adjective, etc. and in the selection of pronouns. Note the distinction between natural gender where the sex of the referent is taken into account and grammatical gender where the classification is arbitrary. *Elle est belle, le nouveau professeur* illustrates both sorts.

genetic classification The classification of **languages** according to their historic relatedness, illustrated by a family-tree of related languages.

genitive In **inflecting** and **agglutinating languages**, the **case** expressing possession or origin and related concepts, e.g., *the dog's bone, a night's fishing.*

genizah Hebrew term for a storeroom, usually attached to a synagogue, where damaged or heretical manuscripts are stored.

glossolalia 'Speaking in tongues', the production of pseudo-linguistic utterance in certain religious sects.

glottal Of a **consonant**, made in the larynx by narrowing or closure of the **glottis**.

glottalic Applied to an airstream in the mouth and pharynx which is generated by a rapid upward or downward movement of the closed **glottis**.

glottis The aperture between the vocal cords.

government In **inflecting** and **agglutinating languages**, the morphological control imposed by a word (class) on another, e.g., in Latin, **prepositions govern** or determine the case of the following **noun**: *ad Romam* but *ab Roma*.

grammar 1 The study of **language** and the rules that govern its usage. **2** A description of the forms of **words** and the manner in which they combine to form **phrases**, **clauses** or **sentences**, = **morphology** + **syntax**. **3** A systematic and explicit account of the structure of (a) language according to the tenets of one or other of the theories of modern linguistics.

grammatical meaning The aspect of meaning conveyed in the grammatical parts of linguistic structures, e.g., in the form *-ing* (**verbal** + **nominal** or + **participial**), *-ed* (**past tense**), *-s* (**plural**), etc.

graph The smallest discrete segment of written or printed material, e.g., *g*, *G*, etc.

group see **foot**

habitual Describes a form or **aspect** expressing repetition, e.g., *He comes frequently*, *He leaves at six*.

Hamitic A term (deriving from Ham, one of the sons of Noah) formerly applied to some non-Semitic members of the **Afroasiatic** family.

Hamitosemitic, **Hamito-Semitic** Another name for **Afroasiatic**, also **Semito-Hamitic**.

Hebraism A locution in a language other than Hebrew, modeled on a Hebrew **construction** or **idiom**, e.g. *All flesh shall see it together.*

hieroglyphic Describes a pictorial writing system used esp. in ancient Egypt.

hiragana, katakana The Japanese **syllabic** writing systems, collectively known as **kana.**

hollow verb A Hebrew **verb** whose **root** contains two **consonants** separated by a Yod (= *y*) or Waw (= *w*), e.g. *SYM* 'to put', *MWT* 'to die'.

homographs Words which have the same spelling but different pronunciation or meaning, e.g., *row* (a boat)/*row* (quarrel) or *tear* (rend)/*tear* (as in tear-drop).

homonymy The circumstances of two lexical items which have the same spelling and pronunciation but differ in meaning, e.g., *bear* (the animal/carry).

homophones Words with the same pronunciation but differing in meaning, e.g., *rough/ruff.*

hypotaxis A variety of **subordination,** specif. of clauses, where a dependent **construction** is connected to the main **clause** by a subordinating **conjunction**, e.g., *I will go home when the bus comes.* (Contrasts with **parataxis**.)

ideogram, ideograph A symbol in a writing system representing a **word** or concept.

idiom A phrase or other sequence of **words** which has a meaning beyond or other than the sum of the meanings of the individual words, e.g., *throw over the traces* (= free oneself of restrictions); *fly off the handle* (= become angry), and which do not participate in the usual possible range of variations, e.g., *He threw over the traces* but **He threw over the trace.*

illocutionary act, speech act In the theory of speech acts, an act performed in saying something, i.e., making a promise, asking a question, giving a name; the **illocutionary force** of an utterance is its status as a promise, inquiry, etc. Cf. **locutionary act, perlocutionary act.**

imperative 1 The inflectional **mood** which expresses the will to control or influence, e.g., in Latin *ama*, the command 'love!' Cf. **indicative, subjunctive**, etc. **2** The **sentence** type or **verb** form typically used in commands, exhortations, entreaties, etc.

imperfect A form of the **verb** in some languages expressing past time usually with some **aspectual** element of duration or continuity. Cf. **perfect, aorist**.

imperfective An **aspect** of the **verb** indicating non-completion or continuation of an action. (Contrasts with **perfective**.)

implosive Describes a (usu. voiced) **consonant** made on a glottalic airstream by lowering of the closed **glottis** which creates an ingressive airstream, e.g., /ɓ/, /ɗ/, etc. Cf. **ejective**.

inceptive A type of **aspect** where the beginning of an action is marked grammatically, indicated in English by e.g., *be on the point of.*

indefinite article see **article**

indicative The inflectional **mood** expressing factivity and simple assertion used in the **verb** forms of statements and questions (declarative and **interrogative** sentence types), e.g., in Latin *amat* (he is loving). Cf. **imperative, subjunctive,** etc.

indirect object The recipient or beneficiary of the action of the **verb**, usu. so termed when no preposition is present, as *I gave/got my daughter a cat*, the equivalent of or equated with *to/for my daughter* in *I gave/got a cat to/for my daughter* (= **dative** function in **inflecting** and **agglutinating languages** and sometimes trad. so termed in English).

infinitive The nonfinite form of the **verb** regarded as the unmarked or base form and used to cite a particular verb, e.g., the verb *go* (= the bare or **zero infinitive**) or, in English, with the particle *to*, the verb *to go* (= the *to*-**infinitive**).

infix *gram* An **affix** inserted within a root or stem, e.g., in Tagalog *sumulat* (wrote) < *sulat* (write).

inflecting language A language in which **words** cannot be readily separated into **morphs**, the **inflections** indicating **grammatical** changes being to some extent fused with the **stem**.

inflection, **inflexion** A change made in the form of a **word** (chiefly by the addition of a **suffix** or **prefix**) to indicate variations in the grammatical relations between words in a **sentence** without changing the class to which they belong, e.g., in the **declension** of **nouns** and **conjugation** of **verbs**.

ingressive A sound made on an inward-moving or **ingressive airstream**, e.g., an **implosive**. (Contrasts with egressive.)

inherent vowel In Northern Indian **alphabets**, the **vowel** traditionally employed in pronouncing the names of **consonant** letters.

instrumental The **case** taken by a noun phrase expressing 'by means of.'

International Phonetic Alphabet (IPA) The symbol system devised by the **International Phonetic**

Association to allow the accurate transcription of any spoken language.

interrogative The **sentence** type or **verb** form typically used in asking a question e.g., *Is John coming*?

intonation The systematic rise and/or fall in the pitch of the voice in speaking.

intransitive verb A **verb** which combines with only one nominal, e.g., ***Betsy*** *sneezed.*

isolating language A type of language in which the **words** are invariable, **syntactic** relationships being organized chiefly through word order, e.g., Vietnamese. (Contrasts with **agglutinating language, inflecting language**.)

iterative A type of **aspect** which expresses the repeated occurrence of an action on a single occasion, e.g., *He kept on bouncing the ball, The ball kept bouncing*.

Japhetic Formerly applied to the Indo-European languages (from Japheth, one of the sons of Noah).

kana see **hiragana**

katakana see **hiragana**

koiné 1 Spoken or written Greek of the eastern Mediterranean in the Hellenistic and Roman periods. **2** The **dialect** or **language** of a locality which has become the standard language of a larger area.

labialized Produced with a **secondary articulation** of an approximation of the lips; it need not necessarily mean that the lips are **rounded**, though the term is often so used.

labial-palatal Applied to a speech-sound produced with closure or the same degree of narrowing both of the lips and between the **front** of the tongue and the palate, e.g. [ɥ] in French *lui* [lɥi].

labial-velar Applied to a speech-sounds produced with closure or the same degree of narrowing both of the lips and between the **back** of the tongue and the **velum**, e.g., [w] as in English *we* [wi].

labiodental Articulated with closure or some degree of narrowing between the upper teeth and the lower lip, e.g. [f], [v].

laminal Articulated with the **blade** of the tongue against e.g. the upper teeth or the **alveolar ridge**; often contrasted with **apical**.

language 1 also **natural language** The principal signaling-system or instrument of communication used by humans for the transmission of information, ideas, etc., the central element of which is verbal but which contains as an essential component a substantial non-verbal element, e.g., intonation, stress, punctuation, etc. Communication by means of language is carried out in a number of **media** (see **medium 1**), viz., speech (regarded by modern linguists as primary), writing and traditionally less centrally, signing (sign language). Human language may be distinguished from the signaling systems of other species chiefly by its grammatical and semantic complexity and flexibility and by its descriptive and creative function but whether this is a difference of degree or kind is open to argument. **2** A variety of speech, writing, etc. used in particular circumstances, e.g., the language of literature, the courts, the streets, science, etc. **3** Non-verbal or artificially constructed communicative symbol systems, e.g., the language of bees, mathematics, computers. **4** An instance of **1** above, the verbal means of communication of a particular community; definable in linguistic or (in part) political terms, i.e., a language is the dialect of a nation, usu. (but not always) different enough from other languages to preclude mutual comprehensibility, e.g., English, Latin, Chinese. **5** The characters, conventions and rules used to convey information, e.g., in a programming language like BASIC or a machine language.

laryngeal Of a speech sound, produced in the **larynx**.

larynx The upper part of the **trachea**, containing the vocal folds.

lateral A **consonant** produced with central closure between the **tip** or **blade** of the tongue and the teeth or **alveolar ridge**, but with one side or both sides of the tongue lowered, leaving a passage clear for an **ingressive** or an **egressive** airstream.

lateral approximant A **lateral** in which the side of the tongue is in **open approximation** with the roof of the mouth, so that no **friction** is heard, e.g. [l].

lateral fricative A **lateral** in which the side of the tongue is in **close approximation** with the roof of the mouth, so that **friction** is heard, e.g. [ɬ] in Welsh *llan* [ɬan].

lateral release Applied to the release of a plosive not centrally but laterally, i.e. by lowering one side of the tongue, as [t^{L}] in *battle* when pronounced [ˈbat^{L}l̩].

lenis see **fortis**

lexeme The minimal distinctive unit in the semantics of a language, a **word** in the sense of a unit of meaning incorporating all the grammatical variations or forms in which it is liable to occur, e.g., the **verb** *sing* (incorporating *sings*, *singing* the present participle, *sang*, *sung* but not *song*, *singer* or *singing* the verbal noun); *good* (including *better*, *best*).

lexical item An item of vocabulary, commonly used as an equivalent of **lexeme**.

lexicography The process of editing a dictionary; the principles and practice of dictionary making.

lexicology The study of the meanings and applications of words.

lexicon The vocabulary or word-stock of a language, a listing of this, as in a dictionary.

lexis The vocabulary of a language.

lingua franca A language used as a means of communication between speakers who have no native language in common, e.g., English and French in Africa, Hausa in West Africa.

linguistics The study of language according to scientific principles.

linguolabial Produced with the **tip** or **blade** of the tongue against the upper lip.

lip-rounded see **rounded**

lip-spread see **unrounded**

loan translation, **calque** A compound or phrase borrowed into a language by translation of its constituent parts item by item, e.g., German *Fernsprecher* < *telephone*.

loan (word), **borrowing** A word etc. taken from one language and assimilated into another, e.g., English *formidable* < French.

locative In **inflecting** and **agglutinating languages**, the **case** expressing place.

locutionary act In the theory of speech acts the production of a meaningful utterance by the physical act of uttering words. Cf. **illocutionary** and **perlocutionary acts**.

lowered A sound produced with a greater degree of opening than the symbol used to notate it would indicate.

majuscule A style of writing consisting of capital letters; a capital letter.

mantra *see attached list*

masculine see **gender**

maxims of conversation, conversational maxims In the theory of speech acts, principles regulating communication, specif, quantity, quality, relation and manner, i.e., that a speaker's contribution to a conversation should be (a) as informative as is required but not more so; (b) truthful; (c) relevant; (d) perspicacious, avoiding obscurity, ambiguity, prolixity and muddle.

medium 1 The means used in a communication, i.e., whether it is spoken, written, symbolic, color coded, etc., e.g., phonic, aural, visual medium. **2** A channel of communication, as in mass media.

minuscule 1 A style of writing, e.g., Carolingian minuscule, consisting of small letters. **2** A small or lower-case letter.

modernism A literary movement which rejected the traditional view of language and story telling, emphasizing instead the nature of language itself as a part of the literary creation, e.g., in the conscious use of unconventional syntax, ambiguity, etc.

modification The limiting of a linguistic element by another dependent linguistic element (the **modifier**), restricted to the use of **adjectives** and **adverbs**, or extended to any dependent structure, e.g., in *the small house on the prairie*, *house* is **modified** by *small*, also, in some approaches, by *on the prairie*.

modifier A limiting dependent structure, see **modification**.

monolingual Having only one language.

mood The category whereby the attitude of the speaker towards what is said (uncertainty, etc.) is expressed by **verbal inflections** or the use of **modal (auxiliary) verb** forms, e.g., *would*, *should*, *ought*, etc. See **indicative**, **imperative**, **subjunctive**, etc.

morph The substantial exponent of a **morpheme**, e.g., in *kicked* two morphs represent the morphemes 'kick' and past tense 'ed', in *went* one morph represents 'go' and past tense.

morpheme The minimal unit of grammatical analysis one or more of which make up a **word** (sense **1**), e.g., *cat* is one morpheme, *cats* (*cat* + *s*), *catkin* (*cat* + *kin*) two.

morphology The study of the **grammatical** structure of **words**.

nasal release Applied to the release of a **plosive** not centrally through the mouth but through the nasal cavity by a lowering of the **velum**, as [pᴺ] in *open* when pronounced [ˈopᴺm̩]

nasal Of a sound, produced with **nasality**, i.e., passage of the airstream through the nasal **cavity** and closure of the oral cavity, e.g., [m], [n], [ŋ].

nasalization An alteration in the quality of a sound caused by part of the airstream passing through the nasal cavity, due to a lowering of the **velum**, during its production.

negation The process of denial or contradiction of or dissent from something asserted, in English freq. by means of the **negative particle** *not*.

negative Describes a word (**adjective**, **pronoun**, **adverb**), **particle**, **sentence**, etc. which exhibits **negation**, e.g., *no*, *nobody*, *nothing*, *nowhere*, *not at all*, *I never went there*, etc.

neologism A recently devised word or usage.

neuter see **gender**

Nicene Applied to the statement of Christian **Trinitarian** beliefs issued by the Council of Nicaea in 325 to combat the **Arian** doctrine, which it condemned.

nominative also **subjective** In **inflecting** and **agglutinating languages**, the **case** of the **subject** of a **verb**.

nonfinite A form of the **verb** capable of functioning only in dependent **clauses**. In English, the **infinitive**, past and present **participles**, e.g., ***To go*** *to school John passed the park*, ***Going*** *to school John...*, ***Gone*** *to school by eight John went through the park*.

noun A member of the word class trad. defined as 'naming a person, place or thing', or, in modern linguistics, with reference to its distribution (preceding the **predicate**, etc.), function (as **subject**, **object**, etc. of a **verb**) and the **morphological** properties it displays (inflecting for **case**, **number**, etc.).

number A grammatical category dealing with the analysis of word forms in so far as they express **singularity**, **plurality** or **duality**.

object 1 also **direct object** The **noun** (**phrase**) following and dependent on a finite **transitive verb**, in simple declarative **sentences** freq. identified with the patient or goal, e.g., *The cat chased the mouse*. In **inflecting** and **agglutinating languages** freq. identified by the **accusative** case. Cf. **indirect object**. **2** The noun (phrase) governed by or following a **preposition**, e.g., *between* ***us***, *down* ***the street***.

oblique In **inflecting** and **agglutinating languages**, applied to any **case** except the **nominative.**

open approximation A degree of narrowing between two **articulators** which imparts a quality to the speech-sound produced, but without **friction.**

open Of a syllable, ending in a vowel. (Contrasts with **closed**.)

open vowel A **vowel** produced with the greatest degree of opening between the highest point of the tongue and the roof of the mouth, e.g. [a], [ɑ] as in *hat* and *hard*; contrasts with **close**, **close-mid**, and **open-mid**.

open-mid vowel A vowel in which the degree of opening between the highest point of the tongue and the roof of the mouth is not as great as in an **open** vowel, but greater than in a **close-mid** or a **close** vowel, e.g. [ɛ], [ɔ] as in *help* and *awed*.

oral tradition The expression of a culture maintained in spoken form and transmitted by word of mouth, e.g., in songs and folktales.

orthography The spelling system of a language or dialect.

palatal Of a speech sound, produced with the front of the tongue in contact with or approaching the hard palate, e.g., [ç], [ɲ] as in German *ich* and French *vigne* respectively.

palimpsest Parchment or other writing material which has been used a second time after the erasure of previous writing.

paradigm An example of pattern illustrating the **inflectional** forms of a part of speech, usu. set out in a table.

parataxis The linking of clauses by juxtaposition, e.g., *Go home. It's already dark*. (Contrasts with **hypotaxis**.)

participle A form of the verb which participates in some characteristics of **verb** and **adjective**, e.g., in *He was running* and *He was cheated, running* and *cheated* are respectively present and past participles, or *ing-* and *ed-* **forms**.

particle An **invariable** word with a grammatical function and difficult to classify in terms of parts of speech, includes, e.g., the **negative particle** (see **negation**), *not*, *to* in the **infinitive** form *to go*, the adverbial component in phrasal **verbs**, e.g., *away* in *Go away*, etc.

passive In the analysis of **voice** (sense **2**), a **sentence** or **clause** in which the **subject** is the **patient** or **recipient** in relation to the action, e.g., *The car was driven by Mary*; the **verb** form in such a sentence or clause.

past (tense) see **tense**

perfect, present perfect A form of the **verb**, sometimes regarded as a **tense**, sometimes as **tense + aspect**, which expresses some variety of past time, in English, the verb form conjugated with *have*, e.g., *He has written*, and regarded as pastness having some relevance to the present, contrasting, e.g., with *He wrote*. Cf. **pluperfect**, **imperfect**, **aorist**.

perfective An **aspect** of the **verb** indicating completion of an action. (Contrasts with **imperfective**.)

perlocutionary act In the theory of speech acts, an effect caused by the way something is said, i.e., by using language to persuade, comfort, move to anger. Cf. **illocutionary act**, **locutionary act**.

person A grammatical category used to identify the participants in a situation: **first person**, **second person**, **third person** referring respectively to the speaker (and associates) (*I*, *we*); hearer(s) (*you*); persons and things other than the speaker and hearer (*it*, *they*, *someone*, etc.).

personal pronoun The **pronoun** referring to **person**, *I*, *me*, *you*, *she*, etc.

pharyngeal 1 Refers to the cavity of the pharynx. **2** Of a **consonant**, produced by a close approximation of the root of the tongue with the wall of the pharynx, e.g., [ħ], [ʕ].

pharyngealized Produced with a **secondary articulation** of narrowing between the **root** of the tongue and the pharynx.

philology The historical or comparative study of language or languages.

phonation The particular activity of the **glottis** in the production of **voiced**, **breathy voiced**, and **creaky voiced** sounds.

phoneme In the theory of **phonemics**, the smallest contrastive unit in the sound system of a **language**.

phonemics An approach to the analysis of the sound system of a **language** based on grouping the sounds or phones of the language into meaningful contrastive units, or **phonemes**, each of which indicates a difference in meaning between words, e.g., /t/, /d/, /s/ differentiate between *tip*, *dip* and *sip*

phonetic Of or pertaining to **phonetics**.

phonetics The study of sounds, esp. the nature and variety of sounds used in speech, particularly in terms of their manner of production (**articulatory phonetics**), acoustic properties (**acoustic phonetics**), and how they are perceived by the hearer (**auditory phonetics**).

phonology The study of the **sound systems** or systems of meaningful distinctions of languages.

phrase Two or more words in a syntactic relationship that function like a **word** (as opposed to a **clause** or **sentence**), specif. **noun phrase**, e.g., *She wore **the red hat***, **verb phrase**, e.g., *They **have gone swimming***, **adjectival phrase**, **e.g.**, *The tramp, **wet and rejected** turned away*, **adverb(ial) phrase**, e.g., *They cooperated **very happily***, **prepositional phrase**, e.g., ***I** saw you **on television***.

pleonasm A type of **redundancy**, the use of more words than are necessary to express a meaning, e.g., *at this moment in time*.

plosive A type of **stop**, a complete closure and sudden release of a pulmonic airstream in an outward movement or **plosion**. Cf. **implosive**.

pluperfect The **perfect** located in past time, i.e., a form of the verb expressing completion of an action in the past, e.g., *He had written*.

plural(ity) A contrast of **number** referring to two or more than two, e.g., *six cats*.

poetic language The sort of language used in poetry, characterized esp. by creativity and, in comparison with other sorts of language, a high degree of deviant or irregular usage, richness of connotation, etc.

pointing (of script) A system of **accents (5)** or diacritics inserted into the **consonantal** text of Hebrew and other Semitic languages to indicate the pronunciation of **vowels**, punctuation, and musical notation. Cf. **vocalization**.

polysemy The circumstance in which a lexical item has more than one meaning, e.g., *rough* (coarse/preliminary drawing). Cf. **homonymy**.

positive The unmarked **degree** of **adjectives** or **adverbs**, implying no level of comparison, i.e., *hot* as opposed to *hotter* and *hottest*.

postalveolar Articulated with the **tip** or **blade** of the tongue just behind the **alveolar ridge**.

postposition A **particle** in, e.g., Japanese, Turkish, etc. which fulfils the functions of a **preposition** in English but comes after the **noun** it modifies, e.g., Japanese *Tokyo e* (to Tokyo).

predicate In the analysis of the sentence, the second part of a two-part analysis: **subject** + **predicate**, specif. the verb + object + adjuncts (some approaches, however, would exclude the adjuncts from the predicate), e.g., in *Susanna fell*, *fell* is the predicate, similarly *ran away*, *ate an apple*, *lay on the grass in the park* might fill that slot.

prefix An **affix** attached to a **root** or **stem** in initial position, e.g., *re-* in *return*; in some languages **inflections** may be **prefixed**, e.g., in ʒe- in Old English or *ge-* in German.

preposition A **particle** which has a grammatical or local function, acting usu. in combination with a following **noun phrase**, e.g., ***in*** *the house*, ***beyond*** *reason*, ***from*** *Venice*, etc.

prepositional pronoun, pronominal preposition A word class in Arabic, Hebrew and Celtic languages containing single words meaning, e.g., 'to me,' 'to you,' 'with you,' etc.

present tense The unmarked **tense** of the **verb**, referring to things as they are at the present moment (now), e.g., *He takes his first extraterrestrial step*, sometimes inclusive of past time, (up to and including now), e.g., *He takes a packed lunch*, and sometimes, also, future time, e.g., *The dodo is extinct*.

primary articulation Applied to the greater degree of narrowing in those cases where a **consonant** is produced with two significant degrees of narrowing, both contributing to the quality of the sound.

progressive assimilation An **assimilation** where a preceding sound causes an alteration in a following sound e.g., in Dutch *opvouwen*, pronounced/ɔpfɔuən/, /v/ > /f/.

progressive, **continuous** An **aspect** of the **verb** (trad. treated as a **tense**), expressing duration or frequency of repetition over time, e.g., *I was traveling to Glasgow for three hours* or *every day*.

pronoun A word that can substitute for a **noun** or **noun phrase** (or **clause**) or words of similar type, e.g., *it* and *what* in *What fell? It did, that clock on the shelf* or *he* in *John left work, he went home*.

proto-language The ancestor language of a family of languages, e.g., 'Proto-Indo-European'.

pulmonic Applied to an airstream, either ingressive or egressive, produced by the lungs.

punctuation A system of standardized marks or **punctuation marks**, used to structure or clarify written text.

rebus principle In pictorial writing systems, the use of the picture of an object which sounds the same as the entity intended, e.g., a picture of a robin = robbing.

reduplication 1 The repetition in a **prefix** or **suffix** of a sound found in the **root**, e.g., in Greek reduplication occurs in perfective forms such as /léluka/(λέλυκα) 'I have loosed' from /lúo:/ (λύω) 'I loose'. **2** The repetition that occurs in reduplicative compounds, e.g., *shilly-shally*.

reference The relationship that obtains between a linguistic expression and what it stands for or **denotes** on any particular occasion of utterance, e.g., *the cat* may mean the cat I own / have just been talking about, etc.

referential meaning The sort of meaning that identifies or **refers** to an entity in the real world (its **referent**), e.g., in *I spoke to the sergeant* whoever is sergeant is intended.

reflexive Describes a **construction** where subject and object refer to the same entity, explicitly with the **reflexive pronoun**, e.g., *John killed himself* or implicitly, e.g., *John never shaves*.

regressive assimilation An **assimilation** where an alteration occurs in a sound because of the influence of a following sound, e.g., in *Edinburgh*, [n] → [m]: [ɛdımbrə].

relative clause A **clause** functioning as a **modifier** within a **noun phrase**, introduced in some languages by a **relative pronoun**, e.g., *the woman* ***that wore the red hat***.

retracted Applied to a sound pronounced further back than the symbol used to notate it would indicate.

retroflex Describes a **consonant** made with the tongue tip curling back to approach or strike the back of the alveolar ridge as in [ʈ], [ɳ], [ʂ], etc.

rhetoric 1 The art of public speaking as a means of persuasion elaborated by stylistic techniques, esp. figures of speech, etc. **2** Applied to technical aspects of discourse or text such as **maxims of conversation**, the techniques of telling a story, etc.

rhoticity 'R-colouring', caused by the **tip** of the tongue being curled back or **retroflected**.

root also **base** The element in a **word** that cannot be further analyzed while still expressing some essential element of the meaning of the word; the core of a word to which affixes are added, e.g., *feel*, *boy*, *-cipe* (in *recipe*). Cf. **stem**.

root of tongue That part of the tongue which, when at rest, faces the back wall of the naso-pharynx or, less technically, the back of the throat.

rounded, **lip-rounded** Applied to a speech-sound produced with a **secondary articulation** of rounding of the lips.

sandhi Phonological alternation in particular environments, specif. **external sandhi** functioning across word boundaries, e.g., English *a*/*an* in *a man* and *an ostrich*, French *pot de terre* [po:dətɛʀ] / *pot au feu* [pɔto:fø]; and **internal sandhi** functioning within words, e.g., *prescribe* as against *prescription*.

script The letter forms of writing systems or styles, e.g., the Roman or hieroglyphic alphabets; uncial, copperplate, etc.

secondary articulation Applied to the lesser degree of narrowing in those cases where a **consonant** is produced with two significant degrees of narrowing, both contributing to the quality of the sound.

semantics The study of meaning as between linguistic expressions and what these expressions describe; the study of the relation between **sentences** and the thoughts they express.

sentence The largest unit of structure in the organization of the grammar of a language, regarded, along with the **word** as one of the two fundamental units of grammatical description. The sentence is classified formally as declarative, exclamative, interrogative, imperative types (corresponding to the functional classifications statement, exclamation, question and command).

sequence 1 A linear succession of interdependent linguistic units, e.g., **phonemes** in /l e t/ (*late*), or words in *the* + *black* + *cat*. **2** Dependency among linguistic units 'following on' from one to another as in the **sequence of tenses** required between successive clauses, e.g., *If I had gone, I would have seen you* / *If I go, I will see you* /* *If I had gone, I will see you*; or the **sequencing** of a question and answer in discourse.

sequence of tenses see **sequence 2**.

sibilant A consonant sound, a **fricative** produced with a narrow groove-like stricture between the blade of the tongue and the alveolar ridge, e.g., [s], [ʃ].

sigmatic Applied to Greek **verbs** or verbal forms that are characterized by the addition of a sigma (= ⟨s⟩), e.g. *lusō* 'I shall loose'.

singular(ity) A contrast of **number** referring to 'one,' e.g., *one*/*a cat*. (Contrasts with **plural(ity)** **(dual(ity)**.)

sociolinguistics, sociology of language The study of how language functions in societies or speech communities, with reference, e.g., to language **varieties**, the linguistic identity of social or racial groups, multilingualism, etc.

speech act = **illocutionary act**

speech act theory An analysis of utterances which recognizes their function in doing something, i.e., that frequently utterances are not statements of truth or falsity, but actions, e.g., *I apologize, I object,* etc. The analysis includes the concepts of constatives, performatives, **illocutionary** acts, **perlocutionary** acts, **locutionary** acts.

spread see **unrounded**

stanza A division of a poem, groups of lines organized in a repeating pattern, typically, four or eight lines.

status absolutus*, absolute state** In Hebrew, Arabic and other Semitic languages, the form of a **noun** not followed by a **genitive**, e.g. Hebrew *bayith* 'house'. Cf. ***status constructus.

status constructus, construct state In Hebrew, Arabic and other Semitic languages, the form of a **noun**

followed by a **genitive**, e.g. Hebrew *bēth hammelekh* 'the king's house'. Cf. ***status absolutus***.

stem The part of a word to which inflections are attached, e.g., *feel/feeling, boy/boyish/boyishly*. Cf. **root**.

stop A **consonant** produced with complete closure of the vocal tract at the place of articulation, e.g., [p], [d].

stress The perceived prominence of a **syllable** relative to those around it due to its greater loudness or increased length or pitch, such a syllable is said to be **stressed**, e.g., *remárkable*. (Constrasts with **unstressed**.)

strong verb A **verb** in which the past tense and past participle are formed by changing the **stem vowel**, e.g., *sing, sang, sung*. (Contrasts with **weak verb** where tense variation is achieved by suffixing, e.g., *knit, knitted.*)

subject A major element of structure which with the **predicate** forms a typical **sentence** or **clause**, e.g., *The cat ate a beetle*, *The beetle was eaten by the cat*. In the latter example *the cat* is sometimes called the **logical** or **underlying subject**.

subjunctive The inflectional **mood** expressing **non-factivity** and possibility, e.g., in Latin *amet* 'let him love'; in English *If I **were** in charge, I would do something about this.*

subordination A type of syntactic linking in which one linguistic unit, the **subordinate** one, is dependent on another, e.g., *He said **that he was ill*** or ***If you don't stop** you will be ill.*

substantive A noun or noun-like item, e.g., *goldfish, the young*; also, sometimes applied to pronouns.

suffix An **affix** added to the end of a **word** or **stem**, e.g., *print**able**, crazi**ly***.

suprasegmental Applied to a feature, such as **intonation**, which characterizes stretches of speech greater than one speech-sound.

surface structure 1 In **transformational grammar**, the stage in the derivation of a **sentence** that comes after the application of **transformational rules** and pro-vides the input for the phonological component. **2** also **surface grammar** More generally, the form an utterance or sentence takes as spoken or as it appears on the page, freq. in relation to the ambiguities evident in such material, e.g., the surface structures of *Germs are too small to see without a microscope* and *They are too much involved in the affair to see without help* are similar (though their **deep-structures** are not).

syllabary A system of writing in which the symbols represent **syllables**.

syllabic Of the nature of a **syllable**.

syllable A minimal unit of sound in the phonological structure of the word; the syllable consists of a **nucleus** and (optionally) two **margins**, the **onset** coming before the nucleus and the **coda** after.

syntax 1 The rules governing how words combine to form sentences. (Contrasts with **morphology). 2** More generally, (the study of) the grammatical relationships entered into by linguistic units at any level, including **morpheme** and **sentence**.

tagmemics An American structuralist model of linguistic description which proposes the **phoneme, morpheme** and **tagmeme** as the basic units, respectively, of phonology, lexicon and grammar, the **tagmeme** being used as a cover term for all grammatical units, which are distinguished in the analysis by differences in **slots** and the **fillers** which can fit into them, e.g., a noun/pronoun or subject in — *wore a hat* (e.g., *She*, *Joan*, *The old man)* or a clause/phrase in *the boy — was caught* (e.g., *who skipped school, running away*).

tap A **consonant** produced by a single rapid contact of the tongue tip with the roof of the mouth, resembling a very short plosive.

target language A **language** or **variety** which is the focus of some linguistic operation, e.g., in teaching or translation, the language being taught or into which material is translated.

tense The category of the **verb** that places the action or state referred to in time, past, present or future in relation to the utterance, e.g., in Latin *scripsi*, *scribo*, *scribam* (I wrote, I am writing, I shall write). In English there are only two grammatical tenses, past and present, e.g., *I wrote*, *I write*; the many other trad. 'tenses', e.g., future, perfect, pluperfect, etc. are formed from combinations of **tense** and **aspect**.

text linguistics The study of aspects of linguistics evident in **texts** (rather than **clauses**, **sentences**, etc,).

text 1 A stretch of writing or utterance, large or small, which by reason of its structure, subject matter, etc. forms a unity, e.g., a story, poem, recipe, road sign, etc. **2** Primarily seen as written material, freq. synonymous with *book*, e.g., '*As You Like It* is a **set text** in second year'.

thesaurus A compilation of **words** arranged according to their meanings, under such headings as, e.g., *recreation*, *plants*, etc.

tip of tongue That part of the tongue which, when at rest, lies under the upper teeth.

tone language A language, e.g., many SE Asian, African and American languages, which uses **tone**, i.e., different levels of pitch or rising or falling pitch in various combinations, to distinguish lexical and/or grammatical meaning.

tone The pitch level of a syllable, specif. in **tone languages, lexical tone** is a means of distinguishing the meanings of words, e.g., in Thai *maa* with a high tone means 'horse', with a rising tone 'dog'.

transformation transformational rule, transform In transformational grammar, one of a number of processes that act on the phrase-structure input (**deep structure)** of the grammar to reorder it in such a way as to produce the **surface structure** output, thereby expressing the perceived linkage between, e.g., active and passive, declarative and interrogative, etc.

transformational grammar In generative grammar, a grammar which includes a **transformational component** in which, by means of **transformations,** elements of structure are reorganized, the **deep structure** of sentences thereby being linked to the **surface structure**; by this process structural relationships are confirmed, e.g., *I love Lucy* is shown to be closely related to *Lucy is loved by me*, and structural ambiguities are resolved, e.g., *Flying planes can be dangerous* is shown to be derivable from either *planes which fly or people who fly planes*.

transitive verb A **verb** which combines with two nominals, e.g., ***James*** *killed* ***Adam***.

transliteration Replacing in a text the characters of one writing system by characters of another with equivalent **phonetic** values.

triliteral Applied to a common type of Semitic **root** that contains three **consonants**, as in Arabic *salām*, *islām*, *muslim*.

trill, roll Describes a consonant made by the rapid tapping of one articulator against another or the vibration of the articulator (excluding that of the vocal folds), e.g., **trilled** or **rolled** *r* [r] or **uvular** *r* [ʀ].

Trinitarian Applied to the Christian doctrine of the Trinity, that is, three Persons in one God: God the Father, God the Son, and God the Holy Ghost; following the Council of Nicaea in 325, this doctrine became orthodoxy in the Roman Empire and the Roman Catholic Church. Cf. **Arian**.

typology, typological linguistics (The study of) the classification of languages according to structural similarities without reference to historical considerations, e.g., in terms of its **inflections** Latin is closer to Finnish than it is to English though historically English and Latin are related, Latin and Finnish are not.

unpointed Applied to texts written in Hebrew and other Semitic scripts in which there are no special signs denoting **vowels**. Cf. **pointing**.

unrounded, lip-spread, spread Articulated with spread, not rounded, lips.

unvoiced = **voiceless**

upstep A gradual rising of the pitch of the high-pitched **tones** throughout a stretch of speech.

Ursprache (German= 'original language') (1)=**proto-language;** (2) the source language in a translation.

uvular Describes a **consonant** made with the **back** of the tongue against the **uvula,** e.g., [q], [ɴ], [ʀ], etc.

variety A general term covering the concepts of **dialect** and **language**: the language of a group of people, or that used for a particular function, distinguished on any grounds and having the widest application, e.g., the language of NE Aberdeenshire, the law, the middle class, etc.

velar Describes a consonant produced by the back of the tongue with the **velum** or soft palate, e.g., [g], [x], [ŋ], etc.

velaric Applied to an airstream produced by making complete closures both (1) between the **back of the tongue** and the **velum** and (2) somewhere towards the front of the mouth (either between the lips or between (1) the tip, blade or front of the tongue and (2) the teeth or the alveolar ridge or the palate); the air thus trapped in the mouth is rarefied by a sucking action; the front closure is then released, resulting in an **ingressive** airstream which produces a

click. An **egressive velaric** airstream can also be produced by compressing the mouth.

velarized Applied to **consonants** produced with a **secondary articulation** of approximation between the **back of the tongue** and the **velum**.

velum The soft palate.

verb A member of the word class trad. defined as a 'doing' word, denoting an action or state, e.g., *Mary dances, Mary knows.* In many languages, the verb is formally identifiable in that it displays contrasts of **tense, aspect, voice** (sense **2**), **mood**, **number** and **person** and is in terms of function the most central element in a clause, able to occur on its own in the imperative, e.g., *Hurry*! and, as a minimal **predicate**, with a single **noun** as **subject**, e.g., *Jane ran.* It is the requirements of the verb that determine the nature of the rest of the predicate, e.g., *give* requires **direct** and **indirect objects**: *Give Mary a present*; *put* requires direct object and prepositional complement: *Put the keys in your pocket*; *break* requires no predicate: *The glass broke.*

vernacular The indigenous language or dialect of a speech community, e.g., *Black English vernacular* (BEV), the language of urban black Americans; *the vernacular of Tyneside, etc.*

vocabulary 1 The range of lexical items evidenced in a text or available to an individual speaker. **2** = **lexicon**

vocalization As applied to **script**, an indication of the pronunciation of **vowels** in Hebrew and other Semitic languages. Cf. **pointing**.

vocative 1 In **inflecting** and **agglutinating languages**, the **case** used when addressing a person or thing, e.g., Latin **Veni**, ***amice*** 'Come, my friend.' **2** Applied to a similar function in non-inflecting languages, e.g., *Come*, ***my friend***, indicated by intonation or punctuation.

voice 1 also **voicing** The sound made by the vibration of the **vocal cords**. **2** The category of the verb which expresses the relationship of the **subject** of the verb to the action expressed by the verb, i.e., in the **active** voice the subject is the **agent** of the action; in the **passive** voice the subject is **recipient** or **patient** in relation to the action.

voiced Describes a sound made while the **vocal cords** are vibrating, specif. voiced consonants, e.g., [b], [z], [m], [l], etc. and vowels. (Contrasts with **voiceless**.)

voiceless, **unvoiced** Describes the absence of **voice**; said of, e.g., voiceless consonants, [p], [s], etc. (Contrasts with **voiced**.)

vowel A speech sound produced without any constriction of the vocal tract sufficient to produce a closure or audible friction. **2** The **nucleus** of a syllable. **3** A symbol or group of symbols representing a vowel sound in a writing system, e.g., *seal*, *sell.*

waw **consecutive**, ***waw*** **conversive** A form of the Hebrew **conjunction** that has the effect of reversing the normal **aspectual** meaning of the **verb** to which it is **prefixed**, e.g. *wayyamot* 'and he died' as opposed to *wĕyamut* 'and let him die'.

weak declension In German and other Germanic languages, a pattern of **nominal** and **adjectival declension** characterized by ⟨n⟩ in **cases** other than the **nominative singular**, and exhibiting little variation according to **gender**, **number**, or **case**.

weak verb (in Germanic languages) *see* **strong verb**.

weak verb (in Hebrew) A **verb** whose **root** contains only two **consonants**, or two **consonants** and one that disappears in some forms, e.g. *natan* 'to give', *yittēn* 'he gives' (with initial *n* **assimilated**).

word 1 One of the two fundamental units of grammar, the other being **sentence**. The linguistic unit that combines to form phrases, clauses and sentences and is otherwise distinguished as the smallest possible sentence unit, e.g., *Hurry!* and by its cohesiveness and by the fixed order of its internal structure, e.g., *impossible* but **possibleim* or **possimible*, **2** The realization in terms of sound or writing of the elements of expression or meaning that make up a word in sense **1**, e.g., /drimd, drɛmt / are phonological realizations, and ⟨dreamed, dreamt⟩ orthographic realizations of the grammatical unit 'dreamed' which is defined as the past tense of the verb 'dream'; or, /rnʌ and ⟨run⟩ are the phonological/ orthographic realizations of the word 'run' in its use as a verb 'to go at a speed faster than a walk' or as a noun 'an act of running,' 'an assembly of migrating fish,' etc.

word-formation The process of forming new words from derivational sources, e.g., affixation, compounding, etc. as opposed to the process of adding inflections, which merely changes the form of the word within the **paradigm**, e.g., *annoyance* < *annoy* + *ance*, in comparison with *annoying*, *annoyed.*

SECTION IX

Transcriptional Conventions and the IPA Alphabet

The pronunciation of the examples of languages used in articles in this Encyclopedia has been notated in such a way as to be as helpful to the reader as possible. All pronunciations are indicated in roman script augmented by special characters. However, it is unrealistic to expect that it would be possible to employ one thoroughly consistent system of symbols to represent the sounds of the languages of the world. There are various reasons for this, chief among them being the fact that slightly different conventions are traditionally employed by scholars in different fields of specialization: it would have been impertinent (and indeed unscholarly) to insist on any deviation from the normal practice of experts. In some traditions there are alternative methods of indicating a given pronunciation: due weight has been given to the predilection of authors in such cases. Within any one article, of course, the system of indicating pronunciation is consistent. The following remarks explain the symbols used in the Encyclopedia.

In the first place it is necessary to distinguish between *transliteration* and *transcription*. Transliteration is the systematic transference of the characters of one writing system into the characters of another. On the other hand transcription is the systematic representation of speech-sounds without any reference to how they may be written conventionally; languages which have no conventional writing system(s)—and such languages are in the great majority—will of necessity be exemplified in transcription.

In articles which touch on spelling or writing systems, letters of the roman alphabet quoted as such are enclosed in angled brackets, thus ⟨a⟩, ⟨b⟩, ⟨c⟩, etc.

1. Transliteration

The conventions used in the transliteration of Arabic, Ancient Greek, Hebrew, and Sanskrit are shown in Tables 1, 2, 3, and 4 respectively. Two slightly different methods of transliterating Cyrillic characters are employed; these are shown in Table 5.

Modern Turkish is written in a roman alphabet which includes the symbols ⟨ı⟩, ⟨ç⟩, and ⟨ş⟩. Because these are not available on some keyboards, they are replaced in certain scholarly writings by ⟨ï⟩ or ⟨ɨ⟩, ⟨č⟩, and ⟨š⟩ respectively.

Table 1. Transliteration of Arabic

Vowels

Short: ـَـ	a	Long: ا or ى	ā	Doubled -iyy- (final form: ī)
ـُـ	u	و	ū	Diphthongs وَ aw (*not* au)
ـِـ	i	ى	ī	ىَ ay (*not* ai)

Consonants

ء	ʾ	ز	z	ق	q
ب	b	س	s	ك	k
ت	t	ش	s̲h̲	ل	l
ث	t̲h̲	ص	ṣ	م	m
ج	j	ض	ḍ	ن	n
ح	ḥ	ط	ṭ	ه	h
خ	k̲h̲	ظ	ẓ	و	w
د	d	ع	ʿ	ى	y
ذ	d̲h̲	غ	g̲h̲	ة	-a (in construct state: -at)
ر	r	ف	f		

Table 2. Transliteration of Ancient Greek

Vowels & Consonants

α	a	ν	n
β	b	ξ	ks
γ	g	ο	o
δ	d	π	p
ε	e	ρ	r
ζ	sd	σ, ς	s
η	ē	τ	t
θ	th	υ	u
ι	i	φ	ph
κ	k	χ	kh
λ	l	ψ	ps
μ	m	ω	ō
		ʽρ	h
			rh

Diphthongs

αι	ai	αυ	au
ει	ei	ευ	eu
οι	oi	ου	ou
υι	ui		
long ᾳ	āi		
long ῃ	ēi		
long ῳ	ōi		

The values of symbols used in transliteration are explained in Sect. 3 below.

Table 3. Transliteration of Hebrew

Consonants

א	ʼ	ל	l
בּ	b	מ	m
ב	bh	נ	n
גּ	g	ס	s
ג	gh (Mod. Heb. g)	ע	ʻ
דּ	d	פּ	p
ד	dh (Mod. Heb. d)	פ	ph
ה	h	צ	ṣ (Mod. Heb. tz)
ו	w (Mod. Heb. v)	ק	q
ז	z	ר	r
ח	ḥ	שׂ	ś
ט	ṭ	שׁ	sh
י	y	תּ	t
כּ	k	ת	th (Mod. Heb. t)
כ	kh		

Note. The vowel letters ה (in final position), ו and י are not represented: e.g., עֵין *ʻen* (not *ʻeyn*), תּוֹרָה *tōrā* (not tôrāh). Final diphthongs are represented thus: *ay*, *oy*, *aw*.

Vowels

ַ	a	ֻ	u
ָ	ā, o	וּ	ū
ֶ	e	ְ	ĕ
ֵ	ē	ֲ	ă
ִ	i, ī	ֱ	ĕ
ֹ	ō	ֳ	ŏ
וֹ	ō		

2. Transcription

2.1 The International Phonetic Alphabet

2.1.1 The 1993 Revision

In some articles the alphabet of the International Phonetic Association is employed to indicate pronunciation; both the alphabet (International Phonetic Alphabet) and the Association are abbreviated as 'IPA.' The alphabet has been revised on several occasions, the most recent revision being that of 1993 (corrected 1996). This version, which appears as Table 6, has been used in the Encyclopedia.

2.1.2 The 1979 Version

However, symbols from the earlier 1979 version are used in a few articles. These are:

(a) a small left-pointing hook attached to the bottom right of the symbol to indicate palatalization, thus m̡, s̡;

(b) a tilde through the middle of the symbol to indicate velarization, thus m̴, s̴;

2.1.3 Alternative Shapes

Some traditions, while adhering to IPA conventions, use slightly different shapes for a very small number of characters. Those appearing in the Encyclopedia are:

(a) η = IPA ŋ;
(b) δ = IPA ð;
(c) γ = IPA ɣ.

2.2 Using the IPA

The IPA alphabet is a notation that provides a phonetic description, in articulatory terms, of each speech-sound transcribed. The consonant symbols appear in boxes on a chart specifying (in horizontal rows) the place of articulation and (in vertical columns) the manner of articulation; where two symbols appear in a box, that on the right indicates a voiced sound. The vowel symbols appear on a diagram that shows front vowels on the left, central vowels in the middle, and back vowels on the right; close vowels appear at the top of the diagram, close-mid vowels under them, open-mid vowels under *them*, and open vowels at the bottom; where symbols appear in pairs, that on the right represents a rounded vowel. It is therefore possible to obtain the information about the articulation of sounds represented simply by locating the symbol on the relevant chart: thus, [ç] represents a voiceless palatal fricative and [ɞ] a rounded open-mid central vowel. Explanations of all the relevant technical terms are to be found in the Glossary of this Encyclopedia. Such information enables the user to understand what is implied by the symbols and to produce the appropriate speech-sounds.

Table 4. Transliteration of Sanskrit

Consonants

क	k	ख	kh	ग	g	घ	gh	ङ	ṅ
च	c	छ	ch	ज	j	झ	jh	ञ	ñ
ट	ṭ	ठ	ṭh	ड	ḍ	ढ	ḍh	ण	ṇ
त	t	थ	th	द	d	ध	dh	न	n
प	p	फ	ph	ब	b	भ	bh	म	m
य	y	र	r	ल	l	व	v	ळ	ḷ
श	ś	ष	ṣ	स	s				
ह	h								

Vowels

अ	a	आ	ā	इ	i	ई	ī	उ	u	ऊ	ū	ऋ	ṛ	ॠ	ṝ
ऌ	ḷ	ॡ	ḹ	ए	e	ऐ	ai	ओ	o	औ	au				

Nasal symbol, called *Anusvāra*, ˙ ṃ. Symbol for the final aspirate, called *Visarga*, : ḥ

Table 5. Transliteration of Cyrillic

Vowels

а	a	я	ja
е	e	э	è, e
и	i	й	j
о	o	ю	ju
у	u		
ы	y		

The soft sign ь is rendered ’ or j.

Consonants

б	b	п	p
в	v	р	r
г	g	с	s
д	d	т	t
ж	zh, ž	ф	f
з	z	х	kh,x
к	k	ц	ts,c
л	l	ч	ch, č
м	m	ш	sh, š
н	n	щ	shch, šč

The same battery of symbols can be used to notate phonemes or speech-sounds. Phonemic symbols (which indicate only distinctions of sound that can differentiate between different words, such as the vowels in *bid* and *bad*) are conventionally enclosed in solidi (/.../); phonetic symbols (which indicate differences of speech-sounds that may or may not distinguish different words, such as the rounded initial consonant in *soon* and the unrounded initial consonant in *seen*) are conventionally enclosed in square brackets ([...]). This convention is observed in the Encyclopedia.

3. Reading Transliterations

For the most part, all transliterations may be interpreted as being in IPA with the following exceptions:

(a) č, ǰ, š, and ž = IPA tʃ, dʒ, ʃ, and ʒ, respectively;
(b) retroflex consonants of Indian languages are indicated with a dot under the symbol for the alveolar consonant articulated in the same manner, thus ṭ, ṇ;
(c) emphatic consonants of Semitic languages are indicated by some writers, not with a symbol for velarization, but with a dot under the symbol for the non-emphatic consonant articulated in the same place and manner, thus ṭ, ṣ;
(d) alternatively, emphatic consonants of Semitic languages are indicated with capital letters instead of lower-case letters with dots subscribed, thus T, S;
(e) ñ = IPA ɲ;
(f) ṇ = IPA ŋ;
(g) ś = IPA ʃ;
(h) ć = IPA ç;
(i) in transliterations from Cyrillic, zh, kh, c, ch, sh, shch, y = IPA ʒ, x, ts, tʃ, ʃ, ʃtʃ, and ɨ, respectively;
(j) uvular articulations may be indicated by a dot under a symbol for velar articulations, thus ḳ = IPA q;
(k) b̲h̲ = IPA v;
(l) d̲h̲ = IPA ð;
(m) g̲h̲ = IPA ɣ;
(n) h̄ = IPA ħ;
(o) ḥ = IPA x;
(p) k̲h̲ = IPA x;
(q) p̲h̲ = IPA f;
(r) s̲h̲ = IPA ʃ;
(s) t̲h̲ = IPA θ;
(t) ’ = IPA ʔ;
(u) ‘ = IPA ʕ;
(v) long vowels may be marked with a macron, thus ā, or with a circumflex, thus â.

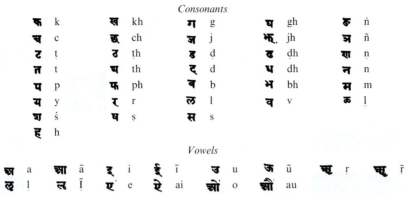

Table 6. The International Phonetic Alphabet (revised to 1993, corrected 1996)

Consonants (Pulmonic)

	Bilabial	Labiodental	Dental	Alveolar	Postalveolar	Retroflex	Palatal	Velar	Uvular	Pharyngeal	Glottal
Plosive	p b			t d		ʈ ɖ	c ɟ	k ɡ	q ɢ		ʔ
Nasal	m	ɱ		n		ɳ	ɲ	ŋ	ɴ		
Trill	ʙ			r					ʀ		
Tap or Flap				ɾ		ɽ					
Fricative	ɸ β	f v	θ ð	s z	ʃ ʒ	ʂ ʐ	ç ʝ	x ɣ	χ ʁ	ħ ʕ	h ɦ
Lateral fricative				ɬ ɮ							
Approximant		ʋ		ɹ		ɻ	j	ɰ			
Lateral approximant				l		ɭ	ʎ	ʟ			

Where symbols appear in pairs, the one to the right represents a voiced consonant. Shaded areas denote articulations judged impossible.

Consonants (Nonpulmonic)

Clicks		Voiced implosives		Ejectives	
ʘ	Bilabial	ɓ	Bilabial	ʼ	Examples:
ǀ	Dental	ɗ	Dental/alveolar	pʼ	Bilabial
ǃ	(Post)alveolar	ʄ	Palatal	tʼ	Dental/alveolar
ǂ	Palatoalveolar	ɠ	Velar	kʼ	Velar
ǁ	Alveolar lateral	ʛ	Uvular	sʼ	Alveolar fricative

Vowels

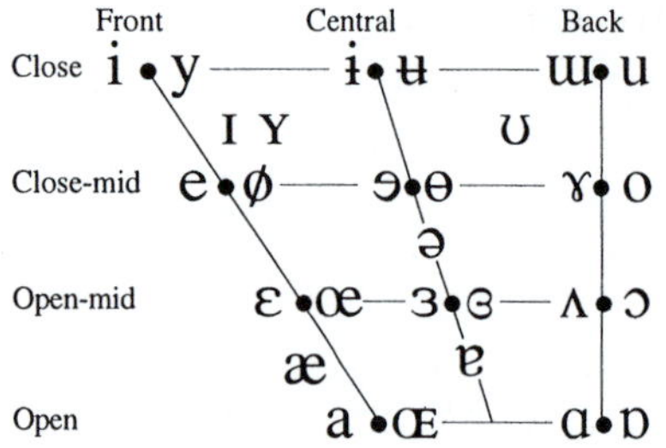

Where symbols appear in pairs, the one to the right represents a rounded vowel.

Other symbols

ʍ Voiceless labial-velar fricative

w Voiced labial-velar approximant

ɥ Voiced labial-palatal approximant

ʜ Voiceless epiglottal fricative

ʢ Voiced epiglottal fricative

ʡ Epiglottal plosive

ɕ ʑ Alveolo-palatal fricatives

ɺ Alveolar lateral flap

ɧ Simultaneous ʃ and x

Affricates and double articulations can be represented by two symbols joined by a tie bar if necessary.

k͡p t͜s

Diacritics Diacritics may be placed above a symbol with a descender, e.g. ŋ̊

̥	Voiceless	n̥ d̥	̤	Breathy voiced	b̤ a̤	̪	Dental	t̪ d̪
̬	Voiced	s̬ t̬	̰	Creaky voiced	b̰ a̰	̺	Apical	t̺ d̺
ʰ	Aspirated	tʰ dʰ	̼	Linguolabial	t̼ d̼	̻	Laminal	t̻ d̻
̹	More rounded	ɔ̹	ʷ	Labialized	tʷ dʷ	̃	Nasalized	ẽ
̜	Less rounded	ɔ̜	ʲ	Palatalized	tʲ dʲ	ⁿ	Nasal release	dⁿ
̟	Advanced	u̟	ˠ	Velarized	tˠ dˠ	ˡ	Lateral release	dˡ
̠	Retracted	e̠	ˤ	Pharyngealized	tˤ dˤ	̚	No audible release	d̚
̈	Centralized	ë	~	Velarized or pharyngealized	ɫ			
̽	Mid-centralized	e̽	̝	Raised	e̝		(ɹ̝ = voiced alveolar fricative)	
̩	Syllabic	n̩	̞	Lowered	e̞		(β̞ = voiced bilabial approximant)	
̯	Non-syllabic	e̯	̘	Advanced Tongue Root	e̘			
˞	Rhoticity	ɚ a˞	̙	Retracted Tongue Root	e̙			

Suprasegmentals

ˈ Primary stress

ˌ Secondary stress

ˌfoʊnəˈtɪʃən

ː Long eː

ˑ Half-long eˑ

̆ Extra-short ĕ

| Minor (foot) group

‖ Major (intonation) group

. Syllable break ɹi.ækt

‿ Linking (absence of a break)

Tones and word accents

Level			Contour		
e̋ or	˥	Extra high	ě or	˩˥	Rising
é	˦	High	ê	˥˩	Falling
ē	˧	Mid	e᷄	˦˥	High rising
è	˨	Low	e᷅	˩˨	Low rising
ȅ	˩	Extra low	e᷈	˧˦˧	Rising-falling
↓		Downstep	↗		Global rise
↑		Upstep	↘		Global fall

Name Index

Hartmann R R K, 336
Hartogs R, 319
Harvery T E, 84
Hastings, 381
Hastings A, 30
Hastings A H, 35
Hastings J, 252
Hastings W, 381
Hattori S, 360
Haugaard W P, 416
Haugen E, 214
Haupt P, 401
Havet L, 479
Hawkes T, 273
Hayes E N, 453
Hayes J H, 405
Hayes T, 453
Haym R, 433
Hayman A P, 286
Hayman P, 72
Haynes R, 93
Haywood J A, 336
Hayyuj J, 431
He Jiu-Ying, 346
Headland P, 468
Healey J F, 161, 224, 226
Heesterman J C, 447
Hegel, 422, 432, 441
Heidegger M, 286, 292, 400, 406, 422, 427, 432, 451
Heiler F, 278
Heinemeyer W, 190
Heintel E, 433
Helgueras A L, 23
Henderson, 44
Henderson I, 197
Henderson J B, 46
Henneke E, 101
Henri Estienne, 374
Henri Meschonnic, 148
Henricus Aristippus, 140
Henry H, 142
Henry VIII, 404
Herbert J, 91
Herbert P, 42
Herder J G, 300, 382, 409, 433, 482
Hermann P, 359
Hermannus Dalmata, 147
Herodotus, 337, 372, 376, 378, 379
Hertz M, 342
Hervás, 381
Herzig, 475
Herzog M I, 490
Hesiod, 267
Hesseling, 464
Hetzron R, 211, 220, 234
Hewitt B G, 189
Heyer E, 459
Heyer G, 240
Heyne C G, 275, 481
Highfield A R, 465
Hildegarde of Bingen, 242
Hintze U, 492
Hinüber O von, 16, 67, 129, 207, 466
HirataAtsutane, 358
Hirschfeld, 443
Hirschfeld, H, 354, 478
Hissmann M, 382
Hjelmslev L, 469
Hobbes T, 34, 268
Hoby T, 142
Hockett, 379, 467
Hodge B, 260
Hodge C T, 162
Hodgeson B, 19
Hoens D J, 264
Hofbauer G, 493
Hoffmann J J, 359
Hoftijzer J, 211
Holdcroft D, 277
Holder W, 434
Hölderlin F, 144
Holding R, 49
Holes, 163, 165
Holes C D, 166
Holeton D R, 436
Holland D T, 280
Holloway S W, 421
Holm J A, 86
Holmer N, 77, 78
Holt P M, 62
Homer, 145, 267, 372, 373, 376, 378
Hong Cheng, 346
Hooper J S M, 41
Hopkins J F P, 57
Hopkins S, 163, 166
Horace, 138, 269
Horace Bénédict de Saussure, 478
Horbury W, 194
Horguelin P, 149
Hospers J H, 220, 228
Houben Jan E M, 298
Houbigant C, 143
Householder F W, 342, 380
Houtman G, 266
Howard I, 360
Howatt A P R, 454
Hoy D, 426
Hsü Shen, 343, 344
Hsüan Tsang, 465
Hu Shih, 346
Hubbard L R, 81, 87, 88
Hübner K, 276
Hubschmann H, 478
Huet P-D, 143
Huffman H R, 168
Huffmon H B, 421

Subject Index

List of Contributors

Contributors are listed in alphabetical order together with their affiliations. Titles of articles which they have written follow in alphabetical order, along with the respective page numbers. Co-authorship is indicated by *; deceased authors are indicated by **.

ADDINGTON, T. G. (University of Arkansas, Fayetteville, AR, USA)
Preaching: 278

AIGNER-FORESTI, L. (Universität Wien, Austria)
Etruscan Religion: 48

AKINER, S. (University of London, UK)
Islam in Central Asia: 57

ALGEO, J. (TSA, Wheaton, IL, USA)
Channeling: 242; *Spiritualism*: 92; *Theosophy*: 95

APPLEYARD, D. L. (Somerset, UK)
Reinisch, Simon Leo (1863–1919): 473

APTE, M. L. (Duke University, Durham, NC, USA)
Taboo Words: 315

ARDEHALI, J. (University of Glasgow, UK)
Persian: 209

ARENDRUP, L. B. (Kobenhavns Universitet, Denmark)
Chinese: 174

ARNOLD, P. P. (University of Missouri, Columbia, MO, USA)
Native American Religions, South: 78

ASHER, R. E. (University of Edinburgh, UK)
Caldwell, Robert (1814–91): 412; **Chinese Linguistic Tradition*: 342; *Gundert, Hermann (1814–93)*: 429; *Postel, Guillaume (1510–81)*: 470; *Renou, Louis (1896–1966)*: 474; *Tamil*: 228; *Trithemius, Johannes (1462–1516)*: 486; *Ziegenbalg, Bartholomäus (1682–1719)*: 501

ASTLEY, I. (University of Edinburgh, UK)
Dhāranī (root dhr, 'to hold'): 244; *Sūtra*: 283

AULD, S. (University of Edinburgh, UK)
Islamic Calligraphy: 252

BAINBRIDGE, W. S. (National Science Foundation, Arlington, VA, USA)
Ecstatic Religion: 46; *Evangelism*: 246; *The Family (Children of God)*: 49; *Jehovah's Witnesses*: 67; *Kwanzaa*: 72; *New Religious Movements*: 81; *Scientology*: 87; *Seventh Day Adventist Church*: 88

BAKALLA, M. H. (King Saud University, Saudi Arabia)
Arab and Persian Phonetics: 322

BARR, J. (Oxford, UK)
Fundamentalism: 293

BEAL, J. C. (University of Newcastle, UK)
Rastafarianism: 85

BEATTIE, T. (University of Bristol, UK)
Irigaray, Luce (1930s–): 439; *Kristeva, Julia (1941–)*: 446

BENDOR-SAMUEL, J. (Buckinghamshire, UK)
Summer Institute of Linguistics: 391

BERNDT, C. H. (University of Western Australia, Nedlands, WA, Australia)
**Australian Aboriginal Religions*: 9

BERNDT, R. M. (Western Australia, Australia)
**Australian Aboriginal Religions*: 9

BEST, W. (University of Virginia, Charlottesville, VA, USA)
American Spirituals: 238

BIRDSALL, J. N. (Durham, UK)
Christianity in the Near East: 37

BREMMER, R. H. JR. (Rijksuniversiteit de Leiden, The Netherlands)
Scaliger, Joseph Justus (1540–1609): 480

BROCK, S. P. (University of Oxford, UK)
Syriac, Christian: 226

BROCKINGTON, J. L. (University of Edinburgh, UK)
Hindu Sacred Texts: 126; *Sanskrit*: 215

BURRIDGE, K. O. L. (University of British Columbia, Nanimo, BC, Canada)
Cargo Cults: 21

**BURSILL-HALL, G. L. (West Vancouver, BC, Canada)
Linguistic Theory in the Later Middle Ages: 361

CAMPBELL, A. T. (University of Edinburgh, UK)
Lévi-Strauss, Claude (1908–): 452; *Malinowski, Bronislaw Kaspar (1884–1942)*: 456

CARTER, M. G. (University of New York, NY, USA)
Sībawayhi (Eighth Century CE): 484

CATHCART, K. J. (University College Dublin, Ireland)
Albright, William Foxwell (1891–1971): 400; *Gordon, Cyrus Herzl (1980–2001)*: 428

Clooney, F. X. (Boston College, Chestnut Hill, MA, USA)
Nobili, Roberto de (1579–1656): 462

COAKLEY, J. F. (Harvard University, Cambridge, MA, USA)
Garshuni: 186

COHEN, A. P. (University of Edinburgh, UK)
Naming: 304

COLLINS, P. J. (University of Durham, UK)
Buddhism, Indian: 15

COLLINS, G. (University of Cambridge, UK)
Derrida, Jacques (1930–): 421

COLLINS, S. (University of Durham, UK)
Cursing: 244; *Performative Utterances*: 277

CONDOMINAS, G. (École des Hautes Etudes en Sciences Sociales, Paris, France)
Buddhism in Southeast Asia: 17

COWARD, H. (University of Victoria, BC, Canada)
Bhartrhari (ca. 500 CE): 410

CRESSWELL, J. (Institute of Oriental Philosophy, Maidenhead, UK)
Buddhism in the West: 19

CRISLIP, A. (Yale University, New Haven, CT, USA)
Gnosticism: 49; *Nag Hammadi Texts*: 128

CRONK, N. E. (University of Oxford, UK)
Bayle, Pierre (1647–1706): 408

CROWN, A. D. (University of Sydney, NSW, Australia)
Samaritan: 214

CUNNINGHAM, A. (Lancaster University, UK)
Mormon, Book of: 127; *Myths About Language*: 298

DANIELL, D. (University College London, UK)
Tyndale, William (1494–1536): 487

DAREAU, M. (University of Edinburgh, UK)
Glossary: 503

DAVIE, M. (University of Exeter, UK)
Dante Alighieri (1265–1321): 419

DEMAIZÈRE, C. (Lyon, France)
Bovelles, Charles de (1479–1566): 412

DENWOOD, P. (University of London, UK)
Tibetan: 231

DINEEN, F. P. (Georgetown University, Washington, DC, USA)
Kilwardby, Robert (ca. 1215–79): 442; *Petrus Hispanus*: 467

DOUGLAS, M. (London, UK)
Religious Symbols: 280; *Taboo, Religious*: 314

DU FEU, V. M. (Leamington Spa, UK)
Dobrovský, Josef (1753–1829): 422

DUNDAS, P. (University of Edinburgh, UK)
Buddhist Hybrid Sanskrit: 173; *Jainism*: 66

ELDERKIN, E. D. (University of London, UK)
Krapf, Johann Ludwig (1810–81): 445

ELWOLDE, J. F. (University of Oxford, UK)
Computers and Religious Studies: 346; *Hebrew, Biblical and Jewish*: 191

EPHREM, ARCHIMANDRITE (St Andrews Monastery, Manchester, UK)
Byzantine Greek: 173; *Cyril and Methodios*: 417; *Mesrob (ca. 361–ca. 439)*: 459

FAIRCLOUGH, N. (Lancaster University, UK)
Language and Power: 254

FLETCHER, P. (Lancaster University, UK)
Agamben, Giorgio (1942–): 400; *Bataille, George (1897–1962)*: 406; *Benjamin, Walter (1892–1940)*: 408; *Levinas, Emmanuel (1906–95)*: 451; *Romanticism*: 313

GANERI, J. (University of Nottingham, UK)

Matilal, Bimal Krishna (1935–91): 457

GAUR, A. (Surrey, UK)
Semitic Scripts: 220

GIBSON, J. C. L. (University of Edinburgh, UK)
Bible: 101

GILBERT, G. G. (Southern Illinois University, Carbondale, IL, USA)
Oldendorp, Christian Georg Andreas (1721–87): 464

GRAVES, M. P. (Regent University, Virginia Beach, VA, USA)
Quakerism: 83

GRAYSON, J. H. (University of Sheffield, UK)
Christianity in East Asia: 30; *Islam in East Asia*: 59; *Korean*: 194; *Ricci, Matteo (1552–1610)*: 475; *Ross, John (1842–1915)*: 476

Groom, S. (Middlesex, UK)
Barr, James (1924–): 405

GROTSCH, K. (Berlin, Germany)
Schlegel, August Wilhelm von (1767–1845): 481

GUTWIRTH, E. (London, UK)
Hayyuj, Judan (ca. 940–1010): 431; *Ibn Ezra, Abraham (ca. 1089–1164)*: 437; *Ibn Janah (ca. 990–1050)*: 437

HAMMOND, G. (University of Manchester, UK)
English Bible: 122

HARDMAN, C. E. (University of Newcastle, UK)
Shamanism: 89

HART, D. B. (Duke University, Durham, NC, USA)
Analogy: 287; *Aquinas, Thomas (1224/5–1274)*: 402

HARVEY, L. P. (Kent, UK)
Arabic and Spanish: Linguistic Contacts: 166

HASTINGS, A. (University of Leeds, UK)
Christianity in Africa: 27

HAYMAN, P. (University of Edinburgh, UK)
Alphabet: Religious Beliefs: 286

HEALEY, J. F. (University of Manchester, UK)
Alphabet: Development: 154

HEMMING, L. P. (Heythrop College, University of London, UK)
Gadamer, Hans-Georg (1900–): 426; *Heidegger, Martin (1899–1976)*: 432

HEWITT, B. G. (University of London, UK)
Armenian: 171; *Georgian*: 188

HILL, T. (Ayrshire, UK)
Weinreich, Uriel (1926–67): 489

HOLES, C. D. (University of Oxford, UK)
Arabic: 162

**HOUSEHOLDER, F. W. (Indiana University, Bloomington, IN, USA)

Aristotle and the Stoics on Language: 336; *Plato and His Predecessors*: 376

HOUTMAN, G. (London, UK)
Meditation: 264

HOWATT, A. P. R. (University of Edinburgh, UK)
Ascham, Roger (1515–68): 404

HULTKRANTZ, Å. (University of Stockholm, Sweden)
Native American Religions, North: 77

HYMAN, G. (Lancaster University, UK)
Postmodernism: 308

IDEL, M. (Hebrew University, Jerusalem, Israel)
Gematria: 294

INGRAM, W. L. (Redford, MI, USA)
British Israelites: 12

IRVINE, A. K. (University of London, UK)
Cerulli, Enrico (1898–1988): 414; *Ullendorff, Edward (1920–)*: 487

JOHNSTONE, W. (University of Aberdeen, UK)
Davidson, Andrew Bruce (1831–1902): 420

KAISER, S. (University of London, UK)
Japanese Linguistic Thought: 355

KATZ, D. (University of Oxford, UK)
Yiddish: 234

KELLEY, D. R. (University of Rochester, NY, USA)
Philology and History: 371

KELLY, L. G. (University of Ottawa, ON, Canada)
Translation: History: 138

KEMP, J. A. (Edinburgh, UK)
Holder, William (1616–98): 433; *Humbolt, Wilhelm von (1767–1835)*: 434; *Lepsius, Carl Richard (1810–84)*: 450

KHAN, G. (University of Cambridge, UK)
Masoretic Tradition: 264; *Talmud*: 137; *Targum*: 138

KILLINGLEY, D. H. (University of Newcastle upon Tyne, UK)
Hinduism: 52

KING, A. (University of Glasgow, UK)
Runes: 211

KIPARSKY, P. (Wissenschaftskolleg zu Berlin, Germany)
Sanskrit (Pāninian) Linguistics: 384

KNOTT, B. I. (University of Glasgow, UK)
Church Latin: 179

KOERNER, E. F. K. (University of Ottawa, ON, Canada)
Saussure, Ferdinand(-Mongin) de (1857–1913): 478; *Schlegel, (Carl Wilhelm) Friedrich von (1772–1829)*: 481; *Whitney, William Dwight (1827–94)*: 492

KRATZ, E. U. (University of London, UK)

Christianity in Southeast Asia: 41; *Islam in Southeast Asia*: 65

KREYENBROEK, P. G. (University of London, UK)
Avestan: 172; *Pashto*: 208

LAMBDEN, G. (University of Newcastle upon Tyne, UK)
**Bahā'ism*: 11

LAMBDEN, S. (University of Newcastle upon Tyne, UK)
**Bahā'ism*: 11

LAMBERT, P.-Y. (Paris, France)
Falc'hun, François (1909–91): 424

LANCASHIRE, D. (Hong Kong)
Buddhism, Chinese: 13; *Taoism*: 93

LANCASTER, L. (University of California, Berkeley, CA, USA)
Apocrypha, Buddhist: 100; *Buddhist Canons: Translations*: 115

LIEU, S. N. C. (Macquarie University, Sydney, NSW, Australia)
Manichaeism: 74

LIM, T. H. (University of Edinburgh, UK)
Dead Sea Scrolls: 122

LIPNER, J. J. (University of Cambridge, UK)
Hindu Views on Language: 295

LLOYD JONES, G. (University of Wales, Bangor, UK)
Coverdale, Miles (1487–1569): 415; *Delitzsch, Friedrich Conrad Gerhard (1850–1922)*: 421; *Gesenius, Wilhelm (1785–1842)*: 427; *Huss, Jan (1372–1415)*: 436; *Jerome (ca. 346–420)*: 440; *Kittel, Gerhard (1888–1948)*: 444; *Reuchlin, Johann (1455–1522)*: 474; *Wycliffe, John (1330–1384)*: 500

LONGACRE, R. E. (Summer Institute of Linguistics, Dallas, TX, USA)
Nida, Eugene Albert (1914–): 461; *Pike, Kenneth Lee (1912–2000)*: 467

LOWE, K. A. (University of Glasgow, UK)
Palaeography: 199

MACQUEEN, J. G. (University of Bristol, UK)
Akkadian: 154

MACROBERT, C. M. (University of Oxford, UK)
Church Slavonic: 180; *Old Church Slavonic*: 197

MAHER, J. C. (Edinburgh, UK)
Batchelor, John (1853–1944): 407; *Foucault, Michel (1926–84)*: 425; *Lacan, Jacques (1901–81)*: 448

MANN, W. M. (University of London, UK)
Guthrie, Malcolm (1903–72): 430

MARTIN SOSKICE, J. (University of Cambridge, UK)
Christian Views on Language: 291

MATTOCK, J. N. (University of Glasgow, UK)
Islam in the Near East: 60; *Arabic Script: Adaptation for Other Languages*: 168

MCDONALD, M. V. (University of Edinburgh, UK)
Silvestre de Sacy, Baron Antoine-Isaac (1758–1838): 485

MCINTOSH, C. (New York, USA)

Magic: 260

McKane, W. (St Andrews, UK)
Andrew of St. Victor: 401; *Black, Matthew (1908–94)*: 411

Menon, A. G. (Rijksuniversiteit te Leiden, The Netherlands)
Kuiper, Franciscus Bernardus Jacobus (1907–): 447

Michael, I. (Bristol, UK)
Lowth, Robert (1710–87): 454; *Priestley, Joseph (1733–1804)*: 471

Moisl, H. (University of Newcastle upon Tyne, UK)
Celtic Religion: 25

Moran, J. (Stirling University, UK)
Jesuit Missionaries to Sixteenth Century Japan: 360

Morgan, D. D. (University of Wales, Bangor, UK)
Hwyl: 250

Mukherjee, A. (Coventry, UK)
Carey, William (1761–1834): 413

Muraoka, T. (Leiden University, The Netherlands)
Bible Translations, Ancient Versions: 104; *Septuagint*: 136

Netton, I. R. (University of Leeds, UK)
Qur'ān: 131

Nguyen, C. T. (George Mason University, Fairfax, VA, USA)
Cao Daī: 24

Norman, K. R. (University of Cambridge, UK)
Pāli: 206

O'Loughlin, T. (University of Wales, Lampeter, UK)
Vulgate: 150

Oakes, G. (Monmouth University, West Long Branch, NJ, USA)
Weber, Max (1864–1920): 488

Onians, I. (University of Oxford, UK)
Buddhism and Language: 288; *Pali Canon*: 129

Parker, R. C. T. (University of Oxford, UK)
Greek Religion: 50

Pearson, J. (The Open University, Milton Keynes, UK)
Incantations: 252

Peel, J. D. Y. (University of London, UK)
Crowther, Samuel Aajayi (1806/08–91): 416

Perrett, R. W. (Charles Sturt University, Barton, ACT, Australia)
Mysticism: 274

Pfister, L. (Hong Kong Baptist College, Hong Kong)
Chinese: Translation of Theological Terms: 118; *Confucianism*: 42

Phiri, I. A. (University of Durban-Westville, Durban, South Africa)
African Traditional Religions: 4

Pickering, W. S. F. (Cambridge, UK)

Blasphemy: 240

POWELL, J. G. F. (University of Newcastle upon Tyne, UK)
Roman Religion: 86

PRABODCHACHRANDAN NAYAR, V. R. (University of Kerala, India)
Rājarājavarma, A. R. (1863–1918): 472

RAY, J. D. (University of Cambridge, UK)
Ancient Egyptian and Coptic: 161; *Champollion, Jean-Francois (1790–1832)*: 415; *Egyptian Hieroglyphs*: 183; *Rosetta Stone*: 134; *Young, Thomas (1773–1829)*: 500

READER, I. (Lancaster University, UK)
Buddhism, Japanese: 16; *Copying*: 243; *New Religions, Japan*: 80; *Shintō*: 89

REDFERN, W. D. (University of Reading, UK)
Euphemism: 245

REIF, S. C. (University of Cambridge, UK)
Cairo Genizah: 118

RIBEIRO DOS SANTOS, C. H. (State University of Rio de Janeiro, Brazil)
Candomblé: 20; *Caribbean Syncretistic Religions 1: Cuban Santeria and Haitian Voodoo*: 22; *Caribbean Syncretistic Religions 2: Jamaican Cumina and Trinidadian Shango*: 23; *Macumba*: 73

**ROBINS, R. H. (Surrey, UK)
Planudes, Maximus (1260–1310): 468

ROBINSON, C. (West Calder, UK)
Ælfric (fl. 987–1010): 399

ROCHER, R. (University of Pennsylvania, Philadelphia, PA, USA)
Sanskrit, Discovery by Europeans: 380

ROGERSON, J. W. (University of Sheffield, UK)
Frazer, James George (1854–1941): 426; *Myth*: 275

SAGE, V. (University of East Anglia, Norwich, UK)
Metaphor: 266

SALMON, P. B, (Oxford, UK)
Herder, Johann Gottfried (1744–1803): 433

SALVESEN, A. G. (University of Oxford, UK)
Peshitta: 130

SANNEH, L. (Yale University, New Haven, CT, USA)
Islam in Africa: 55

SARKAR, P. B. (Calcutta, India)
Sen, Sukumar (1900–92): 483

SAVILLE-TROIKE, M. (University of Arizona, Tucson, AZ, USA)
Silence: 281

SAWYER, D. (Lancaster University, UK)
Daly, Mary (1930s–): 418; Feminism: 248

SAWYER, J. F. A. (Lancaster University, UK)
Allegory: 238; *Apocrypha, Christian*: 100, *Babel*: 287; *Christianity in Europe*: 33; *Driver, Godfrey Rolles (1892–1975)*: 423; *Hymns*: 251; *Introduction: Beliefs About Languages*: 285; *Introduction: Language in the Context of Particular Religions*: 3; *Introduction: Religion and the Study of Language*: 321; *Introduction:*

Religious Languages and Scripts: 153; *Introduction: Sacred Texts and Translations*: 99; *Introduction: Special Language Uses*: 237; *Names: Religious Beliefs*: 302; *Oracle*: 276; *Prayer*: 278; *Pseudepigrapha*: 131; *Word of God*: 319

SCHLADT, M. (Institut fur Afrikanistik, Koln, Germany)
Koelle, Sigismund Wilhelm (1823–1902): 444; *Meinhof, Carl Friedrich Michael (1857–1944)*: 458; *Westermann, Diedrich Hermann (1875–1956)*: 491

SCHUH, R. G. (University of California, Los Angeles, CA, USA)
Welmers, William E. (1916–88): 490

SHACKLE, C. (School of Oriental and African Studies, University of London, UK)
Christianity in South Asia: 39; *Devanagari*: 181; *Granth*: 125; *Gurmukhi*: 190; *Islam in South Asia*: 62; *Panjabi*: 207; *Panjabi (Gurmukhi) Sacred Texts*: 129; *Sikhism*: 91

SHIVTIEL, A. (Leeds, UK)
Bergsträsser, Gotthelf (1886–1933): 409; *Nöldeke, Theodor (1836–1930)*: 463; *Polotsky, Hans (Hayyim) Jacob (1905–91)*: 469

SIMPSON, J. M. Y. (State University of Ceará, Fortaleza-CE, Brazil)
Gothic: 189; *Metrical Psalms and Paraphrases*: 273; *Ogam*: 196; *Wulfila (Ulfilas) (311?–382?)*: 499

SIMS-WILLIAMS, N. (University of London, UK)
Christianity in Iran and Central Asia: 35

SMITH, D. (Lancaster University, UK)
Mantra: 262

SOHNEN-THIEME, R. (University of London, UK)
Müller, Friedrich Max (1823–1900): 460

SOKOLOFF, M. (Bar Ilan University, Jerusalem, Israel)
Aramaic, Jewish: 169

STAAL, F. (Oakland, CA, USA)
Pāṇini: 465; *Ritual*: 310

STAM, J. H. (Uppsala College, Sussex, USA)
Whorf, Benjamin Lee (1897–1941): 493

STEINE, P. C. (United Bible Societies, New York, USA)
Bible Translations: Modern Period: 106

SUBBIONDO, J. L. (California Institute of Integral Studies, San Francisco, CA, USA)
Wilkins, John (1614–72): 494

SULEIMAN, M. Y. I. H. (University of Edinburgh, UK)
Arabic Linguistic Tradition: 326; *Ibn Madā' al-Qurtubī (1120–96)*: 438

SWIGGERS, P. (Leuven, Belgium)
Arnauld, Antoine (1612–94): 403; *Lancelot, Claude (1615/16–95)*: 449

SZUCHEWYCZ, B. G. (University of Toronto, ON, Canada)
Blessings: 241

TÉNÉ, D. (Hebrew University of Jerusalem, Israel)
Hebrew Grammarians: 348

Toolan, M. (University of Washington, Seattle, WA, USA)
Barthes, Roland (1915–80): 405

TRAVIS, C. (Stirling University, UK)

Wittgenstein, Ludwig (1889–1951): 495

TREACY-COLE, D. (University of Bristol, UK)
Christian Science: 27

TROMPF, G. W. (University of Sydney, NSW, Australia)
Melanesian Religions: 75

UHLIG, S. (Norderstedt, Germany)
Ge'ez: 187

VALPEY, K. R. (Oxford Centre for Vaishnava and Hindu Studies, UK)
Hare Krishna Movement: 51

WALES, K. (Royal Holloway and Bedford New College, Surrey, UK)
Archaism: 239

Walker, R. C. S. (University of Oxford, UK)
Kant, Immanuel (1724–1804): 441

WALLS, A. F. (University of Edinburgh, UK)
Missionaries: 368

WANG, W. S.-Y. (University of California, Berkeley, CA, USA)
**Chinese Linguistic Tradition*: 342

WATSON, W. G. E. (University of Newcastle upon Tyne, UK)
Ancient Near Eastern Religions: 6; *Phoenician/Punic*: 210; *Semitic Languages*: 218; *Ugaritic*: 233

WEINBERG, J. (Leo Baeck College, London, UK)
Kimhi, David (1160–1235?): 443; *Levita, Elijah (1469–1549)*: 453; *Saadya Gaon (882–942)*: 477

**WEITZMAN, M. (University College London, UK)
Judaism: 68

WELLS, C. J. (University of Oxford, UK)
Luther, Martin (1483–1546): 455

WILLIAMS, A. V. (University of Manchester, UK)
Pahlavi: 198: *Zoroastrianism*: 95

Williams, C. G. (St David's University College, Lampeter, UK)
Glossolalia: 249

WILLIAMS, P. M. (University of Bristol, UK)
Buddhism, Tibetan: 18; *Kumārajīva*: 448

WINTER, T. (University of Cambridge, UK)
Qur'ān: Translations: 133; *Qur'ān: Versions*: 134

ZVELEBIL, K. V. (Cannes-Minervois, Aude, France)
Tamil Linguistic Tradition: 397